DEATH AND THE AFTERLIFE

DEATH AND THE AFTERLIFE

A CULTURAL ENCYCLOPEDIA

Richard P. Taylor

ABC-CLIO

Santa Barbara, California
Denver, Colorado
Oxford, England

© 2000 by Richard P. Taylor

Library of Congress Cataloging-in-Publication Data

Taylor, Richard P.
  Death and the afterlife : a cultural encyclopedia / Richard Taylor.
    p. cm.
  ISBN 0-87436-939-8 (hard : alk. paper)
  1. Funeral rites and ceremonies—Encyclopedias. 2. Death—Social aspects—Encyclopedias. 3. Future life—Encyclopedias. I. Title.
  GT3150 .T25 2000
  393'.03—dc21
                          00-010926

06 05 04 03 02 01 00 10 9 8 7 6 5 4 3 2 1

ABC-CLIO, Inc.
130 Cremona Drive, P.O. Box 1911
Santa Barbara, California 93116-1911

This book is printed on acid-free paper ∞.

Manufactured in the United States of America

CONTENTS

Preface, ix

DEATH AND
THE AFTERLIFE:
A CULTURAL ENCYCLOPEDIA

PREFACE

I confess I am much disposed to assert the existence of Immaterial natures in the world, and to place my own soul in the class of these beings. It will hereafter, I know not where, or when, yet be proved that the human soul stands even in this life in indissoluble connection with all immaterial natures in the spirit world, that it reciprocally acts upon these and receives impressions from them.

—Immanuel Kant

For as God uses the help of our reason to illuminate us, so should we likewise turn it every way, that we may be more capable of understanding His mysteries; provided only that the mind be enlarged, according to its capacity, to the grandeur of the mysteries, and not the mysteries contracted to the narrowness of the mind.

—Francis Bacon

What has really been preserved in folk and fairy tales and in popular peasant art is, then, by no means a body of merely childish or entertaining fables or of crude decorative art, but a series of what are really esoteric doctrines and symbols. . . . It is not at all shocking that this material should have been transmitted by peasants, for whom it forms a part of their lives, a nourishment of their very constitution, but who cannot explain it; it is not at all shocking that the folk material can be described as a body of "superstition," since it is really a body of custom and belief that "stands over" (*superstat*) from a time when its meanings were understood.

—Ananda K. Coomaraswamy

Religion is, in general, extremely conservative; rituals related to death particularly so. Quite often specific funeral observances are maintained long after the origin and even the meaning of the practice are forgotten. Take, for instance, the modern Western practice of offering a eulogy to the dead: who today recognizes that this practice was in origin an attempt to pacify the soul of the dead in order to prevent him or her from harming the living? Likewise, the ritual funeral procession, common to many religious traditions, originated in the attempt to lead the soul of the dead to follow its body outside the city limits and convince it to *stay there,* bribed by pomp, circumstance, and above all offerings of food, drink, and money.

However, the purpose of this book is not merely to educate or even entertain the reader with information on the practices and beliefs of our allegedly naive ancestors and their "survivals" today. It may be the case that in many quarters the belief in the soul is out of fashion, but perhaps only temporarily. For all the marvelous gifts of technology, there is one thing physical science cannot provide; that is meaning.

Certainly, scientific scrutiny has unveiled in many cases *how* our physical universe works—how, for example, rain clouds form and how blooming flowers follow the path of the sun through the sky each day—but this does not tell us *why* they do so. In fact, the question "why?" is extremely difficult to answer and pausing on this question reveals to us fundamental gaps in our modern understanding of the universe. As the poet T. S. Eliot pointed out, our society tends to substitute knowledge for wisdom, and worse yet, in our technological age, information substitutes for knowledge. Our ancestors certainly had less information at their disposal, but through rituals, myths, and traditions they preserved the wisdom of their culture, a culture representing tens of thousands of generations of human experience, the vast majority of which escapes the current historical record. But the ancient human experience that has been lost is, in some degree, preserved in living tradition, if only it can be laid bare and its meaning penetrated.

Thus, this encyclopedia attempts to be more than a gathering of information, and its study will, it is hoped, produce something greater than just knowledge: the work attempts to draw out the underlying meaning of funeral and afterlife traditions. It makes available a variety of human responses to that most fundamental reality of life—death. Rather than recoiling from death in horror, the thoughtful reader will find that spending time with death is literally life-giving, just as the Underworld (whether the Greek Hades, the Hindu Pātāla, or the Chinese Yellow Springs) is not merely the repository of the dead but the source of tremendous fertility and wealth and—what is more—hidden wisdom bestowed only on the adventurous who have the fortitude to delve deeply.

I have attempted, in each article, to include the insights of thoughtful native authors and commentaries directly related to the cultural topic at hand. These are included out of respect in part for the subject and in part for the indigenous peoples whose experiences through history have gone to form these traditions. In making an effort to use local sources I also had in mind a wish to avoid the reductionism and objectification that can intrude when one group of people studies another. This kind of "cultural imperialism" can be observed when white people tried to study Native Americans even as they were slaughtering them, or when governments and corporations, even today, try to observe the foreign people whom they simultaneously proselytize or capitalize or both. Indeed, much of the current Western "knowledge" of world cultures was gathered during the not-so-distant colonial period, when 85 percent of the inhabited globe was held as property by a few European nations. This fact does not mean that traditional academic knowledge is useless, obviously: often it highlights information that is of interest to observers but overlooked or disregarded by native practitioners. In some cases, sadly, academic studies are all that remain of a vanished or vanishing people. For these reasons, then, in all cases where there was an option, I have chosen to use both academic sources and native informants, with the dual goal of describing the tradition or belief at hand as well as explaining its meaning as understood by practitioners.

Researching and writing this book have been a labor of love. The paramount design was to make available to the thinking public the tremendous variety of deeply interesting traditions around the world related to death and the hereafter. These traditions are often so obscure or so complicated or so little translated into English that they are appreciated by only a few scholars and specialists. An attempt has also been made to contextualize the topics presented, to show how they link up with other traditions in the same culture as well as to compare them with similar practices or beliefs in other cultures. For example, the articles on Heaven, Hell, and Resurrection focus on the Christian understanding of these themes but take pains to show the deep roots of these themes in other earlier traditions, like the Ancient Near East and the Greco-Roman world, and relate Christian traditions to parallels in the other monotheistic religions, namely Zoroastrianism, Judaism, and Islam. Many articles are listed under the native term for the topic, in languages ranging from Chinese to Sanskrit to Hebrew to Celtic. To assist the reader in finding desired articles with foreign titles, a comprehensive index has been included at the back of the book.

Although the material at times may seem daunting, my desire has been to provide maximum benefit for a reader who may have little or no background in comparative religion, folklore, history, archaeology, or linguistics. Likewise, I have used popular translations of classics rather than scholarly editions, so that readers may easily pursue further research on their own. Unless otherwise noted, the following were my sources for the Bible and the Koran: *The New English Bible with the Apocrypha*, general editor Samuel Sandmel, Oxford Study Edition (New York: Oxford University Press, 1976); and *The Koran*, translated by N. J. Dawood, fifth revised edition (New York: Penguin, 1993).

A number of people provided significant help in making this book the useful tool that it is. First of all, I with to thank Lionel Rothkrug for initiating the project and connecting me with ABC-CLIO. Profound thanks are also due to Professor Lewis Lancaster of the East Asian Languages Department of the University of California at Berkeley, for introducing me to Lionel and for invaluable guidance throughout my graduate career. I am also grateful to Professors Robert and Sally Goldman of the South Asian Studies Department at Berkeley for help with Hindu sources and for excellent instruction in various South Asian languages during my graduate study. I was blessed with an incredibly wise and generous acquisitions editor in the person of Todd Hallman, who trusted me with a massive project and without whose vision this encyclopedia never would have happened in the first place. I also wish to thank my project editor, Deborah Lynes, who patiently walked me through the editing and publishing process.

Many of my students at Berkeley also provided valuable assistance and insight. Ananda Sattwa gave excellent bibliographic help for navigating the overwhelming abundance of Native American sources. Josh Clifton and Matt Newton assisted me in finding sources for the article on Near-Death Experience and ventured to share their personal experiences as well. Chandan Narayan helped me keep track of the thousands of volumes I had checked out from various libraries. Ethan Shvartzman read portions of the manuscript and graciously allowed me to expostulate on it regularly. I wish to thank my wonderful Religious Studies class from the summer of 1999 ("Death and Afterlife in World Religion"), who proofread parts of the manuscript and asked critical and penetrating questions that required me to research more deeply in order to answer. I wish to especially thank Beth Glick, my teaching assistant for that class and several others, who helped me think out loud and gave excellent help and feedback in organizing that class.

Finally, I want to offer my profound gratitude to my parents, Dorothy Taylor and Richard A. Taylor, for their constant support and faith in me.

—*Richard P. Taylor*

A

ĀARU (SEKHET-ĀARU)

Literally the "Field of Reeds," Āaru is one of the abodes of the righteous dead in ancient Egyptian belief. Like many underworlds, Āaru is said to be an island far out in the ocean surrounded by deep waters that the dead cannot cross without being ferried over on a boat (by Mā-ha-f, "He Who Looks Behind") or carried by winged gods: "Ye claws of Horus, ye wings of Thoth, carry him over, and do not leave him untransported," one text reads (Erman, p. 94). The island itself is criss-crossed by many canals of running water, which make the land green and abundantly fruitful. Scholars have tried to place this "Field of Reeds" in various geographical regions of Egypt: the oasis of al-Khārgah, the Alexandrian Delta, or Lake Victoria in Central Africa. But such literalism and reductionism is typically modern; much more likely, Āaru is placed well out into the ocean because deep water symbolizes cosmic space—and the afterlife, as is well documented in innumerable texts, was conceived by the ancient Egyptians to be among the stars. The fully resurrected and puri-fied soul hoped to travel the heavens daily on the "boat" of the Sun God, Rā. But such metaphors are difficult to hear with modern ears. There is a synonym for Āaru (or perhaps a subsection of the land), Sekhet-hetep, or "Field of Offerings," where the dead receive their heav-enly sustenance—where food and drink is "offered" to them. Yet the symbolic nature of the name *Sekhet-hetep* and the symbolic characteristics of the plants that grow there (their different sizes indicating different levels of "reward") suggest that Āaru is more than a postmortem paradise; it is also a place of recompense where the dead receive their just desserts. In one of the Pyramid Texts (see BOOK OF THE DEAD, EGYPTIAN) Osiris, lord of the dead, makes the Pharaoh, named Pepi, "plough corn and reap wheat." Ploughing suggests religious work done for the future, and reaping suggests that one receives the benefits of religious work done in the past. Indeed, the Egyptologist E. A. Wallis Budge mentions the Papyrus of Nu (Eighteenth Dynasty, c. 1500 B.C.E.), which says that in Āaru,

> the wheat grew to a height of five cubits, the ears being two cubits long and the stalks three; the barley grew to a height of seven cubits, the ears

being three cubits long and the stalks four. Here lived the spirits of the blessed dead, who were nine cubits high, and the reaping of these crops was, it seems, reserved for them. (Budge, vol. 1, p. 97–98)

Although it is not certain, it appears likely that the souls of the dead "reaping" in the Field of Reeds are actually enjoying the benefits of righteousness (or lack thereof) on earth, with the more righteous distin-guished by higher crops. Similar thinking influenced the Apostle Paul, who says in the Christian New Testament:

> Make no mistake about this: God is not to be fooled; a man reaps what he sows. If he sows seed in the field of his lower nature, he will reap from it a harvest of corruption, but if he sows in the field of the Spirit, the Spirit will bring him a harvest of eternal life. (Gal. 6:7–8)

Because the Egyptian dead first pass through a hall of judgment and have their hearts weighed on a scale against divine justice (Ma'at) and then proceed to the Fields of Āaru, this "reaping" is surely a symbol of heavenly reward.

Purification and ritual cleanliness are also a major concern of the Field of Reeds in the Egyptian Scrip-tures. The goddesses wash the soul with four pitchers of water, and the dead bathes with Rā in the Lake of Āaru. There can be no mystery about the symbolism here: "Pure, pure is the Lake of Āaru. Pure is Rā in the Lake of Āaru, and [the deceased] himself is pure in the Lake of Āaru" (Budge, vol. 2, p. 338). Then various kinds of transfigurations come over the deceased. The sky goddess, Nut, who was often painted on the ceiling of Egyptian tombs, grants the deceased new clothing. The goddess Serqet gives him her breasts: "she places her breasts in his mouth and never does she wean him" so he may live "like a child" (Erman, p. 93). Then the goddess of the Morning Star shaves him.

Certainly, we should not believe that washing, breast-feeding, and shaving are one's literal destiny in the Field of Reeds. Rather one is shedding one's earthly personality, taking on new "garments," and becoming like a child—strangely reminiscent of Jesus' admonition to his disciples to become like children (Matt. 19:14) and to be "born again" (John 3:1). Indeed, Jesus tells Nicodemus, "No one can enter the kingdom of God without being born from water and spirit" (John 3:5). Whereas modern Christianity has taken this literally (as physical baptism), for the ancient Egyptian it was a series of transformations of consciousness, described through symbolism in heaven. Finally, after reaping, changing clothes, breast-feeding, shaving, and in other ways becoming reborn "like a child," the deceased is ready to depart:

> The Two Companies of the Gods tremble before him, and bring him offerings. He is the "nose which breathes" and he appears in the sky from the womb of Amu-apt. He passes through the two heavens, he comes to the two earths, he treads upon the green herbs under the feet of Keb [the earth god], and he walks over the roads of Nut [the sky goddess]. (Budge, vol. 1, p. 132)

See also FUNERARY CUSTOMS, ANCIENT EGYPTIAN; PYRAMID, EGYPTIAN; SOUL, EGYPTIAN.

References

Budge, E. A. Wallis. *Osiris and the Egyptian Resurrection.* 2 vols. 1911. Reprint, New York: Dover, 1973.

Erman, Adolf. *A Handbook of Egyptian Religion.* London: Archibald Constable, 1907.

Frankfort, Henri. *Ancient Egyptian Religion: An Interpretation.* New York: Columbia University Press, 1948.

Morenz, Siegfried. *Egyptian Religion.* Trans. Ann E. Keep. Ithaca, NY: Cornell University Press, 1973.

Quirke, Stephen. *Ancient Egyptian Religion.* London: British Museum Press, 1992.

Spronk, Klaas. *Beatific Afterlife in Ancient Israel and in the Ancient Near East.* Kevelaer: Butzon and Bercker, 1986.

ABHIRATI

One of the "Pure Lands" of later Buddhism, Abhirati (literally "Pleasure") is a purified, heavenly universe far, far to the east of our wicked and material universe. The Abhirati universe is presided over by the Buddha named Akṣobhya, which means "Immovable" or "Imperturbable." The Abhirati cult in Buddhism is now defunct, having been replaced by the much more popular heaven called Sukhāvatī. But in the first few centuries of the common era Buddhists in India practiced to become very pure so that they might be fortunate enough to be reincarnated in Abhirati, for in that universe all obstacles to salvation, or nirvāṇa, were thought to be removed.

The primary source for our knowledge of Abhirati is the Buddhist text the Akṣobhyavyūha Sūtra, which existed as early as the second century C.E., when it was translated into Chinese; in fact, it is probably somewhat older. This text tells of a pious monk who lived innumerable years ago in another universe and made many vows that he would fulfill in order to achieve nirvāṇa. These vows included, among others, never becoming angry, never listening to non-Buddhist doctrines, and always upholding the most perfect morality. Through countless lifetimes this monk kept his vows until he achieved enlightenment and became a perfect Buddha. Then he was able to manifest the heavenly universe called Abhirati and to use his great merits to assist others in achieving salvation.

Those pure Buddhists who enter the path to achieve full Buddhahood, who dedicate all their activities to being reborn in the Abhirati universe, who make vows, meditate, and visualize Abhirati, will find themselves reborn there after death. In the pure Abhirati universe, the Buddha Akṣobhya sits giving spiritual teachings on a raised platform under a great tree. From the tree emanates glorious music surpassing anything on earth. The ground is flat, soft as cotton, and free from any brambles, and the trees are laden with flowers, fruits, and even beautiful garments to wear. There is no sickness, no sadness, no crime, and no sexuality (women become pregnant by the mere intention and glance of a male). Yet the Akṣobhyavyūha Sūtra clearly states that Abhirati is not merely a pleasure ground but is also constructed specifically to remove all obstacles and delays to spiritual practice. With the continual presence of a fully enlightened Buddha and without the passionate distractions of earthly life, one may quickly eliminate all personal impurities and achieve salvation very quickly so that in turn one may save others.

What is quite interesting about this early version of the Pure Land in Buddhism is that it is not timeless and is subject to decay. It is an idealized "earth" and perfect for spiritual gains, but the Scripture indicates that it will eventually decay. The presiding Buddha will pass away, after many years the spiritual teachings will decline, and eventually evil will prevail. This picture is in stark contrast to the current Pure Land ideology of the Sukhāvatī universe now prevalent in China and Japan, where there is no growth, no change or decay, no pregnancy or death—where the Buddhist teachings will prevail for all time.

See also AKṢOBHYA; CHING-T'U; DEWACHAN (TIBETAN BUDDHIST); HEAVENS, BUDDHIST; NIRVĀṆA; PURE LAND; REINCARNATION, EASTERN; SUKHĀVATĪ.

References

Becker, Carl B. *Breaking the Circle: Death and the Afterlife in Buddhism.* Carbondale: Southern Illinois University Press, 1993.

Chang, Garma C. C., ed. *A Treasury of Mahāyāna Sūtras.* Trans. Buddhist Association of the United States. University Park: Pennsylvania State University Press, 1983.

Dantinne, J. *La Splendeur de l'Inébranable (Akṣobhyavyūha),* Vol. 1. Louvain-la-Neuve: Institut Orientaliste, 1983.

Foard, James, Michael Solomon, and Richard K. Payne, eds. *The Pure Land Tradition: History and Development.* Berkeley Buddhist Studies Series no. 3. Berkeley: University of California Press, 1989.

Suzuki, D. T. *Buddha of Infinite Light.* Boston: Shambhala, 1998.

Williams, Paul. *Mahāyāna Buddhism: The Doctrinal Foundations.* New York: Routledge, 1989.

ACHERON

Literally the "Stream of Woe," the name of the mythological Acheron River signifies the nature of death and the Greek Underworld, Hades, in general. Hades was not a hell in the Christian and Muslim sense but a limbo of sadness and separation from the good things of life, like the Jewish Sheol. In some legends it is Acheron that the dead must cross in Charon's boat as they pass from the land of the living to the land of the dead. For example, Dante makes the Acheron the outer limit of Hell in his *Divine Comedy,* and it is so difficult a crossing that Dante falls unconscious from the terror of it. However, in classical Greek tradition the great boundary of the Underworld was the River Styx.

See also AORNUS; COCYTUS; HADES; LETHE; PHLEGETHON; STYX; UNDERWORLD; WATER.

References

Dante Alighieri. *The Divine Comedy.* Trans. John Ciardi. New York: Norton, 1977.

Graves, Robert. *The Greek Myths.* New York: Penguin, 1960.

Turner, Alice K. *The History of Hell.* New York: Harcourt Brace, 1993.

AEDICULA

Literally "little house" in Latin, aediculae were popular in Rome as decorative features on tombs or as miniature tombs in themselves. They were mostly made of brick or stone, were box-shaped with little doors and windows, had small columns supporting a carved pediment, and were topped with gabled or pyramidal roofs. Aediculae ranged greatly in size. Some were only a meter high or smaller and rested on the bare ground, serving as the cinerarium, or ash-chest for poorer burials. House tombs also used aediculae as decorations on either side of the doorway. In temple tombs the cella resting atop the podium was sometimes carved as an aedicula, several meters high.

References

Toynbee, J. M. C. *Death and Burial in the Roman World.* Ithaca, NY: Cornell University Press, 1971.

AKŞOBHYA

As the perfectly enlightened Buddha of the eastern paradise called Abhirati, Akşobhya is pictured as blue in color, crowned on his lotus throne located under a great tree, and sitting in meditation with his right hand touching the earth. Today Akşobhya is important in Tibetan meditation rituals, called *tantra,* involving complex visualizations designed to lead the meditator to union with the divine. However, his cult was quite different in the early centuries of the common era, as the earliest known example of the Pure Land tradition in Buddhism.

As the Sanskrit Buddhist Scripture the Akşobhyavyūha Sūtra tells us, long ago in a different universe a very pious Buddhist monk made solemn vows in order to attain perfect enlightenment. Among other things, he vowed he would

> never in any way bear malice . . . never engage in even the slightest immorality. As a monk he would always be the most perfect monk, austere, eloquent, dignified, mindful in the presence of women, not listening to non-Buddhist doctrines, and so on. This applies not just to the present life but to all lives, with body, speech and mind. He would always save criminals about to be punished, even at the cost of his own life. (Williams's summary, p. 244)

After countless lifetimes, this monk eventually became a perfected human, a Buddha, and was able to create his own universe, called Abhirati ("Pleasure"). Because of his perfect purity over so many lifetimes, his universe, or Buddha-field (Buddha-kşetra), was free from all the impurities that plague most universes. Upon his enlightenment, the great anti-Buddhist demon Māra didn't even try to tempt Akşobhya because he was so pure. Devotees of this Buddha can benefit from his goodness by causing themselves to be reborn in the Abhirati universe after their death on earth.

Although the Akşobhya cult appears to have died out in Indian Buddhism by the medieval period in India (sixth to ninth centuries C.E.), it is striking as a forerunner of the very popular Pure Land traditions in China and Japan today. The Scripture on Akşobhya tells at great length how beautiful the Abhirati universe is and how wonderful it is to be reincarnated there:

> Around the bodhi-tree are rows of palm trees and jasmine trees, which in the gentle breeze, gave forth a harmonious and elegant sound surpassing all worldly music. Furthermore . . . that Buddha-land does not have the three miserable planes of existence. . . . All the sentient beings in that Buddha-land have accomplished the ten good deeds. The ground is as flat as a palm and the color of gold, with no gullies, brambles, or gravel; it is as soft as cotton, sinking as soon as one's foot steps on it and returning to its original state as soon as the foot is lifted. (Dantinne, quoted in Williams, p. 244)

Charon the ferryman rows to collect Dante and his guide, Virgil, to carry them across the River Styx. Illustration by Gustave Dore for Dante's Inferno, *Canto III. Courtesy of Anne Ronan Picture Library.*

Yet unlike most modern Buddhists' practice of the Pure Land, the focus of this early Buddhist Scripture is not on the pleasures and joys of this universe but on the opportunity for spiritual growth there. In Abhirati, "they are said to be [lazy if] they fail to end all their defilements in one sitting." Also unlike current Pure Land practice, the student is not instructed to pray to Akshobhya for rebirth in Abhirati but to learn meditation and visit holy people, visualize the Buddha in his pure land, and vow to be like him. Although this early pure land tradition of Akshobhya is clearly a direct ancestor of modern Pure Land religion, it also sticks fairly closely to early Indian Buddhist emphasis on self-cultivation, avoiding an emphasis on being saved by the power of a saint.

See also ABHIRATI; CHING T'U; DEWACHAN (TIBETAN BUDDHIST); HEAVENS, BUDDHIST; MĀRA; NIRVĀNA; PURE LAND; REINCARNATION, EASTERN; SUKHĀVATĪ.

References

Becker, Carl B. *Breaking the Circle: Death and the Afterlife in Buddhism*. Carbondale IL: Southern Illinois University Press, 1993.

Chang, Garma C. C., ed. *A Treasury of Mahāyāna Sūtras*. Trans. Buddhist Association of the United States. University Park: Pennsylvania State University Press, 1983).

Dantinne, J. *La Splendeur de l'Inébranable (Aksobhyavyūha)*, Vol. 1 Louvain-la-Neuve: Institut Orientaliste, 1983.

Foard, James, Michael Solomon, and Richard K. Payne, eds. *The Pure Land Tradition: History and Development*. Berkeley Buddhist Studies Series no. 3. Berkeley: University of California, 1989.

Suzuki, D. T. *Buddha of Infinite Light*. Boston: Shambhala, 1998.

Williams, Paul. *Mahāyāna Buddhism: The Doctrinal Foundations*. New York: Routledge, 1989.

AL-A'RĀF

Both literally and in Islamic tradition, Al-a'rāf indicates "the Heights" from which inmates can look down upon both the inhabitants of heaven (the Garden of Delights) and hell (Jahannam)—though apparently the people of Al-a'rāf belong to neither.

What is curious about the Heights is that in early Islam one's afterlife was considered to be the just outcome of one's deeds, and there were only two destinations, Paradise or the Fire. Yet there is one verse in the Scripture that has given rise to endless speculation and debate within Islam up to the present. The Qur'ān 7:44–46 states:

> Then the heirs of Paradise will cry out to the inmates of the Fire: "What our Lord promised we have found to be true. Have you, too, found the promise of your Lord to be true?"
>
> "Yes," they will answer, and a herald will cry out among them: "Cursed are the evil-doers who have debarred others from the path of God and sought to make it crooked, and who had no faith in the life to come."
>
> A barrier [al-barzakh] will divide them, and on the Heights [al-a'rāf] there will be men who recognize each one by his look. To those in Paradise they shall say: "Peace be upon you!" But they shall not yet enter, though they long to be there.

The question is, Why can the people of the Heights not enter either location, and what do the words "not yet" mean?

Unlike Catholicism, Islam has no formal teaching of purgatory or of limbo. In every instance but this one, the Qur'ān holds out only two alternatives, thus making every action in one's mundane life profoundly important. Likewise, the Qur'ān reiterates time and again that heaven and hell are eternal, and the Scripture provides no means to exist between them or to move from one to the other. Although the Heights are mentioned only once in the Qur'ān, the idea of the barrier comes up again (57:13), and it seems clearly intended to be a separation, not an in-between state:

> On that [Resurrection] day the hypocrites, both men and women, will say to the true believers: "Wait for us, that we may borrow some of your light." But they will be told: "Go back, and seek some other light!"
>
> A wall with a gate shall be set before them. Inside there shall be mercy, and out, to the fore, the scourge of Hell.

For Muhammed, there was no middle ground. Yet between the seventh century, when the Qur'ān was written down, and the tenth and eleventh centuries, Muslim theology and philosophy grew considerably, and an ever-stronger tendency arose to emphasize God's mercy over God's wrath. Philosophers began to teach that, because of Muhammed's intercession, the Muslims of the top level of hell would eventually be rescued from the flames by God. In a similar vein, some Qur'ānic commentators (such as al-Tabarī and al-Rāzī) interpreted the verses cited previously by claiming that the barrier between heaven and hell was wide and that many people could fit atop it—people who were not so evil as to deserve hellfire and yet not so good as to deserve heavenly pleasure. Jane Smith and Yvonne Haddad report that today the nearly unanimous interpretation of the Heights is to see it as a temporary state where the morally indifferent await God's mercy. In the end, Muslims expect that these people will be saved, but not before they have called out to God in agony for thousands of years to keep them from the Fire.

See also BARZAKH; HEAVEN, HISTORY OF; HEAVEN, ORIGINS OF;

HISĀB; INTERCESSION; JAHANNAM; PURGATORY; QIYĀMA; SĀ'A; SOUL, MUSLIM.

References

Bell, Richard. "The Men on the A'rāf." *Muslim World* 22 (1932).

Dawood, N. J., trans. *The Koran.* 5th rev. ed. New York: Penguin, 1993.

Gardet, Louis. *Dieu et la Destinée de l'Homme.* Paris: Librarie Philosophique, J. Vrin, 1967.

al-Qādī, Imam 'Abd al-Rahīm ibn Ahmad. *The Islamic Book of the Dead.* Trans. 'Ā'isha 'Abd al-Rahmān. Norwich, England: Diwan Press, 1977.

Smith, Jane I. *The Precious Pearl* (A translation of Abū Hāmid al-Ghazālī's *Kitāb al-Durra al-Fākhira if Kashf 'Ulūm al-Ākhira*). Missoula, MT: Scholars Press, 1979.

Smith, Jane I., and Yvonne Yazbeck Haddad. *The Islamic Understanding of Death and Resurrection.* Albany, NY: SUNY Press, 1981.

AMERETAT (AMARDAD)

Ameretat is the personification of immortality and eternal blessedness in the old Persian language called Avestan. In the medieval Iranian language of Pahlavi the name transformed slightly into Amardad.

In the early Zoroastrian Scriptures, or Gathas, the Lord God (Ahura Mazda, literally "Wise Lord") has six personifications of his goodness and energy. These six are referred to as Amesha Spentas, or "Immortal Holy Ones." Though mystically these "beings" are not really separate from the one God, nevertheless the six personifications eventually came to be seen as six independent "gods" who held council in heaven with the Wise Lord God presiding as the seventh and chief. The last of these Holy Ones is Ameretat, or "Immortality." In origin Ameretat is merely a quality of the Divine Being, namely imperishability or eternity, but it is also the gift that God promises to his faithful at the end of time.

Thus in the Gathas, Ameretat is prayed to as a divinity who can bestow his gift on humanity. Usually Ameretat is prayed to along with Haurvatat (literally "Perfection") because they form a pair—the former signifying eternal spiritual life and the latter the blessings in this world that are due to the righteous. Both are metaphorically referred to as the "nectar" that the blest will drink in heaven. Haurvatat and Ameretat have an additional nature as the patron deities of water and plant life, respectively. At the "End Time" they are thought to assuage the thirst and hunger of the righteous during the calamities that will visit humanity. In medieval times (ninth century and later) Zoroastrian theology materialized these "deities" even further by making them indulgent angels who grant food and drink to the living who know the right manthras, or spells, and punish evildoers who misuse or defile water (in Haurvatat's care) or plant life (Ameretat's charge). Each angel was imagined to have a demonic opponent that would be conquered at the final cosmic battle. The symbolic nature of these two "Immortal Holy Ones" was largely lost from medieval times onward, only to be recovered in the nineteenth- and twentieth-century Zoroastrian renaissance (largely under the influence of Western scholarship and Theosophical mysticism).

See also BEHESHT; FRASHO-KERETI; SOUL, ZOROASTRIAN.

References

Boyce, Mary. *A History of Zoroastrianism.* Vol. 1. Leiden, Holland: E. J. Brill, 1975.

Dhalla, M. N. *Zoroastrian Theology from the Earliest Times to the Present Day.* Reprint, New York: AMS Press, 1972.

Jackson, A. V. W. *Zoroastrian Studies.* New York: Columbia University Press, 1928.

Kotwal, Dastur Firoze M., and James W. Boyd, trans. *A Guide to the Zoroastrian Religion.* Studies in World Religion no. 3. Chico, CA: Scholars Press, 1982.

Masani, Sir Rustom. *Zoroastrianism: The Religion of the Good Life.* New York: Collier Books, 1962.

Moulton, James Hope. *Early Zoroastrianism.* London: Williams and Norgate, 1913.

Sethna, Tehmurasp Rustamji. *Book of Instructions on Zoroastrian Religion.* Karachi: Informal Religious Meetings Trust Fund, 1980.

Sidhwa, Ervad Godrej Dinshawji. *Discourses on Zoroastrianism.* Karachi: Ervad Godrej Dinshawji Sidhwa, 1978.

AMPHORA

An amphora was an ancient Greek jug or vase with two high handles and a narrow neck. Plain amphorae were used for storage, and ornamental varieties were given out as prizes in contests or used as decoration. They were also used as grave markers. When amphorae were set partly into the earth with the bottom removed, libations could be poured through the neck into the earth and reach the body buried below.

References

Toynbee, J. M. C. *Death and Burial in the Roman World.* Ithaca, NY: Cornell University Press, 1971.

AMULETS, EGYPTIAN

Funerary amulets are small objects buried on or near the corpse, that are imbued with magical properties to protect or empower the body (or the soul) of the deceased. Amulets appear in vast numbers in Egyptian burials and were often considered the most important kind of security for the preservation of the tomb and its mummy. There were literally hundreds of different kinds of amulets providing every imaginable kind of protection or magical ability to the deceased, from the mundane (providing heat) to the sublime (guaranteeing everlasting life). In the Old Kingdom (c. 2600 to 2100 B.C.E.) a set of seven amulets was considered complete; in later times the "magic" number was 104, and at times an even

Detail from large geometric funerary amphora, Athens, Greece. Courtesy of Anne Ronan Picture Library.

greater number was wrapped up with the mummy. The mummy of Tutankhamen was found with 143.

The amulet had several important aspects: its shape, the material out of which it was carved, any inscriptions it bore, and the kinds of spells that had been recited over it. The principal factor at work in amulets may be termed "sympathetic magic," for it was the relationship between the amulet and the cosmic power it represented that achieved the magical effect for the owner. Many amulets were made in the images of gods or symbolic items associated with them, thus drawing down from heaven their magical abilities.

For example, perhaps the most important funeral amulet was in the shape of the scarab, or dung beetle. The dung beetle lays its eggs within animal dung, and the birth of the small beetles out of feces was symbolic of life coming out of death. For this reason the scarab was also the symbol of the deity Kheperi, who was the rising sun and god of resurrection. Thus the amulet connected the wearer with the power of the rebirth and new life in the afterworld.

A particular kind of scarab amulet was associated with the heart and bore an inscription from The Book of the Dead (spell 30b) preventing the heart from confessing the evil deeds of the owner during the judgment trial in the afterlife. Other amulets took the shape of various body parts, and again, by the principle of sympathetic magic or "like affects like," they empowered or protected the organ they were connected to. Hand and feet amulets both ensured the deceased the use of those parts in the afterlife and could act as substitutes if anything happened to the hands or feet the mummy.

There was also the heart amulet, or ib, of special importance because the seat of a person's identity was, for Egyptians, not the brain but the heart. These amulets preserved one's identity in the Underworld and gave the ba (astral soul) power to come forth upon the earth. The Book of the Dead gives instructions for the production and ritual empowerment of several kinds of heart amulets, stipulating what material each is to be made out of (lapis lazuli, green feldspar, green jasper, gold, carnelian, etc.) and their function in the Underworld.

Amulets existed for at least fifty principal gods, especially the four female benefactors of the dead—Isis, Nephthys, Neith, and Selkis; Anubis, the divine embalmer who also weighed the souls of the dead at judgment; Min, god of fertility and virility; and the four sons of Horus—Imsety, Hapy, Qebhsenuef, and Duamutef—who among other things guarded the organs (see CANOPIC JAR, CHEST).

Amulet of a winged scarab beetle found wrapped in an Egyptian mummy. Often these charms were meant to provide good luck. Courtesy of Kelsey Museum of Archaeology.

The amulet symbolizing the udjat (healthy) eye of Horus connected the wearer with the god Horus, who in his struggle to revive his father Osiris from the dead did cosmic battle with the god Set, lost his eye, and later had it restored. Thus the udjat eye was considered

one of the most powerful of all amulets, preserving the wearer and giving him or her health in the afterlife. The tyet amulet of Isis was made of red material, symbolizing her blood, and conferred strength on the wearer.

"Abstract" amulets, such as the ankh, represented "life," and other amulets derived from hieroglyphics for "good," "truth," "eternity," and so on, which were effective because of the magical property of writing. For the Egyptians writing was not merely convenient or symbolic but was considered the magical power of sound in a stable, permanent form. The hieroglyphic shapes themselves were not considered merely arbitrary shapes but deliberate renditions of the things they represented, and they carried with them the power of those objects or ideas. Belief in this power of images was pervasive, and as much as it was used for the protection of the deceased, there was also a danger in the opposite direction—that hieroglyphic images with their inherent amuletic nature could work harm to the deceased unless disabled. Frequently the hieroglyphics in tombs, particularly of potentially dangerous animals like scorpions or snakes, were left deliberately incomplete and thus magically impotent. Hieroglyphic scorpions might be drawn without their stingers, animals and birds without feet, and humans with only the head and arms—able to convey meaning but without the power to come alive in the afterworld and work mischief.

Loose amulets have been found in the simple burials of the predynastic period (before 3100 B.C.E.) along with pottery, beads, and flint tools, demonstrating that from the earliest times the Egyptians were concerned with the magical power of images and the magical sounds contained in them. Mummies in general have amulets at various places on their body, with each amulet placed over an organ or limb appropriate to it. Amulets were put on the mummy at different intervals in the wrapping process, and Egyptian embalming texts reveal how complex the process was: at each stage of embalming and wrapping the appropriate spells were recited and the empowered amulets were put in their proper places.

See also CANOPIC JAR, CHEST.

References

Hamilton-Paterson, James, and Carol Andrews. *Mummies: Death and Life in Ancient Egypt*. London: William Collins Sons, 1978.

Morenz, Siegfried. *Egyptian Religion*. Trans. Ann E. Keep. Ithaca NY; Cornell University Press, 1973.

Spencer, A. J. *Death in Ancient Egypt*. New York: Penguin, 1982.

Winlock, H. E. *The Rise and Fall of the Middle Kingdom in Thebes*. New York: Macmillan, 1947.

Statue of Oshun, in situ by Oshun River, Oshogbo, Nigeria, 1971. Courtesy of Anne Ronan Picture Library.

ANCESTOR VENERATION

Rituals honoring ancestors are an extremely important part of life in nearly all societies, ancient and modern. In traditional agricultural societies these ancestors are usually one's biological forebears who are responsible for founding or maintaining the family line, whereas in sophisticated urban societies these "ancestors" are usually cultural heroes who played key roles in their society's political, moral, intellectual, or religious development. Most cultures also honor "mythical" ancestors who may or may not have been historical individuals but who became repositories of cultural origins, lore, and values. Whether they were once living and now form the community of the dead or are spirit-beings who never lived (or never died!), ancestors form society's most elevated age group, superior to living elders in wisdom and power. They serve as sources of advice, protection, gifts, and magical aid and, when treated ignobly or improperly, as sources of danger and even wrath.

Much has been made by scholars of ancestor "worship," and controversy has erupted as to whether traditional cultures see their dead actually as gods or merely as spiritual human beings. Certainly the dead are sometimes put into the category of divine beings by traditional peoples. The Japanese may refer to the ancestors as *kami* (which are usually nature spirits or local gods but sometimes the dead), and in the Old Testament, the dead are occasionally referred to as *elohim,* or "gods" (e.g., when Saul conjures up Samuel through the witch of Endor, 1 Samuel 28:13). So too in Assyria the ghosts of the dead were often referred to as *ilani* (gods). But this characterization is not surprising. According to most creation stories around the world, human beings were created partly with divine blood, divine spittle, or divine breath and so partake of some of the divine intelligence or spirit (as in Genesis 2:7, "Then the Lord God formed a man from the dust of the ground, and breathed into his nostrils the breath of life"). At death, this spirit or intelligence leaves the body but retains powers to harm or bless the living.

Not all who die become ancestors, however. As J. Omosade Awolalu writes of the Yorùbá traditions of West Africa, only those who have lived to a ripe old age, died "well," and have left behind good children and a good memory may become venerable ancestors. They are worthy of ritual veneration and respect because they are the Yorùbá's greatest elders, still living, though on another plane of being (p. 61, translations in original):

> In the Yoruba belief, the family is made up of both the living members and the ancestors. The ancestors constitute the closest link between the world of men and the spirit-world and they are believed to

be keenly interested in the welfare of their living descendants. They exercise protective and disciplinary influences on their children. They are the guardians of family affairs, traditions, ethics and activities. Offences in these matters is ultimately an offence against the forefathers who, in that capacity, act as the invisible police of the families and communities. . . . It is believed that witches and sorcerers cannot harm a man and bad medicine can have no effect on him unless his ancestors are "sleeping" or neglecting him. It is a common thing to hear a man in difficulty saying to his ancestors, "Bàbá mi, má sùn o" ("My father, don't sleep").

Without the guidance, support, advice, and correction offered by the ancestors, any society is vulnerable to outside attacks on the whims of capricious gods, witches, foreign deities, and negative forces of nature, all of which are considered conscious and very often opposed to human desires for good climate, enough but not too much rain, and so on.

Because they are now in the spirit world (although generally still in human shape), ancestors have an additional power to parent. They become superparents, as it were. According to E. Bolaji Idowu, author of *African Traditional Religion,*

> In Africa, it is the general belief that a living father or a living mother, by virtue of his fatherhood or her motherhood, is endowed with the power to bless or curse an offspring effectively. That is why every passage of life and every undertaking by the offspring require parental blessing. It is believed that such power in a father or a mother who has passed into the ancestral world has become infinitely enhanced and continues to be actively effective accordingly. (p. 185)

This "parental" aspect of the ancestors is as true for East Asians, Native Americans, medieval Europeans (where ancestors were often Catholic saints), and other traditional societies as it is for Africans. But ancestors in many cultures have another important aspect. They are the pool from which one receives one's children. Awolalu writes (p. 60):

> The Yoruba strongly believe that the departed ancestors have different ways of returning to the living. One of the commonest ways of doing this is for the soul to be reincarnated and to be born as a grandchild to a child of the departed parents. It is believed that the ancestors choose to do this in consequence of their love for the family and of the world. The world, according to the Yoruba, is the best place in which to live. Hence, it has been said

that the Yoruba attitude is world-affirming, not renouncing. . . . There is a strong desire on the part of the living to have their parents reincarnated as soon as possible after their death. Hence well-wishers pray: "Bàbá/Ìyá á yà lówóò re o" ("May your father or mother turn to be a child for you"). And sometimes, in their enthusiasm, they pray saying "Bàbá/Ìyá á tètè yà o" ("May father or mother be reincarnated soon"). The child who is lucky to give birth to the father or mother usually feels particularly happy.

This belief seems to present an interesting paradox, in that traditional societies depend on the ancestors, who are called to be present for personal need and momentous family occasions. How can the ancestors watch over their families "from above" when they are reborn as tiny children?

There is really no paradox because spirits do not exist in only one place at one time. Ancestral souls are not considered purely physical entities, and spiritual beliefs need not follow strict laws of logic. The dead individual may never stand alone for long but is always at some point made to join the society of the ancestors. The Vedas, very early Hindu Scriptures, state this clearly (Macdonell, trans.):

> Unite with the Fathers, unite with Yama . . .
> Leaving blemish behind go back to thy home;
> Unite with thy body, full of vigor.
> (Rig Veda X.14.8)
>
> [The] Creators say: "Let the lower, let the higher,
> Let the Middle Ancestors . . . rise up;
> Let those kind Ancestors, who know cosmic Order,
> Who have gone to eternal life,
> Favor us in our invocations.
> (Rig Veda X.15.1, 10)

The dead are individuals at first, but with time the recently dead become a part of the collective, and indeed the ancestors are often prayed to as a homogeneous group. Thus, even though individual ancestors may have reincarnated (and reincarnation occurs very quickly in Hindu and Buddhist thought), their ancestral energy and perhaps even the ancestral soul remain a benevolent and protective force for the descendants. In East Asia this may be very clearly seen. Each family keeps the soul tablets of the recently dead lined up on the family altar, but the altar itself is a means to contact all the ancestors simultaneously and inform them of births, weddings, and other important family events.

Another important aspect of ancestor veneration is the conception of ancestors not merely as witnesses of the past and keepers of tribal lore but also as guardians of the future. As a collective body, the ancestors pass judgment over the living, accept or reject their descendants' actions, and bless or curse their offspring. A particularly potent example of this occurs at New Year's festivities (the date of which varies from calendar to calendar). The well-known religion scholar Mircea Eliade points out in *The Myth of the Eternal Return* that spirits of the dead play a crucial role in the New Year festivities of almost every culture. The celebrations of the living that accompany the intersection of the old year with the new include the return of the dead en masse to the world of the living. The Greek Anthesteria, Roman Parentalia, Mexican Día de los Muertos, Celtic Samhain, Christian Hallowe'en and All Saints' Day, Festival of Ghosts in China, and Bon Festival of Japan all provide examples of this intimate connection. It is a time of danger and crisis as well as festivity, for the entire coming year's worth of crops, newborn babies, wealth, and health are thought to depend on an auspicious transition from old to new, in large part dependent upon the favor of the ancestors.

A final aspect of the veneration of the dead is reciprocity. Not only do the living regularly need the benefits and blessings of the ancestors, but frequently the dead are thought to need the help of the living. From very early times in Christianity, the prayers and penances of the living were thought to help the dead, long before the Catholic doctrine of Purgatory was formally developed. Tertullian, an African theologian (died c. 220 C.E.), taught that the prayers and sacrifices of the living definitely help the dead, though this was not taught by the Bible:

> We make oblations for the deceased on the anniversary of their death. . . . If you look in Scripture for a formal law governing these and similar practices, you will find none. It is tradition that justifies them, custom that confirms them, and faith that observes them. (*De Corona Militis* 3.2–3, quoted in Le Goff, p. 47)

It is no surprise that Christianity should have been heavily involved in ancestor worship, for it was a major aspect of Israelite, Greek, and Roman religions, just as they in turn inherited such beliefs from Egypt and the ancient Near East. But an important point to note about the ability of the living to improve the condition of the dead is that the dead must deserve such help—otherwise ancestor veneration will be of moral and spiritual benefit to the living, but it will not help the dead. The greatest father of the early Christian church, Augustine (354–430 C.E.), was insistent on this point, and many other cultures agree. In China, the Scripture on the Original Vows of Ti-tsang Bodhisattva states,

> If there is a man or woman who during life did not cultivate good causes or who committed many sins, and if after his or her lifespan has ended, descendants engage in creating good fortune, no matter how much or how little, then of all the religious services, out of seven parts the deceased will receive only one. Six parts of the merit will profit the living. (quoted in Teiser, p. 27)

See also ANTHESTERIA; BON FESTIVAL (JAPAN); DEATH, GOOD; DÍA DE LOS MUERTOS; FESTIVAL OF GHOSTS (CHINA); HALLOWE'EN; SAMHAIN.

References

Awolalu, J. Omosade. *Yoruba Beliefs and Sacrificial Rites.* Brooklyn, NY: Athelia Henrietta Press, 1996.

Eliade, Mircea. *The Myth of the Eternal Return.* Trans. Willard R. Trask. Bollingen Series 46. New York: Pantheon Books, 1954.

Heidel, Alexander. *The Gilgamesh Epic and Old Testament Parallels.* Chicago: University of Chicago Press, 1946.

Hsu, Francis L. K. *Under the Ancestor's Shadow.* New York: Columbia University Press, 1948.

Idowu, E. Bolaji. *African Traditional Religion.* Reprint, Kampala, Uganda. Fountain Publications, 1991.

Janelli, Dawnhee Yim, and Roger L. Janelli. *Ancestor Worship in Korean Society.* Stanford: Stanford University Press, 1982.

Lamm, Maurice. *The Jewish Way in Death and Mourning.* New York: Jonathan David Publishers, 1969.

Le Goff, Jacques. *The Birth of Purgatory.* Trans. Arthur Goldhammer. Chicago: University of Chicago Press, 1984.

MacCulloch, J. A. *The Religion of the Ancient Celts.* Edinburgh: Clark, 1911.

Macdonell, Arthur Anthony. *A Vedic Reader for Students.* Indian ed. Delhi: Motilal Banarsidass, 1995.

Newell, William H., ed. *Ancestors.* The Hague: Mouton, 1976.

Pandey, Raj Bali. *Hindu Samskāras: A Socio-religious Study of the Hindu Sacraments.* Banares: Vikrama Publications, 1949.

Poo, Mu-chou. *In Search of Personal Welfare: A View of Ancient Chinese Religion.* New York: SUNY, 1998.

Shastri, D. R. *Origin and Development of the Rituals of Ancestor Worship in India.* Calcutta: Bookland, 1963.

Teiser, Stephen F. *The Scripture on the Ten Kings and the Making of Purgatory in Medieval Chinese Buddhism.* Honolulu: University of Hawaii Press, 1994.

ANCESTRAL PORTRAIT/BUST

In ancient Rome the upper classes had the interesting practice of making wax portraits or, later, busts of the dead in their families. In the second century B.C.E. Polybius wrote that realistic portrait masks (in Latin, *imago;* in Greek, *eikon*) were displayed in a wooden shrine in the home. In this way families built up considerable galleries of their ancestors (paraphrased in Toynbee, p. 47).

When each member of the family died, those relatives and friends who most resembled the ancestors of the deceased wore the masks during the funeral procession, even speaking and acting as the ancestors themselves. By

ANINUT

Aninut is the state of formal mourning in Orthodox Judaism from the time of a near relative's death until the time of his or her burial. One who is in this state is called an *onen* (pl. *onenim*). Only "near relations" of a deceased person experience aninut, near relations being defined as parents, siblings (including half-siblings), children, or the spouse. Stepbrothers and sisters, divorced spouses, and adoptive children and parents all have the choice of entering aninut but are not required by Jewish religious law to do so.

Because the time between death and burial in Orthodox Judaism is quite short, the state of aninut does not last long, generally no more than twenty-four to forty-eight hours. After the burial of a loved one, mourners enter into a different state of mourning, called *avelut.* This is a longer period, which begins with the seven-day period called *shiva.* There are many ritual restrictions on the person in aninut. For example, one may not eat meat or drink wine (except where such food and drink is prescribed, for example on the Sabbath or certain holidays). One may not engage in celebrations or attend parties (again, excepting participation in public religious celebrations, which is required of Orthodox Jews). One may not study the Torah (Hebrew Scriptures) because traditionally scriptural study is supposed to produce joy—which is out of place during a mourning period. Finally, one may not buy new clothes, wear freshly laundered or pressed clothes, or groom oneself, except in the most necessary and basic fashion. Thus applying cosmetics is generally forbidden, as are wearing perfumes, shaving, cutting hair, bathing for pleasure, and so on. Keri'ah, or the rending of clothes, is performed on one's outer clothing, to be worn throughout the early mourning period (until the end of shiva).

There are exceptions that will exclude certain relatives from entering into aninut. One is an onen only if one participates in arrangements for the funeral or is able to participate in them. Recently married brides are exempted from all funeral arrangements and formal mourning during their designated seven-day honeymoon. Those relatives (even very close ones) who do not learn of the death of their relative before his or her burial, who live too far away to participate in funeral arrangements, or who are not free to do so (being on a military mission, hospitalized, or in prison) do not enter aninut. If the physical body of the deceased is not in the family's possession (for instance, if the deceased is missing and presumed dead), there can be no physical burial, and none of the relatives enter aninut. However, succeeding stages of (postfuneral) mourning do apply.

See also AVELUT; FUNERARY CUSTOMS, JEWISH; KADDISH; KERI'AH; SHIVA (JEWISH).

Bust of Heliogabalus (188–217 C.E.), also known as Elagabalus, born at Emesa in Syria. Roman Emperor (211–217 C.E.). Heliogabalus is the divine name of Caesar Marcus Aurelius Antoninus Augustus. His original name was Varius Avitus Bassianus. Courtesy of Anne Ronan Picture Library.

the first century B.C.E. the funeral masks were sometimes replaced with funerary busts, probably of wax or terracotta, kept in the home in cupboards. At the time of death these images were set around the funerary bed and then carried behind the body in procession.

References

Toynbee, J. M. C. *Death and Burial in the Roman World.* Ithaca, NY: Cornell University Press, 1971.

References

Abramovitch, Henry. "Death." In *Contemporary Jewish Religious Thought,* ed. Arthur A. Cohen and Paul Mendes-Flohr. New York: Charles Scribner's Sons, 1989.

Lamm, Maurice. *The Jewish Way in Death and Mourning.* New York: Jonathan David Publishers, 1969.

Rabinowicz, H. *A Guide to Life.* London: Jewish Chronicle Publications, 1964.

Riemer, Jack, ed. *Jewish Reflections on Death.* New York: Schocken Books, 1974.

ANKOU

In the folklore of Brittany, there is the belief that in each church parish the last person to die the previous year becomes the ankou, or "King of the Dead," for the following year. Like the Irish banshee, the ankou of Brittany is an apparition that warns of impending death. It appears as an emaciated corpse or a ghostly skeleton with trailing white hair, driving a wooden cart to the home of one who is about to die. Whether the ankou stands outside the home and utters heartrending cries or actually knocks on the door and enters, its duty is to call out to the dead and bid them follow. Some legends have the ankou place the dead in its cart, often with the aid of two henchman, and drive off to the netherworld.

References

Evans-Wentz, W. Y. *The Fairy Faith in Celtic Countries.* New York: Carol Publishing, 1990.

ANNWFN (ANNWN, ANNWFYN)

Literally the "Otherworld" or perhaps "Nonworld" of Welsh lore, Annwfn appears most prominently in the Welsh cycle of tales called *The Mabinogi,* wherein several different characters have adventures for good or ill. It is also the center of attention in a poem associated with King Arthur's adventures, called "The Spoils of Annwfn" and ascribed to the Welsh poet-sage Taliesin. There Annwfn is called by many names, including *Caer Siddi,* literally "Fairy Castle." Annwfn serves many roles in these traditions: it is a source of power and royal authority, a source of deception and heroic tests, and a timeless, deathless withdrawal from life marked by endless food and riches, divine music, and the absence of all sorrow.

Like the Irish understanding of the Otherworld, the Welsh Annwfn has no clear physical location: it is neither definitively underground nor over the water, although it *can* be reached through gateways leading into the earth or on islands across the western sea. Sometimes, as in the section Manawydan of the *Mabinogi* cycle, we find Annwfn as a magic castle that appears and disappears; in "The Spoils of Annwfn," it is among other things a "Fortress of Glass" on an island.

In both cases, the Otherworld is essentially a parallel world, near our world, even contained by our world (or vice versa) but invisible and unapproachable except by rare individuals on rare occasions. It is primarily the land of the fairies and other magical creatures, but Annwfn also has profound connections with the dead because it represents essentially "the other," the opposite of living and the known. Whereas the earth has its seasons of summer and winter, change and decay, Annwfn is ever beautiful, ever warm.

The denizens of Annwfn may be met with in the liminal areas of our world—either potentially dangerous areas far from civilization (e.g., islands, woods) or potentially dangerous power centers connected with a distant past undisclosed to contemporary society (e.g., burial mounds). For instance, young Pwyll, lord of the seven cantrefs of the kingdom of Dyfed, enters into the woods on a hunt one day and becomes separated from his companions. After a time Lord Pwyll hears the blowing of horns and the running of hounds that are not his own, and eventually in a forest clearing he sees another hunting party bringing down a stag. The hounds of this party glitter bright white with red ears (the colors marking Otherworld creatures), and their master, Arawn, the lord of Annwfn, is cloaked in gray—symbol of twilight, an intersection of the known and unknown. To make up for a minor offense that he has committed, Lord Pwyll takes the place of Arawn as king of Annwfn for a year and a day, and the reader is offered a glimpse of the Otherworld. It is a realm of magnificence and plenty, with high architecture and ornamented chambers, clothing of shining gold brocade, and the most beautiful people (particularly women) Pwyll has ever seen. The royal court was supplied with more food, drink, gold vessels, and royal treasures than any court on earth, and Lord Pwyll is deeply impressed. After a year he successfully vanquishes Arawn's Otherworld adversary and returns to his own kingdom with the deep gratitude of Arawn and a new title, Pwyll, head of Annwfn. As in so many other cases, a human king has gained in authority through connection with the Otherworld.

Not all encounters with the Otherworld are so pleasant, however. Some years later Lord Pwyll's son Pryderi, his queen, and two friends begin a royal feast on a sacred mound in the same kingdom of Dyfed. In Welsh, Irish, and other northern European traditions, such mounds were usually the burial places of ancestral kings and served as both locations to assert authority and spectator stands for the populace to enjoy entertainments; such a feast was entirely appropriate there. On this occasion, however, the magical nature of the spot asserted itself, and a great thunder and clatter broke out. Simultaneously a profound mist descended, and no one could see anyone else. When the mist lifted moments later, the party of four remained, but all their friends, attendants, councillors, and warriors had disappeared—even the herds of cattle and flocks of birds. Thus began an adventure to rescue all the inhabitants of the kingdom from imprisonment in the Otherworld. Eventually, after much wandering and many side tales, the magical plot is discovered, and the hero Manawydan, son of Llyr, builds a gallows on the same mound. Manawydan intends to hang a pregnant mouse he has caught, which is actually the wife of the Otherworld schemer Llwyd, son of Cil Coed. Through cleverness and persistence, the kingdom's inhabitants are released from sorcery and all is restored.

Besides the site of rewards or sorcery, Annwfn in Welsh tradition may serve as a kind of spiritual resting place or even a symbolic afterlife in which we see its strongest connection with the dead. In the tale "Branwen Daughter of Llyr," only seven Welsh heroes survive a cataclysmic war with Ireland. Returning from their Pyrrhic victory, the seven take the severed head of their former leader (which is still alive and talking) to Wales, only to learn that their own country has been seized by a cousin and all their friends killed. Symbolically, the heroes have "died," and they withdraw to Harlech on the coast of Gwynedd (northwestern Wales) for a "boundless supply of food and drink." They have purposely entered the Otherworld in order to escape from their own realm, and while there they hear the singing of the magical birds of the goddess-figure Rhiannon: "three birds came and began singing songs to them, all the songs they had ever heard were coarse compared to that one. They were a distant vision seen above the waves, yet they were as clear to them as if they were together with them. And they were at that feast for seven years" (Ford, trans.; all quotes from *The Mabinogi* come from Ford unless stated otherwise). Then the heroes removed to Gwales, an island off the coast of Dyfed, which was another gateway to Annwfn. There for another eighty years they withdrew from the world. They spent their time in a royal palace with such pleasure that they were not aware of the passage of time and did not recall any of their former grief until one of their number opened a forbidden door. Suddenly their sorrows came flooding back, and they were "reborn" to the world in order to complete their mission to bury the magical head of their leader at Gwynfryn (literally "White Mount") near London, with the head facing France—clearly a talisman to ward off danger that would come to the British Isles from that direction.

Although it is true that nowhere in extant Welsh literature is Annwfn explicitly called the land of the dead, there are several reasons to believe that it once had such connections. It is the land of immortality, perpetual summer, and joy, a land where magic and magical items may be found, and in all these regards the polar opposite of life on earth. It is also no accident that entrances to Annwfn are in many cases the ancestral burial mounds, as in the second story just summarized. Finally, in one body of tradition King Arthur ventures to Annwfn (most prominently in the cryptic poem *Preiddeu Annwn*, or "The Spoils of Annwn"), which in this case is a castle with a magic cauldron (a prototype of the Grail); and in other references to Arthur and the Otherworld, Annwfn is often directly mentioned as the land of the dead. For instance, in the story "Diu Crône," the king of the magic castle housing the Holy Grail states that he and his folk are dead.

Certainly, if in the distant past Annwfn ever doubled as the land of the dead as well as the land of fairies, it became reduced only to the latter in medieval times, after the advent of Christianity. But again, it is probably not by chance that after the triumph of Christian monks and missionaries in the British Isles, Arawn, the lord of Annwfn, was identified by them with the Devil, lord of Hell. Even then Annwfn retained its magnificence and beauty; only they were spells and illusions, merely the means to lead people to eternal damnation.

See also AVALON; FAIRY MOUND; MOUND; OTHERWORLD, IRISH; SÍD; UNDERWORLD.

References

Ford, Patrick K., ed. *The* Mabinogi *and Other Medieval Welsh Tales*. Berkeley: University of California Press, 1977.

Loomis, Roger Sherman. *Wales and the Arthurian Legend*. Cardiff: University of Wales Press, 1956.

Rees, Alwyn, and Brinley Rees. *Celtic Heritage: Ancient Tradition in Ireland and Wales*. London: Thames and Hudson, 1961.

ANTHESTERIA

In ancient Greek lands the Anthesteria was a three-day festival occurring in the month of February. Although most of the literature that has been preserved from the classical period of Greek culture suggests that the Anthesteria was nothing but a prolonged party—culminating in universal drunkenness—there is ample evidence that originally the festival observed the annual return of the dead, like its Roman counterpart, the Parentalia, which was held during the same time of year.

Jane Harrison suggests that despite the ancient Greek translation of the name Anthesteria as "Blossoming of Flowers," it was in fact too early in the year for blooms, and in any case the name has a much deeper significance. From the root *thes,* meaning "to pray," the festival name probably meant literally "the feast recalling (spirits) by prayer." However, Greek-speaking peoples forgot the early origin of the term and then became hard-pressed to find an etymology. Likewise, the three days of the festival, which would occur in the modern calendar on the eleventh, twelfth,

One of the many activities on the second day of this festival (Choes, literary "Cups") was to sing songs to celebrate the birth of the divine child after his long incubation, as pictured in this ancient Greek relief. Courtesy of Alinari/Art Resource.

and thirteenth of February, also have individual names, which the Greeks translated one way and modern scholars translate another.

The first day of the Anthesteria, called *Pithoigia* (Cask Opening), was taken by ancient Greeks to mean "wine-cask openings" and marked the beginning of the festivities as wine flowed forth. But the term *pithos* used to mean another kind of cask, a great jar or urn dug into the ground in which was stored not only wine, but grain, olive oil, and other things. Furthermore, many communities dug the pithoi into rows and used them to bury the dead. A vase painting from the University Museum of Jena, first published by Paul Schadow in 1897, shows Hermes standing in front of a pithos, an urn, holding a magic wand in his uplifted hand as three winged souls fly out of the urn and one flies back in. In later times, pithoi were less frequently used as burial urns, but the decorative amphora used to mark a grave serves as a reminder of the ancient custom (see AMPHORA). Thus the first day of the Anthesteria, Pithoigia, used to mean the opening of burial urns but came to mean the opening of jars of wine, nothing more than the start of the festival.

The second day of the festival was called *Choes*, literally "Cups." Greeks took it to mean "wine cups," which of course were needed for drinking. On this second day, there was held the annual ritual wedding between the ruler's wife and the god Dionysus, lord of revelry, and the drinking continued. But strangely, the day of "Cups" was also considered a "day of pollution" on the Greek calendar, an unlucky day. One was supposed to take precautions on such a day, such as chewing a sprig of a plant called buckthorn and painting the front doors of homes with pitch. Both actions warded off spirits. Harrison explains the strange precautions that were

taken on a day that was ostensibly a drinking holiday by pointing out that the Greek plural for "cups," *choes,* was probably not the original name of the holiday. Much more likely the second day of the festival was originally called *Choai,* "Funeral Libations." But in time, as wine was poured out to satiate the dead, it was probably poured out to gratify the living as well. Thus, in the original Anthesteria, on the first day the dead rose from their burial urns, and on the second day they were offered wine. Many Greek and Roman graves actually had pipes leading from the surface of the grave to the buried body so that libations could reach the dead, and well-to-do Roman families owned funerary homes on the edge of town, complete with kitchens, in which the living could share a meal and wine with the dead. (Though the dead were thought of as spirit beings, they were in some sense also present in their graves or mausolea.)

Finally, the third day of the Anthesteria was called *Chytroi,* "Pots." On this day of the festival, drama contests were held in which troupes of players acted out ritual plays and dances of Dionysus. A meal of grain and seeds cooked in a pot was also offered to Hermes Chthonios, "Hermes of the Underworld." Again, however, this was likely a late and artificial reconstruction of the festival by the Greeks. The word for ordinary pots in Greek is a feminine noun, in the plural *ai chûtrai,* but the festival is called by the masculine noun, *oi chûtroi,* meaning "natural hollows" in the earth. In ancient Greece earth formations such as caves and chasms were thought of as openings to the Underworld. Ghosts could enter and exit the earth through these openings, and they were sometimes used as convenient spots to bury the funeral urns, or pithoi. The third day of the festival, then, originally referred to the departure of the ghosts to their Underworld dwelling through natural holes in the ground and not to the offering cooked in pots. The proof of this is the formula spoken by revelers at the end of the festival: "Out of the doors you Keres; it is no longer Anthesteria." The Keres were demons and spirits of the dead; the formula clearly identifies them as the focus of the Anthesteria festival and asks them to depart.

How is it possible that a festival, originally a somber commemoration and placation of the visiting dead, turned into a drinking party? As the god of the Underworld, Hades was both the lord of the dead and the lord of that which comes up from the earth, namely plants and animals—so the deceased, particularly family ancestors, were thought to bring both the danger of death pollution and the ability to fertilize the land. It is no accident that both the Greek Anthesteria and the Roman Parentalia were held in February, for February was originally the last month of the year, the month of purification, payment of debts, and most importantly (in the Mediterranean) the first hint of spring. For an agrarian people, the fertility of the earth was of utmost importance, and the blessings and "earth energy" of the earth dwellers (the dead) were needed to awaken the powers of life and growth from sleep (death) in the earth. At the same time, the dead were inherently dangerous because earth energy could also be retrograde, bringing the living "down under" (just as Persephone/Kore, the fertile corn maiden, was kidnapped and dragged to the Underworld). In its origins the Anthesteria, like all festivals of the dead, was an annual ritual to give the dead their due but simultaneously to protect the living from danger. That this solemn ritual became a drinking party is characteristic of the Dionysian aspect of ancient Greek religion.

See also FEBRUARY; FUNERARY CUSTOMS, ANCIENT GREEK; HADES; KER; PARENTALIA; PERSEPHONE; SOUL, GREEK.

References
Fowler, W. Warde. *The Roman Festivals of the Period of the Republic.* London: Kennikat Press, 1969.
Harrison, Jane Ellen. *Prolegomena to the Study of Greek Religion.* Cambridge: Cambridge University Press, 1922.
Schadow, Paul. *Eine Attische Grabekythos.* Inaugural diss., Jena University, 1897.
Toynbee, J. M. C. *Death and Burial in the Roman World.* Ithaca, NY: Cornell University Press, 1971.

AORNUS

Although the name *Aornus* does make sense in the Greek tongue (literally "Birdless"), it is certainly a mistranslation of the early Latin *Avernus.* Aornus refers both to a river in Hades, a tributary of the River Styx, and to a cave, Thesprotian Aornum, located on the middle western coast of Greece through which one could enter the Underworld. Presumably the Greeks called it

Aornus because such fumes poured from the mouth of the cave that no bird (ornus) could fly above unharmed.

See also ACHERON; AVERNUS; HADES; STYX; UNDERWORLD; WATER.

References
Graves, Robert. *The Greek Myths.* New York: Penguin, 1960.

ARCOSOLIUM

Literally "an arch over a throne" in Latin, an arcosolium is a benchlike niche with an arched ceiling cut into or built in front of the wall of a stone tomb. Arcosolia are predominantly a Christian phenomenon, beginning in the third century C.E., but are also found in Jewish tombs in Jerusalem at the end of the Second Temple period (second and first century B.C.E.) and may have been reserved for more expensive burials. Christian arcosolia in fourth-century catacombs were often painted and seem to have been reserved primarily for the bodies of popes and martyrs.

The body was usually placed in a coffin that rested on the arcosolium, but bodies could be laid bare on the benches as well. Typically an arcosolium housed one body only, but in Sicily a larger variety of arcosolia are found with considerably higher arches reaching further into the wall, capable of sheltering five, six, or more bodies.

References
Hertling, Ludwig, and Engelbert Kirschbaum. *The Roman Catacombs and Their Martyrs.* Trans. M. Joseph Costelloe. London: Darton, Longman, and Todd, 1960.
Marucchi, Orazio. *Manual of Christian Archeology* Paterson, NJ: St. Anthony Guild Press, 1935.
Stevenson, James. *The Catacombs.* London: Thames and Hudson, 1978.
Toynbee, J. M. C. *Death and Burial in the Roman World.* Ithaca, NY: Cornell University Press, 1971.

ARENARIUM

Arenarium is the Latin name for quarries, particularly their winding passages, often irregular in shape and size. They were common outside the city walls of Rome where the demand for rock was high, especially a certain kind of rock called *tufa* that was used for mortar. After the arenaria were abandoned commercially, they often became the nuclei for tombs or catacombs. They were utilized by pagans, Jews, and Christians alike, and one may find tombs in arenaria belonging to adherents of these different religions practically side by side. This pattern suggests that, especially in the early days of Christianity, Roman burial practices were not very distinct, and there was little idea that those of another faith would "corrupt" one's final resting place.

References

Hertling, Ludwig, and Engelbert Kirschbaum. *The Roman Catacombs and Their Martyrs*. London: Darton, Longman, and Todd, 1960.

Nash, E. *Pictorial Dictionary of Ancient Rome*. 2nd ed., rev. New York: Praeger, 1968.

Stevenson, James. *The Catacombs: Life and Death in Early Christianity*. London: Thames and Hudson, 1978.

ARŪPA-DHĀTU

The Arūpa-dhātu, or "Immaterial World," is the very highest part of the Buddhist universe, situated beyond the lower "World of Desire" (Kāma-dhātu) and the middle "World of Form" (Rūpa-dhātu). The Immaterial World is placed vertically higher than the other worlds in charts of the Buddhist conception of the universe, but this is a misrepresentation, since it has no dimensions and no location. It is literally formless and does not exist in the gross or subtle material universes.

Access to the four heavens of the Arūpa-dhātu is gained only by those Buddhist saints who have attained the very highest absorptions in meditation during life. Beyond the four meditations mentioned in the entry for RŪPA-DHĀTU, which bring the practitioner beyond selfish desire to states of transcendent calm, there are four higher meditations that take the Buddhist saint higher still. The first of these higher meditations is "infinite space," wherein the meditator realizes that matter is an illusion, that difference between objects is an illusion, and that all sensory experience is merely infinite space. In the second higher meditation, one withdraws from the world further and reaches inward even more. This withdrawal leads one to discover basically the same thing subjectively, that within one's being, beyond discursive thought or emotion, is an infinity of mind or consciousness. The third meditation withdraws even from the mind itself and experiences pure nothingness. Finally, at the fourth stage of the higher meditation, one withdraws even from the experience of nothingness, into a state of neither consciousness nor nonconsciousness, the furthest cessation of human experience.

It is interesting to note that Gautama Shakyamuni, the founder of Buddhism, did not place great stock in these four higher meditations and abandoned his spiritual teachers when these were all they had to offer him. In Buddhism, supernatural spiritual knowledge, like clairvoyance, remembrance of past lives, and insight into reality, is indeed said to follow the experience of the four lower meditations previously mentioned, but from these four higher meditations nothing practical is said to result during life. In the collection of texts called *Abhidharma*, however, those few who have attained these four superhuman higher meditations are said to proceed to the infinite states of being in the Arūpa-dhātu, to experience incredibly long-lasting lives and extreme bliss, and from there usually to attain final salvation or nirvāṇa.

These four immaterial heavens have no names other than the names of the meditations that produce them and differ from each other only in the length of life one is said to experience when reborn in them. In the first immaterial heaven, the infinity of space, one lives for 20,000 cosmic ages, or about eighty-six trillion years. In the next immaterial heaven, the infinity of mind, one lives 40,000 cosmic ages; in the third immaterial heaven, one lives 60,000 cosmic ages; and in the fourth immaterial heaven, one exists for 80,000 cosmic ages. The purely abstract and almost arbitrary nature of these heavens indicates that the early Buddhist scholars, faced with the task of systematizing the Buddha's teachings and setting up a fixed cosmology, were somewhat at a loss as to what to do with the Formless or Immaterial World.

See also HEAVENS, BUDDHIST; KĀMA-DHĀTU; NIRVĀṆA; REINCARNATION, EASTERN; RŪPA-DHĀTU.

References

Becker, Carl B. *Breaking the Circle: Death and the Afterlife in Buddhism*. Carbondale, IL: Southern Illinois University Press, 1993.

Kalupahana, David J. *The Principles of Buddhist Psychology*. Albany: State University of New York Press, 1987.

Kloetzli, Randy. *Buddhist Cosmology: From Single World System to Pure Land*. Delhi: Motilal Banarsidass, 1983.

La Vallée Poussin, Louis de, trans. *L'Abhidharmakosha de Vasubandhu*. Brussels: Mélanges chinois et bouddhiques, 1971.

Law, Bimala Churn. *Heaven and Hell in Buddhist Perspective*. Calcutta: Thacker, Spink, and Co., 1925.

Prebish, Charles S., ed. *Buddhism: A Modern Perspective*. University Park: Pennsylvania State University Press, 1978.

ASPHODEL FIELDS

In Greek myth, the Asphodel Fields (or Meadows) form the atrium of Hades, just inside the entrance, where shades gather after death. In this field the souls wait for the ferryman, Charon, to bring them over the boundary river, the Styx. Odysseus arrived there in his nekyia (his Underworld journey) (Book XI) where he saw many ghosts, including Orion, the hunter giant: "I saw huge Orion in a meadow full of asphodel, driving the ghosts of the wild beasts that he had killed upon the mountains, and he had a great bronze club in his hand, unbreakable for ever and ever" (Homer, *Odyssey,* Butler, trans.).

Asphodel is a kind of plant, related to the lily, that produces beautiful flowers and was an ancient staple food of Greece; it is still used for grazing sheep. Mythologist Robert Graves translates the Greek word *asphodel* as *a* meaning "not," *spodos* meaning "ash," and *elos* meaning "valley," literally "the valley of that which is not reduced to ashes," that is, the shades of the dead rather than their bodies. It may be because of this ultimate derivation that Greek poets associated the asphodel plant with immortality and made it grace the Underworld with its blooms. In the more theologically developed Hades of Roman times, the Asphodel Meadows were not merely the gathering place but the destination of those souls judged by Minos to be neither pure enough for Elysium nor wicked enough for Tartaros. And although it is not mentioned by name, the "meadow" in Plato's *Republic*, where souls congregate before choosing their next lives, is also traditionally identified with the Asphodel Fields.

See also ELYSION, ELYSIUM; HADES; TARTAROS.

References

Graves, Robert. *The Greek Myths*. New York: Penguin, 1960.

Homer. *The Odyssey*. Trans. Samuel Butler. New York: Barnes and Noble, 1993.

Plato. *The Republic*. Trans. Benjamin Jowett. New York: Random House, 1937.

Turner, Alice K. *The History of Hell*. New York: Harcourt Brace, 1993.

Kṛṣhna Teaches about Ātman

The man who believes that it is this spirit which kills, and he who thinks that it may be killed, are both deceived; for it neither kills nor is it killed. The spirit is not a thing of which a man may say "It has been, it is about to be, or it will be in the future," for it is without birth and does not die; it is ancient, constant and eternal, and is not slain when this mortal frame is destroyed. . . . As a man throws away old clothes and puts on new ones, even so the spirit in the body, leaving its old mortal frames, enters into others which are new. The weapon does not cut it, fire does not burn it, water does not corrode it, wind doesn't dry it away; for the spirit is indivisible, inconsumable, incorruptible, and cannot be dried up. It is eternal, universal, permanent, immovable; it is invisible, inconceivable, and unalterable; therefore, knowing it to be so, you should not grieve.

From the Bhagavad-Gita,
Chapter 2, trans. Judge (1986).

ĀTMAN

Simply put, ātman is the eternal spiritual self in Hindu philosophy. Even in the earliest Scriptures of Hindu tradition, the Vedas, the word *ātman* appears, and it already has as one of its meanings "the absolute, the first principle." We read in Rig Veda I.164.4,6 (Sharma, trans.):

Who has seen the primeval (being) at the time of his being born, as the boneless one [spirit] bears one that has bones [flesh]? Where is the [spiritual] breath, blood, and *ātman* of the earth? Who may repair to the sage to ask this? . . .

Not having seen, I ask the poets who have seen for the sake of knowing, not having known. Who has held apart firm these six regions, what then is that, in the form of the unborn?

The word *ātman* originally seems to have meant "spiritual breath," which since ancient times has been thought by many cultures to be the essence of life. In Taoism the spiritual master has control of the "nine breaths" and thus can change shape and become immortal; in the book of Genesis 1:2, "The spirit of God hovered over the waters," where "spirit" is the Hebrew word *ruach,* "wind."

But early on, *ātman* came to mean "breath" and much more. In many Vedic hymns to the gods, *ātman* refers to mind, air, self, essence, intelligence-principle, and so on. It is not surprising, then, that this word was singled out by Indian philosophers who were producing commentaries (Upanishads) on the Scriptures to indicate the absolute, imperishable, unchangeable, immortal part of the human being. Ātman witnesses reincarnation from life to life and experiences life in mortal frame after mortal frame, yet through all this it doesn't change. Rather, it is considered the witness only, that which experiences, but its own nature lies beyond all suffering, pleasure, or confusion. Although Hinduism discerns many "layers" or "sheaths" (koshas) of the human soul, it is best not to translate *ātman* as "soul" at all but rather "supreme spirit," for it is that which transcends all sheaths and conceptions of soul.

Ātman is not merely conceived of as an intangible "something," however; we find it characterized as almost a material object in some cases. Some Upanishadic passages speak of ātman as dwelling in the heart. For example, Katha Upanishad 2.20 (author's translation) states: "The *ātman*, which is subtler than what is subtle, greater than what is great, is seated in the cavity (*guhyam*) of the living being." Upon death, when the life energies of a being are scattering and leaving the body, the ātman is also thought to physically leave the body. Of the various 101 interconnecting "energy channels" (nādīs), only one, through the crown of the head, leads to immortality. If, through ignorance and confusion in the great rush of forces at death, the ātman is expelled from the body through any other opening, reincarnation must result. This is certainly meant on a literal level, and Hindu ascetics, called *yogis*, spend much time training for this important crisis at death. But on a symbolic level, if one does not know the correct channel of departure from the body, it symbolizes continued ignorance of reality and continuing karmic attachments to the world, resulting in the necessity of further life experience.

Finally, ātman is considered identical to the essence of the universe, called *Brahman*—the ultimate reality beyond all gods and ideas of gods. Brahman is *that which is*, and ātman is the ray of Brahman in human beings. To realize this, teach the Upanishads, is to become wise beyond all comprehension. It is ātman that is sought by Hindu meditators, the essence beyond all conception and rational thought: ātman can only be intuited, and directly perceived. To do this completely is to become utterly free of ignorance, personal desires, and the bondage to flesh, space, and time. For this reason, true realization of ātman is called *moksha*, "freedom," and those great masters of Hindu tradition who achieve it are called *jivan-muktas*, "those who have achieved utter freedom while still alive." After death, such beings leave no traces, yet they are said to sometimes aid humanity in its spiritual quest.

It is clear that this concept of ātman finds no corresponding idea in Western thought, except possibly in the "monad" as conceived by the German philosopher Gottfried Wilhelm Leibniz. Christian and Sufi Muslim mystics who have dared to proclaim their intuitive realization of unity with God have most often been branded as heretics and executed. In India, however, this union with the absolute through meditation on and absorption in the ātman is the center around which religion revolves. Although worship of deities and practice of rituals and sacrifices dominates the popular expression of Hindu spirituality, most philosophical treatments of Hinduism (by both practitioners and scholars) see these as symbolic preparations for ultimate union with the divine. By interacting with personifications of the divine (deities) and drawing near them in worship and devotion, one makes steps toward seeing the divine in one's self, and finally experiencing the nonduality of self and divine.

See also FUNERARY CUSTOMS, HINDU; NARAKA; SHIVA (HINDU); SOUL, HINDU; SVARGA; YAMA.

References

Beidler, William. *The Vision of Self in Early Vedānta*. New Delhi: Motilal Banarsidass, 1975.

Judge, William Quan, trans. *Bhagavad-Gita*. Los Angeles: Theosophy Company, 1986.

Keith, Arthur B. *The Religion and Philosophy of the Veda and Upanishads*. London: Oxford University Press, 1925.

Narahari, H. G. *Ātman in the Pre-Upanishadic Vedic Literature*. Madras: Adyar Library, 1944.

Sharma, Baldev Raj. *The Concept of Ātman in the Principal Upanishads*. New Delhi: Dinesh Publications, 1972.

Brut

[While Arthur was fighting the Romans in Burgundy, France, Mordred stole Arthur's kingdom and his queen. Arthur returns and battle ensues.]

Many of the mighty were massacred in that place
Of Arthur's loyal lieges, the high and the low,
And all of the Britons who were attached to his board,
Along with the fosterlings from lands far and wide,
While Arthur was shafted badly by a broad spear;
In fact he received fifteen fatal gashes.
In the greatest of these you could thrust two gloves!
Finally not a single person stood on that plain.
Two hundred thousand were hacked down to the ground,
Except for noble Arthur and two of his knights.
Arthur had been sorely wounded in a serious way.
Then up to him crept a youngster of his kin:
He was the son of Cador, the earl of Cornwall.
His name was Constantine; he was cousinly to the king.
Arthur gazed up at him as he groveled on the ground,
Whispering these words that betokened a woeful heart:
"Dear Constantine, son of Cador, please now hear me.
I bestow upon you now my entire British kingdom.
Please protect my British people for all of your life
And defend the laws that have lasted through my days . . .
I shall go forth to Avalon to the fairest of maidens,
To Argante [Morgan] the queen, the comeliest of fays,
And she shall heal my wounds and make me healthy
And sound, by preparing for me health-giving potions.
And then I shall come again into my own kingdom,
And I shall abide with my Britons in joyous bliss."
A light little boat came lilting over the waters
Even as he spoke, gliding in there from the sea,
And two women were in it of wonderful appearance.
They raised Arthur up and rapidly took him away;
They laid him softly down, and outwardly they sailed.

From Layamon's poem (c. 1200)
on British history, Brut *(verses, 14,256–14,288).*
Translation by Wilhelm (1986).

AVALON (AVALLON, AVILION)

Avalon is best known as the final resting place of King Arthur after he received mortal wounds in a battle with his treacherous nephew Mordred. Like related Celtic Otherworlds, Avalon is a beautiful summer land of goodness and plenty, quite the opposite of the gloomy Greek Hades or the Scandinavian Hel. Late medieval tradition made Morgan le Fay, Arthur's healer in Avalon, his half-sister; and for some centuries all of England was rife with apocalyptic expectations of Arthur's imminent return. Earlier tradition, however, makes Morgan purely a fairy spurned by Arthur in love and makes no mention of Arthur returning to save Britain from Saxon and French invaders. Nor was Avalon the afterlife of Arthur alone; it was the final home of many a hero and in origin was identical to the Celtic Otherworld of fairies and the dead.

Probably the name *Avalon* means "Land of Apples" (possibly from Welsh *afal*, apple), although there has been considerable debate on the etymology for more than a century. Designations in Latin (*Insula Pomorum*) and Welsh (*Ynys Avallach*) can also be literally translated "Apple Island" and thus lend credence to this view. One of the earliest references to Insula Pomorum or Avalon is in *The Life of Merlin*, a long poem by Geoffrey of Monmouth written circa 1150. The author explains that the island is called "fortunate" because "it produces crops in abundance and grapes without help; and apple trees spring up from the short grass in its woods. All plants, not merely grass alone, grow spontaneously; and men live a hundred years or more" (Clarke, trans.; all quotes from *The Life of Merlin* come from Clarke unless stated otherwise).

We also read of nine sister sorceresses, chief among them Morgan, who is greatly skilled at healing, shape shifting, and flying through the air. One of Arthur's assistants, the sage Taliesin, speaks:

> It was here we took Arthur after the battle of Camlan. . . . Morgen received us with due honor. She put the king in her chamber on a golden bed, uncovered his wound with her noble hand and looked long at it. At length she said he could be cured if only he stayed with her a long while and accepted her treatment. We therefore happily committed the king to her care and spread our sails to favorable winds on our return journey.

In this tradition, then, it is not Morgan le Fay herself who brings Arthur to Avalon but his noble aides. And unlike in later tradition, there is no mention of Arthur awakening to save Britain from the Saxon and Norman invaders; rather Merlin predicts that "Conan in his chariot" will arrive from Brittany "and that revered leader of the Welsh, Cadwalader."

Clearly Geoffrey of Monmouth is making up much of his rendition to suit his primary interest, which is with Merlin as patriotic prophet for Britain. However, much in Geoffrey's early tale goes back to even earlier Celtic sources. The Irish war goddess, the Morrigan, is likewise a final helper to her human love, Cú Chulainn, even though for most of his life the Morrigan spent her time opposing him for scorning her love. And in the story "Cú Chulainn's Sick Bed," the hero Cú Chulainn is mortally wounded on one occasion and is transported by boat to the Otherworld, Mag Mell. There Fand, wife of the god Manannán mac Lir, falls in love with him and cures him of his wounds. It is in the Otherworld that Cú Chulainn takes part in a great battle, at which he triumphs. The accounts differ, in that the hero Cú Chulainn is wounded not in combat like King Arthur but by fairy charms; again, the Otherworld is not his final resting place but merely one adventure among many. However, the Otherworld in each case is practically identical, being a land of perpetual summer, beauty, and health, located over the water.

But while dealing with various waves of invasion, the popular culture of the British twelfth century held a very literal belief in King Arthur's imminent return. In a poem by Étienne de Rouen circa 1170, *Draco Normannicus*, we even find that Arthur wrote a letter to King Henry II, chastising Henry and threatening to return and ruin him. As in all popular tradition, however, there was much variation and contradiction regarding Avalon—where was it located, and was that Arthur's true location? Some made Avalon identical to the "Antipodes," referring to a continent that popular belief held to exist in the "lower half" of the globe. Others made Avalon a physical island off the western coast of Britain, such as the Scilly Isles or Glasonbury. On the latter island Christian monks even claimed they had discovered Arthur's tomb. Other accounts stated that Arthur lay in enchanted asleep in a cave or under this or that specific hill or mound, waiting for someone to break the spell. There was even the story that Arthur had been transformed into a raven.

Gradually, however, the artists of elite literature developed and expanded the romantic themes of Arthur and the Knights of the Round Table, and Avalon and its caretakers received their due share of embellishment as well. In the long poem of Layamon (see excerpt), Morgan herself comes to bear Arthur away with her, even though many Arthurian texts, including *Huth Merlin* and *Malory,* go to great lengths to demonstrate Morgan's long-standing hatred of Arthur. We may presume, however, that because Guinevere has defected to the side of Arthur's rival, Mordred, Morgan le Fay is now able to actualize her love. Avalon, too, grew over time and became not merely the respite of Arthur but the final home of other heroes as well. In the English story *Sir Launfal*, the hero Launfal (like so many others) takes a fairy princess to wed and after many victories rides a white steed to Avalon, the home of his bride, the daughter of Avalon's king. Avalon was also the special realm of Morgan, where like a true Celtic fairy she lures many and sundry beautiful heroes into her arms; Lancelot is forced to pay her a visit, as are Arthur's cousin Ogier le Danois and also Renoart and Alisander L'Orphelin, neither of whom was even part of King Arthur's court.

Avalon does not serve merely as a foil for various heroic

Morte D'Arthur, the Death of Arthur—one tile of a set of twelve illustrating the Idylls of the King, *designed by John Moyr Smith for the Minton edition, c. 1875. Courtesy of Glessner House Museum.*

adventures, however; it has a direct connection with death, both literal and symbolic. The writer Gervase of Tilbury related a tale in 1212 in which a man loses his master's horse in the desolate area of Etna (a volcanic and liminal area, far removed from civilization—thus Otherworld events may take place there). The man comes upon a beautiful plain of delights, a magnificent palace, and Arthur on a royal bed. Arthur relates that he has wounds that open annually and thus he must remain in Avalon so that Morgan may tend him with her magic

medicine. But by now, as Loomis has pointed out, the physical battle between Arthur and Mordred has become an allegory of the seasons and Arthur a solar god, for his annual wounds signify the coming of winter and death. His eventual recovery signifies the return of spring and the powers of life. The death and rebirth of Arthur, then, is yet another example of the connection between a king's health and the well-being of his realm, believed in by most ancient peoples. A healthy, moral, and just king ensures a fertile kingdom, whereas an evil king or even one who was merely disfigured or unwhole (like the Irish king Nuada; see TUATHA DÉ DANANN) was unfit and had to be removed from rule. Although the expectation of the literal return of Arthur to save his subjects reified the symbolic meaning of the tale, it was in keeping with the ancient identification of the king and his realm and their mutual death and rebirth.

See also ANNWFN; MAG MELL; MORRIGAN; OTHERWORLD, IRISH; TUATHA DÉ DANANN.

References

Geoffrey of Monmouth. *The Life of Merlin*. Trans. Basil Clarke. Cardiff: University of Wales Press, 1973.

Loomis, Roger Sherman. *Celtic Myth and Arthurian Romance*. New York: Columbia University Press, 1926.

———. *Wales and the Arthurian Legend*. Cardiff: University of Wales Press, 1956.

Paton, Lucy Allen. *Studies in the Fairy Mythology of Arthurian Romance*. Boston: Ginn, 1903.

Wilhelm, James J., ed. *The Romance of Arthur*. Vol. 2. New York: Garland, 1986.

AVELUT

In Orthodox Judaism, the overall period of mourning after the deceased has been buried is called *avelut*, and the mourner is an *avel*. It commences with the recessional from the gravesite and marks a shift from honoring the dead to comforting the survivors. To symbolize this, the mourners march away from the grave through parallel lines of friends and more remote family relations. The friends and relations comfort the mourners who pass between with the following recitation: "Ha'makom yenachem et'chem b'toch she'ar avelei tziyon vi'Yerushalayim," which translates as, "May the Lord comfort you among the other mourners of Zion and Jerusalem." Arriving at the threshold of their home, the mourners wash their hands and enter into the restrictions of avelut.

The first seven days of avelut are called *shiva*, wherein the activities of the mourners are sharply curtailed. During the first three days of avelut, the avel is to receive no guests, refrain from giving or receiving greetings, and refrain from leaving the house except to attend religious services for the Sabbath or a high holiday. During the remaining days the mourner may receive guests, but the other prohibitions of shiva are still in force: no personal enjoyments (including Torah study and sexual relations), no beautification, no work (including most physical labor and chores), no fine or freshly cleaned clothing, and no leather shoes; the avel must wear the ritually torn upper garment, sit on low benches, and avoid most personal bodily care. Mourners attend religious services in the home, if they can be arranged, and say the kaddish prayer daily for the dead.

After shiva has ended, mourners enter into sheloshim, which lasts twenty-three days from the date of burial (after the seven days of shiva). Avels are encouraged to leave the home but to continue to avoid parties. They may now wear newly cleaned clothing but must continue to avoid wearing brand-new clothing, and although personal hygiene begins to return to normal, men are still expected to avoid shaving and cutting their hair. The kaddish is still said daily for the dead. If one is grieving children, siblings, or a spouse, the formal period of mourning ends at the conclusion of sheloshim, on the morning of the thirtieth day after the burial. Sadness may indeed persist long after the month of sheloshim, but ritual observation of grief ceases.

However, if one is mourning one's parents, avelut continues for a full year (twelve months of the Hebrew calendar, which is not always a full solar year), but the restrictions and duties become minimal. The kaddish is still recited as part of all daily, Sabbath, and holiday prayers, and the mourner is still expected to avoid joyous occasions (such as marriages and parties) except religiously required celebrations.

See also FUNERARY CUSTOMS, JEWISH; KADDISH; KERI'AH; SHELOSHIM; SHIVA (JEWISH); SOUL, JEWISH; YAHRZEIT; YIZKOR.

References

Abramovitch, Henry. "Death." In *Contemporary Jewish Religious Thought,* ed. Arthur A. Cohen and Paul Mendes-Flohr. New York: Charles Scribner's Sons, 1989.

Lamm, Maurice. *The Jewish Way in Death and Mourning*. New York: Jonathan David Publishers, 1969.

Rabinowicz, H. *A Guide to Life*. London: Jewish Chronicle Publications, 1964.

Riemer, Jack, ed. *Jewish Reflections on Death*. New York: Schocken Books, 1974.

AVERNUS

Literally "apple land" (from the Indo-European root *abol,* "apple"), Avernus was the primary gateway to the Underworld in the classical world. Near the city of Cumae on the southwestern coast of Italy, the Romans believed there was an entrance to the Underworld. It was a great cave hidden in a shady valley surrounded by dark waters and a thick forest. The Roman epic, the *Aeneid,* describes the place only briefly (Book IV, 318–322; Mandelbaum, trans.):

> There was a wide-mouthed cavern, deep and vast
> and rugged, sheltered by a shadowed lake
> and darkened groves; such vapor poured from those
> black jaws to heaven's vault, no bird could fly
> above unharmed (for which the Greeks have called
> the place "Aornos," or "The Birdless").

Within the forest near Avernus was hidden a tree—girded in mistletoe and growing a golden bough with golden fruit—sacred to Proserpina (in Greek, Persephone), queen of the Underworld. In the *Aeneid,* it was this bough that the prophetess told the hero Aeneas to break off and carry with him if he were to gain entrance to the Underworld. Guided by a pair of doves, birds sacred to Aeneus's mother Venus, the hero found the golden bough. With it he was able to persuade Charon, the Underworld ferryman, to take him across the River Styx ("Hated") and eventually gain entrance into Elysion in order to consult with his father, Anchises.

See also AORNUS; ELYSION, ELYSIUM; GEHENNA; HELL, HISTORY OF; HELL, ORIGINS OF; ISLANDS OF THE BLEST; TARTAROS; UNDERWORLD; WATER.

References

Mandelbaum, Allen, trans. *The* Aeneid *of Virgil*. New York: Bantam Books, 1971.

Turner, Alice K. *The History of Hell*. New York: Harcourt Brace, 1993.

B

BALDACCHINO TOMB

Literally "canopy" in Italian, the baldacchino style of tomb is a particular type of catacomb rare in Rome but popular in parts of Sicily, Malta, and Naples. Absent are the long galleries with carved locculi and arcosolia typical of Roman catacombs; rather the baldacchino are carved in small clusters connected by short passages with large open spaces suitable for Christian meetings. Baldacchino tombs are characterized by pillars of natural rock from floor to ceiling that were left untouched when the chambers were carved out in a honeycomb fashion. In Sicily they are also characterized by unusually large arcosolia capable of housing a number of bodies. To protect the tombs of martyrs and other esteemed dead, the entrance to these tombs was sometimes blocked by a transenna, a grille made of marble or stone and perforated in simple rows. The origin of the baldacchino is probably from surface cemeteries covered by a roof supported by pillars, which was then transferred underground.

References
Stevenson, James. *The Catacombs: Life and Death in Early Christianity*. London: Thames and Hudson, 1978.

BANSHEE

From the Irish *bean sídhe,* literally "fairy woman," this female ghost appears and utters heartrending wails when a death is imminent. Though more often heard than seen, the banshee is said to be old and wan, combing her long white hair as she shrieks. She is said to appear only to those with "Ó" or "Mac" in their surname, that is, those descended from noble Irish families, though banshee traditions are found in the Scottish highlands as well.

Omens of impending death are known worldwide, but the keening female spirit is unique to the Gaelic world, probably having its origin in the ancient Gaelic idea that each region had its own earth/war goddess. Indeed, in some regions the banshee is known as the *Badhbh* (pronounced "bow"), one of the names of the Morrigan. The human king of the region was thought to be mystically mated with the goddess and protected by her. In time each noble family came to have a patron goddess who protected its interests and estate.

In folk tradition the banshee functions purely as an omen of death, but in the literary tradition the banshee preserves some of its more ancient nature, appearing as a muse to inspire poets and encourage kings. It was probably during the difficult sixteenth and seventeenth centuries, when England was seizing land and inflicting great damage on Irish people, that the banshee's shift from muse to omen took place, along with the emphasis that she appeared to Gaelic (not English) families.

See also FUNERARY CUSTOMS, CELTIC; MORRIGAN; SÍD; UNDEAD.
References
Byrne, Patrick. *Irish Ghost Stories*. Cork: Mercier Press, n.d.
Dunne, John J. *Haunted Ireland*. Belfast: Appletree Press, 1977.
Lysaght, Patricia. *The Banshee*. Dublin: Glendale Press, 1986.
Ó hÓgáin, Dáithí. *Myth, Legend and Romance: An Encyclopaedia of the Irish Folk Tradition*. New York: Prentice Hall, 1991.

BARDO

From the Tibetan, *Bardo* may be translated literally as "the Between," with two primary meanings. The most general meaning is the intermediate state in Tibetan Buddhism, after death but before rebirth. The second, more technical meaning is the set of "six betweens": (1) "(ordinary) life," which is between physical birth and physical death; (2) "dream," which falls between waking and deep sleep; (3) "contemplation," which is between regular consciousness and transcendent awareness; (4) "the death point," the hyperconscious period between physical death and existence in an energy body; (5) "reality," which comes between the death point and falling into a new rebirth; and (6) "becoming," which is between the "reality" phase of death and physical conception. Three of these six Bardos are found during physical life; three are found in the afterdeath process.

The most important classical text dealing with the Bardos is the Bardo Thödol, best known in the West under the title the Tibetan Book of the Dead, but better translated as "liberation through understanding in the Between." The main message of the text is that the Bardo states after death are crises of immense importance, for in them one may seek absolute enlightenment, which if achieved would free one from rebirth and re-death. Failing that, one may be drawn again into various rebirths, including heaven, a new human birth, or the very worst kinds of hell. Thus the descriptions of the Bardo states are very detailed, enabling one, it is thought, to recognize the process and thus exert some control over it.

According to the Bardo Thödol, physical death is only the beginning of the death process. The mind and various subtle energies withdraw from the physical body by means of hundreds of channels and then begin to dissolve into each other. The earth energy of the dying person dissolves into the water energy, and there is a corresponding feeling of weakness and loss of sight. Then the water energy of the dying dissolves into the air energy, and the dying person feels as if he or she is "drying out" and suffers a loss of hearing. As each basic energy fades into the next, the dying is said to feel particular unpleasant sensations and lose more physical abilities. After many adventures in consciousness and passages through energy fields, the mind of the dead person finds that it has awakened into a realm of clear light and nondualistic consciousness. There is no longer the distinction between "self" and "other," and all things are one. Now the dead person has truly died and plunged into the deepest nature of mind: a mystical union that is empty of all content.

Failing to recognize that essence, most people do not experience nirvāṇa (Buddhist enlightenment) and continue onward in the Bardo. They find themselves in subtle energy bodies, created spontaneously by the mind and karma, and they wander from plane to plane and experience to experience. They encounter various intensely beautiful sights: peaceful deities and marvelous bright lights that attempt to draw them in. In the Tibetan Book of the Dead, it is described to the deceased:

> Hey noble one! At this time when your mind
> and body are parting ways, pure reality manifests in
> subtle, dazzling visions, vividly experienced,
> naturally frightening and worrisome, shimmering
> like a mirage on the plains in autumn. Do not fear
> them! . . . Whatever sounds, light, and rays may
> come at you, they cannot hurt you. You cannot die.
> It is enough just for you to recognize them as your
> own perceptions. Understand that this is the
> *between.* (Thurman)

If the soul resists being absorbed in the lights, it fails another chance at enlightenment and soon encounters various fear-provoking wrathful deities. There are also visions of family, friends, and the old body of the deceased, provoking nostalgia, longing, and regret. Various other torments, fears, and sufferings arise because of karma.

Finally, perhaps the most terrifying aspect of all looms in the Bardo: the judgment of Yama, god of death. Upon entering his iron hall, without windows or doors, the hapless Bardo traveler unavoidably encounters Yama. He is fearsome to behold: bluish black in color, red eyes ablaze, head like a buffalo's, and in his hand a skull with the spinal cord still attached. Standing naked with phallus erect on the back of a fire-breathing buffalo, Yama personifies both the energies and desires of life and the morbidity and terror of death. As his minions gather about, Yama weighs the good and evil deeds of the deceased and then sends them on to the various heavenly or human realms if their virtue predominates or to the animal and hellish realms if their sins predominate. Then, wandering in view of various couples making love, the soul is attracted to one or another pair and enters into their love act, sparking conception. The soul will feel desire for the male or female partner and, becoming jealous of the other, take on that gender. Thus the soul leaves the Bardo state and reincarnates once more.

Late Indian and Tibetan Buddhist philosophy explains the Bardo states and the various experiences therein as simply manifestations of one's own energy, since one's true nature is ultimately that of an unlimited, enlightened being. The Bardo is no objective reality (any more than earthly life, Buddhist philosophers claim), but the manifestation of one's own nature. In fact, however, most Buddhist lay people take these experiences and the deities encountered in the Bardo, particularly the judgment of the god of death, as very real.

References

Lodö, Lama. *Bardo Teachings*. Ithaca, NY: Snow Lion, 1987.

Mullin, Glenn H. *Death and Dying: The Tibetan Tradition.* Boston: Arkana, 1986.

Rinbochay, Lati, and Jeffrey Hopkins. *Death, Intermediate State and Rebirth in Tibetan Buddhism.* London: Rider and Company, 1979.

Rinpoche, Chokyi Nyima. *The Bardo Guidebook.* Kathmandu: Harper San Francisco, 1991.

Rinpoche, Sogyal. *The Tibetan Book of Living and Dying.* San Francisco: Harper San Francisco, 1992.

Thurman, Robert, trans. *The Tibetan Book of the Dead.* New York: Bantam, 1994.

BARROW

Barrow derives from the Old English *beorh* and Old Norse and German *berg* (mountain) cognate with the Old Irish *brigh* (mountain), and Sanskrit *brihāt* (height). The word *barrow* is synonymous with *tumulus,* but the term *tumulus* is mostly applied to burial mounds in the Mediterranean and Near East, whereas burial mounds in northern and western Europe are called barrows. In Old English *barrow* originally meant a mountain or hill, but today (except in some British dialects) its primary meaning is a round or oblong man-made mound of earth or sometimes piled stones, though the latter is

From *Beowulf*

Then the Geats prepared a pyre for him
on the earth—no petty one, indeed—
hung about with helmets, battle-shields,
bright mail-coats, as he had requested.
In its midst men laid the famous prince,
lamenting their belovéd lord.
On the barrow warriors began to wake
the greatest of funeral-fires; smoke rose
black above the blaze, the roaring flame
mixed with weeping—the wind died away—
till the fire had charred his frame of bone,
hot consumed his heart. Sad in spirit,
they mourned their distress, their liege-lord's death;
likewise, a Geatish woman, with hair
bound up, sang a lament for Beowulf,
dolefully, frequently saying
she feared hard days of mourning lay ahead,
many times of slaughter, war-terror,
harm, captivity. Heaven swallowed the smoke.
Then the people of the Weders built
a mound on the bluff, high and broad,
widely seen by travelers on the waves:
in ten days they built that monument
to the brave warrior, encased in walls
the remnants of the fire, in the most
worthy structure wise men could devise.
In the barrow they set rings and gems,
all such ornaments as warlike men
had earlier taken from the [dragon's] hoard:
they left the wealth of warriors for earth
to hold, gold in the ground, where it still lies,
as useless to men as it ever was.
The battle-brave sons of high-born men,
twelve in all, rode around the mound
to bewail their care and mourn their king,
compose sad lays and speak of the man:
they praised his prowess and applauded
his brave deeds. So is it proper
that a man outwardly honor his lord,
love him in his heart, when his spirit
has been led forth from his body.
Thus his hearth-companions in the host
of the Geats mourned the going of their lord:
they said that of worldly kings he was
the mildest of men and the gentlest,
most kind to his people, most eager for fame.

From Greenfield
(1982, p. 141, verses 3137–3182).

more correctly termed a *cairn.* The cairn is solid stone, but the barrow has a tunnel entrance and one or more inner chambers where the dead and his or her belongings are placed. Larger barrows could accommodate many people, and the entrance tunnel, filled with earth after the last burial, would be dug out again with each successive interment.

A barrow may be great or small, from the huge mounds covering the great megalithic tombs of prehistory to the humble heaps over individual graves, though generally it is only the larger barrows for significant dead that have been preserved into the modern era. Barrows might be raised right where death occurred, over a lonely headland overlooking the sea, or near a river. Dangerous characters especially seem to be buried near water, as in the Icelandic *Eyrbyggia Saga,* in which the undead body of Þórólfr Baegifótr is removed to a ness (promontory) because of his haunting. In quite ancient times it was thought that the souls of the dead departed over water, from whence they could not cross back over (see SOUL). In general, however, the dangerous dead—murdered men and witches—were not given barrows but were covered with turf and stones, presumably to hold them down.

The old Anglo-Saxon hero Beowulf asked to be buried in a mound on a headland, not because he anticipated being a restless ghost but so that his fame might be seen by all passing sailors:

Bid my renowned warriors raise a noble barrow after the burning, on a headland by the sea. It shall be a memorial to my people, as it towers high upon Whale's Ness, so that those who fare across the sea shall in after days name it the mound of Beowulf, when they urge their tall ships far over the misty deep. (Greenfield, trans., 2802–2808)

The barrow was not merely a burial place but literally a *dwelling* for the still-conscious dead, who in Germanic, Scandinavian, Irish, Gaulish, and Anglo-Saxon traditions were thought of as sitting within, keeping jealous watch over their buried treasure and magnificent weapons. The Icelandic *Landnámabók* makes a number of references to prominent Icelandic families who believed that after death, they would pass into particular hills or mountains near their home. The Lapps too seem to have believed that the dead lived in mountains.

Barrows, because of their powerful contents, sometimes became centers of power for the living as well. Some barrows were centers from which kings could make announcements to their people; for instance, to this day on the Isle of Man the Manx Parliament still assembles on the Bronze Age burial mound of Tynwald Hill. Old Irish kings were often consecrated

Newly excavated long barrow (tumulus) near West Kennet, Wiltshire, 1913. This burial chamber contained four skeletons, as well as flint flakes, flint cores, pottery, and a number of artifacts. Courtesy of Anne Ronan Picture Library.

his men sleep beneath the hill of Craig-y-Dinas. Likewise the Irish Fionn and his men rest beneath a hill in the Highlands, only to arise in some future crisis.

See also CAIRN; FAIRY MOUND; MAUSOLEUM; MEGALITHIC TOMB; MOUND; SÍD; TUMULUS.

References

Ashbee, Paul. *The Earthen Long Barrow in Britain*. London: J. M. Dent and Sons, 1970.

Colvin, Howard. *Architecture and the After-Life*. New Haven: Yale University Press, 1991.

Dunning, G. C., and R. F. Jessup. "Roman Barrows." *Antiquity* 10 (1936).

Ellis, Hilda Roderick. *The Road to Hel: A Study of the Conception of the Dead in Old Norse Literature*. Cambridge: Cambridge University Press, 1943.

Greenfield, Stanley B. *A Readable Beowulf*. Carbondale: Southern Illinois University Press, 1982.

Henshall, A. H. *The Chambered Tombs of Scotland*. 2 vols. Edinburgh: Edinburgh University Press, 1963, 1972.

Meaney, Audrey. *A Gazetteer of Early Anglo-Saxon Burial Sites*. London: George Allen and Unwin, 1964.

Piggott, S. *Neolithic Cultures of the British Isles*. Cambridge: Cambridge University Press, 1954.

Powell, T. G. E. *Megalithic Enquiries in the West of England*. Liverpool: Liverpool University Press, 1969.

Twohig, E. Shee. *The Megalithic Art of Western Europe*. Oxford: Clarendon Press, 1981.

on ancestral burial mounds, and heroes of Celtic literature frequently slept overnight on burial mounds, seeking oracles and answers to vexing questions. For instance, when the epic poem *Táin* was lost, two bards slept on the tomb of Fergus MacRoy, the composer, whereupon the poet appeared to them and proceeded to recite it. In the Norse *Volsunga Saga* one king sits on a mound to receive a son, and in the Helgi poems a young prince meets his guardian spirit on a mound, who gives him his name and tells him of his high destiny.

For the elite dead, the goods buried within the sometimes massive mounds could be truly amazing. Often the wives of the heroes and even household servants and friends would be buried along with them. In one saga (not necessarily historically accurate, of course) the Viking Raknar is buried sitting in a chair, along with his ship and 500 men. Furthermore, as warriors were frequently buried with full armor, weapons, and men, their mounds served as a military deterrent to sinister forces seeking to do harm to the community, turning back invading armies and causing the death of their warriors on the field. This protection was not merely symbolic: frequently these mound-dwelling heroes are thought not to have died at all but to be merely asleep, awaiting the hour of their people's need. In some versions of the King Arthur epic, after death Arthur dwells in Avalon, but in other versions of the cycle, Arthur and

BARZAKH

The Arabic word *barzakh* (related to the Persian *farsakh*) means a barrier, hindrance, or separation. Although in the Qur'ān the word *al-barzakh* appears to mean "the barrier" between the living and the dead, in later Islam it came to have more of a cosmic meaning, which should perhaps be translated as "the limbo" where the spirits of the dead exist, awaiting the Hour (Sā'a) when God will bring about the Resurrection (Qiyāma).

Early Islam under the guidance of the Prophet Muhammed was little concerned with the cosmological details of death and any intermediate state. Again and again, the Scripture given form by Muhammed emphasized the necessity of moral behavior during life on earth because of the certainty of future resurrection—whereupon those brought to life again would be judged and sent to heaven or hell. Of the state between physical death and physical resurrection, the Qur'ān and the early traditions say nothing. What the Qur'ān does say is that one's only chance for good deeds is during earthly life, for there will be no chances after death to make up for mistakes. We read in sura 23:100–102:

> When death comes to a wrongdoer, he will say: "Lord, let me go back, that I may do good works in the world I have left behind."
>
> Never! These are the very words which he will speak. Behind them there shall stand a barrier

(al-barzakh) till the Day of Resurrection. And when the Trumpet is sounded, on that day their ties of kindred shall be broken, nor shall they ask help of one another.

Here, the usage of al-barzakh exhorts one to morality but says nothing of what happens before resurrection and judgment. Two other usages of the term relate the same thing, though they don't even have to do with the dead. Suras 25:55 and 55:60 mention the "insurmountable barrier" that God places between the two oceans, salt water and fresh. The term "barrier" in early Islam, then, meant that the dead were irretrievably separated from earthly life, and early Islamic thinkers understood this to mean as well that there could be no communication between the living and the dead. The Qur'ān (35:19–22) specifically affirms this understanding: "The blind and the seeing are not equal, nor are the darkness and the light. The shade and the heat are not equal, nor are the living and the dead. God can cause whom He will to hear Him, but you cannot make those who are in their grave hear you." There is a similar statement at sura 27:80, where the Qur'ān says, "You cannot make the dead hear you, nor can you make the deaf hear your call."

But popular tradition strongly contradicted this teaching. Pre-Islamic beliefs in ghosts and communications with the dead carried on right into the early centuries of Islam, whatever the theologians and philosophers might write. Islam is rich with ghost stories in which the dead in fact do visit the living in person, and the dead are quite "alive" and present during the washing of the corpse and the burial. Families that do not appropriately care for the dead and mourn him or her, according to many popular stories, may expect serious trouble from the dead.

One way Muslim theologians of later times (eleventh to fifteenth centuries) dealt with this recognized conflict was to affirm contact between the living and the dead in the context of dreams while avoiding mention of the actual presence of the spirits of the dead on earth. Eventually, this mix of popular belief and theology was to expand the interpretation of al-barzakh. Rather than simply an "obstacle," it became an actual plane of existence, existing on the boundaries (as a "barrier") between earth, heaven, and hell. There the dead existed spiritually (while still being physically present in their graves) and awaited the coming of the resurrection in full consciousness. Though prevented by the barrier from interacting with the living, it was possible that the living could visit al-barzakh in their dreams and meet with the dead there. This serves to explain, in an orthodox manner, stories of relatives being visited by the dead and given blessings or, more often, reprimands. For example, the twelfth-century theologian

al-Ghazālī, in his book *al-Durra al-fākhirah*, writes:

Someone has related this story: Our father engaged for us a teacher to teach us our lessons at home. Then the teacher died, and after six days we went to his grave to visit him, reminding each other of God's will. Someone passed by us selling a plate of figs, which we bought and ate, throwing the stems onto the grave. When night came, the father saw the dead man in a dream, and said to him, "How are you?" "Fine," he replied, "except that your children took my grave for a garbage pile and spoke about me, saying I was nothing but an infidel." The father reprimanded us, and we said [to each other], "Glory be to God. He continues to bother us in the hereafter just as he did on earth." (Smith, trans., "Concourse Between the Living and the Dead")

One very well known author from the fifteenth century, al-Suyūṭī, describes two kinds of dead, the blest and the punished. The sinful souls are too busy with their temporary punishments (which occupy them until the Final Judgment places them in Jahannam, or hell) to be able to interact with others. But the souls of faithful Muslims are able to travel about, meet with others, and occasionally even visit the living through the "bridge" afforded by their dreams, as shown in the previous quote. Although some authors believe that paradise and hell will only be created by God at the end of time, al-Suyūṭī believed that they exist already and are being experienced in a preliminary way by the dead now. Thus, martyrs exist as green birds in the highest heaven, flying about its meadows and gardens, and true believers (mu'minūn) exist in al-barzakh doing as they please, perhaps able to visit the seven heavens in bird form as well. Meanwhile, the damned (kāfirūn) are devoured by huge black birds in hell. Most often the dead appear to gather into a company (rafīq) of similar spirits to share information and conversation.

The trouble with such later theological explanations that incorporate popular tales and legends is that they not only appear to contradict the original Scriptures but also tend not to make strict logical sense. How is it that the dead are said to be present in the family home for up to a month and in the grave for up to a year or more, while conversing with other spirits in al-barzakh and yet simultaneously enjoying the afterlife as a bird in heaven? Interestingly, al-Suyūṭī addresses this point directly. He writes that it was due to the limited perception of the living that confusion arises. The seen is not like the unseen, and although a physical body can only be in one place at a time, the spirit is not likewise bound.

The spirit there [al-barzakh] is in the likeness of a body and is connected with the body so that it prays in its grave and returns [the] peace [of God, which visitors to the grave offer]. Yet the spirit returns [to the heavens] and is in the highest group [rafīq] and there is no contradiction between these two things; for the condition of the spirits is not the condition of the bodies. (Smith and Haddad, trans.)

Although some mystic elements in Islam have suggested that reincarnation (as a special case or as a general rule) may take place after a "waiting period" in al-barzakh (see the article by Margaret Smith), this is by far a minority view in Islam.

See also ISRĀFĪL; 'IZRĀ'ĪL; JAHANNAM; JUDGMENT, LAST; JUDGMENT, PARTICULAR; PURGATORY; QIYĀMA; SĀ'A; SOUL, MUSLIM.

References

De Vaux, B. Carra. "Barzakh." In *Encyclopedia of Islam.* Leiden: E. J. Brill, 1979.

Eklund, E. *Life between Death and Resurrection according to Islam.* Uppsala: Almquist and Wilksells, 1941.

Macdonald, John. "The Twilight of the Dead." *Islamic Studies* 4, no. 1 (1965).

Smith, Jane I. "Concourse between the Living and the Dead in Islamic Eschatological Literature." *History of Religions* 19, no. 3 (1980).

Smith, Jane I., and Yvonne Yazbeck Haddad. *The Islamic Understanding of Death and Resurrection.* Albany: SUNY Press, 1981.

Smith, Margaret. "Transmigration and the Sufis." *Muslim World* 30 (1940).

Tritton, A. S. "Muslim Funeral Custom." *Bulletin of the School of Oriental and African Studies* 9, no. 3 (1938).

BEHESHT

The Zoroastrian doctrine of Behesht, "heaven" (or rather *seven* heavens), is surprisingly familiar to many Westerners because the Zoroastrian Behesht had a tremendous impact upon the development of the doctrine of heaven in early Judaism, Christianity, and Islam. *Behesht*, a Persian word, is etymologically related to the English word *best:* both mean "most excellent," though the English word became an adjective and the Persian a noun. (The ultimate origin of the word *behesht* is the ancient Avestan word *vahishta,* which became *wahisht* in the medieval Persian language, Pahlavi.) Like the Christian heaven, the Zoroastrian Behesht is the destiny of the good soul whose good deeds at least outweigh any evil ones. (Those whose evil and good are about equal go to neither Behesht nor Dozakh, or hell, but to an intermediate place called *Hamestegān.*) Also like the current Christian understanding of heaven, Behesht is the destiny of the soul, not the body. Zoroastrians, like members of other Western traditions, believe in a future resurrection, but it occurs at the end of time instead of after the death of an individual.

What is significant about the Zoroastrian heaven is that it has seven levels of blessedness, each greater than the one before it. Seven is an extremely important symbol in Zoroastrian doctrine: there are seven aspects to the godhead, seven classes of demonic opponents, and so on. The greater the soul's goodness, the higher the heaven it will enter for its afterlife reward. However, Zoroastrian traditions differ as to exactly what the seven heavens are. According to the great Indian Zoroastrian Sohrabji Meherjirani in his 1869 work *Rehbar-e Din-e Jarthushti,* the seven levels of heaven are as follows (Kotwal and Boyd):

1. *Starpay*	"star station"
2. *Mahpay*	"moon station"
3. *Khorshed pay*	"sun station"
4. *Garothman*	"abode of songs"
5. *Pashum*	"best"
6. *Akhvan*	"existence, being, world"
7. *Anagra Raochah*	"endless lights"

However, a modern Zoroastrian scholar, Dastur Firoze M. Kotwal, commented on Meherjirani's text and explained that according to a more ancient and authoritative text, the ninth-century C.E. text Dadestan-i-Denig (Religious Decisions, written in the priestly language of Pahlavi), a somewhat different listing of the heavens is given (Kotwal and Boyd):

1. *Humat*	"good thoughts"
2. *Hukht*	"good words"
3. *Hwarsht*	"good deeds"
4. *Starpay*	"star station"
5. *Mahpay*	"moon station"
6. *Khorshed pay*	"sun station"
7. *Garothman*	"abode of songs"

According to Kotwal, the other "levels" described by Meherjirani, Pashum (best), Akhvan (existence), and Anagra Raochah (endless lights), are merely descriptions of the highest heaven Garothman (from *Garodemāna* in the early Avestan language). In general, learned Zoroastrians take these heavens to be not physical or ethereal locations but subjective states in the soul.

In any case, many scholars believe that it is through Zoroastrian influence on early Pharisaic Judaism during the exile and diaspora (sixth through first centuries B.C.E.) that the number seven and concepts of *eternal* heavens and hells entered Western apocalyptic thought. For example, this influence can be seen in the New Testament Book of Revelation with its "seven churches" and "seven angels pouring seven pestilences" as well as such phrases as "seventh heaven."

The Soul's Ascent

The first step that the soul of the righteous person made, placed him in the Good Thought paradise; the second step that the soul of the righteous person made, placed him in the Good Word paradise; the third step that the soul of the righteous person made, placed him in the Good Deed paradise; the fourth step that the soul of the righteous person made, placed him in the Endless Lights.

From Yasht 22:15. Translation by Dhalla (1914).

See also AMERETAT; CHINVAT BRIDGE; DOZAKH; FRASHO-KERETI; FRAVASHI; HAMESTEGĀN; RESURRECTION, HEBREW; RISTAKHEZ; SOUL, ZOROASTRIAN.

References

Bode, Dastur F. A. "Man, Soul, Immortality in Zoroastrianism," speech delivered at Portiuncula Firary, Karachi, December 1971.

Dhalla, M. N. *Zoroastrian Theology from the Earliest Times to the Present Day.* Reprint, New York: AMS Press, 1972.

Jackson, A. V. W. *Zoroastrian Studies.* New York: Columbia University Press, 1928.

Kotwal, Dastur Firoze M., and James W. Boyd, trans. *A Guide to the Zoroastrian Religion.* Studies in World Religion no. 3. Chico, CA: Scholars Press, 1982.

Masani, Sir Rustom. *Zoroastrianism: The Religion of the Good Life.* New York: Collier Books, 1962.

Sethna, Tehmurasp Rustamji. *Book of Instructions on Zoroastrian Religion.* Karachi: Informal Religious Meetings Trust Fund, 1980.1

Sidhwa, Ervad Godrej Dinshawji. *Discourses on Zoroastrianism.* Karachi: Ervad Godrej Dinshawji Sidhwa, 1978.

BHAVA-CHAKRA

Literally "the wheel of life" or "the wheel of becoming," the bhava-chakra is a round diagram used by Buddhist teachers to explain to lay Buddhists the nature of birth, death, and reincarnation. The wheel is divided into six compartments, which are the six realms of rebirth ordinarily possible for beings in our world, namely the eight or more hells, the realm of "hungry ghosts" (called *prets* in Sanskrit), the animal kingdom, the human world, the estate of the demigods, and the heavens of the gods. (The six realms are described in more detail in the entry on KĀMA-DHĀTU.) Each of the six compartments contains miniature paintings of the dwellers in each realm and their experiences, happy and unhappy. For instance, in the lowest compartment of the wheel, representing the hells, are pictures of the judgment of the dead by the god Yama; scenes of torment such as dismemberment, burning, and hanging; and colorful pictures of rivers of fire, spiked mountains, and such. The compartment for the hungry ghosts shows their gaunt forms, with huge bellies and pencil-thin necks, searching for food and water to assuage their endless hunger and thirst; sadly, whatever they put in their mouths turns to ashes. The panel for the demigods shows them in rich, brightly colored clothes, making love in their palaces and making war upon the gods higher up in the diagram, of whom they are irrepressibly jealous. Interestingly, in each of the six compartments a Buddha figure is drawn in the center, demonstrating that the wisdom and compassion of the Buddha is present throughout the universe and that through faith and Buddhist practice one can always improve one's future births.

However, the entire wheel with all of its six compartments is surrounded by a massive and horrifying demon, representing the endlessness of desire and craving: its fangs grip the wheel on its top, its claws grasp the wheel on either side, and its ugly feet stick out below. This signifies the fact that in Buddhism, any rebirth, even in the highest heavens, is a temporary state destined to end sooner or later and plagued by the sufferings of aging and death. In Buddhist philosophy, life itself, with its cravings and vain pursuits, inherently involves suffering, and it can be avoided only by seeking the release of nirvāṇa—the goal of the monastic life of moderation and meditation. In popular Buddhism, however, rebirth in one of the heavens is a primary goal of religious practice, and nirvāṇa is largely ignored.

The Buddha's Last Words

[As the Buddha lay dying, he said:] "Have done, Ānanda, do not weep, do not distress yourself! Have I not often told you that it is in the very nature of things that we must eventually be parted from all that is near and dear to us? For how, Ānanda, can it be otherwise? Since everything born, evolved, and organized contains within itself the germs of disintegration, how can it be otherwise than that a being should pass away? No other condition is possible!

"It may be, Ānanda, that some of you will have the idea 'The word of the Teacher is no more, and now we are without a leader!' But, Ānanda, you must not think of it like this. The Dharma, and the Rules for the Sangha which I have expounded and laid down for you, let them after I am gone be your Teacher."

Then the Buddha addressed the monks and said: "This I tell you, Bhikkhus. Decay is inherent in all conditioned things. Work out your own salvation, with diligence."

Adapted from Humphreys (1961, p. 94).

The Tibetan wheel of transmigration. Courtesy of Metropolitan Museum of Art.

Among both monastics and lay Buddhists, however, one teaching is accepted as fundamental, and this is karma, translatable perhaps as "the law of ethical retribution." Briefly stated, death is inevitable to all beings, and one's rebirth is determined entirely by one's good or evil works, words, and thoughts. Thus, after death, those who spent their lives pursuing wealth, slandering neighbors, and thinking evil of others will certainly be reborn in one of the hells, spending many thousands and even millions of years in suffering. Those who spent their lives in altruism, charity, and religious pursuits will surely be reborn in one of the heavens, again to spend nearly innumerable years in bliss. In either case, however, the experience comes to an end, and one is once again reborn, again according to one's past karma. Thus one may whirl endlessly from birth among humans to rebirth in hell to birth again as an animal and again as a demigod. For this reason, the bhava-chakra is painted as a circle or wheel, demonstrating the rotation from life to life. This whirling is called *samsara* and is endless until one attains enlightenment and escapes bhava-chakra altogether. For this reason, Buddhism considers the attainment of enlightenment the pinnacle of life. A Buddha is considered a higher form of life than any of the gods, even the most blissful and longest-lived, because a Buddha has gained insight into the "chain of causation," or the series of twelve mental and physical events that leads to rebirth over and over; as a result a Buddha is enlightened and therefore liberated.

Miniature pictures representing this chain of twelve causes leading to rebirth are painted in twelve smaller compartments along the outer rim of the bhava-chakra diagram. In brief, these twelve causes and their Buddhist Sanskrit terms are as follows:

1. Ignorance (avidyā) (in passing from death into the next life), leading to
2. Mental deposits (saṃskāra) from the last life, leading to
3. Deluded consciousness (vijñāna), leading to
4. Distinctions between "self" and "other" (nāmarūpa), leading to
5. Development of sensory abilities (sadāyatana), leading to
6. Sensory contact with the world (sparśa), leading to
7. Emotions, feelings, and sensations (vedanā), leading to
8. Feelings of desire and thirst for experience (tṛṣṇa), leading to
9. Clinging and grasping thought (upādāna), leading to
10. Sensual life and deluded activity (bhava), leading to
11. Karma and the seeds of rebirth (jāti), leading to
12. Old age, sickness, and death (jarāmaraṇa), leading again to ignorance (cause number one) and a new rebirth

The bhava-chakra, or "wheel of life" diagram, then, serves several purposes for Buddhist teaching simultaneously. It forces the viewer to become aware of the transitory nature of life as well as the theory of karma, that is, that one's actions now are continuously producing the energies leading to one's next life. The diagram also shows the omnipresence of the Buddha and his salvific power. Finally, the diagram colorfully illustrates the endlessness of craving, resulting in birth, suffering, and death, and it shows the minute mental experiences (along the outer rim of the diagram) that prompt the more studious to engage in Buddhist meditation and root out these polluting mental complexes and attachments (āśravas) in order to pursue final salvation.

See also ARŪPA-DHĀTU; HEAVENS, BUDDHIST; HELLS, BUDDHIST; KĀMA-DHĀTU; NIRVĀṆA; PRET; REINCARNATION, EASTERN; RŪPA-DHĀTU; YAMA.

References

Becker, Carl B. *Breaking the Circle: Death and the Afterlife in Buddhism.* Carbondale: Southern Illinois University Press, 1993.

Collins, Steven. *Selfless Persons.* Cambridge: Cambridge University Press, 1982.

Humphreys, Christmas, ed. *The Wisdom of Buddhism.* New York: Random House, 1961.

Kloetzli, Randy. *Buddhist Cosmology: From Single World System to Pure Land.* Delhi: Motilal Banarsidass, 1983.

Law, Bimala Churn. *Heaven and Hell in Buddhist Perspective.* Calcutta: Bhartiya Publishing, 1925.

Prebish, Charles S. *Buddhism: A Modern Perspective.* University Park: Pennsylvania State University Press, 1978.

Waddell, L. Austine. *Tibetan Buddhism.* Reprint, New York: Dover, 1972.

BHŪT (BHŪTA)

Those malevolent ghosts that once were human are generally classed under the term *bhūt* and must be distinguished from malevolent spirits that never were human (rākṣasas, āsuras, yakṣas, etc.) and the ghostly remains of humans that are not usually malevolent (prets, pitris, etc.). This still leaves a wide field for the once-human, evil-minded bhūts.

The modern word *bhūt* descends from the ancient Sanskrit *bhūta* (from a verbal root *bhū*, "to become, to be"), meaning "what has passed, gone." Even in the earliest times from which we have records, Indian philosophers separated the human being into several parts. When the physical body died, there were still several inner, subtle bodies and mental natures remaining, each of which began to separate from the others and go its separate way. In this enumeration, the bhūta was the lower soul or psychic dregs of the deceased, barely conscious, pictured as a shadow. It was carefully distinguished from the eternal spark in man, namely the ātman—the source of spiritual salvation, which never dies but moves from body to body in the course of endless rebirths. This ātman is utterly formless but, accompanied by the conscience and lessons learned over lifetimes, associates soon after death with its new form and nature. Meanwhile, the bhūta, or leftover mental energy, wanders the earth until it begins to weaken and is eventually absorbed by the natural elements. This bhūta, being a collection of one's moral and mental leftovers, is good or evil according to the life one lived. Thus it is not *necessarily* evil, but shorn of its higher ātman becomes unpredictable and irresponsible. Among the modern population, however, such philosophical niceties are not well studied, and *bhūt* is simply the term for an evil ghost whose sole purpose is to harm the living.

In popular Indian belief, as around the world, a deceased human may become a malevolent ghost from many different conditions: (1) the person met with a violent, unexpected, or agonizing death, especially murder or suicide; (2) the funerary rites weren't carried out or weren't carried out properly; (3) the soul of the deceased has been subject to outside evil influences, like witches or other evil forces; (4) the person was unhappy or dissatisfied in life because of being deformed, insane, a woman who died in childbirth, or a man who died without offspring; (5) the person was a foreigner or an Indian native who died in a foreign land; (6) the person was just plain wicked, drunken, or otherwise antisocial. In all these cases, the bhūts have cause to be restless and angry spirits, and although they especially seek out those whom they feel have harmed them, bhūts are also malicious in general and prey on anyone within reach.

Bhūts have many interesting habits and characteristics. They prefer to remain in out-of-the-way places, living in trees and rocks, particularly those of unusual shape. (There is even a species of tree called *bhūtavṛikṣa,* or "demon tree.") Such unusual shapes often become objects of veneration for the local population, who seek to appease the bhūts before they cause trouble. When bhūts do manifest to do harm, they are frequently invisible, recognizable only by the fever and death they leave in their wake. But they may appear to the living as animals or as little goblin figures of twisted shape, dark, with thick limbs, wild hair, huge teeth, and bodies covered in ornaments. The bhūt may also appear exactly as he or she was when alive—so real that the human witness may not be sure whether the apparition is alive or dead. Luckily, certain tests may help one recognize a bhūt. First of all, like most Indian spirits, their feet are turned backward, although this is not a certainty in every case. Second, like the European vampire, bhūts cast no shadows, most likely because they *are* literally

the shadow of their old selves and thus cannot cast an additional shadow. Third, several things may be tried to scare a bhūt, for instance, fire, salt, or burning turmeric. Fourth, a bhūt may not sit on or touch the ground because the earth in India is a holy thing identified with the goddess Pṛithivī, and they are repulsed by it. Thus bhūts must sit on posts, a pile of bricks, or anything else off the ground. Finally, and most telling, a bhūt always speaks with a nasal accent. (This became so proverbial that medieval Indian plays even presented a nasal dialect called "Piṣācha Bhāṣa" or "language of the demons.")

Bhūts are peculiarly attracted to some scents and driven away by others. At the top of the list of ghost attractors are sweets, such that a sweet seller in India always gives a pinch of salt to young children (who are particularly vulnerable to bhūts) so that the salty taste in the mouth may follow the sweets and prevent spirit entry. Likewise, because bhūts are thought to be constantly thirsty, they will drink any kind of water, no matter how filthy and polluted. They are also fond of milk, and no rural Indian mother will let children out of the house after drinking fresh milk. Finally, bhūts are drawn to filth and always prefer a dirty, out-of-the-way location to a clean, well-lighted place. Along with salt, other tastes and smells are repulsive to spirits, like garlic (called in Sanskrit *bhūtaghna*, or "bhūt-killer") and pepper (*bhūtanāshana*, or "destroyer of bhūts").

People in India fear the bhūts entering the body. Because the soul is thought to leave through the crown of the head when a person dies, so too bhūts may try to enter through that secret doorway, and one must take care to guard this sacred spot. A peculiar variety of bhūt called the *vetāl* is fond of entering corpses and reanimating them, causing horror to the living, as told in the cycle of tales called "Vikram and the Vampire." One must take particular care to protect newborns by having a fire constantly burning and by marking black paint (kohl) under the child's eyes to make the child unattractive to hunting bhūts. Bodily orifices are also particularly vulnerable. Yawning is dangerous, both because the soul may escape and because malicious spirits may get in: one should put hand to mouth and say "Nārāyan," that is, a name of God. Likewise, sneezing is a danger because it indicates bhūts are in the nasal passage—though it is not clear if the discomfort is due to bhūts entering or exiting. Thus among various ethnicities of India, it is important to offer a blessing after a sneeze; for example, among Hindus one must say "Live!" or "God bless you," and among Muslims one says "God be praised." If one fails to wash hands or feet, particularly at a ritual occasion like marriage or prayers, bhūts can enter there too. However, pure water, especially that in which an ascetic's feet have been washed, along with loud noises like hand clapping, can fend off this danger. Finally, bhūts can be prevented from

The Exorcism

One morning the dead body of a large and venomous snake, which had been killed near the servants' quarters the night before, was brought to me. It appears that the cold clammy weight of the horrid reptile upon her neck had roused a woman who was sleeping in the open air at the door of one of the out-houses. Instinctively, she flung the snake off, and immediately called for help. Her brother-in-law, the *dhobi* or washerman, ran to her help, and despatched the intruder with a stick. On the following day the dhobi was taken ill, and his work got into arrears. I wanted to know what was the matter with the man, and found out that his illness was due solely to his having neglected to give the customary funeral feast in memory of his deceased wife, who had died in her native village some months previously. The snake which had visited the servants' quarters was none other than the late wife herself, and had come to wreak her vengeance on the woman, who, it would appear, had stood very much in the way of the funeral feast and was, moreover, responsible for the neglect which the deceased had experienced during her lifetime. . . . An exorcist was called in, and immediately commenced operations. In the open air, beside the bed of the sick man, he placed a lighted cheragh, and just before it, drew on the ground a small circle about three inches across, with two diameters at right angles to each other. He put a couple of cloves at one end of each diameter. . . . he gashed his arm with a penknife, and collecting the blood on the blade, wet the cloves with it. Next he took all the cloves in his right hand and, closing his fist, passed it, heavily and slowly, over the sick man, beginning from a little above the knee and going gradually up to and round the head, as if drawing or gathering something up towards the top of the head. Whenever the invalid groaned . . . [the exorcist] expressed his satisfaction, and seemed to coax the spirit to come out. Sometimes the spirit which had taken possession of the sick man would, as it were, struggle under the grasp of the exorcist, and seem as if about to slip away from him. At this the medicine-man's ire would be roused, and, apparently much excited, he would address the enemy in no complimentary terms, while he himself groaned and puffed as if in a severe and exhausting conflict. At length the spirit was safely conducted to the crown of the invalid's head, and was then successfully drawn out of him.

Excerpted from Oman (1972).

entering the ears with ear coverings when it is cold and by means of earrings for both sexes.

Thought to exist in great numbers, bhūts can cause any number of diseases and illnesses ranging from rheumatism and fever to insanity. In ancient Sanskrit, insanity is actually called *bhūtonmāda*, or "spirit madness," of which there are twenty varieties! Thus a great deal of time and energy is spent by the less Westernized classes of Indians in dealing with these malicious spirits. Besides the various apotropaic devices mentioned previously, which are designed to keep these spirits away, one might also try the direct approach: appeasement bordering on worship. One may seek out troublesome bhūts in dark and filthy places and make offerings to them. Or one may build shrines to suicide victims, murdered people, and those who died by snake or animal attack so that by the regular water and food offerings the restless bhūt will remain calm and localized at his or her special little place of worship. Such shrines at crossroads and on hills are quite a common sight in the countryside. There are also shrines to local deities (grāmadevatā) who can defend one from bhūts, particularly in southern India. Here on the outskirts of villages one may find boundary stones, pillars, or little altars given over to various earth mothers (mātā), the earth father Bhairon, or the monkey god Hanuman. There is also the tactic of building a shrine and appeasing the head of the demons, in the hope that he or she can keep his or her "troops" in check. Examples of this are the "honorable father" Aiyanār who rides at night with his horde, the vetāl (vampire) of the Deccan plateau, or chandkaī, eater of children.

Sometimes, however, a physical shrine outside town is not effective because the bhūt is too intimate with the family. For example, during a second marriage, if one believes that the bhūt of the former spouse has become a harassing spirit, one may make offerings or publicly recognize it. For instance, men who marry again after a first wife's death commonly wear a necklace with the image of the goddess Devī on it, to which the second wife must pray and offer presents. In this way the former wife retains her pride of place and may cease her persecutions. In the Punjab, there is even the practice of bird marriage, where a man "marries" a bird, pays the dowry for it, and then divorces it to marry the new (human) wife. In this way the bhūt of the first wife will vent her rage upon the bird bride and leave the "third wife," the human wife, alone. The bhūt may be the restless soul of one who died unmarried, in which case the solution in south India and parts of Burma may be to perform a (mock) marriage ceremony of the bhūt to a living wife. If instead the bhūt is unhappy because his corpse was not available for proper funerary rites, the family can make an effigy of cowrie shells for bones, paste for flesh, and deer hide for skin and perform the cremation and subsequent rites as normal. Sadly, physical torture has also been used to expel bhūts that people think have taken possession of a living person. It may take the shape of beatings, breaking of limbs, and strangulation, accompanied by abusive language and threats. If the bhūt within doesn't speak up, confess, and name conditions of expulsion, the possessed person may be tortured until death, as in the witchcraft trials of Europe and the United States.

See also ĀTMAN; CHUREL; FUNERARY CUSTOMS, ANCIENT INDIAN; PISHĀCHA; PRET; RĀKṢASA; SHIVA (HINDU); SOUL; YAMA.

References

Blavatsky, Helena Petrovna. *The Key to Theosophy*. Point Loma, CA: Aryan Theosophical Press, 1913. Reprint, Los Angeles: Theosophy Company, 1987.

Briggs, George W. *The Doms and Their Near Relations*. Mysore: Wesley Press, 1953.

————. *The Religious Life of India: The Chamars*. Calcutta: Association Press, 1920.

Crooke, William. *The Popular Religion and Folklore of Northern India*. 2nd ed. Delhi: Munshiram Manoharlal, 1968.

Hastings, James, ed. *Encyclopaedia of Ethics and Religion*. Vol. 5: *Demons and Spirits, Indian*. Edinburgh: T. and T. Clark, 1911.

Oman, J. C. *Cults, Customs and Superstitions of India*. Indian ed. Delhi: Vishal Publishers, 1972.

BLACK DEATH

Also known simply as "the plague" or "the pestilence," the Black Death of the fourteenth century was the most virulent and devastating disease known to human history. From one-third to one-half the population of northern Africa, Europe, and Asia, from China to Greenland, perished between the years 1345 and 1350.

History records many epidemics from antiquity to the present. The Old Testament celebrates various plagues, like those visited upon the Philistines (1 Samuel:5, 6), while the Greek historian Thucydides traces the origin of the "Athenian plague" (fifth century B.C.E.) from its alleged origin in Ethiopia through its devastation of the Greek world. The late Roman Empire was harassed by not one but three major waves of infectious diseases. First, from 165–180 C.E., the Romans witnessed the introduction of smallpox to Italy and the western Roman Empire, probably by Roman soldiers returning home from wars on the eastern frontier. Next, in 251 C.E., the Roman world endured the onset of the "Antonine plague," probably measles, which devastated the Roman cities and countryside until about 260 C.E. Fortunately, however, survivors of both epidemics became endowed with relative immunity so that further incursions of smallpox and measles attacked mostly children—damaging to be sure but of reduced impact. Both Roman epidemics, however, pale in comparison to the calamity wrought by the arrival in 541 of the "plague of Justinian," in reality the first wave

A sixteenth-century engraving of a flagellant by Jost Amman. This sect whipped themselves until the blood ran in order to obtain God's mercy and to appease his wrath for the sins of humankind. When disasters such as plague struck, they would march in procession through the streets whipping themselves in the hope that God would lift his punishment from the people. Courtesy of Anne Ronan Picture Library.

of what is now known as the bubonic plague or Black Death. Just as the Emperor Justinian was attempting to reconquer parts of western Europe from Germanic tribes, the plague emanated out, probably from eastern Africa, and swept over central and southern Asia, North Africa and Arabia, and Europe from the Black Sea to Denmark and Ireland. During a four-month span in the Byzantine capital of Constantinople, 200,000 people died, perhaps 40 percent of the total population. Overall, 20–25 percent of the population of Europe south of the Alps perished from "Justinian's plague," and for the next 200 years incidents of plague recurred cyclically every ten to twenty-four years, hampering recovery efforts. Many historians point to the triad of smallpox, measles, and Justinian's plague as a major cause for the fall of Rome and the plunge of Europe into its Dark Ages.

Nevertheless, the second wave of plague that swept the world in the fourteenth century was even more virulent and more widespread than the first wave in the sixth century under Justinian. Although the heavily agrarian Western world had experienced remarkably good weather from c. 800 to c. 1200 C.E., with resultant steady economic improvement and about 300 percent population growth, from 1250 to the time of the plague (1347–1348) the West experienced several natural disasters. Population growth caused a land shortage, which along with steadily worsening weather (dubbed "the little Ice Age") brought particularly severe famines in 1309–1320. This was compounded in western Europe by the ongoing Hundred Years' War, leaving the Western world weak and vulnerable to the scourge from the East.

Justinian's plague almost certainly originated in eastern Africa, but there is little doubt that the Black Death ultimately emanated from northern China in Yunnan province or the nearby Gobi desert. There, carried in the stomachs of fleas infesting the rats of that region, the bacillus that causes plague had been contained for a long time. What exactly caused the primary hosts of the bacilli, the rats, to leave their accustomed dwellings and begin to spread the pandemic is uncertain, but a clue may be found in Chinese records and reports from travelers—that at the time the plague was just beginning to spread, a series of droughts, famines, and earthquakes occurred, followed immediately by severe flooding. This suggests that environmental disruption and ecological imbalance forced the rodents to seek out new sustenance, exposing new populations of animals and humans to their parasites.

Whatever the ultimate cause of the plague, its grim and steady march westward toward the Middle East and Europe and southward toward India and southeast Asia is fairly well documented. In the 1330s and 1340s the Western world began hearing rumors of natural disasters and a so-called miasma or corruption of the air visible as mist or smoke, overtaking Asian countries and killing vast numbers of people. Apparently the plague traveled overland very slowly at first on the inner Asian steppe but soon struck major cities along the Asian trade routes and began to spread rapidly by ship. From the first documentation of the plague, in which a Nestorian Christian community succumbed north of Samarkand deep in central Asia in 1339, after which the plague began to spread outward from China, until its emergence a few thousand miles east among the Golden Horde Mongols in southern Russia at Sarai in 1345, the plague progressed very gradually. From the trade city of Sarai, however, the plague reached the important port of Kaffa on the northern Black Sea, where Italian merchants carried on a brisk sea trade. Late in 1347 plague-bearing rats reached the capital of Byzantium, Constantinople, the gateway to the Mediterranean, and within eighteen months a third—perhaps half—of all Europe and the Middle East would be dead.

In autumn 1347 the plague spread from Constantinople to the islands of Cyprus and Sicily; the central port city of Messina in Italy; and Alexandria, the principle port of Egypt. Like China, Cyprus was wracked with earthquakes and several tidal waves the same year the plague struck. Mortality was so high among the Christian Cypriots that they slaughtered all their Muslim prisoners and slaves, fearing that they would seize power. From Sicily and Messina the disease spread to all of Italy, the commercial center of the Mediterranean, and thence to most of southern Europe by December 1347. By spring 1348 plague had reached all of France and the Spanish peninsula and by fall had reached England and the Netherlands. In 1349 Scandinavia succumbed and then even Iceland and Greenland—the latter having just been colonized the previous century by settlers from Iceland and the mainland. Apparently, mortality among the settlers in Greenland was near 100 percent, for when Norwegian ships put into port in the fifteenth century, only animals were found roaming through deserted villages. From Alexandria, Egypt, another major port and trading city, plague swept up the Nile River, westward toward Gibraltar on the Atlantic, and throughout the hundreds of Mediterranean ports, large and small. At least 200,000 died in Cairo alone, and perhaps 50 percent of the entire Islamic world perished along with them.

It is difficult to overestimate the psychological, economic, and spiritual crises brought on by the plague. Many people in the midst of the pandemic believed it to be the apocalypse. An Italian historian writes,

> The mortality in Siena began in May. It was a cruel and horrible thing; and I do not know where to begin to tell of the cruelty and the pitiless ways. . . . Father abandoned child, wife husband, one brother another. . . . And none could be found to bury the dead for money or friendship. Members of a household brought their dead to a ditch as best they could, without priest, without divine offices. Nor did the death bell sound. . . . And as soon as those ditches were filled, more were dug. And I, Agnolo di Tura . . . buried my five children with my own hands. . . . And so many died that all believed it was the end of the world.

Even the scholars and historians who were recording the events as they were happening themselves took sick and died. One Irish chronicler, John Clyn of Kilkenny, writes, "I . . . waiting till death do come, have put into writing truthfully what I have heard and verified. . . . I add parchment to continue it, if by chance anyone may be left in the future, and any child of Adam escape this pestilence and continue the work thus commenced." In another hand the chronicle continues, "Here it seems that the author died."

Besides horror and bewilderment, reactions to the plague varied widely. In the Muslim world it was widely believed, based on the teaching of the Qurān, that the plague was sent by God as both a beneficial martyrdom for Muslims and a horrible punishment for the infidel. Religious scholars believed that there was no contagion of plague but that it was in fact a corruption of the air, a "miasma" sent by God where he willed. Thus Muslims were instructed neither to flee the plague nor to refrain from entering a plague-stricken land but to stay put and accept God's work with resignation. Nevertheless, many Muslims did flee to the countryside, where the plague lodged a heavy toll, but it appears to have been less than in the cities. Some Muslim scholars disagreed with the normative position and believed that the plague was contagious, citing the existence of isolated individuals, particularly nomads, who stayed away from infected areas and remained healthy.

In Christian lands the plague was widely seen as the final judgment by God and the end of the world. One reaction to this was flight to the countryside, accompanied by widespread banditry and lawlessness, notably in Iberia, despite official attempts to control the situation. Another reaction was hedonism and carelessness; this seems particularly prevalent in areas where mortality was extremely high, for example, in Siena and Florence, Italy, where estimates range from 50 percent to an incredible 75 percent depopulation. People took to drinking, reveling, and spending all of their money; this carelessness often turned to lawlessness as well, with extortion, rape, and murder becoming commonplace. A quite different reaction to the horror and presumed divine judgment was the flagellant movement: troupes of ascetics, headed by a "father" or "master," who gave up all worldly possessions and wandered from village to town beating themselves with spiked whips mercilessly, apparently in the belief that their suffering could appease an angry god. Although this movement sprang up in France, the Low Countries and central Europe, it was most intense in the German Rhineland. There, despite initial popularity, the flagellants became increasingly wild and turned criminal and dangerous; Pope Clement VI eventually issued a bull condemning flagellism and ordering its repression and by 1350 the practice had largely receded.

One of the things preached by flagellism, unfortunately, was anti-Semitism, and in many areas this needed no particular preaching. While the plague raged and immediately afterward, the Jews were convenient scapegoats to blame for God's wrath. This anti-Semitism went far beyond angry feelings: Jews were massacred by the thousands in Iberia, Switzerland, and Germany, particularly, and did not fare much better elsewhere. In Iberia the kings of Castile and Aragon moved quickly to protect their Jewish subjects, although violence continued for years after the plague; likewise Jews were defended in France by the medical faculties of the Universities of Paris and Montpellier. In the German Rhineland, violence against Jews was geno-cidal: entire town populations of Jews were immolated in Basel, Strasbourg, Brussels, Stuttgart, Freiburg, Ulm, Dresden, Worms, Baden, Erfurt, Speyer, and many other places. Some town councils tried to defend the Jewish inhabitants and found themselves ousted by new councilors only too happy to expel or exterminate the Jews. At the end of the pogroms, perhaps one-quarter of the Jewish population remained in the German lands, while most of the survivors had fled to Eastern Europe, to remain there for the following six hundred years.

Ironically, while millenarianism, flagellism, and hysterical anti-Semitism raged, the European economy dramatically improved in the wake of the plague. During the pandemic food became extremely scarce and expensive (since no one was working the fields, nor was there any effective transportation), but immediately afterward so many had died that demand for labor increased sharply; wages rose correspondingly, while food prices dramatically fell. For this reason, the following 150 to 200 years are considered the golden age of the medieval worker. Coupled with this was a weakening of the aristocracy, which lost income because of the high cost of labor, and the emergence of class struggles. The nobility struggled to retain their social superiority in the wake of a lessened gap between noble and commoner, witnessed by the development of somewhat effete codes of chivalry and courtesy, whereas the lower classes discovered a newfound economic power and freedom of thought and travel. This trend ran parallel to the general weakening of the authoritarian church, which lost face with the lay population in light of the clergy's inability to protect mankind from God's wrath. The clergy itself was decimated in many areas, particularly in England, with clerical mortality as high as 65 percent. As the post–Black Death Middle Ages transitioned into the Renaissance, Europe entered a cycle of freer thought, popular mysticism, and a growing idea that individuals had a direct connection to God independent of priest or church, which found articulation in the Reformation. At the same time European culture was sobered by its dreadful plague experience, as can be seen by the growing pessimism of its literature and arts, for example, the ars moriendi, the danse macabre, and an obsession with death, judgment, and salvation.

See also BOOK OF THE CRAFT OF DYING; DANSE MACABRE.

References

Bowsky, William, ed. *The Black Death: A Turning Point in History?* New York: Holt, Rinehart, and Winston, 1971.

Coultan, G. G. *The Black Death.* New York: Macmillan, 1930.

Deaux, George. *The Black Death 1347.* London: Hamilton, 1969.

Dols, Michael W. *The Black Death in the Middle East.* Princeton: Princeton University Press, 1977.

Gottfried, Robert S. *The Black Death: Natural and Human Disaster in Medieval Europe.* New York: Macmillan, 1983.

Helleiner, Karl. "The Population of Europe from the Black Death to the Eve of the Vital Revolution." In *The Cambridge Economic History of Europe*, ed. E. E. Rich and C. H. Wilson. Vol. 4. Cambridge: Cambridge University Press, 1967.

Marks, Geoffrey. *The Medieval Plague*. Garden City, NY: Doubleday 1971.

McNeill, William H. *Plagues and Peoples*. New York: Doubleday, 1976.

Shrewsbury, J. F. D. *A History of Bubonic Plague in the British Isles*. London: Cambridge University Press, 1970.

Sigerist, Henry. *Civilization and Disease*. Chicago: University of Chicago, 1943.

Ziegler, Philip. *The Black Death*. New York: Harper and Row, 1969.

BODY OF LIGHT

Also called the "Rainbow Body," the body of light is a unique mode of death for highly advanced meditators in the Tibetan Buddhist lineage called *Dzogchen* (literally "the Great Perfection"). After many years of practicing meditation, realizing one's true nature (called the "primordial state"), and deepening one's sense of nondualism, or being in union with all things, the meditation master prepares for a living death. Traditionally, the master enters into a cave or secure building, which is then completely sealed for seven days. During this time, the master's body is thought to slowly decompose into the essence of its elements, which is pure light. The body is said to shrink and become smaller and smaller with each passing day as its molecules are transformed into spiritual substance. After the seven-day period, the master's devotees open up the building to find nothing but the clothing of the master and his or her hair and nails, which are considered the impure parts of the body.

The master is not thought to be technically dead, for in Buddhism this means one has left one's earthly body and is headed for rebirth in another. Rather, the master is thought to continue right on in earthly life but simply without a physical body. He or she does not enter the ultimate condition, called nirvāṇa in Buddhism, but continues to exist on earth in an invisible body of light as a Nirmāṇakāya—a technical term for an enlightened being who chooses to remain on earth and try to benefit all the beings who continue to suffer in the delusion of earthly life.

See also BOOK OF THE DEAD, TIBETAN; BURIAL, SKY; NIRMĀṆA-KĀYA; NIRVĀṆA.

References
Norbu, Namkhai. *The Crystal and the Way of Light*. Ed. John Shane. New York: Arkana, 1993.

BON FESTIVAL (JAPAN)

During the seventh month of the Japanese calendar, from the night of the thirteenth to the night of the sixteenth, the dead are believed to return from the other world to the living, and the Bon festival is held to welcome them. Souls arrive first at their tombs, so families visit the graveyard before the festival and take great care to clean up and decorate the tomb. On the thirteenth, bowls of water, rice and other food, and flowers are brought to the grave and offered to the departed one. Likewise, the family home is cleaned and decorated with flowers and ornaments, and the dead are welcomed there.

Early on the morning of the fourteenth, the members of the "branch families" of the greater family clan (dōzoku) gather at the main family's home to prepare the soul tablets for all the dead, which are kept at the altar. This is a time of great clan solidarity, with the various branches acknowledging their subordination to the main family and accepting the main family's hospitality in providing breakfast and lunch. The Bon festival is also a time to visit friends and neighbors who have lost a loved one recently and bring gifts of money, lanterns, food, and incense.

On the afternoon of the last day of the festival, members of the branch families again gather at the main family's home to honor all the ancestors as well as the particular souls dwelling in the soul tablets and bid the dead farewell on their return journey.

See also ANCESTOR VENERATION; FESTIVAL OF GHOSTS; HEAVENS, BUDDHIST; JIZŌ; SOUL TABLET.

References
Habenstein, Robert W., and William M. Lamers. *Funeral Customs the World Over*. Milwaukee: Bulfin Printers, 1963.

Hori, Ichiro. *Folk Religion in Japan: Continuity and Change*. Tokyo: Tokyo University Press, 1968.

BOOK OF THE CRAFT OF DYING

Also known by its Latin title *Ars Moriendi*, this book is the most famous member of a cycle of closely related texts on "dying well," which had an enormous influence on late medieval Europe. There appear to be three principal forms of this book, including an original Latin treatise of unknown authorship loosely called *Ars Moriendi;* the very popular block art books of the *Ars Moriendi,* which can be found translated in nearly every European language, particularly in German, French, and English; and a rare French text, *L'Art de Bien Vivre et Bien Mourire* (The art of living well and dying well), which appears to be directly related to the block books.

Of the Latin text alone, at least three titles are known to us, namely *De Arte Moriendi*, *Tractatus de Arte Moriendi,* and *Speculum Artis Moriendi.* The oldest printed version is ascribed to Mathieu de Cracovie, bishop of Worms, circa 1470, but the text was circulating well before the printing press was available. Three manuscripts of the English version, the *Book of the Craft of*

Dying, exist in the Bodleian Library at Oxford; their exact date is uncertain.

The text is divided into six chapters, the first of which commends death as valuable, both as an escape from this dark world and as a homecoming to God. Death is inevitable, and one may as well welcome it calmly, with resignation:

> And sith, as it is aforesaid, we may not, in no wise, neither flee nor escape, neither change the inevitable necessity and passage of death, therefore we ought to take our death when God will, wilfully and gladly, without any grutching or contradiction, through the might and boldness of the will of our soul virtuously disposed and governed by reason and very discretion; though the lewd sensuality and frailty of our flesh naturally grutch or strive there against. (Comper, pp. 7–8)

The second chapter speaks of the final temptations of the soul that beset one at death: temptations of faith, desperation, impatience, complacence, and worldly distractions. The third chapter contains a list of seven formulaic questions that should be asked of those "that be in their death bed: while they may speak and understand" on topics such as repentance of evil deeds, forgiveness of others, abandonment of all worldly possessions, and acceptance of salvation by Jesus Christ. Chapter 4 reminds one of the final deeds of Jesus on the cross and exhorts the dying to do likewise, namely to pray, cry (in one's heart), weep (out loud), place oneself in God's hands, and freely give up one's life, all of which is accompanied by several prayers to each person of the Trinity and to the Virgin, Queen of Heaven.

Chapter 5 reminds the dying of the grave perils awaiting them after death and exhorts them once more to repent. Images of the crucifix, Virgin, and saints are to be presented, and final prayers offered. Chapter 6 contains prayers to be said over the dying person by family and clergy, concluding with a final oratio:

> Go Christian soul out of this world, in the Name of the Almighty Father that made thee of nought; in the Name of Jesu Christ, His Son, that suffered His passion for thee; and in the Name of the Holy Ghost, that was infounded into thee. Holy angels, Thrones and Dominations, Princehoods, Potentates and Virtues, Cherubim and Seraphim, meet with thee. Patriarchs and prophets, apostles and evangelists, martyrs, confessors, monks and hermits, maidens and widows, children and innocents, help thee. The prayers of all priests and deacons, and all the degrees of Holy Church, help thee; that in peace be thy place, and they dwelling in heavenly Jerusalem everlastingly; by the mediation of Our Lord Jesu Christ, that is Mediator between God and man. Amen. (Comper, pp. 7–8)

References

Comper, Frances M., ed. *The Book of the Craft of Dying.* New York: Arno Press, 1977.

BOOK OF THE DEAD, EGYPTIAN

Although "Book of the Dead" has become the standard title of this collection of Egyptian spells and prayers, the actual title of the work, *Per Em Hru,* is more literally rendered by Book of Coming Forth by Day, or more poetically, Journey to the Light. These latter titles referred to the empowerment granted by the collection of spells that allowed the soul of the deceased to leave the tomb and seek union with the gods, who were stars. The collection was never a specific "book" in the modern sense of the word, for it was a rather loose collection of rituals and incantations from the start. Even in the later period of standardization from the Eighteenth Dynasty on (c. 1500 B.C.E.), the collection still shows some variation in content, probably depending on the wealth of the individual (longer collections required greater expenditure on copyists) and the preferences of the deceased or the family.

Book of the Dead almost certainly originates in the so-called Pyramid texts, very ancient inscriptions in the pyramid chambers of royal burials. In these texts, dating from the Third Dynasty (c. 2700 B.C.E.), the king was considered on a par with the gods and was expected to become associated with one of the circumpolar stars after death. He was often also absorbed by or identified with Osiris, lord and protector of souls during the death process; from the Fifth Dynasty onward the king was also connected with Rā (or Re), the solar god. One typical spell from this early period reads, "O Osiris the King, may you be protected. I give to you all the gods, their heritages, their provisions, and all their possessions, for you have not died" (Pyramid text 775, Spencer).

After the collapse of the Old Kingdom (c. 2181 B.C.E.), Egypt experienced great turmoil for an uncertain length of time. When it was finally unified once more under a single dynasty (c. 2100 B.C.E.), the old afterlife spells that were formerly used only by the kings began to come into widespread use on the wooden coffins of the Eleventh and Twelfth Dynasties—thus their title "coffin texts." Those who could afford spells inscribed on their coffins were still the relatively wealthy. But by the time of the New Kingdom (c. 1500 B.C.E.), a technological breakthrough had enabled the use of papyrus for writing, which made the written word much easier and cheaper to produce. Burials with spells relating to the afterlife became commonplace for

Papyrus from the Egyptian Book of the Dead shows a funeral procession. Courtesy of Anne Ronan Picture Library.

nearly everyone, and a great number of New Kingdom burials have been unearthed containing scrolls of the Book of the Dead. It was also in the New Kingdom period that the practice began of illustrating the Book of the Dead with scenes from the afterlife and at the same time using red ink (instead of the customary black) to highlight titles and other important points. The practice of composing papyri with coffin text spells and burying them with the dead continued unabated down to the Ptolemaic period (c. 100 B.C.E.). Spells from the collection have also been found circulating independently on amulets that were worn by the mummies.

The Egyptian civilization developed an enormous literature dealing with the afterlife. The most important were the Book of Two Ways (found already on coffin texts and describing the Underworld with its canals, streams, islands, blazing fires, and boiling waters); the Book of Gates (depicting Osiris's nightly boat journey through the Underworld bringing light, air, and food to the inhabitants and teaching the reward of the just and the punishment of the wicked); the Book of Am Duat, or That Which Is in the Underworld (describing the twelve sections of the Underworld, each related to an hour of the night); and the Book of Apophis (telling in epic fashion the story of the serpent-enemy Apophis and the Sun God, Rā, doing battle each night).

Yet the Book of the Dead was by far the most influential funerary collection, containing nearly 200 spells covering every conceivable aspect of death, dying, the afterworld, and the funerary gods. Every spell required the name of the deceased, newly called "Osiris (so-and-so)," to be written into the spell for it to be effective. There were spells for how to descend to the land of the dead, avoid various monsters and pitfalls, and silence one's heart from testifying during the judgment before the gods; spells for retaining one's sight and hearing; spells for making one's funerary statues (ushabtis) work for one in the afterlife; and of course, the spell (first in most collections) for how to retain one's ability to move so that one can "go forth into the light" and leave the tomb behind.

It is likely that the whole collection was considered sacred and thus somewhat secret, perhaps the province of priests alone, but in any case, some spells repeatedly stress the secrecy with which they must be treated. Spell 148, for instance, is particularly confidential:

[Title:] Book of Secrets for him who is in the netherworld, (for) initiating the blessed [deceased] into the Mind of Re. . . .

(It contains) secret(s) of the Nether World, mysteries [such as] (how) to cleave mountains and penetrate valleys . . . secrets wholly unknown: (how) to preserve the heart of the blessed one, widen his steps, give him his (powers of) locomotion, do away with his deafness, and reveal his face and (that of) the God. . . .

This roll is a very real secret. No one else is ever to know (it); (it is) not to be told (to) anybody. No eye is to see nor ear to hear (it) except the soul and its teacher. . . . (Allen, pp. 140–141)

In later times, even after the collection of spells had been somewhat standardized, the text was regularly changed both by scribal error and by deliberate intention—to incorporate plays on words, glosses, and even question-and-answer sections. Not unexpectedly, a vast literary and philosophical tradition developed around the spells, and commentaries became attached, either to amplify their power or perhaps just to clarify old ideas that may have become unclear as the centuries passed. For example, spell 17 gives a commentary, which makes rather obvious and redundant points:

> *My words come to pass. (All was) mine when (I) existed alone in the Deep; (I was) Re at (his) dawnings when he began his reign. . . . I am the great god who came into being of himself,*
> —Who is he, "the [great] god who came into being of himself"? (He is) water, he is the Deep, the Father of the gods. He is Re.
> *who created his names, lord (of the Ennead)*
> —Who is he? He is Re when he created the names of his members. So came into being these gods who are in his Train.
> *(most) irresistible of the gods. . . .*
> —He is Re when he rises from the eastern horizon of the sky. (Allen, p. 27)

It seems that the spells were not entirely malleable, for many have explicit directions that their wording is not to be changed, and their efficacy was thought to reside not merely in their intention but in the magical sound of the proper words themselves. Nevertheless, it is clear that from the time of the Pyramid texts down to the spells of the Ptolemaic period, considerable changes had taken place.

See also ĀARU; AMULETS, EGYPTIAN; COFFINS, EGYPTIAN; PYRAMID, EGYPTIAN.

References

Allen, Thomas George, trans. *The Book of the Dead, or Going Forth by Day*. Chicago: Oriental Institute of the University of Chicago, 1974.

Budge, E. A. Wallis. *The Book of the Dead*. New Hyde Park, NY: University Books, 1960.

Hamilton-Patterson, James, and Carol Andrews. *Mummies: Death and Life in Ancient Egypt*. London: William Collins Sons, 1978.

Morenz, Siegfried. *Egyptian Religion*. Trans. Ann E. Keep. Ithaca, NY: Cornell University Press, 1973.

Spencer, A. J. *Death in Ancient Egypt*. New York: Penguin, 1982.

BOOK OF THE DEAD, TIBETAN (BARDO THÖDOL)

Best known in the West as the Tibetan Book of the Dead, a more literal translation of the Tibetan title would run "liberation through understanding in the

---

When the Breath Has Ceased

Hey! Noble one, you named So-and-so! Now the time has come for you to seek the way. Just as your breath stops, the objective clear light of the first between will dawn as previously described to you by your teacher [who instructs the deceased when death is imminent]. Your outer breath stops and you experience reality stark and void like space, your immaculate naked awareness dawning clear and void without horizon or center. At that instant, you yourself must recognize it as yourself, you must stay with that experience. I will describe it again to you at that moment. . . .

Now this mirage you see is the sign of earth dissolving in water. This smoke is the sign of water dissolving into fire. These fireflies are the sign of fire dissolving into wind. This candle's flame is the sign of wind dissolving into consciousness. This moonlit sky is the sign of luminance dissolving into radiance. This dark sky is the sign of radiance dissolving into imminence. This predawn twilight is the sign of imminence dissolving into clear light. . . .

Hey, noble one! Now you have arrived at so-called "death," so you should conduct yourself according to your conception of the spirit of enlightenment. You should conceive your spirit of enlightenment thus: "Alas! I have arrived at the time of death. From now, relying on this death, I will develop my spirit only by contemplating the conception of the spirit of enlightment of love and compassion. For the sake of the whole space-full of beings, I must attain perfect Buddhahood." And especially you should think, "Now for the sake of all beings, I will recognize the death clear light as the body of Truth. Within its experience, I will attain the supreme accomplishment of the Great Seal, and I will accomplish the purposes of all beings. If I don't attain that, then in the time of the between [*bardo*], I will recognize it as the between. I will realize that between as the Great Seal Body of Integration, and I will accomplish the purposes of all the infinite space-full of beings by manifesting whatsoever is needed to tame whatsoever." Thus never losing the willpower of that spiritual conception, you should remember the experience of whatever instructions you have previously practiced.

From The Tibetan Book of the Dead. Translation by Thurman (1994, pp. 122–125).

Between." The title indicates the function of the text for Tibetan Buddhists, which is to help one seek final salvation and enlightenment during the death process, when one is in the "between" state (in Tibetan, *Bardo*) after death but before rebirth. It is often read out loud to people just before they die and during the days immediately after death to guide the soul of the deceased to the best possible rebirth and finally to nirvāṇa if possible.

According to the text itself, the Tibetan Book of the Dead was composed by the great Buddhist adept Padma Sambhava (lotus-born) and dictated to his Tibetan consort Yeshe Tsogyal. This would place the composition of the text perhaps in the eighth century, when Buddhism was just beginning to trickle into Tibet—although Padma Sambhava is an almost mythical figure about whom very little is known for certain. Tibetan legend has it that this far-seeing person realized that Buddhism would be persecuted in Tibet during the ninth century (which it was), and so he hid the text in a cave in a mountain in central Tibet. Tibetan Buddhism has a long-established tradition of such mystically hidden texts, or terma, and in the fourteenth century the great Tibetan scholar Karma Lingpa found the terma and propagated it among the Tibetan people, who were by then thoroughly Buddhist. The text soon became extremely popular among Tibetans, even among the most ordinary, illiterate people.

The actual composition of the Tibetan Book of the Dead varies slightly from place to place but consists of a number of preparatory prayers; exhortations to the deceased to be clear, alert, and detached during the death process; and the main section, which guides the deceased step by step through the complicated and long process of death, teaching him or her what to look for, how to react, and how to attain the best possible station. The various prayers are addressed to the many mentors, gurus, guides, angels, cosmic energies, Buddhas, and bodhisattvas that make up the Buddhist pantheon, asking for assistance and guidance on the perilous journey, since a bad rebirth could lead to the next life as an animal or worse—a very lengthy stay in hell.

The main body of the text, after paying homage to the Buddha of Infinite Light (Amitābha) and his entourage, addresses the deceased in very direct terms:

> Hey! Noble one, you named So-and-so! Now the time has come for you to seek the way. Just as your breath stops, the objective clear light of the first "between" will dawn as previously described to you by your teacher. Your outer breath stops and you experience reality stark and void like space, your immaculate naked awareness dawning clear and void without horizon or center. At that instant, you yourself must recognize it as yourself, you must stay with that experience. (Thurman, trans.)

The cessation of activity in the physical body is only the very first stage of death in Tibetan Buddhism. From there, the soul begins the process of separating from the body, and the various "subtle elements" dissolve into each other. As the earth element dissolves in the water element, the dying person feels the body seem to go weak and shrivel, there is a loss of sight, and everything seems to turn to a mirage. Next, the water element dissolves into air, body fluids seem to dry out, the sense of hearing dies away, and one feels surrounded by smoke.

Then, after the soul has completely separated from the body, various layers of consciousness dissolve away, producing more and more subtle levels of awareness. The various subtle energies of the soul merge into a central channel, coalescing at the heart center (chakra), producing the experience in the dying person of being adrift in a sky full of moonlight, then awash in sunlight, then aware of a sky full of dark light. Finally, after losing (self-) consciousness, one arises in a realm of clear, translucent light with nondualistic consciousness. It is at this point that the Tibetans consider real "death" has occurred, and one then begins the pilgrimage toward rebirth in the next body—whether in human form or that of an animal or in the realms of the gods, antigods, hungry ghosts, or hell beings. Here the Tibetan Book of the Dead attempts to bring the deceased to clarity as to their true nature (nondualistic consciousness and clear light) and prevent rebirth in any realm. Rather, the goal is complete liberation before any rebirth transpires.

Most people, however, are terrified of death and the process of losing all that they know from ordinary life, and so the Tibetan Book of the Dead specifically addresses the several days after death, attempting to guide the deceased to the best possible realm. If enlightenment and nirvāṇa are not options, then perhaps rebirth in a Pure Land of one of the Buddhas may suffice; if not that, then the deceased should try for the best possible judgment from Yama, the god of death, and seek rebirth in the heavens or among humans. There are even careful instructions for how to choose the best continent and the best womb in which to be reborn:

> Choose your continent for rebirth as explained already. Using your clairvoyance, enter a womb in a place where [the Buddhist teaching] has spread. Caution is required, for even if you were to be reborn magically in a heap of dung, you would get the notion that the impure mass smelled delicious and you would be reborn in it by the force of your attraction. Therefore you should not adhere to whatever appearance occurs, and you must discount any signs that trigger attachment or aversion. Then choose a good womb . . . as the child of a holy man,

an adept, or of a clan with an impeccable [Buddhist] lineage. (Thurman, trans.)

The central conception of the Tibetan Book of the Dead, imbedded within its profuse imagery, is a cool detachment and a realization that all of one's postmortem experiences are actually not real but a mere projection of consciousness, a fabrication of one's own mind trapped in ignorance, desire, and confusion. These are what cause birth in the first place, and it is the end of birth and rebirth that is sought by Tibetan Buddhism.

References

Evans-Wentz, W. Y., ed. *The Tibetan Book of the Dead; or, the After-Death Experiences on the Bardo Plane*. Trans. Lama Kazi Dawa-Samdup. 3rd ed. New York: Oxford University Press, 1971.

Hopkins, Jeffrey, and Lati Rinpoche. *Death, Intermediate State and Rebirth*. Ithaca, NY: Snow Lion, 1985.

Mullin, Glenn H. *Death and Dying: The Tibetan Tradition*. Boston: Arkana, 1986.

Rinpoche, Chokyi Nyima. *The Bardo Guidebook*. Kathmandu: Harper San Francisco, 1991.

Thurman, Robert, trans. *The Tibetan Book of the Dead*. New York: Bantam, 1994.

Trungpa, Chögyam, and Francesca Fremantle, trans. *The Tibetan Book of the Dead: The Great Liberation through Hearing in the Bardo*. Berkeley: Shambala, 1975.

BURIAL

The English word *burial* comes from the ancient Anglo-Saxon word *birgan*. Many other related words also come from the same word, including *barrow* (a rounded tomb), *burrow* (tunnel), *berg* (mountain in German), *borough* (district), and *burgh* (district or township). This linguistic relationship is demonstrated in the words of J. Weever, from his book *Ancient Funeral Monuments*, dated 1631:

Close-up of eighteenth-century gravestone, England. Courtesy of CFCL.

[Speaking of the ancient Saxons] . . . the dead bodies of such as were slaine in the field were left lying upon the ground and covered over with turfes, clods, or sods of earth; And the more in reputation the persons had beene, the greater and higher were the turfes raised over their bodies, and this some used to call Byringing, some Beorging, and some Buriging of the dead, which wee now call berying, or burying of the dead, which properly is a shrowding or an hiding of the dead bodie in the earth. . . .

Beries, Baroes, and some Burrowes, which accordeth with the same sence of Byrighs, Beorghs and Burghs. From whence the names of diverse Townes and Cities are originally derived; Places first so called having beene with walls of turfe or clods of earth, fenced about for men to bee shrowded in, as in forts or castles. (cited in P. E. Jackson, pp. 6–7)

Burial proper encompasses not just inhumation (deposition of a corpse in the earth), as commonly believed, but any deliberate interment or enclosure of remains within another substance, including enclosure within stone monuments, in trees, under wooden frames, under piled stones, or even in water. Thus it is proper to speak of tree burial, ship burial, urn burial, and so on, not just of the intact body alone but also of body parts and cremains.

For at least a quarter of a million years, humans have taken great care to perform burials for their dead. Prehistoric humans were certainly not less careful than modern ones, and even the earliest graves often show traces of various weapons, clothing, jewelry and foodstuffs placed in the grave, suggesting a ritual funeral. Furthermore, prehistoric burials almost universally laid the deceased out carefully in a full or extended burial, or else tightly curled up in a fetal or flexed burial, with the knees tucked up to the chest. Prehistoric graves themselves are often clearly oriented to distinct points on the compass, though whether this was north-south or east-west or otherwise varies by region and cultural group.

Except in times of grave calamity (i.e., wars or massive epidemics like the Black Death), there is little evidence that human burials anywhere have ever been other than deliberate, ritualized, and regarded as of the highest importance. According to the Roman conception, if the deceased had not been properly buried, descent into the Underworld was impossible. The Egyptians believed that the body had to be preserved through embalming; otherwise the deceased might lose the prospect of life beyond the grave. Among primitive peoples an unburied body caused great concern. In China no more righteous act could be conceived than

that of burying stray bones and covering up exposed coffins. In Mesopotamian belief, to be left unburied was one of the greatest misfortunes that could befall a person. Such Middle Eastern beliefs persisted in religions that developed in the area subsequently, including Judaism, Christianity, and Islam. The fourth-century church father Ambrose even declared that it was permissible to break up, melt, and sell off the sacred gold and silver vessels of the church if necessary to pay for Christians needing burial. Likewise, there is scarcely a greater sin for an Orthodox Jew than to ignore a passing funeral or to neglect the burial of the dead; rather, Jewish law requires that all witnesses to a funeral procession join it and that even religious study must be interrupted if a body is discovered that requires burying. However, for those who offend against God, the Old Testament prescribes a fate literally worse than death. According to Jeremiah 16:4, 6:

They shall die of grievous deaths; they shall not be lamented; neither shall they be buried, but they shall be as dung upon the face of the earth: and they shall be consumed by the sword and famine; and their carcasses shall be meat for the fowls of heaven, and for the beasts of the earth. . . . Both the great and the small shall die in this land: they shall not be buried, neither shall men lament for them, nor cut themselves, nor make themselves bald for them [i.e., mourning and tearing out of hair].

Improper burial in every traditional culture on the planet is not only a social offense to the living but also disturbs the deceased and risks their return—as vampires, werewolves, and various other undead.

Just what a proper burial is, however, differs starkly from place to place: often what is sacred to one culture is exactly what is most offensive to another. In Hinduism and Buddhism, cremation is the norm, for it disposes of the body quickly and respectably; among early and medieval Christians and Jews, however, cremation was regarded as a great insult and the treatment of last resort against a vampire. Bodily resurrection was expected in these traditions, and so every bone and drop of blood was preserved, if possible, and safely inhumed with the dead. In early Christianity, the veneration of martyrs was so great and the attempts to recover Christian dead so ardent that vindictive Roman officials made every attempt to suppress the Christian movement by tampering with the dead. In 303 C.E. Roman law required that the bodies of imperial servants who were martyrs be exhumed and thrown into the sea, "lest any [Christians], regarding them as actually gods, should worship them as they lay in their tombs." Alternatively, the bodies of Christians might be cremated, with the ashes scattered in a river or in

Burying victims of the plague of London in mass graves, 1665. Courtesy of Anne Ronan Picture Library.

the sea, to thwart the afterlife hopes of the faithful.

There are various treatments of the physical body found in burial traditions around the world. Besides the extended (fully laid out) and flexed (fetal) burial positions mentioned earlier, there are also articulate and disarticulate dispositions of the body. An articulate burial leaves the body intact, whereas a disarticulate burial severs body parts from each other. The latter are occasionally found in medieval graves as attempts to put down bodies suspected of being undead, but generally disarticulate burials show particular respect for the dead. Among some Celtic, Arabic, and Central Asian tribes, heads of warriors were often severed from the rest of the body and buried in rows on hillsides facing the direction of enemy lands: the power of the warrior was thought to reside largely in the head, and its heroic energy was expected to help in undermining the power of adversaries and strengthening the home forces. In medieval Europe, great saints were often dismembered so that their holy relics could be more widely distributed. According to this theology, the whole power of the saint to intercede for the living resides in any single part, so the more parts there were, the more people could benefit from contact with the saint.

Two other kinds of burial are primary and secondary burial. A primary burial is the first deposition of the corpse, after which the body is expected to decay. Most modern cultures today practice only primary burial. Among many ancient cultures and still today among Orthodox Jews, Zoroastrians, some Native Americans, modern Greeks, and others, after enough time has passed that the flesh has thoroughly decayed or separated from the body (generally three to seven years), the bones are disinterred and prepared for the generally more significant secondary burial. In the secondary burial, remains are cleaned, often polished, sometimes painted or stained (red ochre was very widespread among ancient peoples), and, accompanied by appropriate rituals, placed in the family cave, mausoleum, or burial ground. Among cultures that practice secondary burial, it is generally thought that the fleshy remains are impure and corrupting, whereas the cleaned bones are pure, venerable, and contain the real essence of the departed.

Among early peoples, the dead appear to have been placed directly in the earth, although some evidence exists that the dead were in some areas covered with a textile cape or animal skin. In more modern times the shroud became the most common covering for the ordinary dead, with a wooden coffin reserved only for the wealthy. The origin of the coffin is somewhat obscure, but it appears that coffins were developed primarily for three reasons: (1) to protect the corpse from scavengers, (2) to protect it from the elements (at least initially), and (3) to keep the dead from the sight of the living. Although modern funeral directors often emphasize the first two criteria (and try to sell their clients the more costly "protective" coffins), it is generally accepted among researchers that modern coffins serve the needs of the living more than the dead, that is, to present the dead in a socially acceptable way while on display during the funeral and to hide the dead from sight otherwise. A fourth, more modern usage of the coffin is to enhance a family's prestige—a goal that has driven the funeral industry to produce more and more dramatic coffins. The Ghia Gallery of San Francisco, for example, offers everything from brightly colored, biodegradable coffins to leopard print coffins to exorbitantly expensive reproductions of Egyptian sarcophagi.

See also BARROW; BLACK DEATH; CATACOMB; CEMETERY; CENOTAPH; CREMATION; CROSSROADS; DEAD, THE; DEATH, GOOD; FUNERARY CUSTOMS; GARDEN, FUNERARY; HYPOGEUM; MAUSOLEUM; MOUND; RELIQUARY; THOLOS TOMB; TOWER OF SILENCE; TOWER TOMB; URN.

References

Ashbee, Paul. *The Earthen Long Barrow in Britain*. London: J. M. Dent and Sons, 1970.

Dempsey, D. *The Way We Die.* New York: Macmillan, 1975.

Farrell, J. J. *Inventing the American Way of Death 1830–1920.* Philadelphia: Temple University Press, 1980.

Iserson, Kenneth V. *Death to Dust: What Happens to Dead Bodies?* Tucson, AZ: Galen Press, 1994.

Jackson, A. V. W. *Zoroastrian Studies.* New York: Columbia University Press, 1928.

Jackson, P. E. *The Law of Cadavers and of Burial and Burial Places.* New York: Prentice-Hall, 1937.

Jones, Barbara. *Design for Death.* Indianapolis: Bobbs-Merrill, 1967.

Leca, Ange-Pierre. *The Egyptian Way of Death.* Trans. Louise Asmal. New York: Doubleday, 1981.

Meaney, Audrey. *A Gazetteer of Early Anglo-Saxon Burial Sites.* London: George Allen and Unwin, 1964.

Mitford, Jessica. *The American Way of Death.* New York: Simon and Schuster, 1963.

BURIAL, BASKET

Burial in a basket is a variation on the more common exposure burials found in scaffold and tree burials. The practice is chiefly reported among the Cheyenne peoples native to North America who spread out over the vast plains states of Missouri, Oklahoma, Kansas, and the Dakotas. The baskets used for burial (called in English "travois baskets," from the French *travail*) were primarily a means of transportation on the plains but also served as a ready-made kind of platform that could easily be placed high up among tree branches or on an existing scaffold on posts.

In 1927 David I. Bushnell Jr. reported an example of a basket burial in the "United States National Museum." G. M. Sternberg had removed the travois basket from a site in Walnut Creek, Kansas, and discovered that the burial contained the remains of an infant. However, basket burials have been found for adults of both sexes as well. In general, the deceased was dressed in his or her finest clothes, wrapped securely in mats or robes or both to keep off predatory animals and birds, and placed in the basket together with his or her most prized possessions (hunting or cooking implements, pipe, tobacco, beads, and ornaments). Although many Native American tribes later removed exposure burials from their resting places for secondary burials, it appears that the Cheyenne considered such burials final.

See also BURIAL, SCAFFOLD; BURIAL, TREE; FUNERARY CUSTOMS, NATIVE NORTH AMERICAN.

References
Bushnell, David I., Jr. *Burials of the Algonquian, Siouan and Caddoan Tribes West of the Mississippi.* Smithsonian Institution Bureau of American Ethnology, Bulletin 83. Washington, DC: Government Printing Office, 1927.

Yarrow, H. C. *A Further Contribution to the Study of Mortuary Customs of the North American Indians.* Bureau of American Ethnology Annual Report, vol. 1. Washington, DC: Government Printing Office, 1881.

———. *Introduction to the Study of Mortuary Customs among the North American Indians.* Washington, DC: Government Printing Office, 1880.

BURIAL CLOTHES

Traditionally, most societies have buried their dead in their best clothing or at least with a fine robe or fur skin over everyday clothes. Some cultures prescribe particular clothes for the dead to wear, either in place of personal clothing or in addition to it. Among the Amish, who wear black clothing in their daily lives, burial clothing should be white. Mormons who had advanced spiritual instruction in the church, called temple ordinances, are buried in white with a green apron. Among the ancient Romans, officials wore long white robes with purple edging, called *praetextae*. Early Christians objected to fancy burial clothing, however (especially because most early Christians came from the poorer classes), and adopted the simple shroud, essentially a sheet sewed up around the dead and covering the face. Orthodox Jews are likewise covered in a shroud, called a *tachrichim*, though it traditionally goes over the formal burial clothes.

Modern American funeral directors, however, have succeeded in weaning some Americans away from personal clothing or shrouds and since the nineteenth century have provided special burial clothes for sale from the funeral home. Men's burial clothing consists of several choices of dark suits, generally less expensive than a new suit at a department store. Mourners are often more hesitant to purchase burial clothing for women, as women's fashion changes so frequently, but hundreds of styles of women's burial clothes in various fabrics are for sale, including chiffon, crepe, and lace-over-taffeta. Modern American burial clothing opens in the back so that it can be easily placed on a corpse while it is lying down.

References
Dempsey, D. *The Way We Die.* New York: Macmillan, 1975.

Farrell, J. J. *Inventing the American Way of Death 1830–1920.* Philadelphia: Temple University Press, 1980.

Iserson, Kenneth V. *Death to Dust: What Happens to Dead Bodies?* Tucson, AZ: Galen Press, 1994.

Jones, Barbara. *Design for Death.* Indianapolis, IN: Bobbs-Merrill, 1967.

Mitford, Jessica. *The American Way of Death.* New York: Simon and Schuster, 1963.

BURIAL, SCAFFOLD

The "scaffold" or platform burial is a variation on the practice of exposure found mostly among tribal peoples worldwide. Scaffold burial almost certainly originated in each case with tree burials (either placing the corpse in a tree or in the trunk or suspending the body from the branches), and the custom persisted after there were no longer suitable trees to use or after the tribal group relocated to an area without trees, as with the plains tribes of North America.

In a scaffold burial the corpse is placed on a platform propped up on sticks or stilts anywhere from 6 to 20 feet high. The scaffold may also be fixed within the branches of a tree. Although this is a kind of "exposure" burial, the corpse is generally wrapped in blankets or robes that are tightly bound with leather cords or ropes; the elevation prevents wild animals from getting at the corpse, and the coverings keep off birds of prey. After some time, a year or more usually, the remains may be brought down and inhumed in a secondary burial. Scaffold or tree burial was common among the Native American tribes living on the northern plains and prairies of the United States and in the middle part of the Northwest Coast of the United States and Canada, as well as among some aboriginal groups in Australia. (The Native Americans of the Northwest Coast used elevated canoes as their "scaffold," and this practice will be discussed in the article BURIAL, SHIP. Scaffold burial is also occasionally found among some aboriginal groups of Malaysia, Indonesia, and the Pacific Islands, though in general the practice of these Pacific groups is closely tied to tree burial and will be covered in the article BURIAL, TREE.)

One group of Native Americans who practiced scaffold burial was the great Algonquin family of tribes, who were related linguistically more than politically, living from New England to North Carolina and as far west as modern-day Minnesota. The Algonquin tribe known as the Missisauga (located west of the Allegheny mountains along the St. Louis River) were reported by travelers to have practiced scaffold burial for the deaths of ordinary persons very widely in the early eighteenth century, though the bodies of heroes killed in war received special treatment, being cremated and then inhumed. However, among the Ojibway (located around the Great Lakes of the United States) it was the reverse—scaffold burial was a particular mark of respect for chieftains, whereas ordinary people were inhumed. Another Algonquin tribe, the Chippewa, appears to have practiced scaffold burial only occasionally. One traveler named Thomas L. McKenney reported the following in 1826:

> One mode of burying the dead, among the Chippeways [sic], is, to place the coffin, or box, containing their remains, on two cross pieces, nailed, or tied with wattap to four poles. The poles are about ten feet high. They plant near these posts, the wild hop, or some other kind of running vine, which spreads over and covers the coffin. (Bushnell, 1920)

Another linguistic family of Native Americans, the Muskogees (located in the pine lands of the southeastern United States), also practiced scaffold burial on occasion. In 1792 William Bartram reported that the Choctaw tribe of Mississippi and Alabama practiced scaffold burial as the first part of their funerary customs, placing the corpse on a scaffold 18 to 20 feet high in a grove of trees not far from the village. After a time the body was brought down; the flesh was scraped from the bones; and the bones were carefully washed, dried in the air, and then placed in a chest in the "bone house" or ossuary.

Thus among Native Americans of the eastern United States, scaffold burial appears to have been an occasional but widespread custom. Among the Sioux and other great tribes of the prairies and plains (including tribes of the Algonquin family that had been pushed westward, for instance, the Cree and the Cheyenne), scaffold burial was by far the dominant form of disposing of the corpse. The Dakota formed the largest division of the linguistic family of the Sioux, originating in the present state of Minnesota but moving westward and southward into the plains due to the encroachments of the Ojibway. The most common practice for the several tribes of the Dakota was to wrap the body tightly in blankets or to put the corpse in a box made of either a broken canoe or a trunk bought from a trader and place it on a platform 8 to 10 feet high that was propped up on four poles dug firmly into the ground. Generally, a separate scaffold was made for each of the dead, though occasionally several bodies would be placed on one platform. After the body had dried in the wind for several months or a year, relatives returned to remove the remains and prepare them for secondary burial in the ground. (The scaffold burial practice of another tribe related to the Dakota, the Assiniboins, is described in the sidebar.)

One exception to this general pattern was made for the bodies of those who were murdered (not those killed honorably on the battlefield). Murdered persons were buried in the ground, face down, with the head toward the south and a piece of fat in the mouth. This was apparently a defensive measure—since the "natural law" had been broken by means of the murder, steps had to be taken to prevent nature from retaliating by removing the game from the area or to prevent the ghost of the murdered from doing the same.

See also BURIAL, BASKET; BURIAL, TREE; FUNERARY CUSTOMS, NATIVE NORTH AMERICAN; MOUND; TOWER OF SILENCE.

References

Bushnell, David I., Jr. *Burials of the Algonquian, Siouan and Caddoan Tribes West of the Mississippi.* Smithsonian Institution Bureau of American Ethnology, Bulletin 83. Washington, DC: Government Printing Office, 1927.

———. *Native Cemeteries and Forms of Burial East of the Mississippi.* Smithsonian Institution Bureau of American Ethnology, Bulletin 71. Washington, DC: Government Printing Office, 1920.

Driver, Harold E. *Indians of North America.* Chicago: University of Chicago Press, 1961.

MacLeod, W. C. "Certain Mortuary Aspects of Northwest Coast Culture." *American Anthropologist* 27 (1925).

Moss, Rosalind. *The Life after Death in Oceania and the Malay Archipelago.* London: Oxford University Press, 1925.

Yarrow, H. C. *A Further Contribution to the Study of Mortuary Customs of the North American Indians.* Bureau of American Ethnology Annual Report, vol. 1. Washington, DC: Government Printing Office, 1881.

———. *Introduction to the Study of Mortuary Customs among the North American Indians.* Washington, DC: Government Printing Office, 1880.

BURIAL, SHIP

In many cultures around the world ships form part of the physical funeral and gravesite. In some cases the ship, packed with the corpse, offerings, and even sacrificed spouses and slaves, is set adrift on the waters, whereas in other cases the boat with its contents is entirely inhumed or set up on posts, as in a scaffold burial. Despite the obvious diversity, these practices may in fact be related in terms of a complex of themes and symbols that involves transcending ("crossing over") a water barrier on a journey to the other world.

The symbolism of the ship certainly varies culture to culture, but it is instructive that a ship is rarely blamed for its own shipwreck. One may blame the gods, the weather, the unruly nature of water itself, or fate, but tales rarely if ever impugn a ship that sank. Rather, ships generally figure in myth and poetry as romantic, even transcendent symbols—vessels that take humans across danger to places they could never venture unaided. Perhaps for this reason, Greek sailors (who were, of course, male) always chose feminine names for their ships, which signified not only a feminine "vessel" but a thing of beauty. Such ship names included Salvation, Grace, Bringer of Light, Blest, Victorious, Savior, Providence, Peace, Dove, and so on (all feminine nouns in Greek). Again, Noah's Ark was the vessel of salvation for human and animal kind, providing a temporary home and saving a select few from the universal catastrophe. In this sense, then, a boat may be a symbol of transcendence over water, for water very often means "danger," if not "destruction." In this sense too, although the sun is often thought to be pulled by a chariot, frequently (as in ancient Egypt) the sun was carried in or pulled by a ship of the heavens. In general, a ship is a means to "cross over," which is the literal meaning of "transcendence." However, individual cases must be brought to bear on such a general theory in order to test its validity.

Ship burial was widely practiced in ancient Egypt, though authorities do not entirely agree as to why. Entire ships loaded with equipment have been found buried at several ancient Egyptian sites, for instance, around the Great Pyramid. There, four boat-shaped pits were found, and although three were empty, the fourth actually contained the remains of a large wooden ship. To explain this practice, it must be noted that boats served many purposes in the ancient Egyptian funeral. First, the burial site was often across an actual river, so the funeral procession had to be loaded onto boats in order to get there. Second, as the cult of Osiris grew in prominence, the esteemed dead were often taken via the Nile to the cult sites at Busiris and Abydos, the shrines of Osiris, to partake of his death and resurrection. Boats may have been merely instrumental in the funeral—so why bury them? In Egyptian belief, everything connected with the person who died (clothing, embalming tools, personal possessions, often even wives and slaves) was considered "dead" by association and had to be disposed of at the burial ground. Thus the boats that carried the dead may have been routinely buried due to "death pollution." But this belief alone does not explain the fact that from the Old Kingdom period onward (c. 3000 B.C.E.) reliefs of boats, references to boats, and model boats complete with crews and cabins can be found in the tombs. Clearly, these were associated with the funerary boat of Osiris, which both carried him down into the Underworld (in the west) and around

Edwards writes in *The Pyramids of Egypt* (p. 133):

> The burial of boats suitable for navigation, although not uncommon in the enclosures of the large brick Mastabas of the 1st Dynasty, seems to have been limited in the Old Kingdom to the royal Pyramid complexes. Some of these boats may have been used at the time of the funeral, but others were probably intended to provide the dead king with a means of transport in his After-life, the precise region in which they were to be employed being still obscure. In the solar cult, a boat would be required for accompanying the Sun-god on his daily journey across the heavens and his nightly journey beneath the earth; it would also be needed for reaching the region beyond the eastern horizon, where the gods were thought to dwell.

It may be true that whole ship burials were limited to the Old Kingdom (roughly 2800 to 2100 B.C.E. by conservative estimates), but James Hamilton-Paterson and Carol Andrews (p. 93) point out that the ship symbolism carried on in Egypt long after the physical burials of boats ceased: "Model boats appear quite frequently in Middle and New Kingdom tombs. Their purpose was to ferry the dead person up and down the Nile on [ghostly] Osirian pilgrimages to Abydos and Busiris." Clearly, ships were associated with the Egyptian funerary complex from start to finish and must be understood as having a deep religious significance to a people who were so interested in death—not as the end of life but as the beginning of immortality.

Ancient Scandinavians also buried entire boats, with the dead in full regalia sitting upright surrounded by gifts, including animal and even human sacrifices. Ship burial was by no means an everyday affair in Scandinavia, but it does appear to have been a frequent practice for the funerals of nobles or heroic persons. Sometimes the loaded ship was cremated and then buried, and other times it was inhumed intact; in either case the burial site was covered with a large mound. Most ship burials in Norway were vessels less than 10 meters long, and only five have been found larger than 20 meters. The Gokstad ship, found 50 miles south-southeast of Oslo, measures $23^{1}/_{3}$ meters long and had sixteen pairs of oars, sails, a rudder, and an anchor. It and three smaller boats, all covered with a great mound, date to the end of the ninth century. Such a lavish burial indicates the deceased's prominence. Often the boat and its deceased passenger were cremated, and only the discovery of boat rivets in a grave shows that it was a ship burial. Another version of the ship burial in Scandinavia involved outlining the shape of a boat using upright stones over the cremation spot. It is not clear whether the outlined ship and the buried ship were ritually equivalent, or whether

again to the east each day with the rising sun. There can be no doubt that in some cases the deceased (most often a pharaoh) was thought to join or even become Osiris on his Underworld ship drawn by the sun. Thus, burying the boat of an important personage may have had more to do with afterlife hopes than ritual impurity. I. E. S.

some alteration in Scandinavian belief brought on the change in funerary custom.

Yet another variation on the Scandinavian ship burial was the practice of loading a ship up with its dead voyager and equipment and launching it out to sea. In the Norse myth of the death of the beautiful god Balder, this practice appears to be combined simultaneously with cremation. In *Myths of the Norsemen,* H. A. Guerber writes:

> The great ship now drifted out to sea, and the flames from the pyre presented a magnificent spectacle, which assumed a greater glory with every passing moment, until, when the vessel neared the western horizon, it seemed as if sea and sky were on fire. Sadly the gods watched the glowing ship and its precious freight, until suddenly it plunged into the waves and disappeared; nor did they turn aside and return to Asgard until the last spark of light had vanished, and the world, in token of mourning for Balder the good, was enveloped in a mantle of darkness.

Clearly, the ship is not merely a tomb, but an indispensable means of transportation to another world.

One great ship cremation in central Europe was observed firsthand by the Muslim historian Ahmad Ibn Fadhlan, who was serving on an embassy from Baghdad to the Bulgars on the Volga in 922. After a ten-day funeral ceremony, during which there was music and merrymaking, the deceased chieftain was placed on a couch amid a dome of wood on the ship and was cremated along with a slave-girl "wife." Another Arab writer, Ibn Rustah, describes the burial of a ship and chieftain in which the "wife" was buried alive in the grave. It is possible that the persons performing these ship burials in central Europe were Scandinavians abroad, or the custom of ship burial may have migrated to nearby lands. Some Anglo-Saxon tribes are known to have practiced ship inhumation, and an example from myth is recorded in the epic *Beowulf.*

Certain Native American groups also used a boat in funerary customs, mainly those tribes located on the Northwest Coast of the United States. The Chinook, Twana, and Clallam, all tribes of Washington state, used to carry out canoe burials, though this practice faded out after centuries of white influence. H. C. Yarrow (1881) provides several accounts of how this was done. Four holes were punched in old canoes, which were then fitted with four upright beams (or the entire canoe was placed in the branches of a tree) to keep the dead away from wolves and other wild animals. Frequently two canoes were used—one placed upright on the poles, serving as a platform, and a smaller one, inverted and placed on top of the other to protect the dead from birds of prey and other depredations, though a trunk, coffin, or thick blankets were also used as the inner covering. The article "Boats" in the *Encyclopedia of Religion* reports that among the Twana of the Coast Salish group,

> A grieving husband was to spend four days and four nights near the canoe, waiting for his wife to depart for the otherworld. According to Twana belief, the inhabitants of the realm of the dead come in a canoe to claim the newly deceased. Late at night it is said that one can hear their paddles in the water as they come to carry away their new companion.

Burial in a canoe or setting the dead adrift was also practiced at times by other tribal peoples, for instance, the Arctic Eurasian tribes such as the Vogul, the Ostyak, the Sea-Lapps, and the Yakut—all of whom made their living, in part, from the sea.

Using a canoe as a coffin is also common to many parts of Polynesia and greater Oceania, though again this practice has faded greatly because of modernization. In Timorlaut, an island east of Timor, the dead are placed in canoes and exposed on high platforms or tall rocks on the shore, and on the Luang-Sermata and Leti Islands (just off the coast of Timor) miniature boats filled with food and other offerings are either buried in the ground near the deceased or set adrift on the ocean to take the soul of the dead with them to the "island of the dead." The practice of setting the dead adrift on full-sized canoes occurs in Samoa, Fiji, Niue, and the Chatham Islands (all in the Pacific) and was formerly done in Hawaii, Tahiti, and New Zealand, though primarily for chieftains—commoners were simply thrown into the sea, sometimes with weights. In either case, the purpose appears to have been the same: to send the soul "back" to its homeland across the sea. Whether this was a real homeland that these various peoples had migrated from, as maintained by Rosalind Moss, or perhaps just another version of the global belief in a land of the dead to the west (or both) is hard to say.

It is certainly no accident that ship burials take place predominantly among people whose culture revolves around the ocean (such as the Scandinavians and the Twana) or rivers (such as ancient Egyptians on the Nile) or whose "domain" comprises islands (like the people of Indonesia, Polynesia, and Oceania). But the symbolism of the ship burial makes it unlikely that the boat or canoe was merely a convenient coffin—the burial of entire ships beneath the ground is too labor-intensive for mere practicality. Rather, the ship appears to serve the same function for water dwellers as the chariot or horse does for the people of the plains and steppe—it is at once the symbol of the afterlife destination, and the means to get there.

See also BURIAL, SCAFFOLD; FUNERARY CUSTOMS, ANCIENT EGYPT-
IAN; FUNERARY CUSTOMS, NATIVE NORTH AMERICAN; FUNER-
ARY CUSTOMS, SCANDINAVIAN; WATER.

References

Davidson, H. R. Ellis. *The Lost Beliefs of Northern Europe*. London:
Routledge, 1993.

Edwards, I. E. S. *The Pyramids of Egypt*. Rev. ed. New York:
Penguin, 1978.

Ellis, Hilda Roderick. *The Road to Hel: A Study of the Conception of the
Dead in Old Norse Literature*. Cambridge: Cambridge University
Press, 1943.

Guerber, Hélène Adeline. *Myths of the Norsemen from the Eddas and
Sagas*. New York: Dover, 1992.

Hamilton-Paterson, James, and Carol Andrews. *Mummies: Death and
Life in Ancient Egypt*. London: William Collins Sons, 1978.

Kirkby, Michael Hasloch. *The Vikings*. Oxford: Phaidon Press,
1977.

MacLeod, W. C. "Certain Mortuary Aspects of Northwest Coast
Culture." *American Anthropologist* 27 (1925).

Moss, Rosalind. *The Life after Death in Oceania and the Malay
Archipelago*. London: Oxford University Press, 1925.

Nesheim, A. *Traits from Life in a Sea-Lappish District*. Nordnorske
Samlinger Utgitt av Etnografisk Museum Series 6. Oslo:
Etnografisk Museum, 1949.

Sawyer, P. H. *The Age of the Vikings*. London: Edward Arnold, 1962.

Yarrow, H. C. *A Further Contribution to the Study of Mortuary Customs
of the North American Indians*. Bureau of American Ethnology
Annual Report, vol. 1. Washington, DC: Government Printing
Office, 1881.

———. *Introduction to the Study of Mortuary Customs among the North
American Indians*. Washington, DC: Government Printing
Office, 1880.

BURIAL, SKY

Similar to the Iranian and Parsi practice of exposing the
dead in a Tower of Silence, modern Tibetans often practice exposure of the dead in inaccessible high places.
Although cremation is also practiced by Tibetans, the
so-called sky burial is common, particularly where fuel
for a funeral pyre is scarce. At death an astrologer is
called in to determine the appropriate day and time of
burial, and each day until then the family and officiat-
ing lama eat a funeral meal, offering some to the corpse.
On the appointed day of burial the corpse is taken out
of the house by specially appointed caretakers, called
ragyapas. It is the ragyapas who bring the body to a local
mountaintop (often cutting up the body at the joints)
and inviting carnivorous animals and wild birds to eat
the corpse, leaving only the bones. The bodies of criminals, however, are said to be shunned by the bird scavengers. A few days later, the site is visited again to collect the bones, grind them to powder, and mix the
powdered bones with flour to bake bread. The bread is
again left out in the wild for the animals to eat.

There is evidence that in ancient times Tibetans
practiced inhumation, and early chronicles testify to a
long list of kings buried in large pits covered by tumuli.

Sometime after the introduction of Buddhism in the
seventh century, Tibetans appear to have been influenced by the Zoroastrian practice of exposing the corpse
rather than burying it. This conclusion is bolstered by
the tradition of the indigenous Bon religion, which
claims to have been brought to Tibet from Iran centuries before the historical period. In a radical departure
from the Iranian custom, however, the Tibetan practice
shows distinct Buddhist influence. Sky burials, according to Tibetans, are performed not to avoid polluting
the sacred elements of earth, air, fire, and water, as in
Zoroastrianism, but to benefit living creatures. Unless
the body belonged to a high lama or saint, the corpse
is of little account in Buddhism, since the consciousness of the deceased, or *namparshay*, has departed from
the old body en route to a new reincarnation.
Therefore, the remains may as well be used in the most
beneficent way possible, as a final act of self-sacrifice
and *dana,* or charity.

See also KURGAN.

References

Habenstein, Robert W., and William M. Lamers. *Funeral Customs
the World Over*. Milwaukee: Bulfin Printers, 1963.

Stein, R. A. *Tibetan Civilization*. Stanford: Stanford University Press,
1972.

Tucci, Giuseppe. *The Religions of Tibet*. Trans. Geoffrey Samuel.
Berkeley: University of California Press, 1980.

———. *Tibet: Land of Snows*. Trans. J. E. Stapleton Driver. London:
Elek, 1967.

BURIAL, TREE

Although the practice of placing the dead in trees varies
greatly, as Rosalind Moss points out in *The Life after
Death in Oceania* (p. 156), there are only two basic patterns: the temporary placement of bodies in trees
(whether in the branches, on a platform, suspended
from branches, or within the trunk or branch) to be
removed later for secondary burial; and the placement
of the dead in trees as their final resting place.

Many tribal groups in Indonesia, Malaysia, and the
Pacific Islands practiced *temporary* tree exposure until
the advent of industrialization, and some continue to
dispose of their dead in or around trees. New
Caledonians and inland mountain peoples of Borneo
traditionally place their dead erect within the trunks of
trees, replacing the bark over the corpse to hide it from
view. However, among many Oceanic peoples tree burial is less exotic—the dead are simply placed on platforms in trees or laid securely between the branches.
This is practiced on the Andaman Islands and among
the Mafulu of New Guinea, the nomads of Indonesia
and Melanesia, the Orang Kubu peoples of Sumatra,
and the "Sea-Dyaks" of Borneo, to name only a few.

Not many Oceanic peoples appear to have practiced

final tree burial. Some traditional peoples in New Zealand place exhumed bones in hollow trees or on platforms in trees as the secondary burial. Moss reports sporadic final burial in trees among some tribes of the New Hebrides (the Ambryn) and the central islands in the Celebes Sea (the Tolampo). In general, tree burial in Oceania appears to be in decline but is still a mark of honor for important people, especially "medicine men" and shamans who often maintain stronger links with the past than less traditionally educated people.

According to Erminie Voegelin, tree burial was the primary mode of disposing of the dead among some Native American groups, including such eastern woodlands and Great Lakes tribes as the Miami, Sauk, Fox, Potawatomi, Ottawa, Menomini, Huron, Seneca, Nanticoke, Choctaw, Chickasaw, and Omaha (though many other woodlands tribes practiced inhumation). It is important to note that the bodies of the dead were not casually tossed into trees but were dressed in their finest clothes, carefully wrapped from head to foot in mats, and placed upon solidly constructed platforms or between branches, with the intention of protecting the body from marauding animals and birds of prey. For most Native American tribes, tree exposure was not the permanent disposition of the corpse, but was followed after a few months or a year of exposure by a secondary burial in which the remains were inhumed.

See also BURIAL, BASKET; BURIAL, SCAFFOLD; FUNERARY CUSTOMS, NATIVE NORTH AMERICAN.

References

Bushnell, David I., Jr. *Burials of the Algonquian, Siouan and Caddoan Tribes West of the Mississippi.* Smithsonian Institution Bureau of American Ethnology, Bulletin 83. Washington, DC: Government Printing Office, 1927.

————. *Native Cemeteries and Forms of Burial East of the Mississippi.* Smithsonian Institution Bureau of American Ethnology, Bulletin 71. Washington, DC: Government Printing Office, 1920.

Driver, Harold E. *Indians of North America.* Chicago: University of Chicago Press, 1961.

MacLeod, W. C. "Certain Mortuary Aspects of Northwest Coast Culture." *American Anthropologist* 27 (1925).

Moss, Rosalind. *The Life after Death in Oceania and the Malay Archipelago.* London: Oxford University Press, 1925.

Voegelin, Erminie Wheeler. *Mortuary Customs of the Shawnee and Other Eastern Tribes.* Prehistory Research Series, vol. 2, no. 4. Indianapolis: Indiana Historical Society, 1944.

Yarrow, H. C. *A Further Contribution to the Study of Mortuary Customs of the North American Indians.* Bureau of American Ethnology Annual Report, vol. 1. Washington, DC: Government Printing Office, 1881.

————. *Introduction to the Study of Mortuary Customs among the North American Indians.* Washington, DC: Government Printing Office, 1880.

C

CAIRN

From the earlier Celtic word *carn*, the Scottish word *cairn* denotes a mound of stones used as boundary markers and especially as monuments over a significant grave. Although the word is used primarily in Great Britain, the phenomenon of making a pile of stones as a burial monument exists worldwide. In the Old Testament, Absalom, son of King David, was killed by Joab: "They took Absalom's body and flung it into a great pit in the forest, and raised over it a huge pile of stones" (2 Samuel 18:17).

See also BARROW; TUMULUS.

References

Murray, James A. H. et al. *Oxford English Dictionary*. 2nd ed. Oxford: Clarendon Press, 1996.

CANOPIC JAR, CHEST

Canopic jars are stone, pottery, wood, or glazed earthenware vessels, usually vases or urns and often with carved human or animal heads, containing human remains. The word *canopic* comes from an ancient Greek tradition in which a pilot named Canopus was said to have been worshipped in the form of a vase with a human head.

In the pre-Roman civilization of Italy known as Etruria, canopic urns were sometimes used to bury cremation ashes. They were used from the late eighth to the early sixth centuries B.C.E. and took the shape of rudimentary human forms seated on high-backed chairs or thrones. Related cremation vases and urns looked like imitation dwelling huts. However, these canopic urns never took on the mythic and symbolic stature that is found in a similar Egyptian practice dating back many thousands of years.

In the Old Kingdom of Egypt at the beginning of the Fourth Dynasty (c. 2600 B.C.E.), when the science of mummification began in earnest, it was recognized that removing the soft tissue of the internal organs from the corpse helped prevent bodily decay and thus preserved the body better. Because the deceased was thought to need his or her *entire* body in the hereafter, the organs were wrapped in linen for protection and placed near the body, usually in niches carved into the south wall of the tomb. However, the organs of those of the highest rank, for example Queen Hetepheres, were kept in special containers—wooden or alabaster boxes with four inner compartments in which each of the four major organs (lungs, liver, intestines, and stomach) were placed separately. This container was then put outside the coffin but inside the tomb.

By the Fifth and Sixth Dynasties of Egypt (c. 2500 to c. 2100 B.C.E.) the practice of placing the internal organs of the deceased in specialized canopic containers had spread to the lower classes. After removal, each of the four organs was put into heaps of natron (drying salts) for forty days or so until all moisture was removed. They were wrapped in linen for further preservation and placed in a limestone jar, often containing a solution of more natron, and the jars were placed in a special wooden chest.

By the Middle Kingdom period (c. 2100 to c. 1600 B.C.E.), the lids of the jars had acquired the likeness of a human head, and after the Eighteenth Dynasty (1300 B.C.E.), each of the four jars had a different lid dedicated to one of the four sons of Horus. The human-headed Imsety guarded the liver; baboon-headed Hapy guarded the lungs; falcon-headed Qebhsenuef looked after the intestines; and jackal-headed Duamutef watched over the stomach. This new artistic development, however, was not an innovation in thought, for in the funerary texts the four sons of Horus had long been associated with the four internal organs.

In the Twenty-first Dynasty (1085 to 945 B.C.E.) there was a sudden move to retain the corpse completely intact, and although the internal organs were still removed in the embalming process, after being dried by natron they were wrapped in linen and replaced in the body cavity. A little wax figure of the appropriate deity was attached to each organ. Nonetheless, canopic jars were still buried with the coffin in the tomb, even though they were completely empty or were even dummies with entirely solid bodies—another example of the extreme conservatism of Egyptian funerary practices. This continued until the Twenty-sixth Dynasty (c. 660 B.C.E.), at which time the organs were placed between the legs of the mummy and wrapped with it or else returned to the canopic jars. Interestingly, the Egyptians mummified and entombed animals that were significant to them as well, and in

Canopic jars found in the tomb of Tutankhamen. Courtesy of Anne Ronan Picture Library.

the New Kingdom period canopics have been found for the organs of the sacred Apis bulls at Saqqâra.

Not only the jars but the chests in which the jars were stored also became more decorative in the New Kingdom period (Eighteenth to Twenty-first Dynasties). They had extensive inscriptions and relief-work on the exterior, often with blue pigment in the hollows of the carving. The four protective goddesses, each of whom guided one son of Horus (see below), were often carved in relief at the corners of the canopic chest with wings extended to protect the chest's contents. From illustrations of funerary processions, the canopic chest appears to have been mounted on a sledge base in the form of a shrine. It is clear from the inscriptions on the canopic jars and chests that the association of the organs with the various deities was not decorative or coincidental but profoundly significant in Egyptian belief. The inscriptions declare not only that the deities should preserve and guard the organs in the afterworld but that the organs actually *were identical* with the sons of Horus, who in turn were protected by the wings of the four goddesses Isis (over Imsety), Nephthys (over Hapy), Neith (over Duamutef), and Selkis (over Qebhsenuef). Bizarre as this association may seem at first glance, it

had a perfectly consistent rationale: for the Egyptians, as for many ancient peoples, an organ was not merely a mass of tissue as in modern Western medicine but was a conscious entity thought to perform a specific and even occult function. Each function was personified and attributed to a cosmic power or energy that localized itself in the appropriate organ. In much the same way we might imagine that because the brain is the seat of intellect, it must "incarnate" an instance of "cosmic mind." Thus each person's liver *was* Horus's son Imsety, mystically overshadowed by the goddess Isis, thus personifying the human function of the liver and connecting it to the cosmic mythology surrounding Isis. This complex set of beliefs sheds light on the extraordinary concern and investment Egyptian civilization had in the body, alive and especially dead.

See also FUNERARY CUSTOMS, ANCIENT EGYPTIAN; PYRAMID, EGYPTIAN.

References

Garstang, J. *Burial Customs of Ancient Egypt*. London: A. Constable, 1907.

Hamilton-Paterson, James, and Carol Andrews. *Mummies: Death and Life in Ancient Egypt*. London: William Collins Sons, 1978.

Spencer, A. J. *Death in Ancient Egypt*. New York: Penguin, 1982.

Toynbee, J. M. C. *Death and Burial in the Roman World*. Ithaca, NY: Cornell University Press, 1971.

Winlock, H. E. *The Rise and Fall of the Middle Kingdom in Thebes*. New York: Macmillan, 1947.

CATACOMB

A catacomb is a complex of subterranean rock-cut burial chambers linked to each other via small passageways. The word derives from the name of the Christian cemetery, *Ad Catacumbas,* which in turn translates the Greek *kata kumbas,* meaning "at the hollows." The principal Christian catacombs were located on the Via Appia Antica 3 miles south of Rome, and these were the only ones visited in later centuries as pilgrimage sites.

Although Jewish catacombs are found in the late Second Temple period in the Levant, most notably at the necropolis at Beth-shearim, catacombs were by far more common among Christians, particularly in Rome. Forty-two Christian catacombs and six Jewish ones have been discovered in and around that city. They are also found in many major cities that were once ruled by the Roman Empire: Albano, Alexandria, Hadrumetum, Kerch, Naples, Malta, Syracuse, and others. To be sure, catacombs were not the only kind of burials used by the early Christian church; plenty of Christian cemeteries (most often converted from pagan use) have been found, particularly where the ground was not suitable for excavation. Yet the rock-cut tomb of Jesus in the New Testament surely served as an important precedent for Christian burial, and from the mid–third century catacombs became a very popular style of burial among Christians, stretching for at least 350 miles around Rome and housing more than a half million bodies. After Christianity became truly established in the Roman Empire in the fourth century C.E., decoration of the catacombs became quite elaborate.

Catacombs range in size from single-family complexes to multistoried structures administered by the church and housing thousands of tombs. The passageways in the catacombs could be somewhat irregular, particularly if the catacomb was taken over from an abandoned quarry (like many outside the city walls of Rome), but often they were nicely finished, with oil

Catacomb of a Capuchin convent at Palermo, 1833. Courtesy of Anne Ronan Picture Library.

lamps cemented in the walls and vases for holding perfume. Many dead were buried in loculi in the walls of the passageways, and some were in small chambers (cubicula) off the passageways. Each chamber had a number of tombs, either dug into the floor (formae) or cut into the walls (loculi). Whether in the walls of the passageways or the chambers, up to seven rows of loculi recesses could be cut into the walls, each housing from one to four bodies each and sealed with a stone slab or tiles. Some catacomb tombs have been found with wooden or fixed stone tables used for funeral banquets and even Eucharist for the dead. At other times, small rooms were placed at the junctions of corridors, also serving as locations for funeral feasts or housing small altars.

Some of the earliest known Christian art comes from the catacomb decorations. The walls of tombs and the sarcophagi in catacombs were often painted, first with pagan motifs and later more frequently with scenes from the Old and New Testaments. Catacombs usually had a painted or carved inscription identifying the occupant. More elaborate tombs had an arched niche or arcosolium to house popes, martyrs, and other esteemed dead.

Catacombs fell out of use for burial in Rome in the first half of the fifth century C.E. but continued to be visited and embellished as important sites of martyrs and their relics. The increasing practice of removing relics from catacombs for use in churches, as well as the destruction of the cemeteries by the invading Lombards following the siege of 756, caused a decline in the importance of the catacombs during the Middle Ages until they were almost entirely forgotten. By the end of the Middle Ages, however, some of the catacombs were rediscovered and once again became accessible to pilgrims. Dated graffiti show the return of visitors beginning in the 1430s.

In the twentieth century, some scholars thought that early Christians sought prolonged refuge in the catacombs during times of persecution or at least held their regular church services there. Recent scholarship suggests that this was unlikely. Few chambers were larger than 10 feet by 10 feet and so could not hold many people, and the catacombs were subject to dampness and frequent flooding. Although it is certain that many early Christians undertook pilgrimages to the catacombs to visit the martyrs buried there and there is good evidence that funeral rituals and perhaps even annual Eucharist services were held in the catacombs for small groups, there is no evidence that entire churches ever congregated in catacombs on a regular basis.

References

Hertling, Ludwig, and Engelbert Kirschbaum. *The Roman Catacombs and Their Martyrs.* Trans. M. Joseph Costelloe. London: Darton, Longman, and Todd, 1960.

Stevenson, James. *The Catacombs: Life and Death in Early Christianity.* London: Thames and Hudson: 1978.

Tronzo, W. *The Via Latina Catacomb.* University Park: Pennsylvania State University Press, 1986.

CELLA

Literally "small chamber" in Latin, most houses in the Roman world had a cella for storage or as a pen or coop for animals. Whereas in modern English the "cellar" is always underground, beneath the home, in its original usage the cella was often aboveground, inside or outside the house. In a funerary context, the cella was generally the actual resting place of the body or cremains of the deceased in house tombs and temple tombs. It was sometimes one room among several in Roman house tombs or perhaps below the tomb; in the case of the temple tomb, it rested above the podium surrounded by pillars and statuary.

References

Toynbee, J. M. C. *Death and Burial in the Roman World.* Ithaca, NY: Cornell University Press, 1971.

CEMETERY

The word *cemetery* literally means "sleeping place" and comes from the Latin word *coemeterium* and the ancient Greek *koimeterion.* Although many traditional cultures have chosen to bury their dead within the family home (including ancient Greeks and many Native American cultures), most urbanized civilizations have set apart special areas for the final disposition of their dead.

Cemeteries vary widely in form and function around the world. In modern Greece, the dead are first buried in the earth until the flesh falls completely off the bones (generally three to five years); then the bones of the loved one are recovered and reverentially given *secondary* burial in the "cemetery" (kimitiri), which in academic terms is really an ossuary, or "place of bones." Nor are all cemeteries created equal, apparently. Very Orthodox Jews believe that on Judgment Day the resurrection of the dead will take place first at the Mount of Olives in Israel. Thus prices are extremely high for gravesites on the Mount, especially those near an important rabbi's grave (perhaps the rabbi's holiness will transfer to sinners nearby?). Most often, as among modern Chinese, African tribal groups, Muslims, Christians, and many others, cemeteries are placed some distance from human habitation, though close enough for frequent visits. In ancient Rome, burials were required by law to take place outside the city walls, except in the cases of high priests, generals, and emperors. Early Christians had to bury their dead in secret, for they were a proscribed cult and feared spoliation of their remains by Roman authorities. Thus Christians in Rome began using series of catacombs or underground tunnels carved out of soft rock, placing the dead in vertical rows, one above the other, as high as they could reach. After the Roman Empire converted to Christianity, Christians generally followed "civilized" Roman practice and adopted the norms of family cemeteries and mausolea outside the city limits—while Rome's power lasted. After the collapse of Rome, many Christians buried their dead within the walls and floors of the local church, even under the altar or pews. Soon limitations of space and objections of church leaders led to an attempt at reform. The seventh-century Council of Nantes forbade burial inside the sanctuary but allowed it in the atrium of the church—thus the definition of the word *cemetery* became "church atrium." Official proclamations notwithstanding, however, saints were buried within the church by popular demand because their hallowed relics actually contributed to the power and reputation of the church. Other notables—kings, priests, and aristocrats—often managed to get themselves buried within the sanctuary as well. Ordinary Christians were soon buried in the yard surrounding the church.

Thus in time the definition of *cemetery* shifted in medieval Europe to become synonymous with the churchyard. But the medieval cemetery had a great many more uses than in the modern world. First of all, graves in the churchyard cemetery were nowhere near as permanent as they are conceived to be today. Even in medieval times it was known that bodies decay completely in the space of three to seven years, except for bones. Thus graves were regularly opened and new bodies were placed inside, sometimes with the old bones removed and placed in a "charnel house," sometimes not. Because medieval churches often had political power distinct from the state, those in trouble with local authorities could seek asylum in the churchyard, eventually building homes, raising families, and gardening there. Because medieval cemeteries generally lacked the headstones and mausolea that are popular today, the churchyard was also an open space that invited public activity. Fairs, markets, sporting events, theatrical productions, juggling, dancing, and even gambling were everyday uses of the medieval church cemetery. Various church councils attempted to control the activities on church property, but again with little effect—regulations were nearly impossible to enforce when the local clergy themselves gained income and farmland from the diverse cemetery activities.

In the twelfth and thirteenth centuries, Europe began a gradual but massive process of urbanization and population increase, a growth slowed but not stopped by epidemics like the Black Death, which decimated

Northern London cemetery, Highgate, 1838. Courtesy of Anne Ronan Picture Library.

Necropolis in a northern London cemetery, Highgate, 1838. Courtesy of Anne Ronan Picture Library.

Europe beginning in 1347. Overcrowding—first inside the churches, and then in the churchyards—gradually forced the evolution of public cemeteries. These new cemeteries were planned by civil authorities but often administered by religious officials. Civil cemeteries were designed in rigid grid patterns, though from the early Victorian period onward the influence of landscape artists may be seen, with trees and shrubs, garden plots, and sweeping carriageways creating a more inviting atmosphere. Old habits died hard, however, and even until the sixteenth and seventeenth centuries it was the custom for royalty, nobility, and the wealthy to seek burial within church precincts, even if that meant evicting the previous inhabitants for a suitable charge. With the rise of an urban middle class and the gradual use by the wealthy of public cemeteries, engraved headstones and grand monuments became more prominent there and began to spread to the still-functioning churchyard cemeteries.

In modern times, church cemeteries are all but defunct, preserving their dead but not admitting newcomers. Though regulated by government, in Europe and the United States cemeteries and burials have been almost completely taken over by commercial funeral homes, organized into national associations that stridently seek to protect and expand their business. Burial

plots are sold "pre-need" and generally run $100 to $5,000 each, depending on the prestige of the cemetery and the location of the grave site. (Certainly, grave plots on the Mount of Olives or in the Westwood Village Memorial Park in Los Angeles will be considerably more expensive.) Traditional cemeteries with headstones are declining in popularity, largely due to the influence of the funeral associations, which prefer the creation of "memorial parks." A memorial park is simply a cemetery with grave markers (plates or plaques) that are level with the ground, so as to facilitate easier lawn care and groundskeeping. Memorial parks not only are considered more attractive by many visitors but more easily allow other uses of the land, including jogging, bird watching, and even picnicking.

As in the high Middle Ages of Europe, however, the modern world's population growth is also putting the pinch on space in cemeteries and memorial parks. Although "necrotecture" seeks to maximize the usage of cemetery space (for instance, placing one set of graves 12 feet under the surface, so that another layer only 6 feet under may be placed on top), another trend is the relocation of old cemeteries to new space, so that urban and suburban growth may progress unimpeded. The remains of the deceased buried there are generally removed to the new location, but often this is not possible if the bones have turned to dust, or the remains can no longer be identified. According to U.S. law, those who purchase cemetery plots do not own the land but merely the right to use it. "Eminent domain" gives the government the right to take possession of any land (in exchange for reasonable reimbursement), and simple changes in cemetery and civil regulations can mandate changes in the use and location of cemeteries. Kenneth Iserson reports that the cemetery called Potter's Field in New York City

> was established at Madison Square (as in the Gardens) in 1794. As New York City expanded, it was soon moved to Washington Square, then Bryant Square, then Third Avenue and 50th Street, then Ward's Island and finally, in 1870, to Harts Island. The city built up over the old cemeteries and remains were rarely moved. (p. 530)

Likewise, San Francisco banned cemeteries within the city limits in the 1930s and relocated 90,000 graves over ten years to the nearby suburb of Colma, now called "Cemetery City" in local jargon. Another solution to the problem of limited space, of course, is cremation, which is increasingly popular, especially on the West Coast of the United States.

References:

Bassett, S. *Death in Towns: Urban Responses to the Dying and the Dead, 100–1600.* Leicester, UK: Leicester University Press, 1992.

Dempsey, D. *The Way We Die.* New York: Macmillan, 1975.

Farrell, J. J. *Inventing the American Way of Death 1830–1920.* Philadelphia: Temple University Press, 1980.

Geary, Patrick J. *Living with the Dead in the Middle Ages.* Ithaca, NY: Cornell University Press, 1994.

Gilbert, Lionel. *A Grave Look at History: Glimpses of a Vanishing Form of Folk Art.* Sydney: John Ferguson, 1980.

Iserson, Kenneth V. *Death to Dust: What Happens to Dead Bodies?* Tucson, AZ: Galen Press, 1994.

Jones, Barbara. *Design for Death.* Indianapolis: Bobbs-Merrill, 1967.

Mitford, Jessica. *The American Way of Death.* New York: Simon and Schuster, 1963.

Toynbee, J. M. C. *Death and Burial in the Roman World.* Ithaca, NY: Cornell University Press, 1971.

CEMETERY, ANIMAL

One of the most intriguing phenomena of the ancient Egyptian religion is the prominence of animals and animal-headed divinities in the religion. Although scholars may certainly be correct in asserting that later Egyptian religion evolved from early hunter-gatherer religions, where animals figured prominently as the primary means of survival, it would be a mistake to reduce Egyptian concern with animal divinities to purely a superstitious holdover from primitive times. In fact, Egyptian religion must be regarded as philo-sophically complex and rich in symbolism.

The prominence of animals and animal-headed human figures did not so much deify particular animals as associate particular *characteristics* demonstrated by animal species with phenomena in the natural and spiritual worlds. As an example, we may take the prominent scarab beetle amulet found on nearly all mummies: the scarab or dung beetle rolls fecal matter into small balls and lays its eggs inside. The beetle then hatches and breaks out of its tiny prison. To the Egyptian mind, this cycle suggested spiritual transformation and tran-scendence—some even suggest it symbolized reincarnation. Thus it was no supposed magic power of the scarab that was worshipped by the ancient Egyptians but rather the symbolism suggested by the beetle that produced widespread religious usage. Likewise the serpent symbolized duality, the stork the soul, the crocodile the mind, the dog digestion and transformation, and the vulture gestation and completion—each species had its particular symbolic function.

To this end, living animals associated with various deities were kept at their respective temples within the sacred precincts. Sometimes one animal was kept as the divine representative of the deity, or sometimes great numbers were kept: one text refers to food needed for the 60,000 ibises at Saqqâra. When these sacred animals died, they were treated with all the respect of a human who had died—and sometimes more, in the case of the Apis bull at Memphis associated with Osiris. The dead animals were mummified just like human remains and given full burial honors, often including coffins and ceremonies like the Opening of the Mouth (see FUNER-ARY CUSTOMS, ANCIENT EGYPTIAN). Sometimes animal mummies were placed within the wooden statues of the deities they represented, for instance, dogs inside statues of Anubis or cats inside figures of Bastet. More often, however, the animal mummies were placed in special cemeteries.

Animal cemeteries are found scattered throughout the lands of ancient Egypt, particularly near major cities that served as headquarters for specific cults. Extensive underground animal cemeteries have been found at Saqqâra, where more than 400 baboons and several hundreds of thousands of falcons have been found mummified, each in its own coffin, jar, or sar-cophagus, along with bulls, ibises, vultures, snakes, and so on. Large underground ibis and baboon galleries have also been found at Tuna el-Gebel at Hermopolis Magna, with some of the coffins laid out in patterns of eight, which was again symbolic, referring to the eight creative deities of Hermopolis who formed the world. However, at Abydos the ibises were buried in large pots in the earth, and dogs were placed in underground gal-leries. At Dendera extensive tunnels lined with bricks held thousands of mummies of birds, gazelles, cats, ichneumons, and snakes. At Kom Ombos and in the Fayyum, crocodiles were buried along with large numbers of eggs.

References
Spencer, A. J. *Death in Ancient Egypt*. New York: Penguin, 1982.
West, John Anthony. *Serpent in the Sky: The High Wisdom of Ancient Egypt*. New York: Harper and Row, 1979.

CENOTAPH

A cenotaph (from the Greek word *kenotaph*, literally "empty grave"; in Latin, *cenotaphium*) is a tomb erected for one whose body is not available or, in rare cases, for an important person whose body is buried elsewhere. This includes those lost at sea, those killed in battle without their body being recovered, those who died in distant lands, or those who are missing and presumed dead. In ancient times the cenotaph appears intended primarily as a dwelling place for the soul, and the deceased who were missing in body were called upon by name to dwell there. In modern times, a cenotaph is erected primarily to serve as an honorable memorial of the deceased for the living, for example, the "Tomb of the Unknown Soldier" in the United States.

Although the word cenotaph originates in the ancient Greek and Roman world, where it was also called *honorarium sepulchrum* or *honorarius tumulus*, the phenomenon is found worldwide. In Egypt, for example, no body has been discovered in any of the early pyramids, including those that were found undisturbed; additionally, many early Egyptian rulers are known to have had several personal mastabas (large rectangular structures built over subterranean tombs) in various locations.

See also MASTABA; PYRAMID, EGYPTIAN.

References
Edwards, I. E. S. *The Pyramids of Egypt*. 1947. Rev. ed., New York: Penguin, 1978.
Toynbee, J. M. C. *Death and Burial in the Roman World*. Ithaca, NY: Cornell University Press, 1971.

CEPOTAPHIUM (CEPOTAFIUM)
See Garden, Funerary.

CERBERUS

Cerberus is the three-headed (some say fifty-headed) dog-demon who guards the River Styx, which is the entrance to Hades in classical Greek mythology. He has a mane of serpents on each head, a barbed tail, and

Cenotaph in Whitehall, London. Courtesy of CFCL.

Cerberus

Here monstrous Cerberus, the ravening beast,
howls through his triple throats like a mad dog
over the spirits sunk in that foul paste.
His eyes are red, his beard is greased with phlegm,
his belly swollen, and his hands are claws
to rip the wretches and flay and mangle them. . . .
When Cerberus discovered us in that swill
his dragon-jaws yawed wide, his lips drew back
in a grin of fangs. No limb of his was still.
My Guide bent down and seized in either fist
a clod of the stinking dirt that festered there
and flung them down the gullet of the beast.
As a hungry cur will set the echoes raving
and then fall still when he is thrown a bone,
all of his clamor being in his craving,
so the three ugly heads of Cerberus,
whose yowling at those wretches deafened them,
choked on their putrid sops and stopped their fuss.

From Dante's Inferno, *Canto 6:13–33; Dante Alighieri (1977, p. 34), translation by Ciardi.*

Hercules completing the last of his twelve labors and bringing the triple-headed dog, Cerberus, from the Underworld. Courtesy of Anne Ronan Picture Library.

ferocious teeth. According to Robert Graves, the name probably stems from an older, more complete title, *ker berethrou,* or "demon of the pit." The word *ker* in ancient Greek referred to a variety of ghosts, spirits, demons, and Underworld powers, including the winds.

The pedigree of Cerberus is foul indeed, for he is the child of Echidne, a viper-goddess from the sea, and Typhon, the huge god of hurricanes, with countless serpents for hands and feet. Cerberus figures prominently in a number of tales, usually as an obstacle to any living person who would dare to force his or her way into the Underworld. But the truly heroic, of course, find a means to subdue him. Orpheus, seeking his lost love Eurydice, was able to charm the monster with his sweet music, and the twelfth and final labor of Heracles (Hercules) was to capture Cerberus and drag him bodily to the surface to show Eurystheus, his taskmaster. Another technique was to distract him with food, as the Sibyl does in the Roman classic the *Aeneid* and as Virgil does for Dante in the *Inferno.*

The fear of Cerberus was not merely mythological but real in the ancient world. It was not uncommon in burials of the ancient Greek world to include a sop of honey cake or bread in the coffin to placate Cerberus, just as a coin (obulus) was put in the mouth of the corpse to pay the ferryman Charon.

See also HADES; KER; TARTAROS; UNDERWORLD.

References

Dante Alighieri. *The Divine Comedy.* Trans. John Ciardi. New York: Norton, 1977.

Graves, Robert. *The Greek Myths.* New York: Penguin, 1960.

Harrison, Jane Ellen. *Prolegomena to the Study of Greek Religion.* Cambridge: Cambridge University Press, 1922.

Turner, Alice K. *The History of Hell.* New York: Harcourt Brace, 1993.

Virgil. *The Aeneid.* Trans. Robert Fitzgerald. New York: Random House, 1983.

CHEVRA KADDISHA

Unique to Judaism is the chevra kaddisha (literally "holy society"), which is responsible for preparing the dead for burial and ensuring that all the Jewish funerary traditions are carried out. Because mourners are in a profound state of shock and unprepared to handle the body of their loved one and secular authorities are historically unaware of or unconcerned with Jewish law, the local chevra kaddisha was developed. The services provided by the holy society are not considered base or impure; to belong to the society is a rare and honorable privilege. As Rabbi Maurice Lamm puts it, "to assist in the preparation and burial of the dead is one of the great *mitzvot* [religious duties] in our faith" (p. 239).

The chevra kaddisha, as a specialized burial fellowship that provided services to the local Jewish population, only became a widespread phenomenon in Judaism in the late Middle Ages. But the first reference to a local chevra kaddisha appears in the Talmud, a collection of Jewish tradition and law dating to the fourth and fifth centuries C.E. At that time, the burial of the dead was generally the responsibility of the entire community (not just the grieving family), and all work ceased as the town engaged in funerary preparations. But in the Talmud (MK 27b) a passage refers to a Rabbi Hamnuna, who was shocked to find that despite a recent death, the members of the community he was visiting continued on with their ordinary labors. When he protested and threatened to place all the local Jews under a ban, he was informed that they had organized a special chavurah (fellowship) to deal with the dead, and Rabbi Hamnuna permitted them to carry on. However, the earliest mentions of the term *chevra kaddisha* in the Middle Ages denote an exclusive religious society, whose services (whether funerary, charitable, or social) were restricted to its limited membership.

It was not until the sixteenth century in Europe that the term came to its modern usage, namely to indicate a fellowship devoted specifically to burial and whose services were available to the entire local community. Those services today generally include providing a shomer (watcher) for the body between death and burial; washing the body of the dead; purifying the body with poured water in the tohorah ritual; dressing the body in burial clothes (tachrichim); and making arrangements with various officials for the death certificate, funeral service, and burial. However, in the United States (unlike in Europe and in Israel), few Jewish communities have well-organized burial societies, and in many cases Jewish burials are handled by secular authorities and funeral homes without particular regard to ancient Jewish customs.

See also ANINUT; FUNERARY CUSTOMS, JEWISH; SHOMER; TOHORAH.

References

Abrahams, I. *Jewish Life in the Middle Ages.* London: E. Goldston, 1932.

Abramovitch, Henry. "Death." In *Contemporary Jewish Religious Thought,* ed. Arthur A. Cohen and Paul Mendes-Flohr. New York: Charles Scribner's Sons, 1989.

Lamm, Maurice. *The Jewish Way in Death and Mourning.* New York: Jonathan David Publishers, 1969.

Rabinowicz, H. *A Guide to Life.* London: Jewish Chronicle Publications, 1964.

Riemer, Jack, ed. *Jewish Reflections on Death.* New York: Schocken Books, 1974.

CHING-T'U

Ching-T'u is the Chinese heaven that certain Buddhists hope to be reborn in after death here on earth. This heaven is called *ching,* or pure in Chinese, because it is a spiritual abode free from the defilements of life on earth and also because beings who are reborn there are free from the cravings and lower instincts that detract from spiritual growth. It is thought to be at the western edge of the universe, billions and billions of miles from here, full of flowers and trees made of the seven precious substances (gold, silver, etc.), exquisite fragrances, and beautiful rushing waters emitting celestial music and decorated with countless bouquets of flowers. There is no suffering, pain, or misfortune, and all wishes are instantly fulfilled. Ching-T'u is similar to the Christian and Muslim concept of heaven in some ways, for life in Ching-T'u is blissful and unending, and there is a central deity figure there, a cosmic Buddha, who is worshipped. It is the power of this Buddha, called O-mi-t'o Fo, that saves the believer and brings him or her to the heaven of Ching-T'u; the believer can do nothing alone. But unlike the Western conception of heaven, birth in Ching-T'u is something of a halfway house, not an end in itself: Ching-T'u provides the best possible conditions for the attainment of the ultimate goal, which is the final liberation from existence, called by Buddhists *nirvāṇa.*

Buddhist pursuit of rebirth in such a Pure Land is not a part of the original teaching of the historical Buddha, who lived around the sixth century B.C.E. Rather, early Buddhism taught that any rebirth in any world, heavenly or otherwise, was merely another distraction from the ultimate goal of nirvāṇa. Particularly monks, who had renounced personal gain and personal interest, were not supposed to seek happiness in some future world. But we known that Pure Land Buddhism originated in India, for there are texts in the ancient Indian language of Sanskrit, dating from about the second century C.E., that teach their readers how to attain birth in various "pure" heavens, two of which are Abhirati and Sukhāvatī. In these early texts we learn of a powerful saint who, ages ago, vowed to achieve full

This world Ching-T'u . . . which is the world system of the Lord Amitābha, is rich and prosperous, comfortable, fertile, delightful and crowded with many gods and men. And in this world system . . . there are no hells, no animals, no ghosts, no Asuras and none of the inauspicious places of rebirth. . . .

And that world system Ching-T'u . . . emits many fragrant odors, it is rich in a great variety of flowers and fruits, adorned with jewel trees, which are frequented by flocks of various birds with sweet voices, which the Tathāgata's [Buddha's] miraculous power has conjured up. . . . On all sides it is surrounded with golden nets, and all round covered with lotus flowers made of all the precious things. Some of the lotus flowers are half a mile in circumference, others up to ten miles. And from each jewel lotus issue thirty-six hundred thousand milliards of rays. And at the end of each ray there issue thirty-six hundred thousand milliards of Buddhas, with golden-colored bodies, who bear the thirty-two marks of the perfect man, and who, in all the ten directions, go into countless world systems, and there demonstrate Dharma [Buddhist truth].

And further again . . . in the ten directions, in each single direction, in Buddha-fields countless like the sands of the river Ganges, Buddhas and Lords countless like the sands of the river Ganges glorify the name of the Lord Amitābha, the Tathāgata, praise him, proclaim his fame, extol his virtue. And why? Because all beings are irreversible from the supreme enlightenment if they hear the name of the Lord Amitābha, and, on hearing it, with one single thought only raise their hearts to him with a resolve connected with serene faith.

From The Scripture of the Pure Land (adapted from Sommer 1995).

enlightenment only if all other beings could also be freed. Since this saint did become a perfect Buddha named O-mi-t'o, he was also able to create a pure universe where one can be reborn and saved. This Buddha was now able to spiritually transfer his merit to those still struggling on earth and raise them up to his level. Interestingly, the Pure Land tradition never seems to have become widespread in the land of its birth. It is in China that the aim of rebirth in heaven became truly popular among Buddhists, and in China we hear for the first time of a Pure Land "school" of Buddhism that taught its members to forsake all other Buddhist practice and seek rebirth in Ching-T'u alone. The popularity of Pure Land Buddhism in China may relate to the fact that, when Pure Land teachings were introduced in

the fifth and sixth centuries, Chinese religion already had similar traditions. The Chinese were already accustomed to calling on deities to aid their deceased ancestors and were familiar with the idea of "transferring merit" through the offerings they made for their dead.

The first champion of Ching-T'u was a scholar named T'an-luan (488–554), who flourished in the monastery of Hsüan-chung-ssu in the Shanxi Province of China. T'an-luan first identified what would be the three primary Scriptures of Ching-T'u tradition and wrote the first Chinese commentaries on Indian Pure Land texts. In his major work, "A Commentary on the Teaching on Birth [in Ching-T'u]" (*Wang-shêng-lun Chu*), T'an-luan lays out the five "gates" of practice that will lead the faithful to achieve birth after death in Ching-T'u. Those five gates are (1) making prostrations and wishing to be reborn in Ching-T'u; (2) singing the praises and reciting the name of the deity there, "He of Infinite Light," called in Chinese "O-mi-t'o Fo"; (3) making vows to be reborn in Ching-T'u; (4) visualizing O-mi-t'o Fo and his pure land; and (5) transferring the merit attained by these practices to all beings for their salvation as well. T'an-luan laid emphasis on the fourth "gate," visualization, and in his major work T'an-luan goes on at great length about the various decorations of the heaven, the wondrous water, the inhabitants, and a detailed description of the Buddha O-mi-t'o. Presumably, if one is able to completely picture this heaven, then one is actually making contact with that world, and rebirth there after death here will be quite natural.

Later Chinese teachers further refined the tradition of Ching-T'u. The teacher Tao-ch'o (562–645) was the first person to claim that his contemporary Chinese society had entered a period called "the decline of the true teaching" (in Chinese, *mo-fa;* in Japanese, *Mappō*). During such a time of crisis and decline, the world is too corrupt and human understanding and abilities too limited for Buddhism to be practiced the way the historical Buddha gave it out: *only* the "easy" Pure Land path can save one from ignorance and evil rebirth in hell or animal form. The disciple of Tao-ch'o, named Shan-tao (613–681) accepted his teacher's assessment of the world and made Pure Land Buddhism even easier to practice. Shan-tao reduced the "five gates" of entry into Ching-T'u (mentioned previously) to a single all-important practice that was simply chanting the name of the deity, O-mi-t'o Fo, over and over throughout the day and throughout one's life. (This practice is called *nien-fo* in Chinese, *nembutsu* in Japanese). Shan-tao, the great popularizer of Ching-T'u practice in China, claimed that nien-fo was the *only* way to salvation. Chanting the name itself was sufficient for rebirth in Ching-T'u, for it not only called on the assistance of the Buddha but was a magic sound that actually cut through ignorance and manifested wisdom and liberation from this earth. In large part because of the writing, preaching, and art of Shan-tao (including about 300 paintings of Ching-T'u), the Pure Land tradition became a distinct and powerful tradition of Buddhism in China.

The Ch'an tradition of Buddhism in China (known as *Zen* in Japan) found the Ching-T'u tradition powerful enough to criticize, calling rebirth in Ching-T'u a misguided delusion and a distraction from true Buddhist practice. But many Chinese Buddhists who belonged to other traditions of Buddhism (which focused on ascetic practices, study and chanting of Scriptures, and meditation) would use the nien-fo or visualization of Ching-T'u as a supplementary practice to their primary one. By the end of the T'ang dynasty, however (618–907 C.E.) Pure Land Buddhism, like most Buddhist traditions in China, had lost its distinctiveness and blended more or less into the general stream. It was only in the twelfth century in Japan that Pure Land Buddhism would flourish again as an independent school, called Jōdō, under the guidance of such renowned teachers as Hōnen and Shinran.

See also ABHIRATI; AKṢOBHYA; JŌDŌ; NIRVĀṆA; PURE LAND; REINCARNATION, EASTERN; SUKHĀVATĪ.

References

Ch'en, Kenneth. *Buddhism in China*. Princeton: Princeton University Press, 1964.

Foard, James, Michael Solomon, and Richard K. Payne, eds. *The Pure Land Tradition: History and Development*. Berkeley Buddhist Studies Series no. 3. Berkeley: University of California, 1989.

Pas, Julian. *Visions of Sukhāvatī: Shan-Tao's Commentary on the Kuan-Wu-Liang-Shou-Fo Ching*. Albany: SUNY Press, 1995.

Ryosetsu, F. *The Way to Nirvana: The Concept of the Nembutsu in Shan-tao's Pure Land Buddhism*. Tokyo: Kyoiku Shincho Sha, 1974.

Sommer, Deborah. *Chinese Religion: An Anthology of Sources*. New York: Oxford University Press, 1995.

Suzuki, D. T. *Buddha of Infinite Light*. Boston: Shambhala, 1998.

CHINVAT BRIDGE

Translated from the Persian term *Chinvato Peretu* as "the Crossing of the Separator," the Chinvat Bridge is what awaits Zoroastrians after death. At dawn on the fourth day of death, the soul of the deceased is drawn up by the rays of the sun toward heaven, there to meet the daena, literally "she who sees," in the sense of "conscience." The daena appears as a lovely young maiden to those who have been just in life and as a hideous old hag to those who have been unjust. The daena leads the soul to judgment at the heavenly scales, which lie before the Chinvat Bridge. The scales are of a hairbreadth precision and are presided over by three judicial deities: Mithra, lord of the covenant; Sraosha, protector of prayer; and Rashnu, holder of the scales. On these scales the life of the soul is weighed—actions weigh most heavily, then words, then thoughts.

After judgment, the soul is then led by the daena across the Chinvat Bridge, where the judgment plays out: the bridge is as wide as the soul is just. For those who have been found honorable and wise, the bridge is wide and easy to cross, "the width of nine spears"; on the other side lies paradise. For those who were found more wicked than just, the bridge is narrow, for some even as narrow as a razor blade—the soul plunges downward into the abyss. Interestingly, Zoroastrian theology also made a place for those who balanced the scale, those whose wickedness and justice were equal. They were assigned to Misvan Gatu, or "the place of the Mixed Ones," a gray shadowy abode where there was an absence of both joy and sorrow. The souls of the dead do not remain forever in their afterlife abodes but are resurrected at the End Time to endure a *final* judgment. There the evil powers and their helpers are destroyed forever, and what remains is the renewed world for the resurrected righteous.

Some scholars assert that the Zoroastrian concepts of the Chinvat Bridge and final resurrection show traces of being a compromise. There is little evidence of exposure of corpses in ancient times, and it seems instead that the dead were buried in the earth—simple burials for common folk and elaborate tombs for the elite. The implication of this appears to be that all the deceased were assumed to proceed to the Underworld, rather than rise up with the sun's rays to heaven. With the reforms of the prophet Zoroaster around 1400 B.C.E., the ancient belief that all souls went to a netherworld similar to Hades or Sheol was fused with the new ideas of paradise and a final judgment at the End Time. The ancient beliefs were adapted so that the afterlife became only temporary (until the *final* judgment) and differed from person to person depending on how ethical they had been in life. It is also likely that in the Hellenistic period (the first few centuries C.E.) Zoroastrianism was further modified by Jewish, Stoic, and Platonic ideas. At that time it appears that the Zoroastrians intensified their polar views of heaven and hell and took on the apocalyptic notion of an End Time as an ordeal of horrific suffering and final judgment.

Scholars have suggested that although the Chinvat Bridge is certainly taken literally by a majority of Zoroastrians, in symbolic terms it also referred to an actual ordeal of initiation during life. As in the Hindu religion of India, with which Zoroastrianism has much in common, it is probable that certain elite members of society were called upon to pass an initiation ordeal consisting of some ethical tests and trials analogous to the trial of the soul after death.

See also BEHESHT; DOZAKH; FRASHO-KERETI; FRAVASHI; HAMESTEGĀN; RESURRECTION, ANCIENT NEAR EAST; RESURRECTION, HEBREW; AL-SHIRĀT; SOUL, ZOROASTRIAN.

References

Boyce, Mary. *A History of Zoroastrianism.* Vol. 1. Leiden: E. J. Brill, 1975.

Dhalla, M. N. *Zoroastrian Theology from the Earliest Times to the Present Day.* Reprint, New York: AMS Press, 1972.

Jackson, A. V. W. *Zoroastrian Studies.* New York: Columbia University Press, 1928.

Kotwal, Dastur Firoze M., and James W. Boyd, trans. *A Guide to the Zoroastrian Religion.* Studies in World Religion no. 3. Chico, CA: Scholars Press, 1982.

Masani, Sir Rustom. *Zoroastrianism: The Religion of the Good Life.* New York: Collier Books, 1962.

Sethna, Tehmurasp Rustamji. *Book of Instructions on Zoroastrian Religion.* Karachi: Informal Religious Meetings Trust Fund, 1980.

Sidhwa, Ervad Godrej Dinshawji. *Discourses on Zoroastrianism.* Karachi: Ervad Godrej Dinshawji Sidhwa, 1978.

Spronk, Klaas. *Beatific Afterlife in Ancient Israel and in the Ancient Near East.* Kevelaer: Butzon and Bercker, 1986.

CHÖD (TIBETAN SPELLING: gCOD)

From a root meaning "to cut," Chöd is the Tibetan practice of meditating on one's own death and the horrifying deities of death in order to gain detachment from egotistical desires. It may form a complete path to enlightenment for some practitioners, but for most Tibetan meditators it is one religious practice among many in the quest for ultimate freedom from suffering and illusion.

The current form of the practice was developed by a female master, Ma gcig lab sgron ma (pronounced "Machik Labdronma"), in the twelfth century. The Chöd is intended to provoke an emotional crisis in the meditator by summoning up his or her worst fears, and so it is generally performed late at night in lonely places such as caves, graveyards, or charnel grounds (where rotting corpses may be found), especially during the dark of the moon. Under such terrifying circumstances one may contemplate the transitoriness of the body and the imminence of death.

The practitioner first calls upon the patron deity of the death meditation, "She who rejects every process of life" (in Tibetan, Lus srog gzang du bor ba'i ma) as the mother who will give her blessing for what is about to proceed. Then the meditator summons all the beings of the six realms and prepares to make a sacrificial offering of his or her own body.

It is said that in the darkest part of the night, in the midst of corpses, the practitioner actually begins to hallucinate and perceive the arrival of many beings on the scene, particularly the wrathful deities that are described in the Tibetan Book of the Dead. The sacrificial offering of one's own body proceeds in four stages: (1) in "white sharing" one visualizes one's body as nectar and offers it to the Buddhas and Buddhist community; (2) in "multicolored sharing" one visualizes one's body as a garden, as food, as clothes, as all desirable objects, and offers it to the protective deities (Mahāpālas) who help one overcome obstacles on the path to enlightenment; (3) in "red sharing" one visualizes the flesh, blood, and bones of one's physical body being greedily consumed by horrific demons; (4) in "black sharing" one visualizes that one's sins and the sins of all beings are absorbed into one's body, and then it is offered to the demons as a ransom for the sins of all people. After the culmination of these ritual offerings of the body, the meditator understands that these beings, these demons, are projections of one's own consciousness and that all life is transitory and illusory. In this way attachment to the body and fear of death is gradually conquered, freeing (literally, "cutting") the meditator from egotism and other psychological bonds that hold him or her to illusion and suffering in this earthly life.

Various ritual objects are used in this extended meditation. Magical musical instruments, such as the damaru (a handheld two-sided drum) or a trumpet made from a human thigh bone, subdue the demons. An offering bowl made from a human skull is used to help the meditator visualize the bodily offerings and focus on the ever-present reality of human death.

Not surprisingly, practitioners of the Chöd are regarded as quite extraordinary by most Tibetans, and they are generally believed to have special powers over things relating to death. Chöd adepts are called upon to exorcize demons, particularly those demons that are thought to accompany a dead person, obstructing their journey in the afterlife and harassing surviving relatives. Chöd practitioners are also called upon to protect villages from epidemic diseases and exorcize the demons to blame when an epidemic breaks out. Because Chöd practitioners are believed to be immune to any infection, in case of an epidemic they attend the transport of corpses to the cemetery.

See also BHAVA-CHAKRA; BURIAL, SKY; NIRVĀṆA.

References

Edou, Jérôme. *Machig Labdrön and the Foundations of Chöd.* Ithaca, NY: Snow Lion, 1996.

Norbu, Namkhai. *The Crystal and the Way of Light.* Ed. John Shane. New York: Arkana, 1993.

Tucci, Giuseppe. *The Religions of Tibet.* Trans. Geoffrey Samuel. Berkeley: University of California Press, 1980.

CHUREL

The energy of an Indian woman (particularly a poor, low-caste woman) who has died while pregnant, in childbirth, or in the period of impurity directly afterward becomes the hideous churel. Like all bhūts of India, the churel has her feet turned backward, and she is pictured as an old hag, with breasts so long and pendulous that she can and frequently does toss them up over her shoulder. She has horrible teeth sticking out of her thick lips, a black tongue, and wild hair. She has no shadow. The churel lives in dead or deformed trees on the outskirts of the village, crying "kuṭuk, kuṭuk" like a bird, or perhaps in the cemetery, and sometimes she wanders the roads at night. Frustrated in her duties to her family while she was alive, the churel becomes particularly vengeful to her family but also seeks to seduce and destroy all young men, and she may even attack the healthy babies of other women. Like all Indian bhūts and most evil ghosts around the world, nighttime is, of course, her time of operation.

Although her "true" form has been described already, the churel can temporarily, through the illusory magic of the dead, take on other appearances in order to wreak the vengeance she desires. She can appear as a beautiful young woman, at least in front, in order to lure away young men, but often her backside is hollow or filled with putrid flesh, and several young men have escaped by seeing this in time. If she succeeds in luring away her victims, the churel may try to kill them on the spot or lead them away to an Otherworld of her own. In this Otherworld or Underworld, the young man may eat something and then belong to the churel forever. She may also take the form of a bird and attempt to fly over pregnant women or babies in order to cause their destruction. In this case, the child in utero is sure to be stillborn, and babies and children will suffer wasting diseases or fevers that likewise quickly lead to death.

One is not helpless before the churel, however. Besides recognizing her hollow or rotting backside, one may have her exorcised by a village specialist or throw a bone or hot iron at her. (One should not throw a clod of earth, however, because she may take the clod and dissolve it in water, causing one's own flesh to rot.) There are also steps one may take to prevent the churel from forming in the first place. If a woman and fetus have died in childbirth, the mother and child should be buried on opposite sides of a stream (possibly because of the worldwide belief that the soul has trouble crossing water). In any case the body of a churel-candidate should not be cremated—the usual funerary custom of India—but a small fire may be placed on top of the corpse to scare away any evil spirit. The body is buried face downward and the grave covered with heavy stones and thorns to hinder escape. The place where the woman died is sometimes scraped and the topsoil removed, and mustard is planted there. The smell of the blossoms are thought to appeal to the deceased, and the scattered seeds that are produced may prove a time-consuming hindrance as she stoops to pick them up—a variation on the worldwide theme of mazes and other distractions to preoccupy the restless and dangerous dead.

Account of a Churel

There were two high-caste brothers, the stronger of whom slept in the fields at night to guard the crops, while the other remained at home. But the strong man suddenly grew weak and lean. Finally, his brother asked of him the cause of the great physical decline. In reply the other said: "A churel comes to me every night and obliges me to [sleep] with her." Thereupon, the younger brother decided to guard the crops. So, taking a pair of shears he went to the field. That night the churel came and slept with him. In the night he cut her scalp lock very stealthily and concealed it. In the morning the churel awoke a mere naked woman, and she was unable to escape. So he gave her a loincloth, took her home and kept her as his wife. They reared a family, and grandchildren were born to them. Then, one day, she asked her husband for her cuṭiyā [lock of hair]. She said that she wished to dance because she had grandchildren. At first he refused her request; but his friends agreed that, now that she had children and grandchildren to think of, she would not run away. So, at last, he granted her petition. As soon as she had obtained her cuṭiyā she disappeared.

From Briggs (1953, p. 494).

See also BHŪT; FUNERARY CUSTOMS, ANCIENT INDIAN; PISHĀCHA; PRET; RĀKṢASA; SOUL; WATER; YAMA.

References

Briggs, George W. *The Doms and Their Near Relations.* Mysore: Wesley Press, 1953.
———. *The Religious Life of India: The Chamars.* Calcutta: Association Press, 1920.
Crooke, W. *The Popular Religion and Folk-lore of Northern India.* 2nd ed. Delhi: Munshiram Manoharlal, 1968.
Oman, John Campbell. *Cults, Customs and Superstitions of India.* Indian ed. Delhi: Vishal Publishers, 1972.

CINERARIUM

Cinerarium is the Latin word for a receptacle for cremains or a niche in which this receptacle was placed. The cineraria of the ancient Roman world included funerary jars and urns, as well as ash chests made in the forms of altars, small houses, and temples. The cinerarium was buried in a small grave in the ground or placed in a sealed or unsealed niche in the wall or floor of a columbarium.

See also COLUMBARIUM.

CIPPUS

The Latin word for almost any kind of boundary stone marking the limits of a property, in a funerary context cippus refers to a gravestone, particularly that which marks the boundary of any burial space from a full-sized cemetery to merely a family plot. Cippi were used in the Roman world as bases over which to pour libations.

COCYTUS

In the ancient Greek world Cocytus was one of the tributaries of the River Styx, the primary river of Hades. It had little function other than to add yet another descriptive element to the Underworld (the name *Cocytus* literally means "wailing"), along with Acheron (woe) and Phelegethon (burning). However, various cartographers of the Underworld have since tried to find a unique function for each of the bodies of water named in ancient sources. In his Latin classic, the *Aeneid,* Virgil made Cocytus into a deep pool and the Styx into a swamp. But for sheer originality and terrifying power, Dante's medieval work *Inferno* has pride of place. Here Cocytus is a huge frozen lake at the ninth and lowest circle of Hell, an icy prison for the greatest sinners, namely traitors:

> Like a whirling windmill seen afar at twilight,
> or when a mist has risen from the ground—
> just such an engine rose upon my sight
> stirring up such a wild and bitter wind
> I cowered for shelter at my Master's back,
> there being no other windbreak I could find.
> I stood now where the souls of the last class
> (with fear my verses tell it) were covered wholly;
> they shone below the ice like straws in glass.
> Some lie stretched out; others are fixed in place
> upright, some on their heads, some on their soles;
> another, like a bow, bends foot to face.
> (Dante, *Divine Comedy,* Ciardi, trans., p. 182)

The glacial wind is generated by the great batlike wings of Satan, who is stuck chest-deep in the ice, with three heads, each eternally chewing an arch-traitor (Judas, Brutus, and Cassius). Certainly fire was the traditional element of torture in medieval visions of hell, but here Dante has made a persuasive innovation.

See also ACHERON; FUNERARY CUSTOMS, ANCIENT GREEK; HADES; PHLEGETHON; STYX; UNDERWORLD; WATER.

References
Dante Alighieri. *The Divine Comedy.* Trans. John Ciardi. New York: Norton, 1977.
Graves, Robert. *The Greek Myths.* New York: Penguin, 1960.
Harrison, Jane Ellen. *Prolegomena to the Study of Greek Religion.* Cambridge: Cambridge University Press, 1922.
Turner, Alice K. *The History of Hell.* New York: Harcourt Brace, 1993.
Virgil. *The Aeneid.* Trans. Robert Fitzgerald. New York: Random House, 1983.

COFFIN

The word *coffin* is generally synonymous with *casket,* though in the twentieth century a distinction was made between the tapered, wedge-shaped coffin and the clearly rectangular casket. The traditional European- and American-style coffin is eight-sided, including the side marking the head, two sides widening as they approach the shoulders, two straight sides following the shoulders to the elbows, two sides narrowing as they approach the feet, and the side marking the feet. Coffins have most often been made of wood, though stone, baked clay, bronze, and in modern times wrought iron, steel, marble, and even cardboard may be found. In the nineteenth century coffins were made by regular furniture carpenters and sold from their shops, but the emerging funeral industry took over the acquisition and sale of coffins, and most coffins today are now purchased directly from funeral homes, though alternatives exist (including local memorial societies, galleries such as the Ghia gallery in San Francisco, private dealers, and even homemade coffins—with instructions provided, for example, by Ernest Morgan's book *Dealing Creatively with Death* and by pamphlets distributed by Direct Funeral Services of Alameda, California).

Throughout history, coffins have come in a wide variety of styles and shapes, from crude and literally square boxes to the highly refined and decorated anthropoid coffins of ancient Egypt. Modern coffins come in a variety of materials (including cloth-covered pine, hardwood, steel, fiberglass, and marble) but differ little in shape except for decorative style. Throughout the twentieth century, steel has been the material of choice for coffins because it is longer-lasting and actually cheaper than wood. Modern environmental concerns about the vast quantity of buried steel in the earth (200 million pounds each year in the United States alone) and a declining interest in preserving the body from decay as long as possible have resulted in the resurgence of wood as the material of choice for coffins, though steel continues to outrank wood in sales. Coffins come in preset sizes: the standard metal coffin is 6 feet 7 inches by 24 inches, and a standard wooden coffin is 6 feet 3 inches by 22 inches; the "standard oversized" metal coffin is 6 feet 9 inches by 26 to 31 inches, and a "standard oversized" wooden coffin is 6 feet 6 inches by 24 to 28 inches. Finding coffins in sizes other than those listed, say for the deceased who is obese or very tall, is quite difficult, and requires a special order—something few mourners have time or heart for. To handle the very tall, funeral homes routinely place the dead in the coffin without shoes or with bent legs, while for the obese, lifting the elbows as far forward as possible or turning the body partly on its side, allows for a tighter fit.

Retail coffins are quite expensive. Even the cheapest start at about $1,000 and run to well over $15,000 for high-end models. Coffins are marketed as "protective" (keeping the body from decay) and "nonprotective" (cheaper models that are not airtight), though in truth no coffin protects a body from decay. Both aerobic (oxygen-consuming) and anaerobic (non-oxygen-consuming) bacteria are already present in the human body and cannot be kept out of a coffin wherein any corpse is present. Thus an airtight coffin may prevent aerobic bacteria from causing decay to the body of the deceased, but anaerobic bacteria will begin the decay process immediately, whatever sort of coffin one may purchase.

Retail coffins are not required by law for inhumations or cremations in the United States, despite popular opinion to the contrary. Designated as "alternative containers," boxes of corrugated fiber are perfectly legal, as are homemade plywood boxes. However, a good deal of a funeral home's profit comes from the sale of coffins (with a spectacular retail markup of from two and a half to twenty times wholesale prices), so some funeral homes charge mourners several hundred dollars in "handling fees" for funerals using coffins that were purchased elsewhere. Coffins may also be rented just for the duration of a funeral service and the body buried in an alternative container (or, if cremated, in an urn or small wooden box).

See also BARROW; BURIAL; BURIAL, BASKET; BURIAL CLOTHES; BURIAL, SCAFFOLD; BURIAL, SHIP; BURIAL, TREE; CANOPIC JAR, CHEST; CENOTAPH; COFFINS, EGYPTIAN; COMMITTAL SERVICE; MAUSOLEUM; MOUND; MUMMIFICATION; URN.

References

Dempsey, D. *The Way We Die.* New York: Macmillan, 1975.

Farrell, J. J. *Inventing the American Way of Death 1830–1920.* Philadelphia: Temple University Press, 1980.

Iserson, Kenneth V. *Death to Dust: What Happens to Dead Bodies?* Tucson, AZ: Galen Press, 1994.

Jones, Barbara. *Design for Death.* Indianapolis: Bobbs-Merrill, 1967.

Mitford, Jessica. *The American Way of Death.* New York: Simon and Schuster, 1963.

Morgan, Ernest. *Dealing Creatively with Death.* 12th ed. Bayside, NY: Barclay House, 1990.

COFFINS, EGYPTIAN

Coffins were quite simple affairs at the dawn of Egyptian history but came to be enormously important and elaborate over time. The earliest evidence of Egyptian burials shows that the body, arranged in a fetal position, was generally placed in a small container of basketwork or wood and buried in shallow pits dug into the sand at the edge of the community. The first true coffins (c. 3000 B.C.E.) were almost square in shape and made out of small pieces of wood held together by dowels rather than large beams of wood, since good wood was quite scarce in the desert. The corpse within the coffin lay on its side, still in the fetal position but now wrapped with gum-soaked linen. Most of these early coffins were placed directly in the tomb, but even at this early stage royalty or the very rich had their coffin placed within a sarcophagus before interment.

Even the early coffins had elaborate symbolism. Their sides were often recessed with many panels, very much resembling a miniature house with doors. The roof of the coffin was slightly vaulted, just like the buildings of the period. Evidently the coffin, like the tomb itself, represented the cosmos and particularly the heavens, as shown by the identification of the coffin with the sky goddess Nut. She appears frequently on the inside of the coffin lid, looking down at the deceased, and the coffin floor was painted with a picture of Hathor (in the Theban necropolis), Osiris, Isis, or Nut again. The paneled "doors" then allowed the ba (the astral, wandering soul) to enter and exit this world, which had become its new home. By the Old Kingdom (c. 2600 to 2100 B.C.E.), the coffin began to take on many of the characteristics of the tomb. The coffin was often inscribed with spells taken from tomb walls, such as lists of food and other offerings (which materialized in the afterworld through the magical power of writing), and was often painted both inside and out.

The elaboration of the coffin advanced considerably by the Middle Kingdom (c. 2000 B.C.E.). Construction became more skilled, using broad planks of fine imported wood. Inscriptions took on a distinct pattern, beginning with the painting of the two eyes of Horus on the upper left hand side of the coffin. The body within, no longer in fetal position but still arranged on its left (eastern) side, had its face aligned with the painted eyes and could thus magically see outside even while resting inside. Inscriptions ran horizontally along the upper part of the coffin toward the feet (north to south), whereas vertical inscriptions ran at regular intervals down the coffin, between the panels that still served as "doors." The inscriptions generally gave the name and titles of the deceased and invoked the various protective deities: usually Osiris on the east side, Anubis on the west, and Isis and Nephthys on the end boards. The coffin lid again had an inscription running from head to foot, generally invoking the protection of Anubis. The inside of the coffin featured spells to guide and protect the deceased in the afterlife and sometimes even included a map with alternate routes through the Underworld. The lid of the coffin was still identified with the goddess of the sky, Nut, and often had a painted scene of the sky boat of the sun god transporting the deceased through the heavens. Likewise, the floor of the coffin was still associated with the Under-

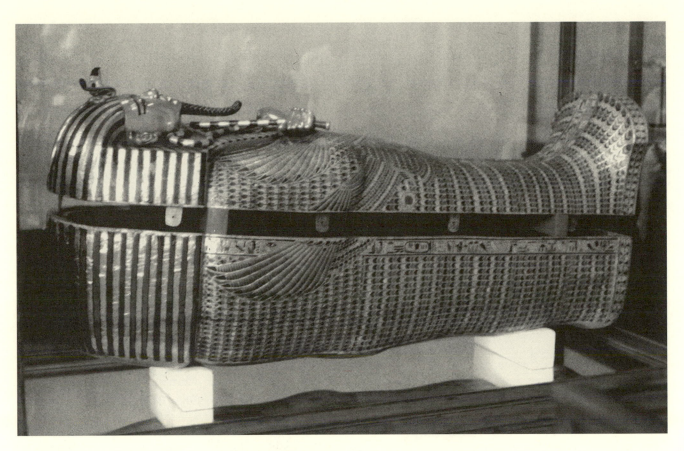

Golden sarcophagus of Tutankhamen, Egypt. Courtesy of Anne Ronan Picture Library.

world and its deities but now included elaborate painted scenes from The Book of the Dead and other funerary literature. The most interesting innovation of the Middle Kingdom period, however, was the use of not one but two coffins nested one inside the other. Furthermore, burials in the Middle Kingdom period began using death masks over the mummy, made of cartonnage (linen strengthened with plaster) and carefully molded and painted to provide the best possible likeness of the dead.

Toward the end of the Middle Kingdom period the inner coffin became more and more closely associated with the mummy and began taking on a distinct anthropoid shape: it lost its customary rectangular shape and took on the shape of a human being. This practice became widespread during the late Second Intermediate Period (c. 1600 B.C.E.) and was perfected in the New Kingdom (c. 1550 to 945 B.C.E.). A pattern of feathers (belonging to winged versions of Isis, Nephthys, the sun disk, serpents, or vultures) is a distinctive feature of these anthropoid coffins, and thus they are known as *rishi* coffins, from the Arabic for feather. The many scenes on these coffins were brightly painted, with either a black background (Eighteenth and Nineteenth Dynasties) or yellow background (Twentieth and Twenty-first Dynasties), and crammed

with afterlife scenes (the resurrection of Osiris, the weighing of the heart at judgment by Anubis, etc.), sacred symbols (such as the scarab; the ankh, which symbolizes life; and other amuletic figures), and inscriptions running in painted strips made to resemble the principal wrapping of the mummy. The overall effect was a lifelike portrait of the deceased, decorated to the hilt with every conceivable protective scene, sign, and deity. In time the outer coffin, too, lost its rectangular shape (which was preserved only in the sarcophagus) and both the inner and outer coffins became virtually wooden mummies. Amazingly, sometimes there were *three* nesting coffins, each more lifelike than the one before, and sometimes even the stone sarcophagus was painstakingly carved to achieve the mummiform anthropoid shape. As the coffin became shaped more and more like a mummy, it is not surprising to find a parallel development, with the mummy becoming more and more like a coffin. From the New Kingdom period onward the mummy might be covered with cartonnage, which was molded and painted to resemble the anthropoid coffin, and fitted with the death mask over its head and shoulders.

Few changes in coffins are seen until the Twenty-fifth and Twenty-sixth Dynasties (c. 750 to 525 B.C.E.), which deliberately harkened back to archaic times, replacing the outer anthropoid coffin with the old rectangular coffin complete with vaulted roof but minus the recessed paneling. The eyes of Horus returned, but only occasionally on the upper left side of the coffin and more often on the headboard. This return to the ancient outer coffin continued through the later dynasties, well into the Ptolemaic period (304 to 30 B.C.E.), retaining the anthropoid inner coffin. By the Greco-Roman period, the quality of decoration had declined considerably, especially as the significance of the various religious motifs began to fade from memory. The coffin lid became gabled, and miniature columns were added to the four corners of the coffin, forming the façade of a shrine. Meanwhile, new motifs entered into Egyptian funerary repertoire, including the Greek zodiac painted inside the coffin lid, maintaining its association with the heavens but now in a Greco-Roman world.

References

Hamilton-Paterson, James, and Carol Andrews. *Mummies: Death and Life in Ancient Egypt.* London: William Collins Sons, 1978.

Morenz, Siegfried. *Egyptian Religion.* Trans. Ann E. Keep. Ithaca, NY: Cornell University Press, 1960.

Spencer, A. J. *Death in Ancient Egypt.* New York: Penguin, 1982.

Winlock, H. E. *The Rise and Fall of the Middle Kingdom in Thebes.* New York: Macmillan, 1947.

COLUMBARIUM

Literally "dove house" in Latin, because doves symbolized the peace of death in the ancient world, a columbarium is a large building (either aboveground or partly or wholly below) carved with hundreds of niches in its walls to hold small vessels containing the ashes of those who have been cremated. There are frequently several rooms and even several storeys to a columbarium, with vaulted ceilings and elaborately decorated walls and floors. Generally only the wealthy or those servants attached to wealthy households were placed in columbaria.

In Rome, several major columbaria have been found in the area between the Via Appia and Via Latina within Rome's Aurelian Walls (but outside the earlier Servian Walls—Roman law forbade burials within the old city limits). These Roman columbaria housed the remains of the imperial family of the Julio-Claudian dynasty and their freedmen and -women in large underground structures with many hundred semicircular and rectangular niches holding the urns (ollae). In the ancient Roman city of Ostia most columbaria were aboveground but were of two architectural designs: one style was roofless with high walls, accessible only by ladder, with the cremation urns sunk in the ground around the inside of the walls; the other style was a rectangular chamber with a barrel-vaulted roof, an entrance in one wall, and urns placed in rows of rec-

tangular niches built into the inner faces of the walls. Both Ostian styles set aside a small area within the structure to perform the actual cremation on the premises.

Columbaria exist even today in many major European and American cities, with a niche costing about U.S.$7,000 dollars and up.

References

Nock, Arthur. "Cremation and Burial in the Roman Empire." In *Essays on Religion and the Ancient World,* ed. Zeph Stewart. 2 vols. Cambridge: Harvard University Press, 1972.

Toynbee, Jocelyn M. C. *Death and Burial in the Roman World.* Ithaca, NY: Cornell University Press, 1971.

Walker, Susan. *Memorials to the Roman Dead.* London: British Museum Publications, 1985.

COMMITTAL SERVICE

Traditional Christianity offers a short religious service for the dead, distinct from the funeral or memorial service held in a church. The committal service is usually held in the cemetery at the side of the grave when the body of a Christian is buried (or, more recently, when ashes from a cremation are "committed" to the ground or sea). The committal is usually much shorter than the funeral and generally includes no scriptural readings unless there was no previous funeral. In the Episcopalian service, the committal opens with an anthem, sung or spoken, which calls on the Lord to "deliver us not into the bitter pain of eternal death." Although God is a judge who is "justly displeased" with human sins, the anthem asks God to "spare us" and "suffer us not, at our last hour, through any pains of death, to fall from thee."

After the anthem, the presiding minister prays,

> In sure and certain hope of the resurrection to eternal life through our Lord Jesus Christ, we commend to Almighty God our *brother/sister* (Name); and we commit *his/her* body to the ground; earth to earth, ashes to ashes, dust to dust. The Lord bless *him* and keep *him,* the Lord make his face to shine upon *him* and be gracious unto *him,* the Lord life up his countenance upon *him* and give *him* peace. (All say) *Amen.* (Bernardin)

The minister concludes the prayer with "The Lord be with you," and the mourners respond, "And with thy spirit." The minister then says, "Let us pray," and all recite the Lord's Prayer, which the Gospels report Jesus taught his disciples at the garden before his arrest (though scholars dispute this account).

The minister then closes the committal service by offering a prayer called the *Dismissal.* The Lutheran version of this prayer states:

Almighty God, by the death of your son, Jesus Christ, you have destroyed death and by this rest in the tomb you have sanctified the graves of all your saints. By his resurrection you have brought life and immortality to light so that all who die in him abide in peace and hope. Give our *brother/sister* peaceful rest until the day when you will raise *him/her* up in glory. Keep us who are still pilgrims in this life in fellowship with all who wait for you on earth and with all around you in heaven, in union with him who is the resurrection and the life, even Jesus Christ our Lord. (All say) *Amen.* (Bernardin)

As in the funeral service, the death and resurrection of Jesus is the cardinal element of the committal service. For Christians, the resurrection of Jesus proves that God has power over death; at some point in the future Jesus will return to earth and raise all the dead for a final judgment.

In some cases, a Christian is buried in a grave that is not in a churchyard or Christian cemetery. In such cases, some traditions have an extra ritual, quite short, called a *Consecration,* in which the burial site is made holy, either just before or just after the burial. The prayer runs as follows:

O God, whose blessed Son was laid in a sepulcher in the garden: Bless, we pray, this grave, and grant that he/she whose body is (is to be) buried here may dwell with Christ in paradise, and may come to thy heavenly kingdom; through thy Son Jesus Christ our Lord. (All say) *Amen.* (Bernardin)

See also CEMETERY; CONSECRATION SERVICE; CREMAINS; FUNERARY CUSTOMS, CHRISTIAN; RESURRECTION, CHRISTIAN.

References

Bernardin, Joseph Buchanan, comp. *Burial Services.* Wilton, CT: Morehouse-Barlow, 1980.

Biddle, Perry H., Jr. *A Funeral Manual.* Grand Rapids, MI: William B. Eerdman's Publishing, 1994.

Inter-Lutheran Commission on Worship. *Burial of the Dead.* Minneapolis: Augsburg, 1976.

Irion, Paul E. *The Funeral: Vestige or Value?* Nashville: Abingdon Press, 1966.

Leach, William H., ed. *The Cokesbury Funeral Manual.* Nashville: Cokesbury Press, 1932.

Lockyer, Herbert. *The Funeral Sourcebook.* London: Pickering and Inglis, 1967.

Mansell, John S. *The Funeral: A Pastor's Guide.* Nashville: Abingdon Press, 1998.

Poovey, William Arthur. *Planning a Christian Funeral: A Minister's Guide.* Minneapolis: Ausburg, 1978.

Searl, Edward. *In Memoriam: A Guide to Modern Funeral and Memorial Services.* Boston: Skinner House, 1993.

CONCLAMATIO MORTIS

Literally "the calling out of the dead," the conclamatio mortis was the ceremonial farewell for the dead in ancient Rome. For those of means, professional mourners were hired; for the poor family, members alone called on the dead by name (conclamare) and loudly grieved their death. This lamentation began after the last breath, with the closing of the deceased's eyes by the nearest relative, and continued at intervals, from lying-in-state (collocare) through funerary procession (pompa) to the final inhumation or cremation of the body and interment of the remains. This practice is known from the earliest records of Roman burial practices and continued in some parts of the Holy Roman Empire through Byzantine times. It is closely akin to the wailing done by women in Greek funerary practices and somewhat more distantly related to the Hebrew *safad* or *misped* (literally "beating of the breast"). Other parallels from around the world abound.

References

Toynbee, J. M. C. *Death and Burial in Ancient Rome.* Ithaca, NY: Cornell University Press, 1971.

CONSECRATION SERVICE

Because commercial and secular institutions now dominate funerary arrangements in the Western world (particularly in the United States), practicing Christians are often buried in a grave that is not in a churchyard or Christian cemetery. Many Protestant denominations have an extra ritual for such cases, called a *Consecration.* (Other denominations, such as Catholic, strongly frown on burials outside previously sanctified ground.) Through the Consecration ritual, the burial site is made holy either just before or just after the burial. The prayer, from Joseph Bernardin's *Burial Services,* runs as follows:

O God, whose blessed Son was laid in a sepulcher in the garden: Bless, we pray, this grave, and grant that he/she whose body is (is to be) buried here may dwell with Christ in paradise, and may come to thy heavenly kingdom; through thy Son Jesus Christ our Lord. (All say) *Amen.*

See also CEMETERY; COMMITTAL SERVICE; CREMAINS; RESURRECTION, CHRISTIAN.

References

Bernardin, Joseph Buchanan, comp. *Burial Services.* Wilton, CT: Morehouse-Barlow, 1980.

Biddle, Perry H., Jr. *A Funeral Manual.* Grand Rapids, MI: William B. Eerdman's Publishing, 1994.

Inter-Lutheran Commission on Worship. *Burial of the Dead.* Minneapolis: Augsburg, 1976.

Lockyer, Herbert. *The Funeral Sourcebook.* London: Pickering and Inglis, 1967.

Mansell, John S. *The Funeral: A Pastor's Guide.* Nashville: Abingdon Press, 1998.

Poovey, William Arthur. *Planning a Christian Funeral: A Minister's Guide.* Minneapolis: Ausburg, 1978.

CREMAINS

The abbreviated form of the words "cremated remains," *cremains* are the ashes and bits of bone left over from a cremation. In the older cultures that practiced cremation, cremains might also include the burned remains of food offerings, eating utensils, gifts to the deceased, and personal possessions—whatever was put on the pyre to be burned with the body. Cremains were placed in funerary vases, urns, chests in the shape of small houses or altars, cylindrical drums, ossuaries, and even reliquaries and have traditionally been interred in columbaria, mausolea, or hypogea or have been treated as unburned human remains and deposited in ordinary tombs or graves. In recent times, when the traditional Jewish and Christian expectation of physical resurrection has lost currency, cremains are not always interred but may be scattered over water, natural scenes, or other meaningful destinations as specified by the deceased.

Sixty percent of bone is inorganic and will not burn—this is the bulk of what remains after cremation. Cremains generally weigh between 4 and 8 pounds. They are usually white or gray but may be slightly tinged with color (yellow, pink, or green) from metals or chemicals in the coffin, tooth fillings, or jewelry. Crematoria are legally required to certify that the ashes presented to mourners after a cremation are in fact those of the deceased, though occasionally mix-ups have been discovered and lawsuits have followed. Once given to the bereaved, ashes are generally scattered (legal restrictions on this practice have been dropped in most states), kept at home or in an urn at a columbarium, or buried in the ground at a cemetery.

See also FUNERARY CUSTOMS, ANCIENT GREEK; FUNERARY CUSTOMS, ANCIENT ROMAN; FUNERARY CUSTOMS, CENTRAL ASIAN; FUNERARY CUSTOMS, ETRUSCAN.

References

Cremation Association of North America (CANA). *Cremation and Percentage of Deaths.* Chicago: CANA, 1989.

———. *Cremation Explained: Answers to Questions Most Frequently Asked.* Chicago: CANA, 1986.

Iserson, Kenneth V. *Death to Dust: What Happens to Dead Bodies?* Tucson, AZ: Galen Press, 1994.

Kubasak, M. W. *Cremation and the Funeral Director—Successfully Meeting the Challenge.* Malibu, CA: Avalon Press, 1990.

CREMATION

Cremation has been the dominant mode of bodily disposal in many cultures since prehistoric times (for example, in Hindu society and many Australian tribes); among other groups it has come in and out of fashion (for example, the Greco-Roman culture); and for some (ancient Egyptians, modern orthodox Jews, Muslims, and Zoroastrians) cremation was and is a horrible, unthinkable practice.

Cremation appears to have been widely practiced at some times in the ancient Near East, particularly in Babylon and among the Phoenicians. Ancient Israelites seem to have frowned upon cremation and reserved it mostly for criminals, in part because bones were regarded as pure objects of veneration once the flesh had decayed. The Torah states repeatedly that the bones of Hebrew patriarchs were "gathered up" and placed with their "fathers"—presumably in family or community tombs. However, cremations of venerated heroes are mentioned in the Old Testament (e.g., 1 Samuel 31:12–13) on rare occasions. Most of Bronze Age Europe appears to have practiced cremation widely though not exclusively, and this tradition was carried on well into Christian times among Germanic and Scandinavian peoples. Aristocratic Greeks and Romans were often cremated (including Julius Caesar), but popular practice appears to have waxed and waned over time, particularly when money was tight (as we shall see, a great deal of wood and a very high temperature are required for effective cremation).

Christianity put an end to Roman cremation practices because intact bodies were desired to facilitate resurrection, a sentiment shared by the other monotheistic religions. Christians were, of course, well aware that bodies gradually disintegrate in the ground and are eventually no more "intact" than cremated bodies, but at least decomposition was a natural process: the "image of God" was not willfully destroyed.

Hinduism practices cremation in all cases save those of very young children and yogis (ascetic mendicants)—neither are considered truly in the world of society and hence are inhumed without formal rites. Buddhism in large part adopted Hindu belief in the transmigration of the soul and the relative unimportance of the body and likewise adopted cremation as the fastest and most hygienic way to dispose of the body, starting with the body of the Buddha himself. His "cremains" were divided into eight parts and placed in eight stūpas, or rounded monuments, at various sacred Buddhist sites in northern India (which are pilgrimage destinations even today). Buddhist cremation practices spread into China, Korea, and Japan as those populations converted to Buddhism; Satī, the sacrifice of a widow on her husband's pyre, is a well-known example (now explicitly forbidden by Indian law).

Cremation is increasingly popular today in European countries and the United States and Canada, after a century of struggle for legal and religious approval. The Catholic Church and most secular authorities in Europe and the United States opposed cremation largely on the

Widow of Brahmin committing satī on husband's funeral pyre. Courtesy of Anne Ronan Picture Library.

grounds that it was not traditional; medical groups such as the International Medical Congress of Florence (Italy) and an interesting array of reformers and occult groups such as the Theosophical Society strenuously promoted the practice. A number of late nineteenth-century pamphlets like Max Levy's "Why Modern Cremation Should Replace Earth Burial" survive, demonstrating in their strong rhetoric what an uphill battle this was at first.

Cremation appears to be gaining ground in the modern world as the most cost-effective means of disposing of the dead; it is also touted for other advantages, such as conserving public land and having less of an environmental impact (compared to the pollution of the ground that might be caused by decaying bodies resting on synthetic fabrics and cushions encased in chemically treated coffins or the seepage of embalming and other fluids into the water table). Cremation is especially popular today in the western United States, where Christian European burial practices did not have as much time to become entrenched. For example, in California and Nevada, cremations now account for more than half of all burials, and a number of cremation societies have sprung up, such as the Telophase Society of San Diego and the Neptune Society in San Francisco.

Although in ancient times (and today in India and elsewhere among people of humble means) cremations were performed in the open air on piles of wood or other combustibles, today cremations in industrialized societies are performed only in crematories, most of which are owned by cemeteries or funeral homes. Usually, crematories also have a columbarium on the premises, which will (for an additional fee of several thousand dollars) permanently store the ashes of the deceased in small drawers or urns placed in niches. There are nearly 2,000 crematories in the United States, with the number expected to grow rapidly in the next few decades. Although most crematories recommend that mourners purchase expensive coffins in which to cremate their loved ones, in fact simple wooden or even sturdy cardboard boxes simplify the combustion process and are all that is legally required in most locations. The temperature of the oven reaches at least 1,600 degrees Fahrenheit (new regulations specify a temperature closer to 2,000 degrees), and the actual combustion of the body takes only half an hour to forty-five minutes, not including preparation, cleanup, and any additional secular or religious ceremony that is requested. The "ashes" that remain are actually made up mostly of tiny bone fragments and weigh from 4 to 8 pounds depending on the size of the body cremated. Often crematories pulverize these remains (sometimes this practice is required by law, as in California). The *total* cost for cremations in the

United States is generally less than $1,000 and through membership in local memorial societies can be as little as $500, though the purchase of extra services and products (embalming, expensive caskets, etc.) can greatly increase the price.

See also COLUMBARIUM; CREMAINS; FUNERARY CUSTOMS, ANCIENT GREEK; FUNERARY CUSTOMS, ANCIENT INDIAN; FUNERARY CUSTOMS, ANCIENT ROMAN; FUNERARY CUSTOMS, CELTIC; FUNERARY CUSTOMS, CHRISTIAN; FUNERARY CUSTOMS, ETRUSCAN; FUNERARY CUSTOMS, HINDU; FUNERARY CUSTOMS, JEWISH; FUNERARY CUSTOMS, MESOPOTAMIAN; FUNERARY CUSTOMS, NATIVE NORTH AMERICAN; FUNERARY CUSTOMS, SCANDINAVIAN; FUNERARY CUSTOMS, ZOROASTRIAN; GARDEN, FUNERARY; MAUSOLEUM; MUMMIFICATION; REINCARNATION, WESTERN; STŪPA.

References
Cook, W. S. "Cremation: From Ancient Cultures to Modern Usage." *Casket and Sunnyside* (1973).
Cremation Association of North America (CANA). *Cremation and Percentage of Deaths*. Chicago: CANA, 1989.
———. *Cremation Explained: Answers to Questions Most Frequently Asked*. Chicago: CANA, 1986.
Iserson, Kenneth V. *Death to Dust: What Happens to Dead Bodies?* Tucson, AZ: Galen Press, 1994.
Kubasak, M. W. *Cremation and the Funeral Director—Successfully Meeting the Challenge*. Malibu, CA: Avalon Press, 1990.
Levy, Max. "Why Modern Cremation Should Replace Earth Burial: An Exposé of the Dangers Caused by Inhumation." San Francisco: San Francisco Cremation Company, 1885.
Neptune Society of Northern California (NSNC). *Disclosures Regarding the Cremation Process*. San Francisco: NSNC, 1993.
Polson, C. J., R. P. Brittain, and T. K. Marshall. *The Disposal of the Dead*. 2nd ed. Springfield, IL: Charles C. Thomas, 1962.

CROMLECH

Called in Irish and Gaelic *cromleac, cromlech* is the Welsh term for the prehistoric megalithic structures fashioned of three or more massive vertical stones weighing upwards of 20 tons each, topped by an equally massive horizontal stone slab, and buried under a great mound of earth or rubble. They all appear originally to have been covered over with a great mound of earth (forming a barrow) with small entrances. Sometimes, over the course of the many thousands of years since their construction, the earthen mound has worn away or has been removed by people, exposing the massive rocks aboveground.

The cultural and religious character of these structures for the people who built them is not entirely understood, but they are thought to have been primarily markers of important burials. In later times when the dead had become conflated (or perhaps purposefully identified) with the gods, the cromlechs developed into centers of religious activity connected with fertility and communication with supernatural powers. They are found in various parts of Great Britain, particularly in

Ancient burial tomb at Benllech, northern Wales. Courtesy of CFCL.

Wales, Devonshire, Cornwall, and Ireland. In Brittany, France, all megalithic structures are called *dolmens,* but in Great Britain the term *cromlech* is used only for a circle of standing stones like Stonehenge, Avebury, and Carnac.

See also BARROW; CAIRN; DOLMEN; MEGALITHIC TOMB.

References
Colvin, Howard. *Architecture and the After-Life*. New Haven: Yale University Press, 1991.
Eogan, G. *Knowth and the Passage-Tombs of Ireland*. New York: Thames and Hudson, 1986.
Henshall, A. H. *The Chambered Tombs of Scotland*. 2 vols. Edinburgh: Edinburgh University Press, 1963, 1972.
Mackie, E. *The Megalith Builders*. Oxford: Phaidon, 1977.
Murray, James A. H. et al. *Oxford English Dictionary*. 2nd ed. Oxford: Clarendon Press, 1996.
O'Kelley, M. *Newgrange*. London: Thames and Hudson, 1982.
Piggott, S. *Neolithic Cultures of the British Isles*. Cambridge: Cambridge University Press, 1954.
Twohig, E. Shee. *The Megalithic Art of Western Europe*. Oxford: Clarendon Press, 1981.

CROSSROADS

The mystery and danger of crossroads, particularly those some distance from cities, form a folk tradition worldwide and are intimately associated with the dead. Crossroads are liminal realms—borderlands—often desolate and belonging neither to one locale nor to another. Thus in myth and legend they are ambiguous, even dangerous intersections of power. This perceived peril probably also arises from the fact that dangerous dead, that is, those in danger of becoming undead, are often buried there, since no locale wants their pollution. Crossroads are a no-man's-land, and the mythology of danger that surrounds them has branches throughout Europe, India, China, and Japan and among Mongols and Native Americans.

There is evidence that among the ancient Greeks and Slavs crossroads were originally considered favorable burial places because of the large number of "visitors" (and thus the increased likelihood of offerings and attention for the dead). However, in general only victims of suicide, murderers, strangers, and the impious have been buried at crossroads. Thus crossroads have predominantly been locations of impurity, fear, witchcraft, demonic forces, and necromancy.

Burial of the dangerous dead at crossroads is probably motivated by several factors. First, the danger is removed from one's habitation and placed in a desolate location betwixt and between. Second, the dead are punished and dishonored by receiving such a despised burial, which satisfies societal norms and serves as an example to others. For Christians in particular, refusing to bury the dead in the sacred ground of the church cemetery might deny them resurrection. In some parts of medieval Europe, it was even customary to bury the dishonored dead with the feet rather than the head toward the east—an explicitly "anti-Christian" burial. Third, burial in such an ambiguous location as a crossroads may be an attempt to isolate the spirits of the dead and confuse them in a maze, as it were, making it difficult for them to return to their old dwellings and harm the living.

Suicides accounted for the largest share of those relegated to a crossroads burial. In Britain suicides were buried near crossroads to rid the township of their presence, doubly ensuring this result by securing the corpse with a stake through the heart lest it should arise as an undead and wander about; this practice continued until forbidden by law in 1823. In Germany no stake was put through the heart, but instead a rope was tied around the foot and the body was buried with a harrow placed on top, presumably to weigh the corpse down and likewise prevent its ambulation. Among the Baganda of Uganda, suicides were taken to crossroads along with wood from their houses or from the trees in which they hung themselves, and everything was burned and buried there. Passersby threw clumps of grass or sticks on the mound to ward off any residual danger.

Plato writes in his *Laws* (Taylor) that criminals were to be taken out to crossroads and buried there, excommunicating them from the city and its respectable dead; likewise, crucifixion—a method of death for the criminal and despised—often took place in the ancient Roman world at crossroads. In Europe and particularly in Britain execution grounds were located outside townships near crossroads, and criminals were buried nearby. This practice carried over to the American colonies and French Canada, where gallows were often put outside the city limits at a crossroads, with murderers left there to hang. In ancient Mayan culture, the spirits of women who died in childbirth, the chichuateteo, were thought to wander about, particularly at crossroads, seeking to devour the children of the living.

They were offered bread in the shapes of butterflies and thunderbolts, pies, and toasted corn in the hopes that they would not be harmful. In Japanese folklore the spirits of gossips are transformed into red-tongued monsters and condemned to haunt crossroads—perhaps a fitting punishment for those too much into the business of others. In India dangerous spirits of the dead— the bhūts—are thought to congregate at crossroads, seeking to waylay the unwary, and in Russia revenants, or reanimated corpses, menace likewise.

Given this connection with death, particularly unwholesome death, crossroads have also been significant in funeral processions. In China spirits who congregate at crossroads are thought to be dangerous to the newly dead, harassing them unless those in the funeral procession make an offering of paper money at each crossroads passed on the way to the burial site. In Wales the funeral procession halts and the bier is set down at each intersection so that the minister might pray and protect the party on the way to the cemetery. In some places in India lamps are placed at each crossroad on the way to the cemetery; after the cremation has been performed, its fire is considered impure, and the embers are taken at sunrise to the nearest crossroads to the south and put out. Indians are also warned not to remain long at crossroads after they have eaten a funerary meal lest the Rakṣasa demons (literally "harmful") or pishācha demons (literally "flesh eaters") should come and torment them.

Properly handled, however, crossroads may be made harmless. Among the Wadschagga tribes of southeastern Africa a sacrifice is performed at crossroads for the lost souls, the varima varekye. Lacking descendants to perform the appropriate funerary rites, these souls can become quite angry, but they are appeased by the offerings from the community as a whole. In pre-Columbian Peru, an annual ceremony was held at the intersection of roads in the town square: a runner with a lance stood posted at each direction, waiting for a herald from the temple of the sun. On approach the herald instructed them that by the authority of the sun evil was to be chased out, and in each direction the runners lowered their lances and chased the evil out to a considerable distance. In Germany, Wales, and much of the rest of Europe, if ghosts harass one during one's travels, the best thing to do is to proceed to the nearest crossroad, even if it is fraught with obstacles—for the dead on all nights except Halloween cannot pass through crossroads and so may be left behind there.

Crossroads can even be sources of protection or help for the pious. In his last discourse the Buddha instructed his disciples to build stūpas with his remains and place them at crossroads so that the greatest number of people would benefit from the holy power of his relics and be reminded of the quest for enlightenment. In ancient Greece, crossroads were considered the

The dead drummer, a legend of Salisbury Plain. Courtesy of Anne Ronan Picture Library.

special domain of the god Hermes, the patron of travelers, among other things. Piles of stones were erected at crossroads in his honor, and each traveler placed a stone on the pile as he or she passed by, asking for protection on his or her journey. Later these piles were replaced with images of Hermes and phallic-shaped stones named for the god, but no matter—Hermes was present all the same and available to those who paid their respects to his symbols. Likewise, at the mountain passes of the Himalayas piles of stones are added to by travelers, for at the intersection of mountain and sky a protective memorial is needed to seek the blessing of the lhas (gods) there. In the Roman world offerings were given to the lares compitales, or "spirits of the crossroads," and an annual festival, the Ludi Compitales, was even held in their honor sometime between December 17 and January 5. In India one may summon demons like the pishāchas to take away diseases (to "eat" the diseased flesh) and the like.

In medieval Christian Europe, small shrines were erected at crossroads to saints and the madonna so that travelers could have their prayers heard. In the eleventh century, we find the church still taking steps to prevent its wards from lighting candles and venerating the saints at crossroads, and even today in modern rural Italy crossroad shrines to certain saints persist. In Japan the chimata no kami, or crossroads spirits, were honored with images built at intersections, and the kami could be invoked for protection by travelers setting out on a journey. In modern times the kami have been replaced by the bodhisattva (Buddhist saint) Jizō, a manifestation of Kwan Yin, protector of all people, particularly children and aborted fetuses. In Central America small idols and clay or stone altars were built at crossroads, where torches and resinous wood were burned, birds were offered along with some of one's own blood, and the powers of the four winds and the four corners of the earth were called upon for protection.

Further, the occult power of crossroads was invoked for more than just obtaining protection—they made good sites for performing divination and other magic of all kinds. In Europe witches were thought to congregate at crossroads and hold their unholy Sabbat revels there, possibly because in ancient Greek tradition Hecate, goddess of the occult, was also a deity of the crossroads and could be appealed to there for her uncanny aid. In Denmark, Iceland, and Norway it was thought that crossroads were centers for prophecy, especially on New Year's Eve. Icelanders were told to take a sharp iron axe and a gray hide to a crossroads where each road led in a straight line to a church. Once there, they were to wrap themselves completely in the hide, tucking it in on all sides, and pronounce spells to raise the dead. Spirits of dead relatives from any of the churches on the roads would appear and reveal the past and the future. If the diviner never took his or her eyes off the edge of the axe or uttered a word, all would be remembered; otherwise, ill was bound to result. In India crossroads were the abode not only of dangerous demons but of Dharmarāja, god of justice, and his haunt was used to try accused criminals in the "ordeal by balance." The accused was placed on a scale at a crossroads and carefully weighed using stones and sand. After he stepped down, the charges were read and placed on his head, and then he was reweighed: if lighter, he was vindicated; if heavier or the same, he was pronounced guilty. Likewise the Hindus have ceremonies for cleansing themselves of sin at a crossroads and using the powers that dwell there to predict the future. European folktales abound that fairies, trolls, demons—even the Devil himself—could be met at a crossroads, whether invited or otherwise, particularly at midnight. If such entities' tricky questions were answered correctly, one might be granted wishes or a heap of money—but of course there was always the danger of losing one's soul. In Arabia, too, the jinn (genies) were thought to haunt crossroads, and although they were indeed dangerous, they could be forced by the wise or audacious to grant powers or treasure.

See also NECROMANCY; UNDEAD; VAMPIRE.

References

Barber, Paul. *Vampires, Burial, and Death: Folklore and Reality*. New Haven: Yale University Press, 1988.

Crooke, William. *The Popular Religion and Folk-lore of Northern India*. 2nd ed. Delhi: Munshiram Manoharlal, 1968.

Davies, Jonathan C. *Folk-lore of West and Mid-Wales*. Aberystwyth: Welsh Gazette Offices, 1911.

Grimm, Jacob. *Teutonic Mythology*. Trans. J. S. Stallybrass. London: G. Bell and Sons, 1883.

Puhvel, Martin. *The Crossroads in Folklore and Myth*. New York: Peter Lang Publications, 1989.

Ralston, W. S. *Russian Folk-tales*. London: Smith, Elder and Company, 1873.

Smith, Grace Partridge. "Crossroads." In *Funk and Wagnalls Standard Dictionary of Folklore, Mythology and Legend*, ed. Maria Leach. New York: Funk and Wagnalls, 1950.

Taylor, A. E., trans. *The Laws of Plato*. London: J. M. Dent and Sons, 1934.

Weule, Karl. *Native Life in East Africa*. Westport, CT: Negro Universities Press, 1970.

CUBICULUM TOMB

Cubiculum is the Latin name for underground, rectangular tomb chambers, usually owned by a single family for a number of generations. Running about 100 to 150 square feet, cubicula are found primarily in the Christian catacombs and are characterized by loculi tombs (tombs carved out of walls in catacombs) and occasionally burials in the floor as well (formae). The wealthier families could afford extensive decorations for their cubicula (including arcosolia, benchlike niches in the walls of stone tombs): the vast majority of early Christian funerary art is to be found in these chambers.

It has sometimes been thought that Christians took refuge in these chambers during persecution or held routine religious services here. As a rule, however, the chambers were too small, damp, and often flooded for such regular usage. It is certain that Eucharist or less formal funerary meals were held in the chamber during the interment of a family member and perhaps annually, since wooden and stone tables (mensa) have been found that served that purpose.

References

Morey, C. R. *Early Christian Art*. Princeton: Princeton University Press, 1953.

Stevenson, James. *The Catacombs: Life and Death in Early Christianity*. London: Thames and Hudson, 1978.

Veidle, W. *The Baptism of Art: Notes on the Religion of the Catacomb Paintings*. London: Dacre, 1950.

D

DAGOBA

The Sri Lankan version of the Buddhist Indian stūpa, a dagoba is an elaborate monument that housed the relics of the Buddha and his disciples. The word *dagoba* is a Sinhalese contraction of the Sanskrit *dhatu-garbha*, which referred originally to the harmika, or altar structure, atop the dome of the monument that held the Buddha's relics and means literally "the womb or container (garbha) that housed the relics (dhatu)." With the passage of time in Sri Lanka, the dome grew larger (sometimes taking the relic box or harmika inside itself), and it came to be called *dhatu-garbha (dagoba)*. Eventually the entire monument was called the *dagoba*.

Although the Sinhalese version of the stūpa is not so different from its Indian predecessor, the interpretation of the elements of the monument is somewhat unique. For instance, the cone-shaped spire rising out of the relic box atop the dome was called *devata kotuva*, or "enclosure of the gods," indicating that the Sinhalese no longer saw the spire as an honorific umbrella, as in India, but as a miniature cosmic mountain (Mount Meru) whereon the gods dwell.

See also MCHOD RTEN; STŪPA.

References

Govinda, Anagarika. *The Psycho-Cosmic Symbolism of the Buddhist Stūpa*. Emeryville, CA: Dharma Publishing, 1976.

DANCE OF DEATH

The dance of death, also known as the danse macabre (French), Totentanz (German), and danza de la muerte (Spanish), is a composition from the late Middle Ages of Europe (fourteenth to fifteenth centuries) portraying the leveling of persons and wealth in the face of death as a ghastly comedy. In fact, the original meaning of the word *macabre* refers to a tragic burlesque dwelling on the details of death (see DANSE MACABRE). Although there is considerable debate regarding the exact origin of the dance of death, it seems likely that it began in France as a pantomime performed in churches, with dialogue added later. There is also an early record of a series of pictures and paintings to which text was probably added later as elucidation. In any case, the dance of death in its many manifestations spread widely throughout late medieval Europe. In the early sixteenth century, the artist Hans Holbein the Younger standardized the pictures of the dance of death in woodcuts with dancing skeletons harassing about forty stereotypical figures and leading them to their deaths.

The overall field of influences that produced the dance of death is ancient and broad. As early as the Babylonian epic *Gilgamesh*, we find characters struggling with death and its mockery of life, physical strength, and social rank. Greek and Roman literature dwells at length on the sad reality of death and a grim afterlife. In the work of the satirist Lucian we find the closest approximation in the ancient world of the tragicomedy of the dance of death, for his *Dialogues of the Dead* pokes grim fun at the humbling of the dead, and he even singles out the skull of Helen of Troy for mockery as an example of the inevitable end of beauty. A more contemporary influence on the dance of death is the twelfth-century monk Hélinant's *Les Vers de la Mort* (Verses on Death), which extols asceticism and features Death in person visiting individuals to warn that their poor behavior will send them to hell. There is also the twelfth-century poem *Le Dit des Trois Mort et des Trois Vifs* (Dialogue between Three Living and Three Dead), accompanied by pictures, in which the living are warned to live good lives because death is their certain end. Perhaps most influential of all is the thirteenth-century poem *Vado Mori*, in which thirty-four classes of people representing society as a whole are sequentially discussed and their end portrayed, beginning with the pope and ending with the hermit. These stereotypical figures, as well as their sequential order, roughly parallel those that appear in the dance of death. There were probably pictures connected with the *Vado Mori*, but unfortunately these have been lost.

The date at which the dance of death was first composed is not known for certain; nor is it known how much it may have changed in the course of its early development. We may certainly assume that the extreme experience of Europe in the course of the plagues of the fourteenth century, beginning in earnest in 1347–1348, made death such an everyday occurrence that grim humor was used as a means to cope with the overwhelming. Representing dying and death in a drama may also have made it more intimate and acceptable. In the archives of the church of Caudebec, a document has been found

Death triumphant, from Hartmann Schedel Liber chroncarum mundi *(Nuremberg Chronicle), Nuremberg, 1493. Courtesy of Anne Ronan Picture Library.*

showing that in 1393 a dramatic religious dance was performed at the church, with actors playing figures of various political or social rank. One by one, the actors disappeared, portraying death's indifference to prestige or power, even to the office of the pope himself. We may assume that the dance of death was first performed well before this date, given its widespread diffusion by the early 1400s.

The most famous pictures illustrating the dance of death are certainly those designed by Hans Holbein the Younger (1497[?]–1543). Holbein's excellent woodcuts were done in the early 1520s in Basel but were not published until 1538, held back probably because of the biting satire. His work included forty-one woodcuts, each illustrating a simple French verse of four lines (with an a-b-a-b rhyme scheme) together with an appropriate quote from the Bible on the subjects of

death and the virtues. The book opened with the chapters "The Creation," "The Temptation," "Expulsion from Paradise," "Birth and Death," and "Death Goes Forth." Then all the principal figures of society are taken up in turn, beginning with the pope, cardinal, bishop, and abbot, running through secular offices (emperor, empress, king, queen, etc.), professions (soldier, judge, lawyer, astrologer), and ending with generic people of various ages (old man, old woman, young child). A later version published in 1547 includes a few more cuts, and the final 1562 edition has a total of fifty-two engravings, including "The Bridegroom and the Bride," originally sketched by Holbein but most likely finished by a student.

In each chapter, the verse holds up the subject facing death for mockery, often with an accusation of a vice stereotypical of their station. The accompanying woodcut supplies a grim but amusing scene with a skeletal figure (occasionally two) harassing the principal character, often foiling the performance of their office or dragging them off by the hand or coat. Nearly every engraving contains an empty hourglass, though often the glass is hidden and the viewer must seek it out as a macabre game. For example, in the chapter "The Duke," we find the following Scripture and verse:

"The prince shall be clothed with desolation ...
I will also make the pomp of the strong to cease."
(Ezekiel 7:27, 24)

Come, potent prince, with me alone—
Leave transient pomps of worldly state;
I am the one who can fling down
The pride and honours of the great.
(Evans, chap. 19)

Meanwhile, the woodcut shows a crowned nobleman with rich clothes turning his head away from a grinning corpse figure "crowned" with a laurel and seizing him by the mantle. The prince's advisers stand about downcast and helpless, while a beggar woman and child grovel at the prince's feet. An empty hourglass is hidden in the wall of the palace in the background.

It is easy to understand why the dance of death would have been spread so enthusiastically by the church, given its constant harping on death and the doom awaiting those who failed to practice virtue. It is interesting, however, that nine of the forty or so subjects of Holbein's woodcuts are church figures who are spared no more than any others.

See also BLACK DEATH.

References

Clark, James M. *The Dance of Death in the Middle Ages and the Renaissance.* Glasgow: Glasgow University Press, 1980.

Evans, Frederick H., ed. *The Dance of Death by Hans Holbein.* London: Temple Sheen Press, 1916.

Kurtz, Léonard P. *The Dance of Death and the Macabre Spirit in European Literature.* Geneva: Slatkine Reprints, 1975.

DANSE MACABRE

The closely related French versions of pictures and texts called the *danse macabre* were probably the source of all later dance of death verses and engravings in Europe. They embody a grim humor toward death, depicting dancing corpses and skeletons disrupting human life and ruining alike emperors and paupers.

There has been considerable controversy over the origin of the word *macabre*, but it first appears in a European language in a poem written in 1376, called *Respit de la Mort* by Jehan Le Fèvre, in connection with a macabre dance. Some scholars have suggested that macabre was the name of the first painter of the danse macabre pictures, whereas others have traced it to a Hebrew root (*macabé*, "the flesh leaves the bones") or the Arabic word *maqabir*, plural of *maqabara* (grave). Another writer notes that the earliest occurrences of the word give *macabré*, not *macabre*, and shows that macabré was a popular pronunciation of the Biblical name Machabees. Three editions of danse macabre works contain the line, "C'est la dance des Macabees." Several European families are known to have carried a version of that name (Macabray, Macabrey). Thus the danse macabre is thought either to have been inspired by the Biblical Machabees and the ghastly sacrifice of the mother and seven sons recorded there or to have been written by a European poet with that family name.

References

Clark, James M. *The Dance of Death in the Middle Ages and the Renaissance.* Glasgow: Glasgow University Press, 1980.

Kurtz, Léonard P. *The Dance of Death and the Macabre Spirit in European Literature.* Geneva: Slatkine Reprints, 1975.

DEAD, THE

In common usage, *the dead* is a collective noun referring to persons who lived and died as human beings. Throughout antiquity, even in our own time, the dead are widely thought to continue living, albeit in more or less altered states, in a variety of locations: in netherworlds, on earth, in heaven, and in other postmortem environments. Ancestors, ghosts, demons, spirits, saints, and often even gods are treated on the one hand as an active and positive class of beings in the world, as important forces to be reckoned with, and as bestowers of good crops, health, and other gifts in the world; and on the other hand as dangerous negative beings to be avoided, since they bring pollution to all they encounter. The dead are still the loved ones that were alive and well only a short time ago but now, connected with the "disease" of death, they can infect others spiritually and bring more death to the community. To reconcile these contradictory but complementary attitudes requires insight into the nature of the social and ritual transformation that begins at physical death.

Almost universally, the dead are thought to move through different stages of death that fall into two broad categories: (1) the recently dead, regarding whom the psychological issue is separation and the ritual issue is pollution; and (2) the established dead, regarding whom the psychological issue is integration and the ritual issue is spiritual power. Very quickly after physical death the body begins to decay, even while the immediate family and larger community are mourning the loss of their member, leading to a tension between supplication of the soul and help on its journey and a sharp rejection of the corpse and the evil spirits associated with it, which

The moneylender visited by death, 1538. Courtesy of Anne Ronan Picture Library.

necessitates that ritual disposal called a *funeral*. Ritual separation, accomplished by preparation of the body, last rites, and physical removal, is handled quite differently around the world. Among the Miao of Southeast Asia, the body lies in state for three to twelve days, whereas in traditional Zoroastrianism, the funeral and disposal of the body must take place on the very day of death unless death occurred near or after sunset.

Failure to properly handle the recently dead results in grave danger to the living. The Synoptic Gospels of the Bible refer frequently to the demons that attend one infected by corpse pollution (e.g., Luke 8:26–33; Matthew 8:28–33; Mark 5:1–14). Likewise, in ancient Persia death pollution appeared in the form of a "corpse fiend" (in Persian, *Druj Nasu*, cf. Greek *Nekus*), the incarnation of the inherent evil of all flesh as envisaged in Zoroastrianism. In India mistreatment of the dead or dabbling in necromancy invited the attention of the bhūts, or the lower psychic remains or doubles of the dead, who vampirize the life energies (prāṇa) of the living.

Yet after some time has passed (from a few weeks to ten years depending on the society), the dangers of corpse pollution diminish, and the dead, if they have been appropriately treated, make the passage to "established dead," marked in almost all traditional societies by a second funeral or ritual observance. Most often the bones are exhumed once the flesh is completely decayed and are treated in various ways. In sub-Saharan Africa, especially among the Bantu-speaking people, the bones of the established dead are pulverized and mixed with ritual beverages. Among the Bamelike of Cameroon, skulls are inherited by surviving clan members, which preserves the memory of the deceased and provides continuity among the clan. Frequently the second funeral is quite jolly and marked by singing, dancing, and copious amounts of food (e.g., among the Famadihana of Madagascar and the Olo Nyadju of Borneo). Most often, when the bones of the dead are not ritually consumed or given away to wild animals (e.g., among the Himalayan peoples, who crush up the bones to bake in bread, which is then given to birds), they are collected and placed in ossuaries, again providing societal continuity and often a final resting place for the dead.

Almost always, the dead retain some semblance of their former social status and may even continue to carry out their former social functions (parents continue to watch over families, holy men continue to actively guide the faithful, kings and princes rule over their netherworld kingdoms). Many cultures see the dead as so present and so active in the world that they are powerful forces to be reckoned with. For example, around 645 B.C.E., the Assyrian monarch Ashurbanipal punished the traitorous Elamites in part by attacking their dead kings. Ashurbanipal described his vengeance: "I have pulled down and destroyed the tombs of their earlier and later kings . . . and I exposed them to the sun. I took away their bones to Assyria. I put restlessness on their ghosts, I deprived them of food offerings and libations of water." This assault on the dead was thought to gravely undermine the power of the Elamites and bring them into submission.

Furthermore, from ancient times in nearly all parts of the world until even today, particularly in China, Korea, and Japan and among most aboriginal peoples, daily care is expected for the dead ancestors of the family. These ancestors frequently include seven or more deceased generations—certainly more if the ancestors had royal or honored military status. Prayers are given for their well-being, accompanied by offerings of food, water, incense, flowers, and so on. Neglect of these duties is not merely disrespectful but downright dangerous, for unpropitiated ancestors might become hungry ghosts and seek vengeance on their selfish descendants. In a proverbial saying among the Chinese, "alive a dead man, dead a *kuei*," *kuei* refers to the ghost of a wronged ancestor who has arisen from the infernal regions to haunt the living as an itinerant and retributive executioner.

References

Abrahamsson, Hans. *The Origin of Death: Studies in African Mythology.* Uppsala: Arno Press, 1951.

Ahern, Emily. *The Cult of the Dead in a Chinese Village.* Stanford: Stanford University Press, 1973.

Ariès, Philippe. *Western Attitudes toward Death: From the Middle Ages to the Present.* Baltimore: Johns Hopkins University Press, 1974.

Bendann, Effie. *Death Customs: An Analytical Study of Burial Rites.* New York: Alfred A. Knopf, 1930.

Bloch, Maurice, and Jonathan Parry, eds. *Death and the Regeneration of Life.* Cambridge: Cambridge University Press, 1982.

Georges, Elaine. *Voyages de la mort.* Paris: Berger-Levrault, 1982.

Hsu, Francis L. K. *Under the Ancestor's Shadow.* New York: Columbia University Press, 1948.

Lewis, Theodore J. "Cults of the Dead in Ancient Israel and Ugarit." *Journal of Biblical Literature* 110 (1991).

Paxton, Frederick S. *Christianizing Death: The Creation of a Ritual Process in Early Medieval Europe.* Ithaca, NY: Cornell University Press, 1990.

Sullivan, Lawrence, ed. *Death, Afterlife and the Soul.* New York: Macmillan, 1989.

Van Gennep, Arnold. *Rites of Passage.* Trans. Monika B. Vizedom and Gabrielle L. Caffe. London: Routledge and Kegan Paul, 1960.

DEATH, GOOD

Although few people look forward to death as an inherently "good" thing, it also becomes clear upon reflection that some kinds of death are far less desirable than others. A "bad" death is generally considered to be full of pain and trauma, long suffering, lonely, or pointless. A "good" death, then, is the opposite experience:

leaving this world in the best and most positive way possible. Since death is absolutely inevitable for all human beings, it behooves us to understand and pursue the "good" death.

Clinical research as well as a comparative study of world religion suggests that several components feed into the experience of what we might call a good or bad death. The first of these is our perceptions, which condition us psychologically from the first moment we clearly grasp that we too shall certainly die—and in the scheme of things relatively soon—until the moment we expire. If we are self-important, perceive death as inherently unfair, or greatly fear to face the beyond, our death will certainly be extremely difficult and psychologically painful. A second important aspect is our sense of completeness in this life. For example, many traditional societies believe that marriage is the essential ritual of life and to die unmarried is almost unthinkable. To remedy this incompleteness, many societies arrange a ritual marriage if one dies single (see later discussion). Third, the "good" death is conditioned by our map of the death process and what the afterlife will require, such as what kind of personal tools, knowledge, and preparations we have to navigate this territory. This component covers both our ethical behavior here in this life as well as our mystical or even magical knowledge (often secret wisdom) that unlocks gates barring our way in the hereafter. If we feel that death is natural, just, and orderly; that we are "done" with this life and ready to go on; and that we have a good sense of what is to come and are ready and able to handle it—this sense of completeness provides for a "good" death and reduces the fear, clinging, and anger we may have about the event.

Clearly our perceptions greatly color the experience of death, which may be seen in poetry. Poets most often gently lead us to the task of coping with death because they have the gift of summing up, in a few sentences, those emotions and thoughts that may be difficult for us to recognize and put into words. In his poem "The Dry Salvages," T. S. Eliot (1888–1965) expresses one view of death that is greatly influenced by his belief that humans are inherently transitory, constantly changing, never the same from moment to moment—death is merely another moment in time:

> Fare forward, travellers! not escaping from the past
> Into different lives, or into any future;
> You are not the same people who left that station
> Or who will arrive at any terminus . . .
> Fare forward, you who think that you are voyaging;
> You are not those who saw the harbour
> Receding, or those who will disembark.
> Here between the hither and the farther shore
> While time is withdrawn, consider the future
> And the past with an equal mind.

This view is in distinct contrast to that of Dylan Thomas (1914–1953), who wrote an address to his dying father, saying:

> Do not go gentle into that good night,
> Old age should burn and rave at the close of day;
> Rage, rage against the dying of the light. . . .
>
> Good men, the last wave by, crying how bright
> Their frail deeds might have danced in a green bay,
> Rage, rage against the dying of the light.

Eliot suggests a stillness, an equanimity, and an acceptance of life and perhaps what is beyond life; Thomas, while calling death that "good" night, protests at the parting and urges us on to burn, rave, and rage at our end.

Elizabeth Kübler-Ross, a psychiatrist who did extensive work with terminally ill patients, found a similar distinction between patients who accepted their deaths and those who felt their death was very unfair and untimely. One patient, after receiving his terminal diagnosis, seemed to have come to peace with his death, and he was willing to die, though he would have preferred to live (p. 132):

> the assisting surgeon told my wife that I had from four to fourteen months to live. I felt nothing. I've been at complete peace with my soul since I found this out. I've had no period of depression. I suppose most anybody in my position would look at somebody else and say, well, why couldn't it have been him. And this crossed my mind several times. But it is only a fleeting passage.

The patient said that his faith in God had produced such calmness and that his death was God's decision to make, not his. In other words, because of his perceptions of himself and his death, he was able to accept his fate. However, a person who has a greater sense of ego, someone who might be called a "control freak," has a very different perception of himself and the event of death. Kübler-Ross writes (p. 67):

> [A] problem patient is the man who has been in control all his life and who reacts with rage and anger when he is forced to given up these controls. I am reminded of Mr. O. who was hospitalized with Hodgkin's disease which, he claimed, was caused by his poor eating habits. He was a rich and successful businessman who had never had any problems in eating, and had never been obliged to diet to lose weight. His account was totally unrealistic, yet he insisted that he, and only he, caused "this weakness." This denial was maintained in spite of

the radiotherapy and his superior knowledge and intelligence.

Certainly, this patient's perceptions of his terminal illness as "weakness" and his rage at all who came near would make it almost impossible to experience a "good" death.

Besides one's perceptions of oneself and the event of death, the experience of a good death also has to do with feeling finished with this life, knowing that one has accomplished what one had to do. Without this psychological and sociological sense of fulfillment, it will be hard to let go and accept death, both on the part of the dying person and on the part of his or her social circle. Feeling this sense of completion certainly varies from person to person and culture to culture. It may involve the certainty that one's children will be okay, one's family will have income, or one's projects (gardening, writing a piece of music, building a home) are finished—or accepting that some things one had hoped for will remain undone. In many cultures, a very important part of fulfilling one's role as an adult and member of the community is to become married (and usually to produce offspring).

There is a time for sex and reproduction and a time for death in the social consciousness. Dying "before one's time" severely disrupts the social order, confusing these separate "times" and producing an unusual amount of anguish over the death, particularly for close-knit, traditional communities. The Chinese of Singapore may arrange a marriage between two dead elder siblings (from different families) so that the younger siblings may fulfill their duty of not marrying before their older brothers or sisters. In Taiwan, the living may marry the dead. In a symbolic marriage, complete with dowry, an unmarried deceased female may be wed to a living married male. He spends one night of sexual consummation with her (presumably also symbolic), and after that she is able to enter the ancestral abode and partake of the reciprocal family structure between the living and the conscious but dead family members. Likewise, contemporary Mormons fear for their dead ancestors if they were not baptized and married according to Mormon rites: in God's eyes, they were not truly married. For this reason Mormons raise their long-dead ancestors (once they have been identified through genealogy) in very complex rituals in order to remarry them in the "proper" way so that they may enjoy the blessings of the highest heaven.

A similar attitude toward the death of unmarried people is found in contemporary Slavic countries. Such a death is considered premature and totally unacceptable. Hence the funeral of a single person (usually a young man or woman) is simultaneously their wedding. A Romanian wedding-funeral hymn, from Gail Kligman's book *Wedding of the Dead* (p. 215), runs as follows:

Oh, good dear young man,
It was not time for you to die;
It was time for you to marry.
Oh, get up and look around,
For at our house there are many people,
Because they thought we had a wedding.
You, well you have married:
You took a daughter of the King.

Most of the mourners wear black, but the stand-in "spouse" and the parents of both the deceased and the living spouse wear wedding attire throughout the funeral. Although the affair is certainly not a happy one, it makes an unacceptable death acceptable and gives a sense of completion to the life of the one who has died.

Finally, an understanding—a map—of what is to come after death greatly assists in providing a good death. Although in the West the belief in "nothingness" after death has become somewhat popular, most other cultures have developed fairly detailed pictures of what happens when we die. The ancient Egyptians and the Tibetan Buddhists are the world's paramount death planners, with their highly developed philosophies, rituals, meditations, and artwork that explain the processes of death and afterlife step-by-step. But every religion attempts to inculcate in its believers a knowledge of what is to come, usually involving some kind of a journey, an ethical judgment in the hereafter, and a final disposition—whether the deceased end up in a heaven or pure land, hell, limbo, or purgatory; among the community of revered ancestors; as ghosts wandering the earth; or reincarnating to enter the whole process once more.

Even when people are aware of and try to meet the preconditions for a "good" death, outside factors may still prevent it. Sometimes death is too sudden, as in a car crash or a murder; in these cases, there is no time for targeted preparation, but the overall tendency of one's life will affect the nature of even an unexpected death. Sometimes it is not the dying who battle with a denial of the reality but the living, who for their own reasons try to prevent the dying from leaving this world. For grieving relatives and friends, Kübler-Ross offers the following sage advice (p. 177):

The most heartbreaking time, perhaps, for the family is the final phase, when the patient is slowly detaching himself from his world including his family. They do not understand that a dying man who has found peace and acceptance in his death will have to separate himself, step by step, from his environment, including his most loved ones. How could he ever be ready to die if he continued to hold onto the meaningful relationships of which a man has so many? When the patient asks to be visited only by a few more friends, then by his children and finally only by his wife, it should be understood that it is his way of separating himself gradually. It is often misinterpreted by the immediate family as a rejection, and we have met several husbands and wives who have reacted dramatically to this normal and healthy detachment. I think we can be of greatest service to them if we help them understand that only patients who have worked through their dying are able to detach themselves slowly and peacefully in this manner. It should be a source of comfort and solace to them and not one of grief and resentment.

See also BOOK OF THE DEAD, EGYPTIAN; BOOK OF THE DEAD, TIBETAN; FUNERARY CUSTOMS.

References

Eliot, T. S. *Four Quartets*. San Diego: Harcourt Brace Jovanovich, 1988.

Kligman, Gail. *Wedding of the Dead*. Berkeley: University of California Press, 1988.

Kübler-Ross, Elizabeth. *On Death and Dying*. New York: Touchstone, 1997.

Thomas, Dylan. "Do Not Go Gentle into That Good Night." In *The Top 500 Poems*, ed. William Harmon. New York: Columbia University Press, 1992.

DEVACHAN (THEOSOPHICAL)

The name *Devachan* (properly spelled "bDe-ba-can") is a Tibetan Buddhist term for a particular Pure Land wherein a devout Buddhist may be reborn. However, in the literature of Theosophy (an occult movement begun in the United States in the late nineteenth century), Devachan has taken on the generalized meaning of the place of rest for all people between reincarnations.

According to Theosophical teachings, after physical death a person's various mortal and immortal souls leave the physical body and manifest on a subtle "astral" plane called *Kāmaloka*. Here, the mortal soul, called *kāmarūpa* (filled with earthly passions and desires), and the immortal soul, which is the real person (composed of higher mind, spiritual energy and the eternal spark, or *ātman*), mingle for a time but gradually begin to separate. Eventually, in a process called "second death," the immortal soul withdraws from the lower soul and is "born again" on a higher plane, called Devachan. Much like the Tibetan Buddhist description of the Bardo, or "in between," this process of separation or second death in Theosophical teaching is long or short, painful or easy, depending on the character of the individual who has died and the degree of spirituality exhibited during life. Again, as in Tibetan Buddhist teaching, Theosophy teaches that the last thought held in the mind during life sums up the "life's meditation" and greatly colors one's experiences in the afterdeath process. One who dies with a final thought of great fear or anger may expect that to dominate in the postmortem state for a time, whereas one dying peacefully and without attachment finds the death process smooth and kindly and the second death separation from the lower soul a quick and easy process.

Once free from the trials and tribulations of earth life and the second death on the plane of Kāmaloka, the immortal soul enters a new stage of joy and comfort. According to Theosophical authors, during life the soul—the immortal, real person—cannot fully actualize its potential, but its unfulfilled hopes and thoughts are real and cannot dissipate unexpressed. Rather they are stored up for later manifestation, as William Q. Judge writes:

> In life we can but to a fractional extent act out the thoughts we have each moment; and still less can we exhaust the psychic energies engendered by each day's aspirations and dreams. The energy thus engendered is not lost or annihilated, but is stored in Manas [the higher mind], but the body, brain and astral body permit no full development of the force. Hence, held latent until death, it bursts then from the weakened bonds and plunges Manas, the thinker, into the expansion, use, and development of the thought-force set up in life.

Thus Devachan is the subjective experience of the higher mind and soul on a higher plane of its own mental creation. Here in this timeless, heavenly state, the soul is able to experience its unfulfilled longings—which differ for each person. The musician exists in a Devachanic world filled with beautiful, perfect music; the abandoned wife finds her long-lost husband, who is now kind and committed to her, and so on. According to Theosophy, these perceptions are all illusions of sorts, for the mind has created this world out of its own energies. But Theosophical writers see the experience of physical life in the same way: illusionary, created by past karma and different for every person.

The duration of Devachan is again an individual affair and depends on the amount of unfulfilled mental energy—particularly spiritual aspirations—of the deceased. For gross materialists, the stay in Devachan is said to be short indeed, a few months or years. For the average person, 1,000 to 1,500 years are to be expected, and deeply spiritual persons may rest in Devachan much, much longer. (It is said that in Devachan the soul feels no passage of time but that time spent there can be measured by equivalent passage of time on earth.) At last, however, one's Devachanic karma runs out, and other, more material karma kicks in, dragging one down to a new birth in a new body. Just before the soul enters into its new life, it is said to have a vision of what has been in its past life, what will be in the immediate future life, and the perfect justice of its circumstances. Then the immortal soul plunges into a new fetus, joined by its lower tendencies, called *skandhas*, left over from the mortal soul in Kāmaloka, which have waited all along and are now magnetically attracted to the returning consciousness. A new astral body is built as the new physical body grows, old traits in the skandhas come alive again to form a new personality along the lines dictated by karma, and earth life begins again for the old soul.

See also ĀTMAN; BARDO; HEAVENS, BUDDHIST; KĀMALOKA; KĀMA-RŪPA; NIRVĀṆA; PURE LAND; REINCARNATION, EASTERN; REINCARNATION, WESTERN; SOUL, BUDDHIST; SOUL, THEOSOPHICAL.

References
Blavatsky, Helena Petrovna. *The Key to Theosophy*. Point Loma, CA: Aryan Theosophical Press, 1913. Reprint. Los Angeles: Theosophy Company, 1987.
———. *The Secret Doctrine*. 2 vols. Reprint. New York: Theosophy Company, 1925.
———. *The Theosophical Glossary*. Reprint. Los Angeles: Theosophy Company, 1973.
Judge, William Quan. *The Ocean of Theosophy*. Los Angeles: Theosophy Company, 1987.

DEWACHAN (TIBETAN BUDDHIST)

Dewachan (spelled more authentically "bDe-ba-can") is the Tibetan translation of the name of an Indian Buddhist heaven called *Sukhāvatī* in Sanskrit. Both Dewachan and Sukhāvatī literally mean "characterized by happiness" and indicate one of the most popular Pure Lands developed by later Buddhist thought.

The Buddha who presides over this western heaven is called 'Od-dpag-med (pronounced Wö-pek-may) in the Tibetan language or Amitābha in the ancient Indian language of Sanskrit. Both names translate as the "(Buddha of) Infinite Light." Through good deeds and prayers to him, a religious person may hope to be reborn in this heaven where the trees are made of gold and silver and the fruits are various kinds of wish-fulfilling jewels.

Because the Buddha is an infinite being, offerings made to him produce infinite merit or good karma. Thus, in the teachings of Pure Land Buddhism, religious people can make offerings to this Buddha of Infinite Light that produce infinite merit, eliminate all negative karma, and after taking birth in Dewachan they need never be reborn again. For this reason Dewachan is considered in popular Buddhism only one step away from nirvāṇa, which is perfect enlightenment and salvation.

See also ABHIRATI; AKṢOBHYA; CHING T'U; DEVACHAN (THEOSOPHICAL); HEAVENS, BUDDHIST; JŌDŌ; NIRVĀṆA; PURE LAND; SUKHĀVATĪ.

References
Becker, Carl B. *Breaking the Circle: Death and the Afterlife in Buddhism*. Carbondale: Southern Illinois University Press, 1993.
Ch'en, Kenneth. *Buddhism in China*. Princeton: Princeton University Press, 1964.
Das, Sarat Chandra. *A Tibetan-English Dictionary*. Calcutta: Bengal Secretariat Book Depot, 1902. Reprint, Kyoto: Rinsen Book Company, 1993.
Foard, James, Michael Solomon, and Richard K. Payne, eds. *The Pure Land Tradition: History and Development*. Berkeley Buddhist Studies Series no. 3. Berkeley: University of California Press, 1989.
Overmyer, D. *Folk Buddhist Religion: Dissenting Sects in Late Traditional China*. Cambridge: Harvard University Press, 1976.
Ryosetsu, F., *The Way to Nirvana: The Concept of the Nembutsu in Sahn-tao's Pure Land Buddhism*. Tokyo: Kyoiku Shincho Sha, 1974.
Suzuki, D. T. *Buddha of Infinite Light*. Boston: Shambhala, 1998.

DÍA DE LOS MUERTOS

The "Day of the Dead" celebrations in Mexico have their roots in pre-Columbian Aztec and other native festivals memorializing the dead, which mixed with the Roman Catholic All Saint's and All Soul's Days imported by Spanish conquistadors. On the Day of the Dead, departed friends and family return from the land of the dead (officially purgatory or heaven but originally the Underworld) to visit with the living for a short time. The living welcome these visitors happily and prepare special offerings on the family altar, or ofrendas, which is usually located in the home but often in the local parish chapel or outside the family cemetery. The ofrendas is laden with incense, candles, water, food (especially sweets), flowers, cigarettes, and liquor—providing a deliberately sensory experience for the dead, who are assumed to be deprived of such things in the afterlife.

In the last days of October the special flowers, breads, sweets, and decorations used for the holiday begin to appear, but the Día de los Muertos does not officially take place until All Souls' Day on November 2. (Frequently, November 1, All Saints' Day, is also seen as part of the "Day.") The traditional flower of the holiday is the zempasuchitl (marigold), which is offered individually as well as in traditional arrangements such as coronas (wreaths) and cruces (crosses). A special sugary "bread of the dead," or pan de muerto, is omnipresent during the festival, shaped in such forms as male and female skeletons, tombstones, and skulls, often in bright colors. Candy skulls and candy tombstones are also extremely popular, both as offerings for the dead and treats for children. As one sign that the Day of the Dead is a time of role reversal and the meeting of opposites, one may note the primarily urban tradition of circulating calaveras (literally "skulls"), poems that mock the living, particularly politicians and celebrities.

Painted skulls displayed during the Mexican festival of the dead, Día de los Muertos. Courtesy of Images Colour Library.

Illustrated with immodest cartoons, these simple rhymes are printed in local papers or circulated throughout neighborhoods.

Recent studies have shown that the Mexican-American observance of the Day of the Dead, as found in Arizona, Texas, and other Mexican immigrant communities, is somewhat different than the Mexican tradition. In the United States, the Day of the Dead appears to put much less of an emphasis on the actual return of the dead and instead focuses on the duty of the living to go out to final resting places of the dead to offer their respects. Bringing food, flowers, candles, and other offerings with them, Mexican-American families visit their loved ones in the cemeteries, often holding picnics and playtime right at the site. The grave itself is cleaned and decorated, usually with plastic flowers that are intended to last all year. Increasingly, the American version of the Day of the Dead is becoming conflated with the American version of Hallowe'en: the Mexican-American pan de muerto is baked in the shape of a bat or pumpkin as often as a skeleton, and black and orange balloons decorate the ancestors' graves alongside the ofrendas.

See also ANTHESTERIA; HALLOWE'EN; LEMURIA; PARENTALIA; SAMHAIN.

References

Gaster, Theodore. *New Year: Its History, Customs and Superstitions.* New York: Abelard-Schuman, 1955.

Green, Judith Strupp. *Día de los Muertos: An Illustrated Essay and Bibliography.* Santa Barbara, CA: Center for Chicano Studies, 1983.

———. *Laughing Souls: The Days of the Dead in Oaxaca, Mexico.* San Diego: San Diego Museum of Man Popular Series no. 1, 1969.

Griffith, James S. *Respect and Continuity: The Arts of Death in a Border Community.* Tucson: Southwest Folklore Center, University of Arizona, 1985.

Toor, Frances. *Mexican Folkways.* New York: Crown Publishers, 1947.

Turner, Kay, and Pat Jasper. "Day of the Dead: The Tex-Mex Tradition." In *Halloween and Other Festivals of Death and Life,* ed. Jack Santino. Knoxville: University of Tennessee Press, 1993.

DILMUN

Although Dilmun was a historical city, well known as an important trade center, in myth it was the Mesopotamian island of the blest, "at the place where the sun rises," that is, in the east. The great hero Gilgamesh traveled there to meet Utnapishtim (in Akkadian, "he found life") when he sought immortality. Utnapishtim (in Sumerian, Ziusudra) and his wife were two of only three humans in Mesopotamian literature who escaped death and the grave. Like the Hebrew Noah, Utnapishtim and his wife rescued humankind from the universal flood. The other human to escape death, Utuabzu, ascended to heaven "to dwell with the gods," like the Hebrew Enoch. There is a close connection between these immortal humans, the god of the sun (Utu or Shamash), and the direction east, the land of the rising sun.

Whereas in Mesopotamian thought the netherworld Kigal was a dark, dismal place where the dead often suffered from hunger and thirst, Dilmun was a bright heavenly island blest with an abundance of fresh water and dates. Like the Garden of Eden, it had a sacred tree:

> In Eridu there is a black *kiskanu*-tree
>   growing in a pure place,
> its appearance is lapis-lazuli,
>   erected on the *Apsu.*
> Enki [god of water], when walking there, filleth
>   Eridu with abundance.
>   In the foundation thereof is the place of the
>   underworld,
> in the resting-place is the chamber of Nammu
>   [ocean].
>   In its holy temple there is a grove, casting its
>   shadow,
> therein no man goeth to enter.

In the midst are the Sun-god and the Sovereign
of heaven,
in between the river with the two mouths.
(Widengren, pp. 5–6)

Unfortunately, there is little evidence that the common person would be admitted to Dilmun after death. Rather, kings and commoners alike dwelled in Kigal.

Some scholars have identified Dilmun with the island of Bahrain in the Persian Gulf, where the more than 150,000 burial mounds (tumuli) suggest that perhaps Mesopotamians moved their remains to Bahrain for a secondary burial in the hope of entering into a beatific afterlife. This hypothesis has been sharply criticized by other scholars, and the lack of Mesopotamian artifacts in the graves greatly weakens the theory.

See also HADES; ISLANDS OF THE BLEST; KIGAL; MOUND; TUMULUS; UNDERWORLD; WATER.

References

Alster, B. "Dilmun, Bahrain, and the Alleged Paradise in Sumerian Myth and Literature." In *Dilmun: New Studies in the Archeology and Early History of Bahrain,* ed. D. T. Potts. Berlin: Berliner Beiträge zur Vorderen Orient 2, 1983.

Armstrong, John. *The Paradise Myth.* London: Oxford University Press, 1969.

Bibby, G. *Looking for Dilmun.* New York: Knopf, 1969.

Delumeau, Jean. *History of Paradise: The Garden of Eden in Myth and Tradition.* Trans. Matthew O'Connell. New York: Continuum, 1995.

Fröhlich, B. "The Bahrain Burial Mounds." *Dilmun* 11 (1983).

Kramer, S. N. *History Begins at Sumer.* New York: Doubleday, 1959.

Lamberg-Karlovski, C. C. "Dilmun: Gateway to Immortality." *Journal of Near Eastern Studies* 41 (1982).

Spronk, Klaas. *Beatific Afterlife in Ancient Israel and in the Ancient Near East.* Kevelaer: Butzon and Bercker, 1986.

Widengren, G. *The King and the Tree of Life.* Uppsala, 1951.

DIS (DIS PATER)

The name *Dis* is the Roman designation for the Greek *Hades,* husband of Proserpina (in Greek myth, Persephone). Dis is probably an alternate form of the old Latin word *Dives,* meaning "the Wealthy," as does the name *Pluto.* Like Hades, Dis is both the Underworld and its lord. In the *Aeneid* (VI:177) the poet Virgil refers to the cave of Avernus, where "day and night the door of darkest Dis is open," clearly referring to the underground region. But some lines later (VI:356–358), Dis is certainly the lord of the underworld, for the hero Aeneas and his sibylline guide

moved along in darkness, through the shadows,
beneath the lonely night, and through the hollow
dwelling place of Dis, his phantom kingdom . . .
(Mandelbaum)

Illustration by Gustave Dore for Dante's Inferno, *1863. Courtesy of Anne Ronan Picture Library.*

Dis is probably better known to modern readers from Dante's *Inferno,* where through Christianization Dis is no longer merely a somber (not evil) underworld ruler but the archfiend Satan, of utterly gigantic proportions. In a caricature of the Christian Trinity, Dante gives Satan/Dis three faces, red, white, and black, with six great bat-wings whose beating freezes all of lower Hell:

It is these winds that freeze all Cocytus.
He wept from his six eyes, and down three chins
the tears ran mixed with bloody froth and pus.
In every mouth he worked a broken sinner
between his rakelike teeth. Thus he kept three
in eternal pain at his eternal dinner.
(Dante, *Divine Comedy,* Canto 34 vv. 52–57, Ciardi, trans., p. 284)

The three sinners being chewed are Judas Iscariot, traitor to Jesus, and Brutus and Cassius, traitors to Caesar. Dante and Virgil climb down the body of Dis and turning around (at the imaginary center of the world's gravity), climb "up" the legs to emerge in a cavern leading up to the mountain of Purgatory.

See also AVERNUS; GEHENNA; HADES; PURGATORY; TARTAROS; UNDERWORLD.

References

Dante Alighieri. *The Divine Comedy*. Trans. John Ciardi. New York: Norton, 1977.

Mandelbaum, Allen, trans. *The Aeneid of Virgil*. New York: Bantam, 1971.

Graves, Robert. *The Greek Myths*. New York: Penguin, 1960.

DOLMEN

Known as a *cromlech* in Great Britain, *dolmen* is the French word for a kind of megalithic tomb found in Spain, Portugal, and France (particularly in Brittany) dating from prehistoric times. The word is possibly from the Breton *tôl* (table) combined with *mean* (stone), meaning "a stone table." Dolmens are primarily huge vertical stone slabs weighing many tons, topped by a horizontal "roof" slab to form a burial chamber. The whole was buried under a great mound of earth or rubble once the bodies (or just bones, if the megaliths served as ossuaries) were interred inside. Dolmens differ from their more western and northern counterparts in that they were smaller and quite often had concave facades forming a semicircle around the entrance to the tomb, though some of the Irish megaliths had this feature as well. Many of the dolmens in France have been found with self-supporting corbelled vaults, that is, the ceilings were made conical by placing rows of tightly fitted stones in ever smaller circles. Some of the later dolmens (even as late as the fourth century B.C.E.) have been found with a central column in the burial chamber supporting a flat roof. In time, however, the tumulus style of tombs, in which a mound of earth is placed over the burial chamber, gave way to freestanding funerary architecture above ground, as in the Roman mausolea that were built from Great Britain to the Black Sea.

See also BARROW; CROMLECH; MAUSOLEUM; MEGALITHIC TOMB; TUMULUS.

Dolmen stone structures in Spain, 300–150 B.C.E. Courtesy of Anne Ronan Picture Library.

References

Colvin, Howard. *Architecture and the After-Life*. New Haven: Yale University Press, 1991.

Daniel, G. *The Prehistoric Chamber Tombs of France*. London: Thames and Hudson, 1960.

Eogan, G. *Knowth and the Passage-tombs of Ireland*. New York: Thames and Hudson, 1986.

Evans, J. D. *Prehistoric Antiquities of the Maltese Islands*. London: University of London, Athlone Press, 1971.

Giot, P. R. *Brittany*. London: Thames and Hudson, 1960.

Guido, M. *Sardinia*. London: Thames and Hudson, 1963.

Henshall, A. H. *The Chambered Tombs of Scotland*. 2 vols. Edinburgh: Edinburgh University Press, 1963, 1972.

Herity, M. *Irish Passage Graves*. New York: Barnes and Noble Books, 1975.

Mackie, E. *The Megalith Builders*. Oxford: Phaidon, 1977.

O'Kelley, M. *Newgrange*. London: Thames and Hudson, 1982.

Piggott, S. *Neolithic Cultures of the British Isles*. Cambridge: Cambridge University Press, 1954.

Twohig, E. Shee. *The Megalithic Art of Western Europe*. Oxford: Clarendon Press, 1981.

DONN

The name of an ancient Irish god of death, the word *donn* may derive from various ancient words for "dark, veiled" similar to Old English *dunn* and Sanskrit *dhvāntas*. Donn might also derive from the Irish *du(i)ne* (Celtic *dunios*), meaning "mortal, man."

Donn is associated with Cnoc Fírinne, a fairy hill in southwestern Ireland in County Limerick. There Donn is called Donn Fírennach, interpreted in popular lore as meaning "Donn the Truthful," and he is said to be the final judge of disputes. Donn is in many ways very similar to Odin in that Donn is a leader of the dead, is the god of wind and storms, and is connected with many hills. It is possible that because of historical contact between Irish and Scandinavian peoples, either during the Hallstatt Period (c. ninth to fourth centuries C.E.) or the Viking period (c. ninth to eleventh centuries B.C.E.), Donn and Odin may actually be two versions of one mythological figure.

His island is Tech Duin, "The House of Donn," also called An Tarbh, "The Bull," off the southwestern corner of Ireland. It is a rocky outpost, steep, grim, and bare, the remnant of a submerged land possibly connected with Ireland. There, in legend, souls are ferried and gathered into the realm of the dead.

See also FAIRY MOUND; FUNERARY CUSTOMS, CELTIC; MORRIGAN; ODIN; OTHERWORLD, IRISH; TUATHA DÉ DANANN.

References

Müller-Lisowski, Kate. "Donn Firine, Tech Duin, An Tarbh." In *Études Celtiques* 6, no. 1 (Paris: Société d'Édition "Les Belles Lettres"), 1953.

DOZAKH

Dozakh is the Zoroastrian hell in the Persian language (Parsi). The word *Dozakh* is derived from the very ancient *Drūjô-demāna,* or "abode of the lie," in the Scriptures called Avesta; this was later condensed to *Drūzôtmān* in the medieval language of Persia, Pahlavi.

In Zoroastrian teaching souls reach Dozakh by attempting to cross the "Bridge of the Separator" (Chinvato-Peretu). The bridge narrows depending on how many sins the deceased committed during life, and the soul may slip and "fall" into the pit of hell. The darkness in Dozakh is said to be so thick that it can be grasped by the hand (see the Zoroastrian Scripture Bundahisn 28:47). Each soul condemned in hell believes it has been abandoned and feels utterly alone, even if in reality the souls are packed together as close "as the hairs in a horse's mane" (Jackson, p. 148).

In the most ancient portions of the Zoroastrian Scripture, Avesta (dated to about 1700 B.C.E.), only one hell appears to be mentioned. But later strata in the Avesta develop four different depths of hell, each one worse than the last. However, these distinctions are probably to be understood as ethically instructive rather than literal. The "four" hells are the literal opposite of the principal divisions of the Zoroastrian heaven, Behesht:

1. *Dushmata*   "evil thought"
2. *Dushukhta*   "evil word"
3. *Dushvarshta*   "evil deed"
4. *Anaghra Temah*   "endless darkness"

Most important, fire is an extremely sacred element to Zoroastrians, related to the sun, and thus has no part in the torments of hell. Rather, Dozakh is cold, lonely, filled with foul stench and spoiled food, and above all profoundly dark. James Moulton suggests that this conception of suffering in hell is drawn from early Zoroastrian struggles with the cold steppes of Central Asia. Another important difference between the Zoroastrian doctrine of hell and that of Judaism, Christianity, and Islam is that nowhere in Zoroastrian writings is hell thought to be a place of eternal torment. True, the souls of the damned may suffer in Dozakh many a long century, but at the end of time, god (Ahura Mazda, the supreme being) will bring about a general resurrection (Ristakhez). The wicked souls, having finished their sentence in hell, will be renovated and purified. At last, all will join the godhead for eternity.

See also AMERETAT; BEHESHT; CHINVAT BRIDGE; FRASHO-KERETI; FRAVASHI; HAMESTEGĀN; RESURRECTION, ANCIENT NEAR EAST; SOUL, ZOROASTRIAN.

References

Bode, Dastur F. A. "Man, Soul, Immortality in Zoroastrianism," speech delivered at Portiuncula Firary, Karachi, December 1971.

Jackson, A. V. W. *Zoroastrian Studies.* New York: Columbia University Press, 1928.

Kotwal, Dastur Firoze M., and James W. Boyd, trans. *A Guide to the Zoroastrian Religion.* Studies in World Religion no. 3. Chico, CA: Scholars Press, 1982.

Masani, Sir Rustom. *Zoroastrianism: The Religion of the Good Life.* New York: Collier Books, 1962.

Moulton, J. H. *Early Zoroastrianism.* London: Williams and Norgate, 1913.

Sethna, Tehmurasp Rustamji. *Book of Instructions on Zoroastrian Religion.* Karachi: Informal Religious Meetings Trust Fund, 1980.

Sidhwa, Ervad Godrej Dinshawji. *Discourses on Zoroastrianism.* Karachi: Ervad Godrej Dinshawji Sidhwa, 1978.

DYSSER
See Megalithic Tomb.

E

EIDOLON

In Greek, *eidolon* refers to the soul or psyche of the dead in the exact likeness of the person as he or she was in life. In the Homeric epics the eidolon plays a prominent role. In one sense it is only the image of the dead, an empty picture of the sad transformation from life to death, but in another sense it is the deceased in propria persona. For example, the eidolon of Patroklos appears to Achilleus at the end of the *Iliad* (23:65–71), described as a ghost but speaking in the first person:

> and there appeared to him the ghost of unhappy Patroklos
> all in his likeness for stature, and the lovely eyes, and voice,
> and wore such clothing as Patroklos had worn on his body.
> The ghost came and stood over his head and spoke a word to him:
> "You sleep, Achilleus; you have forgotten me; but you were not
> careless of me when I lived, but only in death. Bury me
> as quickly as may be, led me pass through the gates of Hades."
> (Lattimore, trans.)

The eidolon was not merely a poetic device meant to provoke sympathy and horror in the audience but reflected an authentic belief, widespread in the ancient world and prominent among many peoples to this day, that after death the psychic remains of the deceased retain the exact image of the body in life. In the *Odyssey* (Book 11, Butler, trans.), the dead appear to Odysseus not only in the clothing they wore in life but still with gaping wounds if they died in battle.

Contrary to some scholarly opinion, in a few instances in Greek literature the eidolon of a person appears while the person is still alive. For example, Herodotus writes:

> They say that the soul of Hermotimos of Clazomenae, wandering apart from the body, was absent for many years, and in different places foretold events such as great floods and droughts and also earthquakes and plagues and the like, while his stiff body was lying inert, and that the soul, after certain periods re-entering the body as into a sheath, aroused it. (*Mirabilia* 3, Bremmer, Trans., p. 27)

Clearly, in this account it is not merely the *image* of the person who wandered about while the body lay still, but the person himself. Yet after death the eidolon no longer seemed to retain the essence of the person and existed only as a shadow or image of the person. The key difference appears to be that in life, according to Homer's epics and later philosophical tradition, there was also the presence of *noos,* or intellect; after death the *noos* either disappeared or carried on to another location—or possibly reincarnated—while the eidolon, bereft of sense, descended to Hades.

See also SOUL, GREEK.
References
Bremmer, Jan. *The Early Greek Concept of the Soul.* Princeton: Princeton University Press, 1983.
Homer, *The Odyssey.* Trans. Samuel Butler. New York: Barnes and Noble, 1993.
Lattimore, Richmond, trans. *The Iliad of Homer.* Chicago: University of Chicago Press, 1951.
Sourvinou-Inwood, Christiane. *"Reading" Greek Death: To the End of the Classical Period.* Oxford: Clarendon Press, 1995.

ELYSION (ELYSIUM)

The warm paradise of Elysion (Elysium in Latin) is first mentioned in the *Odyssey* as the destiny of Menelaos because he has married Helen, daughter of Zeus. Elysion is an island located at the western end of the Earth where there is no snow or rain and the means of life are easy to come by. It appears occasionally in Greek poetry, for instance, in that of Apollonius of Rhodes, third century B.C.E. An alternative name for this paradise is the Islands of the Blest (Nesoi Makaron), which first appears in Hesiod's *Works and Days* (verses 190 ff). Heroes do not die but are magically transported there (cf. DILMUN), "and there they live, free from all care, in the Isles of the Blest, by Ocean's deep stream, blessed heroes for whom the life-giving Earth bears sweet fruit ripening three times a year" (Hesiod, p. 28, trans.

Lombardo). Almost certainly the Greek concepts of both Elysion and the Islands of the Blest were influenced by the Egyptian Āaru fields, where the dead enjoy eternal sunshine and a most pleasant and easy "life."

What is important, however, is that in archaic Greek thought, Elysion was not the destination of the righteous or the just in general, those who perhaps fared well during their judgment in the underworld. Rather paradise appears to have been an exception, the destiny of only those remarkable heroes who were blest with favor from the gods. In common with the rest of the ancient Near East, the Greeks thought the dead were all alike: mindless shades of their former selves condemned to exist forever in Hades, although particular trials awaited sinners like Tantalos and Sisyphos. Only in classical times, from the sixth to fifth centuries B.C.E. and onward, is there clear evidence that ordinary people might experience a paradisiacal afterlife. In his work *Olympian* (2:61–74), the poet Pindar (fifth century B.C.E.) described a land of days and nights of equal length, without weather, and decorated by water and trees of gold blossoms. In *Songs of Mourning* Pindar describes the happy dead playing sports, listening to music, and enjoying the smell of sacrifices made to the gods, all in sunlit meadows full of fruit trees.

This shift in thought is most likely to be attributed to the growing importance of the so-called mystery schools in Greek culture and the corresponding belief in the soul (psyche) as an immortal spirit that will be held accountable for its actions in the future. The mystery teachings were secret, and it is difficult to reconstruct their beliefs, particularly as they might have varied from cult center to cult center. Nevertheless, it seems certain that besides the healing of sickness and worldly woes, the initiate in the mysteries was entitled to a beatific afterlife, whether in Elysion or some other locale. A recently discovered epitaph of a Bythinian initiate states that he has traveled not to dark Acheron (in Hades) but to the "harbor of the blest."

By the fourth century B.C.E., belief in and activity toward a beatific afterlife was quite popular, perhaps strengthened by the influx of Near Eastern and particularly Iranian religions that explicitly taught a paradise after death for the good and just souls. Guidebooks have actually been found in graves of initiates in the Orphic mysteries in the form of hammered gold tablets with guidance for the afterlife. After warnings not to lose one's memory at the spring of Lethe (Forgetfulness), the initiate was instructed to state his or her divine ancestry as a soul and gain entrance into paradise.

By Roman times the idea of an ethical afterlife for all people had become dominant. Rather than needing special initiation into a mystery school, all the deceased were to be judged, with sinners condemned to Tartaros and the virtuous destined for Elysium. In Book VI of the *Aeneid* by Virgil, Elysium is no longer located at the edges of the ocean as in the Greek conception but in its own separate area of Hades, complete with its own sun and stars. Curiously, while in Elysium visiting his father Anchises, the hero Aeneas meets the *future* heroes of Rome, who wait in Elysium for their birth on earth; doctrines of the preexistence of the soul and even repeated reincarnation had become commonplace. Such beliefs also appear in Cicero's work "The Dream of Scipio" at the end of *On the Republic*, in which we find that even the horrific punishment in Tartaros is temporary. After centuries of torturous purification, all souls eventually make their way back to the "celestial sphere" of Elysium, whence they will proceed on again to be reborn in the mortal world. It is obvious that from the original Greek notion of the Elysian Fields for the rare hero, later Greek and Roman speculation took the idea of paradise for all in distinctly ethical directions.

See also ĀARU; DILMUN; HADES; ISLANDS OF THE BLEST; PARADISE; SOUL, GREEK; TARTAROS.

References

Bianchi, U. *The Greek Mysteries*. Leiden: E. J. Brill, 1976.

Burkert, Walter. *Ancient Mystery Cults*. Cambridge: Harvard University Press, 1987.

———. *Greek Religion*. Trans. John Raffan. Cambridge: Harvard University Press, 1985.

Dietrich, B. C. *Death, Fate and the Gods*. London: University of London, Athlone Press, 1965.

Farnell, Lewis R. *Greek Hero Cults and Ideas of Immortality*. Oxford: Clarendon Press, 1921.

Guthrie, W. K. C. *History of Greek Philosophy*. 6 vols. Cambridge: Cambridge University Press, 1962–1981.

Hesiod. Works and Days *and* Theogony. Trans. Stanley Lombardo. Indianapolis: Hackett Publishing, 1993.

Mandelbaum, Allen, trans. *The* Aeneid *of Virgil*. New York: Bantam, 1971.

Richardson, Nicholas J. *The Homeric Hymn to Demeter*. Oxford: Clarendon Press, 1974.

Sourvinou-Inwood, Christiane. *"Reading" Greek Death: To the End of the Classical Period*. Oxford: Clarendon Press, 1995.

EREBUS

The name *Erebus* is a seldom-used (and probably older) name of the abyss, that is, Hades or Tartaros. These were all synonymous in the ancient Greek period. Erebus literally means "the covered" and refers to the covered or hidden pit, the measureless depth under the earth. There, in most ancient cultures, dark powers were thought to reside, and it was the dwelling place of the shades of the dead.

In his creation story, *Theogony* (211–232, in Graves), Hesiod tells how Erebus came to be.

Apparently Darkness was the first of all things, and from her sprang Chaos. Darkness and Chaos together begat Night and Day, Erebus, and the Air. These abstractions are certainly not "gods" in that they have no personalities; they are probably best understood as energies or powers, fundamental building blocks of the unseen and then the visible universe. It is interesting that in Hesiod's story, as in many ancient cosmogonies, it is the hidden female power that comes first: Darkness precedes Chaos, and Night precedes Day.

In either case, Erebus is generally associated with powers inimical to humans. The three terrible spirits of vengeance, the Erinyes (Furies) dwell in Erebus, namely Tisiphone, Alecto, and Megara. The Erinyes were offspring of father Erebus and mother Night, along with Sleep, Dreams, Doom, Old Age, Death, Murder, Discord, Misery, and Nemesis. Importantly, however, Erebus and Night also produced more positive offspring, including Pity, Joy, Friendship, and the Three Hesperides (female personifications of the sun sinking in the west). Thus in Hesiod's time, Erebus was most likely seen not as a place or an evil power per se but as the source of that which is hidden and mysterious.

In later times, however, Erebus lost much of its occult potency and became merely a synonym for Hades. In Virgil's *Aeneid,* the poet uses the various names for the Underworld almost interchangeably. Erebus appears to mean the same as the general names *Hades* and *Dis,* and Avernus, Tartaros, and Elysium have become specific subsections of the subterranean kingdom.

See also AVERNUS; DIS; ELYSION, ELYSIUM; ERINYS; HADES; SLEEP; TARTAROS; UNDERWORLD.

References

Graves, Robert. *The Greek Myths.* New York: Penguin, 1960.

Harrison, Jane Ellen. *Prolegomena to the Study of Greek Religion.* Cambridge: Cambridge University Press, 1922.

Hesiod. Works and Days *and* Theogony. Trans. Stanley Lombardo. Indianapolis: Hackett Publishing, 1993.

Mandelbaum, Allen, trans. *The* Aeneid *of Virgil.* New York: Bantam, 1971.

ERESH

Eresh is an alternative Hebrew name for the netherworld, somewhat less common than Sheol. In its most literal meaning, Eresh is simply the material of the earth extending below to an incalculable depth, containing not only soil and rock but hidden underground waters and the roots of mountains. But Eresh also stands for the particular "land" or "country," a place outside the order of creation, into which the dead pass forever. It is characterized by dust, darkness, and great depth and sometimes as a fortified city (Jonas 2:7;

Sirach 51:9). In Hebrew thought, Eresh signifies the completion of a cycle—the earth to which the dead return, literally and metaphorically, just as it was earth from which they were created.

See also SHEOL.

References

Tromp, Nicholas J. *Primitive Conceptions of Death and the Nether World in the Old Testament.* Rome: Pontifical Biblical Institute, 1969.

ERINYS (PLURAL ERINYES)

Literally "the Angry Ones," these three sisters are also called *the Furies* and euphemistically *the Eumenides* (literally "the Kindly Ones"). Older than the Olympian gods, the Erinyes were born of mother Earth (in Greek, *Gaea;* in Latin, *Terra*) when the blood of her husband Sky (in Greek, *Uranos*) fell to earth after he was castrated by his rebellious son, Cronos (in Latin, *Saturn*).

The three Erinyes are Alecto (the Unresting), Megara (the Jealous), and Tisiphone (the Avenger). They are

One of the Erinyes, the Greek Furies or Eumenides. Courtesy of Anne Ronan Picture Library.

hideous to look at: Robert Graves describes them as old hags with snakes for hair, dogs' heads, coal-black bodies, bats' wings, and bloodshot eyes. Carrying brass-studded scourges, the Erinyes are capable of inciting madness in all who see them but especially in the sinners they pursue. For this reason, people did not mention them by name in conversation, hence their alternate name, *Eumenides*. It is their job to punish crimes, especially those that pervert natural law such as making the sun go off track, altering nature, or murdering one's parents (especially the mother). Greek myths recount the Erinyes punishing Oedipus, Tantalos, Theseus, the Amazonian queen Penthesileia, and above all Orestes for beheading his treacherous mother.

Although the Erinyes appear to represent impersonal divine law (nemesis in Greek philosophy, karma in Eastern thought), they are intensely personified. In many instances, the Erinyes do not appear as abstract goddesses but as specific forces that spring up from the minds of those unjustly murdered. Thus Orestes is not pursued simply by "the Erinyes" but by "the Erinyes of Clytaemnestra," his mother. One interpretation offered by Graves is that the Erinyes were "personified pangs of conscience," which places them within the psyche of the guilty party. However, the ancient Greeks perceived the Erinyes as independent entities (they had shrines dedicated to them) who pursued evildoers even to the ends of the earth. It was possible to shake pursuit of the Erinyes, as Orestes finally did, with the help of prayers, one year's exile, purifications in sacred rivers and temples, and self-mutilation as sin offerings.

Tisiphone, the Avenger, is singled out for special mention in the Roman epic the *Aeneid*. She guards the entrance to Tartaros (the place of punishment in later classical thought) and leads her sisters in violently punishing the wicked with lashes from her whips.

See also EUMENIDES; HADES; KER; TARTAROS; UNDERWORLD.

References

Graves, Robert. *The Greek Myths*. New York: Penguin, 1960.
Harrison, Jane Ellen. *Prolegomena to the Study of Greek Religion.* Cambridge: Cambridge University Press, 1922.
Mandelbaum, Allen, trans. *The Aeneid of Virgil*. New York: Bantam Books, 1971.

EUMENIDES

Literally "the Kindly Ones," the title *Eumenides* is merely a euphemism for the terrible Erinyes of Greek mythology. They are the three homicidal sister-demons who avenge the murders of parents and other crimes against nature (as defined by classical Greek mores). According to an ancient and widespread belief, calling upon supernatural powers by their actual name makes them appear; thus in the classical Greek world, most of the gods and especially the powers of the Underworld had alternate names by which they were indicated without being summoned.

See also ERINYS; HADES; KER; UNDERWORLD.

References

Graves, Robert. *The Greek Myths*. New York: Penguin, 1960.
Harrison, Jane Ellen. *Prolegomena to the Study of Greek Religion.* Cambridge: Cambridge University Press, 1922.

EXEDRA

Also called *niche tombs,* exedrae are ancient Roman tombs, roofed or unroofed, which took the shape of giant hollowed-out niches. Like most Roman tombs, they stood on the roads leading up to the cities and were designed to attract the attention of travelers by providing a bench upon which one could rest. Exedrae were either rectangular or semicircular, from 2 to 4 meters tall, and commonly had an arched entranceway and a vaulted roof (or no roof at all). They usually had seats along their sides, with a tombstone serving as a back wall inscribed with the owner's name and profession and often a portrait, along with a small altar. The urn containing the ashes was buried underneath the altar or below the stone. Exedrae were frequently adorned with stucco or engraved reliefs of pleasant scenes and portraits of the deceased.

References

Toynbee, J. M. C. *Death and Burial in the Roman World*. Ithaca, NY: Cornell University Press, 1971.

F

FAIRY MOUND

Fairy mounds are the hills and knolls in western and northern Europe that serve as the dwelling places of ghosts, fairies from the other worlds, or ancestors—and these categories are often confused. These mounds were sources of both power and danger.

Sometimes fairy mounds are ordinary hills, but frequently they are actually burial mounds dating from prehistory to well past the first Christian conversions—graves heaped over with earth to mark the final resting places of great heroes or kings. Uncovered, these mounds reveal the usual remains of weapons, armor, tools, personal belongings, and even the outlines of disintegrated chariots or ships. But with the passage of time, the growth of legends, and the incursions of foreign settlers, these tombs became the magical dwellings not only of the dead but of fairies, dwarves, and other enchanted beings. Frequently, the fairy mounds were also recognized as entrances to the Otherworld, whether this be the Avalon of Arthur, the Annwfn of the Welsh, or the Mag Mell or Tír n'Aill of the Irish.

The conflation of hills, burial mounds, and fairy dwellings, although in many ways complex, is easily understandable in terms of power. No ordinary dead are buried under the monolithic cairns and barrows of Europe but rather great warriors, kings, and spiritual leaders who were to remain in human memory for many years. Therefore, these sites were known from the first as places of great spiritual and political power, as is discussed in the entry for MOUND. Not surprisingly, perhaps, this power took on supernatural dimensions, and many magical beings came to be associated with such mounds and even certain natural hills.

In Ireland, besides famous heroes and kings, the most prestigious inhabitants of the fairy mounds were the Tuatha Dé Danann, a powerful magical race who inhabited Ireland before humans. These godlike beings were eventually overcome by human heroes, the Milesians or "sons of Mile" (Mile being the mythical ancestor of the Goidelic Irish), in a tremendous battle accompanied by rhyming spells and carnage on both sides. The Tuatha Déa then retreated in invisibility to the caves and hills of Ireland and were granted rule of the underground realms by the human victors (whose poets and sages had "second sight" that enabled them to see invisible beings). To this day, the legends say, these imperishable beings exist in a magical land accessible both through faraway islands across the sea and in the hollow hills and barrows throughout the land. The Tuatha Déa continue to visit humans, most often invisibly, emerging from the barrows to reward heroes and punish evildoers.

Inhabiting the hills and mounds were also lesser but still powerful beings known in Ireland collectively as the *síd* and among the Scandinavians as *hulder* (dwarves) and trolls. Like the gods, the lesser fairies and dwarves sometimes called humans into their realm for purposes of their own. In one such story, the Irish hero Nera was carrying a corpse on his back, traveling on the eve of Samhain, the autumn holiday among the Celts associated with harvest and death. The corpse instructed Nera to enter into an opening in a mound, whereupon Nera found himself in the bright Otherworld and married one of the fairy inhabitants. Although he returned to his own people for a time, like most such heroes he ultimately chose to remain with the fairy folk. Here the corpse and the fairies are distinct entities, yet each seem to be connected to the same mound.

In a story from southern Norway, the hulder carried off a man's wife. One day while chopping wood in the forest, the lonely husband heard a mighty pounding inside a hill and then his wife's voice. Since he looked and looked and could not see her, she told him to hold out his hand to receive a brooch he had once given her. Still invisible, she put the brooch in his hand and told him to let others know that she was fine but that she could never come back to him. Yet other times, the fairies could be helpful entities if treated properly. According to the Icelandic *Kormáks Saga* (12), a man came to a seeress to be healed of his wounds, and she advised him to take a bull that had been sacrificed to a mound "in which dwell elves . . . and redden the outside of the mound with bull's blood, and make the elves a feast with the flesh; and you will be healed" (Davidson, 1988).

It is often difficult to distinguish whether an entity in a mound or hill is a deceased human or a fairy. In the Orkney Islands off the coast of northern Scotland, there is a story of a mound dweller who guarded the luck of

A Norwegian Folktale

On Herre farm, in Heddal, there lived a man name Ole, and he owned a couple of other farms too. Late in the evening, on his way over to Leine farm to go courting, he came to a mound right alongside the road, way up in the parish. There he heard singing and music inside the mound, and sounds of dancing and gaiety and merriment. Ole was not afraid, and stood there listening for a while. When he was about to go on, he said aloud, "There's little use for you to be so happy. You won't share in the glory of God all the same!"

Then they replied from inside the mound, "We hope to share in the glory of God too." But Ole replied, "It's just as impossible for you to share in the glory of God as it is for flowers and leaves to grow on this dry staff I'm holding in my hand!"

Then at once it became silent in there, the dancing and music stopped, and instead he heard them begin to cry and wail. But Ole did not think any more about it. He was completely taken up by thoughts that he would soon see his sweetheart. It was late at night when he came to Leine, and when he went in he left his staff on the porch.

When he was to go home in the morning, he was greatly astonished. There stood his staff, and it was completely covered with flowers and leaves which had grown on it. Then he remembered what had happened the evening before, and he walked as fast as he could to get to the mound. And when he came to it, he heard them still crying and wailing inside there. Then he shouted to them as loud as he could: "You mustn't cry and carry on any more. You can be happy now, for in truth you too will share in the glory of God. Last night leaves and flowers grew out of my staff!"

When he had said that, he heard great rejoicing inside the mound, and they started playing again and shouting to one another.

Christiansen (1964).

the thinnest, the mounds opened up, the evil fairies were most active, and the dead walked about the living in great numbers. In ancient times sacred bonfires were kindled, food was left out at the home hearth, and animal and even human sacrifices were made to appease the dangerous magical entities and ensure the community's survival through the coming long winter. In eleventh-century Sweden a visiting Christian poet named Sigvat complained that near Samhain he could not find lodging because "all of the people in the district were sacrificing to the elves" (Davidson, 1977, p. 156). After the conquest of Christianity in the early Middle Ages, when the pagan new year celebrations of Samhain were moved and incorporated into Christmas, the burning of the Yule log and the food offerings to saints preserved vestiges of the old practice.

The strange location of the Otherworld, accessible both by fairy mound and by overseas journey, points to a close connection between water, earth, and death. For instance, in Irish folklore, one may gain entrance to the Underworld realm of the dark god Donn through a cleft at Knockfierna, where a cairn of stones was raised to him—although one could also enter his realm by journeying over the sea to the island Tech Duin (House of Donn) off the Kelly coast. Norse mythology shows a very similar conception. There too, fallen kings, gods, and nature spirits all may dwell in magical mounds, which frequently give access to a vast magical realm that is both under the ground and under the sea. For example, there is the account of the *Eyrbyggja Saga* from Iceland wherein the great fisherman Thorstein Codbiter went out fishing one night with his crew; all were drowned. Before news of the drowning reached home, a shepherd happened to pass by the mound where Thorstein's ancestors were supposedly buried. The shepherd saw that the hill had opened, with firelight within:

Inside the hill he saw great fires and heard much merriment and noise over drinking horns; when he listened to what was said, he heard that Thorstein Codbiter was being welcomed with his companions, and men were saying that he was to sit in the high seat opposite his father. (Davidson, 1988, p. 115)

Instantly, Thorstein had been transported from a death at sea to his ancestral mound. Yet this is only half true—for the land of the dead, like fairyland, was neither literally under the sea nor underground. In fact, it had no physical location, only a magical one. Along these lines, we find in a great many important Norse burials that the deceased was placed in his ship. This practice was presumably done for a voyage overseas, but the whole was buried underground. Thus horizons in general, whether of water or earth, form the boundary

a family nearby and was given milk and wine offerings. However, when the farmer dug into the mound, the spirit appeared—old and gray-whiskered, dressed in tattered clothes, wearing old horsehide shoes—and struck down six cows in revenge. Whether this was a revenant (one who returns from the dead) or some sort of local land spirit is difficult to say.

The dangerous aspect of the fairy mounds was greatest at the time when the summer and winter halves of the archaic year met in the new year, at the festival of Samhain, beginning the evening of 31 October. Here, the "veil" between this world and the Otherworld was between living and dead, and the question of a physical location is moot.

See also BURIAL, SHIP; CAIRN; MOUND; SAMHAIN; TUMULUS; UNDEAD; WATER.

References

Christiansen, Reidar Th., ed. *Folktales of Norway*. Chicago: University of Chicago Press, 1964.

D'Arbois de Jubainville, H. *The Irish Mythological Cycle and Celtic Mythology*. Trans. Richard Irvine Best. Dublin: Hodges, Figgis, 1903.

Davidson, H. R. Ellis. *Gods and Myths of Northern Europe*. New York: Penguin, 1977.

———. *Myths and Symbols in Pagan Europe*. Syracuse: Syracuse University Press, 1988.

Mac Bain, Alexander. *Celtic Mythology and Religion*. New York: Dutton, 1917.

MacCulloch, J. A. *The Religion of the Ancient Celts*. Edinburgh: Clark, 1911.

Rees, Alwyn, and Brinley Rees. *Celtic Heritage: Ancient Tradition in Ireland and Wales*. London: Thames and Hudson, 1961.

FEBRUARY

February was the last month of the old Roman calendar, a month devoted to purification, placation of spirits and Underworld powers, and preparations for the new agricultural cycle. The name February comes from the Latin *februa,* "instruments of purification," which were used by people during this final month of the year. These included wool, a branch from a pine tree, salted and roasted grain, or any other object that was used ritually to produce catharsis, or release of negativity and growth of fertility. (A few rituals and their februa are described later in this entry.) Some later Roman writers referred to an actual god named *Februus,* which means "god of purification," but this is a fabrication personifying a ritual that was so old that its origins had by then been forgotten.

For the Romans, two spiritual forces converged in the month of February. The first force was backward-looking in fulfillment of the previous year, with all its thoughts, words, and deeds now coming to a close. The end of the year is the time to make restitution, especially for accidental ritual omissions or commissions toward the gods and powers of the earth. The second energy of this time of year was forward-looking: the utter dependence of an (originally) agricultural community upon the willingness of the Underworld to release its powers, which had slept underground all winter. Ancestors were thought to be particularly active at this time of year (as in the Celtic holiday of Samhain, which later evolved into Hallowe'en). Out from their tombs and cisterns and hollows in the earth, the dead returned to the sunlit world during the festival called *Parentalia* on 13–21 February, when they were honored individually by their descendants for most of the festi-

JANUARY PLOUGHING.

FEBRUARY.

MARCH. BREAKING UP SOIL—DIGGING—SOWING—HARROWING.

APRIL. FEASTING.
Eleventh Century.
Calendar. MS. Cott. Jul. A. vi.

Eleventh-century manuscript illustration of the agricultural cycle of the year. Courtesy of Anne Ronan Picture Library.

val and collectively by the entire community on the last day of the festival. Thus feasted and placated, the spirits of the dead promised to aid their living families by keeping forces hostile to growth at bay and ensuring a stable planting in the spring and a good harvest in the fall. Likewise, the Greeks celebrated their festival of ancestors, the Anthesteria, during the same time of year, though the month was not called February but Anthesterion (for obvious reasons) and the month fell eighth, not last, in the Greek calendar.

Other purificatory rituals took place in February besides the Parentalia for ancestors. The Lupercalia (named for its location, the Lupercal, or "Wolf-Cave") was celebrated on 15 February. This rite of spring centered around two young men who sacrificed a goat and a dog, dressed in their skins, and led teams of boys who ran about playfully striking women (and especially young maidens) with strips from the skins of the sacrificed animals. These strips, called *februa,* were thought to literally beat any negative energies out of women and allow fertility to gain ascendance.

The Fornacalia, or "Feast of Ovens" (*fornax* is Latin for oven) was a movable feast that appeared on slightly different days in different years and different communities, but it ended in every case by 17 February. It consisted of baking small cakes made from the ground and roasted seed of the oldest variety of wheat in Italy. During baking, an offering was made to the spirit of the oven, and then the community gathered for a collective meal of these ancient cakes—another ritual, probably, to pray for fertility, directed to yet another of the many spiritual entities in the ancient world.

The last purificatory ritual of the Roman year was the Terminalia, held on 23 February and sacred to Terminus, god of boundaries (and later, god of endings). In country districts, according to the writer Ovid, landowners would decorate the boundary stone between their two properties, each placing a garland or wreath on the stone. Then a temporary altar was made at the boundary, and a fire was kindled using flame brought from the home hearth. A boy of the family held a basket, while a girl took fruits from the basket and three times cast them into the fire, adding cakes of honey as well. All were clothed in white, and after a sacrifice of a lamb and young pig, the festival ended in songs, the sharing of wine, and a communal feast. The original purpose of this ritual appears to have been to stabilize local boundaries (and thus dispel competition and solidify good feelings between neighbors), but later Roman writers believed the Terminalia also referred to the termination of the calendar year and marked the boundary not only of space but of time.

See also ANTHESTERIA; FUNERARY CUSTOMS, ANCIENT ROMAN; LEMURIA; PARENTALIA.

References

Fowler, W. Warde. *The Roman Festivals of the Period of the Republic.* London: Kennikat Press, 1969.

Harrison, Jane Ellen. *Prolegomena to the Study of Greek Religion.* Cambridge: Cambridge University Press, 1922.

Toynbee, J. M. C. *Death and Burial in the Roman World.* Ithaca, NY: Cornell University Press, 1971.

FENG-SHUI

Literally "wind and water," feng-shui is the Chinese science of properly placing objects so as to harmonize with surroundings and not disrupt the natural flow of life energy. Although relevant to all aspects of physical life, feng-shui is considered exceedingly important in the placement of burial sites. An improperly placed grave disturbs the yin and yang energies of an area, disrupting the flow of energy and causing the souls of those buried there to become the restless or even dangerous undead.

References

Ahern, Emily. *The Cult of the Dead in a Chinese Village.* Stanford: Stanford University Press, 1973.

Freedman, Maurice. *Chinese Lineage and Society.* London: Athlone Press, 1966.

Watson, Rubie S. "Remembering the Dead: Graves and Politics in Southeastern China." In *Death Rituals in Late Imperial and Modern China,* eds. James L. Watson and Evelyn S. Rawski. Berkeley: University of California Press, 1988.

FESTIVAL OF GHOSTS (CHINA)

On the full moon of the seventh lunar month (usually in August by Western calendars), the Chinese rite called *Yü-lan-p'en*, or the Ghost Festival, is celebrated. Firecrackers scare off the dangerous dead, and ancestors are welcomed home with bonfire offerings and recitation of Buddhist Scriptures in their honor. The Ghost Festival in China is similar to the Celtic autumn festival of Samhain, in that on this day all the Chinese dead are thought to make their way to the surface of the earth seeking satisfaction from the living. Like Samhain, the day is festive but charged with both power and fear. Unlike Samhain, however, the Chinese festival also includes rituals to spiritually aid the dead, both by sending useful items directly (by burning them) and by "transferring the merit" or good karma of the living to the dead so that the dead may rise to higher estates in the afterlife.

The annual festival to honor and help the dead was widespread in the Chinese countryside by the middle of the sixth century C.E. and hugely popular at every social level from the T'ang Dynasty (618–907) up to the present. Although the Ghost Festival is supported by Buddhist texts that allegedly came from India, in fact the rite is a complex blending of pre-Buddhist Chinese religions, in which ancestor worship plays an enormous role, and imported Buddhist doctrines on karma, hell, and rebirth.

The root text for the Festival of Ghosts in China is *The Transformation Text on Mu-lien Saving His Mother from the Dark Regions.* This is a popular text absent from the Chinese Buddhist canon, which features a wonderful son named Mu-lien, who is an advanced and magically accomplished disciple of the Buddha. Seeking to aid his deceased parents, Mu-lien searches for his mother Ch'ing-t'i in the afterlife realms. Through many journeys, Mu-lien discovers that his mother is not in any of the many Buddhist heavens, nor is she in the Yellow Springs, the Underworld where souls were thought to go before Buddhism arrived in China. Mu-lien delves deeper and deeper into the Underworld, witnessing innumerable grotesque (and for the audience, titillating) sights while meeting Underworld gods such as Ti-tsang and Yama. At last Mu-lien discovers that his mother, because of her evil deeds committed several

Woman meditating with a Chinese Lo Pan Geomancer's Compass. Courtesy of Images Colour Library.

Monk praying during annual Festival of Ghosts, Hong Kong. Courtesy of Images Colour Library.

lifetimes before, has been reborn in the lowest of all hells, Avīci, "the hell without end." There his mother, poor Ch'ing-t'i, is nailed down with forty-nine metal spikes, suffering horribly. At this climax, the Buddha arrives to assist Mu-lien, destroying the prison walls and causing the hell beings to be reborn in a higher realm. Ultimately, Mu-lien's mother is released into heaven.

The tale purports to come from Buddhist texts in India, where Mu-lien finds his origins in the early Buddhist figure of Maudgalyāyana, the disciple of the Buddha most recognized in the Indian Buddhist canon for his supernatural powers. Indeed, Mu-lien's entire journey in hell searching for his mother is for the audience a religiously instructive tale, for Mu-lien at each opportunity uses his magical sight to tell sinners exactly what deeds they committed in the past to bring them to their current woes. The Jātaka Tales (stories of the Buddha's past lives before he became Enlightened) fill a similar role in the Indian sources, teaching the audience through entertainment the basics of Buddhist ethics. Yet much in the tale of Mu-lien cannot be originally Indian. At the end of the story the Buddha insti-

tutes the Festival of Ghosts on the moon of the seventh month (i.e., of a Chinese calendar), instructing his disciples to offer bowls of food to Buddhist monks as they end their three-month summer meditation retreat. It is true that all religious Indians (Buddhist and non-Buddhist) are concerned with the welfare of their deceased ancestors, but the Festival of Ghosts instituted "by the Buddha" in China bears little resemblance to any Indian rite. Therefore, scholars conclude that, whatever the ultimate origins of the Festival of Ghosts, it cannot stem from Indian Buddhist tradition alone.

As Stephen Teiser reports, before Buddhism entered China, the fourteenth day of the seventh month was already an autumnal festival when people gathered under colored canopies for feasting and reciting poetry. A ritual handbook (the *Li-chi cheng-I*, p. 143b) from the early Han period (c. 200 B.C.E.) instructs the Chinese emperor during the seventh month to "devote himself to self-adjustment," for the seventh month marks the inauguration of autumn and the beginning of the cycle of decay. During this month, too, the emperor should reward his ministers for good service and taste the first fruits grown by his populace, offering some of the food to his ancestors. When Buddhism arrived in China, Buddhist monks arranged their three-month meditation retreat to end on the full moon of the seventh month, when they would rejoin the lay populace, who would offer them new robes and a feast. Thus, the Festival of Ghosts, emerging in China in the fifth and early sixth centuries C.E., consolidated Chinese autumnal feasts, imperial reckoning of accounts, and Buddhist monastic rituals with a long-standing Chinese respect for and attachment to the dead.

Even today the Festival of Ghosts in China preserves both its seasonal and its religious roots. For example, as in an autumnal feast, incense, rice, and fruit are offered to the dead, but they are offered to the "soul tablet" of the deceased placed on the altar of a temple. While Buddhist monks are inside the temple reciting

Scriptures in honor of the dead (and ritually "transferring the merit" thus earned to the account of the dead), family members gather in the courtyard of the temple and prepare a bonfire. Various gifts made of paper and purchased from the temple are offered to the dead: paper cars, paper mansions with paper servants, paper clothing, and above all large quantities of special paper money drawn on the Bank of Hell are offered up to the flames. If the deceased have been reborn in hell, they may be able to take the merit and gifts being sent them to "earn" their way to a better rebirth (or else bribe the officials of hell to get released). If the deceased has already been reborn in heaven, this extra "merit" will gain them more happiness and a better rebirth on earth when the time comes.

One ritual of this kind is particularly important, called the "Releasing [Ghosts] with Burning Mouths Ceremony" (in Chinese, Fang Yen-K'ou) and performed by Buddhist monks or Taoist priests in exchange for payment. A family may hire priests to perform this rite at any time of the year to aid their ancestors, but during the Festival of Ghosts it is performed by monasteries and temples as a community service for the dead in general. It is a five-hour ritual for the benefit of those who have been reborn as "hungry ghosts." Called in Chinese e-kuei, these unfortunate creatures have huge bellies but tiny mouths and necks, so they are unable to take in sufficient food and water. Worse, when they try to eat or drink even small quantities, it turns to fire and ashes in the mouth. But by means of this ritual, the priests not only feed but also attempt to save the hungry ghosts:

[The "Release of the Burning Mouths Ceremony" was] always held in the evening, when it [was] easier for hungry ghosts to go abroad. The presiding monks wore red and golden hats in the shape of a five pointed crown. Before them was a collection of magical instruments—mirrors, scepters, spoons, and so on. . . . In the first half of the ceremony the celebrants invoked the help of the Three Jewels [the Buddha, the Holy Teaching, and the Holy Community]. In the second half they broke through the gates of hell, where, with their instruments and magic gestures, they opened the throats of the sufferers and fed them sweet dew, that is, water made holy by reciting a mantra over it. They purged away their sins, administered the Three [Buddhist] Refuges, and caused them to take the bodhisattva resolve [i.e., altruistic vows]. Finally they preached the dharma [Buddhist teaching] to them. If all this was properly done, the ghosts could be immediately reborn as men or even in the Western Paradise. (Welch)

The Festival of Ghosts in China does not have the official sanction of the government as it once did, for example, in the so-called Golden Age, the T'ang Dynasty. Yet observances for the dead on the full moon of the seventh month persist, as they do in Korea, Japan, Hong Kong, Malaysia, and wherever mainland Chinese influence has penetrated. Because devotion to ancestors is so deeply rooted, persisting throughout thousands of years of Chinese culture, it is unlikely that current or future political upheavals will prevent communication between the living and the dead during the autumn festival.

See also FUNERARY CUSTOMS, CHINESE; HEAVENS, BUDDHIST; HELLS, BUDDHIST; PRET; SOUL TABLET; TI-TSANG; YAMA; YELLOW SPRINGS.

References

Bredon, Juliet, and Igor Mitrophanow. *The Moon Year: A Record of Chinese Customs and Festivals.* Shanghai: Kelly and Walsh, 1927.

Duyvendak, J. J. L. "The Buddhistic Festival of All-Souls in China and Japan." *Acta Orientalia* 5, no. 1 (1926).

Granet, Marcel. *Festivals and Songs of Ancient China.* Trans. E. D. Edwards. London: Routledge, 1932.

Huang, Yu-mei. "China's Ghost Festival." *Free China Review* 32, no. 11 (November 1982).

Teiser, Stephen F. *The Ghost Festival in Medieval China.* Princeton: Princeton University Press, 1988.

Welch, Holmes. *The Practice of Chinese Buddhism, 1900–1950.* Cambridge: Harvard University Press, 1967.

Zürcher, Erik. *The Buddhist Conquest of China: The Spread and Adaptation of Buddhism in Early Medieval China.* Rev. ed. Leiden: E. J. Brill, 1972.

FETCH

The word *fetch* is of uncertain origin, possibly from an Old English word *faecce*, though the tradition exists mostly in Irish legend, where the phenomenon is called a *taisch.* The fetch is the apparition or double of the living that appears when the person is not present, though occasionally "fetch-light" will be used to refer to a ghostly light that is interpreted in the same way. Generally, like the banshee, the fetch was not seen as a good omen; rather it presaged a serious accident such as drowning. For instance, one legend relates that witnesses saw a taisch, and not long after a strange ship was wrecked off the coast. Among the dead was a sailor from the ship identical in dress and appearance to the taisch.

By some accounts, to meet one's own fetch was the worst omen of all, indicating certain death. Other accounts call this notion into question, however: if the fetch is seen in the morning, a long life may be expected; if at night, immediate death. Unlike the banshee, which is connected with noble Irish families and is characterized by its piercing wail, the fetch has appeared all over the British Isles and is not known for any particular sound, though some have said it cries or moans as if quite ill. Also unlike the banshee, the fetch

is the double of the individual in question and appears to be identical to him or her. Some have claimed that the fetch is an involuntary "astral projection" of the person in jeopardy, emanating unconsciously from the soul.

See also BANSHEE; UNDEAD.

References

Byrne, Patrick. *Irish Ghost Stories.* Cork: Mercier Press, n. d.

Dunne, John J. *Haunted Ireland.* Belfast: Appletree Press, 1977.

Ó hÓgáin, Dáithí. *Myth, Legend and Romance: An Encyclopaedia of the Irish Folk Tradition.* New York: Prentice Hall, 1991.

FOSSORES (FOSSARII)

Fossores is the Latin term for diggers of graves. It appears that this profession was at first an occupation handed down within family lines and later (third century C.E.) a minor rank of clergy controlled by the Catholic Church. Certainly when Christians were few, the task of digging and burial was carried out by family members and coreligionists (or their servants), but as the early church grew this task was entrusted to professionals. The fossores were responsible not only for digging surface graves but for excavating, inscribing, and possibly even providing the artwork for the catacombs, particularly the cubicula (rectangular tomb chambers) and arcosolia (benchlike niches in the wall of a stone tomb). Artwork in tombs gives a clear idea of what fossores looked like: they wore a short tunic with a pick and a lamp in hand or held a basket or bag with which to excavate the rock and earth. The organization of the fossores was surely complex, but probably they became attached to a particular cemetery. By 357 the Theodosian Code considered fossores clerics and exempted them from certain taxes.

Fossores may also have become the keepers of the cemeteries for some time: inscriptions from the late fourth to early fifth centuries record the purchase of surface graves in cemeteries and spaces in catacombs from fossores. Knowing the right fossor was important because the good burial spaces—those near martyrs—were hard to come by. However, by the mid–fifth century it is clear that the church hierarchy had full control of burial grounds. Tombs were increasingly placed within church structures themselves or in surface cemeteries, and inscriptions referring to fossores disappear.

References

Stevenson, James. *The Catacombs: Life and Death in Early Christianity.* London: Thames and Hudson, 1978.

FRASHO-KERETI (FRASHEN KERENAUM AHUM)

In the ancient Persian religion of Zoroastrianism, frasho-kereti means "renovation." It is the doctrine that at the end of the time allotted for the existence of the world, all things will be consummated and redeemed. A new heaven and a new earth will arise, and the good and evil alike, having been resurrected from the dead, will enjoy God's presence forever after.

The Zoroastrian teachings on the "last things" and the ultimate renovation of the world had a massive impact on the development of eschatology in early Judaism, Christianity, and Islam. The Hebrews came into contact with Zoroastrian doctrines in the sixth century B.C.E., when Judah was conquered and the elite Judaites were exiled to Babylon for generations. Meanwhile, Greek philosophers such as Plutarch show in their writings an awareness of Zoroastrian doctrines as early as the fourth century B.C.E. Thus a grasp of Zoroastrian theology is essential in understanding the origin of Western beliefs in heaven, hell, resurrection, and judgment.

From an early period, Zoroastrianism taught that the universe was finite: it had a definite beginning and would have a definite end. The usual period given for the duration of the world is 12,000 years, divided into four quarters of 3,000 years each. These four cycles are equal in length but unequal in quality. The first, nearest to the Creation, was a Golden Age when humanity was unquestionably obedient to God (Ahura Mazda, "the Wise Lord") and all men were good neighbors to each other. With each subsequent cycle (silver, steel, and iron), mankind suffered a moral decline, due to the evil forces of Druj, "the Lie," active in the world. The last age (the present time) is a time of catastrophe. Nevertheless, Zoroastrians believe that over time humanity is engaged in inner progress, despite the decline in world conditions. Although many succumb to the Lie and suffer in hell after death as a result, nevertheless humanity as a whole grows more mature and spiritual (and all those in hell are eventually saved).

Zoroastrian legend has it that on three occasions during his life, the great Prophet Zoroaster lay with his wife, and his seed fell to the ground. The Prophet's seed was caught and preserved by the angel Neryosangh, who transported it to Ardvisur, the spirit of water. The seed was saved by the water deity in Lake Kans and guarded by 99,999 fravashis (guardian spirits). The legend states that during the last cycle of 3,000 years, our present age, three messiahs will appear 1,000 years apart, each conceived immaculately of a virgin. However, each savior will be of the house of Zoroaster, born of his rescued seed placed in a virgin by angels. Each messiah will usher in a new millennium, each of which will further humanity's spiritual progress. Each savior will make the sun stand still for days on end and through other miracles prove he is a divine messenger come to lead the people back to God. With each savior, poverty will decrease, righteousness and generosity will increase, and the wisdom of the religion will grow. Interestingly, during these last millennia, mankind will gradually cease eating meat and turn to vegetables. After switching from vegetables to milk and from milk to water, finally they will survive on light or nothing at all. Human bodies will gradually become more spiritual and less physical, until they cast no shadows at all. At the end of the last millennium, the last savior or Saoshyant (literally "the Helper") will be born of a virgin named Vispataurvi (literally "the all-triumphant"). The Saoshyant will call fifteen pure men and fifteen pure maidens to him, who will work for the final renovation of humanity and the world.

When the living have been thoroughly spiritualized, the last savior will bring about the general resurrection (Ristakhez). Each of the dead will return from their places in heaven or hell to find themselves rematerialized in bodily form on the exact spot where each died. There will then come a final judgment by God, after which the wicked who fail to pass muster will be condemned to hell once again but only for three excruciating days; although they had suffered in spirit before, now they suffer far worse in conjoined body and soul. At last the earth itself will be deconstructed by God, and the earth and mountains will transform into molten metal, white hot. The torrent of lava washing over the earth will serve as the last ordeal (yah mazishta). It will engulf the righteous aboveground as well as the wicked in hell: to the righteous it will feel like warm milk and for the wicked it will be the pinnacle and culmination of their sufferings. However, this molten fire is literally a purgatorial fire in that it will purge out the last remaining wickedness in all beings, who are then purified and prepared to spend eternity in joy with God. (It is highly likely that this "purgatorial" fire of Zoroastrian thought was the origin of the Greek [Stoic], Christian, and Muslim doctrines of hellfire—though it became more punitive than rehabilitative in their belief and eternal.) After the purifying fire, the earth is swept clean—"renovated"—and God creates a new heaven and a new earth, called *Khshathra Vairya,* literally the "desired kingdom" or "promised land." The Saoshyant gives to each person a magical drink, and their bodies transform into spiritual substance. They will never again experience hunger or thirst or be able to suffer any bodily harm.

The last act to take place in this cosmic drama is the titanic struggle of the spiritual powers of light against the powers of darkness, or "the Lie." Each angel has its nemesis, each god a demonic foe. But in the end, Asha, or Righteousness, triumphs over Druj, with its demonic daevas, priests (kavi), wizards (yatu), and spirits (pairika). Evil incarnate, Angra Mainyu (Ahriman), disappears, and from a dualistic universe, Ahura Mazda (Ormazd) emerges as the only true God, the only real power. All souls now become of one will, which is perfectly in tune with the divine will, and all sing to the glory of God ever after.

See also AMERETAT; BEHESHT; DOZAKH; FRAVASHI; RISTAKHEZ; SOUL, ZOROASTRIAN.

References

Boyce, Mary. *A History of Zoroastrianism.* Vol. 1. Leiden: E. J. Brill, 1975.

Carnoy, A. J. "Zoroastrianism." In *Encyclopaedia of Religion and Ethics,* ed. James Hastings. Vol. 12. Edinburgh: T and T Clark, 1921.

Dhalla, M. N. *Zoroastrian Theology from the Earliest Times to the Present Day.* Reprint, New York: AMS Press, 1972.

Jackson, A. V. W. *Zoroastrian Studies.* New York: Columbia University Press, 1928.

Kotwal, Firoze M., and James W. Boyd, trans. *A Guide to the Zoroastrian Religion.* Studies in World Religion no. 3. Chico, CA: Scholars Press, 1982.

Masani, Sir Rustom. *Zoroastrianism: The Religion of the Good Life.* New York: Collier Books, 1962.

Moulton, James Hope. *Early Zoroastrianism.* London: Williams and Norgate, 1913.

Sethna, Tehmurasp Rustamji. *Book of Instructions on Zoroastrian Religion.* Karachi: Informal Religious Meetings Trust Fund, 1980.

Sidhwa, Ervad Godrej Dinshawji. *Discourses on Zoroastrianism.* Karachi: Ervad Godrej Dinshawji Sidhwa, 1978.

FRAVARDIGĀN

During the last ten days of their calendar year, Zoroastrian communities celebrate the Fravardigān, similar in function to the Christian All-Souls Day on November 2. The fravashis, or spirits of the departed (and by some reckonings, the spirits of the unborn) descend from the heavenly realms and visit their descendants on earth, bringing benefits to the community.

The Zoroastrian calendar is composed of twelve months with exactly thirty days each, plus five sacred days added at the end of the year. Fravardigān begins on the twenty-fifth day (Ashtad, "rectitude") of the twelfth and last month and continues for four more days until the end of the year. The second half of the Fravardigān festival occurs on the five intercalated days, called *gatha* (sacred or hymnal) days. To observe the festival, Zoroastrians set aside a part of their house to be kept meticulously clean and place fresh flowers, pure water, and fruits there as offerings to the fravashis. An oil lamp or small fire is also kept burning, in which incense is burned. Such cleanliness and fragrances attract the spirits, who are accustomed to such things in their heavenly dwellings, and thus they willingly visit the living. To further encourage the fravashis to visit, the living are expected to be on their best behavior and scrupulously observe their religious duties. They are to say their prayers of penance for wrongs committed (patet) and keep themselves very clean in mind, word, and body.

The Fravardigān observances are divided into two parts. During the first five days, a great number of specific rituals are performed. The community recites hymns (yasna) from the sacred text, Avesta, performs a service called *Afrinagan* that blesses the spirits, and offers prayers to God's vice-regent, Srosh. A service called *Dron* is performed before every meal to consecrate bread, as well as a service called *Stum* (from the Avestan word *staomi,* "I praise"), which offers cooked food to the spirits. In a curious ceremony called *Syaw,* a clean set of white clothes, including the sacred kusti thread that initiated Zoroastrians wear around their waist, is ritually offered to the fravashis; but then the clothes are given physically to the local Zoroastrian priest. The spirits seem to gain the benefit of the offered clothing through the agency of the priest, just as in Hinduism, there is a ceremony in which the spirits of the dead enter a brahmin priest's body in order to enjoy the food offerings. Finally, a service called *Geti-kharid* (literally "to purchase this world") is performed. Two Zoroastrian priests perform the ceremony, chanting yasna from the Scriptures, which in effect counteract any evil thoughts, words, or deeds done by the community during the preceding year. In this manner, the souls of those present are made pure and reborn—fitting them for heaven. In this way the "world" of heaven has been "purchased" through the ceremony. During these first five days, the living are also expected to personally say 1,200 repetitions of a prayer called *Ashem Vohu,* which praises righteousness and encourages it in oneself.

During the second five days of the festival, which are officially between the old and the new years, many of the same rituals and prayers are performed. Individuals are expected to say 1,200 repetitions of a prayer called *Yatha Ahu Vairyos,* which has twenty-one words corresponding to the twenty-one volumes of the Scriptures. (Thus, in effect, saying the prayer corresponds to repeating the entire Scriptures.) At dawn on the tenth day of Fravardigān, the fravashis begin to depart back to heaven, or Behesht. The living perform the consecration of bread (Dron) a final time and offer the special prayers (Afrinagan) that bless all the departed. Then the new calendar year begins.

On the nineteenth day (Frawardin) of the ninth month (Adar), a miniature Fravardigān service is observed because on this day as well the fravashis are believed to descend from heaven, though only for a short while. Firoze Kotwal, a very learned Zoroastrian priest, believes that this "mini-observance" exists because in the distant past the ninth month used to begin the New Year, and the day Frawardin is a faint recollection of it (Kotwal and Boyd, p. 162).

See also BEHESHT; FRAVASHI; FUNERARY CUSTOMS, ZOROASTRIAN; SOUL, ZOROASTRIAN.

References

Jackson, A. V. W. *Zoroastrian Studies*. New York: Columbia University Press, 1928.

Kotwal, Firoze M., and James W. Boyd, trans. *A Guide to the Zoroastrian Religion*. Studies in World Religion no. 3. Chico, CA: Scholars Press, 1982.

Masani, Sir Rustom. *Zoroastrianism: The Religion of the Good Life*. New York: Collier Books, 1962.

Moulton, James Hope. *Early Zoroastrianism*. London: Williams and Norgate, 1913.

Sethna, Tehmurasp Rustamji. *Book of Instructions on Zoroastrian Religion*. Karachi: Informal Religious Meetings Trust Fund, 1980.

Sidhwa, Ervad Godrej Dinshawji. *Discourses on Zoroastrianism*. Karachi: Ervad Godrej Dinshawji Sidhwa, 1978.

FRAVASHI (FAROHAR)

The highest, immortal aspect of the human soul in Zoroastrian doctrine is called the *fravashi* (in the ancient Scriptural language, Avesta) or *farohar* (in Middle Iranian). The word *fravashi* refers both to the spirits of the deceased as well as to the spirits of the unborn, suggesting an ancient Zoroastrian belief in reincarnation that has since faded.

For three days immediately after death, the fravashi of the departed remains on Earth, frequenting its place of death as well as the Tower of Silence where its old body has been deposited. During this time the fravashi is somewhat confused and vulnerable. Therefore, surviving friends and relatives engage in ceremonies to comfort the recently deceased spirit, and they repeat a penitential prayer (called *patet*) that allows the soul to repent of past sins and prepare to meet God and receive judgment more advantageously.

After the fravashi has successfully passed judgment and entered heaven (Behesht), it becomes a powerful force for good in the spiritual world (menog) as well as for its family and friends on the material plane (getig). Fravashis are seen by the living as welcome visitors and guardian spirits. Each fravashi visits its descendents on the anniversary of its death each year, and the fravashis collectively descend from heaven to participate in special ceremonies, especially the Zoroastrian equivalent of All Souls' Day called *Fravardigān*, ten days that straddle the old and new year.

To honor and please the fravashis, the living place a metal pot full of water and flowers in a clean space. This is done during the three days' presence of the recently deceased, as well as during memorial services and annual ceremonies. Flowers and water are believed to comfort and please the disembodied soul because of the fragrance and refreshment they provide. A verse from the Zoroastrian Scriptures states: "In that house in which clean and pure water and vegetation is placed, the holy fravashis agree to move about" (Yasht 13:147, Kotwal and Boyd, trans.). An oil lamp is also kept burning because fire keeps away evil spirits and protects the fravashis from pollution. Relatives chant verses (gathas) from the Scriptures, as well as prayers of penitence (patet) and other sacred formulas (called *manthras*, from the Sanskrit *mantras*). These supply the fravashi with "spiritual food." With it, the fravashis are strengthened and can guard the living from danger, ensure fertility in the land, and bring luck. Without such spiritual food, the fravashis depart, leaving the family open to misfortune. However, Zoroastrians are careful to point out that the fravashis themselves do not bring disaster if they are displeased; this is the work of evil spirits.

Each family honors its dead on the individuals' death anniversaries, but the anniversary of the prophet Zoroaster's death is a special occasion for the entire Zoroastrian community. This day is celebrated on the eleventh day of the tenth month (in the Zoroastrian calendar), a day that is dedicated to Khorshed (the Sun). Each local religious community attends a ceremony called *jashan*, which is performed by two or more priests. This jashan honors the spirit of the prophet but also brings benefits to the whole Zoroastrian community. If it is performed correctly in a clean and beautiful place and is attended by pious Zoroastrians, other fravashis by the thousands are also thought to attend, greatly increasing the spirit benefits.

See also AMERETAT; BEHESHT; FRASHO-KERETI; FRAVARDIGĀN; HAMESTEGĀN; SOUL, ZOROASTRIAN.

References

Bode, F. A. "Man, Soul, Immortality in Zoroastrianism." Speech delivered at Portiuncula Firary, Karachi, December 1971.

Jackson, A. V. W. *Zoroastrian Studies*. New York: Columbia University Press, 1928.

Kotwal, Firoze M., and James W. Boyd, trans. *A Guide to the Zoroastrian Religion*. Studies in World Religion no. 3. Chico, CA: Scholars Press, 1982.

Masani, Sir Rustom. *Zoroastrianism: The Religion of the Good Life*. New York: Collier Books, 1962.

Moulton, J. H. *Early Zoroastrianism*. London: Williams and Norgate, 1913.

Sethna, Tehmurasp Rustamji. *Book of Instructions on Zoroastrian Religion*. Karachi: Informal Religious Meetings Trust Fund, 1980.

Sidhwa, Ervad Godrej Dinshawji. *Discourses on Zoroastrianism*. Karachi: Ervad Godrej Dinshawji Sidhwa, 1978.

FUNERARY CUSTOMS

Every human society marks the death of a member with rituals. Most mourners will attest that participating in

Patagonian funeral procession. Wood engraving circa 1880. Courtesy of Anne Ronan Picture Library.

a funeral for a loved one, though difficult, is beneficial—both providing a necessary structure in a time of immobility and providing catharsis, or release of intense emotions that otherwise threaten to overwhelm them. Specifically, whether private or public, these rituals allow the living to accept the finality of their separation from the dead and help the broken group reintegrate as a whole. Most often funerary rituals are additionally intended to help the dead quit their association with the living and illuminate their journey to the final destination.

Obviously, funeral rituals differ widely across the globe, affected by ancient tradition and local custom, wealth or poverty, climate, and beliefs. But a general pattern, abstracted from current cultures and even from records of past civilizations, may be observed. Every element of this pattern may not be present in every funeral of every culture, but the pattern helps in understanding the nature and function of funerals in human life as a whole. In general, funeral rituals begin with the special treatment of the body, usually a very short time after death. The body is almost always bathed in a special manner, clothed (usually in the finest available material), and otherwise made to look presentable, even if it will not be viewed publicly. In most cultures this

is as much for the satisfaction of the dead one who is thought to be looking on as for the comfort of the bereaved. Usually the corpse is considered extremely "impure" (even if perfectly hygienic) and undergoes additionally "purifying" rituals such as prayers, burning of incense, Scriptural readings, and a special orientation within a room or building, such as being placed with the feet facing the doorway.

Sometimes before but usually after the treatment of the body, public expressions of grief take place. This may include wailing, whether spontaneous and personal or formulaic and collective. Mourners who are in immediate relationship to the deceased debase themselves physically (for example, by putting ash in their hair, tearing their clothes, gouging their faces) and enter into seclusion. The body is then conveyed to its final resting place by a public procession in which even casual observers are often expected to participate or at least solemnly observe. Ritual sounds almost always accompany the formal procession, including both instruments and the use of voice in prayers, mantras (sacred spoken formulas), or further wailing.

Upon arrival at the corpse's destination, members of the procession gather for a commemorative ritual that reflects on the life of the loved one and certainly includes praises for the dead. Again, the commemorative ritual is as much for the gratification of the soul of the deceased, who may be angered by an insufficient display of grief or pomp, as it is for the living. Traditionally, the physical interment or disposal of the body is accompanied by a sacrifice of some kind. This sacrifice was most often of something living in ancient times (a goat, bull, horse, or even human dependents), but in modern times the sacrifice is usually food, drink, or merely the burial of valuable goods (often personal possessions) with the deceased. After the disposal of the body, there is a procession of mourners back home, which frequently includes barriers deliberately placed along the way intended to ward off the spirit of the dead, which may attempt to return with the living. Fires, smoke, running water, incantations, and spoken admonishments are thought to keep the dead in their proper place, namely the physical tomb, urn, or grave as well as the spiritual location that they represent (i.e., heaven or the land of the ancestors). As the living return home, they simultaneously undergo various rituals intended to purify themselves from the "corpse pollution" with which they have become contaminated. These purifications most often include washing with water but may also involve seclusion from the society of nonmourners, fasting, changing clothes, and touching certain items like a stone or other natural object.

Once home, the mourners usually enjoy a celebratory feast, quite different in tone from the solemn earlier events. Many cultures include funeral games and amusements, even athletic contests, in addition to an abundance of food. This is probably a deliberate choice that the mourners—or the society they belong to—make as a transition from the negative symbolic world of death to the positive associations of life. Formal mourning periods vary greatly in duration, from several days to a month to one or more years, but they always include various subdivisions in which the restrictions of mourning (humble dress and food, seclusion, abstention from pleasurable activities) gradually diminish, beginning with the period immediately after the funeral. Likewise, frequent returns to the gravesite to honor the dead are traditional in the earlier stages of mourning, followed by a gradually lengthening period between returns. After the formal period of mourning has ended, most cultures mandate visits to the graves of the deceased only on the anniversary of their death and during the general "day of the dead" that most cultures celebrate to honor the dead collectively.

From this generalized pattern of human funeral observances, three main phases distinguish themselves: (1) the severance of the dead from the living; (2) the integration of the deceased individual into his or her new group; and (3) the reintegration of the survivors into a new "whole" social group. In the first phase, the isolation of the dead from the living is critical because around the world, death is considered to be somehow contagious, whether by actual bacteria or other microbes, through emotional or psychical contamination, or through the agency of the dead soul or other spirits. Even if there is no fear of the spread of fatal disease, the living generally feel too threatened in the presence of the dead to remain nearby. Various means accomplish the isolation of the dead from the living. The ritual treatment of the corpse, the collection and isolation of the belongings of the deceased, the funeral procession that takes the corpse out of the habitations of the living, and the barriers placed between the living and the dead on the return trip (especially water and fire)—all these and many other activities are meant to sever the living survivors from the spirit of the deceased, at least temporarily. Many cultures have specific prayers or lamentations addressed to the dead that take great pains to inform them that they are in fact *dead* and that they must depart now. Some such lamentations are quite direct, bribing the spirit of the dead with a sacrificial offering followed by the command, "Take this and no more, and depart. Leave us be."

But the initial phase of isolation is accompanied by or quickly followed by ritual attempts to reintegrate the dead into their new society—the collective dead. There are many ways to accomplish this, for example, by adding the name of the deceased to a roster of venerated ancestors, placing various objects in the grave that will be of use in the new location, reading Scriptures that describe the land of the dead or prayers that give hope for a long and happy life in the new realm, and calling on the ancestors to come and bring this new recruit into their society. Even though the dead are no longer members of the society of the living, they are very much alive in the society of the dead. Nearly every culture, after a period of severance and mourning, actively seeks the presence of the dead and considers the society of the dead a tremendous source of positive energy, wisdom, and even magical benefit. Thus the first phase is characterized by fear and horror, but the second phase is one of hope and altruism, possibly tinged by anxiety that the dead will not integrate into the new society and remain behind to trouble the living.

Finally, the bereaved must repair the psychic damage caused by the loss of the loved one and reintegrate into society again if life is to continue. Traditional cultures are wise indeed to regulate mourning periods and coax the bereaved through gradually diminishing stages of grief until a fully functional life is resumed. Regular repetition of the list of ancestors gives a strong sense of history and collective identity, as does collective mourning through lamentation, religious services, and regular funeral gatherings at the home and gravesite. The loss of loved ones, although certainly a negative emotional experience, may in fact have the lasting effect of further binding families and communities together.

This fact is often recognized and manipulated by political entities who wish to strengthen national identity or galvanize a society to fight a war. They may use loyalty to the national dead as a rallying cry for action (e.g., undertaking migration or war) or may promise universal salvation to a people who will do their political bidding (e.g., a national homeland or a millennium of peace).

FUNERARY CUSTOMS, AFRICAN

The geographical, cultural, and ethnic diversity of the peoples of Africa is truly stunning, and no survey can do justice to the various beliefs and practices prevalent on the continent. Adding to the diversity of indigenous religions, northern Africa has long been influenced by the Christian and Islamic faiths; in recent centuries those two traditions have penetrated deeply even into sub-Saharan Africa. However, this entry will concentrate on what beliefs and practices are generally widespread in Africa as reported by native African sources.

The most common pan-African myth for how death came into the world, according to Hans Abrahamsson, is that a high god, a creator, or the moon sent out a messenger (a chameleon, dog, duck, etc.) to tell humanity that they would be given immortal life or at least resurrection. Whether from miscommunication, vexation, or carelessness, another messenger (a lizard, bird, toad, etc.) appears with the opposite message, that human beings shall surely die. The first messenger is either too slow or, like the dog, distracted by food or relaxation, and the second messenger arrives first, with the result that death becomes a universal aspect of human life. (Other versions, including the Ashanti tale of the women who beat God up and send him on his way, add considerable mirth and variety to the basic myth.) In any case, African traditions recognize that death is the final end of all humans but nevertheless tend to look for supernatural reasons why each particular death should have occurred. Rarely is "old age" an acceptable cause of death; it is much more likely that witchcraft is the real reason or perhaps the curse of a malevolent spirit. When someone is dying, the local oracle or shaman is consulted to discover the source of the malady. If the remedy prescribed does not work and the ill person dies, the natural response is to seek out the human witch who caused the problem and seek murderous revenge. Thus, particularly in village settings, each single death almost always creates a dangerous situation in which many may lose their lives in blood feuds.

Whatever the ultimate cause of death, the treatment of the corpse is generally careful and ritualized. Careless funeral preparations or burial can result in a spiritual

Grave of Zulu chief, with body in sitting position in a stone-lined underground chamber, 1888. Courtesy of Anne Ronan Picture Library.

disaster, with the deceased prevented from joining the benevolent ancestors and instead becoming a dangerous ghost and a grave danger to the family. (Strangers, thieves, murderers, and witches, however, are not given proper burials because their mere presence already presents such danger: their bodies are simply removed far from the community.) Children and pregnant women are not allowed to come near a corpse because of the danger of death pollution, and suspected witches are also kept at bay because they might find further means of spreading their mischief.

Generally the preparation of the body for burial takes place as soon as possible after death, certainly within twenty-four hours, because the African climate encourages rapid decay. Local elders and ritual specialists guide the performance of the rites, but the eldest son should be present and perform or serve as the primary witness to the rites. The corpse is generally washed with pure water, soap and water, or water steeped in medicinal herbs, with hair either nicely trimmed and styled or, particularly with men, shaved off. (An unwashed corpse continues to be polluted by death and will not be accepted by the ancestors. Rather, it becomes undead, called *iwin* or *isheku* among the Yorùbá, according to J. Omosade Awolalu.) In some areas the entire body is anointed with oil or clarified butter, and in some regions the mouth, nostrils, and other bodily openings are stopped up with oil or butter, or the eyes and mouth are covered by strips of cloth tied around the head (for instance, among the Tiv of Nigeria)—no doubt as a preventive measure to keep foreign spirits from entering and animating the "vacated" body. Funeral clothing varies from place to place, but either the corpse is buried in the finest clothes available (and some ritual performances require that the corpse be dressed in several increasingly expensive sets of clothes as the funeral rites progress) or else in natural elements like skins, leather, bark, or leaves.

Funeral rites vary widely among African communities. In some cultural groups, for instance the Yorùbá of West Africa, preservatives are applied to the dead body, which then becomes the focal point of the funeral ceremonies (feasting, music, dancing, and theatrical performances) for several days. Among other groups, however, burial is done right away, and ceremonies are held without the body present, for instance among the Fanti of Ghana. Burial is by far the most common mode of disposing of the dead, though according to John Mbiti (p. 114), exposure of the corpse used to be common, for instance, placing the body in the open bush to be devoured by wild animals, placing the body in a stream to be carried away, or allowing the body to decompose in a funerary shed on the outskirts of the settlement, with the skeletal remains eventually subject to secondary burial. Formerly, the deceased was frequently buried within the floor of his or her own house (which was usually abandoned by the living thereafter), but many African peoples have also long maintained community burial grounds. Often care is taken to conceal the exact place of burial, such as among the Ba Venda of the Transvaal in Southern Africa, because there is some concern that evildoers might try to do harm to the corpse, including stealing a piece of the corpse to perform harmful magic. In older tradition, buried corpses were usually covered in hides (or among the poor, in blankets or cloth), but since industrialization and Christian colonization, particularly in the twentieth century, coffins have come into vogue. Among the many variations in African burial methods, from placing remains in urns to leaving them in caves, special mention must be made of the unique coffin craft now popular among the Ga people of Ghana. There, most famously in the village of Teshi, wooden coffins are made in fanciful shapes and are brightly painted to suit the personalities of the deceased. Examples range from coffins shaped like various fish, mammals, and birds to coffins shaped like Bibles (for the burial of a minister), a sports boot (for a boxer), or an oil drum (for an auto body shop owner).

Personal belongings are generally placed with the dead in the grave, presumably for use in the afterlife, though occasionally these belongings are broken or marred in some way by the mourners. Living sacrifices also form an important part of African funeral customs. Formerly humans were sacrificed upon the death of important persons, such as the wife (or wives) of a chief, along with servants and councilors. Today this is universally replaced by animal sacrifice, which may take place at the time of burial or afterward at the community feast. Often the blood of the sacrificial victim is poured upon the grave, and the deceased is invited to share in the cooked flesh at the feast. This sacrifice is thought to satisfy the dead and strengthen him or her in preparation for the journey to the Otherworld.

After the burial, many different ritual activities take place to help sever the living from the dead. Formal lamentation is made for the dead (performed particularly by women), emphasizing the good qualities of the dead and showing how much he or she is missed. In addition, immediately after the burial many African cultures require that mourners seek purification from their polluting contact with the dead. This process may include washing in a river or stream, jumping over or passing hands and feet through the smoke of a pile of burning grass, or cutting a part of the body to draw blood, for example, the backs of the thumbs. After purification, the community returns to the village for a memorial feast, which often includes much merriment and drinking and may carry on for weeks. In many African communities the direct relatives of the dead fast, shave their heads, abstain from marital relations, and wear outward marks of mourning, including smearing their bodies with white clay or colored paint, refraining from washing, or wearing mourning beads or bracelets or ties around the neck. Work is suspended through the initial mourning period; the fields of the deceased remain untilled and the farm animals unmilked.

Traditionally in Africa, the dead are still very much alive in the minds and daily routines of the living. Unlike Christian and Muslim beliefs, African religions place the dead spirits very near the living, not in a distant heaven or hell, and the dead are frequently contacted in order to honor them or to ask their help. In addition, there are many more "classes" of the dead in traditional African belief than in modern Western thought. Not all the dead become respected ancestors but only those who lived to a ripe old age, did not die through violence or other abnormal means, and left successful and respectable offspring. One's immediate ancestors (those who died recently) provide a deep reservoir of wisdom and supernatural aid to the living and may be contacted on a daily basis. More distant ancestors, forming a yet more senior level of "society," are potentially as powerful as gods, with responsibility for watching over the entire clan or tribe; they are also more liable to anger and must be treated with the utmost care. Add to this pantheon the dangerous ghosts of humans who died by violence or through abnormal means (drowning, burning, lightning, etc.) who must be bribed, warded off by magic, or otherwise guarded against. There are also negative, necromantic spirits—perhaps never human but seen as forces of death—who are a constant threat to crops, childbirth, and other wholesome life-affirming processes. In this complex context of sorcerers, ancestors, ghosts, and spirits, the great importance of correctly performed ritual activity in African life is easily understood. Fortunately, African traditions affirm the place of the seer or "witch doctor" (in the Congo, among the BaNdibu, the term is *ndoki,* a shaman who may be good or evil in utilizing kindoki, or "witch-force"; see Bockie, pp. 41–43), the local religious expert who is able to diagnose the problems caused by sorcerers and spirits and prescribe a cure.

See also ANCESTOR VENERATION; FUNERARY CUSTOMS; FUNERARY CUSTOMS, ANCIENT EGYPTIAN; FUNERARY CUSTOMS, CHRISTIAN; FUNERARY CUSTOMS; MUSLIM; SOUL; UNDERWORLD.

References

Abrahamsson, Hans. *The Origin of Death: Studies in African Mythology.* Uppsala: Arno Press, 1951.

Awolalu, J. Omosade. *Yoruba Beliefs and Sacrificial Rites.* Brooklyn, NY: Athelia Henrietta Press, 1996.

Bockie, Simon. *Death and the Invisible Powers: The World of Kongo Belief.* Indianapolis: Indiana University Press, 1993.

Ephirim-Donkor, Anthony. *African Spirituality: On Becoming Ancestors.* Asmara, Eritrea: Africa World Press, 1997.

Habenstein, Robert W., and William M. Lamers. *Funeral Customs the World Over.* Milwaukee: Bulfin Printers, 1963.

Idowu, E. Bolaji. *African Traditional Religion.* Kampala, Uganda: Fountain Publications, 1991.

Mbiti, John. *Introduction to African Religion.* London: Heinemann, 1975.

Parrinder, Geoffrey. *African Traditional Religion.* 3rd ed. London: Sheldon Press, 1974.

Secretan, Thierry. *Going into Darkness: Fantastic Coffins from Africa.* London: Thames and Hudson, 1995.

FUNERARY CUSTOMS, ANCIENT EGYPTIAN

Death was an elaborate undertaking in ancient Egypt; after all, it was the beginning of eternal life. From earliest times the Egyptians looked forward to the life after death, and an extensive literature prepared the dying for what lay ahead. Yet after physical death many preparations were needed. First of all, the preparation of the body could take the better part of a year, not including the construction or excavation of the final resting place. Equally elaborate, however, were the funeral activities proper, at least for those of middle class and above.

From the decorated walls of tombs and illustrations on funerary papyri comes nearly all our information about Egyptian burial customs. These sources depict an extensive funeral procession with several magical rites performed along the way, culminating in a funerary feast and the sealing of the tomb. Most likely the funeral began in the early morning at the house of the deceased, where the entourage of the procession assembled. As in modern Greece, those Egyptians of means would have hired professional mourners dressed in blue-gray mourning clothes whose job it was to loudly wail, rub themselves with dust and refuse, and tear their clothes and hair. The procession would also contain servants bearing the victuals of the funerary feast (including the foods and beverages that were to be sealed up with the dead), as well as furniture and ritual equipment such as shabtis (ritual statuettes), vases for libations, amulets, and canopic chests.

Behind the servants came the ritual stand-in for the deceased, called the *tekenu,* which served as a scapegoat for the evil deeds committed by the deceased. (This practice was picked up by the Jews during their captivity in Egypt; cf. Leviticus 16:10.) The tekenu was a dressed-up bundle shaped like a human torso and dragged on a sled and would be ritually "killed" near the cemetery along with the animals (usually oxen) that pulled it. Perhaps in very early times the servants were sacrificed as well, although already by the First Dynasty (c. 3100 B.C.E. by orthodox chronology) they were killed symbolically rather than literally.

After the tekenu came a statue of the deceased, which would serve as another kind of stand-in once inside the tomb: a "reserve body" or just a "reserve head" in which the spirit of the deceased could be grounded if (heaven forbid) something happened to the mummy over the course of eternity. The statue was accompanied by the head priest of the service, the sem priest, who was to be distinguished from other religious professionals: the guardians of the deceased's spirit (the ka priests), the reciter (hery priests), and those who oversaw the embalming with prayers and spells (wt-priests).

An engraved boat covered with rich embroideries and mounted on a wooden sled made up the centerpiece of the procession, a physical symbol of the journey the dead person was about to make to the land of eternal life. Inside the boat was the coffin, and inside the coffin were two living women kneeling, playing the role of Isis and Nephthys, goddesses who protected and guided the dead as symbolized by their great wings spread over the mummy in pictures. Finally, behind the coffin came the family, friends, and official representatives of the state, if the deceased was an important person. During the procession, incense was burned, and music might be played.

The whole procession marched toward the Nile, entered into boats, and headed for the cemetery, which was always located on the western side of the river, opposite the side of civilization and life. Chants relating to the journey to the West (i.e., the Underworld) were sung during the passage, and the funeral procession formed once more upon disembarking. At the cemetery musicians might play a dirge while muu dancers performed their solemn act. The sem priest performed a most important ritual at the mouth of the tomb: the "opening of the mouth." Standing in for Horus as well

In this painting from a sarcophagus, Anubis prepares the body of a king. Courtesy of Anne Ronan Picture Library.

as for the deceased's own son, the sem priest watched as the mummy was unloaded from its funeral boat and placed upright, awaiting its quickening. Amid incantations, the priest twice touched the mummy's face with an adze and once with a forked flint rod, repeating his actions on the ka statue, the "reserve body" of the tomb. After the "opening of the mouth," the deceased was once again able to see, hear, eat, and function in the physical world. One of the oxen that pulled the sled carrying the body was ceremoniously slaughtered, and its right foreleg, containing the virility of the animal, was presented to the mouth of the mummy, empowering it with the life energy of the sacrifice.

Finally, it was time to say goodbye to the deceased for good. The widow and family members uttered their (possibly standardized) prayers and farewells, libations were poured, incensed was burned near the mummy for the last time, and at last it was replaced within its nest of coffins and lowered into its tomb, usually a pit grave many meters below the earth; of course, for the pharaoh and the very wealthy, mastabas (large stepped tombs) were more in order. The set of coffins was placed within the sarcophagus, accompanied by the internal organs in canopic jars and the servants' shabtis and surrounded by the tomb furniture and afterlife provisions. Some of the grave goods were ritually "killed" by breaking them so that they might immediately accompany the deceased. Final prayers were offered while the grave shaft was filled with rocks, and then a mason came with mortar and sealed up the tomb for good.

While the mason was doing this job, the funeral party sat down to their final supper, a feast held in honor of the dead in some shade near the tomb. A Theban tomb records a song that was sung on such an occasion:

Bodies pass away since the time of the god and young men come in their place. Re shows himself at dawn, Atum goes to rest in the Western mountain; men beget, women conceive. Every nose breathes the air. Dawn comes, their children are all gone to their tombs. (Hamilton-Paterson and Andrews)

Of course, poorer Egyptians could not afford such an elaborate funeral, but the attempt was made. The mummy would have been of poorer quality, perhaps just wrapped in linen; the coffin of one layer only, made of lower-quality wood; sans furniture and mounds of food, the dead would have gone to their grave with just a few amulets and the tools of their trade. The poor often could not afford even a regular tomb, the grave being only a deep pit wherein many were buried one atop the other with just a layer of dirt in between. But the hope was the same—eternal life in the land of death, joined by the ancestors and the gods of the starry heavens.

See also BOOK OF THE DEAD, EGYPTIAN; MASTABA; MUMMIFICATION; PIT GRAVES, EARLY EGYPTIAN; PYRAMID, EGYPTIAN; SHABTI.

References

Garstang, J. *Burial Customs of Ancient Egypt*. London: A. Constable, 1907.

Hamilton-Paterson, James, and Carol Andrews. *Mummies: Death and Life in Ancient Egypt*. London: Williams Collins Sons, 1978.

Kristensen, W. Brede. *Life Out of Death: Studies in the Religions of Egypt and of Ancient Greece*. Louvain, Belgium: Peeters Press, 1992.

Leca, Ange-Pierre. *The Egyptian Way of Death*. Trans. Louise Asmal. Garden, NY: Doubleday, 1981.

Spencer, A. J. *Death in Ancient Egypt*. New York: Penguin, 1982.

Winlock, H. E. *The Rise and Fall of the Middle Kingdom in Thebes*. New York: Macmillan, 1947.

FUNERARY CUSTOMS, ANCIENT GREEK

Ancient Greek funerals had three primary stages. First came prothesis, or the preparation and laying out of the corpse, which lasted for a day. It was the women's duty to gather at the house of the deceased, wash the body, lay a wreath around the head, and lay the corpse out for viewing. It was also the duty of women to wail for the passing of the deceased, and frequently this task was performed by women hired for the occasion if the family was one of means—women of Caria were famed for their keening. The wailing was accompanied by tearing one's hair, beating one's breasts, and scratching one's cheeks, reminiscent of the Central Asian practice of lacerating the arms and face. At this time the home hearth was put out, to remain unlit for the duration of the mourning period.

The second part of the funeral was the ekphora, or the procession that accompanied the body to the grave. Only on rare occasions were the dead to be buried within the confines of the city—great heroes or political leaders were sometimes buried in the marketplace or in council chambers. However, the pollution associated with death made it imperative that in the vast majority of cases the resting place of the dead was to be clearly set apart from the dwellings of the living. Well-off families hired a funeral wagon, whereas poorer families carried the corpse by hand on a funeral bier, following the roads leading out of the city—thus graves multiplied by the roadside over time. Like the prothesis, the procession was again accompanied by wailing and loud lamentation.

At the gravesite the corpse was either buried or cremated. If it was to be cremated, the funeral pyre was built quite near the gravesite, and it was the duty of the son or nearest relative to gather up the bones afterwards, place them in an urn, and bury the urn properly. In remote times—the Minoan-Mycenaean Bronze Age—tomb burial seems to have been the norm, in great tholoi, or circular stone buildings where entire clans were buried together. However, Greek culture experienced a marked shift in the twelfth century B.C.E. to single burials and cremation, with cremation becoming the dominant mode of disposing of the dead. The grave was marked with a stone stela, called a *sema* or "sign," which was often highly elaborated artistically and seems to have stood for the dead in some sense. At the annual festival of the dead, these stones are washed and anointed and decorated with garlands of flowers and wreaths.

The third part of the funeral involved sacrifices (whether buried with the dead or burned in the pyre) and a funerary banquet. In earliest times burials involved the entombment not only of the corpse but of prodigious wealth as well. As in Central Asian kurgans, the esteemed Greek dead were buried with massive amounts of gold jewelry, equipment, and animals, and a great amount of ash suggests that large animal sacrifices were performed in fiery ceremonies. In later periods sacrifices were still crucial parts of the funeral; earthen vessels containing food and drink are always found with the dead, along with weapons, jewelry, clothing, furniture, and gifts from the mourners. A portion of these gifts were usually burned on the funeral pyre but were thought to go with the dead nonetheless. There were also animal sacrifices and sometimes even human sacrifices: some Greek graves show that a man's servants and wife were slaughtered, and in the *Iliad* Achilles sacrifices twelve Trojan youths from noble families at the funeral of Patroklos, not to mention oxen, sheep, goats, and pigs. The animal sacrifices, whether at the gravesite or later at the funeral banquet, were not only thought to somehow benefit the dead with food and honor but also to mark the grief and loss of the community.

Libations were always poured out for the dead, whether of wine, water, honey, or oil, and occasionally graves are found with pipes in the ground so that libations can be poured directly on the corpse. Libations of water were said to bathe the dead, and others were thought to assuage the terrible thirst that the dead were thought to suffer in Hades. While the liquid was soaking into the earth, a kind of direct contact with the dead was made, and prayers were thought to be most efficacious at that time.

In early times it appears that the funeral banquet (perideipnon) was held directly at the gravesite, but later this feast for the dead was held at home. Three days and nine days after the death, relatives again visit the grave and make food offerings, and after thirty days another feast is held at home to mark the end of the mourning period. Thereafter the dead are remembered with offerings and libations in the annual festival called *nekysia*, or "days of the dead."

There was also the custom of holding funeral games and festivities, called *agones*, after the funeral, especially if the deceased was an important person. Athletes performed, chariots were raced, and poetry was read. By the sixth century B.C.E., these funeral games became more formalized as city or Panhellenic festivals, held in honor of the death anniversaries of local heroes.

During the thirty-day mourning period, the relatives were considered impure and showed outward signs of this inner state—they wore torn or filthy clothes, refrained from bathing, and rubbed ashes or dirt into their hair. Until the end of the mourning period, the family were thus excluded from normal life, and anyone who visited them likewise became impure and had to be purified after leaving by sprinkling themselves with water. At the end of the proscribed period, the family and house had to be purified as well: the family by a bath with water poured over the head and the house by being sprayed with seawater, smeared with earth, and then thoroughly swept out. The home hearth was then relit, usually from the community fire, which burned eternally.

See also ANCESTOR VENERATION; EIDOLON.

References

Alexious, Margaret. *The Ritual Lament in Greek Tradition.* Cambridge: Cambridge University Press, 1974.

Burkert, Walter. *Greek Religion.* Trans. John Raffan. Cambridge; Harvard University Press, 1985.

Humphreys, Sally C., and Helen King, eds. *Mortality and Immortality: The Anthropology and Archeology of Death.* Proceedings of a meeting of the Research Seminar in Archaeology and Related Subjects, London, 1982.

Kurtz, Donna, and John Boardman. *Greek Burial Customs.* Ithaca, NY: Cornell University Press, 1971.

Nilsson, Martin P. *Greek Popular Religion.* New York: Columbia University Press, 1940.

Nock, Arthur. "Cremation and Burial in the Roman Empire." In *Essays on Religion and the Ancient World,* ed. Zeph Stewart. 2 vols. Cambridge: Harvard University Press, 1972.

FUNERARY CUSTOMS, ANCIENT INDIAN

Compared to other cultures, India has an amazing variety of funerary practices, ranging from humble pit and cist graves to huge megaliths to cremation and postcremation burial, all dating from a very early period. For burials from the most ancient times there is no written or pictorial evidence, only the remains discovered by archaeology. From about 2000 B.C.E. the earliest Scriptures, the Vedas, also help shed light on early funerary practices and afterlife beliefs, and this information is supplemented by archaeological work. In later times, Hindu texts such those prescribing the rituals of life, like the Gṛhya Sūtras and the āraṇyaka section of the Krishna-Yajurveda, along with philosophical texts like the Upaniṣads and Purāṇas, demonstrate the massive complexity and change over time that characterizes Indian thinking about death.

The earliest burial sites found in India so far are inhumation graves, with the bodies mostly laid out in extended fashion and a few bodies in a crouched or fetal position. These sites appear to belong to the so-called Late Stone Age in India, roughly the fourth to third millennium B.C.E. Some of the sites show that the dead were buried within the dwellings of the living, whereas others have a demarcated cemetery. These earliest known sites are important for a number of reasons, one being that there is little or no evidence of cremation at this time, which would eventually become the nearly exclusive means of disposing of the dead in India in later times. Also important is that many of the Late Stone Age and Neolithic burials clearly orient the buried bodies to the cardinal directions. A great number of these graves run north to south, with the head of the skeleton pointing north. Again, many of the burials are oriented east to west, with the head pointing east, sometimes west. Although some early burials are exceptions to the rule, the archaeological evidence is clear enough to suggest to scholars that even at this early period, the many diverse cultures living in India may have had afterlife beliefs or "myths of human origin," which caused them to orient the bodies toward the direction where the soul was supposed to go after death. It appears to be no accident that a great many of the graves arrange the head pointing east or west, the directions of the rising and setting sun (for example, the sites at Langhnaj, Lekhahia, and Burzahom). Another important fact is that most of the early sites treat the deaths of infants and children differently, usually placing the corpse in a fetal position in a clay urn that was then buried—suggesting a process of "rewombing," perhaps in expectation of rebirth.

From a slightly later period, called the Chalcolithic (literally "using stone and bone tools"; it dates from 2500 B.C.E. to 1500 B.C.E. in India), there is widespread evidence of cremation, often accompanied by secondary burial of the cremains in pots or urns. This is most noticeable at Baluchistan in the extreme northwest of the Indian subcontinent. Here, possibly under the influence of regular contact with Iranian, Central Asian, and Mesopotamian cultures, a diversity of burial methods were practiced, emphasizing cremation but also including extended inhumation, fractional inhumation, and crouched inhumation. A great diversity of grave goods are discovered with the bodily remains, including gray ware pottery with painted designs, mirrors, decorated hairpins, gems, fragments of glass, copper, and stone tools. Clearly, burials were important ceremonial occasions, but without literary evidence, one may only speculate on the nature of the religion held by these communities.

Beginning from 1000 to 800 B.C.E., according to current scholarly estimations, megalithic tombs were built separately in southern and northern India. The southern megaliths are the most widespread and numerous. They appear to have been the very center of community life, for great tanks of water, presumably for gardens, were built around them, and the discovery of a wide variety of iron and copper-bronze tools, including horse-bits, suggest widespread agriculture centered around the tombs. These megaliths were large and made of heavy stone that was well-chiseled, suggesting large numbers of skilled workers and an organized community to support them. The burials underneath them were of a great architectural variety, including shallow and deep pit burials, passage graves, cist graves, and even multichambered caves, but the bodies beneath were mostly inhumed, not cremated. Frequently, no human remains are found at all, suggesting a religious or magical but not a funerary purpose for the megaliths. Besides metal tools, the tombs contain the characteristic black-and-red ware pottery of all shapes and sizes and objects made from shell, stone, terracotta, gold, and silver.

To this extent can archaeology illuminate India's ancient past. Some scholars see a progression in culture from inhumation to secondary burial of cremains to pure cremation without secondary burial, but the evidence is very scanty and uncertain. It is known for certain that different groups coexisted side by side, and it is very difficult to show whether changes in burial practice are due to changes in the cultural group or to the settlement of new peoples. What is certain is that by the time there is written evidence for ancient India, inhumation burials had nearly completely died out. It may be that those groups practicing inhumation gradually perished, emigrated out of India, or eventually adopted cremation.

References

Bhattacharya, Narendra Nath. *Ancient Indian Rituals and Their Social Contents*. Delhi: Manohar, 1975.

Gupta, S. P. *Disposal of the Dead and Physical Types in Ancient India*. Delhi: Oriental Publishers, 1972.

Shastri, Dakshina Ranjan. *Origin and Development of the Rituals of Ancestor Worship in India*. Calcutta: Bookland, 1963.

Singh, Purushottam. *Burial Practices in Ancient India*. India: Prithivi Prakashan, 1970.

FUNERARY CUSTOMS, ANCIENT ROMAN

The Roman world had several kinds of funeral rites (in Latin, funus) that varied according to the deceased's social rank and services to the state. Ordinary citizens received one kind of funeral (funus translaticum), soldiers another (funus militare), and those who had rendered extraordinary service to Rome yet another (funus publicum). Finally, emperors and their families received the most lavish funerals of all (funus imperatorium). Romans placed a great deal of importance on a proper funeral, both to guarantee a pleasant afterlife for the departed and to maintain family standing in public. Eventually Rome enacted laws that restricted the pomp and expenditures of private funerals.

The person responsible for carrying out the funus was the person designated by will; failing that, the person designated by the deceased's friends; and if none was chosen, the head of the family (or heir, if the deceased was the head of the family). If family were gathered around the body at the moment of death, as was often the case, the nearest relative gave a kiss (witness Anna kissing Dido in the *Aeneid* IV:684–685) to catch the last breath and help free the soul. The eyes were closed, and everyone began the lamentation and called on the deceased by name, which continued at intervals until burial. The body was washed, anointed, and dressed; a wreath was placed on the head, indicating honor; and a coin was placed in the mouth to pay the toll for the ferry of Charon in the Underworld. (This latter practice is found not only in the Mediterranean world but as far west as the Roman settlements in Britain and eastward at least as far as Nabataea, southeast of Palestine.) Then the body was laid upon a funerary bed (lectus funebris) for viewing, which could last from one to seven days.

When it was time to cremate or inhume the body, it was placed upon a cheap bier (for those of small means) or a flamboyant palanquin (for the wealthy) carried by four to eight male relatives or friends, and the funerary procession (pompa) made its way to the body's final resting place. For those who could afford it, musicians and professional mourners were hired—a holdover from Etruscan times.

For the upper classes, portraits in the form of funeral masks were made of the deceased and kept in public view for a time after the body was buried. After a time, the portrait (imago) was returned to the family and placed in the family collection. Interestingly, during the funeral procession, those relatives and friends who most resembled the ancestors of the deceased wore the masks: this practice symbolized the accompaniment by all one's ancestors even as one journeyed to meet them in the afterworld. Toward the end of the Republic period (c. 30 B.C.E.) the funeral masks were sometimes replaced with funerary busts, probably fashioned of wax or terracotta, set around the funerary bed and carried behind the body in procession.

In the most ancient period, burials were performed at night under torchlight, but during most of Roman history all burials (except those of children and the poor) took place by day, though the torches were retained as a ritual element. In any case, all burials had to be outside the city walls because of both sanitation and death pollution, although there were exceptions for emperors and other extraordinary persons. Thus the roads leading to the entrances of all Roman cities were lined with tombs, columbaria, and cemeteries of every sort. At the place of cremation or inhumation a little earth was thrown on the body as a symbolic gesture, and in a cremation a small part of the body was cut off for subsequent burial. Cremation was favored in the ancient Roman world, even among the patrician (upper) classes, although the disposal of the body was a family affair, and many well-known families preferred inhumation.

Cremations took place both in special locations specifically designated as such (ustrina or ustrinum) or at the place where the ashes were to be interred. A rectangular pyre of wood was constructed and mixed with papyrus for easier burning, and the corpse along with its funeral couch was placed within with eyes opened. Gifts and personal possessions were placed within the pyre and even favorite pets were killed, ostensibly for the purpose of accompanying the deceased in his or her journey to the afterworld. The actual burning was normally performed by professionals, called *ustores*. The ashes were drenched with wine and were then gathered into special receptacles (vases, urns, variously shaped chests) and placed in niches in their final locale—columbaria (repositories for ashes) or house and chamber tombs—or simply buried under tumuli (burial mounds) or gravestones.

For inhumation, the actual digging was done by professional gravediggers, called *fossores*. The poor were placed in shallow trench graves (fossae) without coffins, fully extended or in fetal position, and half of an amphora jug was placed over the grave as a marker through which libations could be poured. The bodies of the very poor were tossed into deep pits called *puticuli,* which served as common graves. However, during the Imperial period the bodies of Jews and Christians were placed in loculi tombs in catacombs or hypogea (underground mausolea). The wealthy had elaborate marble

sarcophagi for burial, whereas the less well off were placed in simpler sarcophagi of stone, terracotta, lead, or wood. Sometimes gypsum was poured over the body, forming a mummylike cast of the body. Then a pig was sacrificed, as required by Roman law, in order to make the grave "official."

Ancient Romans ate a funeral meal (silicernium) with the deceased at the place of burial on the day of interment and again on the ninth day after burial, when a libation to the spirit (manes) of the deceased was poured. During these feasts a share was set apart for the dead, and it was customary to leave behind food afterward for the sustenance of the dead, though it is reported that these were frequently stolen and eaten by the hungry. Even after the official period of mourning was over, funerary meals were regularly eaten at the tombs of the deceased, namely on their birthdays and when the annual festivals of the dead (Parentalia or dies Parentales) were celebrated on 13–21 February. It was deemed quite important to provide food for the deceased as attested by hundreds and thousands of funerary inscriptions, and wills set aside a certain sum of money whose interest was to provide regular offerings (food, drink, incense, and flowers). Roses in particular were frequent offerings and were also carved on the vaults and walls of tombs, seeming to indicate the eternal spring of the life after death. Often the dead, whether inhumed or cremated, were provided with eating and drinking vessels in their tombs, and many tombs have been found with lead pipes leading from the surface directly to the remains of the deceased so that they could receive libations. After returning from the funeral, the family had to undergo purification via fire and water (suffitio) and begin a nine-day period of cleansing ceremonies at the home of the deceased, after which time they were free to mingle with society again.

Those killed on the battlefield were collectively buried or cremated, with funeral expenses paid for by their comrades, a special tax being set aside for this purpose. However, the funerals of those who had rendered the state special services (funus publicum) were paid for by the state treasury. These funerals included special honors such as a dirge; a speech praising the deceased's virtues (panegyric); and a funeral procession of senators, magistrates, vestal virgins, musicians, and crowds of soldiers and citizens.

However, most public funerals were reserved for emperors and members of their families. The imperial funeral (funus imperatorium) was, of course, magnificent. The courts were closed (iustitium) while the body (or more often a wax simulacrum), dressed in gold and purple, lay in state for many days on an ivory and gold couch, surrounded by the highest government officials. The funeral procession included all senators and knights with their wives, the praetorian guard, and all citizens who were in Rome. Most emperors whose funerals are recorded had massive cremations in four-, five-, or six-storey funeral pyres, with a chamber at each storey filled with spices, incense, fruits, herbs, and juices and hung with gold, statues of ivory, and elaborate paintings. The cavalry paraded around the pyre while chariots drew around it, containing people in royal purple garments wearing masks of past Roman generals and emperors. The new emperor lit the funeral pyre, and from the topmost storey of the pyre an eagle was released, carrying the emperor's soul upward to the gods.

See also AMPHORA; CATACOMB; CREMATION; FOSSORES; FUNERARY CUSTOMS, ETRUSCAN; HYPOGEUM; LOCULUS TOMB; URN.

References

Cumont, F. V. M. *After Life in Roman Paganism*. New York: Yale University Press 1922.

Hopkins, Keith. *Death and Renewal*. Cambridge: Cambridge University Press, 1983.

Lattimore, Richmond A. *Themes in Greek and Latin Epitaphs*. Urbana: University of Illinois Press, 1942.

Nock, Arthur D. "Cremation and Burial in the Roman Empire." In *Essays on Religion and the Ancient World*, ed. Zeph Stewart. 2 vols. Cambridge: Harvard University Press, 1972.

Stevenson, James. *The Catacombs: Life and Death in Early Christianity*. London: Thames and Hudson, 1978.

Toynbee, J. M. C. *Death and Burial in the Roman World*. Ithaca, NY: Cornell University Press, 1971.

Walker, Susan. *Memorials to the Roman Dead*. London: British Museum Publications, 1985.

FUNERARY CUSTOMS, ARCTIC EURASIAN

The Arctic peoples who inhabit areas from Norway to eastern Siberia carry on a nomadic or seminomadic lifestyle. Roughly west to east across Eurasia, these peoples include the Lapps, Voguls, Ostjaks, Mordvins, Cheremis, Votyak, Ziryene, Samoyeds, Tungus, Lamuts, Yakuts, Yukaghir, Chukchee, Koryaks, Kamchadals, Gilyaks, Kalmuts, and Buryats and even the aboriginal Japanese Ainu. Although these peoples have quite different languages and societies, because of a common geography, lifestyle, and history, their burial traditions and religious beliefs show some marked similarities.

Most Arctic peoples conceive of two souls, though they are sometimes confused and trade functions. The "shadow soul" (ört among the Cheremis, uvi-rit among the Chukchee, sunjesun among the Buryat, wuyil-wuyil among the Koryak, tös among the Yurak-Samoyed, etc.) may leave the body during sleep or unconsciousness and often takes various shapes such as a bee or a butterfly. The "breath soul" (lul, lol, and lil among the Votyak, Ziryene, and Ostjak, respectively; tetkeyun among the Chukchee; amin among the Buryat, wuyuvi among the Koryak, etc.) is the principle of life among both humans and animals, and it is closely connected with the skeleton, vital organs, and blood. Sometimes the life energy in the bones, blood, or vital organs is thought to be able to regenerate the life that has been lost. For this reason, among the Arctic peoples the skeletons of the dead, both animals and humans, are treated with great care, for the new life in the next world (and sometimes the reincarnated life in this world) depends upon proper handling of the bones left behind. Likewise, according to the legends of the heroes, it was a common custom to eat the hearts and livers of the enemies they had slain. In this way their enemies' resurrection was prevented. This idea of resurrection certainly was strengthened after the arrival of Christianity in the thirteenth to sixteenth centuries but cannot be reduced to Christian influence. From very early times children were given the names of deceased ancestors because of the belief that the dead were literally reborn in them. With the coming of Christianity to the northern peoples, reincarnation beliefs were sometimes watered down to the idea that only the "guardian spirit" of the deceased relative came to the newborn child.

When the "breath soul" leaves the body through the mouth or nostrils at the moment of death, the death process has only begun. Though the eyes are shut and covered with coins or buttons and the mouth and nostrils are generally sealed (probably to prevent the breath soul from returning and creating a vampiric condition), the shadow soul is thought to remain near the body for several days, at least three, and this liminal period is a dangerous one because the dead are very much still present and aware. A vigil fire is kept burning in the room where death occurred, serving many purposes. It is said to honor the dead, to keep away evil spirits (who presumably are from the *dark* Underworld), and to serve as a spiritual sign corresponding to the departing spirit. To prevent the soul from returning to the dwellings of the living, the corpse is removed in atypical ways, for example, through a breach in the tent wall, a window, or a hole made in a wall that is later patched up. Food offerings are usually made, but no work should take place other than that associated with funeral preparations. The third day after death is generally reserved for a funeral feast, although those Arctic peoples affected by Russian Orthodox practice generally have moved the feast to three days after the funeral, which in turn comes three days after death. At the feast, great quantities of meat and gin are consumed (if the family can afford it), along with tea and bread. This is then followed by memorials of various sorts on the seventh, twentieth, and fortieth days after death.

Often images of the deceased in the form of wooden images or specially made dolls are kept and treated as if they were the deceased themselves for a period of time after death (generally six months to four years, or until replaced by a more recently deceased relative). They are set in positions of honor and given food offerings; sometimes the wives of the deceased sleep with them in their beds, and they are taken on family journeys. The images are thought to protect against illness and often can express the will of the deceased, which can be discovered by a shaman. Among the Ostjak in particular, their family image (called *tonh*) was treated with great respect and became central to the family's religion. They are thrown out after the requisite time has elapsed, however, unless they represent particularly important dead, like heroes, chiefs, shamans, or important heads of families. In such cases they are kept for generations.

A great variety of funeral goods are placed in the graves intended for use in the Otherworld: weapons, fire-making implements, tools, clothing, eating utensils, sugar, meat, and tobacco. Not only will the dead need their possessions in the hereafter, but the living wish to avoid the death pollution of using the goods of the dead, lest more death should follow. The Lapps bury with the dead the clothes they wore at death but allow themselves to use their other clothing, but some other Arctic people go to greater lengths: the Mordvins place absolutely everything the dead owned in a heap on the grave. Among all the Arctic peoples, however, the funeral goods are generally broken in some way, either to "kill" the goods like their owner so that he or she may receive them or perhaps to more effectively sever the ties between the living and the dead, for the return of the dead or their influence is definitely to be avoided. Therefore, the tools used to dig the grave are left on top or nearby with their blades dulled or their handles broken. Likewise, pots and coins have holes drilled into them; clothing is ritually torn in areas; the runners of the funeral sledge are broken; or the bottom of a boat broken in. A tradition reported among the Finns, which may well speak for other Arctic people, was that when placing the funeral goods in the grave, one is to say to the deceased: "This shall you receive but nothing more" (Storå, p. 182). The import is clear: take your possessions and go to where you belong; leave the living alone. It is clear, however, that the dead are not cut off from all relations with the living but only improper ones. This Cheremis prayer indicates regular visits from the dead: "Farewell (so-and-so). May a light, happy, good and warm life be vouchsafed to you. Do not go away from us forever, but come to us and tell us in dreams how happy and good your life is in the other world" (Pettersson).

In many cases, the grave was seen as a cradle and was decorated as such, presumably because death was a "rebirth" into the next world or even again into this one. The Voguls, for example, place a bed of moss and elk hair in the coffin in which the dead person is laid, just as is done for a newborn child. That death was seen as a journey of some sort is abundantly clear: many dead have been found with reins in their hands, and other burials have been in boats, which resembles ancient Scandinavian custom. Burial places favored by Arctic peoples include secluded forests, hills, river mouths, islets, and mountain gullies. Quite often burial was accompanied by animal sacrifice, including the reindeer that pulled the funeral sled, horses, and even dogs. In recent times it has been thought too costly to sacrifice expensive animals like reindeer, and the principle of substitution can be seen in the carved wooden reindeer figures often placed in graves. Because much of the year the Arctic ground is frozen solid, and advanced tools are not available to dig deeply into the earth, surface or aboveground burials are often practiced. Sometimes these burials are temporary, and in the season when inhumation is possible bodies will be reburied (as in Russia, where in old times bodies were stored in a bohsedom in the outer parts of town until spring arrived). In northern Siberia, corpses are laid on the ground and covered with stones. Among the Samoyeds, Ostjaks, Voguls, and Mordvins, corpses are placed on the ground with rough wooden shelters or "boxes" placed over them, which are covered with snow in the winter and with moss and twigs in the summer. Among the ancient Lapps, surface burials or shallow graves appear to have been the norm until the arrival of Christianity with its prohibitions.

Burial above the ground (aerial sepulture) is also practiced, especially for shamans and other revered dead. A special raised platform might be constructed of wood to allow the body to be exposed to the elements but free from predators until it was ready for secondary burial; this is particularly common in northern Siberia and among the Voguls, Ostjaks, and Samoyeds. Tree burial serves the same purpose, placing the body with or without coffin high in a tree away from bears and wolverines. However, since the arrival of Christianity, inhumation has become popular as well.

Another important but much less frequently mentioned burial custom in the Arctic is the special reverence held for the bear and the practically human burials given bears killed by humans. Among these nomads, bears are thought to have human souls, to have been humans in the past, or at least to have the intelligence of a human. During a feast of freshly killed bear meat, a flap of the tent is left open so that the bear might join in. Likewise, the body of the bear is treated like a human body, with eyes covered as described earlier. Among the Siberians the remains of the body are most often placed on a raised platform as if the animal were an honored dead, and most often among the western peoples (Finns, Lapps, and Samoyeds) the bear is given a careful burial, although the skull may be placed in a tree. Future bears are thought to spring from the bones of the dead (probably not literally but in an occult sense: the life energy in the bones resurrects into a new body). In several human graves, metal figures resembling bears have been found, and it is obvious how important the bear is to the survival of the Arctic people.

See also FUNERARY CUSTOMS, LAPP.

References

Batchelor, J. *The Ainu and Their Folk-lore.* London: Religious Tract Society, 1901.

Christiansen, Reidar Th. *Ecstasy and Arctic Religion.* Studia Septentrionalia no. 4. Oslo: O. Norli, 1953.

Pettersson, Olof. *Jabmek and Jabmeaimo: A Comparative Study of the Dead and the Realm of the Dead in Lappish Religion.* Lund: C. W. K. Gleerup, 1957.

Storå, Nils. *Burial Customs of the Skolt Lapps.* FF Communications No. 210. Helsinki: Suomalainen Tiedeakatemia, 1971.

FUNERARY CUSTOMS, CELTIC

The Celts were a large and militarily successful people of central and western Europe. They are well known in history for their harassment of the Romans and other established groups, their fury in battle, and their spiritual leaders (Druids) whose religion was nature-based and taught doctrines like reincarnation. First entering recorded history in central Europe, they sacked Rome and Delphi in the early centuries of the common era and were known to Paul as the Galatians. They settled widely from Greece and Italy to Spain and the British Isles. Particularly in Ireland and Wales, Celtic traditions lasted the longest, for they were furthest from the reach of Roman and later Christian influences that were to dominate Europe and wipe out much of the preexisting "pagan" beliefs and practices.

It is difficult to know Celtic funerary practices and beliefs with certainty because the various branches of the Celts have for so many centuries been assimilated into other cultures, and their written records come down to us only after centuries of Christian influence and redaction. However, there are several sources of information about ancient Celtic ideas and customs, including Roman observations of Celts around the time of Christ, as well as the heroic legends and myths in the oral (and, much later, written) traditions of Britain, Scotland, Ireland, and Wales. In addition, there is the method of comparing what we suspect of ancient Celtic practice with better recorded traditions from northern Europe. In many cases, since they are distantly related peoples, the Scandinavian and Germanic tales and customs shed light on ambiguous Celtic references.

There is some evidence that Celtic peoples, like many other ancient Indo-European groups, cremated their dead. Caesar wrote in the first century B.C.E. of the Celts of Gaul (modern France and Spain):

Selections from "Cad Goddeu," a Welsh Piece Ascribed to the Poet-Sage Taliesin

I was in many shapes before I was released:
I was a slender, enchanted sword . . .
I was in rain-drops in the air, I was stars' beam;
I was a word in letters, I was a book in origin;
I was lanterns of light for a year and a half;
I was a bridge that stretched over sixty estuaries;
I was a path, I was an eagle, I was a coracle in seas;
I was a bubble in beer, I was a drop in a shower;
I was a sword in hand, I was a shield in battle.
I was a string in a harp enchanted nine years, in the water as foam;
I was a spark in fire, I was wood in a bonfire;
I am not one who does not sing; I have sung since I was small. . . .
The lord produced me when he was quite inflamed;
The magician of magicians created me before the world—
When I had existence, there was expanse to the world.
Fair bard! Our custom is profit; I can put in song what the tongue can utter. . . .
Peoples were made, re-made, and made again.
The brilliant one his name, the strong hand; like lightning he governed the host.
They scattered in sparks from the tame one on high.
I was a snake enchanted in a hill, I was a viper in a lake;
I was a star with a shaft; I was this hunting-shaft. . . .
I lived as a warrior before I was a man of letters; long have I not been a shepherd;
I wandered, I encircled, I slept in a hundred islands, I dwelt in a hundred forts.
Druids, wise one, prophecy to Arthur;
There is what is before, they perceive what has been.

Ford (1977, pp. 184–187).

Their funerals are magnificent and costly, considering their civilization; and all that they think was dear to them [the dead] when alive they put in the fire, even animals; and shortly before this generation the slaves and dependents that they were considered to have loved, were burned along with them in the regular performance of funeral rites. (Mac Bain, trans.)

Another extremely interesting comment comes from the Roman writer Mela Pomponius, who says the Druidic priests of the Celts taught the immortality of the soul and its rebirth in another world:

Reproduction of a warrior's grave found in Marne, France, fifth century B.C.E. Artifacts found in the grave include the skeleton of the warrior's charioteer, his war chariot, a decorated bronze helmet, his weapons, his feasting implements, and even joints of pork and beef. Courtesy of Musée des Antiquités Nationales, Paris.

Accordingly, they burn and bury along with the dead whatever was once useful to them when alive. Business accounts and debt claims used to be transferred to the next world, and some even willingly cast themselves on the funeral pyre of their relatives under the impressions that they would live with them hereafter.

Another Roman writer, Diodorus Siculus, adds that it was customary at funerals for people to write letters to *other* deceased friends and relatives and throw them on the cremation pyre—since the dead person was going to the Otherworld, he or she might as well take along a few letters addressed to others.

To some degree archaeology bears out the Roman observations, for burial mounds that have been excavated at Aulnay-aux-Planche (Marne, France), Yeavering (Northumberland, England), and Libenice (near Kolin, Czech Republic), among many others, have yielded several cremation burials over widely scattered time frames (eighth century B.C.E. to sixth century C.E.). It is clear from these sites that the dead were indeed cremated along with many precious belongings, including animals, and that the dead were buried in regular enclosures, probably ritual sites for festivals or services. However, there are other sites throughout Europe that are clearly Celtic by their artwork and objects but are inhumation burials with no sign of cremation—these

particularly in the British Isles. It is clear, then, that not all Celts practiced cremation, despite the Roman recordings. Indeed, an old Irish poem remembers the death of Mog-Neid, King of Munster, and his honorable inhumation (not cremation):

The grave of Mog-Neid is on Magh Tualaing
With his lance at his shoulder,
With his club, so rapid in action,
With his helmet, with his sword.

In fact, it has often been noted that in Celtic inhumation burials, dead warriors were placed facing the direction that was most vulnerable to attack—having the warrior physically intact and not cremated may have been thought by some to be more effective in warding off danger. Either different groups had different funeral practices from a very early date, or by the time Celtic groups settled in Britain and Ireland, they had given up cremation in favor of inhumation—particularly after the coming of Christianity.

One practice of the Celts argues against cremation, at least in some cases. Archaeology, Roman observations, and Irish legends all tell of the importance of the heads of those slain in battle. At the Celtic sanctuary of Entremont in southern France, dated to about the third century B.C.E., severed heads were carved on pillars and skulls were found throughout the area. Many of the pillars had niches and hooks from which to suspend the heads of enemy warriors. In the second century B.C.E. Posidonius (a Roman writer) recorded that the Celts severed the heads of their enemies and attached them around their horses' necks, riding into battle in triumph. The Celts were also known to have embalmed and carefully preserved the heads of important leaders of their enemies. It was certainly not just bloodlust that allowed the Celts to pursue head hunting, although that was probably part of it for the warrior. There was also the belief, as recorded in Irish legends, that severed heads still retained the personality and wisdom of the slain, and thus keeping and preserving the heads of the slain, particularly of the enemy, gained their power for yourself. One Welsh legend tells of the hero Bendigeidfran, who was slain by the Irish in a cataclysmic battle between clans. Bendigeidfran instructed his men to cut off his head and carry it with them for the next eighty years (heroes lived longer then). His head, Bendigeidfran said, would remain wholesome and continue to provide guidance to his troops, but after that time they were to plant it in a great mound near London, facing France, to ward off the danger that would one day come from that direction. Here the severed head is not a trophy of a slain enemy but a treasured relic of a wise leader, kept for its guidance and protective benefits.

From all that is known of Celtic custom, however, it is certain that neither the head nor the body of the deceased was thought to be that person after death. All accounts, both Roman and native, show that the Celts believed in a very productive and happy afterlife with a new body or the old body made whole and new again. Clearly, it is a very substantial afterlife that will allow the dead to take along their unpaid debts, their personal possessions, letters for dead friends, and even their friends themselves. Diodorus says: "Among them the doctrine of Pythagoras prevailed, that the souls of men were immortal, and after completing their term of existence they live again, the soul passing into another body." Although some scholars believe that the Celts believed in bodily rebirth on this Earth, others believe that the Celts looked forward to a rebirth in a blissful Otherworld. Indeed, both accounts may be true—many ancient peoples believed in an afterlife that was physical and pleasurable, followed after a time by rebirth back on earth (see excerpt from "Cad Goddeu").

In any case, Celtic expectations were not very much like the shadowy, insubstantial Underworld of the Greek Hades or Scandinavian Hel; rather the Celtic afterlife was exuberant, joyful, and intensely material. Appropriately, the Irish and Welsh have almost no "ghost" stories, in the modern sense of a misty specter haunting the living. The dead are certainly thought to return, particularly at Hallowe'en (in ancient times, this festival was called Samhain) but as full flesh and blood characters, though their bodies are somewhat different from those on earth in that they can become invisible. In numerous Celtic folktales, the dead arise in body from the grave, usually a sacred mound. If struck, they bleed, and they eat and make love along with the living. In a great many old stories the dead (particularly heroes) live on in their *síd,* or magical mounds, associating with the other deceased, fairies, and Tuatha Dé Danann, or spirits of ancient Ireland.

As with the Norse, among the Celts the burial mounds of great men, dead kings, or poets were sources of tremendous power. Often in ancient times living kings would be crowned on the burial mounds of their ancestors, and sometimes the burial mounds became gathering places for royal business, such as official meetings and seasonal festivals. Even today on the Isle of Man, the Manx Parliament still assembles on the burial mound of Tynwald Hill. Celtic stories also show the importance of the burial mound, for in many cases it is not only the home of a deceased ancestor or king but also a gateway to magical realms and is therefore useful for provoking adventures. In Ireland particularly, a great many tales tell of a hero (most prominently Finn) sitting or sleeping on a burial mound in the hope of receiving a nocturnal visit from people from the Otherworld or an answer in dreams to some vexing question.

Although Celtic sources place the entrance to the Otherworld in burial mounds, there is also a large body of tradition showing that the land of the dead is in fact over the western waters—and this is true regardless of exactly which western waters are indicated. On the coast of Brittany, France, on a cape that juts into the sea and points toward England, there is an old tradition that fishermen might sometimes be awakened from sleep to ferry the souls of the dead (who apparently cannot cross water) over the seas to "Brittia," the Otherworld. But in Ireland, the land of the dead is off the Atlantic coast, far to the west where the sun sets. It is there where various heroes like Bran travel, to the west where the Plains of Delight or the Land under Wave lie. Coupled with this tradition is the very ancient one of sunken cities such as lost Lyonesse—a tradition that can be found among almost every coastal people of Celtic descent. Whether the myth of Lyonesse is an actual remembrance of a lost land or merely the mythologization of tentative journeys over the vast ocean, one cannot say.

See also FAIRY MOUND.

References

Ford, Patrick K, trans. *The Mabinogi and Other Medieval Welsh Tales.* Berkeley: University of California Press, 1977.

Mac Bain, Alexander. *Celtic Mythology and Religion.* New York: Dutton, 1917.

MacCulloch, J. A. *The Religion of the Ancient Celts*. Edinburgh: Clark, 1911.

Ó hÓgáin, Dáithí. *Myth, Legend and Romance: An Encyclopaedia of the Irish Folk Tradition*. New York: Prentice Hall, 1991.

Rees, Alwyn, and Brinley Rees. *Celtic Heritage; Ancient Tradition in Ireland and Wales.*. London: Thames and Hudson, 1961.

FUNERARY CUSTOMS, CENTRAL ASIAN

Among the nomadic and seminomadic people of the Central Asian and Russian steppes, including the Scythians, Mongols, and Turks, similar funeral and burial customs were followed from at least the seventh century B.C.E. well into the medieval period (fourteenth to fifteenth centuries). Although commoners were buried in fairly ordinary graves, kings and chieftains were buried, usually along with their servants, horses, and even chariots, in roofed underground chambers, sometimes with great mounds called *kurgans* on top.

When the king died, his followers all cut their hair, cropped their ears, and slashed their arms, hands, foreheads, and noses. The king's body was embalmed, stuffed with incense and spices, and put on a wagon. From wherever the leader may have died, the body went on a kind of pilgrimage to visit all the tribes over which the leader ruled, and those people cut their hair and bodies in the same way as the king's followers. The king's body was then transported to the special location where the chieftains were buried. At the site of the burial, a deep grave was dug, often lined with spears. Into it was put the king's body, the bodies of his concubines and servants (who were killed for the occasion), and often cattle or horses, sometimes as many as fifty or a hundred. The grave was then sealed up, and usually a huge mound of earth was piled on top of it, forming an artificial hill topped by a mound of stones.

Among the Mongols in the period after Chinggis (Genghis) Khan, royal funerals and burials became particularly epic events. Many relatives were slain and buried with the khan, along with masses of horses and thousands of gold objects. According to Marco Polo, who recounted the burial of the Mongol leader Mangou Khan, more than 20,000 witnesses to the body as it went on pilgrimage to burial were also killed.

Among commoners the funeral customs were slightly more modest. The deceased was placed on a wagon and for forty days brought around to the nearest kin and friends. Those who hauled the (apparently embalmed) body were feasted by the relatives of the dead, who made sure to give a share to the corpse. Afterward, the deceased was buried, usually in a deep chamber-catacomb, pit grave, or undercut grave. Traces of some of these customs still survive among the Turks of Central Asia.

References

Jettmar, Karl. *The Art of the Steppes*. New York: Crown, 1967.

Kohl, Philip L. *Central Asia: Paleolithic Beginnings to the Iron Age*. Paris: Editions Recherche sur les Civilisations, 1984.

Minns, E. H. *Scythians and Greeks: A Survey of Ancient History and Archeology on the North Coast of the Euxine*. New York: Biblo and Tannen, 1965.

Sinor, Denis, ed. *The Cambridge History of Early Inner Asia*. New York: Cambridge University Press, 1990.

FUNERARY CUSTOMS, CHINESE

Because Chinese culture spans so vast a geographical region and stems from very ancient times, Chinese funerary customs are extremely complex today. Confucian, Taoist, Buddhist, shamanic, and localized customs have mixed, merged, and battled over centuries of interaction, with modern Communist ideology overlaying the whole, smothering some traditions and reifying others. Therefore what follows is an overview, taking some account of regional and cultural variations but on the whole trying to present a unified and systematic account while overlooking much of China's staggering diversity.

In general, death is an event much more accepted and incorporated into family life in China than it is in the West. Elderly persons begin to prepare for death as much in advance as possible. They move back to their native area if they moved away, devote themselves to religious pursuits, and even prepare their own coffin and burial clothes. When it becomes clear that an elderly relative is at death's door, the dying person is moved onto a special bed that is transferred to the main ceremonial room of the house. (This is done both because dying in the communal living area is very unlucky for the surviving family members and because the main ceremonial room is lined with the "soul tablets" of all the family ancestors—thus symbolizing that the dying person is about to join them.)

If possible, close family members gather for the last moments of a dying person, and after the last breath wailing and lamentation begin. The wailing of a daughter is thought to be particularly helpful in dismantling barriers that the dead may encounter as they begin the long journey through the many Underworld realms. Mourners abstain from personal adornment, neglect personal hygiene, and wear plain and somber clothing. If the death has occurred on an inauspicious "double death day" (a day on the calendar in which one death is likely to bring on another) special purification rites are enacted to prevent the spread of the death pollution. In any case, the home is considered impure, and precautions must be taken by all. The death is immediately announced to the outside world, as a family member must hang blue and white lanterns at the front door along with white strips of paper on the left side of the

the coffin, the best time to remove the coffin from the home, the best spot to bury the dead, and the best time to perform the burial, which may be anywhere from a few days to a few months from the moment of death. Finally, the diviner traditionally certifies death in writing so that when it comes time for the funeral procession, the family will be allowed by police to take the body outside the city limits to the cemetery.

As soon as it is practical, the body is prepared for placement in the coffin in a ritual called *hsiao-lien* (dressing the corpse). Water, heated for bathing, is used to wash the body. In Taiwan the body is washed thoroughly three times, whereas in parts of mainland China the auspicious number of washings is seven times in the front and eight times in the back. After bathing, the body is dressed in special new garments called "longevity" clothes, which are silk if the family is wealthy or otherwise plain cotton. Jade (associated with immortality), pearls, gold leaf, or coins are generally placed in the mouth of the dead and around his or her person, along with personal jewelry. The face is covered with a cloth or paper, and after socks and shoes have been placed on the feet, they are bound with colorful string—this last a symbolic measure to prevent the dead from moving around if it should happen to become possessed by evil spirits before burial. Then the body is replaced on its deathbed, shrouded and with a pillow under the head while the coffin is prepared. Meanwhile, a small table is placed against the head of the bed to serve as a personal altar for the dead while he or she lies in state. On the altar is placed a temporary "soul tablet" made of paper (to be replaced later by the real tablet) along with a lantern in the shape of a pagoda, which honors the spirit of the dead thought to hover nearby. For some time, family members will also offer food to the dead on this altar whenever a meal is served.

Pao-sang, or "formal notification," goes out as soon as possible to friends and relations, usually via notices printed on white paper or on yellow paper with a strip of blue, that not only announce the timing of funeral events to come but give a short biography of the dead, birth and death dates, and the names of surviving kin. Wealthy families tend to send out elaborate notices, including extended genealogical information, good deeds, real and invented honors, and so on. Families of means also hire a drummer to stand at the doorway to the home, announcing visitors who have come to mourn. Meanwhile, in less urbanized areas, a family member still notifies the local god(s) by proceeding to their temple or shrine and giving the news through loud lamentation, a ritual called *pao-miao*. Because the local god is responsible for one of the souls of the deceased (the number varies from three to ten, depending on period, region, and religion), this notification

gate (for a deceased male) or the right side of the gate (for a deceased female). White banners are also placed over the lucky red strips of paper (usually printed with auspicious phrases) that were hung outside the home at the previous New Year's festival. White is the color of mourning in East Asia, and bright colors, especially red, are considered joyful and auspicious—qualities that are not at all in keeping with the loss of a family member.

A professional "diviner" (an expert in astrology and feng-shui) is called in by the family as soon as possible to determine the timing of events. The diviner, after examination, tells the family at what time and in which direction the soul will leave the body—at which moment everyone should leave the corpse because witnessing this event is considered very inauspicious. The diviner also predicts the best time to place the body in enlists the deity to help the soul proceed on its way through what is universally perceived in China to be the gauntlet of afterlife trials and difficulties.

When the auspicious time has arrived, the deceased is placed in the coffin in a ritual called *ta-lien.* First the coffin is lined with silk (for the wealthy) along with ashes, lime, and copper coins. Family members lower the body into the coffin, which is then padded with quilts, pillows, and his or her clothing, to prevent the body from slipping around inside. Traditionally, coffins in China are large, made of four half-logs with square panels at each end; they can weigh upwards of 300 pounds. Coffins are generally painted black or black and red, varnished, and highly polished. The wife or eldest son of the deceased wipes the eyes of the dead with k'ai-kuang (cotton floss), and cakes and bread are placed in the coffin to keep off the vicious dogs that wait for the dead in the Underworld. At the right moment, chosen by the diviner beforehand, the coffin is sealed, accompanied by loud wailing and calling out to the dead.

Immediately after a series of complex rituals follows, called in northern China "third-day reception" (chieh-san) and elsewhere "calling back the souls of the dead" (ch'ao-tu wang-hun). In one ritual, Taoist priests hang pictures of the gods near the coffin and pray that the soul be admitted into the Western Paradise, while evil spirits are abjured. Meanwhile, some family members proceed again to the temple of the local deity to ask that the soul in the deity's keeping be returned to the coffin. At the same time, Buddhist monks perform a ritual called "doing the sevens" (tso-ch'i), a series of prayers and scriptural readings that are to be repeated every seven days for seven weeks. In these prayers, the monks cancel out any bad karma of the dead by "transferring the merit" from saints (bodhisattvas) and the monks themselves. The monks also instruct the dead in the Scriptures, which dispels ignorance and allows the deceased a better rebirth. Finally, there is a ritual offering of food, which unlike most offerings can be eaten by the living. Afterward, offerings made of paper are burned outside the home, often at a Buddhist temple. These include great wads of money (called "hell money"), along with paper homes (complete with paper servants, a reference to former human sacrifice among the wealthy), cars, clothes, and all manner of other desirable goods such as cameras or furniture. All this is expected to reach the dead in the Underworld and be used to bribe guards and officials there. (Even though the Taoist priests and Buddhist monks have just finished two separate rituals to ensure that the dead has a clean slate and good fortune, Chinese funerary customs are extremely thorough and attempt to close off all possible avenues of harm.)

For some time, the mourning family receives guests who have come to pay their respects. Visitors are expected to bring offerings to help with the funeral, including food, wine, hell-money, ceremonial objects (incense, candles, etc.) or just cash. All these are displayed in the courtyard outside the home and during the funeral procession. Visitors also pay their respects to the dead by bowing to the coffin while the family surrounds it in carefully ranked groupings, and visitors offer their condolences (k'ai-tiao) to the mourners.

Finally, when the day and time has arrived that the diviner has chosen for the burial, the coffin is taken to the cemetery by means of an elaborate procession (fa-yin or ch'u-pin). The way to the cemetery is lit by lanterns, presumably to ensure that the dead cannot get lost. The procession is lead by women carrying pictures of the deceased, along with musicians, banners, elegiac scrolls, and decorative parasols. Then comes the coffin, traditionally carried by four or even six pallbearers, though a truck is also used in modern times. Just in front of the coffin is an empty chair for the deceased to sit in and join in the procession—another measure to ensure that the dead comes along for the ride and does not remain behind to haunt the living or suffer alone. Trailing behind the pallbearers comes a long stream of mourners, led by the eldest son, each ceremonially dressed very precisely according to which of the twenty-nine grades of mourner he or she may be, including five lineal generations (down to great-great-grandchildren) and five lateral degrees (all the descendants of a common great-great-grandfather). Arthur P. Wolf writes about such processions:

> Seen from a distance, from the top of a building or one of the hills on which most graves are sited, the procession following a Chinese coffin is a colorful sight. The mourners wear long robelike gowns, some of rough dirty-brown sackcloth, others of gray flax or grass cloth, and still others of unbleached white linen or muslin; scattered among these are blue gowns, red gowns, and, on the rare occasion, a yellow gown. Female mourners cover their heads with a hood that almost hides the face and hangs down the back to the waist; men wear a hempen "helmet" over a short hood or one of two kinds of baglike hats of unbleached or dyed muslin. . . . A funeral procession of fifty mourners usually includes twenty or more different combinations of textiles and colors.

Arriving at last at the grave site that the diviner or geomancer picked out, the coffin is slowly lowered into the grave by family members, while music is played, priests chant, and mourners wail. (Burial, or tsang, is the traditional means of disposing of the dead in Chinese areas, though increasingly the Communist Party is encouraging cremation as a way to save land for agricultural use.) After burial, offerings are given to the deceased, including more paper spirit objects that are burned, and offerings are made to the spirit of the soil (hou-t'u) who watches over the land. Finally, an important ceremony takes place, the name of which may be loosely translated as "dotting the chu" and refers to the Chinese character *chu* that means "host" or "master" on the permanent soul tablet for the dead. The soul tablet has previously been prepared by the family for the deceased, but the final dot of the Chinese character is left out so that at the gravesite, the most learned or elevated acquaintance of the family may complete the tablet ritually. Using special vermilion ink, or even blood, the august scholar or dignitary uses a brush to fill in the dot in the character, signifying that the tablet is now the official residence of the soul of the deceased. This tablet will be taken back to the family home and placed in the main ceremonial hall to join all the other ancestors. (Meanwhile, other "souls" of the same deceased person dwell simultaneously in heaven and at the gravesite.) After the disposal of the dead, the procession must return home in the same order as setting out. At home a bonfire is made and all those in the procession must jump through the fire before crossing the threshold. In some places a little water is sprinkled over each person by the Taoist priests.

Mourners observe various restrictions depending on their degree of closeness to the deceased. Those who are in the first degree (closest to the dead) observe mourning customs for two to three years that are rather strict in form at first but gradually relax over time. The historian Chih-p'an (fl. 1258–1269) writes, "Confucius said, 'It is not till a child is three years old that it is allowed to emerge from the arms of its parents.' That is why children must reciprocate with the three-year mourning" (quoted in Teiser [1994], p. 26). Three years is also the time required, in Chinese belief, for all the souls of the deceased to settle into their final places, including the rebirth into another form of the "personal" soul. Observances include giving up all personal hygiene (including bathing, shaving, and hair cutting) for a week to a month and avoiding elegant food, colorful clothing, and joyful occasions and ceremonies.

Regular memorials for the dead are carried out by the family and clergy. For seven weeks after death, Buddhist monks continue to perform the "calling back the souls of the dead" (ch'ao-tu wang-hun) ceremony, and the family performs memorial services that gradually diminish in frequency (although the soul tablet is cared for daily, along with those of all other family ancestors). Three days after the burial, family members return to "round off the grave" (yuan-fen), at which time more earth is piled on the grave, final wailing and lamentation takes place, more offerings are given, and more paper objects and money are burned. Visits to the grave and offerings occur on the sixtieth and hundredth day after death and the anniversary of the death. In addition, rites are observed in the thirteenth month after death, called *hsiao-hsiang* (lesser auspiciousness), and the twenty-fifth month after death, called *ta-hsiang* (greater auspiciousness). Finally, the graves of all one's immediate ancestors are generally visited on New Year's Eve (on the Chinese calendar), and on the summer holiday called *ch'ing-ming,* or "auspicious spirits," which, depending on the year, occurs in the late spring or early summer.

See also SOUL, CHINESE; SOUL TABLET; TEN KINGS OF HELL; YEN-LO WANG.

References

Cormack, J. G. *Everyday Customs in China.* Edinburgh: Moray Press, 1935.

de Groot, J. J. M. *Religion in China.* New York: G. P. Putnam's Sons, 1912.

Habenstein, Robert W., and William M. Lamers. *Funeral Customs the World Over.* Milwaukee: Bulfin Printers, 1963.

Hsu, Francis L. K. *Under the Ancestors' Shadow.* New York: Columbia University Press, 1948.

Jochim, Christian. *Chinese Religions.* Prentice-Hall Series in World Religions. Ed. Robert S. Ellwood. Englewood Cliffs, NJ: Prentice-Hall, 1986.

Johnson, Elizabeth L. "Grieving for the Dead, Grieving for the Living: Funeral Laments of Hakka Women." In *Death Rituals in Late Imperial and Modern China,* ed. James L. Watson and Evelyn S. Rawski. Berkeley: University of California Press, 1988.

Naquin, Susan. "Funerals in North China: Uniformity and Variation." In *Death Rituals in Late Imperial and Modern China,* ed. James L. Watson and Evelyn S. Rawski. Berkeley: University of California Press, 1988.

Teiser, Stephen F. *The Ghost Festival in Medieval China.* Princeton: Princeton University Press, 1988.

———. *The Scripture on the Ten Kings and the Making of Purgatory in Medieval Chinese Buddhism.* Honolulu: University of Hawaii Press, 1994.

Thompson, Laurence. *The Chinese Way in Religion.* Encino, CA: Dickenson Press, 1973.

Watson, James L. "The Structure of Chinese Funerary Rites." In *Death Rituals in Late Imperial and Modern China,* ed. James L. Watson and Evelyn S. Rawski. Berkeley: University of California Press, 1988.

Welch, Holmes. *The Practice of Chinese Buddhism, 1900–1950.* Cambridge: Harvard University Press, 1967.

Wolf, Arthur P. "Chinese Kinship and Mourning Dress." In *Family and Kinship in Chinese Society,* ed. Maurice Freedman. Stanford: Stanford University Press, 1970.

FUNERARY CUSTOMS, CHRISTIAN

In their general structure, funerary rites in the major Christian traditions (Protestant, Roman Catholic, and Eastern Orthodox) do not differ very much, though local ethnic customs create some variety in minor aspects of the services. What does create bewildering funerary variety is the growing secularization of many

Dr. Syntax watching his wife's coffin being lowered into the grave, 1820. Courtesy of Anne Ronan Picture Library.

Christians, who to varying degrees are moving away from established tradition. For example, it is common for Christians today to engage the services of funeral homes rather than churches, read modern poems for the dead rather than Scripture, and cremate rather than bury the body—when the body is not given over entirely to medical science. Such trends from the nineteenth century, which have gained tremendous momentum in this century, make it difficult to say anything exact about how Christians in general observe funerary customs. Thus this entry discusses the elements of "traditional" Christian funerals, noting where possible differences between denominations. At the end, modern trends that are altering or replacing traditions among Christians will be considered.

In times past it was common for the family to hold a "wake," a gathering of friends and family in the home. Although the wake was largely social in function, it was also an ancient ritual designed to guard the body from evil influences night and day; the wake is observed today only by some Roman Catholics and by Orthodox Jews. At the beginning of the twenty-first century, it is much more common for the deceased to be removed from the home very quickly (if he or she is not already away from home, dying in a hospital or hospice). The local coroner or attending physician is called to complete an official certificate of death, and the body is soon transported to a morgue or funeral home. Thus, religious traditions play little part in the funerary customs of Christians today until the body has been handled by secular professionals, cosmetically altered, placed in a coffin, and made ready for transport to the funeral service.

Of course, there are as many distinct funeral services as there are Christian denominations. The Episcopal funeral service, as discussed by Joseph Bernardin (all quotations from funeral services in this entry come from his book), serves as a good example of most mainstream church services in that it falls between the "high church" funeral mass of Roman Catholicism and the "low church" simplicity of denominations such as the Baptist, Presbyterian, United Church of Christ, and Unitarian Universalist. In the Episcopal Church, as in most denominations, observant Christians have the funeral service with the covered body in the church, followed by a short committal service (usually held at the grave side when the body is actually interred). Sometimes a memorial service will follow days or weeks later, particularly for public figures.

Before the congregation arrives in the church the altar candles are lit—fire being an ancient symbol of spirit and, in the Christian case, a symbol of the presence of God. In very traditional ceremonies, the congregation sings an anthem while the casket is carried into the church and placed before the altar. The order of procession begins with the cross, held high on a staff, followed by the paschal candle (the Easter candle, symbolizing resurrection), the presiding minister, assisting ministers, the pallbearers and the coffin, and the mourners, if they choose to participate in the procession. However, in many churches the procession has been abandoned, and the casket is simply placed at the head of the church before the service begins. The casket is always closed and draped with a white or gold pall. If the dead was a clergy member, the casket usually has its head placed toward the altar; if a layperson, the head is placed toward the congregation. In either case, the paschal candle is placed on a stand on the ground at the head of the coffin.

In the formal Episcopal service, the minister opens with a prayer called *the Collect,* during which everyone stands. The minister says "The Lord be with you," and the congregation answers, "And with thy spirit." The minister then says, "Let us pray":

> O God, whose mercies cannot be numbered:
> accept our prayers on behalf of thy servant *(Name),*
> and grant *him/her* an entrance into the land of light
> and joy, in the fellowship of thy saints; through
> Jesus Christ thy Son our Lord, who liveth and
> reigneth with thee and the Holy Spirit, one God,
> now and for ever. (All say) *Amen.* (Bernardin)

An Old Testament reading follows, generally read by a layperson. Frequent selections include verses from the book of Isaiah, Lamentations, Wisdom, and Job. The reader ends by saying, "The word of the Lord," and the congregation responds "Thanks be to God." Next a hymn is sung, or possibly a psalm is recited. Then there is a reading from the New Testament, usually Paul's Epistle to the Romans, 1 Corinthians, 2 Corinthians, or the book of Revelation. Another hymn or psalm follows and then a gospel reading, almost invariably from the Gospel of John. The selections in all of the readings revolve around the theme of the life to come and in particular the promise of resurrection that the suffering and crucifixion of Jesus Christ made possible for all humanity.

A brief homily (sermon) usually comes next, which also focuses on the theme of resurrection and assurance that the just and good in this life will certainly be rewarded in the next life. Although a eulogy is not a traditional part of the Christian funeral service, it has increasingly made an appearance in those denominations that are less ritually formal. If there is a eulogy, it is generally given by one family member representing all the mourners, who offers a brief reflection on and celebration of the deceased. After the homily or eulogy or both, the Episcopalian service includes the Apostle's Creed. The creed was developed in the third and fourth centuries of the common era by the early church, which faced numerous internal disagreements as to the nature and significance of Jesus Christ's life, death, and resurrection. After centuries of argument, the church that emerged as "orthodox" affirmed with the Apostles' Creed that Jesus was a member of a divine Trinity, was crucified, descended into hell (where, legend has it, he liberated deserving pre-Christian pagans), rose again on the third day, and ascended into heaven, from whence he will again descend to judge the living and the dead.

In very traditional funeral services, the Eucharist follows the Apostles' Creed. The Eucharist is the ritual high point of any formal Christian service, for the stage has been set for it by the Scriptural readings (proceeding sequentially from Old Testament to the gospels) and the blessing and spiritual union of the congregation produced by the recital of the communal creed. At the Eucharist, the congregation partakes of the bread (or wafers) and wine (or grape juice), which represent Jesus' resurrected body and blood. (Christian denominations disagree as to whether these elements are symbolic or *literally* become the body and blood of Jesus.) Although oftentimes the Eucharist is not part of the funeral service, particularly in "low church" denominations, it is a suitable component of a funeral because it is intended to reinforce both the individual's ties to a greater force that promises a triumph over death and the communal ties that bind people together—particularly important when a member of the community has ruptured those bonds by departing.

The traditional Episcopalian service is completed by saying a final prayer, called *the Commendation,* which acknowledges the necessity of death even while ultimately denying its final reality. In the Commendation, the congregation says in unison,

> Give rest, O Christ, to thy servant(s) with thy saints,
> where sorrow and pain are no more,
> neither sighing, but life everlasting.

The presiding minister prays:

> Thou only art immortal, the creator and maker of
> mankind; and we are mortal, formed of the earth,
> and unto earth shall we return. For so thou didst
> ordain when thou createdst me, saying, "Dust thou
> are, and unto dust shalt thou return." All we go
> down into the dust; yet even at the grave we make
> our song: Alleluia, Alleluia, Alleluia.

Again, the congregation prays:

Give rest, O Christ, to thy servant(s) with thy saints,
where sorrow and pain are no more,
neither sighing, but life everlasting.

And the minister, facing the casket, responds:

Into thy hands, O merciful Savior, we commend
thy servant *(Name)*. Acknowledge, we humbly
beseech thee, a sheep of thine own fold, a lamb of
thine own flock, a sinner of thine own redeeming.
Receive *him/her* into the arms of thy mercy, into the
blessed rest of everlasting peace, and into the
glorious company of the saints in light. (All say)
Amen. (Bernardin)

The minister concludes by saying, "Let us go forth in
the name of Christ," and the congregation responds
"Thanks be to God." The service ends with a hymn,
anthem, or canticle, and in very traditional services the
anthem accompanies the recessional of the casket from
the church in the same order as the earlier procession,
though the paschal candle remains behind. Sometimes
the mourners proceed with the casket directly to the
cemetery for the committal service, though it may also
be held later or omitted altogether.

More and more frequently, ordained clergy find
themselves in the position of leading funeral services
outside the church building for deceased persons who
were not known to them, who attended no church, or
who were in fact avowed atheists. Funeral services now
take place in funeral homes, hospital chapels, hospices,
at the home of the mourners, at the graveside, and
under other circumstances. Most churches now have
specific instructions on how to alter the traditional
funeral service for the "unchurched," for instance, omit-
ting those prayers that refer to the deceased as "thy
servant." Most churches now find cremation an acceptable way to dispose of the body, and after slightly altering the wording of the committal service, their officials
also preside over the interment of ashes. Organ dona-
tion is an increasingly popular form of social service,
and in some cases the deceased wished his or her entire
body to be donated to medical science. In such a case
the minister may hold an informal service at the home
of the deceased or in the funeral parlor that consists
mainly of the Commendation just described.

Importantly, however, many Christians (perhaps best
referred to as "nominal" Christians) now avoid formal
religious funeral services altogether. Commercial
funeral homes provide a secular ceremony as part of
their services (for an extra charge), and local "memorial
societies" offer alternative funeral arrangements, including disposal of the body as well as simplified ceremonies, for around 20 percent of the cost of services at
traditional funeral homes. These ceremonies are a great
deal more flexible than traditional religious services,
and often allow any number of eulogies and personal
reflections, any type of music, and any kind of structure
that the bereaved prefer. Another trend on the rise is
choosing to design one's own funeral or memorial
observance or allowing one's family and friends to
design it, apart from all organized religion or commercial institutions. Such personal services often take place
at home or in outdoor settings that were special to the
deceased and include favorite songs, poems, and spontaneous remembrances. Regulations surrounding the disposal of the body are not as easily altered, however: both
burial and cremations are regulated by state and federal
law, and remains must be interred on properly designated land under the supervision of authorities.

See also CEMETERY; COMMITTAL SERVICE; CREMAINS; RESURRECTION,
CHRISTIAN; SHOMER.

References
Bernardin, Joseph Buchanan, comp. *Burial Services.* Wilton, CT:
Morehouse-Barlow, 1980.
Biddle, Perry H., Jr. *A Funeral Manual.* Grand Rapids, MI: William
B. Eerdman's Publishing, 1994.
Inter-Lutheran Commission on Worship. *Burial of the Dead.*
Minneapolis: Augsburg, 1976.
Irion, Paul E. *The Funeral: Vestige or Value?* Nashville: Abingdon
Press, 1966.
Leach, William H., ed. *The Cokesbury Funeral Manual.* Nashville:
Cokesbury Press, 1932.
Lockyer, Herbert. *The Funeral Sourcebook.* London: Pickering and
Inglis, 1967.
Mansell, John S. *The Funeral: A Pastor's Guide.* Nashville: Abingdon
Press, 1998.
Poovey, William Arthur. *Planning a Christian Funeral: A Minister's
Guide.* Minneapolis: Ausburg, 1978.
Searl, Edward. *In Memoriam: A Guide to Modern Funeral and Memorial
Services.* Boston: Skinner House, 1993.

FUNERARY CUSTOMS, ETRUSCAN

Etruria was a primary cultural ancestor of the ancient
Roman world, and its funerary practices and beliefs had
a large impact on the developing Roman Republic. The
Roman practice of laying the dead body out for viewing
and ritual lamentation, often with hired mourners, had
its roots at least partly in Etruscan custom. In addition,
Roman civilization gained much of its funerary art,
architecture, and afterlife expectations from its Etruscan
heritage.

As far as can be determined, from the earliest times
Etruria practiced both cremation and inhumation con-
temporaneously. Cremation appears somewhat less frequently than inhumation until the fourth century
B.C.E., when burning human remains gained prevalence,
particularly in the central and northern areas of Italy.
The funeral pyre was near the tomb, and goods such as
offerings and personal possessions were often burned

along with the body. The cremains were placed in terracotta jars and pots as well as in decorated alabaster and terracotta ash chests with effigies in relief or on top. Cylindrical well tombs were cut in the rock or dug in the earth, at the bottom of which were secondary wells covered with a stone slab and housing the jar, urn, or ash chest with the cremains as well as the various foodstuffs and grave goods that were buried along with it. Cremains were also deposited in life-sized stone-carved human figures and in canopic urns of a human form on a high-backed chair or throne.

The earliest Etruscan inhumations were in a plain sarcophagus of wood in shallow trench graves. (Occasionally, cremains have been found in trench graves also.) Chamber tombs, both above and below ground, became common by the end of the seventh century B.C.E., and more elaborate sarcophagi were made of various materials, although sometimes bodies were merely placed in the chamber tomb and left to decompose on a funerary bed sans coffin. Funerary beds ranged from real beds made of wood or metal placed in the tomb in early times to beds carved from the stone walls of rock-cut tombs, sometimes painted to resemble actual beds with legs, pillows, and all.

Chamber tombs with both simple and complex symmetrical layouts have been discovered. Some are entirely underground, cut from the rock, and some are half rock cut from the ground and half built up with masonry. Many famous Etruscan chamber tombs are covered altogether with a massive grassy tumulus (burial mound), but some have just a slight earth covering over a masonry roof. Many tombs, particularly house and temple tombs complete with false "doors," appear to have been constructed in groups, some with walled enclosures, thus forming the predecessors of Roman cemeteries. Some rock-cut tombs are also found carved out of sheer cliff faces or from a steep hill, most with rather plain facades, but there are a few spectacular exceptions with elaborate pillars and entranceways. Finally, although most Etruscan tombs are rectangular in shape, some examples of the round or oval tholos type are found, with the slab or pseudo-vaulted roof upheld by a single pillar.

Early Etruscan funerary art (sixth to fifth century B.C.E.) is almost entirely joyful and peaceful. Scenes painted on the walls of the tombs show the deceased playing games and enjoying food, sports, fishing, music, and other amusements, often in idyllic natural settings. The symposium (drinking party) is a particularly common motif and heavily influenced Roman funerary art. By the Hellenistic period (fourth century B.C.E. onward), the funerary scenes become distinctly darker in tone, with frequent scenes of violent battles taken from myth accompanied by anxious faces, unfriendly spirits, and menacing serpents. There has been much argument in academic circles over whether this dramatic shift in funerary art reflects a change in Etruscan afterlife beliefs based on a worsening political and economic situation or merely an artistic fashion, but the issue has not been resolved. Precious little is known of Etruscan beliefs regarding the afterlife, since nearly all our knowledge comes from archaeological, not textual sources, but it is extremely probable that the Etruscans did not believe all life ended with the grave, given the many food offerings and grave goods (arms, armor, eating vessels, etc.) found in the tombs and graves, whether real or imitated in art.

References

Toynbee, J. M. C. *Death and Burial in the Roman World.* Ithaca, NY: Cornell University Press, 1971.

FUNERARY CUSTOMS, HINDU

The earliest Indian literature, the Vedas, dated by most modern scholars to around 2000 B.C.E., mention only cremation as the way to dispose of the deceased. For example, one hymn (Rig Veda X.16) is addressed entirely to the funeral fires, called *Agni* and *Jātavedas,* who are to burn the corpse and thus carry the dead upward to heaven. A verse of this sacred hymn runs:

> O Jātavedas! When you thoroughly burn this
> [departed person],
> Then may you hand him over to the *pitris* [i.e.,
> heavenly fathers]!
> When he [the deceased] follows this [path] that
> leads on to a new life,
> May he become one that carries out the wishes of
> the gods! (X.16.2; all translations from the Rig
> Veda in this entry are from Kane)

Some scholars have seen in the Vedas vague references to noncremation burials, such as hymns in which the earth is asked to rise over the dead, protecting them, "as a mother covers her child with her skirt" (Rig Veda X.18.10–13). But native interpreters of the Veda, like the medieval scholar Sāyana, state that such verses refer to the burial of cremains (for archaeological evidence, see FUNERARY CUSTOMS, ANCIENT INDIAN). Again, some may object that the Vedas do in fact reveal an ancient practice of inhumation by pointing to one hymn addressed to the ancestors (pitris) as "those . . . burnt and unburnt" (Rig Veda X.15.14). But this passage is quite inconclusive, given that there are different classes of so-called ancestors, some of whom are the spiritual progenitors of the human race—they never lived as humans and were never given funerals. Some of these heavenly beings are symbolized by Fire (Agnishvātta), others by Sacred Grass (Barhishad), and still others by the Moon (Somavant).

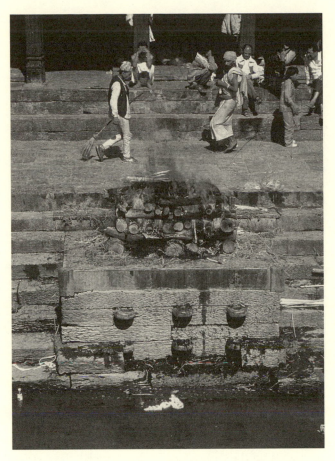

Ritual cremation, Bagmati River, Kathmandu. Courtesy of Images Colour Library.

Thus the only indisputable evidence afforded by the early Scriptures points to cremation as the means of sending the dead on to the next world. Even at the time the Vedas were written, the cult of the dead was quite elaborate. The Heavens (Svarga) were subdivided into at least three realms, and many gods were invoked during the funeral, including Pushan (guide of the dead souls), Yama (king of the heaven reserved for ancestors), and Agni (god of fire and messenger between heaven and earth). The Vedic hymns make reference to an animal (a cow or goat) that accompanied the deceased on the funeral pyre, apparently as a scapegoat. The karmic debt (i.e., sins) of the deceased were transferred to the animal sacrifice, leaving the departed soul free to approach Svarga unimpeded (Rig Veda X.16.4):

O Jātavedas! May you burn by your heat the goat
    that is your share!
May your flame, may your bright light burn that
    goat;
Carry this (departed soul) to the world of those who
    do good deeds
By means of your beneficent bodies [flames]!

There are two terms used in the Vedic period for the path to heaven, namely the *pitriyāna*, or "path of the ancestors," and the *devayāna*, or "path of the gods." Later commentaries, namely the Upanishads, say that the deceased who travel the path of the ancestors dwell in their heaven, eventually to be reborn; whereas the deceased who travel on the path of the gods enter the realm of the sun and *never return*. As for hell, although the later term *Naraka* does not appear in these early Scriptures, there is a clear concept of a dark, lower realm of punishment that is referred to as a "pit" and a realm below the earth. It is not clear if the afterlife realms were conceived by the Vedic Indians as physical places, psychological states, or perhaps both.

Later texts (especially the class of Scriptures called Gṛhya Sūtras, or "Rituals Related to Domestic Life," c. 800 to 300 B.C.E.) describe an even more elaborate funerary cult, although they are careful to constantly refer back to the Vedas. A summary of their instructions is given here, and these rituals are followed by most Hindus even today, though differences in modern tradition are noted.

When it is clear that death is imminent, the dying man is to be taken from his bed and laid facing south on sacred grass strewn on the earth. There the son or other nearest male relative should prepare the dying person for death through several means. All religious vows that have not been completed during life are magically fulfilled by a rite called *vratodyāpana*, or "completion of vows." The dying man (or someone in his name) must make ten gifts, which are the last chance for the dying to acquire merit and thus earn the reward of heaven. Then a ritual should be performed called *sarvaprāyaścitta*, which literally means "atonement for everything." In this rite, the dying man should donate a cow (or its equivalent in cash) after naming the various sins he may by guilty of. It seems that in the past this cow took on the remaining sins of the dying and was slaughtered, but since the slaughter of cows has been prohibited, the cow is now simply given to the priestly caste, with the same ritual effect. This cow is called *Vaitaraṇī*, which is the name of the Underworld river; giving the cow ensures that the dying man will be carried over this river and into Svarga. Finally, the dying should be made ritually pure by bathing in water from the Ganges or other sacred river or, if this is not possible, at least by sipping such holy water. As death occurs, sacred verses from the Vedas should be recited in the dying person's ears.

The Upanishads and other philosophical texts make it clear that one's last thought before death determines the nature of one's afterlife, since the energy given off by the mind at the last minute carries the soul to the corresponding state. Thus angry last thoughts lead to an angry hell, but calm, meditative thoughts lead the soul to a blest heaven. According to the Bhagavad-Gita (8:5), by focusing one's last thoughts on the absolute, one attains final release (mokṣa): "The man, who remembering Me [God] alone in his last moments, departs from this life, and comes to Me; there is no doubt about this." However, it is usually pointed out that one's last thoughts are the result of all that one has thought and done throughout life, so the only guarantee of heaven is to lead a generous and wise life.

The Gṛhya Sūtras lay out the final life ritual, called *antyeṣṭi,* which prescribes the cremation and the concluding sacrifices and purification rituals that follow. All people were cremated at the time these Scriptures were written, except for children and yogis, who were thought too pure to require the purification obtained by cremation. Thus in the ancient period children and ascetics were buried, but in modern times faith in the power of sacred rivers has grown, and now most often the bodies of these two are deposited in the Ganges or another sacred river, if possible. Likewise, victims of epidemics are also placed in a sacred river, but in their case, an effigy is later made of them out of grass and other material, and the entire cremation and rituals are carried out exactly as if the effigy were the original body. Another exception to cremation, and indeed to receipt of proper funeral rites at all, are victims of murder, suicide, and certain other violent deaths. In these cases it is thought that the spirit of the deceased will not rest, funeral or no: the bodies are buried or cast into rivers without rites, and handling them does not cause the mourners to become impure (see discussion later in entry). For all others, however, cremation is an extremely important rite, and if it is not performed, the family will certainly be haunted by the spirit of the deceased, who will become a pret, a ghost suffering extreme hunger and thirst.

In ancient times, most well-to-do families kept sacred fires burning in the home at all times, and so the ancient rituals state that after death, offerings of clarified butter should be made in those fires. In modern times, most families place some leaves of the Tulasi tree in the mouth of the deceased along with a few drops of water. A funeral bed is constructed. Ancient ritual indicates that this bed should be made of the rare udumbara wood, covered by black antelope skin, but nowadays bamboo or other wood is fine, and no animal skin is used. The body is dressed in fresh clothes, and verses are chanted reminding the dead person to give up the old clothes and remember good deeds that were done. The hair, beard, and nails are trimmed, and the thumbs are tied together and bound to the funeral bed. Then the body must be carried to the cremation ground. Ancient ritual prescribed a cart drawn by two bulls, but in modern times blood relations carry the body on the funeral bier themselves, with the eldest son in the lead

carrying a torch lit from the home fire. No doubt this fire was to scare off bhūts and other undead, for in India as elsewhere in the world ghosts cannot abide fire, particularly fire from a sacred source.

Once the procession arrived at the funeral ground, ancient prescriptions directed that the cow donated by the deceased should be slaughtered, while a mantra (sacred verse) was spoken: "Companion of the dead, we have removed the sins of the dead by means of you, therefore no sins or decrepitude may reach us" (Pandey, trans., p. 436). The animal body was then used to cover the human body on the funeral pyre, limb for limb, organ for organ, in a clear attempt to make a double of the human and thus direct all negative energy to the animal victim instead. In modern times, the cow (or goat) is merely led three times around the fire and released or donated to brahmins, while mourners utter similar verses. If the family cannot afford such a substantial expense as donating a cow, money is donated instead. Mantras are spoken to purify the ground and scare away ghosts, and a trench is dug a few inches deep. The hands of the corpse are untied, the cords of the funeral bed are cut, and both bed and body are placed in the trench. In ancient times, the body was disemboweled, fecal matter was removed, and the cavity was filled with a pure substance, namely clarified butter; but this ritual is no longer performed. Gifts and wealth are placed on the corpse, according to social class, especially any items that were personal to the deceased. Their use by the living is certainly inauspicious and could lead to death for them as well. Death is thought to be contagious, and as discussed later in this entry, Indians take extraordinary measures to ensure the separation of the living and the dead.

Finally comes the ancient custom of laying the wife next to the deceased on the funeral pyre. The sacred verse is uttered:

> O mortal, this woman (your wife), wishing to be joined to you in a future world is lying by your corpse; she has always observed the duties of a faithful wife; grant her your permission to abide in this world (of the living), and relinquish your wealth to your descendents. (Pandey, trans., p. 440)

The wife then gets off the pyre and takes the family wealth, and the funeral fire is lit. There can be no doubt that in ancient times the wife was burned along with the husband, and this custom, called *satī,* is still practiced in some parts of India, although it is now officially illegal, and the ritual texts since the time of the Vedas also forbid it. Nevertheless, the most ancient customs tend to persevere despite cultural change. The cremation is understood as a sacrifice to the gods, and mantras invoke the blessing of heaven. The god Pushan is asked to accept the sacrifice and guide the soul of the dead, and the god of fire, Agni, is asked to consume the physical body but create its essence again in heaven. The fire is left to burn itself out, and attention now shifts to the survivors, namely their severance from the dead and their ritual reintegration back into normal society. It is important that both fire and water play a prominent part both in preparing the dead for the funeral and in separating the living from the dead afterward. Around the world, both fire and water are thought to be particularly dangerous and offensive to ghosts and demons.

The members of the procession wash themselves in water that has been poured into three trenches north of the funeral pyre and pass under a yoke propped up by branches. The eldest son or nearest relative is the last to pass under, and taking the yoke, he offers a prayer to the sun. The mourners move off without looking back and refrain from grief because "many tears burn the dead." In the nearest stream or water source, mourners submerge themselves in water and, calling out the name of the dead, offer a handful of water to the dead (a ritual called *Udaka-karma*). Finally, some rice or peas or both are scattered on the earth, allegedly for the birds, but also as a reminder of similar rituals like mazes or scattering of seeds that slow down and confuse the dead if they pursue the funeral party. Then the procession gathers at some pleasant spot and relates stories praising the dead and tales from epics and legend until sunset and the appearance of the first star. At this time, the procession reassembles, again in reverse order, with the youngest in the lead and the eldest son or other funeral leader in the rear. When they reach home, in another act of purification, they should touch several objects in order: a stone on the earth, fire, cow dung, grain, a seed, oil, and water. Only then may they enter the house. Clearly, natural elements, including earth (stone) fire, water, and living things, are thought to counteract the pollution of death. It is interesting to contrast this attitude with Zoroastrian belief, for whereas Hinduism teaches that the natural elements are purifying forces, Zoroastrian belief sees the elements as too pure to be subjected to the pollution of death.

After returning home mourners begin the final period of ritual impurity, called *āśaucha,* which lasts for ten to thirty days depending on social status or caste. Mourners should not cut their hair, study sacred texts, or make ritual offerings, and for the first few days they should also sleep on the ground, not cook their own food, eat only during the day, and abstain from sex. This period includes the ceremony called *pitri-medha,* or "honoring the ancestor," in which the physical remains of the cremation were gathered and ritually buried. In ancient times, a small mound (*śmāsana*) was later built over the postcremation burial site, but today cremains are mostly placed in a sacred river, which is thought to

secure the deceased a very long time in heaven. Finally, at the end of the period of ritual impurity comes a last rite called *shanti-karma,* or "ritual of peace," in which the survivors gather in the morning and kindle a new fire. They sit down, mantras are recited, and four offerings are poured into the fire. Then each person in the assembly in turn touches a red bull. The party walks toward the east, leading the bull. The funeral leader (usually the eldest son) takes a branch and erases the footprints of the bull, while a priest erects a barrier of stones in a circle on the path, saying:

> I place this circle of stones for the living;
> May we and others not go beyond it in life;
> May we all live to a hundred autumns,
> Driving death away from this heap.

The funeral party then proceeds home, extinguishes the old family fire, kindles a new one, and celebrates the end of the period of impurity with a funerary feast. (The ceremony for offerings made to the dead to carry it on to the next life is described separately in the article SHRĀDDHA. The postcremation burial ceremony is described separately in the article PITRI-MEDHA.)

See also ĀTMAN; BHŪT; CREMATION; DEAD, THE; FUNERARY CUSTOMS, ANCIENT INDIAN; FUNERARY CUSTOMS, ZOROASTRIAN; NARAKA; PITRI; PRET; SVARGA; URN; YAMA.

References

Bhattacharya, Narendra Nath. *Ancient Indian Rituals and Their Social Contents.* Manohar, Delhi: 1975.

Crooke, William. *The Popular Religion and Folk-lore of Northern India.* 2nd ed. Delhi: Munshiram Manoharlal, 1968.

Gupta, S. P. *Disposal of the Dead and Physical Types in Ancient India.* Delhi: Oriental Publishers, 1972.

Kane, Pandurang Vaman. *History of Dharmashāstra: Ancient and Medieval Religious and Civil Law in India.* Vol. 4. Poona: Bhandarkar Oriental Research Institute, 1953.

Pandey, Raj Bali. *Hindu Samskāras: A Socio-religious Study of the Hindu Sacraments.* Banares: Vikrama Publications, 1949.

Shastri, Dakshina Ranjan. *Origin and Development of the Rituals of Ancestor Worship in India.* Calcutta: Bookland, 1963.

Singh, Purushottam. *Burial Practices in Ancient India.* India: Prithivi Prakashan, 1970.

FUNERARY CUSTOMS, JEWISH

Because human beings were created in the image of God, according to the Hebrew Bible, the body of the dead is still sacred even when the spirit has departed. Like an impaired Torah scroll, which can no longer be used for religious services but still retains the impression of holiness, the dead are to be treated with great honor and laid in the ground according to exact rites developed through long tradition. Because Jewish funerary customs differ from one community to another, from intensely religious to quite secular, this article will discuss the most ancient and highly developed traditions preserved among Orthodox Jews.

Everything done before the funeral is intended to honor the dead (after the funeral, most mourning customs comfort and assist the survivors). When death is just about to occur, no one may leave the room. This requirement honors the dying and asks the living to witness their passage to the next world. Likewise, immediately after death, the eyes and mouth of the deceased are closed, and a clean sheet is drawn over the head. The feet of the body should face the doorway (perhaps symbolizing the spirit that has departed the home), and if the person died in an awkward position, the body should be gently rearranged to a dignified position. The mourners ask forgiveness from the deceased for anything they may have done to hurt the deceased during life, and then they make ready to depart. From the moment of death until the funeral, the "seven relations" (father, mother, spouse, brothers, sisters, sons, and daughters) are considered onenim (singular, onen), or persons in deep anguish who must enter into formal mourning, which prohibits, among other things, eating meat, taking alcohol, shaving, conducting business, or attending any festivities (except Sabbath).

All the mirrors in the house are covered. Jewish discussion differs on the reasons for this, from discouraging vanity during mourning to respect for the departed "image" of God. (A more academic reading of this tradition may be found in the article SOUL.) A single candle should be lit near the head of the deceased, or many candles may be placed all around the body. This custom originates in the old belief that spirit is akin to fire. A candle near the body stands for what has departed and "guards" the body from possible habitation by negative forces. For the same reason, the body must never be left alone. A "watcher" (called a *shomer*) must be appointed to stay with the body until burial, especially overnight. During this time, Psalms 23 and 91 are recited over the body, but there must be no eating, drinking, or smoking in the room. There is minimal speech, which is limited to praiseworthy remarks about the dead, and no music or singing.

Orthodox Judaism permits no autopsy (except in rare criminal or ambiguous suicide cases) and no embalming of the body. The body is left—unmolested and intact—to the care of the special "holy society" (chevra kaddisha), an organization of local Jews who are trained to prepare deceased members of the community for burial. It is considered a great honor to serve in this society, fulfilling high religious commandments (mitzvot), and it spares the family and friends the painful necessity of dealing with the corpse. Several Biblical statements are taken by Orthodox Jews as indicating that burial should be very rapid. Deuteronomy 21:23, for instance, reads: "His body shall not remain all night" (although the actual context of the verse is the hanging of criminals). Traditionally, burial occurs within twenty-four hours of death, unless the Sabbath (Friday sundown to Saturday sundown) or a major Jewish holiday intervenes. For this reason, the body must be prepared quickly.

The primary task of the holy society is that of washing the body and ritually purifying it. A corpse is considered extremely polluting, but through their ministrations the pollution is reduced. About half an hour after death, the chevra kaddisha begins its work, which is private and not to be viewed by anyone else. They undress the body and cover it with a sheet and address a prayer to the deceased to ask forgiveness for any accidental error or indignity that they may commit. Throughout the process, a series of prayers is read from a book called *maaver yabok*. Straw is cast on the floor and covered with a sheet, and the body is lowered to the ground and placed on it. Any windows in the room are opened (again, probably symbolizing the departure of the soul), candles are lit (if they have not been already) and the shomer watches over the body until just before the funeral.

The casket is brought in, made of wood (not metal or other materials) so that, like the body, the casket may decompose at a natural rate in the earth. After having washed their hands ritually three times, the chevra kaddisha place the body on a special board and begin the washing. Using a large container of lukewarm water, the body is washed part by part in a carefully ordered sequence, beginning with the head, then neck, right hand, other parts of the right side, and the parts of the left side; finally, by gently rolling the body, the back sides are washed in the same order. The body is covered at all times except for the parts being washed. If any blood flows, it is not washed away but simply covered. Blood is considered part of the body, which must be buried "intact." This means that if the person died through accident or violence, even bloody clothes and organs must be buried along with the body; generally they are placed at the foot of the coffin. Next, the nails are trimmed and the hair is combed, and the body is ready for tohorah, or purification.

After washing the body, the chevra kaddisha again wash their hands three times, beginning with the right. Then, straw or wood is again placed on the ground, and the body is raised to a vertical position. Then the burial society members pour 24 quarts (9 Hebrew kavin) of water over the head of the deceased, ensuring that it flows over the entire body in a constant, uninterrupted stream. Then the body is again placed on its tohorah board and covered with a clean, dry sheet. Finally, the chevra kaddisha dress the body in special burial clothing. The order of dressing is prescribed: first the mitznephet, or head covering, is placed on the head, followed by the michnasayim, or trousers; the k'tonet, a long shirt that covers the entire body; the kittel, an overshirt; and the avnet, or special belt wound around the body three times. Finally, the deceased (if male) is wrapped in his tallit or prayer shawl, with at least one tassel cut, followed at last by the sovev, or shroud. The shroud must be hand-sewn of white linen by "pious women" (i.e., observant Jews past the age of menopause). The tachrichim (the burial clothes, including the shroud) should have no pockets (because the dead are not to carry anything with them), nor should there be any binding or knots (which symbolically "hold" the deceased back from the necessary journey). The body is then placed in the casket, along with some broken pottery, called *sherblach* (sometimes the sherblach is placed in the casket at the cemetery). Because the body is not to be viewed by mourners in traditional Judaism, the casket is sealed.

The funeral service may occur at the home, a funeral chapel, or the cemetery. Only great scholars, saints, and leaders have a funeral service within the synagogue, though sometimes the car bearing the body may pull up to the front door, and a special prayer may be said for the benefit of the deceased before the mourners continue on to the cemetery. Because the funeral service may take place elsewhere than the cemetery, the order of events may differ. One of the most prominent features of the Jewish funeral service is the keri'ah, the ritual rending of clothes. Close relations tear their outer clothing to symbolize the grief they feel; the tear can never be repaired. The service itself consists of the reading of prayers and psalms, the hesped, or eulogy, and the recessional—bringing the casket to the hearse.

The processional from hearse to grave is as governed by religious law as every other aspect of Jewish funerary customs. The pallbearers are generally children and brothers of the deceased, though friends and even personal enemies (if their service is a form of regret) are allowed. The processional does not walk directly to the grave but, led by the rabbi, takes a number of pauses, anywhere from five or seven in number to pausing every few feet, symbolizing the hesitation and grief of the event. Once at the graveside, the prayer called *Tzidduk Ha'din,* or "Justification of the Divine Decree," is read, along with psalms and other prayers. At last, it is the family's responsibility to themselves cover the casket with earth, even if cemetery personnel finish filling the grave. Each taking a turn, family members cast earth into the grave and then lay the shovel down—the shovel is not handed person to person, as this would symbolize the "spreading" of the death to others. (This kind of precaution is not unusual: most traditional cultures believe in the "contagion" of death and its concomitant impurity.) Orthodox Jews may not be buried

---

Tzidduk Ha'din, or Justification of Divine Decree

The Rock, his work is perfect, for all His ways are judgment: A God of faithfulness and without iniquity, just and right is He.

The Rock, perfect in every work, who can say unto Him, "What workest thou?" He ruleth below and above; He ordereth death and restoreth to life: He bringeth down to the grave, and bringeth up again.

The Rock, perfect in every deed, who can say unto Him, "What doest thou?" O Thou who speakest and doest, of Thy grace deal kindly with us, and for the sake of him who was bound like a lamb, O hearken and do.

Just in all Thy ways art thou, O perfect Rock, slow to anger and full of compassion. Spare and have put upon parents and children, for Thine, Lord, is forgiveness and compassion.

Just art Thou, O Lord, in ordering death and restoring to life, in whose hand is the charge of all spirits; far be it from Thee to blot out our remembrance. O let Thine eyes mercifully regard us; for Thine, Lord, is compassion and forgiveness.

If a man live a year or a thousand years, what profiteth him? He shall be as though he had not been. Blessed be the true Judge, who ordereth death and restoreth to life.

Blessed be He, for His judgment is true, and His eye discerneth all things, and He awardeth unto man his reckoning and his sentence, and all must render acknowledgment unto him.

We know, O Lord, that Thy judgment is righteous: Thou art justified when Thou speakest, and pure when Thou judgest, and it is not for us to murmur at Thy method of judging. Just are Thou, O Lord, and righteous are Thy judgments.

O true and righteous Judge! Blessed be the true Judge, all whose judgments are righteous and true.

The soul of every living thing is in Thy hand; Thy might is full of righteousness. Have mercy upon the remnant of the flock of Thy hand, and say unto the destroying angel, "Stay thy hand!"

Thou art great in counsel and mighty in deed; Thine eyes are open upon all the ways of the children of men, to give unto every one according to his ways, and according to the fruit of his doings. To declare that the Lord is upright; He is my Rock, and there is not unrighteousness in Him.

The Lord gave, and the Lord hath taken away; blessed be the name of the Lord. And He, being merciful, forgiveth iniquity and destroyeth not. Yea, many a time He turneth His anger away, and doth not stir up all His wrath.

Translation by Lamm (1969, pp. 62–63).

in concrete vaults or mausolea unless the casket is actually *under* the ground, in order to fulfill the words of Genesis 3:19: "Dust you are, to dust you shall return." In general, no artificial means may be used to preserve the body from natural decay or to speed up the process. Cremation is absolutely forbidden for any reason.

Immediately after burial, the prayer known as the kaddish is recited, which looks forward to the resurrection and world to come. A stone is placed on the grave, and then the mourners depart, passing slowly in recession through parallel lines of friends and more remote family relations, who comfort them with a prayer. Upon returning home, all mourners must wash their hands before entering the house (yet another ritual of purification) and then embark upon the very rigorously defined period of formal mourning, namely shiva (for seven days, counted in the Hebrew way) and sheloshim (thirty days, including those of shiva). At the end of one year (from the date of death), the memorial service known as *yahrzeit* is held, and the dead in general are commemorated in the yizkor service held on Yom Kippur and the final days of Passover, Shavuot, and Succot, high Jewish holidays.

See also ANINUT; AVELUT; CHEVRA KADDISHA; KADDISH; KERI'AH; MET MITZVAH; RESURRECTION, HEBREW; SHELOSHIM; SHIVA (JEWISH); SHOMER; SOUL, JEWISH; TOHORAH; YAHRZEIT; YIZKOR.

References

Abramovitch, Henry. "Death." In *Contemporary Jewish Religious Thought,* ed. Arthur A. Cohen and Paul Mendes-Flohr. New York: Charles Scribner's Sons, 1989.

Handcock, P. S. P. *The Archaeology of the Holy Land.* London: T. F. Unwin, 1916.

Lamm, Maurice. *The Jewish Way in Death and Mourning.* New York: Jonathan David Publishers, 1969.

Macalister, R. A. S. *A Century of Excavation in Palestine.* New York: Fleming H. Revell, 1925.

Rabinowicz, H. *A Guide to Life.* London: Jewish Chronicle Publications, 1964.

Riemer, Jack, ed. *Jewish Reflections on Death.* New York: Schocken Books, 1974.

FUNERARY CUSTOMS, LAPP

The Lapps are the ancient inhabitants of the Arctic Circle in what is now upper Norway, Sweden, Finland, and Russia. A nomadic and seminomadic people for millennia, life for the Lapps has traditionally revolved around breeding reindeer and some cows, oxen, and goats. In the past several centuries, a few of the more southerly clans have settled into an agricultural life. The earliest known literary account of the Lapps, under the name *Fenni,* was written in 98 C.E. by the Roman historian Marcus Claudius Tacitus in *Germania,* but in all likelihood they were thriving in Scandinavia long before that. They are generally described as peace loving but also resourceful and even crafty, and among the

ancient Norwegians they had a reputation for sorcery—probably because of their strong shamanic tradition.

Since the advent of Christianity in the sixteenth and seventeenth centuries, the ancient Lapp burial practices have largely been superceded, though traces of them remain. Travel for the Lapps is easiest in the winter, when snow makes the use of a reindeer-drawn sledge possible. In winter Lapps will usually take their dead to a church to have a priest perform last rites, even if it is quite a long distance, by making a funeral sledge and marking the reindeer that pulls it with white cloth or white thread around its ear. If the death occurred too far from a church to make transportation possible, particularly during a long seasonal migration, the dead are often buried where they die, but a bit of earth from the grave is placed in a bag and taken to a priest for blessing when occasion permits, the dirt later being returned to the grave.

As the person is dying, the group gathered may sing psalms, but at the moment of death absolute silence is required so as not to frighten or confuse the dying and cause him or her to be caught for a while between the two worlds, the living and the dead. Although the breath soul (henki) is thought to depart at the moment of death, the shadow soul remains somewhat near the body for a time after death. Death is thus a gradual process and presents certain dangers for the living unless properly handled. Almost everyone leaves the house after a death except the one washing the body. A window in a house or the smoke hole in a tent is opened so the soul may escape. Cats are not allowed to contact the corpse, lest it become vampiric. In addition, the smell of a corpse at the moment of death is considered potentially lethal and to be avoided, as is the gaze of the dead, which is why the eyes are covered. The eyes are closed and covered with coins, particularly the left eye. The mouth is closed (possibly to prevent the breath soul from returning), and among the eastern Lapps, the face is covered by a white cloth. The body is washed, generally by the person closest to the deceased of the same gender; pregnant women are never allowed to wash the corpse. It is then wrapped in white linen (probably due to Christian influence) or put in clean clothes, sometimes made especially for the occasion, with seams on the outside of the garment. The body is then ready for burial and covered with a shroud. Throughout this process, loud wailing and dirges are common.

Burial usually takes place three days after death. The one actually placing the corpse in its coffin is given a brass ring to wear by the nearest relative of the deceased; the ring must remain on the arm until the coffin has been lowered into the grave. The specific reason for wearing the ring, besides its function as an apotropaic device (one that averts evil), is never given, but the representation of the sun on the surface of the ubiquitous magic drums of the Lapps is a ring, with rays pointing out in various directions. Perhaps the power of the sun, symbolized by both the ring and the brass color, helps distinguish the living from the dead.

The intimate possessions of the dead are generally buried with them, including the clothes worn during death, although it is permissible to redistribute their other clothing among relatives or to sell them. The coffin also generally includes various goods such as cheese, fish, butter, tallow, and fire-making implements (among the Umeå Lapps). The funeral goods are generally broken in some way, and even the clothing of the dead is torn in a special way. Likewise, the tools used to dig the grave (generally an axe and a spade) are given decoration, usually by carving their handles, and they are left on or near the grave but broken—either by dulling the sharp edges on a rock or breaking the handle in half. In fieldwork conducted by scholars, several different interpretations are given by the Lapps themselves for this practice: they are broken to prevent their use by the living; they are "killed" so that they can join the dead; or they are destroyed to loosen the ties between the living and the dead. However, the grave goods are not merely apotropaic: the success of the reindeer breeding, the livelihood of most Lapps, depended on proper burial of the dead and their goods. Some Lapps have become very concerned that archaeologists have taken coins and other things from ancient tombs and have blamed poor reindeer breeding seasons on this trend.

Three days after the burial, a reindeer is sacrificed for the deceased and eaten by the relatives in memory of the dead, along with hard liquor. The reindeer chosen for this honor is significant. If there was a funeral sleigh, the reindeer that pulled it is the one chosen. Among the Skolts, a reindeer is chosen with the same sex and "marital" status as the deceased (e.g., a doe who had given birth for married women, a young doe for unmarried women) and is given the deceased's name. After the feast, the reindeer bones are saved and placed in a chest made especially for this occasion and dug down into the earth with a wooden image placed on top. A Lapp with some wealth will have a reindeer sacrificed in like manner annually for several years. Just as Arctic Eurasian peoples invest "bear burials" with great ritual significance, the Lapps bury reindeer bones carefully, for doing so is intimately connected with the production of future reindeer. Disrespect will cause hardship in the future.

Late spring and summer deaths or deaths on a long journey present difficulties for obtaining immediate Christian rites, since travel is so much more difficult. In this case a (temporary) burial according to the old ways will take place, but the body will often be removed to the church when winter comes and travel by sledge is again possible. The deceased's tent is quickly taken down, but the poles are left standing and the fire burning. The area is left alone until the fire is out and grown cold. The deceased is buried on the spot where the ashes lie, usually in a makeshift coffin constructed of planks, a hollowed-out log, or a sledge. The corpse is often covered with birch bark or other tree bark and a little grass, with a stone placed over the grave. In common with other Arctic peoples, the ancient Lapps are known to have practiced at least short-term exposure of the corpse, generally by hoisting the body (with or without the coffin) up in a tree. There the body could be dried by the elements without being destroyed by bears and wolverines. After exposure, when the body has become light, it was transported to its final resting place: an island, a cave, or another remote location (islands seem to have been frequently chosen both because of isolation from scavengers and because the dead are known among most Europeans, as elsewhere, to have difficulty crossing water). Weather permitting, the body was wrapped in bark or skins (depending upon availability) and buried in a hollowed-out log covered by bark, or if the ground was too frozen to dig, a surface grave was made by covering the body and funeral sledge with bark and then grass and stones. Because of the rigors of nomadic life, the Lapps are said to occasionally abandon those who cannot survive the long seasonal migrations: stories are told of the assisted suicide of the old by placing them on sleds and pushing them over steep ravines.

In the nineteenth century and twentieth century, some eastern Lapps developed the habit of making a small wooden structure over the grave, sometimes in the shape of a small house with windows, with a hole always left in the window to allow the soul to escape. Although crosses are usually placed on a grave, sometimes made of crossed skis, a more ancient custom appears to have involved placing a pole over the grave with a piece of white cloth tied to the top. The poles on shamans' graves often had a wooden bird carved on the top—the association of a white cloth or a bird with the soul seems clear. Nowadays, however, under Christian influence the practice is infrequent except in the case of children who drowned or died without baptism, in which case the cloth may be tied to some part of the cross.

Although infant mortality is relatively high, mothers who have lost children appear to recover very quickly. Grief, however intense, is not known to be prolonged among the Lapps for a good reason—the living do not want the dead to remain nearby. Despite all precautions, however, the dead sometimes continue to be a problem: in the case of epidemic or misfortune, the shaman (noaide) with his drum may be called in to determine which of the spirits of the dead is at fault and how they are to be appeased, unless, of course, the problem stems from some angry *ulda*—underground dwarves who are known to be temperamental.

Another ancient tradition persists despite Christian influence, that of making offerings to certain power stones. Carried and shaped by glacial ice, certain stones of pyramidal or other unusual shape (resembling birds, humans, etc.) are recognized by Lapps as sacred and the locus of the energy of the land. Additionally, they are thought to be somehow connected to the ancestors. These stones are consulted for prophecy and treated with great respect, including bowing to them and making offerings such as a carpet of fresh birch or spruce twigs and the sacrifice of cows, hens, fish, and reindeer.

In the nineteenth and twentieth centuries there has been considerable confusion among scholars as to the actual beliefs of the Lapps concerning afterdeath states, which reflects confusion among the Lapps themselves as they attempt to integrate new Christian doctrines with traditional beliefs. It seems clear that originally there was only one realm of the dead among ancient Lapps, called *Jabme-aimo* (literally "the world of the dead"). There, somewhat like the Greek Hades, all the dead went without exception; it appears to have been a world very like this one, but as is typical of northern shamanic traditions, it was reversed or upside-down compared to the land of the living. Since the advent of both Orthodox and Protestant teachings, at least two new realms have appeared, Saivo (Happy) or Radien-aimo, a heavenly realm; and Rutaimo or Mubben-aimo, both meaning "devil's realm" and referring to a dark and foreboding land of shadows (Storå, p. 194). Comparison with other seminomadic Arctic peoples suggests that at one time the current Lapp custom of giving the names of deceased ancestors to children was coupled with the belief that the ancient dead were reincarnated in their newborn descendants.

See also FUNERARY CUSTOMS, ARCTIC EURASIAN; JABMEAIMO; ROTA.

References

Bosi, Roberto. *The Lapps.* Trans. James Cadell. London: Thames and Hudson, 1960.

Collinder, Björn. *The Lapps.* Princeton: Princeton University Press, 1949.

Pettersson, Olof. *Jabmek and Jabmeaimo: A Comparative Study of the Dead and the Realm of the Dead in Lappish Religion.* Lund: C. W. K. Gleerup, 1957.

Storå, Nils. *Burial Customs of the Skolt Lapps.* F. F. Communications no. 210. Helsinki: Suomalainen Tiedeakatemia, 1971.

Turi, Johan. *Turi's Book of Lappland.* Ed. and trans. from Dutch by Emilie Demant Hatt, trans. into English by E. Gee Nash. New York: Harper and Brothers, 1931.

Vorren, Ørnulv, and Ernst Manker. *Lapp Life and Customs: A Survey.* London: Oxford University Press, 1962.

FUNERARY CUSTOMS, MESOPOTAMIAN

As with many ancient cultures, the civilizations of Mesopotamia (Sumeria, Babylonia, Assyria, etc.) placed great importance on the proper burial and regular care of the dead, for the future welfare of the dead depended on it. In the great Gilgamesh epic common to all of Mesopotamia, the hero Gilgamesh summons his lost friend Enkidu from the Underworld to discover what life after death is like. Gilgamesh questions Enkidu as to whether he has seen various kinds of people in the Underworld and what they were like:

He who had one son, hast thou seen him?
I have seen him. He lies prostrate at the foot of the wall and weeps bitterly over it.
He who had two sons, hast thou seen him?
I have seen him. He dwells in a brick-structure and eats bread.
He who had three sons, hast thou seen him?
I have seen him. He drinks water out of the waterskins of the deep. . . .
He whose body lies (unburied) on the steppe, hast thou seen him?
I have seen him. His spirit does not rest in the underworld.
He whose spirit has none to take care of him, hast thou seen him?
I have seen him. What was left over in the pot and the pieces of bread that were thrown in the street he eats. . . . (Heidel, trans.)

Failure to bury the dead denied them rest in the Underworld (Kigal), and failure to make regular food offerings caused the deceased to suffer hunger and thirst. Thus it was the gravest punishment to be denied a proper burial, reserved only for those who were considered the worst of criminals, including women who had an abortion or those who died in childbirth. The deceased had the power to bless descendants and cause their offspring to multiply or to call down upon them the curses of the gods, including Nergal, the god of death and pestilence. Therefore, the dead were provided with food and drink (milk, butter, grain, beer, etc.) at the time of death and regularly thereafter, probably monthly. Much attention was paid to the corpse and the tomb. One Assyrian king says of his father's body:

In royal oil I caused him to rest in goodly fashion. The opening of the sarcophagus, the place of rest, I sealed with strong bronze and uttered a powerful spell over it. Vessels of gold, silver and all the [accessories] of the grave, his royal ornaments which he loves, I displayed before Shamash [the sun god] and placed them in the grave with the father, my begetter. I presented presents to the princely Anunnaki [judges] and the (other) gods that inhabit the underworld. (Ebeling, trans.)

From the earliest known times, even commoners were buried along with objects it was thought they would need in the Underworld. Private graves from as far back as the al-'Ubaid period (circa 5200 B.C.E.) have been found, with the skeletons lying on their backs, hands crossed over the pelvis. The bodies were accompanied by vessels for food and drink, along with weapons. Other bodies, from the Jamdet Nasr period through the Akkadian dynasty (fourth to third millennia B.C.E.), are found on their sides, with the hands holding a cup near the face and the lower body curled up in a tight fetal position. Some scholars (e.g., van der Leeuw, Heidel) suggest that this position indicates a preparation for rebirth, either literally back to Earth again as a child or figuratively into the afterlife.

Some private graves from a later period (c. 2600 to 2000 B.C.E.) were dug in pits reached by rectangular shafts. The bottom of the pit and walls up to about 2 feet high were lined with coarse reed matting, and the dead were likewise wrapped in matting or placed in a coffin made of matting, reeds, wickerwork, wood, or clay. The bodies lay on their side, as if asleep. Cremation was common in some city-states (Surghul, El-Hibba, pre-Sargonic Nippur) but rare in others (Ur and Ashur). In the second millennium it appears to have been as popular to put the dead in pits as to bury them in a family vault built of brick directly below the floor of one's home. It would certainly be easiest to provide for the dead if they were still in some sense "living at home."

Royal tombs, which show a good deal more elaboration, are found from circa 2800 to 2350 B.C.E. in the cities of Ur, Ashur, and Kish. Huge sloping or stepped shafts, as large as 40 feet by 28 feet, descended to the tomb, sometimes as deep as 30 feet underground. The tomb was frequently vaulted and contained one or more large rooms. The body was placed in a wooden coffin or on a wooden bier inside the tomb and provided with rich clothing, jewelry, gaming boards, weapons, and containers of food and drink. (In Ashur the royal tombs were of a considerably later date. They were located actually underneath the palace, and the bodies were buried in stone sarcophagi rather than wooden coffins.) The king's bodyguard, servants, and women, ranging in number from six to eighty people, were killed and interred along with the deceased, often in a chamber separate from the main royal chamber. The bodies of the attendants were not laid out but were placed in crouched positions, as if waiting to provide service. Also, in a few cases, even draft animals yoked to the chariot were found buried with the king, reminiscent of the horse burials of the kurgans (burial mounds) of Central Asia. Clearly, it was thought that life continued beyond the grave much like this one and that the deceased would need the equipment of this life in Kigal, the Underworld.

Although Mesopotamian myths mention the seven fierce judges of the dead, the Anunnaki who dwell in the "palace of justice" in the Underworld, there is no clear evidence that the Mesopotamians looked forward to a happy afterlife even for the righteous. Mesopotamian creation stories state that death was reserved for the humans from the beginning, whereas life was reserved for the gods. (This would appear to contrast with the neighboring Israelites, who describe in the first chapters of Genesis that death was not foreordained for humanity but a tragedy caused by disobedience.) Therefore, the highest blessing among Mesopotamians was a long life on earth, for there seemed little to look forward to in the hereafter.

See also KIGAL; RESURRECTION, ANCIENT NEAR EAST; UNDERWORLD.

References

Charles, R. H. *A Critical History of the Doctrine of a Future Life in Israel*. London: A. and C. Black, 1913.

Clay, A. T. *Documents from the Temple Archives of Nippur*. Philadelphia: University Museum, 1912.

Ebeling, Erich. *Tod und Leben nach den Vorstellungen der Babylonier*. Leipzig: Walter de Gruyter, 1931.

Frankfort, Henri. *Archeology and the Sumerian Problem*. Chicago: University of Chicago Press, 1932.

Heidel, Alexander. *The Gilgamesh Epic and Old Testament Parallels*. Chicago: University of Chicago Press, 1946.

van der Leeuw, G. *Religion in Essence and Manifestation*. New York, 1938.

Watelin, L. C., and S. Langdon. *Excavations at Kish*. Vol. 4. Paris: P. Geunther, 1934.

Wooley, C. L. *Ur Excavations*. Vol. 2: *The Royal Cemetery: Text*. London: Published for the trustees of the two museums, 1927–1976; vol. 2: 1934.

FUNERARY CUSTOMS, MUSLIM

Early Muslims of the seventh and eighth centuries C.E. modeled their behavior in general on that which is prescribed in their sacred text, the Qur'ān, and also on the words and practices of the "Seal of the Prophets" (Muhammed). These two authorities, however, must be viewed in the context of pre-Islamic traditions, namely the traditions of the seminomadic Bedouin tribes as well as the "modernized" practices in fashion in urban centers like Mecca. Thus early Muslims tended to follow the customs of their non-Muslim ancestors except where these were forbidden or supplemented by the teachings of Islam. As Islam spread throughout the Middle East and the world (soon ranging from Spain to Indonesia), funerary customs become more standardized in areas of Muslim stronghold because of advances in

The Cries of the Dead

When [the washer] has finished washing him and he has been laid in his shroud and the places for his feet have been secured, [the deceased soul] calls out to him, "By God, O washer! Do not bind my head shroud too tightly till my face has seen my people, my children and my relations, for this is the last time I shall see them—because this day I shall depart from them and not see them until the Day of Resurrection. . . ."

When he is put on the funeral couch (near the grave) and they take three paces, he calls out so loudly that everything except men and genii hear; he says, "O my friends, my brethren and my children, let not the world beguile you as it beguiled me. Let not time sport with you as it sported with me. Consider me, for I have left what I acquired to my heirs and do not carry anything [but] my sins. God Most High will ask me to account for the worldly gains which you are enjoying now, even then you do not pray for me."

When they have prayed at the funeral and some of his people and friends among those praying have turned away, he says, "By God, O my brethren—if you are friends, do not forget me at this hour. Do not go back before you have properly buried me. O my brethren! If you are [my brethren], know that the dead are colder than the coldest in the hearts of the living. . . ."

When they have put him in the grave, he says, "By God, O my heirs, my people and my brethren! I call you, but you do not call me." When they have put him in his tomb, he says, "By God, O my heirs! I have gathered much wealth in the world which I leave to you. Do not forget me when you have conversation with one another. I taught you the Qur'ān; the recital of it profits! Do not forget me in your petition."

Translation by Macdonald (1965, pp. 62–63).

theology and law and simultaneously more diverse on the peripheries of Islam as more and more regions (with ancient and local customs) converted to the new faith.

According to very ancient Middle Eastern tradition (beginning at least with Zoroastrianism), a corpse brings extreme pollution to home, family, and friends, and thus the funerary preparations are to be carried out with great urgency, often without taking time to inform any but those nearby. Classical Islam largely carried on this tradition, and thus the dead were dealt with posthaste. If the corpse had to stay in the house overnight, a candle was lit, presumably to ward off evil

influences that might attempt to take control of the body and also as a sign of respect to the dead.

When a Muslim has died, the first step is to wash the corpse, on location, because death is considered impure and washing allows the dead to face God in a pure state. (The only exception to this practice is martyrs, who because of their saintly sacrifice are wholly pure and do not need washing; nor does their death bring impurity on their relatives or house.) When Muhammed died, he was washed by his closest relatives according to his wishes, and such is the practice today. Traditionally, men prepare a man for burial, and women prepare the body of a woman. However, there have been many exceptions to this rule: Muhammed's first successor (khalīf) was washed by his widow, and Muhammed's daughter Fatima, considered a saint by tradition, washed herself before death and was washed again by her husband 'Alī after she died. If a woman is washed by relatives of the opposite sex, she is to be washed through her clothes. If a Muslim dies and only strangers (not relatives) are present, only tayammum, or rubbing with sand, is permissible.

Washing begins on the right side of the body; the head is customarily washed with camphor. Since the body is to be washed an uneven number of times (three, five, or sometimes more), the first washing is usually with plain water, the next washing may be with water steeped in acacia leaves, and the last with water and camphor. Sometimes salt is placed in the water as an additional (symbolic) purifier. However, if there is danger of infection from sores or disease, one may simply pour water over the body the requisite number of times. Although orthodox theology teaches that immediately after death the soul (nafs) is taken away from the scene and begins its cycle of trial and judgment, popular tradition has it that the deceased returns to the body very quickly (or never left) and is thus able to watch the proceedings and note the care or carelessness of the mourners in the washing (see excerpt, "The Cries of the Dead").

After the cycle of washings is complete, the deceased is dressed in suitable grave clothes, usually white, though green is allowed. Muhammed was buried in three white garments but without shirt or turban; many of his favorite garments he gave away to family members and close followers, who in turn used them as grave clothes when they died. In general, it is assumed that the dead should be buried in old clothes because the living need the new ones. In classical Islam, spices were often put on the body or between clothes, and sometimes the body was sprinkled with dust. Finally, the dead should be wrapped in a shroud. For this a man's cloak is often used, and if it is not long enough the feet are covered with reeds. A long sheet may be used, either wound around the body or buttoned or sewn over the body. Often there is also a sheet to place between the earth and the body in the grave. As in other funerary preparations, care should be used in clothing and shrouding the dead, for apparently it has some direct effect on their afterlife:

> [The Muslim author al-Suyūtī gives] several reports from the Prophet that disclose the importance of proper shrouding so that the deceased can visit each other in their graves without embarrassment. One delightful story describes a dream in which a man saw several (dead) women, but his own (dead) wife was not with them. He asked them where she was, and they replied that because he had been slipshod in wrapping her in the shroud, she was too shy to go out with them. So with the help of the Prophet the husband found a man of the Anshār who was dying, and he wrapped two saffron robes in his shroud. When night came, the husband again saw the women, and this time his wife was with them, wearing yellow garments. (Smith and Haddad)

After the body is washed and wrapped, it is ready for burial. Because Muhammed was buried at night, this is the preferred time for a Muslim funeral. The Prophet was buried in the quarters of his favorite wife, Ayesha, because that is where he stationed himself when he became gravely ill. To mark the location followers built his green-domed mausoleum, the Gumbad-i-Khizra, which is still a pilgrimage site for millions today. Most Muslims, however, are removed from their homes and first taken in a procession to a mosque for final prayers and then buried in a cemetery on the outskirts of town. The funeral bier is not set down in the mosque during prayers but carried, probably because of the ritual impurity of a corpse. A typical prayer goes as follows:

> O God, he is thy servant, the son of thy servant and thy handmaid; you led him to Islam, you have taken his spirit and know him in secret and in the open. We have come to intercede for him and we have made intercession for him. I take hold of the rope of thy protection for him; he is faithful and under thy care; guard him from the discord of the grave and the punishment of Jahannam. (Tritton)

Martyrs do not require prayers, but for the burials of suicides the usual prayers are said.

After leaving the mosque, the procession continues to the gravesite. It is considered a good deed for Muslims to follow a funeral procession, though in general funerals are private affairs and not celebrations of the person, for that again would be to challenge the centrality of God. Prescriptions for Muslim graves vary quite widely, from niches in brickwork to trenches, square graves, and long graves covered with reeds. In early times coffins were not used, though in modern times they are common. The nearest male relatives (three, five; that is, an uneven number) descend into the tomb and arrange the body, as was done with Muhammed. Women are not allowed to do this. The body is taken into the grave headfirst, laid on the right side, and arranged facing the qibla, the direction of prayer (i.e., Mecca). A brick or stone is placed under the head. However, stonework above the grave is not approved. Men and women in general are not to be buried together or next to each other unless there is some kind of barrier between them.

After a funeral, many different customs relating to mourning and impurity prevail, almost all of which predate Islam and many of which have been frowned upon by it. Some Muslims return to prayer after the burial and then wash away their personal impurity because of association with the dead, or they may wash first and then offer prayers for the dead. In some cases animals are slaughtered and a feast is held; in other cases, relatives fast. Near relatives may wear plain clothes for a month (or even a year), and widows in particular make themselves plain, avoiding perfumes, henna, jewelry, and baths for a time. In some traditions prayers are omitted for a period of time up to a month, and relatives do no work for up to seven days. The water that was used to wash the dead is considered impure, but mourners, particularly women, may pour it over themselves as part of their mourning, along with using ash to dirty themselves and making loud lamentations.

In many ways Islam attempted to overthrow very ancient Middle Eastern customs in its instructions on mourning. Often women are prohibited from funerals altogether, and only men are to carry the funeral bier with the corpse. One reason given for this is that women are prone to excessive grief and wailing, which is an offense to God. If, as Islam teaches, God is all-merciful and just, and if he ordains the times for each person to live and to die, what is there to grieve over? Is not excessive grief a suggestion that some injustice has been done and that one has no faith in God? For this reason, Islam forbids the ancient custom, widespread throughout the Mediterranean and Middle East, of hiring "wailing women" for a funeral (a practice that was meant to ensure that the dead person looking on felt suitably missed and would not need to return to the living for satisfaction). Likewise, Islam forbids mourners (and especially women) to wail over the corpse, to tear their hair, pour ashes over their bodies (as mentioned previously), or blacken their faces with dirt. Such actions anger God and his angels. The treatise called *Kitāb al-Haqā'iq wa'l-Daqā'iq* emphasizes the offensiveness of too much grief:

> It is related that when a man dies, the lamenters gather in his house, and the Angel of Death ('Izrā'īl) stands at the door of his house [and he says to these people], "What is this crying? By God, I have not reduced the life of any one of you. If your crying is on account of me, surely I am (only) a servant under orders. If it is on account of the dead man, surely he is under constraint. If it is on account of God Most High, then you are not believers in God Most High! By God, I shall return time and again among you!" (MacDonald pp. 66–67)

In addition, weeping is thought to torment the dead, and the great Muslim theologian al-Ghazālī says that many times in dreams one hears from the dead that they suffer because of their loved ones' grief (Smith and Haddad). Nevertheless, despite the prohibitions of theology, it is well known that such mourning persists. One text, the *Mudkhal*, disapprovingly describes female mourners who wear black or blue, paint their faces and extremities black, leave their hair loose and disheveled, wail, pour ashes and dust on their heads, and throw ashes around their homes.

After burial, the dead are not forgotten. Many popular traditions indicate that the dead still frequent their old home, especially during the first year after death. Likewise, the dead are thought to reside in their graves, both body and soul, even though the soul is also thought to be residing in the state called *barzakh,* a kind of "barrier" between the living and the dead. Because the soul is a nonphysical entity, its presence in such multiple locations simultaneously does not trouble faithful Muslims. (For more on this idea, see SOUL, MUSLIM.) During the month of Sha'ban, mourners visit the grave or tomb, address the dead on tablets, and sprinkle perfume over the grave. Then the mourners take dust from the grave and return home to light up their houses and remember the dead.

See also BARZAKH; ISRĀFĪL; 'IZRĀ' ĪL; JAHANNAM; JUDGMENT, LAST; QIYĀMA; SĀ'A; SOUL, MUSLIM.

References

Kherie, Altaf Ahmad. *Islam: A Comprehensive Guidebook.* Karachi: Idara Sirat-i-Mustaqeem, 1981.

Macdonald, John. "The Twilight of the Dead." *Islamic Studies* 4, no. 1 (1965).

Smith, Jane I., and Yvonne Yazbeck Haddad. *The Islamic Understanding of Death and Resurrection.* Albany: SUNY Press, 1981.

Tritton, A. S. "Muslim Funeral Custom." *Bulletin of the School of Oriental and African Studies* 9 no. 3 (1938).

FUNERARY CUSTOMS, NATIVE NORTH AMERICAN

It is particularly difficult to discuss the funerary customs of the Native Americans of North America because there are hundreds of tribes ranging from northern Alaska to the Caribbean. Even grouping Native Americans by geographical or linguistic affiliations results in seventeen or eighteen major divisions, according to the authoritative book *Indians of North America* by H. E. Driver (1961). Therefore, this entry can only suggest funerary practices and beliefs in broad strokes and representative examples while begging the indulgence of specialists and Native Americans themselves. To do justice even to a survey of Native American funerary customs would require a volume in itself.

Although most native American tribes that once existed in North America have been destroyed by European colonization, the introduction of foreign diseases, and war, significant records remain detailing Native American ways of life and death. Meanwhile, on government reservations and in small free communities in Alaska, Canada, Mexico, and Meso-America aboriginal American groups continue to observe the customs of their ancient way of life. H. C. Yarrow (1880; 1881) demonstrates the amazing variety of burials that different Native American groups used to practice, including inhumation (in pits, shallow graves, stone-lined cists, and mounds; beneath cabins; in caves), burial in urns or under rocks ("cairns"), cremation, embalmment, mummification, aerial disposal (in trees, on elevated platforms, in suspended canoes, in boxes), and deposition of the corpse in water or adrift in boats.

The historian and ethnologist Erminie Voegelin points out that despite such a wide variety of practices, distinct patterns of funerary customs can be observed in specific regions of North America, and these appear to be quite conservative and constant over centuries in the face of social change and tribal relocation. For example, Voegelin presents a wealth of material on the Shawnee, an Algonquin-speaking group representative of the culture of the eastern woodlands of the United States, even though the remnants of the tribe are now located on reservations in Oklahoma. When a death occurs among the Shawnee, the relatives of the deceased are responsible for the costs of the funeral and appointing a funeral director. The body is left alone for a few hours and then bathed and dressed in new clothes and moccasins provided by relatives. The hair of the deceased is combed and his or her face painted, a man's variously and a deceased woman's with a round red spot on each cheek. The arms of the body are crossed over the chest, and the body is covered with a robe. If death occurred during the day, family members gather in the home and keep a vigil beside the corpse all night. If death occurred at night, the vigil is kept through the rest of the night.

Body left exposed on raised wooden platform by North American Indians in region of Saskatchewan River, 1870. Courtesy of Anne Ronan Picture Library.

When the time comes for burial, the body is removed from the home feet first. Many native peoples around the world break a new exit through the home in order to remove the corpse (presumably to confuse the spirit if it should try to return), but the Shawnee remove the corpse through the ordinary doorway, sweeping the ground or scattering ashes behind the corpse as they go—which appears to serve the same purpose. The body is laid on the ground near the home, head pointed west and feet east, while the grave is dug and the initial funeral ceremonies are held. The gravediggers (which must include a woman) should not be related to the dead person. Wearing a special necklace for the occasion, the diggers prepare a plot 3 to 4 feet deep, and when it is ready, the grave is temporarily "closed" with a shovel or stick laid across it while funeral ceremonies proceed. A speech is directed at the deceased, praising his or her heroic deeds and personal attributes, and then the body is carried to the grave. It is laid extended on its back, head west and feet east, with a pillow under-

neath the head. (Many other Native American tribes tie the bent legs up to the chest and bury the corpse in a seated fetal position.) Some Shawnee place items in the grave with the dead, whereas others do not, but in any case many of the personal items of the dead are given to the gravediggers, cooks, and funeral director after the interment. The funeral director hands each relative a small amount of tobacco, which is thrown into the grave as they circumambulate it slowly in single file. After the funeral the mourners head directly to the home where death occurred, forbidden to look behind as they go. There they wash themselves with a mixture of water and plant juices for purification and enjoy a large feast provided by the blood relatives.

The funeral director and gravediggers initially remain behind with the dead. The director delivers another address to the dead, and then the gravediggers fill up the grave and build a "grave house" over the spot. The diggers and anyone who touched the corpse acquire a "death pollution" and are subject to special purificatory

When life is gone, the body is addressed by some
friend of the deceased in a long speech in which he
begs of him to take courage and boldly pursue his
journey to the great meadow, observing that all his
departed friends and relations are anxiously waiting
to receive him, and that his surviving friends will
soon follow.

The body is then decently dressed and wrapped in
a new blanket, with new shoes garnished, and
painted with vermilion on the feet. It is kept for one
night in the lodge, and is next day buried in the
earth. The nearest relations bear it to the grave, in
which it is wrapped up in birch bark instead of a
coffin, carefully laying his medicine bag under the
head. Some bury kettles, guns, axes and various other
articles with the body, but this custom is not general.
Before the grave is shut, the nearest relation takes a
lock of the deceased's hair and carefully wraps it up
in a piece of cloth or blanket; this they continually
carry with them from place to place and keep many
years as a remembrance. This pledge of their affection
is particularly honored at their feasts and drinking
matches by having the first offerings of their meat
and drink. . . .

They either raise a pile of wood over the grave, or
enclose it with a fence; at the head of the grave a
small post is erected on which they carve the
particular mark of the tribe to whom the deceased
belonged. . . . The bodies of some of their most
celebrated chiefs are raised upon high scaffolds, with
flags flying and the scalps of their enemies, with
other trophies of their prowess, suspended from a
high pole, but all those monuments are not intended
so much to distinguish their great men from the
vulgar as to ensure to their departed souls the same
respectability in the next world which they enjoyed
in this.

It is customary with their warriors at the funeral
of their great men to strike the post and relate all
their martial achievements as they do in the war
dance, and their funeral ceremonies conclude by a
feast around the grave.

*Peter Grant, head of the Red River Department
of the North-West Company, quoted in
Bushnell (1927, pp. 3–4).*

death. The sticks for the fire are laid parallel on an east-
west line, and are meant to guide the spirit of the dead
on its journey.

On the third night after death, the Shawnee hold a
more important vigil for the deceased. This takes place
at the former residence of the dead, where all the mourners gather and prepare a meal that they "share with the
dead," offering a portion for him or her as well. (A
special ceremony for a surviving spouse called a "condolence ceremony" is held at the same time.) Weather permitting, everyone gathers outside, and elders relate
myths and legends until dawn, when the spirit of the
dead is finally thought to depart the earth. Until then,
several taboos are observed by all mourners (in most
Shawnee divisions), and a few additional taboos are
incumbent upon a surviving spouse. All mourners leave
their hair unwashed and disheveled and their faces
unwashed and unpainted. Among some Shawnee bands,
there may be no dancing in the community during the
four-day mourning period, and women may not sew new
material. Additional taboos require that the surviving
spouse eat and drink alone during the initial mourning
period or stay inside alone. For up to a year after the
death, the surviving spouse must avoid looking at young
children or the sick and refrain from gossiping, drinking
liquor, gambling, and dancing.

The day when the spirit of the dead departs is a day
of purification for the mourners. The former residence
of the dead is swept out, the ashes of the old hearth fire
are removed, and a new fire is kindled, signifying a
purification from the death that occurred and a new
start. Water steeped in angelica is sprinkled over the
premises, and cedar wood is burned inside the house.
(Many other tribes feel the pollution at the old residence is too great to purify in this fashion, and the
living actually abandon the home or tear it down and
rebuild it some distance away.) All mourners must wash
their hair, and some Shawnee divisions hold that
mourners must bathe or swim to purify their entire
body. Then any property of the deceased (that was not
used to pay the cooks, diggers, and funeral director) is
divided up among the surviving family members.

What preceded was a brief summary of the funerary
customs of one important tribe, formerly of the eastern
woodlands of the United States. As already stated,
however, the diversity among tribes, especially tribes of
different regions and climates, is vast. For example,
funerals tended to be more elaborate for important
persons such as chiefs, priests, and shamans, particularly
among those tribes in which distinctions between social
ranks were most pronounced, namely on the Northwest
Coast of the United States, on the coastal plain of the
Southeast, in Meso-America, and in the Caribbean. Not
only were such high-ranking ceremonies elaborate and
expensive, but they often included human beings as

rites, including swimming, bathing, and taking a
special tea. They are then fed by the relatives of the
deceased, but separately from the feast for the mourners
because of the temporary pollution they have acquired.
After the feast most mourners leave, but a few close relatives stay with the surviving spouse. One relative lights
a fire at the gravesite each night for three nights after

sacrifices. Victims might be slaves or war captives, and in more southern areas they might include servants, "donated" children, or the widow of the deceased. Among many tribes human sacrifice was never practiced, but a dog or even a horse might have been killed.

Besides distinctions in rank and class, another area of wide divergence among North American tribes was the disposal of the body. Exposure of the corpse above ground was common in Arctic regions because the ground was too frozen nearly all the time to allow digging. Cremation was common in parts of the sub-Arctic, the Northwest Coast, California and parts of the adjacent mountainous areas, and northeastern Mexico (see Driver for more exact locations). Meanwhile, scaffold or tree burial was common in the northern plains and prairies and the middle part of the Northwest Coast. Inhumation appears to have been widely popular among tribes in many areas, though this is difficult to judge because after the coming of the Europeans in 1492, Christian missionaries attempted to force the natives to practice only burial of the dead.

Annual ceremonies for the individual or collective dead were held by many tribes. According to Driver, the Hurons of the northeastern United States and some of their neighbors in the northern prairies held a massive feast for the dead every twelve years. It seems that in some cases the annual ceremonies for the dead marked not only the anniversary of death but the conclusion of the year-long journey of the soul from this world to the next. For example, the Iroquois, mostly situated in present-day New York state, used to believe that the spirit took one year to reach its destination and thus celebrated the successful conclusion of that journey with a feast one year after death (Bushnell 1920). But in more recent history the Iroquois altered their belief in the time required for the journey to just a season and then changed it to merely ten days, with the mourning period shortened correspondingly—suggesting an intimate link between the two.

As for where the land of the dead was located, this also varied by tribe. Among the highly sophisticated and urbanized Aztecs, the inheritors of Mayan culture in many ways, there were up to thirteen vertical levels of heaven, guarded by more than 100 gods. Those who died in war, in childbirth, through human sacrifice, or by drowning or being struck by lightning each went to a special heaven or region of heaven, whereas the ordinary dead proceeded to a dreary Underworld, which at least lacked torture or suffering. By contrast, shamanistic tribes such as the Navajo (southwestern United States), Creek (southeastern United States), Greenland Inuit, and Washington state Sanpoil claimed only one or two different dwelling places for the dead. According to the Creek, good spirits of the dead went to live in the sky, whereas evil ones went west. The Navajo believed

in a single Underworld for all the dead, the Sanpoil believed in only a single land of the dead at the end of the Milky Way, and the Inuit believed in both an Underworld and a Sky World. Up was not always "good," and down was certainly not always "bad." Among the Greenland Inuit, the sky realm of the dead was cold and short of food; therefore they preferred the realm in the Underworld. The American Central Inuit, however, taught that the warm land of plenty (kilivum or adlivum) where there is no ice or snow, is situated in the sky and that the cold, dark land (adilparmiut) is located below in the Earth. The Tlingits of the Northwest Coast believed that the souls of the dead dwell not only in the Underworld far away in the north but also in the sky where only the souls of those killed in battle may go and where, as the flames of the northern lights, they do battle with one another.

See also BURIAL, BASKET; BURIAL, SCAFFOLD; BURIAL, TREE; FUNERARY CUSTOMS, ARCTIC EURASIAN; MOUND.

References

Bushnell, David I., Jr. *Burials of the Algonquian, Siouan and Caddoan Tribes West of the Mississippi.* Smithsonian Institution Bureau of American Ethnology, Bulletin 83. Washington, DC: Government Printing Office, 1927.

———. *Native Cemeteries and Forms of Burial East of the Mississippi.* Smithsonian Institution Bureau of American Ethnology, Bulletin 71. Washington, DC: Government Printing Office, 1920.

Deserontyon, John. *A Mohawk Form of Ritual of Condolence, 1782.* Trans. J. N. B. Hewitt. Indian Notes and Monographs, vol. 10, no. 8. New York: Museum of the American Indian, Heye Foundation, 1928.

Driver, Harold E. *Indians of North America.* Chicago: University of Chicago Press, 1961.

Griffin, James B., Richard E. Flanders, and Paul F. Titterington. *The Burial Complexes of the Knight and Norton Mounds in Illinois and Michigan.* Memoirs of the Museum of Anthropology, no. 2. Ann Arbor: University of Michigan, 1970.

MacLeod, W. C. "Certain Mortuary Aspects of Northwest Coast Culture." *American Anthropologist* 27 (1925).

Morris, Earl H. *Burials in the Aztec Ruin.* Anthropological Papers of the American Museum of Natural History, vol. 26, part 3. New York: American Museum Press, 1924.

Thomas, Cyrus. "Burial Mounds of the Northern Sections of the United States." Smithsonian Institution Bureau of Ethnology, fifth annual report. Washington, DC: Government Printing Office, 1887.

Voegelin, Erminie Wheeler. *Mortuary Customs of the Shawnee and other Eastern Tribes.* Prehistory Research Series, vol. 2, no. 4. Indianapolis: Indiana Historical Society, 1944.

Yarrow, H. C. *A Further Contribution to the Study of Mortuary Customs of the North American Indians.* Bureau of American Ethnology Annual Report, vol. 1. Washington, DC: Government Printing Office, 1881.

———. *Introduction to the Study of Mortuary Customs among the North American Indians.* Washington, DC: Government Printing Office, 1880.

FUNERARY CUSTOMS, SCANDINAVIAN

The characteristics of the prehistoric inhabitants of Scandinavia and the extent of their domain are somewhat uncertain, but at least by the first millennium B.C.E. Teutonic peoples had migrated north from central or eastern Europe and settled in these northern lands. Norse myths and legends hint at the rise and fall of several great Scandinavian epochs, but only one is known to history: during the Middle Ages Scandinavian people, through trade and conquest, controlled a vast territory stretching from Greenland and Iceland to the Upper Volga north of the Caspian Sea. While Viking raiders devastated the coasts of England and France, Scandinavian merchants exchanged fur, weapons, cattle, and Slavic slaves in Constantinople for Muslim silver. With the arrival of Christianity around 1000 C.E., the northern peoples took on Roman Catholic and later Protestant rites, including burial practices.

Throughout the entirety of Scandinavian history up to the Christian period, inhumation and cremation were practiced side by side, although one or the other dominated in different periods. In the very earliest period for which archaeological records exist, it would appear that burial was most widely practiced. Some burials were of groups of people together, whereas others were single burials with the corpse placed in a crouched position (as elsewhere in the ancient world); often a large burial mound was built over the grave. In the middle of what scholars have designated the Bronze Age, however, cremation seems to have suddenly and thoroughly taken hold such that inhumation, with a few notable exceptions, almost disappeared as a funerary practice—until it was reintroduced via Roman influence coming up from the south during the first century C.E. It is not clear what brought about this marked shift toward cremation, though several scholars have noted the simultaneous development of a cult of the sun god and a rise in the practice of burning offerings. Certainly, some dramatic shift in belief took place that influenced funerary practice for so long over such a widely diffused region.

The earliest cremations of the Bronze Age were in human-length stone cists, just like inhumations, but as cremation gained sway as a universal practice, the receptacle for the cremains grew smaller and became a boxlike stone cist holding the urn with the ashes. Burial mounds grew smaller, and sometimes the cremation urns were placed in older mounds or in graves that were completely flat. At first the bones remaining from the cremation were washed and placed in the urn, but gradually the practice grew of burning the body with funerary goods and offerings and placing them en masse into an urn. Together with the cremated body and funerary goods were deposited the weapons and other war gear of the deceased, which had usually been broken (perhaps

---

The Funeral of Balder

The gods hewed and carried down to the shore a vast amount of fuel, which they piled upon the deck of Balder's dragon-ship, Ringhorn, constructing an elaborate funeral pyre. According to custom, this was decorated with tapestry hangings, garlands of flowers, vessels and weapons of all kinds, golden rings, and countless objects of value, ere the immaculate corpse, richly attired, was brought and laid upon it.

One by one, the gods now drew near to take a last farewell of their beloved companion, and as Nanna [his wife] bent over him, her loving heart broke, and she fell lifeless by his side. Seeing this, the gods reverently laid her beside her husband, that she might accompany him even in death; and after they had slain his horse and hounds and twined the pyre with thorns, the emblems of sleep, Odin, last of the gods, drew near. . . .

The great ship now drifted out to sea, and the flames from the pyre presented a magnificent spectacle, which assumed a greater glory with every passing moment, until, when the vessel neared the western horizon, it seemed as if sea and sky were on fire. Sadly the gods watched the glowing ship and its precious freight, until suddenly it plunged into the waves and disappeared; nor did they turn aside and return to Asgard until the last spark of light had vanished, and the world, in token of mourning for Balder the good, was enveloped in a mantle of darkness.

Guerber (1992).

---

to "kill" them so as to make them usable by the dead).

Most interesting from the late Bronze and early Iron Ages is the occasional practice of placing remains (whether inhumed or cremated) in ship-form graves in which the surface of the grave was encircled by upright stones forming the outline of a ship. This practice is the more interesting because it seems to prefigure the medieval practice of actually burying or cremating an entire ship containing the deceased and his or her belongings. Taken together with the many symbolic pictures of ships, sun disks, trees, snakes, and so on found on the walls of tombs, gravestones, and on the mountainsides in Scandinavia, scholars have suggested this Bronze Age interest in funerary ships was connected with fertility and rebirth. In this sense the earlier "crouched" burials suggest a fetal position or return to the womb, whereas the later funerary ship images suggest a belief in travel (physically or metaphorically) to a new life. Indeed, there are several accounts in the Norse epics of lovers born again into human bodies to pursue their love affairs, and there are legends of kings reborn to continue their divinely appointed missions on earth. For instance, there is the apocryphal but popular story of Olaf Geirstadaálfr reborn as Saint Olaf, with the old cloak, bracelet, and sword taken from the burial mound and given to the new king. It is not known how widespread this belief in reincarnation was.

Because of the prestige of Rome at the beginning of the common era, the custom of inhumation again gained ascendancy in Scandinavia, although cremation continued as well. Graves of this period, like Roman burials, were laid out like elaborate banquets, with eating and drinking vessels and stores of food buried along with the dead. The more affluent Denmark was particularly influenced by Roman custom in general and is particularly known during this period for elaborate graves of the banquet-type.

The Roman period is succeeded by the Migration period (200 to 700 C.E.), during which Denmark again more closely followed southern influences and adopted the simplified burial practices of the Merovingians. Meanwhile, in Norway and Sweden a period of simplification in funerary practices can be noted, but again, during the Viking period beginning in the ninth century, burial mounds became popular, growing larger and larger. These barrows were not merely dwelling places for the dead (at least, the terrestrial remains of the dead, see SOUL) but also were monuments to their prestige and memory. The dead were laid within fully clothed (if inhumed) and surrounded by armor, weapons, and household equipment rather than banquet accoutrements. Great care was taken to give the dead, whether male or female, as complete an equipment of personal possessions as possible, including even animal sacrifices. For the wealthy the buried treasures and human sacrifices could be vast: the *Bárdar Saga* tells of the Viking hero Raknar being buried with 500 men. Like the Hindu practice of satī, there is ample evidence in Scandinavian archaeological sites and in its literature that women, particularly wives of eminent leaders, committed suicide (or "died of heartbreak," which is presumably the same thing) on their husband's funeral pyre. The *Eddas* and *Sagas* depict this wifely sacrifice as noble and voluntary, with the women gaining access along with their husbands to Valhalla, the heavenly mansion reserved for heroes; yet there is reason to believe that many women were not pleased with this arrangement. One historical woman, Sigridr the Proud, avoided this fate. Around 990 C.E. she divorced her husband (King Eric Sigrsaell of Sweden) in his old age to avoid going to the grave with him and married the younger Svein of Denmark, thereafter helping him in his conquests.

Also in the Viking period the first physical ships are found, either cremated or inhumed with the deceased and placed in the barrow. Several hundred Scandinavian ship burials have thus far been discovered, some of considerable size; the ship found at Gokstad was over 60 feet long with thirty-two oars, although most ship burials were smaller. Since frequently the boat and its deceased passenger(s) were cremated, sometimes it is only the discovery of metal boat rivets in a grave that alerts the archaeologist to the fact that there was a ship funeral. Indeed, it is quite possible that ship funerals were practiced earlier, as strongly suggested by the stone ship-form graves mentioned above; it has been suggested that evidence for this has not been found because early boats were made without metal rivets and thus leave no remains.

Along with the rise of ship burials, cremation again became the dominant funerary custom, particularly for heroes and other significant dead. The archaeological evidence for this is abundant, but unfortunately most of the original Norse literature has been lost. Only the Icelandic Sagas have survived, but by the time of their composition Scandinavia was already heavily Christianized, and cremations had been stopped. In these *Sagas* inhumation is the primary means of disposal, but there are exceptions: some of the most important heroes (especially Swedish kings) are depicted receiving a magnificent cremation at death, usually in their ships. Likewise in the Icelandic *Eddas,* the death of Balder, son of the high god Odin, occasioned his dramatic cremation in his ship out at sea. Conversion to Christianity in the tenth and eleventh centuries gradually put a stop to all cremations (though the practice was tenacious), since the body was to be needed again, intact, for the resurrection. Since Iceland was colonized by Scandinavia after this period, the practice of cremation never took hold in Iceland. Cremation continued longest in areas like Finland that were farthest removed from Christian civilization, but all finally conformed to the practice of inhumation on holy ground, except for the rare case of cremating a corpse determined to be "undead," as in the rest of Europe.

See also BARROW; BURIAL, SHIP; ODIN; SOUL; TUMULUS; UNDEAD; VALHALLA.

References

Davidson, H. R. Ellis. *The Lost Beliefs of Northern Europe*. London: Routledge, 1993.

Ellis, Hilda Roderick. *The Road to Hel: A Study of the Conception of the Dead in Old Norse Literature.* Cambridge: Cambridge University Press, 1943.

Guerber, Hélène Adeline. *Myths of the Norsemen from the Eddas and Sagas.* New York: Dover, 1992.

Kirkby, Michael Hasloch. *The Vikings*. Oxford: Phaidon Press, 1977.

Nørlund, P. *Viking Settlers in Greenland*. London: Cambridge University Press, 1936.

Sawyer, P. H. *The Age of the Vikings*. London: Edward Arnold, 1962.

Shetelig, Haakan, and Hjalmar Falk. *Scandinavian Archaeology*. Trans. E. V. Gordon. Oxford: Clarendon Press, 1937.

FUNERARY CUSTOMS, ZOROASTRIAN

In the ancient Persian religion of Zoroastrianism, death is thought to be simply the separation of the immortal soul from its mortal coil. After the soul has departed, the body is respected as a vehicle that once contained the sacred, but the corpse is also thought to be extremely polluting. In most cases, unless death occurred near sunset, the body is to be prepared and disposed of on the very day of death, while the sun still shines. The rich and the poor are to be treated in exactly the same way, avoiding social distinctions in burial clothes, elaborate ceremonies, and so on.

If the dying person is able, it is most beneficial for him or her to recite a prayer praising righteousness, namely the Ashem Vohu, and a prayer of penance, patet. If the dying cannot speak or has died suddenly, his or her children or near relatives should say the prayers quietly in the ear of the deceased. At death the corpse is shrouded in a white cotton cloth. After a short time the body is rubbed down with gomez (cow's urine) and then with water. The sacred thread, or kusti, is wrapped around the waist of the deceased with the appropriate prayer, called *nirang-e-kusti bastan.* Finally, the body is clothed in clean but old clothing—it is considered sinful to waste new clothes on the dead, when they could be given to someone in need. For the last time, family members are invited to gather and embrace the dead, for henceforth the body comes under a prohibition due to its extreme ritual pollution. The spirit of decomposition (Druj-i-nasush), thought of as both a foul air and a demon, takes over the now soulless body, and anyone who comes in contact with it becomes impure and must follow elaborate purification rituals, including the nāhn, or sacred bath.

After the family has departed, only special corpse-bearers, called *nassasālārs,* are allowed to touch the body. They must ritually wash their hands, face, and feet; untie and retie their sacred kusti threads in a ritual called *padyab-kusti;* and put on clean but very old clothes—since the clothing the corpse-bearers wear also becomes corrupted by contact with the corpse and must be disposed of with it. While prayers are recited, the corpse is lowered to a clean white sheet placed on the ground, and the corpse-bearers dress the body in a long white robe called a *jāmā.* The body is tied up with white strips of cloth at five locations: the neck, each arm, the waist, the knees, and the toes. The hands are crossed over the chest, and the head is covered with another white cloth. Then the body is placed on slabs of stone or a heap of gravel, which protect the earth from coming into direct contact with the body—to allow the body to touch the earth directly would infect the sacred element of earth. The body should be placed in a corner of the room, with the head not pointing north. Around the body three concentric circles are drawn with a metallic instrument (a nail, bar etc.), which marks off the resting place as contaminated. No one may enter, and the magic metal-drawn circles prevent the death infection from escaping. Finally, both a fire burning sandalwood and other incense and a lamp burning coconut oil are lit. They burn throughout the three-day period when the soul is thought to remain earthbound.

After the body has been thus prepared, a ritual called *sagdid,* literally "dog sight," is performed for the first time. A peculiar-looking dog is brought in to witness that the body is actually deceased. The dog must have eye-shaped spots on the forehead above its actual eyes— a "four-eyed" dog in appearance. Three times the dog is to view the dead: once when the corpse is prepared, once when it is carried away from the house, and finally at the Tower of Silence. If the dog looks at the body, it is surely dead; if the dog looks away or shows no interest in the deceased, there is an investigation as to whether the person is truly dead. The four-eyed dog's gaze is thought to ward off evil, possibly by causing confusion and alarm in nearby evil spirits who are thrown off by the dog's appearance. This unique canine custom also stems from the important role that the figure of the dog plays in Zoroastrian Scriptures, symbolizing the spiritual "witness" in all beings.

About an hour before the body is to be carried out to the Tower of Silence, or "burial" site, two Zoroastrian priests enter the funerary room and perform the geh-sarnu ritual. The first half of the ritual blesses the iron bier (called a *gehān*) that will be used to carry out the dead. The priests begin to chant hymns (or Gathas) from their sacred text, the Avesta, and halfway through the chanting, the priest and all witnesses face away as the corpse-bearers lift the body off its resting place on the stone slabs (or gravel) and place it on the bier. Because this movement of the body is thought to throw off polluting germs, everyone turns to avoid contamination. Sagdid is performed once more, and assured that the deceased is in fact dead, the priests continue with the geh-sarnu, in the latter half offering prayers that bless the dead. Male witnesses line up, approach the dead, and bow, showing their respects one last time (a process that is called *sidjā*); they then prepare to follow the funeral procession out to some distance. Women make salutations where they stand and do not leave the room in procession with the body. At last, the corpse-bearers pick up the bier and proceed to the final resting place of the dead, some distance from civilization. The room where the dead rested is purified by a sprinkling of gomez.

Cremation is almost never practiced by Zoroastrians, and of the two instances in which it is recorded, one was a deliberate act of desecration. Again, because of the belief that the corpse is extremely polluting, burning

At the close of the third night, when the dawn breaks, the soul of the righteous person passes through the trees, inhaling sweet fragrances; it seems as if a wind were blowing from the region of the South; from the regions of the South, of sweet fragrance, of sweeter fragrance than other winds.

And it seems to the soul of the righteous person as if it were inhaling that wind with the nose, and it thinks: "Whence does that wind blow, the wind of the sweetest fragrance that I ever inhaled with my nostrils?"

It seems to him as if his own conscience were advancing to him with that wind in the shape of a maiden, fair, bright, of white arms, courageous, beautiful, tall, with prominent breasts, beautiful of body, noble, of glorious birth, of fifteen years, and of a form as fair as the fairest of creatures.

Then the soul of the righteous person addressed her, asking: "What maiden are thou, the fairest of maidens whom I have ever seen?"

Then replied unto him his own conscience: "O thou youth of good thoughts, good words and good deeds, and of good conscience, everybody love thee for the greatness, goodness, beauty, sweet fragrance, courage, innocence, in which thou dost appear to me.

"Thou didst love me, O youth of good thoughts, good words, good deeds, and good conscience, for the greatness, goodness, beauty, sweet fragrance, courage, innocence, in which I appear to thee. . . .

"Lovely as I was, thou madest me more lovely; beautiful as I was, thou madest me more beautiful; favored as I was, thou madest me more favored; seated as I was on an exalted place, thou madest me sit on a more exalted place, through thy good thoughts, good words and good deeds; and so men will hereafter sacrifice unto me who have long sacrificed unto and have been in communion with Ahura Mazda [the great god of Zoroastrianism].

Yasht 22:7–12, 14, translation by Dhalla (1972).

the dead or burying them corrupts the sacred elements of fire or earth. Therefore, the body is placed in a Tower of Silence, where under the sun's rays the corpse is exposed, and the corrupt flesh is gradually removed from the pure bones, primarily by birds of prey. It is considered extremely meritorious for mourners, dressed all in white, to follow a funeral procession out to the Tower of Silence, but only the specially consecrated nassasalars may enter or touch the tower. The ritual of sagdid is performed one last time, and the corpse-bearers enter the tower and place the corpse inside. All family members are then required to take a ritual bath.

After some time has passed and all of the flesh has been removed from the bones, usually eight months to a year, the family of the deceased returns to gather up the bones and place them in an ossuary.

For three days after death, the soul of the deceased is thought to linger on the Earth, either in the vicinity where death occurred, near the Tower of Silence, or near the sacred flame that burns in Zoroastrian temples. On the third night, three religious offices are said, directed to the god Sraosha, "the protector of prayers" who will soon judge the dead and assign him or her to the correct place in the afterlife. An animal sacrifice is performed on the third day, and at the first light of dawn on the fourth day, when the soul is thought to be drawn up to the sky by the sun's rays, fat from the animal sacrifice is given to the fire. (Among the Parsis of India, however, animal sacrifices were replaced by sandalwood offerings in the twentieth century, probably due to the influence of Hindu and Jain concepts of nonviolence.)

Every day for the first thirty days after death an offering is made for the deceased, after which there is a second animal sacrifice. For the remainder of the year, an offering is made once every month. At the one-year anniversary of the death, another animal sacrifice is performed, along with an offering of food and clothing. In addition, annual ceremonies of food offerings for the deceased take place for thirty years; sometimes the ceremonies for a great person will continue for longer than thirty years. For example, descendants still perform annual services for the great Parsi priest Dastur Meherji Rana, who died in the sixteenth century. Finally, the whole Zoroastrian community performs an annual ceremony for the soul of Zoroaster himself, which has been maintained according to tradition for nearly 4,000 years (Zoroastrians date the life of their prophet to c. 1700 B.C.E., though many modern scholars place him around 600 B.C.E.).

Besides the observances for the individual dead, there is an annual festival for all of the dead that takes place on the last ten days of the year, called *Fravardigān*. Food is put out for the dead, both at home and at the Tower of Silence; houses are meticulously cleaned and filled with juniper incense, and people are on their best behavior. According to a late (ninth-century C.E.) Zoroastrian text, the Saddar Bundahishn, on this day,

During the Fravardegān Holidays, the spirits of the dead revisit this world. They go to their respective houses. There it is necessary for men to burn fragrance over fire during these ten days and remember their dear departed ones. They must . . . recite the Avesta. The spirits of the dead are thereby made felicitous and pleased, and they bless (the living ones). Again it is necessary that during these ten days men must perform works of charity and be free from other ordinary work. The spirits of the dead thereby return (to their mansions in heaven) much pleased, and they bless the living dear ones. (Sidhwa, trans., p. 39)

Among the blessings the dead can bestow are fertility to women as well as to the land; victory in war, health to the sick, and good fortune to all. Failure to give a proper funeral or make appropriate offerings puts the living in danger—not so much from the wrath of the departed but from the dangers that will arise because the connection to the fravashi will be broken and they will not be able to protect the living any longer.

See also BEHESHT; CHINVAT BRIDGE; DOZAKH; FRAVARDIGĀN; FRAVASHI; SOUL, ZOROASTRIAN; TOWER OF SILENCE.

References

Boyce, Mary. *A History of Zoroastrianism.* Vol. 1. Leiden: E. J. Brill, 1975.

Dhalla, M. N. *Zoroastrian Theology from the Earliest Times to the Present Day.* Reprint, New York: AMS Press, 1972.

Jackson, A. V. W. *Zoroastrian Studies.* New York: Columbia University Press, 1928.

Kotwal, Firoze M., and James W. Boyd, trans. *A Guide to the Zoroastrian Religion.* Studies in World Religion no. 3. Chico, CA: Scholars Press, 1982.

Masani, Sir Rustom. *Zoroastrianism: The Religion of the Good Life.* New York: Collier Books, 1962.

Modi, J. J. *The Funeral Ceremonies of the Parsees: Their Origin and Explanation.* Bombay: British India Press, 1923.

———. *The Religious Ceremonies and Customs of the Parsees.* Bombay: British India Press, 1937.

Sethna, Tehmurasp Rustamji. *Book of Instructions on Zoroastrian Religion.* Karachi: Informal Religious Meetings Trust Fund, 1980.

Sidhwa, Ervad Godrej Dinshawji. *Discourses on Zoroastrianism.* Karachi: Ervad Godrej Dinshawji Sidhwa, 1978.

FYLGIE (FYLGJA)

In the pre-Christian Scandinavian and Norse tradition, the fylgie (plural: fylgjur) was the guardian spirit that accompanied each individual throughout his or her life, although in the literature fylgjur are particularly mentioned in association with heroes. The word *fylgie* means literally "to accompany" and appears originally to have been the concept of the higher part of oneself, one's "spirit" as it were, which could speak to the conscious mind and warn of danger. It was generally invisible to all except magicians and other exceptional people and usually spoke only through symbols and dreams. The masses, however, tended to interpret the fylgie as an outside entity that hovers around the individual or as a subtle body-soul that could leave the body and return.

Sometimes this guardian spirit has been pictured as an (invisible) animal, particularly as various kinds of bird, wolf, or bear, which then might become the emblem for a warrior or for a whole clan. This spirit-animal was thought capable of viewing distant lands, communicating with others on an inner plane, or advising in battle. The fylgie was also thought to be a messenger of Orlog (Fate), informing its protégé of what must be. The fylgie has also been pictured as a female spirit, like the Valkyrie but not limited to the battlefield. As a female guardian, however, the fylgie appears less as the guide of an individual and more as the guide of a clan, like the Irish banshee but again, not limited solely to predictions of death.

See also BANSHEE; FUNERARY CUSTOMS, SCANDINAVIAN; NORNS; ODIN; VALKYRIE.

References

Guerber, Hélène Adeline. *Myths of the Norsemen from the Eddas and Sagas.* New York: Dover, 1992.

Lindow, John. "Fylgjur." In *Encyclopedia of Religion,* ed. Mircea Eliade. New York: Macmillan, 1987.

Titchenell, Elsa-Brita. *The Masks of Odin.* Pasadena: Theosophical University Press, 1985.

Turville-Petre, E. O. G. *Nine Norse Studies.* London: Viking Society for Northern Research, University College, London, 1972.

G

GAMES, FUNERAL (GREEK)

From early times in ancient Greece there was a custom of holding games and festivities (epitaphios agon) after a funeral, especially if the deceased was an important person. The earliest evidence for this is found in Homer's description of the funeral games held by Achilles for Patroklos in the *Iliad*, corroborated by Geometric period vase paintings and later inscriptions.

Even Panhellenic ("all the Greek world") games that were connected to calendrical festivals had mythological associations with the deaths of fallen heroes: the Olympic games were said to have been started in honor of the death of either Pelops or Oinomaos. Like the life-denying asceticism practiced by mourners after the loss of a loved one (wearing filthy clothes, abstaining from taking baths, putting ash and earth in one's hair), athletes practiced asceticism for some time before competition, including a vegetarian diet and sexual abstinence.

References

Burkert, Walter. *Greek Religion*. Trans. John Raffan. Cambridge: Harvard University Press, 1985.

Weiler, Ingomar. *Der Agon im Mythos: Zur Einstellung der Griechen zum Wettkampf*. Darmstadt: Wissenschaftliche Buchgesellschaft, 1974.

GAMES, FUNERAL (IRISH)

Called *feis* (feast) and *oenach* (reunion), popular assemblies with games in ancient Ireland were often held on burial grounds in honor of a deceased hero or heroine, possibly as a kind of ancestor worship. Poems and records from all over Ireland indicate such gatherings were extremely common, with the festival and its games fixed in the community's calendar and named after the dead who were so honored.

Legend has it that Tea, daughter of Lugaid and wife of Géide, was buried at Tara, the chief of all places of assembly in Ireland, and gave her name to the palace and assemblies there. Every third year, after the public sacrifices connected with Samhain were completed, the royal assembly gathered at Tara for a public spectacle, the main event being chariot racing.

Another of the most famous assemblies and race-courses in Ireland, Oenach Carman, is named after the goddess Carman, who with her sons used magic to blight the corn of Ireland. Opposing gods, the Tuatha Dé Danann, overthrew Carman and her three sons, and Carman died of grief. The *Book of Leinster* (c. 1079 C.E.) records the origin of the funeral games held in Carman's name:

Hearken, ye Leinstermen of the graves . . .

Carman, gathering place of a hospitable fair,
with level [turf] for courses:
the hosts that used to come to its celebration
conquered in its bright races.

A burial-ground of kings is its noble cemetery,
even specially dear to hosts of high rank;
under the mounds of assembly are many
of its host of a stock ever-honoured.

To bewail queens and kings,
to lament revenges and ill deeds,
there came many a fair host at harvest-time
across the noble smooth check of ancient Carman. . . .

Not men it was, nor wrathful man,
But one fierce marauding woman—
bright was her precinct and her fame—
from whom Carman [field] gets its name . . .
(Ettlinger)

For a week in August every three years, a festival took place at the field of Carman, with seven horse races and other festivities. Interestingly, excavations of the site in County Kildare suggest that the legend is based on facts, for a grave of a woman has been found, with the body in a position that suggests she was buried alive. Whether this live burial was a voluntary self-sacrifice or a punishment is not known.

See also FUNERARY CUSTOMS, CELTIC; GAMES, FUNERAL (GREEK); SAMHAIN.

References

Ettlinger, Ellen. "The Association of Burials with Popular Assemblies, Fairs and Races in Ancient Ireland." *Études Celtiques* 6, no. 1 (Paris: Société d'Édition "Les Belles Lettres," 1953).

Orpen, G. H. "Aenach Carman." *Journal of the Royal Society of the Antiquaries of Ireland* 36 (Dublin, 1906).

GARDEN, FUNERARY

In the ancient Greek and Roman world, the wealthy often endowed a garden around their tombs, to provide both a pleasant place for people to congregate and honor the deceased and an income from the vegetables and fruits produced. Found first in the eastern Greek provinces and most especially in the great city of Alexandria, in the first century B.C.E. funerary gardens (called *cepotaphium* in Latin and *kepotaphion* in Greek) appear to have spread to the western provinces and Rome, becoming quite popular by the second century C.E.

Within walled enclosures surrounding the tomb or mausoleum, the funerary gardens were laid out in geometrical patterns. The few diagrams of the gardens that have survived on marble slabs from cemeteries show neat rows of trees or shrubs lining careful rectangles and squares of lawns, complete with paths for strolling. Wells, pools, and channels provided water for the plants and refreshment for visitors who came to eat their funerary banquet in the dining halls and summer houses provided. Texts from this period describe the gardens as having fruits of every kind, vegetables, vineyards, and various flowers that were not only decorative but could be sold at market, providing a steady source of offerings for the dead and an income for the upkeep of the tomb(s) and the celebration of festivals for the dead (the Parentalia).

References

Toynbee, J. M. C. *Death and Burial in the Roman World.* Ithaca, NY: Cornell University Press, 1971.

GARDENS OF DELIGHT (JANNAT AL-NA'IM)

In Islamic tradition, Paradise is referred to most often as "the Gardens of Delight." It is not difficult to imagine that for the Bedouin tribes of Arabia—who gave birth to Islam—the afterlife imagery of lush shady gardens flowing with streams of water, wine, milk, and honey, would provide welcome relief from the sand and drought that most often characterized their way of life. The gardens are plural because, like the Jewish and Christians traditions (which have shared much common history with Islam), heaven has many levels and subdivisions. With all respect to the integrity of Islam, it is difficult not to notice how much its understanding of the Gardens of Delight parallels and, in some cases, exactly duplicates earlier Christian and especially Jewish tradition, although in a number of respects Muslim traditions of heaven are unique.

There appears to be a preliminary area to the gardens, which receives the newly arrived from their trials and judgment by God and transforms them suitably for heaven. This area is reached after the chosen people pass the final trial, namely a bridge that spans Jahannam (al-Shirāt). There, beyond the bridge, lies a desert containing magnificent trees.

> Beneath each tree are two wells of water, which gush forth from the Garden, one from the right and the other from the left. . . . [The saved] go to that desert and drink from one of the streams. When the water reaches their chests, all the foul matter and blood and urine depart, and they are cleansed of their outer and inner malevolence. Then they come to the other stream and wash their heads in it and their faces become as bright as the moon on the night of the full moon. Their souls become soft like milk and their bodies become sweet like musk. (Macdonald, trans. of *Kitāb al-Haqā'iq wa'l-Daqā'iq*, pp. 355–356)

Much like the rivers encompassing the underworlds of many other cultures (for example, the river of Forgetfulness [Lethe] in Hades), these well-streams appear to mark a boundary between the sacred and profane and transform the blest into new kinds of beings.

The sacred text of Islam, the Qur'ān, gives many such "physical" details about the gardens, especially in the sections that were written earliest in Muhammed's mission. Nowhere, however, does the Scripture give an ordered picture of the overall structure of heaven. One verse of the Qur'ān (23:17) states: "We created above you seven paths . . .," which lends Islamic support to the very ancient Middle Eastern (Sumerian/Babylonian) picture of the heavens as seven-tiered. Many Jewish writings from the third century B.C.E. onward (joined by Christian writings from the first few centuries C.E.) speak of seven heavens and a hero who visits them, including texts such as the Book of Enoch, Testament of the Twelve Patriarchs, IV Ezra, the Apocalypse of Moses, and the Apocalypse of Paul. Even Paul in the New Testament (2 Corinthians 12:2) mentions the "third heaven." No doubt these writings had a great influence on early Muslim thinkers, perhaps even Muhammed. For example, Jane Smith and Yvonne Haddad translate from an eleventh-century Muslim text on the afterlife, *Kitāb ahwāl al-Qiyāma,* wherein the seven levels of heaven are described with corresponding precious materials:

> There are seven gardens [of delight]. The first of them is the abode of the garden and it is of white pearl. The second is the abode of peace and it is of red sapphire. The third is the garden of refuge and it is of green chrysolite. The fourth of them is the garden of eternity and it is of yellow coral. The fifth is the garden of bliss and it is of white silver. The sixth is the jannat al-firdaws [garden of paradise]

Depiction of the garden of Hasan Sabbah, leader of the Syrian branch of the Nizari Isma'ilis, by French traveler Odoric of Pordenone. It is said this garden was modeled on the descriptions of Paradise and was used as an instrument in obtaining the devotion of the Isma'ilis. Courtesy of Bibliothèque Nationale, Paris.

and it is of red gold. And the seventh of the gardens is Eden [jannāt 'adn] and is of white pearl. This is the capital (qasāba) of the Garden and it is elevated over all the gardens. (Smith and Haddad [1981], trans.)

Each garden has its own elaborate gate and appears to be reserved for different classes of the faithful: those who voluntarily gave alms, those who performed pilgrimage (hajj), those who prayed in the right Muslim fashion, and so on. There are different categories of holiness among the inhabitants of the heaven, and only the more deserving may proceed to the higher gardens. The top is reserved for great saints and martyrs, who proceed there directly without trial or judgment on Resurrection Day. Yet John Macdonald points out that as early as the time of Christ, Jewish tradition had already laid out seven heavens, each also associated with

precious objects. Likewise, each level of heaven in Jewish conception had huge decorated gates that admitted only those who through their faith and obedience to God knew the right passwords. Such parallels show the clear influence of early Judaism on Islam.

But because the Qur'ān in different places gives eight separate names for heaven, some Muslim authors have thought that although the heavens proper have seven levels, the actual abode of the blest will be in an eighth level above them. In this eighth level, some say, the Gardens of Delight are technically referred to by the plural noun *Firdaws*. The name *Firdaws* (singular farādis, directly related to the English word *paradise*) appears in the Qur'ān twice as the abode of the particularly blest (18:107, 23:11). Others believe the top level is a new Garden of Eden (in Arabic, 'Adn), while still others believe paradise is one single realm with many names. To this day Muslims debate the point.

On Saturday God Most High will provide drink
[from the water of the garden]. On Sunday [the
inhabitants of heaven] will drink its honey, on
Monday they will drink its milk, on Tuesday they
will drink its wine. When they have drunk, they will
become intoxicated; when they become intoxicated,
they will fly for a thousand years till they reach a
great mountain of fine musk, from beneath which
emanates [the river] Salsabīl. They will drink of it
and that will be Wednesday. Then they will fly for a
thousand years till they reach a place overtopping a
mountain. On it are thrones raised and cups set
out—[as in] the Qur'ān: Every one of them will sit
on a couch. Ginger wine will be brought down to
them and they shall drink. That will be on Thursday.
Then He will rain down upon them vestments from a
white cloud, for a thousand years, and jewels for a
thousand years. Attached to every jewel will be a
black-eyed maiden. Then they will fly for a thousand
years till they reach a perfect level spot. That will be
on Friday. They will be seated on the plateau of
eternity. The finest wine will be brought to them,
sealed with musk. They will drink it.

Translation by Smith and Haddad (1981, p. 90).

Despite later Muslim traditions and ancient Babylonian and Jewish influences, however, the Qur'ān does
not specifically list seven or eight layers of heaven but
merely refers to "the Gardens." At only one point in the
Qur'ān (chap. 55) is there an enumeration of the gardens. One verse (55:46) states: "For those that fear the
majesty of their Lord there are two gardens . . . planted
with shady trees." Later verses add the following: "And
beside these there shall be two other gardens . . . of
darkest green," and then go on to describe all the pleasures and beauties to be found, which are identical in each
garden. There is no indication if these gardens are horizontally adjacent or vertically layered, and the Scripture
does not specify that there are *only* four gardens.

With regard to the nature and content of the
Gardens of Delight, the Qur'ān and later Muslim tradition is more specific and generally more unanimous.
One of the first things the blest will notice about
heaven after arriving is the great banner of praise hung
above the heavens. It will stretch as far as a thousand
years, and its distance will reach the distance from
heaven to earth. The elaborate description is typical of
the Islamic vision of paradise:

It has three pennants of light, some in the East,
some in the West, and others in the center of the

world. On it are three rows of writing: the first row
"In the Name of God Merciful and Compassionate,"
the second "Praise be to God, Lord of the Worlds,"
and the third "There Is Only One God, Muhammed
Is His Apostle."

Each row extends for a thousand years and has
seventy thousand banners; under each banner there
are seventy thousand ranks of angels, and in every
rank there are five hundred thousand angels
praising and sanctifying God Most High.
(Macdonald, trans. of *Kitāb al-Haqā'iq wa'l-
Daqā'iq*)

Separate banners with names of virtues on them
(truth, justice, generosity, etc.) are assigned to various
saints and leaders in Islamic history, who gather to
themselves in heaven faithful Muslims who demonstrated those virtues in life. Until recently, banners
were thought to be a unique tradition in Islamic eschatology, but the recent find of the Dead Sea Scrolls has
shed light on earlier Jewish tradition. One scroll, "The
War of the Sons of Light and the Sons of Darkness,"
contains descriptions of heavenly trumpets and banners
with inscriptions like the Enlisted of God, the Princes
of God, the Rank of God, Offering to God, and
Triumph of God. However, only Islam has decorated
banners stretching across the heavens to welcome the
newcomers.

Again in common with earlier Jewish sources, Islamic
tradition tells of four rivers in paradise, springing from
the great tree that stands beneath the great throne of
God. The rivers are Kawthar, Kāfūr, Tasnīm, and
Salsabīl, and they flow with purest water, milk, wine,
and honey (described in Qur'ān 47:15). Muhammed
claimed to have seen these rivers in the Gardens himself:

One night when I was travelling in heaven the
whole of the Garden confronted me, and I saw there
four rivers, a river of water wholly pure, and a river
of milk, a river of wine and a river of honey.

I said to Jibrā'īl—upon him be peace—whence
come these rivers and wither do they go? Jibrā'īl—
upon him be peace—replied, "To al-Kawthar
[Abundance], but I do not know whence they
come. If you ask God, your Lord will inform you if
you wish." So I petitioned my Lord and an angel
came and greeted me. He said, "O Muhammed—
God bless him and his family and give them
peace—close your eyes." I closed my eyes. Then he
said, "Open your eyes." So I opened them and
behold, I was beside a tree, and I saw a pavilion of
white pearls [the topmost heaven; see earlier
description]. It had a door of green topaz, with a
lock of red gold. If all the Jinn [genies, or fire
spirits] and men in the world were to be put on top

of that pavilion, they would be like a bird sitting on a mountain! (Macdonald, trans., pp. 347–348)

The trees in the Gardens of Delight are also miraculous. Some are made of silver and some of gold, but none decay; even their leaves do not fall. Unlike the trees of our world, which have their roots in the earth and branches in the air, the trees in the gardens have their roots in the air and their branches in the ground (an identical teaching exists in Scandinavia regarding the world tree, Yggdrasil—most likely symbolizing in each case that they are nourished by the spiritual source above and bring their blessings to those below). One tree is particular is said to grow magnificent clothing from its top branches and decorated horses, upon which only the saints may ride, from its side branches. The greatest tree of the garden—of cosmic dimensions—is called Sidrat al-Mutahā, or the Tree of Blessedness. It appears to be the central "energy source" of heaven, and its least aspect is the sun.

> The most abundant of the trees of the Garden is the Tree of Blessedness. Its roots are of pearls, its trunk of mercy, its branches of topaz, its leaves of fine brocade. It has seventy thousand branches, attached to the pedestal of the Throne, and the lowest of its branches are in the lowest heaven.
>
> In the Garden there is neither room nor pavilion nor chamber that does not contain some of its branches and receives their shade. On these branches are the fruits that souls crave for. Their lowest point in the world (itself) is the sun. Their roots are in the sky and their light reaches every level and every place. (Macdonald, trans, p. 350)

There are magical animals in the Gardens of Delight as well and a great abundance of songbirds, which are also to be found in earlier Christian and Jewish conceptions of heaven. But an utterly unique (and controversial) feature of the Islamic Gardens of Delight is the presence of virgins, called *houris,* who are specially created by God to be the "playthings" of men who were abstemious and chaste during life. Although Western critics have sometimes seen these creatures as "whores" (and houri may well be the ultimate source of the English word), Muslims see the houris as the just reward for a good life. (Incidentally, there are no male houris for women in the afterlife.) These maidens are perpetual virgins, although their express purpose is for copulation. Their deep, dark brown eyes are their most prominent feature, set off by silky white skin that actually gives off light. Their faces may be white, red, yellow, or green, and their hair was created by God of cloves. Their bodies are made up completely of perfumes: from their feet to their knees, they are made of saffron; from knees to breasts of musk; from breasts to necks of ambergris, and from their necks to their scalp of camphor, and they are decked out in all manner of ornaments. Their only desire is to give pleasure, for it is written "All the dark-eyed maidens have passions of desire."

Finally, the faithful Muslims who arrive in heaven after resurrection will find themselves somewhat transformed. They will be resurrected to bodies of perpetual youth, and the men will be beardless but will have green mustaches (green being a very auspicious color in Islam). Women and men will be distinguished in this way. (Interestingly, neither Christianity or Judaism appears to make a distinction between the sexes in paradise.) Each person will have seventy delightful garments, each of which changes color seventy times every hour. Personal features considered uncouth will disappear: there will be no hair in the armpits or pubic area, no saliva, and no mucous in the nose. Men will have the strength of a hundred bodies, and all will grow each day more attractive, although there will be no aging. Food will be plentiful without being cooked or prepared and of incredible variety. People will eat one hundred times more than they could on earth and will enjoy it one hundred times more. Game birds will hover in the air, and if anyone wants to taste their flesh, the birds alight in trays and are immediately roasted. But then the bird becomes as it was before, without any of its flesh being consumed. There will be many wonderful alcoholic drinks, but there will be no intoxication, however much is drunk (according to the Qur'ān at least—later tradition taught otherwise; see excerpt.) Music is everywhere, with angels, birds, animals, hills, trees, and men and women joining in.

With all the numerology, gargantuan dimensions, and imaginative delights, one becomes curious how literally the description of the Gardens of Delight should be taken. One leading scholar, Louis Gardet, discusses in his article "Djanna" two important trends in the Islamic interpretation of paradise through the centuries. One direction has been a "traditional exegesis," which accepts the descriptions of the gardens in the Qur'ān literally and multiplies them endlessly. Another direction (including the important philosopher-mystic al-Ghazālī) admits the reality of the delights of heaven but emphasizes the vast difference between the known earthly life and the spiritual realities of the future, such that intellectual and spiritual fulfillment in the hereafter take precedence over the pleasures of the flesh. As Gardet notes, one radical Muslim theologian, Rābi'a, wrote (allegorically) that he wanted "to burn Paradise and drown Hell" so that God might be loved for himself alone and not for his rewards or punishments.

It is this latter tradition that has emphasized most strongly the final blessing of heaven, that of seeing God face to face. According to many traditions (hadīths) tracing themselves back to Muhammed, each Friday (the holy day of the week in Islam) God will present himself for the al-ru'yā, or the "beatific vision." Men follow the Prophet Muhammed, and women follow Muhammed's saintly daughter Fatima, and all approach the throne, which apparently is an inconceivably huge pavilion made of musk. The veil that hides the throne lifts, and God appears in all his glory and says, "Peace be upon you." This spiritual joy exceeds words and is higher than any physical or emotional pleasure:

> While the inhabitants of paradise are in their bliss a light will shine out to them, and raising their heads they will see that their Lord has looked down on them from above. He will then say, "Peace be to you, inhabitants of paradise," the proof of that being the words of God most high, "Peace, a word from a merciful Lord." He will then look at them and they will look at Him, and they will not turn aside to any of their bliss as long as they are looking at Him till He veils Himself from them and His light remains. (Ibn Māja, *Mishkāt al-maṣābīḥ* [II, 1208–1209], in Smith and Haddad, p. 96)

See also BARZAKH; HEAVEN, HISTORY OF; HEAVEN, ORIGINS OF; HISĀB; INTERCESSION; JAHANNAM; JUDGMENT, LAST; PURGATORY; QIYĀMA; SĀ'A; AL-SHIRĀT; SOUL, MUSLIM.

References
Dawood, N. J., trans. *The Koran.* 5th rev. ed. New York: Penguin, 1993.

Evrin, M. Sadeddin. *Eschatology in Islam.* Trans. Sofi Huri. Istanbul, 1960.

Gardet, Louis. "Djanna." In *The Encyclopedia of Islam.* Leiden: E. J. Brill, 1979.

Jenkinson, E. J. "The Rivers of Paradise." *Muslim World* 19 (1925).

Kherie, Altaf Ahmad. *Islam: A Comprehensive Guidebook.* Karachi: Idara Sirat-i-Mustaqeem, 1981.

Macdonald, John. "Paradise." *Islamic Studies* 5, no. 4 (1966).

al-Qādī, Imam 'Abd al-Rahīm ibn Ahmad. *The Islamic Book of the Dead.* Trans. 'ā'isha 'Abd al-Rahmān. Norwich, England: Diwan Press, 1977.

Smith, Jane I. *The Precious Pearl* (A translation of Abū Hāmid al-Ghazālī's *Kitāb al-Durra al-Fākhira if Kashf 'Ulūm al-ākhira*). Missoula, MT: Scholars Press, 1979.

Smith, Jane I., and Yvonne Yazbeck Haddad. *The Islamic Understanding of Death and Resurrection.* Albany: SUNY Press, 1981.

———. "Women in the Afterlife: The Islamic View as Seen from Qur'ān and Tradition." *Journal of the American Academy of Religion* 43, no. 1 (1975).

Taylor, John B. "Some Aspects of Islamic Eschatology." *Religious Studies* 4 (1968).

GEHENNA

A Latin Christian name for Hell, the word *Gehenna* is derived from the Greek *geena*, which comes in turn from the Aramaic *gê-hinnôm*, literally "the valley of Hinnom," a valley on the northern border of Judah. The significance of Gehenna has shifted greatly over time from a physical valley to a bottomless pit to the elaborate seven-tiered hell of Islam (Jahannam), so graphically described in the Qur'ān.

In ancient times the valley is thought to have been the location where Canaanites and apparently some Israelites (including the evil kings Ahaz and Manasseh) sacrificed children to Molech in a fiery ritual (Jeremiah 7:31; 2 Kings 16:3; 2 Chronicles 28:3). Such a sacrifice was expressly forbidden by Yahweh in the Old Testament as a horrendous form of idolatry. The valley was also used as a refuse dump, where fires burned constantly in the heaps of rubbish, and as a mass grave by the Babylonians when they slaughtered the Judeans (Jeremiah 7:29–34; 19:1–15).

Originally, Gehenna had no connection to an afterworld in ancient Judaism but was simply called "the accursed valley" or the abyss. Later, in the intertestamental period (from the 2nd century B.C.E. to the time of Christianity), Gehenna became connected metaphorically with afterlife judgment and eternal fiery torment. According to a text known as the *Sibyllene Oracles,* all the wicked everywhere would be judged and thrown into Gehenna. In the apocrypha 2 Esdras 7:35–36 we read:

> Judgment alone shall remain . . . good deeds shall awake and wicked deeds shall not be allowed to sleep. Then the place of torment shall appear, and over against it the place of rest; the furnace of Gehenna shall be displayed, and on the opposite side the paradise of delight.

This kind of apocalyptic expectation was not unique to first-century Judaism but was widespread throughout the Roman Empire in the Hellenistic era.

In the New Testament, Gehenna appears as the eternal place of fiery punishment for the damned, including lawyers and Pharisees (Matthew 23:15). Yet Gehenna appears to be distinguished from the underworld of Hades. Hades in the New Testament is sometimes mentioned as the temporary resting place of the dead before the End Time and judgment (Acts 2:27, 31; Revelation 20:13), whereas fiery Gehenna was the place of eternal torment for the damned after they had been bodily resurrected (Matthew 10:28). However, in the Gospel of Luke, the wealthy man Dives is said to be suffering torment in Hades, but the beggar Lazarus ascends to "Abraham's bosom," so the distinction between Gehenna and Hades was not exact. But certainly, the early Christians must have been aware that Hades was rarely a place of punishment in Greek tradition, whereas Gehenna was by its nature associated with fire and suffering.

In later Judaism (the Mishnah and Talmud) Gehenna appeared primarily as a temporary purgatory for those Jews who were not pure enough to enter paradise directly, but it also appears occasionally as a place of eternal suffering for criminals and Gentiles.

The sacred book of Islam, the Qur'ān, spares no imagery in describing the torments of Jahannam, which is the name for the collective seven layers of hell, as well as the specific name of the topmost layer. Each layer has a gate with a demon standing guard to torment the damned. The horizon is shrouded in darkness with the sparks and smoke (15:43–44) from the fires, which scorch the victims' skin to a black crisp—only to grow anew so that the torments may be repeated. In Islam Gehenna is also the name of the four-legged beast of Hell—each leg is composed of 70,000 demons, and each demon has 30,000 mouths.

Later Muslim theologians began to assert God's mercy and kindness over his wrath, and the belief developed that the angel Gabriel would rescue the damned after their time of purgation was up. Eventually Jahannam became no more than a temporary purgatory, and it was thought that in time the fires of Jahannam would be extinguished and all sinners pardoned.

See also HADES; HELL, ORIGINS OF (CHRISTIAN); INTERCESSION; JAHANNAM; SOUL, JEWISH; TARTAROS.

References

Dawood, N. J., trans. *The Koran.* 5th rev. ed. New York: Penguin, 1993.

Milikowsky, C. "Which Gehenna? Retribution and Eschatology in the Synoptic Gospels and in Early Jewish Texts." *New Testament Studies* 34: 238–249.

Smith, Jane I., and Yvonne Yazbeck Haddad. *The Islamic Understanding of Death and Resurrection.* Albany: SUNY Press, 1981.

Watson, Duane F. "Gehenna." In *Anchor Bible Dictionary,* ed. David Noel Freedman. New York: Doubleday, 1992.

GIMLÉ (GIMLI)

The name *Gimlé* probably comes from *gim* and *hlé,* or "fire-shelter," meaning the land that has survived the fires and destruction of the End Time, which crushes the nine worlds of old Norse mythology. The name comes to us from only two sources, the *Gylfaginning* of Snorri Sturluson (c. 1220 C.E.) and the Edda poem *Völuspá.* They both state that in Asgard or the realm of the gods rests a hall called Gimlé, "roofed with gold," where it was said righteous people went after death. Because Gimlé is mentioned so rarely, however, and no known artwork depicts it, we must assume that it was much less widely known in ancient Scandinavia than Valhalla or Hel and was probably not the expected afterdeath state of the common person.

According to the legends of the end of the world (Ragnarök), it is not clear at first if anything survives the general destruction in which wolves have swallowed the sun and moon, the three-year winter (fimbulvetr) has destroyed all life on earth, and the universe has been consumed by fire from the world of Múspell. But in time several of the younger gods emerge from the ruins: two sons of Odin, Vidar and Vali, survive, as well as Thor's two sons Magni and Modi with their father's hammer Mjollnir. Hel releases Balder the Beautiful and his brother Höder, and they join the others in the remnants of Asgard. There, sitting in the grass and discussing the past, they find the ancient golden chess pieces of their fathers and begin to play again on the gameboard of life. The mysterious and silent god Hoenir comes out of Vanaheim and brings wisdom to the new godly rulers, and they take up residence in Gimlé. Then new halls rise on the plain of Ida and a new sun shines down brightly on the new worlds. In Midgard, the human world, two humans survived, Lif and Lifthrasir. They hid in a forest called *Hoddmimisholt* during the long, cruel winter preceding Ragnarök, and need only dew for food. They will repopulate the human realm with their children.

The survival of the hall of Gimlé and the youngest of the gods through Ragnarök clearly predicts the rebirth of the world and hints at reincarnation in general. Some have seen in this rebirth merely the Norse echo of the Christian Book of Revelation, wherein the "New Jerusalem" arises with its new heaven and new earth. However, the rebirth of the world is also taught by ancient Indian texts; indeed, in India the regular death and rebirth of the universe is accepted. Among the Hopi tribe in the southwestern United States three worlds are known to have already arisen and fallen away, and in Iranian tradition the wise lord teaches Yima to build an underground shelter to escape the destruction of the End Time and repopulate the world. In such predictions, then, we see a worldwide belief in destruction and rejuvenation and need not seek out specifically Christian influences to explain the Norse belief. Indeed, the cyclic nature of the Earth's seasons itself, with winter followed by spring over and over again, may be enough to suggest cosmic resurrection.

See also ODIN; RAGNARÖK.

References

Crossley-Holland, Kevin, ed. *The Faber Book of Northern Legends.* London: Faber and Faber, 1977.

Guerber, Hélène Adeline. *Myths of the Norsemen from the Eddas and Sagas.* New York: Dover Publications, 1992.

Sturluson, Snorri. *Edda.* Translation by Anthony Faulkes. London: Dent, 1987.

Titchenell, Elsa-Brita. *The Masks of Odin.* Pasadena: Theosophical University Press, 1985.

Turville-Petre, E. O. G. *Myth and Religion of the North: The Religion of Ancient Scandinavia.* Westport, CT: Greenwood, 1964.

H

HADES

Literally "Sightless" in Greek, Hades is both the god of the Underworld and the place itself; the term was later taken over by Roman and then Christian mythology. As a Greek deity, Hades is the son of Kronos and Rhea; full brother of Zeus, Poseidon, Hera, and Demeter; and lord of the dead. In the Homeric epics Hades is called "the unmerciful and irreconcilable" and is for mankind the most hated of gods, yet this description must be recognized as the poetic product of an elite literary tradition. Simultaneously an extensive fertility cult existed in folk tradition from the earliest times, which recognized Hades, with his wife Persephone (also called Kore) as not only the god of the Underworld but the god of the Earth and thus provider of the gifts of the earth: fertility, life, and cyclic order. The Roman counterpart to Hades, Pluto, is even more explicitly connected with fertility and is always depicted with the horn of plenty, giver of all goods. This archaic tension in understanding Hades, god of death, as both "enemy" of life and "renewer" of life seems to have dissolved in the classical period as the Homeric tradition came to dominate popular imagination and Hades gradually became one-sidedly somber and fearsome.

Hades also came to be the name of the land of the dead. In the *Iliad* Hades lies directly beneath the earth, whereas in the *Odyssey* Hades may be reached by ship at the western edge of the world beyond the ocean. These are not necessarily contradictory ideas, for in Greek cosmology, as in most ancient cosmologies, it was thought possible to reach the end of the ocean and go under the edge, into the Earth. Certainly the west was long associated with the dead in ancient Greece, Egypt, Ireland, and elsewhere and connected with it was the idea that the sun, Helios, was thought to set in the west and travel through the Underworld each night before rising in the east by morning. In any case both the *Iliad* and the *Odyssey* place the land of the dead far from human habitation and in close connection with water. The *Iliad* mentions the River Styx, river of hatred, but in the *Odyssey* we find several other rivers as well: Acheron, river of woe; Cocytus, river of wailing, where the unburied dead had to wander for 100 years; Lethe, river of forgetfulness; and Pyriphlegethon, the blazing river. Styx or Acheron or both are generally considered by the ancient sources as the boundary between living and dead, and the "wailing" and "burning" of Cocytus and Pyriphlegethon appear to recapitulate the funeral and cremation of the corpse.

The idea of a watery separation of the land of the living from the dead is common to much of the ancient world and is deeply symbolic. Underground water is not only a reminder of the watery chaos that existed before the world was ordered by the gods; water is connected to the ocean, which is the source of livelihood, transportation, and death for a seafaring people like the Greeks; and water is that mysterious force which brings up vegetation from the earth. Thus it is not coincidental that the ocean borders Hades, land of the dead, or that several rivers provide a massive barrier between the land of the living and the realm of death.

In classical Greek tradition the soul, or psyche of the deceased, may not cross the waters into Hades without burial. In the *Odyssey*, Odysseus is visited by the pathetic shade of his friend Elpenor, who was left "unburied and unwept" on the island of Circe. Elpenor's shade is thus stranded in the no-man's-land between the living and the dead, unable to rest unless Odysseus returns to the world above to provide proper funeral services. Those souls who are able to cross over are greeted by Hermes (in the *Odyssey*; in later tradition, by Charon) in his function as psychopompos (guide of souls) and led through the brass gates into Hades, from which there was no return. In archaic times there was no opportunity for necromancy or communing with the dead on Earth because they were trapped forever in Hades; the only solution was to visit the dead where they resided. This feat was accomplished not only in the epic nekyia of Odysseus (*Odyssey*, Book 11) but later by Herakles in his labors and by Orpheus seeking his lost wife Eurydice.

Among the supernatural inhabitants of the Underworld were the god Hades and his bride Kore/Persephone, rulers of the Underworld; the Erinyes or Furies, which were thought to punish the shades of criminals and oath breakers; King Minos, judge of the Underworld; the great sinners Tityos, Sisyphos, and Tantalos; the shades of epic heroes like Achilles and Patroklos; and far below the Underworld, "as far below Hades as Earth is below the heavens," there lay Tartaros, dwelling place of the anticosmic Titans who once ruled the universe but were defeated by the Olympian gods. In later tradition one also finds the three-headed hound of Hades, Cerberus, and Elysion, a joyous land (or islands) separated from the rest of Hades, where the blest enjoyed their afterlife.

It seems clear that in archaic Greek thought all the dead experienced a similar fate: the shades of the famous heroes of the Trojan war existed in bleak Hades with everyone else. Even the great Achilleus was reduced to nothing, for he says to Odysseus at his visit, "My dear Odysseus, spare me your praise of Death. Put me on earth again, and I would rather be a servant in the house of some landless man, with little enough for himself to live on, than king of all these dead men that have done with life."

This concept of equality and collective existence is somewhat challenged by the belief in Erinyes who punish criminals as well as the eternal torment of infamous sinners such as Tantalos, but it is not until well into the classical period and particularly the time of the writings of Plato that judgment and just desserts for the dead become commonplace. In Plato's myth of Er (*Republic* 10:614 ff., Jowett, trans.), souls in the Underworld no longer endure an eternal stay, but after centuries of reward or punishment, according to their merits they are reborn in new bodies on earth.

Roman mythology further elaborated the Greek conception of Hades, especially with the idea of punishment or reward for all souls. Virgil's *Aeneid* seems to enlarge Hades spatially, for we find in book 6 an outer area of Hades, a kind of limbo for those who are neither punished nor rewarded for their earthly lives. It houses babies, those who died in battle, and suicides. Beyond the encircling river, ferried by Charon, there are many realms of shades. Deeper down, to the left a path leads to Tartaros and to the right Elysium, an Underworld paradise complete with its own sun and stars and identical to the over-water Islands of the Blest. Following on Plato's doctrine of reincarnation, the *Aeneid* likewise teaches that souls "recycle" through the millennia. Much space is allocated in the *Aeneid* to those waiting to return to earth, showing the future heroes of Rome (descendants of Aeneas, fictional ancestor of the Romans) as yet unborn, awaiting in Elysium for their appointed time on earth. And Marcus Tullius Cicero, in his work "The Dream of Scipio" at the end of *On the Republic*, states that even punishment in the horrible Tartaros is temporary; after centuries of torturous purification all souls eventually make their way back to the "celestial sphere" of Elysium. Reincarnation from Hades became a common belief in the Roman Empire, though it was by no means the only conception of the afterlife; a great many tombs are inscribed with the formula "I was not; I was; I am not; I care not," demonstrating a pervasive skepticism as well.

The Christian concept of Hades in the New Testament merges contemporary Jewish notions of Gehenna with archaic Greek and prevailing Roman notions of the afterlife. In the New Testament, the word *Hades* appears ten times and *Gehenna* twelve, but both were conflated into a single Underworld Hell. In early Christianity Hades is no longer a dark, quiet, and shadowy land beyond a barrier river but a blazing inferno where sinners await the eschaton (last things) and final judgment, as we find in the parable of Lazarus and the rich man:

> The poor man died and was carried by the angels to Abraham's bosom. The rich man also died and was buried; and in Hades, being in torment, he lifted up his eyes, and saw Abraham far off, and Lazarus in his bosom. And he called out, "Father Abraham, have mercy upon me, and send Lazarus to dip the end of his finger in water and cool my tongue; for I am in anguish in this flame." (Luke 16:22–24)

Hades/Gehenna was considered to be the realm of eternal punishment by most thinkers of the early church, following the Book of Revelation with its notion of a second death (chap. 20). A minority of theologians contested this doctrine, most notably Origen, who taught (like Cicero before him) that the punishment of Hades was only of sufficient duration to restore the sinner to the presence of God. Both positions were reconciled by the Roman Catholic Church, which maintained the eternal punishment of hell but developed the doctrine of an expiatory purgatory, defined by the Councils of Florence (1439) and Trent (1545–1563). In this way, although few people were worthy to enter heaven directly after death, not everyone was necessarily consigned to the eternal flames. Eastern Orthodox and Protestant Christians, however, rejected the notion of Purgatory, and insisted that directly upon death, God assigns each soul directly to heaven or hell—which in turn problematizes the notion of a final resurrection and judgment at the end of time. Why resurrect souls that have already been judged?

See also ACHERON; AVERNUS; ELYSION, ELYSIUM; GEHENNA; HELL, ORIGINS OF; ISLANDS OF THE BLEST; JUDGMENT, LAST; PURGATORY; REINCARNATION, WESTERN; RESURRECTION, CHRISTIAN; SECOND DEATH; SOUL, GREEK; STYX; TARTAROS; WATER.

References

Bremmer, Jan. *The Early Greek Concept of the Soul*. Princeton: Princeton University Press, 1983.

Burkert, Walter. *Greek Religion*. Trans. John Raffan. Cambridge; Harvard University Press, 1985.

Dietrich, B. C. *Death, Fate and the Gods*. London: University of London, Athlone Press, 1965.

Farnell, Lewis R. *Greek Hero Cults and Ideas of Immortality*. Oxford: Clarendon, 1921.

Graves, Robert. *The Greek Myths*. New York: Penguin, 1960.

Guthrie, W. K. C. *History of Greek Philosophy*. 6 vols. Cambridge: Cambridge University Press, 1962–1981.

Kristensen, W. Brede. *Life Out of Death: Studies in the Religions of Egypt and Ancient Greece*. Louvain, Belgium: Peeters Press, 1992.

Lattimore, Richmond, trans. *The Iliad*. Chicago: Chicago University Press, 1951.

Mandelbaum, Allen, trans. *The Aeneid of Virgil*. New York: Bantam, 1961.

Plato. *The Republic*. Trans. Benjamin Jowett. New York: Random House, 1937.

Rieu, E. V., trans. *The Odyssey*. New York: Penguin, 1945.

Sourvinou-Inwood, Christiane. *"Reading" Greek Death: To the End of the Classical Period*. Oxford: Clarendon Press, 1995.

Turner, Alice K. *The History of Hell*. New York: Harcourt Brace, 1993.

HALLOWE'EN

The name *Hallowe'en* comes from the Scottish version of "All Hallows Evening," the designation of the annual festival assigned by the Roman Catholic Church. In the church's fight against "paganism" in Europe, a consistent effort was made to forbid local religious holidays or, failing that, to replace them with similar rites controlled by the ministers of the church. The old Roman festival for the dead was the Lemuria, held on 9, 11, and 13 May, when the dead were thought to come out of their graves and visit the living; in the seventh century C.E. Pope Boniface IV (608–615) replaced Lemuria with "All Saints' Day" on 13 May. This day was created to honor all the Catholic saints simultaneously (even though all the important saints had their own particular day of honor on the Latin calendar). The peoples of western and northern Europe, however, with their strong Celtic and other "pagan" traditions, proved more of an obstacle to conversion than the people of the collapsed Roman Empire. As part of the assault on native religions, Pope Gregory III (731–741) moved All Saints' Day to 1 November in order to co-opt the Celtic holiday Samhain. The church further designated 2 November "All Souls' Day," on which the ordinary dead were honored at their graves. The Christian suppression of local traditions was never complete, however, and many of the old practices of Samhain continued, albeit under a new name.

The observance of All Hallow's Eve or Hallowe'en has had quite a different history in Europe than in the United States. Because Samhain/Hallowe'en originally marked the end of the Celtic year, a new fire was kindled, often in the form of a bonfire outdoors. Lighted jack-o-lanterns were originally lamps intended to welcome the dead and help them find their way in the dark to their old homes. There, thoughtful relatives left out "treats" in the form of sweet cakes overnight as offer-

Two boys dressed in costume for Hallowe'en. Courtesy of Anne Ronan Picture Library.

ings for the dead. It was this practice that, conjoined with the Irish peasant practice of going door-to-door collecting money and foodstuffs for the community festival of St. Columb Kill, created the modern practice of children's trick-or-treat (though both the tricks and the treats were originally the prerogative of the dead). In modern times, the costumes of the living personify the dead who are thought to return, along with the witches, goblins, and demons who thrive at this most critical of times—the midnight conjunction of the old and new year. Though the official calendar has shifted the New Year to 1 January, the ancient occult associations of the autumnal festival remain.

See also ANTHESTERIA; DÍA DE LOS MUERTOS; LEMURIA; PARENTALIA; SAMHAIN.

References

Bannatyne, Lesley Pratt. *Halloween: An American Holiday, an American History*. New York: Facts on File, 1990.

Gaster, Theodore. *New Year: Its History, Customs and Superstitions*. New York: Abelard-Schuman, 1955.

Santino, Jack, ed. *Halloween and Other Festivals of Death and Life*. Knoxville: University of Tennessee Press, 1993.

HAMESTEGĀN

In Zoroastrian doctrine, those souls that were too wicked in life to go to heaven (Behesht) but not bad enough to go to hell (Dozakh) were consigned to Hamestegān, literally "the balanced place" or "the mixed place." Hamestegān is located between the earth and the heavens, where there is neither joy nor happiness but only the mild suffering of heat and cold because of seasonal changes. Although Hamestegān has been compared to the Roman Catholic doctrine of Purgatory, the parallel does not really work. Souls in Hamestegān do not "work off" any sins or make any spiritual progress; rather, they sit in twilight and await the general resurrection at the end of time—still several thousand years away in the Zoroastrian reckoning of cosmic time.

See also BEHESHT; CHINVAT BRIDGE; DOZAKH; FRASHO-KERETI; RESURRECTION, ANCIENT NEAR EAST; SOUL, ZOROASTRIAN.

References

Jackson, A. V. W. *Zoroastrian Studies.* New York: Columbia University Press, 1928.

Kotwal, Firoze M., and James W. Boyd, trans. *A Guide to the Zoroastrian Religion.* Studies in World Religion no. 3. Chico, CA: Scholars Press, 1982.

Masani, Sir Rustom. *Zoroastrianism: The Religion of the Good Life.* New York: Collier Books, 1962.

Moulton, J. H. *Early Zoroastrianism.* London: Williams and Norgate, 1913.

Sethna, Tehmurasp Rustamji. *Book of Instructions on Zoroastrian Religion.* Karachi: Informal Religious Meetings Trust Fund, 1980.

Sidhwa, Ervad Godrej Dinshawji. *Discourses on Zoroastrianism.* Karachi: Ervad Godrej Dinshawji Sidhwa, 1978.

HEAVEN, HISTORY OF (CHRISTIAN)

Although Christianity has always placed great emphasis on the doctrine of Heaven as the reward for faith, how that Heaven has been conceived has varied widely over the centuries, from Heaven's diverse origins in the ancient world through theological interpretations in the Middle Ages to the visionary experiences of Emanuel Swedenborg and the emergence of the "modern" Heaven.

For some centuries, while Christians were cruelly martyred by periodical Roman persecutions, Heaven was imagined to be reserved for the select few—the small minority of Christians who stood staunchly opposed to "the world" in general. But another vision of Heaven emerged once Christianity became the official religion of Rome (late fourth century C.E.) and the Empire (representing the entire world) had become "holy." The "City of God" described by the theologian Augustine (354–430 C.E.) no longer viewed Heaven as a synagogue, as in early Jewish-Christian accounts such as the Book of Revelation. Instead the picture of Heaven became modeled on the imperial Roman city, complete with walls, pleasure gardens, paved walkways, and elegant buildings, all laid out on a grid. Although in Jerusalem the temple was the center of worship and power, in Roman civilization power emanated from the imperial capital. Augustine and his contemporaries simply replaced the secular Roman Senate seated before the emperor with Christian saints, martyrs, virgins, and the other righteous Christians eternally rapt in the vision of God on the throne. The new imperial Heaven was not completely theocentric, however; Christians, naked and beautiful as God intended people to be, would delight in the reunion of lost loved ones and even conjugal union and procreation, now purified from all selfishness and sin. This, despite the fact that Jesus rebuked the Sadducees regarding Heaven saying, "When they rise from the dead, men and women do not marry; they are like angels in heaven" (Matthew 22:22–33; Mark 12:18–27; Luke 20:26–40).

Later medieval theologies took Heaven in two directions. Farmers and those who renounced worldly life and lived in the country tended to picture Heaven as "nature perfected," that is, a great garden brimming with roses, lilies, and greenery everywhere, along with an absence of great heat or cold, hunger, or thirst. These concerns surely reflected the economic struggles of rural life, including regular famines, harsh weather, and plagues, as well as a theological desire to see the original fall from grace reversed and a restoration of the Garden of Eden. But city dwellers and those peasants who admired the growing wealth and elegance of the urban centers continued to develop the vision of Heaven as a great urban center—increasingly hierarchical, structured and elaborate. Augustine's naked frolickers were replaced with saints, virgins, and other faithful Christians now transformed into regally dressed lords and ladies, complete with their own castles and courts, surrounding God's central palace. In *Heaven: A History,* Colleen McDannell and Bernhard Lang relate revelatory visions of many medieval men and women, including one Gerardesca, a woman living in urban Italy in the thirteenth century (see excerpt). Although Mary, mother of Jesus, is hardly mentioned in the Bible, in medieval theology she became the Queen of Heaven, surrounded by a huge personal entourage clothed in white. Instead of Augustine's imperial City of God, Heaven became the vast countryside of God, the High King, who parceled out fiefdoms to his saints—transformed into heavenly aristocrats.

Another far-reaching development in medieval views of Heaven was the growing interest in science and learning, particularly astronomy. As the first Western universities emerged and scientists began to inquire as to the physical nature of the universe, Heaven again transformed, this time into the cosmos of

The ramparts of God's house. Courtesy of Images Colour Library.

God. Opposed to the dark, material, and sinful earth, layers of heavens reached up toward God with ever more light and knowledge: past the moon and sun, past Jupiter and the "fixed stars" stretched the empyrean, literally "the flaming realm," source of all light, literal and intellectual. In Dante Alighieri's *Paradiso,* the humans in Heaven were seated in a great rose-shaped stadium, absorbed eternally in the "beatific vision" of the nine orders of angels, forming concentric circles above them, which closed around the "Great Light" in three colored circles, symbolizing the Trinity. Growing skill in architecture allowed medieval builders to erect great Gothic cathedrals as the centers of major cities, modeling in their vaulted ceilings and vast stained glass windows the light and grandeur of the new picture of Heaven—God as lord of space, not merely time. In fact, Heaven became so grand and so saintly that it became difficult for ordinary people to imagine themselves there any longer. The doctrine of Purgatory developed as a way for the vast majority of humanity (at least, those who accepted the salvation of Christ as mediated by the Catholic Church) to reach Heaven, but only through a long and difficult purging of personal (not original) sin. That the doctrine of Purgatory also eventually entailed papal

"indulgences" for money and contributed to the Protestant Reformation is well known and is discussed in the entry PURGATORY.

Two great European movements began to chip away at the medieval imagery of Heaven as an incredibly ornate city-state or cosmos, as the critical intellectualism of the Renaissance slowly spread from Italy to the rest of Europe during the fifteenth and sixteenth centuries, and the Protestant Reformation and Catholic Counter-Reformation followed. Scholarly criticism began to challenge the validity of personal and theological "visions" of Heaven, and theological reforms attempted to re-center Heaven on God alone, not the appearance of heavenly clothing, castles, choirs of angels, lush gardens, and layers of cosmic space. From the fifteenth to the seventeenth centuries, speculation on Heaven became increasingly abstract, and there was a marked shift, particularly after the Reformation, to an ascetic and frugal attitude toward sensual pleasures. One's focus, in this life as in the next, was solely on God and not on personal relationships in Heaven or individual activity. This was practically a return to the ancient ascetic philosophies of Plato and Greek Stoicism, which emphasized human beings' *spiritual* nature to the entire exclusion of their physical aspect.

She saw a vast plain called the territory of the Holy City of Jerusalem. There were castles in amazing numbers and very beautiful pleasure-gardens. All the streets of the city-state of Jerusalem were of the purest gold and the most precious stones. An avenue was formed by golden trees whose branches were resplendent with gold. Their blossoms remained rich and luxuriant according to their kind, and they were more delightful and charming than anything we can see in earthly pleasure-gardens. In the middle of this territory lay Jerusalem—holy, sublime, very beautiful and ornate. Nobody lived in the territory, only the city was peopled.

The city was surrounded by seven charming castles with [coats of] arms bearing the glorious Virgin's name. Situated on steep mountains of precious stones, they had stairs leading up and down, made of even more precious gems . . . The castles were furnished with the richest decoration and had banners of victory hoisted, showing the picture of the Blessed Virgin Mary. In the castles were precious chairs, shining with holy radiance, for our Savior and the glorious Virgin, for the angels and archangels, the apostles and prophets, confessors and virgins, and all the saints. All of them were arranged according to their rank. Visited three times a year by the entire celestial court, these castles are filled with ineffable jubilation and incomparable glory.

From the Acta Sanctorum, *quoted in McDannell and Lang, trans. (1988, p. 76).*

These trends were not checked until, in the mid-eighteenth century, Emanuel Swedenborg began to publish his dozens of volumes of remarkably detailed and theologically sophisticated visions of the "invisible world," which included both Heaven and Hell. In their history McDannell and Lang give four characteristics of the "modern" understanding of Heaven, which Swedenborg in the eighteenth century and the spiritualists and occultists in the nineteenth century developed. Briefly, these are (1) that the Otherworld is material, though subtle, and lies very near the known material world, and sensitive people can pierce the veil; (2) rather than an opposite of Earth, Heaven is merely a continuation of earthly virtues and goals on a higher and purer plane; (3) rather than a static heaven, the Otherworld is full of activity, leading to endless spiritual growth of the individual; and (4) there is a renewed focus on human relationships in Heaven, including romantic love—making this conception of Heaven far more anthropocentric than theocentric. Although Swedenborg had little influence on European thought during his life, the door was once again opened to the kind of individual visions that proliferated during the Middle Ages, though now infused with new "scientific" ideas of "progress" and a multidimensional (but still material) universe.

The twentieth century has seen a decline in popular belief in traditional theology and along with it most elaborate conceptions of Heaven. Among those Christians (or quasi-Christians) today who believe in a Heaven, it is largely along the lines that Swedenborg laid down beginning in 1747—people expect to enjoy a Heaven full of activity and pleasurable rewards, though in the current age of communication and diversity it has become very difficult to draw lines between who will and will not be accepted into Heaven. Universalism has grown to such an extent that many in the Western world now believe that any "good" person will go to Heaven—if there is a Heaven—and traditional Christian confession is in marked decline. As one indicator, membership in mainline Protestant churches in the United States has declined for thirty consecutive years. However, evangelical, charismatic, and fundamentalist Christian groups appear to be on the rise and with them a return to the ascetic Heaven of Reformers such as Martin Luther and John Calvin. How the Christian hope of a Heaven after death will transform due to interaction with Islam, Hinduism, Buddhism, and ongoing scientific discoveries in all fields of inquiry remains to be seen. What is clear, however, is that the image of Heaven (and indeed, the idea of what is "perfection") has changed dramatically over the past 2,000 years, closely modeling the economic, political, social, and intellectual trends of each age. Of one thing we can be sure—Heaven will continue to serve as a template for human ideals and hopes, even as those ideals and hopes continue to transform.

See also HADES; HEAVEN, ORIGINS OF; HELL, ORIGINS OF; INTERCESSION; PARADISE; PURGATORY; RESURRECTION, CHRISTIAN.

References

Bultmann, Rudolf. *Theology of the New Testament.* Trans. K. Grobel. London: SCM Press, 1952.

Charles, R. H., ed. "The Book of Enoch." In *The Apocrypha and Pseudepigrapha of the Old Testament.* Oxford: Clarendon Press, 1966.

Dante Alighieri. *The Comedy of Dante Alighieri the Florentine.* Trans. Dorothy L. Sayers. 3 vols. Baltimore, MD: Penguin Books, 1955.

Delumeau, Jean. *History of Paradise: The Garden of Eden in Myth and Tradition.* Trans. Matthew O'Connell. New York: Continuum, 1995.

Gardiner, Eileen, ed. *Visions of Heaven and Hell before Dante.* New York: Italica Press, 1989.

Glasson, T. Francis. *Greek Influence in Jewish Eschatology.* London: SPCK, 1961.

Kirk, K. E. *The Vision of God: The Christian Doctrine of the Summum Bonum.* Bampton Lectures for 1928. Harrisburg, PA: Morehouse Publishing, 1991.

McDannell, Colleen, and Bernhard Lang. *Heaven: A History.* New Haven: Yale University Press, 1988.

Panneton, Georges. *Heaven or Hell*. Trans. Ann M. C. Forster. Westminster, MD: Newman Press, 1965.

Russell, Jeffrey Burton. *A History of Heaven: The Singing Silence*. Princeton: Princeton University Press, 1997.

Simon, Ulrich. *Heaven in the Christian Tradition*. London: Rockcliff, 1958.

Smith, Wilbur M. *The Biblical Doctrine of Heaven*. Chicago: Moody Press, 1968.

HEAVEN, ORIGINS OF (CHRISTIAN)

It is important to realize that Christianity did not originate the doctrine of heaven but rather adopted many of the beliefs current in the time and place where Christ was born, namely Greek-influenced Palestine. Further, as Christianity spread throughout the world, Christian thinkers came into contact with complex and sophisticated alternate theologies. The most direct influence on the foundation of Christian Heaven was certainly Jesus' teaching. However, Greek mind-body dualism, Roman imperialism, and personal visions among believers rapidly drew early Christian thought away from the simple, inner "kingdom of God" (of which Jesus spoke) to a much grander, and eventually less credible "City of God" with thousands of saints, choirs of angels and archangels, and highly elaborate imagery.

Christianity first emerged out of Judaism, but the idea of heaven does not originate with the latter religion. Until Roman times, the religion of the Hebrews was entirely innocent of any such belief; resurrection for the Jews was to take place on a purified Earth, not in an eternal heaven. Even resurrection is only clearly mentioned in the Hebrew Bible by the prophet Daniel, who writes (12:2): "Many of those who sleep in the dust of the earth will awake, some to everlasting life and some to the reproach of eternal abhorrence." But this "everlasting" life was on the Earth, which would return to the paradise that it once was for Adam and Eve. To bring about this radical transformation, God would send a military leader, an "anointed king" (the literal translation of messiah), who would overthrow Israel's oppressors and return Israel to its former prosperity and power, as in the days of King David. A text written down too late to be included in the Hebrew canon, the Book of Enoch (third or second century B.C.E.), describes Jewish expectations of the return to earthly life that the Messiah would bring. Enoch 5:7–9 reads:

> But for the elect there shall be light and grace and peace,
> And they shall inherit the earth.
> And then there shall be bestowed upon the elect wisdom,
> And they shall all live and never again sin . . .
> *But they shall complete the number of the days of their life.*

> And their lives shall be increased in peace.
> And the years of their joy shall be multiplied,
> In eternal gladness and peace,
> All the days of their life.
> (Charles, trans., emphasis added)

At a time when Jews were being mercilessly exiled or killed by foreign oppressors, Jewish leaders were teaching the doctrine of physical resurrection, which would allow Jews whose lives had been cut short to resume their rightful place in a peaceful kingdom. But this earthly paradise was reserved for those Jews alone who were unswerving in their devotion to the God of Israel, even to the point of death.

In radical contrast to the physical and political afterlife hoped for by the Jews, Greek (and later, Roman) philosophy taught that the universe was dualistic and caught in a struggle between spirit and matter. Matter was a corrupting influence on the "real" person, namely the immortal soul—a soul that was purest when furthest from a body. Plato, for instance, relates a near-death experience in the *Republic* wherein earthly life is seen as merely a kind of school; after death the student-souls are judged for their ethical behavior during life. Sinners are punished in an Underworld for a thousand years, while those who lived morally upright lives enjoy a thousand years of bliss in a kingdom of light. Souls return again to new earthly bodies after their allotted time in heaven or hell, and this process goes on indefinitely, "except," Plato writes in the *Phaedrus,*

> [for] the soul of a sincere lover of wisdom, or of one who has made philosophy his favorite. . . . these, in the third period of a thousand years, if they have chosen this [philosopher's] life thrice in succession, thereupon depart, with their wings restored in the three thousandth year. Others are tried, some sentenced to places of punishment beneath the earth . . . others to some region in heaven . . . in the thousandth year they choose their next life. (quoted in Glasson)

Philosophers, of course, were those who eschewed sensual life and adopted celibacy, meditative practice, and a simple life devoted to divine ideas far removed from the concerns of worldly folk.

Plato's ascetic view of life was widely accepted among Greek and Roman thinkers, but among the common people a somewhat less metaphysical afterlife was hoped for. Among ordinary Greeks and Romans the notion of the Islands of the Blest was popular, where food and wine was plentiful, the weather was always temperate, and sickness and death were not known. The Islands of the Blest were generally located over the western ocean, although a similar land that was called

Elysion/Elysium was imagined to lie under the Earth in a warm and sunny part of Hades. Not only philosophers, but also those who served family and country and the morally good were understood to go in soul (not body) to these wonderful realms, where they would be reunited with lost family and friends, engage in athletic contests, and otherwise enjoy themselves.

All of these views were important to the development of the Christian Heaven, and all would have their role to play. It is also certain that Jesus was aware of these various afterlife expectations, and quite strikingly, he clearly distinguished his own teaching from all of them. If the Gospels that have come down to us are at all trustworthy, Jesus believed that a "new age" was near (Matthew 24:8). In the Gospel of Mark (13:28–29), Jesus describes many signs of "the end" and concludes:

> Learn a lesson from the fig tree. When its tender shoots appear and are breaking into leaf, you know that summer is near. In the same way, when you see all this happening, you may know that the end is near, at the very door. I tell you this: the present generation will live to see it all. Heaven and earth will pass away. . . .

But what would follow such turmoil apparently held little interest for Jesus. His concern was to build a "kingdom of God" in his immediate environment during his lifetime, and the way to enter this "kingdom" was to transform oneself from an egocentric, materialistic worldling into a selfless servant of humanity and a knower of the divine within. As is well known, Jesus taught that the last shall be first in the kingdom, namely those who serve others (Mark 10:43–45). Only those who left their families, forsook worldly responsibilities, and made the emerging spiritual community their "family" and their "job" would be a part of the kingdom (Matthew 23:9; Luke 14:26). One had to give up everything material, even concerns for clothes and food (Matthew 6:25–34; 19:23–26). This kingdom was certainly not the new political state of Israel hoped for by some Jews because Jesus realized that he could not stay long with his community. Rather than lead a new state, he expected his followers to become spiritual leaders even greater than he was. In the Gospel of John (14:12), Jesus says: "In truth, in very truth I tell you, he who has faith in me will do what I am doing; and he will do greater things still because I am going to the Father."

Neither did Jesus preach a literal heaven and hell, like common Romans and Greeks. Even though Jesus used the parable of the rich man (Dives) in hell and the beggar (Lazarus) in heaven (Luke 16:19–31), the story has all the hallmarks of Jesus' other *allegorical* teaching and warnings. Another statement of Jesus is much more illuminating (Luke 17:21–22):

> The Pharisees asked him "When will the kingdom of God come?" He said, "You cannot tell by observation when the kingdom of God comes. There will be no saying, 'Look, here it is!' or 'there it is!' For in fact the kingdom of God is within you."

The kingdom of God is a divine potential within each person, which Jesus apparently was already experiencing and wished to share with others. As Jesus experienced divine union with his heavenly father (so much so that Jesus perceived the two becoming "one"), he encouraged his disciples to call no one, even Jesus, "father" or "teacher" but only the spirit itself (Matthew 23:9–10). Just as Jesus said: "The Father is in me, and I in the Father" (John 10:38), Jesus hoped his disciples would find the Christ within themselves, saying: "I am the vine, and you the branches. He who dwells in me, as I dwell in him, bears much fruit; for apart from me you can do nothing."

Teachings on resurrection and punishment in hell are attributed to Jesus in the Gospels, but it is clear that an afterlife resurrection and a heaven and hell were less important to Jesus (counting the sheer number of references to them) than the "kingdom of God" that Jesus attempted to foster on earth. Although at first glance this appears most similar to the Platonic goal, namely producing a spiritual community of philosophers who had renounced wealth and other material concerns, Jesus tried to build a spiritual heaven on Earth, whereas the Greeks expected a spiritual fulfillment only after death, far from bodies and even matter itself. Essentially, Jesus' teaching was that "heaven" was an inner state in the disciple who forsook everything but God and that this state could be achieved on Earth or after death. This perspective was unique in the Mediterranean marketplace of ideas and powerful enough to attract many great minds to the early Christian movement. Unfortunately, because Jesus' views were indeed so unique, they were difficult to maintain in the face of ancient and overwhelming cultural traditions; gradually, students of Jesus began to alter the Christian position. After the death of their leader, Christian teachers began leaning the "kingdom of God" more toward Jewish apocalyptic views, philosophical Greek dualism, or a beautiful land after death depending on their time, place, and often their background before becoming Christian. Either because they could not grasp Jesus' teaching or because the church was forced to adapt to survive, early Christians struggled to integrate such competing visions, and over the centuries Christian beliefs about Heaven took radically different directions that are difficult to reconcile.

Paul is an excellent example of a great personality who was drawn to the life story and message of Jesus, though Paul joined the movement after Jesus had

Then I saw a great white throne, and the One who sat upon it; from his presence earth and heaven vanished away, and no place was left for them. I could see the dead, great and small, standing before the throne; and books were opened. Then another book was opened, the roll of the living. From what was written in these books the dead were judged upon the record of their deeds. The sea gave up its dead, and Death and Hades gave up the dead in their keeping; they were judged each man on the record of his deeds. Then Death and Hades were flung into the lake of fire. This lake of fire is the second death; and into it were flung any whose names were not to be found in the roll of the living.

Then I saw a new heaven and a new earth, for the first heaven and the first earth had vanished, and there was no longer any sea. I saw the holy city, new Jerusalem, coming down out of heaven from God, made ready like a bride adorned for her husband. I heard a loud voice proclaiming from the throne, "Now at last God has his dwelling among men! He will dwell among them and they shall be his people, and God himself will be with them. He will wipe every tear from their eyes; there shall be an end to death, and to mourning and crying and pain; for the old order has passed away!"

Then he who sat on the throne said, "Behold! I am making all things new!" (And he said to me, "Write this down; for these words are trustworthy and true. Indeed they are already fulfilled.") "I am the Alpha and the Omega, the beginning and the end. A draught from the water-springs of life will be my free gift to the thirsty. All this is the victor's heritage; and I will be his God and he shall be my son. But as for the cowardly, the faithless, and the vile, murderers, fornicators, sorcerers, idolaters, and liars of every kind, their lot will be the second death, in the lake that burns with sulphurous flames."

Book of Revelation 20:11–21:8.

already died. Although Paul became an extremely devoted Christian and eventually (it is believed) died for the cause, in many ways Paul never let go of his pre-Christian experience as a Jew, when he belonged to the sect of the Pharisees. The Pharisees held to the common Greco-Roman idea of heaven, which included discrete "levels" or areas. For instance, in 2 Corinthians 12:2, Paul says (probably of himself):

I know a Christian man who fourteen years ago (whether in the body or out of it, I do not know—God knows) was caught up as far as the third heaven. And I know that this same man (whether in the body or out of it, I do not know—God knows) was caught up into paradise, and heard words so secret that human lips may not repeat them.

Not only does heaven have three or more levels, according to Paul, but one does not proceed to heaven immediately after death (despite the report in Luke 23:43 that Jesus said to the thief on the cross, "today you shall be with me in Paradise"). In 1 Thessalonians 4:13–18, Paul writes:

We wish you not to remain in ignorance, brothers, *about those who sleep in death*; you should not grieve like the rest of men, who have no hope. We believe that Jesus died and rose again; and so it will be for those who died as Christians; God will bring them to life with Jesus. For this we tell you as the Lord's word: we who are left alive until the Lord comes shall not forestall those who have died because at the word of command, at the sound of the archangel's voice and God's trumpet-call, the Lord himself will descend from heaven; first the Christian dead will rise, then we who are left alive shall join them, caught up in clouds to meet the Lord in the air. Thus we shall always be with the Lord. (emphasis added)

Jesus taught his students to become like himself, to undergo a radical inner transformation and become "greater than he" in order to form a spiritual kingdom of God on earth. In some ways Paul seems to teach the opposite: rather than focus on this world, Paul condemns the world and looks forward only to Christ's return. Christians are not to *become Christ,* according to Paul, but to *worship Christ* as a redeemer who takes away sin and simply await the end of the world. Until then, the dead sleep, and then they may look forward to the kingdom of God in the clouds (not on Earth)—a Heaven that now has multiple levels and new "spiritual bodies" (1 Corinthians 6:13; 15:43–44). Jesus' original "kingdom of God" was already slipping away.

Meanwhile, the Book of Revelation (which was accepted into the Bible only after centuries of Christian debate and opposition) took the development of the Christian Heaven back in the opposite direction: to the old Jewish apocalyptic hope—a kingly messiah who would restore the earth and raise the dead to enjoy a kingdom on earth. After graphic descriptions of bloodshed, pestilence, famine, and destruction through most of the book, John's Revelation ends by obliterating the distinction between Heaven and Earth altogether. Revelation 21:2–3 prophecies: "I saw the holy city, new Jerusalem, coming down out of heaven from God. . . . Now at last God has his dwelling among men! He will dwell among them and they shall be his people." This picture is diametrically opposed to Paul's teaching: rather than human bodies transforming "in the twinkling of an eye" and rising up to the clouds, Heaven and God himself now permanently descend to the Earth! The Jewish overtones of Revelation are clear: a great altar rests in front of God's throne, surrounded by angels, twenty-four "elders," 144,000 Israelites, and 144,000 celibate men. This heaven is not a cloud but a highly structured synagogue, complete with a liturgy of prayers, hymns, and offerings. It elaborates not on Paul's teaching but on a completely different, Jewish, and non-Greek vision, much more in accord with the temple-centered religion of the Jewish sect of Sadducees.

None of these competing visions of Heaven in early Christianity disappeared in later centuries; rather, each continued to influence the development of Heaven through the Middle Ages and modern period. Whereas mystics like Meister Eckhardt tended to emphasize the inner nature of salvation, the Catholic Church tended to follow Paul's lead in the medieval period and focused on the world to come, on penances and purgation and masses for the dead. Meanwhile, modern millennialists and dispensationalists (largely dependent on Protestant fundamentalists like John Nelson Darby and C. I. Scofield of the early nineteenth and twentieth centuries) continue to predict an end of history and a kingdom of heaven on earth very much in accord with the Book of Revelation. Few Christians realize the very significant differences in these views of Heaven, but the contradictions are so great as to suggest that under the broad banner of "Christianity" there are several almost completely different religions.

References
Bultmann, Rudolf. *Theology of the New Testament.* Trans. K. Grobel. London: SCM Press, 1952.

Charles, R. H., ed. "The Book of Enoch." In *The Apocrypha and Pseudepigrapha of the Old Testament.* Oxford: Clarendon Press, 1966.

Dante Alighieri. *The Comedy of Dante Alighieri the Florentine.* Trans. Dorothy L. Sayers. 3 vols. Baltimore, MD: Penguin Books, 1955.

Delumeau, Jean. *History of Paradise: The Garden of Eden in Myth and Tradition.* Trans. Matthew O'Connell. New York: Continuum, 1995.

Gardiner, Eileen, ed. *Visions of Heaven and Hell before Dante.* New York: Italica Press, 1989.

Glasson, T. Francis. *Greek Influence in Jewish Eschatology.* London: SPCK, 1961.

Kirk, K. E. *The Vision of God: The Christian Doctrine of the Summum Bonum.* Bampton Lectures for 1928. Harrisburg, PA: Morehouse Publishing, 1991.

McDannell, Colleen, and Bernhard Lang. *Heaven: A History.* New Haven: Yale University Press, 1988.

Panneton, Georges. *Heaven or Hell.* Trans. Ann M. C. Forster. Westminster, MD: Newman Press, 1965.

Russell, Jeffrey Burton. *A History of Heaven: The Singing Silence.* Princeton: Princeton University Press, 1997.

Simon, Ulrich. *Heaven in the Christian Tradition.* London: Rockcliff, 1958.

Smith, Wilbur M. *The Biblical Doctrine of Heaven.* Chicago: Moody Press, 1968.

HEAVENS, BUDDHIST

During his lifetime the founder of Buddhism, Gautama Shakyamuni, showed considerable disdain for philosophical speculation that did not directly help one to achieve spiritual enlightenment. He was not interested in mapping out the dimensions of the universe or answering questions about whether the universe was eternal or not. But Buddhist teachings have produced an elaborate picture of the cosmos as it relates to the drama of salvation, that is, the long journey of the soul from reincarnations in hellish realms to heavenly realms to final salvation and escape from rebirth altogether. Because the Buddhist picture of the visible and invisible universe is complex, this entry provides merely an overview of where this picture of the universe came from and the relationship between its parts; the reader may then seek out articles providing more details on each of the various "heavens."

The Earth itself in Buddhism is a huge disk with four continents, supported underneath by a vast circular ocean, which is supported underneath by a mass of "golden earth," which in turn is supported by a huge layer of air, which rests in space. The surface of the Earth consists of a massive central mountain (Mount Meru or Sumeru) whose elevation literally extends into the heavens. Surrounding the central mountain are seven concentric rings of mountain ranges of diminishing heights, with rings of sea in between each mountain range. Around the outer ring of mountains, at the four cardinal points, are the four continents with their minor islands. Surrounding the entire world disk of Earth and ocean is a ring of high mountains made of iron, called Chakravāla, from which the entire world-system gets its name. It is extremely interesting to note that even early Buddhism taught that there were not merely one of these world-systems in space but many of them, all similarly constructed (for example, see the Majjhima Nikāya III:101). Some Buddhist descriptions of the greater universe state that these Chakravāla world-systems, each with their own sun, moon, oceans, and seven concentric mountain ranges, were grouped by thousands, and that the entire universe might contain billions of such groupings of thousands. Regardless of their number, however, the structure of the heavens of each world-system is essentially the same.

Fundamental to the Buddhist view of reality is the belief that all beings are necessarily caused to be born, grow old, die, and be reborn over and over again due to their desires and cravings during life. Exactly what realm in the Chakravāla world-system one is reborn into is determined by one's actions in the preceding life, that is, one's karma. After death, the deceased passes through several experiences, including the harrowing ordeal of judgment. This period between lives is called in Tibetan *Bardo*, or literally "the Between." Then the deceased experiences rebirth into a new body. Ordinarily, there are six possible realms of rebirth, which are situated on, under, or above the Earth. The six states of rebirth in the Buddhist system are represented pictorially as a great "wheel of life" (in Sanskrit, bhava-chakra) because a being is reborn and dies in one state only to be reborn and die in another, depending on karma. One whirls through life after life endlessly until one is "saved" by the release of nirvāṇa.

In the deep bowels of the Earth we find the hells (usually eight in number), each lower hell worse in torment than the last. Those unfortunate beings who are reborn in the hells can expect lifetimes in the millions of years. On the four continents are locations for two other "unfortunate" rebirths, namely as animals and as "hungry ghosts," or prets. Also on the continents live those who are born as humans—the only one of the six states that is thought to produce enough happiness and enough suffering to allow one to achieve the detachment and insight necessary for attaining enlightenment.

The central mountain of the world, Meru, provides the site for the rebirths of the demigods (asuras) and the gods of this world (devas). The demigods are located at the base of the great mountain, pursuing lives of great pleasure but plagued by jealousy over the better lives of the gods who live above them. Therefore, when not carousing and making love, the demigods wage constant war on their superiors, only to lose the battle time and again. Beginning halfway up Mt. Meru at a height of 40,000 leagues and extending to the peak at 80,000 leagues are the dwellings of the gods, or devas, who themselves live in one of six heavens (i.e., vertical stations) based on their degree of blessedness.

This entire set of the six states of rebirth (hell-beings, hungry ghosts, animals, humanity, demigods, and gods) makes up "World of Desire" (in Sanskrit, kāma-dhātu), so called because the beings of all six states pursue physical or emotional goals of one sort or another, whether they are wealth, status, love, security, or peace. Because of their desires, they take rebirth again and again in World of Desire. There are higher heavens in the Chakravāla world-system, however, for those who have mastered Buddhist techniques of meditation. Those who have attained the four lower meditative states of withdrawal and calmness (called *dhyānas*) are reborn after death in a realm where there is form only but no sensual desires, called *Rūpa-dhātu,* which has no less than seventeen distinct heavens. Meanwhile, those who have attained the four higher meditative states are reborn in a world of pure spirit without even form, which has four ascending heavens, called *Arūpa-dhātu*. In these higher heavens, for both those with form only and those with no form, the lifespan is immense, covering cosmic time-spans of billions of years. Even here, however, rebirth is eventually certain as the energy of one's stored-up karma, no matter how pure and blest, runs out. Whether one attains a lifespan of ten years or ten billion, rebirth is certain for everyone in the Chakravāla world-system who has not achieved the total liberation called *nirvāṇa*.

This cardinal doctrine of necessary rebirth, however, underwent a gradual shift as Indian Buddhism evolved over the centuries since its inception; this shift was more dramatic when Buddhism entered East Asia in the first few centuries C.E. The original founder of Buddhism was made into more and more of a god-figure, with more and more amazing powers. Furthermore, as different traditions of Buddhism grew, there also arose the idea that because the universe had so many huge world-systems, surely there were other Buddhas in other "galaxies," as it were, who had the same powers and same abilities as the historical Buddha of our earth. Some of these Buddhas were thought to rule over world-systems much like our own, with hells and heavens and constant reincarnation, whereas other Buddhas presided over world-systems that were thoroughly "pure," meaning there were no unfortunate birth states and no reincarnation. Belief in such otherworldly Buddhas and practices leading to rebirth in their "pure lands" became immensely popular in later Buddhism, particularly in China, Korea, and Japan. Entirely new schools of Buddhism developed around particular Pure Land heavens, such as a heaven called *Sukhāvatī* ruled by the Buddha named Amitābha and a heaven called *Abhirati* ruled by the Buddha Aṣhobhya. In theory, the goal of seeking rebirth in these Pure Lands was to facilitate the pursuit of ultimate salvation, but in popular Buddhism the fact is that most people are more interested in the happiness of heaven than in spiritual liberation. Although modern forms of Buddhism in Tibet, Nepal, Sri Lanka, Thailand, and Burma do not generally accept this form of Buddhism, Pure Land heavens are very popular today in China and Japan.

See also ABHIRATI; ARŪPA-DHĀTU; BARDO; BHAVA-CHAKRA; CHING T'U; HELLS, BUDDHIST; KĀMA-DHĀTU; NIRVĀṆA; PRET; PURE LAND; REINCARNATION, EASTERN; RŪPA-DHĀTU; SUKHĀVATĪ; SVARGA; YAMA.

References

Andrews, Allan. *The Teachings Essential for Rebirth: A Study of Genshin's Ojoyoshu*. Tokyo: Sophia University, 1974.

Becker, Carl B. *Breaking the Circle: Death and the Afterlife in Buddhism*. Carbondale: Southern Illinois University Press, 1993.

Bloom, Alfred. *Shinran's Doctrine of Pure Grace*. Tucson: University of Arizona Press, 1965.

Kloetzli, Randy. *Buddhist Cosmology: From Single World System to Pure Land*. Delhi: Motilal Banarsidass, 1983.

Law, Bimala Churn. *Heaven and Hell in Buddhist Perspective*. Calcutta: Bhartiya Publishing House, 1925.

Stcherbatsky, Th. *The Central Conception of Buddhism*. 1922. Reprint, Delhi: Motilal Banarsidass, 1994.

Thurman, Robert A. F., trans. *The Tibetan Book of the Dead*. New York: Bantam, 1994.

Waddell, L. Austine. *Tibetan Buddhism*. Reprint. New York: Dover, 1972.

Williams, Paul. *Mahāhāna Buddhism: The Doctrinal Foundations*. New York: Routledge, 1989.

HEL

Literally "hiding" or "death," Hel is the old Norse designation for both the realm of the Underworld and the goddess, daughter of Loki, who rules there. Hel herself is described as half blue. She was cast down to Niflheim (the lowest of all Underworlds in Norse mythology) by Odin himself, where she formed her own kingdom and had the power to receive the dead from all the nine worlds. Hel as a figure appears relatively frequently in Norse literature, less as an actual goddess to whom one might sacrifice and more as a metaphor for death. For instance, in the text *Höfudlausn* (Ellis) Hel is said to trample upon corpses in battle, whereas in the *Sonatorrek* (Ellis) she stands on the headland where the poet's son has been buried. In these instances it is clear that poetry and not literal belief inspires the image.

As a place, the descriptions of Hel in Norse literature are vague and incomplete. It is certainly not the only Norse realm of the dead, and in many instances it may simply be a metaphor for the grave itself. *Gylfaginning* (section 33) (Sturlson) speaks of Hel as a place of hunger, illness, and disasters of various kinds and then as a world of shadows. Although most references to Hel denote it simply as the dwelling of the dead, it is described as a hall surrounded by a steep wall through which none of the living can pass—the gates of Hel open for the dead alone. The road to Hel runs downward, is mostly underground, and is well-traveled, passing through several worlds. Its exact location is unclear, but one text, *Grímnismál* (Titchenell), places Hel under the third root of the great ash Yggdrasil, the cosmic tree, beside Jotunheim, the land of the evil giants, and Midgard, the world of humans.

The best description of Hel is given by Snorri Sturluson in *Gylfaginning* (section 49), in which he describes the journey of Hermod, Odin's son, in an attempt to restore to life the tragically slain Balder. On Odin's magical steed Sleipnir, Hermod rode for nine nights "through valleys dark and deep" until he came to a bridge over a river named Gioll. There a maiden named Mödgud gave Hermod directions to his dead brother, "northwards and downwards." Finally Hermod, having geared up Sleipnir, leaped over the gates of Hel and entered the hall, where he found his brother Balder, though he was not ultimately able to secure his release.

Difficulties, however, quickly emerge with this picture of Hel. Balder himself arrived in Hel via water, for he was cremated at sea on his ship, along with his horse and fine possessions. Indeed, the description of Hel as "northwards" from a Scandinavian point of view leads directly to the sea. Yet Hermod rides overland to reach Hel, and other accounts tell of the dead being equipped with "Hel-shoes" in order to make the long journey to Hel over rock and bramble. Meanwhile, other tales of the journey of the living to the land of the dead bring on other ideas. The account of Hadingus has him journey likewise under the Earth but then through a sunny world where fresh plants are growing. In short, there is no one clear picture of Hel as the land of the dead. Rather there are accounts of several realms of the dead that coexisted in Scandinavian tradition.

Some have argued that the Norse Underworld of Hel was influenced by Christian traditions, particularly because its most detailed account was written by Snorri, an avowed convert to the new religion. However, several characteristics of Hel make this theory unlikely. First, there is no record of Hel as a place of retribution. Although a few Norse texts do teach the idea of after-death rewards and punishments, they are associated not with Hel but with Nástrond, the shore of corpses, whose doors face northwards and whose roof is formed of serpents dripping poison (Völuspá). It is said to await perjurers, murderers, and those who beguile the wives of others, and a stern dragon, Níthhoggr, bears away the corpses of the wicked on his wings.

Again, Hel seems originally to have been a temporary resting place for the dead. In one text the wicked are said to "die away from Hel" into Niflheim, an even deeper world of darkness (*Vafthrúdnismál,* section 43 [Ellis]). Meanwhile, reincarnation appears to have been held out as a possible fate for others. A scolding Christian commentary remarks:

> It was the belief in former days that people were reborn after death; but this is now an old wives' tale. Helge and Sigrun are said to have been born again; he was then named Helge Hadingskate and she Kåra Halfdansdotter, as told in the Lays of the Crow; and she was a Valkyrie. (Ellis)

In short, although it is certainly likely that Norse conceptions of death and the afterlife underwent change after the arrival of Christianity, it appears that most of the myths as we now have them stem from earlier traditions.

See also GIMLÉ; NIFLHEIM; ODIN; VALHALLA, VALKYRIE.

References

Ellis, Hilda Roderick. *The Road to Hel: A Study of the Conception of the Dead in Old Norse Literature.* Cambridge: Cambridge University Press, 1943.

Sturluson, Snorri. *Edda.* Trans. Anthony Faulkes. London: Dent, 1987.

Titchenell, Elsa-Brita. *The Masks of Odin.* Pasadena: Theosophical University Press, 1985.

Turville-Petre, E. O. G. *Myth and Religion of the North: The Religion of Ancient Scandinavia.* Westport, CT: Greenwood, 1964.

HELL, HISTORY OF (CHRISTIAN)

Early Christians generally agreed on only a few things regarding the afterlife. One agreement was that except for martyrs (who had passed their test on Earth), everyone would have to pass through a fire to be tested, following Paul's statement in 1 Corinthians 3:13: "For that day dawns in fire, and the fire will test the worth of each man's work." Another point of general agreement among early Christians was that the day of God was at hand. Jesus would return literally any day, for as he had said, "the end is near, at the very door. I tell you this: the present generation will live to see it all" (Mark 13:30–31). Besides a fiery ordeal and the nearness of Christ's return, all else regarding the afterlife was controversial in the early church.

Hell was a particularly thorny problem for the early Christians because the Scriptures are somewhat unclear, even contradictory. The Old Testament offers very few promises of any afterlife at all for the righteous or for the wicked, whereas the apostle Paul taught that "the wage of sin is death," not damnation in the afterlife (Romans 6:23). Meanwhile, the Gospels and the Book of Revelation speak of an eternal place of punishment, though Jesus in the Gospels indicates that this is experienced by the wicked directly upon death (Luke 16:19–31), whereas the Book of Revelation appears to reserve hellfire until after the final judgment and the end of the world. To fill in these gaps, more and more texts appeared in Christian circles claiming apostolic authority, which clarified the nature of Hell, who would go, and what the torments would be like, including the Apocalypse of Peter (included in the Bible until the Council of Carthage in 397), the Apocalypse of Paul, the Apocalypse of Ezra, the Gospel of Nicodemus, and the Gospel of Bartholemew. The last two Gospels in particular were very popular because they describe Jesus' descent into Hell after his crucifixion and before his resurrection. Though neither Gospel was finally retained in the canon of the Bible, nevertheless they made the "harrowing of Hell" a permanent Christian doctrine, included in the official Apostles' Creed.

Adding to the texts circulating under the names of apostles, many Christian theologians wrote in their own names, speculating on the afterlife and Hell in particular. The North African theologian Tertullian (c. 160–230) witnessed much Christian persecution during his lifetime and relished contemplating how his non-Christian enemies would suffer for eternity:

> What a panorama of spectacle on that day! Which sight shall I turn to first to laugh and applaud? Mighty kings whose ascent to heaven used to be announced publicly groaning now in the depths with Jupiter himself who used to witness that ascent? Governors who persecuted the name of the Lord melting in flames fiercer than those they kindled for brave Christians? Wise philosophers, blushing before their students as they burn together, the followers to whom they taught that the world is no concern of God's, whom they assured that either they had no souls at all or that what souls they had would never return to their former bodies? Poets, trembling not before the judgment seat of Rhadamanthus or of Minos, but of Christ—a surprise? Tragic actors bellowing in their own melodramas should be worth hearing! Comedians skipping in the fire will be worth praise! The famous charioteer will toast on his fiery wheel; the athletes will cartwheel not in the gymnasium but in flames. . . . These are things of greater delight, I believe, than a circus, both kinds of theater, and any stadium. (quoted in Turner, pp. 76–77)

Indeed, for Tertullian and many Christians like him, the joys of heaven were made all the more sweet because of the fact that they would be able to witness the endless torments of the pagans and celebrate the "justice" of God—a pleasure labeled the "abominable fancy" by the nineteenth-century Protestant dean, Frederic William Farrar.

But while many texts were celebrating the eternal torments of the damned, important Christian thinkers were challenging the very eternality as well as fundamental purpose of Hell. In contrast to Tertullian, the Alexandrian theologian Clement (fl. 150 to c. 215 C.E.), put forward a proposition that was to influence the debate for centuries, that "God does not wreak vengeance, for vengeance is to return evil with evil, and God punishes only with an eye to the good" (*Stromata* 7.26[Le Goff, p. 53]). Clement's student Origen (c. 180–253 C.E.) was the leading Christian thinker of the third century. Origen developed the notion of divine punishment as education and taught that no soul was ever beyond the bounds of divine compassion and instruction. Origen's doctrine of universal salvation, called *apokatastasis,* taught that suffering, even hellfire, was no more than a purging of sin from the wicked soul, leaving behind a pure entity that might reincarnate on earth and seek final perfection there or perhaps proceed to incarnate on higher spheres of being. Hell could not be eternal (though it might be long-lasting indeed for the truly wicked), for that would indicate a failure on God's part to redeem all of creation, and it would cheapen the crucifixion in a less than universal redemption. This result is unthinkable, according to Origen, for an omnipotent and omniscient being. Origen carried out his interpretation of Hell and Scripture to its logical end, concluding that even the fallen angels and Satan himself would ultimately be saved after eons of suffering and purging—a position that certainly contributed to Origen's ideas being declared heretical by church leaders in the following century.

However, Origen's merciful view carried on for centuries among many followers labeled *misericordes,* or "compassionate ones." Ultimately a kind of theological compromise was reached by the great father of the church, Augustine (354–430 C.E.), who was the last innovative Christian theologian until the Middle Ages. He certainly upheld the doctrine of an eternal Hell, in which he placed a great many people, including atheists and those who had committed serious or "mortal" sins. However, between the time of death and the general resurrection, Augustine believed that those guilty of minor sins (too much laughter, too much affection for family or friends, or overindulgence in food) would ultimately be saved by means of passing through a "purgatorial fire."

In the Middle Ages, the greatest development in the doctrine of Hell and the afterlife was the invention of Purgatory, which attempted to rescue much of Christendom from the clutches of Hell, only to confine them in a hell-like prison marked by the same fire and brimstone but with the important difference of eternal salvation at the end. The medieval period experienced terrific growth in visitations from ghosts, saints, and demons (including a newly invigorated Satan himself) and a corresponding increase in private prayers, masses, almsgiving, penance, and other activities devoted to ameliorating the suffering of the dead. From the time of Pope Gregory the Great (590–604), records of visits to the Otherworld proliferated, both oral and literary, culminating in the supreme poetic vision of Dante's *Divine Comedy* (1314–1321). With its publication, the church lost exclusive control over depictions of Hell and the afterlife. Scenes of Heaven, Hell, and judgment certainly graced cathedrals and church-sponsored public murals from the fourteenth century onward, but such

themes were also favorites of private artists like the Flemish painters Jan van Eyck (c. 1390–1441) and Hieronymus Bosch (c. 1450–1516) and many others independent of church direction. Dante's masterpiece, with its deliberately imaginative, minute detail and fiendishly suitable punishments, likewise inspired an entire genre of secular literature dealing with Hell and its minions.

Helped by the invention of the printing press in the middle of the fifteenth century, hundreds of romances, poems, and plays dealing with Hell circulated throughout Europe, the most famous of which include *Jerusalem Delivered* (1581) by Torquato Tasso, *The Faerie Queene* by Edmund Spenser (1590–1596), *The Tragicall History of Doctor Faustus* (1589) by Christopher Marlowe, and *Paradise Lost* (1667) by John Milton. Miracle plays (ostensibly based on the life of Christ) and "Hell parades" (part of the autumnal festivals from Hallowe'en to St. Stephen's Day on 26 December) gave exaggerated attention to Hell, with troops of actors in demon costumes getting as drunk as their audiences and crudely parodying all things sacred. The violence and chaos that increasingly accompanied such plays and parades led to both being forbidden by religious authorities all over Europe by the beginning of the seventeenth century. But such activities simply divorced themselves from any religious associations and carried on in unsanctioned folk tradition.

These popular depictions—even mockeries—of Hell and other "sacred" topics helped prepare the way for very serious discussions, inside and outside the church. Intellectualism, which had blossomed in the form of Scholasticism in the twelfth and thirteenth centuries, led to critical thinking that began to turn against the Roman Catholic Church itself. This trend eventually led to schism, the Protestant Reformation, the Catholic Counter-Reformation, and a century of bloodshed and religious strife throughout Europe. The Protestants, led by Martin Luther (1483–1546), John Calvin (1509–1564), and Huldreich Zwingli (1484–1531), attempted to wrest control of human salvation from the Catholic Church and place it in God's hands. This meant the end of pardons, indulgences, Purgatory, intercession, and any other kind of human mediation for other humans' destiny. Rather, these Protestant leaders turned to predestination (God determined at creation who would be saved and who would be damned) and a strict Heaven or Hell paradigm, with no middle ground. The Protestants never questioned the existence of a literal Hell, though their Hell was, of course, quickly filling with Catholics. But the Protestants were left with the same problem that the Catholic Church had struggled with since the time of Jesus—what becomes of those who have died as they await the final judgment and dispensation of eternity?

Engraving after miniature in the twelfth-century manuscript "Hortus deliciarum," produced in a monastery at Hohembourg and destroyed in the burning of Strasbourg during Franco-Prussian War, 1870–1871. Courtesy of Anne Ronan Picture Library.

The Protestants largely decided to agree with Augustine's position that the just would await the end of the world in a happy place of refreshment and that the evil would wait in a prison-like environment. However, they found no more Biblical justification for this doctrine than the Catholics had, and they likewise had to accept the doctrine of two judgments, one for individuals at death (to determine in which state they would await the end) and one for all mankind at the end of time.

Although the clash of the Catholic and Protestant titans dominated the sixteenth century, the seventeenth century saw the rise of secular learning or at least intellectual debate that broke free from the constraints of denominational control, often stimulated by pre-Christian writings from Greco-Roman civilization. While modern science was establishing its foundations through the likes of Isaac Newton (1642–1727), Galileo Galilei (1564–1642), and Johannes Kepler (1571–1630), a parallel movement of rational criticism of religious dogma and the birth of modern philosophy began with such thinkers as Thomas Hobbes (1588–1679), René Descartes (1596–1650), and John Locke (1632–1704). All three came to believe that Hell was not eternal but that after the last judgment sinners would simply be destroyed. Locke wrote that sinners in Hell

> shall not live for ever. This is so plain in Scripture, and is so everywhere inculcated—that the wages of sin is death, and the reward of the righteous is everlasting life . . . that one would wonder how the readers could be mistaken (quoted in Walker, p. 94)

This doctrine, which may be called *annihilationism,* was not unique to emerging secular philosophers but was held even among some clergy, including the Reverend John Biddle, who taught annihilationism in his *Twofold Catechism* (1654). Another kind of revolt against the traditional belief in an eternal hell was universalism, the doctrine that all creation would eventually be saved. Cambridge Platonists like Peter Sterry (d. 1672) and Jeremiah White (1630–1707) preached universal salvation, joining this doctrine to the standard predestination believed in by Protestant leaders. Several prominent women also contributed to the rise of universalism, including Jane Lead's 1694 book *Enochian Walks with God,* and Lady Anne Conway's *Principles of the Most Ancient and Modern Philosophy* of 1692, which taught the classical Platonic doctrine of reincarnation as an educational device of the divine. Hell was likewise a tool, which helped sinful souls grow: "All Kinds and Degrees of Sin, have their proper Punishments, and all these Punishments tend to the Creatures Advantage; so

that Grace prevails over Judgment" (quoted in Walker, p. 139).

Interest in physics, astronomy, ancient philosophy, alchemy, and occultism in the seventeenth century steadily drew Europe's finest minds away from church dogma and into the creation of a new physical and spiritual universe. But with the decline of belief among elites in traditional dogmas like the eternality of Hell, there was a strong reaction among the ordinary population fostered by church opposition to secular learning. The decades from 1590 to 1620 saw the first spread of witch hysteria throughout Europe, in which tens of thousands of people were murdered. The Catholic Church itself was fond of burning scientific heretics, for instance, Giordano Bruno in 1600. Such violent reactions succeeded in making secular thinkers more careful of what they published and where, but in the end it only served to drive a further wedge between Christianity and the acquisition of knowledge—a division that has yet to heal completely.

The eighteenth century saw the intellectual abandonment of traditional religion entirely, as educated elites contributed to the rapid expansion of science and philosophy. Heaven and Hell were widely mocked and traced (dismissively) to their primitive origins in Persia, Egypt, and Greece, as in Voltaire's *Dictionnaire Philosophique* of 1764. Christianity slowly lost the battle for minds as the eighteenth century closed and the nineteenth dawned, despite the powerful impact of Emanuel Swedenborg (1688–1772) and his mystical visions of the afterlife. The publication of Swedenborg's mystical journeys indeed influenced millions of people to believe in a literal Heaven and Hell. But mainstream Christianity proved uninterested in firsthand accounts of the afterlife, and the new movement known as "Spiritualism" took shape largely outside the confines of the church. Despite the popularity of Swedenborg's visions, the nineteenth century witnessed the metamorphosis of Hell from a plausible religious doctrine to a nostalgic literary device. In the works of William Blake (1757–1827), Lord Byron (1788–1824), Charles-Pierre Baudelaire (1821–1867), and many other poets and novelists, Satan and Hell became metaphors, tools of Gothic horror, personal allegories of suffering and growth, but never literal truths. By the end of the nineteenth century, as Alice Turner remarks in *The History of Hell,* Hell had virtually disappeared from the popular culture, replaced by fantasy, the occult, and visitors from the Spiritualists' "Summerland."

The twentieth century saw a precipitous drop in the belief in Hell even among the devoutly religious. Fundamentalists and evangelicals attempted to revive a flagging public interest using threats or promises (for instance, Jon E. Braun's *Whatever Happened to Hell?*), but they are generally poorly written and edited and very restricted in readership. Psychoanalysis has replaced confession, ecumenism is gradually eroding denominational and doctrinal boundaries, and universal salvation is popular among all those who still believe in Christianity at all. But the decline in a traditional belief in Hell should not be interpreted as the death of the afterlife in popular culture. Research into "near-death experiences," a rising belief in reincarnation, and the prominence of Eastern and New Age ideology indicates a robust outlook for afterlife adventures in the foreseeable future.

See also GEHENNA; HADES; HELL, ORIGINS OF; INTERCESSION; JUDGMENT, LAST; PURGATORY; UNDERWORLD.

References

Bonner, Hypatia Bradlaugh. *The Christian Hell from the First to the Twentieth Century.* London: Watts, 1913.

Braun, Jon E. *Whatever Happened to Hell?* Nashville: Thomas Nelson Publishers, 1979.

Camporesi, Piero. *The Fear of Hell: Images of Damnation and Salvation in Early Modern Europe.* Trans. Lucinda Byatt. University Park: Pennsylvania State University Press, 1987.

Dante Alighieri. *The Comedy of Dante Alighieri the Florentine.* Trans. Dorothy L. Sayers. 3 vols. Baltimore, MD: Penguin Books, 1955.

Duensing, H. *The Apocalypse of Peter.* In *New Testament Apocrypha,* ed. E. Hennecke and W. Schneemelcher. London: Lutterworth Press, 1965.

Gardiner, Eileen, ed. *Visions of Heaven and Hell before Dante.* New York: Italica Press, 1989.

Himmelfarb, Martha. *Tours of Hell: An Apocalyptic Form in Jewish and Christian Literature.* Philadelphia: University of Pennsylvania Press, 1983.

Kvanig, Jonathan L. *The Problem of Hell.* New York: Oxford University Press, 1993.

Le Goff, Jacques. *The Birth of Purgatory.* Trans. Arthur Goldhammer. Chicago: University of Chicago Press, 1984.

Maurice, Frederick Denison. *Theological Essays.* 3rd ed. London: Macmillan 1871.

Mew, James. *Traditional Aspects of Hell.* London: S. Sonnenschein, 1903. Reprint, Ann Arbor, MI: Gryphon Books, 1971.

Moore, David George. *The Battle for Hell: A Survey and Evaluation of Evangelicals' Growing Attraction to the Doctrine of Annihilationism.* Lanham, MD: University Press of America, 1995.

Paine, Lauran. *The Hierarchy of Hell.* New York: Hippocrene Books, 1972.

Panneton, Georges. *Heaven or Hell.* Trans. Ann M. C. Forster. Westminster, MD: Newman Press, 1965.

Paternoster, Michael. *Thou Art These Also: God, Death and Hell.* London: Society for Promoting Christian Knowledge, 1967.

Turner, Alice K. *The History of Hell.* New York: Harcourt Brace, 1993.

Walker, D. P. *The Decline of Hell: Seventeenth-Century Discussions of Eternal Torment.* Chicago: University of Chicago Press, 1964.

HELL, ORIGINS OF (CHRISTIAN)

The origin and development of Hell provides one of the most interesting and controversial subjects in all of Christian history, for its sheer horror; its potential for abuse; and the passionate debates, schisms, and even bloodshed that it spawned. Christianity has taken the doctrine of Hell in remarkable new directions during 2000 years of religious history, but Christians did not invent Hell. Long before Christianity was born, Egypt, Persia, and India had very sophisticated notions about a place of afterlife punishment for sinners; the beliefs of all three ancient nations likely exerted considerable influence on early Christianity. But the most direct influences on the newborn Christian church were the afterlife beliefs of the Hebrew and Greek peoples.

Early Greek culture appears to have been slow in developing a notion of Hell as a place of punishment for bad humans. To be sure, Hades had long existed in Greek tradition as a dreary land of all the dead, but for Homer (who may have lived in the ninth century B.C.E.) and even for many later poets, it was an afterlife lacking punishment for anyone except a few spectacular criminals from myth, including Tantalos, Ixion, Sisyphos, and Tityos. There was also the realm of Tartaros in the Underworld—situated as far below the earth as an anvil would fall in nine days—where the vanquished Titans were imprisoned after the triumph of the Olympian gods, but it was not a place of mortal punishment. Not until the time of the great philosopher Plato (fourth century B.C.E.) did a complete picture of an afterlife judgment, followed by punishment or reward and then reincarnation, appear in Greek thought. However, from that time forward, expectations of a blissful or horrible afterlife based on one's merits became commonplace in Greek and then Roman thinking.

The Old Testament has absolutely no mention of a retributive Hell in the afterlife, only a Hades-like Underworld named Sheol for all the dead, but in the last few centuries before the birth of Christianity, Judaism became more and more confident of a judgment after death and corresponding bliss or suffering. One text from this intertestamental period, namely the Book of Enoch (c. 200 B.C.E.), discusses the underground "hollows" where various classes of the dead wait for the Last Judgment:

> Then [Enoch] asked [the archangel Raphael] regarding all the hollow places: "Why is one separated from the other?"
> And he answered me saying: "These . . . have been made that the spirits of the dead might be separated. And this division has been made for the spirits of the righteous, in which there is the bright spring of water. And this has been made for sinners when they die and are buried in the earth and judgement has not been executed upon them in their lifetime. Here their spirits shall be set apart in this great pain, till the great day of judgment, scourgings, and torments of the accursed for ever,

so that (there) may be retribution for their spirits for ever. There He shall bind them for ever. (Charles, trans., p. 203)

In the intertestamental period, Judaism also developed a belief in angels, demons, and magic of all kinds, as demonstrated in the apocryphal Book of Tobit. But not all Jews accepted these new doctrines, especially the Sadducees, who tended to hold to the ancient rituals of the Hebrew Bible and deny any resurrection, rebirth, or afterlife (just as ancient Hebrews appear to have done). Thus it is certain the development of an ethical afterlife in Greek philosophy had a direct impact on Hebrew beliefs from the fourth century B.C.E. onward, though it was only partially effective. Even the "new wave" of Hebrew believers were selective in what they accepted, for example, adopting a belief in a future resurrection from the Zoroastrian religion and (by and large) rejecting Greek reincarnation. But many Jews continued to believe that God created humanity for life—to enjoy physical life and to obey and worship God—and that after death the individual was simply dead.

Jesus and his first followers entered into this complex scene where many different religious beliefs coexisted and competed, while the Roman Empire steadily overran and subjugated all territories within reach, including the Near East. Because none of the Gospels that claim to record the teachings of Jesus were written by the eye-witnesses they are named for and because they appear late in the first century (beginning with the Gospel of Mark around 70 C.E.), it is more instructive to take the earliest known documents of Christianity first, namely the letters of the missionary Paul, the earliest of which are dated around 50 C.E. It may surprise some readers who are familiar with the New Testament to discover that Paul does not discuss or teach that sinners after death will go to Hell. To be sure, Paul gives long lists of those who will not be accepted into the kingdom of God, for example, in 1 Corinthians 6:9–10: "Make no mistake: no fornicator or idolater, none who are guilty either of adultery or of homosexual perversion, no thieves or grabbers or drunkards or slanderers or swindlers, will possess the kingdom of God," unless of course such sinners become "justified" through the name of Jesus. But what happens to unrepentant sinners if they are not thrown into the everlasting fire? Paul is a traditional Jew in this matter and teaches that such people will simply die and be dead, forever. Paul writes in Romans 6:20–23:

When you were slaves of sin, you were free from the control of righteousness; and what was the gain? Nothing but what now makes you ashamed, for the end of that is death. But now, freed from the commands of sin, and bound to the service of

God, your gains are such as make for holiness, and the end is eternal life. For sin pays a wage, and the wage is death, but God gives freely, and his gift is eternal life, in union with Christ Jesus our Lord.

If Paul believed that Jesus had taught the existence of Hell for sinners, this would certainly have been the place to put it. But the contrast and the threat here is not between Heaven and Hell; rather, it is between eternal life with God and utter destruction. Paul is consistent in this through every one of his letters (though the Letter to the Hebrews mentions a "fierce fire which will consume God's enemies," scholars universally agree that the letter is not Paul's). Again, in 2 Thessalonians 1:9, Paul writes, "[Sinners] will suffer the punishment of eternal destruction, cut off from the presence of the Lord and the splendour of his might," but again, sinners will apparently not experience Hell.

This attitude of Paul's is generally in contrast to that of the Gospels. Although the Gospel of John does not mention Hell, Mark warns about "the fire that shall never be quenched" and "the undying worm" that will be experienced by the sinner whose hand, or foot, or eye "offends." Clearly, the offending body part was a metaphor for spiritual illness, but most Christians have taken the undying fire and worm literally. Luke's Gospel (16:19–31) has Jesus telling the story of the beggar, Lazarus, and the rich man, Dives, who lead grossly unequal lives on earth. After death they also have very different destinies: Lazarus was "carried up by the angels to be with Abraham," who is apparently in heaven (though his exact location would become a great sticking point), whereas Dives was taken to Hades, "where he was in torment." Interestingly, however, the two can see each other and even communicate. Neither the crimes of Dives nor the virtues of Lazarus are stated; the reader assumes that Dives was selfish and is now denied even a drop of water, but besides the great poverty and suffering of Lazarus on earth, it is not at all clear why he rises "up" with angels. The best way to make sense of Jesus' parable is to see it as a teaching on brotherhood and charity, aimed mostly at the upper class of ancient Israel, though it also appears to give hope to the poor. Because the parable includes passages dealing with the geography of the Otherworld and the chasm that separates Hades from Abraham's bosom, it should be assumed that the audience took Hell literally.

The greatest development of Hell in the New Testament is the Gospel of Matthew, which mentions perdition, the "outer darkness," a furnace of fire, the damnation of Hell, and everlasting punishment frequently (Matthew 7:13; 10:28; 11:24; 13:40–42; 13:50; 23:33; 25:30; 25:41; 25:46; the term used is frequently *Gehenna*, from Hebrew tradition, and not the Greek name *Hades*). Clearly, the writers of the Gospels

Hell in The Apocalypse of Peter

For all things come to pass on the day of decision, on the day of judgment, at the word of God, and as all things came to pass when he created the word of God, and as all things came to pass when he created the world and commanded all that is therein, and it was all done—so shall it be in the last days, for everything is possible with God and he says in the Scripture: "Son of man, prophesy upon the several bones, and say to the bones—bone unto bone in joints, sinews, nerves, flesh and skin and hair thereon." And soul and spirit shall the great Uriel give at the command of God. For him God has appointed over the resurrection of the dead on the day of judgment. . . .

Then will men and women come to the place prepared for them. By their tongues with which they have blasphemed will they be hung up. There is spread out for them unquenchable fire. . . . And behold again another place: this is a great pit filled, in which are those who have denied righteousness; and angels of punishment visit them and here do they kindle upon them the fire of their punishment. And again two women: they are hung up by their neck and by their hair and are cast into the pit. These are they who plaited their hair, not to create beauty but to turn to fornication, and that they might ensnare the souls of men to destruction. And the men who lay with them in fornication are hung up by their [loins] in that burning place, and they say to one another, "We did not know that we would come into everlasting torture."

And the murderers and those who have made common cause with them are cast into the fire, in a place full of venomous beasts, and they are tormented without rest, as they feel their pains, and their worms are as numerous as a dark cloud. And the angel Ezrael will bring forth the souls of them that have been killed and they shall see the torment of those who killed them and shall say to one another, "Righteousness and justice is the judgment of God." For we have indeed heard, but did not believe that we would come to this place of eternal judgment.

And near this flame there is a great and very deep pit and into it there flow all kinds of things from everywhere: judgment, horrifying things and excretions. And the women are swallowed up by this up to their necks and are punished with great pain. These are they who have procured abortions and have ruined the work of God which he has created. Opposite them is another place where the children sit, but both alive, and they cry to God. And lightnings go forth from those children which pierce the eyes of those who, by fornication, have brought about their destruction. Other men and women stand above them naked. And their children stand opposite them in a place of delight. And they sigh and cry to God because of their parents, "These are they who neglected and cursed and transgressed thy commandment. They killed us and cursed the angel who created us and hung us up. And they withheld from us the light which thou hast appointed for all." And the milk of the mothers flows from their breasts and congeals and smells foul, and from it come forth beasts that devour flesh, which turn and torture them for ever with their husbands, because they forsook the commandment of God and killed their children. And the children shall be given to the angel Temlakos. And those who slew them will be tortured forever, for God wills it to be so.

Translation by H. Duensing (1965).

---

were associated with radically different Christian communities, with different values and emphases; only Matthew emphasizes Hell. Yet increasingly, it was Matthew's position on Hell that came to dominate early Christian thinking, particularly as a result of the harsh treatment of early Christians in the first few centuries of the common era. The Jewish community grew increasingly skeptical of the Jesus "cult," as they perceived it, and formally severed ties from the Christians at the council in Jamnia (86 C.E.), where the Hebrew canon of Scriptures was pronounced closed (i.e., no texts written by Christians would be accepted as holy writ). Meanwhile, the Christians were increasingly persecuted by Roman officials, mostly for refusing to participate in Roman worship of the emperor or make homage to any other authority than their "king," Jesus Christ; besides this, for some time Christians refused to serve in the army. Christians became unpopular, were frequently shut out of business deals and high society, and were made into scapegoats for social problems, even poor weather. But it was the Emperor Nero (ruled 54–68 C.E.) who took the persecution to new depths, blaming Roman Christians for a fire with which he was himself suspiciously associated. Nero took delight in using Christians who had been arrested for horrific entertainment, such as feeding them to lions in the arena and even covering them in tar and setting them aflame as torches for his evening parties. It was largely in response to this increasing persecution that the Book of Revelation was written, probably under the reign of another cruel emperor, Domitian (81–96 C.E.). The book is a fascinating example of early Christian apocalyptic writing, with a complex understanding of the events of the end time, but the section most relevant to the present topic is chapter 20, when the tribulations are wrapped up. First, the Devil and the False Prophet are flung into the lake of fire, "there to be tormented day and night for ever" (Revelation 20:10). Then, after the general resurrection, the sea gave up its dead, and Death and Hades gave up the dead in their keeping; they were judged each man on the record of his deeds. Then Death and Hades were flung into the lake of fire. This lake of fire is the second death; and into it were flung any whose names were not to be found in the roll of the living. (Revelation 20:13–15)

It is most curious that Hades, which in most of the New Testament is itself a fiery torment, appears to be thrown into itself; but in any case, the Revelation's development of terrific drama and detail became the hallmark of the Christian doctrine of Hell. These characteristics (drama and detail) only grew over time, spawning an entire genre of visionary literature, such as the Apocalypse of Peter (mid–second century C.E.) and the Apocalypse of Paul (third century C.E.), which are filled for pages and pages with descriptions of the particular kinds of torments for each kind of sinner, in minute detail. As Christian tradition focused more and more on sin as a result of sexual activity (beginning with Adam and Eve), the descriptions of punishments in Hell became more and more obsessed with the genital region. At first such lurid Hells were a psychological balm to the early Christians, allowing them (in literature, at least) to fight back against their oppressors, for the Christians were too numerically inferior to do so militarily (and besides, were committed in the early centuries to pacifism). But after the Roman Empire converted to Christianity in the fourth century, the doctrine of Hell began to be used as a tool against Christians—both to condemn heretics and to keep the masses in line.

As already traced, however, Hell was treated very differently in early Christian communities. Paul's writings in particular must give one pause. If his letters contain the earliest known doctrinal statements of Christianity and yet make no mention of Hell, how trustworthy is the doctrine of Hell in the Gospels, written at the earliest forty years after Jesus' death? But by the time the Gospels and the Book of Revelation were written, the Christian situation had drastically changed. Rome had conquered Israel and destroyed the Hebrews in 70 C.E., as Roman armies had subjugated so many other territories; apocalyptic expectations were on the rise across the newly forged empire; and Christians began to suffer infrequent but very severe persecutions. Thus it was probably not sober theology but fierce experience that drove the Christian doctrine of Hell into ever harsher territory. When the dust settled, so many doctrines had entered Christianity through so many avenues that things had become quite confused, and the early Christian Fathers found themselves in quite a theological quandary: if the dead are sent to Heaven or fierce Hell immediately after death,

as the parable of Dives and Lazarus and other Gospel stories suggest (e.g., Luke 23:43), then what is the point of a resurrection and re-judgment of all the dead? These and other thorny theological issues left much over which succeeding generations of Christians would struggle.

See also DOZAKH; GEHENNA; HADES; HEAVEN, HISTORY OF; HEAVEN, ORIGINS OF; INTERCESSION; JUDGMENT, LAST; PURGATORY; RISTAKHEZ; SHEOL; TARTAROS; UNDERWORLD.

References

Bernstein, Alan E. *The Formation of Hell: Death and Retribution in the Ancient and Early Christian Worlds.* Ithaca, NY: Cornell University Press, 1993.

Bonner, Hypatia Bradlaugh. *The Christian Hell from the First to the Twentieth Century.* London: Watts, 1913.

Braun, Jon E. *Whatever Happened to Hell?* Nashville: Thomas Nelson Publishers, 1979.

Charles, R. H., ed. "The Book of Enoch." In *The Apocrypha and Pseudepigrapha of the Old Testament.* Oxford: Clarendon Press, 1966.

Duensing, H. *The Apocalypse of Peter.* In *New Testament Apocrypha*, ed. E. Hennecke and W. Schneemelcher. London: Lutterworth Press, 1965.

Gardiner, Eileen, ed. *Visions of Heaven and Hell before Dante.* New York: Italica Press, 1989.

Himmelfarb, Martha. *Tours of Hell: An Apocalyptic Form in Jewish and Christian Literature.* Philadelphia: University of Pennsylvania Press, 1983.

Kvanig, Jonathan L. *The Problem of Hell.* New York: Oxford University Press, 1993.

Paine, Lauran. *The Hierarchy of Hell.* New York: Hippocrene Books, 1972.

Panneton, Georges. *Heaven or Hell.* Trans. Ann M. C. Forster. Westminster, MD: Newman Press, 1965.

Paternoster, Michael. *Thou Art These Also: God, Death and Hell.* London: Society for Promoting Christian Knowledge, 1967.

Perrin, Norman, and Dennis C. Duling. *The New Testament: An Introduction.* 2nd ed. New York: Harcourt Brace Jovanovich, 1982.

Turner, Alice K. *The History of Hell.* New York: Harcourt Brace, 1993.

HELLS, BUDDHIST

Hell is only one of six basic possibilities for rebirth after death in Buddhist thought. Unlike Christianity or Islam, Buddhism teaches that hell is only a temporary dwelling for the sinner, although a birth there may last many thousands and even millions of years. Eventually, as the karmic energy of one's sins is "used up," one dies out of hell and is reborn in another state. Even after escaping hell, however, one may perform evil actions in the next life and again die and be reborn in hell. This revolving process of birth and death in various states is called *saṃsāra*. It is important to note that in Buddhism, not only evil actions but evil words and thoughts result in negative karma that can drag one down to hell after death.

Decoration on a building in Hong Kong of a punishment in a Buddhist hell. Courtesy of Images Colour Library.

Although rebirths as an animal or "hungry ghost" (pret) also result from wicked deeds, words, and thoughts, at least such rebirths are on the sunlit world where human beings live. The various hells are obviously the worst possible punishments for sinners, and in the classical Buddhist cosmography (map of the world) the hells are placed directly underneath the Earth, stacked vertically one below the other. Typically the number of Buddhist hells is eight, and like Dante's *Inferno*, they locate the wicked in realms suitable to their crimes, as described later in this entry. However, the names and numbers of the various Buddhist hells multiplied over time as later commentators built on the work of their predecessors, until the number of hells became almost innumerable. Thus we find in northern Buddhism and later in Chinese Buddhism eight "cold" hells in addition to the eight "hot" hells, which are accompanied by 84,000 hells of "outer darkness," and so on.

Although hell is certainly mentioned in the sermons of Gautama Shakyamuni, the founder of Buddhism, it was only after his death that systematic Buddhist philosophy arose and the dimensions and divisions of the cosmos with its heavens and hells were worked out. One of the most extensive of such philosophical presentations of Buddhism is called *Abhidharma* and was developed by what is now known as southern Buddhism. In this system there are eight hells, the uppermost of which begins 1,000 leagues (yojanas) below the surface of the earth. Between each hell are several thousand leagues, and the eighth hell (Avīci), is a full 20,000 leagues under the earth. Each of the eight hells has a specific name, a specific sin that causes a person to be reborn there, a specific duration of suffering, and appropriate "subhells," usually sixteen in number, through which the sinner passes to round out the learning experience. One of the fullest descriptions of the hells comes from a late commentary, the Sūtra of the Remembrance of the True Law (in Sanskrit, *Saddharma-smriti-upasthāna*). Beginning with the uppermost, these hells are as follows:

1. Samjīva, or "Hell of Constantly Reviving," where one is reborn as a consequence of deliberate killing. Such life taking ranges in seriousness from killing insects to murdering holy persons. The torments in this hell, like all the others, reflect the nature of the crime: if one crushed turtles in their shells, one is repeatedly crushed, and those who hunted animals and ate them find themselves eaten from the inside out by sharp-beaked maggots. Sadly, each time one is "killed," one revives, only to undergo new torment.
2. Kālasūtra, or "Black Lines Hell," where one is reborn as a consequence of stealing or using what is reserved for others. Here demons take ropes soaked in black ink and draw them across one's body, which has been nailed down. Then, like butchers carving up meat, one's body is cut up into tiny pieces with burning hot saws. There are also subhells where one is forced to drink molten copper, where one is stabbed with three-pronged spears, and where huge birds pluck out one's eyes.
3. Samghāta, or "Squeezing Hell," where one is reborn because of sexual misbehavior. Here one is led by desires to chase after beautiful sexual objects, only to be squeezed, crushed, cut up, sliced open, and burned up time and time again, never reaching the beloved.
4. Raurava, or "Screaming Hell," where one is reborn to pay for using intoxicants like alcohol and mind-altering drugs. Here demons pry open one's mouth and pour various boiling liquids down the throat, which burns the body from the inside out.

5. Mahāraurava, or "Great Screaming Hell," where one is reborn as a consequence of lying. Here one suffers by having gnawing snakes born within one's body, having one's tongue pulled out, and having one's mouth burned away, and so on.

6. Tāpana, or "Hell of Burning Heat," where one is reborn as a consequence of heretical beliefs. The other hells, which are undoubtedly intensely hot, are said to be as cool as snowflakes compared to this hell. Here one's body is burned up over and over again by searing flames.

7. Pratāpana, or "Hell of Great Burning Heat," the place of rebirth for one who has sexually defiled the religion, for instance seducing or raping a monk or nun. This hell is said to be ten times hotter than the last. A typical torment in the Hell of Great Burning Heat is to be dragged over continents and oceans by demons with iron hooks and then tied to the spiked floor. Here, demons shove sharp-toothed worms up one's anus. The worms devour one's insides as they travel up the body, eventually cracking open one's head and escaping.

8. Avīchi, or "Hell without Cease," where one is reborn in consequence of the gravest of sins, namely premeditated murder of one's mother, father, the Buddha, virtuous Buddhists, or Buddhist saints (arhats). The sufferings of this hell are 1,000 times more awful than the suffering of previous hells, and it is so far below the earth that one is said to fall upside-down for 2,000 years before even reaching it. The sufferings scarcely need to be described; suffice it to say that the wicked born in this hell look up to the other hells and are jealous of what seem to be the lifestyles of the gods.

What is most evident from looking over the list of eight hells is that the first five follow in exact sequence the five vows all Buddhists take, that is, not to kill, steal, engage in sexual misconduct, use intoxicants, or lie; and the last three hells have to do with defending the Buddhist faith from abuse. The hells are thus conveniently arranged for illustrating to the layperson the importance of moral behavior during life, and this fact has prompted some Western students of Buddhism to assume that the hells are nothing more than teaching devices (upāya), ultimately false but useful. More will be said of this later.

Northern Buddhism, born among the lofty Himalayan mountains, also teaches a companion set of eight hells called the "cold" hells—which is not surprising, but in most of India it would be impossible to think of anything cool as "hell." These hells are located on the

---

Buddhist Judgment Scene

The gatekeepers of hell drag the wicked person after death to the throne of the king of hell, Yama, who asks him,

"Did you not when on earth see the five divine messengers sent to warn you—the child, the old man, the sick, the criminal suffering punishment, and the dead corpse?"

And the wicked man answers, "I did see them."

"And did you not think to yourself 'I also am subject to birth, old age, and death. Let me be careful to do good works'?"

And the wicked man answers, "I did not, sire. I neglected in my folly to think of these things."

Then the king, Yama, pronounces his doom. "These, your evil deeds, are not the work of your mother, father, relatives, friends, or advisors. You alone have done them all; you alone must receive the fruit." And the gatekeepers of hell drag him to the place of torment, rivet him to red-hot iron, plunge him in glowing seas of blood, torture him on burning coals, and he does not die until the last residue of his guilt has been atoned.

Adapted from Oldenberg, Deva-dūtta-sutta, quoted in Law (1925).

---

edge of the Buddhist universe and each is colder than the last:

1. Arbuda, or "Chapped," where the naked sinners are constantly submerged in ice and glacier water. Their bodies become covered in blisters caused by ice.

2. Nirarbuda, or "Deeply Chapped," where the cold blisters become open sores.

3. Aṭaṭa, or the sound one makes with chattering teeth. One is too cold here to speak or cry out any more.

4. Hahava, where the tongue is paralyzed, and one can breathe only in gasps.

5. Ahaha, where both jaws and teeth are clenched.

6. Utpala, or "Flower," where the body's sores turn blue like utpala flowers.

7. Padma, or "Lotus," where the body's sores turn red like lotuses.

8. Pundarīka, or "Petal," where the flesh full of raw sores falls away from the bones like the petals of a great lotus. The falling flesh is continually pecked and gnawed by iron-beaked birds and insects.

Even though lay people and many monks and Buddhist teachers have believed literally in these hells for centuries, some scholars argue that the hells were not originally intended to be actual physical locations. Some consider the hells to be useful teaching devices for promoting morality (e.g., Daigan and Alicia Matsunaga); others believe they are psychological states of suffering (e.g., Robert Thurman). A leading Indian Buddhist scholar of the fourth century C.E., Vasubandhu, stated that hell was illusory and that the demons of hell cannot really exist or they would be born in hell to pay for their wicked deeds in punishing sinners. Likewise, the sixth-century Buddhist scholar Chandrakīrti stated that hell is a creation of the human mind (after death), and he compared it to dreams at night. None of this means that hell is not "real" even in scholarly Buddhism, for in Buddhist thought our daily lives are considered to be great illusions, as unreal as dreams. All the six realms are bound up in ignorance and delusion, and only the ignorant and deluded are born in them: the wise seek enlightenment and the great release called *nirvāṇa*.

See also BARDO; BHAVA-CHAKRA; HEAVENS, BUDDHIST; NARAKA; NIRVĀṆA; PRET; REINCARNATION, EASTERN; YAMA.

References

Govinda, Anagarika. *The Psychological Attitude of Early Buddhist Philosophy*. London: Rider, 1961.

Kloetzli, Randy. *Buddhist Cosmology: From Single World System to Pure Land*. Delhi: Motilal Banarsidass, 1983.

Law, Bimala Churn. *Heaven and Hell in Buddhist Perspective*. Calcutta; Bhartiya Publishing House, 1925.

Matsunaga, Daigan, and Alicia Matsunaga. *The Buddhist Concept of Hell*. New York: Philosophical Library, 1972.

Thurman, Robert A. F., trans. *The Tibetan Book of the Dead*. New York: Bantam, 1994.

Waddell, L. Austine. *Tibetan Buddhism*. Reprint, New York: Dover, 1972.

Williams, Paul. *Mahāyāna Buddhism: The Doctrinal Foundations*. New York: Routledge, 1989.

HISĀB

After the Hour (Sā'a) has come, bringing the earth-shaking destruction of the universe and its re-creation by God, Muslims believe that every person will be resurrected bodily from the grave to face God for final judgment. This is the Hisāb, or "the Reckoning."

In truth, the entire conception of death and resurrection in Islam is filled with moments of ethical significance. At the very moment of death, when the angels take the soul of the deceased up to heaven, one knows immediately whether one is allowed to pass through all seven levels of heaven, or is denied entrance and hurled from God's sight. Again, just after burial, Islam teaches that there is a temporary resuscitation of the soul, while angels question the soul as to its nature. The resurrec-

tion itself shows ethical symbolism in that sinners emerge with bodily deformities appropriate to their crimes. The sacred text of Islam, the Qur'ān, stresses over and over that the time for moral behavior and obedience is during earthly life, for in the afterlife all will be decided solely on the soul's merit. The Muslim texts that deal with the afterlife, written by later theologians and commentators, make certain to stress this point at every juncture. The culmination of the ethical drama of Islam is the Hisāb.

After the resurrection, humanity gathers before God in what is called Hashr (Assembly). Then, in al-Ma'mad (the Standing), each person mulls over his or her deeds on earth, thinking over the good and evil and trembling with awe before the majesty of the Almighty. Some sources say that mankind will stand before God a long time, perhaps 1,000 years, perhaps 50,000; there will be such a panic as to their ultimate fate that some people will stand ankle-deep, waist-deep, even neck-deep in their own sweat. Only the martyrs and prophets of Islam are exempt from this dreadful experience because their salvation is assured at death.

After a time (and only God knows exactly how long it will be), God will signal that it is time for prostration. In yet another foreshadowing of final judgment, the faithful Muslims will find that prostration before God is easy, having been practiced five times daily during prayer for their entire lives on earth. Sinners—hypocrites, unbelievers—will find that their vertebrae become rigid and they cannot bend to make obeisance, and their fear will increase.

One by one, people will be called before God to view the records of their earthly sojourn in the great Book of Life, the tablet attached to the throne of God. This tablet records the deeds of every single individual on earth. For those people who were not careful during life nor were aware of Islamic commandments, it will come as a great shock to learn that each day of their lives on earth, angels wrote down their deeds on a new page. They will find that there was a record of their daily activities from birth to death, now presented to them in the form of a book. In yet another symbol of their final destination, those who will be saved are ordered to take their book in their right hand, whereas sinners receive it into their left. The Qur'ān (69:19–31) records this fateful moment and warns those still on earth to take advantage of the knowledge (see excerpt).

In the next sequence of judgment (or perhaps simultaneously with the examination of the books), the resurrected proceed to the great scale (in Arabic, mīzān) whose two sides are operated by the archangels Jibrīl and Mikhā'īl. In some fashion the scales of judgment weigh a person's deeds, but whether they weigh the good and evil pages of that person's book or the actual deeds themselves somehow is not clear. The *Kitāb ahwāl al-qiyāma*, or Book of the Resurrection, states:

The *mīzān* will be set up on the day of resurrection with the length of each of its shafts the distance between the East and West. The scale of the *mīzān* will be like the strata of the earth in length and breadth. One of the two sides will be on the right of the Throne [of God], and it is the scale of good deeds, and the other on the left of the Throne, and it is the scale of wrong deeds. The scales will be piled up like mountains, weighted with good and evil deeds. That day will last for 50,000 years. (Smith and Haddad, trans., pp. 77–78)

What is clear, however, is that the verdict of the scale is self-evident and sinners cannot even try to argue against it. The Qur'ān proclaims, "On that day We shall put a seal on their mouths, and their hands will speak to us and their feet will bear witness to the truth and to the accuracy of the judgment rendered" (sura 36:65).

With so many steps in the judgment process, it would seem that the good and evil could finally be told apart. Yet there is one final test, again seemingly predetermined to ease the process for the faithful and to be impossible for the sinners and non-Muslims. After the ordeal of the scales, all the resurrected are made to march across the great bridge, al-Shirāt, which spans the seven fiery layers of Jahannam (hell), so that they may pass into the eternal Garden of Delights. For the faithful Muslims, Muhammed will be easy to spot, and he and the other prophets and prayer leaders will personally lead their people over the bridge, which will be wide and easy to tread. They will arrive in the Garden of Delights and find all manner of good things. Sinners and unbelievers, however, will flounder in darkness and smoke, unable to see anyone or anything. Arriving at the bridge, they will find that it is as narrow as a hair, yet sharper than a blade. Without a doubt, they will fall headlong into the Fire—as they must, their fate having been foreordained by God. There, according to the Qur'ān, sinners will suffer interminably in one of the seven levels of Jahannam, each level with a hotter fire specifically prepared for each kind of sin. Yet later theologians became increasingly concerned with the person of the Prophet Muhammed and his ability to intercede for his people. Thus a large body of literature that developed in medieval Islam (ninth to twelfth centuries) indicated how many, if not all, of the condemned would eventually be saved by the intercession of Muhammed and other prophets.

See also CHINVAT BRIDGE; INTERCESSION; JAHANNAM; JUDGMENT, LAST; QIYĀMA; SĀ'A; AL-SHIRĀT; SOUL, MUSLIM.

References

Dawood, N. J., trans. *The Koran.* 5th rev. ed. New York: Penguin, 1993.

Evrin, M. Sadeddin. *Eschatology in Islam.* Trans. Sofi Huri. Istanbul, 1960.

Gardet, Louis. "Kiyama." In *Encyclopedia of Islam.* Vol. 5. Ed. C. E. Bosworth. New ed. Leiden: E. J. Brill, 1983.

Kherie, Altaf Ahmad. *Islam: A Comprehensive Guidebook.* Karachi: Idara Sirat-i-Mustaqeem, 1981.

Macdonald, D. B. "The Development of the Idea of Spirit in Islam." *Muslim World* 22 (1932).

Macdonald, John. "The Day of Resurrection." *Islamic Studies* 5, no. 2 (1966).

Smith, Jane I. *The Precious Pearl* (A translation of Abū Hāmid al-Ghazālī's *Kitāb al-Durra al-Fākhira if Kashf 'Ulūm al-ākhira*). Missoula, MT: Scholars Press, 1979.

Smith, Jane I., and Yvonne Yazbeck Haddad. *The Islamic Understanding of Death and Resurrection.* Albany: SUNY Press, 1981.

Taylor, John B. "Some Aspects of Islamic Eschatology." *Religious Studies* 4 (1968).

HOUSE TOMB

Throughout history, tombs have been considered not only figuratively but literally the final "homes" of the deceased or at least the psychic, terrestrial abode of the dead (a divine portion of a person was thought by many ancient peoples to proceed onward to heaven, hell, union with the Godhead, or reincarnation). Although almost all tombs are houses of a sort, many tombs in various cultures were made to look explicitly like houses.

In ancient Roman cities rectangular house tombs were common, lining the roads that approached the city, since with rare exceptions no burials were allowed within the city walls. They were, of course, somewhat costly but popular among those of some means, particularly because a whole family could be buried there as each died in turn. In this way the tomb represented the family honor in public, and a fine house tomb made a good statement. Roman house tombs were made mostly of brick, with either one or two storeys and often with the cella, where the body or ash chest was actually entombed, below ground. The outside facades of the Roman house tombs were quite plain and unimposing, but inside they were often lavishly decorated. On either side of the door might be found elaborate aediculae (literally "little houses") with domed or flat roofs, supported by heavy brackets or put into niches carved in the walls. The walls were often extensively painted in bright colors or had exquisite stucco reliefs, with mythological themes, idyllic natural scenes with animals, and scenes from the daily professional life of the deceased—the tombs under St. Peter's in the Vatican are particularly striking examples of this style. The floors of Roman house tombs were paved—for instance, those at Isola Sacra have black and white or colored mosaics—though later burials in the floor have ruined many of these. The tombs were frequently equipped with dining and living rooms and a kitchen to provide for the funerary meals and family reunions that took place there. The tombs even had small windows, often just small slits in the shape of the capital letter T but giving the distinct impression that someone lived there and might occasionally like to gaze out at the world of the living.

The Roman house tomb became the model for early Christians who wished to give special burials to their martyrs, those who had given their lives for their faith. Called *martyria*, these Christian tombs kept much of the square or rectangular features of the Roman house tomb, including the slanted roof. Martyria became very widespread, especially in Syria during the fourth century C.E., and eventually became the inspiration for the first Muslim tombs a few centuries later. Although Islam formally forbids any marks of superiority among the dead (graves are supposed to be level with the earth, with no mound or marker), the spiritual connotations of the Christian martyria provided religious cover for Muslims to build tombs to their martyrs and saints. These soon became full-scale mausolea and were used not only for saints but increasingly for kings and the wealthy.

In ancient Egypt, mastaba tombs are found from the First Dynasty (c. 3100 B.C.E.), apparently designed in the style of contemporary Pharaonic palaces and wealthy homes. Clearly they were intended to be the home for the departed spirit, given that the Egyptian word for tomb may be translated as "castle of eternity."

In fact, Egyptian sarcophagi were also made to look like miniature houses or palaces, particularly in the Old Kingdom (c. 2600 to 2100 B.C.E.), in which case there is a "house" within a "house." Mastabas had outer walls rising to at least 3 meters, thirty or more interior chambers, and probably a shallow curved roof. The walls were ornately recessed but lacked any doors or windows, and the interior walls were richly painted. The grave lay below the structure, sealed with a slab, and on top was piled a small mound of earth covered with a layer of bricks, probably a holdover from the early pit graves. Aboveground mastabas had defensive walls like a fort and many smaller buildings nearby, presumably duplicating royal compounds. Near the central mastaba have been found the remains of servants who were put to death so that they might serve the pharaoh in his new home.

Central Asian kurgans may also be regarded as house tombs of a sort, in that a "household" is set up appropriate for a nomadic lifestyle, and this portmortem household itself is a microcosm of the earth as a whole. Kurgans have a deep central pit in which is inhumed the chieftain, often with wife or concubine and servants. Frequently, many side chambers are connected with the central grave, holding more servants, horses, golden objects, and other goods; sometimes the grave takes the shape of a massive wheel, with logs radiating out from the central chamber like spokes, dividing the greater kurgan into many compartments. Either wooden stakes or spears were set up in the burial pit, or stone columns were placed atop the burial mound, making a kind of earthen tent. On top of the grave was an earthen mound or tumulus, often rising quite high (30 to 70 feet), sometimes surrounded by smaller mounds, like the encamped tents of a great chieftain's tribe.

See also AEDICULA; HYPOGEUM; KURGAN; MASTABA; MAUSOLEUM; PYRAMID, EGYPTIAN; STŪPA; THOLOS TOMB; TUMULUS.

References

Edwards, I. E. S. *The Pyramids of Egypt*. Rev. ed., New York: Penguin Books, 1978.

Kristensen, W. Brede. *Life Out of Death: Studies in the Religions of Egypt and of Ancient Greece*. Louvain, Belgium: Peeters Press, 1992.

Minns, E. H. *Scythians and Greeks: A Survey of Ancient History and Archeology on the North Coast of the Euxine*. New York: Biblo and Tannen, 1965.

Spencer, A. J. *Death in Ancient Egypt*. New York: Penguin, 1982.

Toynbee, J. M. C. *Death and Burial in the Roman World*. Ithaca, NY: Cornell University Press, 1971.

HUNGRY GHOST

"Hungry ghost" is the English translation of the Chinese term *e-kuei*, which refers to a category of the dead who dwell in the upper echelons of hell. The specific concept of the "hungry" ghosts (detailed later in

Twelve Hungry Ghosts in costume during the Festival of Ghosts, the annual Chinese festival of the dead, in Kowloon, Hong Kong. Courtesy of Images Colour Library.

entry) is borrowed from Indian Buddhism, where such creatures are called Prets. This Buddhist seed found ready soil in China, with its long history of ancestor worship and many different types of undead. Hungry ghosts live in caves, trees, or the earth by day, but they can and often do wander forth at night to seek out the living, mostly to receive aid, sometimes to do mischief. They are particularly abroad during the seventh month, which corresponds to August in the West and is considered the beginning of autumn in China. The seventh month is the time of feasts and festivals, and above all, on the full moon, it is the time of the Festival of Ghosts. During this celebration the hungry ghosts are given food and paper offerings (especially "hell money") by the lay people, while Buddhist and Taoist priests recite Scriptures and perform rituals to improve their sad lot.

The e-kuei are called "hungry" ghosts because they are pictured as shriveled creatures with huge stomachs but pencil-thin necks and tiny mouths: they can never consume enough to keep from starving. Even worse, some descriptions include the fact that even if food or drink were to get in the ghost's mouth, it turns instantly into burning coals and ashes. Through offerings and rituals that transfer the good karma of the

living to the dead, the hungry ghosts are thought to escape their estate. It is far worse for the orphaned souls, or ku-hun, who left no descendants to care for them or whose family neglects their afterlife needs, and for the li-kuei, or the souls of those who died violently before their time: these two classes of spirits are actively dangerous to the living.

See also FESTIVAL OF GHOSTS (CHINA); FUNERARY CUSTOMS, CHINESE; PISHĀCHA; PRET; UNDEAD.

References

Teiser, Stephen F. *The Ghost Festival in Medieval China*. Princeton: Princeton University Press, 1988.

Welch, Holmes. *The Practice of Chinese Buddhism, 1900–1950*. Cambridge: Harvard University Press, 1967.

Zürcher, Erik. *The Buddhist Conquest of China: The Spread and Adaptation of Buddhism in Early Medieval China*. Rev. ed. Leiden: E. J. Brill, 1972.

HYPOCEPHALUS

From the Greek meaning literally "under the head," a hypocephalus was a circular plate made of cartonnage and placed under the heads of Egyptian mummies before burial. Use of the hypocephalus disc grew out of an earlier practice of placing a papyrus with a particular spell (number 162 from the Egyptian Book of the Dead) under the head of a mummy in order to keep it warm in the afterlife. Such papyri have been found in archaeological sites dating from the Twenty-first Dynasty (c. 1085 to 945 B.C.E.), but in all likelihood the practice was considerably older. By the Late Period (c. 660 B.C.E.) the papyrus was mounted on cartonnage to form the more permanent hypocephalus and was painted with both the text of the spell and selected scenes showing the spell being acted out.

See also BOOK OF THE DEAD, EGYPTIAN; FUNERARY CUSTOMS, ANCIENT EGYPTIAN.

References

Allen, Thomas George, trans. *The Book of the Dead, or Going Forth by Day*. Chicago: Oriental Institute of the University of Chicago, 1974.

Garstang, J. *Burial Customs of Ancient Egypt*. London: A. Constable, 1907.

Hamilton-Paterson, James, and Carol Andrews. *Mummies: Death and Life in Ancient Egypt*. London; William Collins Sons, 1978.

Spencer, A. J. *Death in Ancient Egypt*. New York: Penguin, 1982.

Winlock, H. E. *The Rise and Fall of the Middle Kingdom in Thebes*. New York: Macmillan, 1947.

HYPOGEUM

Although the term *hypogeum* (in Greek, an underground chamber) may in theory apply to any type of underground burial facility, in practice its use is confined to larger underground tombs, generally private family sepulchers. Too large to be called cubicula and lacking the interconnecting passageways of catacombs, they are generally structures with good-sized, highly decorated rooms on several levels.

Hypogea first appear among the Etruscans, an early culture of ancient Italy that had a great formative influence on Rome. A famous ancient hypogeum is housed within the Aurelian walls of ancient Rome on the Viale Manzoni. It foundation dates back to 270–275 C.E. but shows additional construction over some length of time. Its ceiling decoration of human figures, peacocks, and seahorses is well-preserved, as is a notable mosaic inscription, a scene of the return of Ulysses, and a depiction of the creation of man not by God but by the demiurges. The various rooms have arcosolia (a niche in a tomb that usually housed one body) and formae (niches for floor burial) and form quite an impressive structure overall. Hypogea are found in great numbers in Sicily and Malta and appear in smaller numbers throughout the ancient Mediterranean world.

See also ARCOSOLIUM; CATACOMB; CUBICULUM TOMB.

References

Gough, M. R. E. *The Origins of Christian Art*. London: Thames and Hudson, 1973.

Nash, E. *Pictorial Dictionary of Ancient Rome*. Rev. ed. London: Thames and Hudson, 1968.

Stevenson, James. *The Catacombs: Life and Death in Early Christianity*. London: Thames and Hudson, 1978.

Toynbee, J. M. C. *Death and Burial in the Roman World*. Ithaca, NY: Cornell University Press, 1971.

I

IBLĪS

The Arabic name *Iblīs* is actually a contraction of the earlier Greek *Diabolos,* or the Devil. As in Jewish and Christian tradition, Muslims believe that one of the mightiest angels of God's creation defied God, was cast out of heaven, and became a tempter and tormenter of human beings along with a host of fallen angels. Iblīs was the tempter in the Garden of Eden, which resulted in death coming into the world. The Islamic understanding of that event, however, differs from contemporary Christian belief in significant details, as well as in the details of the Devil's nature and his final end.

Islamic tradition is somewhat confused as to exactly what kind of being Iblīs is. There are many kinds of nonhuman intelligences in Islam. Two of the most important are the angels, who are said to be created by God out of light (nūr), and the jinn (genies), who are said to have been created out of fire (al-nār). With regard to Iblīs, the sacred text of Islam, the Qur'ān, seems to contradict itself, saying in different places that both are true. And no matter which kind of being the Devil is, a problem is created in Muslim theology. Many verses in the Qur'ān assert that Iblīs is an angel, for instance, when Adam is created in the image of God and the angels are commanded to bow down to Adam (15:30–31): "The angels, one and all, prostrated themselves, except Satan. He refused to prostrate himself with the others." Yet very strong Muslim tradition teaches that the angels were created "obedient" to God, endowed by nature with sinlessness ('ishma). This is one of the reasons that human beings are considered higher beings than the angels, for through free will they may *choose* God. How then can an angel sin?

But many verses in the Qur'ān also assert that Iblīs is among the fire beings, the jinn (18:50): "When [God] said to the angels, 'Prostrate yourselves before Adam,' all prostrated themselves except Iblīs, who was a *jinni* disobedient to his Lord." In another verse (7:12), Iblīs whines, "I am nobler than [Adam]. You created me of fire, but You created him of clay!" Yet if Iblīs belongs to the jinn, how has he come to heaven, and why is he supposed to follow orders given to angels? Commentators have proposed several solutions to these theological problems. Zamakhshari (1075–1144) interpreted the word "angel" in the Qur'ān to mean both actual angels

and jinn and further believed that Iblīs refused to bow to Adam out of reverence to God, not defiance. Another tradition, according to A. J. Wensinck, was that by mistake Iblīs said to God: "You created me out of nār [fire]" instead of "You created me out of nūr [light]" and thus by his own speech condemned himself. Despite all this argument, the kind of being the Devil is remains unsettled in Islamic theology even today.

The function of Iblīs in Islam is not very different from his role in Judaism and Christianity, as his alternate name *Shaytan* shows: it is from the same root as the Hebrew *el-shatan*, "opponent, obstacle." Iblīs tempts people to sin by stirring up arguments and inciting them to be greedy, drink alcohol, gamble, and fall away from God to materialism or worse, to the teachings of false prophets. In the end, Iblīs even leads his own angel followers to hell. In a funerary context, Iblīs tempts the dying, offering the soul after death a drink of water when it is apparently terribly thirsty. He instructs the vulnerable soul: "Say: The Prophet lied." Even after death, apparently, one can still fall into hell. By far the worst deed of Iblīs, however, was to tempt Eve (and thus Adam) in the Garden of Eden and cause humanity to lose its first paradise (Qur'ān 20:116–120):

> "Adam," [God] said, "Iblīs is an enemy to you and to your wife. Let him not turn you both out of Paradise and plunge you into affliction. Here you shall not hunger, or be naked, you shall not thirst, or feel the scorching heat."
> But Iblīs whispered to him, saying, "Adam, shall I show you the Tree of Immortality and an everlasting kingdom?"
> They both ate of its fruit, so that they saw their nakedness and began to cover themselves with the leaves of the Garden. Thus did Adam disobey his Lord and go astray.

Thus Adam and Eve and all humankind became doomed to die, and humanity learned to fear the terrible power of their mortal enemy. Nevertheless, the Qur'ān continues, God promises a resurrection (Qiyāma) for all and a just reward to each for his or her behavior during life.

How is it, in Muslim understanding, that God

permits such literally hellish behavior to go on? Why did God permit Iblīs to fall, and even having permitted him to fall, why allow Satan to tempt humankind away from virtue into everlasting Fire? As we have seen, the sin of Iblīs was that he refused to bow down and worship Adam, who was made in the image of God and higher than the angels. The Qur'ān tells the story of the refusal of Iblīs to worship Adam no less than seven times. Yet the Islamic understanding of this event is drawn from the teachings of an early father of the Christian church, Irenaeus (second century C.E.), who taught that Satan fell because of jealousy for Adam, and his account derives entirely from the even earlier Jewish tradition. Thus, for the origins of the Muslim explanation of why Iblīs fell, we must turn to the text called *The Life of Adam and Eve* dating to the first century C.E. There in chapters 13–17 we read:

> The Devil said, " Adam . . . it is for thy sake that I have been hurled from that place. . . . When God blew into thee the breath of life and thy face and likeness was made in the image of God, [the archangel] Michael also brought thee and made (us) worship thee in the sight of God. . . . I said "Why dost thou urge me? I will not worship an inferior and younger being (than I). . . . It is his duty to worship me. . . . And God the Lord was wrath with me and banished me and my angels from our glory; and on thy account were we expelled from our abodes . . . and hurled on the earth. (Charles, trans.)

Even though this account never made it into the orthodox Jewish or Christian canon, it became a very widespread tradition during the time of the Middle Ages (later Christian tradition, however, was unanimous in making Satan fall *before* the creation of the world out of jealousy for God's might, not Adam's glory). Muhammed, living as he did in Mecca, a major trade center of Arabia, came into contact with many Jews and Abyssinian Christians and was certainly exposed to this account of Satan's fall from their teachings. However, Islamic tradition is innovative in including a further conversation between God and Iblīs, in which the Devil asks for a reprieve of his punishment until the day of judgment (Sā'a, literally "the Hour"), and God sees a use for Iblīs as the tester of humankind. Thus, Iblīs is cast not into the fire of hell (forever) but to Earth to sow his temptations among people; at the end of time, he will be utterly destroyed, and his followers will face eternity in hell. Interestingly, Iblīs is not blamed for human failures, though he is certainly a despised figure. In Islam free will is a constant. The Qur'ān demonstrates that at the end of time, human beings must not blame the Devil for their failings but only themselves. If, at the Reckoning (Hisāb), they

---

The Origin of Satan in Islam

We created man from dry clay, from black molded loam, and before him Satan [We made] from smokeless fire. Your Lord said to the angels: "I am creating man from dry clay, from black molded loam. When I have fashioned him and breathed My spirit into him, kneel down and prostrate yourselves before him."

The angels, one and all, prostrated themselves, except Satan. He refused to prostrate himself with the others.

"Satan," said God, "why do you not prostrate yourself?"

He replied: "I will not bow to a mortal whom You created of dry clay, of black molded loam."

"Begone," said God, "you are accursed. My curse shall be on you till Judgement day."

"Lord," said Satan, "reprieve me till the Day of Resurrection."

[God] answered: "You are reprieved till the Appointed Day."

"Lord," said Satan, "since you have thus seduced me, I will tempt mankind on earth: I will seduce them all, except those of them who are your faithful servants."

[God] replied: "This is the right course for Me. You shall have no power over My servants, only the sinners who follow you. They are all destined for Hell. . . ."

From the Qur'ān 15:25–42.

---

should attempt to complain to Iblīs, he will reproach them: "I had no authority over you except to tempt you, but you listened to me: then reproach not me, but reproach yourselves" (14:22). Only those who by free will can withstand temptation and choose good deserve to attain eternal Paradise—this is considered the justice of God.

There is one final understanding of Iblīs that is unique to Islam and espoused by only a small minority of Muslim mystics, called Sufis. Like Zamakhshari, they had a different and very interesting perspective on Iblīs, seeing him as a strict monotheist who refused to bow to any being but God alone out of fear of blasphemy, not pride. Al-Hallaj (858–922) taught that no one so loved God as Iblīs and for this reason he was chosen as the perfect role model for humans. God set up an impossible task for his most devoted servant in telling him to bow to a mere mortal—just the same, according to al-Hallaj, as if God has cast him into the sea with his hands tied and said "Beware lest you get wet." In choosing exile over blasphemy, Iblīs made the greatest sacrifice to God. The Sufis, however, have never been great in number and in the first few centuries of Islam were persecuted and even martyred for "unorthodox" and mysterious teachings such as this one.

See also HISĀB; 'IZRĀ'ĪL; JAHANNAM; JUDGMENT, LAST; QIYĀMA; SĀ'A.

References

Charles, R. H., ed. *The Apocrypha and Pseudepigrapha of the Old Testament.* Vol. 2: *Pseudepigrapha.* Oxford: Clarendon Press, 1966.

Dawood, N. J., trans. *The Koran.* 5th rev. ed. New York: Penguin, 1993.

Macdonald, John. "The Day of Resurrection." *Islamic Studies* 5, no. 2 (1966).

Russell, Jeffrey Burton. *Lucifer: The Devil in the Middle Ages.* Ithaca, NY: Cornell University Press, 1984.

Smith, Jane I., and Yvonne Yazbeck Haddad. *The Islamic Understanding of Death and Resurrection.* Albany: SUNY Press, 1981.

Wensinck, A. J. "Iblīs." In *The Encyclopedia of Islam,* ed. E. van Donzel. Leiden: E. J. Brill, 1979.

INTERCESSION

Intercession is atonement from sin that is sought on behalf of another person. It may include pleading to a higher power to intervene for the person, bargaining for an exchange of some sort, or even assuming the moral "debt" by a third party, as in the sacrifice of Jesus Christ on the cross. Intercession is best known as a fundamental doctrine of the Roman Catholic Church, but interpreted broadly, intercession is common to most, if not all religions. In all the major world religions and many tribal traditions, prayers to improve the condition of the dead, sacrifices for the benefit of others, and special rituals to transfer the meritorious activity of one person or persons to others are commonplace and form an important part of the function of religion in a community. There are two basic types of intercession, that sought by individuals for other individuals (usually for family members) and that sought on behalf of a community or on behalf of all people, usually performed by ordained clergy. Most religious traditions have both.

In many Asian traditions, particularly in East Asia, intercessory prayers and rituals are a major part of death customs. In China there is a ritual called *tso-ch'i* (doing the sevens), in which Buddhist monks read sacred Scriptures aloud and pray each week for seven weeks after someone has died. This ritual is supposed to generate a great deal of religious merit for the monks, but through a special prayer they "transfer the merit" to the account of the dead to cancel out any bad karma the dead person may have and allow the soul to escape the Underworld. Indeed, the monks also call on Buddhist saints (bodhisattvas) or previous Buddhas themselves to donate some of their immeasurable merit, acquired through many lives of altruism, to the account of the dead. No matter what sins the deceased may have committed, the infinite merits of the saints can certainly overwhelm and cancel them, particularly after the ritual is performed seven times. The fact that the monks are hired to perform such services, even by families with little or no connection to Buddhism, apparently does not lessen the religious merit. But China also practices intercession for the community at large. During the autumnal Festival of Ghosts, called *Yü-lan-p'en,* the dead are thought to return to the world of the living, where they are warmly welcomed. Among the many offerings and prayers for the dead made at this time is a particular ritual called "Releasing [Ghosts] with Burning Mouths Ceremony" (in Chinese, Fang Yen-K'ou) performed by Buddhist monks or Taoist priests. In Chinese belief, sinners may become "hungry ghosts" after death, with burning mouths that leave them unable to eat or drink. By means of this ritual, the priests not only feed but also attempt to save the hungry ghosts. Using special ritual instruments (mirrors, scepters, spoons, etc.) and prayer, the priests magically feed all the dead who are suffering, transfer merit to remove their sin, preach the Scriptures to them, and administer religious vows to them. After this, the ghosts are purified of any remaining sins and able to proceed on to the paradises of the Queen Mother of the West or other deities.

In Judaism there are also prayers of intercession for individuals and rituals that encompass the entire community. The prayer for a deceased individual is called the mourning *kaddish,* which is repeated daily for a deceased person. The mourning kaddish is considered a very meritorious practice that may assist the dead during his or her personal judgment, which is assumed to take place during the first year after death; for this reason it is repeated by family members and in Orthodox communities by the entire synagogue for a full year after death. But on the four high holidays of Yom Kippur (Day of Atonement), Passover, Shavuot, and Succot, a special prayer called *yizkor* is recited for all the dead. According to one scholar cited by Maurice Lamm in *The Jewish Way in Death and Mourning* (p. 197), "the term *Yom Ha'Kippurim* is written in the plural, 'atonements,' because on that day the Jew must seek atonement for both those who are present and those who sleep in the dust." The yizkor is a prayer for all the dead, though most Jews dedicate it to particular relatives as well. It is not known how early the concept of intercession was accepted in Hebrew tradition. Certainly Moses and other prophets are *intermediaries* between God and His people, but there is little evidence that they attempted to use ritual means to alter the moral state of others in the sight of God. One of the earliest examples of true intercession is 2 Maccabees, a popular Jewish text written so late after the other books of the Hebrew Bible that Christians consider it apocryphal. Judas Maccabeus organizes his community to pray for fallen Jewish soldiers, who have apparently committed some unspecified sin, and donate a "sin offering" of 2,000 drachmas to Jerusalem. The prayers and offerings are clearly believed to transfer merit to the dead and improve their condition, as the text itself explains (2 Maccabees 12:45–46):

> For if [Judas Maccabeus] had not been expecting the fallen to rise again, it would have been foolish and superfluous to pray for the dead. But since he had in view the wonderful reward reserved for those who die a godly death, his purpose was a holy and pious one. And this was why he offered an atoning sacrifice to free the dead from their sin.

Certainly by the time Christianity was born from Judaism in the first two centuries of the common era, intercession and the efficacy of prayers for the dead were firmly established. Jesus is himself the primary example of intercession, for by agreeing to be crucified, he took on the sins of the world and made a vicarious atonement for them. All humankind was freed from original sin and forgiven for such sins as they might commit, provided that they accepted Jesus Christ as their savior and tried to live a holy life. But Jesus was not alone in his ability to intercede for others, though he was certainly archetypal. Many early Christian texts demonstrate that, although the dead cannot do any good deeds or earn religious merit on their own, God may accept the prayers and actions of the living toward the benefit of the dead. In one text from the late second century C.E., *The Acts of Paul and Thecla,* a pagan queen named Phalconilla asks the Christian virgin Thecla to pray for the salvation of the queen's dead daughter. Another text, *The Passion of Perpetua and Felicitas* from the early third century, shows the young African martyr Perpetua dreaming that her dead brother Dinocratus is suffering miserably in the afterlife, though he is only a small child. One of the most touching parts of the story shows that Perpetua's prayers improve her brother's condition just before she herself is put to death. And in the Apocalypse of Paul, all of Heaven weeps with Paul when he sees the sinners suffering unceasingly in Hell. Though the sinners are sharply chastised for not making reparations for their sins during life, the archangel Michael, the apostle Paul, and all the angels looking on weep and pray to God to have mercy on the sinners. Suddenly Jesus appears amid tremendous glory and, after chastising the sinners as well, institutes a weekly reprieve in hell from Saturday night to Monday morning, when the dead shall be refreshed "for the sake of Paul, the dearly beloved of God, who has come down to you."

Some early Christian thinkers believed that by the intercession of Jesus or by the acts of others, all sinners would be saved from hell, even the fallen angles and Satan himself. Origen, the dominant theologian of the third century C.E., called this doctrine *apokatastasis.* Though many of Origen's teachings were not accepted by later thinkers, a large group of such believers, called *misericordes,* were still around to harass Augustine in the fifth century. Augustine placed limits on the ability of intercession to save the dead: The very wicked cannot be saved from hell no matter what prayers are said for them. Even the somewhat wicked probably cannot be saved, though perhaps their lot in hell may be improved to a "more tolerable damnation" (tolerabilio damnatio). In *Enchiridion* (Reference manual), Augustine writes:

> during the time which intervenes between a man's death and resurrection at the last, men's souls are reserved in secret storehouses, at rest or in tribulation according to each soul's deserts [sic], according to its lot in the flesh during life. Nor is there room for denial that the souls of the deceased obtain relief through the dutiful service of the friends who are alive, when the Mediator's sacrifice [Eucharist] is offered for them or almsgiving is done in the Church. Such acts, however, are of advantage to those who during their life have deserved that such acts should be of advantage to them. . . . They are not of advantage to everybody. (Le Goff, trans., p. 74)

When Purgatory and the intercession of the saints became part of medieval Catholic doctrine, such cautions were thrown to the wind, and almost any sin, however grave, would be forgiven by the church (through what was called an "indulgence") for a price. The poor would spend their last penny to buy an indulgence for a dead relative thought to be suffering horribly in Purgatory, and the rich could hire out the poor to pray for them—and even flagellate and otherwise torture themselves—to atone for the sins of their wealthy patrons. Those who agreed to engage in the pope's wars (i.e., the various Crusades) were granted "plenary indulgences," which forgave them even those sins that they had not yet committed. The chain of intercession could become very great as the levels of intercessors grew. For example, the mother of a deceased child might pray at a local shrine to a local saint, who would pray to a great saint, who would pray to Mary, mother of God, who would pray to Jesus so that He would ask God's grace for the soul of the lost little one. After the Protestant Reformation and Catholic Counter-Reformation, an attempt was made to bring such excesses under control. The Protestants denied the possibility of intercession at all, as well as the very existence of Purgatory. The Catholics, for their part, greatly reined in the granting of indulgences and concentrated instead on the practices of confession and penance assigned by one's priest.

In Islam intercession is less important than in Judaism and Christianity, except for that practiced by the person of Muhammed. Though Muhammed is not a divine being, as Christians consider Christ to be, Muhammed is considered by Muslims to be the perfect person, the best of God's human creations, and endowed with the ability to mediate (to a degree) for his people. He will be resurrected first on Judgment Day (*Hisāb*) and, prostrate before the throne of God, will win by his prayers the favor of the resurrection of all mankind. As in Christian theology, medieval Islam became increasingly troubled with the eternality of the torments of hell (Jahannam), for it seemed to speak against a truly generous and merciful God. Yet many thought sinners deserved their future punishments. In the fourteenth century the Muslim writer Ibn Qayyim al-Jawzīya, in *Hādī al-Arwāh*, summarized the many arguments for and against eternal punishment but came down on the side of leniency. Like the Christian theologian Origen, Ibn Qayyim believed that there is no use in punishment other than as an aspect of God's care and teaching. If hell were truly eternal, then there would be no possibility of the education and improvement of the soul and no point to the suffering. Today in Islam, as in Christianity, universalism has become a powerful force, and though it is very controversial, the majority of Islamic theologians appear to accept the idea that eventually God's mercy and Muhammed's intercession may save all but the very worst sinners—and perhaps even them.

See also ANCESTOR VENERATION; FESTIVAL OF GHOSTS (CHINA); FUNERARY CUSTOMS, CHINESE; HISĀB; JAHANNAM; JUDGMENT, LAST; KADDISH; PURGATORY; YIZKOR.

References

Lamm, Maurice. *The Jewish Way in Death and Mourning.* New York: Jonathan David Publishers, 1969.

Le Goff, Jacques. *The Birth of Purgatory.* Trans. Arthur Goldhammer. Chicago: University of Chicago Press, 1984.

Macdonald, John. "The Day of Resurrection." *Islamic Studies* 5, no. 2 (1966).

Poo, Mu-chou. *In Search of Personal Welfare: A View of Ancient Chinese Religion.* New York: SUNY, 1998.

Smith, Jane I., and Yvonne Yazbeck Haddad. *The Islamic Understanding of Death and Resurrection.* Albany: SUNY Press, 1981.

Teiser, Stephen F. *The Ghost Festival in Medieval China.* Princeton: Princeton University Press, 1988.

ISLANDS OF THE BLEST

Throughout the world, people once believed in a tropical paradise over the sea. As the story goes, across the great waters exists a land of trees, fruit, flowing water, and endless sun, where only a few inhabitants live, free of work and eternally happy. Although traditionally it was only the rare hero or saint who was allowed to visit the blest island—such as Enoch, Gilgamesh, King Arthur, Osiris, Pwyll, St. Brendan, Chinese immortals—in time the hope for a beatific afterlife spread among ordinary people, influencing the development of "heaven" in modern organized religions (Buddhism, Christianity, Islam, etc.). The symbolism involved in such islands is already complex in its earliest form, involving many individually potent mythic elements: barrier waters, the ship, the journey, the sun, fertility, immortality—all of which feed into later ideas of a collective paradise.

Like the setting or rising sun, the blest islands are almost universally in the far west or far east, depending on the direction of the nearest great body of water. In China, the islands of the immortals exist eastward in the Pacific Ocean, and the Mesopotamian island Dilmun was likewise east, somewhere in the Indian Ocean. In ancient Egypt, Greece, and Celtic lands in Europe (especially England and Ireland), however, the Islands of the Blest lay to the west in the Atlantic Ocean: the Hesperides, Avalon, Atlantis, Mag Mell, Amenti, the Isle of Women, the Land over Wave. The Aztecs, whose civilization lay between two great oceans, had two lands of the blest dead, one in either direction. In the far west lay Tonatiuhilhuicac, or "the house of the sun," which awaited fallen war heroes and women who died heroically in childbirth. In the far east was Tlalocan, or "the land of the god Tlaloc," for his few devotees (special deaths indicated they were chosen by him: drowning, being struck by lightning, or other water-related deaths).

Both Aztec islands were for the exceptional dead, which is an important point: the Islands of the Blest existed *in addition* to a generally dreary Underworld for the common dead. The ordinary Aztec dead had to take the "long, perilous journey under the earth to Mictlan, cold and dark in the north, with grim gods, centipedes, bats, spiders, and owls" (Neumann), but the rare hero was accorded a special place, warm and happy. This pattern exists worldwide: only the particularly blest could hope for immortality. For example, early Egyptian accounts of the fertile Āaru fields left their enjoyment to the Pharaoh alone, though with the passage of time all Egyptians hoped to cross the waters and reach that sacred land. Likewise, the earliest known accounts of the Greek land Elysion show that it was the destiny of only a handful of heroes and kings; but in the Roman epic *The Aeneid*, it finally became merely a section of Hades where all hoped to end up (though Aeneas finds that a fair number were consigned to punishment in Tartaros). The poet Pindar (fifth century B.C.E.), like many Greek mystics a believer in reincarnation, sang of the Islands of the Blest, reserved only for those very few who had three times in a row led blameless lives; in contrast, in early Christianity Heaven was conferred on all who simply placed their faith in Jesus.

Because the Islands of the Blest represent an afterlife, however similar to earthly life, it is fitting that these abodes should be placed across the "great water." For as the islands symbolize eternal life, water symbolizes the boundary between life and death. Water is associated with birth, death, and time everywhere. Nearly all creation stories, including the story of Genesis in the Bible, begin with the "chaos" of waters. Life as we know it is, mythologically, "born" out of water, and hence water is an appropriate symbol for the boundary between life and death. It is significant that worldwide, the souls of the dead are thought to be unable to cross water, particularly running water: the dead must be ferried (or flown) to their destination. And it is only the very few who are able to cross the "great waters" *while alive* in order to visit the paradise of the dead or, rather, the "ever-living." Even such heroes need a ship or some sort of vessel to cross over, to literally "transcend" the boundary between life and death. Heroes from many cultures—Celts such as Bran and Oísin, Pwyll (Welsh), Odysseus (Greek), Rāma (Indian), Aeneas (Roman), and the Pharaohs (Egyptian) have all needed sturdy ships to carry them over the waters of death. In many ancient cultures the source of the earth's water is underground (for instance, the Yellow Springs in Chinese teachings), and water's limit is obviously the ocean's horizon. For this reason sailors may come to the Islands of the Blest by sailing to the edge of the earth, like Osiris, or through a cave leading deep underground, like Odysseus. Both watery horizon and watery cave are equally boundaries, daring heroes to transgress the limit and live to tell the tale.

Such transcendence over water also explains why the sun is recognized as a symbol of immortality and transcendence and why the location of the Islands of the Blest is most often associated with the sun. Such is the case in the *Epic of Gilgamesh,* wherein no mortal can cross the farthest sea, for that is identical to dying. Even to touch those distant waters is to find sudden death. Only the Mesopotamian sun god, Shamash, is able to cross the sea under his own power, and thus his sacred land, Dilmun, lies in the east: symbolically, the sun is immortal in his ability to "rise again" each day. But fortunately for the hero Gilgamesh, who hunts for the secret of eternal life, a deathless ferryman named Urshnabi helps him construct a boat to "cross over." When in search of immortality, one must cross death itself (Sandars, pp. 104–105):

Gilgamesh . . . went into the forest, he cut poles one hundred and twenty; he cut them sixty cubits

long, he painted them with bitumen, he set on them ferrules, and he brought them to Urshnabi. Then they boarded the boat, Gilgamesh and Urshnabi together, launching it out on the waves of the Ocean. For three days they ran on as it were a journey of a month and fifteen days, and at last Urshnabi brought the boat to the waters of death. Then Urshnabi said to Gilgamesh, "Press on, take a pole and thrust it in, but do not let your hands touch the waters. Gilgamesh, take a second pole, take a third, take a fourth pole. Now Gilgamesh, take a fifth, take a sixth and seventh pole. Gilgamesh, take an eighth, and ninth, a tenth pole. Gilgamesh, take an eleventh, take a twelfth pole." After one hundred and twenty thrusts Gilgamesh had used the last pole. Then he stripped himself, he held up his arms for a mast and his covering for a sail. So Urshnabi the ferryman brought Gilgamesh to [the immortal called] Utnapishtim, whom they call the Faraway, who lives in Dilmun at the place of the sun's transit, eastward of the mountain. To him alone of men the gods had given everlasting life.

To live forever on such paradisiacal islands is a boon granted to few, but to visit these lands and return is the more exciting tale. These destinations—whether geographically "real," mythologized, imagined, or visited out of the body or in altered states of consciousness— are charged locations. They are not mere vacation spots but locations of transformation. Here the hero, after an arduous journey, discovers a secret, gains insight, or obtains a gift to bring back to his or her homeland. Osiris was the first to find out the secret of resurrection for his people; Odysseus visited a sage and learned how to rescue his bloodline from destruction; Amitābha Buddha became empowered to offer enlightenment from his western paradise. In this way the Islands of the Blest are not merely comfortable for the fortunate few but redemptive of an entire people.

However, the transformation that the hero undergoes is often so great that the visitor cannot return. King Arthur rests forever in Avalon, though some legends claim he merely "sleeps" until he is needed again. The Celtic heroes—Bran, son of Febal; Loegaire; Connla— did not care to return from the Otherworld. The traveler Oísin tried to return to his homeland, but found upon his return that hundreds of years had passed without his knowing it and that the people of Ireland had become tiny and weak. Despite his fairy wife's warning, he stepped off his magical seagoing horse, immediately aged 300 years, and turned to dust.

See also ĀARU; ANNWFN; AVALON; DILMUN; ELYSION, ELYSIUM; HADES; HEAVEN, ORIGINS OF; MAG MELL; OTHERWORLD, IRISH; TARTAROS; UNDERWORLD; WATER; YELLOW SPRINGS.

References

Erman, Adolf. *A Handbook of Egyptian Religion*. London: Archibald Constable, 1907.

Farnell, Lewis R. *Greek Hero Cults and Ideas of Immortality*. Oxford: Clarendon Press, 1921.

Graves, Robert. *The Greek Myths*. New York: Penguin, 1960.

Leach, Maria, ed. *Standard Dictionary of Folklore, Mythology, and Legend*. Vol. 1. New York: Funk and Wagnalls, 1949.

MacCulloch, J. A. *The Religion of the Ancient Celts*. Edinburgh: Clark, 1911.

Mandelbaum, Allen, trans. *The Aeneid of Virgil*. New York: Bantam, 1961.

Neumann, Frank J. "The Black Man in the Cave in Chapultepec: An Aztec Variant on the Gatekeeper Motif." In *Religious Encounters with Death*, ed. Frank E. Reynolds and Earle H. Waugh. University Park: Pennsylvania State University Press, 1976.

Rees, Alwyn, and Brinley Rees. *Celtic Heritage: Ancient Tradition in Ireland and Wales*. London: Thames and Hudson, 1961.

Sandars, N. K., trans. *The Epic of Gilgamesh*. New York: Penguin, 1972.

ISRĀFĪL

The Muslim angel who sounds the trumpet at the final Hour, the Sā'a, is more than just another of the hundreds of thousands of angels who crowd around God's throne in the seventh heaven. Isrāfīl is the angel nearest to God's throne, one of the last spirits to perish at the cosmic extinction (fanā') and the first spirit to reappear at the great resurrection. Although Isrāfīl is not frightful in appearance, he is mighty indeed, and yet as descriptions are careful to note, he is most humble.

> Isrāfīl has four wings, a wing in the east, a wing in the west, a wing that hides him and a wing with which he covers his head and face from fear of God Most High, bowing his head toward the Throne. He takes the feet of the Throne on his back, so that by the power of God Most High he bears up the Throne. He is, from fear of God, as insignificant as the sparrows. (Macdonald, trans., pp. 133–134)

Isrāfīl has a number of duties, including observing God's commands, which are written in the tablet attached to the throne. In addition to the special spiritual tablet (invisible to all but spiritual eyes) that records each human's good and evil deeds throughout life, this tablet is a kind of "super tablet," the complete record of all that has been or will be. "When God Most High decrees something in the Tablet, Isrāfīl uncovers the veil from his face and he looks at what God Most High has decreed by way of order or command" (Qur'ān, McDonald, trans.). However, Isrāfīl's most important service to God is giving the mighty blast on the trumpet (al-shūr) that signals the final Hour; the trumpet vibrations carry throughout the universe and cause the oceans to drain and the mountains to be cast down into dust.

> None of the Arch-angels is nearer to the Throne than Isrāfīl, peace be upon him; between him and the Throne are seven veils. From one veil to another is a journey of five hundred years. . . . The Trumpet is placed at his right thigh and the head of the Trumpet is at his mouth. He awaits the command of God Most High; when He commands, he blows it. When the world's time is accomplished, the Trumpet is close to the face of Isrāfīl, and Isrāfīl, upon him be peace, gathers his four wings and then blows the Trumpet. (Macdonald, trans.)

After this, God withdraws his breath or spirit (ruh) from the world in an act opposite to the creation, wherein he gave his breath to all things, especially Adam. Then God is utterly alone, and this span of existence is unknown to any being. Eventually, however, God begins to pour out his breath in an act of recreation, and the first spirit to emerge is Isrāfīl. Other invisible spirits follow, and then the heavens and earth are reconstructed. The dead lie again in their graves.

From the Dome of the Rock in Jerusalem, Isrāfīl will give another mighty blast from his trumpet, and the dead will be brought back to life. Beginning at the coccyx (tailbone) or the top of the spine (Muslim traditions differ), the skeletons will regenerate in the grave, gain flesh, and rise up out of the earth, rejoined to their spirits. This is the Qiyāma (Resurrection), which is soon to be followed by the Hisāb, the Reckoning (i.e., final judgment).

See also BARZAKH; IBLĪS; 'IZRĀ'ĪL; JAHANNAM; JUDGMENT, LAST; QIYĀMA; RESURRECTION, CHRISTIAN; RESURRECTION, HEBREW; SOUL, MUSLIM.

References

Dawood, N. J., trans. *The Koran*. 5th rev. ed. New York: Penguin, 1993.

Evrin, M. Sadeddin. *Eschatology in Islam*. Trans. Sofi Huri. Istanbul, 1960.

Gardet, Louis. "Kiyāma." In *Encyclopedia of Islam*, ed. C. E. Bosworth. Vol. 5. Leiden: E. J. Brill, 1983.

Kherie, Altaf Ahmad. *Islam: A Comprehensive Guidebook*. Karachi: Idara Sirat-i-Mustaqeem, 1981.

Macdonald, John. "The Day of Resurrection." *Islamic Studies* 5, no. 2 (1966).

Smith, Jane I., and Yvonne Yazbeck Haddad. *The Islamic Understanding of Death and Resurrection*. Albany: SUNY Press, 1981.

'IZRĀ'ĪL

The angel of death, according to Islamic tradition, was created before Adam, will outlive all the universe, and will be the last remaining thing extinguished when God,

Allāh, withdraws all creation into himself before the final judgment. According to 'Abd al-Wahhāb Sha'rānī (Smith and Haddad, p. 34), a sixteenth-century author, 'Izrā'īl is a terrifying sight to behold. He has four faces and thousands of wings, which encompass both heaven and earth, reaching from the farthest point in the east to the farthest point in the west. His entire body is covered with tongues and eyes, as many as there are living beings. Within his mighty hands the orb of the earth rests lightly. To the faithful Muslim, 'Izrā'īl appears mighty but kind, and he spreads his wings to welcome the obedient souls of the dead. To the souls of the damned (kāfirūn) however, 'Izrā'īl appears as a horrific demon, whose wings become pincers for their torment.

According to A. J. Wensinck, there is a tradition that when God sought to create the first human from a lump of clay, he sent the angel Jibrīl to gather some from the earth. However, the Devil, Iblīs, had so riled up the Earth that Jibrīl could not obtain any clay, even by force. In turn the other archangels were also defeated. 'Izrā'īl, however, was merciless in crushing Iblīs and subduing the Earth, and because of this God appointed him the angel of death. (Obviously, this story contradicts many statements in the Qur'ān, wherein the Devil falls from heaven only *after* Adam is created and God orders the Devil to bow down—he refuses and is cast out.)

It is most interesting that in Islamic tradition, the angel of death is not the same thing as death itself, which is personified separately. The Book of Resurrection (*Kitāb ahwāl al-Qiyāma*, by an anonymous author) states that authority and power over death is given to 'Izrā'īl, though ultimate responsibility belongs to God, who is both merciful and just. When God created death and it spread his wings and flew, all the angles fainted for a thousand years. When they awoke, the angels exclaimed that death was certainly the greatest thing God had ever created. But God replied that death was nevertheless merely his creation, and that God had power over it. Discovering then that it had to submit to 'Izrā'īl, death uttered a mighty cry:

I am death who separates all loved ones! I am death who separates man and woman, husband and wife! I am death who separates daughters from mothers! I am death who separates sons from fathers! I am death who separates brother from his brother! I am death who subdues the power of the sons of Adam. I am death who inhabits the graves. . . . Not a creature will remain who does not taste me. . . . (Smith and Haddad, trans., p. 35)

Thereafter death was brought under the authority of 'Izrā'īl, who watches the great tree under the throne of God for signs when each mortal shall taste death. Forty days before each person's preordained time to die, a leaf with his or her name on it falls from the tree. And at the exact moment of each person's death, the recording angel informs 'Izrā'īl. Then 'Izrā'īl and death descend to the place of the dying and reveal themselves to him or her. Thus 'Izrā'īl is the last sight each mortal sees in this earthly life.

See also BARZAKH; FUNERARY CUSTOMS, MUSLIM; ISRĀFĪL; JAHANNAM; QIYĀMA; SĀ'A; SOUL, MUSLIM.

References

Dawood, N. J., trans. *The Koran.* 5th rev. ed. New York: Penguin, 1993.

Macdonald, John. "The Angel of Death in Late Islamic Tradition." *Islamic Studies* 3, no. 2 (September 1964).

Smith, Jane I., and Yvonne Yazbeck Haddad. *The Islamic Understanding of Death and Resurrection.* Albany: SUNY Press, 1981.

Wensinck, A. J. "'Izrā'īl." In *Encyclopedia of Islam,* ed. E. van Donzel. Leiden: E. J. Brill, 1979.

J

JABMEAIMO (JAMIAIMO, JAMIKASAIMO)

Literally "the land of the dead," Jabmeaimo comes from the Lapp words *jabme* or *jamikas* (a dead person) and *aimo* (realm). Before the coming of Christianity, traditional Lapps believed in a single Underworld/Otherworld where the souls of the dead dwelled; later this belief changed into the Underworld as a kind of resting place or purgatory, followed by an afterlife in heaven or hell. After centuries of mingling with incompletely digested Christian theology, the traditional Lapp beliefs regarding the Underworld have become uncertain and often contradictory.

Typical of northern shamanic traditions, the land of the dead is reversed or upside-down compared to the land of the living, and the dying are said to see upside down. It appears to be quite literally a mirror image of this world, with dark lakes and rivers and forests; people, dogs, and reindeer; hunting and fishing; and so on: life in Jabmeaimo is much like the that of the living Lapps, and so often it is referred to merely as "the Otherworld." We see this as well with other Arctic peoples such as the Vogul, whose word for the land of the dead, *jolkemo,* simply means "Otherworld," as does *tatik tarem* among the Ostjak.

Jabmeaimo is ruled by Queen Jabmeakka, which means "female power (akka) of the dead" (jabme). Sometimes she is accompanied by or replaced by Jami-Ajmo-Ollmaj (literally "the man of the Underworld") or by Rota, a character associated with Odin, usually male but sometimes female. These stern gods of death, paralleled by figures in most other Arctic Eurasian religions, bring sickness and death to the world of humans, but they may be appeased by offerings and particularly by visits from shamans (noaide in Lapp).

The Lapp theology of creation sheds much light on their afterdeath beliefs as well. Originally, Lapp religion appears to have been dualistic: the soul and body come from different places and thus have different destinies. In one creation story the sky god, called Radien-Kiedde, creates the soul, and a more earthy female god, Sarakka, creates the fetus in the womb of the mother; the soul enters the fetus sometime before birth. Thus for the Lapps, the soul is considered a spiritual substance, but the body is made from "dust and dirty water." This dualism is probably not due to Christian influence, at least not in the first instance, for similar dualism of body and soul and the different origins of both are found in almost all Arctic Eurasian shamanic traditions. According to the Vogul, the heavenly father, Numi-Tarem, "the shining one," directed the original creation of humankind, but the earth-mother goddess Joli-Tarem provided them with life. Likewise, the Samoyed show the god Nütja Nuo creating a certain number of souls, which enter into bodies and leave them regularly. Nütja Nuo holds the threads connected to all the souls, and when a person dies the soul is reclaimed and sent back to Earth once more as a newborn child. The Cheremis legends show that humans were made of clay. While the creator god went up to heaven to fetch a soul, an evil power, through the agency of a dog, caused a cold wind to blow, animating the previously inert body. In each of these creation legends the body and soul have different origins and different powers—resulting in their different states after death.

The soul (conceived of variously as breath, a kind of bird, or a shadow) is thought to remain near the body for a time after death and to make only a gradual transition to the world of the dead, thus presenting the potential for danger unless properly handled. For instance, improper burial, speaking ill of the dead, or doing things against the wishes of the dead is literally playing with death because the still-present spirit has the power to wreak vengeance. However, Lapp death practices seem to dwell more on providing a happy afterlife for the deceased than on danger and fear.

Lapps believe that during a serious illness, the astral soul leaves the body for the realm of the dead. To help a person recover from illness requires getting that soul back from Jabmeaimo—either through offerings and bargaining or through the work of trained shamans. Shamans can visit the world of the dead by going into ecstatic trances induced by drumming and sung incantations. During this trance the soul leaves the body and searches out the dead in the Under-, Over-, or Otherworld to try and bring them back. The head of the household makes offerings to the queen of the dead in the hope that she will then be swayed by the visiting shaman. Norwegian Lapps believe that a black cat must be offered, though among Lapps in general any black

Andreas Sivertsen had an only son, Johannes, who, at nineteen, was struck by so severe an illness or fever that nobody thought he would ever recover. His father made use of all the remedies and magic arts that he knew, but all was in vain. Then he decided to call his brother-in-law, a skilled shaman. Having performed the introductory ceremonies, the shaman laid the magic ring on the drum and began beating the magic instrument with the hammer. The magic ring went at once to the painted sign of Jabmeaimo and stayed there no matter how hard the drum was struck, until the father promised to offer a reindeer cow to the dead. At this promise the ring at last moved, but soon returned to the sign for Jabmeaimo again. The father promised to offer in addition a reindeer bull as well, and again the ring moved but ended up returning [to] the sign for the dead. The shaman was very puzzled and went to the river bank to try another type of divination. He hung a consecrated oval stone on a cord, and when it stopped swinging, he prayed and asked the king of the dead why the offerings were not accepted, why the magic drum kept showing the land of the dead. The stone by its swinging gave answer that either the father had to give his promised offerings immediately (which he could not) or that the father had to die himself to replace his son. To this the father agreed, and when the drum was beaten again the ring moved at once to the sign for tents, the land of the living. Soon after the son made a slow but complete recovery while the father sickened and died. The son showed his gratitude by offering a reindeer bull to his father's spirit.

From Pettersson (1957).

animal will do. If no black animal is to be found, an animal may have a black thread drawn through its ear.

Those who do not recover from illness, of course, remain permanently in Jabmeaimo (as least in the earlier, pre-Christian traditions of the Lapps). What this means is unclear: the afterlife in Jabmeaimo may or may not be happy. The Skolt and other eastern Lapps see the aurora borealis (northern lights) as the continuation in the afterlife of violence experienced by those who were murdered or died in battle. Some Lapps teach that a new body is gained in the Underworld with which to enjoy the new life or that the soul itself is the new body for the afterlife. This is distinctly not the Christian teaching of bodily resurrection, for the new body gained in Jabmeaimo is not the reanimation of the deceased one lying in the earthly grave. Other Arctic Eurasian peoples picture the dead in the Underworld as gradually growing smaller and smaller and either disappearing or actually dying from that world and being reborn in another—frequently as reincarnated human beings back on Earth. In general, it may be fairly said that there is no consensus among the Lapps today as to where the dead go after death but rather a confusing host of beliefs often at great variance with one another as the process of cultural assimilation proceeds.

Since widespread Christian conversions in the sixteenth and seventeenth centuries, Lapp beliefs regarding the Otherworld have changed dramatically. Jabmeakka, the queen of the Otherworld, has partially merged with the Virgin Mary as a protector and intermediary, and she may be prayed to for assistance. Meanwhile, Jabmeaimo has become merely a stopping place for the dead on their way to their ultimate destiny, either a heavenly or a hellish realm. Today Skolt Lapps believe that in order to reach tsarsva, or "the heavenly paradise," the dead in Jabmeaimo have to cross the burning river Tolljohk (literally "fire river"). There is a narrow bridge (like the Zoroastrian Chinvat Bridge) from which many fall into the river, but Pedar (Peter, in Finnish, Pietari) with his net will catch those who make the sign of the cross correctly. The destiny of the "saved" is the realm known as Saivo (happy) or Radien-aimo (Radien means "the power of the highest god"), a heavenly realm. Thus many Lapps now call their ancestors the *saivo-olmak*, or "happy men." However, there is also a dark and foreboding land of shadows called *Mubben-aimo* (torment) or *Rutaimo* (land of Ruta), where the fearful demon of disease and death, Rota or Ruto, lives. Rota and Mubben are clearly names for the Christian Devil.

See also FUNERARY CUSTOMS, ARCTIC EURASIAN; FUNERARY CUSTOMS, LAPP; HEL; ODIN; ROTA.

References

Pettersson, Olof. *Jabmek and Jabmeaimo: A Comparative Study of the Dead and the Realm of the Dead in Lappish Religion.* Lund: C. W. K. Gleerup, 1957.

Storå, Nils. *Burial Customs of the Skolt Lapps.* FF Communications no. 210. Helsinki: Suomalainen Tiedeakatemia, 1971.

JAHANNAM

From the Hebrew *gê-hinnôm*, which refers to a valley outside Jerusalem, *Jahannam* is the Islamic word for hell. A great many synonyms and metaphors are used for hell in the Qur'ān (the Scripture of Islam), including al-nār (fire), hāwiya (abyss), sa'īr (punishment), saqar (flame), and al-hutama (the great eater). But Jahannam is by far the most important and most common name, appearing seventy-seven times in the sacred text—a text that Islamic tradition states was revealed gradually over a period of twenty-two years (610 to 632 C.E.) to the final Prophet of God, Muhammed.

Western scholars of the Qur'ān like Thomas O'Shaughnessy have noted that the term *Jahannam* does not appear to have been used at all in the earliest parts of the Qur'ān but only in the later periods, especially in the last period of Muhammed's life in Medina, when he was surrounded by Jews and Jewish scriptures. The earliest parts of the Qur'ān use the term *jahīm* (fire), a corruption of the Ethiopian word *gahannam* (which originates again from the Hebrew). When critics of Muhammed made fun of Muhammed's mispronunciation and lack of education in what he called Scriptures from God, jahīm was replaced in the Qur'ān with the more "authentic" term *Jahannam*. This change is significant, scholars say, because it shows that the Qur'ān was not a purely revealed text but a literary composition by Muhammed himself. Muslim scholars, however, deny the accusation that the Qur'ān was altered after Muhammed received it from God. As proof, they claim that the term *jahīm* was used by pre-Islamic Arabian poets like Umayya ibn Abī'l-Shalt and that Jahannam is merely a synonym.

Whatever the ultimate origin of the term *Jahannam*, its overwhelming significance to Islam is certain. There is scarcely a chapter in the Qur'ān that does not threaten hell for unbelievers, sinners, hypocrites, Jews, Christians, and polytheists. (Interestingly, the sinful spirits called *jinn* will also be consigned to the flames for tempting humans to sin.) Over and over again throughout the Qur'ān, Jahannam is held out as the destiny of all kinds of sinners, including those who refuse to help the poor and oppressed, revel in the luxuries of this world and think nothing of the next world, lie, cheat in buying and selling, commit adultery, eat pork, and so on. At judgment day, hell will approach the sinners as a distant but huge beast, and the roar of its flames will be audible when it is still 1,000 years away. This personified Jahannam will be mind-bogglingly huge, with thirty heads containing 30,000 mouths each, and between each of its four legs, the distance of 1,000 years' travel. At this time, the damned will know their fate and begin to wail.

Their torments will be unending: the damned will be consumed by fire, scorched by black smoke, boiled in water, struck with bars, and cut by knives; they will encounter scorpions and snakes as big as camels; stinking rivers full of slimy creatures will cause them to vomit, and they will find their skin charred and their guts filled with fire. The dwellers in Jahannam will wish to die but continue to exist in torment. The Qur'ān 14:16–17 states: "Hell will stretch behind him, and putrid water shall he drink: he will sip, but scarcely swallow. Death will assail him from every side, yet he shall not die."

But there are particular sins that Islam condemns above all others, and for these the torments of Jahannam are especially severe. They include denying the oneness of God (i.e., polytheism and idol worship) and rejecting the continuing revelation of God through prophets, particularly denying the Qur'ān and its messenger (rasūl), Muhammed. For example, Qur'ān 67: 7–12 warns:

> We have prepared the scourge of Hell for those who deny their Lord: an evil fate!
> When they are flung into its fire, they shall hear it roaring and seething, as though bursting with rage. And every time a multitude is thrown therein, its keepers will say to them: "Did no one come to warn you?" "Yes," they will reply, "he did come, but we rejected him and said: 'God has revealed nothing: you are in grave error.'" And they will say: "If only we listened and understood, we should not now be among the heirs of Hell." Thus shall they confess their sin. Far from God's mercy are the heirs of Hell.

Equally serious is the sin of denying God's resurrection (Qiyāma) of the dead and final judgment (Hisāb), according to Qur'ān 56:40–48:

> As for those on the left hand (wretched shall be those on the left hand!) they shall dwell amidst scorching winds and seething water: in the shade of pitch-black smoke, neither cool nor refreshing. For they have lived in comfort and persisted in the heinous sin, saying: "When we are once dead and returned to dust and bones, shall we be raised to life? And our forefathers too?"

What is noticeable about the descriptions of Jahannam in the Qur'ān, however, is that the chapters received by Muhammed early on in his prophetic mission contain the most intense and graphic descriptions of hellfire, wailing, and torment; whereas the chapters he wrote toward the end of his twenty-two-year mission contain only brief references to hell, with little detail and a more philosophical treatment. Additionally, the early Qur'ān depicts both Jahannam and heaven (called the Garden of Delights) as intensely physical places, and their torments or pleasures are to be experienced—quite literally—in one's physical body. The later Qur'ān, in contrast, gives few details of either destination, referring to heaven at times only as "forgiveness and a rich reward" (5:10). Likewise, hell is toned down in the Qur'ān 2:85–90, where God appears to argue with Jews and Christians, trying to convince them through reason:

> To Moses We gave the Scriptures and after him We sent other apostles. We gave Jesus the son of

Mary veritable signs and strengthened him with the Holy Spirit. Will you then scorn each apostle whose message does not suit your fancies? . . . And now that a Book [the Qur'ān] confirming their own [Old and New Testaments] has come to them from God, they deny it. . . . They have incurred God's most inexorable wrath. An ignominious punishment awaits the unbelievers.

One explanation for this distinct trend toward moderation was given by A. A. Bevan as far back as 1904. Bevan writes that the Judeo-Christian notions of paradise and hell were quite new, and incomprehensible at first, to the Arabs to whom Muhammed preached: "The Arabic language furnished no religious terminology for the expression of such ideas; if they were to be made comprehensible at all, it could only be done by means of precise description, of imagery borrowed from earthly affairs." As Muhammed's mission went on and his followers grasped the basic concepts, Muhammed was able to elevate the focus of his teaching from fear and punishment in hell to a grander philosophical understanding of God in history. Another explanation given is that as the Islamic community grew, the persecution against Muhammed decreased, and he no longer felt the need to threaten his enemies with graphic violence in the hereafter.

The actual structure of Jahannam is incompletely described in the Qur'ān, despite its frequent mention. At one place Jahannam is said to have "seven gates" (15:43) and nineteen guardian angels (not devils) who keep sinners in their place (17:31). Rivers of boiling water run through hell, and at the bottom of the Abyss there is a horrible tree called *Zaqqūm,* whose fruit consists of the heads of devils. Sinners will be forced to eat the fruit, which will burn their throats and stomachs like molten metal (37:62–68). But from the few details like these given in the Scriptures, later Islamic tradition made a great deal. For instance, the eleventh-century Book of Resurrection, the *Kitāb ahwāl al-Qiyāma,* elaborates on the angels of hell:

> The angel of the Fire has as many hands and feet as there are people in the Fire. With each foot and hand he makes [people] stand and sit and puts them in shackles and chains. When he looks at the Fire, the Fire consumes itself in fear of the angel. (Smith and Haddad, trans.)

Likewise, probably under the influence of rabbinic Judaism, later Islamic traditions understood the "seven gates" to indicate seven distinct planes of hell, one on top of another. The overall shape was like a funnel, with the deep and narrow abyss at the bottom. The various synonyms for hell in the Qur'ān (some of whose literal meanings were given earlier in entry) were used to indicate different and increasingly awful levels of punishment suited to different kinds of sinners. In order, these levels are as follows:

Jahannam	The "purgatorial fire" for Muslims
Lazā	The "flaming fire" for Christians
Hutama	The "raging fire" for Jews
Sa'īr	The "blazing fire" for Sabeans, the tribal people of southern Arabia (Yemen)
Saqar	The "scorching fire" for the Magi, the people of Persia (probably Zoroastrians)
Jahīm	The "very fierce fire" for polytheists (Hindus, etc.)
Hāwiya	The "abyss" for the hypocrites of Islam

Over the topmost layer of Jahannam stretches al-Shirāt, literally "the Bridge," which people must cross after resurrection and judgment. The faithful, led first by Muhammed and then other prophets, will find that their way is clear and easy and that the bridge leading to the Garden of Delights is wide. Sinners, however, will find their way dark and smoky, without guidance, and when they arrive at the bridge, it will be as narrow as a hair and sharp as a sword. Without a doubt they will fall into the Fire below and continue falling until they reach their appropriate level.

Despite the fact that all but one of the 114 chapters of the Qur'ān begin with the words: "In the name of God, the Compassionate, the Merciful," the Scripture offers little hope for the eventual rescue of sinners in hell. Statements abound as to the eternality of hell: "Those whom You will cast into the Fire You will put to eternal shame: none will help the evil-doers" (3:192); and "Far from God's mercy are the heirs of Hell" (67:12). Yet later tradition keenly felt the contradiction between God's justice and God's mercy, and wanting to affirm both, theology (kalām) gradually began to erode the endlessness of Hell's punishments. Qur'ānic verses were found that characterized hell as a long torment but not literally eternal, such as, "They will remain in [the Fire] for a long time" (78:23), and the even more suggestive verse, "The Fire shall be your home, and there you shall remain for ever unless God ordain otherwise" (6:128). The first class of those who would eventually be reprieved of eternal torment were the Muslims who were punished for specific sins but not for denying Muhammed, God, or the Qur'ān. Muhammed would intercede for his people, and after sufficient punishment all Muslims in the first layer of hell (Jahannam proper) would be rescued by God's grace. Then Jahannam would cease to exist, leaving only six layers of hell.

This has become the dominant view today in Islam.

Whether all sinners would eventually be saved has continued to vex scholars, however. As early as the fourteenth century, the writer Ibn Qayyim al-Jawzīya, in his work *Hādī al-Arwāh*, summarized the many arguments for and against eternal punishment of non-Muslims and Muslim hypocrites, but eventually he came down on the side of leniency. Using reason, scattered Qur'ānic references, and sayings attributed to the Prophet, Ibn Qayyim pointed out that God is all-powerful and can forgive whomever he pleases; in addition, reason indicates that if God is truly merciful, there is no point to punishment other than as an aspect of God's care and teaching. Eventually, when all tendency to sin has been burned off, even the worst of the worst may enter heaven. Jane Smith and Yvonne Haddad indicate that the majority of Muslims now hold this view, although it still causes much controversy.

See also BARZAKH; GARDENS OF DELIGHT; GEHENNA; HELL, ORIGINS OF; HISĀB; INTERCESSION; JUDGMENT, LAST; PURGATORY; QIYĀMA; SĀ'A; AL-SHIRĀT; SOUL, MUSLIM.

References

Bevan, A. A. "The Beliefs of Early Mohammedans Respecting a Future Existence." *Journal of Theological Studies* (October 1904).

Dawood, N. J., trans. *The Koran.* 5th rev. ed. New York: Penguin, 1993.

Evrin, M. Sadeddin. *Eschatology in Islam.* Trans. Sofi Huri. Istanbul, 1960.

Kherie, Altaf Ahmad. *Islam: A Comprehensive Guidebook.* Karachi: Idara Sirat-i-Mustaqeem, 1981.

Lazarus-Yafeh, Hava. *Some Religious Aspects of Islam.* Leiden: E. J. Brill, 1981.

Macdonald, John. "The Day of Resurrection." *Islamic Studies* 5, no. 2 (1966).

Meier, Fritz. "The Ultimate Origin and the Hereafter in Islam." In *Islam and its Cultural Divergence: Studies in Honor of Gustave E. von Grunebaum,* ed. G. L. Tikku. Urbana: University of Illinois Press, 1971.

O'Shaughnessy, Thomas. "The Seven Names for Hell in the Qur'ān." *Bulletin of the School of Oriental and African Studies* 24, no. 3 (1961).

El-Saleh, Soubhi. *La Vie Future selon le Coran* (The afterlife according to the Qur'ān). Paris: Librarie Philosophique J. Vrin, 1971.

Smith, Jane I. *The Precious Pearl* (A translation of Abū Hāmid al-Ghazālī's *Kitāb al-Durra al-Fākhira if Kashf 'Ulūm al-ākhira*). Missoula, MT: Scholars Press, 1979.

Smith, Jane I., and Yvonne Yazbeck Haddad. *The Islamic Understanding of Death and Resurrection.* Albany: SUNY Press, 1981.

Taylor, John B. "Some Aspects of Islamic Eschatology." *Religious Studies* 4 (1968).

JIZŌ

Among the many deities of the Japanese Buddhist pantheon, Jizō stands out as the figure most closely connected with rescuing people, particularly children, from evil rebirths among animals or in the hells. Of late, Jizō has become most prominent in Japan for his protection of the souls of aborted fetuses, guiding these "rejected souls," or *mizuko*, through the dark regions into a fortunate rebirth.

Technically, Jizō is not a god but rather what is called in Buddhism a *bodhisattva,* or a being who has progressed along the path to perfect enlightenment and salvation (i.e., a saint). Because they are so spiritually advanced and as part of their spiritual work, bodhisattvas choose to convey religious assistance to devout but ordinary mortals. The concept of the bodhisattva and the figure of Jizō himself arose on Indian soil as part of the development of original Buddhism, when people were speculating on the nature of the perfect being (Buddha). Although perfect Buddhas are rare on this earth, surely (the thinking went) there must be many beings who are nearly perfect, who will become Buddhas in the future. These bodhisattvas, or "Buddhas-to-be," became important in Indian Buddhist philosophy and art but were rarely worshipped as individual deities. Although Jizō was known to Indian Buddhism (as Kṣitigarbha), there is little evidence of an independent religious cult around him.

In Central Asia and later in China and Japan, however, as Buddhism spread, bodhisattvas like Jizō gained more attention, and religious associations formed around them that were particularly popular among lay people but were often led by formally trained and well-educated Buddhist masters. In China by the seventh century C.E., Jizō (known as Ti-tsang) gained a reputation for great compassion and the ability to rescue beings from unfortunate rebirths in hell. Ti-tsang was also associated with the "ten kings" who played a role in the judgment of the soul after death.

It is in Japan, however, that the celestial bodhisattva figure now known as Jizō received his most complete development. As part of his activity in rescuing the deceased from unfortunate rebirths, Jizō became specialized in ensuring a good afterlife destiny for children who died young or in utero, and not surprisingly, his worship was largely carried out and developed by women, beginning in the medieval period. Groups of six Jizō images were placed along roadsides, particularly at crossroads, symbolizing two different things simultaneously. First, the group of six Jizō statues represented the six possible realms of rebirth for the dead in Buddhism. But the statues placed along the roadside also symbolized the limbo that deceased children were thought to be in while they awaited another rebirth—roads, especially crossroads, are well known for being "in between" places. Jizō was thought to personally visit this limbo of lost children, which is called *Sai-no-kawara,* or "the Riverbank in the Land of Sai." The children, longing for their parents, could not return to the land of the living, yet they could not immediately cross the river (of rebirth), so they were miserable.

The Riverbank in the Land of Sai became a subject of religious and even melodramatic poetry, where the lost children might be pictured as trying to earn religious merit by building religious structures called stūpas, only to have them knocked down each day by demons (see excerpt). Furthermore, many local areas in Japan that were deserted and austere (i.e., boundary or liminal areas) were popularly called "the Land of Sai," and Jizō images were placed there to assist lost children. One example is the northernmost tip of Sadō island in the Japan Sea, where for many years people have traveled with some difficulty to place Jizō images and children's toys on the rocks by the shore.

Over the centuries, the artistic renderings of Jizō gradually evolved from large, dignified statues to smaller and more and more childlike images. Today, statues of Jizō are about 2 feet tall, are dressed in religious robes as monks but with oversized, perfectly bald heads like those of newborns, and wear red bibs. They are usually decorated and protected from the elements with hand-knit clothing, and the offerings made to them consist of colorful pinwheels, toys, and plastic jewelry. Obviously, these statues are treated with some of the care and joy that would go to a living child. Currently in Japan, the temples that sell or care for cemetery statues of Jizō explicitly identify the Jizō images as both representations of deceased children (mizuko), and the deity who cares for them. Japanese scholar William LaFleur translates a portion of a pamphlet from a Japanese cemetery titled *The Way to Memorialize One's Mizuko*:

> Such a Jizō can do double service. On the one hand it can represent the soul of the *mizuko* [aborted fetus] for parents doing rites of apology to it. Simultaneously, however, the Jizō is the one to whom can be made an appeal in prayer to guide the child or fetus through the realm of departed souls. (LaFleur, p. 221)

Today, as the practice of abortion has grown in Japan, Jizō has grown correspondingly more important. There are huge cemeteries with tens of thousands of small Jizō images on hillside after hillside, placed by parents who are dedicated to caring for the souls of their aborted or otherwise deceased children. Likewise, the "rules" in worshipping Jizō so that he will care for one's lost children are increasingly complex:

> The following pertains to the number of images needed if a person is the parent of more than one *mizuko*. One of each on the home altar and in the cemetery will suffice if all the mizuko were produced by a single couple—whether married or

Hymn for Lost Children

This is a tale that comes not from this world,
But is the story of the Riverbank of Sai
By the road on the edge of Death Mountain.
Hear it and you will know its sorrow.
Little children of two, three, four,
Five—all under ten years of age—
Are gathered at the Riverbank of Sai
Longing for their fathers and mothers;
Their "I want you" cries are uttered
From voices in another world.
Their sorrow bites, penetrates
And the activity of these infants
Consists of gathering river stones
And of making merit stūpas out of them;
The first story is for their fathers
And the second for their mothers,
And the third makes merits for siblings
Who are at home in the land of the living;
This stūpa-building is their game
During the day, but when the sun sets
A demon from hell appears, saying
"Hey! Your parents back in the world
Aren't busy doing memorial rites for you.
Their day-in, day-out grieving has in it
Much that's cruel, sad, and wretched.
The source of your suffering down here is
That sorrow of your parents up there.
So don't hold any grudge against me!"
With that the demon wields his black
Iron pole and smashes the children's
Little stūpas to smithereens.
Just then the much-revered Jizō
Makes an awe-inspiring entrance, telling
The children, "Your lives were short;
Now you've come into the realm of darkness
Very far away from the world you left.
Take me, trust me always—as your father
And as your mother in this realm."
With that he wraps the little ones
Inside the folds of his priest robes,
Showing a wondrous compassion.
Those who can't yet walk are helped
By him to grasp his stick with bells on top.
He draws them close to his own comforting,
Merciful skin, hugging and stroking them,
Showing a wondrous compassion.
Praise be to Life-sustaining
Bodhisattva Jizō!

*Attributed to the Buddhist priest Kūya (903–972 C.E.),
translation by LaFleur (1992).*

not. If, however, the father of a later *mizuko* was different than an earlier one . . . separate Jizō images will be required. . . . [unless] a woman were to discuss this candidly with her second husband and get his permission . . . [and] she requests that the deceased ancestors understand the situation. . . .

When at your home altar you are giving a daily portion of rice and water offerings to your deceased ancestors, be sure to include the *mizuko* too—and let them know of their inclusion. Also pray for the well-being of your *mizuko* in the other world. (LaFleur, p. 222)

To characterize the religious practices centering on Jizō as merely the observance of a complex set of rules, however, does not do them justice. The tradition also emphasizes the seriousness of karmic laws and the consequences of taking life while promoting daily remembrance of the lost child at the family altar and an increase in Buddhist faith.

Some Buddhists (and non-Buddhists) have disapproved of this use of Jizō images and of the apparent religious sanction of abortion. In addition, most Japanese Buddhists have no idea of the historical origin of their Jizō belief; its modification by changing Indian, Central Asian, Chinese, and Japanese conceptions of Buddhism and the bodhisattva figure; and how much current practice differs from original Buddhism. For example, in popular Japanese Buddhism, Jizō is considered merely a special form of another deity of compassion, Kannon—both of whom are entirely separate figures in ancient Indian Buddhism (Kṣitigarbha and Avalokiteshvara), and neither of which was worshipped in order to receive assistance for the dead. Yet these criticisms overlook the nobility of such parental care for the fate of even an unwanted fetus, not to mention consolation and catharsis afforded by the worship of Jizō. The purchase and veneration of a Jizō statue involves considerable expense and effort and indicates something of the high value Japanese society places on each life, however small and seemingly insignificant.

See also BARDO; BHAVA-CHAKRA; CROSSROADS; KṢITIGARBHA; REINCARNATION, EASTERN; STŪPA; TI-TSANG.

References

Ching, Heng, trans. *Sūtra of the Past Vows of Earth Store Boddhisattva: The Collected Lectures of Tripitaka Master Hsüan Hua.* San Francisco: Buddhist Text Translation Society, 1974.

De Visser, M. W. *The Bodhisattva Ti-tsang (Jizō) in China and Japan.* Berlin: Oesterheld and Co., 1914.

Kitagawa, Joseph M. *Religion in Japanese History.* New York: Columbia University Press, 1966.

LaFleur, William R. *Liquid Life: Abortion and Buddhism in Japan.* Princeton: Princeton University Press, 1992.

Williams, Paul. *Mahāyāna Buddhism: The Doctrinal Foundations.* New York: Routledge, 1989.

JŌDŌ

Japanese Buddhists differ as to whether the heaven called Jōdō (Pure Land) exists many billions of miles away from our Earth at the extreme western edge of the universe or whether Jōdō is right here in our hearts. In either case, it is the radiant Buddha named Amida (literally "Infinite Light" or "Infinite Life" or both) who, through his previous vows to save all beings, will cause faithful Japanese Buddhists to be reborn in his heaven. According to this doctrine, salvation comes primarily from faith, not works, for even saying the name of Amida ten times with single-minded reverence is said to be sufficient to attain rebirth there.

The original Buddhist teachings on rebirth in heaven came to Japan (probably during the early seventh century C.E.) from China, where the Pure Land is called *Ching-T'u.* Japanese Buddhists who practice the Pure Land faith still revere the first Chinese patriarchs of the Pure Land tradition. Yet in Japan, pursuit of the Pure Land, or Jōdō, took on new and distinct forms. Although seeking rebirth in the heaven of the Pure Land was most often only a component of Buddhist practice in China, in Japan relatively rigid schools of thought manifested.

It was Hōnen (1122–1212) who first made Pure Land Buddhism an independent and exclusive sect. A great master of meditation, Hōnen secretly wrote that recitation (nembutsu) of the name of the Buddha Amida was sufficient for attaining rebirth in Jōdō. Only after his death were Hōnen's views on chanting made public, and he was strongly criticized by important Buddhist thinkers like Kōben. Nevertheless, Hōnen's disciple Shinran (1173–1262) took the teaching even further, claiming that rebirth in the Pure Land was the *only* means of human salvation and that even nembutsu, a product of human effort, was ineffective: it was through grace alone that people are saved, and all other methods of Buddhist practice were futile and even counterproductive, the result of human hubris. Another teacher, Ryōyo Shōgei (1341–1420), shocked Pure Land Buddhists in Japan by proclaiming in 1385 C.E. that there was no actual Pure Land at the western edge of the universe and no Amida Buddha who saves suffering beings. Rather,

the ordinary conception of the soul's being transported to Paradise and born there [is] merely a figure of speech . . . the fact being that neither Amida, nor the sainted beings . . . are to be conceived as existing "over there" at all, because the Pure Land is the ultimate and absolute reality, and that is everywhere, so that we may be identified with it right here where we are. (quoted in Coates and Ishizuka, pp. 56–57)

This symbolic interpretation of Jōdō has become a popular modern Japanese position.

Although in Chinese forms of Pure Land Buddhism there were many methods of attaining rebirth in paradise with Amida Buddha, including visualization, the making of vows, ethical purity, and prayer, in Japanese Jōdō tradition, the nembutsu (repetition of the Buddha's name) took center stage. Even Shinran's sect, Jōdō Shinshu, taught recitation of the name as a means of devotion while claiming that it did not "cause" salvation. According to the famous Japanese scholar of Buddhism, D. T. Suzuki,

> A name is highly significant in religious life. Amida's name is pronounced in sincerity and with devotion. The saying is NAMU-AMIDA-BUTSU. *Amida-butsu* is Amida Buddha. *Namu* expresses the taking of refuge. Thus, "I take refuge in Amida Buddha." It is a simple formula. . . . When we say NAMU-AMIDA-BUTSU, namu is self-power, or *ki*. *Amida-butsu* is Other-power, or *ho*. Thus, NAMU-AMIDA-BUTSU is the unity of *ki* and *ho*. This unification is the oneness of Amida and ordinary beings, Other-power and self . . . it represents the unification of the two.

In Japan a complex theology evolved regarding "self-power" and "other-power," and Buddhist practices were divided into these two camps. "Self-power," or seeking enlightenment through one's own effort, was characterized as being difficult—especially in such an age as ours when Buddhist teaching is declining (Mappō), causing society as a whole to devolve into immorality, violence, and chaos. Although the original Buddha, Gautama Shakyamuni (sixth century B.C.E.), may have emphasized personal efforts and "difficult" meditation, in much of Japanese Buddhist thought, our age is considered too degenerate to allow any progress at all through one's own means. Rather, reliance should be placed upon the "Other," an infinite being, Amida. Having made and fulfilled "primal vows" (*hon-gan* in Japanese) to save others, his literally infinite good karma can cancel out the effects of any human sins. With one's sins wiped out, one cannot be dragged down to reincarnate in the hell realms or back here on Earth; rather, one is reborn in Jōdō, and free from all karma, one is never reincarnated again.

See also ABHIRATI; AKṢOBHYA; CHING-T'U; NIRVĀṆA; PURE LAND; REINCARNATION, EASTERN; SUKHĀVATĪ.

References

Becker, Carl B. *Breaking the Circle: Death and the Afterlife in Buddhism.* Carbondale, IL: Southern Illinois University Press, 1993.

Bloom, Alfred. *Shinran's Gospel of Pure Grace.* Tucson: University of Arizona Press, 1965.

Coates, H. H., and Ryūgaku Ishizuka. *Hōnen the Buddhist Saint.* Kyoto: Chionon, 1925.

Foard, James, Michael Solomon, and Richard K. Payne, eds. *The Pure Land Tradition: History and Development.* Berkeley Buddhist Studies Series no. 3. Berkeley: University of California Press, 1989.

Suzuki, D. T. *Buddha of Infinite Light.* Boston: Shambhala, 1998.

JUDGMENT, LAST

Also called the "General Judgment," the Last Judgment marks the end of time and the final reckoning of humanity as a whole with God in the Christian and Muslim traditions. (The Muslim tradition is examined in the entry on SĀ'A.) The ultimate origin of the idea of a final judgment—in the Western world—lies in the ancient religion of Zoroastrianism, which teaches that throughout history the supreme power, Ahura Mazda, struggles with the forces of darkness, led by Angra Mainyu. At the end of four world cycles or ages, however, the final conflict will take place between the cosmic powers, and all of mankind will witness the events. The Saoshyant, a descendant of the original prophet Zoroaster, will be born among men. He will be the "Anointed One" (Mashiakh), the king, and will lead the earthly forces to victory over evil. The mountains and hills of the earth will melt and become burning rivers of metal, and all humanity (including all the resurrected dead) will be made to pass through them. The pure will feel in the lava as though they are bathing in warm milk, but the wicked will suffer unspeakable torment as their flesh is melted from their bones. A later doctrine, from post-Sassanian times (seventh century C.E. and onward) taught that after their sufferings the wicked would be purified and able to live in paradise forever, but it seems that the earlier teaching of Zoroaster himself (according to the oldest section of the Avesta, the Gathas) was that the souls of the wicked were utterly destroyed along with all the cosmic powers of darkness, while the just enjoyed a new cosmos of perfect purity.

It is through their contact with Zoroastrian ideas in the Babylonian Exile (587–539 B.C.E.) that the Israelites first began to incorporate such ideas into their teachings. Isaiah 45:1 is the first known text in Israelite literature that uses the term "the anointed one" (Messiah) to refer to a savior. Although Isaiah uses the term to point to Cyrus as the savior of the Israelites in exile, later generations of Jews would expect a messiah to save Israel from various political crises, particularly Roman conquest. (It was this role that many of Jesus' contemporaries saw him as filling—that of political savior who would beat back Roman domination and restore Israel to its former military and ritual glory. The conflict that was produced when Jesus saw himself in an

Apocalypse of Peter

And these things shall come to pass in the day of judgment of those who have fallen away from faith in God and have committed sin: cataracts of fire shall be let loose; and obscurity and darkness shall come up and cover and veil the entire world, and the waters shall be changed and transformed into coals of fire, and all that is in it shall burn and the sea shall become fire; under the heavens there shall be a fierce fire that shall not be put out and it flows for the judgment of wrath. And the stars shall be melted by flames of fire, as if they had not been created, and the fastnesses of heaven shall pass away for want of water and become as though they had not been created. And the lightnings of heaven shall [multiply] and, by their enchantment, they shall alarm the world. And the spirits of the dead bodies shall be like to them and at the command of God will become fire. And as soon as the whole creation is dissolved, the men who are in the east shall flee to the east [and those in the west] to the east; those that are in the south shall flee to the north and those in the [north to the] south, and everywhere will the wrath of the fearful fire overtake them; and an unquenchable flame shall drive them and bring them to the judgment of wrath in the stream of unquenchable fire which flows, flaming with fire, and when its waves separate one from another, seething, there shall be much gnashing of teeth among the children of men.

And all will see how I come upon an eternal shining cloud, and the angels of God who will sit with me on the throne of my glory at the right hand of my heavenly Father. He will set a crown upon my head. As soon as the nations see it, they will weep, each nation for itself. And he shall command them to go into the river of fire, while the deeds of each individual one of them stand before them. [Recompense shall be given] to each according to his work. As for the elect who have done good, they will come to me and will not see death by devouring fire. But the evil creatures, the sinners and the hypocrites will stand in the depths of the darkness that passes not away, and their punishment is the fire, and the angels bring forward their sins and prepare for them a place wherein they shall be punished for ever, each according to his offence. The angel of God, Uriel, brings the souls of those sinners who perished in the flood, and of all who dwell in all idols, in every molten image, in every love and in paintings, and of them that dwell on all hills and in stones and by the wayside, [whom] men call gods: [those gods] shall be burned with [their former habitations] in eternal fire. After all of them, with their dwelling places, have been destroyed, they will be punished eternally.

Translation by H. Duensing, in Charles (1966).

entirely different light is a momentous matter in the history of religions.) Hints of a doctrine of resurrection appear in the book of Isaiah, but not until the book of Daniel (second century B.C.E.) did the first indisputable evidence of Jewish belief in resurrection appear (Daniel 12:2), and even there it is not a universal resurrection in order that humanity stand for God's judgment but rather a partial resurrection of some of the allies and enemies of Israel. Until the advent of developed Christian theology, Jewish notions of a final judgment were scarcely "ethical" in the modern sense but purely politically retributive: Israel was the Promised Land given by God to his chosen people. However poor the fortunes of Israel may *appear* to be in history, fundamental to the Jewish faith is a final political and military triumph of Israel over the world, and the Messiah who will accomplish this through God's power is still to come.

Because early Christians were almost entirely drawn from Jewish circles, they too expected that the coming of the Messiah heralded the end of the known world order. Since the Christians believed that Jesus was the expected Jewish Messiah, the final judgment of the world could not be far behind. Most of the texts in the New Testament indicate that the last judgment was expected literally any day. Studies of the early Christian communities reveal that no thought was taken of long-term planning for the community, of building churches or safeguarding future Christian generations; rather, celibacy was the norm, and personal property was mostly given away or held jointly by the community. These early Christians took the words of Jesus quite literally: "I tell you this: there are some of those standing here who will not taste death before they have seen the kingdom of God already come into power" (Mark 9:1).

The Book of Revelation is certainly the best known of the Christian writings on the last judgment, and it still bears many marks of the Jewish theology that lies immediately behind the Christian doctrine. The focus of the book is certainly devoted to the punishment of sinners, but the bulk of the text is concerned with the signs by which the final judgment will be known, as well as the sequential historical events that comprise it. Rather than going to Heaven or Hell as reward or punishment, those who are faithful to the Christian message will find their reward on an *earth made new,* to which God will descend to dwell. Those who oppose God's Christian purposes, by contrast, are cast into the lake of fire, there to perish (Revelation 20:15); there is no mention of an eternity in hellfire. This closely models Jewish expectations that the final judgment would rid the earth of Israel's enemies, leaving the restored goodness of earth to be enjoyed by God's faithful servants.

As decades passed and the original apostles and

An illustration of the Book of Revelation: the four horsemen of the apocalypse, two of war and one each of famine and pestilence, 1498. Courtesy of Anne Ronan Picture Library.

in history, the doctrine of a final judgment is crucial to Christian theology. The universe and the events therein are perceived as under God's personal protection and guidance, and just as history had a definite and ethical beginning, so must it have a definite and ethical end. What has troubled Christian theology from the second century onward, however, is the connection between the judgment of the individual at death and the judgment of humanity as a whole at the end of the world. Various theories have been proposed through the centuries, which are examined in the entry on JUDGMENT, PARTICULAR.

See also HEAVEN, HISTORY OF; HEAVEN, ORIGINS OF; HELL, HISTORY OF; HELL, ORIGINS OF; INTERCESSION; JUDGMENT, PARTICULAR; PURGATORY; QIYĀMA; RESURRECTION, CHRISTIAN; RESURRECTION, HEBREW; RISTAKHEZ; SĀ'A.

References

Boyce, Mary. *A History of Zoroastrianism.* Vol. 1. Leiden: E. J. Brill, 1975.

Charles, R. H., ed. *The Apocrypha and Pseudepigrapha of the Old Testament.* Vol. 2, *Pseudepigrapha.* Oxford: Clarendon Press, 1966.

Dhalla, M. N. *Zoroastrian Theology.* Reprint, New York: AMS Press, 1972.

Greenspoon, Leonard J. "The Origin of the Idea of Resurrection." In *Traditions in Transformation: Turning Points in Biblical Faith*, ed. Baruch Halpern and Jon D. Levenson. Winona Lake, IN: Eisenbrauns, 1981.

Martin-Achard, Robert. *From Death to Life: A Study of the Development of the Doctrine of the Resurrection in the Old Testament.* Trans. J. P. Smith. Edinburgh: Oliver and Boyd, 1960.

Moore, George Foot. *Judaism in the First Centuries of the Christian Era*, 3 vols. Cambridge: Harvard University Press, 1927–1930. Reprint, New York: Schocken Books, 1971.

Moulton, James. *Early Zoroastrianism.* London: Williams and Norgate, 1913.

Nickelsburg, G. W. E., Jr. *Resurrection, Immortality, and Eternal Life in Intertestamental Judaism.* Cambridge: Harvard University Press, 1972.

disciples died, Christians began to rethink their apocalyptic expectations. It became clear that Jesus was not returning as immediately as was believed and that the world would indeed carry on for at least some while longer. During the sometimes virulent persecutions and martyrdoms of the Christians under the Roman empire, however, apocalyptic thinking would periodically return, and new Christian scriptures were produced demonstrating that God would indeed move swiftly to judge the Romans and rescue the Christians. Such texts include the Apocalypse of Paul and the Apocalypse of Peter, which greatly expanded and developed Christian theology regarding death and the afterlife, punishment, and the work of God and his minions in history. Many of these new texts were considered just as divinely inspired as the texts we now consider the New Testament; indeed, the Apocalypse of Peter was canonical until 397 C.E. But after the conversion of the Roman Empire to Christianity in the early fourth century, oppression against Christians largely ceased, and expectations that the end was near diminished.

In part because of its early oppression and in part because of its close ties to Jewish ideas of God's activity

JUDGMENT, PARTICULAR

From its inception Christianity has accepted the Jewish doctrine of a final judgment carried out by God at the end of the world. In the earliest Christian communities, the question never arose as to what became of the souls of those who died while awaiting the "final" judgment because the end of the world was thought to be very near indeed, any day or even any hour. By the end of the first century of Christendom, however, all the original apostles and disciples of Jesus were dead, and the Lord had not returned—clearly the church was in for far more of a wait than it had ever anticipated, and this realization produced a great number of social, economic, and theological adjustments in the Christian community.

The problem regarding judgment of the dead was this: if the dead are only resurrected and judged by God at the end of the world, what becomes of the dead until then? The problem was more acute because some texts, like the Book of Revelation and the letters of Paul, clearly indicate that at the end of time the righteous will enter into direct fellowship with God and that blasphemers and others will be destroyed; other texts, however, particularly the Gospels, state that directly after death the individual who has died passes on to his or her reward or punishment. The parable of the wealthy man Dives and the beggar Lazarus describes the physical relationship between Heaven and Hell, with Abraham presiding over the saved, and the story of the thief on the cross next to Jesus (Luke 23:43) is explicit in making Jesus say to his companion: "Today you shall be with me in Paradise."

Early church fathers noticed the contradiction in the different texts of the New Testament and attempted various theological solutions. Justin Martyr (c. 100–c. 165) believed that the dead slept or rested until the final judgment, but this teaching was unsatisfactory because it ignored the instances in which Jesus claimed the experience of paradise would be immediate. Another common solution was to have the dead experience *preliminary* pain or happiness until the day of judgment, at which time the *permanent* dispensation of God would be handed down. This meant that each person would be judged as he or she died and his or her soul sent off to a temporary spiritual location. Tertullian, a late second- to early third-century church father (c. 160–c. 230), was one of the first to develop a specific doctrine in this direction, naming the "temporary happiness" of the righteous dead the *refrigerium interim,* an existence in the "bosom of Abraham" mentioned in Jesus' parable of Dives and Lazarus. Meanwhile, evil souls awaited judgment in chains and torment, like prisoners in jail. Another African father, Origen of Alexandria (c. 180–c. 253 C.E.), spoke of paradise, which he distinguished from Heaven. The righteous dead proceeded immediately after death to the earthly paradise from which Adam and Eve were banished and there waited restfully until the resurrection.

By the fourth century C.E. the Christian church had developed another doctrine: that the dead, while they awaited the end, could possibly be helped by the prayers and good deeds of the living—and this view eventually culminated in the doctrine of Purgatory (in the Roman Catholic Church, not in the Eastern Orthodox churches). Meanwhile, trial by fire gained currency in the fourth century as well. Lucius Lactantius (c. 240–320 C.E.), among many others, believed that all the dead would be tried by fire, although not until the end of time:

> When God examines the righteous, he will also do so by means of fire. Those whose sins prevail by

weight or number will be enveloped by fire and purified, while those made ready by unblemished justice or fullness of virtue will not feel this flame, indeed, there is in them something that will repel the flame and turn it back. (Le Goff, p. 59)

Others, including Augustine (354–430 C.E.), were skeptical that serious sins could be "purified," particularly if they prevailed "by weight or number," and believed that such souls were judged unsalvageable immediately upon death and that the final judgment of humanity merely confirmed the earlier, individual one.

To what degree the dead could be "saved" by the living and the exact nature and location of their "waiting" for the final judgment continued to be debated for centuries, even into the late Middle Ages. In 1336 Pope Benedict XII issued a papal bull (entitled "Benedictus Deus") that upheld the doctrine of a "particular judgment" of each soul at death. After this particular judgment, each soul is sent on to Hell, Purgatory, or the presence of God without waiting for the final resurrection of the body. The difficulty with this position is that it leaves little purpose for the final judgment, for each soul in its particular judgment has already been sent to its final destination—except possibly the idea that with a resurrected body (gained in the final judgment) the torments or joys may be more horrific or sweeter. Today, however, the matter has become a nonissue. Protestants largely neglect the theological problem altogether and assume that at death souls are sent directly to Heaven or Hell (because there is no intermediate state) and have only vague notions of the significance of a final judgment, whereas Catholics accept both the doctrines of the "particular judgment" and the "final judgment" and see little contradiction between the two.

See also HEAVEN, HISTORY OF; HEAVEN, ORIGINS OF; HELL, HISTORY OF; HELL, ORIGINS OF; INTERCESSION; JUDGMENT, LAST; PURGATORY; QIYĀMA; RESURRECTION, CHRISTIAN; RISTAKHEZ; SĀ'A.

References

Le Goff, Jacques. *The Birth of Purgatory.* Trans. Arthur Goldhammer. Chicago: University of Chicago Press, 1981.

Nickelsburg, G. W. E., Jr. *Resurrection, Immortality, and Eternal Life in Intertestamental Judaism.* Cambridge: Harvard University Press, 1972.

K

KADDISH

Meaning literally "holy," the kaddish is a Jewish prayer recited frequently in worship; a particular version of it is used in burial and mourning. Generally, the kaddish is recited after any significant sacred event. It is recited after a portion from the Psalms or Torah is read from the Hebrew Bible during a synagogue service, and at the conclusion of the service. It is recited after any study of Talmud (Jewish law and tradition), at the cemetery service, mourning services, and the annual memorial service for the dead (yahrzeit).

The kaddish prayer is in Aramaic, the language of Judaism during the first few centuries of the common era. At its inception (first found in the Talmud) the kaddish was primarily a prayer used by laypeople to end formal worship and by elite scholars to end their study. Because of the prayer's function as an "ending," it gradually came to mark the end of life as well—for each human life in its highest aspect is a period of worship and study of God, suitably ended by such a prayer. In early medieval times, the kaddish began to be used as a formal prayer to end the first, most intense period of mourning after burial (called shiva) for scholars. Gradually, the unsanctioned distinction between mourning a scholar and mourning a layperson was dropped, and the kaddish was recited for all Jews, not only to end the shiva period but to close the grave at the cemetery and at all the monthly mourning services performed for the deceased during the first year after death. In the late medieval period the kaddish became so popular among the common people (who no longer understood the Aramaic language and used the kaddish as a magical spell) that religious authorities had to forbid its overuse, which bordered on necromancy.

Although very few Jews today are able to translate the prayer, the kaddish is still recited in its original language. This practice emphasizes the continuity of modern Judaism (and particularly Jewish funerals) with the distant past. It offers the modern Jew consolation (nechamah) just as it did the ancient Jew and also justifies God's actions, which only temporarily bring suffering to the Jewish people—in the end all will be redeemed, and the Jewish religion and people will be restored. This promise, or covenant, has been the cornerstone of Hebrew faith (in one version or another) since the religion's inception.

The burial kaddish is longer than the mourning kaddish, but it is a prayer, not a formal doxology and thus is uttered outside the synagogue. It is led by the chief male mourner at the gravesite and takes place only after the grave has been covered with earth, or at least a layer of earth. The extra paragraph that begins the burial kaddish states that God will recreate the world, resurrect the dead, reestablish the temple in Jerusalem, and replace the idol worship of the masses with worship of the one true God (Lamm, p. 172):

Yisgadal v'yiskadash shmai rabbah.
Magnified and sanctified be His great name.

B'olmo d'hu asid l'is-chadosho,
In the world which He will renew,

U'lachay'o maisayo, ul'asoko yos'hone lechayai olmo,
Reviving the dead, and raising them to life eternal,

U'lemivnai karto d'yerushalem, u'leshachlel hechalai b'gavah;
Rebuilding the city of Jerusalem, and establishing therein His sanctuary;

U'lemekar pulchana nuchro'o me'aro,
Uprooting idol worship from the land and,

V'la'asovo pulchono d'shmayo le'asrei—
Replacing it with Divine worship—

V'yamlich kudsho b'rich hu b'malchusai vikorai.
May the Holy One, blessed be He, reign in His majestic glory.

Despite the pain of standing at the graveside and burying the body of a loved one, mourners reciting this prayer may feel comfort, too, in the fact that God will bring the deceased back to life, and in the end the entire community of the Jewish people, past and future, will be united.

The mourning kaddish, unlike the burial kaddish, is said not once but frequently during the year-long

Mourner: *Yisgadal v'yiskadash shmai raba.*
Magnified and sanctified be His great name.

Congregation: Amen.

Mourner: *B'olmo deev'ro chir'usai.* In this world
which He has created in accordance with His will,
v'yamlich malchusai, b'chayechon u'vyomechon, may He
establish his kingdom during your lifetime, *u'vchayai
d'chol bais Yisroel,* and during the life of all the House
of Israel, *ba'agolah u'vizman koriv, v'imru amen.*
Speedily, and let us say, Amen.

Mourner: *Y'hai shmai rabah m'varach, l'olam
u'lalmey olmaya!* Let His great name be blessed for
ever and to all eternity!

Congregation: (Repeats above verse.)

Mourner: *Yisborach v'yishtabach v'yispa-er
v'yisromam;* Blessed, praised, glorified and exalted;
v'yisnasai v'yishadar v'yisaleh v'yish-halal, extolled,
honored, magnified and lauded, *shemei d'Kudsha, b'rich
Hu.* Be the name of the Holy one, blessed be He.

Congregation: *B'rich Hu.* Blessed be He.

Mourner: *L'aila min kol birchasa v'shirasa,
tushbechasa v'nechamasa,* He is greater than all
blessings, hymns, praises and consolations, *da'amiron
b'olmo; v'imru, Amen.* Which can be uttered in this
world, and let us say Amen.

Congregation: Amen.

Mourner: *Y'hai shlama raba min shmaya,* May
abundant peace from heaven descend upon us,
v'chayim alenu v'al kol Yisroel; v'imru amen. And may
life be renewed for us and for all Israel; and let us say,
Amen.

Congregation: Amen.

Mourner: *Oseh shalom bimeromav, Hu ya'aseh shalom,*
He who makes peace in the heavens, may He make
peace, *alenu v'al Kol yisroel; v'imru amen.* For us and for
all Israel; and let us say, Amen.

Congregation: Amen.

Translation by Lamm (1969), pp. 149–150.

mourning period after the death of a parent (the mourning period for other close relatives is thirty days). It is considered a very meritorious practice, one that may assist the dead during the judgment of the dead that is assumed to take place during the first year after death. There is an ancient Jewish belief that the parent may be saved "by the merits of their children," even after death. The kaddish is one way to accrue more merit toward the deceased, though it is not the only way. Living a moral life, giving to charity and educational institutions (especially Jewish institutions), studying Scripture, and

raising an upright family are also demonstrations of honor toward one's parents and multiply the merits emanating from the parent's life; the kaddish is meant to summarize such actions, not replace them.

The first time the mourning kaddish is recited is at the first religious service after the burial; it continues daily for one Hebrew calendar year (for parents). Like all recitations of the kaddish, the mourning kaddish may only be performed with a minyan, a quorum of ten adult Jewish males. If it is a parent who has died, the mourning kaddish must be led by the oldest son (not a daughter) even if that son is a minor. The kaddish cannot be transferred to another male relative, and if there is no son, the obligation to recite it ceases. However, another male relative may willingly recite it—often a younger brother of the deceased, a son-in-law, or a grandchild. Sometimes an agent such as sexton or other synagogue personnel is paid to recite the kaddish, but this is considered unorthodox unless no son survives to recite kaddish for his parent.

The mourning kaddish is recited at least three times a day at the conclusion of the morning, afternoon, and evening services, for a full year if a parent has died and for thirty days if another close relative (son, daughter, brother, sister, or spouse) has died. It is also recited by the community for great Hebrew Bible scholars and soldiers killed in war or other service to God. The kaddish is generally recited even for relatives who have committed suicide or were transgressors of Jewish law, but it is not recited for those who have left the Jewish faith. For the recitation of the kaddish, the chief male mourner (as already discussed) steps forward and all the family mourners rise, while the rest of congregation remains seated, and everyone says the prayer in unison. The recitation of the kaddish is considered a short audience with God, so at the end of the prayer, the chief male mourner retreats three steps, symbolizing the end of his audience, and returns to his seat.

See also ANINUT; AVELUT; FUNERARY CUSTOMS, JEWISH; INTERCESSION; RESURRECTION, HEBREW; SHIVA (JEWISH); SOUL, JEWISH.

References

Abramovitch, Henry. "Death." In *Contemporary Jewish Religious Thought,* ed. Arthur A. Cohen and Paul Mendes-Flohr. New York: Charles Scribner's Sons, 1989.

Lamm, Maurice. *The Jewish Way in Death and Mourning.* New York: Jonathan David Publishers, 1969.

Rabinowicz, H. *A Guide to Life.* London: Jewish Chronicle Publications, 1964.

Riemer, Jack, ed. *Jewish Reflections on Death.* New York: Schocken Books, 1974.

KĀMA-DHĀTU

Literally "the World of Desire," this Sanskrit term refers to the six realms of "ordinary" rebirth in Buddhist cosmology (distinguished from the "extraordinary" realms of rebirth for advanced saints). It is called the World of Desire because beings are born again and again because of the karma resulting from their desires and cravings in life. Except for very advanced souls, all beings spend their lives pursuing their individual interests, and whether these are spiritual or intensely selfish, they are, in Buddhist thought, based on desire. Thus even the most devout religious person, without the detachment and impersonality attained by high Buddhist meditations, is considered motivated by "personal" desire and is reborn in a suitable heaven whose rewards fulfill those desires. Buddhist philosophy ultimately aims to remove the craving and clinging aspects from human nature, and thus rebirth in any of the six realms of the World of Desire is considered of little value if it produces no real gain in detachment.

Each of the six realms or stations of life in this World of Desire have their own physical location, subdivisions, and limits of lifespan for those reborn there. The one great distinction between the realms is this: only in the human realm can karma be made, good or wicked. The other five realms of rebirth (in hell or as hungry ghosts, animals, demigods, or gods) are merely realms of "result," meaning that those born there experience the fruits of past karma; they are not capable of original actions and thus do not create any new karma. The human realm is distinct in another way as well, in that it is only in a human life that one may attain final and perfect enlightenment and be released from the necessity of rebirth altogether—the hells and hungry ghost realms produce too much suffering for one to concentrate on meditation, the joys of heaven are too intense to leave one the inclination to pursue study, and rebirth as an animal leaves one too stupid to achieve insight.

Although the six realms are pictured as forming a circle in the Buddhist teaching diagram called the wheel of life, or bhava-chakra, in actual Buddhist cosmology the six realms of rebirth in Kāma-dhātu are located vertically, with hells far below the surface of the earth; humans, animals, and hungry ghosts on the surface; and the demigods and gods dwelling in fine palaces on the heights of the central cosmic mountain. The wheel diagram is meant to emphasize the "whirling" effect of endless reincarnation, whereas the vertical cosmology certainly represents early Buddhist values, where what is considered more valuable is placed "higher" and where the relative worth of different things may be understood immediately. This contrasts with later developments in Buddhism, for example Pure Land traditions in East Asia, where great emphasis is laid on the fact that spectacular and spiritually advanced universes lay in all ten directions (four cardinal directions, four intermediate directions, and up and down).

The eight (and often more) Buddhist hells are described in the entry on HELLS, BUDDHIST, so it is sufficient to say here that they lie many thousands of leagues under the surface of the Earth, one below the other, and each one worse in torment than the last. It is significant that each hell represents a specific violation of the code of ethics to which all Buddhists must adhere (no killing, no stealing, no sexual misconduct, no use of intoxicants, no lying, etc). The hells appear to be places of (painful) learning, for even though horrible and very long in duration, life in hell is temporary, and it is hoped that the lessons learned will stick with the reformed sinner.

The realm of the hungry ghosts (prets) is little better. Rebirth as a hungry ghost is the result of greed, gluttony, and selfishness in a previous life, and in consequence these beings live in constant hunger and thirst, for their mouths are the size of the eye of a needle and their stomachs are the size of huge cauldrons: the hungry ghosts are never able to take in enough food and water to satisfy themselves. They haunt forests and desolate places, crying "Water! Water!" and taking out their misery on any unfortunate humans who happen to be within their reach. Several Buddhist stories, however, teach that beings can be rescued from life as hungry ghosts by appropriate rituals carried out by humans; this teaching had an important impact on ancestor worship throughout the Buddhist world, particularly in East Asia.

Rebirth in the animal realm is considered an unfortunate birth by Buddhist standards. Too stupid to understand the Buddhist teachings leading to salvation (except in rare and one might say "magical" cases, like the Jātaka Tales of Buddha's previous lives), animals exist subject to the cruelty of humans and destruction in the jaws of predators. Rebirth as an animal is due to ignorance, laziness, and apathy in previous lives.

Human rebirth is considered a fortunate birth, particularly because it is considered to have the right balance of suffering and pleasure to prompt one to ponder the facts of existence and discover the facts (in a Buddhist sense) that lead to salvation. Buddhist teachings go to great lengths to describe the sufferings of human life in an effort to goad the audience into religious practice, emphasizing, for example, the sufferings of unfulfilled desires, of losing what is dear, of the struggle for existence, and above all of old age, sickness, and death. Yet only as a human can a being take positive action and produce meritorious karma, and only as a human can one take full advantage of Buddhist teachings and seek final liberation. For this reason, despite almost endless suffering, a human birth is considered the most excellent.

Higher up in the scale of bliss is rebirth as a demigod (called in Sanskrit asura, or literally "antigod"). Rebirth in this state is due to having previously lived a spiritual life but one marred by self-righteousness and pride—thus the leading characteristics of the demigods are arrogance and self-indulgence. They are pictured as dressed in fine silks and dwelling in marvelous palaces at the base of the central cosmic mountain, Meru. Here they spend long lives of hundreds and even thousands of years enjoying their luxuries, but they are tormented by the sight of the gods and insanely jealous of the gods' higher lifestyle. Therefore the demigods are often depicted as warring constantly against the gods who dwell higher up the cosmic mountain and, of course, losing regularly to the superior spiritual and physical power of the gods. Due to arrogance and jealousy, they fail to enjoy the luxuries they have.

The gods (devas) themselves, dwelling variously from the middle of Mount Meru to far above it, are classed by Buddhism into six heavens (deva-loka) depending upon the karmic merits they earned by performing religious activities such as giving charity to monks and nuns, avoiding anger, practicing complete truthfulness, showing respect for parents, being chaste, and so on. From lowest to highest, these heavens are:

1. Cāturmahārājakāyika, or the Realm of the Four Great Kings (of the four cardinal directions), halfway up the slope of Mount Meru. The beings born here guard the heavens from attack and figure prominently in Buddhist cosmic symbolism. A being born here may expect to live up to 500 years, but this is qualified by the fact that fifty human years equal one day in this heaven.
2. Trāyastriṃśa, or the Heaven of the Thirty-Three, which is simply a heavenly realm taken directly from the ancient Hindu Scriptures, the Vedas. Most of the highest gods of Hinduism are here classed as relatively low gods by Buddhism, a clear attempt to declare religious superiority. This heaven rests at the summit of the cosmic world mountain. Life here extends up to 1,000 years, and a day here equals 100 human years.
3. Yama, or the Heaven of Yama, lord of judgment and death. The heaven is placed 80,000 leagues above the cosmic world mountain, and the lifespan is 2,000 years, and one day in this heaven lasts 200 human years.
4. Tuṣita, or the Heaven of Satisfaction, twice as high in the atmosphere as the previous heaven, with four times the longevity. This heaven is special because it is the resting place of a future Buddha before his or her final existence on earth as a teacher and savior of beings.
5. Nirmāṇarati, or the Heaven of Creators, inhabited by gods who create what they desire,

unlike previous heavens where the inhabitants accept what is offered them. The lifespan here is four times that of the heaven below it.
6. Paranirmitavaśavartin, or the Heaven of the Rulers of Creation, the uppermost heaven in the World of Desire, whose gods rule over all others. The span of existence for beings born here is 160,000 years, and one day equals 16,000 human years—these gods witness the rise and fall of cosmic cycles.

Rebirth in these heavens is the result of extraordinary religious merit accrued in previous lives, and the duration of happiness in the upper regions is almost endless. Yet the suffering of a god at the end of its allotted lifespan is tremendous: formerly beautiful, the god grows weak and ugly and avoids being seen by others. Eventually losing its powers and its happiness altogether, the god sinks from heaven, agonizing at the beauty and joy that has been lost—and the being finds itself again being born in the womb of a female in one of the lower realms. For this reason, a Buddha is considered superior to any god because a Buddha is permanently enlightened and liberated from birth and death: there is no regression or fall from bliss.

In the end, the Kāma-dhātu may be understood on two levels: the literal level, intended to induce Buddhists to practice morality, meditate, and study Buddhism; and the symbolic level, intended by the Buddha to criticize human society and the stations of birth among humans. In several Scriptures (such as the Mahāparinibbāna-sutta and the Mahāvastu) the Buddha compares the wealthy princes (the Licchavis) among his students to the "gods" of the Heaven of the Thirty-three and uses them as examples of the happy life experienced there. It is not difficult to see in the figures of beggars and the homeless the suffering of the "hungry ghosts," and the self-righteousness of the "demigods" is only too commonly found in spiritual communities worldwide. Because the Buddha emphasized the ephemeral nature of all the states of rebirth, it is clear that he was also criticizing his human followers, caught up in their own dramas and social circumstances, for even the wealthiest are subject to loss and death. This symbolic reading of the Kāma-dhātu, held by many philosophical Buddhists, does not contradict a more literal view but merely points out the applicability of the doctrine in a variety of settings. For Buddhist skepticism regarding the actual objective existence of the realms of rebirth, see HELLS, BUDDHIST.

See also ARŪPA-DHĀTU; BHAVA-CHAKRA; HEAVENS, BUDDHIST NIRVĀṆA; PRET; REINCARNATION, EASTERN; RŪPA-DHĀTU; YAMA.

References

Becker, Carl B. *Breaking the Circle: Death and the Afterlife in Buddhism*. Carbondale: Southern Illinois University Press, 1993.

Kloetzli, Randy. *Buddhist Cosmology: From Single World System to Pure Land*. Delhi: Motilal Banarsidass, 1983.

La Vallée Poussin, Louis de, trans. *L'Abhidharmakosha de Vasubandhu*. Brussels: Mélanges chinois et bouddhiques, 1971.

Law, Bimala Churn. *Heaven and Hell in Buddhist Perspective*. Calcutta: Bhartiya Publishing House, 1925.

Matsunaga, Daigan, and Alicia Matsunaga. *The Buddhist Concept of Hell*. New York: Philosophical Library, 1972.

Prebish, Charles S., ed. *Buddhism: A Modern Perspective*. University Park: Pennsylvania State University Press, 1978.

Sadakata, Akira. *Buddhist Cosmology: Philosophy and Origins*. Tokyo: Kōsei Publishing Co., 1997.

KĀMALOKA

The term *Kāmaloka*, literally the "place of desire" (corresponding to the originally Buddhist term *kāma-dhātu*, or "World of Desire"), was invented by the founder of the nineteenth-century Theosophical movement, Helena P. Blavatsky. She used the term in her Theosophical teachings to describe the afterdeath state in which the lower energies of a soul gradually dissipate, while the immortal soul (ātman-buddhi-manas) proceeds onward to its rest and eventual reincarnation. This afterdeath separation of the mortal soul and immortal soul is called "second death." The word *Kāmaloka* is apparently coined from two Sanskrit words, *kāma*, meaning "desire" or "craving," and *loka*, meaning "place" or "realm." However, the term *Kāmaloka* does not exist in standard Sanskrit texts in India.

In Blavatsky's *Theosophical Glossary* she defines Kāmaloka as a "semi-material plane, to us subjective and invisible, where the disembodied 'personalities,' the astral forms, called *kāmarūpa*, remain, until they fade out from it by the complete exhaustion of the mental impulses that created [them]." Thus the Kāmaloka appears as a realm of subtle matter, closely attached to the material earth, where the lower soul (astral body) and vital energies (prāna or ch'i) coagulate and slowly decompose into the ether, leaving only essential energy traces (called *skandhas*) that will be picked up again by the soul as it returns to Earth in reincarnation.

The Kāmaloka, then, is the realm of psychic shadows, lower energies, and dangerous spooks; Blavatsky identifies these beings as the dreaded pishāchas and bhūts of Indian belief. Importantly, Theosophy does not teach that these lower souls decomposing in Kāmaloka are the real beings who have recently died—rather, the higher, immortal soul proceeds on to a happy, subjective world of bliss and rest (called *Devachan*). Therefore, Theosophy teaches, contacting the decomposing astral shells of the dead in Kāmaloka, as living mediums and channelers attempt to do, is fruitless, for they possess only the barest glimmer of consciousness that once was. Instead, interacting with these spooks can be quite dangerous

because it invites them into the realm of the living, where they may try to prolong their miserable lives by feeding off the vital energy of those they can reach, becoming psychic vampires.

The Kāmaloka plane is also said by Theosophical authors to be the dwelling of persons who have died prematurely. Deprived of their physical body, they still cannot "die" until their natural lifespan has expired. These include those who have committed suicide, the victims of accidents, and the recipients of capital punishment—all conscious but in unwholesome psychological states, awaiting their eventual "second death" and release from this plane into the resting place between lives called Devachan.

Finally, Theosophy teaches that those who have died with a burning, unfulfilled wish, such as a mother who is now unable to care for her young children, are stranded on the Kāmaloka plane until they or someone on earth fulfills their desperate desire. This, according to Theosophical writers, is the origin of the Christian idea of Purgatory, where the suffering soul cannot be released from its torment without prayers, offerings, and ceremonies from the living.

See also BHŪT; DEVACHAN (THEOSOPHICAL); KĀMARŪPA; PISHĀCHA; SECOND DEATH; SOUL, THEOSOPHICAL; VAMPIRE.

References

Blavatsky, Helena Petrovna. *The Key to Theosophy*. Reprint, Los Angeles: Theosophy Company, 1987.

———. *The Secret Doctrine*. 2 vols. Reprint, New York: Theosophy Company, 1925.

———. *The Theosophical Glossary*. Reprint, Los Angeles: Theosophy Company, 1973.

Judge, William Quan. *The Ocean of Theosophy*. Los Angeles: Theosophy Company, 1987.

KĀMARŪPA

In the teachings of Theosophy (an occult movement begun in the United States in the late nineteenth century), the kāmarūpa is the ghost and psychic shell of a human being left over after death. The name is made up of two Sanskrit words, *kāma*, meaning "desire," and *rūpa*, meaning "body," which when combined may be translated as "the afterdeath repository of desires." The kāmarūpa is distinguished on the one hand from the decaying or cremated physical body, and on the other hand from the immortal soul, called the ātman-buddhi-manas, which ascends to a kind of heavenly rest, called *Devachan*, between lives.

According to Theosophical authors, the human being is multifaceted, made up of more than one kind of body and soul. One of the most important aspects of the human being is the "astral" body, a usually invisible body made of subtle matter, which on rare occasions is capable of leaving the physical body while a person is still alive. After death, while the physical body begins its decay on earth, the various aspects of the soul exit the physical body and transfer to this inner "astral" body for a time. As one Theosophical teacher, William Q. Judge, puts it (p. 99):

The breath leaves the [physical] body and we say the man is dead, but that is only the beginning of death; it proceeds on other planes. When the frame is cold and eyes closed, all the forces of the body and mind rush through the brain, and by a series of pictures the whole life just ended is imprinted indelibly on the inner man not only in a general outline but down to the smallest detail of even the most minute and fleeting impression. At this moment, though every indication leads the physician to pronounce for death and though to all intents and purposes the person is dead to this life, the real man is busy in the brain, and not until his work there is ended is the person gone. When this solemn work is over the astral body detaches itself from the physical and [it and the] remaining . . . [soul] principles are in the plane of Kāmaloka.

The deceased, then, finds himself or herself without a physical body but still quite "alive" and conscious, only on a different plane of existence. Here, on the semimaterial or "astral" plane called Kāmaloka, the various aspects of the soul then begin another separation: the immortal spiritual soul, or ātman (the real person), begins to disentangle itself from the various lower energies of the soul, especially the cravings and personal desires of the previous life collectively referred to as the animal soul, or kāma. This process of disentanglement of the immortal and mortal souls is called "second death" because the real person dies again to its lower soul nature and goes on to a higher state. Depending on whether the deceased was spiritual and elevated of mind or selfish and full of passionate desires, this period of separation may be short and easy or long and painful. In the end, however, the immortal aspect of the deceased "dies" again and proceeds onward to its new resting place, a kind of temporary heaven, clothed in an extremely subtle body of light. From there it will eventually reincarnate back on earth.

Meanwhile, the astral body remains behind and becomes home to the lower mental energies of the deceased, which were stored up during life. It is this leftover mass of passions and desires embodied in the astral shell that is called the kāmarūpa. Like the physical body left on earth, the kāmarūpa of the deceased will also gradually decay and be absorbed by its surroundings but again, the "lifespan" of this soulless spook may be long or short depending on the degree of sensuality in the past life. Left to its own devices, the kāmarūpa slowly dissolves, leaving only energy "deposits" (called

skandhas in Sanskrit), which will be attracted to the immortal soul when it returns again to reincarnate. In Theosophical teachings, as in Buddhism, skandhas serve to build up the new personality, astral form, and physical body at that time.

If disturbed by mediums or channelers, however, the kāmarūpa can be galvanized into activity and return to interaction with the earth plane, according to Theosophy. Retaining the memories and qualities of the deceased but without conscience or higher soul, this kāmarūpa ghost is driven purely by mindless, instinctual desires. It seeks out those things it once wanted in life and, by throwing pictures, memories, and wishes into the minds of sensitive mediums, sets up a kind of artificial communication, seemingly with an intelligent being but actually with an automatic mental operation. The kāmarūpa may be reanimated by the life force (prāṇa or ch'i in Eastern terms) of those sitting at séances or channeling circles, thus slowing its disintegration by draining the living of some of their vitality. Helena P. Blavatsky, the founder of the Theosophical Movement, writes in her *Theosophical Glossary* (p. 172):

Bereft as it is of its higher mind, spirit and physical senses, if left alone to its own senseless devices, it will gradually fade out and disintegrate. But, if forcibly drawn back into the terrestrial sphere, whether by the passionate desires and appeals of the surviving friends or by regular necromantic practices—one of the most pernicious of which is mediumship—the "spook" may prevail for a period greatly exceeding the span of the natural life of its body. Once the *kāmarūpa* has learnt the way back to living human bodies, it becomes a vampire, feeding on the vitality of those who are so anxious for its company. In India these [ghosts] are called Pisāchas, and are much dreaded.

The kāmarūpa may even seek to act out among the living its unfulfilled passions and desires, unchecked by the conscientious, moral qualities that are properties of the higher soul. In this way, sensitive living persons may be used as agents of evil by such ghosts. For this reason, Theosophy (like most spiritual traditions) condemns mediumship and conjuration of the dead.

See also ĀTMAN; BHŪT; DEVACHAN (THEOSOPHICAL); KĀMALOKA; PISHĀCHA; SECOND DEATH; SOUL, BUDDHIST; SOUL, THEOSOPHICAL; VAMPIRE.

References
Blavatsky, Helena Petrovna. *The Key to Theosophy*. Reprint, Los Angeles: Theosophy Company, 1987.
———. *The Secret Doctrine*. 2 vols. Reprint, New York: Theosophy Company, 1925.
———. *The Theosophical Glossary*. Reprint, Los Angeles: Theosophy Company, 1973.

Judge, William Quan. *The Ocean of Theosophy*. Los Angeles: Theosophy Company, 1987.

KER (PLURAL KERES)

In ancient Greek lands, the same term, *Keres,* was used for the souls of the dead; malevolent ghosts; and nature spirits connected with crops, wind, fire, and death. Although the Keres were not in every instance forces of evil, they were always carriers of pollution, which if left untreated could spread through an entire community, bringing pestilence and death to all.

It is difficult to decide for certain the original nature of the Keres. According to the early Greek writer Hesiod (fl. c. 800 B.C.E.), the Keres are the plagues, evil desires, violence, nightmares, and other malevolent urges that rushed forth when inquisitive Pandora opened the forbidden jar. In Homer's *Odyssey* and *Iliad,* the Ker almost always appears in the singular and seems to be fate or doom personified, as in the *Iliad* 18:535–538 (Lattimore, trans.):

and Hate was there [in the battle] with Confusion among them,
and Death [Ker] the destructive;
she was holding a live man with a new wound, and another
one unhurt, and dragged a dead man by the feet through the carnage.
The clothing upon her shoulders showed strong red with the men's blood.

But popular Greek art and legends, humbler than high literature and less abstract, hint at earlier conceptions of Keres. Jane Harrison discusses a vase painting, now in the University Museum in Jena, which shows many small winged beings emerging from a large urn sunk in the earth, while Hermes Psychopompos (Hermes, Guide of Souls) urges them on with a wand. Clearly, these winged beings are the souls of the dead emerging from the Underworld. Popular beliefs that see the Keres as inhabiting wind, fire, and fields further the connection with the dead. In the Orphic *Lithica,* we hear of a magic "lynchis" stone that can avert a hailstorm: "Lynchis, from pelting hail be thou our shield / Keep off the Keres who attack each field." Why a magic stone should avert trouble from the skies is a mystery easily solved: in the ancient world, winds were thought to arise out of caves in the earth and travel across the land, exerting either baleful or lucky influence depending on the direction of their source. Thus, a magic stone would have power over the winds, which were essentially earth energies on the loose.

In art and in folk belief, then, the Keres are chthonic, or earth-related entities—airborne to be sure (thus pictured with wings) but originating underground. Winds were thought to be responsible for fertilizing crops with their life-giving "breath," but winds and Keres could also be "soul snatching" and (like the Norse Valkyrie, possibly from the Greek root *keres*) literally "take one's breath away." It is no coincidence that in Greek (as with many ancient languages) there is one word for breath, wind, and spirit: *pneuma*. But the Keres do not only inhabit the winds and Underworld; they are also spirits of fire—another classic symbol of spirit. An anonymous ancient Greek commentator on the writer Philo stated that no ordinary fire should touch an altar because it might be contaminated with hordes of Keres; ritual fires were always brought from another ritual location or kindled on the spot with appropriate protective incantations.

It is possible that with all their fire, wind, and earth associations, the Keres were originally local earth gods, eventually overcome by the "organized" religion of the Olympians. More likely, however, the Keres were originally the souls of the dead, those "breaths" and "shades" of little consciousness who emerge from the Underworld from time to time (as during annual festivals for the dead such as the Anthesteria and Parentalia) to visit the living. The living took care to appease these ghosts, and if satisfied, the ghosts would bring no harm and could even bring good fortune by using their earth energies to hasten the growth of crops and ward off threatening earth exhalations such as ill winds. But woe to the mortal who dared to break natural law by murdering the living or violating an oath: the ambiguous Keres transform into the hideous and indefatigable Erinyes (Furies), avenging souls who hunt the offender to the ends of the Earth.

See also ANTHESTERIA; ERINYS; FEBRUARY; HADES; PARENTALIA; SOUL, GREEK; UNDERWORLD; VALKYRIE.

References

Fowler, W. Warde. *The Roman Festivals of the Period of the Republic*. London: Kennikat Press, 1969.

Harrison, Jane Ellen. *Prolegomena to the Study of Greek Religion*. Cambridge: Cambridge University Press, 1922.

Lattimore, Richmond, trans. *The Iliad*. Chicago: University of Chicago Press, 1951.

Schadow, Paul. *Eine Attische Grabekythos*. Inaugural diss. Jena University, 1897.

KERI'AH

Keri'ah is the practice of ripping one's garment(s) after the death of a loved one in traditional Judaism. Rending clothes as an outward sign of grief is a very ancient practice in the Hebrew tradition. In the book of Genesis, when the patriarch Jacob learns (falsely) that his son Joseph has been killed by wild beasts, "Jacob rent his clothes, put on sackcloth and mourned his son for a long time" (Genesis 37:34). Likewise, when Job learned that all his children had been killed, he "stood up and rent his cloak; then he shaved his head and fell prostrate on the ground" (Job 1:20). In many ancient cultures, such as Greek and Central Asian, cutting one's flesh was the traditional outward sign of grief; many scholars have suggested that keri'ah originated as a replacement in Hebrew religion for tearing the skin.

Today keri'ah has become formalized by Jewish law (which is only strictly observed by Orthodox Jews). All of the nearest "seven relations" of the deceased must rend their clothing, including the father, mother, spouse, brothers, sisters, sons, and daughters of the deceased. Only adults are required to observe keri'ah; mature children are allowed to participate if they understand the ritual, however.

Generally the cut in the clothing is made by members of the Chevra Kaddisha, the local Jewish burial society. The cut is at least 3 or 4 inches long, along a seam, starting near the neck and proceeding down the chest; it is to be performed while the mourner is standing. For those who are mourning a deceased parent, the cut is made on the left side and must be visible to all viewers; all others wear the keri'ah on the right, and it need not be visible. For men, the clothing to be cut is whatever outer clothing is generally worn: a vest, jacket, suit, or sweater. Many authorities allow keri'ah to be performed on a man's tie (Jewish law stipulates that the article of clothing must be regularly worn and a width of at least three fingers square). For women, keri'ah is performed on the dress, jacket, blouse, or sweater. Frequently mourners change clothing before keri'ah is performed: the goal is not to destroy expensive or new clothes but to express grief visibly in any outer garment.

Keri'ah is generally performed in the funeral chapel before the funeral has begun, but it may also be performed as soon as one learns of the death and as late as the actual burial at the cemetery. For those grieving a lost parent, the rent clothing is worn during the first seven days of mourning after burial, called *shiva*. If they change their clothes during *shiva*, the new clothes must also be rent. After thirty days the rent clothing may be loosely sewn up but never completely—symbolizing the permanent loss felt by the death of one's parent. For those grieving relatives besides parents, only one set of clothes has keri'ah performed, and the rent clothing may be sewn up completely after the thirty-day mourning period of sheloshim has passed.

Traditionally, keri'ah was also practiced when mourning the death of a great scholar, seeing Scripture (Torah) being destroyed by fire, or seeing Jerusalem in ruins. In modern times, the practice of keri'ah appears to be diminishing. Conservative and Reform Jews do not observe the traditional keri'ah but instead wear a torn black ribbon on their lapel for thirty days (mostly in the United States). A number of Orthodox Jews have adopted this practice, though it is widely condemned by Orthodox rabbis.

See also CHEVRA KADDISHA; FUNERARY CUSTOMS, JEWISH; SHELOSHIM; SHIVA (JEWISH).

References

Abramovitch, Henry. "Death." In *Contemporary Jewish Religious Thought,* ed. Arthur A. Cohen and Paul Mendes-Flohr. New York: Charles Scribner's Sons, 1989.

De Sola Pool, David. *The Kaddish.* Jerusalem: Printed by Sivan Press under the auspices of the Union of Sephardic Congregations, New York, 1964.

Lamm, Maurice. *The Jewish Way in Death and Mourning.* New York: Jonathan David Publisher, 1969.

Rabinowicz, H. *A Guide to Life.* London: Jewish Chronicle Publications, 1964.

Riemer, Jack, ed. *Jewish Reflections on Death.* New York: Schocken Books, 1974.

KIGAL

Also called Kur and Kutu, Kigal was "the great place below," the Underworld in the ancient Mesopotamian civilizations of Sumeria, Babylonia, and Assyria. Kigal was ruled over by Ereshkigal, "Queen of the Underworld," joined later by her sometime husband Nergal, god of death and pestilence.

The entrance to Kigal was in the west where the sun set and was guarded by Nedu, the chief gatekeeper. Kigal was also called *eirshitum* (the land of no return) because the lock on the gate was thought to close forever behind the deceased. Through the gate, the dead were met by four-handed Humuttabal (literally, "take away quickly") who ferried them over the River Hubur. Then the dead approached the great city of the Underworld, a metropolis with seven walls and seven gates, each guarded by a demon. At each gate the dead were compelled, like Ishtar in her descent into the Underworld, to shed a piece of their clothing until they arrived within totally naked. Once inside, the dead came to the great lapis lazuli palace of Ereshkigal. There she was in state (sometimes with another god also called her husband, Ninazu, "the powerful robber") surrounded by her attendants, including her scribe Belitsheri as well as her son and messenger Namtar, the herald of death and bringer of the sixty diseases. The many spawn of Kigal, the demons, or utukku limnu, had their home base in the Underworld, though most of their work was in the world above, bringing illness and death to humankind. Thus they were also called *mārê ilitti irshitim,* "children of the Underworld," and *nam-ta-ru,* "bringers of death." The mysterious Anunnaki, the seven fierce judges of the dead, dwelt in their own nearby palace, Egalgina, the hall of justice.

Interestingly, the soul in some Mesopotamian texts is

considered to be in the shape of a bird, reminiscent of
the ba (Egyptian soul). We read in *The Epic of Gilgamesh*
that his friend Enkidu was dying and dreamed of the
Underworld, where he was transformed and his "arms
were covered with feathers like a bird." He was led to
the land of no light, "where they are clad like birds,
with garments of wings." Again, in the myth of Ishtar's
descent into the Underworld, we read that she traveled
likewise to the land where "they see no light, and dwell
in darkness, where they are clad like birds with garments of wings" (Sandars, trans., p. 92).

In one Assyrian tablet from the seventh century
B.C.E., "A Prince's Vision of the Underworld," the
rulers of the Underworld were seen in a dream. Like the
gods of the Egyptians, the Mesopotamian gods of the
Underworld were composite beings, fearsome to look
at. Some gods had human heads, but most appeared
with bird, ox, goat, or serpent heads. Many of the gods
had multiple arms and legs or even wings, and most
were heavily armed with a great variety of deadly
weapons.

Kigal was thought to begin just below the surface of
the earth, as we read when King Nebuchadrezzar II
(630–562 B.C.E.) declared that he built the foundation
of his palace "on the breast of the Underworld" (ina irat
kigalli). Yet we are also told by Assyrian texts that the
Underworld was situated in the lowest part of the earth.
Thus, as with Sheol, the grave itself was part of the
Underworld, as well as an entrance into it.

The question of the status of the dead in the
Underworld is a complex one. We read at the end of the
great Gilgamesh epic that the happiness of the dead
depends on their proper funeral and burial and, most
importantly, on the number of sons left behind to make
offerings after death. The deceased who has no one to
take care of him or her eats leftover crusts of bread in
the street, whereas the deceased with five sons "enters
the palace." What, then, is the function of the
Anunnaki? In many religions, the dead are judged on
their deeds or way of life, but in ancient Mesopotamian
religion their descendants' actions seem to be the deter-
minant of the kind of afterlife the dead will lead.

Likewise, it is an open question whether the shades of
the dead resided forever in the Underworld—most
probably they did. In *The Epic of Gilgamesh,* Utnapishtim
and his wife were exceptional in their immortality; even
Gilgamesh, who was two-thirds divine, failed to escape
a future in Kigal. While many Mesopotamian skeletons
have been found in their graves in a distinct fetal position, suggesting to some scholars the theme of rebirth
(either figuratively or literally), there is no definitive
evidence that anyone ever left the Land of No Return.

See also FUNERARY CUSTOMS, MESOPOTAMIAN; HADES; SHEOL;
    UNDERWORLD.

References

Frankfort, Henri. *Kingship and the Gods.* Chicago: University of
    Chicago Press, 1948.
Heidel, Alexander. *The Gilgamesh Epic and Old Testament Parallels.*
    Chicago: University of Chicago Press, 1946.
Hooke, S. H. *Middle Eastern Mythology.* New York: Penguin, 1963.
Oates, Joan. *Babylon.* Rev. ed. London: Thames and Hudson, 1986.
Pritchard, James B., ed. *Ancient Near Eastern Texts Relating to the Old
    Testament.* 3rd ed. Princeton: Princeton University Press, 1969.
Sandars, N. K., trans. *The Epic of Gilgamesh.* New York: Penguin,
    1972.

KṢITIGARBHA

Literally "Storehouse of the Earth," Kṣitigarbha is an
important deity figure in "northern" or Mahāyāna
Buddhism, more so in East Asia than in India, the land
of his origin. According to a seventh-century C.E.
Indian Buddhist text titled The Scripture on Kṣitigarbha and the Ten Wheels, Kṣitigarbha is the figure
who has been assigned to save sentient beings on Earth
during the vast interval of time between the death of
the previous Buddha, Gautama Shakyamuni, and the
enlightenment of the Buddha Maitreya, who is to come
in the distant future.

Kṣitigarbha is undoubtedly an ancient figure in
Buddhism, though his role has changed dramatically
over the centuries. Originally, he appears to have been
merely an attendant to higher Buddhist personages.
Cave paintings of Kṣitigarbha in the Indian temple at
Ellora and wall paintings in Bezeklik in Central Asia
show him as a monk in humble robes carrying a staff.
Scattered references to Kṣitigarbha are found in some
Indian texts as early as the second century C.E., and quotations exist in some later works from a text, now lost,
specifically about Kṣitigarbha (the Ārya Kṣitigarbha

Sūtra). Yet there are no images or carvings of Kṣiti-garbha as a solitary figure in India or any evidence of any religious cult centering around him. Although Kṣiti-garbha is a popular Buddhist deity in Tibet, where he has the name Sa'i-snying-po, he did not become popular there until after his advent in East Asia.

Later Buddhist Scriptures in Chinese (not Sanskrit) are the only ones that discuss Kṣitigarbha (there called Ti-tsang), as the figure who descends to the realms of the hungry ghosts and hells to save suffering beings. In East Asia, the humble Indian monk has become a celestial bodhisattva, a superhuman being who exists only to serve and save others. The mere name of Ti-tsang being spoken can cause devotees to be reborn in the heavens and cause thirty eons of sins to be wiped out. Because of spiritual vows made in the distant past and the cosmic ages spent in fulfilling them, Kṣitigarbha or Ti-tsang now has the power to do almost anything for suffering humanity. Reciting the eleventh-century Chinese Buddhist Scripture, The Original Vow of Saint Kṣiti-garbha (in Chinese, the Ti-tsang p'u-sa pen-yüan ching) saves one from poverty, sickness, and death. Or the text can be recited in honor of the dead to save one's ancestors from hell or other difficulties. In Japan, under the name Jizō, this figure is particularly concerned with deceased children and aborted fetuses and is thought to protect them in the dark and dangerous passage between lives, called Bardo in Tibetan Buddhism.

See also BARDO; BHAVA-CHAKRA; JIZŌ; REINCARNATION, EASTERN; STŪPA; TI-TSANG.

References

Ching, Heng, trans. Sūtra of the Past Vows of Earth Store Boddhisattva: The Collected Lectures of Tripitaka Master Hsüan Hua. San Francisco: Buddhist Text Translation Society, 1974.

Levering, Miriam. "Kshitigarbha." In Encyclopedia of Religion, ed. Mircea Eliade. New York: Macmillan, 1987.

Welch, Holmes. The Practice of Chinese Buddhism, 1900–1950. Cambridge: Harvard University Press, 1967.

Williams, Paul. Mahāyāna Buddhism: The Doctrinal Foundations. New York: Routledge, 1989.

KURGAN

Central Asian burial pits covered with great mounds of earth and dating from prehistoric times, kurgans are associated with the ancient and diverse Indo-European tribes that later gave rise to Iranian, Indian, Celtic, Scythian, and other Eurasian civilizations. Kurgans and "kurgan culture" have been found in Central Asia from the Black Sea in the east to the Altai mountain region in the west but are particularly associated with the Scythian tribes from the seventh to the first centuries B.C.E. Though kurgans have been found over a wide area, are made of different materials, and have been associated with very different tribes over the centuries, they have several important features in common.

The grave pit is dug into the soil anywhere from 9 feet to a remarkable 42 feet deep (at the Chertomlyk kurgan), with the sides sometimes smoothed and plastered with clay and usually covered with a flat or domed wooden roof. In this central pit is housed the king or chieftain, often with wife or concubine and servants. Frequently, many side chambers, or catacombs, are connected to the central grave, holding more servants, horses, golden objects, and so on. The earthen mound constructed on top of the grave often rises quite high (30 to 70 feet) and is sometimes surrounded by smaller mounds. Most kurgans have an important vertical element, either wooden stakes or spears set up in the burial pit or stone columns placed atop the burial mound. This vertical element appears to symbolize the ability of the deceased, particularly if he or she belongs to the esteemed dead, to rise up from death to the heavens.

Another characteristic of kurgans was their association with the horse. For the Indo-European tribes of Central Asia, the horse was seen as a chthonic creature, that is, closely associated with the power of the Earth and having power over the Earth—a belief that would be expected of a seminomadic steppe-dwelling people. The horse was a major source of a king's power and was connected with chariots and the ability to make war. The horse also served as an intermediary between worlds, conveying the king to heaven in death even as it conveyed the king over the Earth in life. Therefore we find wooden statues of horsemen set up on kurgans (among the Kafir of Nuristan), dolls on a wooden horse (in Central Asia), and quite often mass burials of horse skulls—or even entire horses along with their carts—within the kurgans.

In addition, particularly among the Scythian tribes, a cult of gold is associated with the kurgan. At the Issyk kurgan near Alma-Ata, a princely burial from perhaps the fourth century B.C.E., massive amounts of gold were found. The prince wore a headdress adorned with gold, and his clothing and shoes were almost entirely covered with gold plaques. Meanwhile, more than 4,000 gold objects were buried along with him and his retinue. Likewise, at the Tillya-tepe kurgan in northern Afghanistan, the corpses wore gold crowns and gold embroidered clothing decorated with small gold plaques, about 2,500 to 4,000 plaques per grave. It seems clear that like horses, gold was associated with royal power, but unlike the chthonic symbolism of the horse, gold was a solar symbol. Gold is the color of the gods almost universally and especially among the ancient Indo-Europeans and their descendants. Gold was associated with Agni, the Vedic god of fire, and the Iranian god Vainu. Even the Buddha was said to have golden skin, radiant like the sun. But it is important to recognize that gold was valuable both as a form of wealth and because of its connection to transcendence and divinity—a corpse wrapped in gold was no longer just a mortal but a being from (or headed toward) another world.

Connecting both solar and horse cults, we find some kurgans in the shape of a massive wheel (in Sanskrit, chakra), symbolizing a solar chariot or perhaps the disk of the sun itself. In the Arzhan kurgan (in Tuva) the king and queen are placed in coffins in the center of a square wooden frame (8 by 8 meters) and are surrounded by the coffins of his courtiers, who were killed for the occasion. Logs radiate out from the central chamber like spokes, divided into seventy compartments. Some compartments have mass burials of 15 or 30 horses each; other compartments had humans and horses together. The king, queen, and courtiers were decorated in gold, and horse tails and manes covered the ground. Likewise the Ulug-Khorum kurgan, also in Tuva, formed a huge solar disk—a ring with thirty-two radial spokes. In the center was a semispherical stone 22 meters in diameter, engraved with depictions of horses.

The craftsmanship of the objects buried in the kurgans (weapons, jewelry, clothing, etc.) varies considerably by region, indicating Greek influence, especially around the Black Sea and northward; Iranian influence in the Afghanistan kurgans; and Chinese and Tibetan influence, particularly in the Altaic and Siberian kurgans.

See also BARROW; FAIRY MOUND; MEGALITHIC TOMB; MOUND.

References

Boyce, Mary. *A History of Zoroastrianism.* 3 vols. Leiden: E. J. Brill, 1975–1991.

Herodotus. *The Histories.* Trans. Aubrey de Sélincourt. New York: Crown, 1975.

Jettmar, Karl. *The Art of the Steppes.* New York: Crown, 1967.

Kohl, Philip L. *Central Asia: Paleolithic Beginnings to the Iron Age.* Paris: Editions Recherche sur les Civilisations, 1984.

Litvinskii, B. A. "Prehistoric Religions: The Eurasian Steppes and Inner Asia." In *The Encyclopedia of Religion,* ed. Mircea Eliade. New York: Macmillan, 1987.

Minns, E. H. *Scythians and Greeks: A Survey of Ancient History and Archaeology on the North Coast of the Euxine.* New York: Biblo and Tannen, 1965.

Sarianidi, V. I. *Bactrian Gold: From the Excavations of the Tillya-Tepe Necropolis in Northern Afghanistan.* Leningrad: Aurora Art Publishers, 1984.

L

LEMURIA

Unlike the official Roman commemoration of the dead celebrated each year in February (the Parentalia), the Lemuria was a distinctly gloomy holiday held on 9, 11, and 13 May and designed to chase away evil spirits from the home. It appears to be older in origin than the more "civilized" and urban Parentalia, and indeed in mythology the origin of the Lemuria is said to be a festival held by the first Romans to appease the ghost of one of their founders, Remus, who died violently.

The name *Lemuria* refers to the unquiet ghosts of those who went unburied or were improperly buried, the dead who cannot rest; this ghost is called *lemur*. It was not the well-behaved and even helpful manes (spirit) of one's properly cared for ancestors but an unknown ghost with malevolent intentions. Again, because burials and ritual attention to the dead were standardized and faithfully carried out throughout the period of the Roman Republic (fifth to first centuries B.C.E.), it is difficult to conceive of great numbers of undead spirits haunting the houses of the living—unless this festival is understood to date originally from a time before the urbanization of the Roman world, when unexpected deaths and irregular burial were characteristics of a difficult rural existence. Romans were quite conservative religiously and in other ways, so this festival was kept up even after the addition of the Parentalia and other funerary practices.

During Lemuria, unhappy ghosts brought danger and the pollution of the dead to the living. Only by an occult ritual carefully performed could these dangerous dead be exorcized. The Roman writer Ovid (43 B.C.E. to 17 C.E.) describes the ritual to be carried out by the head of the household:

> At midnight he rises, and with bare feet and washed hands, making a peculiar sign with his fingers and thumbs to keep off the ghosts, he walks through the house. He has black beans in his mouth, and these he spits out as he walks, looking the other way, and saying, "With these I redeem me and mine." Nine times he says this without looking round; then come the ghosts behind him, and gather up the beans unseen. He proceeds to wash again and to make a noise with brass vessels;

and after nine times repeating the formula "Depart, ancient spirits," he at last looks round, and the ceremony is over. (Trans. Warde, edited by Richard Taylor)

Interestingly, the number of days of the month is odd, as is the number of times the saying is repeated; odd numbers signify transition rather than the inherent stability of even numbers. The fact that the ritual takes place at midnight, the moment between the old day and the new, further emphasizes the liminality of the ritual, bridging as it does the worlds of the living and the dead but only to more firmly divide them. Beans, black in color like the black sacrifices offered up at gravesites, were connected in the Greek, Roman, and Persian worlds with life. Ascetics from Pythagoras (sixth century B.C.E.) to Mani (founder of Manichaeism, third century C.E.) refused to eat them as they refused to eat meat, in order to avoid taking "souls" into their bodies. When the heads of households threw beans toward the ghosts, they received the "life energy" they sought through their haunting, and the living humans passed unscathed. (For the same reason blood offerings are thought to satisfy the dead, both at the grave in family offerings and in Hades, where Odysseus uses blood to summon up the seer Tyresias.) Finally, the bare feet and the washing before and after the ritual reinforces the purification aspect of the rite, removing the pollution of the dead from the realm of the living.

See also FUNERARY CUSTOMS, ANCIENT ROMAN; PARENTALIA; SOUL; UNDEAD.

References

Fowler, W. Warde. *The Roman Festivals of the Period of the Republic.* London: Kennikat Press, 1969.

Harrison, Jane Ellen. *Prolegomena to the Study of Greek Religion.* Cambridge: Cambridge University Press, 1922.

Toynbee, J. M. C. *Death and Burial in the Roman World.* Ithaca, NY: Cornell University Press, 1971.

LETHE

One of the minor rivers of the Greek Underworld, Lethe literally means "forgetfulness." It is possible that originally Lethe was the water of forgetfulness drunk by newly arriving shades so that they might forget the cares of their former lives (except when their memories became convenient to visiting heroes like Odysseus). However, at least since the time of Plato, Lethe became the river that the dead drank from as they exited the Underworld to reincarnate on Earth in a new body.

In the last book of Plato's *Republic,* Socrates relates the near-death experience of a soldier named Er, who witnessed the afterlife and saw the souls of the dead, after enjoying the bliss or torture they had merited, choosing their next lives. After this, the souls of the dead

> marched on in a scorching heat to the plain of Forgetfulness, which was a barren waste destitute of trees and verdure; and then toward evening they encamped by the river Lethe, whose water no vessel can hold; of this they were all obliged to drink a certain quantity, and those who were not saved by wisdom drank more than was necessary; and each one as he drank forgot all things. Now after they had gone to rest, about the middle of the night there was a thunderstorm and earthquake, and then in an instant they were driven upwards in all manner of ways to their birth, like stars shooting. (Jowett, trans., pp. 460–461)

The Latin writer Virgil follows Plato's lead in his classic, the *Aeneid,* though for Virgil not all the souls in Hades reincarnate. Here the River Lethe runs through the pleasant area of Hades called Elysium, where the blessed souls who lived morally upright lives stay or even the unborn await their turn. The waters of Lethe are only for those who will reincarnate, for it refreshes them and frees them from previous sorrows.

Like most prominent bodies of water in the ancient world, the River Lethe also had an indwelling spirit, a nymph of the same name. Plato says that the nymph Lethe is the mother of Dionysus, though the modern scholar Robert Graves points out that this connection is probably made because of the heedlessness that revelers experienced in "worshipping" the god of wine.

See also ACHERON; COCYTUS; HADES; PHLEGETHON; STYX; UNDER-WORLD; WATER.

References
Graves, Robert. *The Greek Myths.* New York: Penguin, 1960.
Jowett, Benjamin. *The Essential Plato.* New York: Quality Paperback Books, 1999.
Mandelbaum, Allen, trans. *The Aeneid of Virgil.* New York: Bantam, 1961.

LOCULUS TOMB

A type of tomb found frequently in catacombs, loculi were of two basic types. In the narrow passages of a catacomb, loculi were dug out of the wall itself, lengthwise

(parallel to the passage) just big enough to fit a body, sometimes with and sometimes without a coffin. Since the catacomb passages were generally 7 to 10 feet high, a number of rows of loculi could be carved into each wall. Occasionally the passageways were quite a bit higher, up to 20 feet, with loculi placed even to the very top—indicating that the floor was lowered several times in order to provide more wall space for burial.

The other type of loculi was carved out of small rectangular chambers. These loculi were perpendicular to the wall, and the body was inserted headfirst. Here one, two, or more rows of loculi were carved into each of the three walls, leaving the entrance wall free. These types of loculi are commonly found in family-owned tombs holding several generations.

In either case this arrangement was an economical way to bury the dead because it maximized the number of bodies that could be buried in a single chamber. Loculi are first found among Jewish tombs in Jerusalem and Jericho but are thought to have originated in Egypt. In Jerusalem some loculi tombs had richly decorated facades, and several, probably belonging to prominent Jewish families, have a memorial, or nephesh, in the shape of a pyramid. Among Christians a coffin was not always used, and up to four bodies were placed in each of the loculi chambers. Their loculi were sealed with tile, stone, or marble, frequently stolen from pagan tombs nearby but placed front to back, presumably to hide from view pagan inscriptions and motifs.

References
Hertling, Ludwig, and Engelbert Kirschbaum. *The Roman Catacombs and Their Martyrs.* Trans. M. Joseph Costelloe. Rev. ed. London: Darton, Longman, and Todd, 1960.
Leon, Harry J. *The Jews of Ancient Rome.* Philadelphia: Jewish Publication Society of America, 1960.
Stevenson, James. *The Catacombs: Life and Death in Early Christianity.* London: Thames and Hudson, 1978.

LUCERNARIUM/LUMINARIUM

Lucernaria was the Latin name for narrow shafts (light wells) dug from the earth's surface down into tombs, particularly catacombs. The most important function of the lucernaria was, as their name suggests, providing light in the murky passageways. The church father Jerome (c. 347 to c. 419 C.E.) writes:

> When I was a boy at Rome, and was being educated in liberal studies, I was accustomed, with others of like age and mind, to visit on Sundays the sepulchres of the apostles and martyrs. And often did I enter the crypts, deep dug in the earth, with their walls on either side lined with the bodies of the dead, where everything is so dark that it almost

seems as if the psalmist's words were fulfilled: Let them go down alive into hell (Psalm 55:15). Here and there the light, not entering through windows, but filtering down from above through shafts, relieves the horror of the darkness. (Stevenson)

However the lucernaria had another, almost equally important function, to facilitate excavation. Rather than running back and forth along narrow chambers, carting out the earth and rock removed during the construction of tombs, buckets on ropes could haul debris vertically through these shafts. Footholds were dug into them to facilitate entry and exit.

References

Nash, E. *Pictorial Dictionary of Ancient Rome*. Rev. ed. London: Thames and Hudson, 1968.

Stevenson, James. *The Catacombs: Life and Death in Early Christianity*. London: Thames and Hudson, 1978.

M

MAG MELL

Pronounced "moy mall," this Irish Otherworld name may be translated literally as "the Plain of Happiness." Like all other Irish Otherworlds, it is variously located over the western sea, under the Earth, or even interpenetrating the ordinary human world invisibly. Mag Mell is not a land of the dead per se but an immortal land where special individuals may go and leave human cares behind. In each case, Mag Mell is rarely discovered by human initiative. Rather the Irish hero is called by the *síd*, or Otherworld people, to accomplish some task or to seek a fairy bride.

In *The Voyage of Bran,* the hero Bran (all quotes from Meyer, trans.), son of Febal, awakes one day to the sound of heavenly music sung by a beautiful woman wearing strange clothes. She sings of the splendor of the world beyond the sea, its thrice fifty islands, a land where mortal problems are unknown.

> Unknown is wailing and treachery
> In the familiar cultivated land,
> There is nothing rough or harsh,
> But sweet music striking on the ear.
>
> Without grief, without sorrow, without death,
> Without sickness, without debility.

Though many hear the woman, she is specifically there to call Bran:

> Not to all of you is my speech,
> Thought its great marvel has been made known.
> Let Bran hear from the crowd of the world
> What of wisdom had been told to him.

The beautiful woman departs, leaving Bran with a silver branch of an apple tree from the other world.

Bran sets out with twenty-seven companions (multiples of three are common in Irish lore) and after two days comes upon Manannán mac Lir, one of the banished fairy gods (Tuatha Dé Danann), in this case the god of the sea. Manannán is riding over the open sea in his chariot and says that although Bran sees only open sea, all around him is Mag Mell, a world flush with invisible activity.

> Speckled salmon leap from the womb
> Of the white sea, on which you look:
> They are calves, they are colored lambs
> With friendliness, without mutual slaughter.
>
> Though you see but one chariot-rider
> In Mag Mell of the many flowers,
> There are many steeds on its surface,
> Though you do not see them.
>
> Along the top of a wood
> Your coracle has sailed, over ridges,
> There is a wood of beautiful fruit
> Under the prow of your little skiff.

Bran and his voyagers proceed on to other lands—the Island of Joy, the Land of Women—but when they return to Ireland after a year, they approach in their ship a gathering of people on the shore. Bran announces his return, but no one there has heard of Bran, son of Febal, except in ancient legends. One homesick man jumps ashore, but as soon as he touches the earth he becomes a pile of dust and ashes, as if he had been dead for centuries. Bran leaves the people with his travels set in verse and sails off, never to be heard of again.

In another adventure, Mag Mell is not merely a land of joy and beauty but also a land of strife and struggle. One day the human hero Loegaire, son of King Crimthann, is approached by Fiachna mac Rétach, a síd warrior from the Otherworld. Fiachna requests Loegaire's help in regaining an abducted wife who is being held captive by Goll, son of Dolb, king of the fort at Mag Mell. Loegaire and his fifty men dive into Loch Naneane with Fiachna, and on the other side of the lake is a wonderful land with celestial music and ale for rain. Of course, Loegaire prevails in the battle and is rewarded with marriage to Fiachna's daughter. Loegaire returns to his human family only once for a farewell visit, and his father Crimthann offers him the kingdom of the Three Connachts if he will stay. But Loegaire insists he will return to the Otherworld, for there is

> The noble plaintive music of the *Síd,*
> Going from kingdom to kingdom,

Drinking from burnished cups,
Conversing with the loved one. . .

One night of the nights of the *Síd*
I would not give for your kingdom. (Rees, p. 309)

Finally, the hero Connla is visited by a beautiful goddess from Mag Mell. The goddess's people are housed within a fairy mound (also called a *síd*), which seems to imply that Mag Mell is underground or at least can be entered through the Earth. The goddess gives Connla an apple that sustains him for a month without growing any smaller, but she disappears. Upon her return, the goddess tells Connla that "the Ever-Living Ones" desire him to join them, and Connla steps into a crystal boat and vanishes forever. Here it would seem that Mag Mell is connected with water. In fact, it is both underground and underwater, and neither.

Like many others, the heroes Bran, Loegaire, and Connla are lured by the promise of adventures in Mag Mell, and they are entranced by its unearthly beauty and transcendent music. But the spiritual world is beyond human limits, which is why it often intersects with the human world at junctures, crossroads, and horizons. Thus, once Bran crosses the boundary (in this case, the western sea) he is forever trapped in the Otherworld—not unhappily! But having passed beyond the laws and norms of the mundane world, he truly has "died" and can live only in the Otherworld, here functioning as an "afterlife."

See also ANNWFN; AVALON; CROSSROADS; FAIRY MOUND; OTHER-WORLD, IRISH; SÍD; UNDERWORLD.

References

D'Arbois de Jubainville, H. *The Irish Mythological Cycle and Celtic Mythology*. Trans. Richard Irvine Best. Dublin: Hodges, Figgis, 1903.

Mac Bain, Alexander. *Celtic Mythology and Religion*. New York: Dutton, 1917.

MacCulloch, J. A. *The Religion of the Ancient Celts*. Edinburgh: Clark, 1911.

Meyer, Kuno. Trans. *The Voyage of Bran, Son of Febal, to the Land of the Living*. New York: AMS Press, 1972.

Rees, Alwyn, and Brinley Rees. *Celtic Heritage*. London: Thames and Hudson, 1961.

MĀRA

The Evil One, the Dark One, the Adversary—Māra is the great demon of Buddhism, personifying both passion and death because these two are intimately linked in Buddhist teachings. Māra has three daughters and heads a host of lesser demons, but they are rarely referred to in Buddhist literature. Unlike Christian conceptions of evil incarnate, Buddhist thought depicts no war between armies of angels and demons. Rather, Māra stands alone, representing in his unity the collec-

tive evil, suffering, and death of worldly existence from which Buddhists in their practice are trying to escape. Māra tries and fails to oppose the Buddha and his students, but ultimately it is Māra who holds sway over human existence. By keeping the world in ignorance, he ensures that human passions and lusts grow unchecked, thus condemning humans to death and rebirth.

Māra is a uniquely Buddhist character, having no singular counterpart in other Indian or East Asian religions. His name is etymologically related to that of the Vedic Hindu deity, Mrityu (Death), but Māra's activities go far beyond simply bringing death to living beings. In addition, Hinduism has a host of other demons, such as Namuchi, demon of drought, and Kāma, god of lust. Trevor Ling, in his book *Buddhism and the Mythology of Evil*, points out that the philosophical Māra of Buddhist scriptures and the yakṣas, or demons of folk literature, have much in common. For instance, both Māra and the hosts of yakṣas tend to operate at night, causing fear, especially with loud noises; both haunt lonely places, are shape-shifters, can "possess" human beings, and are hostile to religious rites. But Māra is unique in that he does not belong to a class of demons like himself, and more importantly, he has an eminently symbolic and philosophical value that yakṣas have never held in Indian literature. In representing the evils of the world, human pleasures, and ignorance, the figure Māra negatively teaches the entire Buddhist path: by overcoming Māra, step by step, the Buddhist disciple progresses on the Buddhist "way." Again, just before the culmination of insight into reality, on the eve of the Buddha's enlightenment, the Buddha was assailed by all the powers of Māra; resisting these temptations, the Buddha finally and permanently transcended the world. On that night, "Ignorance was banished and true knowledge arose, darkness was dispelled and light arose, as happens in one who abides diligent, ardent and resolute" (Mahāsaccaka-Sutta, Ñāṇamoli and Bodhi, trans.). The Buddha achieved his perfect enlightenment.

Thus, although Māra's many epithets suggest his roots in folklore—the Evil One, Illness, the Dark One, Death—his most characteristic attribute is ignorance, which throughout Buddhist teachings is the root of evil in human nature, keeping humanity in bondage and suffering. Māra does have a folk religion aspect and, like the European Satan, may appear in people's homes or at crossroads, causing mischief for the common person, but Māra's theologically designed symbolism is transparent, and there can be no doubt that his place in Buddhist literature is due to monastic design and not to the encroachment of popular religion. Māra's three daughters, who attempt to seduce the Buddha during his final approach to enlightenment, are Craving (Tanhā), Discontent (Arati), and

Māra Visits the Buddha

Thus have I heard: The Exalted One, the Buddha, was once staying at Uruvelā, on the banks of the river Nerañjarā, beneath the Goatherds' Banyan tree.

Now on that occasion Māra the evil one, who had been dogging the Exalted One for seven years watching for access, but without obtaining it, approached and addressed the Buddha in verse:

Are you immersed in grief, that in the forest
You meditate? Are you downcast at a loss
Of wealth, or are you wishing it were yours?
Have you committed some crime within the village?
Is there no one who will be your friend?

The Exalted One replied:

Every root of grief has been dragged out of me.
I meditate blamelessly, grieving at nothing.
All lust and longing for new life is cut off,
O You who are related to all that is careless!
So do I meditate, calm and immune.

Māra replied:

Men say of things, "This, that is mine!"
The people who tell you, "This or that is mine!"
For those and these, if you care about them,
O monk, you will never escape me.

The Exalted One replied:

Those things people speak of, they are not for me.
The people who talk, I am not one of them.
Learn this, O evil one, and know,
You don't even see the direction I go.

Māra replied:

If you have thought of a Path that is safe,
By which you can reach the deathless,
Then go, depart on your way, but go alone.
Why give your advice to any other?

The Exalted One replied:

People ask for a land of Immortality
As they seek to cross beyond.
When they ask me, I declare to them
The goal, where there is no basis for rebirth. . . .

Then Māra . . . departed from that place, and seated himself cross-legged upon the earth not far from the Exalted One, silent, discontented, with drooping shoulders, his face downcast, brooding and at a loss, scratching the earth with a stick.

Translation adapted from Rhys-Davids (1917).

Lust (Ragā)—the three principle qualities that Buddhist psychology teaches keep humans in bondage. According to Buddhist literature, Māra spends most of his time attempting to thwart the dharma (spiritual teaching) of the Buddha and the progress of his disciples, not making useless trouble for ordinary people. Māra tries to lure the Buddha into leaving the world with his newfound enlightenment and not spread it through the Buddhist religion (see excerpt). And Māra attempts to claim that because all possible human experience is of the world and Māra controls the world, there is no escape. Addressing the Buddha, Māra is made to say:

Mine, O monk, is the eye, mine are material shapes, mine is the field of visual consciousness. Where can you go, O monk, to escape from me [visually]? Precisely mine, O monk, are the ear, sounds, the field of auditory consciousness; the tongue, tastes, the field of taste-consciousness; the body, objects, the field of tactile consciousness; precisely mine, O monk, is the mind, mine are the mental states, mine is the field of intellectual consciousness. (Kassaka Sutta, trans. Ling)

But the Buddha replies: "Precisely yours, Malign One, is all this. But where there is none of this, there is no coming in for you." This statement is very instructive: early Buddhist scriptures teach students neither to pray to the Buddha to save them from Māra, nor to engage in combat with him, nor to abjure him with spells, all of which may be found in Christianity's conflict with Satan. Rather, the refuge for the Buddhist from the powers of Māra is analytical meditation—thereby ending personal ignorance, stilling the movements of the *āyatanas,* or "gateways to the soul," and entering final liberation. When one knows oneself, when one's personal passions and cravings have been subdued, and when one realizes the ultimate nature of the world and the causes of death and rebirth, then Māra (i.e., the world of illusion and suffering) can have no more effect. One is no longer attached to the eye and what it sees and to the ear and what it hears. Instead, one has attained nirvāṇa and will not be reborn.

Thus Māra is truly a demon and a literal force opposing the Buddhist teaching, but he is not a cosmic Satan or the ruler of hell. Māra is the force of human ignorance of reality, which in itself produces all suffering and death, according to Buddhism. Māra is not the ruler of hell but of the Earth.

See also HELLS, BUDDHIST; NIRVĀṆA; SOUL, BUDDHIST; YAMA.

References

Jones, J. J. *The Mahāvastu.* London, 1949–1956.
Ling, Trevor O. *Buddhism and the Mythology of Evil: A Study in Theravāda Buddhism.* London: Allen and Unwin, 1962.

Nānamoli, Bhikkhu, and Bhikkhu Bodhi, trans. *The Middle Length Discourses of the Buddha.* Boston: Wisdom Publications, 1995.

Rhys-Davids, C. A. F. *The Book of the Kindred Sayings (Samyutta Nikāya).* Pali Text Society Translation Series no. 7. London: Oxford University Press, 1917.

Windisch, E. *Māra und Buddha.* Leipzig: S. Hirzel, 1895.

MASTABA

In the first four dynasties of Egypt (beginning c. 3100 B.C.E. by orthodox chronology), before the pyramid had been developed, large rectangular structures called mastabas were built over subterranean tomb chambers. The word *mastaba* comes from the Arabic word for "bench" because when the structure was engulfed by sand it resembled the low bench built outside present-day Egyptian houses. However, the architectural form of the mastaba (and later the Egyptian sarcophagus) was apparently modeled on the royal palaces used by the early pharaohs, complete with outer walls rising at least 3 meters high, many interior chambers, and probably a shallow curved roof. Indeed, there can be little doubt that the mastabas were intended at least ritually as palaces for the afterlife, for the Egyptian word for tomb may be translated as "castle of eternity." From the earliest period, large boat-shaped pits near the mastaba structure have been found that surely held actual boats at one time; at the pyramids of Giza an actual boat was discovered in 1954. This find strongly suggests that the belief in a postmortem journey to the stars in a solar boat dates from the very beginning of Egyptian civilization.

The outer walls of the mastaba were ornately recessed in a pattern similar to that found in ancient Mesopotamia, and the interior walls were richly painted with a pattern representing ornamental matting used as wall hangings. The inside of the mastaba had thirty or more rooms like a real palace—each probably used to store massive amounts of food and other provisions but lacking any doors or windows. Some have suggested that the absence of doors would facilitate the deceased's entering the storerooms; however, given that false recessed doors were provided for offerings to the deceased in later pyramid tombs, the lack of doors here seems quite odd.

In the center of the structure a deep pit was dug, similar to predynastic pit graves. It was roofed with timber and housed the burial chamber and special storage rooms for more intimate possessions. This subterranean chamber was later (Second and Third Dynasties) protected from robbers with a huge stone slab that could be lowered into the access passage, blocking all entry. Atop the tomb was piled a small mound of earth covered with a layer of bricks, probably a holdover from the early pit graves, which were simple holes in the ground covered with a small mound. In time this central mound became more stylized, supported by four surrounding walls that were in turn surrounded with sloping embankments of sand and rubble cased with bricks laid in a step formation, giving the overall impression of a low, stepped pyramid.

Later mastabas (Second and Third Dynasties) showed considerable development. Those for officials and private persons (not pharaohs) dispensed with the interior chambers aboveground and filled the entire structure with rubble. However, the subterranean tomb became highly developed, with a central hall and a number of side apartments (including closets). An example of this huge underground development is provided by the tomb of Unas, excavated in 1901. At a depth of 21 feet underground, the tomb runs nearly 130 yards in length with about 70 chambers on each side of a central corridor, all hewn out of solid rock.

Aboveground mastabas were surrounded by one and sometimes two defensive walls like those surrounding a fort and were accompanied by many smaller buildings nearby, made of solid stone but presumably duplicating royal compounds. In some cases rows of smaller mastabas have been found with the remains of servants of the royal household who were put to death at the passing of the pharaoh. Some mastabas in Saqqâra were surrounded with a low terrace to which life-sized heads of cattle, modeled in clay but with real horns, were attached.

No actual mummies or coffins have yet been found in any mastabas, though much funerary equipment has turned up. Thus it is not clear if robbers have stolen the physical remains of the kings, or if these structures were for purely ceremonial or ritual use. The problem of actual burial is further complicated by the fact that many early pharaohs are known to have had at least two mastabas erected for them, one in the early Egyptian capital Memphis (or nearby Saqqâra) and one 300 miles south in Luxor or Abydos, old centers of Upper Egyptian power before Egypt was united. Fierce debate continues as to whether one, both, or neither of the duplicate mastabas served as burial places for the actual physical remains of the pharaohs, perhaps modeled after duplicate palaces for the pharaohs during life. Whatever the case, we may certainly assume the early Egyptians would not have gone to the trouble of building duplicate tombs as cenotaphs (tombs for those whose body is lost or elsewhere) unless there were compelling religious or political reasons to do so.

See also KURGAN; MOUND.

References

Edwards, I. E. S. *The Pyramids of Egypt.* Rev. ed., New York: Penguin, 1978.

Fakhry, Ahmed. *The Pyramids.* Chicago: University of Chicago Press, 1961.

Garstang, J. *Burial Customs of Ancient Egypt*. London: A. Constable, 1907.

Kristensen, W. Brede. *Life Out of Death: Studies in the Religions of Egypt and of Ancient Greece*. Louvain, Belgium: Peeters Press, 1992.

Mendelssohn, Kurt. *The Riddle of the Pyramids*. London: Thames and Hudson, 1974.

Spencer, A. J. *Death in Ancient Egypt*. New York: Penguin, 1982.

West, John Anthony. *Serpent in the Sky*. New York: Harper and Row, 1979.

Winlock, H. E. *The Rise and Fall of the Middle Kingdom in Thebes*. New York: Macmillan, 1947.

MAUSOLEUM

Even by the time of the Roman Empire, the word *mausoleum* had become a generic term for any large or ornate tomb aboveground (underground tombs are typically called *hypogea*). The first known usage of the word in this sense is found in the Greco-Roman writer Strabo (c. 64 B.C.E. to c. 23 C.E.). However, there actually was a king named Mausolus, the head of the Persian satrap (province) of Caria near the coast of Anatolia in Asia Minor. His tomb was so spectacular that it drew the attention of the entire ancient world and is mentioned on the majority of ancient lists of the Seven Wonders of the World. In time his name passed into the common vocabulary, and any great tomb became a mausoleum, though few in any age can rival the original.

Mausolus came to power in Caria in 377 B.C.E. and reigned until his death circa 353; his wife Artemisia survived him and ruled two years alone until her death in 351. One of the most important works (erga) of Mausolus was to refound the city of Halikarnassos and lay out its city plan. Because his tomb and the vast artificial hill (temenos) it sat on are integrated into the city plan (placed right in the middle of a major thoroughfare), scholars assume that Mausolus commissioned his own tomb early in his career. Yet written reports from Late Antiquity (by Pliny, Vitruvius, and others) indicate that the tomb was not finished even at Artemisia's death; thus it would appear the tomb took at least ten and possibly up to twenty years to build, at huge expense.

The Mausoleum was an immense structure, which was still standing in the twelfth century C.E., according to eyewitnesses, though apparently it was mostly in ruins a few centuries later and its remains were pillaged by the Knights of St. John in the early sixteenth century to build their castles. Excavations in the nineteenth and twentieth centuries revealed a great deal about the structure, frieze designs, and statuary of the Mausoleum. The structure rose to at least 140 feet and was placed on a foundation of about 120 by 120 feet. The details of the structure are not entirely clear, but the foundation reached well into the ground, and

fifteen layers of immense foundation blocks brought the foundation to ground level. At the bottom of the foundation was the tomb chamber where Mausolus was apparently buried. Excavations have turned up gold appliqués, pieces of Attic pottery, and surprisingly, what appears to be another, earlier tomb chamber. (It may be that Mausolus built on an already somewhat famous site to inherit the prestige.) Above the foundation was a very high base called a *podium*, which was stepped and highly decorated, probably with statues, all around. On top of the podium were thirty-six Ionic columns, providing the peristyle (the interior "chamber") of the Mausoleum. Above the pillars was the cornice, ringed with lions, which formed the base of the twenty-four-step pyramid that rode atop the whole structure. The ancient literary sources have it that four famous artists each chose a different side of the Mausoleum to decorate, though modern scholars have found little evidence of this. But at each level—podium, peristyle, and pyramid—the Mausoleum was highly decorated, particularly with intricate frieze sculptures, though their placement is uncertain. These included sculptures of warring Amazons, a group of centaurs, and a group of chariots (the latter probably on top) whose star was a world-class sculpture called "the Charioteer."

Inside the peristyle of the Mausoleum, probably open to the air, were apparently hundreds of sculptures in the round. These included gods, animals of a great variety, and humans in three sizes: life-size, one-third greater than life-size, and two-thirds larger than life-size. The "colossal" human statues two-thirds greater than life-size appear to be engaged in sacrifice, adoration, and battle, including one that seems to be Mausolus himself holding either a sword or a sacrificial bowl and knife. Few figures of the middle size survive but among them has been found the head of Apollo. The smallest figures, only life-size, appear to be Greeks and Persians enacting one of the interminable real-life battles between those two great empires of the fourth century B.C.E.. The interior ceiling of the peristyle was also highly decorated with reliefs.

For some time scholars have searched for various precursors to the Mausoleum, especially since its design appears to have been influenced by many different—eventually garishly competing—elements. One of the most obvious influences on the Mausoleum is the structure of the Egyptian pyramid, also used (at least later in Egyptian history) as a funerary monument. The pyramids were well known to the ancient world from the *Histories* of the Greek writer Herodotus (c. 484 to 430–420 B.C.E.). Not only the pyramidal summit of the Mausoleum but some of the creatures in the designs bore Egyptian influence, including the head of a sphinx discovered during excavation.

At the Persian capital, Pasargadae, there is the great tomb of Kyros, whose inscription read: "O man, I am Kyros [Cyrus], who founded the empire of the Persians and was King of Asia. Grudge me not this monument." Like the pyramids, Kyros's tomb was also commissioned and planned by its future inmate. Not as massive as the Mausoleum, it was still nearly 40 feet high, drawing on traditional Persian elements with a gable-roofed chamber atop three receding tiers of equal size. Another influence on the Mausoleum was probably the "Nereid Tomb" at Xanthos, also in Asia Minor, built circa 400 B.C.E., a massive tomb whose most impressive features were high columns interwoven with graceful Nereids, mythical goddesses of the sea.

It was the Mausoleum, however, that incorporated elements from Persian, Greek, and Egyptian design, catching the imagination of the ancient world; becoming a household word; sparking competition among Greek, Roman, and Persian rulers for ages to come; and influencing the more humble tombs of early Christians and later Muslims as well.

See also HOUSE TOMB; HYPOGEUM; MAUSOLEUM, ISLAMIC; PYRAMID, EGYPTIAN; THOLOS TOMB.

References

Herodotus. *The Histories*. Trans. Aubrey de Sélincourt. New York: Crown, 1975.

Hornblower, Simon. *Mausolus*. Oxford: Clarendon Press, 1982.

Toynbee, J. M. C. *Death and Burial in the Roman World*. Ithaca, NY: Cornell University Press, 1971.

MAUSOLEUM, ISLAMIC

Orthodox theology in Islam dictates that, as all souls are of equal dignity in the sight of God during life, so they should be in death; only moral merits distinguish one person from another—in theory. Thus according to early Islamic thought and Scripture, graves were to be level with the ground (not mounded), with little or no structure above the grave (no tombstone, stela, etc.). Yet this equality in death apparently did not last long, perhaps because pre-Islamic customs in the Middle East had involved giving the esteemed dead high honors. Islamic literature shows that mausolea were being built as early as the second century of Islam (roughly the eighth century in the Western calendar).

Because of their "heterodoxy," mausolea were often attached to or built within mosques (houses of prayer), madrasas (theological colleges), or caravansarais (courtyards of trade) and made integral to their architecture, thus forming a large complex. As an alternative, free-standing tombs were sometimes built outside the city precincts, occasionally becoming sites of pilgrimage if the entombed was a saint (or if the actual inmate was forgotten and local tradition conjured up a saint instead). Nevertheless, there were occasional uprisings

in various areas of Islam that reacted against such "blasphemy" and damaged or even destroyed all mausolea within reach, for instance, in Baghdad in the tenth and eleventh centuries. Robert Hillenbrand supplies the many native terms for the Islamic mausoleum, which have interesting connotations: *turba* (both "grave" and "dust"), *qabr* (tomb), *marqad* (place of sleep), *madfan* (place of burial), *qubba* (dome), *qasr* (castle), *astana* (threshold), *ziyara* (place of pilgrimage), *mashhad* (shrine), and *rauda* (garden, specifically the Gardens of Delight). The last few terms were especially popular, and it is no accident that such names try to spiritualize what was largely a personal, even egotistical affair: the commemoration of oneself by outward show against the explicit commands of Islamic scripture and the traditions (hadīths) of the Prophet Muhammed.

The first infringements on the austere burial policy appear to have been stelae erected over the graves, oriented toward the holy Islamic city of Mecca, with sacred inscriptions from the Qur'ān such as "In the name of God, the Merciful, the Compassionate," the name of the deceased, and the date of death. Before long, prominent Muslims and devotees of certain saints and religious leaders (particularly in Shi'ite Islam, a minority tradition that honors a succession of divine leaders called *imams*) began looking for better ways to honor the dead. Nearby cultures provided several funerary structures for Islamic use. To the West were the classical Roman and Persian mausolea (named for the original Mausoleum of the fourth century B.C.E.) and the Christian martyrium, which drafted the mausoleum form into service as a shrine for worship and pilgrimage (particularly in Syria). To the East were the Zoroastrian practice of exposing the corpse on tall "Towers of Silence" and the Turkish practice of leaving the bodies of esteemed dead "in state" for a time in their yurts (round tents). From these sources the creative energies of Islam created two basic types of tombs: (1) the "tower tomb," whose height was three to six times the diameter of the round base; and (2) a square (or octagonal) base topped by a dome. As an indication of their quasi-orthodox aspirations, Islamic tombs are always oriented toward Mecca, with a niche in the wall that points in that direction. In addition, most Islamic tombs have one or more inscriptions from the Qur'ān carved or inlaid on the walls or especially on the dome. One common inscription is from sura 21:35: "Every soul must taste death."

From very early times, the "domed-square" style of tomb predominated in Islam, from Egypt to India. (Because the tower tomb was prominent only in Anatolia and Iran for a specific time, it is treated in a separate entry.) In general, the dome represents the canopy of heaven, both because of its distance above the viewer and because of the shade it provides—shade being one of the most-emphasized aspects of the Garden

Turbe, or tomb tower, of Sultan Baiandour at Akhlat, typical of the mausoleum architecture developed by the Seljuk-Turks. Wood engraving, 1853. Courtesy of Anne Ronan Picture Library.

with an octagonal base, four arched doorways at the cardinal points, a second smaller tier, also octagonal, and a simple dome. Here, the eight sides may be symbolic of a Muslim tradition that teaches the existence of eight levels of Paradise.

Somewhat later mausolea began to experiment with new structures and styles. The mausoleum at Tim, dated 977 C.E., introduced a new feature, called a *pishtaq*, which soon became standard: an exaggeratedly arched and deeply framed entranceway, overshooting the height of the base structure and partially obscuring the dome. Other tombs began to amplify the gallery (the stretch of upper walls that encircle the square base) and to elaborate the zone of transition. This trend is particularly noticeable in the Davazdah Imam mausoleum at Yazd (eastern Iran), where atop the square base is a smaller square tier, atop which is a third, even smaller octagonal tier, which in turn supports the dome—geometrically progressing from square to octagon to circle. Another new feature, particularly in Persia and India, was the development of minarets (long, narrow towers topped with domes) at each of the corners of the base, whether square or octagonal. This is demonstrated in the mausoleum of Öljeitü in Sultaniya, the highest in Iran at 173 vertical feet. This tomb has not only a huge gallery above its octagonal base, but a virtual crown of eight minarets surrounding its massive dome—affordable only by the greatest and richest of royal patrons. The culmination of the minaret development can be seen in the Tāj Mahal at Agra in India, where the four huge minarets have become separated from the entire structure and frame the building itself rather than the dome.

In the Fatimid period of Egypt (969–1171 C.E.), when it was ruled by Shi'ites claiming descent from Muhammed's daughter Fatima, tombs were somewhat more acceptable to theology than they were in more eastern territories of Islam. Tombs were very frequently part of larger structures (and were therefore called *intra muros*), either integrated into the city landscape or serving as large and popular pilgrimage sites far from civilization. Indeed, certain main streets in Cairo are practically showrooms for competing mausolea, for instance the Bain al-Qasrain. Here octagonal structures are the norm, the better to accommodate visitors who wish to circumambulate the tomb of the holy saint or martyr inside. However, twelve-sided mausolea are not uncommon either, commemorating the twelve main imams, or perfect leaders, of the "Twelver" sect of Shi'ite Islam. In the cities, mausolea were frequently parts of larger buildings that also contained hospitals (maristan), theological colleges (madrasas) and functional, not decorative minarets (towers from which a caller, or a muezzin, announces the times each day for prayer). In the countryside mausolea were frequently integrated

of Delights, a welcome relief from the arid heat of much of the Islamic world.

Although the earliest mausolea in Islam appear to have been built for the original companions of the Prophet Muhammed and Old and New Testament figures (long after their death), none of these have survived, and in any case they were few. However, one of the earliest surviving tombs, in Bukhara (Central Asia), is thought to represent the type. Dated to about 940 C.E., the "Tomb of the Samanids" (named for an Iranian dynasty of the tenth and eleventh centuries) has the classic square base, with each side containing an inset, arched entranceway. Around the top of the base is an elaborate brickwork pattern topped by a large dome surrounded by four much smaller domes, one on each corner. The entire tomb is highly decorated, except for the dome, which is plain (exactly the opposite was to become the dominant trend, especially in Egypt). The inside is exquisitely carved, particularly the "zone of transition" (the upper area where the square base must gradually give way to the round dome). Another early mausoleum is at Samarra in Mesopotamia and dates to the mid-ninth century. It is a relatively simple tomb,

References
Blair, Sheila S., and Jonathan M. Bloom. *The Art and Architecture of Islam 1250–1800*. New Haven: Yale University Press, 1994.
Ettinghausen, Richard, and Oleg Grabar. *The Art and Architecture of Islam 650–1250*. New York: Viking Penguin, 1987.
Hillenbrand, Robert. *Islamic Architecture: Form, Function and Meaning*. New York: Columbia University Press, 1994.
Hoag, John D. *Islamic Architecture*. New York: Rizzoli, 1987.
Smith, Edmund W. *Akbar's Tomb, Sikandrah, Near Agra, Described and Illustrated*. Allahabad: Archaeological Survey of India, 1909.

into a mosque (for prayer) and caravansarais (for trade caravans). One notable feature developed by the western styles of Islamic mausolea was the muqarnas style of vaulting, a kind of honeycomb of arches, frequently used as the bridging element in the zone of transition. Some western tombs consist of almost nothing but muqarnas, either as the base, topped by an octagonal gallery and then a dome (as at Damascus, Syria, 1174 C.E.), or on top of a square base, replacing the dome altogether (as in the Imam Dur, the tomb of Muslim bin Quraish, in Iraq, 1086 C.E.).

Although Muslim tombs certainly commemorate the lives of prestigious persons, they also frequently served as central religious sites for the living. Sometimes an entire funerary complex—a necropolis—would grow up around the tomb of a particularly holy figure, such as the necropolis at Samarkand in Central Asia. There, in the fifteenth century, royal tombs collected over the decades because of the (probably incorrect) attribution of one of the tombs to Qutham bin al-'Abbas, an original companion of the Prophet. These kings hoped to gain a kind of holiness by association (as when the sick and injured attempted to touch the clothing of Jesus), for in most cases, the closer they could build to the tomb of a saint, the more they would benefit in the afterlife. One final function served by Islamic tombs was to double as pilgrimage centers and military forts on the edges of the territory of Islam (Dar al-Islam) to sanctify the borders Islam held with the heathen and to stave off the regular incursions of the infidels. In this way mausolea became a part of the jihad, or holy war.

See also FUNERARY CUSTOMS, MUSLIM; KURGAN; MAUSOLEUM; TĀJ MAHAL; TOWER OF SILENCE; TOWER TOMB.

MCHOD RTEN

The word *mChod rten* (pronounced chörten) literally means "receptacle of relics" and refers to the Tibetan version of the Buddhist Indian stūpa, or relic monument. Buddhism came to Tibet relatively late compared to other Asian countries (seventh through tenth centuries C.E.) and so the Tibetans inherited the later, highly elaborated version of the Indian stūpa, which they modified even further.

In Tibet the mChod rten has evolved from its origin as a monument that commemorated the esteemed dead and housed their relics to a complex symbol of the Buddhist teachings and their cosmic and psychological correspondences or even just an "auspicious" design. This change was shown in the fact that mChod rten were built not solely as large architectural structures in Tibet but in miniature as well, made of clay and designed for use in homes and monasteries, as sacred decorations, or even as jewelry. Lamas would take miniature mChod rten with small images of deities and folding doors from village to village to display them to the people. Sometimes a modified mChod rten structure, without the same religious significance, was used as an entrance porch at the main entrance to a village or town.

Architecturally, the mChod rten has significantly modified elements found in its earlier cousins, the stūpa and dagoba. To begin with, the base upon which the dome rests became subdivided into three, five, or even more levels and took on a square rather than a round shape. These new foundational levels absorbed the old railings that used to demarcate the sacred space of the stūpa from the profane world and became decorative elements of the surface of each level. Likewise, the gates, or toranas, to the stūpa that marked the four directions and four most important events in the Buddha's life (birth, enlightenment, preaching, and death) were replaced by staircases leading to ever higher levels. The dome changed shape from a nearly perfect hemisphere to a rounded, top-heavy figure, shaped like a pot and perfectly flat on top, and the relic box (harmika) atop the dome became fused with the spire. Meanwhile, the spire became taller, with more carved rings (usually thirteen) symbolizing new stages on the highest spiritual path (the bodhisattva-bhumi). Furthermore, the spire was no longer associated with the honorific umbrella, which symbolized the protection offered by the Buddha; instead, an umbrella shape was added on top of the spire, topped in turn by a crescent moon, a solar disk, and finally a little circle called *bindu,* or drop, symbolizing space (akasha) itself, the absolute essence of spirituality, which pervades all things without obstruction.

As Buddhist doctrine became more elaborate, the different architectural elements of the mChod rten became associated with the various cosmic elements, mystical colors, stages of the path to nirvāṇa, and the corresponding centers of energy or consciousness located in the human frame. The Tibetan Scriptures (Tanjur) describe in detail the significance of each and every element of the mChod rten, which can only be broadly summarized here. The enlarged foundation, with its various levels, symbolized preparatory stages on the spiritual path, including the four foundations of mindfulness, the four efforts, the four mental powers, and so on. All these were associated with solidity and the element of earth because of their foundational character for the devotee. The color associated with the foundation is yellow and corresponds to the lowest human chakra (center of power on the human spine), "root-support" (muladhara).

The dome represents the seven factors or arms (anga) of enlightenment and is associated with the element water, the color white, and the human chakra manipura (navel), the center of life energy. The conical spire was red and corresponded to the cosmic element fire and the radiant heart chakra (anahata). A newly added miniature hemisphere atop the spire corresponded to air, the color green, and the creative throat chakra. These four together represented a unity, a complete manifestation of energy in form.

The next three—the crescent moon, red solar disk, and deep blue bindu, or drop—represent a trinity of rarified spiritualized energies that are a synthesis of the lunar and solar. They are symbolized by abstract space and the highest human chakra, the sahasrara (thousandfold), which sits about a finger's breadth above the head. The devotee who has reached this stage has attained the pinnacle of spiritual development, and enlightenment is complete.

See also DAGOBA, HEAVENS, BUDDHIST; STŪPA.

References

Cook, Elizabeth, ed. *The Stupa: Sacred Symbol of Enlightenment.* Crystal Mirror Series, vol. 12. Berkeley: Dharma Press, 1997.

Dorjee, Pema. *The Stupa and Its Technology: A Tibeto-Buddhist Perspective.* New Delhi: Indira Gandhi National Centre for the Arts and Motilal Banarsidass, 1996.

Govinda, Anagarika. *Psycho-cosmic Symbolism of the Buddhist Stupa.* Berkeley: Dharma Publishing, 1976.

Snellgrove, David. *Himalayan Pilgrimage.* Oxford: B. Cassirer, 1961.

Tucci, Giuseppe. *The Religions of Tibet.* Trans. Geoffrey Samuel. Berkeley: University of California Press, 1980.

MEGALITHIC TOMB

Megalith is Greek for "massive stone," specifically one of the huge burial structures of the Neolithic period that are found by the thousands still standing today throughout Ireland, Britain, Wales, and along the Atlantic seaboard of western Europe from southern Scandinavia to Portugal. A few are found in the western Mediterranean, both on islands and scattered along a few coastlines. They bear different names in each location: dolmens in France and Spain, antas in Portugal, cromlechs in Wales, cairns and barrows in England and Scotland, dysser in Denmark, and tombe di giganti in Sardinia. The largest and most sophisticated megaliths appear to be in Ireland. Although having much in common with the tholos tombs of Minoan, Mycenean, and Greek civilizations, the Irish megaliths in general predate the Mediterranean tombs by many thousands of years and show significant differences in structure and intention.

The megalithic tombs have variations among themselves and appear to belong to different cultures and periods but share several important characteristics: they were made of vertical slabs of natural stone, largely undressed and uncarved, weighing 20, 30, 40, or as much as 100 tons each, and capped by a nearly horizontal slab or slabs of equal or sometimes greater weight without the use of mortar. The vertical slabs were usually positioned to form the soon-to-be underground chambers in a geometric figure, either circular, rectangular, polygonal, or even cruciform or transeptal like medieval churches. Drystone walling was often used, either to fill in gaps between the bigger stones or to form a vaulted ceiling, using overlapping stones to construct smaller and smaller concentric circles. The entire structure was buried under a round, oval, elongated, or trapezoidal tumulus (burial mound) once the dead were in possession, but erosion or human disturbance over thousands of years has sometimes worn away the earthen and rubble covering mound, leaving mysterious and deceptively precarious-looking structures visible aboveground. Scholars estimate that it would have taken 1,000 workers eight years of full-time work to construct the largest of the Irish megalithic tombs, which suggests that the "primitive" human beings we imagine our ancestors to have been were capable of advanced social organization and architectural planning.

The megalithic tombs appear to have served as more than simple, primitive burial places. Often the stones forming the chambers were smoothed down or decorated with patterns chiseled into the rock. In some cases, concave facades were built adjacent to the tumulus at the entrance to the tunnel leading to the burial chambers. These facades were decorated with anticipations of modern columns and occasionally had an upright stone column like an obelisk positioned at the geometric center of the concave figure, as at the Browndod megalith in northern Ireland.

Many factors suggest that the megalithic tombs served not just as simple resting places for the bodies of the dead but also or even primarily as ritual centers. Many of the tombs were clearly ossuaries for secondary burial, for the bones found within had been cleared of flesh before being interred. Likewise, bodies of (supposedly) sacrificed animals are occasionally found buried near the entranceway. Most remarkably, at least some of the megaliths have precise astronomical alignments, like the "henge" monuments of Stonehenge and Avebury in Great Britain and Carnac in Brittany, France. The massive Newgrange megalith in Ireland, measuring 260 feet in diameter and 35 feet in height and constructed of perhaps 200,000 tons of material, has a special aperture aligned precisely to the light from the rising sun at winter solstice, allowing it to shine down the entrance passageway and reach the burial chamber at the heart of the mound. Overall, the megaliths of Europe show much more advanced techniques and served much more sophisticated purposes than was originally thought upon their modern discovery.

See also BARROW; CAIRN; MOUND; THOLOS TOMB.

References

Colvin, Howard. *Architecture and the After-Life*. New Haven: Yale University Press, 1991.

Daniel, G. *The Prehistoric Chamber Tombs of France*. London: Thames and Hudson, 1960.

Eogan, G. *Knowth and the Passage-Tombs of Ireland*. New York: Thames and Hudson, 1986.

Evans, J. D. *Prehistoric Antiquities of the Maltese Islands*. London: University of London, Athlone Press, 1971.

Giot, P. R. *Brittany*. London: Thames and Hudson, 1960.

Guido, M. *Sardinia*. London: Thames and Hudson, 1963.

Henshall, A. H. *The Chambered Tombs of Scotland*. 2 vols. Edinburgh: Edinburgh University Press, 1963, 1972.

Herity, M. *Irish Passage Graves*. New York: Barnes and Noble Books, 1975.

Mackie, E. *The Megalith Builders*. Oxford: Phaidon, 1977.

O'Kelley, M. *Newgrange*. London: Thames and Hudson, 1982.

Piggott, S. *Neolithic Cultures of the British Isles*. Cambridge: Cambridge University Press, 1954.

Twohig, E. Shee. *The Megalithic Art of Western Europe*. Oxford: Clarendon Press, 1981.

MENSA

Mensa is a Latin term with two funerary meanings. First, it was the name for the stone shelf beneath the arch of an arcosolium, upon which the coffin was placed in more elaborate tombs (especially in the underground, rectangular tomb chambers called *cubicula*). These shelves are found often in early Christian catacomb burials. Second, mensa was the name for the wooden or fixed stone table placed in a Christian tomb (or in a small room built at the intersection of passageways in catacombs) to hold the funeral feast or serve as an altar for Eucharist services for the dead.

References

Stevenson, James. *The Catacombs: Life and Death in Early Christianity*. London: Thames and Hudson, 1978.

MET MITZVAH

In Orthodox Judaism, an abandoned corpse or a corpse without a quorum of ten Jews to bury it is called a *met mitzvah*. Jewish tradition considers it essential that all the dead (particularly Jews) be properly buried, not only out of respect for the dead but also because the corpse is a source of tremendous ritual impurity for the entire community. In addition, according to ancient tradition a proper burial complete with all organs, limbs, or blood lost is considered important to one's future physical resurrection.

The met mitzvah, or "abandoned corpse," is not necessarily one that has been literally abandoned. A minyan, or quorum of ten adult Jewish males, is required to carry out a traditional Jewish funeral and burial, and in small Jewish communities (particularly in the Middle Ages) gathering a sufficient number of Jews to form a minyan could be a problem. For this reason Jewish tradition places a very great emphasis on the responsibility of all Jews to assist a met mitzvah—even Jews who are kohens (serving in a priestly role) and who are normally forbidden to handle corpses of any kind are commanded to care for a met mitzvah and accord it a complete and proper funeral. For a similar reason, namely to honor the dead, all Jews of whatever station or rank are commanded to follow any funeral procession that passes them by, even if only for six or eight paces, even if doing so interrupts Scriptural study or other high and important duties. To dishonor the dead by failing to care for an abandoned corpse or failing to follow a funeral procession is considered extremely sinful and grounds for banishment.

See also CHEVRA KADDISHA; FUNERARY CUSTOMS, JEWISH; TOHORAH.

References

Abrahams, I. *Jewish Life in the Middle Ages*. London: E. Goldston, 1932.

Lamm, Maurice. *The Jewish Way in Death and Mourning*. New York: Jonathan David Publishers, 1969.

Rabinowicz, H. *A Guide to Life*. London: Jewish Chronicle Publications, 1964.

MORRIGAN (MÓR-RÍOGHAIN, MÓRRÍGU)

Literally "phantom queen," the Morrigan is the name of a terrifying war goddess of old Ireland, though as protector of various lands and families she also retains aspects of her ancient role as fertility goddess. She sometimes appears as the most prominent of a triad of fierce war goddesses, all sisters, the other two being Badhbh (pronounced "bow") and Macha (pronounced "mokk-uh"), although frequently these are just other names for Morrigan. The Morrigan's roots can be traced back to a Celtic earth goddess whose proper name was Anu or Danu, whence the name of the river Danube. (This name is also cognate with the Sanskrit river goddess Dānu and the Welsh wizard-mother Dôn). Anu or Danu was "the mother of the Irish gods" perhaps both mythologically and literally, for the later goddess Morrigan was identified with her and took on Danu's roles regarding fertility and especially war.

In the epics the Morrigan is the wife of the principal Irish divinity Daghdha (pronounced "daye"), but she may be more powerful than he in the Irish tradition. For instance, in the central battle between the demonic Fomhóire giants and the noble Tuatha Dé Danann, the Morrigan predicted where the enemy would land, terrified the Fomhóire king Inneach ("draining the blood from his heart"), and gathered the wise seer-poets together to sing spells against the foe. Then she and her sisters brought down hail and fierce showers on the giants and cast javelins and flails against them—demonstrating both her fertility and war roles simultaneously.

Less romanticized than the Valkyries of Norse tradition, the Morrigan still shares in the ambiguity of her violent function: like the Valkyries the Morrigan both incites war, seeming to delight in its carnage, and yet protects her chosen heroes, leading them to victory. She may appear as a beautiful maiden, as when she tries to warn her erstwhile nemesis Cú Chulainn of the trap laid for him. But most often she appears as a hideous hag before and during great battles—the original banshee—revealing herself to the side that will be worsted. In these instances, as before the death of the hero Cormac Conn Loingeas and at the historical battle of Corcomroe Abbey in 1317 C.E., she is seen as a hideous red hag washing blood-soaked clothes in a river, turning the waters crimson with gore. She is also seen as a lean, "gray-haired," "red-mouthed" hag leaping speedily over weapons and shields and shrieking in battle lust. Finally, she is said to fly as a black carrion crow over battles, delighting in the corpses and carnage. In these examples the Morrigan is merely a symbol of the destructiveness of war, as in the description of the battle between the troops of Leinster and Ossory in 870 C.E.: "Great indeed was the din and tumult that occurred between them then, and the Badhbh raised her head between them, and there was massive killing between them" (Ó hÓgáin).

Often, however, the Morrigan does not serve such a clear-cut positive or negative role. For instance, in the Ulster cycle the Morrigan actually protects both sides. Under the name Macha she lays a curse on the men of Ulster so that they cannot defend themselves against the encroaching armies of Queen Meadhbh (pronounced "mwai-ev"), yet under the name of Badhbh she shrieks over Meadhbh's army, causing chaos and frightening many soldiers literally to death. Her ambivalent nature is revealed again in the Morrigan's dealings with Irish mythology's preeminent hero, Cú Chulainn. At their first encounter the Morrigan claims she has fallen in love and offers to help him. After he refuses her advances, the Morrigan creates all manner of obstacles in the great hero's path. Yet in the Ulster war she eggs him on to great victory, and just before the treachery that ends his life, the Morrigan attempts to warn him. This ambivalence, even contradiction, reflects both the shifting tides of battle and the many layers of stories incorporated into the Morrigan tradition.

Interestingly, in Welsh and British tradition, the Morrigan enters the cycle of texts connected with King Arthur. There she is Morgan le Fay, the sometime helper, sometime foe of Arthur, but at the end it is Morgan who brings the mortally wounded king to Avalon, one of the many names for the Celtic Otherworld of fairies and gods. Even today he rests there under Morgan's care, but it is said that one day from a fairy mound, King Arthur will return to save Britain in its hour of need.

See also BANSHEE; FAIRY MOUND; FUNERARY CUSTOMS, CELTIC; VALKYRIE.

References

Best, Richard I., and Michael A. O'Brien. *The Book of Leinster 2–3*. Dublin: Dublin Institute for Advanced Studies, 1956–1957.

Hennessy, William M. *Révue Celtique* 1 (Paris, 1870).

Ó hÓgáin, Dáithí. *Myth, Legend and Romance: An Encyclopaedia of the Irish Folk Tradition*. New York: Prentice Hall, 1991.

O'Rahilly, Cecile, ed. *Táin Bó Cuailnge: Recension 1*. Dublin: Dublin Institute for Advanced Studies, 1976.

Royal Irish Academy. *Contributions to a Dictionary of the Irish Language*. Dublin: Royal Irish Academy, 1913–1975.

MOT (MAWET)

The Hebrew word for "death," *mot* is often used like Sheol to refer both to the realm of death and the personification of the god of death. In the second millennium B.C.E., Mot was clearly a personal god, as we see from the Canaanite texts discovered at Ugarit, an ancient city in Syria. He is characterized as being insatiable, with one lip on the Earth and the other reaching to heaven, greedily devouring all. In these texts, Mot struggles mightily and repeatedly with Baal, the god of life. Most scholars see this as a fertility struggle, especially given the fact that after Mot is defeated by Baal, fertility returned to Ugarit: the heavens rained vegetable oil, and the rivers ran with honey.

Centuries later in ancient Judaism, Mot appears less often as the god of death and more often as the realm of death. Occasionally a remembrance of the insatiable, swallowing nature of Mot surfaces in the Bible (e.g., Habakkuk 2:5, Job 18:13), but as Judaism rejected polytheism more and more strongly, Yahweh gradually incorporated into himself all the attributes of earlier gods. Thus it is Yahweh himself who becomes the "swallower" in the relatively late text, Isaiah 25:7–8:

On this mountain the Lord will swallow up
   that veil that shrouds all the peoples,
   the pall thrown over all the nations;
   he will swallow up Death [Mot] forever.

References

Cassuto, U. *The Goddess Anath*. Trans. I. Abrahams. Jerusalem: Magness Press, Hebrew University, 1971.

Kaufmann, Y. *The Religion of Israel*. Trans. M. Greenberg. Chicago: University of Chicago Press, 1960.

Moor, Johannes. C. de. *An Anthology of Religious Texts from Ugarit*. Leiden: E. J. Brill, 1987.

Oldenburg, U. *The Conflict Between El and Ba'al in Canaanite Religion*. Leiden: E. J. Brill, 1969.

Tromp, Nicholas. J. *Primitive Conceptions of Death and the Nether World in the Old Testament*. Rome: Pontifical Biblical Institute, 1969.

Watson, P. L. *Mot, the God of Death, at Ugarit and in the Old Testament*. Ph.D. diss., Yale University, 1970.

MOUND

After the early cave burials, humans next began to bury their dead in mounds of earth or stone or both. As burial sites, mounds are almost identical in function to caves: they protect the dead and offer the same womb-like symbolism (in many mound burials, the body is arranged in a fetal position and the bones are colored red), the same return to earth and origins and night. Indeed, the earliest mounds (which tend to be the largest) appear to have been attempts to create artificial caves: the mound was built over great slabs of stone, which were used to create a protected chamber, within which the body (or bodies, if it was a family grave) was placed. A long tunnel, filled loosely with dirt, kept the chamber in contact with the "outside world."

Yet the mound, to the degree it is artificial and deliberate, adds some additional features in symbolism. Against a flat horizon, nothing could be a more distinct symbol than a giant mound. It is a profound interruption of the environment: the heaped versus the flat, the vertical versus the horizontal. The flat earth speaks of the mundane, whereas the rising earth speaks of transcendence, of heaven and of higher life. Together, they are visual representations of abstract notions, opposites, and boundaries. Thus the mound is a meeting of incompatibles, which is both philosophical and symbolic, as if to say "ponder me" and "notice me" at the same time. All later aboveground funerary structures built on this opposition between flat and elevated.

Mounds have an additional symbolic element, one that comes out most clearly in the pyramid (the most advanced and precise "mound" known to history), in that the mound is often proportioned precisely to mimic the mathematical dimensions of the Earth's hemisphere, both in height-to-width ratio and in orientation to heavenly bodies. Stonehenge is an example of ancient knowledge regarding astronomy, though it was probably never covered with a mound because it was to be used by the living. As the Earth is to heaven, so the flat ground is to the vertical mound. The interior of the mound symbolizes the round Earth, and the outer dome symbolizes the "dome" of heaven and the heavenly bodies therein.

The larger mounds around the world often contain not merely the body of the deceased hero or king but his wife (the two placed in the center), servants, soldiers, royal horses, other animals, and royal equipment (including full-length boats). Clearly, when the leader died, the "world order" died with him, and all his servants and belongings were sent along (voluntarily or involuntarily) into the next world to build a new empire on the "other side." This last point is proved by the fact that such royal burials were often laid out in a carefully geometric fashion, representing local beliefs about the order and pattern of the universe.

Many types of mounds were used by cultures around the globe. Often they differ only slightly in form and function and bear different names merely because of their geographical location or ethnic heritage. Megaliths (literally "massive stones" in Greek) are mounds built over slabs or stone—several slabs placed vertically with one laid on top—so large and weighing so many tons that modern scholars can scarcely understand how they were made.

Tholos tombs are found mainly in the Mediterranean basin. In these tombs, the mound covers a chamber wherein a central stone column holds up the tiered roof—this at a time when the complex architecture of the dome was not perfected. The central column was not merely a necessary architectural element but a symbol of the axis mundi, the "pillar of the world," the central cosmic hub of creation, comparable to the cosmic tree or cosmic mountain or cosmic ladder found in almost every culture. Thus, even more clearly than in the standard mound, in the tholos tomb the dead live within the cosmic mountain at the root of the world.

In Central Asia the kurgan likewise demonstrates a "cosmic" element in its construction. In the greater burials, the chieftain, wife, staff, animals, and equipment were laid out in a circular fashion, with wooden planks separating the various compartments like spokes on a wheel. This arrangement suggests both the round horizon of the earth as well as the solar disk.

The Buddhist stūpas of Asia were intended to be entirely symbolic, since they generally contained no physical body at all but only "spiritual" relics, namely copies of the Buddha's words, the sacred Scriptures, and sometimes other ritual implements. The dome with its spire symbolizes the stages of the Buddhist path to the goal of transcendence (nirvāṇa). Each successive level indicates upward progress cosmically (stretching, like all mounds, toward heaven), ethically (as the base steps represent progress as an altruistic being), and physiologically (as the various elements represent the seven chakras, or centers of power, on the human spine where the "subtle energies" congregate).

Greek, Persian, and Islamic mausolea are likewise deeply symbolic developments of the mound, formalized like the stūpa in classical architecture of brick or stone. The symbolism may draw from religious sources (particularly the Muslim mausoleum), but because such monuments actually contain a physical body (or bodies) their symbolism is often highly personal or political. Like the stūpa, the mausoleum was often designed to invite pilgrims and had built-in areas for offerings, circumambulation, and other activities.

Possibly the Egyptian pyramids represent the ultimate development of burial mounds. Again, like the megaliths, the earliest pyramids are by far the largest and most solidly constructed and have survived throughout the ages. The mathematical precision of the design of many pyramids leaves no doubt as to their cosmically symbolic function, representing the sphere of Earth but pointing (via various internal shafts) toward significant stars and constellations in the sky. Their pointed shape alone tells even the most casual observer that they were intended for the ascent of the dead king or queen into heaven.

In many regions, mounds came to be seen as not just the dwelling places of the esteemed dead but also as centers of power from which radiated all kinds of occult powers, fertile and beneficent as well as necromantic and dangerous. In general, mounds have at least three functions for the living (besides serving as burial places). First, mounds are often perceived as boundary zones between the living and the dead. Mounds can serve as "doorways" to the land of the dead (like caves), which may open during the annual festival of the dead, and they may allow the living and the dead to communicate, often through dreams. Second, mounds may also come to be seen as supernaturally charged boundaries in

general. Thus, besides the dead, burial mounds may be thought to have Otherworld inhabitants—living but nonhuman dwellers such as elves, dwarves, lords of animals, fairies, and so on. The heroes and heroines of many a tale find that, when they pass by a sacred mound, they hear voices inside, which may give threats or invite them inside. Otherworld adventures begin very often at mounds, which may lead underground, across the ocean, into the sky, or into fairy kingdoms that do not perceive time as we know it. Third, mounds are often seen as dangerous spots to be conquered only by the strong. Gifts, including kingship, may come to the hero who passes certain tests or conquers the land around the mound. Taking control of a mound is often synonymous with assuming the powers of the distant past and once again claiming rightful rule or, with the rightful union of territories who share a mound, as a common boundary.

See also BARROW; CAIRN; FAIRY MOUND; KURGAN; MAUSOLEUM; MEGALITHIC TOMB; PYRAMID, EGYPTIAN; STŪPA; THOLOS TOMB; TUMULUS; UNDERWORLD.

References

Ashbee, Paul. *The Earthen Long Barrow in Britain*. London: J. M. Dent and Sons, 1970.

Colvin, Howard. *Architecture and the After-Life*. New Haven: Yale University Press, 1991.

Cook, Elizabeth, ed. *The Stūpa: Sacred Symbol of Enlightenment*. Crystal Mirror Series, vol. 12. Berkeley: Dharma Press, 1997.

Dunning, G. C., and R. F. Jessup. "Roman Barrows." *Antiquity* 10 (1936).

Govinda, Anagarika. *Psycho-cosmic Symbolism of the Buddhist Stūpa*. Berkeley: Dharma Publishing, 1976.

Hillenbrand, Robert. *Islamic Architecture: Form, Function and Meaning*. New York: Columbia University Press, 1994.

Hoag, John D. *Islamic Architecture*. New York: Rizzoli, 1987.

Hornblower, Simon. *Mausolus*. Oxford: Clarendon Press, 1982.

Kohl, Philip L. *Central Asia: Paleolithic Beginnings to the Iron Age*. Paris: Editions Recherche sur les civilisations, 1984.

Longhurst, A. H. *The Story of the Stūpa*. New Delhi: Asian Educational Services, 1979.

Minns, E. H. *Scythians and Greeks: A Survey of Ancient History and Archaeology on the North Coast of the Euxine*. New York: Biblo and Tannen, 1965.

Powell, T. G. E. *Megalithic Enquiries in the West of England*. Liverpool: Liverpool University Press, 1969.

Rees, Alwyn, and Brinley Rees. *Celtic Heritage*. London: Thames and Hudson, 1961.

Toynbee, J. M. C. *Death and Burial in the Roman World*. Ithaca, NY: Cornell University Press, 1971.

MUMMIFICATION

A mummy is simply an embalmed corpse, usually associated with ancient Egyptians. However, the word *mummy,* which comes from the Arabic *mumiya,* was the product of a misunderstanding of how mummies were prepared. In the Late Period of Egypt (c. 664 to 380

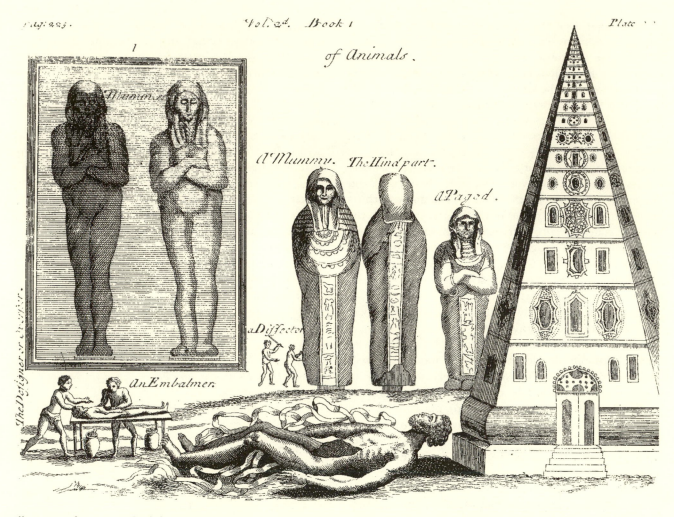

Illustrations of mummies and embalming. From P. Pomet, A Compleat History of Drugs, *London, 1725. Courtesy of Anne Ronan Picture Library.*

B.C.E.), badly embalmed mummies were so black and brittle that people assumed they had been dipped in bitumen. Mumiya is the Arabic word for bitumen.

Archaeological studies since 1800 have revealed a great deal about the gradual evolution of early Egyptian interest in preserving the body. No evidence of artificial attempts to preserve the body after death has been found from the Predynastic Period (before c. 3100 B.C.E.), but the practice of burying the corpse in shallow graves in the sand had the effect of drying and preserving the body very well quite naturally. As the Egyptians gradually turned to coffins and burial chambers with roofs, the bodies were protected from the hot, drying sand and thus decomposed rapidly.

By the time of the First Dynasty (c. 3100 to 2890 B.C.E.), corpses were found wrapped in linen, which did little to preserve the body but had the effect of preserving the body's shape. In the Fourth Dynasty (c. 2600 B.C.E.), the first attempts at true mummification were made, in which the internal organs were removed and the internal cavity was allowed to dry thoroughly. In

royal burials, the four primary internal organs (lungs, liver, stomach, and intestines) were removed to canopic jars, the earliest example of this being Queen Hetepheres, and the cavity inside the body was filled with resin-soaked linen, sawdust, and other fillers. Still, the bodies from this time were not very well preserved, and the Egyptians were clearly aware of this. The bodies went on decaying even after treatment, though at a much slower rate. So the early Egyptians contented themselves with at least giving the mummy as lifelike an appearance as possible by wrapping the body extremely tightly and carefully with fine linen. The earliest mummy found so far, a court musician named Waty from the Fifth Dynasty (c. 2400 B.C.E.), was so expertly wrapped that every facial and body feature is still recognizable, down to the callus on one foot. One mummy was found from the Sixth Dynasty (c. 2100 B.C.E.) wearing a linen dress over her bandaged wrappings, and many are found coated with plaster and adorned with wigs, painted faces, and false mustaches and beards. The effect was that of a portrait, and it was thought to be a more acceptable home for the ba (soul). Interestingly, the facial details were painted using green paint, green being the color associated with resurrection.

After the Old Kingdom had collapsed (c. 2200 B.C.E.) mummification became much more sophisticated, and the entire process from death to burial took seventy days, including ample time for extensive rituals at various points along the way. The whole body was first probably washed with a solution of natron, a preserving salt found in great quantities left behind when the flooding from the Nile dried up in the desert sun. Then the body was coated with resin to help preserve the body while it was being worked on and to help with the undeniable smell of a corpse. An incision was made in the lower left part of the abdomen, and the soft-tissue organs were removed as already described. The heart, however, was always left in place, since it was the seat of intelligence and will, and the deceased needed it to remain in his or her body. A cheaper means of removing the organs, used for poorer clients, was to inject oil and spices through the anus and plug it up, and after the body had been dessicated and the internal organs had decayed and liquefied, the anus was unplugged and the insides of the deceased were allowed to drain out.

Whether the internal organs were removed or not, the body was placed for some forty days under heaps of powdered natron, which drew out nearly all moisture from the body, preventing bacteria from decaying the flesh. Then the body was returned to the embalming table and prepared for wrapping. The internal cavities were rinsed out with spices and palm wine, probably mostly as a deodorant, and restuffed with resin and linen and sewn up again or sealed with gold foil or a tablet of beeswax held in place by pouring molten resin over it. The eyes and nose, now shrunken, were stopped up with linen. Often, especially from the Twenty-first Dynasty (1085 to 945 B.C.E.) on, artificial eyes made from alabaster or other material and complete with painted pupils were placed over the original (sunken) eyeballs. The whole body was rubbed with a lotion of juniper oil, beeswax, spices, and natron and then painted with molten resin to toughen the skin and make it waterproof. Cosmetic additions with paint were added, and often the entire body was painted with ochre, red for men and yellow for women.

Finally, the body was wrapped. The fingers and toes were wrapped first, individually, and then each limb. The mummy mask was placed over the head and shoulders, followed by at least one shroud, and then the whole body was very carefully and tightly wrapped. At various layers amulets, onions, spells from the Book of the Dead, and jewelry were placed on the body. Each stage of wrapping, like the previous stages of preparation, was accompanied by the appropriate magical recitations. In the final stages, the mummy of the deceased was told that he or she had regained the use of each section (head, arms, legs, etc.). After the wrapping was completed, the body was delivered to the family or priests for the funeral. Interestingly, every single thing that had come into contact with the mummy over the course of embalming—rags, oil, sawdust, instruments, anything that might have a speck of the body's flesh on it—was collected and preserved. After the funeral, at the entombment, all of this was put into a great number of pots and buried near the tomb, often accompanied by the embalming table and the four wooden blocks that supported it. The Egyptians expected the body to magically resurrect on the other side of death, and every piece of flesh would need to be nearby to facilitate that process.

Despite the Egyptian concern with timelessness and changelessness, it is clear that mummification practices changed over time. An innovation in the New Kingdom (c. 1550 to 945 B.C.E.) was the removal of the brain, which as reported by the Greek historian Herodotus (c. 484 to 430–420 B.C.E.) was a difficult procedure and costly enough to be performed only for wealthier clients. A small chisel was used through the left nostril to break through the ethmoid bone into the skull, the brain was removed bit by bit by an iron probe, and the cranial cavity washed out with water and oils. It was then restuffed, either with linen soaked in resin or with sawdust. Another innovation was the care taken to preserve fingernails and toenails, either by binding them on with the linen wrap or securing them with little tubes of metal placed over the tips. In the Eighteenth Dynasty (c. 1300 B.C.E.), the placement of the arms changed, first from having them lie flat against the sides of the body, to having the hands cross over the pelvic region, to crossing the arms over the chest, which lasted until the end of the Twentieth Dynasty. Then, for some reason, the position of the arms returned to the sides.

The Twenty-first Dynasty marked the peak of perfection in the science of mummification. The Egyptians developed subcutaneous stuffing: the practice of padding the shrunken and dessicated body with linen, sawdust, or sand under the skin, molded to the shape of the body, to return it to an appearance of plump health. In addition to the incision made to remove the internal organs, incisions were made at the base of the feet, in the back, and elsewhere to allow almost every part of the body to be reached. Also, to increase the perfection of the body, the internal organs were no longer placed in canopic jars but after drying were wrapped and replaced inside the body, although the canopic jars were retained for purely traditional reasons. The priests of the Twenty-first Dynasty also tried to restore the mummies of ancient kings that had been damaged by grave robbers, often using wooden splints to repair broken or missing limbs and then rewrapping and reburying the bodies in secret places.

There are also extensive mummies of animals, of nearly every kind that was native to Egypt. Mummies have been found of snakes, baboons, fish, birds, cats, dogs, and most spectacularly of the Apis bulls from the Egyptian city of Memphis, which were treated as pharaohs. In the long course of Egyptian history a highly sophisticated theology developed, and each species of animal took on cosmic symbolism.

After the New Kingdom the art of mummification steadily declined, and there were no innovations, except for the remarkably intricate geometric patterns that developed in the wrapping of the Roman Period (beginning in 30 B.C.E.). Crude embalming practices lingered among the early Egyptian Christians until the rise of Islam in the seventh century, which halted mummification entirely. Nevertheless, the mummies of Egypt continued to be regarded with awe by later cultures, and in Arabia and medieval and renaissance Europe a brisk trade in "mummy powder" developed—it was thought to cure everything from colds to bleeding to broken bones. So great was the demand, even into the twentieth century in some places, that it led to the widespread sale of fake mummy powder made from local corpses of beggars and criminals.

See also AMULETS, EGYPTIAN; BOOK OF THE DEAD, EGYPTIAN; FUNERARY CUSTOMS, ANCIENT EGYPTIAN; PIT GRAVES, EARLY EGYPTIAN; PYRAMID, EGYPTIAN; SOUL, EGYPTIAN.

References

Budge, E. A. W. *The Mummy.* New York: Causeway Books, 1972.

Garstang, J. *Burial Customs of Ancient Egypt.* London: A. Constable, 1907.

Hamilton-Paterson, James, and Carol Andrews. *Mummies: Death and Life in Ancient Egypt.* London: William Collins Sons, 1978.

Harris, J. E., and K. R. Weeks. *X-Raying the Pharaohs.* London: MacDonald and Company, 1973.

Leca, Ange-Pierre. *The Egyptian Way of Death.* Trans. Louise Asmal. Garden City, NY: Doubleday, 1981.

Lucas, A. *Ancient Egyptian Materials and Industries.* 4th ed. Revised by J. R. Harris. London: E. Arnold, 1962.

Montet, P. *Everyday Life in Egypt.* London; E. Arnold, 1958.

Smith, G. E. *Egyptian Mummies.* London: G. Allen and Unwin, 1924.

Spencer, A. J. *Death in Ancient Egypt.* New York: Penguin, 1982.

N

AL-NAR
See Jahannam.

NARAKA

In more than 5,000 years of history, Hinduism has developed more hells than any other culture on earth. Not only are the number and types of hells carefully inventoried and elaborated (although different native sources are wildly contradictory in this regard), but also the exact descriptions of which sins lead to which hell and for how long give evidence of a philosophy of ethical retribution that long predates that of every other known society. Even in the most ancient Hindu Scriptures, the Vedas (dated variously from 4000 to 2000 B.C.E. by modern scholars), there is a clear teaching that those who commit evil will be punished in their afterlife, and this belief continues to have a strong hold over the followers of all Indian religions today, whether they are Hindu, Buddhist, Jain, or Sikh. To be sure, conceptions of the afterlife and particularly of Naraka, or hell, have evolved over the centuries, and opinions differ as to whether the hells are literal, even physical locations or perhaps penitential but psychological and spiritual states of being. But the essential ethical aspect of the philosophy has remained constant throughout.

In the earliest known text, the Rig Veda, the conception of hell is vague, and the later word *Naraka* does not appear. Western scholars explain this absence by pointing out that the idea of hell was not developed at such an early time, whereas traditional Indian scholars say that because the Vedas had a different purpose than laying out systematic cosmography, they did not discuss it. But the Rig Veda does show clearly that evil-doers were to be punished, for there is reference to sinners being "hurled below the three earths," and Rig Veda verse VII.104.3 states:

O [gods] Indra-Soma, dash the evil-doers down
Into the pit, the gloom profound and bottomless,
So that not one of them may ever thence emerge;
Such be your wrathful might to overpower them.
(Griswold, trans.)

Other sacred hymns from the Rig Veda refer briefly to this "bottomless pit" that sinners create for themselves, but there is little information as to its nature, location, or the extent of time a sinner might endure existence there. Rather, many hymns relating to the afterlife define the correct performance of sacrifice, the pursuit of spiritual knowledge, the paths of the ancestors to follow, and immortality. Yet even so these hymns already contain an idea of a cosmology with dark realms below the "three earths" and realms of light above.

Most traditional scholars in the West have insisted that early Scriptures like the Vedas do not have a developed philosophy of karma or reincarnation, but some verses suggest the opposite; for example, one hymn of the Rig Veda (X.16.3) blesses the cremated departed and discusses their "merit" and new abodes: "The Sun receives your eye, the wind your spirit [ātman]. Go as your merit is, to earth or heaven. Go, if it is your lot, unto waters; go, make your home in plants with all your members" (Oldenberg, trans.). This verse agrees with worldwide conceptions of a multipart soul, each segment of which departs to different states after death (cf. Homer's notion that the shade of Hercules lives in Hades, while simultaneously his "self" dwells with the gods on Olympos). Thus, given the Vedic understanding of ethics, afterlife, and soul, when later texts discuss the hells as punishments for specific sins, they are not so much inventing a "new" idea but fleshing out what existed from the very beginning of Indian thought.

This "fleshing out" was prodigious. By the time the Purāṇas were written (300 to 600 C.E.), the number of heavens and hells enumerated had multiplied dramatically, with at least seven heavens (Svargas) above the earth; seven nether-regions (called *talas*) below the Earth; and the 7, 14, 21, 28, or more hells (Narakas) placed even below the talas. The hells are carefully distinguished from the talas in that the hells are specifically places of suffering for beings who have committed sins in past lives, whereas the talas are simply Underworlds that are the natural home to various races of beings, such as serpent men (nāgas), titans (asuras, dānavas, daityas), and demons (rākṣasas, prets, bhūts). These races are morally dubious, but in the later philosophical systems and epic tales they can exercise free will and are not inherently evil. For their crimes, however, they too will suffer in the hells below, like beings of all other races, human and nonhuman.

Although the Purāṇas state that their information was gained by direct spiritual vision on the part of great saints, the clever suitability of sufferings paired to specific crimes and graphic descriptions suggest great literary embellishment. For instance, the Agni Purāṇa enumerates 144 hells and gives copious examples: the soul of a man who has eaten sweets by himself without sharing with others is doomed to the hell called *Kākola* (literally "Crows") where he must eat excrement and the parasites that infest excrement while being fed on by crows. One who kills his mother sinks to one of the lowest of hells, Asipatravana ("Forest of Sword Blades"). Here hell is a dense forest where the leaves of the trees are razor-sharp blades, and the sinner continually runs about being cut to ribbons. Again, the soul of a tyrant who oppressed others is himself oppressed in the hell of boiling oil. Other hells feature continual drowning (Avīchi), sinners baked in clay pots (Kumbhīpāka), a multitude packed into a tiny space (Sanghāta), suffocation (Niruchvāsa), great burning (Mahājvāla), the pitcher of undigested bile (Amakumbha), terrible smells (Ugragandha), and blinding darkness (Andhatāmisra). The time spent in such hells varies from as little as 100,000 years to a length of time called a *kalpa*. A kalpa is a great age of the universe, the period of time it would take to wear down the Himalayas to sea level if, once each century, one were to take a silk scarf and lightly brush their peaks—in short, some sinners need not even think of *ever* getting out of hell, although in theory, all existence is temporary and rebirth is inevitable, for gods as well as sinners.

It is obvious that a great deal of effort has been spent in Hindu literature in examining the hells and bringing out their dreadfulness; this is apparent not only in the philosophical literature but in the most popular of tales, such as those in the great collection *The Ocean of Story*. Death and the fear of hells are major themes, and the common Hindu is much concerned about the lasting consequences of sin. Not surprisingly, sin itself has been thoroughly developed in Indian literature, with nine major kinds of sins enumerated; sin is defined not merely as evil actions but as even the desire to commit selfish or evil actions. Thus, in Indian thought, control of the mind is absolutely essential to spiritual knowledge and progress. Once a sin is committed, however, in thought, word, or deed, karma has been set in motion, and only the equal and opposite karma of penance and reparations (prāyaśchitta) in this life can save one from a (nearly) endless future in Naraka. Thus devout Hindus are very careful to tally their sins and make amends in whatever way prescribed by the village priest (brahmin).

The Torments of Naraka

Sinners guilty of having committed [one or more of the nine kinds of] sins have to endure terrible sufferings when they have left this life and reached the path of [the god] Yama. Being dragged hither and thither by the fierce servants of Yama, they are led [to Naraka] by them with frightening gestures. [In Naraka] they are devoured by dogs, jackals, crows, herons, cranes and other birds eating raw flesh, by snakes and scorpions that have [poison] in their mouths. They are scorched by fire, pierced by thorns, divided into parts by saws and oppressed by thirst. They are afflicted with hunger and by terrible hordes of tigers and they faint away at every step on account of the stinking smell of pus and blood. Desiring to secure the food and drink of others they are beaten by the servants whose faces are similar to . . . crows, herons and cranes. In some places they are boiled in oil, in others they are pounded with pestles or ground down in iron or stone vessels. In some places they eat what is vomited or pus or blood or excrements, and hideous meat smelling like pus. In one place they have to stay in terrible darkness, and are devoured by horrible worms having flames in their mouths. In some places they are overwhelmed by cold or have to pass through the midst of unclean things and in other places the departed devour each other, thus becoming most horrible. In some places they are beaten on account of their former deeds and are suspended in other places [from trees, etc.] or are struck with heaps of arrows or are cut into pieces. In other places they have to tread upon thorns and they are encircled by the hoods of serpents, they are tormented with machines and are dragged to their knees. Their backs, heads and necks are fractured, they become terrible [to look at]. . . . Sinners are being tormented in this way and having suffered intense pain undergo various further sufferings in their passage through animal bodies [in which they are reborn].

From Vishnu Dharma Sutra; translation by P. V. Kane (1953).

The perception of the ordinary Hindu does not necessarily match the conception of the philosopher, however. The great scholar P. V. Kane, in his massive work *History of Dharmashāstra*, suggests that from very early times there has been debate on whether the Narakas—or Svargas for that matter—are really physical locations "beyond" the Earth. To be sure, many native Indian thinkers have interpreted the Narakas in a literal manner throughout Indian history, but there have also been voices of dissent. A recent scholar,

Ananda Coomaraswamy, has shown the manifestly metaphorical nature of the Vedic hymns and how much more sophisticated the Vedas are when read symbolically rather than literally. Thus heaven and hell in the Vedas are metaphysical postulates about forces in nature and not physical places of human pleasure or torment. A much earlier critic, named Shabara, stated his belief that heaven is joy "and not a thing (dravya) which brings joy" (quoted in Kane). Logically, then, hell would be a state of suffering, not a geographical place where suffering occurs. Thus there has been the suggestion among some Indian philosophers that the Narakas are in fact the states of mind that are the indubitable result of evil, experienced either here or in the hereafter; but meanwhile the literal belief in the place of the Narakas below the earth is allowed to continue even by the symbolically minded because it helps the uneducated grasp moral standards more tangibly and avoid the real but "psychological" effects of sin.

See also BHŪT; FUNERARY CUSTOMS, HINDU; NIRVĀṆA; PĀTĀLA; PRET; RĀKṢASA; SHIVA (HINDU); SVARGA; YAMA.

References

Coomaraswamy, Ananda K. *Rig Veda as Land-Náma-Bók*. Delhi: Bharatiya Publishing House, 1980.

Griswold, H. D. *The Religion of the Rigveda*. Indian ed. Delhi: Motilal Banarsidass, 1971.

Hastings, James, ed. *Encyclopaedia of Religion and Ethics*. Vol. 4: "Cosmogony and Cosmology (Indian)." Edinburgh: T. and T. Clark, 1911.

Kane, Pandurang Vaman. *History of Dharmashāstra: Ancient and Medieval Religious and Civil Law in India*. Vol. 4. Government Oriental Series, Class B, no. 6. Poona: Bhandarkar Oriental Research Institute, 1953.

O'Flaherty, Wendy Doniger. *The Origins of Evil in Hindu Mythology*. Berkeley: University of California Press, 1976.

Oldenberg, Hermann. *The Religion of the Veda*. Trans. Shridhar B. Shrotri. Indian ed. Delhi: Motilal Banarsidass, 1988.

Shastri, Manmatha Nath Dutt, trans. *Agni Purānam*. Varanasi: Chowkhamba Publications, 1967.

Tawney, C. H., trans. *The Ocean of Story*. Indian ed. Delhi: Motilal Banarsidass, 1968.

Wilson, H. H. *Vishnu Purāna*. Vol. 1. London Trübner, 1864.

NEAR-DEATH EXPERIENCE

In recent decades, the near-death experience (NDE) has gained great notoriety and generated tremendous controversy, largely stemming from Raymond A. Moody's 1975 book, *Life after Life,* wherein he summarizes the experiences of nearly 150 people who believed they had clinically died and shortly thereafter had been resuscitated. Moody postulated that although NDEs may be uncommon, they were probably much more common than suspected due to the reticence of survivors to discuss their often mystical experiences before a skeptical public. In fact, a 1982 Gallup poll appears to have borne Moody out: the poll found that 5 percent of

---

An Archetypal Near-Death Experience

A man is dying and, as he reaches the point of greatest physical distress, he hears himself pronounced dead by his doctor. He begins to hear an uncomfortable noise, a loud ringing or buzzing, and at the same time feels himself moving very rapidly through a long dark tunnel. After this, he suddenly finds himself outside of his own physical body, but still in the immediate physical environment, and he sees his own body from a distance, as though he is a spectator. He watches the resuscitation attempt from this unusual vantage point and is in a state of emotional upheaval.

After a while, he collects himself and becomes more accustomed to his odd condition. He notices that he still has a "body," but one of a very different nature and with very different powers from the physical body he has left behind. Soon other things begin to happen. Others come to meet and to help him. He glimpses the spirits of relatives and friends who have already died, and a loving, warm spirit of a kind he has never encountered before—a being of light—appears before him. This being asks him a question, nonverbally, to make him evaluate his life and helps him along by showing him a panoramic, instantaneous playback of the major events of his life. At some point he finds himself approaching some sort of a barrier or border, apparently representing the limit between earthly life and the next life. At this point he resists, for by now he is taken up with his experiences in the afterlife and does not want to return. He is overwhelmed by intense feelings of joy, love and peace. Despite his attitude, though, he somehow reunites with his physical body and lives.

Later he tries to tell others, but he has trouble doing so. In the first place, he can find no human words adequate to describe these unearthly episodes. He also finds that others scoff, so he stops telling other people. Still, the experience affects his life profoundly, especially his views about death and its relationship to life.

From Moody (1975), pp. 21–23.

Americans reported having at least one near-death experience.

Certainly, the near-death experience appears to be a rare but not unheard-of condition as old as humanity. Accounts of NDEs and deathbed visions were told in the West by Plato, Pope Gregory the Great, the eighth-century historian Bede, Leo Tolstoy, Native American leader Black Elk, Admiral Richard Byrd, Ernest Hemingway, and Carl Jung, to name only a few (not to mention the plethora of Eastern accounts such as the Tibetan Book of the Dead), long before Moody published his research. Indeed, even academic studies of near-death experiences were known before Moody's work. A Swiss geologist, Albert von St. Gallen Heim, published a study in 1892 of the near-death experiences of Alpine climbers who had nearly fatal falls ("Notizen über den Tod durch Absturz," or "Remarks on Fatal Falls"; see Basford), and Richard Kalish published "Experiences of People Reprieved from Death" in 1969, in which he examined 127 near-death accounts. Nevertheless, Raymond Moody's *Life after Life* was the first examination of near-death experiences to thoroughly lay out a common sequence of experiences among those who "died," and it was the first such work to be read by millions of people. A study of the history of near-death literature itself tells the story: about seventy-five articles (and a few books) about near-death experiences were published in the West in the many centuries preceding Moody's work, and well over 1,000 studies have been completed in the few decades since. Therefore, any account of the modern near-death experience movement must pay careful attention to the seminal work *Life after Life.*

Moody's first book was important because it presented a carefully ordered sequence of events in the near-death experience. Although Moody admits that no one account includes every single element of his composite sequence, most NDEs appear to include the majority of events he describes. Briefly, Moody's sequence of events includes the following:

1. Noting ineffability of the NDE: it cannot adequately be put into words
2. Hearing the news (from doctors, bystanders, etc.) that one is dead
3. Experiencing peace and quiet
4. Hearing a buzzing or ringing noise
5. Passing through a long, dark tunnel
6. Finding oneself out of one's body
7. Being greeted by other beings, including relatives and friends who have died previously
8. Encountering a tremendous light, which appears to be a being
9. Experiencing a rapid but detailed review of one's life
10. Approaching a border or limit (water, a mist, a door, a field)
11. Coming back into the body and being resuscitated

In his later work, *Reflections on Life after Life,* Moody added a few more elements to this sequence: experiencing a "vision of knowledge" (a complete understanding of past, present, and future), seeing cities of light, encountering bewildered spirits, and witnessing "supernatural rescues" of people who died prematurely. Signi-

ficantly, Moody found no "hellish" near-death experiences (later researchers would beg to differ), and Moody spent some time fending off criticisms that NDEs were merely chemical reactions in a dying brain, hallucinations, or the result of drugs administered for treatment (the latter view would become a source of controversy in years to come).

One of the most interesting things about Moody's revolutionary publication was the public reaction to it. Many representatives of Christianity, especially those of fundamentalist persuasion but also mainstream clergy, initially reacted to reports of near-death experiences with hostility. Christian authors such as John Weldon, Mark Albrecht, and Father Albert Moraczewski tended to emphasize the fact that accounts of NDEs did not appear to support the details of the afterlife that Christian Scriptures teach, including afterlife judgment and resurrection, and noted that NDEs appeared to be leading people into embracing New Age and Eastern forms of spirituality rather than traditional organized religion. A number of Christian authors deemed that near-death experiences were neither biological reactions to dying nor hallucinations but actually destructive visions sent by demonic forces to turn people away from the church. Meanwhile, medical professionals tended to dismiss the NDE as biochemical in origin and irrelevant, and psychoanalytic commentary focused on the "denial of death" and wish-fulfillment aspects of the near-death encounters. As a result of the widespread and widely varying public reaction, hundreds of articles and full-length studies were produced, including many books by people who claimed to have had NDEs themselves. Within a decade of publication of Moody's *Life after Life,* the International Association for Near-Death Studies was founded, with its own quarterly publication, the *Journal of Near-Death Studies.*

Important advances have been made in studying the near-death experience since the 1970s. One of the most powerful discoveries was that not all NDEs were positive, world-affirming, "heavenly" visions. Rather, as P. M. H. Atwater (1992) has pointed out, "hellish" near-death experiences are far more common than previously known. These include encountering lifeless or threatening apparitions; barren or ugly expanses; threats, screams, or silence; feelings of danger and the possibility of torture; and temperature extremes, often extreme cold. However, in Atwater's experience, "hellish" or terrifying near-death experiences are never reported by children, suggesting that what is currently known about NDEs is but the tip of a very large and mysterious iceberg. What may be more definitively known, according to Atwater (1996), are the psychological and physiological aftereffects of experiencing a near-death event, including an increased capacity for unconditional love, a new acceptance of differences among people, less regard for time and schedules, psychic ability, a belief in immortality, less reliance on logic and rationality, heightened sensitivity, reduced stress, and lowered blood pressure.

It is difficult to know how to interpret the significance of near-death experiences. Are they definitive proof of life after death? Few researchers, even the boldest, would go this far. Are NDEs merely daydreams of an oxygen-starved brain? Although this view is popular among medical researchers, it does not seem to do justice to the complex content of the near-death experience or explain why many people have reported near-death experiences (or out-of-body experiences) even when there was no physical trauma or lack of oxygen. Hostility toward NDE research from religious groups is curious when one considers that every major religion teaches that the soul survives death. Furthermore, every major religion teaches that ethical behavior, love toward other beings, and the acquisition of spiritual knowledge on this plane of existence are extremely important in determining one's future state. The current understanding of NDEs does not appear to support in full the specific teachings of any one religion, but it does appear to support them all in a broad sense.

Clearly, the near-death experience suggests that there is more to human consciousness than previously suspected. Although Moody was not able to include cross-cultural samples in his work, much research since that time has done so, demonstrating that very similar experience is had by people all over the world. Further, Melvin Morse and P. Perry demonstrated that even small children report much the same near-death experiences as adults, suggesting that cultural conditioning would seem to play little role in determining the events encountered near death. It is premature to determine that near-death experiences actually reveal what it will be like to die, since none of those reporting NDEs were dead for long; in one sense none of them truly died. As the Tibetan master Sogyal Rinpoche states in *The Tibetan Book of Living and Dying* (pp. 331–332), it is also premature "to try to link the near-death experience too precisely with the [Tibetan] bardo descriptions, because the person who has survived the near-death experience has only been—literally, 'near death.'" Thus, although it is difficult to accept near-death experiences as literal descriptions of exactly what will happen to us when we die, they are powerfully suggestive that the mind may be separate from the body and that some kind of conscious experience may carry on after bodily death, probably in radically different fashion from the consciousness experienced while "alive."

See also BARDO; BOOK OF THE CRAFT OF DYING; BOOK OF THE DEAD, EGYPTIAN; BOOK OF THE DEAD, TIBETAN; SOUL.

References

Atwater, P. M. H. *Coming Back: The After-Effects of the Near-Death Experience.* New York: Dodd, Mead, 1988.

———. "Is There a Hell? Surprising Observations about the Near-Death Experience." *Journal of Near-Death Studies* 10, no. 3 (Spring 1992).

———. "What Is Not Being Said about the Near-Death Experience." In *The Near-Death Experience: A Reader*, ed. Lee W. Bailey and Jenny Yates. New York: Routledge: 1996.

Bailey, Lee W., and Jenny Yates, eds.. *The Near-Death Experience: A Reader.* New York: Routledge, 1996.

Basford, Terry K. *Near-Death Experiences: An Annotated Bibliography.* New York: Garland Publishing. 1990.

Black Elk, with John G. Neihardt. *Black Elk Speaks.* Lincoln: University of Nebraska, 1972.

Greyson, B., and N. E. Bush. "Distressing Near-Death Experiences." *Psychiatry* 55 (1992).

Kalish, Richard A. "Experiences of People Reprieved from Death." In *Death and Bereavement,* ed. Austin H. Kutscher. Springfield, IL: Charles C. Thomas, 1969.

Kastenbaum, Robert, ed. *Between Life and Death.* New York: Springer Publishing, 1979.

Kellehear, Allan. *Experiences near Death: Beyond Medicine and Religion.* New York: Oxford University Press, 1996.

Moody, Raymond A., Jr. *Life after Life.* New York: Bantam, 1975.

Morse, M., and P. Perry. *Closer to the Light: Learning from the Near-Death Experiences of Children.* New York: Villard, 1990.

Pace, James C., and Deborah L. Drumm. "The Phantom Leaf Effect and Its Implications for Near-Death and Out-of-Body Experiences." *Journal of Near-Death Studies* 10, no. 4 (Summer 1992).

Ring, Kenneth. *Life at Death: A Scientific Investigation of the Near-Death Experience.* New York: Coward, McCann and Geoghegan, 1980.

Rinpoche, Sogyal. *The Tibetan Book of Living and Dying,* ed. Patrick Gaffney and Andrew Harvey. San Francisco: Harper San Francisco, 1992.

NECROMANCY

Necromancy is the use of the dead (or items relating to the dead) in magical rituals. Such use is not always destructive in intent: in many times and places it has been believed that the touch of a dead person heals sickness or brings good luck (although without ritual protection, contact with the dead is almost universally polluting). Sometimes the dead are also thought to bestow knowledge, longevity, political success, or magical powers on the beneficiary.

Clearly, necromancy has a very long history, for it is specifically prohibited in the Bible. Deuteronomy 18:9–13 reads:

When you come into the land which the Lord your God is giving you, do not learn to imitate the abominable customs of those other nations. Let no one be found among you who makes his son or daughter pass through fire, no augur or soothsayer or diviner or sorcerer, no one who casts spells or traffics with ghosts and spirits, and no necromancer. Those who do these things are abominable to the Lord, and it is because of these abominable practices that the Lord your God is driving them out before you.

Nevertheless, much against the will of Jahweh, apparently, many Israelites did call up the "shades" from Sheol and consult them in times of crisis. We find Saul consulting the dead Samuel via the witch of Endor (1 Samuel 28:8–20), and the text places no reprimand on him. In fact, the dead Samuel is called one of the elohim (gods), not rephā'im (the dead). Isaiah twice mentions the noises ghosts make when consulted (8:19, 29:4) though the text does not condone their visitations.

Another ancient type of necromancy popular in Europe was the use of "mummy powder." During Roman times, the population was fascinated by the funerary rites of the Egyptians, who were considered ancient and mysterious even then. It is not clear how the belief originated, but Romans and, after them, European Christians believed that the powder made from mummified corpses would cure illness when swallowed. A great demand for this "mummy powder" developed, and every available Egyptian tomb was ransacked and its inhabitant ground down to powder. Of course, the supply of mummies was extremely limited compared to the demand, so entrepreneurs readily produced fake mummy powder, which was "real" in the sense that it was made from the dead. The local corpses of beggars and criminals were much easier and cheaper to obtain than mummies from Egypt!

The human head has been an object of necromancy in several cultures. The ancient Celts were famous for placing the heads of deceased warriors in rows on hillsides facing the direction from which enemies might arise: the power of the Celtic heroes continued even in death, warding off danger and protecting the living. The Jibaros of South America are well-known for their head-hunting and head-shrinking techniques. Because they believe that the soul resides in the head, capturing, shrinking, and wearing the head of an enemy allows them to acquire his or her spiritual power and add it to their own. Ralph Karsten, an early twentieth-century explorer, was an eyewitness to Jibaro practice, and reported on the shrinking process in great detail, at the end of which,

By this treatment the Jibaros are able to gradually reduce the head to such an extent that it is not larger than an orange, or about one-fourth of its normal size, becoming at the same time completely hard and dry. Through both lips, shrunk in proportion to the rest of the head, three small chonta pins, about 5 centimeters in length and painted red with roucu, are passed parallel with each other, and round these pins a fine cotton string, which is also painted red, is wound. . . . Lastly, the whole trophy, even the face, is dyed black with charcoal. (cited in Iserson, p. 384)

Besides hunting, ritual human sacrifice is another way for the living to acquire the virility or strength of the dead or dying. Many ancient cultures (e.g., Central Asian, Egyptian, Chinese, Mesopotamian, Celtic, Greek, Scandinavian, Central American, African, etc.) buried the servants, wives, children, and even pets of an important person when he died so that they could accompany the deceased on his journey to the next life and continue in their supporting roles. The Aztecs of Central America organized much of their religion around human sacrifice, and estimates suggest that up to 1 percent of their population (a total of 250,000 victims in the fifteenth century) was sacrificed annually. Typically, captives were taken atop a step pyramid temple structure, their hearts ("the precious eagle-cactus fruit") were torn out (and sometimes eaten), and the bodies were rolled down the sides of the temple to be dismembered and eaten, primarily by the warriors. Such ritual cannibalism not only satisfied the gods and caused the rain to fall, but also supplemented a protein-deficient diet. In Tibetan Buddhism there are no reports of cannibalism or ritual murder, but as part of the meditation on death (chöd), which allows practitioners to break free of attachment to life, human thigh bones are used as musical instruments and skulls as ritual cups. The human parts for these ritual implements are gathered from abandoned corpses or from local spots for "sky burial" where corpses were "buried" by being exposed to the elements. In parts of Africa today, authorities battle surviving cults that prey upon young children, seeking to kill them and sell their parts as fetishes and charms.

In medieval Europe, necromantic beliefs flourished among rich and poor alike, despite the intense persecution of those suspected of witchcraft and diablerie. The cult of the relics of saints is itself a kind of necromancy, in that the population believed in the magic powers of the body parts of the dead, even dividing the bodies of famous saints up among several competing churches and placing these relics on display. Relics were so sought-after that quite a problem developed with churches attempting to steal each others' relics to increase their own reputations (Geary). In England it was believed that touching a still-warm corpse cured diseases, and public executions were often well-attended for that reason. In what has to be one of the most gruesome accounts of European necromancy, the Hungarian Countess Elisabeth de Báthory was famous in the early 1600s for acquiring virgins. The countess believed that the blood of virgins was a potion of youth and bathed each

SAUL AND THE WITCH OF ENDOR

יהוה

Saul perceived that it was Samuel, & he
stooped with his face to the ground, &
bowed himself.
1 Samuel. ch. 28. v. 14.

Pub. by Hogg & Co. Paternoster row.

Saul uses the Witch of Endor to communicate with dead Samuel. She brings Samuel "out of the earth" (necromancy) after Saul has promised to take no action against her as a witch, 1804. Courtesy of Anne Ronan Picture Library.

morning in the blood of a virgin that she had killed. R. Tannahill reports that the countess went through at least 650 such virgins before she was caught.

See also CHÖD; MUMMIFICATION; REPHĀ'IM; SHEOL; VAMPIRE.

References

Edou, Jérôme. *Machig Labdrön and the Foundations of Chöd.* Ithaca, NY: Snow Lion, 1996.

Geary, Patrick J. *Furta Sacra: Thefts of Relics in the Central Middle Ages.* Princeton: Princeton University Press, 1978.

Hamilton-Paterson, James, and Carol Andrews. *Mummies: Death and Life in Ancient Egypt.* London: William Collins Sons, 1978.

Heidel, Alexander. *The Gilgamesh Epic and Old Testament Parallels.* Chicago: University of Chicago Press, 1946.

Iserson, Kenneth V. *Death to Dust: What Happens to Dead Bodies?* Tucson, AZ: Galen Press, 1994.

Sanday, Peggy. *Divine Hunger: Cannibalism as a Cultural System.* Cambridge: Cambridge University Press, 1986.

Tannahill, R. *Flesh and Blood: A History of the Cannibal Complex.* New York: Stein and Day, 1975.

NETHERWORLDS, CHINESE

The evolution of afterlife beliefs in China is a long and fascinating process, involving organized religious speculation from Taoist and Buddhist sources as well as more ambiguous traditions arising through shamanic experience and localized cults. Because of the scarcity of evidence, especially in ancient times, many of the important details of this history are presently unknown, but some general outlines can be drawn.

The earliest burial sites in China for which we have relatively sound dating (Shang Period, c. 1700 to c. 1100 B.C.E.) contain ritual bronze vessels placed in the grave pits, with inscriptions demonstrating filial piety and asking boons of deceased ancestors. From the late Shang Period a ritual bronze bucket has been excavated, with an inscription telling of a leader who has been rewarded by the state for good service (Sommer, p. 15):

> Tzu gloriously presented Feng with two strings of cowrie shells and said, "The cowries are to recognize your accumulated merit." Feng used them to make a sacrificial vessel for Mother Hsin. This was in the twelfth month, when Tzu said, "I command you to go to the Jen region."

Here, the official named Feng uses his good fortune to thank his female ancestor and make an offering for her. There are also scattered references from this early period indicating that descendents of the imperial line could expect after death to ascend and dwell on the left and right of Ti, the Lord of the Heavens, accompanied by servants sacrificed for the occasion. Thus it seems that deceased rulers had a happy and comfortable afterlife. What exactly the state of the common dead might have been in this period and where (if anywhere) they dwelled are a mystery.

By the later part of the Chou Dynasty (1122–256 B.C.E.), some people began to believe that many of the dead went underground. An inscription on a tripod states that its owner, the nobleman Ai-ch'eng-shu, was to "die underneath the earth to serve prince Kang-kung." This inscription would suggest, as Mu-chou Poo points out, that here both the lesser and higher nobles were thought to go under the Earth after death. Whether this was the general expectation is uncertain. Not long after, in the Warring States period of China (403 to 221 B.C.E.), "Yellow Springs" is spoken of as the resting place of the deceased, although it is not clear whether this was a poetic metaphor for the grave or an actual realm of the dead. In this period references were also made to a "Dark City" underground ruled by a monstrous Governor of the Earth (T'u-po or T'u-pai), whose hideous appearance was supposed to scare people off. According to the *Ch'u {Kingdom} Anthology* (Thompson, trans., p. 32) no matter what direction the soul goes after death, horrors await (for everyone—there is no hint of ethical judgment yet). "Down" is particularly bad:

Go not down to the Land of Darkness (*yu-tu*),
Where the earth God lies, nine-coiled,
With dreadful horns on his forehead
And a great humped back and bloody thumbs,
pursuing men, swift-footed:
Three eyes he has in his tiger's head,
and his body is like a bull's.

Better documentation from the Han Dynasty (206 B.C.E. to 220 C.E.) makes us aware of an increasingly defined and bureaucratic Underworld, meaning a realm of the dead below the Earth that was compartmentalized and ruled by various levels of infernal magistrates. The great mountain, T'ai Shan, in present-day Shandong, was by the later Han period (c. 200 C.E.) considered both a deity and the primary residence of the dead. According to Edouard Chavannes (quoted in Thompson, p. 34),

T'ai Shan . . . is also called younger brother of Heaven; this means that he is the younger brother of the celestial Emperor; he presides over summoning the souls of men; he is the East, [principle] of existence for all beings; this is why he decides upon the length or brevity of the life of men.

Here, we see that the Lord T'ai Shan is a powerful relative of the deity who rules heaven—not only does T'ai Shan receive the dead into his kingdom, but from the very beginning he determines the length of each human's life. Far more bureaucratic, however, was a Taoist cult's vision of the afterlife netherworld and its effect on human beings, according to Michel Strickmann:

[Human] illness was . . . a sentence pronounced by the *San Kuan* (Three Officials), judges and custodians of the dead. The sentence was carried out by the spectral hordes of the Six Heavens (*Liu T'ien*), a posthumous dwelling place of all unhallowed mortals. Against such judicial severity, only formal appeal to higher authority might avail. Using the rising flame and smoke of the incense burner in the center of the oratory to transmit the . . . the libationer [priest] submitted petitions to the appropriate bureau of the three Taoist heavens. The Taoist canon contains long lists of the "officials and generals," each specializing in a different sort of complaint, who would respectively pronounce on the appeal and marshal the celestial forces against the offending demons.

For the Taoists, the realm of the dead was thus a complex of several ideas, including "sin," illness, and supernatural help—influenced more and more over the years by growing Buddhist incursions into China (see also THE SIX HEAVENS).

By the T'ang Dynasty (618–907 C.E.) Buddhist ideas on karma (the consequences in future lives of good and evil actions committed during this life) had permeated Chinese consciousness so thoroughly that nearly every Chinese person expected to face judgment in purgatory in the afterlife. Before the dead could reach the "Six Heavens" of Mount Lo-feng or any other "dwelling" in the afterlife, however, they had to pass through the extremely important trials of the "Earth-prisons" (ti-yü). These dark and frightening places of judgment were variously located under the ocean, under rivers (especially China's two major river systems, the Yellow and the Yangtze), under Mount T'ai-shan (mentioned previously), and of course, in the vast realm of the Ten Kings under the Earth itself. For a period of forty-nine days (sometimes up to three years), the dead were shuttled from official to official, making bribes and standing trials, before they were assigned to an afterlife destination in one of the hells, released into a heaven, or reborn in a human or other form on earth. Due to this Buddhist emphasis on purgatory and judgment, indigenous Chinese practices relating to offerings for the dead took on even more urgency, and funerary cults blossomed practically into full-fledged religions (see ANCESTOR VENERATION; FESTIVAL OF GHOSTS, CHINA; and SOUL TABLET.)

The astounding variety of Chinese afterlife beliefs is only hinted at in this entry. Competing Buddhist sects, along with several different Taoist traditions, developed many sets of heavens, purgatories, and Pure Lands led by various saints and deities. This, combined with a pursuit of spiritual or physical immortality and elaborate Confucian, Buddhist, and Taoist rites for ancestor worship, makes Chinese beliefs regarding the netherworld probably the most diverse and complex in the world.

See also ANCESTOR VENERATION; CHING-T'U; FESTIVAL OF GHOSTS (CHINA); FUNERARY CUSTOMS, CHINESE; PURE LAND; THE SIX HEAVENS; SOUL, BUDDHIST; SOUL, CHINESE; SOUL TABLET; TEN KINGS OF HELL; TI-TSANG; YELLOW SPRINGS; YEN-LO WANG.

References
Chan, Wing-tsit, ed. and trans. *A Source Book in Chinese Philosophy*. Princeton: Princeton University Press, 1963.
Chavannes, Edouard. *Le T'ai Chan*. Paris, 1910.
Loewe, Michael. *Ways to Paradise: The Chinese Quest for Immortality*. London: Allen and Unwin, 1979.
Poo, Mu-chou. *In Search of Personal Welfare: A View of Ancient Chinese Religion*. New York: SUNY Press, 1998.
Sommer, Deborah, ed. *Chinese Religion: An Anthology of Sources*. New York: Oxford University Press, 1995.
Strickmann, Michel. "Taoism, History of." *Encyclopaedia Britannica*. Vol. 3. Chicago: Encyclopaedia Britannica, 1974.

Teiser, Stephen F. *The Ghost Festival in Medieval China*. Princeton: Princeton University Press, 1988.

Thompson, Laurence G. "On the Prehistory of Hell in China." *Journal of Chinese Religions*, no. 17 (Fall 1989).

NIFLHEIM (NIFLHEIMR, NIFLHEL)

Literally meaning "the misty Underworld" of Norse mythology, Niflheim existed before the Earth or any of the other nine worlds were formed, according to the tale laid out by Scandinavian writer Snorri Sturluson (c. 1220 C.E.). It was a dark world and brutally cold, but nearby was the flaming hot world of Muspell. From a well in Niflheim, called *Hvergelmir* (Resounding Kettle), sprang eleven rivers. They flowed out of Niflheim and froze, piling up ice and rime to an incredible extent in the Ginnungagap (the Deep). But sparks from the hot world of Muspell mixed with the piles of ice and created a slushy mixture. From this material, the giant Ymir emerged. When the first gods were born later from a cosmic cow, they killed Ymir and fashioned the present universe.

Niflheim is thus a primordial plane of undeveloped matter, having much in common with other Indo-European planes of cosmic matter like the Prakriti of ancient Indian philosophy and the Hyle of the Greeks. After Odin and his friends created the nine worlds, Niflheim remained below them all and became known as the realm of permanent death, deeper and darker even than Hel. It was said to be the realm where the wicked went after dying out of Hel (*Vafthrúdnismál*, section 43, quoted in Davidson), but it had its positive uses in the mythology as well. The text *Baldrs Draumr* tells how Odin's son Balder had evil, foreboding dreams. Odin mounted his horse Sleipnir and rode to the lowest world, Niflheim, to inquire of a dead seeress the meaning of the dreams and what the future held. There the seeress gave him the answers to all of his questions about how the world was formed and how it would end in Ragnarök.

See also HEL; ODIN; RAGNARÖK.

References

Davidson, H. R. Ellis. *Gods and Myths of Northern Europe*. New York: Penguin, 1964, 1977.

Guerber, Hélène Adeline. *Myths of the Norsemen from the Eddas and Sagas*. New York: Dover Publications, 1992.

Sturluson, Snorri. *Edda*. Trans. Anthony Faulkes. London: Dent, 1987.

Titchenell, Elsa-Brita. *The Masks of Odin*. Pasadena: Theosophical University Press, 1985.

Turville-Petre, E. O. G. *Myth and Religion of the North: The Religion of Ancient Scandinavia*. Westport, CT: Greenwood. 1964.

NIRMĀṆAKĀYA

Nirmāṇakāya is a Sanskrit term in Mahāyāna Buddhism indicating an enlightened being who after death chooses not to accept the final rest of nirvāṇa—where one is utterly inaccessible to unenlightened beings—but to remain on Earth serving all beings in an active role. The compound word *nirmāṇa-kāya* literally means "manifestation" (nirmāṇa) "body" (kāya), which is thought to be a subtle or spiritual body that an enlightened being consciously creates after death. It is considered the highest perfection, the most subtle form of existence outside absolute *nirvāṇa*, and it is the only way in which a being may be in perfect and constant contact with the absolute truth, or Dharmakāya.

According to Mahāyāna Buddhism, enlightened beings are totally free from samsāra (the tiresome round of rebirth and suffering) and need not reappear on Earth any more. They have dissolved all karmic ties and have nothing to gain personally from any more reincarnations on Earth. But these beings are said to be able to choose to remain on Earth in order to continue to perform service, which may be done in several ways. An enlightened being may deliberately reincarnate in a human body in the ordinary way in order to bring the Buddhist teachings to humans, but this is accompanied by all the limitations of bodily life, including eventual death. The nirmāṇakāya, or magical manifestation body, however, being composed of the essence of the elements and not the gross elements of the physical body, is perfect and beyond decay and death, thus serving as a permanent vehicle for service. However, this body is ordinarily invisible to mortals except on rare occasions, so nirmāṇakāyas, like Christian intercessor saints, are thought to be visible only to the spiritually advanced, even though they strive to serve all in a general way.

References

Govinda, Anagarika. *Foundations of Tibetan Mysticism*. York Beach, ME: Samuel Weiser, 1991.

Norbu, Namkhai. *The Crystal and the Way of Light*. Ed. John Shane. New York: Arkana, 1993.

NIRVĀṆA (PALI: NIBBĀNA)

Of all words used by Indian philosophers, *nirvāṇa* is the most difficult to define. It is described both as an eternal, blissful life beyond all suffering and as a transcendental state utterly beyond thought or description, an ineffable absolute. *Nirvāṇa* is said to be experienced only when a person has eliminated all selfishness, worldliness, and attachment to objects. The word itself comes from the Sanskrit root *nir* plus *vā*, meaning "to blow out, to be extinguished" and referring to human passions, desires, and attachments. When these "burning" passions are "blown out," then the grace and bliss of nirvāṇa is won. Very seldom are positive descriptions made of nirvāṇa. Few try to say what it is; rather, most descriptions say what it is not: the absence of desire, craving,

Hindu Nirvāṇa

Learn from me [Krishna] in brief, in what manner the man who has reached perfection attains to the Supreme Spirit, which is the end, the aim, and the highest condition of spiritual knowledge.

Embued with pure discrimination, restraining himself with resolution, having rejected the charms of sound and other objects of the senses, and casting off attachment and dislike; dwelling in secluded places, eating little, with speech, body and mind controlled, engaging in constant meditation and unwaveringly fixed in dispassion; abandoning egotism, arrogance, violence, vanity, desire, anger, pride, and possession, with calmness ever present, a man is fitted to be the Supreme Being. And having thus attained to the Supreme, he is serene, sorrowing no more, and no more desiring, but alike towards all creatures he attains to supreme devotion to me. By this devotion to me he knows fundamentally who and what I am and having thus discovered me he enters into me without any intermediate condition [after death].

From The Bhagavad-Gītā, chap. 18,
translation by Judge (1986).

---

suffering, and pain; the absence of loneliness and separation from god or the infinite; it is not temporary, not incomplete, not partial. It is all-encompassing immortality, but it is also the end of separate, personal existence.

Although some scholars of Hindu and Buddhist thought have made nirvāṇa a late development in Indian philosophy, it seems clear that even the earliest Indian Scriptures, the Vedas, refer to a transcendent state like nirvāṇa. They describe many spiritual sages (called *muni*) experiencing ecstatic bliss (e.g., Rig Veda X.136) and ascetics practicing penances and becoming "men-gods," like the character named Ekavrātya (Atharva Veda XV.1). Additionally, these early texts describe two carefully distinguished afterdeath paths. One is the path of the ancestors (pitriyāna), by which most of the dead enjoy the heaven of the god Yama. The other is the path of the gods (deva-yāna), which is a higher path for the elect only and is associated with the sun and immortality. Later commentaries on these early texts make it clear that the souls who go to the heaven of the ancestors (pitriyāna) eventually reincarnate and return to Earth; but others, possessing supreme spiritual knowledge, go to dwell with the immortal gods and remain out of incarnation permanently—one definition of nirvāṇa:

Now whether people perform funeral ceremonies [shrāddha] for him or not, he goes to light . . . [traveling] from the sun to the moon, from the moon to lightning. There is a person who is not human that leads him to Brahman [the Absolute]. This is the path of the Devas [gods], the path that leads to Brahman. Those who proceed on that path do not return to the life of man, yes, they do not return. (Chāndogya Upanishad IV.15.5–6; trans. Taylor)

Thus in Hinduism and later in the younger religion of Buddhism, nirvāṇa is understood as a kind of "superdeath." In Indian thought all things continually die and are reborn, from plants and animals to humans, worlds, and galaxies. This whirling from life to death to life again is called saṃsāra and is seen as very unpleasant, the basis for continual attachment and consequent suffering. Nirvāṇa is the "death" of death and rebirth and thus the ultimate goal of Hindus—absolute freedom, or moksha. Hindus tend to see this freedom from death and rebirth as a merging of the personal self (i.e., the spiritual practitioner) with the cosmic self (i.e., God), as the reunion of the dewdrop with the ocean. Although Buddhists will usually speak of nirvāṇa in somewhat different, more impersonal terms, for Hindus the path to perfection and nirvāṇa is usually theistic and understood as the return of an individual soul to the universal Godhead.

Modern Hinduism has developed many techniques for the spiritual practitioner to merge with the divine and thus achieve nirvāṇa. Most of these systems of effort may be called *yoga,* although there is a great variety among them, ranging from body postures (hatha yoga) thought to free the mind from attachment, to following a path of righteous action (karma yoga), to meditation and concentration on the infinite (rāja yoga), to the pursuit of mystical knowledge (jñāna yoga). There are esoteric practices of ecstatic contemplation called *tantra,* there is the control of breath (prānayama), the awakening of mystical energies (for example, siddha yoga and kundalini yoga), and there is the path of pure faith in a supreme being (bhakti yoga). Hinduism has cast its net very wide, and a huge diversity of schools, spiritual masters (gurus), texts, and ascetic practices promise to lead the student to absolute freedom, which is nirvāṇa. However, this perfection is not the task of a lifetime or even several lifetimes but the unremitting spiritual striving of hundreds, even thousands of human rebirths before the individual is released from suffering, birth, and death. As the god Krishna says in the classic Hindu Scripture, the Bhagavad-Gītā, "Among thousands of mortals a single one perhaps strives for perfection, and among those so striving perhaps a single one knows me as I am"

The death of Buddha. Courtesy of Anne Ronan Picture Library.

(Judge, trans., p. 53). Clearly, the attainment of the ultimate goal is rare in human life and the fruit of almost endless labor.

Buddhism holds a similar view regarding the path to nirvāṇa but a slightly different conception of what the final result may be. Like practitioners of Hindu yoga systems, the founder of Buddhism, Gautama Shakyamuni, taught that endless birth, death, and rebirth were a nightmare of insecurity and suffering and that the ultimate goal was to transcend this samsāra. This transcendence is often referred to as enlightenment, and the Buddha is not a god but an example of a perfectly enlightened human being. The Buddha's philosophy is traditionally summed up in what are called the Four Noble Truths:

1. Life is suffering. Samsāric existence is inextricably bound up with unhappiness, loss, and death.
2. The cause of this suffering is human craving after the goods and experiences of mortal life.
3. There is an end to this craving that produces suffering, called *nirvāṇa*.
4. There is a spiritual path or system of effort that leads to this ultimate goal.

The spiritual path taught by Buddhism is essentially similar to several yoga systems in Hinduism, with a few crucial distinctions. Hinduism teaches an unchanging essence to each individual called *ātman*; it is this mysterious entity that is the true immortal self and that transmigrates from life to life, rebirth to rebirth. But Buddhism teaches a doctrine called *anātman,* or "no-self." One of the primary causes of suffering, according to Buddhism, is grasping after permanence when none can be had—resulting inevitably in suffering as one's hopes are frustrated time and again. Buddhists see the doctrine of an "unchanging self" as quite dangerous, leading a person to imagine that they truly "exist" and will always exist. Rather, the outer personality and even the inner nature of a person are constantly changing along with everything else in the universe: nothing has an essential, unchanging nature. Accepting this fact, according to Buddhist teaching, leads to letting go of false ideas, including a "self," which promotes tranquility and acceptance of the way of the universe. The difficulty is that Buddhism likewise teaches the twin doctrines of reincarnation and karma—but if there is no essential nature to a human being, no permanent self (ātman), what is reborn, what receives its karma from past actions, and most important of all, who or what is it that achieves enlightenment in nirvāṇa after so many lifetimes of effort?

The last question is recognized as being of the utmost importance by Buddhists, for nirvāṇa is the entire reason for being in Buddhist spirituality. But different schools of Buddhism have come up with quite diverse teachings regarding the nature of nirvāṇa. Frustrated by the diversity of views, Western scholars have sought out the very earliest Buddhist texts to provide a definitive answer, for according to Western thinking, the earliest teaching is closer to the "source" and therefore the most authoritative. But what the "original" Buddhists believed is not clear because the early texts themselves admit to different interpretations. The Buddha is known to have varied the phrasing of his teaching for different audiences, and he could also be elusive when it served him. Once when a student asked the Buddha whether a "perfected one" exists after death, the Buddha remained silent; he later told one of his closest disciples, Ānanda, that any answer he could have given would have further confused the poor student and would have led to false views. At another time, the Buddha taught a student named Vipasyin about the path to perfection. He concluded by saying "Finally, Vipasyin, the completely perfect Buddha, after having performed the totality of obligations of a Buddha, was like a fire of which the fuel is consumed, entirely annihilated in the element of *nirvāṇa* in which nothing remains of that which constitutes existence."

Here, nirvāṇa sounds like absolute annihilation, and the spiritual practitioner who achieves enlightenment simply ceases to exist (although "existence" itself is a suspect term). Several Buddhist schools and many Western scholars tend toward this view. Southern Buddhist tradition (e.g., Abhidharma) and a widespread philosophical tradition in northern (Mahāyāna) Buddhism called *Mādhyamika* teach of nirvāṇa in purely negative terms. Enlightenment is the total dying away of all aspects of human existence (skandhas) "without remainder."

However, on another occasion, the Buddha instructed his disciples not to think of nirvāṇa as annihilation. Although it is true that all temporary things must eventually fall apart, there is something beyond what is temporary and can be destroyed (Udāna 2.98, trans. Taylor):

> There is, O monks, something not born, something not manifested, not created, not composite; because, if there were not something which is not born, not manifested, not created, not composite, there would not be any salvation for that which is born, which is manifested, created, composite.
>
> But since, O monks, there is something not born, therefore there is taught salvation from what is born, from what is manifested, created, and composite.

Despite avoiding any substantial description of nirvāṇa, the Buddha clearly distinguishes between the ephemeral and the absolute, and it is because of the absolute that what is ephemeral (like the human being) may be saved. Some Western scholars (Max Müller, Caroline Rhys-Davids, LaVallée Poussin) have held this view that nirvāṇa in Buddhism is some kind of *impersonal* but eternal life of bliss. A late Indian school of Buddhism called *Yogācāra* and most of Tibetan Buddhist tradition tend to emphasize the positive nature of nirvāṇa and do not shy away from words like "absolute," "essential," and "eternal." For instance, a Tibetan meditation verse from the text *The Vast Clear Liberation Path* teaches:

> I and the infinite multitude of sentient beings
> Are the Absolute [Buddha] from the beginning.
> Realizing this as our essential identity,
> Let us generate this mind of Supreme
>   Enlightenment!

Quite different from the negative description of nirvāṇa as the absence of suffering and the end of existence, the Yogācāra and Tibetan descriptions announce a radical new existence for the enlightened being:

possessed of superhuman powers and omniscient knowledge, the person who achieves nirvāṇa becomes in turn a Buddha and seeks to lead others on the path. Yet both the negative and the positive views of nirvāṇa trace their origins to teachings of the historical Buddha himself and not merely later tradition.

Does the Buddha contradict himself when speaking of nirvāṇa, or is he unsure of the nature of nirvāṇa himself? These are not the only possibilities. Buddhist traditions in India (and by all accounts the Buddha himself) have shied away from theoretical constructions and verbal descriptions; they have tended to emphasize spiritual practice and practical experience. It seems quite likely that the ultimate human experience of salvation, or nirvāṇa, in Buddhist thought is simply inexpressible. One neither "exists" nor does not exist after attaining nirvāṇa, simply because such a state is so beyond human categories and thought that the term "existence" no longer applies or carries any meaning. It seems certain that Buddhists (or Hindus for that matter) would not deliberately spend their lives pursuing utter annihilation, particularly when the path to nirvāṇa consists of kindness, charity, and other life-affirming virtues. But neither can it be said exactly what the end result of all this striving will be. The casual inquirer may never know, but the spiritual practitioner seeks to *experience* it firsthand.

See also ĀTMAN; NIRMĀṆAKĀYA; PURE LAND; REINCARNATION, EASTERN; SUKHĀVATĪ.

References

Becker, Carl B. *Breaking the Circle: Death and the Afterlife in Buddhism.* Carbondale: Southern Illinois University Press, 1993.

Eliade, Mircea. *Yoga: Immortality and Freedom.* New York: Pantheon, 1958.

Judge, William Quan, trans. *Bhagavad-Gita.* Los Angeles: Theosophy Company, 1986.

Keith, A. B. "The Doctrine of the Buddha." *Bulletin of the School of Oriental Studies* 6 (1930–1932).

McDermott, James P. "Nibbāna as a Reward for Kamma." *Journal of the American Oriental Society* 93, no. 3 (1973).

Obermiller, Eugéne. *Nirvāna in Tibetan Buddhism.* Ed. Harcharan Singh Sobti. Delhi: Classics India Publications, 1988.

Palden, Kunzang, trans. *Vast Clear Liberation Path: A Recitation Text of the Foundation Practices.* San Francisco: Enlightened Heart Meditation Center, 1996.

Shukla, Karunesh, ed. *Nature of Bondage and Liberation in Buddhist Systems.* Gorakhpur, India: Nagarjuna Buddhist Foundation, 1988.

Sobti, Harcharan Singh. *Nibbāna in Early Buddhism.* Delhi: Eastern Book Linkers, 1985.

Stcherbatsky, Th. *The Central Conception of Buddhism.* 1922. Reprint, Delhi: Motilal Banarsidass, 1994.

Welbon, Guy Richard. *The Buddhist Nirvāna and Its Western Interpreters.* Chicago: University of Chicago Press, 1968.

NORNS

Like the Greek Moirai, the Norns were the three sisters who wove the fabric of Fate in ancient Scandinavian tradition. Beyond the control of humans or gods, it was they who decreed life and death and who knew the ultimate result of all things. Odin, the All-father, consulted with them regularly, but there was much they would not share.

Their names are significant as well as the manner in which they are portrayed. The eldest, Urd (also Wyrd, hence "weird"), symbolized the past. Pictured as an old crone looking back in contemplation, her name means "origin" or "cause." The name of the second, Verdandi, means "becoming," and she is pictured as looking straight ahead fearlessly. The youngest, Skuld, whose name means "debt," is represented as veiled and holding a book or scroll as yet unopened. This last Norn was particularly associated with death.

Soon after the close of the golden age of the world, these three sisters took up residence at one of the roots of the cosmic tree, Yggdrasil. Although Odin planted the great tree of life, it was the Norns who watered it daily from the Urdar fountain and pressed fresh clay around its roots to keep it strong; for the death of the cosmic tree was equivalent to the end of the universe. The Norns are most famous, however, for their endless weaving, spinning out huge webs stretching from the mountains to the sea. These webs are the destinies of all things, great and small, and the colors of the threads signify the character of what is to be. Interestingly, Urd and Verdandi were considered beneficent Norns, spinning out beautiful webs that were continually undone

---

Odin's Last Ride to the Norns

Rode he long and rode he fast.
First beneath the great Life Tree,
At the sacred Spring sought he
Urdar, Norna of the Past;
But her backward seeing eye
Could no knowledge now supply.
Across Verdandi's page there fell
Dark shades that ever woes foretell;
The shadows which 'round Asgard hung
Their baleful darkness o'er it flung;
The secret was not written there
Might save Valhal, the pure and fair.
Last youngest of the sisters three,
Skuld, Norna of Futurity,
Implored to speak, stood silent by—
Averted was her tearful eye.

From Jones (1878).

by Skuld; not infrequently, it was said, she would angrily tear a work to shreds when nearly finished, perhaps symbolizing the necessary bitterness of a future dependent on the deeds of the past. But in any case, it appears the Norns did not weave according to their fancy but reluctantly, according to the decrees of a still higher power, Orlog or "Fate" itself. At Ragnarök, or "the Twilight of the Gods," Odin rode down to the Urdar fountain one last time, where under the toppling Yggdrasil, the Norns sat silent with veiled faces, their last web lying torn at their feet.

The Norns were also depicted as caring for two swans in the Urdar fountain at Yggdrasil's roots, from which all swans on earth were supposed to be descended. At times the Norns themselves were believed to take swan shape and fly to earth, sporting or bestowing prophecies on mankind, in particular at childbirth. Indeed, there is evidence of an actual cult of the Norns in northern Europe, which was slow in giving way to Christianity. The eleventh-century Bishop of Worms chastised women for worshipping the three goddesses who determined the fate of children and even setting three places at the table for them.

There was also a sorority of women known as *Norns* or *Vala* (meaning "Prophetess"), who officiated as priestesses at forest shrines in sacred groves. These women were apparently much respected and feared, for the Roman general Drusus actually retreated before Veleda, one such Norn, who warned him not to cross the Elbe River in his attack. Whether these women were worshipers of the three Norns in Asgard or rather were identified with them, they left a deep impression on the European mind. After the encroachment of Christianity such prophetesses were degraded to the status of "witches," as they appear in William Shakespeare's *Macbeth,* but even then they were held in high regard or at least feared.

See also NIFLHEIM; ODIN.

References

Davidson, H. R. Ellis. *Myths and Symbols in Pagan Europe.* Syracuse: Syracuse University Press, 1988.

Guerber, Hélène Adeline. *Myths of the Norsemen from the Eddas and Sagas.* New York: Dover, 1992.

Jones, Julia Clinton. *Valhalla.* New York: R. Worthington, 1880; San Francisco: E. Bosque and Company, 1878.

Mackenzie, Donald A. *Teutonic Myth and Legend.* New York: Wise, 1934.

Sturluson, Snorri. *Edda.* Trans. Anthony Faulkes. London: Dent, 1987.

Titchenell, Elsa-Brita. *The Masks of Odin.* Pasadena: Theosophical University Press, 1985.

O

ODIN (OðINN)

Like most gods in ancient history, the Norse figure Odin is complex, confusing, and contradictory. He is simultaneously the god of death, battle, kings, runes, magic, wisdom, trickery, poetry, and inspiration. He is said, in the prose Edda *Gylfaginning,* to be the All-father of the gods: he made heaven and Earth and made human beings with a soul, he rules all nine worlds, and he lives throughout the ages. Yet in other myths his horrible death is recorded at the Twilight of the Gods (Ragnarök) in the jaws of the Fenris wolf. He takes form among the Danish as Othon, among the old Germans as Wodan, in Sweden as Othin, and among the Anglo-Saxons as Woden, and in each geographical region he appears as a similar but not identical figure. For instance, his Germanic name *Wodan* comes from the noun *wut,* meaning "fury, intoxication, or possession," whereas the Scandinavian version *Odin* comes from *óðr,* meaning "raging, drunk, inspired": the meanings are nearly the same but from different roots.

In the poems and myths, Odin was pictured as tall, about fifty years old, with a long beard and a gray cloak with a blue hood. His blue mantle was flecked with gray, undoubtedly representing the sky and the clouds as he ruled from the seat of the gods at Asgard. As the high king, Odin had three halls. His hall of government was Gladsheim, which contained the seats of the twelve Aesir (high gods); but Odin's own hall was Válaskjálf, roofed with silver, with his vast throne Hlidskjalf, the highest spot in the universe. From his throne he looked down and saw with his (literally) eagle eye the activities of all the nine worlds. As lord of war he also had the hall of the fallen, Valhalla, with 540 doors attended by the virgin Valkyries; from there he was commander of thousands of warriors. The historical kings of Sweden claimed descent from Odin, recalling the Irish myth that all of Ireland was descended from their god of death, Donn. Kings devoted to Odin hoped to receive his blessing and enjoy a long and victorious reign, yet Odin, as god of wisdom, was also untrustworthy: he knew the cycles of rising and falling and could withdraw his support as quickly as he gave it. He was more than once accused of faithlessness and treachery, and so his name was synonymous with luck and sudden reversals. According to Danish historian Saxo Grammaticus (Davidson), Odin supported King Harald Wartooth of Denmark, instructing him in war and granting him many victories. Yet in the battle of Brávalla against King Ring, Odin magically took the place of Harald's charioteer and in spite of the old king's pleas flung him down and slew him with his own sword as he fell. Odin handed out weapons to favorite warriors but later broke or withdrew them when their time came. He gave a magical sword to Sigmund the Volsung but then shattered the sword into pieces at a critical juncture. Later the pieces of the sword were reforged for Sigmund's son, Sigurd, who also received battle spells and a marvelous horse from Odin. Eventually, Odin struck down Sigurd as well and carried him off to the hall of fallen heroes.

As god of kings, then, Odin was necessarily god of war, and for this he is primarily known. His equipment was certainly that of a kingly warrior: he had two ravens, one perched on each shoulder, named Hugin (thought) and Munin (memory). They traveled the earth each day, returning at dusk to give Odin the news of the world, and like ravens and hawks throughout Europe symbolized battle, for they were birds of prey and scavengers of battlefield corpses. There were two wolves at his feet, Geri and Freki, fed by Odin himself at the table in Valhalla. These again represented war, for even in prehistory wolves have been seen as dangerous foes and symbols of violence. There was even a class of warriors who worshipped Odin, called in English *berserkers* but known in the *Hrafnsmál* as *wolf-coats*; these Odin inspired with battle madness, and they were feared even as far away as Rome. Odin's horse was the magical Sleipnir of the eight legs, which has been interpreted by H. R. Ellis Davidson as a funeral casket borne by four men. His infallible spear was called Gungnir, which he threw to begin a conflict. This practice was carried out among Norse warriors at the start of battles—they would throw a single spear over the heads of the enemy and give the battle cry, "Odin take you all." Odin's spear was so sacred a symbol that oaths were sworn over its point, and it was said that they could never be broken.

Because Odin was the god who granted victory or defeat, he was also the god of death. He knew the way to Hel, for he saw the future at his son Balder's death in

Odin or Woden, the Scandinavian god of wisdom, poetry, war, agriculture, magic, and the dead, presiding over Valhalla. Courtesy of Anne Ronan Picture Library.

Baldrs Draumar. Sometimes Odin is also psychopomp, or "guide of souls." In the *Volsunga Saga* he carries away the dead son of Sigmund in his boat, and in the poem *Hárbardsljód* he is again represented as a ferryman for souls, carrying them across the sea. Norse warriors (particularly the berserkers) were said to be such formidable foes in battle because they had no fear of death: either Odin would grant them victory, or else he would grant them defeat and his Valkyries would escort them to the blessed Valhalla, where until the end of the age they would eat, drink, and be merry. This sentiment was summed up in these words, put into the mouth of Odin in the *Hávamál*:

> Cattle die, kinsfolk die,
> oneself dies the same.
> I know one thing only which never dies—
> the renown of the noble dead.

Warriors dedicated to him received cremation and the highest honors the Norse culture could offer.

Odin was also lord of death because of the vast sacrifices that were associated with his worship. In the eleventh century, Adam of Bremen recorded that every ninth year at Uppsala, Sweden, a massive sacrifice was made to Odin and the powers of the Underworld in return for victory in the years ahead. The sacrifice lasted for nine days, with a human and one of each species of animal or bird offered every day. In volume 4 of *Danish History*, Saxo Grammaticus tells the story of a King Vikar who decided on a human sacrifice in return for a favorable wind. When the king himself was chosen by lot for this sacrifice, he decided on a mock sacrifice only, but "prompted by Odin," a follower named Starkad made sure that the sacrifice was real. Victims sacrificed to Odin were generally hanged while being impaled by a spear on a tree.

Although it is difficult to say whether myth or practice came first, Odin himself hung for nine days, pierced by a spear, on the world tree named Yggdrasil, voluntarily suffering in order to receive the secret of runes, the key to all wisdom. We read Odin's words again in *Hávamál*:

> I know I hung
> on the windswept Tree,
> through nine days and nights.
> I was struck with a spear
> and given to Odin,
> myself given to myself . . .
> They helped me neither
> by meat nor drink.
> I peered downward,
> I took up the runes,
> screaming, I took them—
> then I fell back.

In another ritual of suffering in exchange for knowledge, Odin also sacrificed one of his eyes to the giant Mimir, who guarded the spring of the Underworld, in order to gain permission to drink from the spring and gain its wisdom. In this way Odin was also closely associated with wisdom and redemptive suffering, not unlike Christ on the cross.

Like other seers and shamans, Odin was given to shape-shifting in his quest for knowledge. His helmet was crested with the eagle, and he was known as the god of the eagle eyes, for in several myths he becomes an eagle. In one myth, often represented in art, the Aesir and Vanir gods ended a long strife and brewed a magical mead as a signal of their everlasting truce. The mead gave inspiration and thus knowledge and power. The giants, representatives of primordial chaos like the Titans of Greek myth, tried to steal the mead and thus conquer the world. But Odin recovered it from its hiding place within a mountain by transforming into a serpent and crawling through the rock. After drinking the mead, he shape-shifted into an eagle and flew off, vomiting the mead up for the gods into special vessels.

Despite all his wisdom—he knew the end of the world and the exact events leading up to it, beginning with his son's death—Odin was not able to delay or prevent the end of the world. He knew that when the cock Gollinkambi crowed three times, the end was near. It was his destiny to be swallowed by Loki's offspring the wolf, while Thor would perish in slaying the poisonous world serpent. Yet Odin also foresaw the events after Ragnarök and saw that some few would be saved in the hall of Gimlé from the general destruction and would populate a new Earth under new gods.

In truth, Odin did live on for many years after the conversion of Scandinavia to Christianity. Legends all over Europe told of the Great Huntsman who, preceded by his supernatural hounds and traveling on the wind, would ride the storms and sweep up the souls of all he chanced to meet.

See also FUNERARY CUSTOMS, SCANDINAVIAN; HEL; RAGNARÖK; VALHALLA; VALKYRIE.

References

Craigie, William Alexander. *The Religion of Ancient Scandinavia.* 1906. Reprint, New York: Books for Libraries Press, 1969.

Davidson, H. R. Ellis. *Gods and Myths of Northern Europe.* New York: Penguin, 1964, 1977.

———. *The Lost Beliefs of Northern Europe.* London: Routledge, 1993.

Guerber, Hélène Adeline. *Myths of the Norsemen from the Eddas and Sagas.* New York: Dover Publications, 1992.

Sturluson, Snorri. *Edda.* Trans. Anthony Faulkes. London: Dent, 1987.

Titchenell, Elsa-Brita. *The Masks of Odin.* Pasadena: Theosophical University Press, 1985.

Turville-Petre, E. O. G. *Myth and Religion of the North: The Religion of Ancient Scandinavia.* Westport, CT: Greenwood. 1964.

ORCUS

Among the many names for Hades, lord of the Underworld, *Orcus* is the most confusing. The Latin name *Orcus* has two possible derivations from Greek, neither of which directly denote the Underworld. The first possibility comes from the Greek *horkios,* which means "he of the oath." The ancient writer Pausanias (fl. 143–176 C.E.) informs us that in the Bouleterion at Elis there was an image of Zeus called *Horkion,* before which athletes had to swear an oath to obey the athletic rules while standing on pieces of an animal sacrifice. At other locations in the ancient Greek world, such oaths were also sworn, with the understanding that oath breakers would be sacrificed like the animal they stood on—and thus descend into Hades. This circumstantial evidence indicates that Hades had, as part of his character, a responsibility to uphold sacred oaths and punish violators; thus Orcus should be translated as "He of the Oath."

The more likely derivation of the Roman epithet *Orcus* is from the Greek *phorcys,* which means boar or pig (hence the English word *pork*). The pig was sacred to the goddess of the corn all over the ancient world, most notably to Demeter, and by extension, to her daughter/double Persephone. Pigs were sacrificed to the Corn Goddess, often herself called Phorcis, in order to make the corn sprout each year. And because

Persephone spent half her time in the Underworld with her husband Hades, he may have taken on the masculine form of the name, hence Phorcys (in Latin, Orcus). James Frazer reports several Greek myths in support of this hypothesis, for instance, that when Hades kidnapped Persephone, a swineherd named Eubuleus and his swine were caught up in the chasm that opened into the Underworld. In the autumn festival in Attica, called *Thesmophoria,* pigs, cakes of dough, and pine branches were thrown into the "chasm of Demeter and Persephone" (a nearby cave) in commemoration of this event. Later, the decayed remains would be gathered up and used as fertilizer to make the crops grow. To further the connection between pigs, corn, and Underworld fertility, Frazer notes that "the swineherd Eubuleus was a brother of Triptolemus, to whom Demeter first imparted the secret of the corn," in one version as a reward for telling Demeter where her daughter could be found. Thus the Roman title *Orcus* for the lord of the dead should be translated "Boar," commemorating his role in Greco-Roman fertility myths and rites.

See also DIS; HADES; PLUTO; TARTAROS.

References

Frazer, James George. *The New Golden Bough.* Ed. Theodor H. Gaster. New York: Criterion Books, 1959.

Graves, Robert. *The Greek Myths.* New York: Penguin, 1960.

Harrison, Jane Ellen. *Prolegomena to the Study of Greek Religion.* Cambridge: Cambridge University Press, 1922.

OSIRIS BED

Boxes made of wood or pottery in the shape of the Egyptian god Osiris have been found in tombs beginning with the Eighteenth Dynasty and occur frequently throughout the rest of the New Kingdom period (c. 1550 to 945 B.C.E.). The boxes were wrapped in linen just as if they contained the mummified body of a king but instead were filled with fertile silt from the Nile. Corn was planted in the Osiris bed, which sprouted but, without sunlight, could not continue to grow.

These boxes were yet another symbolism of resurrection, for the sprouting of the corn represented the resurrection of the Earth each spring, which in turn corresponded to the resurrection of Osiris. In the later periods of Egyptian history, the deceased was identified with this god of the dead and his or her name was actually changed after death to "Osiris (so-and-so)." Therefore, through sympathetic magic and simply by suggestion and symbolism, the sprouting corn in the coffin of Osiris added to the deceased's hopes for a pleasant afterlife.

See also FUNERARY CUSTOMS, ANCIENT EGYPTIAN; MUMMIFICATION; PYRAMID, EGYPTIAN.

References

Garstang, J. *Burial Customs of Ancient Egypt*. London: A. Constable, 1907.

Hamilton-Paterson, James, and Carol Andrews. *Mummies: Death and Life in Ancient Egypt*. London: William Collins Sons, 1978.

Spencer, A. J. *Death in Ancient Egypt*. New York: Penguin, 1982.

Winlock, H. E. *The Rise and Fall of the Middle Kingdom in Thebes*. New York: Macmillan, 1947.

OSSUARY

From the Latin *ossuarium* (literally "for bones"), ossuaries are small containers, usually in the shape of chests, miniature altars, or urns, designed to hold the bones for secondary burial. When the flesh had decayed from the body, leaving only the skeleton, the bones—now purified—were gathered up and placed in the ossuary for final interment. One ossuary has been found in Palestine dating to the Chalcolithic age (c. 4000–3300 B.C.E.). Ossuaries were much in use in ancient Judaism, at least from the early Roman period, as evidenced by the hundreds of limestone boxes found in the vicinity of Jerusalem, frequently in the loculi tombs there. They are inscribed in Hebrew, Aramaic, or Greek with the personal name of the deceased and decorations such as rosettes (symbolizing spring).

In Zoroastrianism the flesh of the human body—the playground of the evil one—is one of the most impure things imaginable, but the clean bones are quite pure and sacred and worthy of being laid to rest. Even today, ossuaries are used after the dead body has been exposed on the dakhma (tower of silence) and all the impure flesh has been eaten by birds and animals of prey. The ancient Scripture Vendidad instructs the mourners to construct an ossuary (uzdana) in the form of a small casket or urn and to place the bones "out of reach of dogs and foxes and wolves, not to be rained on from above. . . . If they are able . . . let it be among stones or chalk or clay." Although some modern Zoroastrians cut a cist out of a mountain or hillside and place the bare bones inside, ossuaries are still very much in use, in a variety of styles.

Ossuaries are common worldwide among those cultures that practice cremation or secondary burial, either as the ordinary funerary custom or as a special treatment of elite remains. Frequently, the remains of chiefs and priests are buried in special elevated or aboveground ossuaries, whereas the corpses of the common folk are buried underground.

See also CREMAINS; FUNERARY CUSTOMS, JEWISH; FUNERARY CUSTOMS, ZOROASTRIAN; LOCULUS TOMB; TOWER OF SILENCE; URN.

References

Boyce, Mary. *A History of Zoroastrianism*. Vol. 1. Leiden: E. J. Brill, 1975.

Meyers, E. M. *Jewish Ossuaries: Reburial and Rebirth*. Rome: Biblical Institute Press, 1971.

OTHERWORLD, IRISH

Conceptions of a parallel world inhabited by spiritual beings, fairies, or only beautiful women and where death and suffering are unknown are extremely common in Irish folklore and myth. From Mag Mell (Plain of Happiness) to Tīr-na-n'Og (Land of the Living) to Tīr fa Tonn (Land under Wave) (and many more besides), Irish literature gives many, often conflicting descriptions of a marvelous world beyond, under, or invisibly adjacent to our mundane land. In the tales, these other worlds are rarely identified explicitly with the land of the dead; rather they are parallel worlds, places of magic and adventure. Yet there is reason to believe that before the coming of Christianity (and the Christian editing of Irish myths) these worlds were in fact one or more lands of the dead, which only great heroes could visit while still alive.

In the folklore of the people dwelling on every prominent Celtic cape, from France to England to Ireland, there are legends of buried cities off the coast. These cities, or entire civilizations, whether they are called the sunken district of Lyonesse or the lost island of Atlantis, experienced some great upheaval, usually because of some great sin, and sank beneath the waves. At rare intervals, they become visible, sometimes in outline underwater and sometimes in full physical form above the horizon. Some even claim to have visited these lands, while they were manifest for only a few short minutes or hours.

The writer Procopius records a legend in the sixth century C.E. regarding fishermen off the coast of France (Brittany), at Cape Raz, which is called the Bay of Souls. There, around midnight, ordinary fishermen are awakened by strange sounds and the irresistible urge to ferry the dead souls to Brittia, the land of the dead identified hazily with Britain:

> At night they perceive the door to be shaken, and they hear a certain indistinct voice summoning them to do their work. They proceed to the shore under compulsion of necessity they cannot understand. Here they perceive vessels—not their own—apparently without passengers. Embarking, they take the oars, and feel as if they had a burden on board in the shape of unseen passengers, which sometimes sinks the boat to within a finger-breadth of the water. They see no one. After rowing for an hour, they reach Brittia, really a mortal journey of over twenty-four hours. Arrived at Brittia, they hear the names of their passengers and their dignities called and answered; and then on the ghosts' landing, they are wafted back to the habitable world.

The Celts who settled in Ireland put the land of the dead, or the Plain of Happiness, even further west, over *their* sea, the Atlantic. Obviously it is an ancient tradition among the Celts that a land of the dead lies over the *western* water. Perhaps because the ancient Celts were believers in immortality and the transmigration of the soul, no single land of the dead has come down in the standard cycle of Celtic heroic tales. Rather, various heroes go to a great variety of mystical lands, and in other tales many characters are reborn here on this Earth, and the tales follow them from incarnation to incarnation. Thus it is clear that whatever original tradition regarding the land of the dead may have existed long ago, it became atomized and shaped by a variety of local traditions, especially after Christian acculturation. The priests frowned on traditional pagan speculation, and because for many centuries only the Christian monks were literate, their written record of the legends with an official Christian stamp outlasted the native oral tradition. Unlike writing, oral cycles of tales rely on an unbroken stream of believers from generation to generation, and this tradition slowly died out over the centuries under the new theological regime.

Nevertheless, the theme of the Otherworld in general (suitably altered) remained extremely prominent even in the written tradition, and it figures in an extraordinary number of tales. It is a source of romance, adventure, and physical danger to the world of humans; it is a land of endless summer, opposed to the cycles of growth and decay in the mortal world; and, on a higher plane, it is an inner realm of mystical initiation, wisdom gathering, and soul evolution. In many cases the heroes who have ventured into the Otherworld are never able to return (see MAG MELL). In other cases, the hero returns with a gift of wisdom or aid for humanity.

Many journeys of Irish heroes into the Otherworld begin on Samhain (later called Hallowe'en), that is, on the evening of 1 November. Here, at the turning of the seasons, at the temporal boundary between summer (life) and winter (death) and between the human world of light and the superhuman, nocturnal world of dark (because the night was unknown and mysterious), the separation between the two worlds is said to be particularly thin. Even into the eighteenth century, on this night thoughtful country families in Ireland and Britain would leave the front door unlocked, a fire burning in the hearth, and the chairs arranged around the fire, welcoming the dead who were returning after all were asleep. Likewise, on this night the fairies came out of their mounds (síd) and were likely to cause mischief.

On one such Samhain, the hero Nera encounters a talking corpse hanging from a gallows. After assuaging the thirst of the corpse through various adventures, Nera returns to his village Cruachan and sees the whole town in flames. He is horrified when he comes upon a great heap of the heads of his neighbors and relatives. Nera then follows the fairy warriors who have done this into a

---

Oísin Meets the Fairy Maiden

[The beautiful maiden from the Otherworld, who has fallen in love with the hero Oísin, says:]

I place you under obligations (gessa) which no true heroes break through—to come with me on my white steed to Tīr-na-n'Og, the most delightful and renowned country under the sun. Jewels and gold there are in abundance, and honey and wine; the trees bear fruit and blossoms and green leaves all the year round. Feasting and music and harmless pastimes are there each day. You will get a hundred swords, and robes of richest loom; and a hundred steeds, and hounds of keenest scent; numberless herds, and sheep with fleeces of gold; a hundred maidens merry and young, sweeter of mouth than the music of birds; a hundred suits of armor, and a sword, gold-handled, that never missed a stroke. Decline shall not come on you, nor death, nor decay. These, and much more that passeth all mention, shall be yours, and myself as your wife!

From MacBain (1917).

---

cave and meets with the king of the síd (which is the name for the fairy folk as well as their mounds). The king makes Nera a servant and sets him to bring in firewood each day from the house of a single woman. Time goes by, and unknown to the king of the síd, Nera and the woman become married, and she helps him undo his fate. She tells Nera of the well where the golden crown of the fairy king—one of the three wonders of Ireland—has been hidden and that what he has seen of his town being destroyed is nothing but a vision—but that it would indeed come true by the next Samhain. She advises him to return to his people with the warning that they should destroy the fairy mound where the síd lives before it can destroy them, and she instructs Nera to take the fruits of summer from the fairy land to prove to his people (now in winter) that he is telling the truth. Nera then returns to his own people and discovers that only moments have passed. All is done as his fairy wife instructed: the mound is destroyed, the town is saved, and the golden crown of the fairy king is discovered in the well and given to the rightful (human) heir.

In another tale (not on Samhain) the hero-bard Oísin, son of Fionn, is in the company of his relations when suddenly a woman of the síd presents herself. She is Niam of the Golden Hair and proclaims her love for Oísin (see excerpt). At last, Oísin is persuaded to go with her to the Otherworld (here called Tīr-na-n'Og, or "the Land of the Living"), which is described as marvelous and without death or sorrow. The two mount her steed and dash magically across the ocean. Time passes for him as in a dream, until at last Oísin sets his foot on a stone that his fairy-wife has warned him against. Suddenly he is seized with homesickness and, despite Niam's pleading, insists on visiting his native Ireland. At last his wife gives him a horse but forbids him from dismounting on Irish soil. Returning to his home, he finds that all has changed, and he is dismayed. He sees only tiny people, who are trying helplessly to raise a great stone; they ask the giant Oísin to help them. He jumps down from his horse and easily tosses the stone aside—but turning, he sees that the horse has vanished, and he has been transformed into a frail old man. Three hundred years have passed!

In his study of ancient Celtic beliefs, J. A. MacCulloch points out that there are at least four basic types of Otherworld in Irish tales. They do not necessarily describe different Otherworlds but perhaps different visions of the Otherworld and different locations for it. What follows is an extension of his discussion, with examples added:

1. *The síd, or fairy Otherworld.* An example of this conception is the tale of Nera, who makes contact with a parallel world first through a cave and then later realizes the source of the danger to his town stems from the fairy mound. In a great many tales, the hero accomplishes his task by entering or digging up an earthen mound, as when King Eochaid recovers his stolen wife Etain. Again, many heroes pursue some villain, fairy, or beautiful Otherworld woman, only to catch them just as they are entering the síd. In later, Christian times, mounds became the source of hauntings and the dwelling places of the dead—which may have brought the nature of the fairy mounds full circle, back to their original form. In almost all cases, heroes entering the Otherworld through a mound or cave are able to return.

2. *The island Otherworld.* The Land of Women, the Island of Joy, and Mag Mell (Plain of Happiness) are examples of the Otherworld as an island (or huge continent) in the sea far off the western coast of Ireland—west, not coincidentally, where the sun sets. In this case, heroes like Oísin, Bran, or Maeldoein set sail for the west, either by Otherworld invitation or on the advice of a Druid to attain some goal—in Maeldoein's case, to avenge a slain father. Only rarely are heroes who have entered the Otherworld via sea able to return.

3. *The Land under Waves.* This is a variation of the island theme in which the Otherworld exists *under* the water. The entry on MAG MELL gives

examples of this, such as when Bran is told by the sea god that his boat has just sailed over underwater ridges, forests, and towns. Likewise, Loegaire plunges through a lake to fight his Otherworld battle and win a bride. Again, the heroes tend to remain forever under the waves or perish upon trying to return to Ireland.

4. *An Otherworld adjacent to and co-extensive with this world.* Like the Welsh Annwfn, some Irish tales show the Otherworld adjacent to our own but impossible to get to without a special knowledge or object. It is sometimes a kingdom but frequently a four-cornered castle (sometimes of glass) that magically appears and vanishes. The hero Cormac goes in search of the Otherworld to find his abducted family, and after several adventures finds his family with the hero Manannán mac Lir, one of the fairy gods called *Tuatha Dé Danann.* Manannán entertains Cormac for one night and presents Cormac with two magical items as boons. They are a branch of golden apples that when shaken produces a music dispelling all sorrow and a cup that breaks when a lie is told but becomes whole again when a true word is spoken. Cormac falls asleep and awakens the next morning in his own palace at Tara, with family, branch of music, and cup of truth.

In every case, the Irish tales locate the entrance to the Otherworld as some kind of boundary or horizon (fairy mound, lake, distant sea), as if to indicate that the spiritual realms do not exist in the physical three-dimensional realm but only where a fourth and unknown dimension intersects with the human world. Time dilation or shrinkage also indicates that the Otherworld is not bound by physical laws and is more a realm of the mind or soul, like the dreaming state. Here, from the inner world (or inner mind), human beings may be tested, triumph, and receive boons that aid them, their families, or their people. Psychologically, the Otherworld serves not only as the occult source of inspiration or rejuvenation but also as a sort of feminine counterpart to the active, warlike world of men in ancient times. In many descriptions the Otherworld (or a part of it) is peopled primarily or entirely with women or female fairies, and a great many heroes have obtained their brides as rewards for adventures in the Otherworld. In their work *Celtic Heritage,* the Rees brothers have pointed out that in many ways, the Irish Otherworld functions as an unconscious mind, a passive source of ideas and knowledge for the conscious, active mind (world) of waking humans.

It may be that in ancient times, every deceased person was thought to pass time in the Otherworld and then be reborn again on Earth. Unfortunately, the beliefs of the common people in the distant past have not been preserved, only the tales of the unusual man, the hero, and the supernaturally beautiful woman. These tales may well shed light on the actual beliefs of ancient people and their afterlife, but they are also characterized by the exaggerations and plot twists that make good oral literature, and they are not to be trusted literally, however valuable they are symbolically.

Again, Christianization was taking place in Ireland for many centuries while the tales were still being told, such that it is almost impossible to get back to a pre-Christian original. One example is "The Voyage of Snegdus and Mac Riagla," in which a tyrannical king has been assassinated by the Men of Ross. The king's brother imprisons the guilty parties and intends to burn them alive, but two clerics of St. Colum Cille of Iona suggest that instead the guilty be cast out to sea on small boats, so that God himself may pass judgment upon them. Two clerics, Snegdus and Mac Riagla, decide to sail along voluntarily with the prisoners, but the two are swept away by the sea to several islands and adventures. At the sixth island they come to, they find the Men of Ross dwelling happily without sin and joined by Enoch and Elijah, who in the Old Testament were likewise carried from Earth without dying. The tale is entertaining in its own right and joins several ancient themes with medieval Christian ones, for example, setting to sea those who are ambiguously guilty only to pair them with Old Testament heroes awaiting final judgment on an island in the western sea. Whether this tale has a pre-Christian origin and whether it reflects literal pre-Christian belief about the state of the dead are impossible to say. Clearly, like the Lappland Underworld, called Jabmeaimo, the Irish Otherworld was changed by Christianization into a mere stopping place on the way to eternal salvation in heaven or damnation in hell—a radically different form of belief in immortality than native Celtic transmigration.

See also ANNWFN; FAIRY MOUND; JABMEAIMO; MAG MELL; SAMHAIN; SÍD; TUATHA DÉ DANANN; UNDERWORLD.

References

D'Arbois de Jubainville, H. *The Irish Mythological Cycle and Celtic Mythology*. Trans. Richard Irvine Best. Dublin: Hodges, Figgis, 1903.

Loomis, Roger Sherman. *Celtic Myth and Arthurian Romance*. New York: Columbia University Press, 1927.

Mac Bain, Alexander. *Celtic Mythology and Religion*. New York: Dutton, 1917.

MacCulloch, J. A. *The Religion of the Ancient Celts*. Edinburgh: Clark, 1911.

Rees, Alwyn, and Brinley Rees. *Celtic Heritage*. London: Thames and Hudson, 1961.

P

PALL

Traditionally, a pall is any long cloth used for ceremonial purposes, such as a magistrate's or cleric's robe, a cloth covering an altar, or a canopy. A funeral pall is a long cloth, usually of black, purple, or white velvet, that is draped over a coffin, hearse, or tomb, particularly during funeral services and processions. Often the pall is kept by the family of the deceased after the funeral as a memorial of the dead.

Use of the funeral pall is an ancient tradition dating back to Greek and Roman times in the Western world. An innovation in modern times is the practice of mourners attaching personal items to the pall of the deceased. Frequently, ribbons, personal messages, photographs, and broaches are fixed to the pall, which increases its value as a memento.

References

Dempsey, D. *The Way We Die.* New York: Macmillan, 1975.

Farrell, J. J. *Inventing the American Way of Death 1830–1920.* Philadelphia: Temple University Press, 1980.

Iserson, Kenneth V. *Death to Dust: What Happens to Dead Bodies?* Tucson, AZ: Galen Press, 1994.

Jackson, A. V. W. *Zoroastrian Studies.* New York: Columbia University Press, 1928.

Jones, Barbara. *Design for Death.* Indianapolis: Bobbs-Merrill, 1967.

Mitford, Jessica. *The American Way of Death.* New York: Simon and Schuster, 1963.

PARADISE

As a theme in myth worldwide, paradise has a rich history and holds many different meanings for different peoples. In Islam, Paradise, or "the Gardens of Delight," is a synonym for heaven, and it has at least seven or eight levels. Many ancient cultures, including Greek, Mesopotamian, Celtic, and Chinese, believed that paradisiacal islands existed far to the East or West, where unique heroes, prophets, or sages lived in bliss. Meanwhile, medieval Europe believed in an earthly paradise—located deep in the ocean, high on a mountain, or hidden in a remote location—well into the age of global exploration and European colonization.

In Western myth and tradition, paradise is generally quite distinct from the idea of heaven. The word *paradise* literally means "walled garden" and comes from the Pahlavi (Old Persian) word *pairidaêza*. The word entered Hebrew as *pardês* and the Greek version of the Scriptures (the Septuagint) as *paradeisos* (which translated both *pardês* and the more mundane Hebrew word for garden, *gan*). Paradise in Hebrew tradition is almost universally interpreted as a delightful earthly enclosure, as in Genesis 2:8–14:

Then the Lord God planted a garden in Eden away to the east, and there he put the man whom he had formed. The Lord God made trees spring from the ground, all trees pleasant to look at and good for food; and in the middle of the garden he set the tree of life and the tree of the knowledge of good and evil.

There was a river flowing from Eden to water the garden, and when it left the garden it branched into four streams. The name of the first is Pishon, that is the river which encircles all the land of Havilah, where the gold is. The gold of that land is good; bdellium and cornelians are also to be found there. The name of the second river is Gihon; this is the one which encircles all the land of Cush. The name of the third is Tigris; this is the river which runs east of Ashur. The fourth river is the Euphrates.

Because of the seemingly specific geographic details, Hebrew tradition (as well as traditional Christianity and Islam) interpreted this story literally. Furthermore, since the Bible nowhere specifically mentions the deliberate destruction of the Garden of Eden by God (rather, Genesis 3:24 states that God stationed an angelic guard to bar the way), Western religious tradition until the age of global exploration continued to assume that the earthly paradise remained somewhere hidden on the earth. In fact, two Hebrew prophets Enoch and Elijah are spoken of in the Bible as not dying but proceeding bodily to God—oral tradition named these worthies as the sole inhabitants of Eden/paradise. The word *pardês/paradeisos* occurs elsewhere in the Hebrew Scriptures (e.g., Nehemiah 2:8; Ecclesiastes 2:5; Song of Songs 4:13), each time referring to one or more earthly gardens or orchards, reinforcing the interpretation of paradise as a place on Earth, not a heavenly realm.

Most early fathers of the Christian church accepted

The last judgment, as described in Revelation 20:11. Courtesy of Anne Ronan Picture Library.

the Hebrew tradition that ancient Eden survived the flood. Further, they believed that since Christ's crucifixion, Eden/paradise had been reopened and was in use again as a place of waiting or "refreshment" for the faithful between death and the last judgment (see REFRIGERIUM). A third-century Christian document, *The Passion of Perpetua and Felicitas,* reveals Christian expectations of the time:

> We had died . . . and had put off our flesh, and we began to be carried towards the east by four angels who did not touch us with their hands. . . . While we were being carried by these four angels, a great open space appeared, which seemed to be a garden, with rose bushes and all manner of flowers. . . . The trees were as tall as cypresses, and their leaves were constantly falling. . . . And there we began to recognize many of our brethren, martyrs among them. All of us were sustained by a most delicious odour that seemed to satisfy us. (quoted in Delumeau, p. 28)

This place is not heaven, the African theologian Tertullian (c. 160–230 C.E.) assured his readers. Rather it was an earthly paradise, prepared only for martyrs and saints to await the end; the ordinary dead went to the old Hebrew Sheol, and "the heavenly realms . . . shall be opened [only] at the end of the world." Not all teachers and texts agreed: the cycle of Pauline texts, such as The Apocalypse of Paul, asserted that heaven, composed of various levels, was currently in use and that the Apostle Paul had been there himself, as described in 2 Corinthians 13:1–5. But the majority of Christians seem to have agreed with Tertullian's view, though just where paradise was located was a topic for debate.

Christian tradition focused on the four rivers flowing out of paradise, identifying Pishon as the Ganges and Gihon as the Nile. However, the sources of the four rivers were known even in antiquity, and they did not originate anywhere near the same place. This was explained by the fact that some rivers travel underground before surfacing, so the four rivers of paradise originated from some high place, probably a mountain (placing paradise on a high mountain also explained how it escaped the flood), and plummeted with such force toward the Earth that they ran underground and surfaced in different areas. Of course, the mountain of paradise could not be located either, but it was assumed to be deliberately obscured by God. Medieval maps frequently placed paradise across a vast expanse of water, connected to the inhabited (flat) world only by a narrow stretch of land, if at all. Others, like Isidore of Seville (560–636) placed paradise in Asia or at least somewhere in the Far East (probably under the influence of

the statement in Genesis that God placed Eden "away to the east"). Dante Alighieri was quite creative in placing paradise atop the mountain of Purgatory in the *Divine Comedy,* directly opposite the city of Jerusalem on a *spherical* earth. The 1568 edition of John Calvin's Protestant Bible included a map of the world that placed the earthly paradise squarely between Assyria and Babylon.

Christopher Columbus, like many explorers of his time, believed in the earthly paradise and thought that he had drawn near it when he reached the mouth of the Orinoco River in the South American Gulf of Paria:

> I do not hold that the earthly Paradise has the form of a rugged mountain, as it is shown in pictures, but that it lies at the summit of what I have described as the stalk of a pear, and that by gradually approaching it one begins, while still at a great distance, to climb towards it. As I have said, I do not believe that anyone can ascend to the top. I do believe, however, that, distant though it is, these waters may flow from there to this place which I have reached, and form this lake [gulf]. (Cohen, trans., p. 221)

Many explorers, including Amerigo Vespucci, for a time identified Brazil with the earthly paradise, citing the longevity of the native inhabitants, the lush vegetation and abundance of amazing fruits, and even the colorful parrots who spoke with human voices as evidence that this was God's kingdom. At nearly the same time, British settlers in North America thought that Virginia, Maryland, and Georgia might be the original paradise or at least close to it, as described by George Williams in *Wilderness and Paradise in Christian Thought.* Within a few decades of colonization, however, the globe had been largely mapped out, and except for a faint hope that "St. Brendan's Isle" might still exist somewhere in the Pacific Ocean, belief in an earthly paradise had largely vanished.

See also ĀARU; AVALON; DILMUN; ELYSION; GARDENS OF DELIGHT; GIMLÉ; HEAVEN, HISTORY OF; HEAVEN, ORIGINS OF; ISLANDS OF THE BLEST; MAG MELL; OTHERWORLD, IRISH; PURE LAND; PURGATORY; REFRIGERIUM; RESURRECTION, CHRISTIAN; RESURRECTION, HEBREW; SUKHĀVATĪ; SVARGA.

References

Armstrong, John. *The Paradise Myth.* London: Oxford University Press, 1969.

Cohen, J. M., ed. and trans. "Narrative of the Third Voyage." In *The Four Voyages of Christopher Columbus.* New York: Penguin, 1969.

Delumeau, Jean. *History of Paradise: The Garden of Eden in Myth and Tradition.* Trans. Matthew O'Connell. New York: Continuum, 1995.

Heinberg, Richard. *Memories and Visions of Paradise: Exploring the Universal Myth of a Lost Golden Age.* Los Angeles: Jeremy P. Tarcher, 1989.

Le Goff, Jacques. *The Birth of Purgatory.* Trans. Arthur Goldhammer. Chicago: University of Chicago Press, 1984.

Lincoln, Andrew T. *Paradise Now and Not Yet: Studies in the Role of the Heavenly Dimension in Paul's Thought with Special Reference to His Eschatology.* Cambridge: Cambridge University Press, 1981.

McClung, William Alexander. *The Architecture of Paradise: Survivals of Eden and Jerusalem.* Berkeley: University of California Press, 1983.

Smolinski, Reiner, ed. *The Threefold Paradise of Cotton Mather: An Edition of "Triparadisus."* Athens: University of Georgia Press, 1995.

Sylvia Mary, Sister. *Nostalgia for Paradise.* London: Darton, Longman, and Todd, 1965.

Williams, George. *Wilderness and Paradise in Christian Thought: The Biblical Experience of the Desert in the History of Christianity and the Paradise Theme in the Theological Idea of the University.* New York: Harper and Brothers, 1954.

PARENTALIA (DIES PARENTALES)

The Parentalia, or festival of dead ancestors, was observed in the Roman world from 13 to 21 February. The first eight days were reserved for private family celebrations and feasting, but 21 February, the Feralia, was the day of public ceremony. All nine days were dies religiosi, that is, days reserved for religious observance: temples were closed, marriages were not performed, officials appeared without their insignia, and commerce and administration ceased.

Unlike the older and more macabre festival of Lemuria, held in May, the Parentalia was festive and gay. It was a happy remembrance of departed kin, not a time of gloom or fear of angry spirits. As one inscription records,

> Sprinkle my ashes with pure wine and fragrant oil
> of spikenard:
> Bring balsam, too, stranger, with crimson roses.
> Tearless my urn enjoys unending spring.
> I have not died, but changed my state.
> (Toynbee, trans.)

Families at the middle class level and above had their regular family tomb in a "city of the dead" (necropolis) outside the city walls, and the dead (manes) were familiar and well cared for. In general, their living relatives had little to fear. It was not uncommon for those with some wealth to set aside large sums in their wills to help their descendants finance their afterdeath care. The family used the interest on this estate to bring regular offerings to the dead (on the anniversary of death, on the birthday of the deceased, etc.), keep up the tomb, and light lamps on the grave each month during the new moons (kalends), the first quarters (nones), and the full moons (ides).

But the time for such loving visits was above all the Parentalia. Food was certainly the most important of the ritual offerings for the dead and is mentioned in nearly every surviving inscription and will. The dead, whether cremated or inhumed, were nearly always accompanied by eating and drinking vessels in their tombs, some with lead pipes leading from the surface directly to the remains of the deceased so that they could receive libations or fluid offerings. During the Parentalia, meals were brought out for the dead and eaten right on the spot, the dead taking part along with the living. Some large family tombs, constructed like actual houses, were even equipped with kitchens to facilitate these joint meals. In addition, there were offerings of incense, fruits, and flowers to decorate the tomb (especially violets and roses) and in some reports the blood of black-colored animals (sheep, goats, etc.). Through these offerings, the living family members and the dead shared for a time their old intimacy. Because February was the final month of the old Roman calendar, the living family members also took advantage of this annual meeting to ask the dead, with their Otherworld powers, for help and protection in the new year to come.

The Parentalia was sanctioned by the state and, by the time of the Roman Republic (fifth century B.C.E.), was mostly systematized for city dwellers and stripped of earlier cultic behavior. But records show some surviving practices that were probably from an earlier period of the festival of the dead, perhaps from a more rural time when the family dead were considered dangerous. In one of these bizarre rituals, an old hag accompanied by young women performed rituals to prevent harm from evil spirits. The old woman would burn incense at a mouse hole, utter spells while holding seven black beans in her mouth, sew up the mouth of a fish, roast it, eat it, and share wine with the young women, claiming that "the mouth of the enemy has been bound."

The Parentalia festival of the dead closed, appropriately, with a ceremony for the living. On 22 February was the Caristia, a feast day only for the living members of the family. It was a kind of reunion of the family after they had completed their rites for the dead and was supposed to be a loving and harmonious celebration: all quarrels were to be forgotten, and no guilty or cruel member could be present.

See also ANTHESTERIA; FEBRUARY; FUNERARY CUSTOMS, ANCIENT ROMAN; HOUSE TOMB; LEMURIA; MAUSOLEUM; SOUL, GREEK.

References

Fowler, W. Warde. *The Roman Festivals of the Period of the Republic.* London: Kennikat Press, 1969.

Harrison, Jane Ellen. *Prolegomena to the Study of Greek Religion.* Cambridge: Cambridge University Press, 1922.

Toynbee, J. M. C. *Death and Burial in the Roman World.* Ithaca, NY: Cornell University, 1971.

PĀTĀLA

In the ancient description of the universe found in Hindu texts, Pātāla is the collective name for the seven Underworlds located above hell (Naraka) and below the Earth (Bhūloka) and heaven (Svarga). Like all things Indian, the root idea of the Underworld is found in the earliest spiritual texts, the Vedas, but it is vastly developed in later speculative philosophy.

In the most ancient period, that of the Vedas, the Indian map of the world contained three broad divisions, which were loosely the Earth (Prithivī), the Atmosphere or Middle Region (Antariksha), and Heaven or Sky (Dyaus). Even at this early time, however, the plane or realm of Earth was thought to be subdivided, for one Vedic hymn refers to "the six earths, the one great [world]" (Rig Veda X.14.16), and another implores that sinners be deprived of their bodies and cast *below* the "three earths" (Rig Veda VII.104.11). Thus, in the first Scriptures (dated by scholars variously from 4000 to 2000 B.C.E.), a concept existed of multiple "layers" or planes of Earth and an evil space below them. Given the metaphorical and symbolic nature of the Vedas, we need not assume that the three Earths were necessarily placed one atop the other like pancakes; perhaps they were different planes of existence, different states of being embodied, or centers of mystical contemplation similar to the shamanic journeys of many ancient peoples.

In much later texts, however, the physical and vertical nature of the universe is made abundantly clear, for measurements are given from one physical layer to the next. The Vishnu Purāṇa places the first Underworld 10,000 yojanas under the surface of the earth—about 90,000 miles. The next is 10,000 yojanas below that and so on down to the lowest plane of the Underworld, called Pātāla (which is also the name of the combined Underworld system), at 70,000 yojanas below the earth, or about 630,000 miles. Again, philosophers have sometimes taken these measures of "distance" below the Earth as symbols of the great debasement of the planes of the Underworld or their difference from the kind of physical matter on Earth. But there can be no mistake that in the popular imagination of India the netherworlds have been understood quite literally as existing in the dark layers of the universe far below our sunlit Earth.

The seven talas (literally "lower layers") are given individual names in various lists, such as in Vyāsa's *Yogabhāṣya,* where they are laid out as Rasātala, Mahātala, Atala, Sutala, Vitala, Talātala, and Pātāla, but in most cases they are scarcely distinguished in nature or inhabitants and are simply referred to by the name of the lowest plane. Although in earlier times the seven Underworlds may have been identical with the seven hells (Naraka), by later times they are clearly distinguished, for although Pātāla is described as gloomy and dangerous, only Naraka is ever said to be the place of rebirth for punishment of sin. Upon their deaths, the inhabitants of Pātāla are reborn for punishment in hell if they deserve it.

The seven-layered Pātāla is home to a great many fascinating nonhuman creatures, some possessing superhuman wisdom and many possessing superhuman strength, magic, or skills. One such race is the Nāgas, the "Serpent-People," who in tales are sometimes dangerous and evil. But in religious symbolism, serpents stand for wisdom and magic and shed their skin in a physical "reincarnation." Thus the Nāgas were also powerful magicians, secretive but beneficial to humankind. When they took over Hindu cosmology, Indian and Tibetan Buddhists made the Nāgas a powerful race of spiritual masters who could come to earth to deliver sermons, restore long-lost Scriptures, and train spiritual initiates. Other races include the demonic Rākṣasas (literally "harmful"), who represent the dark side of humanity, our lower nature of greed, lust, and above all pride, as seen in the epic antihero Rāvaṇa, star of the long poem the Rāmāyaṇa. There live also the pishāchas, flesh-eating demons who are sometimes identified as human ghosts, the soul remains of great sinners. Bhūts, or regular ghosts, also dwell in Pātāla but come to the surface of the Earth each night to prey upon the living. On one of the planes of Pātāla also live the daityas, powerful demons who make war upon the gods but are known to have beautiful daughters. In sum, popular legend and spiritual tradition make a home in the seven Underworlds for all creatures of darkness, secrecy, and the occult.

But Pātāla has its charms. Though it is under the Earth and thus shrouded in darkness, it glows with the supernatural radiance of gems and precious metals. Like the dwellers on the surface of Earth, the races of Pātāla have their temples, particularly to Shiva, god of the occult (among other things), and the holy river Ganges has a tributary that runs through the Underworld as well. Scented trees, piles of flowers, and delicious fruits grow there, though their touch and taste is dangerous to those wishing to return to the surface, and there are many other dangers. The strange combination of Otherworld beauty and necromantic horror make Pātāla a fertile ground for romance and adventures.

One tale in *The Ocean of Story* tells of a king, Bhūnandana, who seeks in the Underworlds a beautiful Daitya maiden whom he loves. Led by a magical ascetic and his disciples, the king performs various magic rites to keep away demons and enters Pātāla through a cave in Kashmir. The party walks downward for five days and five nights until they cross the Ganges of the lower regions and behold the lower world spread out for them in all its beauty. Despite the warning of the magician, one of the disciples eats some fruit there and becomes immobilized. The rest pass through a gate composed of precious gems, guarded by two rams with bodies of iron. Eventually, passing by beautiful palaces and women of indescribable beauty and delicacy, the king finds his love. Yet that magical world is a curious combination of sensual delights and horror, for his maiden lover would have him drink from a potion of wine and the fat and blood of corpses. When he refuses, the maiden dumps the potion on his head, and he is instantly transported back to the surface alone but finds that the drink has made him irresistibly fragrant. In time, however, and through spiritual austerity the king again finds his love, and the tale ends piously that "after he had lived with her a long time in happiness, he attained salvation."

See also BHŪT; NARAKA; PISHĀCHA; RĀKṢASA; SHIVA (HINDU); SVARGA; YAMA.

References

Hastings, James, ed. *Encyclopaedia of Religion and Ethics.* Vol. 4: "Cosmogony and Cosmology (Indian)." Edinburgh: T. and T. Clark, 1911.

Kane, Pandurang Vaman. *History of Dharmashāstra: Ancient and Medieval Religious and Civil Law in India.* Vol. 4. Government Oriental Series, Class B, no. 6. Poona: Bhandarkar Oriental Research Institute, 1953.

Tawney, C. H., trans. *The Ocean of Story.* Indian ed. Delhi: Motilal Banarsidass, 1968.

Wilson, H. H. *Vishnu Purāna.* Vol. 1. London: Trübner, 1864.

PERSEPHONE

With a name that literally means "bringer of destruction" (as in the death of vegetation in the autumn), Persephone is the wife of Hades, the god of the Underworld. She is also known as Kore (maiden) and in Roman sources as Proserpina (fearful one).

Later Greek tradition makes Persephone the daughter of the fertility goddess Demeter, who searches for her abducted daughter until she learns that she has been hidden in the Underworld by Hades. Demeter withholds all fertility from the earth, and every living thing is in danger of extinction until Zeus brokers a deal, according to which Persephone spends part of the year aboveground with her mother (which explains the Earth's fertility in summer) and part of her time underground with her husband (which is why the Earth is barren in winter).

But Persephone is a goddess in her own right, appearing frequently in art and myth as both corn maiden and also as queen of the underworld. Poplar trees are sacred to her, and her black poplar grove marks the entrance to Hades. Persephone also has a starring role in the stupid adventure of Theseus and Peirithous, who descend to Hades in an attempt to abduct her. However, arriving in the Underworld, Hades offers them a seat, with which their flesh merged—and they were stuck fast until Herakles visited years later.

But in a more symbolic reading, Persephone is also an integral part of a triple or quadruple goddess, the earth mother Gaia, whose aspects are that of virgin (kore) and bride (nymph), mother (meter) and crone (maia), represented as Kore (corn maiden), Persephone, Demeter, and Hecate (witch and moon goddess). In some sense, these are not separate beings but the same female energy of fertility in different aspects of maturation, reflecting the life stages of women, who were in the ancient past responsible for agriculture and its ritual. Persephone as virgin, then, represents the energy of untilled land ripe with potential, whereas Persephone the underworld queen represents the Earth, who receives her dead children back into her womb.

See also ANTHESTERIA; BANSHEE; ERINYS; HADES; HEL; MORRIGAN; SÍD; UNDERWORLD.

References

Bremmer, Jan. *The Early Greek Concept of the Soul.* Princeton: Princeton University Press, 1983.

Burkert, Walter. *Greek Religion.* Trans. John Raffan. Cambridge: Harvard University Press, 1985.

Dietrich, B. C. *Death, Fate and the Gods.* London: University of London, Athlone Press, 1965.

Farnell, Lewis R. *Greek Hero Cults and Ideas of Immortality.* Oxford: Clarendon Press, 1921.

Graves, Robert. *The Greek Myths.* New York: Penguin, 1960.

Harrison, Jane Ellen. *Prolegomena to the Study of Greek Religion.* Cambridge: Cambridge University Press, 1922.

Kristensen, W. Brede. *Life Out of Death: Studies in the Religions of Egypt and Ancient Greece.* Louvain, Belgium: Peeters Press, 1992.

Lattimore, Richmond, trans. *The Iliad.* Chicago: University of Chicago Press, 1951.

Mandelbaum, Allen, trans. *The Aeneid of Virgil.* New York: Bantam, 1961.

Rieu, E. V., trans. *The Odyssey.* New York: Penguin, 1945.

Sourvinou-Inwood, Christiane. *"Reading" Greek Death: To the End of the Classical Period.* Oxford: Clarendon, 1995.

PHLEGETHON (PYRIPHLEGETHON)

Literally the "burning" river, Phlegethon probably originally referred in a poetic way to the ancient Roman practice of cremating the dead. The name entered into the popular imagination, however, and made a regular appearance in classical visionary literature about the land of the dead. Phlegethon encircles the hellish part of the Roman Underworld, triple-walled Tartaros, in Virgil's classic, the *Aeneid*—terrifying the hero Aeneas who must pass by it to see his father in Elysium. In Dante's great work, *The Divine Comedy,* Phlegethon is no longer a fiery river but a purple river of boiling blood in which violent sinners are steeped up to their waists, shoulders, or even throats. Packs of thousands of centaurs roam the banks, shooting any who try to escape.

See also ACHERON; COCYTUS; HADES; LETHE; STYX; UNDERWORLD; WATER.

References

Dante Alighieri. *The Divine Comedy*. Trans. John Ciardi. New York: Norton, 1977.

Graves, Robert. *The Greek Myths*. New York: Penguin, 1960.

Jowett, Benjamin. *The Essential Plato*. New York: Quality Paperback Books, 1999.

Mandelbaum, Allen, trans. *The Aeneid of Virgil*. New York: Bantam, 1961.

PISHĀCHA

The pishāchas (literally "flesh-eaters," from the Sanskrit word *pishita,* or flesh) are mentioned from the remotest period of Indian history in the first book of the Indian Scriptures called the Vedas. There, along with the titanic asuras and demonic Rākṣasas, the pishāchas are pictured not as ghosts but instead as a race of nonhuman beings who seem to exist solely to cause grief for the pious and god-fearing. Only later are they thought to be the souls of the damned, described as yellowish of skin and of hideous, misshapen appearance. Possibly they are the personification of the eerie, glowing swamp gas that Europeans called *will-o'-the-wisp,* or *ignis fatuus.*

The pishāchas are now a class of Indian ghosts or demons like the bhūts, who are irrational and malevolent toward human beings. Although bhūts are said to form from the souls of those who were murdered or died unhappily, the pishāchas are ghosts of those who were evil and malicious in life: the pishācha is literally the lower mental embodiment of sins like anger, jealousy, greed, and lust. They are considered an extremely dangerous kind of spirit and are thought to possess their hapless victims, bringing on illness and insanity as they attempt to carry on their sinful way of life through a new body.

In some cases, however, like all creatures of the occult, the pishāchas are thought to have some ability to take away the very conditions that they can bring on. Thus if one is able to charm a pishācha or bind it magically, then it may be forced to do one's bidding. William Crooke recounts a tale from the Indian collection *The Ocean of Story* in which a sufferer is told:

> Rise up in the last watch of the night, and with dishevelled hair, and naked, and without rinsing your mouth, take two handfuls of rice as large as you can grasp with the two hands, and, uttering a form of words [mantra], go to a place where four roads meet and there place the two handfuls of rice, and return in silence without looking behind you. Do so always until that Pishācha appears and says, "I will put an end to your ailment." Then receive his aid gladly, and he will remove your complaint.

In this case it seems that appearing wild and unkempt, like a demon oneself, helps in securing demonic assistance—which is surely an instance of sympathetic magic.

See also CHUREL; CROSSROADS; FUNERARY CUSTOMS, ANCIENT INDIAN; PRET; RĀKṢASA.

References

Crooke, William. *The Popular Religion and Folk-lore of Northern India*. 2nd ed. Delhi: Munshiram Manoharlal, 1968.

Hastings, James, ed. *Encyclopaedia of Ethics and Religion*. Vol. 5: "Demons and Spirits, Indian." Edinburgh: T. and T. Clark, 1911.

Monier-Williams, Sir Monier. *A Sanskrit-English Dictionary*. Indian ed. Delhi: Motilal Banarsidass, 1995.

Oman, J. C. *Cults, Customs and Superstitions of India*. Indian ed. Delhi: Vishal Publishers, 1972.

PIT GRAVES, EARLY EGYPTIAN

Well before the first dynasties of Egypt (c. 3100 B.C.E. by orthodox dating methods), pit graves on the desert fringes of Egyptian civilization testify to an early belief in an afterlife. The early graves were simple affairs, merely shallow rectangular, oval, or circular pits, sometimes lined with wooden boards lashed together by leather thongs at the corners, making a kind of primitive coffin. The body was placed in a contracted position, with the knees drawn up under the chin and the hands lying before the face. The body posture, commonly referred to as "fetal position," may be suggestive of a belief in reincarnation because the body was placed in such a way as to prepare it to reenter the womb.

The body was buried with a few possessions: a necklace or other jewelry, pots that probably stored limited food and drink for the after-death journey, and a weapon or tool of the deceased's trade. Some items found in these early graves seem to be ritual objects, probably early amulets.

There is some evidence that attempts were made, even at this early period, to preserve the body by wrapping it in a reed mat or animal skin and sometimes by placing a woven basket over the face, presumably to protect it from sand. In some cases, a simple wooden roof was put on top of the grave to further protect it from the elements, leading perhaps in time to the first actual coffins.

References

Edwards, I. E. S. *The Pyramids of Egypt*. Rev. ed. New York: Penguin, 1978.

Fakhry, Ahmed. *The Pyramids*. Chicago: University of Chicago Press, 1961.

Garstang, J. *Burial Customs of Ancient Egypt*. London: A. Constable and Company, 1907.

Kristensen, W. Brede. *Life Out of Death: Studies in the Religions of Egypt and of Ancient Greece*. Louvain, Belgium: Peeters Press, 1992.

Mendelssohn, Kurt. *The Riddle of the Pyramids*. London: Thames and Hudson, 1974.

Spencer, A. J. *Death in Ancient Egypt*. New York: Penguin, 1982.

PITRI

In the ancient Indian language of Sanskrit, the word *pitri* means "male ancestor," like the Latin *pater* and Spanish *padre*. Ancestors, or pitris, play a very large role in the religious life of the common Hindu person. Not only are a proper funerary ritual and cremation exceedingly important to the immediate welfare of the deceased, but also after the cremation, regular rituals called *shrāddha* are required to insure that the deceased escapes painful states in the ghostly afterlife and arrives safely in Svarga (heaven). Food, water and kind words offered to the dead are thought to reach them whether they are in heaven or have reincarnated elsewhere, removing obstacles and increasing their store of good karma. In return, many blessings such as health, long life, and the birth of baby boys come to the living descendants. To be sure, there is not only the hope of blessings but some elements of fear in dealing with one's deceased ancestors. Even in an ancient Hindu text, Rig Veda III.55.2, there is the prayer: "May the gods and the ancient *pitris* who know the place not injure us here," and certainly modern Indians are very concerned about ghosts.

Many ancient Hindu texts say that the pitris move about as birds, which is similar to the beliefs of many nations, for instance, ancient Egypt, which indicated the word *soul* in hieroglyphics with a human-headed bird. Yet there is some confusion in Hindu thought as to whether the dead remain for some time in an intermediate, "between lives" state in an aerial form moving about over the Earth, or whether the dead quickly incarnate into new bodies either in heaven, in hell, or on the Earth as insects, animals, or humans according to their karma. Some texts, like the *Auśāsana-smriti*, indicate that during sacrifices and rituals meals held in their honor, the pitris in their aerial forms actually enter into the bodies of the brahmin "priests" leading the ceremony. In the bodies of the priests, the pitris physically enjoy what the brahmin priests eat, smell what the priests smell, and are satisfied when the brahmins are satisfied. In this way, the spirits of the departed satisfy the hunger and thirst that characterize the recently dead.

But funerary rituals are not performed only for the very recently dead; they are considered extremely important rituals for relatives as distant as one's great-grandfather. Furthermore, Hindu religious texts emphasize that even ancestors who died long ago may benefit from funerary offerings—but how so if they have been physically reborn? Do those who are reincar-

nated and living happily in new bodies suddenly take aerial forms and fly to the place of a funerary ritual? One text, the *Shrāddhakalpalatā,* states that through the mediation of spiritual beings, namely the gods classed as Vasus, Rudras, and Ādityas, the benefits of the offerings are brought to one's ancestors, wherever they might be. The same deities then bring rewards to the family that performs the ritual with devotion. Often, however, this answer is seen even by Hindus as rather farfetched, and the ritual becomes merely one of faith: it is done because the Scriptures say so. Scholars suggest that a more ancient rite of placating dangerous spirits of the dead has come into conflict with the more philosophical doctrine of reincarnation, and Hinduism has forced the two religious positions into coexistence. Another possibility arises when one examines the literary origin of the concept of pitris, who in the ancient texts are not the recently departed but the ancient ancestors and instructors of the human race.

The earliest known Hindu Scriptures, the Vedas, show a great concern for the pitris, but at this time pitris were understood more as the creators and early sage-heroes of the human race, not as one's immediately departed ancestors. In the Rig Veda, a very ancient Hindu compilation of sacred hymns addressed to gods and cosmic powers, one hymn (X.15.1, 10) addressed to the pitris seems to clarify their nature:

> Let the lower, let the higher,
> Let the middle Ancestors, loving Soma, rise up;
> Let those kind Ancestors, who know cosmic Order,
> Who have gone to eternal life,
> Favor us in our invocations. . . .
>
> They who are true, consuming the offering,
> Having the same nature as Indra and the gods,
> Come O Agni [Lord of Fire], with those thousand Ancestors,
> Those remote, early Ancestors, sitting at the heating vessel,
> Praising the gods. (Adapted from Macdonell)

These ancestors are relatively few in number and are associated with the spiritual enlightenment of the mysterious substance called *soma*. In addition, they are equated with the gods and Indra and are expressly called "remote" and "early." The ritual seems designed to call upon humanity's remote ancestors in order to receive benefits from these wise, departed sages. They might be called "cosmic" or "spiritual" pitris. The Shatapatha-brāhmana commentary on the Vedic Scriptures classifies the "cosmic" ancestors into three groups, Agniśvātta (Consumed by Fire), Barhiṣad (Placed on Sacred Grass), and Somavant (Characterized by the Magic Soma). Other texts have seven or even twelve groups, suggesting astrological correspondences.

But the souls of the recent human dead differ from these ancient entities or gods: the "human" pitris dwell in a separate (and lower) heaven than the gods, namely the third, and they tend to be associated with the moon and the dark halves of the months and the years, whereas the gods dwelling in high heavens are associated with the sun and the light halves of months and years. If the ordinary Hindu ever knew of the distinction between cosmic and human ancestors, it is certainly not the case now, and pitris exist in popular consciousness purely as the souls of the recent dead, that is, up to three generations removed. Thus, it is possible to suggest that an ancient philosophical concept of "spiritual" ancestors devolved by contact with popular belief into a cult of ancestors "validated" by half-understood Scriptures.

See also BHŪT; FUNERARY CUSTOMS, HINDU; NARAKA; PITRILOKA; PRET; REINCARNATION, EASTERN; SHRĀDDHA; SVARGA.

References

Kane, Pandurang Vaman. *History of Dharmashāstra: Ancient and Medieval Religious and Civil Law in India*. Vol. 4. Government Oriental Series, Class B, no. 6. Poona: Bhandarkar Oriental Research Institute, 1953.

Macdonell, Arthur Anthony. *A Vedic Reader for Students*. Indian ed. Delhi: Motilal Banarsidass, 1995.

Pandey, Raj Bali. *Hindu Samskāras: A Socio-religious Study of the Hindu Sacraments*. Banares: Vikrama Publications, 1949.

Shastri, Dakshina Ranjan. *Origin and Development of the Rituals of Ancestor Worship in India*. Calcutta: Bookland, 1963.

PITRILOKA

Literally, "the place of the ancestors," Pitriloka is the Hindu heaven in which the departed enjoy their rest between lives. Exactly where this heaven fits into Hindu cosmography, however, is cause for some debate. In the Scriptural commentary Taittirīya-brāhmana, it is stated that the pitris (ancestors) dwell in the third world from this one. Our Earth is called *Bhūloka*, followed by the atmosphere (or "intermediate region") called *Antariksha*, and higher still the heaven of *Pitriloka*. However, in the commentary titled Brihadāranyaka-upaniṣad, the only worlds mentioned are the ascending worlds of human beings, pitris, and gods, with no atmosphere or intermediate region between humans and the souls of the departed ancestors.

In popular Hindu literature, like the great Indian epic the *Mahābhārata,* heaven is merely one realm, referred to as *Svarga,* and all the dead are received into bliss there. Yet philosophical Hindu texts develop a seven-planed universe, where at the end of every cosmic age (called a *kalpa*) the three lower worlds are destroyed by fire along with the visible universe.

In short, we cannot be certain as to the exact location of Pitriloka in the earliest Scriptural commentaries. However, in developed Hinduism it seems clear that Pitriloka is identical with Svarloka, the third of seven heavens (counting from the bottom up), with the higher four heavens being reserved for the high gods. At the end of each cosmic age, the heaven of the ancestors (along with the Earth and the heaven below Pitriloka) is destroyed and its inhabitants reborn among the gods for a time—only to descend again into human (or lower) bodies at the reemergence of the material universe after the immense period of cosmic rest called *pralāya*.

See also FUNERARY CUSTOMS, HINDU; NARAKA; PITRI; PRET; REINCARNATION, EASTERN; SHRĀDDHA; SVARGA.

References

Kane, Pandurang Vaman. *History of Dharmashāstra: Ancient and Medieval Religious and Civil Law in India*. Vol. 4. Government Oriental Series, Class B, no. 6. Poona: Bhandarkar Oriental Research Institute, 1953.

Macdonell, Arthur Anthony. *A Vedic Reader for Students*. Indian ed. Delhi: Motilal Banarsidass, 1995.

Pandey, Raj Bali. *Hindu Samskāras: A Socio-religious Study of the Hindu Sacraments*. Banares: Vikrama Publications, 1949.

Shastri, Dakshina Ranjan. *Origin and Development of the Rituals of Ancestor Worship in India*. Calcutta: Bookland, 1963.

PITRI-MEDHA

In India the collection and burial of bones left after a cremation is called *pitri-medha*, or "the sacrifice (honoring) ancestors." There is evidence that some early version of this rite was performed even in the ancient Indus Valley civilization, for example, at Mohenjo-Daro, dated by scholars from 3500 to 2500 B.C.E. The principal sources for the current rules of its performance are the Gṛhya Sūtra by Āśvalāyana and the Antyeṣti-paddhati (although older texts like the Taittirīya Āraṇyaka and the Shatapatha-brāhmana contain other prescriptions that were used in more ancient times). It is clear from this rite that the bones of the deceased are considered extremely impure, hence the many precautions such as closing eyes and making regular use of water and milk, both purifying elements in Indian belief.

Generally ten days after the cremation of the body (although in modern cities, it may be immediately), the family members go to the cremation ground to gather the cremains, wash them, and ritually bury them. Some authorities allow women to take part in the rite, but others do not. The performer(s) of the rite should sip water, call out the name and clan of the deceased, and announce the intention to collect the bones. The performer(s) should then walk three times around the spot (with the left side facing the dead) and sprinkle the cremains with purifying milk and water using a tree branch, while mantras (sacred formulas) are spoken. The ashes are collected and thrown away to the south, the cosmic direction of death and the god of death, Yama.

Then the intact bones are gathered. Again, this must be done according to specific directions. The gatherers should crouch on a stone or have at least the left foot on a stone, symbolic of the purifying force of sacred Earth. With closed eyes and using only the thumb and fourth finger of the left hand, the gatherers should collect the bones, beginning with the bones of the feet and proceeding systematically toward the head. The urn itself is specific to gender, the bones of a dead man being placed in an urn without protuberances and the bones of a woman placed in one with protuberances. In either case the bones should be placed in the urn silently, without clinking and jostling. Finally, the bones are winnowed in a basket to remove dust, washed, and replaced in the urn.

The urn is covered with a lid and buried in a pure spot where there is no danger of a river flowing in; for the same reason the burial should not take place during the rainy season. With hands folded, the performer repeats the mantra "approach this mother, Earth" (from Rig Veda X.18.10). The family should then depart without looking back, bathe, and perform the rite of shrāddha for the soul of the deceased. In some texts the family is later instructed to build a small mound (śmāśāna) over the spot, but this practice is dying out in modern times, along with the whole rite of postcremation burial, as the belief in the purifying power of sacred rivers has grown. It is frequent nowadays, especially for those living in northern India, to perform cremations on ghats, or platforms, right on the Ganges or other sacred river. After the cremation the family deposits the cremains in an urn, as already indicated, but the urn is then placed in the river and allowed to float away.

See also FUNERARY CUSTOMS, HINDU; PITRI; SHRĀDDHA.

References

Bhattacharya, Narendra Nath. *Ancient Indian Rituals and Their Social Contents*. Delhi: Manohar, 1975.

Kane, Pandurang Vaman. *History of Dharmashāstra: Ancient and Medieval Religious and Civil Law in India*. Vol. 4. Government Oriental Series, Class B, no. 6. Poona: Bhandarkar Oriental Research Institute, 1953.

Pandey, Raj Bali. *Hindu Samskāras: A Socio-religious Study of the Hindu Sacraments*. Banares: Vikrama Publications, 1949.

Shastri, Dakshina Ranjan. *Origin and Development of the Rituals of Ancestor Worship in India*. Calcutta: Bookland, 1963.

PLUTO (PLUTUS)

One of the many epithets for the Greco-Roman lord of the Underworld, Pluto means "Wealth." It would be natural for the Underworld god to be given this title because of the vast gems and precious metals that lie under the Earth and presumably rest in his power. Hades/Pluto was also worshipped in shrines all over the ancient world for his role in bringing fertility "up from the Earth" each growing season—grain and veg-etation being another kind of "wealth."

The mythological explanation for why the name Pluto was given to Hades is as follows: Hades (literally "Sightless") once abducted Kore (Maiden) from her mother Demeter (Barley Mother). After Demeter brought destruction to the world (and Kore's name was changed to Persephone, or "Bringer of Destruction") Hades consented to release the corn maiden to her mother for part of the year. Thus Hades, in bowing to his mother-in-law Demeter's wishes, became like a son to her and was called by (or confused with) her other son's name, Plutus. This entire cycle of myth was acted out ritually on a yearly basis in many parts of the ancient world, along with prayers and animal sacrifice to the two great powers: Hades, keeper of hidden wealth, and Demeter, bringer of wealth to the sunlit world.

See also DIS; HADES; TARTAROS.

References

Frazer, James George. *The New Golden Bough*. Ed. Theodor H. Gaster. New York: Criterion Books, 1959.

Graves, Robert. *The Greek Myths*. New York: Penguin, 1960.

Harrison, Jane Ellen. *Prolegomena to the Study of Greek Religion*. Cambridge: Cambridge University Press, 1922.

POLTERGEIST

Literally "knocking spirit" (from the German words *poltern* and *geist*), the poltergeist is traditionally thought to be a ghost who takes delight in frightening the living in their homes. Whereas vampires and other undead actively seek to harm the living (or like the banshee, presage impending disaster), the poltergeist merely seems to demand attention. The phenomena associated with the poltergeist are generally physical disturbances: noises such as doorbells ringing or knocking or stomping on walls and ceilings; damage such as broken windows; terrible smells; and dislocation of small objects (including rocks, dirt, and knickknacks used as projectiles). Occasionally, more complex or larger-scale disturbances are reported: heavy furniture is rearranged, phones continually dial certain numbers, loud voices are heard, lights go on and off, and residents are attacked (hair-pulling, scratching, pinching, even sexual assault). In most cases the phenomena appear to be random and unrelated to particular events in the environment; rarely have any patterns of disturbance been reported, and fewer still are the cases of communication between the poltergeist and the victim(s) or investigators.

Hauntings of the poltergeist type have been widely reported in Europe from the earliest times but are also known to various cultures around the world, particularly China and Japan, where a complex demonology and deep-rooted belief in ghosts rivals anything in the West.

Until recent times, poltergeist phenomena were assumed to be caused by spirits of the dead or by demonic or even Satanic possession. Modern investigators have proposed a variety of parapsychological theories that tend to focus on the living. Among the interesting data turned up by such studies, one observation is of particular interest: poltergeist hauntings rarely last longer than a few months (although rare cases such as the Amityville haunting carry on for many years, most unusually, through successive inhabitants of a house). In addition, the poltergeist phenomena often appear to revolve around particular individuals and do not occur when that individual is not in the area. This has caused most modern investigators to speculate that the poltergeist disturbances are caused not by an undead spirit but by psychic energy generated unconsciously by the victim(s) themselves.

References

Gauld, Alan, and A. D. Cornell. *Poltergeists*. London: Routledge and Kegan Paul, 1979.

Rogo, S. Scott. *On the Track of the Poltergeist*. Englewood Cliffs, NJ: Prentice-Hall, 1986.

Roll, William. *The Poltergeist*. Garden City, NY: Nelson Doubleday, 1972.

Stevenson, Ian. "Are Poltergeists Living or Are They Dead?" *Journal of the American Society for Psychical Research* 66 (1972).

Winer, Richard, and Nancy Osborn. *Haunted Houses*. New York: Bantam Books, 1979.

POOKA (PHOOKA, PUCK)

The pooka is a mischievous, usually malicious, spirit that may take many frightening forms and was once blamed for many unlucky accidents in western and northern Europe. It is unclear whether the word is ultimately of Old English or Old German origin, for well before the year 1000 C.E. variations on the word *pooka* are found in writings and place-names in both Old English (*púca*) and Old Norse (*púki*). (Modern versions of the word are the Welsh *pwca*, Irish *púca*, and English *pooka* or *puck*.) Although in more recent folklore the pookas are a class of beings, in Middle English "the Pooka" (or Puck) equated with the Devil. In the unique sense the pooka is also sometimes called Hobgoblin or Robin Goodfellow.

Sometimes in folklore, the pooka may be found in the household as a kind of harmless, even helpful spirit, like the brownie. It may live in the roof, cellar, or seldom-used corners of the house and live off the crumbs of the table. If annoyed, the pooka may upset containers of milk or cause strange noises, but it is also known occasionally to help with chores and clean up after itself. More frequently in folk legend and fairy tales, however, the pooka takes on a much more serious aspect, causing fatal or near-fatal accidents and haunting the countryside as a maleficent ghost, associated with death and decay. When seen at all, the pooka takes on various dark or shadowy shapes, such as a black goat, horse, or bat, sometimes using a fairy light (i.e., *ignis fatuus*, or will-o'-the-wisp) to lead a stranger all night through forest or marsh to his death. For this reason the Irish call rocky pits and caverns *Poula Phooka*.

A good example is the tale of Morty Sullivan, an Irish pilgrim on his way to a chapel in Ballyvourney. One night, as he traveled, he saw a light that he mistook for a campfire, and he began to follow it, though it led off the beaten track. After the fire kept retreating and Morty kept following, he finally met an old hag with glowing red eyes. The hag grabbed Morty's arm and dragged him to the spirit-horse:

> "Mount, Morty, Mount!" cried she, seizing him with supernatural strength, and forcing him upon the back of the horse. Morty finding human power of no avail, muttered, "O that I had spurs!" and tried to grasp the horse's mane; but he caught at a shadow, which nevertheless bore him up and bounded forward with him . . . rushing like the dark midnight storm through the mountains. The following morning Morty Sullivan was discovered by some pilgrims . . . lying on the flat of his back, under a steep cliff, down which he had been flung by the Phooka. (Croker)

William Shakespeare, however, seems to portray the lighter side of the mischievous pooka when he has a fairy say in *A Midsummer Night's Dream* (2.1.40):

> Either I mistake your shape and making quite,
> Or else you are that shrewd and knavish sprite,
> Called Robin Good-fellow: are you not he,
> That fright the maidens of the villagery;
> Skim milk; and sometimes labour in the quern,
> And bootless make the breathless housewife churn;
> And sometime make the drink to bear no barm;
> Mislead night-wanderers, laughing at their harm?
> Those that Hobgoblin call you, and sweet Puck,
> You do their work, and they shall have good luck.

Shakespeare keeps up the ancient tradition of referring to possibly dangerous spirits as "good" and "sweet"; this is certainly a way of trying to avoid potential harm by using reverse psychology. For the same reason fairies, though notoriously dangerous and unpredictable, are often referred to as "the good people" in the hopes of getting them on one's side.

References

Croker, T. Crofton. *Fairy Legends* London: William Tegg, 1862.

PRET (PRETA, PETA)

In India a pret is a ghost, often of the recently dead, who may or may not be dangerous. It is thought to be the size of a person's thumb and to remain in its family home. *Pret* was originally the name of the recently dead, who would within a year proceed on to a more permanent heaven with the divine ancestors. In this sense, the pret is merely a benign household spirit, sometimes helping the family it has left behind in various ways. However, in folk belief, the word *pret* is also used for the malevolent ghost of an abused or unhappy person, for example, a child who has died prematurely due to parental neglect of sacred rites or a deformed or crippled person. In this case, the pret does not soon depart the Earth, and it harbors great resentment against the living. It may be dangerous indeed.

The word *pret* descends originally from the ancient Indian language of Sanskrit. From the prefix *pra* and the verbal root *i,* meaning "to depart," the word *preta* is derived, meaning "one who has departed, died." In ancient times the preta was not a ghost exactly but merely a soul undergoing the normal process of death, which involved remaining on Earth in a limbo between physical death and the completion of proper funeral rites. These ritual offerings go on for a year or more. At the end of one year, the preta gains a new spiritual body and ascends "by the paths of the fathers" on to the realm of the ancestors, or pitris. In the meantime the preta is completely dependent on its family, particularly a son, to carry out the absolutely essential funerary rituals. Of course, if the offerings are not made properly or on time, the preta may not be able to transform into a pitri and proceed onward to heaven—in which case it is condemned to remain a preta on Earth indefinitely. Most Hindu families are quite careful to avoid this danger.

Spiritual texts, such as the collection dealing with domestic rituals (Gṛhya Sūtras) and those concerned with life duties in general (Dharmaśāstras), detail the necessary funeral steps to assist the preta. After cremation, the dead person is thought to arise in an invisible body made entirely of light (tejas), air (vayu), and extremely subtle matter (ākāśa). In this subtle bodily form, called *ātivāhika śarīra,* or "faster-than-wind body," the deceased is extremely vulnerable, and suffers terribly from heat, cold, and wind. However, on each day after the cremation, a family member makes a ritual offering of a rice ball (called *piṇḍa*) mixed with honey, fruits, milk, and butter and an offering of water and sacred leaves, accompanied by appropriate utterances (mantras). Each of the ten days of offerings is thought to build up a part of a new body, still invisible but more hardy, so that the intense suffering of the preta may cease and the journey to the Otherworld begin. On the first day, the piṇḍa offering builds the subtle head, the second day builds the subtle ears, nose, and eyes, and so on down to the tenth day,

which completes the new subtle body. The intense suffering from wind, heat and cold ceases, but the new, more solid body brings on new sufferings: hunger and thirst. To compensate, the deceased is given food offerings every month until the first anniversary of his or her death. Then a final grand offering is made at a ceremony called *sapiṇḍakaraṇa,* whereupon the preta graduates to a new, elevated form called *pitri* and ascends to the world of the ancestors for enjoyment—until the time comes for rebirth. The family no longer makes monthly offerings to the individual dead but only annual offerings to the collective ancestors residing in heaven

The situation is quite similar in Buddhism, which also originated in India and gained a great many things from its Hindu parent religion, but enough differences remain to warrant a closer view. In the Buddhist language of Pali, the word is *peta,* and a large body of Buddhist writings concerns these unhappy creatures, such as the southern Indian Buddhist work called the *Petavatthu,* written by Dhammapāla, in the larger cycle of texts called Khuddaka Nikāya.

In the Buddhist view, the death of a human being is merely the occasion of the inner nature, or skandhas, taking a new birth, often almost immediately. This rebirth may return the deceased to Earth or send him or her to a great variety of heavens and hells. Wicked people, particularly those neglectful of (Buddhist) religion, can be reborn in one of the hells as a peta. Here we see a significant difference from the Hindu conception in that the peta is not an intermediate state prior to ascension to heaven; for Buddhists, the peta itself is the rebirth of the soul, and its lifespan is very much longer than a year. In Buddhism the peta is pictured as a miserable creature with a monstrously huge potbelly but a pitifully small mouth and neck—thus, as in Hinduism but more graphically, we see that the petas suffer endlessly from hunger and thirst.

Usually, the peta is confined to his or her state for a great length of time measured in thousands of years, but eventually this karma will be fulfilled and fade out, hopefully to be replaced by another, better karma that has been stored up from the past and will lead to a more fortunate rebirth. The efforts of family members for the deceased, such as offerings of food and water, can ease their suffering. The family may also make donations to Buddhist monasteries and shrines, transferring the merit thus obtained to the deceased and shortening the length of time spent suffering as a peta.

See also BHŪT; FUNERARY CUSTOMS, HINDU; PITRI; SHRĀDDHA; YAMA.

References

Crooke, William. *The Popular Religion and Folk-lore of Northern India.* 2nd ed. Delhi: Munshiram Manoharlal, 1968.

Gupta, A. P. *Disposal of the Dead and Physical Types in Ancient India.* Delhi: Oriental Publishers, 1972.

Kane, Pandurang Vaman. *History of Dharmashāstra: Ancient and Medieval Religious and Civil Law in India*. Vol. 4. Government Oriental Series, Class B, no. 6. Poona: Bhandarkar Oriental Research Institute, 1953.

Keith, Arthur Berriedale. *The Mythology of All Races*. Vol. 6: *Indian Mythology*. New York: Cooper Square, 1964.

Pandey, Raj Bali. *Hindu Saṃskāras: A Socio-religious Study of the Hindu Sacraments*. Banaras: Vikrama Publications, 1949.

Shastri, Dakshinaranjan. *Origin and Development of the Rituals of Ancestor Worship in India*. Calcutta: Janakinath Basu, 1963.

PURE LAND

In later Buddhism (from around 200 C.E. onward), particularly in China and then Japan, a religious practice emerged that focused less on the early Buddhist ideal of nirvāṇa and more on a blest rebirth after death in heaven. This heaven is called *pure* (in Chinese, *ching*) because it is free from all base passions and desires, from sin, and from all the distractions and defilements that prevent a perfect spiritual life on Earth. It is described as everything Earth is not: always pleasant, with no hunger or disease, and fragrant with scents in the air. The entire heaven is responsive to its inhabitants' slightest desire, and life there is unending. Even quite ordinary people can gain rebirth there simply through faith and devotion to the deity. Although Pure Land Buddhism is one of the most important religious movements in East Asia, it is also controversial. Pure Land teachings in their developed form cannot be found in the undisputed early teachings of the Buddha, and the new focus on "faith" is a radical departure from the self-reliance everywhere prevalent in the early Buddhist Scriptures. Yet today, belief in an afterlife existence in the pure field of a radiant cosmic Buddha is the primary faith of millions of Buddhists.

Early Buddhism, as described in the Nikāya Scriptures of the third to first centuries B.C.E., taught that any rebirth into a body—human, nonhuman, heavenly, worldly, pleasant, or unpleasant—merely prolongs the suffering inherent in existence. Such whirling from death to rebirth to death to rebirth is called *saṃsāra* and is caused by constant desires for more sensory experience and more gratification of the ego, or false sense of "self." The original, historical Buddha appears to have taught very clearly that there is but one escape from craving that leads to human suffering and but one spiritual goal worthy of the name: the complete liberation of enlightenment, called in Sanskrit *nirvāṇa*. The perfect release of nirvāṇa is directly opposed in early Buddhist texts to activity that builds up merit for future rewards, such as a happy birth (see, for instance, the *Khuddaka-pāṭha* VI.14). Yet early Buddhism recognized that such a path of sensual withdrawal from the world and cutting off craving for rewards is very difficult and not attainable by many, at least not for many

lifetimes to come. As we read in the Dhammapada (85–86), "Only a few reach the farther shore. Most people go their rounds on this one. Those, however, who listen to the Teaching and live up to its precepts cross over to the farther shore. This crossing over the dominion of [the demon] Māra is difficult indeed." Thus in early Buddhism, those who were not capable of full liberation in this present human life were encouraged to follow the ascetic path in preparation for nirvāṇa, which would only be reached after many, many lifetimes of hard work on Earth.

This view is quite different from the popular and largely nonascetic Pure Land Buddhist movement, which developed in India many centuries after Buddhism was founded in the sixth century B.C.E. Rather than many lifetimes of self-reliance, the emerging Pure Land tradition used faith and all-consuming devotion to a transhistorical Buddha to gain rebirth in a heaven called *Sukhāvatī*—where there will be no more suffering and no more reincarnation and where, in the presence of a cosmic deity, one will attain nirvāṇa quickly and easily. (For a very early and slightly less faith-centered version of the Pure Land movement, see the entry on ABHIRATI.) Rebirth in the Pure Land results from having a strong faith and practicing devotions such as chanting the name of a Buddha and visualizing his heavenly paradise. The Pure Land practice is said to be "easy," and rebirth in the pure heaven is attainable by anyone who repeats the name of the deity (Amitābha in India; Amida in Japan; O-mi-t'o Fo in China) up to ten times, even if the practitioner is a great sinner. How can the Pure Land tradition be reconciled with early, established Buddhism or even be called Buddhism at all?

Textually, Pure Land Buddhists justify their movement by relying on two Sanskrit Scriptures, the Larger and Smaller Sukhāvatī-vyūha-sūtras (Pure Land Scriptures) composed around the second century C.E. and a Chinese Scripture, the Wu-liang-shou ching (Meditation Scripture), dating to around the fifth century C.E. None of these texts may reasonably be dated back to the historical Buddha; the Meditation Scripture was not even written in India, the original land of Buddhism. But Pure Land Buddhism cannot be fairly criticized on account of "made up" Scriptures because all Buddhist schools base their Scriptures on oral traditions from the historical Buddha as well as later written compilations. At least two of the Pure Land texts are clearly Indian in origin and point to a relatively early development of religious practice aimed at rebirth in heaven, though there is every reason to believe such practice was relatively unpopular at first. Also, Pure Land tradition asserts that several immensely important Buddhist thinkers in India supported Pure Land teachings, including Nāgārjuna from the second century C.E. and Vasubandhu from the fourth century C.E. Unfortunately, only the Chinese versions of their Pure Land works exist, not the alleged Sanskrit originals, so it is not clear if the support of these two great philosophers is a fact or a later, pious fabrication.

Philosophically, Pure Land Buddhism is grounded in coherent principles that merely extend religious ideas accepted by all Buddhists. One such universal Buddhist idea is that a perfectly enlightened Buddha is an infinite being with the power to lead less realized beings to enlightenment. Another universal Buddhist idea is the power of making a gift with sincerity and devotion— making gifts generates good karma for the giver and sets up conditions for a happy future. Finally, there is the Buddhist belief, drawn from established Indian tradition, in the magical power of making a vow; sincere vows over time naturally tend to their fulfillment. Pure Land philosophy extends these ideas, claiming that a being may make a vow that he or she will attain perfect spiritual realization but not without saving all beings. Eventually, when after countless eons the vow is fulfilled, the being who made the vow becomes a perfect Buddha—which implies that the means have also been created to save all other beings. Thus, in Pure Land teaching, upon enlightenment, such a vow-fulfilling Buddha may act as a deity, generating an entire universe (in Sanskrit, *buddha-kṣetra*) that is utterly pure (unlike our defiled world) with qualities perfect for the attainment of freedom. Meanwhile, impure, sinful beings, by making gifts, offering praise, or simply focusing thought on such a Buddha, gain the attention of that Buddha. At the death of the devotee, the Buddha causes that person to be reborn in his personal heaven, and through transferring part of his infinite merit to the sinful person, all of that person's bad karma is wiped out, and he or she can stay in the Buddha's heaven without rebirth, practicing spirituality until full enlightenment dawns.

Pure Land Buddhism was far more influential in East Asia than it was in India. Under the missionary efforts of such pioneers as T'an-luan (c. 488–c. 554 C.E.), Tao-ch'o (562–645), and his disciple Shan-tao (613–681), rebirth in the Pure Land (called Ching-T'u) gained tremendous popularity in the East. In early Chinese Buddhist history and probably in India as well, Pure Land devotion was seen as a somewhat remedial practice for the weak. By the sixth and seventh centuries C.E. in China, however, faith in the Buddha aimed at rebirth in heaven became a practice that stood alone and was respectable to many. Although the Pure Land movement eventually lost strength in China, it remained an important part of the thinking and practice of many Buddhist schools. Later, in the Kamakura period of Japanese history (twelfth to fourteenth centuries C.E.), Pure Land spirituality again rose to great prominence and today remains the most popular form of Japanese Buddhism.

Although it is grounded in established Buddhist principles, Pure Land theology is controversial among Buddhists who follow earlier Buddhist practice and Scriptures. Some Buddhists question where this Pure Land might exist, for there is no room in the traditional Buddhist picture of the universe for such a state. The Pure Land appears to lie beyond the karmic laws of the known universe of saṃsāra but below the perfectly enlightened state of nirvāṇa. Likewise, the practice of relying almost entirely upon the power of a Buddha seems to undermine many early Buddhist teachings that emphasize constant attention to one's thoughts and behavior and the gradual attainment of enlightenment. Even some prominent East Asian Buddhist thinkers have been critical of Pure Land hopes, such as Ching-ying Hui-yuan, who stated, "Although this land is pure, it is generated by erroneous thoughts and hence is as empty and unreal as what is seen in a dream" (Foard). Yet in the final analysis, Pure Land Buddhists rely not on texts, philosophy, or consent from other Buddhist traditions but on personal spiritual experience. The Pure Land is seen and known in meditative experience; the love of the Buddha is felt by practitioners reciting his name; and at death, the devotee receives a vision of his or her acceptance into the Pure Land.

See also ABHIRATI; AKṢOBHYA; CHING T'U; DEWACHAN (TIBETAN BUDDHIST); HEAVENS, BUDDHIST; JŌDŌ; NIRVĀṆA; REINCARNATION, EASTERN ; SUKHĀVATĪ.

References

Becker, Carl B. *Breaking the Circle: Death and the Afterlife in Buddhism*. Carbondale, IL: Southern Illinois University Press, 1993.

Cappell, David. "Chinese Buddhist Interpretations of the Pure Lands." In *Buddhist and Taoist Studies*, ed. David Chappell and Michael Saso. Honolulu: University Press of Hawaii, 1977.

Chang, Garma C. C., ed. *A Treasury of Mahāyāna Sūtras*. Trans. Buddhist Association of the United States. University Park: Pennsylvania State University Press, 1983.

Ch'en, Kenneth. *Buddhism in China*. Princeton: Princeton University Press, 1964.

Dantinne, J. *La Splendeur de l'Inébranable (Akshobhyavyūha)*. Vol. 1: *Tripitaka Sūtrapitaka Akṣobhyatathāgatavyūha*. Louvain-la-Neuve: Institut Orientaliste, 1983.

Foard, James, Michael Solomon, and Richard K. Payne, eds. *The Pure Land Tradition: History and Development*. Berkeley Buddhist Studies Series no. 3. Berkeley: University of California Press, 1989.

Overmyer, D. *Folk Buddhist Religion: Dissenting Sects in Late Traditional China*. Cambridge: Harvard University Press, 1976.

Ryosetsu, F. *The Way to Nirvana: The Concept of the Nembutsu in Sahn-tao's Pure Land Buddhism*. Tokyo: Kyoiku Shincho Sha, 1974.

Suzuki, D. T. *Buddha of Infinite Light*. Boston: Shambhala, 1998.

Williams, Paul. *Mahāyāna Buddhism: The Doctrinal Foundations*. New York: Routledge, 1989.

PURGATORY

In Catholic belief, Purgatory is the place after death where sinners go if they are not so wicked as to deserve eternity in Hell but not pure enough to enter Heaven: in other words, the vast majority of humanity. There, for hundreds, even thousands or tens of thousands of years, the souls of sinners are punished and purged, often by fire and terrible, hell-like tortures. Over time they gradually become lighter and cleaner and may finally ascend to heaven. Fueled by thousands of personal visions of the afterlife as well as an increasingly rational theology, the doctrine of Purgatory was a gradual invention of the Roman Catholic branch of Christianity. It is a commonsense doctrine, answering the needs of ordinary people who cannot possibly live up to the standards set by Jesus in the Gospels: it provides a means by which they could "work off" inevitable human sins and still enter Heaven eventually. The doctrine of Purgatory also supports the natural beliefs of the majority of humanity that the living can help the dead through offerings, sacrifices, and prayers: these shorten the stay of loved ones in Purgatory and make their sufferings there easier to bear. However, the doctrine of Purgatory is also easily abused, for it gives the church tremendous power over the dead as well as the living. To this day, the Catholic Church reserves for itself the power to determine who goes to Heaven, who goes to Purgatory, and who is consigned to everlasting Hell. Priests hear confessions, absolve sins, and prescribe penances, and they also excommunicate and condemn. The opportunities for abuse are real and have been frequent in history. Meanwhile, the Biblical basis for the existence of Purgatory is slim at best. For these and similar reasons, Roman Catholicism is alone among the Christian denominations in teaching a Purgatory; Protestants and the Eastern Orthodox Churches do not accept the doctrine.

Purgatory evolved very gradually over centuries, in response to changing human needs and growing intellectual unrest. A major problem for the early Christians was the extreme dualism of Heaven and Hell. As long as Christians were in the minority in the Roman Empire and survived in small, tightly knit groups, it was easy for them to declare that all Christians were destined for Heaven and that their Roman persecutors were consigned to Hell. But when Christianity became the dominant religion in the ancient world—its adherents widespread and quite different by geographical region and social class—and Jesus still did not return as expected, Christianity was forced to accept new political, social, and intellectual roles. Gradually, the simplistic Heaven/Hell dichotomy began to be troubling, and new questions arose. What happened after death to "heretics," those Christians who did not think like the majority? What happened after death to faithful, bap-

tized Christians who still committed many sins? Since the world apparently was not ending immediately, as predicted in the New Testament, then what happened in the long period between an individual's death and the eventual Last Judgment of the world? To answer these new questions, Christians took a closer look at their own Scriptures, as well as the beliefs and philosophies of their older and (sometimes) wiser neighbors.

In many matters theological, the early Christians had their roots in Jewish traditions. In the Book of Enoch, dated from around 200 B.C.E., the prophet Enoch sees the various kinds of dead awaiting the Last Judgment in mountain caverns. The righteous await the resurrection in a pleasant area, while some of the wicked suffer; others, who were punished during life, apparently will not be resurrected at all. This is no Purgatory, for no sins are removed here. Nevertheless, the Book of Enoch raised the question of what the souls of the dead experience between the time of their own deaths and the end of the world. Another Jewish text, 2 Maccabees, suggested that prayers of the living could help the dead. Judas Maccabeus ordered all his people to pray for Jewish soldiers and collected a "sin offering" of 2,000 drachmas, which he sent to Jerusalem. How this was supposed to have helped the dead, the author of the text himself explains (2 Maccabees 12:45–46):

> For if [Judas Maccabeus] had not been expecting the fallen to rise again, it would have been foolish and superfluous to pray for the dead. But since he had in view the wonderful reward reserved for those who die a godly death, his purpose was a holy and pious one. And this was why he offered an atoning sacrifice to free the dead from their sin.

Such a belief became increasingly important in early Christianity as church doctrines were forced to come to grips with the tenacious belief of common people that the dead can be helped by actions specifically dedicated to them and performed by the living. Such a transference of merit eventually became a central concept in the new doctrine of Purgatory.

Another important purgatorial component was the ancient Greek belief in reincarnation and afterdeath punishment for sin, summed up very well by Plato in the *Republic* and other dialogues. The basic teaching was this: between lives, the souls of the dead are rewarded or punished for their actions but only temporarily and only as part of the soul's education. Repeatedly, all souls came back to new bodies on Earth, until at last perfected souls were released from bondage to the material world altogether and ascended to the Good. Many early Christians were persuaded by this "education" theory and chose to believe that after death, even sinners (or some of them, anyway) could suffer and be thus purged of their sins—though there is little evidence that reincarnation ever became popular in Christianity. One of the greatest Christian thinkers, however, was Origen of Alexandria (c. 180 to c. 253 C.E.), who probably accepted reincarnation and taught as well that even the worst sinners in Hell—even Satan himself!—would eventually be purged of their sins, and all of God's creation would be reunited eventually in Heaven, even if it took millions of years. Within a century after his death, however, Origen's views were condemned by the new authorities in the church.

So if *all* the dead were not saved, then, the trouble remained for Christian doctrine: which sinners, exactly, can be saved after death, either through their own personal suffering or through the aid of the living? This problem was made more difficult by the slim yet contradictory testimony of the Bible. All the statements reported of Jesus offer only two afterlife conditions: one is either saved, or one is lost (i.e., condemned to Gehenna, a lake of fire). Scholars continue to debate whether we should metaphorically understand Jesus regarding Heaven and Hell; nevertheless, only two destinations are provided. The story of the rich man Dives and the pauper Lazarus gives the same impression: the sinful rich man finds himself in Hell after death and cries out to Lazarus, who sits in a heaven-like place called "the bosom of Abraham" (Luke 16:19–26). There is no middle place. Strangely, the great apostle Paul, author of most of the letters in the New Testament, does not teach the doctrine of Hell at all: but he also seems to indicate only two possibilities: the righteous will be resurrected into new spiritual bodies, and sinners will be destroyed, plain and simple. As Paul is famously quoted, "the wage of sin is death" (Romans 5:6). Yet Paul makes one solitary statement that was tantalizingly ambiguous enough to provide a foothold for a "middle place," and indeed this single statement became almost the sole Scriptural basis for Purgatory. It is found in 1 Corinthians 3:11–15:

> There can be no other foundation beyond that which is already laid; I mean Jesus Christ himself. If anyone builds on that foundation with gold, silver, and fine stone, or with wood, hay, and straw, the work that each man does will at last be brought to light; the day of judgement will expose it. For that day dawns in fire, and the fire will test the worth of each man's work. If a man's building stands, he will be rewarded; if it burns, he will have to bear the loss; and yet he will escape with his life, as one might from a fire.

The ambiguities are many: is Paul speaking of a real fire after death? Probably not—but most early and even medieval Christians understood him this way.

What does Paul mean that even he who loses his foundation "yet will escape with his life"? Does this mean that even after death and the day of judgment, sinners may be forgiven or may somehow rectify their situation? The interpretation of this verse became key in the many debates that attended the development of Christian beliefs regarding death, the afterlife, and Purgatory.

Although he was not the first, Augustine (354–430 C.E.) was the most successful of the church fathers in systematizing Christian beliefs about the state of the dead and the possibility of cleansing or purging sins after death. According to Augustine, there were not two or three but four fundamentally different kinds of persons; each will lead a categorically different kind of "life" in the next world. Atheists and grievous sinners proceed directly to Hell; they need not await the foregone conclusion of the Last Judgment. Sinners who are not altogether wicked also go to Hell, but acts of the living (prayers, charity in their name, etc.) may help them—if not to escape Hell, at least to lessen its fury as far as they are concerned. The perfectly pure saints and martyrs form a third class, who proceed directly to Heaven. Finally, those Christians who are guilty of numerous "minor" sins might possibly be saved by means of an ordeal after death, that is, suffering miserably in a purgatorial fire but eventually arriving at Heaven. Augustine is clear that the aid of the living does not necessarily help the dead unless the dead have done things to merit such aid. And even at this early date, Augustine was concerned about the routinization of forgiveness of sins, later sold by the church as "indulgences." Augustine leaves the ultimate fate of the dead in God's hands and warns against human attempts to abuse God's mercy:

> Of course we must take care that no one should think that those outrageous crimes, the commission of which excludes from possession of the kingdom of God, may be perpetrated every day, and every day bought off by almsgiving. Rather should there take place an amendment of life: and by means of almsgiving God should be brought to pardon sins past, and not in some sort of way bribed to allow them to be continually committed with impunity. (Augustine, *Enchiridion,* sections 69–70, quoted in Le Goff)

On careful analysis, it becomes clear that Augustine did not teach the existence of a literal place called *Purgatory,* but rather offered the hope that some few Christians, less than perfect, might eventually be saved by the actions of their pious relatives and, most of all, through God's grace. The great theologian was careful, however, to leave the details of purgation to God.

penitential burden. The latter, whose life was beyond reproach, accepted, and though he thought he had a great deal of time remaining in which to carry out his promise, he soon died. A few days after his death, he appeared in a dream to the penitent monk, who asked about his condition. The dead monk told him that on his account he had suffered a fate hard and cruel. Delivered from his own sins, he was still laden down with those of his companion. He asked for help from his living brother and from the entire convent. All the monks submitted to penance, and the dead man reappeared, this time with a serene and even happy look. Thanks, he said, to the prayers of his brothers he had not only been delivered from the pain of punishment but by a miraculous decision of the right hand of the Most High, he had recently been transported among the elect. (Le Goff, pp. 179–180)

This emphasis on purgation—and the possibility of transferring merit recorded in such visions—eventually came to dominate thinking about the afterlife. Entire monasteries were formed to pray for society as a whole (or paid to pray for wealthy patrons and carry out their penances), and the church increasingly saw its public services, especially the mass, as primarily for the benefit of the dead rather than the living. Special locations on the Earth became associated with purgation and were the focal point of massive pilgrimages, such as the volcano Mount Etna in Sicily and Saint Patrick's Purgatory, a cave in Ireland. Local heroes and saints, and above all, Mary, the mother of God, grew more important because they could pray to Jesus to intercede with God for the forgiveness of sins. (The prominence of Mary veneration in the High Middle Ages of western Europe can scarcely be overstated.) In addition, visionary literature began to impress the newly forming intelligentsia of the twelfth and thirteenth centuries, prompting the Catholic Church to make Purgatory official doctrine at the Second Council of Lyons in 1274. The triumph of visionary literature came with Dante Alighieri's *Divine Comedy,* the first part of which was published in 1314 and which offered a complete geography of the afterlife. From vague notions of caves and chasms, Purgatory emerged as a great mountain, stretching from Hell as its base to the earthly paradise at its summit and pointing to the vast empyrean of the heavens. Dante's imagery gave permanent shape to Purgatory.

The subsequent theological and even military struggles over papal indulgences, the intercession of saints, so-called Maryolatry, and other issues that led to the Reformation are well known to students of history. Beginning with Martin Luther (1483–1546),

After Augustine, the Western world rapidly slipped into the intellectual and economic eclipse of the Middle Ages, and little changed theologically in the Christian church from the fifth to eleventh centuries. During this decline in learning, however, popular culture continued to evolve and gradually wrought fundamental changes in the church. One of the most important developments was the rise to prominence of "visions," either of people who had themselves somehow seen the afterlife or visions of people who had been visited by dwellers in the realms beyond. Augustine cited a few visions to give clout to his version of the afterlife, but in the Middle Ages, testimonials from ghosts and spirits of all sorts clinched the fact that prayers, charity, and church services (masses) performed by the living for the dead did indeed help the suffering dead. Popular visionary literature tended toward the dramatic and emphasized the horrendous sufferings of Purgatory; but such tales also emphasized the fact that in every case, after receiving spiritual help from the living, the suffering dead were able to escape hell-like tortures and join the blest in Heaven. Apparently, one could not only transfer merit from the living to the dead, but one could also transmit both merit and sin between the living, as one story from Peter Damian (a prominent monk and then cardinal of the late eleventh century) relates:

In the monastery *ad Pinum,* near the sea, there was a monk who, weighed down by sin, had been given a long, hard penance. He asked a brother who was a close friend of his to help him and share his the reforming Protestants systematically excised from their belief all doctrines that did not have an extremely clear source in the Bible, and of course Purgatory, buttressed weakly with 1 Corinthians 3:13–15 and Matthew 12:32 was quickly cut out. There can be no doubt that many unscrupulous members of the Catholic Church hierarchy did indeed abuse the doctrines of Purgatory and intercession, economically and spiritually; great wealth was made by selling writs of forgiveness of sin, and not infrequently the wealthy hired out the poor to complete their own penances. Certainly the medieval church relished its newfound ability to dictate the fate of the dead as well as the living and intimidate ordinary people and even great rulers with portrayals of a near-eternity of unspeakable sufferings. Nevertheless, it must not be overlooked that Purgatory provides considerable comfort to the believer. Rather than an eternity in Hell, even serious sinners have at least a hope of working off their spiritual debts in Purgatory and eventually entering Heaven; meanwhile, those who have lost loved ones take heart in the belief that through their prayers, vigils, and masses for the dead, their loved ones may be helped. After death, most Catholics hope that they too will be remembered in the prayers of the people they left behind. For all its abuses, the Catholic Church has shown in the doctrine of Purgatory at least the intention of being a good shepherd to its people.

See also ANCESTOR VENERATION; BARZAKH; GEHENNA; HEAVEN, ORIGINS OF; HELL, HISTORY OF; HELL, ORIGINS OF; INTERCESSION; JUDGMENT, LAST; JUDGMENT, PARTICULAR; UNDERWORLD.

References

Bosing, Walter. *Hieronymous Bosch: Between Heaven and Hell.* Cologne: Benedikt Taschen, 1987.

Catherine of Genoa. *Catherine of Genoa, Purgation and Purgatory.* New York: Paulist Press, 1847.

Dante Alighieri. *The Purgatorio: Dante's Timeless Drama of an Ascent through Purgatory.* Trans. John Ciardi. New York: New American Library, 1961.

Fenn, Richard K. *The Persistence of Purgatory.* Cambridge: Cambridge University Press, 1995.

Gardiner, Eileen, ed. *Visions of Heaven and Hell before Dante.* New York: Italica Press, 1989.

Gurevich, Aron. *Medieval Popular Culture: Problems of Belief and Perception.* Trans. James M. Bak and Paul A. Hollingworth. New York: Cambridge University Press, 1990.

Le Goff, Jacques. *The Birth of Purgatory.* Trans. Arthur Goldhammer. Chicago: University of Chicago Press, 1984.

Owen, D. D. R. *The Vision of Hell: Infernal Journeys in Medieval French Literature.* New York: Barnes and Noble, 1971.

PYRAMID, EGYPTIAN

Pyramids are the quintessential symbols of Egypt, not merely for the curious modern traveler but equally for the ancient Egyptians themselves. For the pyramids—demonstrating in their construction a sophisticated mathematical, astronomical, and philosophical development—were meant to serve as permanent architectural testaments to Egyptian values and thought, and they provide the modern researcher a cultural legacy well worth careful investigation.

Pyramids appear precipitously in Egyptian history with no antecedents and remarkably little experimentation. One would expect a gradual development of architectural skill and a prolonged period of perfection, but the reverse is the case. At the start of the Third Dynasty (around 2700 B.C.E. by orthodox chronological accounts), the earlier Egyptian tombs (see MASTABA) were no longer being built, and pyramids of immense scale appeared, almost without transition. The only transitional monuments are a few so-called step pyramids, discussed later. Even more puzzling, the largest, best-executed pyramids belong to the early dynasties, but as Egyptian history progressed, the size and quality of new pyramids steadily decreased until they were no longer built at all. A satisfactory explanation for this phenomenon has yet to gain widespread approval among researchers, although several theories are in circulation. One theory is that Egypt was invaded in the early dynastic period, and the invaders brought advanced mathematical and architectural skills with them; but this theory merely pushes the origin of the problem to another geographical region without solving it. Another theory proposes that Egypt did not develop its early culture by itself but rather inherited much from previous culture(s) that left few traces, unless one accepts recent attempts to re-date the Sphinx to a much earlier period.

In either case, one can only marvel at the scope and grandeur of the pyramid-building project. The Greek historian Herodotus (c. 484 to 430–420 B.C.E.) states that the great pyramid of Khufu took thirty years to construct, using 100,000 workmen rotated every three months; this might be taken as a typical example. It has been suggested that immense ramps were built encircling the pyramids in order to lift the huge blocks up to ever greater heights as the work on a pyramid progressed. The several million stone blocks used in each pyramid weighed 8 to 10 tons each. (Stones of even greater size were routinely used in ancient Egypt: the colossus of Ramses II weighed at least 1,000 tons and was cut from a single block.) The ramp theory has come under criticism, however, because the material needed to form the ramp would itself be eight or nine times as massive as the material of the pyramid itself. Other theories of construction involve complex systems of pulleys and levers or perhaps balancing machines using counterweights to lift each stone. In short, no one is quite certain exactly how the pyramids were built.

The first pyramid-like structure found so far in

The pyramids at Giza. Courtesy of Anne Ronan Picture Library.

Egypt and the first structure to be made entirely of stone rather than mud bricks, are the step pyramids at Saqqâra and Zawiyet ed-Aryan, which are actually quite different from later pyramids. The most important of these step pyramids is at Saqqâra, attributed to the pharaoh Zoser and built by his architect Imhotep (twenty-seventh century B.C.E.), whom later tradition deified as the father of medicine, astronomy, and magic. It was clearly built in stages, probably beginning with an unusually shaped mastaba, of square design rather than the usual rectangle. Each side of the base was oriented to one of the four cardinal directions and faced with dressed stone. However, the base was enlarged and made into the bottom of a six-stepped pyramid (paralleling the six steps of Osiris's tomb at Abydos described later in entry) giving the pyramid a total height of 204 feet, with a base 411 feet wide by 358 feet long. It was surrounded by a great wall and a large complex of mortuary temples and related buildings connected with the afterlife of the king. Near Zoser's pyramid in Saqqâra lies another step pyramid, belonging probably to the pharaoh Sekhemkhet, and a short distance from Saqqâra, another step pyramid has been found, belonging possibly to the pharaoh Khaba. Neither of these two

pyramids came close to being finished but seem clearly to have been modeled after Zoser's remarkable prototype.

In the Fourth Dynasty (c. 2600 B.C.E.), by current accounts, the "true" pyramid style emerged. Each of the five known pharaohs of this dynasty built for himself massive pyramids of superlative quality, including the so-called Great Pyramid of Khufu (Cheops in Greek) and the three different pyramids ascribed to Seneferu. Although many Egyptologists are content to consider the early pyramids merely grandiose tombs, several facts make this identification problematic and lead the careful scholar to distinguish between the probable function(s) of the massive and precise early pyramids and the smaller and shabbier pyramids of later dynasties.

First, among all the early true pyramids, only three (probably ritual) sarcophagi have been found, without a single coffin or mummy—but later, smaller pyramids, which were indisputably used as tombs, have yielded a plethora of both coffins and mummies. Also, the walls of tomb chambers of all later pyramids are richly decorated in funerary motifs, loaded with food and food vessels for the afterlife journey, and stuffed with various furniture and servant statuary. The "tomb" chambers of the first ten large pyramids (c. 2600–2180 B.C.E.) have none of this. They are stark and unadorned and have almost no funerary supplies (with the exception of Zoser's step pyramid, which has a maze of underground burial chambers and funerary supplies, like the mastabas it was modeled on). I. E. S. Edwards writes of the early pyramids: "No traces of carving in relief [has] been found in any of the 4th Dynasty Pyramids or in their adjoining buildings, although they were certainly included in some of the contemporary private Mastabas." Although the tomb function of mastabas is well documented, the early pyramids were probably cenotaphs (monuments for those whose bodies are elsewhere) rather than actual tombs.

Second, the internal and external symbolism of the early pyramids suggests that they were used as living religious centers concerned with the afterlife rather than mere silent cemeteries. One can scarcely overemphasize the astronomical and mathematic precision of the early true pyramids, the Great Pyramid in particular. The sides of each pyramid were oriented almost exactly (even by modern standards) to the four cardinal directions. The entrance to the pyramid was *always* in the north face, and sharply sloping tunnels and shafts (at angles routinely greater than 20 degrees) point directly at various stars and constellations and appear to take note of zodiacal shifts as the axis of the Earth slowly circles over thousands of years. Clearly, funerary processions carrying a heavy coffin with the mummy of the pharaoh could scarcely have been accommodated by such sharply sloping walkways. By contrast, in the later period the entrance to a pyramid could be on the south or sometimes even the west side, and there were no sharply sloping tunnels in the interior of the pyramid.

In the early pyramids, the angles of the square base are almost perfect 90 degree angles, and the huge sides of each pyramid are of almost equal length—and even this divergence may be symbolically significant. The slope of most pyramids ascending toward the top is a constant 51 degrees, 52 inches, which causes the peculiar characteristic of the height standing in the same ratio to the circumference of its base as the radius of a circle to its circumference, that is, one-half π. In effect, the early pyramids mathematically symbolize hemispheres. This is no coincidence, for the pyramids were meant to serve as symbols of the Northern Hemisphere of the Earth, with which Egypt was identified. The minor discrepancy of a few inches in construction corresponds exactly to the flattening of the Earth's globe at the North Pole.

What this evidence suggests is that the first pyramids were not merely architectural improvements over earlier mastabas but in fact radically different religious monuments altogether—connected with death and the afterlife to be sure but not primarily by housing physical remains. They reflect new and powerful spiritual concerns that necessitated an entirely new architectural symbolism.

But what of Zoser's step pyramid, which was clearly used for funerary purposes? It appears to stand in between this great shift in thinking, very reminiscent of the mastaba yet reflecting quite different sensibilities. As Edwards remarks, "With the exception of the Mortuary Temple . . . the buildings surrounding the Step Pyramid are without any known precedent or parallel." Further, he adds, "It is impossible to divine with any certainty the archetype by which Imhotep was guided when designing this Mortuary Temple." Clearly, the step pyramid marks a major shift, not only in architectural style but in religious thinking, that married the pyramid's shape to its spiritual function. Like the mathematical and astronomical design of the early pyramid, this spiritual function can be known with some certainty.

The symbolism of the pyramid is profound and multifaceted but above all is related to resurrection and eternal life. The underground tomb of Osiris at Abydos is mentioned in Egyptian texts from the earliest period and prefigures the development of the pyramid. This tomb where Osiris experienced resurrection was an island in the middle of the Nile River that represented the first bit of land to appear at the creation—the primordial cosmic mountain—the first triumph of order out of disorder. Surrounded by primordial waters, the island represents pre-creation or, in a word, death. Stairs are carved on both sides of the island and go down deep into the water, while the sanctuary of Osiris lies underground. The stairs on either side of the tomb form a pyramidal shape and represent the ascent of Osiris to resurrection after being "reborn" from death in the primordial deep. What was once underground (the stepped tomb) became placed aboveground in the grand tombs of the pyramids; that is, the pyramids are in one sense an actual "stairway to heaven" for the deceased pharaoh, recreating the resurrection of Osiris.

The hemispheric symbolism of the pyramids now becomes clear. The size of the Great Pyramid corresponds to the size of the Northern Hemisphere precisely on a scale of 1:43,200—the number of seconds in twenty-four hours (86,400) divided in half: one half for daylight and the other half for when the sun is "underground" in the kingdom of death. The ratio symbolizes not only a "day" but also the cosmic "year" of life and death—itself a cipher for "eternity."

Both the tomb stairway of Osiris and the pyramid get their triangular shape from the symbol (benben) of the young sun god (Bennu), which is related to the Greek word *phoenix*. Bennu was understood to rise out of the ashes of his own dead body and is often depicted above a pyramid-shaped benben symbol, signifying his (daily) rebirth and resurrection. Thus the primordial cosmic mountain arising out of the chaotic deep and the triangular benben symbol connected with solar rays and ascension create a powerful religious imagery when combined in the symbol of the pyramid.

Finally, in Egyptian symbolism, direction is of utmost importance. "Up" stands for life, and "down" is death. To stand up, rise up, or be placed in an upright position symbolizes activity and life, particularly eternal life, but to lie down prone symbolizes passivity and death. Ancient pyramid texts call upon the deceased king to arise, to stand up "because you are not dead." Like Osiris, the king is "the great one [who falls] and lies on his side; he stands up because behold, he is a god. His power is with him, and his crown is on his head. King, stand up!" (spell 178p, Allen, p. 188). The mummy was placed upright in its tomb while the "opening of the mouth" and other empowerment ceremonies were performed, and the stela representing the soul of the deceased was placed upright within the tomb, receiving offerings for the departed. In addition, obelisks were erected throughout Egypt, their upright position universally symbolizing Re together with his transcendent height. In every known Egyptian temple from the entrance gallery to the interior "holy of holies," there is a successive elevation in the floor from room to room, usually by one or more steps up as one goes inward. Likewise, the pyramids have a steady ascent and serve as the ultimate symbols of rising up or standing up, culminating in a point high in the sky from which one might ascend to the starry heavens themselves.

It is most likely that the pyramids served primarily as living symbols of the triumph of eternal life over evanescent death. The presence of empty sarcophagi within a few of the early pyramids is not evidence of a tomb function but rather of a cenotaph, saying, in effect, the spirit of the king dwells here but not his body. Likewise, the astronomical and mathematical symbolism connected to the Earth's globe connects the mere mortal with the eternal heavens and the distant stars, providing the ritual center for a solar cult. It seems entirely possible that the early pyramids, along with their surrounding temples, boats, and causeways, provided sacred space within which to perform regular solar and astronomical rituals, initiate new recruits into the solar mysteries, and worship the transcendent living dead.

See also BARROW; CENOTAPH; FUNERARY CUSTOMS, ANCIENT EGYPTIAN; MASTABA.

References

Allen, Thomas George, trans. *The Book of the Dead, or Going Forth by Day*. Chicago: Oriental Institute of the University of Chicago, 1974.

Edwards, I. E. S. *The Pyramids of Egypt*. Rev. ed., New York: Penguin, 1978.

Fakhry, Ahmed. *The Pyramids*. Chicago: University of Chicago Press, 1961.

Garstang, J. *Burial Customs of Ancient Egypt*. London: A. Constable and Company, 1907.

Kristensen, W. Brede. *Life Out of Death: Studies in the Religions of Egypt and of Ancient Greece*. Louvain, Belgium: Peeters Press, 1992.

Mendelssohn, Kurt. *The Riddle of the Pyramids*. London: Thames and Hudson, 1974.

Spencer, A. J. *Death in Ancient Egypt*. New York: Penguin, 1982.

West, John Anthony. *Serpent in the Sky*. New York: Harper and Row, 1979.

Winlock, H. E. *The Rise and Fall of the Middle Kingdom in Thebes*. New York: Macmillan, 1947.

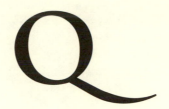

QIYĀMA (KIYAMA)

Literally "Resurrection" in Arabic, Qiyāma refers to the Muslim understanding of the restoration of all life at the end of time, followed by the final judgment. The word *Qiyāma* occurs seventy times in the Qur'ān, the sacred text of Islam, each time in the phrase *Yawm al-Qiyāma,* or "Day of Resurrection." At the end of time, Muslims believe, the angel Isrāfīl, who is nearest the throne of God, will blow his mighty trumpet. The universe will rapidly be withdrawn into God, and there will be a universal extinction. For a long time—unknowable to any creature, for none exists any more—God remains alone in his oneness (tawhīd). Eventually, however, he re-creates the angel of Resurrection, Isrāfīl, and then the other angels, led by Jibrīl, Mikhā'īl, and 'Izrā'īl. Then preparations are made to resurrect humanity as a whole.

First, the winged horse of Muhammed will be resurrected, named al-Burāq because he is as fast as lightning (in Arabic, *al-barq*). Muhammed rode this horse on his fantastic night journey to Jerusalem, where he met Moses and Jesus and led them in prayer (the event is called the *Mi'rāj,* source of the French and English word *mirage*). The angels saddle him up in regal fashion and then seek out the tomb of Muhammed. This proves difficult because the Earth is now a featureless plain, but then a pillar of light manifests from Muhammed's tomb, reaching to heaven. The archangels then call out to Muhammed in turn, but it is only when 'Izrā'īl, the angel of death, calls out that the Prophet answers:

Then Isrāfīl, peace be upon him, cries out, "O pleasing spirit, enter into the pleasant body," but there is no reply. Next, 'Izrā'īl, upon him be peace, cries out, "O pleasing spirit, arise for the last part of the Judgment and the reckoning and the compensation by the Merciful One."

Then the tomb splits open, and lo! Muhammed sits in his tomb, shaking the earth from his head and beard. Jibrā'īl, peace be upon him, presents him with two vestments and al-Burāq, and Muhammed says, "O Jibrā'īl (peace be upon him), "what day is this?" Jibrā'īl (peace be upon him) says, "This is the day of the Resurrection. This is the day of assembly and convocation. This is the day of promise and the day of threat. This is the day of separation. This is the day of meeting." (Macdonald, trans., 1966, p. 151)

Muhammed then proceeds to God and prostrates himself. God welcomes his prophet and grants Muhammed's request to bring forth his people. In many ways, the following events recapitulate the creation of the world described in the Bible, which most Muslims accept as factual history. While God goes about restoring the world and creating the new structures of heaven and hell, the dead literally regrow their bodies in their graves, waiting for God to

---

The Blowing of the Trumpet and the Resurrection

Then God Most High says: "O Isrāfīl, arise and give the Resurrection blast on the Trumpet!" Isrāfīl does so and proclaims, "O departed spirits, torn off bones, decayed bodies, severed veins, torn off skins and fallen out hairs, stand up for the part of the judgment." This is in accordance with the Most High's statement [in the Qur'ān]: "And they shall rise and gaze around them," that is, they shall gaze at the heavens which had split and at the earth which had changed, and at their companions who had become destitute, and at the wild beasts which had been destroyed, and at the seas which had become swollen, and at the souls which had been paired, and at the avenging angels which had been brought in, and at the sun which had been brought down, and at the scales which had been set up, and the Garden which had been brought near. A soul realized what had been prepared!

This is in accordance with what the Most High said: "'Woe to us!' they shall say. 'Who has roused us from our resting-place?'" [Qur'ān 36:52] The believer answers them: "This is what the Lord of mercy promised; the apostles have preached the truth!" They will come forth from the tombs alive and naked.

Translation by Macdonald (1966) of Kitāb al-Haqā'iq wa'l-Daqā'iq, *p. 156.*

The Miraj Buraq, the horse that carried Muhammed from Jerusalem to heaven. Islamic tapestry. Courtesy of Anne Ronan Picture Library.

breathe their spirits back into them. This regeneration, apparently, begins either from the base of the spine (the coccyx) or the top vertebra of the spine, from which the rest of the spine and then the entire skeleton will manifest.

The re-creation begins with water, recalling fundamental themes in Genesis, both the "Spirit of God moving over the waters" (Genesis 1:2–3) and the destruction witnessed by Noah (Genesis, chaps. 6–9):

> Then God Most High gives command to heaven that it should rain water, (which is life-giving) like men's seed, for forty days and the water lies upon everything up to twelve cubits. Then the creatures will grow up through that water as plants grow up, until their bodies are complete as they were before. Then the heaven and earth will roll up. . . .
>
> Then the mountains become like ruffled wool, and He transforms the earth, on which the disobedient labored, and He raises up Jahannam [Hell] upon it. He brings up a land of white silver

and He establishes the Garden upon it. (Macdonald, trans., 1966, p. 154)

When all is prepared, the angel of resurrection, Isrāfīl, blows mightily on his trumpet, as he did previously to herald the end of the world. Spirits reenter the full-grown bodies and rise up out of the grave, marveling at the changes the Lord has made. Resurrected humanity appears to rise up in waves, prefiguring the Reckoning (Hisāb) that is to come. The faithful Muslims are resurrected whole and healthy and joyful, but those who were judgmental in life find themselves raised up from the dead blind. The legal scholars (called *'ulamā'* in Islam) who were hypocrites have pus running from their mouths, traitors are resurrected to resemble pigs, and the vain find themselves deaf and mute. But in another sense, all are reborn as equals under God, without any of the advantages they had on Earth; humanity must now be judged solely on its moral merit. The mystic and scholar al-Ghazālī says: "At that moment everyone is equal, each sitting upon his grave;

among them are the naked and the clothed, the black and white" (Smith and Haddad, p. 74). Another tradition states, "At the resurrection you will be assembled barefoot, naked and uncircumcised," that is, exactly as one is when born (al-Bagawī, *Mishkāt al-Masābīḥ*, cited by Ibn 'Abbās, in Smith and Haddad, p. 74). Animals too are resurrected and face the coming judgment, but curiously the only settlement is to be made between animals who have harmed other animals with their horns. After their settlement, they appear to fade away and do not receive destinies in heaven or hell. (The animals that do appear in heaven apparently exist purely for the pleasure of the faithful and are created specially for that purpose by God.)

After the resurrection, the great Gathering (Hashr) takes place when all assemble before God. This is followed by the Standing (al-Ma'mad), in which the pious and impious contemplate their lives on Earth and endure the waiting (some Muslim traditions say up to 50,000 years) that precedes the final judgment. (For the Muslim understanding of postmortem judgment, see the entry on HISĀB.)

See also BARZAKH; CHINVAT BRIDGE; IBLĪS; ISRĀFĪL; 'IZRĀ'ĪL; JAHANNAM; JUDGMENT, LAST; SĀ'A; AL-SHIRĀT; SOUL, MUSLIM.

References

Dawood, N. J., trans. *The Koran*. 5th rev. ed. New York: Penguin, 1993.

Evrin, M. Sadeddin. *Eschatology in Islam*. Trans. Sofi Huri. Istanbul, 1960.

Gardet, L. "Kiyāma." In *Encyclopedia of Islam,* ed. C. E. Bosworth. Vol. 5. Leiden: E. J. Brill, 1983.

Kherie, Altaf Ahmad. *Islam: A Comprehensive Guidebook*. Karachi: Idara Sirat-i-Mustaqeem, 1981.

Macdonald, D. B. "The Development of the Idea of Spirit in Islam." *Muslim World* 22 (1932).

Macdonald, John. "The Day of Resurrection." *Islamic Studies* 5, no. 2 (1966).

Smith, Jane I. *The Precious Pearl* (A translation of Abū Hāmid al-Ghazālī's *Kitāb al-Durra al-Fākhira if Kashf 'Ulūm al-ākhira*). Missoula, MT: Scholars Press, 1979.

Smith, Jane I., and Yvonne Yazbeck Haddad. *The Islamic Understanding of Death and Resurrection*. Albany: SUNY Press, 1981.

Taylor, John B. "Some Aspects of Islamic Eschatology." *Religious Studies* 4 (1968).

R

RAGNARÖK

Ragnarök is usually translated "the Twilight of the Gods," but according to one scholar, the word *Ragnarök* is a compound word made up of the Icelandic *Ragna*, plural of *regin* (god, ruler), and *rök* (cause, origin), or "the time when the ruling gods return to their origin."

In common with other northern and western European traditions and with Indo-European legends in general, the Norse believed that the world had a definite beginning and would have a definite end. Not human beings alone but even the very foundations of the universe would one day be consumed in fire and flood. The gods themselves, born of a mixture of divine and giant elements, were imperfect, as one scholar has put it, and thus were bound ultimately to destruction and perhaps rebirth.

There are many sources for the description of the End Time, as much of Norse literature calls it. The most famous and complete account is the poem *Völuspá* (trans., Titchenell), but there are also rather full accounts in the prose *Edda* of Icelandic writer Snorri Sturluson and in the lays *Grímnismál* (Titchenell) and *Vafthrúdnismál* (Ellis). In these we read of the long and joyful Golden Age, when the gods were young and innocent. But soon there are signs of the coming of Ragnarök: tensions rise between the pastoral gods (the Vanir) and the high gods (the Aesir) until a war between them breaks out. Then the wall of Asgard (the world of the gods) is broken, and finally there is the account of the god Loki's final betrayal. He arranges the murder of Odin's son Balder, and for this Loki is bound to three rocks on an island with his own son's intestines as ropes; poison drips down on Loki from a serpent stationed above. These signs presage greater chaos to come, which will at last engulf all the worlds.

On the mortal plane below Asgard, the evil of men increases during the Knife Age, the Axe Age, and the Age of Cloven Shields. Brothers slay one another, and sin increases in the world until at last the Age of Northern Winds comes and with it the Fimbul Winter (fimbulvetr), a three-year winter without break. Evil and murder increase, the world of humankind is gripped in ice, and no food can be grown. The dragon Nidhug chews on the roots of the cosmic tree, Yggdrasil, until at last he gnaws all the way through, and the entire tree quivers, sending shocks throughout the nine worlds.

At this, the Goldcomb cock, perched atop the world tree, crows in Asgard; in the depths of the Underworld (Hel), the red Firecock crows in response; and likewise in Midgard, the mortal world, on a hilltop in Ironwood the Storm Eagle flaps his wings and crows—these are the final signs of the end. The wolf-sons of Fenris swallow the sun and moon, and the traitor Loki and his three evil children, the Fenris wolf, the world-serpent Jörmungandr, and the death goddess Hel, break their bonds and approach the world of the gods. Loki captains the ship that brings the sons of Múspell from the east, arriving on the battlefield with the giant Hrym and all the frost giants who have long calculated the destruction of the gods. The waves caused by the awakening of the cosmic serpent Jörmungandr cause the ship of death, Nagelfar, to set sail. This ghastly ship is built entirely of the fingernails of the men who were improperly buried through the ages—a symbol of the cumulative sins of humankind.

The guardian of the rainbow entrance to Asgard, Heimdall, now blows his mighty horn for the last time to warn of the oncoming enemy, and the dwellers in heaven, the Underworld, and the realm of humans prepare for the final onslaught of good and evil. It is for this that the mighty fallen heroes of old, the Einheriar, were gathered by Odin's Valkyries to Valhalla, according to ancient Scandinavian belief, and it is known that this belief encouraged warriors to look forward to their deaths on the battlefield, for in death they were glorified and chosen for a greater purpose. In *Eiríksmál*, when Odin condemns his favorite hero Erik to death in battle, this reason is given: "The grey wolf watches the abodes of the gods."

In the immense battle that follows between the monsters and giants on one side and the gods of Asgard on the other, each figure has his own destiny. Odin is swallowed by the Fenris wolf, but the wolf in turn is killed by Odin's son Vidar. Heimdall kills Loki, but in death Loki falls upon Heimdall and slays him in turn. The fire giant Surtr kills the Vanir god Freyr, but the great Thor slays the huge serpent Jörmungandr who encircles the world—only to drown in the sea of poison that is released. In the end, the final combatant standing, the fire giant Surtr, releases a conflagration that consumes the world tree Yggdrasil and envelopes the nine worlds, including the high palaces of the gods. At last the Earth sinks into the oceans, making them boil.

All is not lost, however. Eventually, out of the ruins come the youngest of the gods, who apparently survive the general destruction and find the ancient golden chessmen of their fathers and begin to play again on the game board of life. New palaces are built in a higher heaven called Gimlé, and a new beginning comes. Likewise, in Midgard, a man and a woman hid in a forest during the long winter, surviving only on dew.

This powerful account of cosmic destruction and renewal has by many scholars been linked to Christian missionary influences during the Middle Ages, and much has been made of the "resurrection" of the world through a chosen few. There is even a line of the *Völuspá*

that refers to "another, mightier god" whose name one dare not mention, who is thought to rule over Gimlé and judge humankind. Surely this is a Christian interpolation if ever there was one. However, there is reason to believe that the Norse account is inherently consistent, and in any case it bears resemblances to many older Indo-European accounts of the end of the world. Indeed, Christian influence on the Norse story of Ragnarök may be rather the Christian packaging of more ancient, eastern thought.

The Scandinavian legends bear particular similarities not only to Christian apocalyptic writings but also to the Irish account of the Second Battle and Indian, Iranian and Greek accounts of the end of the world. In the Irish account of the great Second Battle for Ireland, the high gods of war struggle with primordial giants, the Formorians; the hero Núadu loses his hand as Tyr (god of war) does while binding the wolf, and Bres (one-time king of the Tuatha Dé Danann) deserts the gods as Loki does. Likewise, the Irish prophetess, the Badhbh, gives prophecies of coming carnage that resemble the *Vǫluspá*. The Iranian account shares with the Norse a long, horrible winter of three years, when only a few humans survive by building an underground shelter while the world is destroyed; and the Indian account mentions the śiṣṭa, or "seed" of humanity, which is secluded in a secret valley when all other life perishes. The ruin of the world through fire and water is common to most oriental mythologies, especially those of India, in which the cosmos is regularly burned up to, but not including, the highest heavens, from which planes the new cosmos will reincarnate, like the rebirth of the Norse through Gimlé. The Greek account, too, shows a few humans, namely Deucalian and Pyrrha, surviving the flood, and Delphi alone, like Gimlé, has the power to withstand the onslaught of general destruction. The Greek Fates, like the Scandinavian Norns, lay out the entire end of the cosmos in prophetic verse well before the event. Further parallels could easily be found.

Even so, Christian influence upon later Scandinavian thought was profound and ultimately triumphant. The apparently later Norse tradition that good humans would be reborn after death in Gimlé and that evil would wind up in the "hell" of Nastrond, all due to the judgment of "the one" who could not be named, certainly has a monotheistic, Christian ring. Yet deeper inspection reveals that this possibly later tradition maintains more than two "worlds," good and evil: the giants have their heavenly mansion, Brimer, and the dwarves are said to dwell in Nida. Whatever changes the Norse myth may have undergone at Christian hands before it was swept away altogether as a living faith, the process of assimilation was undoubtedly a complex and subtle interaction, for the overall framework and inherent Indo-European motifs remained intact.

See also GIMLÉ; HEL; ODIN; VALHALLA; VALKYRIE.

References

Davidson, H. R. Ellis. *Gods and Myths of Northern Europe*. New York: Penguin, 1964, 1977.

Ellis, Hilda Roderick. *The Road to Hel: A Study of the Conception of the Dead in Old Norse Literature*. Cambridge: Cambridge University Press, 1943.

Guerber, Hélène Adeline. *Myths of the Norsemen From the Eddas and Sagas*. New York: Dover, 1992.

Mackenzie, Donald A. *Teutonic Myth and Legend*. New York: Wise, 1934.

Sturluson, Snorri. *Edda*. Trans. Anthony Faulkes. London: Dent, 1987.

Titchenell, Elsa-Brita. *The Masks of Odin*. Pasadena: Theosophical University Press, 1985.

Turville-Petre, E. O. G. *Myth and Religion of the North: The Religion of Ancient Scandinavia*. Westport, CT: Greenwood, 1964.

RĀKṢASA

Literally "one who harms," the Rākṣasa is an Indian blood-drinking demon connected with death and a shadowy Otherworld. The Rākṣasas are not the ghosts of dead humans but a fully self-conscious race (for the most part invisible to us) with their own society, caste, religion, occupations, families, and so on. Generally, they are thought to live and have kingdoms in the wild parts of our world, but frequently they are pictured as living in a parallel world that borders on our own. Although Rākṣasas are universally considered magical beings who create illusions, shape shift, and perform other spells, in their natural form they are said to be hideous, with massive, deformed bodies, wild hair, red eyes, a huge mouth stretching from ear to ear, and ears pointed like spears.

The Rākṣasas are pervasive in Indian literature, appearing in everything from the earliest known texts (the Vedas) to current folk legends and modern novels. In the two great epics of India, the *Mahābhārata* and especially the *Rāmāyaṇa*, they have starring roles. But what is most fascinating about Rākṣasas is that they have never been one-dimensional evildoers who merely moved the plot along; instead, they are complicated, often thoughtful beings with their own social ethics, pieties, strengths, and weaknesses. Something of this complexity is seen even in vulgar folktales in which Rākṣasas frequently appear. Although the evil male Rākṣasa serves as the target of the human hero's valor, the female Rākṣasī is a beautiful maiden who often marries the successful hero, bearing him many gifts and equally heroic offspring. Other tales have a Rākṣasī demanding daily tribute from a city. When the gallant human king offers himself as a victim in place of the usual sacrifice, the Rākṣasī is moved by pity and gives up eating human flesh.

Such concessions do not generally have the effect of making demonic Rākṣasas sympathetic characters, however, for Rākṣasas as a rule are still ghastly evil-minded ogres. Their fingernails contain a deadly poison, and their ravenous hunger for human flesh is proverbial. From their endless marauding the Rākṣasas are thought to have gained enormous wealth, and they are regarded as the demonic architects of many of the great ruins of India, for in the popular imagination these mysterious edifices could only have been erected through evil sorcery. Rākṣasas prefer darkness, and they are unconquerable at midnight. However, they greatly fear light, and in the ancient Indian language of Sanskrit, one of the words for "lamp" is *rakṣogna*, or "destroyer of demons." In many cases Rākṣasas seem to be a psychological projection of lower human nature. That is, they represent "the Other": whatever we do not approve of in ourselves, whatever base desires, lust, greed, or pride we feel, are embodied in the demonic

A Rākṣasa Encounter in the Woods

While [the five Pāndava heroes] were sleeping . . .
a Rākṣasa by the name of Hidimba was living in a
shāla-tree not very far from the wood. He was a cruel
Rākṣasa who ate human flesh—powerful and strong,
malformed, yellow-eyed, tusked, and loathsome to
the eye. He was hungry and looking for flesh when
he happened to see them. Fingers pointed upward, he
scratched his unkempt hair and shook it, yawned,
big-mouthed, as his eyes kept returning to them.
Then this evil, large-bodied, powerful devourer of
human flesh, sniffing the smell of humans, said to his
sister, "Now—and how long has it been?—I have
found my favorite food! My tongue is slavering with
appetite and licks around my mouth! I'll sink my
eight sharp-pointed tusks, impatient after all this
time they had nothing to bite, into these bodies and
their delicious flesh. I'll get on their human throats,
cut the artery, and guzzle the plentiful, fresh, warm,
foaming blood! Go and find out who they are who
are lying in the wood—the powerful smell of humans
alone seems to sate me! Kill all those humans and
bring them to me. . . . We'll cook the flesh of these
humans the way we like it and gorge ourselves on it
together! Now hurry and do as I tell you!"

From The Mahābhārata, *Vol. 1:*
The Book of the Beginning,
translated by van Buitenen (1973, pp. 294–295).

Rākṣasa for the hero to valiantly slay. In this way, particularly when this situation is turned into a play, the audience experiences catharsis, a purging of unwanted feelings and a restoration of moral purity.

Certainly the great epic the *Rāmāyaṇa* proves this point. The antihero, Rāvaṇa, was the most powerful Rākṣasa in the world. He had ten heads and twenty arms, symbols of his gargantuan strength and rulership. He was as tall as a mountain and could stretch out his arms and stop the sun and moon in their course, and he was known for all kinds of vice, including raiding other kingdoms and stealing others' wives and wealth. Interestingly, by following the rules for gaining spiritual power, Rāvaṇa amassed tremendous karmic merit and was able to force the greatest of gods to grant him boons. In time, through guile and "spiritual" power, this great demon managed to enslave most of the Hindu pantheon: Yama, the god of death, had the job of washing the dirty clothes, and Vayu, the Vedic god of the atmosphere, was reduced to sweeping the floor; the other gods had their menial tasks as well. In this way, the epic story sets up Rāvaṇa as the embodiment of pride par excellence; the importance of humility and

obedience to law is the insight the audience gains at his destruction. Reinforcing the theme of demonic complexity mentioned above, Rāvaṇa's youngest brother, Vibhīshana, ends up turning against his fellow Rākṣasas and siding with the human hero Rāma (who is actually an incarnation of Viṣṇu, "the Preserver"). Vibhīshana is one of the few Rākṣasas known for his purity and goodness.

In the *Mahābhārata*, Rākṣasas also show this dual aspect, though the demonic predominates. The cruel Rākṣasa Hidimba, dwelling in a tree in the deep woods, tries to kill the hero Bhima and is duly slaughtered, but his Rākṣasī sister, representing the other side of Rākṣasa nature, is impressed by the valor of the human hero and not only marries the human slayer of her brother but bears him a heroic child, named Ghaṭotkaca.

Such duality makes the Rākṣasas most interesting in the literature: like humans, they too have free will to make moral choices, though they usually choose wrongly and thus teach the listening audience piety through negative example. However, Indian literature was sophisticated even in very early times and enjoyed the complexity of role reversal and challenges to preestablished categories. For instance, one Rākṣasa, Sukeshin by name, convinces many of the demons to turn from their evil ways and follow a path of goodness and justice, preeminently by worshipping the supreme god Shiva (the Destroyer). Eventually their city becomes so virtuous that it shines like the heavens:

their brilliant luster paralyzed the sun, moon and
stars; night was like day; the night-blooming
lotuses did not bloom, thinking that it was still
day; owls came out and crows killed them. People
thought that the city of the demons was the moon,
and that it had overcome the sun. (O'Flaherty,
trans.)

Eventually great chaos ensues because the demons are not acting like demons, and the universe is becoming unraveled. The sun decides to destroy the Rākṣasas, but Sukeshin calls out to his god Shiva, who responds by casting down the sun. Eventually the other gods prevail upon Shiva to restore the sun, and they agree to take the Rākṣasa Sukeshin up to heaven, where presumably he sheds his Rākṣasa form and becomes a deva, or god. Thus the role of the Rākṣasas in Indian literature is complex. They serve not only as embodiments of night terror and flesh-eating personifications of the wilderness and impiety but also as models of the possibility of role reversal and transcendence.

See also BHŪT; PRET.

References

Crooke, William. *The Popular Religion and Folk-lore of Northern India.*
2nd ed. Delhi: Munshiram Manoharlal, 1968.

Goldman, Robert P., and Sally Sutherland Goldman, trans. *The Rāmāyana of Vālmīki*. Princeton: Princeton University Press, 1984.

Kane, Pandurang Vaman. *History of Dharmashāstra; Ancient and Medieval Religious and Civil Law in India*. Vol. 4. Government Oriental Series, Class B, no. 6. Poona: Bhandarkar Oriental Research Institute, 1953.

Keith, Arthur Berriedale. *The Mythology of All Races*. Vol. 6: *Indian Mythology*. New York: Cooper Square Publishers, 1964.

Moor, Edward. *The Hindu Pantheon*. Ed. W. O. Simpson. Madras: J. Higginbotham, 1864.

O'Flaherty, Wendy Doniger. *The Origins of Evil in Hindu Mythology*. Berkeley: University of California Press, 1976.

Oldenberg, Hermann. *The Religion of the Veda*. Trans. Shridhar B. Shrotri. Indian ed. Delhi: Motilal Banarsidass, 1988.

van Buitenen, J. A. B., trans. *The Mahābhārata*. Vol. 1: *The Book of the Beginning*. Chicago: University of Chicago Press, 1973.

RED

Although many colors have special associations with death and the afterlife, particularly black in the Western world and white in the Far East, red has both a biological and a cross-culturally magical relationship with death. Red is most poignantly and importantly the color of blood—including the blood spilling from mortal wounds, the cyclical blood of menstruation, and the blood of childbirth. According to George Thomson,

> It is a worldwide custom for menstruating or pregnant women to daub their bodies with red ochre, which serves at once to warn the men away and to enhance their fertility. In many marriage ceremonies the bride's forehead is painted red . . . a sign that she is forbidden to all men save her husband and a guarantee that she will bear him children. . . . Among the Valenge, a Bantu tribe, every woman keeps a pot of red ochre, which is sacred to her sex and used to paint her face and body for ceremonial purposes. Of the many occasions for which she needs it, the following may be noted. At the end of her confinement both mother and child are anointed with it: in this way the child will live and the mother is restored to life. At initiation the girl is painted red from head to foot. So she is born again and will be fruitful. At the conclusion of mourning, after stepping over a fire, the widow is painted the same color: so she returns from the contamination of death.

Red is also an auspicious color used to mark many beginnings. In India, during the New Year festival of Holi (celebrated on the day of the first full moon of spring, usually in March), the most important rite is the smearing of red powder on the bodies of friends and relatives. During the Chinese New Year, lucky red strips of paper (usually printed with auspicious phrases) are

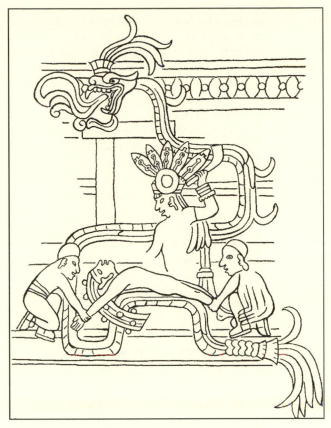

Typical representation of human sacrifice found in Mayan wall paintings, monuments, and codices. The color red was tremendously charged with meaning, in part because of the importance of blood in rituals. Courtesy of Anne Ronan Picture Library.

hung outside the family doorposts, but they are covered with white should a death occur during the year.

Thus it is most intriguing to find that primitive humans nearly worldwide, in prehistoric India, across Europe, and even in North America, frequently retrieved the buried bones of the deceased, painted or stained them with red ochre, and then carefully replaced the treated bones in the ground in a secondary burial. According to Macalister,

> The symbolism becomes quite clear when we find, as we commonly do, that the skeleton has been laid in the contracted or uterine posture. Smeared with the color of life, curled up like a babe in the womb—what more could the primitive man do to ensure that the soul of the departed would be born again?

To paint the bones with the ruddy coloring of life was the "nearest thing to mummification that the paleolithic peoples knew; it was an attempt to make the body again serviceable for its owner's use" (Macalister).

Not all red-stained bones found worldwide have been placed in a fetal position. Some were arranged in an extended position, and red-stained bones have even been found in fragmented burials. In some cases only the skulls were reburied and in other cases apparently all the bones except the skulls. It is certainly going too far to claim that primitive humans around the world practiced exactly the same funerary customs or held exactly the same beliefs regarding the state of the dead and their eventual fate. But the widespread use of red coloring in both primitive and modern rituals of death and renewal, from New Year's rites to menstruation to burial, certainly points to a very early origin of humanity's hopes for a postmortem resurrection or reincarnation.

References

Bhattacharya, Narendra Nath. *Ancient Indian Rituals and Their Social Contents.* Delhi: Manohar, 1975.

Macalister, R. A. S. *Textbook of European Archaeology.* Vol. 1. Cambridge: Cambridge University Press, 1921.

Thomson, George. *Studies in Ancient Greek Society.* Vol. 1. London: Lawrence and Wishart, 1949.

REFRIGERIUM

Literally meaning "refreshment," the Latin word *refrigerium* was given a more specific usage by early Christian writers to refer to the "refreshment of souls" who awaited the judgment of God after death. In the early Christian church it was believed that most of the dead did not go immediately to Heaven or to Hell but awaited the final judgment at the end of time (martyrs were believed to be an exception and proceeded directly to heaven after death without any trial or judgment). Some Christian thinkers believed that the dead waited in dreamless slumber until they were awakened by the trumpet call of the angel and the general resurrection; others believed that the souls of the dead waited— somewhere, perhaps in Hades—in full consciousness for the end to come. One such thinker was the African theologian Tertullian (fl. c. 160 to 220 C.E.), who believed that *all* the dead waited in Hell for the end. However, those disembodied souls who would be saved by God in the future were not suffering in Hell but even in that dismal place were already experiencing some measure of Heaven's "refreshment." (Tertullian was unique in creating a new level of Hell in accordance with this doctrine. See REFRIGERIUM INTERIM.)

According to Jacques Le Goff, it was common for inscriptions on early Christian tombs to look forward to the coming "refreshment" of the righteous, whether this was expected to occur immediately or only later in Heaven. Such inscriptions read, for example, "in pace et refrigerium" (in peace and refreshment), "esto in refrigerio" (may he be in refreshment), "deus refrigeret spiritum tuum" (may God refresh his spirit), and so on. They attest to one of the most important aspects of the new Christian religion, namely that after the death and

resurrection of Jesus, immortality and refrigerium were open to all who would only believe, whereas traditional Greeks and Romans could only anticipate gloomy Hades or the vague promise of Elysium.

Refrigerium was not merely the refreshment of those who would be saved but also referred to the temporary refreshment of those who were suffering in the afterlife. Several early Christian texts taught that the prayers of the righteous, either those still living or the prayers of angels and saints in Heaven, could intercede for the dead and help them or at least reduce their suffering. One early text, titled *The Passion of Perpetua and Felicitas* and dating from the very beginning of the third century C.E., told the story of several Christians who were martyred. In the story, the young woman Perpetua, who was imprisoned by the Romans for her faith and scheduled to die in the bloodthirsty "games," had a vision of her younger brother who was suffering in the place of the dead (where exactly this was, the text leaves vague). The young boy was in a place of darkness, covered in rags and filth, burning and parched with thirst. In Perpetua's vision her brother was trying to reach a fountain in order to take a drink, but the fountain was too high for his small frame. Perpetua realized that because of her great faith and the fact that she was about to be martyred, she had the power to intercede for her brother and began to pray "night and day, wailing and crying that my prayers be granted." Due to her intercession, Perpetua had another vision a few days later, in which her brother was clean, dressed, and most importantly, "refreshed" (refrigerantem) because the fountain had been lowered. Perpetua said that "he began playing happily with the water, as children do. I awoke and I understood that his penalty [probably that of not being baptized] had been lifted" (Le Goff, pp. 49–50).

Another, grander text discussing intercession for the dead and refrigerium is the mid–third century Apocalypse of Paul, an apocryphal Christian text that purports to describe Paul's journey to the "third heaven" described in 2 Corinthians 12:2–4. In the Apocalypse, Paul is fortunate enough to accompany angels through the various heavens, as well as the regions of darkness "beyond the Ocean," and witness the judgment of souls as they leave their mortal bodies. After witnessing an incredible number of horrible tortures that the wicked were experiencing, Paul and the Archangel Michael and all the dead begin to pray that, despite their iniquity and failure to repent during life, the wicked might somehow be granted "refreshment." Immediately Christ came down out of Heaven, and after chastising the dead for refusing to repent despite all of his sufferings on their behalf, he grants them a temporary refreshment from their sufferings every Sunday to commemorate the day on which he rose from the tomb.

The teaching of refrigerium was certainly controversial in the early church, and many church fathers did not believe that the ordinary dead either suffered or rejoiced between the time of death and the resurrection. Nevertheless, the doctrine of refrigerium met a need among early Christian believers to somehow help their long-dead ancestors or recently deceased family members who may not have converted to the new faith or who may have led less than ideal Christian lives. Refrigerium also reinforced preexisting "pagan" beliefs (still strong among many early Christians) that the dead were still "present" and required regular offerings and prayers. In time, the doctrines of suffering in the afterlife, intercession, refrigerium, and the growing cult of martyrs and saints would combine into the full-blown Catholic doctrine of Purgatory, though this did not take firm shape until the twelfth century.

See also ELYSION, ELYSIUM; FUNERARY CUSTOMS, CHRISTIAN; HADES; INTERCESSION; ISLANDS OF THE BLEST; JUDGMENT, LAST; JUDGMENT, PARTICULAR; PURGATORY; REFRIGERIUM INTERIM; SHEOL.

References

Dodds, E. R. *Pagan and Christian in an Age of Anxiety*. Cambridge: Cambridge University Press, 1965.

Duensing, H., trans. "Apocalypse of Paul." In *New Testament Apocrypha*, ed. E. Hennecke and W. Schneemelcher. Vol. 2. London: Lutterworth Press, 1965.

Le Goff, Jacques. *The Birth of Purgatory*. Trans. Arthur Goldhammer. Chicago: University of Chicago Press, 1984.

REFRIGERIUM INTERIM

"Temporary [place of] refreshment," or refrigerium interim, was a phrase coined by the early African church father Tertullian (fl. c. 160–220 C.E.) to describe the "new level of Hell" that he essentially created. As in many other matters of doctrine, it was the author Marcion (d. c. 160 C.E.) who provoked this development in early church thinking. Marcion (considered by many early church thinkers to be a heretic, though he nearly became pope) began teaching that after death not only martyrs but also good Christians went directly to Heaven, which directly contradicted nearly unanimous second-century church opinion. Marcion based this belief on the words of Jesus on the cross to the thief near him (Luke 23:43): "Today you shall be with me in Paradise." Likewise, in Luke 16:19–31 Jesus taught that after death the beggar Lazarus was carried by angels to "the bosom of Abraham," from which vantage point he could see and converse with the damned soul of Dives, the rich man, suffering in what Luke explicitly calls "Hades." Marcion, drawing from the Gospels, was able to make a clear case for immediate judgment and disposition of the dead in Heaven or Hell after death. By contrast, church doctrine from the time of Paul was summed up in 1 Thessalonians 4:13–18, that

the dead "sleep" until the final judgment and were in neither Heaven nor Hell; nor were they conscious of anything.

To reconcile this seeming contradiction in the Bible that the dead sleep and yet appear to be already in Heaven, Tertullian taught that all the dead went to Hades (which paralleled the old Jewish belief that all the dead went to Sheol) but that all the dead were not treated the same there. Hell had different levels, one in which the wicked were punished even while they awaited their (somewhat redundant) "final condemnation," and one in which those who were destined to be saved experienced a foretaste of heaven in the refrigerium interim, a temporary place of coolness and comfort. It was this place, asserted Tertullian, that Jesus meant by "the bosom of Abraham": "This place, the bosom of Abraham, though not in heaven, and yet above hell, offers the souls of the righteous an interim refreshment [refrigerium interim] until the end of all things brings about the general resurrection and the final reward" (*Adversus Marcionem* 4.34, quoted in Le Goff, p. 47).

Ultimately, Tertullian's solution to Biblical contradiction did not convince other architects of church doctrine. Instead, Christianity began to accept that the dead did in fact go to Heaven or Hell directly from the point of death. However, Tertullian paved the way for a "third place" between Heaven and Hell, which medieval theologians would point to as confirmation for yet a new afterlife destination, that of Purgatory.

See also FUNERARY CUSTOMS, CHRISTIAN; HEAVEN, HISTORY OF; HEAVEN, ORIGINS OF; INTERCESSION; ISLANDS OF THE BLEST; JUDGMENT, LAST; JUDGMENT, PARTICULAR; PURGATORY; REFRIGERIUM.

References

Dodds, E. R. *Pagan and Christian in an Age of Anxiety*. Cambridge: Cambridge University Press, 1965.

Duensing, H., trans. "Apocalypse of Paul." In *New Testament Apocrypha*, ed. E. Hennecke and W. Schneemelcher. Vol. 2. London: Lutterworth Press, 1965.

Le Goff, Jacques. *The Birth of Purgatory*. Trans. Arthur Goldhammer. Chicago: University of Chicago Press, 1984.

Mohrmann, Christine. "Locus refrigerii." In *L'Ordinaire de la messe: Texte critique, traduction et études*, ed. B. Botte and C. Mohrmann. Paris-Louvain, 1953.

REINCARNATION, EASTERN

A belief in reincarnation is a cornerstone of most Asian religions. Not humans only but all things reincarnate, from microbes to mammals to universes, in neverending cycles (yugas and kalpas) of manifestation and cessation. In Asia, the doctrine of reincarnation is often used to explain the obvious discrepancies among people in economic, social, intellectual, and moral status, for one's situation in the current life is thought to depend heavily upon one's activities in previous incarnations. In popular belief reincarnation also provides a means for advancement, either in material prosperity or in personal growth and spiritual insight. Among Asian philosophers, however, reincarnation is generally not seen as something positive, but rather a snare that catches those who do not perceive reality as it truly is.

Western scholars debate when and how reincarnation took root in the religions of the Indian subcontinent, but Indian theologians themselves have no doubt that reincarnation is as old as India itself and was present as a central tenet even in the earliest portion of the oldest Scriptures, the Vedas, in circulation since at least 2000 B.C.E. In any case, every single religion of India has accepted reincarnation as a fundamental—if sad—truth about life. (Only the ancient materialist school of thought, the Cārvaka, denied reincarnation, but in truth such thinking had little influence in traditional India.) Reincarnation, called *punarjanman* (repeated birth) or more pertinently *punarmrityu* (repeated death) is dreaded by Indian ascetics and philosophers, who seek to become enlightened and achieve complete liberation (mokṣa) and thus escape the tedious round of birth, old age, and sickness.

Although the many traditions of Hinduism are quite diverse in their teachings, the dominant Hindu position is that of eternalism, called *śhāśavatavāda* in the ancient language of Sanskrit. This position means that reality (called *Brahman* in a cosmic sense, though the absolute dwells within each person as the ātman) is unchanging and does not appear or disappear, grow or lessen, punish or reward. Rather, reality simply "is" eternally and does not require prayers or sacrifices or worship to become actuated in the world. However, Hindu teachings recognize that the masses do not perceive this ultimate reality and do not know how to get in touch with it. Humankind is caught up in the appearance of constant change; people perform innumerable actions, even in the course of a single day, as if each person were a separate being, not part of a whole. Such behavior creates consequences (karma) ad infinitum in a limitless, self-perpetuating web of actions and reactions. Thus, Hindu Scriptures compare life, as ordinarily perceived, to a dream in which all manner of things may happen that have little relevance to the true nature of things. This world of appearances and the state of infinite beings whirling from life to death to life again is called *saṃsāra,* and its root cause is spiritual ignorance, or avidyā. Thus it is the goal of Hindu teachings to help individuals attain wisdom and cease their existence as a whirling beings trapped in causes of their own making. As the Supreme Lord Krishna says to his disciple Arjuna in the most popular Hindu Scripture, the Bhagavad-Gītā,

Do not say
"God gave us this delusion."
You dream you are the doer,
You dream that action is done,
You dream that action bears fruit.
It is your ignorance,
It is the world's delusion
That gives you these dreams.
(Prabhavananda and Isherwood, trans., p. 59)

Various systems of effort (yogas) help to acquire the spiritual wisdom that frees one from the bonds of karmic retribution and rebirth, including devotion to a higher being (bhakti yoga); scriptural study and meditation (jñāna yoga); or the performance of charity, penance, and austerity (karma yoga). The "royal path" (rāja-yoga) includes them all. But since liberation is highly unlikely for most people in the present incarnation, whatever yogas one chooses, a simple life of kindness, few desires, and devotion to the ultimate goal is recommended. In this way, the entire tendency of one's life moves toward liberation, and in succeeding incarnations one may eventually reach the goal.

The last thought of the dying is believed to be particularly powerful in determining that person's next life, and for this reason the dying and the recently dead are treated very carefully. The atmosphere surrounding the deathbed should be one of meditative calm and reading or chanting of Scriptures rather than noise and disturbance. As the last chance to earn merit in this life, those on their deathbed are encouraged to give away their property as a final act of charity and to have performed a rite called *vratodyāpana,* or "completion of vows," which prevents one from dying in the negative karmic state of having vows unfulfilled. There is also a ritual called *sarvaprāyaścitta* (literally "atonement for everything") Despite all this, Hindu tradition points out that one's last thoughts at death are the result of all that one has thought and done throughout life, and no last-minute rituals can completely erase an evil, selfish life.

Perhaps too much has been made of the distinction between the Hindu belief in an essential "self," or ātman, that reincarnates and the Buddhist belief, called *anātman*, that there is no such thing as a "self," an unchanging, personal entity that moves from body to body. Although the distinction is, loosely, accurate, nevertheless reincarnation plays a similar role in both religions. Both Buddhism and Hinduism regard transmigration as an undesirable event, something that the individual needs to take action to avoid. In Buddhism the goal is generally called *nirvāṇa,* which means "to be extinguished." However, very much like the Hindu concept of mokṣa, it does not necessarily mean annihilation but rather the cessation of personal desire, the grasping such desire produces, and the inevitable result, suffering (duhkha).

Buddhism appears to reject the Hindu view of eternalism, teaching instead the exact opposite that everything is in flux, but the differences may be more semantic than theological and functional. For although Buddhism teaches that every compounded thing in the universe ultimately changes and falls apart, it is this very universe of "suffering" that the teachings of the Buddha are designed to enable one to escape. Throughout its history Buddhism has been extremely reluctant to embrace the eternalism of Hindu thought, and nirvāṇa is not considered at all comparable to some eternal paradise of bliss located somewhere (unlike Jainism, which teaches that liberated "victors," or tirthankaras, ascend to the highest point of the universe and remain there in bliss). But then again, neither is mokṣa presented as a spatially or temporally located heaven. Both the Buddhist and the Hindu systems of effort have as their goal an escape from the delusion that life as ordinarily perceived is ultimately satisfying. Offering very similar yogic techniques of asceticism, meditation, and the acquisition of wisdom, both religions attempt to foster a disengagement from the perceived world and a reorientation to a spiritual reality that is best perceived by attaining it inwardly. Buddhism refuses to designate ultimate reality with a name, calling it vaguely "thatness" or "suchness" (tathatā), whereas Hinduism is willing to identify ultimate reality with the Godhead (Mahā Viṣṇu) or by pantheistic terms like *Brahman*. But it is clear that both systems hold out such a reality as the only possible escape from the otherwise endless round of reincarnation.

Reincarnation was certainly not unknown to the other cultures of Asia before the missionary zeal of Buddha's followers brought that doctrine forcibly to their attention in the first centuries of the common era, but reincarnation appears to have been less emphasized and less widely accepted in China, Korea, and Japan, for example, before the arrival of Buddhism. Confucian sources make no mention of the doctrine, but many Taoists, with their focus on natural energies and rhythms, appear to have accepted the idea. On the whole, however, Taoism seems much less distressed over the passage of the inner nature from body to body than Hinduism and Buddhism. Chuang-tzu, an early systematizer of Taoist philosophy who lived around 300 B.C.E., is quoted as saying:

> To have attained to the human form must be always a source of joy. And then, to undergo countless transitions, with only the infinite to look forward to—what incomparable bliss is that! Therefore it is that the truly wise rejoice in that

which can never be lost, but endures always. (quoted in Giles, p. 83)

After the success of Buddhist missionary work, reincarnation became a very widely accepted doctrine throughout East Asia and Southeast Asia, though it never succeeded in eradicating indigenous forms of belief. For example, many Chinese to this day continue to offer incense and prayers to their ancestors in "heaven" in the traditional Confucian manner, even though according to traditional Buddhist teachings, these ancestors would have long since reincarnated into new bodies. This seeming contradiction is easily resolved, however, by the popular Chinese belief in multiple souls within each person. The problem was resolved differently in India, where some Hindu thinkers criticized similar ancestor veneration by claiming that the ancestors no longer exist as spirits but have reincarnated. The canonical response, according to Hindu scholar Pandurang Vaman Kane, was that wherever the ancestors may be, such offerings from devoted relatives will help them, either in some other world as spiritual food and blessings or as additional good karma in their new life in this world.

See also ĀTMAN; BHAVA-CHAKRA; FUNERARY CUSTOMS, CHINESE; FUNERARY CUSTOMS, HINDU; NARAKA; NIRVĀṆA; SVARGA; YAMA.

References

Becker, Carl B. *Breaking the Circle: Death and the Afterlife in Buddhism.* Carbondale: Southern Illinois University Press, 1993.

Eliade, Mircea. *The Myth of the Eternal Return.* Trans. Willard R. Trask. Bollingen Series 46. New York: Pantheon Books, 1954.

———. *Yoga: Immortality and Freedom.* New York: Pantheon, 1958.

Giles, H. A., trans. *The Musings of a Chinese Mystic.* London: John Murray, 1955.

Head, Joseph, and Sylvia Cranston. *Reincarnation: The Phoenix Fire Mystery.* New York: Julian Press/Crown Publishers, 1977.

Kane, Pandurang Vaman. *History of Dharmashastra; Ancient and Medieval Religious and Civil Law in India.* Vol. 4. Government Oriental Series, Class B, no. 6. Poona: Bhandarkar Oriental Research Institute, 1953.

McDermott, James P. "Nibbāna as a Reward for Kamma." *Journal of the American Oriental Society* 93, no. 3 (1973).

Mittal, Kewal Krishnan, ed. *Perspectives on Karma and Rebirth.* Delhi: Delhi University, 1990.

Prabhavananda, Swami, and Christopher Isherwood. *The Song of God: Bhagavad-Gītā.* 1954. Reprint, New York: Penguin, 1972.

Rinpoche, Sogyal. *The Tibetan Book of Living and Dying,* ed. Patrick Gaffney and Andrew Harvey. San Francisco: Harper San Francisco, 1992.

Shukla, Karunesh, ed. *Nature of Bondage and Liberation in Buddhist Systems.* Gorakhpur, India: Nagarjuna Buddhist Foundation, 1988.

Stevenson, Ian. *Cases of the Reincarnation Type.* Charlottesville: University Press of Virginia, 1975.

REINCARNATION, TRIBAL

The belief in reincarnation in one form or another was extremely widespread if not universal in antiquity, and it continues to be popular in many areas of the world today, including the modern West. For many believers, the regular re-embodiment of the soul is suggested by nature's rhythms in which the tides, the phases of the moon, the seasons, and the constellations all recur in predictable intervals. Because a human being is a microcosm or "small universe," the same cycles govern the human soul. Others see reincarnation as the result of divine revelation or sometimes even personal experience. It is a cardinal doctrine of most of the great religions of Asia, but it is less widely known that reincarnation is a common belief among tribal peoples in many parts of the world, possibly from a very ancient period.

Archaeological evidence from the earliest periods of the human race suggests, albeit somewhat ambiguously, that reincarnation may have been a primal belief of humankind. Very ancient humans—in such disparate locations as North America, Europe, ancient Egypt, and India—usually placed the dead in a crouched position (some have said a "fetal" position) with the legs drawn up to the chin and the arms placed tightly over the chest. In many cases the bones were dug up years later and stained or painted with red ochre. This practice may be interpreted (hesitantly) as a "re-wombing" of the dead in "Mother Earth," preparing the deceased to return in a new body; the red color in particular is associated with blood, especially the blood of sacrifice and (re-)birth. Such a belief continues among many peoples at the turn of the twenty-first century, including, for example, the Vogul, an Arctic Eurasian tribe, who place a bed of moss and elk hair in the coffin in which the dead person is laid, exactly as they treat the cradle of a newborn child.

Whether or not the scanty evidence proves that very ancient humans believed in reincarnation, many tribal cultures did, at least at the beginning of the twentieth century. Nearly a century ago anthropologists Baldwin Spencer and F. J. Gillen wrote of the aboriginal cultures of northern Central Australia (p. 145):

> In every tribe without exception there exists a firm belief in the reincarnation of ancestors. Emphasis must be laid on the fact that this belief is not confined to tribes such as the Arunta, Warramunga, Binbinga, Anula and others, amongst whom descent is counted on the male line, but is found just as strongly developed in the Urabunna tribe, in which descent, both of class and totem, is strictly maternal.

According to James Frazer, the pattern of Australian

belief in reincarnation suggests that the doctrine was once universal among all the Australian aborigines but has declined over the millennia, a change hastened by contact with white Christian settlers. Likewise, many African tribes believe that after death, the spirit is reincarnated in the family line. For example, the Ewe believe in an original "home of souls" to which the soul returns on the body's death to be born again in a new fetus. Children are very important and must be respected, not only because they are the future of the tribe but because they literally represent the venerated ancestors of the past. J. Omosade Awolalu (p. 60) writes of the Yoruba tribe:

> The Yoruba strongly believe that the departed ancestors have different ways of returning to the living. One of the commonest ways of doing this is for the soul to be reincarnated and to be born as a grandchild to a child of the departed parents. It is believed that the ancestors choose to do this in consequence of their love for the family and of the world. The world, according to the Yoruba, is the best place in which to live. Hence, it has been said that the Yoruba attitude is world-affirming, not renouncing. . . . There is a strong desire on the part of the living to have their parents reincarnated as soon as possible after their death. Hence well-wishers pray: "Bàbá/Ìyá á yà lówóò re o" ("May your father or mother turn to be a child for you"). And sometimes, in their enthusiasm, they pray saying "Bàbá/Ìyá á tètè yà o" ("May father or mother be reincarnated soon"). The child who is lucky to give birth to the father or mother usually feels particularly happy.

The situation is complex, however, because the living continue to pray to the dead, who apparently continue to exist with the ancestors "in heaven" even after they have reincarnated in a descendant (or in more than one descendant simultaneously).

Reincarnation of the elderly into the children of the family line has been a common pattern of belief among many tribal peoples, including many Australians, Africans, native North American tribes, the people of Melanesia, New Guinea, Arctic peoples, and others (see Head and Cranston). These tribal peoples also commonly believe that one can be reborn as a creature other than human or can remain in the world of the dead and experience reincarnation into various forms there. The north Asian Gilyak, for example, believe that in the realm of the dead the souls live for a time much as they do on Earth, but they may also grow sick and die there, be transformed afterward into Otherworld birds and gnats and finally ashes, and sometimes be reborn in this world to begin the whole process over again.

See also ANCESTOR VENERATION.

References

Awolalu, J. Omosade. *Yoruba Beliefs and Sacrificial Rites.* Essex, UK: Longman, 1979.

Christie-Murray, David. *Reincarnation: Ancient Beliefs and Modern Evidence.* London: Newton-Abbot, 1981.

Eliade, Mircea. *The Myth of the Eternal Return.* Trans. Willard R. Trask. Bollingen Series 46. New York: Pantheon Books, 1954.

Ephirim-Donkor, Anthony. *African Spirituality: On Becoming Ancestors.* Trenton, NJ: Africa World Press, 1997.

Frazer, James G. *The Belief in Immortality and the Worship of the Dead.* London: Macmillan, 1913.

Garstang, J. *Burial Customs of Ancient Egypt.* London: A. Constable, 1907.

Harva, U. *Mythology, Finno-Ugric, Siberian.* Mythology of All Races Series. Boston: Archaeological Institute of America: Marshall Jones Company, 1927.

Head, Joseph, and Sylvia Cranston. *Reincarnation: The Phoenix Fire Mystery.* New York: Julian Press/Crown Publishers, 1977.

Pettersson, Olof. *Jabmek and Jabmeaimo: A Comparative Study of the Dead and the Realm of the Dead in Lappish Religion.* Lund: C. W. K. Gleerup, 1957.

Spencer, Baldwin, and F. J. Gillen. *Northern Tribes of Central Australia.* London: Macmillan, 1904.

REINCARNATION, WESTERN

Reincarnation has a long and honorable history in the Western hemisphere, not among ancient tribal peoples alone but also in Western philosophy, in the myths and legends of pre-Christian Europe, and among certain early Christian church fathers.

In premodern Europe, heroes and even kings were frequently thought to be the reincarnations of their namesakes, often very distant ancestors in the family line. Norse scholar E. O. G. Turville-Petre tells a story (from around the year 1220 C.E.) of a Christian convert who was bothered by the persistence of such "heathen" beliefs (p. 194):

> It is told that once when King Olaf (the Saint) was riding with his bodyguard past the [burial mound] of Olaf the Elf of Geirstadir, one of his followers . . . questioned him: "tell me, Lord, were you buried here?" The King answered: "never did my soul have two bodies, and it never will have, neither now nor on the day of resurrection, and if I say anything else, then the common faith is not truly implanted in me." Then the courtier said: "people have said that when you came to this place before, you exclaimed 'here we were, and here we go.'" The King answered: "I never said that and I never will." The King was deeply disturbed at heart; he pricked his horse and sped from the place as fast as he could. It was easy to see that King Olaf wished to uproot and blot out this heretical superstition.

The Myth of Er

Well, I will tell you a tale . . . of what once happened to a brave man, Er, who, according to the story, was killed in battle. . . . On the twelfth day after his death, as he lay on the funeral pyre, he came to life again, and then proceeded to describe what he had seen in the other world. . . . Those [souls] who were come from [under the] earth told their tale with lamentations and tears, as they bethought them of all the dreadful things they had seen and suffered in their subterranean journey . . . while those who were come from heaven described enjoyments and sights of marvellous beauty.

[The gathered souls drew lots for their next lives, and were addressed:] "Ye short-lived souls, a new generation of men shall here begin the cycle of its mortal existence. Your destiny shall not be allotted to you, but you shall choose it for yourselves. . . . Virtue owns no master. He who honors her shall have more of her, and he who slights her, less. The responsibility lies with the chooser. Heaven is guiltless."

It was a truly wonderful sight, he said, to watch how each soul selected its life—a sight at once melancholy, and ludicrous, and strange. The experience of their former life generally guided the choice. . . . It so happened that the soul of Odysseus had drawn the last lot of all. When he came up to choose the memory of his former sufferings had so abated his ambition that he went about a long time looking for a quiet retired life, which with great trouble he discovered lying about, and thrown contemptuously aside by the others. As soon as he saw it, he chose it gladly, and said that he would have done the same if he had even drawn the first lot. . . .

Now, when all the souls had chosen their lives . . . they all travelled into the plain of Forgetfulness. . . . each, as he drinks, forgets everything. When they had gone to rest, and it was now midnight, there was a clap of thunder and an earthquake; and in a moment the souls were carried up to their birth, this way and that, like shooting stars. Er himself was prevented from drinking any of the water; but how, and by what road, he reached his body, he knew not; only he knew that he suddenly opened his eyes at dawn, and found himself laid out upon the funeral pyre.

And thus, Glaucon, the tale has been saved and has not perished, and will save us if we are obedient to the word spoken; and we shall pass safely over the river of Forgetfulness and our soul will not be defiled. Wherefore my counsel is that we hold fast ever to the heavenly way and follow after justice and virtue always, considering that the soul is immortal and able to endure every sort of good and every sort of evil. Thus shall we live dear to one another and to the gods . . . and it shall be well with us both in this Life and in the pilgrimage of a thousand years [between incarnations] which we have been describing.

From Plato's Republic, *Book 10 (quoted in Head and Cranston, 1977, pp. 215–216).*

In Celtic tales reincarnation also makes a regular appearance. In their volume *Celtic Heritage,* Alwyn Rees and Brinley Rees give several such accounts, identifying them as examples of a "heroic essence" that moves from form to form (p. 230):

> When Daolgas son of Cairril lay dying, his daughter stooped over him and kissed him. As she did so, a spark of fire flew from his mouth to hers and she became pregnant. In due time she gave birth to a broad-crowned boy, and, since no other name was found for him, he was called by his father's name, Daolgas.

Another example is Tuan, the sole survivor of Patholón's company (the original mythological human settlers of Ireland), who after successive transformations into a deer, a boar, and an eagle was eventually eaten in the form of a salmon by the wife of King Cairell and reborn of her. He was called Tuan, son of Cairell, but he bore within him the whole history of Ireland since the coming of Partholón (Rees and Rees, p. 229).

In the Welsh story of Taliesin, the witch Ceridwen prepares in her cauldron a magic brew, which, after a year's boiling, will yield three blessed drops. Whoever swallows these drops will know all the secrets of the past, the present, and the future, and she intends them for her ugly son Morfran ("Sea-crow") who is nicknamed Afagddu ("Blackness"). The drops fly out of the cauldron and fall on the finger of Gwion Bach, the boy who has helped to tend the fire underneath the cauldron. He puts his finger in his mouth, and then, realizing his danger, flees. Ceridwen sets out in pursuit. Gwion transforms himself successively into a hare, a fish, a bird, and a grain of wheat; she gives chase in appropriate forms—a greyhound, an otter-bitch, a hawk, and a hen. In this last form, she swallows the grain of wheat, and in the fullness of time, Gwion Bach is reborn of her as the wizard-poet Taliesin.

In Western philosophy, reincarnation has been widespread, though less so than in the East, and has been variously perceived as a marvelous fact of nature or a horrible curse, depending on the social and historical context. The Greek philosopher Plato believed that reincarnation was a burden to humankind, but at least it provided a chance for moral learning and spiritual growth. For Plato, humanity's ultimate goal was to transcend the process of migration by three lifetimes in a row choosing to become a philosopher, eschewing a life of pleasure, and dedicating oneself to contemplation and moral perfection. A number of early Christian leaders, under the influence of Plato and especially the Neoplatonists, taught reincarnation to their followers without particularly celebrating or bemoaning the idea. For example, Origen (c. 180 to c. 253), who was considered the greatest theologian in Christendom in his time, appears to have taught that reincarnation provided necessary lessons for God's creatures, but soon, he hoped, perfected souls would no longer need physical bodies and would move on to higher things. Jerome (c. 347 to c. 419 C.E.), a more orthodox Christian, wrote around the year 410 his "Letter to Avitus" criticizing Origen:

> If it can be shown that an incorporeal and reasonable being has life in itself independently of the body and that it is worse off in the body than out of it; then beyond a doubt bodies are only of secondary importance and arise from time to time to meet the varying conditions of reasonable creatures. Those who require bodies are clothed with them, and contrariwise, when fallen souls have lifted themselves up to better things, their bodies are once more annihilated. They are thus ever vanishing and ever reappearing. (Quoted in Head and Cranston, pp. 147–148)

By the fifth century, reincarnation was considered by the Christian church to be a heretical doctrine, and in the Middle Ages reincarnationists like the Cathars of France would be put to death.

Reincarnation is also a minority tradition in Judaism, but it has never been considered heretical. In fact, reincarnation has been taught continuously in mystical Jewish circles for well over 2,000 years. Probably because Judaism is world affirming in general and celebrates the material universe created by a caring God, reincarnation has not been interpreted as a curse that must be escaped, as Indian traditions and Neoplatonists saw it. Instead, reincarnation has been seen by Judaism, as by most other organized traditions, as a tool of God or the soul to achieve perfection. By moving through different forms, beginning with the mineral kingdom, progressing to the vegetable and animal kingdoms, and finally arriving in the human kingdom, the imperishable soul is able to experience the fullness of God's creation and achieve all that the divine has in store for it. Reincarnation is discussed in detail in an eleventh-century text called the *Zohar,* which served as the great fountainhead of both medieval Jewish and Christian occultism (Kabbalah). There reincarnation is called *gilgul,* which may be translated as "the wheel" (similar to Buddhism's doctrine of the wheel of rebirth). Interestingly, an influential sixteenth-century text called *Shaar HaGilgulim* (The Gate of the Wheels) by Rabbi Chaim Vittal Calibrese used the doctrine of reincarnation to interpret social trends and personal idiosyncrasies:

> Know that the reason the sages of our time are overpowered by their wives is because these holy

men are the reincarnated souls of the generation of the Exodus, specifically of those who did not try and stop the dissidents from making the Golden Calf. However, the women of that time declined complicity and refused to surrender their jewelry to the Golden Calf builders. Therefore, these women now reign over their husbands. (quoted in Winkler, p. 35)

The belief in reincarnation is even found among Muslims. An early sect of Islam was called *tanāsukhiyya* because its members believed in reincarnation (in Arabic, tanāsukh), and medieval theologians such as Ibn Rushd (1126–1198; also known as Averroës) considered reincarnation perfectly consistent with the Qur'ān, though not specifically taught by that Scripture (Waugh, pp. 59–62). Reincarnation has also been a common doctrine among the mystical brotherhoods in Islam, called Sufis, from the earliest period of Islam up to the present. Finally, the powerful Shi'ite minority in Islam also believes in reincarnation, although only for revered prophets called *imams* (particularly the last and greatest imam, the Mahdī) and not for the common person. This belief was probably borrowed from Samaritanism, an early religion closely related to Judaism, and the same belief in the reincarnation of great prophets is also found today in the new religion known as Baha'i, founded in the last quarter of the nineteenth century as a breakaway Islamic sect.

A number of important Western thinkers accepted reincarnation, even in the eighteenth and nineteenth centuries, including Ben Franklin, Johan Wolfgang von Goethe, Johann Gottlieb Fichte, William Wordsworth, Ralph Emerson, and Henry David Thoreau. Napoléon Bonaparte (1769–1821) believed he was the reincarnation of Charlemagne, who founded the Holy Roman Empire in 800 C.E. Walt Whitman (1819–1892) writes:

> I know I am deathless. No doubt I have died myself ten thousand times before. I laugh at what you call dissolution, and I know the amplitude of time. This day before dawn I ascended a hill and looked at the crowded heaven. And I said to my spirit, When we become the enfolders of those orbs, and the pleasure and knowledge of everything in them, shall we be filled and satisfied then? And my spirit said, No, we but level that lift to pass and continue beyond. ("Song of Myself," *Leaves of Grass*)

Although reincarnation was accepted by a few great figures before the twentieth century, it became surprisingly popular among the masses in that century. Two major sources of this resurgence of belief in rebirth are (1) the great success of traditional Buddhism, Hindu-

ism, and Taoism in the West in the twentieth century and (2) the rise of the New Age movement. Both of these phenomena may be traced to the pioneering work of Helena P. Blavatsky (1831–1891), founder of the Theosophical Society in New York City in 1875. Blavatsky stated that she had been sent to the West by Indian sages to popularize Eastern metaphysics and combat scientific materialism, and to this end she published hundreds of newspaper and magazine articles and several large volumes, including *Isis Unveiled* (1877) and *The Secret Doctrine* (1888). These books dealt extensively with what she considered the "twin doctrines" of reincarnation and karma, along with many other teachings she claimed belonged to a "universal religion" or "perennial philosophy" that she hoped would gradually be restored to the world. By Blavatsky's death in 1891 reincarnation and karma had indeed become household words in the United States and Europe. Meanwhile, Theosophical efforts in India, Sri Lanka, and Japan were organized to repulse Christian missionaries and reassert native religious traditions.

In the twentieth century Asian religious leaders gained a foothold in Western cities and rapidly established a considerable following, in large part because of groundwork performed by the Theosophical movement. (The success of Buddhist missionaries and their frequent connections to Blavatsky or her followers is documented in Rick Field's book *How the Swans Came to the Lake*.) The influx of Eastern religions rapidly led to an amalgamation with Western occultism, including Theosophy, the Rosicrucian movement, Kabbalah, and Native American shamanism, resulting in the incredible diversity of the New Age movement. Interest in reincarnation shows no sign of waning, judging by the number of popular books and academic research currently being published covering everything from near-death experiences, past-life regression, and past-life therapy to the impact of Eastern thought on Western traditions, such as in the recent volume *The Original Jesus: The Buddhist Sources of Christianity*. The twenty-first century promises to be an exciting time for comparative religion.

See also REINCARNATION, EASTERN; REINCARNATION, TRIBAL.

References
Christie-Murray, David. *Reincarnation: Ancient Beliefs and Modern Evidence.* London: Newton-Abbot, 1981.
Eliade, Mircea. *The Myth of the Eternal Return.* Trans. Willard R. Trask. Bollingen Series 46. New York: Pantheon Books, 1954.
Fields, Rick. *How the Swans Came to the Lake: A Narrative History of Buddhism in America.* Boston: Shambala, 1992.
Frazer, James G. *The Belief in Immortality and the Worship of the Dead.* London: Macmillan, 1913.
Garstang, J. *Burial Customs of Ancient Egypt.* London: A. Constable, 1907.

Gruber, Elmer R., and Holger Kersten. *The Original Jesus: The Buddhist Sources of Christianity* Rockport, MA: Element, 1995.

Head, Joseph, and Sylvia Cranston. *Reincarnation: The Phoenix Fire Mystery.* New York: Julian Press/Crown Publishers, 1977.

Rees, Alwyn, and Brinley Rees. *Celtic Heritage: Ancient Tradition in Ireland and Wales.* London: Thames and Hudson, 1961.

Stevenson, Ian. *Cases of the Reincarnation Type.* Charlottesville: University Press of Virginia, 1975.

Titchenell, Elsa-Brita. *The Masks of Odin.* Pasadena: Theosophical University Press, 1985.

Turville-Petre, E. O. G. *Myth and Religion of the North: The Religion of Ancient Scandinavia.* Westport, CT: Greenwood, 1964.

Waugh, Earl. "Persistent Fragments: The Trajectories of Reincarnation in Islam." In *Concepts of Transmigration,* ed. Steven J. Kaplan. Studies in Comparative Religion, vol. 6. Lewiston, NY: Edwin Mellen Press, 1996.

Whitman, Walt. "Song of Myself." In *Leaves of Grass.* New York: Modern Library, 1950.

Winkler, Gershon. *The Place Where You Are Standing Is Holy: A Jewish Theology on Human Relationships.* Northvale, NJ: J. Aronson, 1994.

RELIQUARY

In the most general sense, reliquaries are receptacles for the earthly remains (relics) of a deceased person (or occasionally, a deceased animal). This definition would include all coffins, sarcophagi, funerary pots, urns, and even the tombs, mausolea, and columbaria (structures with niches for the burial of ashes) that housed such remains. However, the more common and technical usage of the term *reliquary* refers to a spiritually charged container for the remains (ashes, bones, personal belongings) of special, saintly figures. The relics of these figures are thought either to maintain a personal, conscious connection between the deceased figure and this world or else to preserve some of the sanctity of the deceased, which can benefit those who come into contact with their relics.

Reliquaries from the Christian world are preserved from the fourth century C.E. onward, becoming quite massive after the eighth century as the cult of relics grew to great proportions and tombs of martyrs in the catacombs were raided for their saintly remains. Reliquaries in Buddhism (in the form of stūpas) are found from around the beginning of the common era and became enormously popular in Tibet, China, and Japan during the succeeding 1,000 years. In Egypt, besides the coffins and sarcophagi serving as reliquaries for mummified people, reliquaries for animals are also found in great numbers in extensive animal cemeteries.

Reliquaries were designed to sanctify either a physical location such as a church (specifically, an altar in a church) or a person. Portable Christian reliquaries took the shape of small amulets or medallions containing ashes or small bits of bone and worn by devotees. Reliquaries containing bits of the True Cross were often cruciform in shape. Fixed reliquaries often took the

The relic hand of St. James of Compostela, which resides in the Church of St. Peter, Marlow, England. Courtesy of Images Colour Library.

shape of miniature coffins resembling gabled buildings and were called reliquary *chasses* (from Latin capsa, "coffin"). There were also reliquaries containing bones that took the shape of the appropriate limb, such as the brachium, which contained an arm bone and was made in the shape of an arm.

Medieval Christian reliquaries could be made of intricately decorated wood, precious metals, or ivory, and the value of the container often reflected the precious cargo within. It was essential that reliquaries could be opened in order to provide physical access to the relic; thus reliquaries are found with either lids or panels with hinges or in some cases with a view of the relic within via a grill or rock crystal covering.

Buddhist stūpas served as fixed reliquaries that sanctified the ground, sometimes in deliberate geomantic designs intended to lay down lines of spiritual force. They were built in the shape of temples symbolizing the world mountain and worldly transcendence and were made of mud brick and or stone.

Egyptian reliquaries for animal remains were rectangular in shape, were built of wood or bronze, and held a few bones from an animal rather than the mummified remains one might expect. Atop the box was fixed a figure of the appropriate creature; at Saqqâra reliquaries for falcons have been found in great numbers, as well as some for ibises, ichneumons, snakes, and scarab beetles.

See also COLUMBARIUM; MAUSOLEUM; STŪPA.

References

Brubaker, Leslie. "Reliquary." In *Dictionary of the Middle Ages,* ed. Joseph R. Strayer. Vol. 10. New York: Charles Scribner's Sons, 1982–1989.

Govinda, Anagarika. *The Psycho-cosmic Symbolism of the Buddhist Stupa.* Berkeley: Dharma, 1976.

Spencer, A. J. *Death in Ancient Egypt.* New York: Penguin, 1982.

Weitzmann, Kurt, ed. *Age of Spirituality: Late Antique and Early Christian Art, Third to Seventh Century.* New York: Metropolitan Museum of Art, 1979.

REPHĀ'IM

Rephā'im is the Hebrew name for the dead, who are said to dwell in darkness in Sheol (also called Mot). The word *rephā'im* appears eight times in the Hebrew Bible, with different but related meanings. God's might is said to reach down beneath the oceans, even to the rephā'im who "writhe in fear" in Sheol and Abaddon (Job 26:5–6). Here the word appears to refer generically to all the dead. More specifically, the rephā'im also appear as an ancient and deceased lineage of kings in the Bible. Addressing the hated king of Babylon, Isaiah 14:9 says:

Sheol below was all astir
to meet you at your coming;
she roused the Rephaim to meet you,

all who had been leaders on earth;
she made all who had been kings of the nations
rise from their thrones.

But we find a different meaning in Genesis 14:5, where the king of the Elamites, Kedorlaomer, defeated the rephā'im who lived in Ashteroth-karnaim. Again, in Deuteronomy 2:14 the rephā'im are referred to as a race of giants.

Both usages (rephā'im as the dead and as giants) go back to the second millennium B.C.E., before the Canaanite and Israelite tribes became separated. At that time, in ancient Ugarit, the word *rephā'im* referred to the line of dead kings and heroes and meant "esteemed ancestors." Later on in Israel's history, the original usage was forgotten (although Isaiah 14:9 hints at it), and the word took on two different meanings.

Ancient Judaism makes almost no suggestions about a future life of bliss for the dead, with the exception of Psalm 73. Rather, the dead dwell in silence (Psalms 94:17; 115:17), in dust (Genesis 3:19; Psalm 104:29; Ecclesiastes 3:20; Job 34:15), and in destruction (literally "Abaddon"). In fact, some scholars have suggested that for the ancient Jews, the breath of life (ru'ach) that was first breathed into Adam (Genesis 2:7) was thought to be reabsorbed by God at death, and the dead simply ceased to exist at all. Yet the cult of the dead and the practice of necromancy seem prevalent enough in ancient Israel and in the ancient Near East in general to make this position unlikely.

See also MOT; SHEOL.

References

Heidel, Alexander. *The Gilgamesh Epic and Old Testament Parallels.* Chicago: University of Chicago Press, 1946.

L'Heureux, C. E. *Rank Among the Canaanite Gods: El, Ba'al, and the Rephaim.* Missoula, MT: Scholars Press, 1979.

Pope, M. H. "Notes on the Rephaim Texts." In *Essays on the Ancient Near East in Memory of Jacob Joel Finkelstein*, ed. M. de Jong Ellis. Hamden, CT: Archon, 1977.

Rosenberg, R. *The Concept of Biblical Sheol within the Context of Ancient Near Eastern Beliefs.* Ph.D. diss., Harvard University, 1980.

RESERVE HEAD/BODY

In ancient Egypt considerable care was taken to preserve the body by mummification and burial in secure coffins within locked sarcophagi. Nonetheless, Egyptians knew that the body sometimes perished despite the greatest efforts and that tombs were broken into and ransacked by unscrupulous grave robbers who often damaged the human remains.

For this reason a magical double was constructed of the deceased, either a statue or merely a figure carved in relief, which could stand in as a dwelling for the soul (ba) should anything happen to the body. It could also serve the soul even while the body was intact, for instance, by being carved into the tomb walls, thus facilitating the soul's entry into and exit from the tomb. These doubles, or "reserve bodies," are found from the First Dynasty (c. 3100 B.C.E.) carved of wood, but Egypt soon switched to stone for greater durability. In the Fourth and Fifth Dynasties, reserve heads were entombed with the mummy, sometimes to supplement and sometimes to replace full-body statues and reliefs.

Although this practice follows the well-known Egyptian principle of "substitution" (that any ritual item made to resemble the real thing, such as painted or carved servants or food items, could stand in for it), it is unclear why most of the surviving reserve heads should have the ears broken off and a strange incision made from the top of the skull down to the back.

References

Edwards, I. E. S. *The Pyramids of Egypt*. Rev. ed., New York: Penguin, 1978.

Garstang, J. *Burial Customs of Ancient Egypt*. London: A. Constable, 1907.

Hamilton-Paterson, James, and Carol Andrews. *Mummies: Death and Life in Ancient Egypt*. London: Williams Collins Sons, 1978.

RESURRECTION, ANCIENT NEAR EAST

The belief that the dead will physically resurrect, or "rise again" to life, is an extremely important and ancient doctrine in all the religions that stem from the ancient Near East; it is also found among many tribal peoples around the world. There are two basic forms of the belief in resurrection, one related to the cyclical death and rebirth of fertility in nature and the other related to a final judgment by a personal god.

The resurrection of the dead as a part of the cyclical rebirth of nature may be termed a "primitive" belief—in the sense of being ancient and primal, not in the sense of being shallow or ignorant. A great many of Earth's cultures have believed that mortal creatures will live in new bodies after death. Among the Arctic Eurasian peoples, for instance, the bones of hunted game (particularly bears) are carefully buried with the understanding that in time the game will resurrect—possibly to be hunted and eaten again. This belief in resurrection reveals that the dead are thought to return to life again in this (unchanged) world or a world much like it, often called the Otherworld. The resurrected do not proceed to a heaven or hell but carry on much as before.

A much more theological understanding of resurrection may be found among the ancient Egyptians. In some ways Egyptian resurrection depended on a favorable judgment being passed on the dead, after which the dead (at first only kings) would rise up to a new life.

> Rise up, O Teti.
> Take your head,

> collect your bones,
> gather your limbs,
> shake the earth from your flesh.
> Take your bread that rots not,
> your beer that sours not.
> (Spronk, trans., p. 90)

Yet Egyptian resurrection was not a one-time event for each individual. It was closely tied to the cycles of the sun. The land of the dead lay in the West where the sun set, and the resurrected and "justified" dead rode along with Osiris in the solar boat. Each day the dead rose again in the East. The key phrase associated with the "justified" dead was "going out by day" (the real name of the so-called Egyptian Book of the Dead), which demonstrated the cyclical associations of the resurrection—each "night" at least the ba-soul returns to the tomb (even if the ab, the immortal soul, remains among the stars). Frequently, seeds of wheat were planted in the tomb with the dead; the wheat soon sprouted (though without sunlight it did not survive), symbolizing in yet another way the close connection between natural rhythms, fertility, and resurrection for the ancient Egyptian.

Another example of a theologized understanding of natural and cyclic resurrection is Canaanite belief, which had a marked impact on the Judeo-Christian-Muslim tradition. Very ancient texts discovered at Ugarit (on the Mediterranean coast north of Israel) have given scholars a much better picture of the warrior and fertility god of the Canaanites, Baal, whose worship was much opposed by the prophets of orthodox Judaism. Baal was praised by his Canaanite (and heterodox Israelite) devotees for conquering various monsters and bringing fertility back to the land. During his mythic battles, nature itself was held hostage: rains were withheld from the Earth and everything seemed to die.

> Seven years Baal failed,
> Eight years the Cloud Rider;
> no dew nor shower,
> No surging of the double-deep,
> Nor goodly sound of Baal's voice.
> (Greenspoon, p. 270)

After Baal's victory, however, nature sprang to life again:

> The heavens are raining oil,
> The *wadis* [ravines] run with mead.
> (Greenspoon, trans., p. 270)

Baal's consort, Anat, was famous for conquering death itself, personified in the god Mot:

She seized El's son Mot.
With a sword she sliced him;
With a sieve she winnowed him;
With a fire she burnt him;
With millstones she ground him.
(Greenspoon, trans., p. 269)

Thus the Canaanite gods Baal and Anat had power over life and death. In the annual New Year's festival, the two gods were actually thought to (temporarily) resurrect all the dead, called *rp'um* (compare the Hebrew *rephā'im*), who appeared on their descendants' farms and threshing floors—no doubt to reconsecrate the sites of fertility and guarantee their harvest in the coming year. An important part of the ritual celebration was the fact that for two days the "dead" gods (and nature) were imagined to be underground, but on the third day they rose again to life. Clearly, the idea of resurrection occurring on the "third day" permanently influenced Judeo-Christian thought (Jesus too was said to have resurrected on the third day after his death).

At first Hebrew tradition (at least that part of it represented by the orthodox prophets and priests) vehemently opposed such ideas of resurrection because they tied Yahweh too closely to Baal. The Book of Hosea 6:1–3 indicates that some northern Israelites had begun to see the god of Israel as having the same power as Baal:

Come, let us return to the Lord;
for he has torn us and will heal us,
he has struck us and he will bind up our wounds;
after two days he will revive us,
on the third day he will restore us,
that in his presence we may live.
Let us humble ourselves, let us
strive to know the Lord,
whose justice dawns like morning light,
and its dawning is as sure as the sunrise.
It will come to us like a shower,
like spring rains that water the earth.
(emphasis added)

But the prophet Hosea angrily rejects the idea that the Lord might restore the Hebrews as Baal restores the Canaanites (Hosea 6:4–6):

O Ephraim, how shall I deal with you?
How shall I deal with you, Judah?
Your loyalty to me is like the morning mist,
like the dew that vanishes early.
Therefore have I lashed you through the prophets
and torn you to shreds with my words;
loyalty is my desire, not sacrifice,
not whole-offerings but the knowledge of God.

Ezekiel's Vision

The hand of the Lord came upon me, and he carried me out by his spirit and put me down in a plain full of bones. He made me go to and fro across them until I had been round them all; they covered the plain, countless numbers of them, and they were very dry. He said to me, "Man, can these bones live again?" I answered, "Only thou knowest that, Lord God." He said to me, "Prophesy over these bones and say to them, O dry bones, hear the word of the Lord. This is the word of the Lord God to these bones: I will put breath [or spirit] into you, and you shall live. I will fasten sinews on you, bring flesh upon you, overlay you with skin, and put breath in you, and you shall live; and you shall know that I am the Lord."

I began to prophecy as he had bidden me, and as I prophesied there was a rustling sound and the bones fitted themselves together. As I looked, sinews appeared upon them, flesh covered them, and they were overlaid with skin, but there was no breath in them. Then he said to me, "Prophecy to the wind, prophesy, man, and say to it, These are the words of the Lord God: Come, O wind, come from every quarter and breathe into these slain, that they may come to life."

I began to prophecy as he had bidden me: breath came into them; they came to life and rose to their feet, a mighty host. He said to me, "Man, these bones are the whole people of Israel. They say, 'Our bones are dry, our thread of life is snapped, our web is severed from the loom.' Prophecy, therefore, and say to them, These are the words of the Lord God: O my people, I will open your graves and bring you up from them, and restore you to the land of Israel. You shall know that I am the Lord when I open your graves and bring you from them, O my people. Then I will put my spirit [or breath] into you and you shall live, and I will settle you on your own soil, and you shall know that I the Lord have spoken and will act. This is the very word of the Lord."

Ezekiel 37:1–14.

Orthodox Hebrew prophets such as Hosea certainly did not want to deny that Yahweh had the power to resurrect whomever he chose; indeed, the prophets Elijah and Elisha are credited with no less than three individual resurrections through the power of God, the last performed solely by Elisha's bones (1 Kings 17:17–24; 2 Kings 4:31–37; 13:20–21). But such examples are very rare, and in general Yahweh was not concerned with the dead but with his living chosen people. Sheol, the land of the dead, was a place of dust and darkness, "far removed" from Yahweh, Lord of Israel, who had no contact with the dead shades (rephā'im) there. It was a "land of no return" (Job 7:9–10; 16:22). Psalm 88:10–12 reads,

> Does thou work wonders for the dead?
> Shall their company rise up and praise thee?
> Will they speak of thy faithful love in the grave,
> of thy sure help in the place of Destruction?
> Will thy wonders be known in the dark,
> thy victories in the land of oblivion?

The answer, obviously, is no. Death is the end of meaningful existence, and the writer of the psalm prays to God for help *now*, during life (see also Psalms 6:5, 30:9). Most of the Old Testament does not mention a general resurrection and in many places actually denies the possibility of it.

This picture changes only during the period of exile at the beginning of the sixth century B.C.E. The Israelite capital Jerusalem was destroyed, its central temple pulled down, and the entire upper echelon of Israelites dragged off as captives to Babylon. There—in utter despair that their god would allow so many righteous Hebrews to die, while their "wicked" captors so obviously enjoyed wealth and long lives—the Hebrews came into contact with the highly apocalyptic and ethical Zoroastrian religion.

For centuries in the Middle East, Zoroastrianism had taught that during life, the forces of evil held sway; final compensation for the just and unjust generally occurred not in life but after death. In a final cosmic moment, "time" would stop. All would be resurrected (ristakhez) from the dead, the wicked would be renovated, and all human souls would join God. A messiah known as the Saoshyant would bring on this final reckoning between the true god (Ahura Mazda) and the god of the lie (Angra Mainyu). All of this was new to the Hebrews, but after several generations in exile such ideas came to affect their theology profoundly and to explain why God, apparently without cause, had taken away the Holy Land and allowed evildoers to prosper. The Zoroastrian Scripture, the Avesta, contains material that is difficult to date; estimates range from 1700 B.C.E. (Boyce) to 600 B.C.E. or later; but modern Biblical scholarship freely admits the profound Persian/Zoroastrian influence on the development of later Hebrew religion, particularly Hebrew eschatology. The Persian scholar Ernst Herzfeld reconstructed one passage from the Avesta that is very clear on resurrection (Herzfeld, p. 299, from Yasht 19.88f.):

> Astvarta will set forth
> from the water of Kansaviya
> the champion of Ahura Mazdāh
> and his other companions,
> that they make humanity *frasham* [transcendent],
> not-aging, not-dying,
> not-decaying, not-rotting,
> ever-living, ever-flourishing.
> When the dead will rise up,
> the reviver, the imperishable will come,
> he will make humanity *frasham,* please God!

One of the first indications that the Hebrews were absorbing such Zoroastrian ideas comes from the book of the sixth-century prophet Ezekiel, whose mission was in Babylon with the Hebrew people. In chapter 37, Ezekiel has a grand vision of the resurrection of all the Hebrews killed in exile (see excerpt). The majority of Biblical scholars believe Ezekiel intended this prophecy as a *metaphorical* restoration of the "house of Israel," not a literal resurrection. (For instance, the bones of all the exiled Hebrews never lay around in one great plain.) Nevertheless, later generations took Ezekiel's vision literally and joined it to a vision of the end of time. Another passage from the sixth century, Isaiah 26, reveals a Hebrew expectation of resurrection, but as in Ezekiel, only those devoted to the god of Israel will be brought back to life: "the bitter enemies of thy people do not see it . . . [those] dead will not live again" (Isaiah 26:11, 14), Clearly, at the time, resurrection was a new idea prophesied only for the few as well as a response to the unprecedented destruction of Israel. When many Israelites believed that God had at last abandoned them, the new theology held out a hope that God would rectify all things after death.

See also GEHENNA; HADES; HEAVEN, HISTORY OF; HEAVEN, ORIGINS OF; HELL, HISTORY OF; HELL, ORIGINS OF; JUDGMENT, LAST; JUDGMENT, PARTICULAR; MOT; QIYĀMA; REINCARNATION, EASTERN; RISTAKHEZ; SHEOL; SOUL.

References

Boyce, Mary. *A History of Zoroastrianism.* Vol. 1. Leiden: E. J. Brill, 1975.

Charles, R. H., ed. *The Apocrypha and Pseudepigrapha of the Old Testament.* Vol. 2: *Pseudepigrapha.* Oxford: Clarendon Press, 1966.

Cross, Frank Moore. *Canaanite Myth and Hebrew Epic: Essays in the History of the Religion of Israel.* Cambridge: Harvard University Press, 1973.

Eklund, R. *Life between Death and Resurrection according to Islam.* Uppsala: Almquist and Wilksells, 1941.

Glasson, T. Francis. *Greek Influence in Jewish Eschatology.* London: SPCK, 1961.

Greenspoon, Leonard J. "The Origin of the Idea of Resurrection." In *Traditions in Transformation: Turning Points in Biblical Faith,* ed. Baruch Halpern and Jon D. Levenson. Winona Lake, IN: Eisenbrauns, 1981.

Guignebert, Charles. *The Jewish World in the Time of Jesus.* New York: University Books, 1965.

Herzfeld, Ernst. *Zoroaster and His World.* Vol. 1. Princeton: Princeton University Press, 1947.

Martin-Achard, Robert. *From Death to Life: A Study of the Development of the Doctrine of the Resurrection in the Old Testament.* Trans. J. P. Smith. Edinburgh: Oliver and Boyd, 1960.

Moore, George Foot. *Judaism in the First Centuries of the Christian Era.* 3 vols. Cambridge: Harvard University Press, 1927–1930; New York: Schocken Books, 1971.

Moulton, James Hope. *Early Zoroastrianism.* London: Williams and Norgate, 1913.

Nickelsburg, G. W. E., Jr. *Resurrection, Immortality, and Eternal Life in Intertestamental Judaism.* Cambridge: Harvard University Press, 1972.

Perkins, P. *Resurrection: New Testament Witness and Contemporary Reflection.* Garden City, NY: Doubleday, 1984.

Robinson, J. M. "Jesus from Easter to Valentinus (or to the Apostles' Creed)." *Journal of Biblical Literature* 101 (1982): 5–37.

Smith, Jane I., and Yvonne Yazbeck Haddad. *The Islamic Understanding of Death and Resurrection.* Albany: SUNY Press, 1981.

Spronk, Klaas. *Beatific Afterlife in Ancient Israel and in the Ancient Near East.* Kevelaer: Verlag Butzon, 1986.

RESURRECTION, CHRISTIAN

Christianity struggled at first to distinguish itself from its parent religion, Judaism, in part because it was rejected by Jewish leaders. A turning point came in 86 C.E. when the Hebrew canon of Scripture was closed by a council of Jewish scholars in the city of Jamnia. These leaders decided that the Scriptures were complete (thus locking out the "unorthodox" texts being written by the Christians about their messiah, Jesus), and the Christians were thrown out of the synagogues. Nevertheless, Christianity continued to accept many of the basic teachings of Judaism, and stories told about Jesus and his miraculous deeds closely resemble traditions surrounding previous Hebrew prophets. Thus it is not a surprise that Christianity also accepted the doctrine of resurrection, though it came to be transformed in the light of systematic Greek philosophy (an encounter that never occurred on a deep level between the Hebrew and Greek traditions).

Like the ancient prophets Elijah and Elisha, Jesus showed his power over death by resurrecting not only the dead but himself. Such an event was unprecedented in Hebrew history and, for an increasing number of Jews of the period, proved that the Messiah had in fact come and that a new age was about to begin. But what is most remarkable about the earliest Christian traditions, according to the majority of Biblical scholars, is that they originally contained no resurrection story about Christ. The early source on which the Gospels of Matthew and Luke drew, called *Q* by scholars (from Quelle, "source"), contains parables and teachings of Jesus but no stories of his birth or death. Most scholars of the early church now believe that the resurrection and apocalyptic emphasis of Christianity was not part of Jesus' teaching but was added by later Jewish Christians, who projected onto Jesus centuries of Jewish hopes for salvation after death (as surveyed in RESURRECTION, HEBREW).

Certainly, by the time of the apostle Paul (flourished c. 35 to c. 65 C.E.), the resurrection of Jesus had become the very foundation of Christian belief and salvation. Paul believed that the resurrection of Christ signified not only the potential salvation of all humankind (in a quasi-physical resurrection leading to eternal life) but that it would occur very, very soon—within the lifetimes of those hearing him. Many early Christians sold their homes, gave away their property, and lived in small communities, awaiting the imminent return of the resurrected son of God. Faith, for Paul, became far more important than works. This marks an important shift from early Hebrew belief, which saw a coming resurrection as a vindication of those who did right in the eyes of the Lord and a punishment for those who behaved wickedly. But for Paul, faith in Jesus and belief in the salvific power of his resurrection was everything; besides, there was little time for good works. In 1 Thessalonians 1:10 Paul tells his flock "to wait expectantly for the appearance from heaven of his Son Jesus, whom he raised from the dead." The Christians were expected to do little but pray, live conscientiously with regard to each other, and wait, calling "Marana tha— Come, O Lord!" (1 Corinthians 22).

But as years turned into decades and Jesus did not return, a Christian theology developed, which is reflected in the four Gospels and later epistles of the New Testament (all dating from after Paul's death, from c. 65 to c. 180 C.E. and even later). Stories about Jesus' resurrection (with somewhat conflicting details) were added to stories of his birth and travels and interspersed with teachings from Q and other (probably oral) sources. Because the Christians drew from widely diverse Jewish sources and theology, the New Testament writings give different interpretations of the significance of the resurrection of Jesus and humankind. The three synoptic Gospels, Matthew, Mark, and Luke, have Jesus predicting a great number of elaborate catastrophes before the Kingdom of Heaven will appear, whereas the Gospel of John seems to indicate that the arrival of the Kingdom *has already happened* for those who understand. John 5:24 states: "In very truth, anyone who gives heed to what I say and puts his trust in him who sent me has hold of eternal life, and does not come up for judgement, but has already passed from death to life." (Limited verses in other Gospels faintly

Jesus raising Lazarus from his tomb, John 11:43. Courtesy of Anne Ronan Picture Library.

echo John's point of view: Mark 1:15; Luke 17:21; Luke 11:20; Matt 12:28.) Yet the Gospel of John (5: 28–29) also mentions that the dead will be raised for judgment: "the time is coming when all who are in the grave shall hear his voice and come out: those who have done right will rise to life; those who have done wrong will rise to hear their doom." But Luke indicates that the righteous are *already* in paradise and the evil already in Hell, having proceeded to their afterlife destinations immediately after death. Luke 16:23 has Jesus describe a rich man who died, was buried, appeared in Hades in torment, and cried out to Abraham to give him even a drop of cool water; Lazarus, meanwhile, was in heaven. Likewise, in Luke 23:43, Jesus says to the thief who hangs on a cross near him: "I tell you this: today you shall be with me in Paradise."

Neither Christian nor Jewish theology ever resolved the discrepancy between individual judgment immediately after death and a general resurrection and judgment in the distant future. The Christian Book of Revelation goes to great pains to describe in detail the activities and signs at the end of the world and the final judgment and dispensation of souls; but if the individual dead are already judged and placed in Heaven or Hell immediately after death, there is little sense in resurrecting all the dead only to rejudge them and place them back in their previous afterlife situations! For centuries early church fathers struggled with this conundrum without reaching a unanimous decision. But Islam, which took over Jewish and Christian doctrines on resurrection, resolved this conflict by describing the *temporary* pleasure or pain of the individual dead in their graves—these experiences in the grave are "presentiments" of the real judgment, which is only to come at the end of time. (For more information on the Muslim doctrine of resurrection, see SĀ'A and QIYĀMA.)

For some reason this theological controversy, which was hotly debated among early Jewish and Christian scholars, never gained widespread public notice. Under the influence of long-held Israelite apocalyptic belief, early Judaism and early Christianity continued to teach that there would be a resurrection only at the end of time, when all humankind would be judged. Rabbinic Judaism, beginning in the first century of the common era, triumphed over the skeptical Sadducees, who denied the resurrection or the world to come. The Hebrew text Mishnah (c. 200 C.E.) accepts resurrection and heaven as a commonplace: the Mishnah Sanhedrin 10:1 states,

> All of Israel has a portion in the world to come . . .
> [but] the following have no portion in the world to come:
> one who says, "There is no resurrection of the dead."

Similarly, early Christians expected to wait for some time after their deaths until the resurrection; indeed, one of the greatest motivations to be a martyr for God during Roman persecutions was the belief that martyrs proceeded directly after death to heaven, unlike the common believers, who had to bide their time until the end of the "age." Gradually, however, this belief began to shift; in modern times, most Jews and Christians believe that the dead proceed directly to Heaven or Hell (or elsewhere) immediately after death, leaving the doctrine of a future *physical* resurrection and judgment largely forgotten or only hazily understood.

See also GEHENNA; HADES; HEAVEN, HISTORY OF; HEAVEN, ORIGINS OF; HELL, HISTORY OF; HELL, ORIGINS OF; JUDGMENT, LAST; JUDGMENT, PARTICULAR; PURGATORY; QIYĀMA; SOUL.

References

Charles, R. H., ed. *Apocrypha and Pseudepigrapha of the Old Testament.* Vol. 2: *Pseudepigrapha.* Oxford: Clarendon Press, 1966.

Glasson, T. Francis. *Greek Influence in Jewish Eschatology.* London: SPCK, 1961.

Greenspoon, Leonard J. "The Origin of the Idea of Resurrection." In *Traditions in Transformation: Turning Points in Biblical Faith,* ed. Baruch Halpern and Jon D. Levenson. Winona Lake, IN: Eisenbrauns, 1981.

Guignebert, Charles. *The Jewish World in the time of Jesus.* New York: University Books, 1965.

Martin-Achard, Robert. *From Death to Life: A Study of the Development of the Doctrine of the Resurrection in the Old Testament.* Trans. J. P. Smith. Edinburgh: Oliver and Boyd, 1960.

Moore, George Foot. *Judaism in the First Centuries of the Christian Era.* 3 vols. Cambridge: Harvard University Press, 1927–1930. Reprint, New York: Schocken, 1971.

Nickelsburg, G. W. E., Jr. *Resurrection, Immortality, and Eternal Life in Intertestamental Judaism.* Cambridge: Harvard University Press, 1972.

Perkins, P. *Resurrection: New Testament Witness and Contemporary Reflection.* Garden City, NY: Doubleday, 1984.

Robinson, J. M. "Jesus from Easter to Valentinus (or to the Apostles' Creed)." *Journal of Biblical Literature* 101 (1982): 5–37.

Smith, Jane I., and Yvonne Yazbeck Haddad. *The Islamic Understanding of Death and Resurrection.* Albany: SUNY Press, 1981.

Spronk, Klaas. *Beatific Afterlife in Ancient Israel and in the Ancient Near East.* Kevelaer: Verlag Butzon and Bercker, 1986.

RESURRECTION, HEBREW

A careful study of the Old Testament and other ancient documents of the Hebrew religion shows that resurrection was not originally accepted by the ancient Israelites. In contrast to their Canaanite and Egyptian neighbors, who appear to have believed in a resurrection of the dead based on the seasonal rhythms of nature, the Hebrews sharply distinguished Yahweh from comparable fertility deities and denied any connection between their god and the dead. After prolonged exposure to ancient Near Eastern ideas, however, and particularly

Elijah raising the widow's son from apparent death, circa 1860. Courtesy of Anne Ronan Picture Library.

after the exile of the Israelites to Babylon and exposure to Zoroastrian ideas (c. 600 B.C.E.), Hebrew texts began to show a greater and greater acceptance that at least some of the dead might be resurrected and judged.

An extra-Biblical book from about 200 B.C.E., 1 Enoch, shows how deeply belief in a literal resurrection had penetrated Israelite thought. For the first time, the dead in the Underworld of Sheol (now placed in the west) were conceived as still conscious and grouped into separate cells to be "brought forth" for judgment at a later time. 1 Enoch 22:3–4 reads:

> Then Raphael . . . said unto me: "These hollow [three or four] places have been created for this very purpose, that the spirits of the souls of the dead should assemble therein, yea that all the souls of the children of men should assemble here. And these places have been made to receive them till the day of their judgment and till their appointed period, till the great judgment comes upon them."
> (Charles, trans., p. 202)

The righteous wait near a bright spring of water, whereas the wicked, whose "judgment has not been executed upon them in their lifetime," wait in torment. Importantly, there is a third group: those who are unrighteous *and* who suffered for it in their lifetime will not be raised from the dead. Theologically, then, the doctrine of resurrection became not merely a reward for Israelites who suffered unjustly in life but also a means of vengeance on the wicked who escaped punishment in life. Nevertheless, a general resurrection of all humans was still not contemplated. Even the second-century B.C.E. prophet Daniel, the first Biblical prophet whom scholars believe spoke of a literal resurrection, only states that "many of those who sleep in the dust of the earth will wake, some to everlasting life and some to the reproach of eternal abhorrence" (Daniel 12:2). "Many" is still not "all." In addition, no Jews of the time thought that the resurrection would be to immortal life—merely to a life temporarily restored while just desserts were meted out.

The period between the time of the writing of the Old Testament and the time of the writing of the New Testament was an intense and confusing time politically and theologically. Many Jews expected the end of the world to come in their lifetime, and speculations about a final judgment and an afterlife ran wild, as can be seen in the mutually contradictory religious texts produced in this period: 2 Maccabees describes a future time of general judgment, when the righteous will be resurrected bodily (and temporarily), while the unrighteous will remain in the grave (7:14). But 4 Maccabees describes no general judgment of the human race or any physical resurrection at all: it speaks of the eternal life of the soul, which begins for each person at the moment of death. Like the aforementioned 1 Enoch, 2 Baruch states that everyone, not only the righteous, will be resurrected from Sheol in a future judgment; meanwhile, the Hymn Scroll from the Dead Sea Scrolls tells the reader that the resurrection has already happened: those who join the life of the religious community already possess the state of resurrection. It was the outside social world (not an Underworld) that was Sheol, the land of the "dead" (Qumran Hymn Scroll 3:19–23; 11:3–4). In general, however (especially among the Pharisees), the belief was growing that the resurrection would be for all people, it would take place at the holy city of Jerusalem, and the righteous who passed judgment would enjoy a restored earthly kingdom, though not eternal life. The Jews did not share the later Christian doctrine that the blest would share a vision of God or dwell in heaven. Rather, the resurrection would restore lives that had been cut short against God's will. After each person's God-given term of life had expired, he or she would die again permanently.

See also GEHENNA; HADES; HEAVEN, ORIGINS OF; HELL, ORIGINS OF; JUDGMENT, LAST; JUDGMENT, PARTICULAR; MOT; QIYĀMA; REINCARNATION, WESTERN; RISTAKHEZ; SHEOL; SOUL.

References

Charles, R. H., ed. *The Apocrypha and Pseudepigrapha of the Old Testament.* Vol. 2: *Pseudepigrapha.* Oxford: Clarendon Press, 1966.

Cross, Frank Moore. *Canaanite Myth and Hebrew Epic: Essays in the History of the Religion of Israel.* Cambridge: Harvard University Press, 1973.

Eklund, R. *Life between Death and Resurrection according to Islam.* Uppsala: Almquist and Wilksells, 1941.

Glasson, T. Francis. *Greek Influence in Jewish Eschatology.* London: SPCK, 1961.

Greenspoon, Leonard J. "The Origin of the Idea of Resurrection." In *Traditions in Transformation: Turning Points in Biblical Faith*, ed. Baruch Halpern and Jon D. Levenson. Winona Lake, IN: Eisenbrauns, 1981.

Guignebert, Charles. *The Jewish World in the Time of Jesus.* New York: University Books, 1965.

Martin-Achard, Robert. *From Death to Life: A Study of the Development of the Doctrine of the Resurrection in the Old Testament.* Trans. J. P. Smith. Edinburgh: Oliver and Boyd, 1960.

Moore, George Foot. *Judaism in the First Centuries of the Christian Era*, 3 vols. Cambridge: Harvard University Press, 1927–1930. Reprint, New York: Schocken Books, 1971.

Moulton, James. *Early Zoroastrianism.* London: Williams and Norgate, 1913.

Nickelsburg, G. W. E., Jr. *Resurrection, Immortality, and Eternal Life in Intertestamental Judaism.* Cambridge: Harvard University Press, 1972.

Spronk, Klaas. *Beatific Afterlife in Ancient Israel and in the Ancient Near East.* Kevelaer: Verlag Butzon, 1986.

RISTAKHEZ

The Zoroastrian doctrine of ristakhez is the first theological presentation of resurrection in the Near East.

Originating hundreds of years before the Jewish or Christian doctrine of the bodily resurrection of the dead, Zoroastrianism taught that after the last millennium God has allotted to the Earth, a savior will appear to initiate the final act of the cosmic drama, the struggle of good (Asha) and evil (Druj, or "the Lie").

Although in Zoroastrian belief each soul is sent to heaven (Behesht) or hell (Dozakh) immediately after death, this is only a temporary reward or punishment, a natural result of the life each person lived on Earth. However, it is God's nature as an infinitely good creator that none of his creation will ultimately suffer or perish, but all will be restored in a final Redemption or Renovation (Frasho-kereti). God will resurrect the dead to the very place on Earth where they died and call each to final judgment. There will then be a final purgation of evil from the Earth (through a tidal wave of molten metal) and a purgation of evil from the heavens (through a cosmic battle of spiritual forces). In the end good will triumph, and each person will find himself or herself transformed into a spiritualized body and soul. Those who died as adults will be transformed into healthy adults of forty years of age, and those who died young will find themselves permanently youthful, about age fifteen. In these new spiritual bodies, humans will live without food, without hunger or thirst, and without weapons (or possibility of bodily injury). The material substance of the bodies will be so light as to cast no shadow. All humanity will speak a single language and belong to a single nation without borders. All will experience immortality (Ameretat) and will share a single purpose and goal, joining with the divine for a perpetual exaltation of God's glory.

See also AMERETAT; BEHESHT; DOZAKH; FRASHO-KERETI; SOUL, ZOROASTRIAN.

References

Boyce, Mary. *A History of Zoroastrianism.* Vol. 1. Leiden: E. J. Brill, 1975.

Dhalla, M. N. *Zoroastrian Theology.* Reprint, New York: AMS Press, 1972.

Jackson, A. V. W. *Zoroastrian Studies.* New York: Columbia University Press, 1928.

Kotwal, Firoze M., and James W. Boyd, trans. *A Guide to the Zoroastrian Religion.* Studies in World Religion no. 3. Chico, CA: Scholars Press, 1982.

Masani, Sir Rustom. *Zoroastrianism: The Religion of the Good Life.* New York: Collier Books, 1962.

Moulton, James Hope. *Early Zoroastrianism.* London: Williams and Norgate, 1913.

Sethna, Tehmurasp Rustamji. *Book of Instructions on Zoroastrian Religion.* Karachi: Informal Religious Meetings Trust Fund, 1980.

Sidhwa, Ervad Godrej Dinshawji. *Discourses on Zoroastrianism.* Karachi: Ervad Godrej Dinshawji Sidhwa, 1978.

ROTA (RUTA)

Rota is the Lappish god of the Underworld, a demonic character heavily influenced by the Christian Devil. Rota is sometimes a female deity, as among Finnish Lapps, but is primarily pictured as a male. Rota lives in the depths of the Earth and receives the incoming souls of the dead who have failed to pass on to the heavenly realm, usually called *Saivo,* or "Happy." Some have said that Rota is a Lapp version of the Norse sky god Odin, given the two gods' mutual connection with death, dogs, blue clothing, and horses. However, Odin has never been seen among the Norse as a deity associated exclusively with death (although he is the deity who determines fortunes on the battlefield), nor has Odin been pictured as quite so bloodthirsty and vengeful as Rota.

Like the Christian Devil, however, Rota is not content merely with tormenting the souls of the lost but also takes pleasure in bringing pestilence and other suffering upon the living. Thus, when the Lapps are not able to get assistance from more benevolent, protective figures, they are forced to turn to Rota and appease him with offerings. One such ritual is extremely expensive for a nomadic community, involving the sacrifice of both a reindeer and a horse—hefty commodities for a small community. To begin with, a feast is held during which the head, spine, and feet of a specially slaughtered reindeer are eaten by the friends and family who have been summoned. The bones, a piece of tongue, a part of the lungs, and pieces of the ears, heart, and tail of the reindeer are placed on an altar made for the occasion, and wooden figures made in honor of Rota are sprinkled with the blood and set up near the altar. Finally, after making their request of Rota to cease whatever evil he has been up to, the Lapps slaughter a horse and place it in the Earth so that on this animal Rota would ride away from the dwellings of the living to his home, the hellish world of Rotaimo.

See also FUNERARY CUSTOMS, LAPP; HEL.

References

Pettersson, Olof. *Jabmek and Jabmeaimo: A Comparative Study of the Dead and the Realm of the Dead in Lappish Religion.* Lund: C. W. K. Gleerup, 1957.

Storå, Nils. *Burial Customs of the Skolt Lapps.* FF Communications no. 210. Helsinki: Suomalainen Tiedeakatemia, 1971.

RŪPA-DHĀTU

The Rūpa-dhātu heavens are among the highest heavens in the Buddhist system of death and rebirth, a system that was developed primarily in the collection of philosophical texts titled Abhidharma. Although Buddhism teaches that most people are reborn after death in one of the six realms of bhava-chakra (wheel of life), those who have attained extraordinary degrees of spirituality and meditative ability are reborn in transcendent realms of bliss.

The difference between the high heavens of the lower universe (the Kāma-dhātu, or "World of Desire") and the higher heavens of the Rūpa-dhātu, or "World of Form," is profound and necessary to grasp in order to understand the Buddhist philosophy of salvation. However spiritual one may be—perhaps spending one's life in charity, fasting, and service to others—as long as one retains desire or craving for anything, one is bound by karma to Kāma-dhātu. Desire leads one inevitably to attachment, wishful thinking, and activities aimed at achieving one's goal, which create karma binding one to death and rebirth in the material world.

For those who have achieved a high level of detachment and spiritual maturity through intense meditation, Buddhism holds out a special afterlife, namely a world of subtle matter or "form" utterly without personal desire. Buddhism teaches that the bliss experienced in such a state far outstrips the transitory happiness of any lower, worldly heaven. In the Rūpa-dhātu, lifespans are truly immense, measuring in the billions of years, and the rebirth afterward is guaranteed to be among a family of spiritual people, so that one may continue pursuing the path to liberation (nirvāṇa).

There are four specific meditations that one must master during life on the way to final liberation, each of which brings one to higher and higher levels of peacefulness and detachment from worldly desires and goals. It is important to note that in Buddhism these meditations are practiced not in order to attain particular heavens after death but to pursue the path to nirvāṇa. Rebirth in the higher heavens after the meditator's death is merely a by-product of achieving such profound depth of mind. The first meditation consists of being entirely free from personal desire and from unwholesome ideas (akusala dharma). One in this state experiences joy throughout the whole body caused by freedom and detachment. At the second stage of meditation, one transcends even the reasoning process of the waking mind (vitarka) and attains a state of consciousness free from trains of thought or dwelling on objects. The joy permeating one's body grows even more intense. At the third state of meditation, one transcends even this joy and experiences great calmness and alertness, greeting each experience in the world with transcendent peacefulness. The bodily joy of the previous stages passes into quiet happiness throughout the body. Finally, at the fourth stage of meditation, the practitioner rises above even this quiet happiness into a neutral state of equanimity (adukkham-asukham), in which one has control of one's mind and can use it to penetrate the nature of phenomena in the world.

Buddhism carefully distinguishes these states of meditation from each other and prescribes a specific heavenly afterlife for those who have attained each stage. The Buddhist teachings distinguish whether one has attained only a little of the meditative experience, has become absorbed in it, or has totally mastered it. The degree of practice determines in which of the subdivisions of each heaven one will be reborn. For example, if one has attained only a little experience in the first meditation, one is reborn merely in the company of the god Brahmā, whereas one who has attained great experience in the first meditation is reborn as a priest of Brahmā in his heaven. Finally, one who has completely mastered the first meditation is reborn as one of the great gods who are even higher than Brahmā. The following table lists each meditation achieved during life and the subdivisions of each corresponding heaven one may attain after death:

1. Free from Desire
   a. Retinue of Brahmā
   b. Brahmā's Priests
   c. Great Brahmās

2. Free from Thinking
   a. Limited Splendor
   b. Immeasurable Splendor
   c. Radiant Gods

3. Free from Disruptive Joy
   a. Limited Beauty
   b. Immeasurable Beauty
   c. Complete Beauty

4. Equanimity
   a. Cloudless
   b. Merit-Born
   c. Abundant Fruit
   d. Effortless
   e. No Heat
   f. Beautiful
   g. Well-Seeing
   h. Superior

Situated vertically above the heavens of the Kāma-dhātu, the seventeen heavens of the Rūpa-dhātu carry on the same incremental increases in lifespan and size of the beings born there. Thus, a being born in the lowest realm of the first meditation, the heaven of the Retinue of Brahmā, has a lifespan of one-fourth of a cosmic age, or about 1 billion years, and the height of such a being is one-half league. A being born in the next higher realm, the heaven of Brahmā's Priests, lives in that realm for more than 2 billion years and stands a league tall, and so on. Each heaven is larger than the one before, which reflects the systematic expansion of heavens that began with Kāma-dhātu.

The fact that Buddhism prescribes a specific heaven even for subdivisions of meditative attainment suggests that these seventeen heavens of the Rūpa-dhātu are purely symbolic of the states of consciousness one experiences during life while engaged in these meditations. This interpretation of the Rūpa-dhātu heavens would also accord with the Buddha's warning not to engage in useless cosmological speculation but rather to pursue salvation directly. During life, the practice of the four stages of meditation lead the meditator directly along the path to nirvāṇa, but the afterlife experience of billions of years in "heaven" would seem to slow down the process without any meaningful gain. For this reason it seems likely that the early compilers of the Abhidharma texts were overzealous in building up their "vertical" cosmology. In attempting to emphasize the paramount value of the higher states of meditation, the Abhidharmists appear to have reduced the spiritual attainments of meditation to mere figures and measurements.

See also ARŪPA-DHĀTU; HEAVENS, BUDDHIST; KĀMA-DHĀTU; NIRVĀṆA; REINCARNATION, EASTERN.

References

Beck, Carl B. *Breaking the Circle: Death and the Afterlife in Buddhism.* Carbondale: Southern Illinois University Press, 1993.

Kalupahana, David J. *The Principles of Buddhist Psychology.* Albany: State University of New York Press, 1987.

Kloetzli, Randy. *Buddhist Cosmology: From Single World System to Pure Land.* Delhi: Motilal Banarsidass, 1983.

La Vallée Poussin, Louis de, trans. *L'Abhidharmakosha de Vasubandhu.* Brussels: Mélanges chinois et bouddhiques, 1971.

Law, Bimala Churn. *Heaven and Hell in Buddhist Perspective.* Calcutta: Bhartiya Publishing House, 1925.

Prebish, Charles S., ed. *Buddhism: A Modern Perspective.* University Park: Pennsylvania State University Press, 1978.

S

SĀ'A

In Arabic, Sā'a means "the Hour" of the end of the world, when the Earth and heavens are destroyed and all is extinguished (fanā') in God. There are many signs (ishārāt) by which the Hour may be known, but like all apocalyptic religions, Islam has trouble pinpointing the exact sequence and time of the events it describes. For this reason, there is little agreement among Muslims about how or when the Sā'a will begin, but this imprecision does not matter, for the Qur'ān says (33:63): "People ask you about the Hour of Doom. Say: 'God alone has knowledge of it. Who knows? It may well be that the Hour is near at hand.'" In any case, although the exact day and time may not be known, the end is known with certainty: the righteous will be saved.

In general, the moral degeneration of the world is a major sign of the Hour. Works such as the *Mishkāt al-Mashābīh* offer specifics on this point. When Muslims are persecuted, when each man has to provide for fifty women, or when people eat like cows and have hearts like wolves, one may know Sā'a approaches. Ignorance and fornication will become the hallmarks of humankind. Into the midst of this turmoil will come a religious leader, a savior from the house of the Prophet Muhammed, who will gather together the Muslim faithful and establish a true kingdom of peace. This savior is called the Mahdī, and his coming will be marked by the rising of the sun in the west and a triple eclipse of the moon. The great Mahdī will radically alter the moral degeneration and depravity of humanity: "He will possess all the world, as did Alexander and Solomon. . . . He will return to Muslims their blessedness and well-being and will fill the world with justice. . . . He will accumulate extensive wealth and divide it equally among people in heaven and earth. Birds, beasts and all creatures will be pleased with him" (Muhammed ibn Rasū al-Husaynī al-Barzinjī, *al-Ishā'a li-ishrāt al-sā'a*, quoted in Smith and Haddad, p. 67).

Predictions vary as to how long the Mahdī will rule—five, seven, or nine years are all regularly given. In a short while, grave dangers will arise to present humanity with its final trials (fitan). First will come two huge creatures, sometimes described as beasts and sometimes described as giant human cannibals and called Yājūj and Mājūj (known in the Bible as Gog and Magog; see Genesis 10:2; Ezekiel 38:2; 1 Corinthians 1:5; and Revelation 20:8). Although these terrible creatures had been held in check by a dam in the far northeastern corner of the world, at the coming of the Hour they will break through and, multiplying greatly, sweep down on the Earth bringing plague and wreaking havoc. The Qur'ān (21:96–97) records God as saying:

> It is ordained that no nation We have destroyed shall ever rise again. But when Yājūj and Mājūj are let loose and rush headlong down every hill; when the true promise nears its fulfilment; the unbelievers shall stare in amazement, crying: "Woe to us! Of this we have been heedless. We have done wrong."

Then another danger will arise to trouble mankind even more seriously: al-Dajjāl, "the false messiah," a beast in the form of a human figure. He is described as one-eyed (or blind in one eye), reddish in color, with the word *kafīr* (damned) on his forehead. Al-Dajjāl will establish a mighty kingdom and bring much ruin to the world, both within and without the Muslim umma (brotherhood). He will reign for a time (some say forty days, others forty years) and attempt to ruin all that the Mahdī has wrought. But eventually he will be overthrown by a hero sent by God.

In much Muslim tradition, that hero is thought to be Jesus, who is called 'Īshā in Arabic (which is related to the Hebrew version of that name, Yeshu). Islam has always accepted 'Īshā/Jesus as a true prophet of God, but the Muslim view of Christianity is that it developed out of great disfigurement of the teachings of Jesus. In Islam, 'Īshā supports the Muslim understanding of God, and thus expectations of his second coming are somewhat different than the expectations of Christians for Jesus' return. When 'Īshā returns, he will help the Mahdī kill the Dajjāl and likewise trample all false traditions, including Christendom—its followers and its places of worship—in order to prepare the way for the final triumph of Islam.

The last sign of Sā'a will be the famous trumpet blast by the angel nearest to God, Isrāfīl, a cosmic being who represents the center of the universe. Likewise, the

> ### The Cessation
>
> When the sun ceases to shine; when the stars fall
> down and the mountains are blown away; when
> camels big with young are left untended, and the
> wild beasts are brought together; when the seas are
> set alight and men's souls are reunited, when the
> infant girl, buried alive, is asked for what crime she
> was slain [because baby girls may be rejected by
> families]; when the records of men's deeds are laid
> open, and heaven is stripped bare; when Hell burns
> fiercely and Paradise is brought near; then each soul
> shall know what it has done.
>
> I swear by the turning planets, and by the stars
> that rise and set; by the night, when it descends, and
> the first breath of morning: this is the word of a
> gracious and mighty messenger, held in honor by the
> Lord of the Throne, obeyed in heaven, faithful to his
> trust.
>
> *Qur'ān 81:1–21.*

trumpet (al-Shūr) is no ordinary trumpet but symbolizes the entirety of creation. One of the sayings, or
hadīths, of the Prophet Muhammed states:

> It is on the authority of Abū Hurayrah that he
> said: The Apostle of God, God bless him and give
> him peace, said: God Most High created the
> Trumpet and it has four branches, one in the West,
> one in the East, one under the seventh earth, one
> above the seventh heaven. In the Trumpet are gates
> corresponding to the number of spirits; and each
> contains seventy houses. In one are the spirits of the
> prophets, in another the spirits of the angels, in the
> third the spirits of the *jinn* [the "genies" made by
> God from fire] and in the fourth are the spirits of
> humans, in the fifth the spirits of the devils and in
> the sixth the spirits of the reptiles—down to the
> ant, and so on, including all seventy species.
> (Macdonald, trans., p. 137)

This, finally, is the moment of the Hour. Isrāfīl will
give a mighty blast on the cosmic trumpet, signaling
the eschaton, or end, and rapidly the universe begins to
experience a literal "undoing" of all creation.

The process is not merely one of great destruction,
however, but also one of ethical revelation. Humanity
will have run out of time for deceit as well as for prayer.
All things come to an end, and each person must now
taste death and then prepare to meet the maker (Qur'ān
69:13–18):

When the Trumpet sounds a single blast; when
earth with all its mountains is raised high and with
one mighty crash is shattered into dust—on that
day the Dread Event will come to pass.

Frail and tottering, the sky will be rent asunder
on that day, and the angels will stand on all sides
with eight of them carrying the throne of your Lord
above their heads. On that day you shall be utterly
exposed, and all your secrets shall be brought to
light.

Likewise, God now exposes the Devil, Iblīs, for what he
is. God sends the angel of death, 'Izrā'īl, along with
70,000 well-armed angels, to draw Iblīs out, chase him
from east to west, and finally carry out his death sentence, which has been postponed since the creation of
Adam. The stars begin to fall from the heavens, the
mountains flatten, and mountains rise up where none
stood before. The Earth will be shaken to its very core,
and all things that God made will be taken apart. First
the seas, then the mountains, and finally the Earth itself
will be visited by 'Izrā'īl. He announces to each their
destruction, they lament the loss of their powers, and
then they are no more. The heavens roll up like a scroll.
Finally, the spirits of all things—human beings, angels,
jinn, beasts, everything—are taken by 'Izrā'īl, brought
to God, and they are extinguished utterly.

Then God asks 'Izrā'īl what of creation remains. "O
my God," answers the angel of death, "you are the
living who never dies. Only Jibrīl and Mikā'īl and
Isrāfīl and the eight bearers of the throne and I, your
weak servant, remain." Then God says, "Seize their
spirits!" and they too perish completely. Finally, God
takes away the only remaining soul, that of the angel of
death himself. This is the final extinction, the fanā',
where absolutely nothing but God remains. It fulfills
the Qur'ānic statement, "There is no god but Him. All
things shall perish except Himself. His is the judgement, and to Him you shall return" (28:88). Time
ceases, and there is only the utter oneness (tawhīd) of
God. Eventually, however, comes the miracle of
Qiyāma (Resurrection).

See also BARZAKH; IBLĪS; ISRĀFĪL; 'IZRĀ'ĪL; JAHANNAM; JUDGMENT,
LAST; QIYĀMA; SOUL, MUSLIM.

References
Dawood, N. J., trans. *The Koran.* 5th rev. ed. New York: Penguin,
1993.
Evrin, M. Sadeddin. *Eschatology in Islam.* Trans. Sofi Huri. Istanbul,
1960.
Gardet, L. "Kiyāma." *Encyclopedia of Islam,* ed. C. E. Bosworth. Vol.
5. Leiden: E. J. Brill, 1983.
Kherie, Altaf Ahmad. *Islam: A Comprehensive Guidebook.* Karachi:
Idara Sirat-i-Mustaqeem, 1981.
Macdonald, John. "The Day of Resurrection." *Islamic Studies* 5, no. 2
(1966).

Smith, Jane I., and Yvonne Yazbeck Haddad. *The Islamic Understanding of Death and Resurrection*. Albany: SUNY Press, 1981.

Taylor, John B. "Some Aspects of Islamic Eschatology." *Religious Studies* 4 (1968).

SALLEKHANĀ (JAINA)

Literally "properly thinning out," sallekhanā is the practice of deliberately fasting unto death in the Jain religion of India. In Jainism, nonviolence and self-restraint are the highest moral imperatives, and Jains take great pains to avoid injury to any living creature by, among other things, refusing to engage in any profession that might cause such injury such as working as a farmer, butcher, tanner, or soldier. Jain monks even sweep the path before they walk and strain their drinking water to rescue insects. Even so, it is evident that however careful one may be, the very process of living as a human being involves the death of countless creatures, even the bacteria that perish in the mucous membranes of our lungs as we breathe. Therefore, when one is prepared by years of meditation and discipline, the ideal culmination of the Jain spiritual life is to renounce life itself and slowly fast until death.

Making the vow of sallekhanā is not the same as committing suicide, however. Padmanabh Jaini (p. 229) delimits the four traditional conditions under which the holy death fast may be performed: (1) calamity such as capture by an enemy, which prevents living life according to Jain spiritual discipline; (2) famine; (3) extreme old age, characterized by the failure of bodily organs or limbs (becoming blind, crippled, senile, etc.); and (4) terminal illness in which death is imminent. One may not perform the death fast because one wishes to escape the rigors or pains of life or to attain heaven or any other reward: such suicides are believed only to increase one's selfishness and personal passions, not to lead to a holy death or spiritually conducive rebirth. But under the direction of a Jain teacher, the student takes the sallekhanā vow, often on the deathbed or when it is obvious that death is close at hand. The student calls for the teacher and says:

> Please instruct me, sir. I have come forward to seek . . . sallekhanā (the vow of) which will remain in force as long as I live. I am free of all doubts and anxieties in this matter. I renounce, from now until the moment of my last breath, food of all kinds. (Jaini, p. 230)

If the teacher determines that the monk or layperson has sufficient spiritual maturity and discipline, he agrees to supervise the fast. Nourishing food is gradually restricted until the student takes only liquids.

Death with One's Will

These two ways of life ending with death have been declared: death with one's will, and death against one's will.

Death against one's will is that of ignorant men, and it happens (to the same individual) many times [through reincarnation]. Death with one's will is that of wise men, and at best it happens but once. . . .

Full of peace and without injury to any one is, as I have heard (from my teachers), the death of the virtuous who control themselves and subdue their senses. . . .

To the highest regions, in due order, to those where there is no delusion, and to those which are full of light, where the glorious (gods dwell)—who have long life, great power, great lustre, who can change their shape at will, who are beautiful as on their first day, and have the brilliancy of many suns—to such places go those who are trained in self-control and penance, monks or householders, who have obtained liberation by absence of passion.

From the Jain Scripture Uttarādhyayana, translation by Jacobi (1968), pp. 20–23.

Then nourishing liquids are reduced from milk to juice to plain water. Through prayer, meditation, and discipline, the student prepares for death (strongly supported by the Jain community), hoping that at the final moment of death, the mind will be tranquil and absorbed in nonviolence and devotion, leading to a holy rebirth in which the final freedom (mokṣa) may occur.

Though it is primarily celibate monks who undertake the discipline of sallekhanā, laypersons are permitted to engage in the holy fast. All are greatly respected for such spiritual efforts and are even thought to develop paranormal powers of perception and wisdom. At the end of a long life of kindness, charity, self-restraint, and devotion to escaping the bonds of karma, the holy fast of sallekhanā is considered the crowning achievement: maintaining control even over one's death.

References

Jacobi, Hermann, trans. *Jaina Sutras*. Reprint from *The Sacred Books of the East*. New York: Dover Publications, 1968.

Jaini, Padmanabh S. *The Jaina Path of Purification*. Berkeley: University of California Press, 1979.

Renou, Louis. *Religions of Ancient India*. London: University of London, Athlone Press, 1953.

SAMHAIN (SAMHUINN)

The festival of Samhain (possibly from *sam*, "summer," and *fuin*, "sunset" or "end", in Old Gaelic) is the old

Celtic observance of the new year and the predecessor of modern Hallowe'en, when the green powers of life faded into winter, burial mounds opened, and the dead walked for a time among the living.

The earliest Celtic calendar had two divisions corresponding to agricultural rhythms, the winter half of the year and the summer half. Each half was marked by two major festivals. As the Celts counted their days beginning with the evening, so they reckoned their calendar beginning with the winter half of the year. Geimredh, the winter half of the year, began with the festival of Samhain (1 November) and included the festival of Oimelc (1 February), and Samhradh, the summer half of the year, had the festivals of Beltane (1 May) and Lugnasadh (1 August). The new year began with Samhain, from the evening of 31 October into the day of 1 November.

As the end of the old year and the beginning of the new, Samhain was the most liminal of the four festivals, the time when the harvest was threshed, the days were growing dark, most vegetation was dying and retreating underground, and the signs of death were all around. Therefore the veil between this world and the Otherworld was thinnest, and supernatural and occult powers were at their zenith. Witches, fairies, and the dead were at their most active, and special rituals were needed to protect against them. And as the "transitional" holiday, Samhain was the date assigned for many important political and spiritual transitions in Celtic mythological history.

It was on Samhain each year that the first rulers of Ireland, demonic giants known as the Fomorians, required sacrifices from their subjects. On the plain called Mag Cetne, two-thirds of the crops grown each year and two-thirds of the children born were to be delivered to these cruel tyrants. This continued, the mythical history says, until one year, also on the day of Samhain, when a great battle began between the Fomorians and a new, invading race of fairy gods, the Tuatha Dé Danann. The battle allegedly took place at the plain of Mag Tured (now pronounced "moytura"), and after several days of horrible slaughter the Fomorians were routed and retreated across the sea. In the arrangements of their surrender, however, the Fomorians were allowed to continue to receive sacrifices, much reduced in quantity and only in exchange for ensuring the success of the following harvest.

The Fomorians were probably the fertility gods of an indigenous people who were displaced by the belief system of the arriving Celts. Conquered but not vanished, the original fertility gods became hostile to growth, destroying corn and milk unless appeased. They required sacrifices from their new location "across the sea," that is, the land of the dead, or else they would release the powers of death upon the living. In time, even the new fairy race of the Tuatha Dé Danann was conquered, this time by human heroes, and they too retreated underground and into the hills and burial mounds of the land. Maintaining the pattern, on Samhain each year the Tuatha Dé Danann's burial mounds opened, and these fairy gods reemerged, dangerous like their predecessors the Fomorians unless appeased.

Thus, in the most ancient celebrations, the Samhain festival already served a dual function: to strengthen the powers of life and fertility through the winter and to ward off the potential evils associated with the transition from light to dark. In more physical terms, Samhain was held at the time after the threshing of the harvest when farm animals were slaughtered, for their meat would be needed throughout the winter. This task was followed by feasts, particularly of animals thought to be sacred to the season, like the boar and wren. The scent of blood attracted the dead, who were thought to seek some passing vigor from absorbing the life energy of the slain, and the wise tamed these potentially dangerous visitors with some of what they sought. Thus Samhain was also the time of sacrifice, both to the dead and, as already described, to the ancient and uncertain lords of growth and fertility.

It was necessary to secure the aid of the powers that would safely bring the community through the often difficult winter, as well as to ensure that the needed forces would awaken again from slumber in spring for a new season of growth. The last sheaf of corn cut that year was called the "maiden" or the "mother," and with it the harvest was done for the year—the corn spirit was "dead." To ensure that this spirit would be reborn, offerings of corn, animals, and even humans representing this corn mother or maiden were sacrificed; by substituting their deaths for the spirit of the corn, "she" would then be empowered to return at the end of winter. In his book on the Celts in Gaul (modern France and Spain), Caesar remarked on their human sacrifices, and the Greco-Roman historian Strabo quoted the Druid priests as saying that the harvest would be rich in proportion to the richness of the harvest of death. The extent and frequency of human sacrifice at Samhain is impossible to ascertain, but it is not uncommon for a conquering people like the Romans to demonize their native foes. In any case, receiving her due, the mother or maiden of the corn retreated underground, and like the powers of most vegetative life, she slept.

The Celts were aware, however, that not all vegetation slept during winter. Mistletoe, holly, ivy, and evergreen trees testified to the continuing presence of life energy and became symbols of this festival. These symbols were retained with the arrival of Christianity, and much of the meaning of Samhain was absorbed into

Christmas, when mistletoe, evergreen wreaths, and sprigs of holly mark the holiday season.

On the eve of Samhain, a new fire, freshly kindled by friction, was set in a large public place to provide a completely pure fire suitable to a new year. No doubt in one sense this bonfire represented the heat and light of the failing sun, and thus the failing powers of life were symbolically strengthened. Simultaneously, the fire served an apotropaic function, warding off the powers of darkness and purifying the community. In North Wales people even rushed to jump through the fire to be strengthened and purified, although it was said that the "black sow," a creature of evil, brought up the rear. That evening each family took a torch from the public fire and used it to rekindle the home hearth. At bedtime the fire was left burning, and food was laid out for the dead, who would return that night and seek welcome from the living.

Despite Christian attempts to suppress old pagan practices and replace them with Christian holidays, many of the rituals survived anyway, and the church was forced to make adjustments. For instance, the pagan holiday Samhain on 1 November was replaced with "All Saints' Day," but the practices observed for the dead continued the previous evening anyway under the new names "All Hallow's Eve" or Hallowe'en. Thus the church was obliged to add "All Soul's Day" to the calendar on 2 November to create a Christian day for remembrance of the dead. And when the Christian church attempted to replace the "new year" festivities of Samhain with Christmas and the birth of Christ, the rituals of fire continued until quite recently in many parts of Europe in the guise of lighting the Yule log. The offerings for the dead transformed into food left out for Saint Nicholas, or Santa Claus as he is more commonly known now. But in some cases the more original forms of the traditions survive. For example, the Celts of Brittany, France, still put cakes and sweetmeats on the graves of their ancestors during the day of Samhain and in the evening light the fire and leave the leftovers of dinner on the table so that the visiting dead may feel at home.

See also ANTHESTERIA; FAIRY MOUND; HALLOWE'EN; ISLANDS OF THE BLEST; LEMURIA; PARENTALIA.

References

D'Arbois de Jubainville, H. *The Irish Mythological Cycle and Celtic Mythology.* Trans. Richard Irvine Best. Dublin: Hodges, Figgis, 1903.

Mac Bain, Alexander. *Celtic Mythology and Religion.* New York: Dutton, 1917.

MacCulloch, J. A. *The Religion of the Ancient Celts.* Edinburgh: T. and T. Clark, 1911.

Slade, Paddy. *Encyclopedia of White Magic: A Seasonal Guide.* New York: Mallard, 1990.

SECOND DEATH

Various traditions around the world use the expression "second death" with quite contrary meanings. In all cases, the deceased experiences another death after the physical body has died, but what experiences the second death and the significance of this event vary widely.

In an anthropological sense, bodily death is only the beginning of death as experienced by the survivors who endure the loss of the loved one. The period between the onset of physical death and the complete decay of the corpse is a critical time for the soul and for the community grieving its loss and attempting severance. It is first of all a *dangerous* time, for the deceased is not *fully* dead yet and still has many ties to the world of the living. Apparently, the departed soul is often tempted to return and is usually propitiated with things from the world of the living, such as its old possessions and offerings of wine, honey, milk, water, and foodstuffs.

Along with the active and rather gruesome (and thus "dangerous") changes to the physical body after death, the soul or life energy of the deceased remains active as well and is nearly always perceived as at least potentially dangerous. The dead can not only scare and harass the living, but because death by its nature is thought to be "contagious," the presence of the recently deceased is polluting and even potentially lethal. The work implements, clothing, and other personal possessions of the deceased are generally not to be used and are frequently destroyed (often ritually "killed") or placed in the grave with the deceased. However, the final reduction of the corpse to dry bones, even ash, marks the "second death" of the deceased when he or she goes to the final resting place, perhaps joining the ancestors, going to heaven (or hell), or being reincarnated. On this occasion, the remains are often dug up or recovered from wherever they have been deposited (in an exposure-type burial, for example) and, after treatment, ritually reburied. Such practices continue among modern Orthodox Jews and Zoroastrians, to name but two examples.

Among many tribal peoples, however, the second death refers to an extinction of individuality. Typically, if the departed has lived to a ripe old age, lived a "good" life (in the estimation of neighbors and kin), and left respectable offspring, he or she is entitled to become a venerated ancestor and receive the special offerings and rites due a member of an "elder" station in society. When the memory of the departed as an individual has faded among the living—when all direct descendants have died out, and no living person knew the ancestor personally—it is called the second death, and the dead ceases to exist as an individual and is remembered only as part of the collective ancestors.

Islamic doctrine refers to a "second death," unfortunately ambiguously, in the sacred text, the Qur'ān, which says (2:28; 40:11) that human beings live and die twice. Most Qur'ānic commentators understand the second life and death to be that of the tomb, although the issue is debated. According to L. Gardet, writing in the *Encyclopedia of Islam* (p. 237):

What is being discussed is a first and transitory resuscitation, at once corporeal and spiritual, which is not a true resurrection. It is not necessary, say some authors, that the entire body should revive; it is enough that some fundamental part or other, heart, kidney, etc., be animated afresh. Moreover, if the body has been completely devoured or reduced to ashes, it will not be difficult for God to reassemble it and restore to life a sufficient quantity of matter. Besides, this survival of the tomb is brief. After being thus examined [by the two angels] and punished (or rewarded), the man experiences "the second death." It is also declared that the prophets and martyrs who have died fighting for God are excused from the interrogation and from the punishment of the tomb.

Thus the Islamic second death is only the temporary resurrection that believers expect to occur in the grave, when the two angels, Munkar and Nakīr, awaken the dead in order to question and try them in a fashion preliminary to God's final judgment. After this short "second life" in the grave, there follows the second death.

Christianity defines second death in a completely contrary way, as an event occurring after the resurrection of all the dead at the day of judgment. Those who are worthy find that they have been raised to life eternal, but those who fail God's examination realize to their horror that they are condemned to the lake of fire: "This lake of fire is the second death; and into it were flung any whose names were not to be found in the roll of the living" (Revelation 20:15). A curious reference to a second death is found in Scandinavian religion, in which Niflheim (a shadowy Underworld) was said to be the realm where the wicked went after dying out of Hel (*Vafthrúdnismál*, section 43 [Ellis]), although there is no clarification available as to what exactly this meant.

Finally, an occult definition of second death exists in New Age literature, instigated by the Theosophical writings of Helena Blavatsky in the late nineteenth century. For Blavatsky (and her spiritual descendants) physical death merely ends the life of the physical body, which is nothing more than a material envelope or sheath of the complex psychic and spiritual energies of the inner person. Upon physical death, these psychic and spiritual constituents gradually withdraw from the corpse and experience a short quasi-life on the astral plane. After a time, the immortal, spiritual elements of the deceased separate from the lower personality, which

is characterized by passions, desires, and animal instincts. This separation (and eventual destruction of the lower elements) constitutes the Theosophical second death.

See also ANCESTOR VENERATION; KĀMALOKA; NIFLHEIM; SOUL, MUSLIM.

References

Blavatsky, Helena P. *The Key to Theosophy.* Reprint, Los Angeles: Theosophy Company, 1987.

Ellis, Hilda Roderick. *The Road to Hel: A Study of the Conception of the Dead in Old Norse Literature.* Cambridge: Cambridge University Press, 1943.

Gardet, L. "Kiyāma." In *Encyclopedia of Islam,* ed. C. E. Bosworth. Vol. 5. Leiden: E. J. Brill, 1983.

Lowie, Robert H. *Primitive Religion.* New York: Boni and Liveright, 1924.

Smith, Jane I., and Yvonne Yazbeck Haddad. *The Islamic Understanding of Death and Resurrection.* Albany: SUNY Press, 1981.

SHABTI (USHABTI, SHAWABTI)

A shabti is a small funerary statuette shaped like a mummy and used in Egyptian burials, especially from the Middle Kingdom period (c. 2100 to 1600 B.C.E.) onward. They were designed and especially inscribed to stand in for the deceased in the next world if the deceased should be called upon by the Underworld government to perform labor or services.

The practice of using shabtis originated in the Old Kingdom (c. 2600 to 2100 B.C.E.) with the use of life-sized reserve heads made from limestone, which were buried with the mummy. These "reserve heads" stood in for the body of the deceased if anything should happen to it and served as a substitute home to which the ba (soul) could return each night. By the Middle Kingdom, this substitute head was replaced by a single small wooden shabti—an entire body, in miniature, to be used as the "reserve body." Often the little shabti had its own coffin and was carefully made to look lifelike.

In time the shabtis lost their "reserve body" status and were reconceived as servants in general—especially since the practice of actually slaughtering several servants and burying them with the deceased had fallen off. Thus not one but several shabtis were needed to perform all the necessary work in the afterlife: sow seeds, breach dykes, water fields, shift sand, and carry baskets. By the New Kingdom (1550 to 945 B.C.E.), hundreds of shabtis were buried along with the corpse, and the practice grew from a primarily royal custom to one widespread among ordinary people. The standard number of shabtis became 401: one for each day of the year (365) and 36 overseers, whose statues carried whips to ensure that none of the servant-shabtis were lazy. They were all crammed into large square shabti-boxes with vaulted tops that were decorated with funerary

Egyptian shabti funerary doll, Cairo Museum of Antiquities, Cairo, Egypt. Courtesy of Anne Ronan Picture Library.

bits of rounded glaze ware with a vaguely human shape.

What made the shabtis effective, however, was not their artistry but the power of inscription, or writing. Among the Egyptians, writing was thought to magically transform thoughts and wishes into actions, particularly if it was performed in the right way. Thus it was essential that the shabtis bore the owner's name, and very often, especially in the New Kingdom, they also bore in hieratic script a formula invoking them to action: "O you shabti, if the deceased is called upon . . . in the necropolis to do any work which is to be done there, you are charged with it: to cultivate the fields, breach the dykes, or transport sand to the west or to the east. 'I will do it; here I am' you will say." Likewise, when the shabtis were bought from the temple workshops, the contract of their sale recorded not only the price paid but an invocation from their maker that they were to quickly work for Osiris and his servant called so-and-so, saying "we are ready" whenever they were summoned for service.

It must be kept in mind that the little statuettes themselves were not imagined to work for the deceased, since there were no fields to be cultivated or dykes to be breached in the burial vault. Rather, just as the mummy of the deceased together with the soul was transformed and transported into a new life in the Underworld necropolis, so too were the shabtis mere symbols of the servants that would manifest and unquestioningly obey.

See also FUNERARY CUSTOMS, ANCIENT EGYPTIAN; MUMMIFICATION; SOUL, EGYPTIAN.

References

Allen, Thomas George. *The Book of the Dead, or Going Forth by Day.* Chicago: Oriental Institute of the University of Chicago, 1974.

Hamilton-Paterson, James, and Carol Andrews. *Mummies: Death and Life in Ancient Egypt.* London: William Collins Sons, 1978.

Spencer, A. J. *Death in Ancient Egypt.* New York: Penguin, 1982.

Winlock, H. E. *The Rise and Fall of the Middle Kingdom in Thebes.* New York: Macmillan, 1947.

SHELOSHIM

In Orthodox Judaism, sheloshim is the thirty-day period of formal mourning, counted from the day of burial (not the day of death) of the deceased. For most of the "seven relatives" (father, mother, brother, sister, and spouse of the deceased) sheloshim is the last period of mourning, but if one grieves a parent, son, or daughter, formal mourning continues for a full year (twelve Hebrew months). The first seven days of mourning are called *shiva*, during which Orthodox mourners observe strict positive and negative regulations. Many of these are lifted during the remainder of mourning in sheloshim. One no longer keeps a candle lit for the deceased, covers the mirrors in the home, or continues

scenes and inscribed. Simultaneously with the increase in their number, the craftsmanship of the shabtis declined because they were mass-produced with blank spaces for the owner's name. By the late Ptolemaic period (c. 100 B.C.E.) they were little more than little to sit on a low stool or bench ("sitting shiva"). During sheloshim, one may again study the Torah, engage in sexual relations, wear leather shoes and freshly cleaned clothing, and return to work and household chores.

However, several regulations of shiva are still observed during sheloshim. Mourners continue to avoid cutting their hair, trimming their nails, buying or wearing brand new clothing, attending parties, accepting gifts, or getting married. Likewise, mourners continue to recite the kaddish prayer daily in honor of the dead. But in modern times even many of the sheloshim observances are lifted due to a rabbinic innovation called "social reproach." For example, although sheloshim regulations forbid mourners from cutting their hair, the first time someone mildly "reproaches" them for their appearance, the mourners may begin to trim their hair or shave. Thus many sheloshim observances have been reduced to formalities: kind friends and neighbors "reproach" the grieving family at the earliest opportunity so that they may resume ordinary hygiene and personal care. Social reproach applies only to sheloshim regulations, however, not to those in place during shiva. As with shiva, sheloshim observances are suspended during the Sabbath and cancelled entirely if a major holiday intervenes.

See also ANINUT; AVELUT; FUNERARY CUSTOMS, JEWISH; KADDISH; KERI'AH; SHIVA (JEWISH); YAHRZEIT; YIZKOR.

References

Abramovitch, Henry. "Death." In *Contemporary Jewish Religious Thought,* ed. Arthur A. Cohen and Paul Mendes-Flohr. New York: Charles Scribner's Sons, 1989.

Lamm, Maurice. *The Jewish Way in Death and Mourning.* New York: Jonathan David Publishers, 1969.

Montefiore, C. G., and H. Loewe, eds. *A Rabbinic Anthology.* New York: Schocken Books, 1974.

Rabinowicz, H. *A Guide to Life.* London: Jewish Chronicle Publications, 1964.

Riemer, Jack, ed. *Jewish Reflections on Death.* New York: Schocken Books, 1974.

SHEOL

Sheol is the old Hebrew name for the Underworld, probably formed from the Hebrew root *sh'l,* meaning "to ask, to inquire" and referring either to necromancy or possibly to postmortem judgment. Sheol was variously conceived of as dark (e.g., Job 17:13), possessed of barred gates (e.g., Isaiah 38:10), dusty and earthy (e.g., Job 17:16), watery (e.g., Jonah 2:3–6), and most especially, like Tartaros, very, very far beneath the earth (e.g., Deuteronomy 32:22).

Sheol is an ambiguous word, the more so because it was used most often as a poetic device: of the sixty-five occurrences of the word "Sheol" in the Hebrew Bible, fifty-seven of them are in poetic compositions. There are times when Sheol appears to be a full-blown

---

Sheol, the Land of Death

But remember this: wise men must die;
stupid men, brutish men, all perish.
The grave is their eternal home,
their dwelling for all time to come;
They may give their own names to estates,
but they must leave their riches to others.
For men are like oxen whose life cannot last,
they are like cattle whose time is short.
Such is the fate of foolish men
and of all who seek to please them;
Like sheep they run headlong into Sheol, the land of
     Death;
he is their shepherd and urges them on;
Their flesh must rot away
and their bodies be wasted by Sheol, stripped of all
     honor.
But God will ransom my life,
he will take me from the power of Sheol.

Psalm 49:10–15.

Underworld (with inhabitants called *Rephā'im*) comparable to the Underworlds of Greece, Rome, Mesopotamia, and Egypt, and other times when the writer(s) simply used Sheol as a metaphor for the physical grave (e.g., dark, narrow, dusty, etc.). Sheol is also personified occasionally as an intelligent entity with a tremendous appetite, as in Isaiah 5:14:

Therefore Sheol gapes with straining throat
and has opened her measureless jaws:
Down go nobility and common people,
their noisy bustling mob.

In such personification Sheol, like Hades for the Greeks and Hel for the Scandinavians, serves as both a place and a person (the god of the Underworld).

Despite the occasional personification of Sheol, ancient Judaism, unlike Christianity, does not appear to have conceived of a heaven for the righteous and a hell for the wicked. Rather, the "shades" (rephā'im) of all the dead appear to have "gone down" to Sheol together, there to remain forever, as this passage from Psalms 89:48 indicates: "What man shall live and not see death, or save himself from the power of Sheol?" Even celebrated figures, such as Jacob and Samuel, went to Sheol after death. There are hints of a judgment after death and possibly rescue for the righteous (Psalm 73:24), but there is nothing in Judaism like the later developed doctrine of Heaven found in Christianity.

Life in Sheol seems to carry on like a faded and grim version of earthly life. Samuel, when summoned from the dead, appears "distinguished by his mantle" (1 Samuel 28:14); kings appear in their crowns (Isaiah 14:9); and the uncircumcised still have their foreskins (Ezekiel 32:18–32). Even those slain with a sword will bear forever the tokens of a violent death (Ezekiel 32:25).

Much against the will of Yahweh (according to orthodox Hebrew priests and prophets of the time), many Israelites would call up the "shades" from Sheol and consult them in times of crisis, as we find Saul consulting the dead via the witch of Endor (1 Samuel 28:8–20). Also, despite Biblical injunctions, Israelites seem to have maintained an extensive cult of the dead, making regular offerings at family tombs and burying many household items, including food, along with the dead.

After the Babylonian captivity, however, starting in 597 B.C.E. under the Assyrian ruler Nebuchadrezzar II, Zoroastrian ideas slowly began to take root in Judaism and altered Jewish ideas of the afterlife. These new ideas included a belief in an apocalyptic judgment by Yahweh at the end of time, and resurrection (ristakhez for Zoroastrians) for those who were found to be righteous. It was not until quite late, however—the time of the Maccabean crisis in the second century B.C.E.—that these ideas began to become widespread. Thus we read in Daniel 12:2 (dated to the mid–second century B.C.E.), "Many of those who sleep in the dust of the earth will wake, some to everlasting life and some to the reproach of eternal abhorrence." This is the only clear reference to resurrection in the entire Hebrew Bible. Throughout most of Jewish history, Sheol was considered the dreary but final abode of all the dead, as in Job 7:9–10:

> he that goes down to Sheol never comes back;
> he never returns home again,
> and his place will know him no more.

When the idea of postmortem judgment began to take root, Jewish interest in the Underworld transformed the dreary shadowland of Sheol into the burning hell of Gehenna (and later, to the Christian Hell and Muslim Jahannam).

This shift was gradual, however. By the time of the apocryphal Book of Enoch, the work of an anonymous writer(s) circa 200 B.C.E., Sheol had evolved into something like a "holding tank," wherein the righteous and unrighteous dead were unequal. They do not sleep or wander around as lifeless shades (as in the old Sheol) but await a resurrection and judgment. In chapter 22 of the Book of Enoch, the prophet Enoch is made to visit the Underworld in spirit. He perceives "a great and high mountain of hard rock" enclosing a number of hollow places. Enoch inquires as to the nature of these vast caves, and the angel Raphael responds that they "have been made that the spirits of the dead might be separated." The righteous spend their time near a bright spring of water, whereas sinners suffer in great pain until the time of judgment. A third group consists of the unrighteous who were already punished in their lifetimes—these will not be resurrected because they have already been judged.

What makes the Enochian vision of Sheol important is that it is a halfway mark between the old Hebrew conception of Sheol as an indiscriminate Underworld of all the dead and the later Christian idea of an eternal Heaven and Hell wherein the dead are separated eternally. In the Book of Enoch, resurrection does not lead to eternal life in Heaven but merely a restoration of life *on Earth* for those who were good but suffered unjustly and for those who were evil but did not suffer appropriately. Sheol in Enoch was an afterlife divided ethically into separate regions; only later did entirely different afterlives emerge for the saints and sinners. Heaven became removed from the Underworld to the sky, and the Underworld Sheol became embellished with fire and brimstone.

See also GEHENNA; HADES; HEAVEN, HISTORY OF; HEAVEN, ORIGINS OF; HELL, HISTORY OF; HELL, ORIGINS OF; JAHANNAM; JUDGMENT, LAST; JUDGMENT, PARTICULAR; KIGAL; MOT; REPHA'IM; RESURRECTION, HEBREW; RISTAKHEZ; TARTAROS.

References

Bailey, L. R., Sr. *Biblical Perspectives on Death*. Philadelphia: Fortress Press, 1979.

Charles, R. H. "Book of Enoch." In *The Apocrypha and Pseudepigrapha of the Old Testament*. Vol. 2: *Pseudepigrapha*. Oxford: Clarendon Press, 1966.

Fohrer, G. *History of Israelite Religion*. Trans. D. E. Green. Nashville: Abingdon Press, 1972.

Kraus, H. J. *Theology of the Psalms*. Trans. K. Crim. Minneapolis: Augsburg, 1986.

Lewis, Theodore J. *Cults of the Dead in Ancient Israel and Ugarit*. Atlanta: Scholars Press, 1989.

Rosenberg, R. *The Concept of Biblical Sheol within the Context of Ancient Near Eastern Beliefs*. Ph.D. diss., Harvard University, 1980.

Spronk, K. *Beatific Afterlife in Ancient Israel and in the Ancient Near East*. Kevelaer: Butzon and Bercker, 1986.

Tromp, N. J. *Primitive Conceptions of Death and the Nether World in the Old Testament*. Rome: Pontifical Biblical Institute, 1969.

SHIRĀT (AL-SHIRĀT AL-JAHĪM)

The word *al-shirāt* (literally "the path") appears frequently in the Qur'ān to indicate the "straight path" that faithful Muslims must follow. However, there is a particular al-shirāt that must be traveled in the afterlife, which reflects the religious path (or lack thereof) that one followed in life. This is al-Shirāt al-Jahīm, "the

Bridge over the Fire," the span that crosses over the topmost layer of hell (Jahannam), called *Gehenna*.

The Scriptural sources for this afterlife bridge are weak in the Qur'ān. One verse frequently cited in support of the real existence of such a bridge is Qur'ān 36:66, which reads, "Had it been Our will, We [God] could have put out [the sinners'] sight: yet even then they would have rushed headlong upon their wonted path." Here, the word *al-shirāt* appears as "path," but there is no reference to the fires of hell or even an afterlife context. The other Qur'ānic verse that Muslim scholars use is sura 37:23–24, which reads, "We [God] shall say: 'Call the sinners, their spouses, and the idols which they worshipped besides God, and lead them to the path of Hell.'" Again, the word *al-shirāt* is used in the context of hell but does not refer to a bridge. Western scholars of Islam are thus fairly certain that the original Prophet of Islam, Muhammed, intended no "bridge" that crossed over hell.

How, then, did such an idea enter Islam so thoroughly as to become almost universally accepted among the Muslim faithful? The historical source was undoubtedly the Zoroastrian teaching of the Chinvato Peretu, "the Bridge of the Separator." The borrowing is all the more certain when one considers that for more than a thousand years Zoroastrianism and Islam have coexisted together in the Middle East in the lands of the old Persian empire. In Zoroastrian belief, after death each soul must cross this bridge that spans the abyss of hell: those with the spiritual power of a life righteously lived find that the bridge opens wide before them and they cross over into heaven; the wicked find that the bridge narrows, even to a razor's edge, and they pitch headlong into the depths.

There are key differences between the Zoroastrian and Islamic teachings regarding this bridge, however. In Zoroastrian belief, nurtured on the cold, dark steppes of Central Asia, hell (Dozakh) is a frigid place where the darkness is so thick one may grasp it by the hand. Furthermore, the Zoroastrian hell is not eternal but lasts only until the final cataclysm between the god of truth and the god of the lie; at that time all souls are raised from the dead, purified, and joined in the Godhead. By contrast, in Islam, which was born in the hot deserts of Arabia and Persia, hell (Jahannam) is a hot place, likewise dark but also eternal (at least in early Islamic theology). Whereas Zoroastrians are saved from hell by the resurrection, Muslims are condemned to hell only after the resurrection. Another important difference is that in Zoroastrian belief, the Bridge of the Separator is something that each soul has to face alone after death. In Islam, however, the Prophet Muhammed himself leads his faithful followers over the bridge en masse, and there is no chance of them getting lost; but the wicked find that smoke and ash cloud their vision and cannot find the path, at last tumbling into the flames, falling through as many layers of hell as their sins take them to.

Thus it is clear that once the idea of a bridge over hell entered into Islamic thought, it developed in ways that met Islamic theology's needs. For example, in the visionary text of the afterlife, the *Kitāb ahwāl al-Qiyāma* (trans. Smith and Haddad), the al-Shirāt al-jahīm is huge and highly elaborated. The bridge has seven arches, each 3,000 years' travel in length, corresponding to the seven religious requirements that Islamic teaching demands of its followers. At each great arch, an angel will question the believer as to his or her faith, daily prayers, and charity before allowing the deceased to pass. How this will be done when the resurrected dead pass through in droves led by Muhammed is an open question and seems to recall the Zoroastrian emphasis on individual passage across the bridge. Islamic thinkers also came to believe that the torment of the wicked who fell from al-Shirāt al-jahīm would not be eternal; those Muslims in the top layer of hell, at least, would eventually be rescued, either because they will have been sufficiently punished or because of the intercession (shafā'a) of the Prophet. In this way Islamic thinking also came to resemble Zoroastrian doctrine, though Islam has yet to unanimously decide whether non-Muslims may eventually be saved from hell.

See also BARZAKH; GARDENS OF DELIGHT; JAHANNAM; JUDGMENT, LAST; JUDGMENT, PARTICULAR; QIYĀMA; SĀ'A; SOUL, MUSLIM.

References

Bevan, A. A. "The Beliefs of Early Mohammedans Respecting a Future Existence." *Journal of Theological Studies* (October 1904).

Dawood, N. J., trans. *The Koran*. 5th rev. ed. New York: Penguin, 1993.

Evrin, M. Sadeddin. *Eschatology in Islam*. Trans. Sofi Huri. Istanbul, 1960.

Kherie, Altaf Ahmad. *Islam: A Comprehensive Guidebook*. Karachi: Idara Sirat-i-Mustaqeem, 1981.

Lazarus-Yafeh, Hava. *Some Religious Aspects of Islam*. Leiden: E. J. Brill, 1981.

Macdonald, John. "The Day of Resurrection." *Islamic Studies* 5, no. 2 (1966).

O'Shaughnessy, Thomas. "The Seven Names for Hell in the Qur'ān." *Bulletin of the School of Oriental and African Studies* 24, no. 3 (1961).

Smith, Jane I. *The Precious Pearl* (A translation of Abū Hāmid al-Ghazālī's *Kitāb al-Durra al-Fākhira if Kashf 'Ulūm al-Ākhira*). Missoula, MT: Scholars Press, 1979.

Smith, Jane I., and Yvonne Yazbeck Haddad. *The Islamic Understanding of Death and Resurrection*. Albany: SUNY Press, 1981.

Taylor, John B. "Some Aspects of Islamic Eschatology." *Religious Studies* 4 (1968).

SHIVA (HINDU)

In Hinduism, Shiva is the lord of death, destruction, and regeneration. It is instructive that Shiva's name

Chloa bronze, sixteenth-century representation of Shiva in the dance of creation. Courtesy of Anne Ronan Picture Library.

phallus and horns, and surrounded by wild animals. In the earliest Scriptures of India, the Vedas (dating to at least 2000 B.C.E. and probably much earlier), Shiva is called *Rudra,* "the Howler," a fearsome deity (or demon) of storm and physical activity. Even in remote times, Shiva holds his later character as one outside the pale of civilization and its established religious rituals and sacrifices. Shiva is solitary, a wanderer, an ascetic, and a holder of occult wisdom.

Thus in classical and medieval Indian texts Shiva is the lord of ascetics, those seeking spiritual enlightenment through harsh bodily and spiritual practices far from cities and royal courts. In this aspect Shiva is called *Kapālin,* "User of Skulls," for part of the meditations of ascetics, or yogis, consists of meditating on death and using human skulls as ritual bowls. In this meditative, world-renouncing aspect Shiva is also called *Bhūtnath,* "Lord of Ghosts and Vampires." He is associated with cemeteries and desolate spots where insight into reality (i.e., death and what lies beyond it) may occur. Not just human death, but cosmic death is his realm: as Mahā-Kāla (Great Time or Eternity), Shiva brings about the final dissolution of the entire universe at the end of time only to reform and recreate it. He is death and beyond death and thus is known as *Yamāntaka,* the "Ender of Yama," for Yama is the god of death.

Perhaps the most famous image of Shiva in the Western hemisphere is in his four-armed pose as Natarāja, or "Lord of the Cosmic Dance." As typically depicted, Shiva is white in color or more accurately ashen, the color of renunciation, and his face is absolutely serene. Wearing a garland of skulls, he dances rhythmically, hypnotically, trampling underfoot a small black dwarf named *Apasmāra Purusha,* who represents human pride, attachment, and worldliness. Each of his four arms and two feet strikes an important, symbolic pose, representative of his many aspects. Shiva's upper right hand holds a small two-sided drum, symbolizing with its beat not only cosmic time and the rhythm of universal ages but also sound, the first cosmic element in creation and source of all others, for it is the word or speech (vāk) with its magic power that creates and destroys all manifestation. Shiva's upper left hand bears a flame, symbol of spirit and destruction: the two upper hands strike a balance between the rhythm of manifestation and the combustion leading to silence. Shiva's lower right hand has palm upturned toward the viewer, in the symbol (mudrā) called *fearlessness* (abhāya), representing the spiritual quality necessary to transcend the world of appearances, the world of emanation and decay. While his right foot dances on the dwarf of ignorance, Shiva's lower left hand, angled like an elephant's trunk, points to his left foot, which is raised in the air, signifying the possibility of being

means "the Gracious, the Benevolent," for he is a protective deity even in his ferocious aspect as the destroyer of the universe at the end of the cosmic age. He is an ancient Indian deity, central to Indian religion from the remotest times to the present and demonstrating both horrific power and perfect enlightenment.

One entire wing of Hindu tradition (called Shaivism) is focused on Shiva as the supreme deity, he who transcends time, who existed before the universe came into being and who will continue to exist undisturbed after the universe returns to the nonbeing called *pralāya.* As the absolute principle of the universe, Shiva is called *Mahādeva,* or Great Lord, who emanates from his own being all lesser gods, who in turn produce the spiritual and material universes. But Shiva, who is called by 100 names and more by his devotees, has many aspects.

Shiva is known even in Indian prehistory from archaeological findings from the Indus Valley civilization (c. 3500–2500 B.C.E.) as Pashupati, Lord of Animals (and Souls, pashu), pictured in meditation posture, with erect

The Descent of the Ganges

Once there was a mighty king by the name of Sagara. His sons disturbed a great sage, Kapila, in his austerities. The sage cursed them, and they were burned to ashes. As they had died in this unceremonial manner, their souls could not go to heaven. Sagara pleaded with the sage Kapila, and Kapila ultimately relented, and said that if the heavenly river, Mandakini ("Slow-Flowing"), or Ganga (the Ganges), came to the earth and flowed over the ashes, the souls of the dead princes would go to heaven. Several generations went by. No one knew how to bring Ganga down. At last King Bhagiratha decided to do so by great austerities. So severe were his penances that ultimately Ganga decided to come down to earth. She descended in a torrential mass of water. The volume would have engulfed the whole world if Shiva had not interposed his head, with its matted hair, in between heaven and earth. Shiva thus took the shock of the fall of the heavenly Ganga to earth. For several years the waters of the Ganges were imprisoned in Shiva's ascetic knots of coiled hair. Ultimately Shiva divided the water into seven streams and released them. They fell on the world like thunder. Flowing over the ashes of Sagara's sons, they released their souls from eternal damnation. The fields were also now well cultivated and there was neither drought nor hunger. Everyone was pleased and worshipped the sacred Ganges river as the goddess, Mother Ganga.

Adapted from Ghosh.

released from the universe, land of illusion. As he dances Natarāja is surrounded by a circle of flames, symbolizing the energy of primordial wisdom.

Yet less appreciated in the Western world is Shiva's primary iconographic representation, the lingam (erect phallus). This signifies nothing other than Shiva's primary role as the potent center of the universe, the pillar around which all revolves. This point is underscored by the fact that most stone lingam in Indian temples are surrounded by and arise out of a base that represents the female sexual organ, called *yoni* in Sanskrit. The yoni represents Shiva's important female consort, who has many names and many human incarnations—Durga, Kali, Sati, Umā, and Parvati. Together the phallus and yoni symbolize the essence of the universe, the seed and ground of being.

The dual nature of Shiva is often overlooked, probably because his terrific aspect is so powerful and attractive. But in Hindu thought, death is ever temporary, like its inseparable twin, life. Shiva destroys, but doing so is the same as transforming, which is the same as preserving,

for those who have eyes to see. One of Shiva's many names is Nīlakantha, or "Blue-throat," which comes from one of the many instances when Shiva saved the universe. Once, when the gods were stirring the universal ocean to produce the nectar of immortality (amrita), they used the cosmic serpent as a spoon. In the usual Hindu pairing of evil and good, the serpent in protest spewed forth a torrent of poison, which threatened to dissolve the world. But Shiva swallowed the entire stream, and although his throat turned permanently blue from the poison, the world was saved. When the world was overrun by demons (asuras) who consolidated the power of the three worlds into one fortress called Tripura, Shiva became Tripurāntika, their destroyer, and saved the gods from ruin. Again, when the extremely potent sacred river, the Ganges, was called down to Earth, its power would have decimated the humble Earth had not Shiva sheltered the world with his matted locks, absorbing and taming the too-powerful river and letting it fall to earth gently for human benefit. Shiva's sons, too, symbolize his many-faceted nature. One son, Ganesha of the elephant head, is the god of learning and wisdom and the remover of (spiritual) obstacles; the other son is Karttakeya, god of war.

What is the meaning of this complex figure of death and rebirth, this god of renouncers and ascetics, this world savior? Shiva defies easy compartmentalization, but the basic aspect that emerges to his devotees is one of insight, which sees behind the kaleidoscope of the ever-changing universe with calmness and spiritual understanding. Magician, demon, guide of souls, Shiva is the psychological key to that which keeps humanity in bondage.

See also FUNERARY CUSTOMS, HINDU; NIRVĀṆA; REINCARNATION, EASTERN; YAMA.

References

Agrawala, V. S. *Shiva Mahādeva, the Great God.* Varanasi: Veda Academy, 1966.

Ghosh, Oroon K. *The Dance of Shiva and Other Tales from India.* New York: New American Library, 1965.

Marshall, Sir John. *Mohenjo-Daro and the Indus Civilization.* London: A. Probsthain, 1931.

Moor, Edward. *The Hindu Pantheon.* Ed. W. O. Simpson. Madras: J. Higginbotham, 1864.

O'Flaherty, Wendy Doniger. *Asceticism and Eroticism in the Mythology of Shiva.* London: Oxford University Press, 1973.

Rao, T. A. G. *Elements of Hindu Iconography.* Varanasi: Indological Book House, 1971.

Zimmer, Heinrich. *Myths and Symbols in Indian Art and Civilization.* Ed. Joseph Campbell. Bollingen Series 6. New York: Random House, 1946.

SHIVA (JEWISH)

Meaning literally "seven," shiva is the seven-day period of mourning in Judaism that follows the burial of the loved one. (Before burial there is a different period of mourning known as *aninut*.) This seven-day period of mourning is also called *sitting shiva* because one of the requirements of the mourners is to forsake their regular seats and sit on low stools, benches, or the ground, symbolizing their abasement in grief. Shiva is most strictly observed in Orthodox Judaism.

After a Jew is buried, all the "seven relatives" (mother, father, daughter, son, brother, sister, and spouse) enter into a long mourning period called *avelut;* shiva is merely the first (and most intense) part of that period. Each relative is required to observe the positive and negative regulations of mourning, whether they were personally close to the deceased or not. In-laws, divorced spouses, adopted parents and children, half-siblings, and stepchildren and stepparents have the option of observing formal mourning if they choose, but they are not required to do so by Jewish law. Recent brides and grooms are forbidden to observe mourning rituals until after their seven-day honeymoon period (upon which time they observe the full period of shiva).

Shiva appears to be a very ancient custom in Judaism. The high priest Aaron refused to eat the sacrificial offering, even though it was his duty, when he was mourning the death of his two sons (Leviticus 10:20), but it is not clear how long his period of mourning lasted. Although Jewish sages from around the beginning of the common era claim that Moses himself instituted the seven-day period, there is little evidence for this other than their assertion. There is, however, a passage in the book of Genesis in which Joseph mourns his father Jacob's death in Egypt. According to the (unlikely) tale, Joseph and his entire household left Egypt and traveled to Canaan to bury Jacob in his homeland. But the relevant passage reads: "When they came to the threshing floor of Atad beside the river Jordan, they raised a loud and bitter lament; *and there Joseph observed seven days' mourning for his father*" (Genesis 50:10; emphasis added). Genesis was certainly not put into writing in the days of Joseph (c. sixteenth century B.C.E.); it was written well before the common era and gives some credence to the view that shiva or some version of it is many thousands of years old.

Today, shiva begins at the end of the funeral, when the grave of the deceased is completely covered with earth. The burial kaddish is recited, and the seven relatives recess from the grave through two parallel lines of friends and family, who recite a prayer of comfort. Mourners proceed directly home and wash their hands before crossing the threshold of their homes. The washing is a symbolic way of acknowledging the impurity of being closely associated with death and of preventing its spread—a variation on the ancient belief in the "contagion" of death. Once inside, mourners formally indicate that they have entered into shiva by removing their shoes and sitting on a low bench, stool, or the ground. (Sometimes, however, mourners temporarily remove their shoes and sit on a low seat even in the cemetery after the funeral, before they proceed home.)

The duration of shiva is strictly defined as seven *Hebrew* days. Because nearly all burials will take place during the day, this counts as the first day of shiva. The second day begins that night (as Hebrew days begin at nightfall), and shiva continues until after the morning religious service (called *shacharit*) five days later. For example, if the burial was on a Monday, that is the first day, and Monday night begins the second day, Tuesday night the third, Wednesday night the fourth, Thursday night the fifth, Friday night the sixth, and Saturday night the beginning of the seventh day. After the first service on Sunday morning, the seventh "day" is considered completed. In general, Orthodox Jews follow the seven days of shiva strictly, but Conservative and Reformed Jews often alter the time period to conform to individual needs or to coincide with a weekend. (In the latter Jewish traditions, formal shiva may not be observed at all.)

Sitting shiva includes a number of observances related to the home and to the persons of the bereaved. Immediately upon returning from the cemetery, candles are lit in memory of the deceased (symbolizing the soul), and all the mirrors in the home are covered. All the mourners avoid work, both employment and chores around the home (unless in doing so irreparable financial harm would be caused), especially during the first three days of shiva. Personal hygiene is at a minimum, and nothing may be done for personal pleasure or unnecessary adornment. No new clothes are worn, nor even those that are freshly washed or pressed. Wearing leather shoes is forbidden, and mourners may go outside the home only to attend to religious duties that cannot be performed by anyone else. There is no haircutting, shaving, applying cosmetics, perfumes, or scented oils, and bathing is discouraged except when required for hygiene and then only in cold water. Meat and wine are forbidden, except during the Sabbath and holidays. Sexual relations cease during shiva. Mourners do not exchange greetings (such as "shalom," or "peace be with you") with each other or with visitors because Jewish law recognizes that it is ridiculous to ask those plunged in grief, "How are you?" Mourners are to sit on low stools or benches during shiva, except in the case of those who are seriously ill, elderly, or pregnant—but even then, sitting on a low seat in order to receive visitors is considered important. Finally, mourners do not accept gifts, attend parties, or even study Torah (Scripture) because all are associated with joy—which is unseemly during a period of grief.

The first three days of shiva are considered the most intense, and mourners have very few social contacts. An important exception is the meal of condolence that neighbors prepare for the bereaved, consisting of bread, hard-boiled eggs, and cooked vegetables. Friends and neighbors are certainly expected to pay a visit during shiva (indeed, this is considered a sacred duty in Orthodox communities), but it is generally delayed until the latter half of shiva because the mourners are assumed to be in no state to receive guests until then. Another exception are the three daily religious services observed by the Orthodox. These services are held in the home of the deceased during shiva if at all possible. This is done to honor the dead, and includes the very important recitation of the kaddish prayer (which can only be recited for the dead by a group). However, holding services in the home requires the presence of a quorum of adult Jewish males, ten in number (called a *minyan*). If a minyan cannot be gathered, the mourners may (in some communities) leave the home to attend services at the synagogue, but only if in doing so they can avoid breaking the observances of shiva (such as wearing leather shoes).

Most important, shiva is considered by Jewish law to be a time of intensely *personal* grief. It is overshadowed by the requirement of the greater community to observe festivities during the Sabbath (Friday night to Saturday night) and high holidays (Passover, Shavuot, Succot, Rosh Hashanah, and Yom Kippur). Thus shiva observances are suspended during the Sabbath, except for those that cannot be seen in public. Thus for the evening Sabbath service, mourners may bathe, put on new or freshly cleaned clothes, wear leather shoes, and leave the house to attend synagogue, but candles are kept burning in the home, the mirrors remain covered, and marital relations are still taboo. Unlike the suspension of regulations during the Sabbath, if a major holiday occurs during shiva, the shiva is cancelled entirely. This is only the case if the mourners had already begun to observe shiva before the holiday began (even if the holiday commenced on the evening of the day of burial). If a death occurs *during* a holiday, shiva is postponed until after the holiday period is over, and then shiva regulations are observed for a full seven Hebrew days.

After the week of shiva has passed, avelut (formal mourning) continues on for three more weeks in a lessened form, called *sheloshim*. Many of the restrictions of shiva are lifted, but during sheloshim mourners continue to avoid haircutting and shaving, bathing and wearing new clothes, going to parties, and getting married (as these are all associated with excessive joy or adornment). As with shiva, sheloshim regulations are suspended during the Sabbath and cancelled entirely if a major holiday intervenes.

See also ANINUT; AVELUT; FUNERARY CUSTOMS, JEWISH; KADDISH; KERI'AH; SHELOSHIM; YAHRZEIT; YIZKOR.

References

Abramovitch, Henry. "Death." In *Contemporary Jewish Religious Thought,* ed. Arthur A. Cohen and Paul Mendes-Flohr. New York: Charles Scribner's Sons, 1989.

Lamm, Maurice. *The Jewish Way in Death and Mourning.* New York: Jonathan David Publishers, 1969.

Montefiore, C. G., and H. Loewe, eds. *A Rabbinic Anthology.* New York: Schocken Books, 1974.

Rabinowicz, H. *A Guide to Life.* London: Jewish Chronicle Publications, 1964.

Riemer, Jack, ed. *Jewish Reflections on Death.* New York: Schocken Books, 1974.

SHOMER

Literally, "the watcher," the shomer guards the corpse until the funeral according to Jewish tradition. Guarding the body is an important mitzvah (a religious commandment in Orthodox Judaism), and the shomer is exempt from all other religious duties. The shomer is expected to stay with the body at all times or, if this is not possible (as in a morgue), to stay within line of sight of the body (through a window or door.) The shomer remains awake all night and as often as possible recites psalms from the Hebrew Bible over the body. This recitation is thought to comfort the dead (if still present) as well as to protect the body from harm. Smoking, eating, and casual conversation are forbidden in the room with the deceased, and enforcing these restrictions is also the shomer's responsibility.

The importance placed on guarding the body until its proper burial probably dates back to very ancient times, when it was generally believed that evil spirits were anxious to possess a freshly dead corpse and when fear of the undead was widespread. For this reason, Jewish tradition prescribes many apotropaic practices (measures to ward off evil) related to the body: keeping a shomer in the room, keeping a candle lit, covering the mirrors in the home, orienting the feet of the deceased toward the door, and so on. After a religious funeral and burial, however, the body is generally considered inert and free of danger.

See also ANINUT; CHEVRA KADDISHA; FUNERARY CUSTOMS, JEWISH; SOUL; SOUL, JEWISH; VAMPIRE.

References

Abramovitch, Henry. "Death." In *Contemporary Jewish Religious Thought,* ed. Arthur A. Cohen and Paul Mendes-Flohr. New York: Charles Scribner's Sons, 1989.

Lamm, Maurice. *The Jewish Way in Death and Mourning.* New York: Jonathan David Publishers, 1969.

Riemer, Jack, ed. *Jewish Reflections on Death.* New York: Schocken Books, 1974.

SHRĀDDHA

In India the daily and then monthly ceremonies held to honor and help the recently deceased after cremation are called *shrāddha,* as is the annual ritual to honor and help the ancestors in general. This word is derived from the ancient Sanskrit word *shraddhā,* meaning "faith, loyalty, devotion." Immediately after cremation, the dead are thought to exist in very vulnerable spiritual bodies subject to extreme heat, cold, and fear. Only the love and faith expressed in this ceremony by their surviving family members, particularly the eldest son, rescue the deceased from fate as an undead and release them to the bliss of heaven. Likewise, in the annual rite one's ancestors for three generations back are honored by offerings, and their afterlife experience is thought to be made better.

The Vedas (the earliest Indian Scriptures dated to about 2000 B.C.E. or earlier) provide little evidence that the dead were imagined to suffer after death unless they were cast into "the pit." Rather, early texts like the Rig Veda celebrate the immediate journey of the dead, now called a *pitri* (ancestor), to the heaven of the ancient ancestors or, for the particularly fortunate, to the heaven of the gods by way of the sun.

Unite with the Fathers, unite with Yama
With the reward of thy sacrifices and good works in
    the highest heaven.
Leaving blemish behind go back to thy home;
Unite with thy [new] body, full of vigour.
(Rig Veda X.14.8, Macdonell, trans.)

In the early texts there is no discussion of a delay before making this journey to the ancestors' realm. Although silence does not equal proof that the doctrine was not held, it may at least be said that it was not worth discussing.

The situation changed in later times, when intermediate stages after death are much discussed. In the ritual texts called Gṛhya Sūtras (c. 800 to 300 B.C.E., according to Pandurang Vaman Kane) the doctrine is put forward that after death the deceased does not immediately become a pitri but is first a suffering ghost (pret). Only after a year, having received the proper cremation ceremonies and food offerings, does the pret become an ancestor spirit and cease to experience the sufferings of hunger and thirst while being bound to Earth's atmosphere. At a later stage, in the Purāṇa texts (300 to 600 C.E.), there is another intermediate stage between death and the eventual afterlife. As soon as the physical body is cremated, the deceased is thought to arise in an invisible body called *ātivāhika śarīra,* or "faster-than-wind body" (also called *linga śarīra,* or "subtle body"). In this body the miserable ghost is thought to suffer terribly from extreme heat, cold, hunger, and thirst. Only through offerings made by the surviving family can the dead pass through this stage to pret, where suffering is less intense, and again through (less frequent) offerings, the dead finally becomes a pitri and departs to the higher world.

Depending on the "stage" of the soul of the deceased, the shrāddha ceremonies are of several types, but all the shrāddhas are extremely important in Indian life. It is no exaggeration to say that much of Hindu popular religion revolves around proper shrāddhas, with hundreds of texts addressing the ceremony. Hindu fathers see the production of a son as perhaps the single most important accomplishment in their life because only a son can perform the shrāddha ceremonies at maximum power. Failure to produce a son is one of the greatest causes of misery in Hindu families, for without proper shrāddha one may literally be trapped after death as a suffering pret indefinitely. (It might be added that this emphasis on male offspring has contributed to higher abortion rates for female fetuses as well as female infanticide.) Many texts praise the shrāddha highly, teaching that it not only benefits the deceased but brings long life, happiness, and male offspring to the family; what's more, the world at large benefits. The Smriticandrika states: "Nothing else is declared to be more beneficial than *shrāddha*" (Kane, trans.); and the Viṣṇu Purāṇa adds: "If a man performs *shrāddha* with faith, he thereby propitiates Brahmā, Indra, Rudra and the other gods, sages, birds, men, beasts, creeping animals, hosts of *pitris* and whatever else is styled a 'being' in the whole world" (Kane, trans.).

The initial shrāddha ceremony begins on the first day of death and is repeated each day for ten days. Any family member may perform this daily rite, which goes as follows. On a bed of sacred kusha grass, a stone is placed. Facing south, the family member takes a handful of water mixed with sesame and pours it over the stone, and then a large ball of cooked rice (called *pinda*) mixed with honey, fruits, milk, and butter is placed on the stone as an offering. More water mixed with sesame is poured over the pinda along with sacred leaves, and sacred formulas called *mantras* are spoken. Then the ball of rice is disposed of by throwing it into water, and the performer goes away and bathes for purification. This ten-day ritual frees the deceased from the extreme suffering of the ātivāhika body because for each ball or pinda offered, the deceased soul gains a part of a new subtle body. On the first day, the offering builds the subtle head; the second day builds the subtle ears, nose, and eyes; and so on down to the tenth day, which completes the new subtle body. Thus after ten days the deceased has developed a new ghostly body, called *preta,* in which suffering is not as intense.

After the initial ceremony begin the more elaborate monthly rites of shrāddha (called *ekodiṣṭa*). Almost any direct family member may lead these rites, but the eldest son is preferred. As in the ten-day ritual, the center of this rite involves offering the deceased a piṇda, but a water offering and ritual meal for guests are included as well. The performer of the ceremony should, after washing hands and feet, sip water, take up sacred kusha grass in hand, seat himself facing south, name the deceased, and pour out a water oblation while saying: "May this be acceptable to thee." Then he presents a cushion made of the sacred kusha grass and, after naming the deceased, pours out water mixed with sesame, perfumes, and flowers. Finally, again naming the deceased, rice, clarified butter (called *ghee*), and water are offered. All the while, sacred formulas are spoken.

The rite continues by seating the invited brahmins (members of the highest caste in India). While reciting verses from sacred texts, the family should serve these educated men a special dinner consisting of milk, butter, sesame oil, fruits, vegetables, certain grains, and salt. Garlic, onions, leeks, certain beans, dark cereals, and possibly flesh are forbidden, though debate continues over the last item. The texts are very specific about which brahmins are to be invited and which should not be invited. In the Manusmriti, ninety-three categories of people are listed as unfit to be called to dinner at a shrāddha ceremony, including those with skin diseases or with deformed nails, those who neglect sacrifice, wine drinkers, hypocrites, skeptics of Scriptures, and so on. Which foods are offered and who to invite are central considerations because the deceased is thought to actually enter into the bodies of the brahmins and spiritually partake of the food. There are equally strict regulations about what kinds of vessels to serve the food in, time of day, and so on, all of which may be passed over here. Finally, after offering ghee in the fire and feeding the brahmins, the hosts place a piṇḍa on a bed of sacred grass on the table near the brahmins' plates. This ball of flavored rice, like the food eaten by the brahmins, reaches the dead and helps him or her move on to the next stage of life as a deceased person.

After twelve monthly rituals like the one already described (possibly with a few others at the halfway point), the deceased person is ready to be transformed from a preta into a full-fledged pitri. The final rite for the individual dead person (called *sapiṇḍīkaraṇa*) is the most important of all, for only afterward can the dead be received into the world of light, the heaven (Svarga) of blest ancestors. The rite is quite similar to the monthly one, but at the end of the meal, four vessels should be prepared containing water, sandalwood paste, and sesame grains. The first three vessels represent the father, grandfather, and great-grandfather of the deceased, and the fourth vessel with water represents the ghost of the recently dead. Reciting the formula, "I shall unite the vessel for the *preta* with the vessels for his three paternal ancestors," the eldest son pours the water of the fourth vessel into the other three. Then four piṇḍas are prepared, representing the same persons as

the four vessels of scented water. The fourth piṇḍa is divided into three parts and merged into the three piṇḍas representing the paternal ancestors. With this, the ghost of the recently dead is released into the world of the ancestors and suffers no more.

The final type of shrāddha to be discussed is the annual rite (called *pārvana*) performed for the collective benefit of one's three most recent paternal ancestors (father, grandfather, and great-grandfather), and it may only be performed by a son. The rules about when to hold this annual rite are extremely complex and may be passed over here, except to note that days of the new moon, eclipses, and other special astronomical events are favored. The rite may also be performed more often than annually (up to ninety-six times in a year) if one seeks to earn extra merit for oneself and one's ancestors, but this is rare, for the rite is expensive. It is exactly like the ekodiṣṭa ceremony, but more brahmins must be invited, representing each of the three ancestors being honored as well as superintendent gods. This ritual begins by pouring ghee into the sacred fire, if the family is orthodox and keeps a sacred fire in the home; otherwise, the ghee should be poured into the open hands of a brahmin. Uttering mantras somewhat different from those used for the ekodiṣṭa ceremony, the ritual feast is held as before, and afterward three pindas are offered, one for each of the ancestors being honored. The three ancestors are thought to actually enter into the bodies of the brahmins representing them and thus partake of the feast directly.

Several sacred Indian texts report doubts about shrāddha expressed by skeptics. These persons questioned the value of the ceremony, wondering how ancestors, who presumably have been reborn in new material bodies (in heaven, hell, or again on Earth) could be present at the ceremony. Questions were also raised regarding karma: if one must suffer the rewards or punishments of one's own deeds, how can the actions of another change one's personal fate, which has been fairly earned? The standard reply is that several classes of gods (specifically, the Vasus, Rudras, and Ādityas, representing each of the three generations being honored in the annual rite) serve as mediators, delivering the benefits of the shrāddha food to one's ancestors wherever they might be. Meanwhile, the same classes of gods reward the performers of the shrāddha with long lives, healthy offspring, wisdom, happiness, and even final liberation (mokṣa).

See also BHŪT; FUNERARY CUSTOMS, HINDU; NARAKA; PITRI; PRET; SVARGA.

References

Crooke, William. *The Popular Religion and Folklore of Northern India.* 2nd ed. Delhi: Munshiram Manoharlal, 1968.

Kane, Pandurang Vaman. *History of Dharmashāstra: Ancient and Medieval Religious and Civil Law in India.* Vol. 4. Government Oriental Series, Class B. no. 6. Poona: Bhandarkar Oriental Research Institute, 1953.

Macdonell, Arthur Anthony. *A Vedic Reader for Students.* Indian ed. Delhi: Motilal Banarsidass, 1995.

Pandey, Raj Bali. *Hindu Samskāras: A Socio-religious Study of the Hindu Sacraments.* Banares: Vikrama Publications, 1949.

Shastri, Dakshina Ranjan. *Origin and Development of the Rituals of Ancestor Worship in India.* Calcutta: Bookland, 1963.

SHROUD

Early Christians appear to have invented the shroud in the Western Hemisphere. On both economic grounds (generally the first Christians were of humble means) and spiritual grounds, Christians objected to distinguishing their dead on the basis of their fancy burial clothing or lack thereof. Kenneth Iserson quotes Saint Jerome's *Vita Pauli,* which asks: "Does a desire for appearance exist amid mourning and tears? Why should the dead be clothed in sumptuous vestments? Cannot the rich rot away unless in the same gorgeous apparel that decorated them while alive?" (Iserson, p. 451).

Traditionally, shrouds were made of plain cloth, often linen (a cheap material in pre-modern Europe), though sometimes authorities tried to impose the use of certain materials. In 1666, the English passed a law requiring shrouds to be made of wool in an attempt to preserve rag linen for the paper industry; allegedly 200,000 pounds of rag linen were saved every year. In 1707, the Scottish government passed a similar law, though this was a blatant attempt to promote the wool industry. In the Middle Ages, "cerecloth" was developed, which was fine cloth soaked in wax or other adhesive. In fashion among the wealthy, cerecloth made an airtight shroud and helped slow the onset of bodily decay.

Traditionally, shrouds were made to cover the whole body, and the edges were sewn up so that the dead person was effectively sealed in a cloth sack. In some cases, however, shrouds were made with holes at the top to fit over the head because it was thought that on resurrection day these holes would make it easier for the newly risen to emerge.

See also BURIAL; BURIAL CLOTHES; FUNERARY CUSTOMS, CHRISTIAN; FUNERARY CUSTOMS, JEWISH.

References
Dempsey, D. *The Way We Die.* New York: Macmillan, 1975.

Farrell, J. J. *Inventing the American Way of Death 1830—1920.* Philadelphia: Temple University Press, 1980.

Iserson, Kenneth V. *Death to Dust: What Happens to Dead Bodies?* Tucson, AZ: Galen Press, 1994.

Jackson, A. V. W. *Zoroastrian Studies.* New York: Columbia University Press, 1928.

Jones, Barbara. *Design for Death.* Indianapolis: Bobbs-Merrill, 1967.

Mitford, Jessica. *The American Way of Death.* New York: Simon and Schuster, 1963.

SÍD

Pronounced "shee," the Irish term *síd* refers both to the Otherworld fairy race and to the green knolls and mounds where they are supposed to dwell. More often than not, these mounds are simultaneously the burial mounds of ancient kings and heroes, which is no accident. In Irish lore, the fairies, the gods, and the dead are all conflated.

Properly, síd (in modern Gaelic, *sith* and *sithean*) refers to the ancient mounds of the Celtic world—the cairns, dolmens, and barrows of Ireland, Great Britain, and parts of continental Europe. These mounds are extremely ancient and long predate the people now known as the Celts, but their worship was taken up by these settlers and incorporated into a complex belief system of kingship, magic, and the Otherworld. Very often these mounds house megalithic tombs under their grassy turf, sometimes with skeletal remains accompanied by funerary offerings like bowls, weapons, and precious jewelry. Sometimes the síd lack burial remains but have become important landmarks in local myths and pseudohistory, as the spot where an ancient hero was crowned king or where a magnificent battle was fought. More than likely, the Celtic settlers inherited many of the ancient myths of the peoples who proceeded them, merely changing the names.

In addition, síd has come to mean the nonhuman race of the Otherworld, the fairies ("people of the síd") who inhabit the mounds, as well as the godlike Tuatha Dé Danann, sorcerer-heroes who were long ago banished underground, legends say, by conquering humans. The people of the síd have many special characteristics. They are usually thought to be immortal and invisible, though on rare occasions like Samhain (modern Hallowe'en), the lucky adventurer might catch a glimpse of them. The fairy race is divinely beautiful and accomplished in Otherworldly music, dance, shape shifting, and all manner of spells, both beneficial and harmful to humans. Angered, the people of the síd can increase strife among humans, sour milk, harm crops, and even deprive entire regions of their fertility. Yet treated with respect, the síd can offers favors, locate missing people or objects, and even invite the rare individual into their weird realm. A year in the Otherworld may turn out to be 300 years in human time, whereas several years with the fairies may be only seconds on earth. From the fairy world some have been known to come back with beautiful brides and riches; others never return at all.

Interestingly, much of the folklore surrounding the people of the síd warns of interaction with them because one might recognize a dead relative among them, which implies a connection between the human dead and the Otherworld race. What has happened is that, over time, two separate ideas have been confused and become practically one. Both the dead and the fairies are thought to dwell in a happy realm of sensual delights, a realm that is often considered to lie underground or over the waters; both are invisible except in rare circumstances; and both are thought to possess superhuman abilities and can bring trouble to the living if angered. It seems natural then that the dead would be thought to transform into fairies or at least be accepted by the fairies and proceed to live in their realm. This last may have been the actual Celtic belief in prehistory, before the theological revisions enforced by Christian missionaries and monks. There is evidence that in ancient times the Celts believed in reincarnation, and so perhaps the dead recuperated in the fairy Otherworld before returning again to Earth.

The story of Étain Echraide, beautiful daughter of the king of Ulster in Ireland, strongly implies belief in a concept of reincarnation. Étain is given as a wife to a certain Midir, who takes her to his home. But Midir's first wife Fuamnach grows jealous and with a magic rod turns Étain into a pool of water. Étain emerges from the pool as a purple fly and finds her way to Midir, but the jealous first wife finds her again and through magic traps Étain, the fly, in a wind that carries her over the ocean for many years. Eventually, poor Étain lands in a golden goblet and is swallowed by another woman, the wife of Étar—Étain is reborn as their daughter. When Étain grows up this time, she is engaged to a new husband. But soon her old husband Midir shows up and steals her away, escaping her pursuers by hiding in a síd. Only when every síd in Ireland is dug up is Midir found, and he promises to give Étain back to her fiancé in this life. Midir has the last laugh, however, when through magic he passes off Étain's daughter as Étain herself, for they look identical.

Tracing Étain's journey through several incarnations, this tale seems to suggest that the dead are not really "dead," as in "vanished forever," but merely transformed. Midir's first wife certainly killed Étain, though the tale uses the metaphors of transformation into a pool of water and a purple fly. Being sent out to sea by a magic wind is a metaphor for the afterlife in the Otherworld, which in Irish folklore is frequently placed over the sea (see MAG MELL). After being reborn, Étain has to face the conflict between her husband in her past life and her suitor in her current incarnation. Eventually she is born yet again through her "identical" daughter, and both gentlemen are happy, for each gets to keep a version of Étain. A crucial point in all this is that Étain's problems are solved only after her discovery and transformation within the síd. Her time underground is certainly a reference to her afterlife in the Otherworld.

Countless other tales demonstrate the transformative powers of the síd mounds, thus connecting the immortality of the people of the síd with the mortality of humans. Suggesting that all fairies in their mounds are merely once and future humans awaiting rebirth goes too far because the folklore is nothing like a systematic theology, and fairies and the dead maintain somewhat separate identities in popular thought. Yet the conflation of the two is remarkable, and on Hallowe'en night, both the dead and the fairies emerge from the very same síd to visit the living.

See also CAIRN; DOLMEN; FAIRY MOUND; MOUND.

References
MacCulloch, J. A. *Religion of the Ancient Celts*. Edinburgh: T. and T. Clark, 1911.
Ó hÓgáin, Dáithí. *Myth, Legend and Romance: An Encyclopaedia of the Irish Folk Tradition*. New York: Prentice Hall, 1991.
Paton, Lucy Allen. *Studies in the Fairy Mythology of Arthurian Romance*. Boston: Ginn, 1903.
Rees, Alwyn, and Brinley Rees. *Celtic Heritage*. London: Thames and Hudson, 1961.

THE SIX HEAVENS

The "Six Heavens" are relatively well-known to scholars through the "spirit-writing" of the Taoist Yang Hsi (fl. 350–400 C.E.), who apparently visited them under trance. The Six Heavens were associated with Mount Lo-feng (Lo-feng Shan) in the North Sea. Mount Lo-feng apparently had six exterior palaces (kung-shih) on its slopes and six interior caverns, each a thousand leagues in circumference. An early Taoist commentator (T'ao Hung-ching, 456–536 C.E.) informs us that the outer palaces are the offices where documents are controlled, and the interior palaces are "residences and places where interrogations are carried out" (quoted in Thompson, p. 40). The dead residing in the interior palaces of the mountain had some merit but had not yet attained the physical immortality sought by the Taoist. Through services such as chasing illness-causing demons, the spirits of the dead could earn the merit that would lead to their celestial transformation.

See also FUNERARY CUSTOMS, CHINESE; SOUL, CHINESE; TEN KINGS OF HELL.

References
Loewe, Michael. *Chinese Ideas of Life and Death*. Boston: Allen and Unwin, 1982.
Poo, Mu-chou. *In Search of Personal Welfare: A View of Ancient Chinese Religion*. New York: SUNY Press, 1998.
Teiser, Stephen F. *The Ghost Festival in Medieval China*. Princeton: Princeton University Press, 1988.
———. *The Scripture on the Ten Kings and the Making of Purgatory in Medieval Chinese Buddhism*. Honolulu: University of Hawaii Press, 1994.
Thompson, Laurence G. "On the Prehistory of Hell in China." *Journal of Chinese Religions*, no. 17 (Fall 1989).

SLEEP

Many cultures have recognized a close connection between sleep and death, probably because in sleep and especially in dreams, an altered state of consciousness is experienced while the body lies inert, suggesting an analogy with the consciousness imagined to be obtained after death.

Often, however, sleep is not considered a real analogy to death but merely a polite or comforting euphemism for death, particularly in modern Western culture in which death has become something to be hidden from sight and avoided in daily life. The use of sleep as a euphemism is not unique to modern times but is found even in the ancient world. For example, the word *cemetery* comes from the ancient Greek word *koimeterion*, literally "sleeping place." Continuing the Greek usage, inscriptions on early Christian tombstones (especially from the fourth to sixth centuries C.E.) frequently refer to the grave as *koimeterion*. Today those who grieve may content themselves with this denial, and it is not uncommon to tell grieving children that "Mommy is sleeping now." Though cross culturally widespread, it is a denial of the reality of death.

In early Christianity, however, and in Islam and some Jewish traditions today, this "sleeping" is a literal sleep. The early Christians, probably borrowing the tradition from an even earlier Jewish one, believed that the dead were literally lying in rest, perhaps with pleasant dreams or perhaps with nightmares, but waiting for the real life to come—the physical resurrection followed by judgment. This belief made martyrdom (i.e., dying for the faith) very popular in early Christianity—martyrs were an exception to the general rule. Rather than sleeping for ages while awaiting judgment, martyrs went straight to heaven after their heroic deaths. Eventually, Islam took on both ideas (the sleep of the common dead and the instant translation to heaven of martyrs) as it drew its traditions largely from the Judaism and Christianity that had gradually spread throughout the Middle East. Unlike Islam, however, medieval Christianity began to popularize the idea that everyone could proceed directly to Heaven or Hell (or Purgatory) after death; indeed, after the Reformation the Protestants even did away with Purgatory. Today hardly any Christians believe in the literal sleep of the dead or waiting until the end of the world before experiencing an afterlife. But this change in Christian belief has produced new theological problems. For if one proceeds *immediately* to Heaven or Hell after death, why believe in a final resurrection and judgment, the purpose of which is supposedly to send one to Heaven or Hell?

More common than either euphemism or literalism is sleep's function as an instructive analogy to death. A great many cultures believe that sleep is a kind of death, a minor death wherein the dead may be contacted and something of the afterlife may be experienced. Among their many, many words for death, ancient Egyptians, included many "sleep" words, which seems to have had a suggestive purpose. Words for death included *wrd,* "to

Daniel's vision of the beasts: "Four great Beasts came up from the sea, diverse one from another." Daniel 7:3, from an evangelical illustrated Bible, 1804. Courtesy of Anne Ronan Picture Library.

be tired," *bān,* "to sleep," *mā',* "to be laid out," *shbāgi,* "to make tired," and *shkd,* "to make sleep." The corpse was placed on its left side, the position of sleep, but drawings often showed the corpse turned onto its right, the symbolic position of waking. Thus, after the "sleep" of death, the ancient Egyptian expected to "awake" in resurrection. Like later Muslims, Egyptians often emphasized the "awakening" of Osiris in the Underworld and his reemergence from sleep with the rising sun.

Ancient Hebrew tradition also used words for sleep to indicate death but carefully distinguished a "good death" from a violent or bad death. The Hebrew Bible makes kings who died a natural death "lay down" or "go to sleep" (wayyishkab), whereas kings who died a violent death, like Azariah, Jehoahaz, Jehoram, Ahab, Josiah, Amaziah, and Amon—all the kings despised by the writers of the Hebrew Bible—do not "fall asleep" but "die" (wayyāmot). Most important, revered kings were "gathered to their fathers" (wayyê'āsep) both figuratively and quite literally because their bones were gathered up and placed in the family tomb after three to seven years when all the flesh had fallen off, a process called "secondary burial." For example, in the Wisdom of Solomon, a first-century B.C.E. text of the Apocrypha, Moses makes sure to take the bones of Joseph from Egypt on the exodus to Canaan.

Likewise, although Islam believes in the literal sleep of the dead, it also clearly juxtaposes sleep and death for purposes of instruction. The Qur'ān 39:42 states: "God takes away men's souls upon their death, and the souls of the living during their sleep. Those that are doomed He keeps with Him, and restores the others for a time ordained. Surely there are signs in this for thinking men." The obvious analogy, then, is that God takes whom he will—the living for a time, the dead for eternity—but the "sign" (aya) is that just as one wakes from sleep, one will "wake" from death to resurrection. This promise recurs over and over in Islam, and the analogy of sleep is a frequent object lesson.

The ancient Greeks also made an important analogy between sleep and death. In Hesiod's poetic account of creation, the *Theogony* (c. 800 B.C.E.), he makes Hypnos (Sleep) and Thanatos (Death) twin brothers, sons of Father Erebus (the Abyss, Darkness) and Mother Night. In Greek cosmology, as in every other ancient cosmology (even the Hebrew), Night existed before Day. Semitic nations even count their days from sundown to sundown. The message in the Greek myth—or one of the messages—is that death and sleep belong to the original nature of the universe and human beings, the same nature that underlies all of manifestation. Before the universe was and after it ends, cosmic space and the endlessness of night still exist, which is the reality behind appearances. To know sleep is to taste death as well as something of our deeper nature that creeps out in twilight but is hidden by the fierce light of day.

The Hindus promote much the same idea when they teach the "three states" of consciousness (sometimes adding a fourth, turiya, as the great sage Shankaracarya does). These three states are waking (jagrata), dreaming (svapna), and dreamless sleep (sushupti). In waking life a person falls victim to the cosmic illusion (maya), and lives only according to ego and desire and ignorance unless he or she is an advanced soul. In dreams, however, not only can one commune with the hidden powers of nature but, more importantly, with the higher self within, the ātman. In dreamless sleep, a person is utterly out of touch with his or her outer *persona*—a Latin word that means "mask"—and fully one with one's deepest self. Because the brain has utterly ceased to function, a person retains no memory of this kind of sleep, but it is considered the true life of the soul, the most real and only permanent part of oneself that will not be freed until that person is "dead" to this sunlit life (either literally or figuratively) and off the wheel of repeated birth

(punarjanman), and worse, repeated death (punarmrityu). Such, briefly, is the Hindu conception.

Because of the analogy with death, the state of sleep often functions as more than a mere symbol or analogy of death but as an activity that requires participation, even action, on the part of the sleeper to understand fundamental things about life and death. Especially in Western religions, instruction during dreams can help dreamers improve their lives because an immoral life leads to eternal damnation or simply extinction (unlike in Hinduism and Buddhism, in which karma rectifies things over much time and many births). The Book of Job (33:15–18) mentions the importance of dreams:

In dreams, in visions of the night,
When deepest sleep falls upon men,
While they sleep on their beds,
God makes them listen,
and his correction strikes them with terror.
*To turn a man from reckless conduct,
to check the pride of mortal man,*
at the edge of the pit he holds him back alive,
and stops him from crossing the river of death.
(emphasis added)

Sleep also allows the dreamer to gain hidden knowledge, some of which may be useful in the world and some of which is reserved for initiates and those who prepare to participate in the mysteries of God. Very often the dreamer gains a vision of what is to come in the afterlife, and often it is very good. In 2 Corinthians 12:1–5, Paul writes:

I am obliged to boast. It does no good; but I shall go on to tell of visions and revelations granted by the Lord. I know a Christian man who fourteen years ago (whether in the body or out of it, I do not know—God knows) was caught up *as far as the third heaven.* And I know that this same man (whether in the body or out of it, I do not know—God knows) was caught up into paradise, and *heard words so secret that human lips may not repeat them.*
(emphasis added)

Paul may not have been able to share the secret words, but he could share with Christians the ancient Hebrew and ultimately Babylonian map of the world with its seven heavens and seven hells. Many modern near-death experiences are similarly positive, showing heavens waiting for humans after death.

Jewish tradition also records the connection between sleep and death, and many Jewish stories describe the dead coming to the living in dreams, either to teach a lesson, request a favor, or warn the living. The collection called the *Mimekor Yisrael* reports:

A well-known Hasid who used to live in an inn near the city of Lubavitch used to tell how one day was the anniversary of his mother's death, and he studied the Mishnah texts that night for the ascent of her soul. While he studied, he fell asleep and heard a voice calling him by name from outside. He went out at once and saw two dead people standing there in white garments. One of them he recognized as his mother. He did not recognize the other, but she was his mother's mother. His mother told him: "My son, we have come to inform you that there have been great charges brought against you in the court on high, and they have sentenced you to death. All our family pleaded for you but it has not helped. Therefore, my son, see what you must do about it." His grandmother said, "The only remedy for him is to go to the holy rabbi of Lubavitch, for he is held in very high esteem on high. When his name is mentioned in the upper world the whole court trembles." And after they had finished speaking, they vanished.

The Hasid went home and sat wondering until daylight. Then he went to the rabbi of Lubavitch at once and told him the whole story. The holy rabbi was silent for quite a long while, then he said, "Have no fear, you will not die." He asked him whether it had been the practice of the Hasid to visit his father Rabbi Schnoeur Zalman. "Yes," said the other, "I was in his holy presence several times."

Then the rabbi asked, "Have you carried out the *tikkun* that he gave you?" And the Hasid remembered that in the course of time he had become ill and had been unable to carry out all the fasts that he had been commanded to keep.

"See to it," the rabbi said, "that you keep all the fasts as he instructed you, and you will live for full term and have nothing to worry about." With the aid of His Blessed Name he completed the tikkun and remained alive and, furthermore, his name and fame and fortune all increased. (Gorion pp. 1011–1012)

References

Gorion, Micha Joseph Bin. *Mimekor Yisrael*. Vol. 2. Trans. I. M. Lask. Tel Aviv: n.p., 1938–1940.

Hesiod. Works and Days *and* Theogony. Trans. Stanley Lombardo. Indianapolis: Hackett Publishing, 1993.

Smith, Jane I. "Concourse between the Living and the Dead in Islamic Eschatological Literature." *History of Religions* 19, no. 3 (1980).

Zandee, Jan. *Death as an Enemy according to Ancient Egyptian Conceptions*. New York: Arno Press, 1977.

SOTOBA
See Stūpa.

SOUL

The word *soul* is one of the most difficult in the English language because of its many different meanings. Understanding what the word means in English is hard enough, but the problem is compounded when the ambiguous word *soul* is forced to translate complex ideas from around the world.

In English the word *soul* is often used to indicate one's sense of oneself at the deepest level, identity, or true self; often the word is also used to represent the part of oneself—whether within or beyond the body—that one dares to hope will survive the physical trauma and decay of death. But the *Oxford English Dictionary*, the most scholarly and authoritative dictionary of English, demonstrates how complex such notions are. The word *soul* dates back to the early centuries of the common era and is found in the seventh-century epic poem *Beowulf* as *sawol*. The *Oxford English Dictionary* lists many meanings, only a selection of which can be provided here:

1. The principle of life in man or animals; animate existence
2. The principle of thought and action in man, commonly regarded as an entity distinct from the body; the spiritual part of man in contrast to the purely physical
3. The seat of the emotions, feelings or sentiments . . .
8. The essential, fundamental, or animating part, element or feature of something
9. The spiritual part of man considered in its moral aspect or in relation to God and His precepts
10. The spiritual part of man regarded as surviving after death and as susceptible to happiness or misery in a future state . . .
12. The disembodied spirit of a deceased person, regarded as a separate entity and as invested with some amount of form and personality

Clearly, the same word can refer to many various invisible aspects of a living person as well as the eternal identity or even the ghost of the deceased. In modern times the word *soul* often denotes no particular entity at all but merely the physical life of the body, which perishes at death. But such materialistic thinking, brought on by Western scientific skepticism, is very uncommon among the world's traditional cultures. Indeed, creation stories from around the globe demonstrate that not only is the soul conceived of as quite distinct from the body, with an "inner" life of its own, but that the soul itself nearly always has distinct parts or aspects that separate after death and continue on to different destinies.

Most cultures believe that the soul and body are

distinct because they were originally made of different substances. In the creation story in the Bible (Genesis 2:7), God formed Adam's body out of clay, but Adam was not *alive* until God breathed into his nostrils "the breath of life" (in Hebrew, *nephesh*). What is most remarkable about this creation story is that variations of it occur widely all over the world, even among isolated tribes who are very unlikely to have been influenced by the Hebrew tradition in the distant past when each of their creation stories came into being. For example, among the Arctic Eurasians, the soul and body are made by different gods, the body usually of clay and the soul out of snow or the breath of a god. Australian aborigines believe that the god Pundjel, the creator, modeled human beings out of clay. Then he lay down on them and breathed into their mouths, nostrils, and navels, and then they stirred. The Bagobos of southeastern Mindanao teach that the creator god took two lumps of earth and spat on them to make a man and a woman. The Toradjas of Sulawesi, Indonesia, say that humans were made by the god iKombengi out of wood; then the god iLai went to heaven to bring eternal breath for man and woman, but in the meantime common wind animated them, thus making humankind mortal. The Maoris of New Zealand believe that Tiki, the creator god, took red clay, kneaded it with his own blood, made a human figure, and then breathed into its mouth and nostrils. The Inuit of Alaska tell that a spirit made a clay man, stood him on the shore to dry, and then breathed into him. In Africa, too, soul and body were thought to have different origins: the Ewe believe that the human body was originally made of potter's clay, but the soul comes from the "heavenly land of souls," whereas the Songe tribe teaches that humankind is made of earth but gets life from God's saliva. Meanwhile, the Natchez tribe of Native Americans (from Louisiana) believe that the creator took clay into his hands, mixed with the sweat of his own body, and kneaded it into a lump into which he breathed.

Clearly then, around the globe, traditional peoples (i.e., those who are unaffected by modern philosophical materialism) believe that the body and soul are distinct in origin, and therefore after death the body returns to its origin, and the soul is "liberated" from its sheath and can wander about (or under) the Earth, join the ancestors, cross over the great waters, or proceed "upward" to some sort of heaven. Beliefs as to what happens to the soul after death are very complex because notions about what entity or entities constitute the "real" person are often vague and confused in cultures around the world, just as ideas about the meaning of the world *soul* are vague and confused in English. But a cross-cultural study of ideas about the soul (meaning the inner nature or natures of a human being) reveals something very interesting indeed: almost every culture has a concep-

tion of at least a dual soul, even though the two are often confused, particularly upon the arrival of an organized dogmatic religion like Christianity.

Even when they are not named separately, the symbolism and folklore of the soul around the world clearly reveals this duality in conception and function. There is generally a higher soul or higher life essence connected with the heart and breathing, which departs to the land of the blest or the land of the ancestors (if deserving). And there is always a lower soul, which may be termed a "shadow" soul or a "body" soul (perhaps what the New Age traditions refer to as the "astral" soul), which is connected with the physical life of the body. It is this lower soul, very much like a shadow or reflection of the physical body, which hangs around the corpse and has the potential to haunt and harm the living.

Many languages use the same word for soul, shadow, reflection, and even photograph (for example, in the Tungusic language family, the Mordvins, the Kiwai Papuans of New Guinea, and many others) because the lower soul is almost universally conceived of as the duplicate image of the physical body, a "double" (hence one German term for a ghost, *Doppelgänger,* means "double-goer.") Yet, even though it is closely connected to the physical body, the lower soul is in fact incorporeal and thus often able to change shape, fly, appear in dreams, and so on. When the soul of the deceased appears to the living, it may in theory come in almost any shape (for example, any number of animal or bird forms, bees, and even butterflies), but in the vast majority of cases the lower soul appears in the exact likeness of the deceased during life, even if the corpse has been disfigured or indeed cremated. In Book 11 of *The Odyssey*, when Odysseus sails down into Hades, it is clear that the images of the dead appear just as they did while alive but frozen, apparently, at their last moment of life. Odysseus says:

> When I had prayed sufficiently to the dead, I cut the throats of the two sheep and let the blood run into the trench, whereupon the ghosts came tromping up from Erebus—brides, young bachelors, old men worn out with toil, maids who had been crossed in love, and brave men who had been killed in battle, with their armor still smirched with blood; they came from every quarter and flitted round the trench with a strange kind of screaming sound that made me turn pale with fear. (Butler, trans.)

It is clear that these apparitions are merely images or shades of the deceased, but they appear to replicate exactly the physical body at the moment of death, including clothing and blood.

Because the soul is thought to take form in the image

Figure incarcerated in tomb (see circle), absorbing the black crow (symbolizing death), with soul and spirit leaving (two boy-headed birds). 1624. Courtesy of Anne Ronan Picture Library.

of the body, it is related to or even identified with projections of the physical body in water, mirrors, polished metal, or shadows. For this reason many tribal peoples dislike having their pictures taken because it detracts from, wounds, or even captures the soul, which is in its essence an image. In much of medieval Europe mirrors had an important relationship with the soul: it was many years' bad luck—even potentially lethal—to break a mirror because it "injured" one's reflection and thus one's soul. Similarly, throughout medieval Europe mirrors were turned to face the wall after a death in the house because, like water, they might catch a reflection of the dead, radiating out that image or essence to the living and spreading death like an infection. But mirrors are apparently dangerous to the sick as well: among Bombay Muslims all mirrors in the house should be covered during an illness lest the patient look within and his or her soul be absorbed. In a similar "reflective" way, the gaze of the dead is dangerous to the living, and around the world the eyes of the dead must be closed after death, probably because of the reflective property of the eyes: looking into the eyes of the dead, one may see one's own tiny image and thus see oneself in the dead, which is surely inauspicious.

Like a mirror, water is both a barrier and a danger to the lower soul. Apparently the lower soul is by nature hydrotropic—that is, involuntarily drawn toward water—because of the soul's nature as a reflected image of the body. Since water reflects, it may "capture" the soul and trap or "drown" it, preventing the dead from

continuing on their afterlife journey. For this reason, in many cultures standing water in the house of the recently dead must either be covered or poured out. But water also forms a useful barrier between the living and the dead. In many funeral ceremonies, most noticeably in Hindu rites, water is poured across the path when the mourners leave the gravesite after the burial, preventing the lower soul of the deceased from following. Among the Celts, Scandinavians, Greeks, Melanesians, and many other maritime cultures, the land of the dead was thought to be an island over a great water. The deceased had to be ferried there by boat (for example, by the ancient Greek figure Charon) and once there could not return.

As an image, the lower soul is also closely tied to sleeping and especially dreaming. In many cultures it is thought that in sleep the soul travels about, receiving instruction or visiting friends and family. It is unwise to wake a sleeping person too rapidly, for the soul may not have time to return from its travels, and the person will die. Likewise, after death, the soul continues this dream-like function but is able to travel to the dreams of the living. Thus it is an extremely common phenomenon around the world for the living and dead to communicate in dreams (see SLEEP). In addition, the undead are known to haunt people in their dreams at least as often as in waking life, for the dream state is a liminal realm between life and death. One example is the Slavic undead creature called the *mora,* which sends slumber to unsuspecting persons and then enters their dreams, causing terrible nightmares, choking them, and sucking their blood. In Russia before the Bolshevik revolution, children were instructed not to look into mirrors before bed because they would suffer bad dreams, and in Hungary everyone had to observe this rule.

In another aspect of its nature as an image, the lower soul is also frequently likened to the shadow of the body; sometimes the two are even considered as one and the same thing. In Nigeria the shadow cast by a living person is said to be the shape of his soul but compressed for the time being into a small space. On the Amboyna and Uliasse Islands (in the equatorial region), people feared to go out of their houses at noon, for having no shadow they might lose their soul. On the Malay Peninsula one may not bury a body at noon for the same reason: short shadows equals short lives, particularly where a recent death is concerned. Among the Javanese and Malaysians, food that has been touched by the shadow of another must not be eaten, lest the soul's substance be consumed. Likewise in Malaysia, according to folklorist Maria Leach, writing in the 1970s, "the soul must not fall on graves, trees or other objects inhabited by spirits which might consume the shadow and thus cause death." In Romania the shadow of a person is traced onto the foundation of a building to make sure that it will be steady; this is almost certainly the remnant of a custom in the distant past when humans were sacrificed so that their souls would enter into and protect the building. Leach adds that "passersby are warned not to come near a house while it is being built lest their shadows be caught and they die." In a similar line of thinking, in Poland folklore has it that murderers may be recognized because they have no shadow (i.e., they have no soul, having lost it in committing heinous crimes). In India one must avoid stepping on the shadow of someone else, particularly the head.

It is, then, almost universally the case that the lower soul is deeply connected to the physical body, and the lower soul has the most trouble severing its connection to this plane of existence. The higher soul (to be discussed in a moment) is like breath or fire and quickly goes on to join the ancestors or gods; it is the lower, shadowlike soul that may cause trouble as a ghost or undead being after the body has died. After death, the physical body, lower soul, and higher soul separate, and the lower soul is left without full mind or conscience—for this departed with the higher soul. Robbed of its higher nature, the lower soul embodies all of the unrestrained passions and desires of the deceased but remains attached to its old body and tends to hover around it or places it stayed in life—alternating (or bilocating) between the graveyard and the family home and quite frequently causing difficulties for the surviving friends and family. Childlike, the lower soul becomes angry at the slightest provocation and must be propitiated.

In time, however, the total and final decomposition of the corpse finally frees or destroys the lower soul or causes it to be absorbed, though in some cultures this "liberation" occurs ritually before complete dissolution of the body. In modern Greece the time between burial and ritual safety is forty days, whereas for most cultures the point of safety is not reached until every last bit of flesh has fallen off the bones. Some peoples, like the Jews, wait until nature takes its course over several years. They then disinter and gather up the now "purified" bones to place them in a family sepulcher; the authority for this is found in the Hebrew Bible, where the white bones of various patriarchs are each in turn said to be "gathered unto their fathers." The Zoroastrians and Tibetans speed this process along by exposing the corpse to predators and the elements in the wilderness; Indians and others cremate; and the fastest method of all, practiced by the Caribs, is to take the flesh off the corpse by hand. In any case, each culture has specific funerary rituals for pacifying the danger posed by the fresh corpse and the newly dead lower soul and raising the dead to the status of a revered ancestor.

So far this entry has examined only the lower soul, but in many cultures the body is distinguished from not

one but two souls, both a lower and a higher soul. Traces of a belief in two (or even more) distinct souls for each person are clearly visible from even a cursory glance at world traditions. For instance, Paul, the founder of organized Christianity, closes his first letter to the Thessalonians with these words (1 Thessalonians. 5:23): "May God himself, the God of peace, make you holy in every part, and keep you sound in spirit, soul, and body, without fault when our Lord Jesus Christ comes!" Few Christians today have ever given thought to the difference between "spirit" and "soul," though the words in the Greek original are strikingly distinct, namely *pneuma* (spirit, breath) and *psyche* (mind, soul).

Belief in a second, higher soul was commonplace in the ancient world and among believers in non-Western traditions (though even there, as may be seen with Paul, a few traces remain). Most important, this higher soul is almost never given a particular shape or conceived as an image of the body; rather it is immaterial and shapeless, compared to breath, wind, light, fire, heat, a spark, or a star. It is the "higher" soul in the sense that it usually represents the moral nature, the intellectual, the spiritual, the more "human" part of the human; the other kind of soul is more animal, associated with passions and desires and with darkness, earth, blood, bone, the shadow, and danger.

The Romans used the word *animus* (breath or wind) to refer to the higher nature, the "animating" spirit that actually gives life. In Poland the soul is breath or more condensed as a puff of fog. Among the Lapps, at death the higher soul, the "breath soul" leaves for higher realms, but the "free shadow soul" remains behind animating the dead body. Commonly, the breath soul leaves through mouth or nostrils. In Russia the wind of the steppe blowing over the body may cause vampirism because the wind may "reanimate" the corpse. The Arctic tribe known as the Koryak believe in two souls, one of which goes up to the sky and the other to the Underworld. Likewise, the Buryat have bjeje, the body; amin, the breath soul; and sunjesun, the high soul. Among Lapps prior to the arrival of Christianity, there were two souls: the breath spirit (jieG'Ga) situated in or near the heart literally gave "life" and departed (Finnish: hengenlähtö) through the mouth or nose upon death. (In German this spirit is called *atem*, literally "breath" or "breathing.") The other soul was the "shadow soul," which may leave the body during sleep and remains near the body during the period just after death. The same higher soul idea surfaces with the Scandinavian word *fylgie*.

Not in Europe alone but around the world the distinction between the two souls is clear, as Table 1 suggests. Most tribes in Africa, as well as most Native American and Australian aboriginal tribes, also have distinct words for the "shadow" or "body" soul and the

Table 1 Words for Higher and Lower Souls

Tradition	Lower Soul (body double)	Higher Soul (akin to light)
1. Arctic peoples	Orrt, uvi-rit, wuyil, etc.	Lul, lol, lil, tetkeyun, etc.
2. Roman	Manes/lares	Anima/animus
3. Early Christian	Soul	Spirit
4. Hebrew	Nephesh	Ru'ach
5. Muslim	Nafs	Ruh
6. Ancient Egyptian	Akh and ka	Ba and ab
7. Ancient Greek	Psyche and eidolon	Pneuma
8. Persian	Urvan	Fravashi
9. Hindu	Linga sharīra	Manas and ātman
10. Chinese	P'o (yin)	Hun (yang)

higher "breath" or "light" soul. (Some cultures even have conceptions of three or more souls, including ancient Egyptian and modern Hindu cultures, not to mention the very complex conception of the individual held by Buddhists—for details, see the relevant entries on Buddhist, Chinese, Egyptian, and Hindu souls.)

What is most interesting about the belief in two souls is that in most cultures, these two souls experience different afterlife destinies. After death the higher soul is released into a realm of light and becomes an ancestor or joins the gods or the divine, perhaps after a time reincarnating (as in Africa, India, China, and elsewhere). But the lower soul is tied to the body for a time, and even after its "release" it is earthbound, thus posing a danger to survivors: hence the great variety of protective rituals to deal with the recently dead. The lower soul, if not carefully and respectfully treated, may become undead (if the body is intact) or an angry ghost (if bodiless). This important distinction between the two souls explains how the living can conceive of the dead as existing simultaneously at the burial site (as the dead body) and in the family home (as a lower soul, possibly dangerous) and yet again as a benevolent ancestor, saint, or god (as a higher soul). Few religious believers in any tradition may be able to explain such diverse conceptions coherently, but the important point is that conceiving of the dead as existing in more than one place simultaneously is not inherently contradictory but grounded in a very widespread and ancient tradition.

References

Homer. *The Odyssey*. Trans. Samuel Butler. New York: Barnes and Nobles, 1993.

Leach, Maria, ed. *Standard Dictionary of Folklore, Mythology and Legend*. New York: Funk and Wagnalls, 1972.

Simpson, J. A., and E. S. C. Weiner, eds. *The Oxford English Dictionary*. Oxford: Clarendon Press, 1989.

Storå, Nils. *Burial Customs of the Skolt Lapps*. FF Communications no. 210. Helsinki: Suomalainen Tiedeakatemia, 1971.

SOUL, BUDDHIST

From its inception Buddhism has taken a unique position among world religions regarding the soul. Buddhism admits many unseen energies and aspects to human nature, many of which survive bodily death, and even names and describes these various "parts" of the soul. But it denies any unchanging essence in human nature (see ĀTMAN). This belief is all the more interesting, since like Hinduism, Buddhism teaches reincarnation and the transmission of sin and merit (collectively called *karma*) from life to life.

It is most important to recognize that Buddhist teachings were not designed to answer philosophical or speculative questions. Buddhism was first and foremost designed to be a vehicle of salvation for suffering beings, and its teachings focus on how to reduce suffering and attain salvation, or nirvāṇa, while avoiding the temptation to waste time on philosophy and verbiage that does not tend toward salvation. Although over the centuries Buddhism developed many doctrines regarding the nature of the universe and the soul, it is by nature an experiential system, and its descriptions of the soul and the world around it are provisional, designed to aid meditative experience, and not intended as absolute realities.

One of the most general Buddhist terms for the human soul is *nāmarūpa*, or "mind-body." In the mind-body duality, neither exists independently. The mind (or nāma, including intellect, emotion, and experiences) is shaped by the sensations and experience of the body (i.e., rūpa, which includes not merely physical matter but vital energy currents and other subtle natures). Likewise, the body (with its subtle energy complex) is shaped and directed by the mind. This teaching helps the Buddhist practitioner watch the body and mind interact, analyze thought patterns and moral behavior, and realize that neither mind nor body is "I." There is no essence, no eternal "thing" that can be called "me," for the nāmarūpa is constantly changing and growing older

On No-Self

"What do you think, O monks; is the body static or subject to growth, old age, and death?"

"The body is subject to growth, old age, and death, Lord."

"And is that which is subject to growth, old age and death—painful or pleasant?"

"Painful, Lord."

"Is it appropriate to think of what is subject to growth, old age, and death, what is painful and impermanent—as "mine," as "I," as "myself"?

"Certainly not, Lord."

"What do you think, O monks; is sensation [vedanā] . . . is perception [saññā] . . . are mental deposits [sankhārā] . . . is consciousness [viññāna] . . . static or subject to growth, old age and death? [and so on, as above with the body]

"Therefore the body, past, future or present, subjective or objective, outer or inner, low or exalted, whether near or far, is to be perceived by one who clearly and rightly understands as: "This body is not 'mine,' it is not 'I,' I am without 'self.'"

"[Just so with] sensation [vedanā] . . . perception [saññā] . . . mental deposits [sankhārā] . . . consciousness [viññāna]. This consciousness is not 'mine,' it is not 'I,' I am without 'self.'"

"Comprehending this, the noble disciple turns away from the body, from the sensations, from perceptions, from the mental tendencies and conditions, from consciousness. Being thus detached, he is free from desire-attachment; being free from desire-attachment he is liberated, and he experiences the freedom of liberation [nirvāna]. For he knows that for him there will be no rebirth, that the holy life has reached its culmination, and has accomplished that which he set out to accomplish; he is free."

Adapted from Humphreys (1961, p. 78).

3. Saññā, or perceptions (both physical observations and concepts)
4. Sankhārā, or mental deposits, that is, deep tendencies that shape experience and consciousness
5. Viññāna, or stream of consciousness

These five aspects of human nature are called *skandhas,* or "heaps" of energy, because Buddhism sees them as merely accumulated piles of physical and psychological material: human beings pile them up in life after life, and they constantly change, forming a "stream of experience" but again no permanent essence. No one of these skandhas is the "self," and all five, mutually affecting each other in each moment of life, survive death and (eventually) produce a new physical life. Again, the Buddhist meditator is supposed to learn detachment by observing him- or her-"self" and seeing it work in these five interrelated ways.

A third way in which Buddhism describes the mind-body complex involves explaining how consciousness arises and how it too is devoid of any permanent nature. In this teaching, twelve "gateways" (āyatanas) of experience are examined. These gateways pair the sense organs with their corresponding sense objects:

1. The power of sight paired with physical forms
2. The power of hearing paired with sounds
3. The power of smell paired with smells
4. The power of taste paired with tastes
5. The power of touch paired with tangible objects
6. The power of thought paired with concepts

These twelve "gateways" produce the experiences of sight, sound, smell, taste, touch, and thought in the human stream of consciousness; but as quickly as each experience arises in the stream of consciousness, it is replaced by others. This whirl of sensation and thought gives rise to the illusion of a permanent, lasting self or soul, but, according to Buddhism, this perception is merely samsāra, or "whirling experience," which produces grasping, clinging, attachment, and inevitable loss, resulting in suffering. After death, one is merely reborn again to continue whirling and suffering endlessly—unless the cords binding one to delusion and craving are cut.

To explain how one can ultimately escape from the endless experience, craving, and suffering produced by the mind-body complex, however, is not easy; nor is it easy to explain how the elements making up the mind-body complex can be transmitted from life to life. Early Buddhism relied rigidly on the previous descriptions and merely explained that when a person experienced physical death, each mind-body element produced "causes" that led to new elements arising upon rebirth:

(and, it is hoped, wiser). This teaching is supposed to lead to detachment and hence a reduction in suffering.

Another, better known word for "soul" in Buddhism is *pañcakkandha* or "the five heaps" in Pali (ancient Indian scriptural language). Here the mind-body complex is separated into five (pañca) different "collections" or "heaps" (skandha) that interact to produce the human personality. In brief, the five heaps are as follows:

1. Rūpa, or (again) the body and subtle vital energies
2. Vedanā, or feelings and sensations (pleasant, unpleasant, and indifferent)

a new body (rūpa), new sensation (vedanā), new perception (saññā), new mental deposits (sankhāra), and new consciousness (viññāna). As a result, when a person dies, his or her energies are "thrown off," only to coagulate after a time into new energies in a new body. So the person being reborn is directly related to the person who recently died, but the two persons are neither exactly the same nor completely different. This view is not very surprising, however, for Buddhism holds the same attitude toward people when they are alive: because new sensations produce rapidly changing experiences, a person is never exactly the same from second to second. Salvation is simply and mysteriously explained as "cessation" of impure experiences.

However, some later Buddhist groups felt dissatisfied with this simple explanation and went further in describing the inner workings of human consciousness. In addition to the six kinds of momentary consciousnesses already described (sight, sound, smell, taste, touch, and thought) brought about by the āyatanas, a major school in Buddhism called "Mind-Only" (originating in India around the third century C.E. and spreading to Tibet and China) proposed two more kinds of consciousness: "tainted" (klishta-manas) and "storehouse" (ālaya-vijñāna). "Tainted" mind is the layer of consciousness behind momentary sensations and thoughts that unifies experiences and imagines that there is a single "self." "Storehouse" consciousness is the deepest level of human experience, which "stores" the energies created by sensations and thoughts as seeds (bīja). These daily energies "ripen," each in its own time, and reemerge as karma, producing happiness or sadness later. The "storehouse" consciousness passes from life to life—like everything else it is always changing but at a slower rate; thus it is mistaken by "tainted" consciousness for a "soul." In this way the "Mind-Only" school of Buddhism felt it more precisely explained the human *feeling* of "self" (a feeling contradicted by dogma) as the psychic process of rebirth.

Salvation still proved difficult to explain, however, for how can consciousness that is momentary, tainted, or full of karma-seeds be made into something pure, eternal, and nonchanging, that is, the experience of nirvāna? Here the Mind-Only school experienced a disagreement. One group, led by the teacher Paramārtha in China (sixth century C.E.), taught a ninth type of consciousness called *immaculate consciousness* (amala-vijñāna), which is always present, shining in its own nature, but covered by the previously mentioned impurities. When the impurities are gradually wiped away by meditation and other Buddhist practices, the "immaculate consciousness" emerges, and one is "saved." Another group led by the teacher Hsüan-tsang (602–664 C.E.) in China, disagreed, stating that there is no "ninth" consciousness; rather the "storehouse" con-

sciousness is itself eternal and when emptied of karma seeds transforms permanently into a pure and transcendent nature. Another similar explanation for salvation popular in Tibet and China revolved around the idea that all beings already possess the nature of the perfectly enlightened Buddha (tathāgata-garbha) within them and that salvation consists not in seeking something new but uncovering what is already there in our innermost being. Both the Mind-Only schools and the tathāgata-garbha school of Buddhism have been accused of smuggling a "self" concept into Buddhism, which originally taught no permanent self.

Because of differences in teachings about the soul and about how salvation is achieved, modern Buddhists hold quite different views of what becomes of consciousness after death. Many schools of Buddhism, particularly the popular Buddhism of the masses, believe quite literally in rebirth in various heavens, hells, or animal realms following physical death. (The various realms of Buddhist rebirth are explained in the entry on BHAVA-CHAKRA.) Theravāda Buddhism, dominant in Sri Lanka, Thailand, and Burma, teaches that only by good deeds and meditation in this life can one avoid a gloomy fate after death. Pure Land Buddhism, dominant in China, Japan, and Korea, teaches that by faith in a Buddha figure, a person may be saved from his or her evil deeds and brought to a pure realm of beauty and happiness after death. All the Tibetan Buddhist schools of thought agree that immediately after death, the deceased must pass through the intense condition known as "the between" (bardo) before being reborn in a new body. Different Buddhist schools emphasize charity, prayer, recitation, visualization, study of Scriptures, or homage to ancestors for happy rebirth. All Buddhists can agree on one thing, however: rebirth in any realm after death is temporary until one achieves nirvāna. Without liberation, one is liable to be born again and again and again, continuing the whirl of experience, craving, and suffering.

See also BARDO; BHAVA-CHAKRA; BOOK OF THE DEAD, TIBETAN; NARAKA; NIRMĀNAKĀYA; NIRVĀNA; PURE LAND; REINCARNATION, EASTERN.

References

Collins, Steven. *Selfless Persons: Imagery and Thought in Theravāda Buddhism*. Cambridge: Cambridge University Press, 1982.

Griffiths, Paul J. *On Being Mindless*. La Salle, IL: Open Court, 1986.

Humphreys, Christmas. *The Wisdom of Buddhism*. New York: Random House, 1961.

Kalupahana, David J. *The Principles of Buddhist Psychology*. Albany: SUNY Press, 1987.

Kloetzli, Randy. *Buddhist Cosmology: From Single World System to Pure Land*. Delhi: Motilal Banardsidass, 1983.

Stcherbatsky, Th. *The Central Conception of Buddhism*. 1922. Reprint, Delhi: Motilal Banarsidass, 1994.

Williams, Paul. *Mahāyāna Buddhism: The Doctrinal Foundations*. London: Routledge, 1989.

SOUL, CHINESE

After Buddhism was assimilated by Chinese culture (roughly during the second to sixth centuries C.E.), the Indian Buddhist view of the soul became the "official" doctrine in Buddhist circles. But ancient China had considered the nature of life, death, and the soul for long centuries before Buddhism arrived.

For the Confucians, humans formed but a link in the chain of beings from inorganic material to heaven: the human soul is but one grade among many. Confucius, or K'ung Fu-tzu (552–479 B.C.E.), laid out the place of humans in relation to each other and heaven, but later Chinese commentators elaborated Confucian teaching on the souls of all things. Hsün Ching (third century B.C.E.) placed humankind at the pinnacle of nature's soul energies, incorporating all "below" them in rank.

> Water and fire have subtle [energy] (ch'i) but not life (seng). Plants and trees have life (seng) but not perception (chih); birds and animals have perception (chih) but not a sense of justice (i). Man has spirit, life, and perception, and in addition the sense of justice; therefore he is the noblest of earthly beings. (Needham, trans.)

Later commentators like Wang Khuei (fourteenth century) took this hierarchy of "souls" even further, but still human beings incorporate all the energies of the universe and thus have tremendous potential in the Confucian view.

For the Taoists, the body and the inner nature of humans were not radically different: the body with its energy and the subtle inner energies of the human constitution formed a single continuous system. Ultimately, all manifest things in the universe result from the action of two cosmic energies, yin and yang, and it is easiest to understand the energies that make up humanity as a microcosm (small world) that in many ways exactly replicates the energies of the macrocosm (larger universe).

This "law of correspondence" between the great universe and the little world of each human being seems to date from the earliest period of Chinese history. But judging from the available evidence, in earlier times the enumeration of energies was simpler. Besides the body, human beings were thought to have two basic energies or soul aspects (ch'i) in ancient China. One kind of energy, the hun-soul, corresponded to the bright, expansive, masculine, active universal energy called *yang*. At death, the human hun-soul was thought to return to its native element, heaven, but was able to visit the ancestral tablet (kept in the home or the temple) regularly to receive offerings, news, and requests. The lower human soul was called *p'o,* the "bone soul" or energy, which corresponded to the cosmic yin energy—dark, contractive, feminine, receptive nature. At death, the p'o-soul also returned to its native element, Earth, and it retained a connection with the physical burial site.

This duality of energy, or yin-yang theory, is associated with the *I-Ching*, or *Book of Changes*, an extremely ancient philosophical text to which no date can be assigned. From that manual one learns that all things, even plants and stones, are penetrated by one life energy, or ch'i, although it has two aspects, expansive and contractive. Both are necessary for the creation, maintenance, and transformation of all things, and both aspects of ch'i are mutually dependent and interpenetrate each other. There is no war of opposing energies here but rather the ceaseless play of cosmic forces. Likewise, the human soul is but the temporary embodiment of natural forces, yet humans in their great complexity embody the finest aspects of these essences. The common person may know nothing of such things, but the initiate into the mysteries of nature and the human body may learn to manipulate natural forces, become invisible, fly, know the future, and even transcend death, becoming an immortal. Much of Chinese religious history may be summed up as the pursuit of physical immortality, either through esoteric alchemy, breath control and spiritual meditation, or worship of ancestors and divine forces.

After the beginning of the common era, a movement called philosophical Taoism gained in strength and publicly introduced a more complex system detailing human energies. In a manual dated to circa seventh century C.E., called *Oral Instructions for Breathing Exercises* (T'ai-ch'ing fu-ch'i k'ou-chüeh, quoted in Schipper, pp. 34–35), we read that the single, whole tao (cosmic force) becomes manifested in thousands of ways in the human being. We also see that the number of "souls" has crept up to ten (three hun-souls and no less than seven p'o-souls):

> Five viscera and six receptacles,
> seven directors and nine palaces,
> skin and veins,
> muscles, bone, marrow, and brains,
> nine openings to watch and protect,
> twelve abodes for the gods,
> on the left three hun,
> on the right the seven p'o,
> three levels of the body,
> with eight effulgences each,
> making up twenty-four gods,
> one thousand two hundred projections,
> twelve thousand vibrations,
> three hundred sixty articulations,
> and eighty-four thousand pores.

Here the human body has become the abode of almost countless gods, which is merely a symbolic way of describing the various energies and potencies locked in human consciousness.

In popular thought, however, the soul energies are understood less as secret embodiments of cosmic energy and more as "entities" that survive after death in various heavenly palaces (often on Earth) or Underworlds associated with spiritual mountains. In very early times the p'o-soul was thought to sink down to the source of water in the Earth, called the Yellow Springs, or to travel to a Dark City ruled by an Earth Lord, although there is no evidence that these souls were "judged" for their deeds there. After the advent of Buddhism, however, ethical judgment became a crucial component of the afterdeath journey. Adopting the traditional Indian Buddhist understanding that rebirth into a new form occurred forty-nine days after death, the Chinese nevertheless gave their own form to the postmortem trials. Ten Kings were known by the Chinese to judge souls in Underworld realms called *ti-yü* (Earth prisons), after which the dead would be sent on to any number of hells or heavens, each associated with a particular deity. The heaven of the Queen Mother of the West was a particularly famous heaven among Taoists, whereas Buddhists hoped for rebirth in the Pure Land of Amitābha Buddha (O-mi-t'o Fo). In general, afterlife hopes were quite diverse, and there was often no clear distinction between Taoist, Buddhist, and Confucian teachings; this is still the case today, although the reign of communism has attempted to dampen religious belief and practice.

Sometimes in China the deceased fail to journey on through the Earth prisons to their final destinations. Rather, souls of the dead may remain on Earth, harassing the living or suffering all alone. Although it is most characteristic of the earthbound (yin) soul, the p'o, to haunt places on the Earth and to cause trouble if made angry, in truth much Chinese literature makes no philosophical distinction between hun and p'o. There are many ghost and vampire tales that tell of the souls of the dead (hun or p'o) being made angry by their offspring or by their graves being disturbed. These negative spirits are of several types, but often no clear distinction is made: all are "ghosts." There are the ku-hun, or "orphaned souls," who left no descendants to make offerings to the dead or whose family neglect them; to compensate, they may accept offerings made by the community, and there are many such rites performed in China for the dead in general. Then there are the li-kuei, or "vengeful ghosts," who have been made angry by some specific acts against them or who died in a violent, sudden, or allegedly "unjust" manner. These ghosts need to be appeased through offerings or overcome by magic or exorcism.

The Wraith of Po-yu

The people of Cheng were all frightened of Po-yu, and if someone said, "Po-yu is here!" they would all run away heedless of where they went. In the second month [March], when the punishments were being decided, someone dreamed that Po-yu appeared in armor and walked around, saying, "On the day *jen-tzu* I will kill Ti, and next year, on the day *jen-yin*, I will kill Tuan." When the day *jen-tzu* arrived and Ti did actually die, the people became even more frightened; when Kung-sun Tuan died on the day *jen-yin* in the month when the states Ch'i and Yen made peace, they became absolutely terrified. In the next month, Tzu-ch'an gave appointments to Kung-sun Hsieh and to Liang Chih, the son of Po-yu, to placate the wraith. The incidents stopped. When Tzu-t'ai Shu asked Tzu-ch'an why he did this, he replied, "When ghosts have a place to return to, they do not become wraiths, and now I have given them a place to return to. . . ."

When Tzu-ch'an went to Chin, Chao Ching-tzu asked him whether it was possible that Po-yu really had become a ghost. Tzu-ch'an replied, "It is possible. When humans are born, they first develop what is called the corporeal soul. When the yang force develops, then there is the anima soul. By interacting with things their subtle energies increase, and the corporeal and anima souls strengthen. Eventually their energies intensify until they become numinous and bright. If average men or women should die violently, they are able to linger near people as malevolent wraiths. . . . Po-yu was from a family that held political power for three generations. He had access to many things, and his subtle energies were strong. He came from a great and distinguished clan. Doesn't it stand to reason that it was possible for him to become a wraith when he suffered a violent death?"

From Master Tso's Commentary on the Spring and Autumn Annals, *fifth century* B.C.E., *in Sommer (1995, pp. 25–26).*

Finally, there are the e-kuei, or "hungry ghosts" (the prets of Indian Buddhism), who have actually been reborn in this ghostly form as karmic punishment for their misdeeds. With swollen bellies and needle-thin necks, these horribly suffering spirits wander the Earth, frequenting crossroads, doorposts, and other "boundary" areas trying to assuage their hunger and thirst and sometimes taking vengeance on the living who do not perform the ritual called "Releasing [Ghosts] with Burning Mouths Ceremony" (Fang Yen-K'ou), which allows them to be fed (see FESTIVAL OF GHOSTS [CHINA]). Unlike Indian prets, these hungry ghosts are sometimes thought to live in a part of hell; high-ranking ones serve as officers and executioners of the god of death in hell (Yen-lo in Chinese, Yama in Sanskrit).

Despite all its fascination with the dead, Chinese culture has always placed a very high value on human life and especially long life. Even in bronze inscriptions from the Chou Dynasty (1122–256 B.C.E.), the character *shou* (longevity) is by far the most popular term in prayers for blessings. In Confucian tradition, immortality is attained by means of moral, cultural, and political achievements, for example, bestowing on the world a great classic of literature or serving as an upright servant of the state. In Taoist tradition, physical immortality can be gained through moral activity, diet, prayer, and inner transformation. In some sense, those who have died have failed: death is not an unavoidable fate. Yet even in death, there is the hope of transcendence, perhaps on the Eastern Isles or in the paradise of the Queen Mother of the West.

See also CROSSROADS; FUNERARY CUSTOMS, CHINESE; HELLS, BUD-DHIST; SOUL, BUDDHIST; SOUL TABLET; TEN KINGS OF HELL; TI-TSANG; YELLOW SPRINGS; YEN-LO WANG.

References

Chan, Wing-tsit, ed. and trans. *A Source Book in Chinese Philosophy*. Princeton: Princeton University Press, 1963.

Loewe, Michael. *Chinese Ideas of Life and Death*. London: Allen and Unwin, 1982.

Needham, Joseph. *Science and Civilisation in China*. Vol. 2: *History of Scientific Thought*. Cambridge: Cambridge University Press, 1962.

Schipper, Kristofer. *The Taoist Body*. Trans. Karen C. Duval. Berkeley: University of California Press, 1982.

Sommer, Deborah, ed. *Chinese Religion: An Anthology of Sources*. New York: Oxford University Press, 1995.

Thompson, Laurence G. "On the Prehistory of Hell in China." *Journal of Chinese Religions*, no. 17 (Fall 1989).

Tu, Wei-ming. *Confucian Thought: Selfhood as Creative Transformation*. Albany: SUNY Press, 1985.

Welch, Holmes. *The Practice of Chinese Buddhism, 1900–1950*. Cambridge: Harvard University Press, 1967.

Yü, Ying-Shih. "Life and Immortality in the Mind of Han China." *Harvard Journal of Asiatic Studies* 25 (1964).

SOUL, EGYPTIAN

The civilization of Egypt lasted for many thousands of years, and it is clear that over time popular religious attitudes toward the soul and the afterlife shifted. At no period, however, do we find a simple dichotomy of soul and body so widespread in later Western religion. From earliest times the Egyptians were mightily concerned with death and the afterlife, and their understanding of the nonphysical dimension of human beings was sophisticated. In Egyptian thought, no single entity can rightly be called the soul; that name belongs to an entire complex of psychic and subtle energies taken together.

Considerable disagreement exists in the academic community over how to interpret Egyptian thought on the afterlife, largely because of the scarcity of explicit texts describing the soul. No papyri survive from the Old Kingdom (c. 2600 to 2100 B.C.E.), and we must rely for the most part on coffin and pyramid inscriptions supported by what little of Egyptian myth has come down to us. It seems clear that the Egyptians believed that life continued on after death as vigorously as before but transformed. It was generally conceived that ethical living had much to do with a successful afterlife, as one text from the interior of a coffin indicates:

> One generation of men passes to another, and God, who knows characters, has hidden Himself, . . . so worship God upon his way. . . . The soul goes to the place it knows. . . . Beautify your mansion in the West, embellish your place in the necropolis with straightforwardness and just dealing; . . . more acceptable is the good character of the straightforward man than the [sacrificial] ox of the wrongdoer. . . . Provide for men, "the cattle of God," for He made heaven and earth at their desire.

But it seems a meritorious earthly life by itself did not guarantee the deceased a happy afterlife. Especially toward the New Kingdom period of Egyptian civilization (c. 1550 to 945 B.C.E.), the population became increasingly concerned with magical spells and formulas to prepare for the afterlife journey and pacify various deities who might have a complaint. With the proper spells and preparations in life, the Egyptian expected to become an akh aper, or an "equipped spirit" or "perfect spirit," after death.

Scholars disagree about Egyptian ideas of the parts of the soul and their persistence after death, and Egyptian texts disagree among themselves. Some scholars claim that the Egyptians believed in four aspects of the human soul existing after death, whereas others say six, seven, or even eight. This entry considers those parts of the deceased that are widely described in Egyptian texts and inscriptions, with the caveat that the discussion is incomplete.

The ka, or "vital force," was represented iconographically in Egyptian art as the body double of a person. If the pharaoh is depicted in some scene, perhaps conversing with the gods, an exact duplicate of him will stand nearby, often behind him. The gods too have their kas as do all living beings (people, animals, etc.), but during life the ka is an integral part of the being and cannot be separated from it. After death the ka appears to become an independent force, and the deceased must be ritually prepared to "go to the ka," at which point it will become alive again, "master of one's ka." The ka

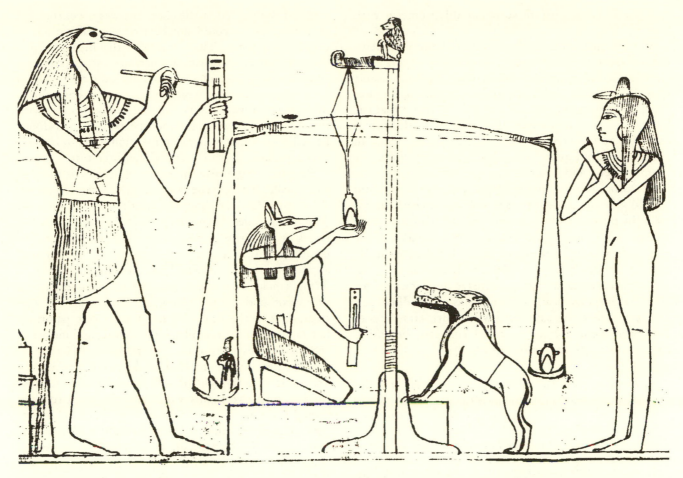

The jackal-headed god Anubis (center) weighs the heart of Princess Nesitanebtashru (right). The heart in its casket is on the right-hand pan of the balance, and the goddess of truth and righteousness on the left-hand pan. From the Greenfield Papyrus, tenth century B.C.E. *Courtesy of Anne Ronan Picture Library.*

appears to be a sort of astral body or life force, giving life while alive and protecting the deceased after death like a guardian spirit. It is the ka that emerges from a false door (stela) in the tomb to receive the offerings left by the living.

The ba was represented in hieroglyphics first as a wading bird and, later, beginning in the Eighteenth Dynasty (1300 B.C.E.), as a bird with a human head, arms, and hands. The ba may come closest to Western notions of a "soul," though this identification must be made cautiously. It represents self-consciousness, perception, and memory in the deceased, as well as his or her presence. For instance, the ba is not tied to the mummy and may leave the tomb, traveling up to the heavens or becoming present in statues, amulets, and so on. It is correct to say that the deceased is the ba, not that the deceased has a ba. Yet the ba is not unique to people but is possessed likewise by gods and animals. It is never mentioned in texts dealing with living beings but seems only to refer to the transformation of the individual after death.

The akh was represented in hieroglyphics as a bird, the crested ibis. It may be translated as "ghost" and is related to the root word for "shining" or "luminous." The akh appears to be the psychic remains of the deceased, similar to the bhūt of India or manes of Rome, and at times its actions could be malevolent. Letters have been found written to deceased persons' akhs urging them to desist from their evil ways.

Finally, the ab (or ib) was represented by the glyph for the human heart. The ab was the deepest nature of the deceased person, the seat of his or her creative power, spiritual knowledge, and courage, thus well symbolized by the heart. Egyptian texts also state that the "god who lives in human beings" dwells in the ab, though it is not clear if the word refers to a particular god using human beings as a vehicle or simply to an immortal principle or "higher self" in everyone. After death, Anubis and Thoth judge the ab and weigh it in a great scale against Ma'at (cosmic justice and order), symbolized by a feather. If the ab is lighter, it is allowed to pass on to the realm of Osiris (often associated with the sun), possibly to merge with him.

It is not clear whether the Egyptians believed in reincarnation or the transmigration of souls at any time during their long history. Many modern scholars assert that they did not, but Greek sources, including the later Neoplatonists, state that they did. It is certain that the Egyptian gods themselves were subject to death and rebirth, and cemeteries for the gods have been found in certain parts of Egypt. The well-known story of the dismemberment and resurrection of Osiris and his constant association with the cyclic journey of the sun should give the student pause. Although in early Egypt only the pharaohs were mummified and identified with the gods in their cyclic journeys, death and afterlife processes became more democratized as time passed. By the time of the collapse of the Old Kingdom (c. 2181 B.C.E.), commoners made extensive preparations for death with spells, nearly everyone was mummified, and nearly everyone was associated with Osiris and the sun. Even the names of the deceased changed, becoming hyphenated with the prefix "Osiris."

References

Allen, T. G. *The Book of the Dead, or Going Forth by Day.* Chicago: Oriental Institute of the University of Chicago, 1974.

Cerny, Jaroslav. *Ancient Egyptian Religion.* London: Hutchinson University Library, 1952.

Frankfort, Henri. *Ancient Egyptian Religion: An Interpretation.* New York: Columbia University Press, 1948.

Goedicke, H. *The Report about the Dispute of a Man with His Ba.* Baltimore: Johns Hopkins University Press, 1970.

Griffiths, J. G. *The Origins of Osiris and His Cult.* Leiden: E. J. Brill, 1980.

Morenz, Siegfried. *Egyptian Religion.* Trans. Ann E. Keep. Ithaca, NY: Cornell University Press, 1973.

Mueller, D. "An Early Egyptian Guide to the Hereafter." *Journal of Egyptian Archeology* 58 (1972).

Piankoff, A. *The Wandering of the Soul.* Princeton: Princeton University Press, 1974.

Sandman, M. "Texts from the Time of Akhenaton." *Bibliotheca Aegyptica* 8 (1938).

Spencer, A. J. *Death in Ancient Egypt.* New York: Penguin, 1982.

Zabkar, L. V. *A Study of the Ba Concept in Ancient Egyptian Texts.* Chicago: University of Chicago Press, 1968.

SOUL, GREEK

The concept of the soul in ancient Greece transformed over time. In the earliest times of which we have written records, there are several "souls" or aspects of the soul, each with its own name and function. Thymos was the emotional center of the person, where hope, courage, grief, anger, fear, and joy were located. It was thought to reside primarily in the chest and appears to have been conceived of as a material substance. The noos or nous was the mind or a thought or purpose of the mind. It too resided in the chest but was never thought of as material. It could not be struck or blown out as could the thymos. There was also the menos, which appears to have constituted a person's mental strength and also the power of the warrior. Aion referred to a person's vital energy, which is mentioned particularly in connection with the young and rarely, if ever, with the old. All of these "souls" or aspects of the self disappeared at death, or at least no mention of them is made after a person's death in early Greek literature.

But most prominent in ancient Greek writings was the psyche. The psyche was an unconscious, breathy shade that left the body at death, only to proceed directly to Hades, from which there was no escape. The Greek word *psyche* is related to the verb *psychein,* "to breathe." This meaning is appropriate for how the soul appears in the Underworld of the Homeric epics: a wispy, smoky image (eidolon) of the deceased lacking the vigor and consciousness of the person in life. Beginning in the sixth century B.C.E., vase paintings portray the soul as a small winged figure, and indeed in the *Iliad* the psyches of both Patroklos and Hector are described as "flying" to Hades (*Iliad* 16:856; 23:362). The souls were thought of as weak and unable to cross the barrier between this world and the other (usually thought of as dark water) without a guide (psychopompos), Hermes in ancient Greek thought and the ferryman Charon in Roman times. Yet even in the earliest times the psyche, for all its impotence, was clearly distinguished from the body; this idea is demonstrated by the opening lines of the *Iliad*, addressed to the Muse:

Sing, goddess, the anger of Peleus' son Achilleus
and its devastation, which put pains thousandfold
    upon the Achaians,
hurled in their multitudes to the house of Hades
    strong souls
of heroes, but gave their bodies to the delicate
    feasting
of dogs, of all birds. (Lattimore, trans.)

Once in the Underworld the soul is thought to exist only as a memory of itself, carrying out mechanically the primary activities it enjoyed during life: Orion the hunter hunts; Achilles is surrounded by his men. Yet the souls are portrayed as practically mindless, and only when Odysseus offers a blood sacrifice and places the bowls of blood before the shades do they revive and become aware enough to speak with him. If there were other ideas of the soul in early times, no record has been preserved for us.

There is some tension, however, between the concept of the soul and the idea of judgment after death, which appears from time to time in ancient Greek literature. The Furies (Erinyes) are thought to pursue and punish the souls of the dead, and in the *Odyssey* great evildoers such as Sisyphos, Tantalos, and Tityos endure eternal punishment. Surely, the mindless shades would not be punished unless it were thought that some aspect of the conscious personality remained? And what becomes of those who lived virtuous lives? Do they receive a reward in the afterlife? There are the exceptional few who, after death, go to Elysion—Menelaus, Achilles, and Diomedes. Only quite late in Greek history, however, is there clear evidence that ordinary people believed that a happy afterlife was possible.

These tensions were developed and resolved by the eschatological teachings of the mystery schools on the one hand and the rise of systematic theology/philosophy on the other. It is not clear how ancient the mystery schools were—the cult at Eleusis that achieved the most prominence claimed for itself an immense antiquity that is difficult to verify. Certainly, however, by the sixth century the mysteries had become well known and influential in Greek culture. Because the teachings were secret and reserved only for the initiates (mystes), reconstructing their beliefs poses problems. Nevertheless it seems clear that the souls of the initiates, at least, were destined for a better afterlife than the common lot in Hades, which implies that the afterdeath state was imagined as somewhat more than that of a mindless shade. We read at the end of the Eleusinian *Hymn to Demeter* (479–482) that the initiates in the mysteries become obloi (blest ones), whereas the uninitiated will fade away under the misty darkness, and an epitaph of an initiate found at Bythinia proclaims that he has traveled not to dark Acheron (in Hades) but to the "harbor of the blest." What kind of heavenly state this might be or its duration is never explicitly stated. The regular reliance in the mysteries on the myth of Persephone suggests a reincarnation theme, for this Underworld goddess lived one-half of the year in the Underworld, and one-half on the sunlit Earth, in a regular cyclic rise and fall. The same idea plays out with the death and rebirth of gods such as Zeus, suggesting that initiates somehow bonded with divinity and experienced a rebirth, though it is not clear where this rebirth might take place. Both Plato (c. 428 to 348/347 B.C.E.) and the poet Pindar (fifth century B.C.E.) state that transmigration of souls was a central doctrine in the mysteries, but they may be using the concept in an allegorical way.

The afterlife teachings of the mysteries are joined by the philosophical speculations on the soul in the Archaic and Classical periods. Pre-Socratic thinkers, such as Parmenides (born c. 515 B.C.E.) and Diogenes of Apollonia (fifth century B.C.E.), broke with the ancient poetic conception of the soul as a mindless, "gibbering shade" and saw the psyche as a superior, spiritual kind of natural element that was indestructible and gave order to the world. A small part of the great soul resided in each person where it became the source of consciousness and moral reasoning. At death the body returned to the Earth, whereas the spiritual psyche returned to the ether (Euripides, *Helena* 1014 [Guthrie]).

Living in the fourth century B.C.E., Plato built his philosophy on pre-Socratic thought but undoubtedly drew as well on the traditions of the mysteries, to which he alluded frequently. He developed the concept of an immortal soul in human beings to such a degree that he influenced all subsequent Western philosophy. According to Plato, the soul is not only divine in origin but is by nature of a higher order of reality than the body and the material world. Through its contact with eternal, spiritual ideas (eidos) the soul gains innate knowledge, which it can manifest in earthly life in the body if only it will reach up to its innate greatness, study philosophy, and summon up the memory of wisdom gained from its past lives. Rising above life and death, the soul grasps justice, goodness, and beauty and possesses true wisdom. After death, Plato tells us, those truly in love with wisdom ascend to the highest station in the universe, while in the *Republic* he says that after death, most people meet their punishment or reward and after a number of centuries are reborn in human form on Earth.

From the fourth century B.C.E. on, popular interest in the afterlife became more apparent in Greek culture, the more so as interest in the mysteries spread, including Mithraism and other Near Eastern cults. Members of the Orphic mysteries were buried with hammered gold tablets inscribed with guidance for the afterlife. There was a warning not to drink from an icy spring in the Underworld—as mentioned by Plato, this spring called Lethe would cause forgetfulness and lack of discrimination—and to pass on to the river of memory, explaining to the gods that they were children of Earth and starry night, of ancient divine ancestry, so that the gods would allow them to bypass Lethe. Belief in reincarnation became widespread, and Plato's notion of the soul as the essential, conscious aspect of humans achieved dominance.

See also ELYSION, ELYSIUM; HADES.

References

Bianchi, U. *The Greek Mysteries*. Leiden: E. J. Brill, 1976.

Bremmer, Jan. *The Early Greek Concept of the Soul*. Princeton: Princeton University Press, 1983.

Burkert, Walter. *Ancient Mystery Cults*. Cambridge: Harvard University Press, 1987.

———. *Greek Religion*. Trans. John Raffan. Cambridge: Harvard University Press, 1985.

Caird, E. *The Evolution of Theology in the Greek Philosophers*. Glasgow: J. MacLehose and Sons, 1904.

Crombie, I. M. *An Examination of Plato's Doctrines*. New York: Humanities Press, 1962.

Dietrich, B. C. *Death, Fate and the Gods*. London: University of London, Athlone Press, 1965.

Farnell, Lewis R. *Greek Hero Cults and Ideas of Immortality*. Oxford: Clarendon Press, 1921.

Guthrie, W. K. C. *History of Greek Philosophy*. 6 vols. Cambridge: Cambridge University Press, 1962–1981.

Homer. *The Odyssey*. Trans. Samuel Butler. New York: Barnes and Noble, 1993.

Lattimore, Richmond, trans. *The Iliad*. Chicago: University of Chicago Press, 1951.

More, P. E. *The Religion of Plato*. Princeton: Princeton University Press, 1921.

Plato. *The Republic*. Trans. Benjamin Jowett. New York: Random House, 1937.

SOUL, HINDU

Like other cultures that stretch back thousands of years, Hindu tradition has a complex understanding of the soul and its several parts. A funeral hymn from the Rig Veda dated to around 2000 B.C.E. shows this complexity even in the ancient period of Indian culture, for the soul of the deceased is expected to go on to the world of the fathers, yet various parts of the soul merge with the natural world:

> When you cook him perfectly, [O Agni, God of Fire],
> Then give him over to the fathers [ancestors].
> When he goes on the path that leads away the breath of life,
> Then he will be led by the will of the gods.

> May your eye go to the sun, your life's breath to the wind.
> Go to the sky or to the earth, as is your nature;
> Or go to the waters, if that is your fate.
> Take root in the plants with your limbs.
> (Rig Veda 10.16.2–3, O'Flaherty, trans.)

The "real" man goes to dwell with the ancestors in the heaven of the first man, called Yama (who later becomes the fearsome lord of death). But while in heaven, some aspect of the soul symbolized by "eye" journeys to a physical or spiritual sun, while the life energy joins the wind. Although scholars dispute whether the Vedic Scriptures taught reincarnation as long ago as 2000 B.C.E., no one disputes that these Scriptures teach that human beings have an essence, an imperishable entity that survives death. Called in ancient Sanskrit *ajobhāga* (unborn), *amartya* (undying), and other names, this immortal spirit flees the dead body like a bird made of light and goes to dwell in a radiant heaven. Later philosophical commentaries, called *Upanishads*, termed this immortal essence *ātman* and considered it identical with the absolute first principle of the universe (called *Brahman*). Realizing this truth, one becomes free from the bonds of matter and avoids rebirth.

But if Hindus thought that the "soul" or nonphysical aspects of human beings consisted of simply the imperishable principle ātman, everyone would be godlike already. Rather Hindu philosophy has conceived of the soul as a series of layers, or more exactly as sheaths (kośas) that cover up the immortal essence in people. Not only is the immortal soul weighed down with a physical body, but it also has an energy body (linga śarīra), a rational mind (manas), any number of wishes and desires, and the consequences of actions performed in any number of past lives (karma). These psycho-physiological layers are not unique to humankind but partake, each in its own way, of an aspect of the universe. Quite directly in Hindu thought, the human being in mind, body, and soul forms a microcosm (miniature universe) that corresponds in detail to the layers of the macrocosm (large universe).

One of the most important Hindu philosophical works, the Taittirīya Upaniṣad, sets out one of the classical formulations of the "soul complex" in Hinduism. There exists the supreme spirit, ātman, and five successively more subtle "layers" that cover it. In order from gross to subtle, these are as follows:

1. Annakośa, the sheath made of food (the body)
2. Prāṇakośa, the sheath made of bio-energy (as in Chinese, ch'i, the subtle body)
3. Manahkośa, the sheath made of mental energy (the mind)

4. Vijñānakośa, the sheath made of subtle mind (intuition, wisdom)
5. Ānandakośa, the sheath made of pure bliss (ātman's own radiance)

Each kośa is the superior and director of the one before it. The body is senseless without bio-energy enlivening it, but likewise prāṇa is directionless without thoughts to guide it. The ātman, most subtle and important of all, serves as the god of this little universe and is the only aspect that is considered ultimately "real," for the others change over time. Through meditation, Hinduism teaches, one is increasingly able to self-actualize the higher levels of the soul complex and thus achieve greater and greater wisdom, insight, and peace.

In Hinduism, this model of the soul's structure is considered a testable hypothesis. Different levels of the soul complex are said to come into awareness in different human states of consciousness, and so the dead can observe them going to their respective "sources" in the cosmos. For example, it is obvious enough that in waking life, human consciousness is focused in the physical body and its physical senses and experiences the material plane of the cosmos. In various dream states, however, humans live a mental life and have experiences only through a temporary dream body, made up of prāṇa (bio-energy) without strict physical limits. Here, humans are thought to exist on an energy level of the universe in transition between physical matter and the spiritual reality experienced after death. In deep, dreamless sleep, however, both mental and bodily energies sleep quiescent, while consciousness activates on the level of vijñāna, or "spiritual wisdom." This spiritual awakening each night is so far removed from waking life and brain activity that almost no impression is retained by the person passing into dream consciousness and then waking consciousness. A fourth state of consciousness, unknown in Western thought but called turīya in Sanskrit, is utterly beyond thought or language. It is said to be beyond even the bliss of deep sleep, for in this consciousness ātman is said to function on its own plane of bliss, unconscious of any sense of "self" or ego—the person is merged in union with "God."

At death, the sheaths of the soul break apart and separate, each going its own way. The body begins to decay and join the matter of the Earth, the "energy sheath" dissolves into the life energy of the Earth itself, and the essences of the mental sheath and wisdom sheath withdraw into the sheath of bliss, said to be seated in the heart center of the human being. From here, the ātman prepares to exit the body along the various energy routes that are too occult to be enumerated here. Then, depending upon one's karma and spiritual development, various afterdeath states are experienced, either hellish or heavenly, as the soul prepares for a new birth in a new form.

A Spell to Retain One Who Is Dying

If your spirit has gone to Yama the son of Vivasvan far away, we turn it back to you here to dwell and to live.

If your spirit has gone to the sky or to the earth far away, we turn it back to you here to dwell and to live.

If your spirit has gone to the four-cornered earth far away, we turn it back to you here to dwell and to live.

If your spirit has gone to the four quarters of the sky far away, we turn it back to you here to dwell and to live.

If your spirit has gone to the billowy ocean far away, we turn it back to you here to dwell and to live.

If your spirit has gone to the flowing streams of light far away, we turn it back to you here to dwell and to live.

If your spirit has gone to the waters, or to the plants, far away, we turn it back to you here to dwell and to live.

If your spirit has gone to the sun, or to the dawns far away, we turn it back to you here to dwell and to live.

If your spirit has gone to the high mountains far away, we turn it back to you here to dwell and to live.

If your spirit has gone to this whole moving universe far away, we turn it back to you here to dwell and to live.

If your spirit has gone to distances beyond the beyond, far away, we turn it back to you here to dwell and to live.

If your spirit has gone to what has been and what is to be, far away, we turn it back to you here to dwell and to live.

From the Rig Veda 10:58, translation by O'Flaherty (1981, pp. 57–58).

According to Hindu philosophy, rebirth is inexorable for all beings except those who have absolutely sundered all ties to and desires for earthly life and have achieved complete conscious union with ātman and the universal absolute, Brahman, at the time of death. Such freedom, called *mokṣa*, is ostensibly the goal of every Hindu, but in fact liberation from birth and death is said to be extremely rare and achieved only after countless lifetimes of effort. For the majority, the best that can be hoped for is a good, charitable life leading to rebirth in one of the blissful Svargas (heavens).

See also ĀTMAN; FUNERARY CUSTOMS, HINDU; NARAKA; REINCARNATION, EASTERN; SHRĀDDHA; SOUL, BUDDHIST; SVARGA; YAMA.

References

Aurobindo, Shri. *Eight Upanishads*. Pondicherry: Sri Aurobindo Ashram, 1953.

———. *Life Divine*. New York: Greystone Press, 1949.

Beidler, William. *The Vision of Self in Early Vedānta*. Delhi: Motilal Banarsidass, 1975.

Mahony, William K. "Soul: Indian Concepts." In *Encyclopedia of Religion*, ed. Mircea Eliade. New York: Macmillan, 1987.

O'Flaherty, Wendy Doniger. *The Rig Veda: An Anthology*. New York: Penguin, 1981.

Shankara. *The Brihadāranyaka Upanishad with the Commentary of Shankaracarya*. Trans. Swami Madhavananda. 2nd ed. Calcutta: Almora Advaita Asram, 1941.

Sharma, Baldev Raj. *The Concept of Ātman in the Principal Upanishads*. New Delhi: Dinesh Publications, 1972.

SOUL, JEWISH

Jewish conceptions of the soul have undergone massive change over time. To trace this development is to take in the scope of Hebrew and Jewish history from its origin to the present; to witness the successive impacts of foreign civilizations and the rise and fall of the fortunes of the state of Israel; and above all to observe Jewish people doubt, believe, and doubt again that an eternal life awaits them after death.

There is no conception of an eternal soul in the Hebrew Bible (at least, not until the Book of Daniel, dated to the second century B.C.E. or later). It is not even clear that early Hebrew religion (c. 1200 to c. 800 B.C.E.) conceived of a "soul" in anything like the terms associated with that word today. In Genesis, it is clear that when man was created by God, he was a composite of both flesh and life essence: "Jahweh God formed man of the dust of the ground; he breathed into his nostrils the breath of life, and man became a living soul" (Genesis 2:7). The phrase for "living soul" in Hebrew is *nephesh chayyah,* and it appears to be connected not only with the breath but with the blood. For this reason, Charles Guignebert suggests, Hebrews were forbidden to eat meat with the blood still in it: Genesis 9:4 states, "But the flesh with the life thereof shall ye not eat." Even today, Orthodox Jews hang slaughtered animals up until the blood has thoroughly drained from them—only then is the meat fit for consumption.

Given the identity of nephesh with breath and blood, it becomes obvious how closely related body and "soul" are: there can be no postmortem survival of the vitality alone. At physical death, at least in *early* Hebrew religion, the human being ceases to exist. The physical body decays, and the nephesh scatters (like breath) or sinks into the ground (like blood). There are various poetic references to the grave (later Underworld), Sheol, wherein the nephesh is thought to exist among the shades (rephā'im), but until the fourth to third centuries B.C.E., life after death appears to be nothing more

---

The Nature of Human Beings

Rabbi Tafdai in the name of Rabbi Aha said: The upper beings [angels] are created in the image and likeness of God, but they do not increase and multiply [procreate]. The lower beings [animals] increase and multiply, but they are not created in the image and likeness of God. So God said, "I will create man in the image and likeness of the angels, but he shall increase and multiply like the animals." And God said, "If I were to create him entirely according to the nature of the angels, he would live for ever, and never die; if I were to create him entirely according to the nature of the animals, he would die, and not live again; so behold I will create him with something of the natures of both; if he sins, he shall die, if he does not sin, he shall live."

From Genesis Rabbah, Bereshit, VIII, 11, translation by Montefiore and Loewe (1974).

---

than metaphor. Occasionally other words are used to describe the vitality of the body, for instance, ru'ach (breath, often metaphoric), neshamah (literal respiration of the body), or lêb (the heart). But until very late in Hebrew history, under the influence of Greek views of the soul's dichotomy or even trichotomy, these other Hebrew words were largely synonyms for nephesh—at least in the Orthodox literature (the Torah and Prophets) preserved by the priestly leadership.

Death was the end for the ancient Hebrew, and for this reason, the focus of a person's religious activity and his or her hopes for reward were all in this life. Wealth, many children, a long happy time on Earth—these were the blessings of God, a result of a faithful Hebrew life lived in obedience to Jahweh; after death, the dead lived on merely in the memory of their descendants. There are scattered references in the Hebrew Bible to a cult of ancestors or even worship of the dead, as when Saul consults the witch of Endor and conjures up the shade of Samuel (1 Samuel 28:7–14). This story suggests that even in ancient times Sheol was, for some Hebrews, an actual Underworld rather than a metaphor for the grave. Such a belief in Sheol may even predate Hebrew religion. But as a whole the orthodox Hebrew tradition in ancient times strictly forbade such ancestor worship (Leviticus 19:31; 20:6, 27; Deuteronomy 18:10–11; 2 Kings 23:24), perceiving it as idolatry and deviance from the worship of the tribal god Jahweh.

Such focus on the present and such a naive view that the obedient would be rewarded and the disobedient would be punished—in this life—worked well enough for the Hebrew community as long as the nation of Israel held military and political power in the ancient

Near East; occasional exceptions when bad things happened to good people could be ignored or left as isolated mysteries, though they were recorded (for instance, the Book of Job). Gradually, however, the fortunes of Israel diminished, and more and more it became obvious that the faithful did not always prosper, whereas foreign evil doers triumphed; it appeared that Jahweh was increasingly handing the Hebrews over to their enemies. The prophetic tradition explained this as a moral failure among Hebrews, who (they said) had abandoned Jahweh and his covenant for foreign gods; the prophets increasingly hoped for a coming king (Messiah) from the line of David to restore Israel's obedience to Jahweh and hence Israelite power. But a growing minority among the Israelites proclaimed that only in an afterlife would justice be done, and this belief required development of the idea of the soul—it had to become something that could survive bodily death.

Although the prophet Ezekiel does not believe in the afterlife, he acknowledges the separate life of the soul. Apparently his visions take him out of his body (Ezekiel 8:1–3):

> On the fifth day of the sixth month in the sixth year, I was sitting at home [in Babylon] and the elders of Judah were with me. Suddenly the hand of the Lord God came upon me, and I saw what looked like a man. . . . He stretched out what seemed a hand and seized me by the forelock. A spirit lifted me up between heaven and earth, carried me to Jerusalem in a vision of God and put me down at the entrance to the inner gate [of the Temple] facing north.

Ezekiel does not explicitly challenge then-current notions about the soul in his writings, but his experiences demonstrate that the soul is separable from the body. At the end of chapter 11, he is reunited with his body and writes, "I told the exiles [in Babylon] all that the Lord had revealed to me [in Jerusalem]."

Through contacts with Egyptians and Persians in the fifth, fourth, and third centuries B.C.E., many Jews (particularly those in Diaspora, i.e., those forced to live outside Israel) came to believe in a coming resurrection in which the body and nephesh of each faithful person would be reunited. It took many centuries, but this popular view eventually grew even among the keepers of orthodoxy. Evildoers would not be resurrected, however; the Earth would be left solely to the faithful to live out the happy lives denied them before. For instance, the Mishnah Sanhedrin 11:3 reads, "The generation of the Flood will have no part in the next world, and will not be raised for the judgment"; the text goes on to list other sinners who will not be resurrected either. (This idea contrasts with later Jewish and Christian views of

a resurrection of all leading to salvation for some and damnation for others.) In this view, even though the physical body and nephesh were scattered, the resurrection brought them together again, maintaining the ancient understanding that there was no life without both body and nephesh. Likewise, the newly resurrected "living beings" (nephesh chayyah) were still subject to all the laws of life and death: the resurrection was a temporary affair, another life on Earth meant to compensate those faithful Hebrews who did not receive their just rewards in their first life because of their oppression by the enemies of Israel. After living out a long and prosperous resurrected life, death would come once more. Body and nephesh would separate again, and as in the ancient period, the Hebrews envisioned no afterlife (see RESURRECTION, HEBREW).

Other Hebrews who came under Greek and Roman influence (in the fourth through first centuries B.C.E.) believed in a heaven apart from the Earth where those faithful to Jahweh would be eternally rewarded (in the underground Sheol or, later thinkers taught, in a paradise in the sky). In this view, the soul had to become something eternal or at least conditionally eternal (if God saw fit to grant immortality). Hence, immediately upon death, the faithful were assigned to heaven, whereas evildoers were annihilated or consigned to a hell in a newly conceived Sheol.

Some Hebrews believed both in a coming resurrection on Earth and then a later celebration in heaven; contrarily, some believed that resurrection itself immediately determined who would go to heaven or hell. The situation became confused, with many different parties (Zealots, Pharisees, Sadducees, Essenes, and others) teaching conflicting doctrines regarding the soul and immortality; this confusion was passed on to early Christianity.

Roughly by the time of Jesus, however, the understanding that the human person had aspects that could separate and even live separate "lives" after death had become dominant. The body (in Hebrew, *basar;* in Greek *sôma, sarkos*) was quite distinct from the soul (in Hebrew, *nephesh;* in Greek, *psyche*) and from the more vague spirit (in Hebrew, *ru'ach;* in Greek, pneuma). After death, the body began to decompose, but the soul descended into Sheol, which by this time, like the Greek Hades, had developed compartments—felicitous housing for the blest and infernal torment for the wicked. The mysterious ruach (literally "wind") flew back to God, according to Guignebert. In this way of thinking, the nephesh became a kind of vessel that could be filled by either of two substances: material influence carried by the body (which tended toward passions, desires, and wrongdoing) or spiritual influence carried by the ru'ach (which tended toward God). The soul had become a battleground where two armies fought for dominance. It is easy to see how, in this period, the doctrine of Satan could have received such enormous development, for if God tried with all his might to bring souls to his side, what on earth could oppose him? Although the more priestly class of Jews, the Sadducees (in political power during the Roman period) held no such notions, the Pharisees championed this trichotomous view of the soul. According to the Jewish historian Josephus, the Pharisees

> believe that souls are endowed with immortal power (*athanoton te ischun tais psychais*) and that somewhere under the earth rewards and punishments will be meted out to them, according to whether they have loved vice or virtue. The former will be condemned to perpetual imprisonment, but the others will be allowed to return to life [in resurrection]. (Josephus, *Antiquities*, quoted in Guignebert)

This same trichotomy appears in early Christian thinking, as in 1 Thessalonians 5:23, in which Paul asks that God keeps his people sound in "body, soul, and spirit." The "sinful flesh" became the view of the body among Greco-Roman Jews and Christians, and rather than being called to obedience to the tribal god Jahweh, Jews now found themselves embroiled in a cosmic war with eternity at stake.

In medieval Judaism a new view of the soul began to take shape as part of a movement called Kabbalah (best translated as "esoteric Judaism"). In the Kabbalistic view, the soul was truly created in God's image—spiritually—and thus participated in the complexity and grandeur of the invisible heavenly world. Not moral behavior alone but also wisdom, knowledge of the secrets of the world and its invisible hierarchy of beings and powers (sefirot), and above all mystical devotion (devekut, "clinging") to God would save the soul from the lower passions of the body and raise it to perfection, like God above. Through intense prayer and meditation, the soul could reach up to God, and the divine could reach down to it, forming a harmonious whole. As Kabbalah scholar Rachel Elior writes (p. 893):

> the kabbalah arrived at a most important conclusion: man's relationship with God could not be reduced to [man's] one-sided need for heavenly mercy; it was characterized, rather, by reciprocal influence and mutual assistance. . . . Man was sustained by the downward flow from the world of the sefirot, but he also extended an upward influence of his own. . . . the harmonious interplay of the spheres of divine life depends upon the actions of man. . . . This conception of the soul as a spiritual power that brought man into communion

with God and exerted its own influence upon the divine was of crucial importance in shaping the kabbalistic interpretation of the worship of God, according to which the purpose of all the commandments is to enable the soul to unite with God and to bring about a union of the elements of the divine.

The human being went from being a sinner in need of salvation to an important player in cosmic evolution. Because the ultimate purpose of God in creating human souls was to bring about greater perfection in the world and because so few humans die truly perfect in God's eyes, the ancient Greek idea of reincarnation, called in Hebrew *gilgulim,* or "revolutions (of the soul)," replaced resurrection in the Kabbalah. Human souls are to reincarnate life after life until perfection is achieved.

Needless to say, Kabbalistic theology was a radical departure from the Judaism of the Greco-Roman period, let alone that of Biblical times, and the Kabbalah has never been more than a minority tradition among Jews, although a powerful and fertile one. The majority of Jews continued to believe in a soul separable from the body. At death the soul was immediately consigned by God to heaven or hell. The doctrine of a future Messiah, resurrection, and final judgment became somewhat confused during the Middle Ages because it was not clear what the purpose of a resurrection would be if the dead were already experiencing their just desserts in heaven or hell. The rightly famous medieval theologian Maimonides (1135–1204 C.E.) reconciled the two conflicting views, that of the eternality of the disembodied soul and the temporary resurrection of the body-soul complex. In his view, according to Allan Arkush, the resurrection was a temporary, intermediate stage in the drama of the soul followed by a second death. After the second death, the wicked would be destroyed forever, and the faithful would exist with God forever as bodiless souls. This view became widely accepted, though in practice the conflict between the older and newer views continued.

Modern Judaism moves along many different paths. Orthodox Jews continue to believe in a physical resurrection wherein the nephesh and body are reunited, after which they cannot say what happens. A more liberal tradition was inaugurated by Moses Mendelssohn (1729–1786), wherein the indestructibility of the soul (nizhiyut ha-nephesh) was affirmed along with the ultimate restoration of all souls to God's presence after a period of purgation for the wicked. There is also a high degree of skepticism among modern Jews, who find it hard to believe in an afterlife of any kind. This latter view, induced for the most part by modern scientific materialism, is ironically closer to the very ancient Hebrew position than either the Orthodox or liberal view. The skeptical view also raises again the question faced by the early Hebrews: How can the wicked prosper while the good suffer and die young? In the wake of the Holocaust, such concerns are all the more pointed and troubling.

See also FUNERARY CUSTOMS, JEWISH; GEHENNA; HADES; REPHĀ'IM; RESURRECTION, HEBREW; SHEOL; SOUL, GREEK.

References

Arkush, Allan. "Immortality." In *Contemporary Jewish Religious Thought,* ed. Arthur A. Cohen and Paul Mendes-Flohr. New York: Charles Scribner's Sons, 1989.

Elior, Rachel. "Soul." In *Contemporary Jewish Religious Thought,* ed. Arthur A. Cohen and Paul Mendes-Flohr. New York: Charles Scribner's Sons, 1989.

Glasson, T. Francis. *Greek Influence in Jewish Eschatology.* London: SPCK, 1961.

Guignebert, Charles. *The Jewish World in the Time of Jesus.* New York: University Books, 1965.

Montefiore, C. G., and H. Loewe, eds. *A Rabbinic Anthology.* New York: Schocken Books, 1974.

Moore, George Foot. *Judaism in the First Centuries of the Christian Era.* 3 vols. Cambridge: Harvard University Press, 1927–1930. Reprint, New York: Schocken Books, 1971.

Riemer, Jack, ed. *Jewish Reflections on Death.* New York: Schocken Books, 1974.

Scholem, Gershom. *On the Kabbalah and Its Symbolism.* New York: Schocken Books, 1965.

Spronk, Klaas. *Beatific Afterlife in Ancient Israel and in the Ancient Near East.* Kevelaer: Butzon and Bercker, 1986.

Twersky, Isadore, ed. *A Maimonides Reader.* New York: Behrman House, 1972.

SOUL, MUSLIM

The Arabic term *nafs* (cognate to the Hebrew *nephesh*) may be simply translated as "soul" and is roughly equivalent to the Christian understanding of soul. However, the discussion of nafs in Islamic theology, especially the possible distinction of a "soul" (nafs) from God's "spirit" or "breath" (ruh), has been long and complex. Whether the soul in Islam has different parts or aspects, exactly what survives death, and exactly what is resurrected at the day of judgment have been hotly debated questions.

The earliest use of nafs was in Arabic poetry, where it meant the self or individual person, whereas ruh referred generically to breath and wind. In the sacred text of Islam, the Qur'ān, both terms are used and altered slightly from pre-Islamic use. Nafs becomes human conscience and inner nature, and ruh is a mysterious force associated with angels and God. In theological usage (after the Qur'ān), the terms are frequently interchanged, and various philosophers have spilled much ink either in identifying the two terms (as names for the same spiritual entity) or in attempting to distinguish them.

For most Islamic thinkers the nafs is definitely a material substance, not a pure abstraction or dimensionless phantom. However, the substance of the nafs is very subtle, light, and generally invisible to the eye, whereas the body (badan) is grossly material and dense. In common with all Semitic tradition, the Islamic nafs and the body make up a whole person that is not easily divided into pieces: the body and the soul were both created by God out of the material of the universe; both are mortal; and both "die" at death to be resurrected by God on judgment day, called *Sā'a* (the Hour). However, the nafs has unique properties that distinguish it from the body to some degree. It is the nafs and not the body that contains rationality and is called "the knower" ('allāma). The nafs must determine whether to act for good or evil in life and will be questioned in the grave at death—but interestingly, both nafs and body will suffer or be rewarded in the resurrection.

However, some Muslim thinkers, including Sufis, other philosophers known as Mu'tazila, and some Muslim theologians influenced by Greek philosophy denied that the nafs was material at all and taught that it was pure immortal spirit. To these minority thinkers, the nafs was the real person, not the body-soul union; the nafs is only temporarily associated with a material body during earthly life, for it existed before birth and exists still after death. Ibn Hazm (994–1064 C.E.) used nafs and ruh interchangeably and taught that the souls of all humans were created at the same time as Adam. Souls exist in a place called *barzakh* (literally "the barrier" between life and death) until angels place them (literally "blow them") into embryos.

According to all Islamic theology, the soul undertakes a kind of journey on Earth through three states of spirituality. The first state of the soul, in which it carelessly pursues sensual gratification like an animal, is called that which is "prone to evil" (ammara bi'l-su). Subject to the urgings of the shayatin (satans, i.e., the various demons headed by Iblīs, the Devil), the soul in this first state is mired in sin except as the Lord shows mercy.

A soul in the second state of spirituality perceives its sinfulness and actively strives to overcome its evil nature. Aware of the inevitable judgment and resurrection to come, this nafs is "self-reproaching" (al-nafs al-lawwama) and actively seeks God's help in righteousness. The Qur'ān, in the sura (chapter) entitled "Resurrection" (Qiyāma) says in its first two verses, "I swear by the Day of Resurrection, and by the self-reproaching soul! Does man think We shall never put his bones together again? Indeed, We can remould his very fingers!"

Finally, there is the third spiritual state of the nafs, which is devoid of base instincts, totally centered in God, and "at peace" (al-nafs al-mutma'inna). Most Muslims believe this state is only possible after death and resurrection, when the soul is through with worldly temptation and has been allowed to enter the Gardens of Delight by God. The mystical tradition of Sufism within Islam, however, has taught that through intense self-sacrifice, devotion, and meditative absorption (fana) in God, such a state is possible even on Earth.

Except for martyrs, who go directly to God at death, most Muslims expect to experience a complex series of events after physical death—all of which revolve around the ethical state of the soul during life. Popular traditions have mixed with orthodox theology for fourteen centuries, and what follows is a reconstruction of major afterlife events, though the order and importance of each tends to vary with each author. One tradition has it that exactly forty days before each person's death (which is preordained by God in his infinite wisdom), a leaf falls from the great tree called the *Sidrat al-Muntahá,* which stands beneath the throne of God. On that leaf is written the name of the person who is to die, and the angel of death, ʿIzrāʾīl, sees it and makes preparations. At the moment of death that angel appears to the dying and informs him or her that there is no escape and preliminary judgment will immediately follow.

Although orthodox Islam teaches that the dead are never able to return to communicate with the living, the recently deceased is keenly aware of what is taking place for both the body and soul. (Meanwhile, popular tradition has contradicted orthodox teachings in providing many ghost stories and dreams in which the deceased chastises the living for shabby treatment; see excerpt.) In any case, immediately upon the death of the body, one feels one's soul being drawn out of the body by four angels clothed in white, and at this time there may be a vision of the invisible worlds beyond this one. Al-Ghazālī (1058–1111 C.E.), one of the most famous and respected Sufi mystics and theologians in Islam, describes the deathbed scene from the dying person's perspective (from his work *Kitā al-Durra al-Fākhira*):

> And when one's destiny approaches . . . then four angels descend to him: the angel who pulls the soul from his right foot, the angel who pulls it from the left foot, the angel who pulls it from his right hand, and the angel who pulls it from his left hand. Some of the circumstances of the Malakūtī [higher] world may be unveiled to the dying person before he expires, so that he sees those angels, not the way they actually appear in their own world, but according to the extent of his understanding. If his tongue is unhampered [by the angels] he may tell about their existence [to the living who are near him as he dies]. . . . Then he is silent so that his tongue is tied, while they pull the soul from the

tips of his fingers. The good soul slips out like the jetting of water from a waterskin, but the profligate's spirit squeaks out like a skewer from wet wool. (Smith and Haddad, trans., pp. 36–37)

Then the released soul, about the size of a bee but still with human characteristics, is said to shimmer like a drop of mercury in the hand of the angel.

Once out of the body, a great grief comes upon the soul, which sees his or her body being wept over and prepared for burial by washing and wrapping. The soul also feels a great thirst, and thereupon is tempted by Iblīs or one of his minions, who appear on the left side of the head and offer the deceased water, if only he or she will say, "The Prophet (Muhammed) lied." However, God determines the answer the soul gives, with the faithful denying Satan and the sinful accepting the bargain. Those present with the dead are said to be able to see the results of this first of the soul's trials, according to Al-Ghazālī:

> When you look at the dying person and his mouth waters, his lips contract, his face turns black and his eyes become bluish, then know that he is miserable. The reality of his wretchedness in the hereafter has been unveiled to him. And when you see the dying person and his mouth is hollow as if he were laughing, his face beaming, his eyes cast down, then know that he has been told the good news of the joy that will come to him in the hereafter; the reality of his blessedness has been revealed to him.

The soul is then escorted up to heaven, accompanied either by the angels who coaxed the soul out of the body or, in some accounts, by Jibrīl, the angel who recited the Qurʾān to Muhammed. At the doors to each of the seven levels of heaven, the angels knock, and when asked "Who are you?" the angels lavish praise on the soul they bring (if a faithful Muslim) or condemn the soul for its sins and are barred progress through heaven. The evil soul is barred from the gates of the seven heavens, wrapped in a hair shirt, and flung back to Earth. But the good soul arrives at last in the highest heaven (named *ʿIliyīn*) and the beatific presence of God and takes in the majesty and glory of God. There God determines the fate of the soul until resurrection. Some Muslims believe that the good soul remains with God until the final judgment, but widespread popular belief claims that the soul (whether good or evil) soon finds itself reunited with the corpse, so quickly that the washers are still at their work, just beginning to prepare the body for burial.

Many Muslims assert that once the body is sealed into the grave and after the journey described in the

Abū Qalāba's Dream

It is related from Abū Qalāba that he saw in a dream a cemetery, and it was as if the graves were split open and the dead came out of them. They sat on the edges of the graves and each one had before him a light. He saw among them one of his neighbors with no light in front of him and he asked him about it, saying, "Why do I not see any light in front of you?" The dead person said, "These others have children and friends to pray for them and give alms for them and their light is produced by that. I have only one son and he is no good. He does not pray for me and does not give alms on my behalf, therefore I have no light. And I am ashamed in front of my neighbors." When Abū Qalāba woke up he called the man's son and told him what he had seen. So the son said, "I will mend my ways and will no more do what I have been doing." And he was obedient and prayed for his father and gave alms on his behalf. And sometime later when Abū Qalāba saw the graveyard in his dream he saw the same man with a light brighter than the sun and greater than the light of his companions. And the man said, "O Abū Qalāba, may God reward you well for me. Because of what you said [to my son], I am saved from shame in front of my neighbors.

From the Muslim treatise on resurrection,
Kitāb ahwāl al-Qiyāma, *translation by Smith and Haddad (1981, pp. 60–61).*

---

previous paragraph, it finds itself temporarily rejoined with the nafs and brought to life again or at least a quasi-life, referred to as the "second life." The Qur'ān twice mentions that humans experience two lives and two deaths (2:28; 40:11). Soon the soul finds itself questioned by two angels, Munkar and Nakīr, who are black with green eyes and of a very fearsome appearance, though some authorities indicate that they appear frightening only to the wicked. These angels ask the dead such questions as "Who is your Lord?" and "What (spiritual) knowledge do you have?" After this test, the soul is visited by a personage who may be lovely or ugly in appearance and smell sweet or foul. This character is the personification of the soul's good or evil deeds in life, who then speaks with the dead and announces what will be the soul's state in the grave while it awaits final judgment. The benevolent and faithful Muslim will then find that even while in the grave awaiting the resurrection, a window opens on its right, and breezes and sweet odors waft in from Paradise (though some tradi-

tions maintain that even the most faithful soul will suffer somewhat in the grave for minor offenses committed during life). The damned soul, however, wails in misery as the tongues of fire lap up on the left from hell. A story (hadīth) traced back to the Prophet Muhammed claims that his camel refused to walk near graveyards because it could hear the shrieks of souls suffering in their tombs. After a time, however, all became darkness, the soul slept, and it seemed merely the wink of an eye until the end arrived and all were brought before God for the last time. Al-Ghazālī states that this sleep overtakes the soul in the grave "when its individuality fades away." Most Muslim theologians consider this the "second death."

The exact location of the soul after death, as previously shown, appears to vary considerably, no doubt because of the many layers of popular tradition as well as ambiguity in the Qur'ān. Some consider that after the initial visit to heaven, the soul remains there with God awaiting the end of time, but others place the soul in the grave, experiencing a taste of what is to come in its temporary "second life." Still other traditions have the soul hanging about its former habitation for a month or a year, and some believe the soul can visit the dead in dreams—or rather, both the dead and the living who sleep can meet together in "the barrier land," or barzakh.

See also BARZAKH; FUNERARY CUSTOMS, MUSLIM; ISRĀFĪL; 'IZRĀ'ĪL; JAHANNAM; JUDGMENT, LAST; QIYĀMA; SĀ'A; SECOND DEATH.

References

Al-Ahouani. "Treatise Concerning Our Knowledge of the Rational Soul and Its Different States." In *Islamic Philosophy*. Cairo: Anglo-Egyptian Bookshop, 1957.

Calverley, E. E. "Doctrines of the Soul (*nafs* and *ruh*) in Islam." *Muslim World* 33 (1943).

———. "Nafs." In *Encyclopedia of Islam*, ed. C. E. Bosworth. Vol. 7. Leiden: E. J. Brill, 1993.

Dawood, N. J., trans. *The Koran*. 5th rev. ed. New York: Penguin, 1993.

Evrin, M. Sadeddin. *Eschatology in Islam*. Trans. Sofi Huri. Istanbul, 1960.

Macdonald, D. B. "The Development of the Idea of Spirit in Islam." *Muslim World* 22 (1932).

Smith, Jane I. *The Precious Pearl* (A translation of Abū Hāmid al-Ghazālī's *Kitāb al-Durra al-Fākhira if Kashf 'Ulūm al-Ākhira*). Missoula, MT: Scholars Press, 1979.

Smith, Jane I., and Yvonne Yazbeck Haddad. *The Islamic Understanding of Death and Resurrection*. Albany: SUNY Press, 1981.

———. "The Understanding of *Nafs* and *Ruh* in Contemporary Muslim Considerations of the Nature of Sleep and Death. *Muslim World* 49 (1979).

Tritton, A. S. "Man, *Nafs, Ruh, 'Aql*." *Bulletin of the School of Oriental and African Studies* 34, no. 3 (1971).

SOUL, PERSIAN

There are two primary terms for soul in Iranian belief, which became synonymous in later Zoroastrian Scriptures. In archaic times (1,000 B.C.E. to the time of Christ) the term *urvan* appears to have been used for the lower souls—the shades—of men (and animals), which at death went to the Underworld. The term *fravashi* may have originally meant the highest essence of a person, which if honorable and just went to "paradise" after death to dwell in the sky or with the sun. In the historical period (from the ninth century C.E.), however, the two terms are used almost identically, but one trace of difference remains: among the living, prayers are made *for* the urvan, but prayers are made *to* the fravashi. This seems to indicate that the urvan is somehow more earthbound and needing assistance, while the fravashi is godlike and able to bestow blessings.

In Persian thought the fravashi is immortal not only after death but before birth, from the beginning of time. The fravashi are considered the preexistent souls of those not yet born as well as the souls of those who have died. They were present at the beginning of the world and participated in the six creations with the good god Ahura Mazda, and it is through them that the world is kept in growth and motion. Ahura Mazda is even made to say of them: "If the mighty fravashis of the just had not given me help, there would not now have been cattle and men" (Yasht 13:12). In a sense, then, every person now alive has already had an immense past as a spirit being. After a short sojourn on Earth, the spirit is released again to its cosmic life.

At death the soul remains on Earth for three days, either near the place of death, the burial tower (dakhma), or the Zoroastrian sacred fire. At the first light of dawn on the fourth day the soul is drawn up with the sun's rays to its new abode, where it is pictured as a bird, winged, able to fly about. But quickly the soul is greeted by a maiden, called *daena* (literally "conscience"), who will appear to be beautiful if the deceased has been just and hideously ugly if the deceased has been unjust. The daena guides the soul to the scales where it will be weighed for judgment and then to the crossing of the Chinvat Bridge. For the just, the bridge is wide, "the length of nine spears," but for the unjust it is barely the width of a razor's edge. Those souls who cross over find themselves in paradise, whereas those who fail pitch headlong into the torments of hell. Although the portrayal of postmortem judgment is certainly graphic enough to produce a very literal belief, it is also easy to see the underlying ethical and psychological statement that after death, guided by "conscience," one harvests the fruits of one's life.

On Earth the survivors of the deceased continue to make ritual offerings for the dead: daily for thirty days, monthly for a year, and annually for thirty years, even though the deceased is thought to have crossed over to the Otherworld. It is believed that the souls of the departed benefit from these offerings, and they help the dead maintain a connection with the living so that they can bestow blessings on their descendants. The dead have the power to bring fertility to both land and people, to aid in war and sickness, and to bring good luck. Failure to give a proper funeral or make appropriate offerings puts the living in danger—not so much from the wrath of the departed but from the dangers that will arise because the connection to the fravashi will be broken and they will not be able to protect the living any longer.

For the first year after death, the soul is considered to be in an intermediate period: not fully dead while the flesh is still on the bones but certainly not living in the usual sense. After a year, souls are thought to fully join the community of the dead but still continue to exist as individuals. After thirty years, offerings are no longer made for the individual soul: as far as the living are concerned, the soul has merged entirely with the collective dead, "the fravashis" as a whole, who are honored with an entirely different set of ceremonies. The fravashis collectively are venerated on special occasions like marriage as well as at an annual festival, called *Fravardigān,* during which food, incense, and good deeds are offered in the hopes of receiving blessings.

It is difficult to determine which Persian beliefs about the soul reach back to very ancient times and which stem from the religious reforms made by the great prophet Zoroaster, probably around 1400 B.C.E. One belief that most likely dates from the period after Zoroaster concerns a resurrection and final judgment. According to this teaching, which began to gain widespread popularity in the Middle East after the fall of the Assyrian empire in the sixth century B.C.E., the final messiah will come to proclaim the End Time. At that point, the mountains and hills of the Earth will melt and become molten rivers of metal. The souls of all the dead will be resurrected to endure the final judgment, namely being immersed in these molten rivers to test their purity. The pure will feel as though they are bathing in warm milk, but the wicked will suffer unspeakable torment as their flesh melts from their bones. A later doctrine from post-Sassanian times (seventh century C.E. and onward) taught that after their sufferings the wicked would be purified and live in paradise forever, but the earlier teaching of Zoroaster himself was that the souls of the wicked were utterly destroyed along with all the cosmic powers of darkness (Angra Mainyu), while the just enjoyed a new cosmos of perfect purity.

See also JUDGMENT, LAST; JUDGMENT, PARTICULAR; SOUL, ZOROASTRIAN.

References

Boyce, Mary. *A History of Zoroastrianism.* Vol. 1. Leiden: E. J. Brill, 1975.

Frye, Richard Nelson. *The Heritage of Persia.* Cleveland: World Publishing Company, 1963.

Herzfeld, E. *Zoroaster and His World.* Princeton: Princeton University Press, 1947.

Spronk, Klaas. *Beatific Afterlife in Ancient Israel and in the Ancient Near East.* Kevelaer: Butzon and Bercker, 1986.

SOUL TABLET

Traditionally the Chinese people believe that several energies, or "souls," exist in each person; after death these souls go their separate ways. The higher energy is the hun-soul, corresponding to the active energy of yang. Although the hun-soul dwells permanently in heaven with the ancestors after death, it is also connected to the ancestral tablet that relatives keep on the family altar (or, if the family is wealthy, in an ancestral hall dedicated to ritual performance). Chinese do not believe that the soul of the departed actually dwells *in* the tablet as the living dwell in a house; rather the name of the deceased is inscribed on the tablet, and the name represents and manifests the soul, especially when called forth by the veneration of descendants.

The soul tablet is one of the most crucial aspects of Chinese religion. All those who die have a tablet prepared for them, except perhaps infants or wandering strangers. Immediately after death a temporary tablet with the name of the dead on it is placed on the family altar along with a lantern in the shape of a pagoda to honor the spirit of the dead, which is thought to hover nearby. Throughout the funeral preparations, family members and visitors kneel before the temporary tablet to offer condolences, good wishes, and material gifts such as uncooked food.

Meanwhile, another tablet is prepared that will replace the cheaper temporary one. The name of the deceased is also inscribed on the permanent tablet, but it lacks part of one Chinese character, *chu,* which means "host" or "master." The funeral procession to the gravesite brings along the permanent soul tablet, set up in a place of honor, as well as an empty seat in which the deceased may accompany the proceedings. Only after the burial is completed and the grave is sealed will the final character be placed on the tablet in an important ceremony called "dotting the chu." The most learned or politically connected acquaintance of the family uses special ink or even blood to fill in the dot in the character, signifying that the tablet is now the official residence of the soul of the deceased. In the funeral procession back to the home, the tablet is treated as the person himself or herself and is placed in the main ceremonial hall of the home with all the other ancestors.

The importance placed on the soul tablet in the home does not mean that the dead is associated with it and nothing else. Although the relatives (especially the matron of the family) make daily offerings to the departed directed at the tablet on the family altar, visiting the actual gravesite is considered another kind of ritual connection with the dead, especially on holidays dedicated to honoring the dead and the anniversary of death. Meanwhile, during the annual Festival of Ghosts, the spirits of the dead are thought to return to the family home in propria persona, even though the deceased are apparently already present through their soul tablets. Clearly, different qualities and degrees of presence are associated with different ritual implements and ritual activities for the dead. In some schools of Taoism up to ten different souls are counted, making Chinese religion and particularly ancestor veneration one of the most complex religious systems on the planet.

See also FESTIVAL OF GHOSTS (CHINA); FUNERARY CUSTOMS, CHINESE; HEAVENS, BUDDHIST; PURE LAND; SOUL, CHINESE; TEN KINGS OF HELL; TI-TSANG; YEN-LO WANG.

References

de Groot, J. J. M. *Religion in China.* New York: G. P. Putnam's Sons, 1912.

Hsu, Francis L. K. *Under the Ancestor's Shadow.* New York: Columbia University Press, 1948.

Jochim, Christian. *Chinese Religions.* Prentice-Hall Series in World Religions. Ed. Robert S. Ellwood. Englewood Cliffs, NJ: Prentice-Hall, 1986.

Naquin, Susan. "Funerals in North China: Uniformity and Variation." In *Death Rituals in Late Imperial and Modern China,* ed. James L. Watson and Evelyn S. Rawski. Berkeley: University of California Press, 1988.

Teiser, Stephen F. *The Ghost Festival in Medieval China.* Princeton: Princeton University Press, 1988.

Thompson, Laurence. *The Chinese Way in Religion.* Encino, CA: Dickenson Press, 1973.

Watson, James L. "The Structure of Chinese Funerary Rites." In *Death Rituals in Late Imperial and Modern China,* ed. James L. Watson and Evelyn S. Rawski. Berkeley: University of California Press, 1988.

Welch, Holmes. *The Practice of Chinese Buddhism, 1900–1950.* Cambridge: Harvard University Press, 1967.

SOUL, THEOSOPHICAL

The Theosophical Movement was launched by Helena P. Blavatsky (1831–1891) at the end of the nineteenth century to study human beings' inner nature and relationship to the spiritual world. Although Blavatsky and other authors compared Theosophical teachings on the human soul and destiny to various world religions, still they claimed that the Theosophical teachings were actually the "perennial philosophy," which was older than any religion on the planet and served to unify and explain differences among religions.

When Madame Blavatsky first published Theosophical teachings on the nature of the soul in her 1877 work *Isis Unveiled*, she divided the human being into three parts, namely body, soul, and spirit. "Soul" she defined as the personal consciousness of a person, which reincarnates from life to life, whereas "spirit" is that absolute, eternal spark of the divine (ātman) that overshadows each person but is beyond anything personal or limited. She compared this division to that made by many religious traditions, including Paul in his letter to the Thessalonian church (1 Thessalonians 5:23): "May God himself, the God of peace, keep you holy in every part, and keep you sound in spirit, soul, and body." The ancient Greek philosopher Plutarch (c. 46 to c. 119 C.E.) also divided the human being into three principles, spirit (noos or nous), soul (psyche), and body, as did many other ancient thinkers.

However, later in her career, Blavatsky expanded her analysis of the inner nature, keeping the three main divisions as before but breaking these down further into a total of seven "aspects" of the human being. In her 1889 work, *The Key to Theosophy*, Blavatsky summed up these seven human principles, with their Indian Sanskrit equivalents, as follows:

The Lower Human Nature
1. Physical body, or rūpa
2. Life, vital principle, or prāṇa
3. Astral body, or linga-śarīra
4. Animal soul, passions, kāma

The Higher Human Nature
5. Mind, intelligence, or manas
6. Spiritual soul, or buddhi

The Eternal Divine Essence
7. Spirit, or ātman

These terms hold somewhat complex meanings in Theosophical teachings, although the nature of the physical body is clear enough. The life force or vital principle, better known in the Western world today by its Chinese name, *ch'i,* is that part of the energy of the earth's sphere that circulates in each material body, whether human, animal, or plant. The "astral" body is much discussed today in the New Age scene, though the term was first popularized in the nineteenth century by the Theosophists to describe the "inner body" made of subtle material, which on rare occasions may actually leave the physical body while the latter is still alive. This conception is the source of modern interest in "out-of-body" experiences. The passionate nature, or animal soul, is that aspect of human nature that moves us with desire. It is this part of a person that both Theosophy and traditional Buddhism seek to suppress because it is thought to degrade humanity and cloud more spiritual perceptions. In Theosophical teachings, none of the four "lower" aspects of people carry on much beyond death: they slowly dissipate and decay, leaving only subtle deposits called *skandhas* that carry some of a person's karma and rejoin the higher soul when it returns from its heavenly rest. For more information on the death process, see DEVACHAN (THEOSOPHICAL) and KĀMARŪPA.

The higher division of human nature may properly be called the real soul because it is the seat of consciousness and the aspect of human beings that reincarnates. In Theosophical teachings, mind (or *manas* in Sanskrit) is not merely the thinking mind of waking humans but all of the unconscious and untapped powers of the mind ranging from material logic to psychic ability to spiritual union with the divine. The "spiritual" soul, or buddhi in Indian terminology, is higher still than the mind and therefore difficult to define. In *The Ocean of Theosophy,* William Q. Judge calls it "the vehicle of universal spirit," and elsewhere in Theosophical literature the spiritual soul is referred to as "spiritual discrimination" or "intuition." The spiritual soul has such intuition and inherent wisdom because it is that divine nature in human beings that stores all experiences from all past lives and gathers to itself the collective understanding gained from those lives.

Finally, the eternal essence that overshadows humanity, called in Indian terminology *ātman,* is not really individual at all but a ray of the absolute infinite spirit. It does not incarnate in human beings, at least not in the ordinary human full of passions and desires; but for the rare individual who attains perfect enlightenment, the mind and buddhi are said to bond completely and permanently with the divine essence, or ātman, making that person a godlike being, consciously immortal and beyond birth and death. This union of the human and eternal natures is said by Theosophical writers to be the goal of human existence (though it is a distant one for most people), leading to a state called *nirvāṇa.*

Clearly, Theosophical teachings on the soul bear a great similarity both to the fivefold analysis of the soul (skandhas) in Buddhism and the sixfold analysis of the soul (kośas) in Vedantic Hinduism. Blavatsky herself pointed to these similarities as proof that Theosophical ideas were valid, but she claimed that her source of knowledge was an ancient tradition far predating either of these schools of thought. Theosophical teachings on the soul do differ significantly from both Buddhism and Vedantic Hinduism as well. Whereas Buddhism is extremely careful to teach no eternal "self," Theosophy clearly teaches the eternality of the spirit, or ātman, though it is not a *personal* self. Likewise, although Theosophy teaches reincarnation for all beings, it differs from both Buddhism and Hinduism in that Theosophy denies the possibility of humans being reborn into animal bodies or other "lower" forms. Theosophy also denies the literal heavens and hells of Buddhism and Hinduism, explaining these as merely the passages of the soul through Kāmaloka and Devachan, temporary states of consciousness of the soul between human lives. However, the overall similarities between Theosophy and these Indian schools are clear, and Theosophists sometimes identify themselves with esoteric rather than "popular" Buddhism, particularly the esoteric Buddhism of Tibet.

See also ĀTMAN; DEVACHAN (THEOSOPHICAL); KĀMALOKA; KĀMA-RŪPA; NIRVĀṆA; REINCARNATION, EASTERN; REINCARNATION, WESTERN; SOUL, BUDDHIST.

References

Blavatsky, Helena Petrovna. *Isis Unveiled.* 2 vols. Reprint, Pasadena: Theosophical University Press, 1976.

———. *The Key to Theosophy.* Reprint, Los Angeles: Theosophy Company, 1987.

———. *The Secret Doctrine.* 2 vols. Reprint, New York: Theosophy Company, 1925.

Judge, William Quan. *The Ocean of Theosophy.* Reprint, Los Angeles: Theosophy Company, 1987.

SOUL, ZOROASTRIAN

In Zoroastrianism, the ancient religion of the Middle East and Central Asia, we find one of the oldest analytical understandings of the soul on the planet. Rather than the simple mind-body dualism believed in by many modern religions such as Christianity and Islam or even the tripartite constitution of human beings of ancient Greece (body, soul, and spirit), Zoroastrianism teaches no fewer than nine essential components in all humans: three physical aspects, three subtly material ones, and three aspects that may only be termed "spiritual." In the Zoroastrian Scripture, the Avesta (dated by tradition to 1700 B.C.E.), the following terms are used (Yasna Hā 55.1):

1. Gaethā, bodily matter and sensation
2. Tanu, the physical frame of the body and nervous system
3. Azdi, skeleton and sinews
4. Ustāna, life energy, "heart's heat"
5. Kehrpa, astral body, capable of leaving the physical body
6. Tevishi, subtle material, ethereal substance
7. Baodhangha, consciousness, a bridge between bodily sensation and the "soul"
8. Urvāna, soul, inner self, human spirit
9. Fravashi, divine spark, indwelling holy spirit

During life the nine elements on their three "planes" (physical, subtle, and spiritual) all work together to produce and maintain the human being. "Death" is nothing other than the separation of the elements,

---

Invocation to the Spirits

The living, the departed, the to-be born, those yet-unborn, of this land, of other lands, those pious men and women, infants and adolescents, whosoever are of this land of the Aryans and belonging to the Good Religion that have departed, all those Righteous Fravashis together from Gayomard [first man] to Saushyant [messiah], do we hereby invoke now!

From Dibāche āfringān, translation by Sidhwa (1978).

which then go their separate ways. After this separation, the physical elements dissolve more or less rapidly into their material elements; likewise, the subtle material elements dissolve into the ethereal plane and general pool of life energy. The final three elements are all immortal, and after death they are generally considered to be one entity, even though technically the urvāna is considered the morally responsible agent. Only the urvāna has free will and must act for good or ill, though it is influenced by the baodhangha and fravashi.

For three days the immortal soul is believed to remain earthbound, visiting its place of death, family, and "burial" spot (the Tower of Silence). During this time, the family members say prayers for the dead, perform charity on her or his behalf, and remember him or her, which is thought to be helpful to and comforting for the deceased. At dawn on the fourth day after death, the soul is drawn up by the rays of the sun to its judgment, and no living being is able to help it further (although the living continue the ceremonies to make the spirits happy, so that they will benefit the living). The soul faces the Chinvat Bridge, "the Separator," which grows wide or narrow depending on the quality of the life just lived. For the wicked, the bridge grows too narrow to cross, and they fall down into hell (Dozakh). The kind and generous souls, however, pass on to one of the seven paradises, collectively called *Behesht.* For those whose deeds are neither particularly good nor particularly evil, there is an intermediate place of gloom, called *Hamestegān.*

Despite the view of Western scholars, largely Christian-influenced, that the bridge, heaven, and hell are literal places, native sources unanimously affirm that these descriptions of afterlife judgment and locations are metaphorical. This does not suggest that after death Zoroastrians do not expect a real judgment and a real bliss or suffering, but that they are internal states of the soul, which are incomprehensible except by means of such allegorical descriptions. In addition to the afterlife judgment for individual souls, Zoroastrian doctrine maintains that there will also be a great day of reckoning, when the 12,000-year struggle between the cosmic forces of good and evil comes to a close and the great god Ahura Mazda overcomes the god of the lie, Angra Mainyu, once and for all. At that time of Frasho-kereti (Renovation), all souls will be resurrected (ristakhez) and given a final dispensation. All people may then expect to experience an eternal life with God, called *ameretat,* or "ultimate immortality."

See also AMERETAT; BEHESHT; DOZAKH; FRASHO-KERETI; FRAVASHI; FUNERARY CUSTOMS, ZOROASTRIAN; HAMESTEGĀN; RISTAKHEZ.

References

Boyce, Mary. *A History of Zoroastrianism.* Vol. 1. Leiden: E. J. Brill, 1975.

Jackson, A. V. W. *Zoroastrian Studies.* New York: Columbia University Press, 1928.

Kotwal, Firoze M., and James W. Boyd, trans. *A Guide to the Zoroastrian Religion.* Studies in World Religion no. 3. Chico, CA: Scholars Press, 1982.

Masani, Sir Rustom. *Zoroastrianism: The Religion of the Good Life.* New York: Collier Books, 1962.

Modi, J. J. *The Funeral Ceremonies of the Parsees: Their Origin and Explanation.* Bombay: British India Press, 1923.

———. *The Religious Ceremonies and Customs of the Parsees.* Bombay: British India Press, 1937.

Sethna, Tehmurasp Rustamji. *Book of Instructions on Zoroastrian Religion.* Karachi: Informal Religious Meetings Trust Fund, 1980.

Sidhwa, Ervad Godrej Dinshawji. *Discourses on Zoroastrianism.* Karachi: Ervad Godrej Dinshawji Sidhwa, 1978.

STRIGOÏ

Strigoï, from the Latin root *striga,* or "witch," represents not only the type of vampire found in Romania but also ghost, witch, and wizard—all being but various phases of one state, namely a connection with uncanny magical power. In Romania, lore of the strigoï is plentiful and complex, forming a reservoir that has been drawn on by other European nations. Whereas western Europe has largely attributed vampirism to the machinations of the Devil, Romanian tradition sees vampirism as a natural result of the unrest of the individual soul and generally looks for no higher animating principle of evil. The Inquisition and witch hunting experienced in other parts of Europe during the late Middle Ages and Renaissance largely bypassed Romania, which thus finds the strigoï considerably less horrible. One's next-door neighbor, or the local tavern owner, or even the priest may be a strigoï (witch) while he or she is alive, but this is no cause for uncivil relations, only caution, especially after they die. The use of the word *strigoï* is frequent, even casual in Romania; in some contexts it merely means talent or uncanny power (e.g., "He's a strigoï for making money!").

Furthermore, witches, wizards, vampires, and werewolves have a productive function and are not solely loci of danger in Romania. Following on the Greek and Roman purification rites held in February (from februa, a cleansing object) and in particular the Anthesteria (the annual festival of the return of the dead), Romanians believe that the liminal period from Christmas to Easter (i.e., winter solstice to vernal equinox), with its long nights and dark days, is a time of renewal, regeneration, and fertility. It is also the time of magical influence and the return of the dead. Traditionally, Romanians have held costumed celebrations during this period, particularly from Christmas to Epiphany, in which animal forms, especially wolves, are prevalent, and the activity of the dead is thought to be particularly intense. Romanians also believe that the period after midnight is the most occult period of the twenty-four-hour day and the time of the greatest activity of magic and the undead in Romania—ended, of course, by dawn (or by 3 A.M.—accounts differ), when strigoï are back in their graves and the world is ordered again. For all these reasons, strigoï (both living witches and undead vampires) are looked upon as dangerous but also natural and acceptable.

Certain attributes may predispose one to be a strigoï in life as well as in death. These include the standard European attributions of being born with the caul (amniotic membrane) on one's head, particularly one that is red with blood, or being born with some physical abnormality (an extra nipple, teeth, a birthmark, a tail extension of the spinal cord, etc.). In Romania, however, the causes are considerably more diverse: being weaned twice as a child, being the seventh child, being a third-generation illegitimate child, or having one's godparents stumble while reciting the Apostle's Creed at the baptism. A less visible cause is being born with two hearts: the human one, which dies at death, and the vampiric one, which enables the strigoï to live on. (It is this second heart, when a stake is driven through it, that bursts and sends blood gushing high into the air.) There are also activities that might turn one into a strigoï even if one was not a witch while alive: having one's corpse buried with an open wound, having the blood of the living dropped on one's grave in a cemetery, converting from Christianity to Islam, being a priest who says mass in a state of mortal sin, or that old favorite, having a cat or other animal jump over (or sometimes under) one's corpse before burial.

In Romania strigoï, alive or dead, do not merely suck the blood of the living: they are users of self-serving black magic in general, taking milk from cattle and sheep, stealing and eating sheep and cattle outright, or taking the life energy from wheat and the life force from animals. They bring bad weather, cause drought, or make uncanny noises to frighten others. Fortunately, there are a host of apotropaic funerary practices designed to prevent a strigoï from manifesting in the first place. These include covering mirrors immediately after a death; opening windows in the house a crack so the soul may escape (but not wide enough to let in corpse-jumping cats); and placing incense over the nostrils, ears, and eyes. Sharp objects are generally kept near the corpse—sickles are placed over or near a body if it is ever left alone before burial, and thorns and needles are placed in the coffin along with the deceased. It is unwise to cry over the dead in the region of Vrancea in Romania because doing so will attract evil spirits just waiting to pounce on their next victim; rather the mourners should sing and dance so that onlooking spirits will imagine they are seeing a celebration, not a funeral. In most other regions, however, not only does the family wail and lament, but (according to ancient Mediterranean tradition) professional mourners are hired so that the dead will not feel neglected and be tempted to seek revenge on the living. Seven weeks after burial, an offering of forty-four jars of water is made to the corpse, thought to aid in decomposition (and therefore to reduce the danger that the dead will be able to return).

If a person seems particularly disposed to becoming a strigoï, the body should be placed face down in the coffin and a sickle placed around its neck—for automatic beheading should it try to arise. The same principle is behind the practice of driving a sharpened stake or group of stakes right into a potentially threatening grave so that if the dead should try to rise up, he or she will automatically be impaled. Unmarried people run a greater risk of vampirism, presumably because their sexuality has not been ritually tamed and thus they may go on a rampage after death; occasionally no chances are taken and a sickle is plunged into their heart before burial. If all preventatives have failed, then the aspen stake through the heart is employed, with garlic to be used in the meantime, rubbed in the form of the cross on doors, windows, and animals. This precaution should be taken especially on the eve of Saint Andrew's Day (Andrew is the patron saint of wolves, and his feast day is 30 November), but garlic is good to have in one's pocket in general or around one's neck.

See also UNDEAD; VAMPIRE; VRYKOLAKAS.

References

Barber, Paul. *Vampires, Burial, and Death: Folklore and Reality*. New Haven: Yale University Press, 1988.

Kmietowicz, Frank. *Slavic Mythical Beliefs*. Windsor, Ontario: F. Kmietowicz, 1982.

Murgoci, Agnes. "The Vampire in Romania," *Folk-Lore* 27, no. 5 (1926).

Perkowski, Jan Louis. *Vampires of the Slavs*. Cambridge: Slavica Publishers, 1976.

Senn, Harry A. *Were-Wolf and Vampire in Romania*. East European Monographs no. 17. New York: Columbia University Press, 1982.

STŪPA

Also called a *caitya* (from the Sanskrit word *cita,* or funeral pyre) and a *sotoba* (by the Buddhist Shingon sect in Japan), the stūpa (Sanskrit; in Pali, thupa) has a long and important history in all lands where Buddhism has flourished. Originally the stūpa was a relatively simple Buddhist monument, reminiscent of tumuli and central Asian kurgans and almost certainly influenced by them historically. Stūpa were first erected in order to commemorate the Buddha and his disciples and house their relics, whether those were actual physical remains or "spiritual remains" in the form of copies of the sacred texts (called *sūtras*).

It appears that the Buddha himself asked that stūpas be built, for in the earliest Buddhist Scriptures the Buddha says to Ānanda, his favorite disciple:

> Ānanda, the remains of a wheel-turning [universal] monarch are wrapped in a new linen cloth. This they wrap in teased cotton wool, and this in a new cloth. Having done this five hundred times each, they enclose the king's body in an oil-vat of iron, which is covered with another iron pot. Then having made a funeral-pyre of all manner of perfumes they cremate the king's body, and they raise a stūpa at a crossroads. That, Ānanda, is what they do with the remains of a wheel-turning monarch, and they should deal with the Tathāgata's [Buddha's] body in the same way. A stūpa should be erected at the crossroads for the Tathāgata. And whoever lays wreaths or puts sweet perfumes and colours there with a devout heart, will reap benefit and happiness for a long time. . . . And why is a [Buddha] worthy of a stūpa? Because, Ānanda, at the thought "This is the stūpa of a Tathāgata" . . . people's hearts are made peaceful, and then, at the breaking-up of the body after death they go to a good destiny and rearise in a heavenly world. That is the reason. . . . (pp. 264–265 of a dialogue called "The Buddha's Last Days," in Walshe)

What is interesting about the Buddha's statement is that the stūpa is not constructed in order to glorify him but to bring inspiration to all who might see it and remind people of the possibility of transcendence of this world. Certainly, Buddhists believe that the presence of physical remains or even just the Scriptures of the Buddha housed inside the stūpa give tremendous energy to the monument and make it worthy of pilgrimage. But unlike prehistoric tumuli, where the soul of the deceased is thought to remain inside or at least maintain some direct connection with the mound, the stūpa is not thought by Buddhists to house the soul of the Buddha or his disciples.

The earliest stūpas had as their most prominent

feature a hemisphere (called *garbha*, "dome," or *anda*, "egg") on a circular base topped by an altarlike structure (the gala or harmika), which in turn was crowned by a tapering pillar (the cudamani) symbolizing an honorific umbrella. The whole was surrounded by a fence (sucaka or vedika) separating the sacred space of the stūpa structure from the profane space of the outside world. This fence was often decorated with auspicious symbols to protect against evil influences and had four gates opening to the four quarters of the world and symbolizing the universal aspect of Buddhism. The physical relics (usually ashes) of the Buddha or his disciples and copies of the Buddhist Scriptures were housed in the harmika atop the dome. The oldest stūpas were covered with hundreds of niches for oil lamps so that when lit, the monument glowed.

The holy power of the stūpa is thought to come not only from the relics housed within but from the sacred architecture of the monument itself. Thus the symbolism of the stūpa's design, although complex, is of enormous significance for Buddhist beliefs about the nature of life and death. The architecture of the stūpa may be read on many levels, but only three will be considered here: the stūpa's cosmic symbolism, its symbolism of the subtle human energy system, and its representation of basic Buddhist teachings.

Cosmically, the anda signifies the vast expanse of the heavens and the Earth and symbolizes immanence, this-worldliness (laukika), austerity, and concentration. Anagarika Govinda indicates that the anda thus has a lunar significance. The crowning vertical spire, which became with time longer and more and more slender, signifies transcendence of the cosmos and karma, intellect, wisdom, and enlightenment, thus demonstrating a solar heritage. The harmika in between the dome and the spire demonstrates the union of the two, imminence and transcendence, saṃsāra and nirvāṇa together, personified by the Buddha, whose relics the harmika houses.

Govinda also points out that in Nepal human eyes are regularly painted on the harmika. With the addition of the eyes, one may almost see in the stūpa's shape a human figure sitting in meditation posture: the crossed legs the base, the body up to the shoulders in the hemisphere, and the head with its eyes in the harmika. This symbolism is most appropriate, for on another level the stūpa represents the Indian belief in the occult energies and consciousness embodied in human beings, written in the language of architecture. In Indian thought, the human body has centers of force, called *chakras,* all situated near the spine. Each center has its own unique energy and corresponding level of consciousness, and this is symbolized in the various vertical aspects of the stūpa. (See MCHOD RTEN for a fuller discussion.)

Likewise, numerological elements incorporated into the architecture display in physical form crucial ele-

Shrines around the Shwedagon Pagoda, Burma, Rangoon. Courtesy of CFCL.

ments of Buddhist teaching. For instance, taking the vertical dimension, the heights of various parts of the stūpa form proportions in relation to each other based on three; furthermore, the surrounding railing is formed by three bars, symbolizing the fundamental Buddhist trinity of Buddha, dharma (truth), and sangha (Buddhist community). There are also the three marks of all manifested things (impermanence, suffering, and lack of self) and the three planes of the universe (Kāma-dhātu, or World of Desire; Rūpa-dhātu, or World of Form; and Arūpa-dhātu, or the Immaterial World). The horizontal dimension incorporates a four-cornered ground plan with four gates and a four-cornered altar housing the relics. Four is the central number in Buddhist morality and practice, with the four noble truths, four great efforts, four fundamental meditations, four trances, four psychic powers, and four foundations of mindfulness.

Nevertheless, the architecture of the stūpa was not constant through time but closely followed the elaborations and transformations of Buddhism as it spread to new regions. Early Buddhism may be characterized as "realistic," focused on the historical person of the Buddha and interested in freedom from this world with its snares and suffering. Thus the focus of the early stūpas was on the dome situated on a round base: the sphere is a symbol of concentration and the dome signifies Earth and groundedness.

Even today Sri Lanka, which preserved the doctrinal positions of early Buddhism, manifests stūpas (called dagobas) that have changed relatively little in shape from the earliest period. But in other lands, with the passage of time more and more scholastic elaboration took place in Buddhism, resulting in various changes in the basic shape of the stūpa: the base was elevated; the harmika enlarged, and the spire prolonged or subdivided or both, thus changing the numerological significance of the architecture. With the rise of Mahāyāna doctrine in Buddhism came a much greater emphasis on transcendence and cosmic speculation. Correspondingly, the Tibetan version of the stūpa, called the *mchod rten* (pronounced chörten), has a reduced aṇḍa, no longer in a hemispheric shape, along with a greatly elaborated spire topped with abstract symbols for sun and moon. The pagoda of China displays similar elaboration.

Eventually stūpas were built not only to house relics but to mark the locations where significant events in the Buddha's biography took place: at Lumbini, Nepal, where the Buddha was born; at Bodh Gaya, India, where the Buddha meditated under the bodhi tree and attained perfect enlightenment; at the Deer Park in Sarnath, India, where the Buddha preached his first sermon; and at Kusinagara, where the Buddha died. These locations became enormously important as pilgrimage sites for centuries, until Buddhism was destroyed by the arrival of Islam in India—though in the twentieth century these sites are once again becoming popular destinations for tourists and pilgrims.

It is important to recognize that stūpas were built not merely as monuments to be looked at but as miniatures of the cosmos and the process of enlightenment: they were meant to be engaged and directly experienced by circumambulation, prayer, and offerings. By circling the stūpa, one engages bodily in a kind of three-dimensional mandala, or meditation diagram. The vertical rise of the stūpa, which is ascended gradually by the pilgrim circumambulating on a higher terrace each time, symbolizes the gradual rise from saṃsāra (the round of suffering) to nirvāṇa (eternal peace).

See also ARŪPA-DHĀTU; DAGOBA; KĀMA-DHĀTU; KURGAN; MCHOD RTEN; RŪPA-DHĀTU; TUMULUS.

References
Cook, Elizabeth, ed. *The Stupa: Sacred Symbol of Enlightenment*. Crystal Mirror Series, vol. 12. Berkeley: Dharma, 1997.

Dorjee, Pema. *The Stupa and Its Technology: A Tibeto-Buddhist Perspective*. New Delhi: Indira Gandhi National Centre for the Arts and Motilal Banarsidass Publishers, 1996.

Gómez, Luis O., and Hiram W. Woodward Jr., eds. *Barabudur: History and Significance of a Buddhist Monument*. Ann Arbor: University of Michigan Press, 1974.

Govinda, Anagarika. *The Psycho-cosmic Symbolism of the Buddhist Stupa*. Berkeley: Dharma, 1976.

Grünwedel, A. *Buddhist Art in India*. Trans. Agnes C. Gibson. London: B. Quaritch, 1901.

Longhurst, A. H. *The Story of the Stupa*. New Delhi: Asian Educational Services, 1979.

Pant, Sushila. *The Origins and Development of Stupa Architecture in India*. Varanasi: Bharata Manisha, 1976.

Tucci, Giuseppe. *The Religions of Tibet*. Trans. Geoffrey Samuel. Berkeley: University of California Press, 1980.

Walshe, Maurice, trans. *The Long Discourses of the Buddha: A Translation of the Dīgha Nikāya*. Boston: Wisdom Publications, 1995.

STYX

The River Styx (whose name means "hated") is the best known of the rivers of Hades. Apparently the Styx was at one time a real river in Greek Arcadia, whose waters were considered poisonous (Graves, vol. 1, p. 124). Traditionally, however, the Styx encircled Hades, forming a great barrier between the living and the dead; one could cross only with the help of the ferryman Charon, and he was loathe to transport any but the dead. However, the many rivers of the Greek Underworld are often confused. Virgil makes Acheron the boundary river and Styx a swamp (*Aeneid,* Book 6), and Dante makes Acheron, Styx, and Phlegethon encircle progressively lower levels of Hell. The Styx is also the habitation of a nymph by the same name, the eldest daughter of Oceanus and Tethys. The ancient writer Apollodorus claims that Persephone is the daughter of Zeus and the nymph Styx.

Because it flows through the Underworld, the Styx has magical properties; Achilleus was dipped bodily into the Styx by his mother Thetis, which conferred invulnerability on all but his heel (though some versions have Thetis burning her sons in a fire to achieve the same end). Great heroes appear to have little trouble crossing the Styx (Herakles, Odysseus, Theseus, Orpheus, Aeneas, and Dante all succeed in forcing their way onto Charon's boat). But the fundamental nature of the Styx is archetypal, and it serves the same function as Underworld rivers in every nation's mythology: to symbolize the boundary between the living and the dead. To cross it means to die, and even successful heroes find that when they return from the Underworld they are "reborn." The Styx is more a symbolic than a real boundary as shown in the Greek belief that without a proper ritual burial the shades of the dead may not cross the Styx but are forced to wait 100 years or even longer. Thus Odysseus in his Underworld adventure found his comrade Elpenor wandering miserably on the near shore, for no one had known of his death and he was stranded in limbo without a

SUKHĀVATĪ

Literally meaning "the Land of Bliss," *Sukhāvatī* is the Buddhist Sanskrit name for the "Pure Land" ruled by the Buddha Amitābha. It is first discussed in Indian Buddhist texts from around the second century C.E. as a glorious "heaven" at the western edge of the universe, billions and billions of miles from Earth, full of jeweled trees and all good things. There is no sin, craving, passions, or suffering, but all wholesome desires are instantly fulfilled (see excerpt). Belief in this Pure Land (called in Tibetan *Dewachan,* in Chinese *Ching-T'u,* and in Japanese *Jōdo*) died out in India and Southeast Asia and is mainly popular now in China, Korea, and most especially in Japan. Pure Land Buddhist devotees hope to be reincarnated in this spectacular heaven, and so they spend their earthly lives in practices that have the land of Sukhāvatī as their goal. However, many Pure Land teachers in East Asia have held that reincarnation in Sukhāvatī comes not from works but from faith alone: it is not through "self-power" but only through the "other-power" of a godlike Buddha that one may be saved.

It is interesting that in Pure Land Buddhist belief Sukhāvatī has not always existed in the universe: it was created by a perfect being as the result of a vow. The primary Indian text on this heaven teaches that many universal ages ago, a spiritual being named Dharmakāra vowed not to enter into the perfect liberation and joy of nirvāṇa himself unless all sentient beings were likewise saved. Although his vow, as recorded in Buddhist Scriptures, has twenty-four, forty-seven, or forty-eight parts, the important parts (taken from the Larger Sukhāvatī-vyūha Scripture) run as follows:

> All beings in ten directions with sincere profound faith who seek to be born in my land and call upon my name ten times, except those who have committed the five cardinal crimes or injured the true dharma, shall be born in my land.
> I will appear at the moment of death to all beings of the ten directions committed to enlightenment and the practice of good deed, who seek to be born in my land.
> All beings of the ten directions who hear my name, desire the Pure Land, and practice virtue in order to attain the Pure Land will succeed.
> (Matsunaga and Matsunaga)

After making this "original vow," the bodhisattva Dharmakāra strove for many cosmic eons to attain enlightenment; when he finally achieved his goal, the force of his "original vow" was fulfilled. Having become the perfect Buddha Amitābha (literally "infinite light"), he was now able to create the heaven called *Sukhāvatī* on the western edge of the universe, where anyone who had

Hades, showing Charon the ferryman; Cerberus, the three-headed guardian of the infernal regions; Pluto, King of the underworld and his queen Persephone; and the River Lethe. From Andrew Tooke, The Pantheon, *London, 1798. Courtesy of Anne Ronan Picture Library.*

funeral. The Styx was not only symbolic, however: many ancient Greeks placed a coin in the mouth of the dead before burial as a very real offering to fierce Charon.

See also ACHERON; FUNERARY CUSTOMS, ANCIENT GREEK; HADES; UNDERWORLD; WATER.

References
Dante Alighieri. *The Divine Comedy.* Trans. John Ciardi. New York: Norton, 1977.
Graves, Robert. *The Greek Myths.* Vol. 1. New York: Penguin, 1960.
Harrison, Jane Ellen. *Prolegomena to the Study of Greek Religion.* Cambridge: Cambridge University Press, 1922.
Turner, Alice K. *The History of Hell.* New York: Harcourt Brace, 1993.
Virgil. *The Aeneid.* Trans. Robert Fitzgerald. New York: Random House, 1983.

faith in him could be reborn after death. Even in this earthly life, during meditation, Sukhāvatī may be seen, and at the death of a truly devoted believer, the Buddha Amitābha is said to appear at the deathbed and personally escort the devotee to Sukhāvatī.

Sukhāvatī is not a heaven in the Christian sense, however; those who are reborn in Sukhāvatī are there for a purpose, not merely to enjoy themselves for eternity. The delights of Sukhāvatī are certainly described at length, but in the final analysis they are not real, any more than this Earth with its suffering is "real" in Buddhist philosophy. Rather, both this Earth and Sukhāvatī are but shades of the same illusion. The fact that everything in Sukhāvatī is responsive to every whim of the inhabitants shows that it is actually a mental realm created by the mutual energy of its presiding deity—Amitābha—and the spiritual residents reborn in Amitābha's heaven because of their intense devotion. Sukhāvatī is nothing but a mental projection under the guidance of a Buddhist master, with optimal conditions for achieving full enlightenment. It is this aspect of Sukhāvatī that makes it distinctly Buddhist, not theistic like Christianity or Islam.

However, popular practice rarely emphasizes the goal-oriented aspect of this heaven. The focus instead is on what life in this heaven is like and what one must do to get reborn there. Many works of art have portrayed Sukhāvatī with Amitābha pictured, golden in color, sitting "in state" in the center of his Pure Land and accompanied by his saintly companions, Avalokiteshvara and Mahasthamaprapta. A tremendous iconography has developed around these three figures, and much literature is devoted to describing life with them after death. Certainly, for the illiterate lay Buddhist who might have trouble grasping such abstract concepts as nirvāṇa, a detailed description of Sukhāvatī with its Buddha is probably an effective incentive to lead a spiritual life.

The tradition of Sukhāvatī, and reincarnation in a Pure Land, became one of the largest and most influential movements in East Asian Buddhism, but interest in a Pure Land was certainly known in early India, where Buddhism began. Even then, however, the Sukhāvatī movement must have been controversial, as it is today. There is no mention of Sukhāvatī or the Buddha Amitābha in the earliest Buddhist texts, and the "southern" or Theravāda school of Buddhism accepts nothing of the kind. However, the paradigm for the Pure Land Sukhāvatī appears to have been Kusavati, the capital city of the semilegendary king Mahasudassana, who is frequently mentioned in the Pali Scriptures of the southern Buddhists. Several important "northern" or Mahāyāna Buddhist Scriptures (the Larger and Smaller Sukhāvatīvyūha, the Avataṃsaka, and the Gandhavyūha sūtras) developed the "earthly paradise" of Kusavati into the heavenly paradise of Sukhāvatī. These later Indian Scriptures teach about rebirth in a Pure Land heaven after death, although it seems clear that these teachings never gained widespread appeal in India. However, carried along the trade routes of Central Asia, Buddhist faith centered around Sukhāvatī entered China by the third century C.E., spread to Korea and Japan by the Nara period (710–794 C.E.), and then entered Tibet. It is in Japan, many say, that the Sukhāvatī tradition received its fullest development, and even today, under the name *Jōdo,* faith in the Pure Land is the most powerful tradition of Buddhism in Japan.

See also ABHIRATI; AKṢOBHYA; CHING T'U; DEWACHAN (TIBETAN BUDDHIST); JŌDŌ; NIRVĀṆA; PURE LAND.

References

Becker, Carl B. *Breaking the Circle: Death and the Afterlife in Buddhism.* Carbondale: Southern Illinois University Press, 1993.

Foard, James, Michael Solomon, and Richard K. Payne, eds. *The Pure Land Tradition: History and Development.* Berkeley Buddhist Studies Series no. 3. Berkeley: University of California Press, 1989.

Gómez, Luis O. *The Land of Bliss: The Paradise of the Buddha of Measureless Light*. Honolulu: University of Hawaii Press, 1996.

Matsunaga, Daigan, and Alicia Matsunaga. *The Buddhist Concept of Hell*. New York: Philosophical Library, 1972.

Müller, Max, ed. *Sacred Books of the East*. Vol. 49: *The Larger Sukhāvatī-vyūha-sūtra*. Oxford: Clarendon Press, 1894.

Williams, Paul. *Mahāyāna Buddhism: The Doctrinal Foundations*. New York: Routledge, 1989.

SVARGA

The expectation of meeting heaven after death is a belief found in the most ancient Hindu Scriptures, the Vedas. In these earliest Indian texts, there is already a division of heaven into at least three levels, namely the lowest, "rich in water," the middle, "the empire of pīlu-trees," and the highest, "where the fathers sit" (Atharva Veda XVIII.2.4). Svarga holds special places for those of high achievements, particularly those who have advanced "to the sun" through ascetic practices (Rig Veda X.154.2). And life there is said to be "immortal," though as Hermann Oldenburg states, there are many indications that "immortality" means simply "a very long duration." Contrary to much Western scholarly opinion, it is most likely that reincarnation was the cardinal doctrine even in the earliest period of Indian religion. There is no evidence of reincarnation being introduced as a "new" faith and coming into conflict with "older" practice.

A curious substance called *soma,* which appears to have been a ritual drink that induced spiritual experience, was known in ancient India. In one hymn (Rig Veda IX.113) praising this drink (and the god) soma, there is a wonderful account of Svarga:

> Where radiance inexhaustible
> Dwells, and the light of heaven is set,
> Place me, clear-flowing one, in that
> Imperishable and deathless world. . . .
>
> Make me immortal in that realm,
> Wherein is movement glad and free,
> In the third sky, third heaven of heavens,
> Where are the lucid worlds of light.
>
> Make me immortal in the place
> Where loves and longings are fulfilled,
> The region of the ruddy sphere,
> Where food and satisfaction reign.
>
> Make me immortal in the place
> Wherein felicity and joy,
> Pleasure and bliss together dwell,
> And all desire is satisfied.

In this hymn heaven is described in quite material terms, though it would not be difficult to see symbolic references as well. Proper funeral rites, including cremation, were considered extremely important in order to secure the joys of heaven, and the ancient texts mention the dead surviving on the transformed food offered up at sacrifices. Because of the rituals performed by the priestly caste, called brahmins, "With pools of butter, with shores of honey, with brandy instead of water, full of milk, water, curdled milk: honey-sweet shall such rivers flow surging towards you in the heavenly world. May lotus-ponds surround you on all sides" (Atharva Veda IV.34). The body in heaven is mentioned in the Vedas frequently as becoming perfect, having left diseases behind, with limbs strong and "not twisted." Obviously, the conception here is of earthly suffering and imperfection being done away with and the maturation in heaven of the hopes one had during one's life on Earth. Also frequently mentioned is joining the ancestors, or pitris, in heaven, though this probably means more than simply reuniting with one's ancestors—certain classes of pitris have cosmological significance as the creators and shapers of the material universe.

Later Hindu religion considerably expanded this already rich body of tradition, especially as speculation proceeded on the nature and dimensions of the universe. By the period of the Purāṇas, texts composed circa 300 to 600 C.E., a rigidly structured picture of the universe had emerged, with no less than seven heavens placed vertically one atop the other. Below the surface of the Earth, at very great depths, seven Underworlds were stacked, called Pātāla. Below even these were located the hells, seven, fourteen, twenty-one, or even more. From highest to lowest, the names of the seven heavens are:

7. Satyaloka, whose inhabitants never experience death
6. Taparloka, the heaven of the fruits of asceticism
5. Janarloka, the heaven of divine men and sons of the god Brahmā
4. Maharloka, the lowest heaven which escapes destruction each cosmic age
3. Svarloka, reaching from the sun to the pole star
2. Bhuvaloka, stretching from the earth's atmosphere to the sun
1. Bhūloka, the Earth with its various continents and atmosphere

At the end of each cosmic age, called a *kalpa,* the material universe is destroyed by fire (or sometimes water). The destruction reduces all forms to empty space, up to and including the third heaven, Svarloka. The heat is said to be so intense that even the beings in the fourth heaven, Maharloka, are scorched, and though their world is not destroyed, they retreat to the fifth heaven while the fires blaze. During this time of pralāya, or cessation, there is no activity in the lower

From the Ascent to Heaven

Causing heaven and earth to tremble, the god Indra came to the hero Yudhishthira on a chariot and asked him to ascend it. Seeing his brothers fallen on the earth, and burning with grief, Yudhishthira said to Indra, "My brothers have all fallen here! They must go with me. Without them I do not wish to go to heaven, O lord! My wife, the delicate princess Draupadī, should also go with us. Please permit this."

"You will behold your family in the celestial region," the god Indra replied. "They have reached there before you." They ascended by chariot to heaven.

Though he could not see his wife Draupadī or his brothers anywhere in heaven, Yudhishthira saw the evil warlord Duryodhana radiant with prosperity and seated on an excellent seat. Then Yudhishthira was suddenly overcome with anger and turned away. "O you gods," he said, "I have no wish to see the evil Duryodhana! What is heaven to me if I am separated from my brothers?"

The god Nārada replied, "O king of kings! This is heaven, there can be no enmities here! But if you wish to see your brothers, you may go there." Yudhishthira and the celestial messenger went together to see Yudhishthira's brothers and wife. The path was difficult, trodden by sinners, fetid with the stench of rotting flesh. Corpses smeared with fat and blood, with arms and thighs cut off, or with entrails torn out and legs severed, lay along the path which was skirted all along with a blazing fire.

Yudhishthira was distressed and stupefied by the foul stench. Resolved to return, he began to retrace his steps.

Just then he heard the piteous cries of his brothers, wife, friends and instructors, calling out for help. Hearing the pleas for help, Yudhishthira asked, "What perverse destiny is this? What are the sins which were committed by these great heroes, that they should suffer in hell?" With great anger and a sense of injustice, the hero Yudhishthira told his companion, "Go back to those whose messenger you are. Tell them that I shall not return to them, but shall stay here to bring comfort to these suffering brothers of mine."

Then Indra, lord of gods, appeared and said, "O mighty Yudhishthira, join the ranks of the gods who are pleased with you. These illusions have ended. You once deceived the general Drona on the battlefield, lying to him that his son was dead, and have therefore been shown hell by an act of deception. But let the fever of your heart be dispelled. Here is the celestial river, sacred and sanctifying the three worlds. It is called the celestial Ganges. Plunging into it, you will attain your proper place."

Having bathed in the celestial Ganges, and renouncing his human form, Yudhishthira obtained the form of a celestial. Through that bath, he became divested of all his enmities and grief. Surrounded by the gods, he then went away from there, and reached the place where those heroes, his brothers and their earthly foes, freed from human wrath, were each enjoying their respective place in heaven.

Adapted from Narasimhan, The Mahābhārata, *Book 18 (1965).*

---

realms, and all are reborn for a time among the gods of the higher heavens. Eventually, however, from the force of karma, the universe itself is reborn and beings begin to repopulate the lower realms.

Not merely cosmological speculations but philosophical and ethical speculations also engaged with the tradition of Svarga. In one such story, we find that at one time the god Shiva, in his infinite mercy, created on Earth a shrine that could send people to heaven directly when they visited it. Soon everyone on Earth had come to see it and had been saved by their faith and pilgrimage alone—they went to heaven without any of the usual religious practices, without real spiritual knowledge, and in spite of their evil actions.

Sacrifices, asceticism, donations to brahmins (priests), and all the other prescribed rites ceased, and heaven became crowded with men, old and young, those skilled in the Vedas and those ignorant of them. Sacrifice was destroyed, earth became empty, and heaven was so overfull that

people had to stand holding their arms up. . . . Yama, king of Dharma, is struck dumb when he contemplates the record of their evil deeds and the seven hells, which are empty. (Skanda Purāṇa, O'Flaherty, trans., p. 254)

The gods, feeling crowded, decide to create a new god, Ganesh, lord of wealth, who would introduce material craving and desire into human minds, by which they would fall from heaven into hell.

Did this story arise as a reaction against the sect of Shiva worship, or did its authors take a perverse delight in the suffering of others? Probably neither: the authors appear to be skeptical of the value of a heaven so easily attained and mock the grossly physical conception of heaven as a place with so little space that people must stand "holding their arms up." Furthermore, in Hindu tradition, ritual sacrifices on the Earth paralleled divine sacrifices performed by the gods, which literally kept the world turning and the vital essences of the world circulating. If humans, through such an easy "out," were to cease to perform their prescribed duties, the world would become seriously imbalanced, and nature itself would be thrown into disarray. This story is a philosophical lesson in duty and the value of laborious religious practice.

Today Svarga is a living reality for the nearly one billion people who call themselves Hindu. Evil deeds that produce negative karma prevent one from entering heaven, and Hindu teachers prescribe strict rites for the expiation of sins (see Kane, *History of Dharmashāstra*). Performance of duty (called *dharma*), charity, reverence for elders, and study of Scriptures are among the many ways by which the common person may hope to attain Svarga. Rites for deceased ancestors up to three generations past are also considered of the utmost importance to many Hindu families, for their ancestors depend on these offerings, called shrāddha, for their enjoyment in heaven; in addition, the correct performance of the rites ensures that the living family members will also in their time experience heavenly bliss. Although philosophical Hindu literature clearly teaches that Svarga is merely a temporary rest between lives, however long it may last—up to millions of years!—still, everyone must eventually reincarnate in a lower realm because of the force of unexpended karma. At such time, one must take up a new form, enter a new life, and once again experience death and rebirth. Mokṣa, or liberation, is held out by philosophical Hinduism as the only true

and lasting happiness and escape from the suffering of death and rebirth (saṃsāra). But for the majority of Hindus, Svarga is the near goal, and mokṣa or perfect freedom a distant hope.

See also FUNERARY CUSTOMS, HINDU; NARAKA; PĀTĀLA; REINCARNATION, EASTERN; SHIVA (HINDU); SHRĀDDHA; YAMA.

References

Griswold, H. D. *The Religion of the Rigveda*. Indian ed. Delhi: Motilal Banarsidass, 1971.

Hastings, James, ed. *Encyclopaedia of Religion and Ethics*. Vol. 4: "Cosmogony and Cosmology (Indian)." Edinburgh: T. and T. Clark, 1911.

Kane, Pandurang Vaman. *History of Dharmashāstra: Ancient and Medieval Religious and Civil Law in India*. Vol. 4. Government Oriental Series, Class B, no. 6. Poona: Bhandarkar Oriental Research Institute, 1953.

Narasimhan, Chakravarthi V. The Mahābhārata: *An English Version Based on Selected Verses*. New York: Columbia University Press, 1965.

O'Flaherty, Wendy Doniger. *The Origins of Evil in Hindu Mythology*. Berkeley: University of California Press, 1976.

Oldenberg, Hermann. *The Religion of the Veda*. Trans. Shridhar B. Shrotri. Indian ed. Delhi: Motilal Banarsidass, 1988.

Shastri, Manmatha Nath Dutt, trans. *Agni Purānam*. Benares: Chowkhamba Publications, 1967.

Wilson, H. H. *Vishnu Purāna*. Vol. 1. London: Trübner, 1864.

T

TAISCH
See Fetch.

TĀJ MAHAL

The name of this famous Indian mausoleum literally means "the Crown of the Palace," another name for Emperor Shāh Jahān's favorite wife, Arjuman Banu Begum. (She was also known as Mumtaz Mahal, or "Light of the Palace.")

Shihab al-Din Shāh Jahān ruled from 1628 to 1658 C.E. He succeeded his father Jahāngīr to the Mughal throne in India and stepped up his ancestors' patronage of Islamic architecture and arts. He was a cruel ruler but cunning enough to realize that the creation of monumental works greatly legitimizes a government in the eyes of others. Immediately upon his father Jahāngīr's death in 1627, Shāh Jahān ordered the seven-year construction of his tomb, which was only one storey tall but colossal in scope. His father's tomb emphasized the extremely tall tower (minaret) at each corner, which would later contribute to the great beauty and distinctiveness of the Tāj Mahal.

Only four years into his reign, in 1631, Shāh Jahān's favorite wife died. Demonstrating his love for her (and simultaneously his wealth and power), the emperor hired three master architects to plan her fabulous tomb. The Tāj Mahal required the services of thousands of workers and sixteen years to construct; it was completed in 1649. Like previous Mughal monuments, the Tāj Mahal is situated in a garden, which is divided into four equal portions by four shallow canals radiating out at right angles from a central point. The four canals symbolize the four rivers of paradise. This style of park is called a *chahr bagh,* introduced from Persia by the first Mughal Emperor, Bābur (ruled 1526–1530). The Tāj Mahal is unique because it is situated in the center of the north side of the park (against a riverbank on the other side) rather than in the middle of the chahr bagh. On the south edge of the park stands a large arched gatehouse, facing the great mausoleum and creating a sense of balance in the garden. Meanwhile, just west of the Tāj Mahal and facing it is a mosque; just east is a mirror image of the mosque but designated as a guesthouse. All three—the gatehouse, guesthouse, and mosque—have a facade in the traditional red sandstone of the region, and they present a stark contrast to the gleaming white polished marble of the Tāj Mahal.

The plan of the Tāj Mahal largely follows that of the tomb of the second Mughal Emperor, Humāyūn (d. 1586), though refined in many details. Like Humāyūn's tomb, the Tāj Mahal is on a huge low platform that stretches far beyond the actual mausoleum east and west. Unlike the tomb of Humāyūn, to each of the four corners of this platform Shāh Jahān added a tall, slender tower called a minaret, which in mosques were used by the caller (muezzin) to "call" (or sing, really) the faithful to prayer five times a day. On the Tāj Mahal the minarets are purely decorative, but they add to the religious symbolism of the tomb. This design and the positioning of a mosque nearby comes from the Middle East, where it probably originated as an attempt to religiously justify the building of grandiose tombs, even though the Qur'ān explicitly forbids doing so.

The main body of the Tāj Mahal is built on a plan called *hasht behisht,* "eight Paradises," also modeled on the tomb of Humāyūn and inherited from Persian architectural style. These eight regions of the Muslim conception of Paradise were symbolized both by the octagonal shape of the four flanking towers and the fact that the four towers (called *chahr taqs*), each with two storeys, present eight pavilions or inner "gardens." The central square tower or "drum," with the great bulbous dome atop it, symbolizes the throne of God, which in Muslim tradition is set above the eight Gardens of Delight but is visible from them. Four smaller domed gazebo-like structures (called *chatris*) stand atop the four flanking octagonal towers, surrounding the higher central dome. The overall effect of symmetry, height, and proportion is truly beautiful.

Adding to the grandeur of the "Crown of the Palace" are the reliefs and inlaid semiprecious stones that cover much of the exterior and interior marble. The designs are in the shapes of flowers and vines, recalling for the viewer the Gardens of Delight and giving the effect of setting the entire structure in a field of flowers, as John D. Hoag remarks in his work, *Islamic Architecture.* From a Persian poem about the Tāj Mahal written by Emperor Shāh Jahān himself, Hoag (p. 185) quotes,

Photograph of the Tāj Mahal showing just a fragment of the lush ornamentation. Courtesy of Anne Ronan Picture Library.

Like the garden of heaven a brilliant spot,
Full of fragrance like paradise fraught with
   ambergris.
In the breadth of its court perfumes from the
   nose-gay
of sweet-heart rise.

To further the religious associations, long verses from the Qur'ān are inlaid in black marble running along the roof and all the arches, reminding the spectator (who can read Arabic) of the Resurrection (Qiyāma) and judgment day to come.

See also FUNERARY CUSTOMS, MUSLIM; GARDENS OF DELIGHT; KURGAN; MAUSOLEUM, ISLAMIC; QIYĀMA; TOWER TOMB.

References
Begley, Wayne E. "The Myth of the Taj Mahal and a New Theory of Its Symbolic Meaning." *Art Bulletin* 56, no. 1 (1979).
Blair, Sheila S., and Jonathan M. Bloom. *The Art and Architecture of Islam 1250–1800*. New Haven: Yale University Press, 1994.
Hoag, John D. *Islamic Architecture*. New York: Rizzoli, 1987.
Jairazbhay, R. A. "The Taj Mahal in the Context of East and West: A Study in the Comparative Method." *Journal of the Warburg and Courtauld Institute* 24 (1961).
Lowry, Glenn D. "Humayun's Tomb: Form, Function, and Meaning in Early Mughal Architecture." *Muqarnas* 4 (1987).
Pal, Pratapaditya. *Romance of the Taj Mahal*. Los Angeles: Los Angeles County Museum of Art, 1989.
Smith, Edmund W. *Akbar's Tomb, Sikandrah, Near Agra, Described and Illustrated*. Allahabad: Archaeological Survey of India, 1909.

TARTAROS

According to Greek scholar Robert Graves, the root *tar* means west; thus *tartaros* means "far west." It was one of the names of the land of the dead in the ancient Greek world and was located ambiguously over the water as well as under the Earth. In this way it was possible for Odysseus to sail to Tartaros without descending, though in general the land of the dead is placed far underground.

At first Tartaros was the dwelling not of the human dead but the banished primordial gods. According to Hesiod in *Theogony* (c. eighth century B.C.E.), Tartaros is the dwelling place of the Titans after their defeat at the hands of the Olympians. There they are ruled over by Kronos, the former leader of heaven and Earth (although in another piece by Hesiod, *Works and Days*, Kronos rules over the heroic dead on the Islands of the Blest). In the *Iliad* (8:10–16) Homer makes Zeus threaten the gods on Olympos with a similar fate:

any one I perceive against the gods' will attempting
to go among the Trojans and help them, or among
   the Danaans,
he shall go whipped against his dignity back to
   Olympos;

or I shall take him and dash him down to the murk
   of Tartaros,
far below, where the uttermost depth of the pit lies
   under
earth, where there are gates of iron and a brazen
   doorstone,
as far beneath the house of Hades as from earth the
   sky lies.
(Lattimore, trans.)

In later Greek mythology, when Hades had become considerably more developed theologically, murky Tartaros became the lowest of the regions of the Underworld, a place of punishment for especially vile sinners (which, later interpretations explained, was *why* the rebellious Titans were down there). It was said that an anvil would fall for nine days and nights before it reached Tartaros. At first, it was only the most horrible of criminals, mythic in scale, who were punished in Tartaros: Tantalos, for feeding his son to the gods for dinner; Sisyphos, for playing the gods for fools; Theseus and Peirithous, for attempting to rape Persephone, and so on. In time, however, the concept of universal afterlife judgment gained force in the Greco-Roman world, and Tartaros became a general place of punishment.

This later Tartaros is described as a prison with gates, guarded by Tisiphone, cruelest of the Erinyes, and locked so tightly that no visitor to hell may even observe the torments within. In the Roman epic the *Aeneid* (VI:824–832), the hero Aeneas has a prophetess-guide to report to him what awaits sinners consigned to Tartaros:

Here is one who sold his fatherland for gold
and set a tyrant over it; he made
and unmade laws for gain. This one assailed
the chamber of his daughter and compelled
forbidden mating. All dared horrible evil
and reached what they had dared. A hundred
   tongues,
a hundred mouths, an iron voice were not
enough for me to gather all the forms
of crime or tell the names of all the torments.
(Mandelbaum, trans.)

The *Aeneid*, written just decades before the Christian era, demonstrates that already the Romans had fully accepted the reality of ethical judgment in the afterlife.

See also ERINYS; HADES; ISLANDS OF THE BLEST.

References
Frazer, James G. *The New Golden Bough*. Ed. Theodor H. Gaster. New York: Criterion Books, 1959.
Graves, Robert. *The Greek Myths*. New York: Penguin, 1960.
Harrison, Jane Ellen. *Prolegomena to the Study of Greek Religion*. Cambridge; Cambridge University Press, 1922.

Dante and Virgil at the edge of the abyss. Illustration by Gustave Doré for Dante's Inferno, *1861, Canto XVI. Courtesy of Anne Ronan Picture Library.*

Hesiod. *Works and Days* and *Theogony*. Trans. Stanley Lombardo. Indianapolis: Hackett Publishing, 1993.

Lattimore, Richmond, trans. *The Iliad*. Chicago: University of Chicago Press, 1951.

Mandelbaum, Allen, trans. *The Aeneid of Virgil*. New York: Bantam, 1961.

Sourvinou-Inwood, Christiane. *"Reading" Greek Death: To the End of the Classical Period*. Oxford: Clarendon Press, 1995.

West, M. L. *Early Greek Philosophy and the Orient*. Oxford: Clarendon Press, 1971.

TEMPLE TOMB

This kind of tomb, whether rock-cut, free-standing, or underground, was designed in the form of a temple or shrine to honor the esteemed dead and serve as a center for their cults. The Greeks made their dead into heroes, the Romans regarded theirs as minor supernatural powers, giving them the title of *di Manes,* and the Egyptians regarded their deceased pharaohs as full-blown divinities. Thus it is not surprising that the more respected dead should be accorded temples as their rightful homes.

In the Hellenistic world, temple tombs often took the shape of rectangular tombs with high podiums as their base and steps leading up on at least one side and sometimes on all four sides. Columns rested upon this base and supported the domed, conical, or pyramidal roof. Set within the columns was the cella, often with a false door facing front, in which the body or more often cremains were placed. Sometimes the tomb had only two pillars and a back wall carved with a false door leading to a nonexistent cella. Other temple tombs had actual doors leading inside the cella or to a stairway that led downward to the cella below, either in the podium or actually underground. The decoration of these Hellenistic temple tombs was almost always ornate, with elaborately carved and capped pillars, relief carvings on the podium or pediment above the pillars, family busts ranged on tiers on the insides of the walls, and the cella carved and decorated to look like an aedicula, or small house.

Egyptian pyramids must also be seen as temple tombs, even though in the first nine or ten great pyramids of the early dynasties (the Fourth and Fifth Dynasties, c. 2600–2200 B.C.E.) no physical remains of the deceased or any coffin have been found. The pyramid, with its upward-pointing architecture and elaborately painted inner chambers, served as the focal point of a solar cult in which the deceased pharaoh served as patron deity, accompanied by the Underworld Osiris, god of the dead, and the heavenly god Re, whose chariot pulled the sun on its daily rounds. Egyptian pyramids, especially the greatest and earliest of them, were surrounded by various temple structures clearly indicating that they were centers of living cults,

although their exact initiations and rituals are difficult to determine.

Many medieval Christian churches can be viewed as temple tombs, for as the cult of relics grew, especially from the eighth century C.E. onward, and the catacombs were raided for the remains of the martyrs, churches came more and more to serve as shrines for the esteemed dead. God was a distant and unapproachable figure, but "living" relics energized a Christian church with their holy and supernatural power, making the prayers of the faithful likewise powerful and able to be heard and acted upon.

References
Toynbee, J. M. C. *Death and Burial in the Roman World*. Ithaca, NY: Cornell University Press, 1971.

TEN KINGS OF HELL (SHIH-WANG)

In Chinese belief, after death the soul must undergo ten rites of passage in the Underworld in order to win a happy afterlife. The first forty-nine days after death, the soul undergoes seven trials, each one seven days after the last, passing from one dreary bureaucratic office to the next and being judged by the officials at each station. Three more trials soon follow: one hundred days after death, thirteen months after death, and twenty-five months after death. For each trial in the Underworld there is a presiding judge, called a *wang,* or "king" in Chinese, who reads one's merit and decides one's fate. Taken together, these are the Ten Kings of hell.

During the first few centuries of the common era, Buddhism imported from Central Asia and India began to compete and eventually mingle with indigenous Chinese traditions (Confucian and Taoist) to produce rather new and unique ideas about death and the afterlife. The Indian god of death, Yama, took his place as Yen-lo wang among a host of important Chinese deities who were thought to have influence over the dead, and dozens of competing Indian and Chinese paradises and hells produced a very complicated religious scene. By the seventh century C.E., however, a single, organized understanding of the death process and journey rose to dominance in Chinese religion. Three powerful strands of belief were synthesized to make up the ten realms of the Ten Kings: (1) the early Chinese belief in an Underworld existence after death, most famously under the sacred Mount T'ai Shan; (2) the Buddhist teaching of karma, including postmortem judgment for one's behavior in life; and (3) worship of ancestors and belief in rituals to better their lot in the afterlife. Now, in a single Underworld bureaucracy composed of many departments with their documents and their officials, souls were ushered through a long process of examinations and waiting periods, during which their descendants could send offerings to influence the Ten Kings and secure the deceased a better lot. After this three-year ordeal, souls were then sent along to their "final" destination, either to be reborn in a new form on Earth or to be sent to one of the many stratified hells, the paradises of the Eastern Sea, or the blest realm of the Queen Mother of the West.

The combination of Buddhist and native Chinese ideas that produced the Ten Kings system is difficult and tedious to draw out; suffice it to say that Chinese Buddhism sanctioned the karmic judgments of the Ten Kings, and Buddhist monks became renowned for their performance of funerals. Meanwhile, Confucian reverence for the dead was incorporated in the ten memorial services designed to help the dead at their ten judgments.

A noncanonical but widely influential Buddhist text, The Scripture on the Ten Kings, tells us the names and positions of the ten kings.

1. The Far-Reaching King of Ch'in: first 7 days after death
2. The King of the First River: 8–14 days after death
3. The Imperial King of Sung: 15–21 days after death
4. The King of the Five Offices: 22–28 days after death
5. King Yama: 29–35 days after death
6. The King of Transformations: 36–42 days after death
7. The King of Mount T'ai: 43–49 days after death
8. The Impartial King: 100 days after death
9. The King of the Capital: 13 months after death
10. The King of the Cycle of the Five Paths: 25 months after death

Here we see that the Buddhist lord of the dead, Yama, has become the head king of the whole system but has as his many assistants powerful Chinese deities, including the magistrate of the Underworld at Mount T'ai. The Chinese belief in crossing a river, called Nai-ho, in the afterlife has become codified as the domain of the King of the First River, where ox-headed jailers force people to cross over. In each of the ten realms, the dead stand practically naked, humbled by the judgments pronounced upon them, and utterly dependent upon the officials who preside—though the Ten Kings may be persuaded to see more "merit" and good deeds in a person whose grieving family manages to send great amounts of hell money, clothing, and equipment (by burning them at memorial services).

As the realms of the Ten Kings became more rigid over time, Chinese believers began to feel more and more terrified by the harsh justice meted out in the Underworld. Not coincidentally, the saint Ti-tsang

soon became a very prominent guest in hell because he was the Buddhist figure responsible for saving all beings until the future Buddha should arrive. Visiting hell often, Ti-tsang was empowered to receive the prayers and offerings of those suffering in hell and grant absolution by his grace. Silk paintings of the Ten Kings, recovered this century from the Chinese border town of Tun-Huang on the old Silk Route, show the kings in very subservient positions, whereas the saint Ti-tsang is in the center, clearly portrayed as the master of the realm. The cult of Ti-tsang gained considerable prominence in China, mediating with forgiveness the paperwork and convictions handed down by the Ten Kings.

See also SOUL, CHINESE; TI-TSANG; UNDERWORLD; YELLOW SPRINGS.

References

Loewe, Michael. *Chinese Ideas of Life and Death*. London: Allen and Unwin, 1982.

Poo, Mu-chou. *In Search of Personal Welfare: A View of Ancient Chinese Religion*. New York: SUNY Press, 1998.

Teiser, Stephen F. *The Ghost Festival in Medieval China*. Princeton: Princeton University Press, 1988.

———. *The Scripture on the Ten Kings and the Making of Purgatory in Medieval Chinese Buddhism*. Honolulu: University of Hawaii Press, 1994.

Thompson, Laurence G. "On the Prehistory of Hell in China." *Journal of Chinese Religions*, no. 17 (Fall 1989).

THOLOS TOMB

A Minoan-Mycenaean-Greek type of tumulus, also called a *rotunda,* a tholos tomb is a large circular stone building, often beehive-shaped, with a domed masonry roof, that might serve as the burial place for an entire clan over many generations. They are nearly always underground or partially underground where the artificial earth mound has eroded away. Although many of the tholoi tombs have much in common structurally with the Neolithic-period megaliths of Ireland, England, and western Europe, the tholoi are mostly several thousands of years younger and generally of better construction due to the availability of bronze tool technology. The stonework is still without mortar, like that in the megalithic structures, but is professionally dressed and fitted, accurately laid out, and beautifully built to a regular profile. Over 100 tholos tombs are still standing on the Greek mainland and on various Aegean islands.

The tholos tomb is first found in the early Minoan civilization (third millennium B.C.E.) in southern Crete, where there are paved places for dancing near the tombs, possibly indicating their use as centers for a cult of the dead. In the late Mycenaean period (c. 1500 to 1300 B.C.E.) the tholoi tombs of Crete began to be imitated on the mainland, becoming more and more massive. Great facades were built around the entrance-way with early columns and massive lintels over the doorway, often weighing many tons.

The most famous and most massive tholos tomb is the thesauros (treasury) of Atreus at Mycenae, the royal tomb from the fourteenth century B.C.E. A passageway (dromos) led inward to the actual entrance (stomion), which was filled with earth after the dead were interred inside; it had to be dug out for each burial and refilled afterward. Besides the grave chamber inside, there was a massive vault that served ritual purposes and probably symbolized the Underworld. Animal bones and ash are regularly found in excavated tholoi, indicating that funerary sacrifices were performed in the vault, probably accompanied by a funeral banquet. Horses and even entire chariots have been found buried in the tholoi tombs, as in the kurgans of Central Asia.

After the mysterious collapse of Minoan-Mycenaean culture (as well as the civilizations of the rest of the eastern Mediterranean) around 1200 B.C.E., tholoi tombs were seldom built. Lesser quality tholos tombs are found late into the Iron Age in Thessaly (1000–800 B.C.E.) and in the Etruscan period of Italy (c. 700 B.C.E.) with single pillars supporting their pseudodomed roofs. Gradually the tholos-style tombs in the Greek and Roman Mediterranean world were replaced by above-ground autonomous mausolea for the elite, and single-burial graves and cremation predominated for the masses. Nevertheless, some tholos tombs continued to be built well into the Hellenic period, as fourth-century B.C.E. tombs have been found in various reaches of the Greek-influenced world, including in Thrace (modern Bulgaria), Scythian territory around the Black Sea, and Anatolia.

See also FUNERARY CUSTOMS, ANCIENT GREEK; FUNERARY CUSTOMS, ANCIENT ROMAN.

References

Burkert, Walter. *Greek Religion*. Trans. John Raffan. Cambridge: Harvard University Press, 1985.

Colvin, Howard. *Architecture and the After-Life*. New Haven: Yale University Press, 1991.

Hutchinson, R. W. *Prehistoric Crete*. Baltimore: Penguin, 1962.

Mylonas, G. *Mycenae and the Mycenaean Age*. Princeton: Princeton University Press, 1966.

Nilsson, Martin P. *The Minoan-Mycenaean Religion and Its Survival in Greek Religion*. 2nd ed. Lund: C. W. K. Gleerup, 1950.

Taylour, W. *The Mycenaeans*. New York: Praeger, 1964.

Xanthoudides, S. *The Vaulted Tombs of Mesará*. Liverpool: University Press of Liverpool, 1924.

TI-TSANG

Ti-tsang is the Chinese Buddhist deity (bodhisattva) associated with rescuing one's ancestors from unfortunate states after death. Imported from India, where his name was Kṣitigarbha, Ti-tsang was originally an advanced saint, mentioned in Mahāyāna Buddhist Scriptures, such as the seventh-century Indian Buddhist text called *The Scripture on Kṣitigarbha and the Ten Wheels* (Daśa-chakra-kṣitigarbha-sūtra). It was Kṣitigarbha's job to lead beings to salvation during the immense period of time between the death of the last Buddha, Gautama Shakyamuni, and the Buddha Maitreya, who will appear on Earth many thousands of years from now. This "salvation" was understood—in early Indian Buddhism—as leading beings to final liberation and enlightenment, called *nirvāṇa*. In China, however, Ti-tsang was seen more as a shepherd of one's ancestors' souls, rescuing them from rebirth in the hells and ghostly wastelands and thereby securing benefits for their descendants living on Earth. Particularly as the Underworld became more bureaucratized, governed by ten separate kings led by the fearsome Yen-lo wang, Ti-tsang became an extremely important mediator and allowed indigenous Chinese belief in the efficacy of funerary offerings to alleviate the strictness of karmic law imported from India.

This new role of Ti-tsang in China is announced in The Scripture on the Original Vows of Ti-tsang Bodhisattva (in Chinese, *Ti-tsang P'u-sa Pen-yüan Ching*). In this work, Ti-tsang's immense and glorious past is revealed, along with his miraculous powers to assist all beings, especially those in the Underworld, or "earth prisons." This Scripture purports to be from an Indian original, translated into Chinese in the seventh century C.E.. Certainly, however, the text was composed in China by Buddhists many centuries later, when Pure Land Buddhism and the worship of a great variety of saints was growing popular among the masses. In Chinese Buddhist thinking, the world had grown dramatically worse since the time of the historical Buddha, around 500 B.C.E., so it was no longer possible to achieve salvation through one's own power. One must rely on the other-power of great saints who had spent eons building up their spiritual abilities and infinite good karma in order to rescue beings from decaying worlds such as Earth. Thus prayer, recitation, visualization, and pilgrimage became common practices among Buddhists in China, who sought favor with Buddhist deities. This practice largely replaced the traditional Indian goal of self-liberation through self-control, calmness, and meditation (vipaśyana).

An entire tradition of Buddhism evolved in China centering around the worship of Ti-tsang, saint of compassion. Worship of Ti-tsang led to all kinds of benefits for ordinary Buddhists, including long life, freedom from poverty and sickness, increase in memory and intelligence, and good fortune to the family and especially newborns. But more important, Ti-tsang was the protector of one's deceased ancestors. The mere recitation of his special Scripture on the Original Vows of Ti-tsang Bodhisattva, was enough to free one's ancestors from judgment in hell and release them into heaven. Ti-tsang is pictured as physically descending into the hells (and there are many of them) to rescue those suffering there. Whenever he appears, the hot hells grow cool, the frigid hells warm up, and beautiful scents and sounds pacify the souls suffering there. Even if one's ancestors were in a fortunate rebirth, services held in their name to honor Ti-tsang improved their karma in general and served as a very widespread form of filial piety. Although fear of the Ten Kings of Hell played a large role in the popular conception of the deceased's post-mortem fate, Chinese art (such as silk paintings discovered this century in the border city of Tun-Huang) shows Ti-tsang as a huge central figure dominating the Ten Kings and reassuring the viewer that compassion and devotion to Ti-tsang were more powerful than even the collective judgment of the Underworld kings.

At the beginning of the twenty-first century, this tradition is as important as ever. In the seventh lunar month, Ti-tsang's Scripture is widely recited across the country (mostly by monks hired to do so), and offerings are made to thank Ti-tsang for his attention to the ancestors. As part of the funeral rites performed by a family for one who has recently died, Buddhist monks may be hired to recite this Scripture to ensure a good rebirth. The Scripture is often recited on the anniversary of the death each year and on the first and fifteenth day of each lunar month. Some Chinese temples contain columbaria, where families can have their ancestors' urns taken out and placed on an altar sacred to Ti-tsang for extra benefit. But Ti-tsang still has a religious function outside death and dying. Mount Chiu-hua in Anhwei province is sacred to Ti-tsang and is one of the "four famous mountains" in the Chinese Buddhist pilgrimage circuit that devout Buddhists hope to visit in their lifetime.

See also BHAVA-CHAKRA; HELLS, BUDDHIST; JIZŌ; KṢITIGARBHA; NIRVĀṆA; PURE LAND; REINCARNATION, EASTERN; SOUL, CHINESE; STŪPA; YEN-LO WANG.

References

Ching, Heng, trans. *Sūtra of the Past Vows of Earth Store Boddhisattva: The Collected Lectures of Tripitake Master Hsüan Hua*. San Francisco: Buddhist Text Translation Society, 1974.

De Visser, M. W. *The Bodhisattva Ti-tsang (Jizō) in China and Japan*. Berlin: Oesterheld, 1914.

Kitagawa, Joseph M. *Religion in Japanese History*. New York: Columbia University Press, 1966.

LaFleur, William R. *Liquid Life: Abortion and Buddhism in Japan*. Princeton: Princeton University Press, 1992.

Welch, Holmes. *The Practice of Chinese Buddhism, 1900–1950*. Cambridge: Harvard University Press, 1967.

Williams, Paul. *Mahāyāna Buddhism: The Doctrinal Foundations*. New York: Routledge, 1989.

TOHORAH (TAHARAH)

In Judaism, the ritual preparation and cleansing of the corpse before burial is called *tohorah* (also spelled *taharah*). In traditional Judaism this task was performed by the local burial society called the *chevra kaddisha*; in modern times, particularly among Reform Jews, the preparation of the body for burial is often performed by the staff of a funeral home, and tohorah is dispensed with. (Because tohorah is not mentioned in the Bible but was developed by rabbinic tradition beginning in the first centuries of the common era, such a modern shift in funerary customs is not as innovative as it may seem.)

Generally men perform the ritual for men, and women perform it for women. The tohorah begins about half an hour after death, when the chevra kaddisha undress the deceased, cover him or her with a clean sheet, and place the body on a special tohorah board. The body on the tohorah board is lowered to the ground (which has been strewn with straw or wood shavings and also covered with a sheet). The body is straightened, with the feet oriented toward the door so that the death impurity may escape the room; likewise, the windows are opened and candles are lit. (Whether the presence of a "physical" impurity literally "escapes" is a matter of personal belief.) Throughout these preparations specific prayers are to be said, which are read from a book called the maaver yabok.

Since the actual bathing and tohorah ritual are to be performed as close to the actual funeral and burial as possible, a shomer (watcher) is appointed to guard the body, particularly overnight. Just before the funeral the chevra kaddisha must ritually wash the body and then perform the actual purification of tohorah. This requires at least four members of the chevra kaddisha, none of whom may be the deceased's father-in-law, mother's husband, or brother-in-law (if the deceased is male) or parallel relations for a female.

The chevra kaddisha first wash their hands, washing first the right and then the left, three times in succession. A large container of water is used for the bathing, and smaller cups are employed to pour water upon various parts of the body. The entire body is washed in the following order: head, neck, right hand, right upper half of the body, right lower half of the body, right foot, left hand, left upper half of the body, left lower half of the body, and left foot. Then, rolling the body gently to one side and then the other, the right side of the back is washed and then the left. At no time is the body to be placed face down, as this would signify dishonor to the dead. The very Orthodox then rub a beaten egg mixed with wine or water over the head and front part of the body because in Jewish tradition the egg represents the round of life, death, and new life. After the bathing, the fingernails and toenails are trimmed and the hair is combed.

Finally, the deceased is ready for the purification ritual, which alone is properly called *tohorah*. The chevra kaddisha again wash their hands three times, right and left. The body is lifted from the ground vertically until it stands up straight, and more straw or wood shavings are placed on the ground where the body stands. Nine kavin (about 24 quarts) of water are then poured in a continuous stream over the dead without interruption. In some Orthodox circles this is repeated, or alternately the body may even be soaked in a mikveh, or ritual bath. In any case, after the tohorah the body is then replaced upon the dry tohorah board and dressed in burial clothes and covered with a shroud (called *tachrichim*). The body is then placed in its casket, often with some broken pieces of pottery (called *sherblach*), and the casket is sealed.

See also CHEVRA KADDISHA; FUNERARY CUSTOMS, JEWISH; SHOMER.

References

Abrahams, I. *Jewish Life in the Middle Ages.* London: E. Goldston, 1932.

Abramovitch, Henry. "Death." In *Contemporary Jewish Religious Thought,* ed. Arthur A. Cohen and Paul Mendes-Flohr. New York: Charles Scribner's Sons, 1989.

Lamm, Maurice. *The Jewish Way in Death and Mourning.* New York: Jonathan David Publishers, 1969.

Rabinowicz, H. *A Guide to Life.* London: Jewish Chronicle Publications, 1964.

Riemer, Jack, ed. *Jewish Reflections on Death.* New York: Schocken Books, 1974.

TOMBE DI GIGANTI
See Megalithic Tomb.

TOWER OF SILENCE

A tower of silence (in Persian, *dakhma*) is a round stone tower used in Iranian Zoroastrianism (and later among Parsis in India) to dispose of corpses by exposure to carnivorous animals, vultures, and the elements. Although a great many cultures practice exposure of corpses rather than burial or cremation, towers of silence are unique to Zoroastrianism in that they are permanent structures placed almost without exception in arid lands far from civilization for the sole purpose of eliminating all flesh from the bones of the deceased. When the process is complete, the bones—now only so many particles of dust—are traditionally gathered up and placed in sacred ossuaries (burial structures for bones).

The sacred texts of Zoroastrianism, the Avesta, Vendidad, and Zand, indicate that the human corpse is the essence of impurity. Zoroastrianism teaches a strict dualism between the forces of good and evil, and because the corpse is composed of flesh, it belongs wholly to the forces of evil. The fleshly corpse is the medium of infec-tion by demons and the source of temptation inflicted on humans by the god of supreme evil, Angra Mainyu. Bones, however, are purified of contaminating human energies and flesh, and they are therefore associated with the deity of supreme good, Ahura Mazda.

Since the corpse is, above all other objects, the essence of pollution, it is unthinkable for Zoroastrians to bury the corpse in the ground or burn it. Burial or cremation would allow the corpse to pollute the earth, fire, atmosphere, and plants that are the holy creations of Ahura Mazda. However, the body must be disposed of quickly lest it contaminate the place where death occurred. Unless the death took place late in the day near or after sundown, the preparation of the body, funeral, and transportation to the tower of silence must be accomplished immediately on the very day of death.

The Persian term *dakhma* appears to originate from the Indo-European root *dhmbh* and seems to have referred originally to a simple tomb or grave. Yet even as early as the Achaemenid period of the Middle East (circa 500 B.C.E.) there is evidence that ritual exposure of corpses was widely practiced by Zoroastrians—prob-ably at first just on the ground or on a bier—in common with the Parthians and the ancient nomads of the Arctic north and Central Asia in general, preemi-nently among the Mongols. Soon, however, the ritual exposure of the corpse became more elaborate, and dakhma began to indicate the specialized tower of silence. The first literary reference to constructed towers of silence appears in the eighth century C.E., but they were probably in use well before that time. The popu-larity of towers of silence appears to have peaked in Iran in the seventeenth century C.E., and towers of silence are declining in popularity today.

The structure of the tower of silence is relatively simple. The entry door is traditionally to the east so that the sun's rays may draw the soul up to heaven and away from the rotting corpse. There are no stairs inside, only a ladder leading up to the raised platform on top of the tower. There, cells (pavis) in three concentric circles provide space for the corpses: men in the outer circle, women in the middle, and children in the innermost circle. In the center of the tower is a deep pit, often extending downward 6 or more feet below the surface of the Earth. There, after the corpses have been relieved of their polluted flesh by wild animals, vultures, and the rays of the sun and moon, the bones are pushed into the central pit. Sun and lime placed in the pit transform the bones into dust. The pit branches into four canals to drain off rainwater that is received in four subterranean cisterns where carbon and sand purify it. In ancient times, the remains were removed from the central pit periodically and after a second funeral rite placed in sacred ossuaries, though this practice seems to have mostly fallen away in recent times. With the rise of

Islam, the towers of silence were constructed to be taller and removed to remote locations, and locks were placed on the doors to prevent spoliation—the Muslims found the Zoroastrian dakhmas revolting and occasionally attempted to disrupt their contents.

Because the Zoroastrians are so attentive to purity and ritual, the towers of silence receive special treatment—after all, they are the centers wherein the most impure objects in the world, corpses, are transformed into pure and honorable remains. The ceremonies for the construction of a tower of silence are therefore complex, including rituals for the excavation of the site, for construction of the foundation, and for the consecration of the tower. Traditionally, towers of silence may only be used for 100 years; after this period too much impurity may have accumulated in one spot, and a new tower of silence must be constructed elsewhere, provided the local community can afford it.

Frequently, a small cluster of buildings are constructed nearby a tower of silence for ritual use. In one building may be kept lightweight biers for transporting corpses up the ladder and in another a sacred and everburning flame symbolizing the spiritual state of the soul and the eternality of Ahura Mazda and his heaven. Many Zoroastrian communities hold annual or septennial services and feasts at their towers of silence to commemorate the dead.

See also FRAVARDIGĀN; FUNERARY CUSTOMS, ZOROASTRIAN; OSSUARY; SOUL, ZOROASTRIAN.

References

Boyce, Mary, *A History of Zoroastrianism.* 3 vols. Leiden: E. J. Brill, 1975–1991.

———. *A Persian Stronghold of Zoroastrianism.* Oxford: Clarendon Press, 1977.

———. *Zoroastrians: Their Religious Beliefs and Practices.* London: Routledge and Kegan Paul, 1979.

Gnoli, Gherardo. "Dakhma." In *Encyclopedia of Religions,* ed. Mircea Eliade. New York: Macmillan, 1987.

Thomas, Louis-Vincent. "Funeral Rites." In *Death, Afterlife and the Soul,* ed. Lawrence Sullivan. New York: Macmillan, 1989.

TOWER TOMB

A uniquely Muslim architecture for the dead, the tower tomb was composed of a tall cylinder with a domed or conical roof and with a height usually four or five times its width. The Muslim tower tomb was never as popular or as widespread as the mausoleum style of tomb. It was generally confined to northern Iran and Anatolia during the Seljuk dynasty (eleventh to thirteenth centuries C.E.), and the style virtually died out by the sixteenth century.

Although the fully developed tower tomb in the Middle East demonstrated purely Islamic principles in its design and placement, it is clear that the inspiration for the tower form came from pre-Islamic religious trends. The first known tower tomb, the gigantic Gunbad-i Qabus in northern Iran, shows clear Zoroastrian influence. It was built far from civilization, recalling the Zoroastrian practice of placing the dead as far from habitation as practical (which is not the norm in Muslim burials). The tomb's inscription dates the structure to the year 397 of the Muslim calendar (1006 C.E.) but also lists the alternate date of the old Persian (Yazdigirdi) calendar. Robert Hillenbrand mentions the tradition (from Muslim historian al-Jannabi) that the body of the prince "buried" in the tower was actually suspended from the roof in a glass coffin, with the head turned toward the only window, facing the rising sun—all of which strongly recalls the Zoroastrian dakhma, which did not allow the corpse (considered dreadfully polluting) to touch the sacred earth (see TOWER OF SILENCE).

Other early tower tombs, such as the two (somewhat smaller) structures in the remote plains of Kharraqan, strongly recall the tents used by Turkish nomads, and indeed the area was traditionally nomadic grazing land. Dated to 1067 and 1093 C.E., the tombs have very prominent thin, round columns (similar to poles) girding the outside of the structure, and the conical roofs and "woven" brickwork lattices are all strongly reminiscent of a large tent. The corpses were placed in a crypt underneath the structure, but there is a chamber above the surface that was probably used to expose the body for a time in state before burial—again duplicating the pre-Muslim Turkish practice of exposing the body of the chief for a time in his tent before burying it later.

Unlike the Islamic mausoleum, which tends to emphasize internal space and welcome pilgrims, the tower tomb emphasizes sheer height, and its main purpose appears to be to prominently mark the burial site (thus even more directly violating the Qur'ān's prohibition on marking graves and making distinctions among the dead). Hillenbrand points out that the use of flanges (deep grooves that run from top to bottom) enhances the perception of height, as do the vaulted ceilings within. In contrast to the dome on the square or octagonal mausoleum, which represents the dome of heaven, most tomb towers have conical roofs, again emphasizing the upward motion of the whole. Inscriptions from the Qur'ān may encircle the tower near the roof, but they are too far away to be read; the interior may be elaborately decorated, but is too small to hold services or a significant number of people. This demonstrates again the predominantly monumental (and nonfunctional) nature of the tower tomb, and it may explain why this type of tomb never caught on in much of the Muslim world or survived as a living style today—only those tombs with a more explicitly religious function were able to garner the support of the entire community and survive the occasional but devastating purges of Muslim purists.

See also FUNERARY CUSTOMS, MUSLIM; GARDENS OF DELIGHT; KURGAN; MAUSOLEUM, ISLAMIC.

References

Blair, Sheila S., and Jonathan M. Bloom. *The Art and Architecture of Islam 1250–1800*. New Haven: Yale University Press, 1994.

Ettinghausen, Richard, and Oleg Grabar. *The Art and Architecture of Islam 650–1250*. New York: Viking Penguin, 1987.

Hillenbrand, Robert. *Islamic Architecture: Form, Function and Meaning*. New York: Columbia University Press, 1994.

Hoag, John D. *Islamic Architecture*. New York: Rizzoli, 1987.

Smith, Edmund W. *Akbar's Tomb, Sikandrah, Near Agra, Described and Illustrated*. Allahabad: Archaeological Survey of India, 1909.

TUATHA DÉ DANANN

Literally "the people of the goddess Danann," the Tuatha Dé Danann were originally the gods of old Celtic Ireland, later reduced in Christian times to the status of kingly heroes, then fairies, and finally demons. They are closely connected with the Celtic fairy race known in Ireland as the *síd*, and thus the Tuatha Dé Danann are sometimes referred to as the rulers of the síd, or even *Aes-Síd,* which is cognate with the collective name of the Norse high gods, the *Aesir.*

In the distant past the Tuatha Dé Danann were simply the gods of the Celts, and they had a home, like Asgard of the Norse or Olympos of the Greeks, that later became an Otherworld to be visited by select heroes. Despite the later transformation of the Tuatha Dé Danann after the conquest of Christianity, they retained for long centuries their godlike status. Even in the eighth century C.E., an Irish monk wrote his prayers to Goibniu and Diancecht, the two Tuatha Dé Danann associated with protection and healing. Among the leaders of these gods were Lug, patron of all arts, culture, sports, and the sun; Nuada, the military leader of the Tuatha Dé Danann, most famous for losing his hand in the first battle of Mag Tuired; Dagda, "the great god" and overall leader of the Tuatha Dé Danann, connected with fertility, as seen in his cauldron that is never empty and his swine that when killed and eaten are replenished the next day (see VALHALLA); Manannán, a sea and storm god who gave the Tuatha Dé Danann their invisibility and immortality after their defeat at human hands; and Brigit, goddess of wisdom, art, poetry, fire, and fertility.

In Christian times all these and the other gods of the Celts were reduced to merely great wizards and heroes whose adventures figure in the cycles of tales. In the current versions of the myths, only faint traces of the divinity of the Tuatha Dé Danann remain, for instance, their immortality, magic possessions (Lug's spear that never misses, Dagda's cauldron that never empties, the stone that proclaims the rightful man king, etc.), and connection to invisible realms under Earth and sea. Brigit was fortunate enough to be proclaimed a saint by the new Christian regime, and the old Celtic *Imbolc,* the evening of 1 February, which announced the beginning of Celtic spring, was renamed St. Brigid's day. The Tuatha Dé Danann continue to represent the spiritual, fructifying element in nature and human life, but it is conditional, and it resides literally in the land of the dead, for the realm of the Tuatha Dé Danann is underground, and the primary entrances are the burial mounds of ancestral kings.

Even though the mythology surrounding the Tuatha Dé Danann has been heavily Christianized and euhemerized (that is, forced to fit quasi-historical ideas) it is still a fascinating saga. The legends relate that Ireland has had several successive waves of "invasions" by various races (all descended from Noah, pious Christian authors record). The Tuatha Dé Danann were the fifth wave of settlers and forcibly displaced the earlier inhabitants, the Firbolg and Fomorians, described as misshapen, often one-eyed, monstrous giants. But whereas all preceding groups reached Ireland by ship, the Tuatha Dé Danann came riding in dark clouds in the sky and landed on the mountain called Conmaicne Réin, casting a darkness over the sun for three days. They were known as the most powerful race of wizards in history, commanding the atmosphere and the sea, with the particular specialty of casting illusions to thwart their enemies. (Thus their identification as demons by Christian monks is easy to understand.) The Tuatha Dé Danann were supernaturally beautiful, with magnificent clothing and equipment. Their music was the most gifted on Earth and was preternaturally alluring, and with their command of the sciences and arts they could accomplish almost any feat. In short, they were masters of all wisdom.

What is particularly relevant to the study of death is that the Tuatha Dé Danann are said to have landed in Ireland on 1 May, which is Beltaine in the Celtic calendar, the festival beginning the summer half of the year. They gave battle to the Firbolg giants and Danann succeeded handily in ousting the monsters. This certainly points to a seasonal motif in which the powers of life, sunlight, and growth banish the winter powers of death and darkness. As if to solidify the point, we find that after twenty-seven years (Irish myth is very fond of multiples of threes), the Fomorians, a very similar giant race, gave battle to the Tuatha Dé Danann again in the same place, this time on 1 November eve, that is, Samhain, which is the first day of the winter months. At this battle many of the Tuatha Dé Danann lost their lives, and although they won, they were certainly put in abeyance. These two battles signal that the Tuatha Dé Danann are, among other things, symbolic of the powers of life and summer, whereas their foes are the powers of death and winter.

This distinction is important, for when humans

finally arrive in Ireland to take control, the Tuatha Dé Danann are on the losing side despite their magic and wisdom. After the victory, the human poet-seer Amairgen was elected to divide Ireland in two, giving one half to the Tuatha Dé Danann and the other half to the humans, the sons of Mile (the first human patriarch of Ireland, according to myth). However, the half given to the Tuatha Dé Danann was the underground half, and the sons of Mile, of course, took over the surface. For this reason the Tuatha Dé Danann are now thought to live in the Otherworld, which has entrances in the hills and the fairy regions. Manannán mac Lir, the overlord of the Tuatha Dé Danann, is said to have distributed the ten great síd (fairy mounds) among the Tuatha Dé Danann before he went to dwell over the sea.

But these fairy mounds are often simultaneously recognized as the burial mounds of ancestral kings. Why should the two be equated?

It is simply a matter of a transfer of power from one to another. Once the Tuatha Dé Danann lost their status as gods (for Christianity is insistent on monotheism), they were banished underground but retained a great deal of power in the Irish psyche. So they were remodeled as the powers of nature, the invisible powers of life and summer and growth. From there, it is but a step to identifying their world as the world of the dead and connecting the Tuatha Dé Danann with all things hidden and occult: invisible realms, the fairies, and even one's dead ancestors. The Tuatha Dé Danann, prevented from being thought of as gods, became lords of the "other."

For this reason, the Tuatha Dé Danann (or their fairy subjects) are now thought to have control over crops, cow's milk, weather patterns, and other natural phenomena out of human control. If humans displease these invisible powers, they will find that life-giving energy is withheld, milk is spoiled, crops wither, and storms or drought manifest. Likewise, if an ancestral burial mound, also home of the fairies, is disturbed, the Otherworld is liable to break into the human world and wreak havoc.

Yet the Tuatha Dé Danann are not merely powers of danger but hidden "powers" in general. In the Irish cycles of tales, the Tuatha Dé Danann often provide wives or mothers for humans in the tales. Particularly the heroes of the Fenian cycle of texts (starring the hero Finn or his relatives) have mothers who are Tuatha Dé Danann. These beings also serve as the spiritual spark or "third agent" necessary in the creation of life (the first two being the mother and father, obviously). In many stories Lug, Manannán, or another of the Tuatha Dé Danann are called the "true" fathers of a hero, even though it is recognized that the hero in question is physically the son of his human father and mother. In some cases the Tuatha Dé Danann are reborn in human children as themselves, furthering the subtle reincarnation theme throughout Irish legends.

Any contact with the Tuatha Dé Danann can lead to permanent changes in one's life. In one story the hero Finn pursues an ogre to the door of a fairy mound and jams his thumb in the door as it closes. When he puts his thumb in his mouth because it smarts, he realizes he now has the power to know hidden things, and this ability figures in all future tales of him. Likewise, journeys to the Otherworld of the Tuatha Dé Danann can bring back boons for humankind, but they often result in permanent changes to the human hero, who is never again allowed to return.

The Celtic scholar Alexander MacBain has pointed out that the Tuatha Dé Danann, as the ancient gods of the Gaelic Celts, gave their names to many widely scattered places in Ireland and Scotland. For example, the Isle of Man is called after the sea god Manannán mac Lir, and the whole of Ireland is named after the Tuatha Dé Danann queen Eire. Even though the living belief in the Tuatha Dé Danann is dying out, their influence remains in Irish stories and even on the land itself.

See also FAIRY MOUND; FUNERARY CUSTOMS, CELTIC; MAG MELL; MORRIGAN; ODIN; OTHERWORLD, IRISH; SAMHAIN; SÍD.

References

Mac Bain, Alexander. *Celtic Mythology and Religion*. New York: Dutton, 1917.

MacCulloch, J. A. *The Religion of the Ancient Celts*. Edinburgh: T. and T. Clark, 1911.

Ó hÓgáin, Dáithí. *Myth, Legend and Romance: An Encyclopaedia of the Irish Folk Tradition*. New York: Prentice Hall, 1991.

Rees, Alwyn, and Brinley Rees. *Celtic Heritage: Ancient Tradition in Ireland and Wales*. London: Thames and Hudson, 1961.

TUMULUS

Originally just a naturally occurring round hill or knoll, in a funerary context the word *tumulus* refers to the artificial earthen burial mounds made over graves, megaliths, tholos tombs, and hypogea. Tumuli are truly omnipresent in ancient human history: they are found the world over and include the megaliths of Neolithic Europe; the legend-inspiring mounds of the Celts and Teutons; the kurgans of Central Asia and the stūpas of Buddhist India, Tibet, and East Asia; the mounds of many Native American tribes; and the tumuli of the ancient Greek and Roman world. Those too poor or too limited in cemetery space to erect actual mounds mimicked them symbolically with piles of stones, headstones, or a broken amphora (vase). One may even consider the pyramids of Egypt the ultimate architectural development of the prehistoric tumulus. Frequently, tumuli rest on a wooden or masonry roof that shelters the tombs below. Tumuli may have low walls surrounding them or may be built atop such walls.

Tumulus at Mycenae. Courtesy of Anne Ronan Picture Library.

In the Greek and Roman worlds, the ancient tumulus form was gradually replaced with the free-standing mausolea, at least for elite burials. As late as the second century B.C.E., massive tumuli were being built in Ionia, Anatolia, Thessaly, and Scythian territory on the Black Sea. One of the largest tumuli ever built was for King Alyattes of Lydia (d. 560 B.C.E.), more than 2,400 yards in circumference. At Pergamon the tumuli of the third and second century B.C.E. Attalid kings had a circumference of 1,700 feet and rose 100 feet above the plain. Alexander the Great built a massive tumulus in Bactria for his friend Demaratus in 327 B.C.E., and Alexander's father Philip II himself lay buried beneath a tumulus.

Tumuli may be taken to symbolize the Earth as a whole or just the Underworld and may serve as the physical or spiritual dwellings of the deceased but very much "alive" inhabitants. Frequently, goods are buried in the tumulus that were associated with the dead while they were alive, including not just personal items but tools of their trade and nourishment for the afterlife. The elite might have entire households full of servants, guards, and wives buried along with them, making up an afterlife society in the new world to come.

See also AMPHORA; BARROW; CAIRN; HYPOGEUM; KURGAN; MAU-
SOLEUM; MOUND; PYRAMID, EGYPTIAN; STŪPA; THOLOS TOMB.

References

Colvin, Howard. *Architecture and the After-Life*. New Haven: Yale University Press, 1991.

Davidson, H. R. Ellis. *The Lost Beliefs of Northern Europe*. London: Routledge, 1993.

U

UNDEAD

There are a vast multitude of undead beings, rising from the experiences and imaginations of every culture on Earth. Even the categories of undead are numerous, including (to name just a few) apparitions, screaming banshees, doppelgängers, ghosts, ghouls, poltergeists, shades, vampires, and zombies. Despite their various natures, the undead share a number of characteristics, including their earthly origin and their necromantic activities.

The undead is almost always one who died an unhappy or uncertain death or was improperly handled after death, even if he or she has been deliberately re-animated for nefarious purposes by a witch, a sorcerer, or the Devil himself—these are the very victims chosen by the occult professionals because they are so apt to return from the dead. In some cases the subject died suddenly, "before his time," by lightning, suicide, murder, or disease. The victim could not live out his or her allotted lifespan and is now unwilling or unable to continue on. Sometimes the undead is simply one who was known to be disagreeable in life and now seeks to continue to make life difficult from the hereafter. Or the person died with unfinished business in this world (like leaving orphaned children behind) and cannot rest without completing it, as in this example from second-century C.E. Greece:

There was a house in Athens haunted by a spectre who came out at night rattling his chains; an old man, skinny and dirty, with scruffy hair and beard, wearing fetters on his legs and chains at his wrists. A philosopher decided to spend a night there to find out what was going on. As he read his book he heard the noises, then saw the figure. It beckoned him; he followed it into the garden where the ghost suddenly vanished. The scholar picked up some grass and leaves and marked the place of disappearance. Next day he had the local magistrates dig there, and a skeleton in chains was found; after proper burial rites the haunting ceased. (from a letter of Pliny the Younger, in Finucane, p. 2)

Because of tales like this one, from prehistory to the present, in every known culture, the proper handling of the dead is considered of the utmost importance, whether those services are simple or enormously complicated. The danger is twofold: improper postmortem rituals may hinder the dead from obtaining his or her next state, and such mistakes in turn may cause the dead to remain near the earthly plane, bringing havoc and death to the living. But a proper funeral carried out with all culturally prescribed precautions (and these vary enormously) will guarantee the safety of the public and the grieving family . . . well, usually.

The way in which one initially handles the body is important in protecting it from reawakening. First of all, it must never be left alone but always watched over by a sympathetic person, night and day. This tradition is found the world over, from Hindu to Jewish to Native American death rituals. Second, various substances in the environment can affect the body. Light or flame is thought to be a positive element, drawing the soul out as desired and preventing anything else from getting in. Lighted candles are therefore frequently placed around the body and nearly always accompany traditional funeral processions (although in Christianity the sign of the cross often substitutes for lit candles). No flame must pass over the body, however, or any breath, wind, or even a cat or other animal because of their sympathetic connection to spirit. (In many languages, the words for breath, wind, and spirit are the same.) To pass a symbol of life or animation over the inert corpse is to invite possession. In Russia even the wind from the steppe might bring about vampirism. Another potent substance is water, both for its reflective quality (which is related to mirrors) and for its formless, shapeless quality. Souls around the world appear to be hydrotropic—drawn irresistibly to water—and thus water is often used as a barrier to newly deceased souls, preventing their passage toward the corpse or hindering the return of the dead from the graveyard to the home. Smoke and incense serve a similar purpose.

Finally, the corpse must be removed from the place of death with care and deliberation. It is commonly believed that when the undead seek to return to their family home, they must go by the exact way in which they left; fortunately, it is easy to make this practically impossible for them. One method is simply to lift the threshold and take the corpse out of the house under it. Others involve taking the corpse out of the house by means of a window or specially made hole in the wall, removing the corpse feet first, or pouring water behind the coffin to create a magical barrier. Corpses in danger of becoming undead (i.e., people dying early or having unfinished business, murder victims, known witches) may also be quarantined by having the corpses removed from the world of the civilized (including the cemetery) and cast into water, a bog, a ravine, or a distant cave or by reburying them at boundary zones between districts or at a crossroads—all of which serve to dislocate and "unmake" the formerly human being.

The very sight of the rotting corpse may be dangerous to the living, because it sometimes appears to be in motion, that is, changing, while spiritually it is supposed to be absolutely inert. Perceiving this "contradiction" is not only frightening for the living, but the act of perception itself may generate a reanimation. Thus corpses must be covered from the moment of death until safely buried in the ground or otherwise disposed of. Breaking this rule leads to dire consequences. In Japan, for instance, the god Izanagi went down to the Underworld to reclaim his dead wife Izanami prematurely; he found her rotting corpse, was horrified, and fled, pursued by demons. The moral: the corpse is not fully "dead" until the flesh is off the bones, and it is extremely dangerous until this "second death," that is, after three to seven years. After this time, however, secondary burial is safely practiced by many cultures, in which the bones are gathered up and moved to a final resting place, often in a family tomb. (See, for example FUNERARY CUSTOMS, JEWISH.) Meeting the gaze of the dead is also very dangerous, and for this reason the eyes (or the entire head and body) are usually covered or even stopped up with wax or pinned shut with needles. Likewise, to avoid the gaze of the dead or even the sight of the reflection of the corpse, mirrors are turned against the wall after someone has died.

Corpses have particular "danger spots" that, if mishandled, can lead to reanimation of the dead body. These spots include all orifices (mouth, nose, ears, eyes, and private areas) as well as hands, feet, and the heart. Bodily openings provide means of ingress to wandering spirits, including the newly departed soul itself. Meanwhile, the extremities provide the reanimated corpse a means of mobility and harmful activity. For example, in Greek folklore murder victims and executed criminals are considered extremely prone to returning from the dead and reportedly had their extremities cut off and strung on a chain around their neck to prevent them from doing so. The general rule in handling corpses appears to be like the proverb "an ounce of prevention is worth a pound of cure."

The mouth is the preeminently dangerous zone;

therefore, it is often stopped up, even before trouble has a chance to arise. Techniques for this vary around the world, but the purpose appears to be the same. Among the Kashubes of western Prussia, a potsherd was put in the revenant's mouth so that the corpse would have something to chew on that would not magically bring death to others—as chewing one's shroud or limbs would do. In Poland a priest was called in to deal with an undead corpse. He took the revenant out of his grave, put a slip of paper under his tongue with his name on it, and laid him face down in his grave. In Egypt the mummy's mouth was filled with wool, whereas in rural Greece wax or cotton is often placed on the lips of the corpse. One scholar has even reinterpreted the obolus, or coin placed in the mouth of the dead in ancient Greece. Usually it is believed to be for the fare Charon charges to ferry souls across the river into Hades; but John Lawson believes that it was originally intended as a charm to keep evil spirits from entering the corpse via the mouth, possibly including the spirit of the deceased. The mouth might also be filled with dirt, tied shut, or propped shut with a brick, a chunk of sod, or even a songbook. In China jade is frequently put into the mouth of the corpse and other orifices of the body, and in Australia soft plant fibers were used. Some Gypsies in the Balkans are said to use wool in the mouth for the same reason, as is done with Peruvian mummies. Among the Slavs thorns, nails, and knives may be inserted under the tongue to prevent the mouth from chewing or sucking blood.

One way to prevent the creation of a revenant is to give the dead something to do in the grave. For example, many cultures place objects in the grave that are either expected to satisfy the dead, render it incapable of returning, or satisfy/thwart any demonic force that might try to reanimate it. Food and water offerings are especially thought to please the dead and, it is hoped, obviate its need to return to feed upon or drink from the living. Many creatures are believed to do so, such as the lilats of ancient Babylonia and Assyria, the khu of Egypt, the modern molong of Malaysia, and the penangelam of Indochina; in addition, the Finnish lord of the Underworld, the Bohemian mora, and the German alp all suck human blood. In many parts of medieval Europe, poppy seeds were among the food offerings, chosen for their value as narcotics that would bring on sleep. The actual narcotic contained in poppy seeds is extremely small, but again it is symbolic magic that works in these circumstances. The deceased was thought to eat the poppy seeds at the rate of one per year and either be simply occupied or put to sleep.

Besides making food offerings, providing other activities is common around the world. In northern Germany, for example, the undead were thought to be obsessed with untying knots: therefore nets or stockings were buried in the grave to occupy the dead, who could apparently untie only one knot per year. But in Greece this was unacceptable, for any knots in the grave were thought, by the occult law of correspondence, to bind the soul to the body and prevent its being loosed. Although the Greeks too had the corpse bound and the mouth tied up, these bonds were made powerful through symbolic magic, not physical presence: they were cut just before burial to allow the soul to go free but not the body. In Bulgaria and Pomerania a lit candle was provided in the grave to illuminate the deceased's way to the other world; apparently it is a dark and confusing trip.

Sharp objects are also useful for preventing or, if worse comes to worst, "re-killing," a revenant. In eastern Serbia a hawthorn peg may be driven into the grave beside the cross, whereas in Romania and Hungary a sickle may be placed in the grave: if the corpse starts to bloat, a sure sign of it becoming a vampire, the sharp sickle will puncture the body, foiling the Devil's plans. In Yugoslavia the sickle is placed around the neck—should the body try to rise, it will decapitate itself. In Morocco a dagger or other sharp object of iron or steel is placed on the abdomen of the corpse. In Slavic burials all kinds of sharp objects have been found, even in urns holding cremains: iron knives, hair needles, or awls. The apotropaic principle is the same. In Hungary thorns or a piece of a saw may be put in with the corpse in the hopes that if it should try to return the sharp objects will catch its shroud and prevent it. In Iceland nails are driven through the soles of a revenant corpse to prevent it from walking; likewise, Serbians habitually cut the knee ligaments for the same purpose. Finally, there is the most famous use of a sharp object for a vampire, a stake through the heart, practiced when necessary throughout Europe.

Cremation is thought to be a particularly effective means (in Europe) of preventing one from becoming undead, but it is very expensive, time-consuming, and difficult to get enough heat and oxygen to the body. Even in modern times cremation takes about 90 minutes in a special furnace at 1600 degrees Fahrenheit; using wood or oil it would take considerably more effort and time. However, many stories of the undead culminate when the corpse of the offender is finally cremated as a last resort.

See also ANCESTOR VENERATION; ANKOU; BANSHEE; BHŪT; CHUREL; CROSSROADS; ERINYS; HUNGRY GHOST; KER; MUMMIFICATION; PISHĀCHA; POOKA; PRET; RĀKṢASA; SÍD; SOUL; UNDERWORLD; VALKYRIE; VAMPIRE; WATER.

References

Barber, Paul. *Vampires, Burial, and Death*. New Haven: Yale University Press, 1988.

Finucane, R. C. *Appearances of the Dead: A Cultural History of Ghosts*. Buffalo, NY: Prometheus Books, 1984.

Lawson, John Cuthbert. *Modern Greek Folklore and Ancient Greek Religion*. 1910. Reprint, New York: University Books, 1964.

Máchal, Jan. *Slavic Mythology*. New York: Cooper Square Publishers, 1918.

Masters, Anthony. *The Natural History of the Vampire*. New York: G. P. Putnam's Sons, 1972.

Ramos, Maximo. *The Creatures of Midnight*. Quezon City, Philippines: Island Publishers, 1967.

Senn, Harry A. *Were-Wolf and Vampire in Romania*. East European Monographs, no. 17. New York: Columbia University Press, 1982.

Summers, Montague. *The Vampire: His Kith and Kin*. New Hyde Park, NY: University Books, 1960.

Westermarck, Edward. *Ritual and Belief in Morocco*. London: Macmillan, 1926.

UNDERWORLD

The Underworld is the mysterious universe secreted away beneath the surface of the Earth and believed in by almost every ancient or traditional culture. The Underworld is many things to many people and is not necessarily the same for all. Often it is the land of the dead, or their cousins, inhuman spirits. It is also the source of agricultural fertility and often other kinds of wealth: pure water, gems and gold, even wisdom. As a liminal realm sharing some territory with the known world, the Underworld may offer experiences that push the boundaries of our perceptions—it is the dwelling place of dwarves, gnomes, fairies, and elves, a mirror realm that reverses or reflects "surface" realities, a realm where time dilates or shrinks and soul-enhancing adventures are to be had. Farther down, grander secrets lie hidden: a world in itself, a universe in miniature, with its own gods, physical and spiritual laws, history, and reality. Deep down, the Underworld is a place of eerie transformation from which it is difficult or impossible to return, and the transformation is rarely a positive one. As the Greek hero Achilles says to Odysseus during the latter's visit, "I would rather be a slave on the earth than the king of the dreary undead" (Homer).

Nevertheless, in most cultures the dead *must* pass down to the Underworld and stay there forever, while despite its dangers countless heroes and heroines *choose* to venture down and attempt to return. These include the Chinese monk Mu-lien, the Hindu king Bhūnandana, the Japanese god Izanagi, the Roman hero Aeneas, the Italian poet Dante Alighieri, the Norse god Odin and the Norse hero Hermod, the Welsh hero Pwyll, the crucified Jesus, and countless others—but not all are successful, as Theseus' abortive attempt to kidnap Persephone shows. In either case, whether by destiny or choice, the descending soul or hero pursues simultaneously a physical, psychological, and spiritual journey to complete some task or gain some crucial knowledge. The tale of Mesopotamian goddess Inanna's trials in the "Great Below" are representative of

Dante, guided by Virgil, in the third gulf of the eighth circle of hell, observes those guilty of simony burning, buried headfirst with just their legs and feet exposed. Illustration by Gustave Doré for Dante's Inferno, *1861, Canto XIX. Courtesy of Anne Ronan Picture Library.*

Underworld journeys in general, although the specific purpose of her journey is not clear:

Inanna decided to visit her sister, Ereshkigal, Queen of the Underworld. From the Great Above, she set her mind to the Great Below. Prudently, she informs her visier, Ninshubur, of her intentions, instructing him as to what to do should she not return. Dressed in her most splendid clothes and jewels, she is halted by an officious guardian at the first lapis lazuli gate to the Underworld, and the crown is removed from her head. At each of six following gates, an article of her apparel is taken, till, naked and furious, she confronts Ereshkigal, at whom she "flies." Her sister stops her in midflight, releasing on her the "sixty miseries" (in the Akkadian version) or hanging her from a stake (the Sumerian text). Three days and nights pass, or, in the Akkadian version, a season in which "the bull springs not upon the cow, the ass impregnates not the jenny . . . the man lies down in his own chamber, the maiden lies down on her side." The Akkadian version marks this as a fertility myth; the Sumerian version may interest people looking for parallels to Christ's sacrifice, or the sacrifice of Attis hung on his tree, or Odin crucified on his.

Alarmed by her absence, the faithful vizier petitions the gods for his mistress's rescue. Reluctantly, Ereshkigal permits Inanna to return to the Great Above, provided she can provide a substitute or ransom for herself (this theme will turn up again in a number of guises, one of them important to Christianity). A brace of escort goblins is sent topside to make sure she keeps her word. The ransom she sends is Dumuzi (Tammuz in Akkadian), Inanna's shepherd consort. Eventually a political compromise is reached by requiring Dumuzi to stay below for only six months of the year if his sister will stand in for him during the other six months. (Turner)

Certainly from one vantage point, this is a vegetation/seasonal/fertility myth—seen again in the Hittite Telepinus and Kamrusepas, the Canaanite Baal and Anath, the Egyptian Osiris and Isis, the Middle Eastern Attis and Cybele, the Greek Persephone and Demeter, and the Roman Adonis and Aphrodite. But Inanna's descent is also a very early version of the heroic journey, in which the heroine loses herself and then finds herself again: a symbolic rebirth or resurrection. One of the primary uses of the Underworld, now understood in-depth by psychology, is as a means of "shedding" the old self and rebuilding a new one. At each successive "gate," Inanna has to shed some of her clothing—symbols of her self on the surface—until at last she is stripped naked and vulnerable. Gilgamesh is naked at the last, just before he obtains the secret of immortality, and Odysseus arrives home at last after twenty years wandering the Underworld and the open seas in a similar condition.

Other structural elements are so common worldwide in Underworld myths that they demand our attention:

1. A passage through a cave, gate, or other boundary
2. The psychopomp (guide of the soul)
3. Water
4. The ferryman who provides a vehicle to "cross over"
5. Gatekeepers, for example, Cerberus or demons
6. Many perilous and literally "trying" ordeals
7. Various levels, always odd in total number
8. The final confrontation

Passing the initial boundary indicates that one has definitely left the sunlit world of order and reason, and the psychopomp is essential for one's safety as well as education, as Dante discovers with his guide Virgil. Water provides a formidable spiritual obstacle to any Otherworld journey and without a ferry or vehicle is utterly impassable (even the Buddha provided his followers the greater and lesser yāna to cross the symbolic "waters" of saṃsāra, that is, impermanence and death).

The focus of the heroic journey, however, is the increasingly difficult ordeals the hero/soul must surmount in the succession of gates and trials. Few can stand the trial, however, and most will meet the same end in the Great Below as countless other Underworld souls—they simply die and recycle through nature's secret interior processes. This is because most people die unconsciously, unaware of their great secret power, and enter the Underworld wearing only their lower soul: the body double, shade, or reflection. Unsatisfied, it has the danger of becoming caught between the various boundaries of the living and the dead, but properly treated through culturally determined funerary customs, the lower soul proceeds to its rightful location under the Earth (which is its element, whereas the higher soul is related to breath, wind, and fire). There in the early Chinese Yellow Springs, Hebrew Sheol, Greek Hades, or Hindu Pātāla, passing through danger after danger and level after level, the lower soul settles into the Earth, eventually to disintegrate and add its constituents to the collective world soul from which life is regenerated.

This is the meaning behind the various numbered levels of the descent, for the Mesopotamian Underworld had seven levels, the Scandinavian Hel was placed below three or seven or nine great worlds; the Hindu Pātāla has seven levels, and Dante's Inferno and the

Aztec Mictlan were composed of nine. All are odd numbers, hence uneven (denoting instability) and thus magical numbers of *potential* transformation but only for those possessed of the higher soul of power and self-determination. For the ordinary soul, then, the descent into the Underworld is a gradual disintegration of ego and self often followed by involuntary rebirth, whereas for the hero the journey is deliberately redemptive of self and mankind.

See also ĀARU; ANNWFN; AVERNUS; BARROW; ERESH; FAIRY MOUND; GEHENNA; HADES; HEL; MOUND; NIFLHEIM; PĀTĀLA; SHEOL; YELLOW SPRINGS.

References

Chan, Wing-tsit, ed. and trans. *A Source Book in Chinese Philosophy*. Princeton: Princeton University Press, 1963.

Downing, Christine. "Journeys to the Underworld." *Mythosphere* 1, no. 2 (1998).

Ford, Patrick K., ed. *The Mabinogi and Other Medieval Welsh Tales*. Berkeley: University of California Press, 1977.

Homer. *The Odyssey*. Trans. Samuel Butler. New York: Barnes and Noble, 1993.

Kristensen, W. Brede. *Life out of Death: Studies in the Religions of Egypt and of Ancient Greece*. Louvain: Belgium: Peeters Press, 1992.

Loewe, Michael. *Ways to Paradise: The Chinese Quest for Immortality*. Boston: Allen and Unwin, 1979.

MacCulloch, J. A. *The Religion of the Ancient Celts*. Edinburgh: T. and T. Clark, 1911.

Mandelbaum, Allen, trans. *The Aeneid of Virgil*. New York: Bantam, 1961.

Ó hÓgáin, Dáithí. *Myth, Legend and Romance: An Encyclopaedia of the Irish Folk Tradition*. New York: Prentice Hall, 1991.

Rees, Alwyn, and Brinley Rees. *Celtic Heritage: Ancient Tradition in Ireland and Wales*. London: Thames and Hudson, 1961.

Rieu, E. V., trans. *The Odyssey*. New York: Penguin, 1945.

Spronk, K. *Beatific Afterlife in Ancient Israel and in the Ancient Near East*. Kevelaer: Butzon and Bercker, 1986.

Thompson, Laurence G. "On the Prehistory of Hell in China." *Journal of Chinese Religions*, no. 17 (Fall 1989).

Tromp, N. J. *Primitive Conceptions of Death and the Nether World in the Old Testament*. Rome: Pontifical Biblical Institute, 1969.

Turner, Alice K. *The History of Hell*. New York: Harcourt Brace, 1993.

URN

Used by the ancient Celtic, Greek, Etruscan, and Roman peoples, an urn is a narrow-necked, full-bodied jar or vase used for storage, ritual, or funerary purposes. Urns used for storage typically held liquids or grain, whereas those employed in religious rituals held wine or even blood from sacrifices. Smaller urns were also used as decorative items. From ancient times to the present, however, urns are widely used to hold cremains or goods for burials. They might be sealed and buried right in the ground, placed in a niche in a columbarium, or placed in a cemetery and sheltered by a brick or stone tomb. In modern times, with the increasing popularity of cremation and decreasing cemetery space, urns are sometimes kept in the family home.

The most remarkable funerary urn yet discovered is that of the Vix grave in the upper valley of the Seine, found with the remains of a woman about thirty-five years old and fine funeral goods including a wagon. What is remarkable about this urn is both its huge size (1.64 meters high, able to hold about 1,200 liters of liquid) and rich decoration. The immense handles are in the form of gorgon heads, around the neck is a frieze of warriors marching and riding chariots, and the lid has the figure of a woman wearing a veil over her head and shoulders with one arm outstretched. The grave dates from the sixth century B.C.E.

V

VALHALLA (VALHÖLL)

The most accepted derivation of this name comes from *valr* (battle corpses) and *höll* (hall), literally "the hall of the slain," although another possible etymology is discussed later in the entry. Valhalla is the Norse paradise for heroes slain in battle (or in sacrifice). Their time having arrived, fallen warriors are lifted up by the Valkyries and carried to Odin's realm, where they eat, drink, and fight until the end of the world; then they will fight at Odin's side. From all sources it appears that Valhalla was never the destiny of the common man or woman but the reward only of the chosen few.

The poetic descriptions of Valhalla in Norse literature (*Grímnismál, Gylfaginning,* etc.) are majestic and massive. The hall stands in Gladsheimr, the World of Joy, near Asgard, the realm of the gods. The roof is made of shields, and shafts of spears form the rafters. There are 540 huge doors to the hall, and through each door 800 warriors can pass side by side. A wolf guards west of the entrance, and an eagle perches atop the building. This is the favorite dwelling place of Odin, god of the dead, battle, poetry, and wisdom. He lives on mead alone but feeds his two wolves, Gere and Freke, meat from his plate. Also present are Odin's two ravens, named Hugin (thought) and Munin (memory), reporting to their master the news they have gathered from traveling over the Earth by day.

Inside the warriors are waited on by the virginal Valkyries and have an endless supply of meat and wine. The boar Saehrímnir is stewed every day and arises whole in the evening, and the mead from the udders of the goat Heidrún, fed by the leaves of the tree Laeradr, never gives out. All day on the plain of battle called Vigridsslätten, Odin's chosen warriors, now called *einherjar,* or "soldiers of one army," fight each other, inflicting horrific wounds. But at the sound of the bell for dinner all are magically healed and at peace, ready to feast and fight another day.

It is unclear if this image of Valhalla is merely a poetic transformation of the grave or burial mound, or if Valhalla was the actual hope of the Norse warriors. The widespread cult of Odin in northern Europe, which included human and animal sacrifice, would seem to indicate an actual religious adherence to him and therefore his afterdeath paradise. Carved memorial stones from all over ancient Scandinavia show a figure on a horse being greeted by a woman with a horn. This is described in early poems such as *Eiríksmál* and *Hákonarmál* as a Valkyrie greeting the fallen king or hero at Odin's hall with a horn of ale. The stylized hall on these carved stones bears a great resemblance to a burial mound, and such barrows (sometimes including a full-size ship) again seem to indicate a real belief in an afterlife journey.

Theories on the ultimate origins of Valhalla are various. Some scholars have seen foreign influence in the detailed description of Valhalla, and others have pointed out its similarity to a Roman amphitheatre or the Colosseum, suggesting that descriptions may have been brought back by travelers. Others view Valhalla merely as a glorified chieftain's hall and the warriors there living out no more than a glorified version of their lives on Earth. It is a fact that the name *Valhall* is applied to certain rocks in Sweden believed to be dwelling places of the dead, and thus it is possible that originally the name *Valhalla* meant "rock of corpses," from *valr* (battle corpses) and *hallr* (rock). The mythic Valhalla thus was nothing more than a poet's glamorization of the grave. Finally, some authorities have seen Valhalla as a complex, esoteric symbol wherein various obstacles (the hounds of Odin, the wolf, the eagle) are to be overcome, representing a series of personal transformations leading to spiritual initiation. In this connection, a link is shown between the numbers of doors and warriors (540 × 800 = 432,000) and a sacred number known to ancient Babylon and India (also 432,000). Such esoteric symbolism is entirely plausible, but it is unlikely to have been understood by the common warrior, who undoubtedly thought of Valhalla as a well-deserved paradise signifying not only honor but duty. For indeed, in the tenth-century poem *Hákonarmál,* Odin is asked why he allows noble kings to fall in battle, and he replies, "The grey wolf watches the abodes of the gods." Not far from Asgard, the home of the gods, was Jotunheim, the land of the frost giants. One day, according to the prophecies, they would rise up and attack the gods, attempting to bring about the total destruction of the world. For this purpose, it was said, Odin gathered up the warriors and encouraged them to fight all day in preparation for the end time when their aid would be sorely needed.

See also BARROW; BURIAL, SHIP; FUNERARY CUSTOMS, SCANDINAVIAN; ODIN; RAGNARÖK; VALKYRIE.

References

Davidson, H. R. Ellis. *The Lost Beliefs of Northern Europe.* London: Routledge, 1993.

Guerber, Hélène Adeline. *Myths of the Norsemen from the Eddas and Sagas.* New York: Dover Publications, 1992.

Titchenell, Elsa-Brita. *The Masks of Odin.* Pasadena: Theosophical University Press, 1985.

Turville-Petre, E. O. G. *Myth and Religion of the North: The Religion of Ancient Scandinavia.* Westport, CT: Greenwood, 1964.

VALKYRIE

Literally the "choosers of the slain," in origin, Valkyries seem to be a convergence of local guardian spirits with war goddesses from national epics. By the time they appear in ancient Scandinavian sagas, they are the winged warrior women of the Norse who do Odin's bidding on Earth, directing the course of battles and tending to the spirits of the slain heroes. Few images in world mythology are more poetic and inspiring than the description of the beautiful Valkyrie carrying a slain warrior in her tender arms over the Rainbow Bridge to his final resting place in Valhalla. Yet the Valkyries, three, nine, or even twenty-seven in number, are also known for their ferocity, which can bring about the ruin of entire armies.

The association of a group of female deities with war is an ancient one in European religion; the late Norse figure of the Valkyrie appears against the background of earlier Teutonic, Celtic, and Roman images. Inscriptions from the Housesteads fort at Hadrian's Wall in northern England are dedicated to Mars and various warrior goddesses, including Baudihillie (ruler of battle) and Friagabi (giver of freedom), names very similar to later Valkyrie names like Brynhild (battle armor).

The word *Valkyrie* is related to the Old English word *Waelcyrge,* found as early as the eighth century C.E. in word lists, meaning like Valkyrie "chooser of the slain" but referring to the three Furies (in Greek, *Erinys*: Tisiphone, Megara, and Alecto). Likewise the Old English poem *Exodus* contains the adjective *waelceasig,* which means "choosing the slain," in describing a raven, a bird of prey long associated with battlefields. The Irish goddess of war, the Morrigan, took the form of a raven or crow and feasted on corpses. In part the winged Valkyries are probably a development of bird imagery related both to the carnage of battle and the release of the soul.

But Valkyries, bearing the dead to Valhalla and waiting upon them at Odin's table, also appear to incorporate certain traditional activities of actual women. There is evidence of a class of professional women, perhaps priestesses, who officiated at sacrifices of prisoners of war and at cremations: the tenth-century Muslim traveler Ibn Fadlan tells of an old woman called the *Angel of Death* who organized the funeral ceremonies of an important Swedish trader on the Volga. Additionally, like the Hindu practice of sati, in which a wife is burned on her husband's funeral pyre, there was a Norse custom, apparently widespread in ancient times, of a wife throwing herself upon her husband's burning corpse; countless passages in the *Eddas* and *Sagas* refer to a woman being laid next to her mate on the funeral pyre. In later times this practice was reduced to a ritual with a sacrificial "wife," often a slave girl, chosen for the occasion.

Thus the Valkyrie is a complex figure filling many roles. They form a link between the will of the distant god Odin and the needs and hopes of mortals. Like the Norns they decide men's fate; like angels they may protect. On Earth Valkyries serve as an explanation for victory or defeat; they do the will of Odin, carrying out his role as the binder and looser of men, granting and withdrawing success and power as he directs from his all-seeing chair. Defeat in battle, however, was not seen by ancient Norse warriors as necessarily negative. Rather than a punishment from the Valkyries, death on the battlefield could be seen as the Valkyries choosing the great heroes, by a "kiss of death," whose time had come to ascend to Valhalla. There the honored dead would join Odin in preparations for the last day, Ragnarök, when their assistance would be much needed against the invading giants. In heaven, then, the Valkyrie serves as the constant inspiration of the warrior, the consummation of his earthly dreams: a virginal maid dressed in white serving endless horns of mead and attending to his every need.

Brunhilde bearing a wounded warrior to Valhalla, painted by Rolf Delitz after Richard Wagner's Ride of the Valkyries. Courtesy of Anne Ronan Picture Library.

One must be cautious, however, in gauging the extent to which Valkyries figured in actual Scandinavian beliefs of the afterlife. The Valkyries may also function as a simple metaphor, as their names in the works of ninth- and tenth-century poets show: Hildr, Hlokk, and Guor are all synonyms for battle and demonstrate the romanticization of war. Likewise a Valkyrie name like *Herfjoturr* (war-fetter) explains the hesitation or paralysis of a warrior in battle as the will of Odin. Dressed in shining armor and helmets and riding swiftly on pure white horses over land and sea, the Valkyries may be no more than a poetic device to describe wars and explain the triumph or defeat of its leading participants. The tragic humanity of Brynhild and Sigurd in the *Volsunga Saga* (i.e., Brunhild and Siegfried in the German *Nibelungenlied* and Richard Wagner's *Ring Cycle*) give credence to the purely mythological and poetic view of the Valkyries. Nevertheless, extensive carved grave-

stones found throughout Scandinavia, particularly Sweden, depict Valkyries with horns greeting riders on horses, suggesting a real role played by Valkyries in Scandinavian afterlife beliefs.

See also BANSHEE; FUNERARY CUSTOMS, SCANDINAVIAN; MORRI-GAN.

References

Crossley-Holland, Kevin, ed. *The Faber Book of Northern Legends*. London: Faber and Faber, 1977.

Davidson, H. R. Ellis. *Gods and Myths of Northern Europe*. New York: Penguin, 1964, 1977.

———. *The Lost Beliefs of Northern Europe*. London: Routledge, 1993.

Guerber, Hélène Adeline. *Myths of the Norsemen from the Eddas and Sagas*. 1909. Reprint, New York: Dover, 1992.

Mackenzie, Donald A. *Teutonic Myth and Legend*. New York: Wise, 1934.

VAMPIRE

In English-speaking countries, under the influence of fictional works like Bram Stoker's *Dracula* and popular movies, the "vampire" has become an international figure of horror:

> I saw the Count [Dracula] lying within the box upon the earth, some of which the rude falling from the cart had scattered over him. He was deathly pale, just like a waxen image, and the red eyes glared with the horrible vindictive look which I knew too well. As I looked, the eyes saw the sinking sun, and the look of hate in them turned to triumph. But, on the instant, came the sweep and flash of Jonathan's great knife. I shrieked as I saw it shear through the throat; whilst at the same moment Mr. Morris' bowie knife plunged into the heart. It was like a miracle; but before our very eyes, and almost at the drawing of a breath, the whole body crumbled into dust and passed from our sight. (Stoker)

But in fact the European experience of vampires, not to mention the vampiric traditions of other world cultures, by far predates their dramatization in modern literature. The word *vampire* comes from the Slavic *upir* and is a particular kind of revenant tied to eastern European traditions (see STRIGOÏ), but vampiric creatures are known in India, China, the Philippines, Africa, Central America, and South America as well. In each culture the vampire has a distinct name and distinct characteristics: not all vampires attempt to drink the blood of the living, for example. In general the "vampire" type has the following characteristics: it is the spirit, or more frequently the reanimated corpse, of one who recently died or was buried improperly and who returns from the dead with necrotic intent, that is, to curtail fertility and interfere with natural rhythms and order.

In Europe, particularly the old Slavic regions of Europe, vampires have many different names (*mora* in Yugoslavia; *strigoï* in Romania; *nachzehrer* and *blutsauger* in Germany; *vrykolakas* in the Balkans; *wieszczy* and *montwiec* in Poland; *kruvnik* in Bulgaria; *oboroteen* in Russia, etc.), but they seem to have similar descriptions. Generally they do not match the Hollywood-inspired image of pale but suave aristocrats seeking to molest young females. Usually they are peasants: short, dark, unkempt, hugely bloated, and ugly. Furthermore, unlike the vampires of modern fiction, the vampires of folklore are miserable loners. They do not purposely seek to create more vampires in order to rule over an undead kingdom; their creation of more vampires is but a byproduct of their lust for blood, more life, and wreaking havoc on the living.

Unlike the living, the undead do not appear to be integrated beings. They are dislocated in body and soul and restless in their duality. Although on occasion corpses are thought to physically leave the grave to disturb the living, it is most often the case that the corpse remains in the grave while the spirit double (see SOUL) roams about the Earth or invades the dreams of the living, seeking blood or life energy to bring back to the grave in order to prolong the quasi-life of the body.

Although the population of vampires in Europe seems to have waxed and waned in accord with the outbreak of plagues and social crises (e.g., a pronounced vampire craze struck Germany in the 1730s), in general a great many categories of deceased are prone to vampirism. Some people appear to be predisposed to becoming vampires because of physical abnormalities, such as being born with teeth (Upper Silesia and Kashubes, Poland), an extra nipple (Romania), a split lower lip (Russia), a red birthmark, or a red caul (amniotic membrane) on one's head (in much of medieval Europe). Some are predisposed to vampirism by their lifestyle, either because it is criminal (robbers, arsonists) or looked down upon (prostitutes, alcoholics, unwed mothers, "deceitful" barmaids, "witches,")—the opportunity for scapegoating during a social crisis is obvious. Others may become vampires because of they ways in which they died, usually grisly or sudden (by suicide, murder, drowning, or plague); because their burial was inept, insincere, or lacking altogether; because they died on a battlefield (Hungary); because they died as a baby before baptism; and most especially because their death was brought on by another vampire. Again, some vampires may return from the dead to finish tasks left undone: to care for orphaned children, punish unfaithful spouses or family members who have taken advantage of one's death, or reclaim lost property. One may become a vampire through magical means, such as the attentions of a witch or sorcerer, or because an animal, bat, bird, or even a candle passed over one's corpse while it lay in state before burial, reanimating it. Finally, there is the broad (though often unspoken) idea that everyone has an allotted lifespan (either peculiar to themselves or the seventy years promised in Psalm 90), and if that predetermined length of life is cut short for any reason, the deceased is unwilling or actually *unable* to proceed to the other world until that span of time expires.

What does a vampire do? Their activities vary from Africa to Europe to China, but generally their trouble-making takes place at night, especially between midnight and dawn, and frequently in dreams. Vampires are in essence the opposite of fertility, productivity, and order, causing drought and draining the life out of crops, the milk out of animals, and the blood out of people. In some tales, however, they are simply quarrelsome and refuse to remain quietly dead. Vampires can appear as wolves, horses, donkeys, goats, cats, owls, mice, frogs, and most remarkably, butterflies and haystacks. In Slavic regions the vampire is thought to suck blood and indulge in other troublesome behaviors: suffocating people, throwing rocks and making horrifying noises, eating other corpses, and spreading pestilence and death (especially epidemics). In Iceland, rather than suck blood, vampires tend to bang on the roofs; the sight of them causes unconsciousness or even insanity, as reported in *Grettir's Saga.* Among Gypsies, vampires turn over caravans. In general the vampire can serve as the cause of almost any misfortune.

Signs that one may be dealing with a vampire are equally numerous, complex, and even contradictory. The presence of a plague is enough to prove that a vampire is present: the first person to die of plague is certainly a vampire who infects the blood of all within reach—a variation of the modern idea of contagion. If mourners are having visions of the deceased, if death comes to other members of the family, if bad weather has come, or if the community is experiencing general difficulties, quite likely a vampire is at the root of the trouble. But the only way to be sure is to disinter the body and examine it for any of the following telltale signs:

1. The grave has holes in the earth
2. The grave mound has sunk or has cracks
3. The body, or part of the body, has managed to come to the surface
4. The body is undamaged and has not decayed
5. The limbs are flexible
6. The body has changed position since burial
7. The body is bloated
8. The body, particularly the face, is dark or red-cheeked
9. The blood is liquid, not coagulated

10. There is a lot of blood around, particularly on the mouth and nose
11. There are new fingernails or skin growing under the old
12. The beard or hair has continued to grow
13. The mouth is open
14. The eyes are open (especially the left eye)
15. The liver is white

There are two methods of dealing with vampires: apotropaic measures to keep existing vampires away and neutralization methods to "kill" the vampire's body (repeatedly if necessary) when it is found. Strong smells are almost universally considered effective, possibly because they counteract the supernatural stench of the corpse. Garlic is popular in Slavic countries, especially if worn around the neck, as are green nutshells, cow dung that has been found on a hawthorn bush (combining smell with a sharp object), or tar smeared across a doorway in the form of a cross. Sometimes the blood of a vampire is considered apotropaic (in the spirit of homeopathy?). In Pomerania (present-day Poland) a would-be vampire slayer could dip part of a shroud in the blood of the undead, let it set in brandy, and drink the potion to become resistant to all vampires. At other times the blood of a vampire in itself *causes* vampirism and is to be avoided at all costs; this attitude is seen when the exhumed body of a vampire is covered before being staked to prevent lethal splatter. Sharp objects are also useful for preventing someone from becoming a vampire: hawthorn is an especially effective apotropaic in Serbia, either under the tongue or as a peg driven into the top of the grave. In Romania, Hungary, and Yugoslavia, sickles, thorns, or pieces of a saw are placed in the grave, whereas in Morocco a dagger or other sharp object of iron or steel is placed on the corpse.

It is also said that when vampires seek to return to their family home, they must go by the exact way they left; this provides another possibility for defense. In Slavic cultures the lintel of the doorway is temporarily raised and corpses are often carried out underneath on their bier, or they are taken out through a window or a hole knocked in the wall and later repaired. Likewise among the Lapps, the body is taken out under the tent at the spot where death occurred rather than the door flap. It is also known that human souls are hydrotropic—drawn to water—and so open containers of water are covered up or emptied out after a death in the household. Various explanations for this are given by informants in field research, either that the soul may be drawn into the water and thus be unable to leave the household or else that the soul may drown in the water and be unable to continue on. Similarly, the undead are thought to have difficulty crossing water, so water is often emptied on the funeral route or between the home and the cemetery so that the deceased will not be able to return. Other customs throughout Europe, in some areas continuing to this day, include covering mirrors or turning them toward the wall after a death and stopping the clocks. The former practice likely arose from the belief that the soul of the dead may be reflected in a mirror and that the gaze of a dead soul is lethal. The latter practice probably relates to assisting the deceased on the journey from the land of the living to the land of the dead: normal time ceases while the sometimes difficult and reluctant crossing is made into the "other world."

Finally the various "danger spots" of the human body must be neutralized on a newly dead corpse (see UNDEAD). Since the gaze of the dead can kill, eyes must be shut; in Poland, as elsewhere, coins are traditionally used to weigh down the eyelids. Likewise, the mouth is dangerous, not only because the soul is connected with breath and thus enters and exits through the mouth but because the chewing of a vampire is the magical source of much of its power; stories abound of corpses chewing off their limbs or their shrouds and thus spreading death among the living. Thus the mouth must be shut, in some cases tied shut or sealed with cotton or wax, as among ancient Egyptians and Babylonians. Romanians have traditionally covered eyes, ears, nose, and mouth with incense. Because vampires are preternaturally ambulatory, in medieval times legs or feet were tied. In sum, vampires are to be prevented by burials carried out in the (culturally) appropriate way and by removing attractions that might cause the deceased to remain with the living.

Despite all precautions, a vampire may arise nonetheless, in which case the half-dead body must again be "killed," although finding the vampire can be difficult, especially because they tend to become invisible. In the Balkans the vampire is compelled to remain in his or her grave on Saturdays, for he is visible on that day to his or her son or to anyone born on a Saturday—thus this is a safe day to search out the grave and destroy the corpse. The stake-through-the-heart method has become popularized in modern fiction, and in fact innumerable exhumed corpses were staked throughout medieval Europe. It is important to get the *right* heart, however, for vampires are often thought to have two. (The stake should be made of ash in Russia and the Baltic states, oak in Germany, and hawthorn in Serbia.) But other sharp objects have proven equally effective. In Iceland nails are driven through the soles of a revenant corpse to prevent it from walking, and Serbians habitually cut the knee ligaments of corpses for the same purpose. In Poland, Germany, and among the western Slavs the head may be cut off and reburied, with a layer of dirt between body and head—presumably then the vampire will be unable to reach its head and will remain inert. Fire is also "lethal" to vampires and has often been combined

A Russian Vampire

About the beginning of the 18th century, there occurred in Russia one of the most frightful cases of vampirism on record. The governor of the Province of Tch— was a man of about sixty years, of malicious, tyrannical, cruel and jealous disposition. Clothed with despotic authority, he exercised it without stint, as his brutal instincts prompted. He fell in love with the pretty daughter of a subordinate official. Although the girl was betrothed to a young man whom she loved, the tyrant forced her father to consent to his having her marry him; and the poor victim, despite her despair, became his wife. His jealous disposition exhibited itself. He beat her, confined her to her room for weeks together, and prevented her seeing any one except in his presence. He finally fell sick and died. Finding his end approaching, he made her swear never to marry again; and with fearful oaths, threatened that, in case she did, he would return from his grave and kill her. He was buried in the cemetery across the river; and the young widow experienced no further annoyance, until, nature getting the better of her fears, she listened to the importunities of her former lover, and they were again betrothed.

On the night of the customary betrothal-feast, when all had retired, the old mansion was aroused by shrieks proceeding from her room. The doors were burst open, and the unhappy woman was found lying on her bed, in a swoon. At the same time a carriage was heard rumbling out of the courtyard. Her body was found to be black and blue in places, as from the effect of pinches, and from a slight puncture on her neck drops of blood were oozing. Upon recovering, she stated that her deceased husband had suddenly entered her room, appearing exactly as in life, with the exception of a dreadful pallor; that he had upbraided her for her inconstancy, and then beaten and pinched her most cruelly. Her story was disbelieved; but the next morning, the guard stationed at the other end of the bridge which spans the river, reported that, just before midnight, a black coach and six had driven furiously past them, toward the town, without answering their challenge.

The new governor, who disbelieved the story of the apparition, took nevertheless the precaution of doubling the guards across the bridge. The same thing happened, however, night after night; the soldiers declaring that the toll-bar at their station near the bridge would rise of itself, and the spectral equipage sweep by them despite their efforts to stop it. At the same time every night, the coach would rumble into the courtyard of the house; the watchers, including the widow's family, and the servants, would be thrown into a heavy sleep; and every morning the young victim would be found bruised, bleeding, and swooning as before. The town was thrown into consternation. The physicians had no explanations to offer; priests came to pass the night in prayer, but as midnight approached, all would be seized with the terrible lethargy. Finally the archbishop of the province came, and performed the ceremony of exorcism in person, but the following morning the governor's widow was found worse than before. She was now brought to death's door.

The governor was finally driven to take the severest measures to stop the ever-increasing panic in the town. He stationed fifty Cossacks along the bridge, with orders to stop the spectre-carriage at all hazards. Promptly at the usual hour, it was heard and seen approaching from the direction of the cemetery. The officer of the guard, and a priest bearing a crucifix, planted themselves in front of the toll-bar, and together shouted: "In the name of God, and the Czar, who goes there?" Out of the coach window was thrust a well-remembered head, and a familiar voice responded: "The Privy Councillor of State and Governor, C—!" At the same moment, the officer, the priest, and the soldiers were flung aside as if by an electric shock, and the ghostly equipage passed by them, before they could recover their breath.

The archbishop then resolved, as a last expedient, to resort to the time-honored plan of exhuming the body, and pinning it to the earth with an oaken stake driven through its heart. This was done with great religious ceremony in the presence of the whole populace. The story is that the body was found gorged with blood, and with red cheeks and lips. At the instant that that the first blow was struck upon the stake, a groan issued from the corpse, and a jet of blood spurted high into the air. The archbishop pronounced the usual exorcism, the body was reinterred, and from that time no more was heard of the vampire.

How far the facts of this case may have been exaggerated by tradition, we cannot say. But we had it years ago from an eye-witness; and at the present day there are families in Russia whose elder members will recall the dreadful tale.

Blavatsky (1976, vol. 1, pp. 454–455).

---

with sharp objects; for example, piercing the heart with a glowing stake. In extremis the heart may be physically cut out of the body and burned or cremated (called *excoriation*). In general, cremation is the last resort, whether of the heart, head, or (what is more expensive) entire body, although this is the preferred method for the Greek *vrykolakas*. When killed, the body of the vampire is frequently said to squirm, writhe in agony, scream out or utter a blood-curdling groan, and spurt blood high into the air (see excerpt for a thrilling example). Finally, after adequate treatment, the body must be specially reburied. Frequently this means no more than replacing the vampire in his or her grave face down (an example of "widdershins," or reversal of normal practices when dealing with the occult), but the body may also be thrown in water or a desolate spot (Russia).

See also POLTERGEIST; SOUL; STRIGOÏ; UNDEAD; UNDERWORLD; VRYKOLAKAS; WATER.

References

Barber, Paul. *Vampires, Burial, and Death*. New Haven: Yale University Press, 1988.

Blavatsky, Helena Petrovna. *Isis Unveiled*. 2 vols. Reprint, Pasadena: Theosophical University Press, 1976.

Florescu, Radu, and Raymond T. McNally. *Dracula: A Biography of Vlad the Impaler*. New York: Hawthorn Books, 1973.

Máchal, Jan. *Slavic Mythology*. New York: Cooper Square Publishers, 1918.

Masters, Anthony. *The Natural History of the Vampire*. New York: G. P. Putnam's Sons, 1972.

Perkowski, Jan Louis. *Vampires of the Slavs*. Cambridge: Slavica Publishers, 1976.

Ramos, Maximo. *The Creatures of Midnight*. Quezon City, Philippines: Island Publishers, 1967.

Stoker, Bram. *Dracula*. Edited by Glennis Byron. Peterborough, Ontario: Broadview, 1998.

Summers, Montague. *The Vampire: His Kith and Kin*. New Hyde Park, NY: University Books, 1960.

———. *The Vampire In Europe*. New York: University Books, 1968.

Wright, Dudley. *Vampires and Vampirism*. London: Will Rider and Son, 1924.

VRYKOLAKAS

A vrykolakas is a specific type of vampire in Greece and the Balkans. The word *vrykolakas,* like its cognates (the Russian *volkodlak,* Bulgarian and Serbian *vukodlac,* and Czech *vilkodlak*), was originally the term for werewolf (from the Indo-European word for "robber"), and its etymology underscores the historical fact that in Slavic and Balkan belief magicians, lycanthropes, and vampires are all versions of the same phenomenon. The symbolic history of the wolf in European legend and myth has been well studied: as European peoples gradually shifted from nomadic or marauding bands to settled pastoral societies, the wolf moved from a positive symbol of war and honorable power to a threatening symbol of danger from outside forces. The association of wolf with death magic and the undead is thus a natural one in agrarian medieval European history: anyone who is in touch with "the other side" of nature, the occult, is symbolically a wolf, connected to death and danger. The magician is able to change shape (figuratively and literally) between human and animal states and to function in both the mundane and occult worlds. He or she is thus likely to continue such ambiguous, if not nefarious, activity after death, that is, become a vampire.

Interestingly, of all the European countries that have strong vampire beliefs, the vrykolakas in Greece has possibly the most amiable nature. True, there are horror stories of the evil revenant who comes to suck the milk out of cows and the blood out of humans. But there are also a great many stories of quite amiable vampires— they return from the dead to mend their children's shoes, plough fields, and chop wood for the family. Greeks are even known for their frequent "vampiric" curses, such as "May the earth not receive you" or "May the ground refuse to digest." Clearly, the overwhelming fear of the undead experienced in much of Europe did not take the same hold in Greece. Perhaps Greece did not inherit all of its beliefs regarding the vrykolakas from Slavic tradition, nor did the Orthodox Christian history of Greece expose it to the Inquisition and witch burning of more westerly Catholic countries.

From ancient Greek religion, modern Greece has inherited the belief that certain classes of people are likely to become a vrykolakas: those without full and proper burial rites, those who died a violent death, and those who lived extremely immoral lives. Later, Slavic traditions about the strigoï mixed with Greek beliefs: one may become a vrykolakas in rural Greece today if anything jumps over the corpse (animal, bird, insect) or even if a lighted candle is passed over the corpse; if one eats the flesh of sheep killed by a wolf; or if one is cursed by a priest. The handling of the vrykolakas in Greece also differs somewhat from practices in other parts of Europe: while driving a stake or nail through the heart is certainly known, it is much more frequent in Greece to burn the body of a suspected revenant. In some cases prayers recited by the priest take care of the problem. There is also the unique Greek tradition of firing a shot from a revolver into the casket, not to mention acroteriazein: cutting off the feet, hands, nose, and ears of a vampire and tying them to the elbows.

References

Blum, Richard, and Eva Blum. *The Dangerous Hour: The Lore of Crisis and Mystery in Rural Greece.* New York: Charles Scribner's Sons, 1970.

Lawson, John Cuthbert. *Modern Greek Folklore and Ancient Greek Religion*. 1910. Reprint, New York: University Books, 1964.

Lee, D. Demetracopoulou. "Greek Accounts of the Vrykolakas." *Journal of American Folklore* 55 (1942).

WATER

Untamed water is the most terrifying element known to humankind. Fire can and does consume human works—at times uncontrollably—but fire has by and large been tamed. Wind can blow things over or even tear trees out of the earth, but it is infrequently destructive. And although the Earth may move underneath us, it is by and large a stable element and the source of many good things, including produce. But water, particularly the deep, seemingly bottomless waters of a lake or ocean, terrifies. Salvation Army and Red Cross volunteers have verified that floods produce greater anxiety and shock in victims than any other kind of natural disaster. One may sink and disappear from view forever, though still bodily intact. The ocean, however placid it may look, is a constant source of danger, as sailors and swimmers know. The old fisherman's adage is "never turn your back on the sea." Thus it is not surprising that, symbolically, water is everywhere associated with those powerful transformations of birth, death, and time.

By nature unformed, water can take any shape yet holds none. For this reason water is a suitable symbol for primordial chaos and danger and preexistent death, even though it is out of chaos that law and life arose. In ancient Mesopotamia, the original chaos is symbolized by Tiamat, a fearsome water dragon; only when she is slain by the hero Ea (or later, the Babylonian Marduk) can the lawful human order of creation begin. In India, the high god Indra slays the serpent demon Vritra, who (among other things) represents water. The demon holds back the necessary rains and prevents fertility, but his death unleashes a welcome thundershower. In the Hebrew tradition, only by command after command of Jahweh is the unformed water gradually made into an ordered universe. Whenever a body of water appears in myth, one of the echoes it should produce in the reader's or listener's mind is that of primordial time.

In its role as origin and chaos—and thus death—it is only natural that water should serve as a primary boundary between the living and the dead. It represents the periods before and after existence, the hidden, and the unknown—in contrast to the land of the living, the sunlit world of order, growth, and linear time. Dry land is the realm of production; water is or leads to the realm of disintegration and the dead, or separates that realm from the living. Time and again, interactions between this world and the other take place in and around water. In the Welsh Otherworld, the hero Pwyll slays his opponent Hafgan at a ford, and many Irish versions of the Otherworld are islands (or castles) located over the western sea or reached by diving through a lake. Thus water as a symbol also divides the known from the unknown.

Water functions as a symbol of division in a variety of situations: surrounding the Underworld, holding mysterious Islands of the Blest at its horizon, and serving as a literal mirror or curtain between the order of time and the timeless. In a myth from the Native American Zuñi tribe, a young man follows his dead wife to the land of the dead, hoping at some point he will be able to save her and return with her to the living. The man follows the red feather on his invisible wife's head until it plunges at last into a large deep lake, and the husband discovers that truly, he is cut off from her ("The Spirit Wife," in Erdoes and Ortiz).

In every known Underworld, a river (or several rivers) provides the boundaries to the land of the living. Both Homer's the *Iliad* and the *Odyssey* place the land of the dead far from human habitation and in close connection with water. The *Iliad* mentions the River Styx, but in the *Odyssey* we find several other rivers as well: Acheron, river of woe; Cocytus, the river of wailing, where unburied dead had to wander for 100 years; Lethe, river of forgetfulness; and Phlegethon, the blazing river. Water is likewise prominent in the Scandinavian Underworld, Hel; the Chinese Yellow Springs; the Mesopotamian Kigal; the Latin Avernus; and the Egyptian Amenti and Āaru. Underground water is not only a reminder of the watery chaos that existed before the world was ordered by the gods; water is connected to the ocean, which is the source of livelihood, transportation, and death for a seafaring people like the Greeks; and water is that mysterious force that brings up vegetation from the Earth. Thus it is not coincidental that the ocean borders Hades and other subterranean lands of the dead; the ambiguity of water is a perfect component of the dual nature of the Underworld—a source of danger as well as fertility and wealth. Often water is represented by a goddess or other powerful female, who in her persona demonstrates both the fierceness and motherly generosity of water. Examples from the Celtic world include the Irish Morrigan (who meets her hero/nemesis Cú Chulainn at a ford); Matrona the Gaullish water divinity; the Welsh Modron, goddess of river crossings; and the medieval French and British Morgan Le Fay, sometime enemy of Arthur and guardian of Avalon, the paradisiacal island across the sea. The Greek Circe is another such dangerous water goddess, first the foe and then the friend of Odysseus; it was Circe who provided Odysseus with the maritime passage to Tartaros, the Underworld.

Likewise, water frequently separates the ordinary world of humans from fantastic worlds "beyond the sea." Such islands are, in actuality, prototypes of heaven and offer a more blessed afterlife than the typical Underworld. Literature from many cultures contains countless voyages of heroes across the ocean to the Otherworld wherein dwell the dead or the fairies (who are often merely the dead transformed). In this fairy/spirit world time is distorted: a fairy year can be hundreds of humans years or no longer than an instant. For example, in Celtic legend Bran, son of Febal, visited Emain, an immortal land across the waters inhabited only by women. After staying only a year he returned home to find that hundreds of years had passed, and he turned to dust. Likewise in Japan, Urashima Taro married the Sea King's daughter and was away for three centuries. Such voyages are thus fraught with danger and may literally as well as symbolically be equated with death. Traditionally, Indians were forbidden to cross the "great black waters" for fear of losing caste, thus becoming ritually dead. Even in the nineteenth century, Mahatma Gandhi was forbidden to board a ship from India to study law in England; he was forced to undergo a terrible ordeal upon returning to his homeland in order to regain his caste (Gandhi, 1957).

Additionally, water has another important symbolic connection to death: water has an uncanny and important relation to the soul in nearly all parts of the world. First of all, the soul is itself a reflection. For this reason, it often looks like the body—it is the psychic projection of how one thinks one looks. Ghosts, doppelgängers, banshees, and most other undead appear as the physical body did during life. Even out-of-body and near-death experiences had by the living persons, though allegedly taking place in "the soul," are experienced as taking place with a subtle "astral" body that looks like the physical one. Probably in part because of its reflective quality, water, like mirrors, has the property of absorbing soul energy, especially of the dead. The soul, itself a reflection, is "captured" by being reflected in water (and, by extension, mirrors).

Water, being in this way "absorptive" of soul energy, can be used to keep the dead in their place (i.e., in the grave) or form a barrier. Undead can almost never cross water, and possibly because they have no soul (and thus cast no reflection), the dead are powerless against water. Dangerous dead (those likely to become vampires in local opinion) were frequently removed to islands or buried there in the first place to prevent their travels altogether. In eastern Prussia the water used to bathe the corpse (leichenwasser) was poured out between the coffin and the house as the funeral procession departed, forming a barrier against the return of the dead, and then the container was broken. Likewise, the Wends in Lausitz returned from a burial by crossing over water. Interestingly, vampires were thought in Russia (and elsewhere in medieval Europe) to cause droughts, possibly related to their fear of water and inability to cross it. In Serbia, Croatia, and Bulgaria it is important to pour out any standing water after someone in the house has died, sometimes because the dead is thought to have bathed in the water or simply to avoid the possibility that it might have reflected the dead soul—for the sight of the dead soul by the living could bring death to others in the household. In Romania it is important to cover any containers of water after a death, because the soul might fall into it and drown. In Macedonia after the exhumation of a corpse, a container of water is left in the empty grave, probably to capture the soul and avoid any trouble that might be caused by it. Likewise in Bulgaria a jar of water is left at the grave, and in Hungary and medieval Prussia, the bloating of the corpse (which apparently is caused by evil souls creeping in) can be prevented by putting a container of water under the bier.

The last necromantic power of water to be investigated is its ability to cleanse. Water is regarded in many parts of the world as a great purifier, in part perhaps because it has the observable quality of dissolving almost anything, given enough time. In India and the Himalayan regions it is the highest honor to be cremated and have the ashes placed in the sacred river Ganges (or any stream that eventually terminates in the Ganges). The poor are only able to afford a partial burning, and the very poor simply place the entire corpse into the water. It does not matter: the Ganges accepts and purifies everything, and daily all along its shores millions continue to bathe in it, while newly purified corpses float by.

In medieval Europe, however, something of the opposite practice developed, though for the same reason: water was thought, like the Earth, to be thoroughly pure. Water would only receive the righteous dead and would reject evildoers or the undead. The corpses of the undead were believed to rise up, especially if placed in water. This belief led to the iudicium aquae, or "trial by water," which was used primarily to interrogate women for witchcraft. The theory, articu-

From "The Dry Salvages"

The sea howl
And the sea yelp, are different voices
Often together heard: the whine in the rigging,
The menace and caress of wave that breaks on water,
The distant rote in the granite teeth,
And the wailing warning from the approaching
    headland
Are all sea voices, and the heaving groaner [buoy]
Rounded homewards, and the seagull:
And under the oppression of the silent fog
The tolling bell
Measures time not our time, rung by the unhurried
Ground swell, a time
Older than the time of chronometers, older
Than time counted by anxious worried women
Lying awake, calculating the future,
Trying to unweave, unwind, unravel
And piece together the past and the future,
Between midnight and dawn, when the past is all
    deception,
The future futureless, before the morning watch
When time stops and time is never ending;
And the ground swell, that is and was from the
    beginning,
Clangs
The bell.

Eliot (1988).

lated by no less an authority than King James, was that "the water shall refuse to receive them in her bosom, that have shaken off them the sacred water of baptism and wilfully refused the benefit thereof" (Barber). In such a water trial, the innocent were supposed to sink (and die), the guilty, having been rejected by the waters, floated and were promptly killed. Less macabre is the old Japanese belief in the purity of water. If one is suffering from a skin disease, one dons a hat and submerges in a river, lake, or the sea until the hat floats; the disease will be carried away with the hat.

Mythologically, any water—even a small quantity—represents all water. It is associated with purity and danger, fertility and death. Water reminds us not only of measureless depth (what the Greeks called the *abyss*) but of measureless time. From humanity's perspective, it is always moving yet always stays the same; thus in a symbolic, in a cosmic, even in a Darwinian sense, water is our home, a source that existed long before humans.

See also ĀARU; ANNWFN; AVALON; BURIAL, SHIP; DILMUN; ELYSION; HADES; HEL; ISLANDS OF THE BLEST; OTHERWORLD, IRISH; UNDERWORLD; YELLOW SPRINGS.

References

Barber, Paul. *Vampires, Burial, and Death: Folklore and Reality*. New Haven: Yale University Press, 1988.

Eliot, T. S. *Four Quartets*. San Diego: Harcourt Brace Jovanovich, 1988.

Erdoes, Richard, and Alfonzo Ortiz, eds. *American Indian Myths and Legends*. New York: Pantheon, 1984.

Farnell, Lewis R. *Greek Hero Cults and Ideas of Immortality*. Oxford: Clarendon Press, 1921.

Gandhi, Mohandas K. *An Autobiography: The Story of My Experiments with Truth*. Boston: Beacon Press, 1957.

Homer. *The Odyssey*. Trans. Samuel Butler. New York: Barnes and Noble, 1993.

Lattimore, Richard, trans. Homer. *The Iliad*. Chicago: University of Chicago Press, 1951.

Loomis, Roger Sherman. *Celtic Myth and Arthurian Romance*. New York: Columbia University Press, 1926.

Mandelbaum, Allen, trans. *The Aeneid of Virgil*. New York: Bantam, 1961.

Rees, Alwyn, and Brinley Rees. *Celtic Heritage: Ancient Tradition in Ireland and Wales*. London: Thames and Hudson, 1961.

Sandars, N. K., trans. *The Epic of Gilgamesh*. New York: Penguin, 1972.

Y

YAHRZEIT

The anniversary of a loved one's death is called *yahrzeit* in Judaism. The special observances of yahrzeit are especially directed toward remembrance of deceased parents, but they are occasionally performed for other loved ones if they were very close to the bereaved: children, spouse, other relatives, or friends. For Orthodox Jews, the anniversary of death is calculated on the Hebrew lunar calendar, which causes the yahrzeit to fall on different days on the standard solar calendar. Many Jews simply observe the anniversary on the standard calendar, however.

The yahrzeit is not as highly regulated as other Jewish mourning rituals (for example, shiva), which may indicate that yahrzeit has a later origin, although it is mentioned in the Talmud, a collection of Jewish wisdom and law that dates to the early centuries of the common era. In any case, mourners who observe yahrzeit have considerable freedom in how to do so. Some mourners commit themselves to a fast on the anniversary of their parent's (or other relative's) death; if this is done it is obligatory annually. Exceptions are made for the weak or sick, who reduce the fast to merely avoiding meat and wine, associated in Judaism with festivity. Likewise, fasting is avoided if yahrzeit falls on a major religious holiday. Because Hebrew days begin in the evening, the fast begins the night before the anniversary and continues until nightfall of the day of yahrzeit.

Another common observance of yahrzeit is to light a candle for the deceased and let it burn throughout the anniversary. Since ancient times the candle has been a symbol in Judaism for the human being: the body is the wick, and the soul is the flame. A separate candle is lit for each deceased relative (if one is commemorating more than one person at the same time). Likewise, several people commemorating a single relative, for example, several children of the same parent, also generally light separate candles. Orthodox Jews, however, do not light a candle if the yahrzeit falls on the Sabbath (Friday evening to Saturday evening) because lighting a fire (among many other kinds of "work") is forbidden on the day of rest.

A third popular observance of yahrzeit is study of Scripture (including the Hebrew Mishnah, a collection of religious law), which may even be carried out at the gravesite of the deceased. Because a visit to the grave is also a traditional part of yahrzeit and such visits are ordained in the Mishnah, it is particularly fitting to study religious law even as one observes it in honor of the dead. Psalms are also typically recited, with the mourner(s) even placing one hand on the tombstone as he or she reads. A standard memorial prayer is also recited, called *El Malei Rachamim* (literally "O God, full of compassion").

Finally, it is typical to have the El Malei Rachamim prayer recited by the entire synagogue on the Sabbath prior to the yahrzeit. Orthodox Jews, who observe three daily religious services, are invited to lead all the services on the day they are observing yahrzeit. An important part of these services is the recitation of the mourner's kaddish, a prayer that honors the dead and is even thought to be of benefit to them in the afterlife.

See also ANINUT; AVELUT; FUNERARY CUSTOMS, JEWISH; INTERCESSION; KADDISH; SHIVA (JEWISH); SOUL, JEWISH; YIZKOR.

References
Abramovitch, Henry. "Death." In *Contemporary Jewish Religious Thought,* ed. Arthur A. Cohen and Paul Mendes-Flohr. New York: Charles Scribner's Sons, 1989.
De Sola Pool, David. *The Kaddish.* Jerusalem: Printed by Sivan Press under the auspices of the Union of Sephardic Congregations, New York, 1964.
Lamm, Maurice. *The Jewish Way in Death and Mourning.* New York: Jonathan David Publishers, 1969.
Rabinowicz, H. *A Guide to Life.* London: Jewish Chronicle Publications, 1964.
Riemer, Jack, ed. *Jewish Reflections on Death.* New York: Schocken Books, 1974.

YAMA

The lord of death in Hinduism and Buddhism, Yama dramatically changed in character from his benevolent first appearance in the earliest Hindu literature, the Vedas (c. 4000 to 2000 B.C.E.), to his frightening and seemingly evil aspect in Buddhist texts. Along the way he is a heroic man, a king, a god, a demon, and an illusion—a most fascinating figure in religious history.

The earliest of Indian texts, the Rig Veda, finds Yama, son of Vivasvant (the luminous) to be a heroic man and pioneer of higher worlds. Yama is the first

The god and goddess of death and karmic judgment, Yama and Yami, riding on a bull that stamps on a human corpse. Yama is horned, naked, and surrounded by wisdom flames. Four demon gods (in the colors of the four basic elements) accompany both, who help them in catching the souls of the dead. At the top are pictured the Tibetan guru Tsongkhapa and his two main disciples, Gyaltshab and Khaedup. Courtesy of Taeger Collection.

mortal to choose to die out of the realm of Earth and seek out the higher worlds of the heavenly fathers, called *pitris*. There Yama makes offerings to the gods and sets up a special kingdom of light for the deceased mortals who will follow his lead in ages to come. Thus Yama is called "a gatherer of men," and a good many early hymns celebrate Yama and his deeds, such as Rig Veda X.14.1d–2:

> [O sacrificer,] present Yama the king with an
> offering!
> Yama first showed us the way;
> This kingdom is everlasting.
> Where our heavenly fathers have gone,
> There mortals pass away by their many paths.
> (Richard P. Taylor, trans.)

In Vedic death rituals Yama is called on to come to the funeral and bring the deceased directly to his kingdom, guided by Agni, the god of fire. Certainly, the physical process of cremation coupled with the symbolism of "arising" in a "car of flames" is a powerful religious image of leaving this world for another, but very little in the Vedic literature makes Yama a dreadful or evil figure; he is a hero who has provided for his "flock." His kingdom is full of song and the music of the flute, and it is clearly located near the realm of the highest gods, for Yama is constantly associated with the sun, Agni, and the immortal fathers. It is true that the path to Yama's kingdom is said to be guarded by two dogs, one striped, one brown, each with four eyes; and Yama is sometimes treated as a personification of destruction, and called *Mrityu* (Death). There are hints that Yama's kingdom of light was not the automatic destination of the dead, that perhaps there were some trials and tribulations. But at this early time he was a powerful human spirit or even a symbol of humanity as a whole but not a god. The very early Indians had a good and beneficent relationship with Yama.

In the Zoroastrian Scripture the Avesta, a similar figure appears. Yima, son of Vīvanghvant, is a heroic man or a god but is shown to communicate directly with the high god, Ahura Mazda. He is said to be the first and highest of men, and Ahura Mazda asks Yima to guard the world and defend it from coming cataclysms. Yima says, "Yes, I will rule and watch over thy world. There shall be, while I am King, neither cold wind nor hot wind, neither disease nor death." Thus although Yima is somewhat more "mortal" than the Hindu Yama, he is still a very beneficial figure and likewise a leader and path maker for human beings.

It is most interesting, then, that later literature begins to chip away at Yama, or as he is increasingly called, *Mrityu*. The text Aitareya Brāhmana (c. 1500–1000 B.C.E.) says that Mrityu has fetters and wooden clubs for catching sinful men, and Yama's messenger has become the owl, an evil omen in Indian thought. There is a doctrine in Indian religion that as time passes the world slips into a worse and worse condition, until it approaches the absolute bottom of morality in the Kali Yuga, or (present) Black Age. Thus it may be that Indians felt their sins increasing and anticipated a less and less bright afterlife—so death, represented by the figure Yama, became a more foreboding journey. Indeed, in the more recent texts called the *Purāṇas* (dated 300 to 600 C.E.), Yama is assisted by a recording spirit, a dreadful judge of souls called Chitragupta, who is portrayed as only too happy to cast sinners into the most awful Naraka (hell). Chitragupta drags the wicked with ropes around their necks over rugged terrain; "his heart is hard," and he casts people headlong into the abyss. In this way Yama is increasingly associated with ethical judgment, and so he is also called Dharmarāja, or King of Justice.

Buddhism arose in India around the time of the earliest Purāṇas, and so their hideous vision of Yama, lord of death, prevailed in Buddhist literature. The recently dead enter Yamapur, "the city of Yama," an iron hall without windows or doors. There they take in the fearful sight of their new lord: Yama is bluish black in color, red eyes ablaze, head like a buffalo's, and in his hand is a skull with the spinal cord still attached. Standing naked with phallus erect on the back of a fire-breathing buffalo, Yama personifies both the energy and desires of life and the morbidity and terror of death. Yama weighs the good and evil deeds of the deceased and then sends them on to their karmic fate in heaven or hell.

This same image, originally Hindu and now Buddhist, was carried by Buddhist missionaries to Tibet, where under his new Tibetan name *gShin-rje* (pronounced "Shin-jay") Yama terrifies true believers to this day. He is pictured as holding the wheel of life with its six realms of birth in his jaws, surrounded by his clawed arms and feet, symbolizing the fact that wherever one may be reborn, even in heaven, karma dictates that eventually one must die and be reborn, again and again and again. Thus death is omnipresent:

the entire universe is Yama's abode, and one is subject to death and rebirth until one escapes from the cycle by attaining enlightenment. Thus it is only by wisdom and compassion, the spiritual attributes leading to release from rebirth, that death is conquered. Tibetan Buddhists demonstrate this belief in festivals in which individuals masquerade as Yama in colorful costumes with ogre bodies and bull heads, performing a fierce dance. Yet Yama is always tamed in the end by one of the Buddhist saviors, representing the ultimate liberation of the soul.

See also BARDO; DEWACHAN (TIBETAN BUDDHIST); FUNERARY CUSTOMS, ANCIENT INDIAN; NARAKA; PURE LAND; REINCARNATION, EASTERN; SVARGA.

References

Blavatsky, H. P. *The Secret Doctrine.* 2 vols. Reprint, New York: Theosophy Company, 1925.

Carnoy, Albert J. *The Myths of All Races.* Vol. 6: *Iranian.* Ed. L. H. Gray. New York: Cooper Square Publishers, 1964.

Griswold, H. D. *The Religion of the Rigveda.* Indian ed. Delhi: Motilal Banarsidass, 1971.

Kane, Pandurang Vaman. *History of Dharmashāstra: Ancient and Medieval Religious and Civil Law in India.* Vol. 4. Government Oriental Series, Class B, no. 6. Poona: Bhandarkar Oriental Research Institute, 1953.

Keith, Arthur Berriedale. *The Mythology of All Races.* Vol. 6: *Indian Mythology.* Ed. L. H. Gray. New York: Cooper Square Publishers, 1964.

Moor, Edward. *The Hindu Pantheon.* Ed. W. O. Simpson. Madras: J. Higginbotham, 1864.

Oldenberg, Hermann. *The Religion of the Veda.* Trans. Shridhar B. Shrotri. Indian ed. Delhi: Motilal Banarsidass, 1988.

Thurman, Robert. *The Tibetan Book of the Dead.* New York: Bantam, 1994.

YELLOW SPRINGS (HUANG-CH'UAN)

From very early times in China, reference was made to an underground after-death destination called the *Yellow Springs.* A text dated to the third century B.C.E. states: "Those who are killed go to the yellow springs; they die but do not perish" (quoted in Teiser, p. 169). To be sure, it was not the spiritual hun aspect of the soul that descended underground but rather the p'o element of the soul, called the *animal* soul and related to earthly (yin) energy.

Because the underground Yellow Springs was conceived of as the source of earthly waters and possibly as the source of yin energy in the world, it may be that the p'o soul, in journeying to the Yellow Springs, was only returning to its ultimate source. In support of this theory, we find that one of the alternative names for Yellow Springs is "Nine Sources" (chiu-yuan). But the first known references to the Yellow Springs make it the place of death, not life. It is dark and cold like a physical grave, and it appears to be the destination of *all* souls, as was the Greek Hades, Scandinavian Hel, and Hebrew Sheol. Only later, in the first century C.E., do sources refer to the Yellow Springs as the source of life. Laurence Thompson (p. 29) quotes one text that makes the Yellow Springs part of the mystical geography of the Earth: "The position of Water is in the northern quadrant. In that quadrant the vital *yin*-breath is beneath the Yellow Springs, where it nourishes the myriads of beings." Unlike later Chinese cosmology (after the advent of Buddhism, particularly), this early Underworld has no reference to punishment—although in later Chinese religion Yellow Springs becomes one of the names of Purgatory.

In one early tale about the Yellow Springs, *Master Tso's Commentary on the Spring and Autumn Annals* (Sommer), dating to the Warring States period (403–221 B.C.E.), we find Duke Chuang who seeks his mother after her death. He is advised to dig a tunnel to the Yellow Springs, which he does. His mother is able to ascend the tunnel a short distance, and they meet. In another Chinese text, dating much later, to the advent of Buddhism in China (c. third to sixth centuries C.E.), a certain Mu-lien also seeks his mother, and not finding her in heaven, he seeks her in the hells below the Earth. Here we find that ancient Chinese images have been fully absorbed by Buddhist cosmography, and the Yellow Springs has become nothing more than the gateway to the Buddhist Underworld of torment.

See also HADES; HEL; HELLS, BUDDHIST; SHEOL; SOUL, CHINESE; TI-TSANG.

References

Chan, Wing-tsit, ed. and trans. *A Source Book in Chinese Philosophy.* Princeton: Princeton University Press, 1963.

Loewe, Michael. *Ways to Paradise: The Chinese Quest for Immortality.* Boston: Allen and Unwin, 1979.

Maspero, Henri. *Les religions chinoises.* Paris: Civilisations du Sud, SAEP, 1950.

Sommer, Deborah, ed. *Chinese Religions: An Anthology of Sources.* New York: Oxford University Press, 1995.

Teiser, Stephen F. *The Ghost Festival in Medieval China.* Princeton: Princeton University Press, 1988.

Thompson, Laurence G. "On the Prehistory of Hell in China." *Journal of Chinese Religions,* no. 17 (Fall 1989).

YEN-LO WANG

Since the introduction of Buddhism to China from the first to the fourth centuries C.E., the god Yen-lo wang has been one of the central deities concerned with death. His name is a half-translation, half-transliteration of that of the Indian deity of death, *Yama-rāja,* or "king Yama." The Chinese monks who brought Buddhist ideas to China, taking the Indian sounds of Yama-rāja, transliterated it as "Yen-mo lo-she" or Yen-lo for short. In case this was unclear to a Chinese audience, the word "wang" (king) was added; so the final product "Yen-lo wang" reads something like "king Yama king." Yen-lo

wang is usually depicted as a well-groomed king in Chinese art, unlike the demonic appearance given Yama in India. However, Yen-lo wang is no less fearsome in China, for it is he who judges mortals in their Underworld purgatory and condemns the dead to hell if they fail to pass muster.

When Buddhism entered China, it encountered an already highly developed religious sensibility. From the ancient and vague Chinese concept of the Yellow Springs, where the shades of the dead gathered at an underground water source, the Chinese had evolved a large and highly bureaucratized Underworld government, largely resembling the imperial system that governed the living in medieval China. In one or another of these underground "Earth prisons" (*ti-yü*) the souls of the dead were ruled by powerful magistrates. Alongside this understanding, some Chinese were beginning to develop hopes of paradisiacal realms in the west or among islands in the east, and other Chinese, influenced by Taoism, pursued various alchemical and religious devices to induce actual physical immortality. It was in this complex milieu that Buddhist notions of death arrived.

In Buddhist India, Yama is the complete lord of his realm, and it is he who judges the dead (with a few minor assistants) according to karma from their past lives. In China, he found that he had competition. At first, Yen-lo wang (formerly Yama) appears not to have been well integrated into Chinese thought. A second-century C.E. Chinese text, the *Scripture of Questions on Hell,* portrays Yen-lo wang acting alone in the Earth prisons, but one must assume that this picture was accepted only by the (so far) very small Buddhist community, whereas Taoist and Confucian ideas of the afterlife were still quite different. From the *Scripture of Questions on Hell,* comes:

> To the north, south, east and west of Yen-lo wang's city are arrayed all of the hells. Although there is light from the sun and moon, it is not bright; the prisons are so black that light does not illuminate them. . . . Sinners take on a body composed of intermediary aggregates [a subtle body] and enter the city of Naraka, which is where all those who have not yet received punishment gather together. Blown about by the winds of fortune according to the severity of their karma, they receive bodies either large or small. Blown by ill-odored winds, people who have committed evil receive coarse, ugly forms. Blown by fragrant winds, people who have performed good receive fine, ethereal bodies. (quoted in Teiser, 1988, pp. 185–186)

In this description, there is no mention of native Chinese deities, mortuary offerings by relatives, or a bureaucracy with ministers in the Underworld. The fate of the dead hangs solely on their balance of karma, good or evil, and they are soon reborn into one of the "six realms" of the Buddhist cosmology (see BHAVA-CHAKRA).

A few centuries later, however, the Chinese picture is quite different. Yen-lo wang still holds a high position, but he finds himself only part of the huge Underworld bureaucracy, ruled by not one but ten kings. The idea of rebirth had largely been accepted by the Chinese people during the medieval period (fifth to tenth centuries C.E.), according to which the dead were reincarnated after a short time in the Underworld in between lives. Shuttled every seven days from realm to realm and king to king, the dead were judged for their actions while alive, but meanwhile they were hoping for large memorial offerings from living relatives to "assist" the ten kings in making their decisions. In this system Yen-lo wang became the fifth king, who greeted the dead on the twenty-ninth day after their death and held them until the thirty-fifth day.

For Chinese Buddhists, of course, Yen-lo wang was seen as the high king in this scheme, and he is pictured in Chinese Buddhist scriptures receiving his grisly task of judgment directly from the historical Buddha. In *The Scripture on the Ten Kings*, Stephen Teiser relates that Indian and Chinese deities gathered centuries ago to hear one of the Buddha's last sermons before he died. At that time, the Buddha stated that one's descendants should make funerary offerings to the ten kings after a relative has died in order to generate the good karma that the deceased will need to escape punishment. The schedule of such offerings was explained by the Buddha—one rite for each of the ten kings—and Yen-lo wang agreed to send messengers riding black horses to the homes of grieving families to see whether they made the necessary offerings. Furthermore, the Buddha explained that Yen-lo wang, the most feared deity of the dark places, will himself someday attain perfect enlightenment and Buddhahood, for his harsh punishments were actually an aspect of his compassion for sinners in bringing them to knowledge of a better way of life.

That this Buddhist Scripture was composed in China and not India is abundantly clear, for it shows the integration of the strong Chinese belief in the efficacy of mortuary rituals and offerings to aid the dead, joined with the Buddhist concept that one's own karma determines one's fate. Likewise, the Underworld bureaucracy has become so huge and even unwieldy that a new figure, the bodhisattva (enlightening being) Ti-tsang, becomes an integral part of the Chinese Underworld, likewise assisting beings from escaping judgment by accepting offerings from them. The tension between harsh judgment (meted out by the ten stern kings headed by Yen-lo wang) and compassion (generated by Ti-tsang and offerings made by grieving family members) is the hallmark of medieval Chinese thinking on death and the afterlife.

See also ANCESTOR VENERATION; BHAVA-CHAKRA; HEAVENS, BUDDHIST; HELLS, BUDDHIST; SOUL, BUDDHIST; SOUL, CHINESE; YAMA.

References

Teiser, Stephen F. *The Ghost Festival in Medieval China*. Princeton: Princeton University Press, 1988.

———. *The Scripture on the Ten Kings and the Making of Purgatory in Medieval Chinese Buddhism*. Honolulu: University of Hawaii Press, 1994.

Thompson, Laurence G. "On the Prehistory of Hell in China." *Journal of Chinese Religions*, no. 17 (Fall 1989).

YIZKOR

Four times a year, on the high holidays of Yom Kippur, Passover, Shavuot, and Succot, Jews perform a memorial service for the dead called *yizkor*. The service is held in the synagogue and is intended for the collective dead, but individuals are invited to offer prayers for any specific loved ones they wish. Candles are lit to symbolize the souls of the departed, and two prayers for the benefit of the dead (hazkarat neshamot) are offered. The rabbi or cantor recites the prayer called *El Malei Rachamim* (God, full of compassion), and individuals silently repeat the yizkor prayer (see excerpt).

Jewish tradition teaches that, although parents are responsible for bringing children into the world and teaching them right from wrong, parents cannot by their own acts redeem their children from error and sin. However, the converse is not true: children who lead meritorious lives can elevate their parents spiritually, even after the parents are dead, according to Maurice Lamm. In his work *The Jewish Way in Death and Mourning,* he quotes the Talmud, saying "bera mezakeh aba," "the son endows the father." The yizkor memorial service is considered an important part of honoring one's parents and adding to their spiritual merit after death. It does not replace upright, moral living—which is the most important way to honor a parent and bring merit to them even after death—but performing yizkor forms part of such a life, and it is thought to have a very real benefit for those in the world to come (olam ha'ba).

The yizkor first entered Jewish tradition in the Middle Ages, when it became a part of the religious service performed on Yom Kippur, the Day of Atonement. Yom Kippur became not only a day for living Jews to atone for their sins before God but for the living to seek atonement for the dead as well. At first the yizkor was probably recited only for deceased parents, but today it is considered appropriate to offer the prayer for any family or friends who have died, if one wishes. One may offer a single prayer collectively for all the dead or repeat it for each individual loved one. Although the yizkor is part of the synagogue service and requires a minyan (a quorum of ten adult Jewish males) to perform it, if one is ill and cannot attend synagogue, yizkor may be offered privately at home. (This sets yizkor apart from the kaddish, another prayer for the benefit of the dead, which may *only* be recited in a minyan.)

The yizkor prayer contains a promise that the living members of the deceased's family will make charitable donations to be counted toward the benefit of the deceased. In time this aspect of charity began to be emphasized as much as the aspect of atonement, and so

the yizkor service was added to the three high holidays associated with pilgrims and charity, namely Passover, Shavuot, and Succot. Each person who attends synagogue on these holidays is expected to bring an offering. "Each of you shall bring such a gift as he can," Deuteronomy 16:17 says (which is read as part of the holiday service), and the merit that accrues from such charity is dedicated to the deceased. Yizkor prayers are offered for a loved one beginning with the first high holiday after their death and continue to be offered at each holiday thereafter as long as one lives.

See also FUNERARY CUSTOMS, JEWISH; INTERCESSION; KADDISH; SHIVA (JEWISH); SOUL, JEWISH; YAHRZEIT.

References

Abramovitch, Henry. "Death." In *Contemporary Jewish Religious Thought,* ed. Arthur A. Cohen and Paul Mendes-Flohr. New York: Charles Scribner's Sons, 1989.

De Sola Pool, David. *The Kaddish.* Jerusalem: Printed by Sivan Press under the auspices of the Union of Sephardic Congregations, New York, 1964.

Lamm, Maurice. *The Jewish Way in Death and Mourning.* New York: Jonathan David Publishers, 1969.

Rabinowicz, H. *A Guide to Life.* London: Jewish Chronicle Publications, 1964.

Riemer, Jack, ed. *Jewish Reflections on Death.* New York: Schocken Books, 1974.

BIBLIOGRAPHY

Abrahams, I. *Jewish Life in the Middle Ages.* London: E. Goldston, 1932.

Abrahamsson, Hans. *The Origin of Death: Studies in African Mythology.* Uppsala: Arno Press, 1951.

Abramovitch, Henry. "Death." In *Contemporary Jewish Religious Thought,* ed. Arthur A. Cohen and Paul Mendes-Flohr. New York: Charles Scribner's Sons, 1989.

Agrawala, V. S. *Shiva Mahādeva, the Great God.* Benares: Veda Academy, 1966.

Ahern, Emily. *The Cult of the Dead in a Chinese Village.* Stanford: Stanford University Press, 1973.

Al-Ahouani. "Treatise Concerning Our Knowledge of the Rational Soul and Its Different States." In *Islamic Philosophy.* Cairo: Anglo-Egyptian Bookshop, 1957.

Alexander, H. B. *Latin American Mythology.* Mythology of All Races Series. Boston: Marshall Jones, 1920.

———. *North American Mythology.* Mythology of All Races Series. Boston: Marshall Jones, 1916.

Alexiou, Margaret. *The Ritual Lament in Greek Tradition.* Cambridge: Cambridge University Press, 1974.

Allen, Thomas George, trans. *The Book of the Dead, or Going Forth by Day.* Chicago: Oriental Institute of the University of Chicago, 1974.

Alster, B. "Dilmun, Bahrain, and the Alleged Paradise in Sumerian Myth and Literature." In *Dilmun: New Studies in the Archeology and Early History of Bahrain,* ed. D. T. Potts. Berlin: Berliner Beiträge zur Vorderen Orient 2, 1983.

Andrews, Allan. *The Teachings Essential for Rebirth: A Study of Genshin's Ojoyoshu.* Tokyo: Sophia University, 1974.

Ariès, Philippe. *The Hour of Our Death.* New York: Oxford University Press, 1981.

———. *Western Attitudes toward Death: From the Middle Ages to the Present.* Baltimore: Johns Hopkins University Press, 1974.

Arkush, Allan. "Immortality." In *Contemporary Jewish Religious Thought,* ed. Arthur A. Cohen and Paul Mendes-Flohr. New York: Charles Scribner's Sons, 1989.

Armstrong, John. *The Paradise Myth.* London: Oxford University Press, 1969.

Ashbee, Paul. *The Earthen Long Barrow in Britain.* London: J. M. Dent and Sons, 1970.

Atwater, P. M. H. *Coming Back: The After-Effects of the Near-Death Experience.* New York: Dodd, Mead, 1988.

———. "Is There a Hell? Surprising Observations about the Near-Death Experience." *Journal of Near-Death Studies* 10, no. 3 (Spring 1992).

Aurobindo, Shri. *Eight Upanishads.* Pondicherry: Sri Aurobindo Ashram, 1953.

———. *Life Divine.* New York: Greystone Press, 1949.

Awolalu, J. Omosade. *Yoruba Beliefs and Sacrificial Rites.* Essex, UK: Longman, 1979.

Bailey, L. R., Sr. *Biblical Perspectives on Death.* Philadelphia: Fortress Press, 1979.

Bailey, Lee W., and Jenny Yates, eds. *The Near-Death Experience: A Reader.* New York: Routledge, 1996.

Bannatyne, Lesley Pratt. *Halloween: An American Holiday, an American History.* New York: Facts on File, 1990.

Barber, Paul. *Vampires, Burial, and Death: Folklore and Reality.* New Haven: Yale University Press, 1988.

Basford, Terry K. *Near-Death Experiences: An Annotated Bibliography.* New York: Garland Publishing, 1990.

Bassett, S. *Death in Towns: Urban Responses to the Dying and the Dead, 100–1600.* Leicester, UK: Leicester University Press, 1992.

Batchelor, J. *The Ainu and Their Folk-lore.* London: Religious Tract Society, 1901.

Becker, Carl B. *Breaking the Circle: Death and the Afterlife in Buddhism.* Carbondale: Southern Illinois University Press, 1993.

Begley, Wayne E. "The Myth of the Taj Mahal and a New Theory of Its Symbolic Meaning." *Art Bulletin* 56, no. 1 (1979).

Beidler, William. *The Vision of Self in Early Vedānta.* Delhi: Motilal Banarsidass, 1975.

Bell, Richard. "The Men on the A'rāf." *Muslim World* 22 (1932).

Bendann, Effie. *Death Customs: An Analytical Study of Burial Rites.* New York: Alfred A. Knopf, 1930.

Bernardin, Joseph Buchanan, comp. *Burial Services.* Wilton, CT: Morehouse-Barlow, 1980.

Bernstein, Alan E. *The Formation of Hell: Death and Retribution in the Ancient and Early Christian Worlds.* Ithaca, NY: Cornell University Press, 1993.

Best, Richard I., and Michael A. O'Brien. *The Book of Leinster 2–3.* Dublin: Dublin Institute for Advanced Studies, 1956–1957.

Bevan, A. A. "The Beliefs of Early Mohammedans Respecting a Future Existence." *Journal of Theological Studies* (October 1904).

Bhattacharya, Narendra Nath. *Ancient Indian Rituals and Their Social Contents.* Delhi: Manohar, 1975.

Bianchi, U. *The Greek Mysteries.* Leiden: E. J. Brill, 1976.

Bibby, G. *Looking for Dilmun.* New York: Knopf, 1969.

Biddle, Perry H., Jr. *A Funeral Manual.* Grand Rapids, MI: William B. Eerdman's Publishing, 1994.

Black Elk, with John G. Neihardt. *Black Elk Speaks.* Lincoln: University of Nebraska Press, 1972.

Blair, Sheila S., and Jonathan M. Bloom. *The Art and Architecture of Islam 1250–1800.* New Haven: Yale University Press, 1994.

Blavatsky, Helena Petrovna. *Isis Unveiled.* 2 vols. 1877. Reprint, Pasadena: Theosophical University Press, 1976.

———. *The Key to Theosophy.* Reprint, Los Angeles: Theosophy Company, 1987.

———. *The Secret Doctrine.* 2 vols. Reprint, New York: Theosophy Company, 1925.

———. *The Theosophical Glossary.* Reprint, Los Angeles: Theosophy Company, 1973.

Bloch, Maurice, and Jonathan Parry, eds. *Death and the Regeneration of Life.* Cambridge: Cambridge University Press, 1982.

Bloom, Alfred. *Shinran's Doctrine of Pure Grace.* Tucson: University of Arizona Press, 1965.

Blum, Richard, and Eva Blum. *The Dangerous Hour: The Lore of Crisis and Mystery in Rural Greece.* New York: Charles Scribner's Sons, 1970.

Boas, F. *The Central Eskimo.* Reports of the Bureau of Ethnology (Washington) no. 6. Washington, DC: 1888.

———. *The Doctrine of Souls and of Disease among the Chinook Indians.* New York, 1893.

Bockie, Simon. *Death and the Invisible Powers: The World of Kongo Belief.* Indianapolis: Indiana University Press, 1993.

Bode, F. A. "Man, Soul, Immortality in Zoroastrianism." Speech delivered at Portiuncula Firary, Karachi, December 1971.

Bonner, Hypatia Bradlaugh. *The Christian Hell from the First to the Twentieth Century.* London: Watts, 1913.

Bosi, Roberto. *The Lapps.* Trans. James Cadell. London: Thames and Hudson, 1960.

Bosing, Walter. *Hieronymous Bosch: Between Heaven and Hell.* Cologne: Benedikt Taschen, 1987.

Bowsky, William, ed. *The Black Death: A Turning Point in History?* New York: Holt, Rinehart, and Winston, 1971.

Boyce, Mary. *A History of Zoroastrianism.* 3 vols. Leiden: E. J. Brill, 1975–1991.

———. *A Persian Stronghold of Zoroastrianism.* Oxford: Clarendon Press, 1977.

———. *Zoroastrians: Their Religious Beliefs and Practices.* London: Routledge and Kegan Paul, 1979.

Braun, Jon E. *Whatever Happened to Hell?* Nashville: Thomas Nelson Publishers, 1979.

Bredon, Juliet, and Igor Mitrophanow. *The Moon Year: A Record of Chinese Customs and Festivals.* Shanghai: Kelly and Walsh, 1927.

Bremmer, Jan. *The Early Greek Concept of the Soul.* Princeton: Princeton University Press, 1983.

Briggs, George W. *The Doms and Their Near Relations.* Mysore: Wesley Press, 1953.

———. *The Religious Life of India: The Chamars.* Calcutta: Association Press, 1920.

Brubaker, Leslie. "Reliquary." In *Dictionary of the Middle Ages,* ed. Joseph R. Strayer. Vol. 10. New York: Charles Scribner's Sons, 1982–1989.

Budge, E. A. Wallis. *The Book of the Dead.* New Hyde Park, NY: University Books, 1960.

———. *The Mummy.* New York: Causeway Books, 1972.

———. *Osiris and the Egyptian Resurrection.* 2 vols. 1911. Reprint, New York: Dover, 1973.

Bultmann, Rudolf. *Theology of the New Testament.* Trans. K. Grobel. London: SCM Press, 1952.

Burkert, Walter. *Ancient Mystery Cults.* Cambridge: Harvard University Press, 1987.

———. *Greek Religion.* Trans. John Raffan. Cambridge: Harvard University Press, 1985.

Bushnell, David I., Jr. *Burials of the Algonquian, Siouan and Caddoan Tribes West of the Mississippi.* Smithsonian Institution Bureau of American Ethnology, Bulletin 83. Washington, DC: Government Printing Office, 1927.

———. *Native Cemeteries and Forms of Burial East of the Mississippi.* Smithsonian Institution Bureau of American Ethnology, Bulletin 71. Washington, DC: Government Printing Office, 1920.

Byrne, Patrick. *Irish Ghost Stories.* Cork: Mercier Press, n.d.

Caird, E. *The Evolution of Theology in the Greek Philosophers.* Glasgow: J. MacLehose and Sons, 1904.

Callaway, H. *The Religious System of the Amazulu.* London: Trübner, 1870.

Calverley, E. E. "Doctrines of the Soul (*nafs* and *ruh*) in Islam." *Muslim World* 33 (1943).

———. "Nafs." In *Encyclopedia of Islam,* ed. C. E. Bosworth. Leiden: E. J. Brill, 1983.

Camporesi, Piero. *The Fear of Hell: Images of Damnation and Salvation in Early Modern Europe.* Trans. Lucinda Byatt. University Park: Pennsylvania State University Press, 1987.

Cappell, David. "Chinese Buddhist Interpretations of the Pure Lands." In *Buddhist and Taoist Studies,* ed. David Chappell and Michael Saso. Honolulu: University Press of Hawaii, 1977.

Carnoy, Albert J. *Myths of All Races.* Vol. 6: *Iranian.* Ed. L. H. Gray. New York: Cooper Square Publishers, 1964.

———. "Zoroastrianism." In *Encyclopaedia of Religion and Ethics,* ed. James Hastings. Vol. 12. Edinburgh: T. and T. Clark, 1921.

Cassuto, U. *The Goddess Anath.* Trans. I. Abrahams. Jerusalem: Magness Press, Hebrew University, 1971.

Catherine of Genoa. *Catherine of Genoa, Purgation and Purgatory.* New York: Paulist Press, 1847.

Cerny, Jaroslav. *Ancient Egyptian Religion.* London: Hutchinson University Library, 1952.

Chan, Wing-tsit, ed. and trans. *A Source Book in Chinese Philosophy.* Princeton: Princeton University Press, 1963.

Chang, Garma C. C., ed. *A Treasury of Mahāyāna Sūtras.* Trans. Buddhist Association of the United States. University Park: Pennsylvania State University Press, 1983.

Charles, R. H. *A Critical History of the Doctrine of a Future Life in Israel.* London: A. and C. Black, 1913.

Charles, R. H., ed. *The Apocrypha and Pseudepigrapha of the Old Testament.* Vol. 2: *Pseudepigrapha.* Oxford: Clarendon Press, 1966.

———. "The Book of Enoch." In *The Apocrypha and Pseudepigrapha of the Old Testament,* ed. R. H. Charles. Oxford: Clarendon Press, 1966.

Chavannes, Edouard. *Le T'ai Chan.* Paris, 1910.

Ch'en, Kenneth. *Buddhism in China.* Princeton: Princeton University Press, 1964.

Ching, Heng, trans. *Sūtra of the Past Vows of Earth Store Boddhisattva: The Collected Lectures of Tripitaka Master Hsüan Hua.* San Francisco: Buddhist Text Translation Society, 1974.

Christiansen, Reidar Th. *Ecstasy and Arctic Religion.* Studia Septentrionalia no. 4. Oslo: O. Norli, 1953.

———, ed. *Folktales of Norway.* Chicago: University of Chicago Press, 1964.

Christie-Murray, David. *Reincarnation: Ancient Beliefs and Modern Evidence.* London: Newton-Abbot, 1981.

Clark, James M. *The Dance of Death in the Middle Ages and the Renaissance.* Glasgow: Glasgow University Press, 1980.

Clay, A. T. *Documents from the Temple Archives of Nippur.* Philadelphia: University Museum, 1912.

Coates, H. H., and Ryūgaku Ishizuka. *Hōnen the Buddhist Saint.* Kyoto: Chionon, 1925.

Cohen, J. M., trans. "Narrative of the Third Voyage." In *The Four Voyages of Christopher Columbus.* New York: Penguin, 1969.

Collinder, Björn. *The Lapps.* Princeton: Princeton University Press, 1949.

Collins, Steven. *Selfless Persons: Imagery and Thought in Theravāda Buddhism.* Cambridge: Cambridge University Press, 1982.

Colvin, Howard. *Architecture and the After-Life.* New Haven: Yale University Press, 1991.

Comper, Frances M. M., ed. *The Book of the Craft of Dying.* New York: Arno Press, 1977.

Cook, Elizabeth, ed. *The Stupa: Sacred Symbol of Enlightenment.* Crystal Mirror Series, vol. 12. Berkeley: Dharma, 1997.

Cook, W. S. "Cremation: From Ancient Cultures to Modern Usage." *Casket and Sunnyside* (1973).

Coomaraswamy, Ananda K. *Rig Veda as Land-Náma-Bók.* Delhi: Bharatiya Publishing House, 1980.

Cormack, J. G. *Everyday Customs in China.* Edinburgh: Moray Press, 1935.

Coultan, G. G. *The Black Death.* New York: Macmillan, 1930.

Craigie, William Alexander. *The Religion of Ancient Scandinavia.* 1906. Reprint, New York: Books for Libraries Press, 1969.

Cremation Association of North America (CANA). *Cremation and Percentage of Deaths.* Chicago: CANA, 1989.

———. *Cremation Explained: Answers to Questions Most Frequently Asked.* Chicago: CANA, 1986.

Croker, T. Crofton. *Fairy Legends.* London: William Teg, 1862.

Crombie, I. M. *An Examination of Plato's Doctrines.* New York: Humanities Press, 1962.

Crooke, William. *The Popular Religion and Folk-lore of Northern India.* 2nd ed. Delhi: Munshiram Manoharlal, 1968.

Cross, Frank Moore. *Canaanite Myth and Hebrew Epic: Essays in the History of the Religion of Israel.* Cambridge: Harvard University, 1973.

Crossley-Holland, Kevin, ed. *The Faber Book of Northern Legends.* London: Faber and Faber, 1977.

Cumont, F. V. M. *After Life in Roman Paganism.* New York: Yale University Press, 1922.

Curl, J. S. *The Victorian Celebration of Death.* Detroit: Partridge Press, 1972.

Czaplicka, M. A. *Aboriginal Siberia.* Oxford: Clarendon Press, 1914.

Daniel, G. *The Prehistoric Chamber Tombs of France.* London: Thames and Hudson, 1960.

Dante Alighieri. *The Comedy of Dante Alighieri the Florentine.* Trans. Dorothy L. Sayers. 3 vols. Baltimore, MD: Penguin Books, 1955.

———. *The Divine Comedy.* Trans. John Ciardi. New York: Norton, 1977.

———. *The Purgatorio: Dante's Timeless Drama of an Ascent through Purgatory.* Trans. John Ciardi. New York: New American Library, 1961.

Dantinne, J. *La Splendeur de l'Inébranable (Akṣobhyavyūha).* Vol. 1: *Tripitaka Sūtrapitaka Akṣobhyatathāgatavyūha.* Louvain-la-Neuve: Institut Orientaliste, 1983.

D'Arbois de Jubainville, H. *The Irish Mythological Cycle and Celtic Mythology.* Trans. Richard Irvine Best. Dublin: Hodges, Figgis, 1903.

Darmesteter, J. *The Zend Avesta.* 3 vols. Oxford: Clarendon Press, 1880–1887.

Das, Sarat Chandra. *A Tibetan-English Dictionary.* Calcutta: Bengal Secretariat Book Depot, 1902. Reprint, Kyoto: Rinsen Book Company, 1993.

Davidson, H. R. Ellis. *Gods and Myths of Northern Europe.* New York: Penguin, 1964, 1977.

———. *The Lost Beliefs of Northern Europe.* London: Routledge, 1993.

———. *Myths and Symbols in Pagan Europe.* Syracuse: Syracuse University Press, 1988.

Davies, Jonathan C. *Folk-lore of West and Mid-Wales.* Aberystwyth: *Welsh Gazette* Offices, 1911.

Dawood, N. J., trans. *The Koran.* 5th rev. ed. New York: Penguin, 1993.

de Groot, J. J. M. *Religion in China.* New York: G. P. Putnam's Sons, 1912.

De Sola Pool, David. *The Kaddish.* Jerusalem: Printed by Sivan Press under the auspices of the Union of Sephardic Congregations, New York, 1964.

De Vaux, B. Carra. "Barzakh." In *Encyclopedia of Islam,* ed. E. van Donzel. Leiden: E. J. Brill, 1979.

De Visser, M. W. *The Bodhisattva Ti-tsang (Jizō) in China and Japan.* Berlin: Oesterheld, 1914.

Deaux, George. *The Black Death 1347.* London: Hamilton, 1969.

Delumeau, Jean. *History of Paradise: The Garden of Eden in Myth and Tradition.* Trans. Matthew O'Connell. New York: Continuum, 1995.

Dempsey, D. *The Way We Die.* New York: Macmillan, 1975.

Deserontyon, John. *A Mohawk Form of Ritual of Condolence, 1782.* Trans. J. N. B. Hewitt. Indian Notes and Monographs, vol. 10, no. 8. New York: Museum of the American Indian, Heye Foundation, 1928.

Dhalla, M. N. *Zoroastrian Theology from the Earliest Times to the Present Day.* Reprint, New York: AMS Press, 1972.

Dietrich, B. C. *Death, Fate and the Gods.* London: University of London, Athlone Press, 1965.

Dodds, E. R. *Pagan and Christian in an Age of Anxiety.* Cambridge: Cambridge University Press, 1965.

Dols, Michael W. *The Black Death in the Middle East.* Princeton: Princeton University Press, 1977.

Dorjee, Pema. *The Stupa and Its Technology: A Tibeto-Buddhist Perspective.* New Delhi: Indira Gandhi National Centre for the Arts and Motilal Banarsidass, 1996.

Downing, Christine. "Journeys to the Underworld." *Mythosphere* 1, no. 2 (1998).

Driver, Harold E. *Indians of North America.* Chicago: University of Chicago Press, 1961.

Duensing, H., trans. "The Apocalypse of Paul." In *New Testament Apocrypha*, ed. E. Hennecke and W. Schneemelcher. Vol. 2. London: Lutterworth Press, 1965.

———. "The Apocalypse of Peter." In *New Testament Apocrypha*, ed. E. Hennecke and W. Schneemelcher. Vol. 2. London: Lutterworth Press, 1965.

Dunne, John J. *Haunted Ireland.* Belfast: Appletree Press, 1977.

Dunning, G. C., and R. F. Jessup. "Roman Barrows." *Antiquity* 10 (1936).

Duyvendak, J. J. L. "The Buddhistic Festival of All-Souls in China and Japan." *Acta Orientalia* 5, no. 1 (1926).

Ebeling, Erich. *Tod und Leben nach den Vorstellungen der Babylonier.* Leipzig: Walter de Gruyter, 1931.

Edou, Jérôme. *Machig Labdrön and the Foundations of Chöd.* Ithaca, NY: Snow Lion, 1996.

Edwards, I. E. S. *The Pyramids of Egypt.* Rev. ed., New York: Penguin, 1978.

Eklund, E. *Life between Death and Resurrection according to Islam.* Uppsala: Almquist and Wilksells, 1941.

Eliade, Mircea. *The Myth of the Eternal Return.* Trans. Willard R. Trask. Bollingen Series 46. New York: Pantheon Books, 1954.

———. *Yoga: Immortality and Freedom.* New York: Pantheon, 1958.

Elior, Rachel. "Soul." In *Contemporary Jewish Religious Thought,* ed. Arthur A. Cohen and Paul Mendes-Flohr. New York: Charles Scribner's Sons, 1989.

Eliot, T. S. *Four Quartets.* San Diego: Harcourt Brace Jovanovich, 1988.

Ellis, A. B. *The Ewe-Speaking Peoples of the Slave Coast of West Africa.* London: Chapman and Hall, 1890.

Ellis, Hilda Roderick. *The Road to Hel: A Study of the Conception of the Dead in Old Norse Literature.* Cambridge: Cambridge University Press, 1943.

Eogan, G. *Knowth and the Passage-Tombs of Ireland.* New York: Thames and Hudson, 1986.

Ephirim-Donkor, Anthony. *African Spirituality: On Becoming Ancestors.* Asmara, Eritrea: Africa World Press, 1997.

Erdoes, Richard, and Alfonzo Ortiz, eds. *American Indian Myths and Legends.* New York: Pantheon, 1984.

Erman, Adolf. *A Handbook of Egyptian Religion.* London: Archibald Constable, 1907.

Ettinghausen, Richard, and Oleg Grabar. *The Art and Architecture of Islam 650–1250.* New York: Viking Penguin, 1987.

Ettlinger, Ellen. "The Association of Burials with Popular Assemblies, Fairs and Races in Ancient Ireland." *Études Celtiques* 6, no. 1 (Paris, Société d'Édition "Les Belles Lettres," 1953).

Evans, Frederick H., ed. *The Dance of Death by Hans Holbein.* London: Private printing by Arthur K. Sabin at the Temple Sheen Press, 1916.

Evans, J. D. *Prehistoric Antiquities of the Maltese Islands.* London: University of London, Athlone Press, 1971.

Evans-Pritchard, E. E. *Witchcraft, Oracles and Magic among the Azande.* Oxford: Clarendon Press, 1950.

Evans-Wentz, W. Y. *The Fairy Faith in Celtic Countries.* New York: Carol Publishing, 1990.

———, ed. *The Tibetan Book of the Dead; or, the After-Death Experiences on the Bardo Plane.* Trans. Kazi Dawa-Samdup. 3rd ed. New York: Oxford University Press, 1971.

Evrin, M. Sadeddin. *Eschatology in Islam.* Trans. Sofi Huri. Istanbul, 1960.

Fakhry, Ahmed. *The Pyramids.* Chicago: University of Chicago Press, 1961.

Farnell, Lewis R. *Greek Hero Cults and Ideas of Immortality.* Oxford: Clarendon Press, 1921.

Farrell, J. J. *Inventing the American Way of Death 1830–1920.* Philadelphia: Temple University Press, 1980.

Fenn, Richard K. *The Persistence of Purgatory.* Cambridge: Cambridge University Press, 1995.

Finucane, R. C. *Appearances of the Dead: A Cultural History of Ghosts.* Buffalo, NY: Prometheus Books, 1984.

Florescu, Radu, and Raymond T. McNally. *Dracula: A Biography of Vlad the Impaler.* New York: Hawthorn Books, 1973.

Foard, James, Michael Solomon, and Richard K. Payne, eds. *The Pure Land Tradition: History and Development.* Berkeley Buddhist Studies Series no. 3. Berkeley: University of California Press, 1989.

Fohrer, G. *History of Israelite Religion.* Trans. D. E. Green. Nashville: Abingdon Press, 1972.

Ford, Patrick K., ed. *The Mabinogi and Other Medieval Welsh Tales.* Berkeley: University of California Press, 1977.

Fowler, W. Warde. *The Roman Festivals of the Period of the Republic.* London: Kennikat Press, 1969.

Frankfort, Henri. *Ancient Egyptian Religion: An Interpretation.* New York: Columbia University Press, 1948.

———. *Archeology and the Sumerian Problem.* Chicago: University of Chicago Press, 1932.

———. *The Birth of Civilization in the Near East.* Bloomington: Indiana University Press, 1951.

———. *Kingship and the Gods.* Chicago: University of Chicago Press, 1948.

Frazer, James G. *The Belief in Immortality and the Worship of the Dead.* London: Macmillan, 1913.

———. *The New Golden Bough.* Ed. Theodor H. Gaster. New York: Criterion Books, 1959.

Freedman, Maurice. *Chinese Lineage and Society.* London: Athlone Press, 1966.

Fröhlich, B. "The Bahrain Burial Mounds." *Dilmun* 11 (1983).

Frye, Richard Nelson. *The Heritage of Persia.* Cleveland: World Publishing Company, 1963.

Gandhi, Mohandas K. *An Autobiography: The Story of My Experiments with Truth.* Boston: Beacon Press, 1957.

Gardet, Louis. *Dieu et la Destinée de l'Homme.* Paris: Librarie Philosophique, J. Vrin, 1967.

———. "Djanna." In *The Encyclopedia of Islam,* ed. E. van Donzel. Leiden: E. J. Brill, 1979.

———. "Kiyāma." In *The Encyclopedia of Islam,* ed. C. E. Bosworth. Vol. 5. Leiden: E. J. Brill, 1983.

Gardiner, A. H. *The Attitude of the Ancient Egyptians to Death and the Dead.* Cambridge: Cambridge University Press, 1935.

Gardiner, Eileen, ed. *Visions of Heaven and Hell before Dante.* New York: Italica Press, 1989.

Garstang, J. *Burial Customs of Ancient Egypt.* London: A. Constable, 1907.

Gaster, Theodore. *New Year: Its History, Customs and Superstitions.* New York: Abelard-Schuman, 1955.

Gauld, Alan, and A. D. Cornell. *Poltergeists.* London: Routledge and Kegan Paul, 1979.

Geary, Patrick J. *Furta Sacra: Thefts of Relics in the Central Middle Ages.* Princeton: Princeton University Press, 1978.

———. *Living with the Dead in the Middle Ages.* Ithaca, NY: Cornell University Press, 1994.

Geoffrey of Monmouth. *The Life of Merlin.* Trans. Basil Clarke. Cardiff: University of Wales Press, 1973.

Georges, Elaine. *Voyages de la mort.* Paris: Berger-Levrault, 1982.

Ghosh, Oroon. K. *The Dance of Shiva and Other Tales from India.* New York: New American Library, 1965.

Gilbert, Lionel. *A Grave Look at History: Glimpses of a Vanishing Form of Folk Art.* Sydney: John Ferguson, 1980.

Giles, H. A., trans. *The Musings of a Chinese Mystic.* London: John Murray, 1955.

Giot, P. R. *Brittany.* London: Thames and Hudson, 1960.

Glasson, T. Francis. *Greek Influence in Jewish Eschatology.* London: SPCK, 1961.

Gnoli, Gherardo. "Dakhma." In *Encyclopedia of Religion,* ed. Mircea Eliade. New York: Macmillan, 1987.

Goedicke, H. *The Report about the Dispute of a Man with His Ba.* Baltimore: Johns Hopkins University Press, 1970.

Goldman, Robert P., and Sally Sutherland Goldman, trans. *The Rāmāyana of Vālmīki.* Princeton: Princeton University Press, 1984.

Gómez, Luis O. *The Land of Bliss: The Paradise of the Buddha of Measureless Light.* Honolulu: University of Hawaii Press, 1996.

Gómez, Luis O., and Hiram W. Woodward Jr., eds. *Barabudur: History and Significance of a Buddhist Monument.* Ann Arbor: University of Michigan Press, 1974.

Gordon, A. *Death Is for the Living.* Edinburgh: Paul Harris, 1984.

Gorion, Micha Joseph Bin. *Mimekor Yisrael.* Vol. 2. Trans. I. M. Lask. Tel Aviv: n.p., 1938–1940.

Gottfried, Robert S. *The Black Death: Natural and Human Disaster in Medieval Europe.* New York: Macmillan, 1983.

Gough, M. R. E. *The Origins of Christian Art.* London: Thames and Hudson, 1973.

Govinda, Anagarika. *Foundations of Tibetan Mysticism.* York Beach, ME: Samuel Weiser, 1991.

———. *The Psycho-cosmic Symbolism of the Buddhist Stupa.* Berkeley: Dharma, 1976.

———. *The Psychological Attitude of Early Buddhist Philosophy.* London: Rider, 1961.

Granet, Marcel. *Festivals and Songs of Ancient China.* Trans. E. D. Edwards. London: Routledge, 1932.

Graves, Robert. *The Greek Myths.* Vol. 1 and 2. New York: Penguin, 1960.

Green, Judith Strupp. *Día de los Muertos: An Illustrated Essay and Bibliography.* Santa Barbara, CA: Center for Chicano Studies, 1983.

———. *Laughing Souls: The Days of the Dead in Oaxaca, Mexico.* San Diego: San Diego Museum of Man, Popular Series no. 1, 1969.

Greenfield, Stanley B. *A Readable Beowulf.* Carbondale: Southern Illinois Press, 1982.

Greenspoon, Leonard J. "The Origin of the Idea of Resurrection." In *Traditions in Transformation: Turning Points in Biblical Faith,* ed. Baruch Halpern and Jon D. Levenson. Winona Lake, IN: Eisenbrauns, 1981.

Greyson, B., and N. E. Bush. "Distressing Near-Death Experiences." *Psychiatry* 55 (1992).

Griffin, James B., Richard E. Flanders, and Paul F. Titterington. *The Burial Complexes of the Knight and Norton Mounds in Illinois and Michigan.* Memoirs of the Museum of Anthropology, no. 2. Ann Arbor: University of Michigan, 1970.

Griffith, James S. *Respect and Continuity: The Arts of Death in a Border Community.* Tucson: Southwest Folklore Center, University of Arizona, 1985.

Griffith, Ralph T. H., trans. *The Hymns of the Atharva-Veda.* New Delhi: Munshiram Manoharlal Publishers, 1985.

Griffiths, J. G. *The Origins of Osiris and His Cult.* Leiden: E. J. Brill, 1980.

Griffiths, Paul J. *On Being Mindless.* La Salle, IL: Open Court, 1986.

Grimm, Jacob. *Teutonic Mythology.* Trans. J. S. Stallybrass. London: G. Bell and Sons, 1883.

Griswold, H. D. *The Religion of the Rigveda.* Indian ed. Delhi: Motilal Banarsidass, 1971.

Gruber, Elmer R., and Holger Kersten. *The Original Jesus: The Buddhist Sources of Christianity.* Rockport, MA: Element, 1995.

Grünwedel, A. *Buddhist Art in India.* Trans. Agnes C. Gibson. London: B. Quaritch, 1901.

Guerber, Hélène Adeline. *Myths of the Norsemen from the Eddas and Sagas.* 1909. Reprint, New York: Dover, 1992.

Guido, M. *Sardinia.* London: Thames and Hudson, 1963.

Guignebert, Charles. *The Jewish World in the Time of Jesus.* New York: University Books, 1965.

Gupta, S. P. *Disposal of the Dead and Physical Types in Ancient India.* Delhi: Oriental Publishers, 1972.

Gurevich, Aron. *Medieval Popular Culture: Problems of Belief and Perception.* Trans. James M. Bak and Paul A. Hollingworth. New York: Cambridge University Press, 1990.

Guthrie, W. K. C. *History of Greek Philosophy.* 6 vols.. Cambridge: Cambridge University Press, 1962–1981.

Habenstein, Robert W., and William M. Lamers. *Funeral Customs the World Over.* Milwaukee: Bulfin Printers, 1963.

Hamilton-Paterson, James, and Carol Andrews. *Mummies: Death and Life in Ancient Egypt.* London: William Collins Sons, 1978.

Handcock, P. S. P. *The Archaeology of the Holy Land.* London: T. F. Unwin, 1916.

Harris, J. E., and K. R. Weeks. *X-Raying the Pharaohs.* London: MacDonald and Company, 1973.

Harrison, Jane Ellen. *Prolegomena to the Study of Greek Religion.* Cambridge: Cambridge University Press, 1922.

Hartmann, Franz. *Buried Alive: An Examination into the Occult Causes of Apparent Death, Trance, and Catalepsy.* Boston: Occult Publishing, 1895.

Harva, U. *Mythology, Finno-Ugric, Siberian.* Mythology of All Races Series. Boston: Archaeological Institute of America: Marshall Jones Company, 1927.

Hastings, James, ed. *Encyclopaedia of Religion and Ethics.* Vol. 4: "Cosmogony and Cosmology (Indian)." Edinburgh: T. and T. Clark, 1911.

———. *Encyclopaedia of Religion and Ethics.* Vol. 5: "Demons and Spirits, Indian." Edinburgh: T. and T. Clark, 1911.

Head, Joseph, and Sylvia Cranston. *Reincarnation: The Phoenix Fire Mystery.* New York: Julian Press/Crown Publishers, 1977.

Heidel, Alexander. *The Gilgamesh Epic and Old Testament Parallels.* Chicago: University of Chicago Press, 1946.

Heinberg, Richard. *Memories and Visions of Paradise: Exploring the Universal Myth of a Lost Golden Age.* Los Angeles: Jeremy P. Tarcher, 1989.

Helleiner, Karl. "The Population of Europe from the Black Death to the Eve of the Vital Revolution." In *The Cambridge Economic History of Europe,* ed. E. E. Rich and C. H. Wilson. Vol. 4. Cambridge: Cambridge University Press, 1967.

Hennessy, William M. *Révue Celtique* 1 (Paris, 1870).

Henshall, A. H. *The Chambered Tombs of Scotland.* 2 vols. Edinburgh: Edinburgh University Press, 1963, 1972.

Herity, M. *Irish Passage Graves.* New York: Barnes and Noble Books, 1975.

Herodotus. *The Histories.* Trans. Aubrey de Sélincourt. New York: Crown, 1975.

Hertling, Ludwig, and Engelbert Kirschbaum. *The Roman Catacombs and Their Martyrs.* Trans. M. Joseph Costelloe. Rev. ed. London: Darton, Longman, and Todd, 1960.

Herzfeld, Ernst. *Zoroaster and His World.* Vol. 1. Princeton: Princeton University Press, 1947.

Hesiod. Works and Days *and* Theogony. Trans. Stanley Lombardo. Indianapolis: Hackett Publishing, 1993.

Hillenbrand, Robert. *Islamic Architecture: Form, Function and Meaning.* New York: Columbia University Press, 1994.

Himmelfarb, Martha. *Tours of Hell: An Apocalyptic Form in Jewish and Christian Literature.* Philadelphia: University of Pennsylvania Press, 1983.

Hoag, John D. *Islamic Architecture.* New York: Rizzoli, 1987.

Homer. *The Odyssey.* Trans. Samuel Butler. New York: Barnes and Noble, 1993.

Hooke, S. H. *Middle Eastern Mythology.* New York, 1963.

Hopkins, Jeffrey, and Lati Rinpoche. *Death, Intermediate State and Rebirth.* Ithaca, NY: Snow Lion, 1985.

Hopkins, Keith. *Death and Renewal.* Cambridge: Cambridge University Press, 1983.

Hori, Ichiro. *Folk Religion in Japan: Continuity and Change.* Tokyo: Tokyo University Press, 1968.

Hornblower, Simon. *Mausolus.* Oxford: Clarendon Press, 1982.

Howitt, A. W. *The Native Tribes of South-East Australia.* London: Macmillan, 1904.

Hsu, Francis L. K. *Under the Ancestors' Shadow.* New York: Columbia University Press, 1948.

Huang, Yu-mei. "China's Ghost Festival." *Free China Review* 32, no. 11 (November 1982).

Hultkrantz, Å. *Conceptions of the Soul among North American Indians.* Ph.D. diss., Stockholm, Ethnographical Museum of Sweden, 1953.

Humphreys, Christmas, ed. *The Wisdom of Buddhism.* New York: Random House, 1961.

Humphreys, Sally C., and Helen King, eds. *Mortality and Immortality: The Anthropology and Archeology of Death.* Proceedings of a meeting of the Research Seminar in Archaeology and Related Subjects, London, 1982.

Hutchinson, R. W. *Prehistoric Crete.* Baltimore: Penguin, 1962.

Idowu, E. Bolaji. *African Traditional Religion.* Reprint, Kampala, Uganda: Fountain Publications, 1991.

Inter-Lutheran Commission on Worship. *Burial of the Dead.* Minneapolis: Augsburg, 1976.

Irion, Paul E. *The Funeral: Vestige or Value?* Nashville: Abingdon Press, 1966.

Iserson, Kenneth V. *Death to Dust: What Happens to Dead Bodies?* Tucson, AZ: Galen Press, 1994.

Jackson, A. V. W. *Zoroastrian Studies.* New York: Columbia University Press, 1928.

Jackson, P. E. *The Law of Cadavers and of Burial and Burial Places.* New York: Prentice-Hall, 1937.

s'Jacob, Henriette Eugénie. *Idealism and Realism. A Study of Sepulchral Symbolism.* Leiden: E. J. Brill, 1954.

Jacobi, Hermann, trans. *Jaina Sutras.* Reprint from *The Sacred Books of the East.* New York: Dover Publications, 1968.

Jaini, Padmanabh S. *The Jaina Path of Purification.* Berkeley: University of California Press, 1979.

Jairazbhay, R. A. "The Taj Mahal in the Context of East and West: A Study in the Comparative Method." *Journal of the Warburg and Courtauld Institute* 24 (1961).

Janelli, Dawnhee Yim, and Roger L. Janelli. *Ancestor Worship in Korean Society.* Stanford: Stanford University Press, 1982.

Jastrow, M. *The Religion of Babylonia and Assyria.* Boston: Ginn and Company, 1898.

Jenkinson, E. J. "The Rivers of Paradise." *Muslim World* 19 (1925).

Jeremias, A. *The Babylonian Conception of Heaven and Hell.* London: D. Nutt, 1902.

Jettmar, Karl. *The Art of the Steppes.* New York: Crown, 1967.

Jochim, Christian. *Chinese Religions.* Prentice-Hall Series in World Religions. Ed. Robert S. Ellwood. Englewood Cliffs, NJ: Prentice-Hall, 1986.

Johnson, Elizabeth L. "Grieving for the Dead, Grieving for the Living: Funeral Laments of Hakka Women." In *Death Rituals in Late Imperial and Modern China,* eds. James L. Watson and Evelyn S. Rawski. Berkeley: University of California Press, 1988.

Jones, Barbara. *Design for Death.* Indianapolis: Bobbs-Merrill, 1967.

Jones, J. J. Trans. *The Mahāvastu.* 3 Vol. London: Pali Text Society, 1949–1956.

Jones, Julia Clinton. *Valhalla.* New York: R. Worthington, 1880; San Francisco: E. Bosque and Company, 1878.

Jowett, Benjamin. *The Essential Plato.* New York: Quality Paperback Books, 1999.

Judge, William Quan, trans. *Bhagavad-Gita.* Los Angeles: Theosophy Company, 1986.

———. *The Ocean of Theosophy.* Los Angeles: Theosophy Company, 1987.

Kalish, Richard A. "Experiences of People Reprieved from Death." In *Death and Bereavement,* ed. Austin H. Kutscher. Springfield, IL: Charles C. Thomas, 1969.

Kalupahana, David J. *The Principles of Buddhist Psychology.* Albany: State University of New York Press, 1987.

Kane, Pandurang Vaman. *History of Dharmashāstra: Ancient and Medieval Religious and Civil Law in India.* Vol. 4. Government Oriental Series, Class B, no. 6. Poona: Bhandarkar Oriental Research Institute, 1953.

Kastenbaum, Robert, ed. *Between Life and Death.* New York: Springer Publishing, 1979.

Kaufmann, Y. *The Religion of Israel.* Trans. M. Greenberg. Chicago: University of Chicago Press, 1960.

Keith, Arthur Berriedale. "The Doctrine of the Buddha." *Bulletin of the School of Oriental Studies* 6 (1930–1932).

———. *The Mythology of All Races.* Vol. 6: *Indian Mythology.* New York: Cooper Square Publishers, 1964.

———. *The Religion and Philosophy of the Veda and Upanishads.* London: Oxford University Press, 1925.

Kellehear, Allan. *Experiences Near Death: Beyond Medicine and Religion.* New York: Oxford University Press, 1996.

Kherie, Altaf Ahmad. *Islam: A Comprehensive Guidebook.* Karachi: Idara Sirat-i-Mustaqeem, 1981.

Kirby, W. F. *The Land of Heroes.* Ed. Kalevala. Vols. 1–2. London: J. M. Dent and Sons, 1907.

Kirk, K. E. *The Vision of God: The Christian Doctrine of the Summum Bonum.* Bampton Lectures for 1928. Harrisburg, PA: Morehouse Publishing, 1991.

Kirkby, Michael Hasloch. *The Vikings.* Oxford: Phaidon Press, 1977.

Kitagawa, Joseph M. *Religion in Japanese History.* New York: Columbia University Press, 1966.

Kligman, Gail. *Wedding of the Dead.* Berkeley: University of California Press, 1988.

Kloetzli, Randy. *Buddhist Cosmology: From Single World System to Pure Land.* Delhi: Motilal Banarsidass, 1983.

Kmietowicz, Frank. *Slavic Mythical Beliefs.* Windsor, Ontario: F. Kmietowicz, 1982.

Kohl, Philip L. *Central Asia: Paleolithic Beginnings to the Iron Age.* Paris: Editions Recherche sur les Civilisations, 1984.

Kotwal, Firoze M., and James W. Boyd, trans. *A Guide to the Zoroastrian Religion.* Studies in World Religion no. 3. Chico, CA: Scholars Press, 1982.

Kramer, S. N. *History Begins at Sumer.* New York: Doubleday, 1959.

Kraus, H. J. *Theology of the Psalms.* Trans. K. Crim. Minneapolis: Augsburg, 1986.

Kristensen, W. Brede. *Life Out of Death: Studies in the Religions of Egypt and of Ancient Greece.* Louvain, Belgium: Peeters Press, 1992.

Kubasak, M. W. *Cremation and the Funeral Director—Successfully Meeting the Challenge.* Malibu, CA: Avalon Press, 1990.

Kübler-Ross, Elizabeth. *On Death and Dying.* New York: Touchstone, 1997.

Kurtz, Donna, and John Boardman. *Greek Burial Customs.* Ithaca, NY: Cornell University Press, 1971.

Kurtz, Léonard P. *The Dance of Death and the Macabre Spirit in European Literature.* Geneva: Slatkine Reprints, 1975.

Kvanig, Jonathan L. *The Problem of Hell.* New York: Oxford University Press, 1993.

La Vallée Poussin, Louis de, trans. *L'Abhidharmakosha de Vasubandhu.* Brussels: Mélanges chinois et bouddhiques, 1971.

LaFleur, William R. *Liquid Life: Abortion and Buddhism in Japan.* Princeton: Princeton University Press, 1992.

Lamberg-Karlovski, C. C. "Dilmun: Gateway to Immortality." *Journal of Near Eastern Studies* 41 (1982).

Lamm, Maurice. *The Jewish Way in Death and Mourning.* New York: Jonathan David Publishers, 1969.

Lattimore, Richmond, trans. *The Iliad.* Chicago: University of Chicago Press, 1951.

———. *Themes in Greek and Latin Epitaphs.* Urbana: University of Illinois Press, 1942.

Law, Bimala Churn. *Heaven and Hell in Buddhist Perspective.* Calcutta: Bhartiya Publishing House, 1925.

Lawson, John Cuthbert. *Modern Greek Folklore and Ancient Greek Religion.* 1910. Reprint, New York: University Books, 1964.

Lazarus-Yafeh, Hava. *Some Religious Aspects of Islam.* Leiden: E. J. Brill, 1981.

Le Goff, Jacques. *The Birth of Purgatory.* Trans. Arthur Goldhammer. Chicago: University of Chicago Press, 1984.

Leach, Maria, ed. *Standard Dictionary of Folklore, Mythology, and Legend.* New York: Funk and Wagnalls, 1972.

Leach, William H., ed. *The Cokesbury Funeral Manual.* Nashville: Cokesbury Press, 1932.

Leca, Ange-Pierre. *The Egyptian Way of Death*. Trans. Louise Asmal. Garden City, NY: Doubleday, 1981.

Lee, D. Demetracopoulou. "Greek Accounts of the Vrykolakas." *Journal of American Folklore* 55 (1942).

Leon, Harry J. *The Jews of Ancient Rome*. Philadelphia: Jewish Publication Society of America, 1960.

Levering, Miriam. "Kshitigarbha." In *Encyclopedia of Religion*, ed. Mircea Eliade. New York: Macmillan, 1987.

Levy, Max. *Why Modern Cremation Should Replace Earth Burial: An Exposé of the Dangers Caused by Inhumation*. San Francisco: San Francisco Cremation Company, 1885.

Lewis, Theodore J. *Cults of the Dead in Ancient Israel and Ugarit*. Atlanta: Scholars Press, 1989.

L'Heureux, C. E. *Rank Among the Canaanite Gods: El, Ba'al, and the Rephaim*. Missoula: Scholars Press, 1979.

Lincoln, Andrew T. *Paradise Now and Not Yet: Studies in the Role of the Heavenly Dimension in Paul's Thought with Special Reference to His Eschatology*. Cambridge: Cambridge University Press, 1981.

Lindow, John. "Fylgjur." In *Encyclopedia of Religion,* ed. Mircea Eliade. New York: Macmillan, 1987.

Ling, Trevor O. *Buddhism and the Mythology of Evil: A Study in Theravāda Buddhism*. London: Allen and Unwin, 1962.

Litvinskii, B. A. "Prehistoric Religions: The Eurasian Steppes and Inner Asia." In *Encyclopedia of Religion*, ed. Mircea Eliade. New York: Macmillan, 1987.

Lockyer, Herbert. *The Funeral Sourcebook*. London: Pickering and Inglis, 1967.

Lodö, Lama. *Bardo Teachings*. Ithaca: Snow Lion, 1987.

Loewe, Michael. *Chinese Ideas of Life and Death*. London: Allen and Unwin, 1982.

———. *Ways to Paradise: The Chinese Quest for Immortality*. London: Allen and Unwin, 1979.

Longhurst, A. H. *The Story of the Stupa*. New Delhi: Asian Educational Services, 1979.

Loomis, Roger Sherman. *Celtic Myth and Arthurian Romance*. New York: Columbia University Press, 1926.

———. *Wales and the Arthurian Legend*. Cardiff: University of Wales Press, 1956.

Lowie, Robert H. *Primitive Religion*. New York: Boni and Liveright, 1924.

Lowry, Glenn D. "Humayun's Tomb: Form, Function, and Meaning in Early Mughal Architecture." *Muqarnas* 4 (1987).

Lucas, A. *Ancient Egyptian Materials and Industries*. 4th ed. Revised by J. R. Harris. London: E. Arnold, 1962.

Lysaght, Patricia. *The Banshee*. Dublin: Glendale Press, 1986.

Mac Bain, Alexander. *Celtic Mythology and Religion*. New York: Dutton, 1917.

Macalister, R. A. S. *A Century of Excavation in Palestine*. New York: Fleming H. Revell, 1925.

———. *Textbook of European Archaeology*. Vol. 1. Cambridge: Cambridge University Press, 1921.

MacCulloch, J. A. *The Religion of the Ancient Celts*. Edinburgh: T. and T. Clark, 1911.

Macdonald, D. B. "The Development of the Idea of Spirit in Islam." *Muslim World* 22 (1932).

Macdonald, John. "The Angel of Death in Late Islamic Tradition." *Islamic Studies* 3, no. 2 (September 1964).

———. "The Day of Resurrection." *Islamic Studies* 5, no. 2 (1966).

———. "Paradise." *Islamic Studies* 5, no. 4 (1966).

———. "The Twilight of the Dead." *Islamic Studies* 4, no. 1 (1965).

Macdonell, Arthur Anthony. *A Vedic Reader for Students*. Indian ed. Delhi: Motilal Banarsidass, 1995.

Máchal, Jan. *Slavic Mythology*. New York: Cooper Square Publishers, 1918.

Mackenzie, Donald A. *Teutonic Myth and Legend*. New York: Wise, 1934.

Mackie, E. *The Megalith Builders*. Oxford: Phaidon, 1977.

MacLeod, W. C. "Certain Mortuary Aspects of Northwest Coast Culture." *American Anthropologist* 27 (1925).

Mahony, William K. "Soul: Indian Concepts." In *Encyclopedia of Religion*, ed. Mircea Eliade. New York: Macmillan, 1987.

Mandelbaum, Allen, trans. *The Aeneid of Virgil*. New York: Bantam, 1961.

Mansell, John S. *The Funeral: A Pastor's Guide*. Nashville: Abingdon Press, 1998.

March, H. C. "Polynesian Ornament, a Mythography. Or, a Symbolism of Origin and Descent." *Journal of the Royal Anthropological Institute* 22 (London, 1893).

Marks, Geoffrey. *The Medieval Plague*. Garden City, NY: Doubleday, 1971.

Marshall, Sir John. *Mohenjo-Daro and the Indus Civilization*. London: A. Probsthain, 1931.

Martin-Achard, Robert. *From Death to Life: A Study of the Development of the Doctrine of the Resurrection in the Old Testament*. Trans. J. P. Smith. Edinburgh: Oliver and Boyd, 1960.

Marucchi, Orazio. *Manual of Christian Archeology*. Patterson, NJ: St. Anthony Guild Press, 1935.

Masani, Sir Rustom. *Zoroastrianism: The Religion of the Good Life*. New York: Collier Books, 1962.

Maspero, Henri. *Les religions chinoises*. Paris: Civilisations du Sud, SAEP, 1950.

Masters, Anthony. *The Natural History of the Vampire*. New York: G. P. Putnam's Sons, 1972.

Matsunaga, Daigan, and Alicia Matsunaga. *The Buddhist Concept of Hell*. New York: Philosophical Library, 1972.

Maurice, Frederick Denison. *Theological Essays*. 3rd ed. London: Macmillan, 1871.

Mbiti, John. *Introduction to African Religion*. London: Heinemann, 1975.

McClung, William Alexander. *The Architecture of Paradise: Survivals of Eden and Jerusalem*. Berkeley: University of California Press, 1983.

McDannell, Colleen, and Bernhard Lang. *Heaven: A History*. New Haven: Yale University Press, 1988.

McDermott, James P. "Nibbāna as a Reward for Kamma." *Journal of the American Oriental Society* 93, no. 3 (1973).

McNeill, William H. *Plagues and Peoples*. New York: Doubleday, 1976.

Meaney, Audrey. *A Gazetteer of Early Anglo-Saxon Burial Sites.* London: George Allen and Unwin, 1964.

Meek, Charles Kingsley. *Tribal Studies in Northern Nigeria.* London: K. Paul, Trench, Trübner and Company, 1931.

Meier, Fritz. "The Ultimate Origin and the Hereafter in Islam." In *Islam and Its Cultural Divergence: Studies in Honor of Gustave E. von Grunebaum,* ed. G. L. Tikku. Urbana: University of Illinois Press, 1971.

Mendelssohn, Kurt. *The Riddle of the Pyramids.* London: Thames and Hudson, 1974.

Mew, James. *Traditional Aspects of Hell.* London: S. Sonnenschein, 1903. Reprint, Ann Arbor, MI: Gryphon Books, 1971.

Meyers, E. M. *Jewish Ossuaries: Reburial and Rebirth.* Rome, 1971.

Milikowsky, C. "Which Gehenna? Retribution and Eschatology in the Synoptic Gospels and in Early Jewish Texts." *New Testament Studies* 34, nos. 238–249.

Minns, E. H. *Scythians and Greeks: A Survey of Ancient History and Archaeology on the North Coast of the Euxine.* New York: Biblo and Tannen, 1965.

Mitford, Jessica. *The American Way of Death.* New York: Simon and Schuster, 1963.

Mittal, Kewal Krishnan, ed. *Perspectives on Karma and Rebirth.* Delhi: Delhi University, 1990.

Modi, J. J. *The Funeral Ceremonies of the Parsees: Their Origin and Explanation.* Bombay: British India Press, 1923.

———. *The Religious Ceremonies and Customs of the Parsees.* Bombay: British India Press, 1937.

Mohrmann, Christine. "Locus refrigerii." In *L'Ordinaire de la messe: Texte critique, traduction et études,* ed. B. Botte and C. Mohrmann. Paris-Louvain, 1953.

Monier-Williams, Sir Monier. *A Sanskrit-English Dictionary.* Indian ed. Delhi: Motilal Banarsidass, 1995.

Montefiore, C. G., and H. Loewe, eds. *A Rabbinic Anthology.* New York: Schocken Books, 1974.

Montet, P. *Everyday Life in Egypt.* London: E. Arnold, 1958.

Moody, Raymond A., Jr. *Life after Life.* New York: Bantam, 1975.

Moor, Edward. *The Hindu Pantheon.* Ed. W. O. Simpson. Madras: J. Higginbotham, 1864.

Moor, Johannes C. de. *An Anthology of Religious Texts from Ugarit.* Leiden; E. J. Brill, 1987.

Moore, David George. *The Battle for Hell: A Survey and Evaluation of Evangelicals' Growing Attraction to the Doctrine of Annihilationism.* Lanham, MD: University Press of America, 1995.

Moore, George Foot. *Judaism in the First Centuries of the Christian Era.* 3 vols. Cambridge: Harvard University Press, 1927–1930. Reprint, New York: Schocken Books, 1971.

More, P. E. *The Religion of Plato.* Princeton: Princeton University Press, 1921.

Morenz, Siegfried. *Egyptian Religion.* Trans. Ann E. Keep. Ithaca, NY: Cornell University Press, 1973.

Morey, C. R. *Early Christian Art.* Princeton: Princeton University Press, 1953.

Morgan, Ernest. *Dealing Creatively with Death.* 12th ed. Bayside, NY: Barclay House, 1990.

Morgan, K. W. *The Religion of the Hindus.* New York: Ronald Press, 1953.

Morris, Earl H. *Burials in the Aztec Ruin.* Anthropological Papers of the American Museum of Natural History, vol. 26, part 3. New York: American Museum Press, 1924.

Morse, M., and P. Perry. *Closer to the Light: Learning from the Near-Death Experiences of Children.* New York: Villard, 1990.

Moss, Rosalind. *The Life after Death in Oceania and the Malay Archipelago.* London: Oxford University Press, 1925.

Moulton, James Hope. *Early Zoroastrianism.* London: Williams and Norgate, 1913.

Mueller, D. "An Early Egyptian Guide to the Hereafter." *Journal of Egyptian Archeology* 58 (1972).

Müller, Max, ed. *Sacred Books of the East.* Vol. 49: *The Larger Sukhāvatī-vyūha-sūtra.* Oxford: Clarendon Press, 1894.

Müller-Lisowski, Kate. "Donn Firine, Tech Duin, An Tarbh." In *Études Celtiques* 6, no. 1 (Paris, Société d'Édition "Les Belles Lettres," 1953).

Mullin, Glenn H. *Death and Dying: The Tibetan Tradition.* Boston: Arkana, 1986.

Murgoci, Agnes. "The Vampire in Romania," *Folk-Lore* 27, no. 5 (1926).

Murray, James A. H. et al. *Oxford English Dictionary.* 2nd ed. Oxford: Clarendon Press, 1996.

Mylonas, G. *Mycenae and the Mycenaean Age.* Princeton: Princeton University Press, 1966.

Nadel, S.F. *Nupe Religion.* London: Routledge and Kegan Paul, 1954.

Ñānamoli, Bhikkhu, and Bhikkhu Bodhi, trans. *The Middle Length Discourses of the Buddha.* Boston: Wisdom Publications, 1995.

Nansen, F. *Eskimo Life.* London: Longmans, Green and Company, 1893.

Naquin, Susan. "Funerals in North China: Uniformity and Variation." In *Death Rituals in Late Imperial and Modern China,* ed. James L. Watson and Evelyn S. Rawski. Berkeley: University of California Press, 1988.

Narahari, H. G. *Ātman in the Pre-Upanishadic Vedic Literature.* Madras: Adyar Library, 1944.

Narasimhan, Chakravarthi V. *The Mahābhārata: An English Version Based on Selected Verses.* New York: Columbia University Press, 1965.

Nash, E. *Pictorial Dictionary of Ancient Rome.* Rev. ed. London: Thames and Hudson, 1968.

Needham, Joseph. *Science and Civilisation in China.* Vol. 2: *History of Scientific Thought.* Cambridge: Cambridge University Press, 1962.

Neptune Society of Northern California (NSNC). *Disclosures Regarding the Cremation Process.* San Francisco: NSNC, 1993.

Nesheim, A. *Traits from Life in a Sea-Lappish District.* Nordnorske Samlinger Utgitt av Etnografisk Museum Series 6. Oslo: Etnografisk Museum, 1949.

Neumann, Frank J. "The Black Man in the Cave in Chapultepec: An Aztec Variant on the Gatekeeper Motif." In *Religious Encounters with Death,* ed. Frank E. Reynolds and Earle H. Waugh. University Park: Pennsylvania State University Press, 1976.

Newell, William H., ed. *Ancestors*. The Hague: Mouton, 1976.

Nickelsburg, G. W. E., Jr. *Resurrection, Immortality, and Eternal Life in Intertestamental Judaism*. Cambridge: Harvard University Press, 1972.

Nilsson, Martin P. *Greek Popular Religion*. New York: Columbia University Press, 1940.

———. *The Minoan-Mycenaean Religion and Its Survival in Greek Religion*. 2nd ed. Lund: C. W. K. Gleerup, 1950.

Nock, Arthur. "Cremation and Burial in the Roman Empire." In *Essays on Religion and the Ancient World*, ed. Zeph Stewart. 2 vols. Cambridge: Harvard University Press, 1972.

Norbu, Namkhai. *The Crystal and the Way of Light*. Ed. John Shane. New York: Arkana, 1993.

Nørlund, P. *Viking Settlers in Greenland*. London: Cambridge University Press, 1936.

Ó hÓgáin, Dáithí. *Myth, Legend and Romance: An Encyclopaedia of the Irish Folk Tradition*. New York: Prentice Hall, 1991.

Oates, Joan. *Babylon*. Rev. ed. London: Thames and Hudson, 1986.

Obermiller, Eugéne. *Nirvāna in Tibetan Buddhism*. Ed. Harcharan Singh Sobti. Delhi: Classics India Publications, 1988.

O'Flaherty, Wendy Doniger. *Asceticism and Eroticism in the Mythology of Shiva*. London: Oxford University Press, 1973.

———. *The Origins of Evil in Hindu Mythology*. Berkeley: University of California Press, 1976.

———. *The Rig Veda: An Anthology*. New York: Penguin, 1981.

O'Kelley, M. *Newgrange*. London: Thames and Hudson, 1982.

Oldenberg, Hermann. *The Religion of the Veda*. Trans. Shridhar B. Shrotri. Indian ed. Delhi: Motilal Banarsidass, 1988.

Oldenburg, U. *The Conflict between El and Ba'al in Canaanite Religion*. Leiden: E. J. Brill, 1969.

Oman, J. C. *Cults, Customs and Superstitions of India*. Indian ed.. Delhi: Vishal Publishers, 1972.

O'Rahilly, Cecile. *Táin Bó Cuailnge: Recension 1*. Dublin: Dublin Institute for Advanced Studies, 1976.

Orpen, G. H. "Aenach Carman." *Journal of the Royal Society of the Antiquaries of Ireland* 36 (Dublin, 1906).

O'Shaughnessy, Thomas. "The Seven Names for Hell in the Qur'ān." *Bulletin of the School of Oriental and African Studies* 24, no. 3 (1961).

Overmyer, D. *Folk Buddhist Religion: Dissenting Sects in Late Traditional China*. Cambridge: Harvard University Press, 1976.

Owen, D. D. R. *The Vision of Hell: Infernal Journeys in Medieval French Literature*. New York: Barnes and Noble, 1971.

Pace, James C., and Deborah L. Drumm. "The Phantom Leaf Effect and Its Implications for Near-Death and Out-of-Body Experiences." *Journal of Near-Death Studies* 10, no. 4 (Summer 1992).

Paine, Lauran. *The Hierarchy of Hell*. New York: Hippocrene Books, 1972.

Pal, Pratapaditya. *Romance of the Taj Mahal*. Los Angeles: Los Angeles County Museum of Art, 1989.

Palden, Kunzang, trans. *Vast Clear Liberation Path: A Recitation Text of the Foundation Practices*. San Francisco: Enlightened Heart Meditation Center, 1996.

Pandey, Raj Bali. *Hindu Samskāras: A Socio-religious Study of the Hindu Sacraments*. Banares: Vikrama Publications, 1949.

Panneton, Georges. *Heaven or Hell*. Trans. Ann M. C. Forster. Westminster, MD: Newman Press, 1965.

Pant, Sushila. *The Origins and Development of Stupa Architecture in India*. Varanasi: Bharata Manisha, 1976.

Pardi, M. M. *Death: An Anthropological Perspective*. Washington, DC: University Press of America, 1977.

Parrinder, Geoffrey. *African Traditional Religion*. 3rd ed. London: Sheldon Press, 1974.

Pas, Julian. *Visions of Sukhāvatī: Shan-Tao's Commentary on the Kuan-Wu-Liang-Shou-Fo Ching*. Albany: SUNY Press, 1995.

Paternoster, Michael. *Thou Art These Also: God, Death and Hell*. London: SPCK, 1967.

Paton, Lucy Allen. *Studies in the Fairy Mythology of Arthurian Romance*. Boston: Ginn, 1903.

Pavry, J. D. C. *The Zoroastrian Doctrine of a Future Life*. Columbia University Indo-Iranian Series 11. New York: Columbia University Press, 1926.

Paxton, Frederick S. *Christianizing Death: The Creation of a Ritual Process in Early Medieval Europe*. Ithaca, NY: Cornell University Press, 1990.

Perkins, P. *Resurrection: New Testament Witness and Contemporary Reflection*. Garden City, NY: Doubleday, 1984.

Perkowski, Jan Louis. *Vampires of the Slavs*. Cambridge: Slavica Publishers, 1976.

Perrin, Norman, and Dennis C. Duling. *The New Testament: An Introduction*. 2nd ed. New York: Harcourt Brace Jovanovich, 1982.

Pettersson, Olof. *Jabmek and Jabmeaimo: A Comparative Study of the Dead and the Realm of the Dead in Lappish Religion*. Lund: C. W. K. Gleerup, 1957.

Piankoff, A. *The Wandering of the Soul*. Princeton: Princeton University Press, 1974.

Piggott, S. *Neolithic Cultures of the British Isles*. Cambridge: Cambridge University Press, 1954.

Plato. *The Republic*. Trans. Benjamin Jowett. New York: Random House, 1937.

Polson, C. J., R. P. Brittain, and T. K. Marshall. *The Disposal of the Dead*. 2nd ed. Springfield, IL: Charles C. Thomas, 1962.

Poo, Mu-chou. *In Search of Personal Welfare: A View of Ancient Chinese Religion*. New York: SUNY Press, 1998.

Poovey, William Arthur. *Planning a Christian Funeral: A Minister's Guide*. Minneapolis: Ausburg, 1978.

Pope, M. H. "Notes on the Rephaim Texts." In *Essays on the Ancient Near East in Memory of Jacob Joel Finkelstein*, ed. M. de Jong Ellis. Hamden, CT: Archon, 1977.

Powell, T. G. E. *Megalithic Enquiries in the West of England*. Liverpool: Liverpool University Press, 1969.

Prabhavananda, Swami, and Christopher Isherwood, trans. *The Song of God: Bhagavad-Gītā*. 1954. Reprint, New York: Penguin, 1972.

Prebish, Charles S., ed. *Buddhism: A Modern Perspective*. University Park: Pennsylvania State University Press, 1978.

Pritchard, James B., ed. *Ancient Near Eastern Texts Relating to the Old Testament.* 3rd ed. Princeton: Princeton University Press, 1969.

Puhvel, Martin. *The Crossroads in Folklore and Myth.* New York: Peter Lang Publications, 1989.

al-Qādī, Imam 'Abd al-Rahīm ibn Ahmad. *The Islamic Book of the Dead.* Trans. 'Ā'isha 'Abd al-Rahmān. Norwich, England: Diwan Press, 1977.

Quirke, Stephen. *Ancient Egyptian Religion.* London: British Museum Press, 1992.

Rabinowicz, H. *A Guide to Life.* London: Jewish Chronicle Publications, 1964.

Ralston, W. S. *Russian Folk-tales.* London: Smith, Elder, and Company, 1873.

Ramos, Maximo. *The Creatures of Midnight.* Quezon City, Philippines: Island Publishers, 1967.

Rao, T. A. G. *Elements of Hindu Iconography.* Varanasi: Indological Book House, 1971.

Rees, Alwyn, and Brinley Rees. *Celtic Heritage: Ancient Tradition in Ireland and Wales.* London: Thames and Hudson, 1961.

Renou, Louis. *Religions of Ancient India.* London: University of London, Athlone Press, 1953.

Rhys-Davids, C. A. F. *The Book of the Kindred Sayings (Samyutta Nikāya).* Pali Text Society Translation Series no. 7. London: Oxford University Press, 1917.

Richardson, Nicholas J. *The Homeric Hymn to Demeter.* Oxford: Clarendon Press, 1974.

Ridley, W. "Report on Australian Languages and Traditions." *Journal of the Royal Anthropological Institute* 2 (London, 1873).

Riemer, Jack, ed. *Jewish Reflections on Death.* New York: Schocken Books, 1974.

Rieu, E. V., trans. *The Odyssey.* New York: Penguin, 1945.

Rinbochay, Lati, and Jeffrey Hopkins. *Death, Intermediate State and Rebirth in Tibetan Buddhism.* London: Rider and Company, 1979.

Ring, Kenneth. *Life at Death: A Scientific Investigation of the Near-Death Experience.* New York: Coward, McCann and Geoghegan, 1980.

Rinpoche, Chokyi Nyima. *The Bardo Guidebook.* Kathmandu: Harper San Francisco, 1991.

Rinpoche, Sogyal. *The Tibetan Book of Living and Dying,* ed. Patrick Gaffney and Andrew Harvey. San Francisco: Harper San Francisco, 1992.

Robinson, J. M. "Jesus from Easter to Valentinus (or to the Apostles' Creed)." *Journal of Biblical Literature* 101 (1982): 5–37.

Rogo, S. Scott. *On the Track of the Poltergeist.* Englewood Cliffs, NJ: Prentice-Hall, 1986.

Roll, William. *The Poltergeist.* Garden City, NY: Nelson Doubleday, 1972.

Roscoe, J. *The Northern Bantu.* Cambridge: Cambridge University Press, 1915.

Rosenberg, R. *The Concept of Biblical Sheol within the Context of Ancient Near Eastern Beliefs.* Ph.D. diss., Harvard University, 1980.

Roy, S. Chandra. *Oraon Religion and Custom.* Ranchi: *Man in India* Office, 1928.

Royal Irish Academy. *Contributions to a Dictionary of the Irish Language.* Dublin: Royal Irish Academy, 1913–1975.

Russell, Jeffrey Burton. *A History of Heaven: The Singing Silence.* Princeton: Princeton University Press, 1997.

———. *Lucifer: The Devil in the Middle Ages.* Ithaca, NY: Cornell University Press, 1984.

Ryosetsu, F. *The Way to Nirvana: The Concept of the Nembutsu in Shan-tao's Pure Land Buddhism.* Tokyo: Kyoiku Shincho Sha, 1974.

Sadakata, Akira. *Buddhist Cosmology: Philosophy and Origins.* Tokyo: Kōsei Publishing Co., 1997.

El-Saleh, Soubhi. *La Vie Future selon le Coran* (The afterlife according to the Qur'ān). Paris: Librarie Philosophique J. Vrin, 1971.

Sandars, N. K., trans. *The Epic of Gilgamesh.* New York: Penguin, 1972.

Sanday, Peggy. *Divine Hunger: Cannibalism as a Cultural System.* Cambridge: Cambridge University Press, 1986.

Sandman, M. "Texts from the Time of Akhenaton." *Bibliotheca Aegyptica* 8 (1938).

Sandmel, Samuel, ed. *The New English Bible with the Apocrypha.* Oxford Study Edition. New York: Oxford University Press, 1976.

Santino, Jack, ed. *Halloween and Other Festivals of Death and Life.* Knoxville: University of Tennessee Press, 1993.

Sarianidi, V. I. *Bactrian Gold: From the Excavations of the Tillya-Tepe Necropolis in Northern Afghanistan.* Leningrad: Aurora Art Publishers, 1984.

Sawyer, P. H. *The Age of the Vikings.* London: Edward Arnold, 1962.

Schadow, Paul. *Eine Attische Grabekythos.* Inaugural diss., Jena University, 1897.

Schipper, Kristofer. *The Taoist Body.* Trans. Karen C. Duval. Berkeley: University of California Press, 1982.

Scholem, Gershom. *On the Kabbalah and Its Symbolism.* New York: Schocken Books, 1965.

Searl, Edward. *In Memoriam: A Guide to Modern Funeral and Memorial Services.* Boston: Skinner House, 1993.

Secretan, Thierry. *Going into Darkness: Fantastic Coffins from Africa.* London: Thames and Hudson, 1995.

Senn, Harry A. *Were-Wolf and Vampire in Romania.* East European Monographs, no. 17. New York: Columbia University Press, 1982.

Sethna, Tehmurasp Rustamji. *Book of Instructions on Zoroastrian Religion.* Karachi: Informal Religious Meetings Trust Fund, 1980.

Shakespeare, William. *The Complete Works of William Shakespeare.* Volume III. Edited by David Bevington. New York: Bantam, 1988.

Shankara. *The Brihadāranyaka Upanishad with the Commentary of Shankaracarya.* Trans. Swami Madhavananda. 2nd ed. Calcutta: Almora Advaita Asram, 1941.

Sharma, Baldev Raj. *The Concept of Ātman in the Principal Upanishads.* New Delhi: Dinesh Publications, 1972.

Shastri, Dakshina Ranjan. *Origin and Development of the Rituals of Ancestor Worship in India.* Calcutta: Bookland, 1963.

Shastri, Manmatha Nath Dutt, trans. *Agni Purānam.* Varanasi: Chowkhamba Publications, 1967.

Shetelig, Haakan, and Hjalmar Falk. *Scandinavian Archaeology.* Trans. E. V. Gordon. Oxford: Clarendon Press, 1937.

Shrewsbury, J. F. D. *A History of Bubonic Plague in the British Isles.* London: Cambridge University Press, 1970.

Shukla, Karunesh, ed. *Nature of Bondage and Liberation in Buddhist Systems.* Gorakhpur, India: Nagarjuna Buddhist Foundation. 1988.

Sidhwa, Ervad Godrej Dinshawji. *Discourses on Zoroastrianism.* Karachi: Ervad Godrej Dinshawji Sidhwa, 1978.

Sigerist, Henry. *Civilization and Disease.* Chicago: University of Chicago Press, 1943.

Simon, Ulrich. *Heaven in the Christian Tradition.* London: Rockcliff, 1958.

Simpson, J. A., and E. S. C. Weiner, eds. *The Oxford English Dictionary.* Oxford: Clarendon Press, 1989.

Singh, Purushottam. *Burial Practices in Ancient India.* India: Prithivi Prakashan, 1970.

Sinor, Denis, ed. *The Cambridge History of Early Inner Asia.* Cambridge: Cambridge University Press, 1990.

Slade, Paddy. *Encyclopedia of White Magic: A Seasonal Guide.* New York: Mallard, 1990.

Smith, E. W., and A. M. Dale. *The Ila-Speaking Peoples of Northern Rhodesia.* 2 vols. London: Macmillan, 1920.

Smith, Edmund W. *Akbar's Tomb, Sikandrah, Near Agra, Described and Illustrated.* Allahabad: Archaeological Survey of India, 1909.

Smith, G. E. *Egyptian Mummies.* London: G. Allen and Unwin, 1924.

Smith, Grace Partridge. "Crossroads." In *Funk and Wagnalls Standard Dictionary of Folklore, Mythology and Legend,* ed. Maria Leach. New York: Funk and Wagnalls, 1950.

Smith, Jane I. "Concourse between the Living and the Dead in Islamic Eschatological Literature." *History of Religions* 19, no. 3 (1980).

———. *The Precious Pearl* (A translation of Abū Hāmid al-Ghazzālī's *Kitāb al-Durrah al-Fākhirah if Kashf 'Ulūm al-Ākhirah*). Missoula, MT: Scholars Press, 1979.

Smith, Jane I., and Yvonne Yazbeck Haddad. *The Islamic Understanding of Death and Resurrection.* Albany: SUNY Press, 1981.

———. "The Understanding of *Nafs* and *Ruh* in Contemporary Muslim Considerations of the Nature of Sleep and Death. *Muslim World* 49 (1979).

———. "Women in the Afterlife: The Islamic View as Seen from Qur'ān and Tradition." *Journal of the American Academy of Religion* 43, no. 1 (1975).

Smith, Margaret. "Transmigration and the Sufis." *Muslim World* 30 (1940).

Smith, Wilbur M. *The Biblical Doctrine of Heaven.* Chicago: Moody Press, 1968.

Smolinski, Reiner, ed. *The Threefold Paradise of Cotton Mather: An Edition of "Triparadisus."* Athens: University of Georgia Press, 1995.

Snellgrove, David. *Himalayan Pilgrimage.* Oxford, 1961.

Sobti, Harcharan Singh. *Nibbāna in Early Buddhism.* Delhi: Eastern Book Linkers, 1985.

Sommer, Deborah. *Chinese Religion: An Anthology of Sources.* New York: Oxford University Press, 1995.

Sourvinou-Inwood, Christiane. *"Reading" Greek Death: To the End of the Classical Period.* Oxford: Clarendon Press, 1995.

Spencer, A. J. *Death in Ancient Egypt.* New York: Penguin, 1982.

Spencer, Baldwin, and F. J. Gillen. *Northern Tribes of Central Australia.* London: Macmillan, 1904.

Spronk, Klaas. *Beatific Afterlife in Ancient Israel and in the Ancient Near East.* Kevelaer: Butzon and Bercker, 1986.

Stcherbatsky, Th. *The Central Conception of Buddhism.* 1922. Reprint, Delhi: Motilal Banarsidass, 1994.

Stein, R. A. *Tibetan Civilization.* Stanford: Stanford University Press, 1972.

Stevenson, Ian. "Are Poltergeists Living or Are They Dead?" *Journal of the American Society for Psychical Research* 66 (1972).

———. *Cases of the Reincarnation Type.* Charlottesville: University Press of Virginia, 1975.

Stevenson, James. *The Catacombs: Life and Death in Early Christianity.* London: Thames and Hudson: 1978.

Stoker, Bram. *Dracula.* Edited by Glennis Byron. Peterborough, Ontario: Broadview, 1998.

Storå, Nils. *Burial Customs of the Skolt Lapps.* FF Communications no. 210. Helsinki: Suomalainen Tiedeakatemia, 1971.

Strickmann, Michel. "Taoism, History of." *Encyclopaedia Britannica.* Vol. 3. Chicago: Encyclopaedia Britannica, 1974.

Strömbäck, D. "The Realm of the Dead on Lappish Magic Drums." *Studia Ethnographica Upsaliensia* 10 (Uppsala, 1956).

Sturluson, Snorri. *Edda.* Trans. Anthony Faulkes. London: Dent, 1987.

Sullivan, Lawrence, ed. *Death, Afterlife and the Soul.* New York: Macmillan, 1989.

Summers, Montague. *The Vampire: His Kith and Kin.* New Hyde Park, NY: University Books, 1960.

———. *The Vampire in Europe.* New York: University Books, 1968.

Suzuki, D. T. *Buddha of Infinite Light.* Boston: Shambhala, 1998.

Sylvia Mary, Sister. *Nostalgia for Paradise.* London: Darton, Longman and Todd, 1965.

Tannahill, R. *Flesh and Blood: A History of the Cannibal Complex.* New York: Stein and Day, 1975.

Tawney, C. H., trans. *The Ocean of Story.* Indian ed. Delhi: Motilal Banarsidass, 1968.

Taylor, A. E., trans. *The Laws of Plato.* London: J. M. Dent and Sons, 1934.

Taylor, John B. "Some Aspects of Islamic Eschatology." *Religious Studies* 4 (1968).

Taylour, W. *The Mycenaeans.* New York: Praeger, 1964.

Teiser, Stephen F. *The Ghost Festival in Medieval China.* Princeton: Princeton University Press, 1988.

———. *The Scripture on the Ten Kings and the Making of Purgatory in Medieval Chinese Buddhism*. Honolulu: University of Hawaii Press, 1994.

Thomas, Cyrus. "Burial Mounds of the Northern Sections of the United States." Smithsonian Institution Bureau of Ethnology, fifth annual report. Washington, DC: Government Printing Office, 1887.

Thomas, Dylan. "Do Not Go Gentle into That Good Night." In *The Top 500 Poems*, ed. William Harmon. New York: Columbia University Press, 1992.

Thomas, Louis-Vincent. "Funeral Rites." In *Death, Afterlife and the Soul,* ed. Lawrence Sullivan. New York: Macmillan, 1989.

Thompson, Laurence G. *The Chinese Way in Religion.* Encino, CA: Dickenson Press, 1973.

———. "On the Prehistory of Hell in China." *Journal of Chinese Religions,* no. 17 (Fall 1989).

Thomson, George. *Studies in Ancient Greek Society.* Vol. 1. London: Lawrence and Wishart, 1949.

Thurman, Robert. *The Tibetan Book of the Dead.* New York: Bantam, 1994.

Titchenell, Elsa-Brita. *The Masks of Odin.* Pasadena: Theosophical University Press, 1985.

Toor, Frances. *Mexican Folkways.* New York: Crown Publishers, 1947.

Toynbee, J. M. C. *Death and Burial in the Roman World.* Ithaca, NY: Cornell University Press, 1971.

Tritton, A. S. "Man, *Nafs, Ruh, 'Aql.*" *Bulletin of the School of Oriental and African Studies* 34, no. 3 (1971).

———. "Muslim Funeral Custom." *Bulletin of the School of Oriental and African Studies* 9, no. 3 (1938).

Tromp, Nicholas J. *Primitive Conceptions of Death and the Nether World in the Old Testament.* Rome: Pontifical Biblical Institute, 1969.

Tronzo, W. *The Via Latina Catacomb.* University Park: Pennsylvania State University Press, 1986.

Trungpa, Chögyam, and Francesca Fremantle, trans. *The Tibetan Book of the Dead: The Great Liberation through Hearing in the Bardo.* Berkeley: Shambala, 1975.

Tu, Wei-ming. *Confucian Thought: Selfhood as Creative Transformation.* Albany: SUNY Press, 1985.

Tucci, Giuseppe. *The Religions of Tibet.* Trans. Geoffrey Samuel. Berkeley; University of California Press, 1980.

———. *Tibet: Land of Snows.* Trans. J. E. Stapleton Driver. London: Elek, 1967.

Turi, Johan. *Turi's Book of Lappland.* Ed. and trans. from Dutch by Emilie Demant Hatt, trans. into English by E. Gee Nash. New York: Harper and Brothers, 1931.

Turner, A. W. *Houses for the Dead.* New York: David McKay, 1976.

Turner, Alice K. *The History of Hell.* New York: Harcourt Brace, 1993.

Turner, Kay, and Pat Jasper. "Day of the Dead: The Tex-Mex Tradition." In *Halloween and Other Festivals of Death and Life,* ed. Jack Santino. Knoxville: University of Tennessee Press, 1993.

Turville-Petre, E. O. G. *Myth and Religion of the North: The Religion of Ancient Scandinavia.* Westport, CT: Greenwood, 1964.

———. *Nine Norse Studies.* London: Viking Society for Northern Research, University College, London, 1972.

Twersky, Isadore, ed. *A Maimonides Reader.* New York: Behrman House, 1972.

Twohig, E. Shee. *The Megalithic Art of Western Europe.* Oxford: Clarendon Press, 1981.

van Buitenen, J. A. B., trans. *The Mahābhārata.* Vol. 1: *The Book of the Beginning.* Chicago: University of Chicago Press, 1973.

van der Leeuw, G. *Religion in Essence and Manifestation.* Trans. J. E. Turner. Princeton: Princeton University Press, 1986.

Van Gennep, Arnold. *Rites of Passage.* Trans. Monika B. Vizedom and Gabrielle L. Caffe. London: Routledge and Kegan Paul, 1960.

Veidle, V. *The Baptism of Art: Notes on the Religion of the Catacomb Paintings.* London: Dacre, 1950.

Virgil. *The Aeneid.* Trans. Robert Fitzgerald. New York: Random House, 1983.

Voegelin, Erminie Wheeler. *Mortuary Customs of the Shawnee and Other Eastern Tribes.* Prehistory Research Series, vol. 2, no. 4. Indianapolis: Indiana Historical Society, 1944.

Vorren, Ørnulv, and Ernst Manker. *Lapp Life and Customs: A Survey.* London: Oxford University Press, 1962.

Waddell, L. Austine. *Tibetan Buddhism.* Reprint, New York: Dover, 1972.

Walker, D. P. *The Decline of Hell: Seventeenth-Century Discussions of Eternal Torment.* Chicago: University of Chicago Press, 1964.

Walker, G. A. *Gatherings from Graveyards.* London: Longman, 1839. Reprint, New York: Arno Press, 1977.

Walker, Susan. *Memorials to the Roman Dead.* London: British Museum Publications, 1985.

Walshe, Maruice, trans. *The Long Discourses of the Buddha: A Translation of the Dīgha Nikāya.* Boston: Wisdom Publications, 1995.

Watelin, L. C., and S. Langdon. *Excavations at Kish.* Vol. 4. Paris: P. Geunther, 1934.

Watson, Duane F. "Gehenna." In *Anchor Bible Dictionary,* ed. David Noel Freedman. New York: Doubleday, 1992.

Watson, James L. "The Structure of Chinese Funerary Rites." In *Death Rituals in Late Imperial and Modern China,* ed. James L. Watson and Evelyn S. Rawski. Berkeley: University of California Press, 1988.

Watson, P. L. *Mot, the God of Death, at Ugarit and in the Old Testament.* Ph.D. diss., Yale University, 1970.

Watson, Rubie S. "Remembering the Dead: Graves and Politics in Southeastern China." In *Death Rituals in Late Imperial and Modern China,* ed. James L. Watson and Evelyn S. Rawski. Berkeley: University of California Press, 1988.

Waugh, Earl. "Persistent Fragments: The Trajectories of Reincarnation in Islam." In *Concepts of Transmigration,* ed. Steven J. Kaplan. Studies in Comparative Religion, vol. 6. Lewiston, NY: Edwin Mellen Press, 1996.

Weiler, Ingomar. *Der Agon im Mythos: Zur Einstellung der Griechen zum Wettkampf.* Darmstadt: Wissenschaftliche Buchgesellschaft, 1974.

Weitzmann, Kurt, ed. *Age of Spirituality: Late Antique and Early Christian Art, Third to Seventh Century.* New York: Metropolitan Museum of Art, 1979.

Welbon, Guy Richard. *The Buddhist Nirvāna and Its Western Interpreters.* Chicago: University of Chicago Press, 1968.

Welch, Holmes. *The Practice of Chinese Buddhism, 1900–1950.* Cambridge: Harvard University Press, 1967.

Wensinck, A. J. "Iblīs." In *The Encyclopedia of Islam,* ed. E. van Donzel. Leiden: E. J. Brill, 1979.

———. "'Izrā'īl." *Encyclopedia of Islam,* ed. E. van Donzel. Leiden: E. J. Brill, 1979.

West, John Anthony. *Serpent in the Sky: The High Wisdom of Ancient Egypt.* New York: Harper and Row, 1979.

West, M. L. *Early Greek Philosophy and the Orient.* Oxford: Clarendon Press, 1971.

Westermarck, Edward. *Ritual and Belief in Morocco.* London: Macmillan, 1926.

Weule, Karl. *Native Life in East Africa.* Westport, CT: Negro Universities Press, 1970.

Whitman, Walt. "Song of Myself." In *Leaves of Grass.* New York: Modern Library, 1950.

Widengren, G. *The King and the Tree of Life in Ancient Near Eastern Religion.* Uppsala: Lundequistska bokhandeln, 1951.

Wilhelm, James J., ed. *The Romance of Arthur.* Vol. 2. New York: Garland, 1986.

Williams, George. *Wilderness and Paradise in Christian Thought: The Biblical Experience of the Desert in the History of Christianity and the Paradise Theme in the Theological Idea of the University.* New York: Harper and Brothers, 1954.

Williams, Paul. *Mahāyāna Buddhism: The Doctrinal Foundations.* New York: Routledge, 1989.

Wilson, H. H. *Vishnu Purāna.* Vol. 1. London: Trübner, 1864.

Windisch, E. *Māra und Buddha.* Leipzig: S. Hirzel, 1895.

Winer, Richard, and Nancy Osborn. *Haunted Houses.* New York: Bantam, 1979.

Winkler, Gershon. *The Place Where You Are Standing Is Holy: A Jewish Theology on Human Relationships.* Northvale, NJ: J. Aronson, 1994.

Winlock, H. E. *The Rise and Fall of the Middle Kingdom in Thebes.* New York: Macmillan, 1947.

Wolf, Arthur P. "Chinese Kinship and Mourning Dress." In *Family and Kinship in Chinese Society,* ed. Maurice Freedman. Stanford: Stanford University Press, 1970.

Wooley, C. L. *Ur Excavations.* Vol. 2: *The Royal Cemetery: Text.* London: Published for the trustees of the two museums, 1927–1976; vol. 2, 1934.

Wright, Dudley. *Vampires and Vampirism.* London: Will Rider and Son, 1924.

Xanthoudides, S. *The Vaulted Tombs of Mesará.* Liverpool: University Press of Liverpool, 1924.

Yarrow, H. C. *A Further Contribution to the Study of Mortuary Customs of the North American Indians.* Bureau of American Ethnology Annual Report, vol. 1. Washington, DC: Government Printing Office, 1881.

———. *Introduction to the Study of Mortuary Customs among the North American Indians.* Washington, DC: Government Printing Office, 1880.

Yü, Ying-Shih. "Life and Immortality in the Mind of Han China." *Harvard Journal of Asiatic Studies* 25 (1964).

Zabkar, L. V. *A Study of the Ba Concept in Ancient Egyptian Texts.* Chicago: University of Chicago Press, 1968.

Zandee, Jan. *Death as an Enemy according to Ancient Egyptian Conceptions.* New York: Arno Press, 1977.

Ziegler, Philip. *The Black Death.* New York: Harper and Row, 1969.

Zimmer, Heinrich. *Myths and Symbols in Indian Art and Civilization.* Ed. Joseph Campbell. Bollingen Series 6. New York: Random House, 1946.

Zürcher, Erik. *The Buddhist Conquest of China: The Spread and Adaptation of Buddhism in Early Medieval China.* Rev. ed. Leiden: E. J. Brill, 1972.

INDEX

keri'ah and, 216
  work of, 136–37
Ch'i, 341, 358
Chimata no kami, honoring, 79
Ching-T'u, 64–66, 203, 364
  T'an-luan and, 65
  Tao-ch'o and, 65
  vision of, 65
Chinggis Khan, royal funerals/burials and,
  125
Ch'ing-t'i, 102, 104
Chinvat Bridge, 66–67, 198, 356, 359
Chinvato Peretu, 66, 93, 324
Chloa bronze, 325 (photo)
Choctaw
  scaffold burials and, 48
  tree burial and, 53
Chöd, 67
Choes, 15, 15 (photo)
Christian Fathers, theological quandry for,
  180
Christianity
  ancestor worship and, 11
  intercession and, 192
  Irish Underworld and, 261
  Judaism and, 167
  Roman Empire and, 180
Chthonic, 215, 218
Chu, 128, 357
Chuang, Duke: on Yellow Springs, 404
Chuang-tzu, reincarnation and, 297
Ch'u Anthology (Thompson), 247–48
Churel, 67–68
Cicero, Marcus Tullius, 96
  on afterlife, 162
Cinebarium, 68
Cippus, 69
City of God, 164, 167
Class struggles, emergence of, 38
Clement VI, 173
  flagellism and, 38
Clothes
  burial, 47, 64, 137–38, 139, 150, 157,
    331
  funeral, 112–13, 120, 216
  longevity, 126
  rending of, 137
Cocytus, 69, 161, 397
Codbiter, Thorstein, 100
Coffins, 69–70, 228, 302, 303
  anthropoid, 69, 71
  boat, 51, 114
  Chinese, 127
  Egyptian, 70–72, 281
  Lapp, 139
  origin of, 46
  palls for, 263
  renting/retail, 70
  styles/shapes of, 69, 113
  symbolism of, 70

Columbarium, 72, 119, 302, 388
  cremation and, 74, 75
Columbus, Chrisopher: paradise and, 265
Commemorative rituals, 110–11
Commendation, 130
"Commentary on the Teaching on Birth"
  (T'an-luan), 65
Committal service, 72–73, 131
Conclamatio mortis, 73
Condolences, 127, 146
Confucius, 341
  funeral customs and, 125
  on mourning, 128
  Ten Kings and, 373
Conjuration, 214
Connla, 194, 226
Consecration service, 73–74
Consumed by Fire, 270
Conway, Lady Anne, 176
Coomaraswamy, Ananda K., v
  Vedic hymns and, 243
Corn Goddess, 257
Corpse pollution, 85, 111
  cremation/burial and, 377
Corpses
  dangers of, 384
  neutralizing, 393
  treatment of, 111, 112
  undead, 384
Cosmography, Buddhist, 181
Council of Florence (1439), 162
Council of Trent (1545–1563), 162
Counter-Reformation, 165
  Hell and, 174
  intercession and, 192
Creation, Lapp theology on, 197
Cremains, 74
  Etruscans and, 132
  secondary burial of, 118
Cremation, 61, 74–76, 75 (illus.), 119,
    134, 135
  Celts and, 123
  corpse pollution and, 377
  crossroads and, 77
  Etruscan, 131
  Greeks and, 116
  Hindus and, 74
  Indian, 117, 118, 133 (photo)
  Islam and, 74
  Jews and, 74
  monotheistic religions and, 74
  Native American, 144, 147
  popularity of, 75
  Roman, 74, 119
  Scandinavian, 148, 149
  ship, 51
  total costs of, 75–76
  undead and, 385
  vampires and, 394
  Zoroastrians and, 150–51

Crimthann, Three Connachts and, 225
Cromlech, 76, 233
Crooke, William, 269
Crossing of the Separator, 66
Crossing over, 49, 387
Crossroads, 76–77, 78 (illus.), 79, 384
  Buddhism and, 201
  burial at, 77
Crossroads spirits, honoring, 79
Crown of the Palace, 369
Cubiculum tomb, 58, 79–80, 106, 187,
  234
Cú Chulainn, 20, 398
  Morrigan and, 235
Cyrus
  Isaiah and, 204
  tomb of, 230

Daena, 66, 356
Dagoba, **81**, 383
Dakhma, 356, 377, 378
Damian, Peter, 279
Dance of death, 81–83, 82 (illus.)
Daniel, 167
  resurrection and, 311
  vision of, 333 (illus.)
Danish History (Saxo Grammaticus), 256
Danse macabre, 81, **83**
Dante Alighieri, 3, 63, 69, 279, 363, 372
    (illus.), 385, 386 (illus.)
  on Cerberus, 62
  Dis and, 91
  on Heaven, 165
  Hell and, 174, 181
  Inferno of, 387–88
  on Purgatory, 265
Darby, John Nelson, 170
Dark City, 247, 343
Darkness, Erebus and, 97
Davazdah Imam, mausoleum of, 231
Davidson, H. R. Ellis, 255
Day of Atonement, 191, 405
Day of Resurrection, 29, 142, 285, 353
Day of the Dead, observing, 90
Dead, 83–85
  baptism/marriage of, 87
  blessings by, 152
  collective, 111
  dangerous, 398
  judgment of, 206–7
  land of, 397
  memories of, 85, 144
  mistreatment of, 85
  politeness to, 105
  sleep of, 334
  spirit of, 111
  veneration of, 11
  visions of, 392
Dead drummer, 78 (illus.)
Dead Sea Scrolls, 156